LAROUSSE

MINI

SPANISH-ENGLISH
ENGLISH-SPANISH

DICTIONARY

W9-AAA-610

LAROUSSE

Realizado por / Produced by

LAROUSSE

Redacción/Editors

JOAQUÍN BLASCO, ISABEL BROSA SÁBADA
CARMEN ZAMANILLO, ZÖE PETERSEN
ANA CARBALLO VARELA, ELENA PARSONS
MALIHE FORGHANI-NOWBARI, LESLEY KINGSLEY
CALLUM BRINES, WENDY LEE

MINI PLUS

Agradecer
- (Muchas) gracias.
- Gracias, igualmente.

- Le agradezco su ayuda.

Saying thank you
- Thank you (very much).
- Thank you. The same to you too.
- Thank you for your help.

Devolver las gracias
- No hay de qué.
- No es nada.
- De nada.

Replying to thanks
- Don't mention it.
- Not at all.
- You're welcome.

Aceptar disculpas
- Discúlpeme. Disculpe. [polite form]
- Discúlpame. Disculpa. [to a friend]
- Lo siento. Lo lamento.
- Perdón. Disculpas.
- Perdóneme. Perdone. [polite form] Perdóname. Perdona. [to a friend]
- Siento llegar tarde/ molestarlo (molestarla).
- Lo siento (mucho).

Apologizing
- Excuse me.

- Excuse me.

- I'm sorry.
- Sorry!
- Pardon me.

- I'm sorry I'm late/to bother you.
- I'm (terribly) sorry.

Aceptar excusas
- No importa.
- Está bien.
- No se preocupe. No es nada.

Accepting an apology
- It doesn't matter.
- That's all right.
- No harm done.

LAROUSSE

MINI
DICCIONARIO

ESPAÑOL-INGLÉS
INGLÉS-ESPAÑOL

LAROUSSE

El diccionario MINI Larousse está pensado para principiantes y viajeros.

Con más de 30.000 voces y 40.000 traducciones, esta nueva obra presenta una amplia cobertura del vocabulario básico, así como un tratamiento exhaustivo del léxico propio de carteles, letreros y menús de restaurante.

El texto incluye una gran cantidad de indicadores de sentido claros y precisos. Se ha puesto especial cuidado en la redacción de las palabras más básicas, con numerosos ejemplos de uso y una atractiva presentación.

De consulta rápida y eficaz, esta obra práctica y completa será la herramienta indispensable para estudiantes y turistas. Esperamos que disfruten con él y no duden en ponerse en contacto con nosotros si tienen cualquier observación que hacernos.

EL EDITOR

The Larousse MINI dictionary has been designed with beginners and travellers in mind.

With over 30,000 references and 40,000 translations, this new dictionary gives thorough coverage of general vocabulary plus extensive treatment of the language found on street signs and menus.

Clear sense markers are provided throughout, while special emphasis has been placed on basic words, with many examples of usage and a particularly user-friendly layout.

Easy to use and comprehensive, this handy book packs a lot of wordpower for users at school, at home and on the move. We hope you enjoy using this dictionary, and don't hesitate to send us your comments.

THE PUBLISHER

ABBREVIATIONS

ABREVIATURAS

abbreviation	*abbr/abrev*	abreviatura
adjective	*adj*	adjetivo
adverb	*adv*	adverbio
American English	*Am*	inglés americano
Latin American Spanish	*Amér*	español latinoamericano
anatomy	*ANAT*	anatomía
before noun	*antes de s*	antes de sustantivo
article	*art*	artículo
automobile, cars	*AUT(OM)*	automóviles
auxiliary	*aux*	auxiliar
British English	*Br*	inglés británico
commerce, business	*COM(M)*	comercio
comparative	*compar*	comparativo
computers	*COMPUT*	informática
conjunction	*conj*	conjunción
continuous	*cont*	continuo
culinary, cooking	*CULIN*	cocina
sport	*DEP*	deporte
juridical, legal	*DER*	derecho, jurídico
pejorative	*despec*	despectivo
economics	*ECON*	economía
school, education	*EDUC*	educación
exclamation	*excl*	interjección
feminine noun	*f*	sustantivo femenino
informal	*fam*	familiar
figurative	*fig*	figurado
finance, financial	*FIN*	finanzas
formal	*fml*	formal, culto
inseparable	*fus*	inseparable
generally	*gen*	generalmente
grammar	*GRAM(M)*	gramática
informal	*inf*	familiar

computers	*INFORM*	informática
exclamation	*interj*	interjección
invariable	*inv*	invariable
juridical, legal	*JUR*	derecho, jurídico
masculine noun	*m*	sustantivo masculino
mathematics	*MATH*	matemáticas
medicine	*MED*	medicina
military	*MIL*	militar
music	*MUS/MÚS*	música
noun	*n*	sustantivo
nautical, maritime	*NAUT*	náutica, marítimo
numeral	*num/núm*	número
oneself	*o.s.*	
pejorative	*pej*	despectivo
plural	*pl*	plural
politics	*POL(ÍT)*	política
past participle	*pp*	participio pasado
preposition	*prep*	preposición
pronoun	*pron*	pronombre
past tense	*pt*	pasado, pretérito
registered trademark	®	marca registrada
religion	*RELIG*	religión
noun	*s*	sustantivo
someone, somebody	*sb*	
school, education	*SCH*	educación
Scottish English	*Scot*	inglés escocés
separable	*sep*	separable
singular	*sg*	singular
something	*sthg*	
subject	*subj/suj*	sujeto
superlative	*superl*	superlativo
technology	*TECH/TECN*	tecnología
television	*TV*	televisión
transport	*TRANS(P)*	transportes
verb	*vb/v*	verbo
intransitive verb	*vi*	verbo intransitivo

impersonal verb	*v impers*	verbo impersonal
pronominal verb	*vpr*	verbo pronominal
transitive verb	*vt*	verbo transitivo
vulgar	*vulg*	vulgar
cultural equivalent	≃	equivalente cultural

SPANISH ALPHABETICAL ORDER

This dictionary follows international alphabetical order. Thus entries with **ch** appear after **cg** and not at the end of **c**. Similarly, entries with **ll** appear after **lk** and not at the end of **l**. Note, however, that **ñ** *is* treated as a separate letter and follows **n**.

ENGLISH COMPOUNDS

A compound is a word or expression which has a single meaning but is made up of more than one word, e.g. **point of view, kiss of life, virtual reality** and **West Indies**. It is a feature of this dictionary that English compounds appear in the A-Z list in strict alphabetical order. The compound **blood test** will therefore come after **bloodshot** which itself follows **blood pressure**.

LA ORDENACIÓN ALFABÉTICA EN ESPAÑOL

En este diccionario se ha seguido la ordenación alfabética internacional. Esto significa que las entradas con **ch** aparecerán después de **cg** y no al final de **c**; del mismo modo las entradas con **ll** vendrán después de **lk** y no al final de **l**. Adviértase, sin embargo, que la letra **ñ** *sí* se considera letra aparte y sigue a la **n**.

LOS COMPUESTOS EN INGLÉS

En inglés se llama compuesto a una locución sustantiva de significado único pero formada por más de una palabra; p.ej. **point of view, kiss of life, virtual reality** o **West Indies**. Uno de los rasgos distintivos de este diccionario es la inclusión de estos compuestos con estricta propia y en riguroso orden alfabético. De esta forma **blood test** vendrá después de **bloodshot**, el cual sigue a **blood pressure**.

PHONETIC TRANSCRIPTION

TRANSCRIPCIÓN FONÉTICA

English vowels

[ɪ]	pit, big, rid
[e]	pet, tend
[æ]	pat, bag, mad
[ʌ]	run, cut
[ɒ]	pot, log
[ʊ]	put, full
[ə]	mother, suppose
[i:]	bean, weed
[ɑ:]	barn, car, laugh
[ɔ:]	born, lawn
[u:]	loop, loose
[ɜ:]	burn, learn, bird

Vocales españolas

[i]	piso, imagen
[e]	tela, eso
[a]	pata, amigo
[o]	bola, otro
[u]	luz, una

Vocales catalanas

[ɛ]	fresc

English diphthongs

[eɪ]	bay, late, great
[aɪ]	buy, light, aisle
[ɔɪ]	boy , foil
[əʊ]	no, road, blow
[aʊ]	now, shout, town
[ɪə]	peer, fierce, idea
[eə]	pair, bear, share
[ʊə]	poor, sure, tour

Diptongos españoles

[ei]	ley, peine
[ai]	aire, caiga
[oi]	soy, boina
[au]	causa, aula
[eu]	Europa, deuda

Semi-vowels

you, spaniel	[j]
wet, why, twin	[w]

Semivocales

hierba, miedo	
agua, hueso	

Consonants

pop, people	[p]
bottle, bib	[b]
	[β]
train, tip	[t]
dog, did	[d]
come, kitchen	[k]
gag, great	[g]
	[ɣ]

Consonantes

papá, campo	
vaca, bomba	
curvo, caballo	
toro, pato	
donde, caldo	
que, cosa	
grande, guerra	
aguijón, bulldog	

chain, wretched	[tʃ]	ocho, chusma
jet, fridge	[dʒ]	
fib, physical	[f]	fui, afán
vine, live	[v]	
think, fifth	[θ]	cera, paz
this, with	[ð]	cada, pardo
seal, peace	[s]	solo, paso
zip, his	[z]	
sheep, machine	[ʃ]	
usual, measure	[ʒ]	
	[x]	gemir, jamón
how, perhaps	[h]	
metal, comb	[m]	madre, cama
night, dinner	[n]	no, pena
sung, parking	[ŋ]	banca, encanto
	[ɲ]	caña
little, help	[l]	ala, luz
right, carry	[r]	atar, paro
	[rr]	perro, rosa
	[ʎ]	llave, collar

The symbol ['] indicates that the following syllable carries primary stress and the symbol [ˌ] that the following syllable carries secondary stress.

Los símbolos ['] y [ˌ] indican que la sílaba siguiente lleva un acento primario o secundario respectivamente.

The symbol [ʳ] in English phonetics indicates that the final "r" is pronounced only when followed by a word beginning with a vowel. Note that it is nearly always pronounced in American English.

El símbolo [ʳ] en fonética inglesa indica que la "r" al final de palabra se pronuncia sólo cuando precede a una palabra que comienza por vocal. Adviértase que casi siempre se pronuncia en inglés americano.

Spanish Verbs

Key: A = present indicative, **B** = imperfect, **C** = preterite,
D = future, **E** = conditional, **F** = present subjunctive,
G = imperfect subjunctive, **H** = imperative, **I** = gerund,
J = past participle

N.B. All forms of the **imperfect subjunctive** can also take the
endings: -se, -ses, -se, -semos, -seis, -sen

acertar: A acierto, acertamos, etc., **F** acierte, acertemos, etc., **H** acierta, acertemos, acertad, etc.

adquirir: A adquiero, adquirimos, etc., **F** adquiera, adquiramos, etc., **H** adquiere, adquiramos, adquirid, etc.

AMAR: A amo, amas, ama, amamos, amáis, aman, **B** amaba, amabas, amaba, amábamos, amabais, amaban, **C** amé, amaste, amó, amamos, amasteis, amaron, **D** amaré, amarás, amará, amaremos, amaréis, amarán, **E** amaría, amarías, amaría, amaríamos, amaríais, amarían, **F** ame, ames, ame, amemos, améis, amen, **G** amara, amaras, amara, amáramos, amarais, amaran, **H** ama, ame, amemos, amad, amen, **I** amando, **J** amado, -da

andar: C anduve, anduvimos, etc., **G** anduviera, anduviéramos, etc.

avergonzar: A avergüenzo, avergonzamos, etc., **C** avergoncé, avergonzó, avergonzamos, etc., **F** avergüence, avergoncemos, etc., **H** avergüenza, avergüence, avergoncemos, avergonzad, etc.

caber: A quepo, cabe, cabemos, etc., **C** cupe, cupimos, etc., **D** cabré, cabremos, etc., **E** cabría, cabríamos, etc., **F** quepa, quepamos, cabed, etc., **G** cupiera, cupiéramos, etc., **H** cabe, quepa, quepamos, etc.

caer: A caigo, cae, caemos, etc., **C** cayó, caímos, cayeron, etc., **F** caiga, caigamos, etc., **G** cayera, cayéramos, etc., **H** cae, caiga, caigamos, caed, etc., **I** cayendo

conducir: A conduzco, conduce, conducimos, etc., **C** conduje, condujimos, etc., **F** conduzca, conduzcamos, etc., **G** condujera, condujéramos, etc., **H** conduce, conduzca, conduzcamos, conducid, etc.

conocer: A conozco, conoce, conocemos, etc., **F** conozca, conozcamos, etc., **H** conoce, conozca, conozcamos, etc.

dar: A doy, da, damos, etc., **C** di, dio, dimos, etc., **F** dé, demos, etc., **G** diera, diéramos, etc., **H** da, dé, demos, dad, etc.

decir: A digo, dice, decimos, etc., **C** dije, dijimos, etc., **D** diré, diremos, etc., **E** diría, diríamos, etc., **F** diga, digamos, etc., **G** dijera, dijéramos, etc., **H** di, diga, digamos, decid, etc., **I** diciendo, **J** dicho, -cha.

dormir: A duermo, dormimos, etc., **C** durmió, dormimos, durmieron, etc., **F** duerma, durmamos, etc., **G** durmiera, durmiéramos, etc., **H** duerme, duerma, durmamos, dormid, etc., **I** durmiendo

errar: A yerro, erramos, etc., **F** yerre, erremos, etc., **H** yerra, yerre, erremos, errad, etc.

estar: A estoy, está, estamos, etc., **C** estuve, estuvimos, etc., **F** esté, estemos, etc., **G** estuviera, estuviéramos, etc., **H** está, esté, estemos, estad, etc.,

HABER: A he, has, ha, hemos, habéis, han, **B** había, habías, había, habíamos, habíais, habían, **C** hube, hubiste, hubo, hubimos, hubisteis, hubieron, **D** habré, habrás, habrá, habremos, habréis, habrán, **E** habría, habrías, habría, habríamos, habríais, habrían, **F** haya, hayas, haya, hayamos, hayáis, hayan, **G** hubiera, hubieras, hubiera, hubiéramos, hubierais, hubieran, **H** he, haya, hayamos, habed, hayan, **I** habiendo, **J** habido, -da

hacer: A hago, hace, hacemos, etc., **C** hice, hizo, hicimos, etc., **D** haré, haremos, etc., **E** haría, haríamos, etc., **F** haga, hagamos, etc., **G** hiciera, hiciéramos, etc., **H** haz, haga, hagamos, haced, etc., **J** hecho, -cha

huir: A huyo, huimos, etc., **C** huyó, huimos, huyeron, etc., **F** huya, huyamos, etc., **G** huyera, huyéramos, etc., **H** huye, huya, huyamos, huid, etc., **I** huyendo

ir: A voy, va, vamos, etc., **C** fui, fue, fuimos, etc., **F** vaya, vayamos, etc., **G** fuera, fuéramos, etc., **H** ve, vaya, vayamos, id, etc., **I** yendo

leer: C leyó, leímos, leyeron, etc., **G** leyera, leyéramos, etc., **I** leyendo

lucir: A luzco, luce, lucimos, etc., **F** luzca, luzcamos, etc., **H** luce, luzca, luzcamos, lucid, etc.

mover: A muevo, movemos, etc., **F** mueva, movamos, etc., **H** mueve, mueva, movamos, moved, etc.

nacer: A nazco, nace, nacemos, etc., **F** nazca, nazcamos, etc., **H** nace, nazca, nazcamos, naced, etc.

oír: A oigo, oye, oímos, etc., **C** oyó, oímos, oyeron, etc., **F** oiga, oigamos, etc., **G** oyera, oyéramos, etc., **H** oye, oiga, oigamos, oíd, etc., **I** oyendo

oler: A huelo, olemos, etc., **F** huela, olamos, etc., **H** huele, huela, olamos, oled, etc.

parecer: A parezco, parece, parecemos, etc., **F** parezca, parezcamos, etc., **H** parece, parezca, parezcamos, pareced, etc.,

PARTIR: A parto, partes, parte, partimos, partís, parten, **B** partía, partías, partía, partíamos, partíais, partían, **C** partí, partiste, partió, partimos, partisteis, partieron, **D** partiré, partirás, partirá, partiremos, partiréis, partirán, **E** partiría, partirías, partiría, partiríamos, partiríais, partirían, **F** parta, partas, parta, partamos, partáis, partan, **G** partiera, partieras, partiera, partiéramos, partierais, partieran, **H** parte, parta, partamos, partid, partan, **I** partiendo, **J** partido, -da

pedir: A pido, pedimos, etc., **C** pidió, pedimos, pidieron, etc., **F** pida, pidamos, etc., **G** pidiera, pidiéramos, etc., **H** pide, pida, pidamos, pedid, etc., **I** pidiendo

poder: A puedo, podemos, etc., **C** pude, pudimos, etc., **D** podré, podremos, etc., **E** podría, podríamos, etc., **F** pueda, podamos, etc., **G** pudiera, pudiéramos, etc., **H** puede, pueda, podamos, poded, etc., **I** pudiendo

poner: A pongo, pone, ponemos, etc., **C** puse, pusimos, etc., **D** pondré, pondremos, etc., **E** pondría, pondríamos, etc., **F** ponga, pongamos, etc., **G** pusiera, pusiéramos, etc., **H** pon, ponga, pongamos, poned, etc., **J** puesto, -ta

querer: A quiero, queremos, etc., **C** quise, quisimos, etc., **D** querré, querremos, etc., **E** querría, querríamos, etc., **F** quiera, queramos, etc., **G** quisiera, quisiéramos, etc., **H** quiere, quiera, queramos, quered, etc.

reír: A río, reímos, etc., **C** rió, reímos, rieron, etc., **F** ría, riamos, etc., **G** riera, riéramos, etc., **H** ríe, ría, riamos, reíd, etc., **I** riendo

saber: A sé, sabe, sabemos, etc., **C** supe, supimos, etc., **D** sabré, sabremos, etc., **E** sabría, sabríamos, etc., **F** sepa, sepamos, etc., **G** supiera, supiéramos, etc., **H** sabe, sepa, sepamos, sabed, etc.

salir: A salgo, sale, salimos, etc., **D** saldré, saldremos, etc., **E** saldría, saldríamos, etc., **F** salga, salgamos, etc., **H** sal, salga, salgamos, salid, etc.

sentir: A siento, sentimos, etc., **C** sintió, sentimos, sintieron, etc., **F** sienta, sintamos, etc., **G** sintiera, sintiéramos, etc., **H** siente, sienta, sintamos, sentid, etc., **I** sintiendo

SER: A soy, eres, es, somos, sois, son, **B** era, eras, era, éramos, erais, eran, **C** fui, fuiste, fue, fuimos, fuisteis, fueron, **D** seré, serás, será, seremos, seréis, serán, **E** sería, serías, sería, seríamos, seríais, serían, **F** sea, seas, sea, seamos, seáis, sean, **G** fuera, fueras, fuera, fuéramos, fuerais, fueran, **H** sé, sea, seamos, sed, sean, **I** siendo, **J** sido, -da

sonar: A sueno, sonamos, etc., **F** suene, sonemos, etc., **H** suena, suene, sonemos, sonad, etc.

TEMER: A temo, temes, teme, tememos, teméis, temen, **B** temía, temías, temía, temíamos, temíais, temían, **C** temí, temiste, temió, temimos, temisteis, temieron, **D** temeré, temerás, temerá, temeremos, temeréis, temerán, **E** temería, temerías, temería, temeríamos, temeríais, temerían, **F** tema, temas, tema, temamos, temáis, teman,

G temiera, temieras, temiera, temiéramos, temierais, temieran, **H** teme, tema, temamos, temed, teman, **I** temiendo, **J** temido, -da

tender: A tiendo, tendemos, etc., **F** tienda, tendamos, etc., **H** tiende, tendamos, etc.

tener: A tengo, tiene, tenemos, etc., **C** tuve, tuvimos, etc., **D** tendré, tendremos, etc., **E** tendría, tendríamos, etc., **F** tenga, tengamos, etc., **G** tuviera, tuviéramos, etc., **H** ten, tenga, tengamos, tened, etc.

traer: A traigo, trae, traemos, etc., **C** traje, trajimos, etc., **F** traiga, traigamos, etc., **G** trajera, trajéramos, etc., **H** trae, traiga, traigamos, traed, etc., **I** trayendo

valer: A valgo, vale, valemos, etc., **D** valdré, valdremos, etc., **E** valdría, valdríamos, etc., **F** valga, valgamos, etc., **H** vale, valga, valgamos, valed, etc.

venir: A vengo, viene, venimos, etc., **C** vine, vinimos, etc., **D** vendré, vendremos, etc., **E** vendría, vendríamos, etc., **F** venga, vengamos, etc., **G** viniera, viniéramos, etc., **H** ven, venga, vengamos, venid, etc., **I** viniendo

ver: A veo, ve, vemos, etc., **C** vi, vio, vimos, etc., **G** viera, viéramos, etc., **H** ve, vea, veamos, ved, etc., **I** viendo, etc., **J** visto, -ta

VERBOS IRREGULARES INGLESES

Infinitive	Past Tense	Past Participle	Infinitive	Past Tense	Past Participle
arise	arose	arisen	blow	blew	blown
awake	awoke	awoken	break	broke	broken
be	was/ were	been	breed	bred	bred
			bring	brought	brought
bear	bore	born(e)	build	built	built
beat	beat	beaten	burn	burnt	burnt
begin	began	begun		/burned	/burned
bend	bent	bent			
bet	bet	bet	burst	burst	burst
	/betted	/betted	buy	bought	bought
			can	could	–
bid	bid	bid	cast	cast	cast
bind	bound	bound	catch	caught	caught
bite	bit	bitten	choose	chose	chosen
bleed	bled	bled	come	came	come

Infinitive	Past Tense	Past Participle	Infinitive	Past Tense	Past Participle
cost	cost	cost	kneel	knelt	knelt
creep	crept	crept		/kneeled	/kneeled
cut	cut	cut	know	knew	known
deal	dealt	dealt	lay	laid	laid
dig	dug	dug	lead	led	led
do	did	done	lean	leant	leant
draw	drew	drawn		/leaned	/leaned
dream	dreamed	dreamed	leap	leapt	leapt
	/dreamt	/dreamt		/leaped	/leaped
drink	drank	drunk	learn	learnt	learnt
drive	drove	driven		/learned	/learned
eat	ate	eaten	leave	left	left
fall	fell	fallen	lend	lent	lent
feed	fed	fed	let	let	let
feel	felt	felt	lie	lay	lain
fight	fought	fought	light	lit	lit
find	found	found		/lighted	/lighted
fling	flung	flung	lose	lost	lost
fly	flew	flown	make	made	made
forget	forgot	forgotten	may	might	–
freeze	froze	frozen	mean	meant	meant
get	got	got (*Am* gotten)	meet	met	met
			mow	mowed	mown
give	gave	given			/mowed
go	went	gone	pay	paid	paid
grind	ground	ground	put	put	put
grow	grew	grown	quit	quit	quit
hang	hung	hung		/quitted	/quitted
	/hanged	/hanged	read	read	read
have	had	had	rid	rid	rid
hear	heard	heard	ride	rode	ridden
hide	hid	hidden	ring	rang	rung
hit	hit	hit	rise	rose	risen
hold	held	held	run	ran	run
hurt	hurt	hurt	saw	sawed	sawn
keep	kept	kept	say	said	said

Infinitive	Past Tense	Past Participle	Infinitive	Past Tense	Past Participle
see	saw	seen	spoil	spoiled	spoiled
seek	sought	sought		/spoilt	/spoilt
sell	sold	sold	spread	spread	spread
send	sent	sent	spring	sprang	sprung
set	set	set	stand	stood	stood
shake	shook	shaken	steal	stole	stolen
shall	should	–	stick	stuck	stuck
shed	shed	shed	sting	stung	stung
shine	shone	shone	stink	stank	stunk
shoot	shot	shot	strike	struck	struck
show	showed	shown			/stricken
shrink	shrank	shrunk	swear	swore	sworn
shut	shut	shut	sweep	swept	swept
sing	sang	sung	swell	swelled	swollen
sink	sank	sunk			/swelled
sit	sat	sat	swim	swam	swum
sleep	slept	slept	swing	swung	swung
slide	slid	slid	take	took	taken
sling	slung	slung	teach	taught	taught
smell	smelt	smelt	tear	tore	torn
	/smelled	/smelled	tell	told	told
sow	sowed	sown	think	thought	thought
		/sowed	throw	threw	thrown
speak	spoke	spoken	tread	trod	trodden
speed	sped	sped	wake	woke	woken
	/speeded	/speeded		/waked	/waked
spell	spelt	spelt	wear	wore	worn
	/spelled	/spelled	weave	wove	woven
spend	spent	spent		/weaved	/weaved
spill	spilt	spilt	weep	wept	wept
	/spilled	/spilled	win	won	won
spin	spun	spun	wind	wound	wound
spit	spat	spat	wring	wrung	wrung
split	split	split	write	wrote	written

A

a *prep* **1.** *(tiempo):* **a las pocas semanas** a few weeks later; **al mes de casados** a month after marrying; **a las siete** at seven o'clock; **a los once años** at the age of eleven; **dos veces al año** twice a year; **al oír la noticia se desmayó** on hearing the news, she fainted.

2. *(frecuencia)* per, every; **cuarenta horas a la semana** forty hours a week.

3. *(dirección)* to; **voy a Sevilla** I'm going to Seville; **llegó a Barcelona/la fiesta** he arrived in Barcelona/at the party.

4. *(posición, lugar, distancia):* **a la salida del cine** outside the cinema; **está a cien kilómetros** it's a hundred kilometres away; **a la derecha/izquierda** on the right/left.

5. *(con complemento indirecto):* **dáselo a Juan** give it to Juan; **dile a Juan que venga** tell Juan to come.

6. *(con complemento directo):* **quiere a su hijo** she loves her son.

7. *(cantidad, medida, precio):* **a cientos/docenas** by the hundred/dozen; **¿a cuánto están las peras?** how much are the pears?; **vende las peras a 150 pesetas** he's selling pears for 150 pesetas; **ganaron por tres a cero** they won three nil.

8. *(modo, manera):* **a la gallega** Galician-style; **escribir a máquina** to type; **a mano** by hand.

9. *(finalidad)* to; **entró a pagar** he came in to pay; **aprender a nadar** to learn to swim.

abad, -desa *m, f* abbot (*f* abbess).

abadía *f* abbey.

abajo *adv (de situación)* below; *(en edificio)* downstairs; *(de dirección)* down; **allí ~** down there; **aquí ~** down here; **más ~** further down; **para ~** downwards; **de ~** *(piso)* downstairs.

abalear *vt (Amér)* to shoot.

abandonado, -da *adj* abandoned; *(lugar)* deserted.

abandonar *vt (persona, animal, proyecto)* to abandon; *(coche, lugar, examen)* to leave; *(prueba)* to drop out of □ **abandonarse** *vpr* to let o.s. go.

abandono *m (dejadez)* neglect.

abanicarse *vpr* to fan o.s.

abanico *m* fan.

abarcar *vt (incluir)* to include; *(ver)* to have a view of.

abarrotado, -da *adj* packed.

abarrotero, -ra *m, f (Amér)* grocer.

abarrotes *mpl (Amér)* groceries.

abastecer *vt* to supply ❑

abastecerse de *v + prep* to get, to buy.

abatible *adj* folding.

abatido, -da *adj (desanimado)* dejected.

abatir *vt (muro)* to knock down; *(árbol)* to flatten.

abdicar *vi* to abdicate.

abdomen *m* abdomen.

abdominales *mpl* sit-ups.

abecedario *m (alfabeto)* alphabet.

abeja *f* bee.

abejorro *m* bumblebee.

aberración *f (disparate)* stupid thing.

abertura *f (agujero)* opening.

abeto *m* fir.

abierto, -ta *adj* open; *(de ideas)* open-minded; **estar ~ a** to be open to.

abismo *m* abyss.

ablandar *vt (materia)* to soften; *(persona)* to mollify.

abofetear *vt* to slap.

abogado, -da *m, f* lawyer.

abolición *f* abolition.

abolir *vt* to abolish.

abollar *vt* to dent.

abonado, -da *adj (tierra)* fertilized; **está ~ a la televisión por cable** he subscribes to cable TV.

abonar *vt (tierra)* to fertilize; *(cantidad, precio)* to pay ❑ **abonarse a** *v + prep (revista)* to subscribe to; *(teatro, fútbol)* to have a season ticket for.

abono *m (del metro, autobús)* sea-son ticket; *(para tierra)* fertilizer.

abordar *vt* to tackle.

aborrecer *vt* to loathe.

abortar *vi (espontáneamente)* to have a miscarriage; *(intencionadamente)* to have an abortion.

aborto *m (espontáneo)* miscarriage; *(intencionado)* abortion; *(fam: persona fea)* freak.

abrasador, -ra *adj* burning.

abrasar *vt (suj: incendio)* to burn down; *(suj: sol)* to burn.

abrazadera *f* brace.

abrazar *vt* to hug ❑ **abrazarse** *vpr* to hug.

abrazo *m* hug.

abrebotellas *m inv* bottle opener.

abrecartas *m inv* paper knife.

abrelatas *m inv* tin opener *(Br)*, can opener *(Am)*.

abreviar *vt (texto)* to abridge; *(discurso)* to cut.

abreviatura *f* abbreviation.

abridor *m* opener.

abrigar *vt (del frío)* to keep warm ❑ **abrigarse** *vpr* to wrap up.

abrigo *m (prenda)* coat; **al ~ de** *(roca, árbol)* under the shelter of.

abril *m* April; → **setiembre**.

abrillantador *m* polish.

abrillantar *vt* to polish.

abrir *vt* to open; *(grifo, gas)* to turn on; *(curso)* to start; *(agujero)* to make; *(ir delante de)* to lead ♦ *vi (comercio)* to open ❑ **abrirse** *vpr*: **~se a alguien** to open up to sb.

abrochar *vt* to do up ❑ **abrocharse**: **~se el pantalón** to do up one's trousers; **abrón-**

se los cinturones please fasten your seatbelts.

abrumador, -ra *adj* overwhelming.

abrumarse *vpr (agobiarse)* to be overwhelmed.

abrupto, -ta *adj (accidentado)* rough; *(empinado)* steep.

ábside *m* apse.

absolución *f (DER)* acquittal; *(RELIG)* absolution.

absolutamente *adv* absolutely.

absoluto, -ta *adj* absolute; **en ~** *(de ninguna manera)* not at all; **nada ~** = nothing at all.

absolver *vt*: **~ a alguien (de)** *(DER)* to acquit sb (of).

absorbente *adj (material)* absorbent; *(actividad)* absorbing; *(persona)* domineering.

absorber *vt (líquido)* to absorb; *(tiempo)* to take up.

absorto, -ta *adj*: **~ (en)** engrossed (in).

abstemio, -mia *m, f* teetotaller.

abstención *f* abstention.

abstenerse: **abstenerse de** *v + prep* to abstain from.

abstinencia *f* abstinence; **hacer ~** to fast.

abstracto, -ta *adj* abstract.

absuelto, -ta *pp* → **absolver**.

absurdo, -a *adj* absurd.

abuelo, -la *m, f (familiar)* grandfather *(f grandmother)*; *(fam: anciano)* old man *(f old woman)* ❑

abuelos *mpl* grandparents.

abultado, -da *adj* bulky.

abultar *vi* to be bulky.

abundancia *f* abundance.

abundante *adj* abundant.

aburrido, -da *adj (que aburre)* boring; *(harto)* bored.

aburrimiento *m* boredom.

aburrir *vt* to bore ❑ **aburrirse** *vpr (hastiarse)* to get bored; *(estar aburrido)* to be bored.

abusar: **abusar de** *v + prep (excederse)* to abuse; *(aprovecharse)* to take advantage of.

abusivo, -va *adj (precio)* extortionate; *(Amér: que abusa)* who takes advantage of; *(Amér: descarado)* cheeky.

abuso *m* abuse.

a/c *(abrev de a cuenta)* as a down payment.

acá *adv (aquí)* here ◆ *pron (Amér)*: **~ es mi hermana** this is my sister.

acabar *vt* 1. *(concluir)* to finish. 2. *(provisiones, dinero, gasolina)* to use up; *(comida)* to finish. ◆ *vi* 1. *(concluir)* to finish; **~ de hacer algo** to finish doing sthg; **~ bien/mal** to end well/badly; **acaba en punta** it ends in a point. 2. *(haber ocurrido recientemente)*: **~ de hacer algo** to have just done sthg. 3.: **~ con** *(violencia, etc)* to put an end to; *(salud)* to ruin; *(paciencia)* to exhaust. 4. *(volverse)* to end up. ❑ **acabarse** *vpr (agotarse)* to run out.

academia *f (escuela)* school; *(de ciencias, arte)* academy.

académico, -ca *adj* academic ◆ *m, f* academician.

acalorado, -da *adj (por el*

acalorarse

acalorarse *calor)* hot; *(enfadado)* worked-up; *(apasionado)* heated.

acalorarse *vpr (por un esfuerzo)* to get hot; *(enfadarse)* to get worked-up.

acampada *f* camping; **ir de ~** to go camping.

acampanado, -da *adj* flared.

acampar *vi* to camp.

acantilado *m* cliff.

acaparar *vt (mercado)* to monopolize; *(comida)* to hoard.

acápite *m (Amér)* paragraph.

acariciar *vt* to stroke.

acaso *adv* perhaps; **por si ~** just in case.

acatarrarse *vpr* to catch a cold.

acaudalado, -da *adj* well-off.

acceder *vi*: **~ a** *(lugar)* to enter □ **acceder a** *v + prep (petición)* to agree to.

accesible *adj (lugar)* accessible; *(persona)* approachable.

acceso *m (a un lugar)* entrance; *(a poder, universidad)* access; **"~ pasajeros"** "passengers only beyond this point".

accesorio *m* accessory.

accidentado, -da *adj (viaje)* bumpy; *(carrera)* eventful; *(terreno)* rough.

accidental *adj (encuentro)* chance *(antes de s)*.

accidente *m* accident; *(de avión, coche)* crash; **por ~** by accident; **~ geográfico** geographical feature; **~ laboral** industrial accident.

acción *f (acto, hecho)* deed, act □ **acciones** *fpl (en bolsa)* shares.

acechar *vt* to observe secretly.

aceite *m* oil; **~ de girasol** sunflower oil; **~ de oliva** olive oil.

aceitoso, -sa *adj* oily.

aceituna *f* olive; **~s rellenas** stuffed olives.

acelerador *m* accelerator.

acelerar *vt* to speed up ◆ *vi* to accelerate.

acelga *f* chard.

acento *m* accent; *(intensidad)* stress.

acentuación *f* accentuation.

acentuar *vt (vocal)* to put an accent on; *(destacar)* to stress.

aceptable *adj* acceptable.

aceptación *f* acceptance.

aceptar *vt* to accept.

acequia *f* irrigation channel.

acera *f* pavement *(Br)*, sidewalk *(Am)*.

acerca: **acerca de** *prep* about.

acercamiento *m* approach.

acercar *vt*: **~ algo a alguien** to pass sb sthg, to pass sthg to sb; **~ algo a algo** to move sthg closer to sthg □ **acercarse** *vpr (suj: tiempo)* to be near; *(suj: persona, animal)* to come closer; **~se a** *(lugar)* to be near; **acercarse a** *v + prep (solución, idea)* to be closer to.

acero *m* steel; **~ inoxidable** stainless steel.

acertado, -da *adj* right.

acertar *vt (respuesta, solución)* to get right □ **acertar con** *v + prep (hallar)* to get right; *(elegir bien)* to choose well; **acertar en** *v + prep (dar en)* to hit; *(elegir bien)* to choose well.

acertijo *m* riddle.

achinado, -da *adj (Amér)* low-class (used of Indians).

ácido, -da adj (sabor) sour ◆ m acid.

acierto m (respuesta, solución) right answer; (habilidad) skill.

aclamar vt to acclaim.

aclarar vt (ropa, cabello, platos) to rinse; (dudas, problemas) to clear up; (situación) to clarify ◆ v impers (tiempo) to clear up ❑ **aclararse** vpr (entender) to understand.

aclimatación f acclimatization.

aclimatar vt to acclimatize ❑ **aclimatarse** vpr to become acclimatized.

acogedor, -ra adj (lugar) cosy.

acoger vt (suj: persona) to welcome; (suj: lugar) to shelter ❑ **acogerse a** v + prep (ley) to have recourse to; (excusa) to resort to.

acogida f welcome.

acomodado, -da adj (rico) well-off.

acomodador, -ra m, f usher (f usherette).

acomodarse vpr (aposentarse) to make o.s. comfortable ❑ **acomodarse a** v + prep (adaptarse a) to adapt to.

acompañamiento m (en música) accompaniment.

acompañante mf companion.

acompañar vt (hacer compañía) to accompany; (adjuntar) to enclose; **le acompaño en el sentimiento** to my condolences.

acomplejado, -da adj with a complex.

acondicionado, -da adj (establo, desván) converted.

acondicionador m (en peluquería) conditioner.

acondicionar vt (establo, desván) to convert; (local) to fit out.

aconsejable adj advisable.

aconsejar vt to advise.

acontecer v impers to happen.

acontecimiento m event.

acoplar vt (encajar) to fit together; (adaptar) to adapt.

acordar vt to agree on; ~ **hacer algo** to agree to do sthg ❑ **acordarse** vpr to remember; **~se de hacer algo** to remember to do sthg.

acorde adj (conforme) in agreement ◆ m chord; ~ **con** in keeping with.

acordeón m accordion.

acortar vt to shorten.

acosar vt (perseguir) to hound; (molestar) to harass.

acoso m harassment.

acostar vt to put to bed ❑ **acostarse** vpr (irse a dormir) to go to bed; **~se con alguien** (fam) to sleep with sb.

acostumbrar vt: ~ **a alguien a** (habituar) to get sb used to; **no acostumbro a hacerlo** I don't usually do it ❑ **acostumbrarse** vpr: **~se a** to get used to.

acreditado, -da adj (con buena reputación) reputable.

acreditar vt (con documentos) to authorize.

acrílico, -ca adj acrylic.

acrobacia f acrobatics (pl).

acróbata mf acrobat.

acta f (de reunión) minutes (pl).

actitud f (del ánimo) attitude;

activar

(postura) posture.

activar *vt* to activate.

actividad *f* activity ❑ **actividades** *fpl* activities.

activo, -va *adj* active.

acto *m* act; ~ **seguido** straight after; **en el** ~ *(llaves, arreglos)* while you wait; *(multar)* on the spot; "**paga sus consumiciones en el** ~" sign indicating that customers should pay for their order immediately.

actor, -triz *m, f* actor (*f* actress).

actuación *f (conducta)* behaviour; *(en el cine, teatro)* performance.

actual *adj* current, present.

actualidad *f (momento presente)* present time; **de** ~ topical; **en la** ~ nowadays.

actualizar *vt* to bring up to date.

actualmente *adv (en este momento)* at the moment; *(hoy día)* nowadays.

actuar *vi* to act.

acuarela *f* watercolour.

acuario *m* aquarium ❑ **Acuario** *m* Aquarius.

acuático, -ca *adj (animal, planta)* aquatic; *(deporte)* water *(antes de s)*.

acudir *vi (ir)* to go; *(venir)* to come; ~ **a alguien** to turn to sb.

acueducto *m* aqueduct.

acuerdo *m* agreement; **de** ~ all right; **estar de** ~ to agree; **ponerse de** ~ to agree.

acumulación *f* accumulation.

acumular *vt* to accumulate.

acupuntura *f* acupuncture.

acusación *f (increpación)* accusation; *(DER)* charge.

acusado, -da *m, f*: **el/la** ~ the accused.

acusar *vt*: ~ **a alguien (de)** to accuse sb (of).

acústica *f (de un local)* acoustics *(pl)*.

adaptación *f* adaptation.

adaptador *m* adapter.

adaptarse *vpr*: **adaptarse a** *v + prep (medio, situación)* to adapt to; *(persona)* to learn to get on with.

adecuado, -da *adj* suitable, appropriate.

adecuar *vt* to adapt ❑ **adecuarse** *vpr (acostumbrarse)* to adjust.

a. de J.C. *(abrev de antes de Jesucristo)* BC.

adelantado, -da *adj* advanced; *(pago)* advance; **ir** ~ *(reloj)* to be fast; **por** ~ in advance.

adelantamiento *m* overtaking.

adelantar *vt (sobrepasar)* to overtake; *(trabajo, cita, reunión)* to bring forward; *(reloj)* to put forward ◆ *vi (reloj)* to be fast ❑ **adelantarse** *vpr (anticiparse)* to be early.

adelante *adv* ahead ◆ *interj (pase)* come in!; **más** ~ later; **en** ~ from now on.

adelanto *m* advance; *(en carretera)* overtaking.

adelgazante *adj* slimming.

adelgazar *vt* to lose ◆ *vi* to lose weight.

además *adv (también)* also; *(encima)* moreover; ~ **de** as well as.

adentro *adv* inside.

adherente *adj* adhesive.

adherir *vt* to stick ❑ **adherirse** *a v + prep (propuesta, idea, opinión, etc)* to support; *(asociación, partido)* to join.

adhesión *f (unión)* sticking; *(apoyo)* support; *(afiliación)* joining.

adhesivo, -va *adj* adhesive ♦ *m (pegatina)* sticker.

adicción *f* addiction.

adición *f* addition.

adicional *adj* additional.

adicto, -ta *adj:* ~ **a** addicted to.

adiós *m* goodbye ♦ *interj* goodbye!

adivinanza *f* riddle.

adivinar *vt (solución, respuesta)* to guess; *(futuro)* to foretell.

adivino, -na *m, f* fortuneteller.

adjetivo *m* adjective.

adjuntar *vt* to enclose.

administración *f (de productos)* supply; *(de oficina)* administration ❑ **Administración** *f:* **la Administración** the Government (Br), the Administration (Am).

administrar *vt (organizar, gobernar)* to run; *(medicamento)* to give.

administrativo, -va *adj* administrative ♦ *m, f* office worker.

admiración *f (estimación)* admiration; *(sorpresa)* amazement.

admirar *vt (estimar)* to admire; *(provocar sorpresa)* to amaze.

admisible *adj* acceptable.

admitir *vt* to admit.

admón. *(abrev de administración)* admin.

adobe *m* adobe.

adolescencia *f* adolescence.

adolescente *adj & mf* adolescent.

adonde *adv* where.

adónde *adv* where.

adopción *f (de un hijo)* adoption.

adoptar *vt* to adopt.

adoptivo, -va *adj (padre)* adoptive; *(hijo)* adopted.

adoquín *m* cobblestone.

adorable *adj* adorable.

adoración *f (culto)* worship; *(amor, pasión)* adoration.

adorar *vt (divinidad)* to worship; *(persona, animal, cosa)* to adore.

adornar *vt* to decorate.

adorno *m* ornament.

adosado, -da *adj:* ~ **a** against; **casa adosada** semi-detached house; **chalé** ~ semi-detached house.

adquirir *vt (comprar)* to purchase; *(conseguir)* to acquire.

adquisición *f* purchase.

adquisitivo, -va *adj* purchasing.

adrede *adv* deliberately.

aduana *f* customs *(sg)*; **pasar por la** ~ to go through customs.

aduanero, -ra *adj* customs *(antes de s)* ♦ *m, f* customs officer.

adulterio *m* adultery.

adúltero, -ra *adj* adulterous.

adulto, -ta *adj & m, f* adult.

adverbio *m* adverb.

adversario, -ria *m, f* adversary.

adverso, -sa *adj* adverse.

advertencia *f* warning.

advertir *vt (avisar)* to warn; *(notar)* to notice.

aéreo, -a *adj* air *(antes de s).*

aerobic (æˈroʊbɪk) *m* aerobics *(sg).*

aeromodelismo *m* airplane modelling.

aeromoza *f (Amér)* air hostess.

aeronave *f* aircraft.

aeropuerto *m* airport.

aerosol *m* aerosol.

afán *m (deseo)* urge.

afear *vt* to make ugly.

afección *f (formal: enfermedad)* complaint.

afectado, -da *adj (afligido)* upset; *(amanerado)* affected; **~ de** *por (enfermedad)* suffering from.

afectar *vt* to affect □ **afectar a** *v + prep* to affect; **afectarse** *vpr:* **~se por** o **con** to be affected by.

afectivo, -va *adj (sensible)* sensitive.

afecto *m* affection.

afectuoso, -sa *adj* affectionate.

afeitado, -da *adj (barba)* shaven; *(persona)* clean-shaven ♦ *m* shave.

afeitarse *vpr* to shave.

afeminado, -da *adj* effeminate.

afiche *m (Amér)* poster.

afición *f (inclinación)* fondness; *(partidarios)* fans *(pl).*

aficionado, -da *adj (amateur)* amateur; **~ a** *(interesado por)* fond of.

aficionarse: aficionarse a *v + prep (interesarse por)* to become keen on; *(habituarse a)* to become fond of.

afilado, -da *adj* sharp.

afilar *vt* to sharpen.

afiliado, -da *adj:* estar **~ a** to be a member of.

afiliarse: afiliarse a *v + prep* to join.

afín *adj* similar.

afinar *vt (instrumento)* to tune; *(puntería)* to perfect ♦ *vi* to be in tune.

afinidad *f* affinity.

afirmación *f* statement.

afirmar *vt (decir con seguridad)* to assert □ **afirmarse en** *v + prep (postura, idea)* to reaffirm.

afirmativo, -va *adj* affirmative.

afligido, -da *adj* upset.

afligir *vt (apenar)* to upset □ **afligirse** *vpr* to get upset.

aflojar *vt (cuerda)* to slacken; *(nudo)* to loosen ♦ *vi (en esfuerzo)* to ease off; *(ceder)* to die down.

afluencia *f (de gente)* crowds *(pl).*

afluente *m* tributary.

afónico, -ca *adj:* quedar **~** to lose one's voice.

aforo *m* seating capacity.

afortunadamente *adv* fortunately.

afortunado, -da *adj (con suerte)* lucky, fortunate; *(oportuno)* happy; **~ en** lucky in.

África *s* Africa.

africano, -na *adj & m, f* African.

afrodisíaco *m* aphrodisiac.

afrutado, -da *adj* fruity.

afuera *adv* outside ❏ **afueras** *fpl:* **las ~s** the outskirts.

agacharse *vpr* to crouch down.

agarrar *vt (con las manos)* to grab; *(fam: enfermedad)* to catch ❏ **agarrarse** *vpr (pelearse)* to fight; **agarrarse a** *v + prep (oportunidad)* to seize.

agencia *f* agency; **~ de viajes** travel agency.

agenda *f (de direcciones, teléfono)* book; *(personal)* diary; *(actividades)* agenda.

agente *mf* agent; **~ de policía** police officer.

ágil *adj (movimiento)* agile; *(pensamiento)* quick.

agilidad *f (del cuerpo)* agility; *(de la mente)* sharpness.

agitación *f* restlessness.

agitado, -da *adj (líquido)* shaken; *(persona)* restless.

agitar *vt (líquido)* to shake; *(multitud)* to stir up ❏ **agitarse** *vpr (aguas)* to get choppy; *(persona)* to get restless.

agnóstico, -ca *adj* agnostic.

agobiado, -da *adj* overwhelmed.

agobiar *vt* to overwhelm ❏ **agobiarse** *vpr* to be weighed down.

agosto *m* August, → **setiembre**.

agotado, -da *adj (cansado)* exhausted; *(edición, existencias)* sold-out; **el dinero está ~** the money has run out.

agotador, -ra *adj* exhausting.

agotamiento *m (cansancio)* exhaustion.

agotar *vt (cansar)* to exhaust; *(dinero, reservas)* to use up; *(edición, existencias)* to sell out of ❏ **agotarse** *vpr (cansarse)* to tire o.s. out; *(acabarse)* to run out.

agradable *adj* pleasant.

agradar *vi* to be pleasant.

agradecer *vt (ayuda, favor)* to be grateful for; **agradecí su invitación** I thanked her for her invitation.

agradecido, -da *adj* grateful.

agradecimiento *m* gratitude.

agredir *vt* to attack.

agregado, -da *adj* added ♦ *m, f (en embajada)* attaché (*f* attachée).

agregar *vt* to add.

agresión *f* attack.

agresivo, -va *adj* aggressive.

agresor, -ra *m, f* attacker.

agreste *adj (paisaje)* wild.

agrícola *adj* agricultural.

agricultor, -ra *m, f* farmer.

agricultura *f* agriculture.

agridulce *adj* sweet-and-sour.

agrio, agria *adj* sour.

agrupación *f* group.

agrupar *vt* to group.

agua *f (líquido)* water; *(lluvia)* rain; **~ de colonia** eau de cologne; **~ corriente** running water; **~ mineral** mineral water; **~ mineral con/sin gas** sparkling/still mineral water; **~ oxigenada** hydrogen peroxide; **~ potable** drinking water; **~ tónica** tonic water ❏ **aguas** *fpl (mar)* waters.

aguacate *m* avocado.

aguacero *m* shower.

aguafiestas *m inv* wet blanket.

aguamiel *f* (*Amér*) drink of water and cane sugar.

aguanieve *f* sleet.

aguantar *vt* (*sostener*) to support; (*soportar*) to bear; (*suj: ropa, zapatos*) to last for; **no lo aguanto** I can't stand it ❏ **aguantarse** *vpr* (*risa, llanto*) to hold back; (*resignarse*) to put up with it.

aguardar *vt* to wait for ◆ *vi* to wait.

aguardiente *m* liquor.

aguarrás *m* turpentine.

agudeza *f* (*de ingenio*) sharpness.

agudo, -da *adj* (*persona, dolor*) sharp; (*sonido*) high; (*ángulo*) acute; (*palabra*) oxytone.

águila *f* eagle.

aguinaldo *m* Christmas box.

AGUINALDO

In Spain, it is traditional for deliverymen and postmen to go from house to house over the Christmas period with Christmas cards for the occupiers. In return, they receive an "aguinaldo": a gift or a small amount of money in recognition of their services over the year.

---

aguja *f* (*de coser*) needle; (*de reloj*) hand; (*de pelo*) hairpin; **~ hipodérmica** hypodermic needle.

agujerear *vt* to make holes in.

agujero *m* hole.

agujetas *fpl*: **tener ~** to feel stiff (after running).

ahí *adv* there; **por ~** (*en un lugar indeterminado*) somewhere or other; (*fuera*) out; (*aproximadamente*) something like that; **de ~ que** that's why.

ahijado, -da *m, f* (*de un padrino*) godson (*f* goddaughter); (*en adopción*) adopted son (*f* adopted daughter).

ahogado, -da *adj* (*sin respiración*) breathless ◆ *m, f* drowned man (*f* drowned woman).

ahogarse *vpr* (*en el agua*) to drown; (*jadear*) to be short of breath; (*por calor, gas, presión*) to suffocate.

ahora *adv* now; **por ~** for the time being; **~ bien** however; **~ mismo** right now.

ahorcar *vt* to hang ❏ **ahorcarse** *vpr* to hang o.s.

ahorita *adv* (*Amér*) right now.

ahorrar *vt* to save.

ahorro *m* saving ❏ **ahorros** *mpl* (*dinero*) savings.

ahuecar *vt* (*vaciar*) to hollow out; (*pelo, colchón, almohada*) to fluff up.

ahumado, -da *adj* smoked.

aire *m* air; (*viento*) wind; (*gracia, garbo*) grace; (*parecido*) resemblance; (*descubierto*) exposed; **al ~ libre** in the open air; **se da ~s de artista** (*despec*) he fancies himself as a bit of an artist; **estar/quedar en el ~** to be in the air; **hace ~** it's windy; **~ acondicionado** air conditioning.

airear *vt* to air.

airoso, -sa *adj* (*gracioso*) graceful; (*con éxito*) successful.

aislado, -da *adj* isolated.

aislamiento m isolation.

aislante adj insulating.

aislar vt (persona, animal) to isolate; (local) to insulate ❏ **aislarse** vpr to cut o.s. off.

ajedrez m chess.

ajeno, -na adj: **eso es ~ a mi trabajo** that's not part of my job; **~ a** (sin saber) unaware of; (sin intervenir) not involved in.

ajetreo m bustle.

ají m (Amér) (pimiento picante) chilli; **ponerse como un ~** (fam: ruborizarse) to go red.

ajiaco m (Amér) chilli, meat and vegetable stew.

ajillo m: **al ~** in a garlic and chilli sauce.

ajo m garlic; **estar en el ~** to be in on it.

ajuar m trousseau.

ajustado, -da adj (cantidad, precio) reasonable; (ropa) tight-fitting.

ajustar vt (adaptar) to adjust; (puerta, ventana) to push to; (precios, condiciones, etc) to agree ❏ **ajustarse a** v + prep (condiciones) to comply with; (circunstancias) to adjust to.

al → a, el.

ala f wing; (de sombrero) brim.

alabanza f praise.

alabar vt to praise.

alabastro m alabaster.

alacena f recess for storing food.

alambrar vt to fence with wire.

alambre m (de metal) wire; (Amér: brocheta) shish kebab.

alameda f (paseo) tree-lined avenue.

álamo m poplar.

alardear: alardear de v + prep to show off about.

alargar vt (falda, pantalón, etc) to lengthen; (situación) to extend; (acercar) to pass ❏ **alargarse** vpr (en una explicación) to speak at length.

alarma f alarm; **dar la (voz de) ~** to raise the alarm.

alarmante adj alarming.

alarmar vt to alarm ❏ **alarmarse** vpr to be alarmed.

alba f dawn.

albañil m bricklayer.

albarán m delivery note.

albaricoque m apricot.

albatros m inv albatross.

albedrío m: **elija el postre a su ~** choose a dessert of your choice.

alberca f (Amér) swimming pool.

albergar vt (personas) to put up; (odio) to harbour; (esperanza) to cherish ❏ **albergarse** vpr to stay.

albergue m (refugio) shelter; **~ juvenil** youth hostel.

albóndiga f meatball; **~s a la jardinera** meatballs in a tomato sauce with peas and carrots.

albornoz (pl -ces) m bathrobe.

alborotado, -da adj (persona) rash; (cabello) ruffled.

alborotar vi to stir up ✦ vt to be rowdy ❏ **alborotarse** vpr to get worked up.

alboroto m (jaleo) fuss.

albufera f lagoon.

álbum m album; **~ familiar** family album; **~ de fotos** photo album.

alcachofa f (planta) artichoke; (de ducha) shower head; **~s con jamón** artichokes cooked over a low heat with chopped "jamón serrano".

alcaldada f (abuso) abuse of authority.

alcalde, -desa m, f mayor.

alcaldía f (cargo) mayoralty.

alcalino, -na adj alkaline.

alcance m (de misil) range; (repercusión) extent; **a su ~** within your reach; **dar ~ a** to catch up; **fuera del ~ de** out of reach of.

alcanfor m camphor.

alcantarilla f (cloaca) sewer; (boca) drain.

alcanzar vt (autobús, tren) to manage to catch; (persona) to catch up with; (meta, cima, dimensiones) to reach; (suj: disparo) to hit; **~ a** (lograr) to be able to; **~ algo a alguien** to pass sthg to sb □ **alcanzar para** v + prep (ser suficiente para) to be enough for.

alcaparra f caper.

alcayata f hook.

alcázar m fortress.

alcoba f bedroom.

alcohol m alcohol; **sin ~** alcohol-free.

alcohólico, -ca adj & m, f alcoholic.

alcoholismo m alcoholism.

alcoholizado, -da adj alcoholic.

alcoholizarse vpr to become an alcoholic.

alcornoque m cork oak.

aldea f small village.

aldeano, -na m, f villager.

alebestrarse vpr (Amér) (ponerse nervioso) to get worked up; (enojarse) to get annoyed.

alegrar vt (persona) to cheer up; (fiesta) to liven up □ **alegrarse** vpr to be pleased; **~se de** to be pleased about; **~se por** to be pleased for.

alegre adj happy; (local) lively; (color) bright; (fam: borracho) tipsy; (decisión, actitud) reckless.

alegremente adv (con alegría) happily; (sin pensar) recklessly.

alegría f happiness.

alejar vt to move away □ **alejarse** vpr: **~se de** to move away from.

alemán, -ana adj, m, f German.

Alemania s Germany.

alergia f allergy; **tener ~ a** to be allergic to.

alérgico, -ca adj allergic; **ser ~ a** to be allergic to.

alero m (de tejado) eaves (pl).

alerta adv & f alert ◆ interj watch out!; **estar ~** to be on the lookout; **~ roja** red alert.

aleta f (de pez) fin; (de automóvil) wing; (de nariz) flared part □ **aletas** fpl (para nadar) flippers.

alevín m (de pez) fry; (en deportes) beginner.

alfabético, -ca adj alphabetical.

alfabetización f (de personas) literacy.

alfabetizar vt (personas) to teach to read and write; (palabras, letras) to put into alphabetical order.

alfabeto m alphabet.

alfarero, -ra *m, f* potter.

alférez (*pl* -ces) *m* = second lieutenant.

alfil *m* bishop (*in chess*).

alfiler *m* (*aguja*) pin; (*joya*) brooch; ~ **de gancho** (*Amér*) safety pin.

alfombra *f* (*grande*) carpet; (*pequeña*) rug.

alfombrilla *f* (*de coche*) mat; (*felpudo*) doormat; (*de baño*) bath-mat.

alga *f* seaweed.

álgebra *f* algebra.

algo *pron* (*alguna cosa*) something; (*en interrogativas*) anything ♦ *adv* (*un poco*) rather; ~ **de** a little; ¡~ **más?** is that everything?; **por** ~ for some reason.

algodón *m* cotton; **de** ~ cotton; ~ **hidrófilo** cotton wool.

alguien *pron* (*alguna persona*) someone, somebody; (*en interrogativas*) anyone, anybody.

algún → **alguno**.

alguno, -na *adj* (*indeterminado*) some; (*en interrogativas, negativas*) any ♦ *pron* (*alguien*) somebody, some people (*pl*); (*en interrogativas*) anyone, anybody; **no hay mejora alguna** there's no improvement.

alhaja *f* (*joya*) jewel; (*objeto*) treasure.

aliado, -da *adj* allied.

alianza *f* (*pacto*) alliance; (*anillo de boda*) wedding ring; ~ **matrimonial** marriage.

aliarse: aliarse con *v* + *prep* to ally o.s. with.

alicates *mpl* pliers.

aliciente *m* incentive.

aliento *m* (*respiración*) breath; **quedarse sin** ~ to be out of breath; **tener mal** ~ to have bad breath.

aligerar *vt* (*peso*) to lighten; (*paso*) to quicken.

alijo *m* contraband.

alimentación *f* (*acción*) feeding; (*régimen alimenticio*) diet.

alimentar *vt* (*persona, animal*) to feed; (*máquina, motor*) to fuel ♦ *vi* (*nutrir*) to be nourishing ❏ **alimentarse de** *v* + *prep* to live on.

alimenticio, -cia *adj* nourishing.

alimento *m* food.

alinear *vt* to line up ❏ **alinearse** *vpr* (*DEP*) to line up.

aliñar *vt* (*carne*) to season; (*ensalada*) to dress.

aliño *m* (*para carne*) seasoning; (*para ensalada*) dressing.

alioli *m* garlic mayonnaise.

aliviar *vt* (*dolor, enfermedad*) to alleviate; (*trabajo, carga, peso*) to lighten.

alivio *m* relief.

allá *adv* (*de espacio*) over there; (*de tiempo*) back (then); ~ **él** that's his problem; **más** ~ further on; **más** ~ **de** beyond.

allegado, -da *m, f* (*pariente*) relative; (*amigo*) close friend.

allí *adv* (*de lugar*) there; ~ **mismo** right there.

alma *f* soul.

almacén *m* (*para guardar*) warehouse; (*al por mayor*) wholesaler ❏ **almacenes** *mpl* (*comercio grande*) department store (*sg*).

almacenar *vt* (*guardar*) to store; (*acumular*) to collect.

almanaque _m_ almanac.

almejas _fpl_ clams; ~ **a la marinera** clams cooked in a sauce of onion, garlic and white wine.

almendra _f_ almond.

almendrado _m_ round almond paste sweet.

almendro _m_ almond tree.

almíbar _m_ syrup; **en ~** in syrup.

almidón _m_ starch.

almidonado, -da _adj_ starched.

almidonar _vt_ to starch.

almirante _m_ admiral.

almohada _f_ (para dormir) pillow; (para sentarse) cushion.

almohadilla _f_ small cushion.

almorranas _fpl_ piles.

almorzar _vt_ (al mediodía) to have for lunch; (a media mañana) to have for brunch ♦ _vi_ (al mediodía) to have lunch; (a media mañana) to have brunch.

almuerzo _m_ (al mediodía) lunch; (a media mañana) brunch.

aló _interj_ (Amér) hello! (on the telephone).

alocado, -da _adj_ crazy.

alojamiento _m_ accommodation.

alojar _vt_ to put up ◻ **alojarse** _vpr_ (hospedarse) to stay.

alondra _f_ lark.

alpargata _f_ espadrille.

Alpes _mpl_: **los ~** the Alps.

alpinismo _m_ mountaineering.

alpinista _mf_ mountaineer.

alpino, -na _adj_ Alpine.

alpiste _m_ birdseed.

alquilar _vt_ (casa, apartamento, oficina) to rent; (coche, TV, bicicleta)

to hire; "**se alquila**" "to let".

alquiler _m_ (de casa, apartamento, oficina) renting; (de coche, TV, bicicleta) hiring; (precio de casa, etc) rent; (precio de TV) rental; (precio de coche, etc) hire charge; **de ~** (casa, apartamento) rented; **~ de coches** car hire.

alquitrán _m_ tar.

alrededor _adv_: **~ (de)** (en torno a) around; **~ de** (aproximadamente) about ◻ **alrededores** _mpl_: **los ~es** the surrounding areas (sg).

alta _f_ (de enfermedad) (certificate of) discharge; (en una asociación) admission; **dar de ~** to discharge.

altar _m_ altar.

altavoz (pl -ces) _m_ (para anuncios) loudspeaker; (de tocadiscos) speaker.

alteración _f_ (cambio) alteration; (trastorno) agitation.

alterado, -da _adj_ (trastornado) agitated.

alterar _vt_ (cambiar) to alter; (trastornar, excitar) to agitate ◻ **alterarse** _vpr_ (excitarse) to get agitated.

altercado _m_ argument.

alternar _vt_: **~ algo con algo** to alternate sthg with sthg ◻ **alternar con** _v + prep_ (relacionarse con) to mix with.

alternativa _f_ alternative.

alterno, -na _adj_ alternate.

Alteza _f_: **su ~** His/Her Highness.

altibajos _mpl_ (de comportamiento, humor) ups and downs; (de terreno) unevenness (sg).

altillo _m_ (de vivienda) mezzanine; (de armario) small cupboard to use up the space near the ceiling.

altiplano m high plateau.

altitud f (altura) height; (sobre el nivel del mar) altitude.

altivo, -va adj haughty.

alto, -ta adj high; (persona, edificio, árbol) tall ◆ m (interrupción) stop; (lugar elevado) height ◆ adv (hablar) loud; (encontrarse, volar) high ◆ interj halt!; **a altas horas de la noche** in the small hours; **en lo ~ de** at the top of; **mide dos metros de ~** (cosa) it's two metres high; (persona) he's two metres tall.

altoparlante m (Amér) loudspeaker.

altramuz (pl -ces) m (fruto) lupin seed (formerly eaten as snack).

altruismo m altruism.

altruista adj altruistic.

altura f (medida) height; (elevación) altitude; **tiene dos metros de ~** (cosa) it's two metres high; (persona) he's two metres tall; **estar a la ~ de** to match up to □ **alturas** fpl: **me dan miedo las ~s** I'm scared of heights; **a estas ~s** now.

alubias fpl beans.

alucinación f hallucination.

alucinar vi to hallucinate.

alud m avalanche.

aludido, -da adj: **darse por ~** (ofenderse) to take it personally.

aludir: **aludir a** v + prep to refer to.

alumbrado m lighting.

alumbrar vt (iluminar) to light up ◆ vi (parir) to give birth.

aluminio m aluminium.

alumno, -na m, f (de escuela) pupil; (de universidad) student.

alusión f reference; **hacer ~ a** to refer to.

alza f rise; **en ~** (que sube) rising.

alzar vt to raise □ **alzarse** vpr (levantarse) to rise; (sublevarse) to rise up.

a.m. (abrev de ante meridiem) a.m.

amabilidad f kindness.

amable adj kind.

amablemente adv kindly.

amaestrado, -da adj performing.

amaestrar vt to train.

amamantar vt (animal) to suckle; (bebé) to breastfeed.

amanecer m dawn ◆ vi (en un lugar) to wake up ◆ v impers: **amaneció a las siete** dawn broke at seven.

amanerado, -da adj affected.

amansar vt (animal) to tame; (persona) to calm down.

amante mf (querido) lover; **ser ~ de** (aficionado) to be keen on.

amapola f poppy.

amar vt to love.

amargado, -da adj bitter.

amargar vt to make bitter ◆ vi to taste bitter □ **amargarse** vpr (alimento, bebida) to go sour; (persona) to become embittered.

amargo, -ga adj bitter.

amarillear vi to turn yellow.

amarillo, -lla adj & m yellow.

amarrar vt (embarcación) to moor.

amarre m mooring.

amasar vt (pan) to knead; (fortuna) to amass.

amateur (ama'ter) adj & mf amateur.

amazona f horsewoman.

Amazonas m: el ~ the Amazon.

amazónico, -ca adj Amazonian.

ámbar m amber.

ambición f ambition.

ambicioso, -sa adj ambitious.

ambientador m air freshener.

ambiental adj (ecológico) environmental.

ambiente m (aire) air; (medio social, personal) circles (pl); (animación) atmosphere; (Amér: habitación) room.

ambigüedad f ambiguity.

ambiguo, -gua adj ambiguous.

ámbito m confines (pl).

ambos, -bas adj pl both ◆ pron pl both (of them).

ambulancia f ambulance.

ambulante adj travelling.

ambulatorio m state-run surgery.

amén adv amen; **decir ~ (a todo)** to agree (with everything) unquestioningly.

amenaza f threat; ~ **de bomba** bomb scare.

amenazar vt to threaten ◆ v impers: **amenaza lluvia** it's threatening to rain; ~ **a alguien (con o de)** to threaten sb (with).

amenizar vt to liven up.

ameno, -na adj entertaining.

América s America.

americana f jacket.

americanismo m Latin Americanism.

americano, -na adj & m, f American ◆ m (lengua) Latin American Spanish.

ametralladora f machine gun.

ametrallar vt to machinegun.

amígdalas fpl tonsils.

amigo, -ga m, f friend; **ser ~s** to be friends.

amistad f friendship □ **amistades** fpl friends.

amnesia f amnesia.

amnistía f amnesty.

amo, ama m, f (dueño) owner; **ama de casa** housewife; **ama de llaves** housekeeper.

amodorrado, -da adj drowsy.

amoldarse: **amoldarse a** v + prep to adapt to.

amoníaco m ammonia.

amontonar vt to pile up □ **amontonarse** vpr (problemas, deudas) to pile up.

amor m love; **hacer el ~** to make love; ~ **propio** pride □ **amores** mpl love affair (sg).

amordazar vt (persona) to gag; (animal) to muzzle.

amoroso, -sa adj loving.

amortiguador m shock absorber.

amortiguar vt (golpe) to cushion; (ruido) to muffle.

amparar vt to protect □ **ampararse en** v + prep to have recourse to.

amparo *m* protection; **al ~ de** under the protection of.

ampliación *f* (de local) extension; (de capital, negocio) expansion; (de fotografía) enlargement.

ampliar *vt* (estudios, conocimientos) to broaden; (local) to add an extension to; (capital, negocio) to expand; (fotografía) to enlarge.

amplificador *m* amplifier.

amplio, -plia *adj* (avenida, calle) wide; (habitación, coche) spacious; (extenso, vasto) extensive.

amplitud *f* (de avenida, calle) width; (de habitación, coche) spaciousness; (extensión) extent.

ampolla *f* (en la piel) blister; (botella) phial.

amueblado, -da *adj* furnished.

amueblar *vt* to furnish.

amuermarse *vpr* (fam) to get bored.

amuleto *m* amulet.

amurallar *vt* to build a wall around.

analfabetismo *m* illiteracy.

analfabeto, -ta *adj & m, f* illiterate.

analgésico *m* analgesic.

análisis *m inv* (de problema, situación) analysis; (de frase) parsing; **~ (de sangre)** blood test.

analítico, -ca *adj* analytical.

analizar *vt* (problema, situación) to analyse; (frase) to parse.

analogía *f* similarity.

análogo, -ga *adj* similar.

ananás *m inv* (Amér) pineapple.

anaranjado, -da *adj* orange.

anarquía *f* (en política) anarchism; (desorden) anarchy.

anárquico, -ca *adj* anarchic.

anarquista *adj* anarchist.

anatomía *f* anatomy.

anatómico, -ca *adj* anatomical.

anca *f* haunch.

ancho, -cha *adj* wide ◆ *m* width; **tener dos metros de ~** to be two metres wide; **a sus anchas** at ease; **quedarse tan ~** not to bat an eyelid; **venir ~** (prenda de vestir) to be too big.

anchoa *f* anchovy.

anchura *f* width.

anciano, -na *adj* old ◆ *m, f* old man (f old woman).

ancla *f* anchor.

anda *interj* gosh!

Andalucía *s* Andalusia.

andaluz, -za *adj & m, f* Andalusian.

andamio *m* scaffold.

andar *vi* 1. (caminar) to walk.
2. (moverse) to move.
3. (funcionar) to work; **el reloj no anda** the clock has stopped; **las cosas andan mal** things are going badly.
4. (estar) to be; **anda atareado** he is busy; **creo que anda por ahí** I think she's around somewhere; **~ haciendo algo** to be doing sthg.
◆ *vt* (recorrer) to travel.
◆ *m* (de animal, persona) gait.
❑ **andar en** *v + prep* (ocuparse) to be involved in; **andar por** *v + prep*: **anda por los cuarenta** he's about forty; **andarse con** *v + prep*: **~se con cuidado** to be careful; **andares** *mpl* (actitud) gait (sg).

ándele interj (Amér) (vale) all right; (venga) come on!

andén m platform.

Andes mpl: los ~ the Andes.

andinismo m (Amér) mountaineering.

andinista mf (Amér) mountaineer.

andino, -na adj Andean.

anécdota f anecdote.

anecdótico, -ca adj incidental.

anemia f anaemia.

anémico, -ca adj anaemic.

anémona f anemone.

anestesia f anaesthesia.

anestesista mf anaesthetist.

anexo, -xa adj (accesorio) attached ◆ m annexe.

anfetamina f amphetamine.

anfibios mpl amphibians.

anfiteatro m (de teatro) circle; (edificio) amphitheatre.

anfitrión, -ona adj & m, f Anglo-Saxon.

anguila f eel.

angula f elver.

angular adj angular.

ángulo m angle.

angustia f anxiety.

angustiado, -da adj distressed.

angustiarse vpr to get

worried.

angustioso, -sa adj (momentos) anxious; (noticia) distressing.

anhelar vt (ambicionar) to long for.

anhelo m longing.

anidar vi to nest.

anilla f ring □ **anillas** fpl (en gimnasia) rings.

anillo m ring.

ánima m o f soul.

animación f (alegría) liveliness.

animado, -da adj (divertido) lively; ~ a (predispuesto) in the mood for.

animal m animal ◆ adj (bruto, grosero) rough; (exagerado) gross; ~ de compañía pet; ~ doméstico (de granja) domestic animal; (de compañía) pet.

animar vt (alegrar) to cheer up; (alentar) to encourage □ **animarse** vpr (alegrarse) to cheer up; ~se a (decidirse a) to finally decide to.

ánimo m (humor) mood; (valor) courage ◆ interj come on!

aniñado, -da adj childish.

aniquilar vt to annihilate.

anís m (grano) aniseed; (licor) anisette.

aniversario m (de acontecimiento) anniversary; (cumpleaños) birthday.

ano m anus.

anoche adv last night.

anochecer m dusk ◆ v impers to get dark; al ~ at dusk.

anomalía f anomaly.

anómalo, -la adj anomalous.

anonimato m anonimity.

anónimo, -ma adj anonymous ♦ **m** anonymous letter.

anorak *m* anorak.

anorexia *f* anorexia.

anotar *vt* to note down.

ansia *f* (*deseo, anhelo*) yearning; (*inquietud*) anxiousness.

ansiedad *f* (*inquietud*) anxiety.

ansioso, -sa *adj*: ~ **por** impatient for.

Antártico *m*: **el** ~ the Antarctic.

ante *prep* (*en presencia de*) before; (*frente a*) in the face of ♦ **m** (*piel*) suede.

anteanoche *adv* the night before last.

anteayer *adv* the day before yesterday.

antebrazo *m* forearm.

antecedentes *mpl*: **tener** ~ (**penales**) to have a criminal record.

anteceder *vt* to precede.

antecesor, -ra *m, f* predecessor.

antelación *f*: **con** ~ in advance.

antemano: **de antemano** *adv* beforehand.

antena *f* (*de radio, TV*) aerial; (*de animal*) antenna; ~ **parabólica** satellite dish.

anteojos *mpl* (*Amér*) glasses.

antepasados *mpl* ancestors.

antepenúltimo, -ma *adj* last but two.

anterior *adj* (*en espacio*) front; (*en tiempo*) previous.

antes *adv* **1.** (*en el tiempo*) before; ~ **se vivía mejor** life used to be better; ¿**quién llamó** ~? who rang earlier?; **mucho/poco** ~ much/a bit

earlier; **lo** ~ **posible** as soon as possible; ~ **de hacerlo** before doing it; **llegó** ~ **de las nueve** she arrived before nine o'clock.
2. (*en el espacio*) in front; **la farmacia está** ~ the chemist's is in front; ~ **de** o **que** in front of; **la zapatería está** ~ **del cruce** the shoe shop is before the crossroads.
3. (*primero*) first; **yo la vi** ~ I saw her first.
4. (*en locuciones*): **iría a la cárcel** ~ **que mentir** I'd rather go to prison than lie; ~ (**de**) **que** (*prioridad en el tiempo*) before; ~ **de nada** first of all.
♦ *adj* previous; **llegó el día** ~ she arrived on the previous day.

antesala *f* waiting room.

antiabortista *mf* antiabortionist.

antiarrugas *m inv* anti-wrinkle cream.

antibiótico *m* antibiotic.

anticiclón *m* anticyclone.

anticipado, -da *adj* (*prematuro*) early; (*pago*) advance.

anticipar *vt* (*noticias*) to tell in advance; (*pagos*) to pay in advance ❑ **anticiparse** *vpr*: ~**se a alguien** to beat sb to it.

anticipo *m* (*de dinero*) advance.

anticoncepción *f* contraception.

anticonceptivo *m* contraceptive.

anticuado, -da *adj* old-fashioned.

anticuario *m* antique dealer.

anticuerpo *m* antibody.

antidepresivo *m* antidepressant.

antier adv (Amér: fam) the day before yesterday.

antifaz (pl -ces) m mask.

antiguamente adv formerly.

antigüedad f (en el trabajo) seniority; (época): en la ~ in the past ❑ **antigüedades** fpl (muebles, objetos) antiques.

antiguo, -gua adj (viejo) old; (inmemorial) ancient; (pasado de moda) old-fashioned; (anterior) former.

antihistamínico m antihistamine.

antiinflamatorio m anti-inflammatory drug.

Antillas s: las ~ the West Indies.

antílope m antelope.

antipatía f dislike.

antipático, -ca adj unpleasant.

antirrobo adj antitheft ◆ m (en coche) antitheft device; (en edificio) burglar alarm.

antiséptico m antiseptic.

antitérmico m antipyretic.

antojitos mpl (Amér) Mexican dishes such as tacos served as snacks.

antojo m (capricho) whim; **tener ~ de** to have a craving for.

antología f anthology.

antónimo m antonym.

antorcha f torch.

antro m (despec) dump.

anual adj annual.

anuario m yearbook.

anulado, -da adj (espectáculo) cancelled; (tarjeta, billete, etc) void; (gol) disallowed.

anular m ring finger ◆ vt (espectáculo) to cancel; (partido) to call off; (tarjeta, billete) to validate; (gol) to disallow; (personalidad) to repress.

anunciar vt to announce; (en publicidad) to advertise.

anuncio m (notificación) announcement; (en publicidad) advert; (presagio, señal) sign.

anzuelo m (fish) hook.

añadidura f addition; **por ~** what is more.

añadir vt to add.

añicos mpl: **hacerse ~** to shatter.

año m year; **hace ~s** years ago; **¿cuántos ~s tienes?** how old are you?; **tengo 17 ~s** I'm 17 years old); **~ nuevo** New Year; **los ~s 50** the fifties.

añoranza f (del pasado) nostalgia; (del hogar) homesickness.

añorar vt to miss.

aorta f aorta.

apache adj & mf Apache.

apacible adj (persona, carácter) gentle; (lugar) pleasant; (tiempo) mild.

apadrinar vt (en bautizo) to act as godparent to; (proteger, ayudar) to sponsor.

apagado, -da adj (luz, fuego) out; (aparato) off; (persona, color) subdued; (sonido) muffled.

apagar vt (luz, lámpara, televisión, etc) to turn off; (fuego) to put out; (fuerzas) to sap ❑ **apagarse** vpr (morirse) to pass away.

apagón m power cut.

apaisado, -da adj oblong.

apalabrar vt to make a verbal

agreement regarding.

apalancado, -da *adj* comfortably installed.

apañado, -da *adj* clever.

apañarse *vpr* to manage; **apañárselas** to manage.

apapachado, -da *adj (Amér)* pampered.

apapachar *vt (Amér)* to stroke fawningly.

aparador *m* sideboard.

aparato *m (máquina)* machine; *(de radio, televisión)* set; *(dispositivo)* device; *(electrodoméstico)* appliance; *(avión)* plane; *(digestivo, circulatorio, etc)* system; *(ostentación)* ostentation.

aparcamiento *m (lugar)* car park; *(hueco)* parking place; *(de un vehículo)* parking; "**~ público**" "car park".

aparcar *vt (vehículo)* to park; *(problema, decisión, etc)* to leave to one side; "**no ~**" "no parking"; "**~ en batería**" *sign indicating that cars must park at right angles to the pavement.*

aparecer *vi (de forma repentina)* to appear; *(lo perdido)* to turn up; *(publicación)* to come out.

aparejador, -ra *m, f* quantity surveyor.

aparejar *vt (embarcación)* to rig.

aparejo *m (de embarcación)* rigging.

aparentar *vt (fingir)* to feign; *(edad)* to look.

aparente *adj (fingido)* apparent; *(vistoso)* showy.

aparición *f* appearance; *(de lo sobrenatural)* apparition.

apariencia *f* appearance; **en ~** outwardly; **guardar las ~s** to keep up appearances.

apartado, -da *adj (lejano)* remote; *(separado)* separated ◆ *m* paragraph; **~ de correos** P.O. Box.

apartamento *m* apartment; "**~s de alquiler**" "apartments (to let)".

apartar *vt (separar)* to separate; *(quitar)* to remove; *(quitar de en medio)* to move out of the way; *(disuadir)* to dissuade ❏ **apartarse** *vpr (retirarse)* to move out of the way; **~se de (alejarse de)** to move away from.

aparte *adv (en otro lugar)* to one side; *(separadamente)* separately; *(además)* besides ◆ *adj (privado)* private; *(diferente)* separate; **~ de (además de)** besides; *(excepto)* apart from.

aparthotel *m* holiday apartments *(pl)*.

apasionado, -da *adj* passionate; **~ por (aficionado)** mad about.

apasionante *adj* fascinating.

apasionar *vi*: **le apasiona el teatro** he loves the theatre ❏ **apasionarse** *vpr (excitarse)* to get excited; **apasionarse por** *v + prep (ser aficionado a)* to love.

apdo. *(abrev de apartado)* P.O. Box.

apechugar *vi*: **~ con (fam)** to put up with.

apego *m*: **tener ~ a** to be fond of.

apellidarse *vpr*: **se apellida Gómez** her surname is Gómez.

apellido *m* surname.

apenado, -da *adj (Amér)* embarrassed.

apenar vt to sadden.

apenas adv hardly; (escasamente) only; (tan pronto como) as soon as.

apéndice m appendix.

apendicitis f inv appendicitis.

aperitivo m (bebida) aperitif; (comida) appetizer.

APERITIVO

Before their main midday meal, Spanish people often go to a bar, where they sit outside and have a glass of vermouth, wine or some other drink and some "tapas", to whet their appetite. It is also common for them to have an aperitif at home, whilst finishing the cooking.

apertura f (inauguración) opening.

apestar vi to stink.

apetecer vi: ¿te apetece un café? do you fancy a coffee?

apetecible adj appetizing.

apetito m appetite; **abrir el ~ to** whet one's appetite; **tener ~ to** feel hungry.

apetitoso, -sa adj appetizing.

apicultura f beekeeping.

apiñado, -da adj packed.

apiñarse vpr to crowd together.

apio m celery.

apisonadora f steamroller.

aplanar vt to level.

aplastar vt (chafar) to flatten.

aplaudir vt & vi to applaud.

aplauso m round of applause;

~s applause (sg).

aplazar vt to postpone.

aplicación f application.

aplicado, -da adj (alumno, estudiante) diligent; (ciencia, estudio) applied.

aplicar vt to apply □ **aplicarse** vpr: ~se en to apply o.s. to.

aplique m wall lamp.

aplomo m composure.

apoderarse: apoderarse de v + prep to seize.

apodo m nickname.

apogeo m height; **estar en su ~ to** be at its height.

aportación f contribution.

aportar vt to contribute.

aposta adv on purpose.

apostar vt & vi to bet □ **apostar por** v + prep to bet on.

apóstol m apostle.

apóstrofo m apostrophe.

apoyar vt (animar) to support; (fundamentar) to base; (respaldar) to lean □ **apoyarse** vpr (arrimarse): ~se (en) to lean (on). •

apoyo m support.

apreciable adj (perceptible) appreciable; (estimable) worthy.

apreciación f appreciation.

apreciado, -da adj (estimado) esteemed.

apreciar vt (sentir afecto por) to think highly of; (valorar) to appreciate; (percibir) to make out.

aprecio m esteem.

apremiar vt (dar prisa) to urge ♦ vi (tiempo) to be short.

aprender vt to learn ♦ vi: ~ a to learn to.

aprendiz (*pl* -ces) *m* apprentice.

aprendizaje *m* (*proceso*) learning.

aprensión *f* (*miedo*) apprehension; (*escrúpulo*) squeamishness.

aprensivo, -va *adj* (*miedoso*) apprehensive; (*escrupuloso*) squeamish; (*hipocondríaco*) hypochondriac.

apresurado, -da *adj* hurried.

apresurarse *vpr* to hurry; **~ a** to hurry to.

apretado, -da *adj* (*cinturón, ropa, etc*) tight; (*victoria, triunfo*) narrow; (*agenda*) full.

apretar *vt* (*presionar*) to press; (*gatillo*) to pull; (*ajustar*) to tighten; (*ceñir*) to be too tight for; (*en los brazos*) to squeeze ◆ *vi* (*calor, hambre*) to intensify □ **apretarse** *vpr* (*apiñarse*) to crowd together; **~se el cinturón** to tighten one's belt.

apretujar *vt* (*fam*) to squash □ **apretujarse** *vpr* to squeeze together.

aprisa *adv* quickly.

aprobado *m* pass.

aprobar *vt* (*asignatura, examen, ley*) to pass; (*actitud, comportamiento*) to approve of.

apropiado, -da *adj* suitable.

apropiarse: apropiarse de *v* + *prep* (*adueñarse de*) to appropriate.

aprovechado, -da *adj* (*tiempo*) well-spent; (*espacio*) well-planned.

aprovechar *vt* (*ocasión, oferta*) to take advantage of; (*tiempo, espacio*) to make use of; (*lo inservible*) to put to good use ◆ *vi*: **¡que**

aproveche! enjoy your meal! □ **aprovecharse de** *v* + *prep* to take advantage of.

aproximación *f* (*acercamiento*) approach; (*en cálculo*) approximation.

aproximadamente *adv* approximately.

aproximar *vt* to move closer □ **aproximarse** *vpr*: **~se a** to come closer to.

apto, -ta *adj*: **~ para** (*capacitado*) capable of; **~ para menores** suitable for children; **no ~ para menores** unsuitable for children.

apuesta *f* bet.

apuesto, -ta *adj* dashing.

apunarse *vpr* (*Amér*) to get altitude sickness.

apuntador, -ra *m, f* prompter.

apuntar *vt* (*escribir*) to note down; (*inscribir*) to put down; (*arma*) to aim; (*con el dedo*) to point at □ **apuntarse** *vpr* (*inscribirse*) to put one's name down; **apuntarse a** *v* + *prep* (*participar en*) to join in with.

apunte *m* (*nota*) note; (*boceto*) sketch □ **apuntes** *mpl* notes; **tomar ~s** to take notes.

apuñalar *vt* to stab.

apurar *vt* (*agotar*) to finish off; (*preocupar*) to trouble □ **apurarse** *vpr* (*darse prisa*) to hurry; **~se por** to worry about.

apuro *m* (*dificultad*) fix; (*escasez económica*) hardship; **me da ~ (hacerlo)** I'm embarrassed (to do it); **estar en ~s** to be in a tight spot.

aquel, aquella *adj* that.

aquél, aquélla *pron* (*lejano en*

el espacio) that one; *(lejano en el tiempo)* that; ~ **que** anyone who.

aquello *pron neutro* that; ~ **de su mujer es mentira** all that about his wife is a lie.

aquellos, -llas *adj pl* those.

aquéllos, -llas *pron pl* those.

aquí *adv (en este lugar)* here; *(ahora)* now; ~ **arriba** up here; ~ **dentro** in here.

árabe *adj & mf* Arab ◆ *m (lengua)* Arabic.

Arabia Saudí *s* Saudi Arabia.

arado *m* plough.

arandela *f* washer.

araña *f* spider.

arañar *vt* to scratch.

arañazo *m* scratch.

arar *vt* to plough.

arbitrar *vt (partido)* to referee; *(discusión)* to arbitrate.

árbitro *m* referee.

árbol *m* tree; ~ **de Navidad** Christmas tree.

arbusto *m* bush.

arca *f (cofre)* chest.

arcada *f* arcade ◻ **arcadas** *fpl (náuseas)* retching *(sg)*.

arcaico, -ca *adj* archaic.

arcángel *m* archangel.

arcén *m (en carretera)* verge; *(de autopista)* hard shoulder.

archipiélago *m* archipelago.

archivador *m* filing cabinet.

archivar *vt* to file.

archivo *m (lugar)* archive; *(documentos)* archives *(pl)*.

arcilla *f* clay.

arcilloso, -sa *adj* clayey.

arco *m (de flechas)* bow; *(en arqui-*

tectura) arch; *(en geometría)* arc; *(Amér: en deporte)* goal; ~ **iris** rainbow; ~ **de triunfo** triumphal arch.

arder *vi* to burn; **está que arde** *(fam)* he's fuming.

ardiente *adj (que arde)* burning; *(líquido)* scalding; *(apasionado)* ardent.

ardilla *f* squirrel.

área *f* area; "~ **de descanso**" "rest area"; "~ **de recreo**" ≈ "picnic area".

arena *f* sand; ~**s movedizas** quicksand.

arenoso, -sa *adj* sandy.

arenque *m* herring.

aretes *mpl (Amér)* earrings.

Argelia *s* Algeria.

Argentina *s* Argentina.

argentino, -na *adj & m, f* Argentinian.

argolla *f (Amér: fam)* ring.

argot *m (popular)* slang; *(técnico)* jargon.

argumentar *vt (alegar)* to allege.

argumento *m (razón)* reason; *(de novela, película, etc)* plot.

aria *f* aria.

árido, -da *adj* dry.

Aries *m* Aries.

arista *f* edge.

aristocracia *f* aristocracy.

aristócrata *mf* aristocrat.

aritmética *f* arithmetic.

arlequín *m* harlequin.

arma *f* weapon; **ser de ~s tomar** *(tener mal carácter)* to be a nasty piece of work.

armada *f (fuerzas navales)* navy.

armadillo *m* armadillo.

armadura *f (coraza)* armour.

armamento *m (armas)* arms *(pl)*.

armar *vt (ejército)* to arm; *(pistola, fusil)* to load; *(mueble)* to assemble; *(tienda)* to pitch; *(alboroto, ruido)* to make ◆ **armarse** *vpr* to arm o.s.; **armarse de** v + prep *(valor, paciencia)* to summon up.

armario *m (de cajones)* cupboard; *(ropero)* wardrobe; **~ empotrado** fitted cupboard/wardrobe.

armazón *f (de cama, tienda de campaña)* frame; *(de coche)* chassis.

armisticio *m* armistice.

armonía *f* harmony.

armónica *f* harmonica.

armonizar *vt* to match.

aro *m (anilla)* ring; *(juguete)* hoop.

aroma *m (olor)* aroma; *(de vino)* bouquet; **~ artificial** artificial flavouring.

arpa *f* harp.

arqueología *f* archeology.

arqueólogo, -ga *m, f* archeologist.

arquero *m (Amér)* goalkeeper.

arquitecto, -ta *m, f* architect.

arquitectónico, -ca *adj* architectural.

arquitectura *f* architecture.

arraigar *vi* to take root.

arrancar *vt (del suelo)* to pull up; *(motor)* to start; *(de las manos)* to snatch ◆ *vi (iniciar la marcha)* to set off; *(vehículo)* to start up; **~ de** to stem from.

arranque *m (ímpetu)* drive; *(de ira, pasión)* fit.

arrastrar *vt (por el suelo)* to drag; *(convencer)* to win over ❏

arrastrarse *vpr (reptar)* to crawl; *(humillarse)* to grovel.

arrastre *m* dragging; **estar para el ~** to have had it.

arrebatar *vt* to snatch.

arrebato *m (de ira, pasión)* outburst.

arreglar *vt (ordenar)* to tidy up; *(reparar)* to repair; *(cita)* to do up ❏ **arreglarse** *vpr (embellecerse)* to smarten up; *(solucionarse)* to sort itself out; **arreglárselas** to manage.

arreglo *m (reparación)* repair; *(de ropa)* mending; *(acuerdo)* agreement.

arrendatario, -ria *m, f* tenant.

arreos *mpl* harness *(sg)*.

arrepentirse: arrepentirse de v + prep to regret.

arrestar *vt* to arrest.

arriba *adv (de situación)* above; *(de dirección)* up; *(en edificio)* upstairs; **allí ~** up there; **aquí ~** up here; **más ~** further up; **para ~** upwards; **de ~** *(piso)* upstairs; **de ~ abajo** *(detenidamente)* from top to bottom; *(con desdén)* up and down.

arriesgado, -da *adj* risky.

arriesgar *vt* to risk ❏ **arriesgarse** *vpr* **~se a** to dare to.

arrimar *vt* to move closer; **~ el hombro** to lend a hand ❏ **arrimarse** *vpr:* **~se a** to move closer to.

arrodillarse *vpr* to kneel down.

arrogancia *f* arrogance.

arrogante *adj* arrogant.

arrojar *vt (lanzar)* to hurl; *(vomi-*

tar) to throw up; **~ a alguien de** *(echar)* to throw sb out of ❑ **arrojarse** *vpr (al vacío)* to hurl o.s.; *(sobre una persona)* to leap.

arroyo *m* stream.

arroz *m* rice; **~ blanco** boiled rice (with garlic); **~ a la cazuela** dish similar to paella, but cooked in a pot; **~ chaufa** *(Amér)* chop suey; **~ a la cubana** boiled rice with fried egg, tomatoes and fried banana; **~ con leche** rice pudding; **~ negro** rice cooked with squid ink.

arruga *f (en piel)* wrinkle; *(en tejido)* crease.

arrugado, -da *adj (piel)* wrinkled; *(tejido, papel)* creased.

arrugar *vt* to crease ❑ **arrugarse** *vpr* to get creased.

arruinar *vt* to ruin ❑ **arruinarse** *vpr* to be ruined.

arsénico *m* arsenic.

arte *m o f* art; **tener ~ para** to be good at; **con malas ~s** using trickery; **por ~ de magia** as if by magic ❑ **artes** *fpl* arts.

artefacto *m* device.

arteria *f* artery.

artesanal *adj* handmade.

artesanía *f* craftsmanship; **de ~** handmade.

artesano, -na *m, f* craftsman *(f* craftswoman).

ártico, -a *adj* arctic ◆ **Ártico** *m*: **el Ártico** the Arctic.

articulación *f* joint; *(de sonidos)* articulation.

articulado, -da *adj* articulated.

articular *vt* to articulate.

articulista *mf* journalist.

artículo *m* article; *(producto)* product; **~s de consumo** consumer goods; **~s de lujo** luxury goods.

artificial *adj* artificial.

artificio *m (dispositivo)* device; *(habilidades)* trick.

artista *mf* artist; *(de espectáculo)* artiste.

artístico, -ca *adj* artistic.

arveja *f (Amér)* pea.

arzobispo *m* archbishop.

as *m* ace.

asa *f* handle.

asado, -da *adj & m* roast; **carne asada** *(al horno)* roast meat; *(a la parrilla)* grilled meat; **pimientos ~s** baked peppers.

asador *m* roaster.

asalariado, -da *adj* salaried ◆ *m, f* wage earner.

asaltar *vt (robar)* to rob; *(agredir)* to attack.

asalto *m (a banco, tienda, persona)* robbery; *(en boxeo, judo, etc)* round.

asamblea *f (de una asociación)* assembly; *(en política)* mass meeting.

asar *vt (al horno)* to roast; *(a la parrilla)* to grill ❑ **asarse** *vpr* to be boiling hot.

ascendencia *f (antepasados)* ancestors *(pl)*.

ascendente *adj* ascending.

ascender *vt (empleado)* to promote ◆ *vi (subir)* to rise ❑ **ascender a** *v + prep (suj: cantidad)* to come to.

ascendiente *mf* ancestor.

ascenso *m (de sueldo)* rise *(Br)*, raise *(Am)*; *(de posición)* promotion.

ascensor *m* lift *(Br)*, elevator *(Am)*.

asco *m* revulsion; **ser un ~** to be awful; **me da ~** I find it disgusting; **¡qué asco!** how disgusting!; **estar hecho un ~** (*fam*) to be filthy.

ascua *f* ember; **estar en ~s** to be on tenterhooks.

aseado, -da *adj* clean.

asear *vt* to clean ❑ **asearse** *vpr* to get washed and dressed.

asegurado, -da *adj* insured ◆ *m, f* policy-holder.

asegurar *vt* (*coche, vivienda*) to insure; (*cuerda, nudo*) to secure; (*prometer*) to assure ❑ **asegurarse de** *v* + *prep* to make sure that.

asentir *vi* to agree.

aseo *m* (*limpieza*) cleaning; (*habitación*) bathroom; "**~s**" "toilets".

aséptico -ca *adj* aseptic.

asequible *adj* (*precio, producto*) affordable.

asesinar *vt* to murder.

asesinato *m* murder.

asesino, -na *m, f* murderer.

asesor, -ra *adj* advisory ◆ *m, f* consultant.

asesorar *vt* to advise ❑ **asesorarse** *vpr* to seek advice.

asesoría *f* consultant's office.

asfaltado, -da *adj* tarmacked ◆ *m* road surface.

asfaltar *vt* to surface.

asfalto *m* asphalt.

asfixia *f* suffocation.

asfixiante *adj* (*olor*) overpowering; (*calor*) suffocating.

asfixiar *vt* to suffocate ❑ **asfixiarse** *vpr* to suffocate.

así *adv & adj inv* like this; **~ de**

grande this big; **~ como** just as; **~ es** that's right; **~ es como** that is how; **~ y todo** even so; **y ~ sucedió** and that is exactly what happened.

Asia *s* Asia.

asiático, -ca *adj & m, f* Asian.

asiento *m* seat.

asignatura *f* subject.

asilado, -da *adj* living in a home.

asilo *m* (*para ancianos*) old people's home; **~ político** political asylum.

asimilación *f* assimilation.

asimilar *vt* (*conocimientos*) to assimilate; (*cambio, situación*) to take in one's stride.

asistencia *f* (*a clase, espectáculo*) attendance; (*ayuda*) assistance; (*público*) audience.

asistir *vt* (*suj: médico, enfermera*) to attend to ❑ **asistir a** *v* + *prep* (*clase, espectáculo*) to attend.

asma *f* asthma.

asmático, -ca *adj* asthmatic.

asno, -na *m, f* ass.

asociación *f* association.

asociar *vt* to associate ❑ **asociarse** *v* + *prep* to become a member of; **asociarse con** *v* + *prep* to form a partnership with.

asolar *vt* to devastate.

asomar *vi* to peep up ◆ *vt* to stick out ❑ **asomarse** *vpr*: **~se a** (*ventana*) to stick one's head out of; (*balcón*) to go out onto.

asombrar *vt* (*causar admiración*) to amaze; (*sorprender*) to surprise ❑ **asombrarse de** *v* + *prep* (*sentir admiración*) to be amazed at; (*sor-*

prenderse) to be surprised at.

asombro *m (admiración)* amazement; *(sorpresa)* surprise.

asorocharse *vpr (Amér)* to get altitude sickness.

aspa *f (de molino de viento)* arms *(pl)*.

aspecto *m (apariencia)* appearance; **tener buen/mal ~** *(persona)* to look well/awful; *(cosa)* to look nice/horrible.

aspereza *f* roughness.

áspero, -ra *adj (al tacto)* rough; *(voz)* harsh.

aspiradora *f* vacuum cleaner.

aspirar *vt (aire)* to breathe in ❑ **aspirar a** *v + prep* to aspire to.

aspirina® *f* aspirin.

asqueado, -da *adj* disgusted.

asquerosidad *f* filthiness.

asqueroso, -sa *adj* filthy.

asta *f (de lanza)* shaft; *(de bandera)* flagpole; *(de toro)* horn; *(de ciervo)* antler.

asterisco *m* asterisk.

astillero *m* shipyard.

astro *m* star.

astrología *f* astrology.

astrólogo, -ga *m, f* astrologer.

astronauta *mf* astronaut.

astronomía *f* astronomy.

astronómico, -ca *adj* astronomical.

astrónomo, -ma *m, f* astronomer.

astuto, -ta *adj (sagaz)* astute; *(ladino)* cunning.

asumir *vt (problema)* to cope with; *(responsabilidad)* to assume.

asunto *m (tema general)* subject;

(tema específico) matter; *(problema)* issue; *(negocio)* affair.

asustar *vt* to frighten ❑ **asustarse** *vpr* to be frightened.

atacar *vt* to attack.

atajo *m (camino)* short cut; *(despec: grupo de personas)* bunch; **un ~ de** a string of.

ataque *m (agresión)* attack; *(de ira, risa, etc)* fit; *(de fiebre, tos, etc)* bout; **~ al corazón** heart attack.

atar *vt (con cuerda, cadena, etc)* to tie; *(ceñir)* to tie up.

atardecer *m*: **al ~** at dusk.

atareado, -da *adj* busy.

atasco *m (de tráfico)* traffic jam.

ataúd *m* coffin.

ate *m (Amér)* quince jelly.

ateísmo *m* atheism.

atención *f (interés)* attention; *(regalo, obsequio)* kind gesture; **~ al cliente** customer service; **llamar la ~ to** be noticeable ❑ **atenciones** *fpl (cuidados)* attentiveness *(sg)*.

atender *vt (solicitud, petición, negocio)* to attend to; *(clientes)* to serve; *(enfermo)* to look after ♦ *vi (escuchar)* to pay attention; **¿le atienden?** are you being served?

atentado *m* attempt *(on sb's life)*.

atentamente *adv (en cartas)* Yours sincerely.

atento, -ta *adj (con atención)* attentive; *(amable)* considerate.

ateo, -a *m, f* atheist.

aterrizaje *m* landing; **~ forzoso** emergency landing.

aterrizar *vi* to land.

aterrorizar *vt* to terrify.

atestado, -da *adj* packed.

atestiguar vt to testify to.

ático m penthouse.

atinar vi to guess correctly.

atípico, -ca adj atypical.

Atlántico m: el ~ the Atlantic.

atlas m inv atlas.

atleta mf athlete.

atlético, -ca adj athletic.

atletismo m athletics.

atmósfera f atmosphere.

atmosférico, -ca adj atmospheric.

atole m (Amér) thick drink of maize flour boiled in milk or water.

atolondrarse vpr to get flustered.

atómico, -ca adj nuclear.

átomo m atom.

atónito, -ta adj astonished.

atontado, -da adj dazed.

atorado, -da adj (Amér) (atascado) blocked; (agitado, nervioso) nervous.

atorar vt to block □ **atorarse** vpr (Amér) (atascarse) to get blocked; (atragantarse) to choke.

atracador, -ra m, f (de banco, tienda) armed robber; (de persona) mugger.

atracar vt (banco, tienda) to rob; (persona) to mug ◆ vi (barco) to dock □ **atracarse de** v + prep to eat one's fill of.

atracción f attraction □ **atracciones** fpl fairground attractions.

atraco m robbery.

atractivo, -va adj attractive ◆ m (de trabajo, lugar) attraction; (de persona) attractiveness.

atraer vt to attract ◆ vi to be attractive.

atragantarse vpr to choke.

atrapar vt to catch.

atrás adv (de posición) behind; (al moverse) backwards; (de tiempo) before.

atrasado, -da adj (reloj, tarea, proyecto) delayed; (pago) overdue; (en estudios) backward; ir ~ (reloj) to be slow.

atrasar vt (llegada, salida) to delay; (proyecto, cita, acontecimiento) to postpone; (reloj) to put back ◆ vi (reloj) to be slow □ **atrasarse** vpr (persona) to be late; (tren, avión, etc) to be delayed; (proyecto, acontecimiento) to be postponed.

atraso m (de evolución) backwardness □ **atrasos** mpl (de dinero) arrears.

atravesar vt (calle, río, puente) to cross; (situación difícil, crisis) to go through; (objeto, madero, etc) to penetrate □ **atravesarse** vpr to be in the way.

atreverse vpr: ~ a to dare to.

atrevido, -da adj (osado) daring; (insolente) cheeky; (ropa, libro) risqué; (propuesta) forward.

atribución f (de poder, trabajo) responsibility.

atribuir vt to attribute; (poder, cargo) to give.

atributo m attribute.

atrio m (de palacio) portico; (de convento) cloister.

atropellar vt (suj: vehículo) to run over; (con empujones) to push out of the way □ **atropellarse** vpr (hablando) to trip over one's words.

atropello m running over.

ATS mf (abrev de Ayudante Técnico Sanitario) qualified nurse.

atte abrev = **atentamente**.

atún m tuna; ~ **en aceite** tuna in oil.

audaz (pl -ces) adj daring.

audiencia f audience.

audiovisual adj audiovisual ♦ m audiovisual display.

auditivo, -va adj ear (antes de s).

auditor m auditor.

auditoría f (trabajo) auditing; (lugar) auditor's office.

auditorio m (público) audience; (local) auditorium.

auge m boom; **en ~** booming.

aula f (de universidad) lecture room; (de escuela) classroom.

aullar vi to howl.

aullido m howl.

aumentar vt to increase; (peso) to put on.

aumento m increase; (en óptica) magnification.

aun adv even ♦ conj: ~ **estando enferma, vino** she came, even though she was ill; ~ **así** even so.

aún adv still; ~ **no han venido** they haven't come yet.

aunque conj although.

aureola f (de santo) halo; (fama, éxito) aura.

auricular m (de teléfono) receiver ❑ **auriculares** mpl (de radio, casete) headphones.

ausencia f absence.

ausente adj (de lugar) absent; (distraído) absent-minded.

austeridad f austerity.

austero, -ra adj austere.

Australia s Australia.

australiano, -na adj & m, f Australian.

Austria s Austria.

austríaco, -ca adj & m, f Austrian.

autenticidad f authenticity.

auténtico, -ca adj (joya, piel) genuine; (verdadero, real) real.

auto m (automóvil) car.

autobiografía f autobiography.

autobús m bus.

autocar m coach; ~ **de línea** (long-distance) coach.

autocontrol m self-control.

autóctono, -na adj indigenous.

autoescuela f driving school.

autógrafo m autograph.

automáticamente adv automatically.

automático, -ca adj automatic.

automóvil m car.

automovilismo m motoring.

automovilista mf motorist.

autonomía f autonomy; ~ **de vuelo** range.

autonómico, -ca adj (región, gobierno) autonomous; (ley) devolution.

autónomo, -ma adj (independiente) autonomous; (trabajador) freelance.

autopista f motorway; ~ **de peaje** toll motorway (Br), turnpike (Am).

autopsia f autopsy.

autor, -ra m, f (de libro) author; (de cuadro, escultura) artist; (de acción, hecho) perpetrator.

autoridad f authority; **la ~ the** authorities (pl).

autoritario, -ria adj authoritarian.

autorización f authorization.

autorizado, -da adj authorized.

autorizar vt to authorize.

autorretrato m self-portrait.

autoservicio m self-service.

autostop m hitch-hiking; **hacer ~** to hitch-hike.

autostopista mf hitch-hiker.

autosuficiente adj selfsufficient.

autovía f dual carriageway (Br), divided road (Am).

auxiliar adj auxiliary ♦ mf assistant ♦ vt to assist; **~ administrativo** office clerk; **~ de vuelo** flight attendant.

auxilio m help ♦ interj help!; **primeros ~s** first aid (sg).

aval m (persona) guarantor; (documento) guarantee.

avalador, -ra m, f guarantor.

avalancha f avalanche.

avalar vt (crédito) to guarantee; (propuesta, idea) to endorse.

avance m (de tecnología, ciencia, etc) advance; (de noticia) summary; (de película) preview.

avanzado, -da adj advanced.

avanzar vi to advance.

avaricioso, -sa adj avaricious.

avaro, -ra adj miserly.

avda (abrev de avenida) Ave.

AVE m (abrev de Alta Velocidad Española) Spanish high-speed train.

ave f bird.

avellana f hazelnut.

avellano m hazel tree.

avena f oats (pl).

avenida f avenue.

aventar vt (Amér) to throw.

aventón m (Amér) shove; **dar un ~ a alguien** to give sb a lift.

aventura f adventure; (de amor) affair.

aventurar vpr: **~ a hacer algo** to risk doing sthg.

aventurero, -ra adj adventurous ♦ m, f adventurer (f adventuress).

avergonzado, -da adj (abochornado) embarrassed; (deshonrado) ashamed.

avergonzarse: avergonzarse de v + prep (por timidez) to be embarrassed about; (por deshonra) to be ashamed of.

avería f (de coche) breakdown; (de máquina) fault.

averiado, -da adj (coche) broken-down; (máquina) out of order.

averiarse vpr to break down.

averiguar vt to find out.

aversión f aversion.

avestruz (pl -ces) m ostrich.

aviación f (navegación) aviation; (cuerpo militar) airforce.

AVIACO f charter flight division of Iberia, the Spanish state airline.

aviador, -ra m, f aviator.

avión m plane; **en ~** by plane; **por ~** (carta) airmail.

avioneta f light aircraft.

avisar vt (llamar) to call ❑ **avisar de** v + prep (comunicar) to inform of; (prevenir) to warn of.

aviso m (noticia) notice; (advertencia) warning; (en aeropuerto) call; **hasta nuevo ~** until further notice; **sin previo ~** without notice.

avispa f wasp.

avituallarse vpr to get provisions.

axila f armpit.

ay interj (expresa dolor) ouch!; (expresa pena) oh!

ayer adv yesterday; **~ noche** last night; **~ por la mañana** yesterday morning.

ayuda f (en trabajo, tarea, etc) help; (a otros países, etc) aid.

ayudante mf assistant.

ayudar vt: **~ a alguien a** to help sb to; **~ a alguien en** to help sb with.

ayunar vi to fast.

ayuntamiento m (edificio) town hall; (corporación) town council.

azada f hoe.

azafata f air hostess; **~ de vuelo** air hostess.

azafrán m (condimento) saffron.

azar m chance; **al ~** at random.

azotea f terraced roof.

azúcar m o f sugar; **~ glass** icing sugar; **~ moreno** brown sugar.

azucarado, -da adj sweet.

azucarera f sugar bowl.

azucena f white lily.

azufre m sulphur.

azul adj & m blue; **~ marino** navy (blue).

azulado, -da adj bluish.

azulejo m (glazed) tile.

azuloso, -sa adj (Amér) bluish.

B

baba f saliva.

babero m bib.

babor m port.

babosa f slug.

baboso, -sa adj (caracol) slimy; (bebé) dribbling; (fam: infantil) wet behind the ears; (Amér: tonto) stupid.

baca f roof rack.

bacalao m cod; **~ a la llauna** dish of salt cod cooked in a metal pan with garlic, parsley, tomato, oil and salt; **~ al pil-pil** Basque dish of salt cod cooked slowly in an earthenware dish with olive oil and garlic; **~ con sanfaina** Catalan dish of salt cod in a ratatouille sauce; **~ a la vizcaína** Basque dish of salt cod baked with a thick sauce of olive oil, garlic, paprika, onions, tomato and red peppers.

bacán adj (Amér) elegant ♦ m (Amér) dandy.

bachillerato m (former) course of secondary studies for academically orientated 14 to 16-year-olds.

bacinica f (Amér) chamber pot.

bádminton m badminton.

bafle m loudspeaker.

bahía f bay.

bailar vt & vi to dance; **el pie me baila en el zapato** my shoe is too big for me.

bailarín, -ina m, f. (de ballet) ballet dancer; (de otras danzas) dancer.

baile m (danza) dance; (fiesta) ball.

baja f (por enfermedad) sick leave; **dar de ~** (en empresa) to lay off; (en asociación, club) to expel; **darse de ~** to resign; **estar de ~** to be on sick leave.

bajada f descent; **~ de bandera** minimum fare.

bajar vt (lámpara, cuadro, etc) to take down; (cabeza, mano, voz, persiana) to lower; (música, radio, volumen) to turn down; (escalera) to go down ♦ vi (disminuir) to go down ❑ **bajar de** v + prep (de avión, tren) to get off; (de coche) to get out of.

bajío m (Amér) low-lying land.

bajo, -ja adj (persona) short; (objeto, cifra, precio) low; (sonido) soft ♦ m (instrumento) bass ♦ adv (hablar) quietly ♦ prep (físicamente) under; (con temperaturas) below ◘ **bajos** mpl (de un edificio) ground floor (sg).

bala f bullet.

balacear vt (Amér) to shoot.

balacera f (Amér) shootout.

balada f ballad.

balance m (de asunto, situación) outcome; (de un negocio) balance; **hacer ~ de** to take stock of.

balancín m (mecedora) rocking chair; (en el jardín) swing hammock.

balanza f (para pesar) scales (pl).

balar vi to bleat.

balcón m balcony.

balde m bucket; **de ~** free (of charge); **en ~** in vain.

baldosa f (en la calle) paving stone; (en interior) floor tile.

Baleares fpl: **las (islas) ~** the Balearic Islands.

balido m bleat.

ballena f whale.

ballet [ba'le] m ballet.

balneario m (con baños termales) spa; (Amér: con piscinas, etc) = lido.

i BALNEARIO

In South America, a "balneario" is a place where there are several open-air swimming pools and cheap facilities for sunbathing, eating and drinking etc.

balón m ball.

baloncesto m basketball.

balonmano m handball.

balonvolea m volleyball.

balsa f (embarcación) raft; (de agua) pond.

bálsamo m balsam.

bambú m bamboo.

banana f banana.

banca f (institución) banks (pl); (profesión) banking; (en juegos) bank.

banco m (para dinero) bank; (para sentarse) bench; (de iglesia) pew; (de peces) shoal; **~ de arena** sandbank.

banda f (cinta) ribbon; (franja) stripe; (lado) side; (en fútbol) touchline; (de músicos) band; (de delincuentes) gang; **~ sonora** soundtrack.

bandeja *f* tray.

bandera *f* flag.

banderilla *f* (*en toros*) banderilla, *barbed dart thrust into bull's back*; (*para comer*) *hors d'oeuvre on a stick*.

banderín *m* pennant.

bandido *m* (*ladrón*) bandit; (*fam: pillo*) rascal.

bando *m* (*en partido*) side; (*de alcalde*) edict.

banjo *m* banjo.

banquero *m* banker.

banqueta *f* stool.

bañador *m* (*para mujeres*) swimsuit; (*para hombres*) swimming trunks (*pl*).

bañar *vt* (*persona*) to bath; (*cosa*) to soak; (*suj: luz*) to bathe; (*suj: mar*) to wash the coast of □ **bañarse** *vpr* (*en río, playa, piscina*) to go for a swim; (*en el baño*) to have a bath.

bañera *f* bath (tub).

bañista *mf* bather.

baño *m* (*en bañera, de vapor, espuma*) bath; (*en playa, piscina*) swim; (*espacio, habitación*) bathroom; (*de oro, pintura*) coat; (*de chocolate*) coating; **al ~ maría** cooked in a bain-marie; **darse un ~** to have a bath □ **baños** *mpl* (*balneario*) spa (*sg*).

bar *m* bar; **~ musical** *bar with live music*.

baraja *f* pack (of cards).

cards each. The symbols of the four suits are gold coins, wooden clubs, swords and goblets. In each suit, the cards called "sota", "caballo" and "rey" correspond roughly to the jack, queen and king in a standard deck.

barajar *vt* (*naipes*) to shuffle; (*posibilidades*) to consider; (*datos, números*) to marshal.

baranda *f* handrail.

barandilla *f* handrail.

baratija *f* trinket.

barato, -ta *adj* cheap ♦ *adv* cheaply.

barba *f* beard; **por ~** per head.

barbacoa *f* barbecue; **a la ~** barbecued.

barbaridad *f* (*crueldad*) cruelty; (*disparate*) stupid thing; **una ~** loads; **¡qué ~!** how terrible!

barbarie *f* (*incultura*) barbarism; (*crueldad*) cruelty.

bárbaro, -ra *adj* (*cruel*) cruel; (*fam: estupendo*) brilliant.

barbería *f* barber's (shop).

barbero *m* barber.

barbilla *f* chin.

barbudo, -da *adj* bearded.

barca *f* small boat; **~ de pesca** fishing boat.

barcaza *f* lighter.

Barcelona *s* Barcelona.

barco *m* (*más pequeño*) boat; (*más grande*) ship; **~ de vapor** steamboat; **~ de vela** sailing ship.

barítono *m* baritone.

barman *m* barman.

barniz (*pl* **-ces**) *m* varnish.

barnizado, -da *adj* varnished.

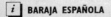

BARAJA ESPAÑOLA

The Spanish deck contains 48 cards divided into 4 suits of 12

barnizar vt (madera) to varnish; (loza, cerámica) to glaze.

barómetro m barometer.

barquillo m cone.

barra f bar; (de turrón, helado, etc) block; ~ **de labios** lipstick; ~ **de pan** baguette; ~ **libre** unlimited drink for a fixed price.

barraca f (chabola) shack; (para feria) stall.

barranco m (precipicio) precipice.

barrendero, -ra m, f road sweeper.

barreño m washing-up bowl.

barrer vt to sweep.

barrera f (obstáculo) barrier; (de tren) crossing gate; (en toros) low wall encircling central part of bullring.

barriada f area.

barriga f belly.

barril m barrel.

barrio m (de población) area; (Amér: suburbio) poor area; ~ **chino** red light district; ~ **comercial** shopping district.

barro m (fango) mud; (en cerámica) clay.

barroco, -ca adj & m baroque.

bártulos mpl things, stuff (sg).

barullo m (fam) racket.

basarse: basarse en v + prep to be based on.

bascas fpl (náuseas) nausea (sg).

báscula f scales (pl).

base f (de cuerpo, objeto) base; (de edificio) foundations (pl); (fundamento, origen) basis; **a** ~ **de** by (means of); ~ **de datos** database.

básico, -ca adj basic.

basta interj that's enough!

bastante adv (suficientemente) enough; (muy) quite, pretty ♦ adj (suficiente) enough; (en cantidad) quite a few.

bastar vi to be enough; **basta con decírselo** it's enough to tell him; **basta con estos dos** these two are enough ❑ **bastarse** vpr: ~**se para hacer algo** to be able to do sthg o.s.

bastardo, -da adj bastard.

bastidores mpl: **entre** ~ behind the scenes.

basto, -ta adj coarse ❑ **bastos** mpl (naipes) suit in Spanish deck of cards bearing wooden clubs.

bastón m (para andar) walking stick; (de mando) baton.

basura f rubbish (Br), garbage (Am).

basurero, -ra m, f dustman (f dustwoman) (Br), garbage collector (Am) ♦ m rubbish dump.

bata f (de casa) housecoat; (para baño, etc) dressing gown; (de médico, científico) coat.

batalla f battle; **de** ~ everyday.

batería f battery; (en música) drums (pl); ~ **de cocina** pots and pans (pl).

batido m milkshake.

batidora f mixer.

batín m short dressing gown.

batir vt (nata) to whip; (marca, huevos) to beat; (récord) to break.

batuta f baton.

baúl m (caja) trunk; (Amér: maletero) boot (Br), trunk (Am).

bautismo m baptism.

bautizar vt (en religión) to baptize; (dar un nombre) to christ-

bautizo m (ceremonia) baptism; (fiesta) christening party.

baya f berry.

bayeta f cloth.

bayoneta f bayonet.

bazar m bazaar.

beato, -ta adj (santo) blessed; (piadoso) devout; (fam: tonto) simple-minded.

beba f (Amér: fam) little girl.

bebé m baby.

beber vt & vi to drink.

bebida f drink.

bebido, -da adj drunk.

bebito, -ta m, f (Amér) new-born baby.

beca f (del gobierno) grant; (de fundación privada) scholarship.

becario, -ria m, f (del gobierno) grant holder; (de fundación privada) scholarship holder.

becerro, -rra m, f calf.

béchamel f béchamel sauce.

bedel m caretaker (Br), janitor (Am).

begonia f begonia.

beige [beɪʒ] adj inv beige.

béisbol m baseball.

belén m crib.

belga adj & mf Belgian.

Bélgica s Belgium.

bélico, -ca adj war (antes de s).

belleza f beauty.

bello, -lla adj (hermoso) beautiful; (bueno) fine.

bellota f acorn.

bendecir vt to bless.

bendición f blessing.

bendito, -ta adj holy ♦ m, f (bobo) simple soul.

beneficencia f charity.

beneficiar vt to benefit ❑ **beneficiarse de** v + prep to do well out of.

beneficio m (bien) benefit; (ganancia) profit; **a ~ de** (concierto, gala) in aid of.

benéfico, -ca adj (gala, rifa) charity (antes de s); (institución) charitable.

benevolencia f benevolence.

benévolo, -la adj benevolent.

bengala f flare.

berberechos mpl cockles.

berenjena f aubergine; **~s rellenas** stuffed aubergines (usually with mince or rice).

bermudas mpl Bermuda shorts.

berrinche m tantrum.

berza f cabbage.

besar vt to kiss ❑ **besarse** vpr to kiss.

beso m kiss; **dar un ~ to** give a kiss.

bestia adj (bruto) rude; (ignorante) thick ♦ mf brute ♦ f (animal) beast.

besugo m sea bream.

betún m (para calzado) shoe polish.

biberón m (baby's) bottle.

Biblia f Bible.

bibliografía f bibliography.

biblioteca f library.

bibliotecario, -ria m, f librarian.

bicarbonato m bicarbonate of soda.

bíceps m inv biceps.

bicho m (animal pequeño) creature, beast; *(insecto)* bug; *(pillo)* little terror.

bici *f (fam)* bike.

bicicleta *f* bicycle.

bicolor *adj* two-coloured.

bidé *m* bidet.

bidón *m* can.

bien *m* 1. *(lo que es bueno)* good. 2. *(bienestar, provecho)* good; **hacer el ~** to do good.
♦ *adv* 1. *(como es debido, correcto)* well; **has actuado ~** you did the right thing; **habla ~ inglés** she speaks English well. 2. *(expresa opinión favorable)* well; **estar ~** *(de salud)* to be well; *(de aspecto)* to be nice; *(de calidad)* to be good; *(de comodidad)* to be comfortable. 3. *(suficiente)*: **estar ~** to be enough. 4. *(muy)* very; **quiero un vaso de agua ~ fría** I'd like a nice, cold glass of water. 5. *(vale, de acuerdo)* all right.
♦ *adj inv (adinerado)* well-to-do.
♦ *conj* 1.: **~ ... ~** either ... or; **entrega el vale ~ a mi padre, ~ a mi madre** give the receipt to either my father or my mother. 2. *(en locuciones)*: **más ~** rather; **¡está ~!** *(vale)* all right then!; *(es suficiente)* that's enough; **¡muy ~!** very good!
□ **bienes** *mpl (patrimonio)* property *(sg)*; *(productos)* goods; **~es de consumo** consumer goods; **~es inmuebles** O **raíces** real estate *(sg)*.

bienal *adj* biennial.

bienestar *m* wellbeing.

bienvenida *f* welcome.

bienvenido, -da *adj* welcome

♦ *interj* welcome!

bife *m (Amér)* steak.

bifocal *adj* bifocal.

bigote *m* moustache.

bigotudo, -da *adj* moustachioed.

bigudí *m* curler.

bilingüe *adj* bilingual.

billar *m (juego)* billiards; *(sala)* billiard hall; **~ americano** *m* americano pool.

billete *m (de dinero)* note *(Br)*, bill *(Am)*; *(de transporte)* ticket; *(de lotería)* lottery ticket; **~ de ida y vuelta** return ticket *(Br)*, roundtrip (ticket) *(Am)*; **~ sencillo** single (ticket) *(Br)*, one-way (ticket) *(Am)*.

billetero *m* wallet.

billón *m* billion *(Br)*, trillion *(Am)*.

bingo *m (juego)* bingo; *(sala)* bingo hall.

biodegradable *adj* biodegradable.

biografía *f* biography.

biográfico, -ca *adj* biographical.

biología *f* biology.

biopsia *f* biopsy.

bioquímica *f* biochemistry.

biquini *m* bikini.

birlar *vt (fam)* to swipe.

birra *f (fam)* beer.

birria *f (fam: persona)* sight; *(fam: cosa)* monstrosity; *(Amér: carne)* barbecued meat.

bisabuelo, -la *m, f* greatgrandfather *(f* great-grandmother).

biscuit *m* sponge; **~ con chocolate** chocolate sponge cake; **~ glacé** ice cream made with eggs, milk, *flour and sugar.*

bisexual *adj* bisexual.

bisnieto, -ta *m, f* great-grandson (*f* great-granddaughter).

bisonte *m* bison.

bistec *m* steak; ~ a la plancha grilled steak; ~ de ternera veal cutlet.

bisturí *m* scalpel.

bisutería *f* imitation jewellery.

bíter *m* bitters.

bizco, -ca *adj* cross-eyed.

bizcocho *m* sponge.

blanca *f*: estar sin ~ (*fam*) to be broke, → **blanco.**

blanco, -ca *adj & m, f* white ◆ *m* (*color*) white; (*diana, objetivo*) target; **dar en el ~** (*acertar*) to hit the nail on the head; **en ~** (*sin dormir*) sleepless; (*sin memoria*) blank.

blando, -da *adj* soft; (*carne*) tender; (*débil*) weak.

blanquear *vt* (*pared*) to whitewash; (*ropa*) to bleach.

blindado, -da *adj* (*puerta, edificio*) armour-plated; (*coche*) armoured.

blindar *vt* to armour-plate.

bloc *m* (*de notas*) notepad; (*de dibujo*) sketchpad.

bloque *m* block; ~ de pisos block of flats.

bloquear *vt* (*cuenta, crédito*) to freeze; (*por nieve, inundación*) to cut off; (*propuesta, reforma*) to block ❏

bloquearse *vpr* (*mecanismo*) to jam; (*dirección*) to lock; (*persona*) to have a mental block.

bloqueo *m* (*mental*) mental block; (*económico, financiero*) blockade.

blusa *f* blouse.

bluyines *mpl* (*Amér*) jeans.

bobada *f* stupid thing; **decir ~s** to talk nonsense.

bobina *f* (*de automóvil*) coil; (*de hilo*) reel.

bobo, -ba *adj* (*tonto*) stupid; (*ingenuo*) naïve.

boca *f* mouth; ~ a ~ mouth-to-mouth resuscitation; ~ de incendios hydrant; ~ de metro tube entrance (*Br*), subway entrance (*Am*); ~ abajo face down; ~ arriba face up.

bocacalle *f* (*entrada*) entrance (*to a street*); (*calle*) side street.

bocadillo *m* sandwich.

bocado *m* (*comida*) mouthful; (*mordisco*) bite.

bocata *m* (*fam*) sarnie.

boceto *m* (*de cuadro, dibujo, edificio*) sketch; (*de texto*) rough outline.

bochorno *m* (*calor*) stifling heat; (*vergüenza*) embarrassment.

bochornoso, -sa *adj* (*caluroso*) muggy; (*vergonzoso*) embarrassing.

bocina *f* (*de coche*) horn; (*Amér: de teléfono*) receiver.

boda *f* wedding; ~s de oro golden wedding (*sg*); ~s de plata silver wedding (*sg*).

bodega *f* (*para vinos*) wine cellar; (*tienda*) wine shop; (*bar*) bar; (*de avión, barco*) hold; (*Amér: almacén*) warehouse.

bodegón *m* (*pintura*) still life.

bodrio *m* (*despec: porquería*) rubbish; (*comida*) pigswill.

bofetada *f* slap (in the face).

bogavante *m* lobster.

bohemio, -mia *adj* bohemian.

bohío m (Amér) hut.

boicot (pl **boicots**) m boycott; **hacer el ~ a** to boycott.

boicotear vt to boycott.

boina f beret.

bola f (cuerpo esférico) ball; (fam: mentira) fib; (fam: fam: rumor) racket; (Amér: fam: lío) muddle; **hacerse ~s** (Amér: fam) to get into a muddle.

bolera f bowling alley.

bolero m bolero.

boletería f (Amér) box office.

boletín m (informativo) bulletin; (de suscripción) subscription form.

boleto m ticket.

boli m (fam) Biro®.

bolígrafo m Biro®.

Bolivia s Bolivia.

boliviano, -na adj & m, f Bolivian.

bollería f (tienda) cake shop.

bollo m (dulce) bun; (de pan) roll.

bolos mpl (juego) skittles.

bolsa f (de plástico, papel, tela) bag; (en economía) stock market; **~ de basura** bin liner; **~ de viaje** travel bag.

bolsillo m pocket; **de ~** pocket (antes de s).

bolso m (de mujer) handbag.

boludez f (Amér) stupid thing.

boludo, -da m, f (Amér) idiot.

bomba f (explosivo) bomb; (máquina) pump; **~ atómica** nuclear bomb; **pasarlo ~** to have a great time.

bombardear vt to bombard.

bombardeo m bombardment.

bombero m fireman.

bombilla f light bulb.

bombo m (de lotería, rifa) drum; (tambor) bass drum; **a ~ y platillo** with a lot of hype.

bombón m (golosina) chocolate; (persona) stunner.

bombona f cylinder; **~ de butano** gas cylinder.

bombonería f sweetshop.

bonanza f (de tiempo) fair weather; (de mar) calm at sea; (prosperidad) prosperity.

bondad f goodness; **tenga la ~ de** (formal) please be so kind as to.

bondadoso, -sa adj kind.

bonificación f discount.

bonificar vt to give a discount of.

bonito, -ta adj (persona, cosa) pretty; (cantidad) considerable ◆ m (pescado) tuna; **~ con tomate** tuna in a tomato sauce.

bono m (vale) voucher.

bonobús m multiple-journey ticket.

bonoloto f Spanish lottery.

BONOLOTO

In this Spanish state-run lottery, participants try to guess a combination of six numbers between one and forty-nine. A ticket contains eight grids of forty-nine boxes, each grid being equivalent to one entry. The "bonoloto" is drawn four times a week.

bonsai m bonsai.

boñiga f cowpat.

boquerones *mpl* (fresh) anchovies.

boquete *m* hole.

boquilla *f* (del cigarrillo) cigarette holder; (de flauta, trompeta, etc) mouthpiece; (de tubo, aparato) nozzle; ~ insincere.

borda *f* gunwale.

bordado, -da *adj* embroidered ◆ *m* embroidery; **salir ~** to turn out just right.

bordar *vt* (en costura) to embroider; (ejecutar perfectamente) to play to perfection.

borde *m* (extremo) edge; (de carretera) side; (de vaso, botella) rim ◆ *adj* (despec) grouchy, miserable; **al ~ de** on the verge of.

bordear *vt* (rodear) to border.

bordillo *m* kerb.

bordo *m*: **a ~ (de)** on board.

borla *f* (adorno) tassel; (para maquillaje) powder puff.

borrachera *f* drunkenness; **coger una ~** to get drunk.

borracho, -cha *adj & m, f* drunk.

borrador *m* (boceto) rough draft; (goma) rubber (Br), eraser (Am).

borrar *vt* (con goma) to rub out (Br), to erase (Am); (en ordenador) to delete; (en casete) to erase; (dar de baja) to strike off.

borrasca *f* thunderstorm.

borrón *m* blot.

borroso, -sa *adj* blurred.

bosque *m* (pequeño) wood; (grande) forest.

bostezar *vi* to yawn.

bostezo *m* yawn.

bota *f* (calzado) boot; (de vino) small leather container in which wine is kept; **~s de agua** wellington boots; **ponerse las ~s** to stuff o.s.

botana *f* (Amér) snack, tapa.

botánica *f* botany.

botar *vt* (Amér) to throw away.

bote *m* (de vidrio) jar; (de metal) can; (de plástico) bottle; (embarcación) boat; (salto) jump; **~ salvavidas** lifeboat; **tener a alguien en el ~** to have sb eating out of one's hand.

botella *f* bottle.

botellín *m* small bottle.

botijo *m* earthenware jug.

botín *m* (calzado) ankle boot; (tras un robo, atraco) loot.

botiquín *m* (maletín) first-aid kit; (mueble) first-aid cupboard.

botón *m* button ❏ **botones** *m inv* bellboy.

bouquet [bu'ke] *m* bouquet.

boutique [bu'tik] *f* boutique.

bóveda *f* vault.

bovino, -na *adj* (en carnicería) beef (antes de s).

boxear *vi* to box.

boxeo *m* boxing.

boya *f* (en el mar) buoy.

bragas *fpl* knickers.

bragueta *f* flies (pl) (Br), zipper (Am).

bramar *vi* to bellow.

brandada *f*: **~ de bacalao** thick fish soup made with cod and milk.

brandy *m* brandy.

brasa *f* ember; **a la ~** barbecued.

brasero *m* brazier.

brasier *m* (Amér) bra.

Brasil s Brazil.

brasilero, -ra adj & m, f (Amér) Brazilian.

bravo, -va adj (toro) wild; (persona) brave; (mar) rough ◆ interj bravo!

braza f (en natación) breaststroke.

brazalete m bracelet.

brazo m arm; (de lámpara, candelabro) branch; **con los ~s abiertos** with open arms; **de ~s cruzados** without lifting a finger; **~ de gitano** ≃ swiss roll.

brebaje m concoction.

brecha f (abertura) hole; (herida) gash.

brécol m broccoli.

breve adj brief; **en ~** shortly.

brevedad f shortness.

brevemente adv briefly.

brezo m heather.

bricolaje m do-it-yourself.

brida f bridle.

brigada f (de limpieza) team; (de la policía) brigade.

brillante adj (material) shiny; (persona, trabajo, actuación) brilliant ◆ m (cut) diamond.

brillantina f Brylcreem®.

brillar vi to shine.

brillo m shine; **sacar ~ a** to polish.

brilloso, -sa adj (Amér) shiny.

brindar vi to drink a toast ◆ vt to offer; **~ por** to drink to ◆ **brindarse** vpr: **~se a** to offer to.

brindis m inv toast.

brío m spirit.

brisa f breeze.

británico, -ca adj British ◆ m,

f British person; **los ~s** the British.

brizna f (de hierba) blade.

broca f (drill) bit.

brocal m parapet (of well).

brocha f (para pintar) brush; (para afeitarse) shaving brush.

broche m (joya) brooch; (de vestido) fastener.

brocheta f (plato) shish kebab; (aguja) skewer.

broma f (chiste) joke; (travesura) prank; **gastar una ~ a alguien** to play a joke on sb; **ir en ~** to be joking; **tomar algo a ~** not to take sthg seriously; **~ pesada** bad joke.

bromear vi to joke.

bromista adj fond of playing jokes ◆ mf joker.

bronca f (jaleo) row; **echar una ~ a alguien** to tell sb off.

bronce m bronze.

bronceado m tan.

bronceador m suntan lotion.

broncearse vpr to get a tan.

bronquios mpl bronchial tubes.

bronquitis f inv bronchitis.

brotar vi (plantas) to sprout; (lágrimas, agua) to well up.

brote m (de planta) bud; (de enfermedad) outbreak.

bruja f (fam: fea y vieja) old hag, → **brujo**.

brujería f witchcraft.

brujo, -ja m, f wizard (f witch).

brújula f compass.

brusco, -ca adj (repentino) sudden; (grosero) brusque.

brusquedad f (imprevisión) suddenness; (grosería) brusqueness.

brutal *adj* (*salvaje*) brutal; (*enorme*) huge.

brutalidad *f* (*brusquedad*) brutishness; (*salvajada*) brutal act.

bruto, -ta *adj* (*ignorante*) stupid; (*violento*) brutish; (*rudo*) rude; (*peso, precio, sueldo*) gross.

bucear *vi* to dive.

buche *m* (*de ave*) crop.

bucle *m* (*de cabello*) curl; (*de cinta, cuerda*) loop.

bucólico, -ca *adj* country (*antes de s*).

bueno, -na (*compar, superl* mejor) *adj* good ♦ *adv* (*conforme*) all right ♦ *interj* (*Amér*: al teléfono) hello!; ¡buenas! hello!; ¡buen día! (*Amér*) hello!; ¡buenas noches! (*despedida*) good night!; ¡buenas tardes! (*hasta las cinco*) good afternoon!; (*después de las cinco*) good evening!; ¡~ días! (*hola*) hello!; (*por la mañana*) good morning!; hace buen día it's a nice day.

buey *m* ox; ~ **de mar** spider crab.

búfalo *m* buffalo.

bufanda *f* scarf.

bufete *m* (*despacho*) lawyer's practice.

buffet *m* buffet; "~ **libre**" "eat as much as you can from the buffet".

buhardilla *f* (*desván*) attic; (*ventana*) dormer (window).

búho *m* owl.

buitre *m* vulture.

bujía *f* (*de coche*) spark plug; (*vela*) candle.

bula *f* (*papal*) bull.

bulbo *m* bulb.

bulerías *fpl* Andalusian song with lively rhythm accompanied by clapping.

bulevar *m* boulevard.

Bulgaria *f* Bulgaria.

bulla *f* racket.

bullicio *m* (*actividad*) hustle and bustle; (*ruido*) hubbub.

bullicioso, -sa *adj* (*persona*) rowdy; (*lugar*) busy.

bulto *m* (*volumen*) bulk; (*paquete*) package; (*en superficie*) lump; (*en piel, cabeza*) lump; "**un solo ~ de mano**" "one item of hand luggage only".

bumerang [bume'ran] *m* boomerang.

bungalow [buŋga'lo] *m* bungalow.

buñuelo *m* = doughnut; ~ **de bacalao** type of cod dumpling; ~ **de viento** = doughnut.

BUP *m* (*abrev de Bachillerato Unificado Polivalente*) academically-orientated secondary school course taught in Spain for pupils aged 14-17.

buque *m* ship.

burbuja *f* (*de gas, aire*) bubble; (*flotador*) rubber ring.

burdel *m* brothel.

burgués, -esa *adj* middle-class ♦ *m, f* middle class person.

burguesía *f* middle class.

burla *f* taunt.

burlar *vt* (*eludir*) to evade; (*ley*) to flout □ **burlarse de** *v* + *prep* to make fun of.

buró *m* (*Amér*) bedside table.

burrada *f* stupid thing.

burro, -rra *m, f* (*animal*) donkey; (*persona tonta*) dimwit.

buscar vt to look for; **ir a ~** (*personas*) to pick up; (*cosas*) to go and get.

busto m (*en escultura, pintura*) bust; (*parte del cuerpo*) chest.

butaca f (*asiento*) armchair; (*en cine, teatro*) seat.

butano m butane (gas).

butifarra f type of Catalan pork sausage; **~ con judías** barbecued "butifarra" with haricot beans.

buzo m (*persona*) diver; (*traje*) overalls (*pl*).

buzón m letterbox.

C

c/ (abrev de calle) St; (abrev de cuenta) a/c.

cabales mpl: **no está en sus ~** he's not in his right mind.

cabalgada f mounted expedition.

cabalgar vi to ride.

cabalgata f procession.

caballa f mackerel.

caballería f (*cuerpo militar*) cavalry; (*animal*) mount.

caballero m (*persona, cortés*) gentleman; (*formal: señor*) Sir; (*de Edad Media*) knight; **"~s"** (en aseos) "gents"; (en probadores) "men"; (en tienda de ropa) "menswear".

caballete m (*para mesa, tabla*) trestle; (*para cuadro, pizarra*) easel.

caballito m: **~ de mar** sea horse; **~ de totora** (*Amér*) small fishing boat made of reeds used by Peruvian and Bolivian Indians ❑

caballitos mpl (*tiovivo*) merry-go-round (*sg*).

caballo m (*animal*) horse; (*en la baraja*) = queen; (*en ajedrez*) knight; **~s de vapor** horsepower.

cabaña f cabin.

cabaret m cabaret.

cabecear vi (*negando*) to shake one's head; (*afirmando*) to nod one's head; (*durmiéndose*) to nod off; (*barco*) to pitch; (*coche*) to lurch.

cabecera f (*de la cama*) headboard; (*en periódico*) headline; (*en libro, lista*) heading; (*parte principal*) head.

cabecilla mf ringleader.

cabellera f long hair.

cabello m hair; **~ de ángel** sweet consisting of strands of pumpkin coated in syrup.

caber vi (*entrar*) to fit; (*ser posible*) to be possible; **no cabe duda** there is no doubt about it; **no me caben los pantalones** my trousers are too small for me.

cabestrillo m sling.

cabeza f head; **~ de ajos** head of garlic; **~ de familia** head of the family; **~ rapada** skinhead; **por ~** per head; **perder la ~** to lose one's head; **sentar la ~** to settle down; **traer de ~** to drive mad.

cabezada f: **dar una ~** to have room.

cabida f: **tener ~** to have room.

cabina f (*booth*); **~ telefónica** phone box (*Br*), phone booth.

cable m cable; **por ~** by cable; **~**

eléctrico electric cable.

cabo m (en geografía) cape; (cuerda) rope; (militar, policía) corporal; **al ~** de after; **atar ~s** to put two and two together; **~ suelto** loose end; **de ~ a rabo** from beginning to end; **llevar algo a ~** to carry sthg out.

cabra f goat; **estar como una ~** to be off one's head.

cabré v → **caber**.

cabrear vt (vulg) to piss off ❑ **cabrearse** vpr (vulg) to get pissed off.

cabreo m (vulg): **coger un ~** to get pissed off.

cabría v → **caber**.

cabrito m kid (goat).

cabrón m (vulg) bastard (f bitch).

cabronada f (vulg) dirty trick.

caca f (excremento) pooh; (suciedad) dirty thing.

cacahuete m peanut.

cacao m (chocolate) cocoa; (fam: jaleo) racket; (de labios) lip salve.

cacarear vi to cluck.

cacería f hunt.

cacerola f pot.

cachalote m sperm whale.

cacharro m (de cocina) pot; (fam: trasto) junk; (fam: coche) banger.

cachear vt to frisk.

cachemir m cashmere.

cachete m slap.

cachivache m knick-knack.

cacho m (fam: trozo) piece; (Amér: cuerno) horn.

cachondearse: cachondearse de v + prep (fam) to take the mickey out of.

cachondeo m (fam): **estar de ~** to be joking; **ir de ~** to go out on the town.

cachondo, -da adj (fam: alegre) funny.

cachorro, -rra m, f puppy.

cacique m local political boss.

cactus m cactus.

cada adj (para distribuir) each; (en frecuencia) every; **~ vez más** more and more; **~ vez más corto** shorter and shorter; **~ uno** each one.

cadáver m corpse.

cadena f chain; (de televisión) channel; (de radio) station; (de música) sound system; (de montañas) range; **en ~** (accidente) multiple.

cadencia f rhythm.

cadera f hip.

cadete m cadet.

caducar vi (alimento) to pass its sell-by date; (ley, documento, etc) to expire.

caducidad f expiry.

caduco, -ca adj (persona) very old-fashioned; **de hoja caduca** deciduous.

caer vi to fall; (día, tarde, verano) to draw to a close; **~ bien/mal** (comentario, noticia) to go down well/badly; **me cae bien/mal** (persona) I like/don't like him; **cae cerca de aquí** it's not far from here; **dejar ~ algo** to drop sthg ❑ **caer en** + prep (respuesta, solución) to hit on, to find; (día) to be on; (mes) to be in; **~ en la cuenta** to realize; **caerse** vpr (persona) to fall down.

café m (bebida, grano) coffee;

(establecimiento) cafe; **~ descafeinado** decaffeinated coffee; **~ irlandés** Irish coffee; **~ con leche** white coffee; **~ molido** ground coffee; **~ solo** black coffee.

CAFÉ

Spanish coffee is usually of the strong, expresso variety, served in very small cups. A small cup of black coffee is called "un solo". A "solo" with a tiny amount of milk added is called "un cortado". "Un carajillo" is a black coffee with a dash of liqueur. "Café con leche" is a large cup filled half with coffee and half with hot milk and is usually drunk at breakfast. In South America, "café de olla", which contains sugar, cinnamon and other spices, is also common.

cafebrería f *(Amér)* *cafe cum bookshop.*

CAFEBRERÍA

The South American "cafebrería" is a cafe which, in addition to serving drinks and snacks, also sells books, magazines and records. "Cafebrerías" are often the venue for "tertulias", poetry readings, conferences and concerts.

cafeína f caffeine.
cafetera f *(para servir)* coffee pot; *(en bares)* expresso machine; *(eléctrica)* coffee machine.
cafetería f cafe.

cagar vi *(vulg)* to shit ◆ vt *(vulg)* to fuck up.
caída f fall.
caído, -da adj *(abatido)* downhearted; **los ~s** the fallen.
caiga v → **caer**.
caimán m alligator.
caja f *(recipiente)* box; *(para transporte, embalaje)* crate; *(de banco)* cashier's desk; *(de supermercado)* till; *(de instrumento musical)* body; **~ de ahorros** savings bank; **~ de cambios** gearbox; **~ de herramientas** tool-box; "**~ rápida**" = "handbaskets only", *sign at till for customers with only a small number of items;* **~ registradora** cash register.
cajero, -ra m, f *(de banco)* teller; *(de tienda)* cashier; **~ automático** cash point.
cajetilla f packet ◆ m *(Amér: despec)* city slicker.
cajón m *(de mueble)* drawer; **~ de sastre** muddle.
cajonera f chest of drawers.
cajuela f *(Amér)* boot *(Br)*, trunk *(Am)*.
cal f lime.
cala f *(ensenada)* cove.
calabacín m courgette *(Br)*, zucchini *(Am)*; **~ relleno** courgette stuffed with mince.
calabaza f pumpkin.
calabozo m cell.
calada f drag.
calamar m squid; **~es a la plancha** grilled squid; **~es a la romana** squid rings fried in batter; **~es en su tinta** squid cooked in its own ink.
calambre m *(de un músculo)* cramp; *(descarga eléctrica)* shock.

calamidad f calamity; **ser una ~** (persona) to be a dead loss.

calar vt (suj: lluvia, humedad) to soak; (suj: frío) to penetrate ◻ **calar en** v + prep (ideas, sentimiento) to have an impact on; **calarse** vpr (mojarse) to get soaked; (suj: vehículo) to stall; (sombrero) to jam on.

calato, -ta adj (Amér) naked.

calaveras fpl (Amér) rear lights.

calcar vt (dibujo) to trace; (imitar) to copy.

calcáreo, -a adj lime.

calcetín m sock.

calcio m calcium.

calcomanía f transfer.

calculador, -ra adj calculating.

calculadora f calculator.

calcular vt (cantidad) to calculate; (suponer) to reckon.

caldear vt (local) to heat; (ambiente) to liven up.

caldera f boiler.

calderilla f small change.

caldo m broth; **~ gallego** thick soup with meat.

calefacción f heating; **~ central** central heating.

calefactor m heater.

calendario m calendar; (de actividades) timetable.

calentador m heater.

calentamiento m (en deporte) warm-up.

calentar vt (agua, leche, comida) to heat up; (fig: pegar) to hit; (fig: incitar) to incite ◻ **calentarse** vpr (en deporte) to warm up; (excitarse) to get turned on.

calesitas fpl (Amér) merry-go-round (sg).

calibrar vt to gauge.

calibre m (importancia) importance.

calidad f quality; (clase) class; **de ~** quality; **en ~ de** in one's capacity as.

cálido, -da adj warm; (agradable, acogedor) friendly.

caliente adj hot; **en ~** in the heat of the moment.

calificación f (en deportes) score; (de un alumno) mark.

calificar vt (trabajo, examen) to mark; **~ a alguien de algo** to call sb sthg.

caligrafía f (letra) handwriting.

cáliz m (de flor) calyx; (de misa) chalice.

callado, -da adj quiet.

callar vi to be quiet ◆ vt (secreto) to keep; (respuesta) to keep to o.s. ◻ **callarse** vpr (no hablar) to keep quiet; (dejar de hablar) to be quiet.

calle f (de población) street; (de carretera, en natación) lane; **dejar a alguien en la ~** to put sb out of a job; **~ abajo/arriba** down/up the street.

callejero, -ra adj street (antes de s) ◆ m street map.

callejón m (calle estrecha) alley; (en toros) passageway behind low wall encircling bullring; **~ sin salida** cul-de-sac.

callejuela f side street.

callo m (de pies) corn; (de manos) callous ◻ **callos** mpl tripe (sg); **~s a la madrileña** tripe cooked with black pudding, smoked pork sausage, onion *and peppers.*

calloso, -sa *adj* calloused.

calma *f* calm.

calmado, -da *adj* calm.

calmante *m* sedative.

calmar *vt* to calm ◆ **calmarse** *vpr* to calm down.

calor *m o f (temperatura elevada, sensación)* heat; *(tibieza, del hogar)* warmth; **hace ~** it's hot; **tener ~** to be hot.

caloría *f* calorie.

calumnia *f (oral)* slander; *(escrita)* libel.

calumniar *vt (oralmente)* to slander; *(por escrito)* to libel.

caluroso, -sa *adj (caliente)* hot; *(tibio, afectuoso, cariñoso)* warm.

calvario *m (sufrimiento)* ordeal.

calvicie *f* baldness.

calvo, -va *adj* bald ◆ *m* bald man.

calzada *f* road (surface); **"~ irregular"** "uneven road surface".

calzado *m* footwear; **"reparación de ~s"** "shoe repairs".

calzador *m* shoehorn.

calzar *vt (zapato, bota)* to put on; **¿qué número calza?** what size (shoe) do you take? ❏ **calzarse** *vpr* to put on.

calzoncillos *mpl* underpants.

calzones *mpl (Amér)* knickers.

cama *f* bed; **guardar ~** to be confined to bed; **~ individual** single bed; **~ de matrimonio** double bed.

camaleón *m* chameleon.

cámara[1] *f (para filmar)* camera; *(de diputados, senadores)* chamber; *(de neumático)* inner tube; **~ fotográfica** camera; **~ de vídeo** video (camera).

cámara[2] *m* cameraman *(f* camerawoman*)*.

camarada *mf (en el trabajo)* colleague.

camarero, -ra *m, f (de bar, restaurante)* waiter *(f* waitress*)*; *(de hotel)* steward *(f* chambermaid*)*.

camarón *m* shrimp.

camarote *m* cabin.

camastro *m* rickety bed.

cambiar *vt* to change; *(ideas, impresiones, etc)* to exchange ◆ *vi* to change; **~ de** *(coche, vida)* to change; *(domicilio)* to move ❏ **cambiarse** *vpr (de ropa)* to change; **~se de** *(casa)* to move; **~se de camisa** to change one's shirt.

cambio *m (de ideas, propuestas, etc)* exchange; *(valor de moneda)* exchange rate; **en ~** on the other hand; **~ de marchas** gear change; **"~ (de moneda)"** "bureau de change"; **"~ de sentido"** *sign indicating a slip road allowing drivers to change direction on a motorway.*

camello *m* camel.

camellón *m (Amér)* central reservation.

camembert [kamember] *m* camembert.

camerino *m* dressing room.

camilla *f (para enfermo, herido)* stretcher.

caminante *mf* walker.

caminar *vi* to walk ◆ *vt* to travel.

caminata *f* long walk.

camino *m (vía)* road; *(recorrido)* path; *(medio)* way; **a medio ~** halfway; **~ de** on the way to; **ir**

por buen/mal ~ *(ruta)* to be going the right/wrong way; **ponerse en ~** to set off.

camión m *(de mercancías)* lorry (Br), truck (Am); *(Amér: autobús)* bus.

camionero, -ra m, f lorry driver (Br), trucker (Am).

camioneta f van.

camisa f shirt.

camisería f outfitter's (shop).

camisero, -ra adj with buttons down the front.

camiseta f *(de verano)* T-shirt; *(ropa interior)* vest.

camisola f *(Amér)* shirt.

camisón m nightdress.

camomila f camomile.

camorra f trouble.

campamento m camp.

campana f *(de iglesia)* bell; *(de chimenea)* chimney breast; *(de cocina)* hood.

campanario m belfry.

campaña f campaign.

campechano, -na adj good-natured.

campeón, -ona m, f champion.

campeonato m championship; **de ~** terrific.

campera f *(Amér)* jacket.

campesino, -na m, f *(agricultor)* farmer; *(muy pobre)* peasant.

campestre adj country.

camping ['kampin] m *(lugar)* campsite; *(actividad)* camping; **ir de ~** to go camping.

campista mf camper.

campo m field; *(campiña)*

countryside; *(de fútbol)* pitch; *(de golf)* course; **~ de deportes** sports ground; **dejar el ~ libre** to leave the field open.

Campsa f Spanish state petrol company.

campus m campus.

camuflar vt to camouflage.

cana f grey hair; **tener ~s** to be going grey.

Canadá m: **(el) ~** Canada.

canadiense adj & mf Canadian.

canal m *(para regar)* canal; *(en geografía)* strait; *(de televisión)* channel; *(de desagüe)* pipe.

canalla mf swine.

canapé m canapé.

Canarias fpl: **(las islas) ~** the Canary Islands.

canario, -ria adj of/relating to the Canary Islands ♦ m, f Canary Islander ♦ m *(pájaro)* canary.

canasta f basket; *(en naipes)* canasta.

canastilla f *(de recién nacido)* layette.

cancela f wrought-iron gate.

cancelación f cancellation.

cancelar vt to cancel; *(cuenta, deuda)* to settle.

cáncer m cancer ❑ **Cáncer** m Cancer.

cancerígeno, -na adj carcinogenic.

cancha f court.

canciller m chancellor.

canción f song.

cancionero m songbook.

candado m padlock.

candela f (Amér) fire.

candelabro m candelabra.

candidato, -ta m, f: ~ (a) candidate (for).

candidatura f candidacy.

candil m (lámpara) oil lamp; (Amér: araña) chandelier.

candilejas fpl footlights.

caneca f (Amér) rubbish bin (Br), trashcan (Am).

canela f cinnamon.

canelones mpl cannelloni.

cangrejo m crab.

canguro m (animal) kangaroo ◆ mf (persona) babysitter.

caníbal mf cannibal.

canica f marble □ **canicas** fpl (juego) marbles.

canijo, -ja adj sickly.

canilla f (Amér) (grifo) tap; (pierna) leg.

canje m exchange.

canjeable adj exchangeable.

canjear vt to exchange; ~ **algo por** to exchange sthg for.

canoa f canoe.

canon m (de belleza, perfección) ideal.

canónico, -ca adj canon.

canoso, -sa adj grey-haired.

cansado, -da adj (fatigado, aburrido) tired; (pesado) tiring; **estar ~ (de)** to be tired of.

cansador, -ra adj (Amér) tiring.

cansancio m tiredness.

cansar vt to tire □ **cansarse** vpr: **~se (de)** (fatigarse) to get tired (from); (hartarse) to get tired of.

cantábrico, -ca adj Cantabrian □ **Cantábrico** m: el Cantá-

brico the Cantabrian Sea.

cantante mf singer.

cantaor, -ra m, f flamenco singer.

cantar vt (canción) to sing; (premio) to call (out) ◆ vi to sing; (fig: confesar) to talk.

cántaro m large pitcher; **llover a ~s** to rain cats and dogs.

cantautor, -ra m, f singer-songwriter.

cante m: ~ **flamenco** □ **jondo** flamenco singing.

cantera f (de piedra) quarry; (de profesionales) source.

cantidad f (medida) quantity; (importe) sum; (número) number ◆ adv a lot; **en ~** in abundance.

cantimplora f water bottle.

cantina f (en fábrica) canteen; (en estación de tren) buffet, station café.

canto m (arte) singing; (canción) song; (borde) edge; **de ~** edgeways; ~ **rodado** pebble.

canturrear vt & vi to sing softly.

caña f (tallo) cane; (de cerveza) small glass of beer; ~ **de azúcar** sugarcane; ~ **de pescar** fishing rod.

cáñamo m hemp.

cañaveral m sugar-cane plantation.

cañería f pipe.

caño m (de fuente) jet; (tubo) pipe; (Amér: grifo) tap.

cañón m (arma moderna) gun; (arma antigua) cannon; (de fusil) barrel; (entre montañas) canyon.

cañonazo m gunshot.

caoba f mahogany.

caos *m inv* chaos.

caótico, -ca *adj* chaotic.

capa *f* (*manto*) cloak; (*de pintura, barniz, chocolate*) coat; (*de la tierra, sociedad*) stratum; (*de torero*) cape; ~ **de ozono** ozone layer; **a ~ y espada** (*defender*) tooth and nail; **andar de ~ caída** to be doing badly.

capacidad *f* (*de envase, aforo*) capacity; (*habilidad*) ability.

capacitado, -da *adj*: **estar ~ para** to be qualified to.

caparazón *m* shell.

capataz (*pl* **-ces**) *mf* foreman (*f* forewoman).

capaz, -ces *adj* capable; **ser ~ de** to be capable of.

capazo *m* large wicker basket.

capellán *m* chaplain.

capicúa *adj inv* reversible.

capilar *adj* hair (*antes de s*).

capilla *f* chapel.

capital *adj* (*importante*) supreme ◆ *m & f* capital.

capitalismo *m* capitalism.

capitalista *adj & mf* capitalist.

capitán, -ana *m, f* captain.

capitanía *f* (*edificio*) = field marshal's headquarters.

capitel *m* capital (*in architecture*).

capítulo *m* chapter.

capó *m* bonnet (*Br*), hood (*Am*).

capón *m* (*animal*) capon; (*golpe*) rap.

capota *f* hood (*Br*), top (*Am*).

capote *m* (*de torero*) cape.

capricho *m* whim; **darse un ~** to treat o.s.

caprichoso, -sa *adj* capricious.

Capricornio *m* Capricorn.

cápsula *f* capsule.

captar *vt* (*sonido, rumor*) to hear; (*persona*) to win over; (*explicación, idea*) to grasp; (*señal de radio, TV*) to receive.

capturar *vt* to capture.

capucha *f* (*de prenda de vestir*) hood; (*de pluma, bolígrafo*) cap.

capuchino, -na *adj & m, f* Capuchin ◆ *m* cappuccino.

capullo *m* (*de flor*) bud; (*de gusano*) cocoon.

cara *f* (*rostro*) face; (*de página, tela, luna, moneda*) side; ~ **a** ~ face to face; **de** ~ **a** (*frente a*) facing; ~ **o cruz** heads or tails; **echar algo a ~ o cruz** to toss a coin for sthg; **dar la ~** to face the consequences; **echar en ~ algo a alguien** to reproach sb for sthg; **esta comida no tiene buena ~** this meal doesn't look very good; **plantar ~ a** to stand up to; **tener (mucha) ~** to have a cheek.

carabela *f* caravel.

carabina *f* (*arma*) rifle; (*fam: persona*) chaperone.

caracol *m* snail; ~**es a la llauna** snails cooked in a pan with oil, garlic and parsley.

caracola *f* conch.

caracolada *f* dish made with snails.

carácter *m* (*modo de ser*) character; (*tipo*) nature; **tener mal/buen ~** to be bad-tempered/good-natured; **tener mucho/poco ~** to have a strong/weak personality.

característica *f* characteristic.

característico, -ca adj characteristic.

caracterizar vt (identificar) to characterize; (representar) to portray ❑ **caracterizarse por** v + prep to be characterized by.

caradura adj inv (fam) cheeky.

carajillo m coffee with a dash of liqueur.

caramba interj (expresa sorpresa) good heavens!; (expresa enfado) for heaven's sake!

carambola f cannon (in billiards); **de ~** (de casualidad) by a fluke; (de rebote) indirectly.

caramelo m (golosina) sweet; (azúcar fundido) caramel.

carátula f (de libro, revista) front cover; (de disco) sleeve; (de casete) inlay card.

caravana f (en carretera) tailback; (remolque) caravan; **hacer ~** to sit in a tailback.

caravaning [kara'βanin] m caravanning.

caray interj (expresa sorpresa) good heavens!; (expresa enfado, daño) damn it!

carbón m coal.

carboncillo m charcoal.

carbono m carbon.

carburador m carburettor.

carburante m fuel.

carcajada f guffaw; **reír a ~s** to roar with laughter.

cárcel f prison; **en la ~** in prison.

carcoma f woodworm.

cardenal m (en religión) cardinal; (morado) bruise.

cardíaco, -ca adj cardiac.

cardinal adj cardinal.

cardiólogo, -ga m, f cardiologist.

cardo m (planta) thistle; (fam: persona) prickly customer.

carecer: carecer de v + prep to lack.

carencia f (ausencia) lack; (defecto) deficiency.

careta f mask.

carey m (de tortuga) tortoiseshell.

carga f (de barco, avión) cargo; (de tren, camión) freight; (peso) load; (para bolígrafo, mechero, pluma) refill; (de arma, explosivo, batería) charge; (responsabilidad) burden; **"~ y descarga"** "loading and unloading".

cargado, -da adj (cielo) overcast; (habitación, ambiente) stuffy; (bebida, infusión) strong; **~ de** (lleno de) loaded with.

cargador, -ra m, f loader ♦ m (de arma) chamber; (de batería) charger.

cargar vt (mercancía, arma) to load; (bolígrafo, pluma, mechero) to refill; (tener capacidad para) to hold; (factura, deudas, batería) to charge ♦ vi (molestar) to be annoying; **~ algo de** (llenar) to fill sthg with ❑ **cargar con** v + prep (paquete) to carry; (responsabilidad) to bear; (consecuencia) to accept; **cargar contra** v + prep to charge; **cargarse** vpr (fam: estropear) to break; (fam: matar) to bump off; (fam: suspender) to fail; (ambiente) to get stuffy; **cargarse de** v + prep (llenarse de) to fill up with.

cargo m charge; (empleo, función) post; **estar a ~ de** to be in charge of; **hacerse ~ de** (responsabilizarse) to take care of; (asumir el control) to take charge of; (comprender) to understand.

cargosear vt (Amér) to annoy.

cargoso, -sa adj (Amér) annoying.

cariado, -da adj decayed.

Caribe m: el ~ the Caribbean.

caribeño, -ña adj Caribbean.

caricatura f caricature.

caricia f (a persona) caress; (a animal) stroke.

caridad f charity.

caries f inv tooth decay.

cariño m (afecto) affection; (cuidado) loving care; (apelativo) love.

cariñoso, -sa adj affectionate.

carisma m charisma.

caritativo, -va adj charitable.

cariz m appearance.

carmín m (para labios) lipstick.

carnal adj (pariente) first.

Carnaval m Shrovetide.

carne f (alimento) meat; (de persona, fruta) flesh; ~ **de cerdo** pork; ~ **de cordero** lamb; ~ **de gallina** goose pimples (pl); **picada** mince (Br), mincemeat (Am); ~ **de ternera** veal; ~ **de vaca** beef.

carné m (de club, partido) membership card; ~ **de conducir** driving licence (Br), driver's license (Am); ~ **de identidad** identity card.

carnear vt (Amér: reses) to slaughter; (fig: reses, personas) to butcher.

carnero m ram.

carnicería f (tienda) butcher's

(shop); (matanza) carnage.

carnicero, -ra m, f butcher.

carnitas fpl (Amér) snack of spicy, fried meat in taco or bread.

caro, -ra adj expensive ♦ adv at a high price; **costar** ~ to be expensive.

carpa f (de circo) big top; (para fiestas) marquee; (pez) carp.

carpeta f file.

carpintería f (oficio) joinery; (arte) carpentry; (taller) joiner's workshop.

carpintero m (profesional) joiner; (artista) carpenter.

carrera f (competición) race; (estudios) degree course; (profesión) career; (en medias, calcetines) ladder (Br), run (Am); **a la** ~ at full speed.

carrerilla f (carrera corta) run-up; **de** ~ (fam) by heart.

carreta f cart.

carrete m (de fotografías) roll; (de hilo) reel.

carretera f road; ~ **de circunvalación** ring road; ~ **comarcal** minor road; ~ **de cuota** (Amér) toll road; ~ **nacional** = A road (Br), = state highway (Am).

carretilla f wheelbarrow.

carril m (de carretera, autopista) lane; (de tren) rail; ~ **de aceleración** fast lane; ~ **bici** cycle lane; ~ **bus** bus lane; ~ **de los lentos** (fam) crawler lane.

carrito m (de la compra) trolley; (para bebés) pushchair (Br), buggy (Am).

carro m (carruaje) cart; (Amér: coche) car; ~ **comedor** (Amér) dining car; ~ **de la compra** trolley.

carrocería f bodywork.

carromato m covered wagon.

carroña f carrion.

carroza f coach, carriage.

carruaje m carriage.

carrusel m (de feria) carousel.

carta f (escrito) letter; (de restaurante, bar) menu; (de la baraja) card; ~ **de vinos** wine list.

cartabón m set square.

cartearse vpr to correspond.

cartel m poster.

cartelera f (de espectáculos) entertainments section; (tablón) hoarding (Br), billboard (Am); **estar en** ~ (película) to be showing; (obra de teatro) to be running.

cartera f (para dinero) wallet; (de colegial) satchel; (para documentos) briefcase; (sin asa) portfolio; (de mujer) clutch bag.

carterista mf pickpocket.

cartero, -ra m, f postman (f postwoman).

cartilla f (para aprender a leer) first reading book; ~ **de ahorros** savings book; ~ **de la Seguridad Social** ≈ National Insurance card.

cartón m (material) cardboard; (de cigarrillos) carton.

cartucho m cartridge.

cartulina f card.

casa f (edificio) house; (vivienda, hogar) home; (familia) family; (empresa) company; **en** ~ at home; **ir a** ~ to go home; ~ **de campo** country house; ~ **de huéspedes** guesthouse.

---

casadero, -ra adj marriageable.

casado, -da adj married.

casamiento m wedding.

casar vt to marry ◻ **casar con** v + prep (colores, tejidos) to go with; **casarse** vpr: ~**se (con)** to get married (to).

cascabel m bell.

cascada f waterfall.

cascado, -da adj (fam: persona, ropa) worn-out; (voz) hoarse.

cascanueces m inv nutcracker.

cascar vt (romper) to crack; (fam: golpear) to thump.

cáscara f (de huevo, frutos secos) shell; (de plátano, naranja) peel.

casco m (para la cabeza) helmet; (envase) empty (bottle); (de caballo) hoof; (de barco) hull; ~ **antiguo** old (part of) town; ~ **urbano** town centre; ~**s azules** Blue Berets.

caserío m (casa de campo) country house.

caserita f (Amér) housewife.

casero, -ra adj (hecho en casa) home-made; (hogareño) home-loving ◆ m, f (propietario) landlord (f landlady).

caseta f (de feria) stall; (para

perro) kennel; *(en la playa)* bathing hut.

casete *m (aparato)* cassette player ◆ *m o f (cinta)* cassette, tape.

casi *adv* nearly, almost; ~ **nada** almost nothing, hardly anything; ~ **nunca** hardly ever.

casilla *f (de impreso)* box; *(de tablero, juego)* square; *(de mueble, caja, armario)* compartment; ~ **de correos** *(Amér)* P.O. Box.

casillero *m (mueble)* set of pigeonholes; *(casilla)* pigeonhole.

casino *m* casino.

caso *m* case; **en ~ de** in the event of; **(en) ~ de que venga** if he comes; **en todo ~** in any case; **en cualquier ~** in any case; **hacer ~ a alguien** to take notice of sb; **ser un ~** *(fam)* to be a case; **no venir al ~** *(fam)* to be irrelevant.

caspa *f* dandruff.

casquete *m* skullcap.

casquillo *m (de bala)* cartridge case; *(de lámpara)* socket.

casta *f (linaje)* stock; *(en la India)* caste.

castaña *f (fruto)* chestnut; *(fam: golpe)* bash.

castaño, -ña *adj (color)* chestnut ◆ *m (árbol)* chestnut tree.

castañuelas *fpl* castanets.

castellano, -na *adj & m, f* Castilian ◆ *m (lengua)* Spanish.

castidad *f* chastity.

castigar *vt* to punish.

castigo *m* punishment.

castillo *m* castle.

castizo, -za *adj* pure.

casto, -ta *adj* chaste.

castor *m* beaver.

castrar *vt* to castrate.

casualidad *f* coincidence; **por ~** by chance.

catacumbas *fpl* catacombs.

catalán, -ana *adj, m, f* Catalan.

catálogo *m* catalogue.

Cataluña *s* Catalonia.

catamarán *m* catamaran.

catar *vt* to taste.

cataratas *fpl (de agua)* waterfalls, falls; *(en los ojos)* cataracts.

catarro *m* cold.

catástrofe *f* disaster.

catastrófico, -ca *adj* disastrous.

catear *vt (fam)* to flunk.

catecismo *m* catechism.

cátedra *f (en universidad)* chair; *(en instituto)* post of head of department.

catedral *f* cathedral.

catedrático, -ca *m, f* head of department.

categoría *f* category; **de ~** top-class.

catequesis *f inv* catechesis.

cateto, -ta *m, f (despec)* dimwit.

catire, -ra *adj (Amér)* blond (blonde).

catolicismo *m* Catholicism.

católico, -ca *adj & m, f* Catholic.

catorce *núm* fourteen, → **seis.**

catre *m* campbed.

cauce *m (de río)* riverbed; *(de lluvia, artificial)* channel.

caucho *m* rubber.

caudal *m (de un río)* volume,

flow; **~es** (dinero) wealth (sg).

caudaloso, -sa adj with a large flow.

caudillo m leader.

causa f cause; **a ~** de because of.

causante m (Amér) taxpayer.

causar vt to cause.

cáustico, -ca adj caustic.

cautela f caution; **con ~** cautiously.

cautivador, -ra adj captivating.

cautivar vt (seducir) to captivate.

cautiverio m captivity; **en ~** in captivity.

cautivo, -va adj & m, f captive.

cauto, -ta adj cautious.

cava f (bodega) wine cellar ♦ m Spanish champagne-type wine; **al ~** in a sauce of single cream, shallots, "cava" and butter; **~ brut** brut "cava".

cavar vt to dig.

caverna f (cueva) cave; (más grande) cavern.

caviar m caviar.

cavidad f cavity.

cavilar vi to ponder.

cayera v → **caer**.

caza f (actividad) hunting; (presa) game; **andar** o **ir a la ~ de** to chase; **dar ~** to hunt down.

cazador, -ra m, f hunter (f huntress).

cazadora f (bomber) jacket, → **cazador**.

cazar vt (animales) to hunt; (fam: marido, esposa) to get o.s.; (captar, entender) to catch.

cazo m (vasija) saucepan; (cucharón) ladle.

cazuela f (de barro) earthenware pot; (guiso) casserole; **a la ~** casseroled.

cazurro, -rra adj (obstinado) stubborn.

CC (abrev de código civil) civil code in Spanish law.

c/c (abrev de cuenta corriente) a/c.

CE f (abrev de Comunidad Europea) EC.

cebar vt (animales) to fatten up ❏ **cebarse en** v + prep to take it out on.

cebo m bait.

cebolla f onion.

cebolleta f spring onion.

cebra f zebra.

cecear vi to lisp.

ceder vt (sitio, asiento, etc) to give up ♦ vi (puente) to give way; (cuerda) to slacken; (viento, lluvia, etc) to abate; **"ceda el paso"** "give way".

cedro m cedar.

cédula f document; **~ de identidad** (Amér) identity card.

cegato, -ta adj (fam) shortsighted.

ceguera f blindness.

ceja f eyebrow.

celda f cell.

celebración f celebration.

celebrar vt (cumpleaños, acontecimiento, misa) to celebrate; (asamblea, reunión) to hold.

célebre adj famous.

celebridad f fame; **ser una ~** to be famous.

celeste adj (del cielo) of the sky.

celestial *adj* celestial.

celo *m* *(cinta adhesiva)* Sellotape®; *(en el trabajo, etc)* zeal; **estar en ~** to be on heat ❑ **celos** *mpl* jealousy *(sg)*; **tener ~s** to be jealous.

celofán® *m* Cellophane®.

celoso, -sa *adj* *(en el amor)* jealous.

célula *f* cell.

celulitis *f* inv cellulitis.

cementerio *m* cemetry; **~ de coches** breaker's yard.

cemento *m* cement; **~ armado** reinforced concrete.

cena *f* dinner.

cenar *vt* to have for dinner ◆ *vi* to have dinner.

cencerro *m* cowbell; **estar como un ~** *(fig)* to be mad.

cenefa *f* border.

cenicero *m* ashtray.

ceniza *f* ash ❑ **cenizas** *fpl* *(restos mortales)* ashes.

censado, -da *adj* recorded.

censar *vt* to take a census of.

censo *m* census; **~ electoral** electoral roll.

censor *m* censor.

censura *f* *(de película, libro, etc)* censorship.

censurar *vt* *(película, libro, etc)* to censor; *(conducta, etc)* to censure.

centena *f* hundred; **una ~ de** a hundred.

centenar *m* hundred; **un ~ de** a hundred.

centenario, -ria *adj* *(persona)* hundred-year-old ◆ *m* centenary.

centeno *m* rye.

centésimo, -ma *núm* hundredth, → **sexto**.

centígrado, -da *adj* centigrade.

centímetro *m* centimetre.

céntimo *m* *(moneda)* cent; **no tener un ~** not to have a penny.

centinela *mf* sentry.

centollo *m* spider crab.

centrado, -da *adj* *(en el centro)* in the centre; *(persona)* well-balanced; *(derecho)* straight; **~ en** *(trabajo, ocupación)* focussed on.

central *adj* central ◆ *f (oficina)* head office; **~ eléctrica** power station.

centralismo *m* centralism.

centralita *f* switchboard.

centrar *vt* *(cuadro, mueble)* to centre; *(miradas, atención)* to be the centre of ❑ **centrarse en** *v + prep* to focus on.

céntrico, -ca *adj* central.

centrifugar *vt* *(suj: lavadora)* to spin.

centro *m* centre; *(de ciudad)* (town) centre; **en el ~ de** in the middle of; **ir al ~** to go to town; **ser el ~ de** to be the centre of; **~ comercial** shopping centre; **~ juvenil** youth club; **~ social** community centre; **~ turístico** tourist resort; **~ urbano** town centre.

Centroamérica *s* Central America.

centuria *f* century.

ceñido, -da *adj* tight.

ceñir *vt* *(ajustar)* to tighten; *(rodear)* to surround ❑ **ceñirse a** *v + prep* to stick to.

ceño *m* frown.

cepa f (vid) vine.

cepillar vt (pelo, traje, etc) to brush; (fam: elogiar) to butter up ▫

cepillarse vpr (fam) (acabar) to polish off; (matar) to bump off.

cepillo m brush; **~ de dientes** toothbrush.

cepo m (de animales) trap; (de coches) wheelclamp.

CEPSA f Spanish petrol company.

cera f wax.

cerámica f (objeto) piece of pottery; (arte) pottery; ◆ ~ ceramic.

ceramista mf potter.

cerca f (valla) fence ◆ adv near; **~ de** (en espacio) near; (casi) nearly; **son ~ de las cuatro** it's nearly four o'clock; **de ~** from close up.

cercanías fpl (alrededores) outskirts.

cercano, -na adj (en espacio) nearby; (en tiempo) near.

cercar vt (vallar) to fence off; (rodear) to surround.

cerco m (de vallas) fence.

cerda f bristle, → **cerdo**.

cerdo, -da m, f (animal) pig (f sow); (despec: persona) pig ◆ adj (despec) filthy ◆ m (carne) pork.

cereal m cereal ▫ **cereales** mpl (para desayuno) breakfast cereal (sg).

cerebro m (del cráneo) brain; (persona inteligente) brainy person; (organizador, responsable) brains (pl); **~ electrónico** computer.

ceremonia f ceremony.

ceremonioso, -sa adj ceremonious.

cereza f cherry.

cerezo m (árbol) cherry tree.

cerilla f match.

cerillo m (Amér) match.

cero m núm (número) zero, nought; (en fútbol) nil; (en tenis) love; **bajo ~** below zero; **sobre ~** above zero; **ser un ~ a la izquierda** (fam: ser un inútil) to be useless, → **seis**.

cerquillo m (Amér) fringe (Br), bangs (Am) (pl).

cerrada f (Amér) cul-de-sac (on estate).

cerrado, -da adj (espacio, local, etc) closed; (tiempo, cielo) overcast; (introvertido) introverted; (intransigente) narrow-minded; (acento) broad; (curva) sharp; **"~ por vacaciones"** "closed for the holidays".

cerradura f lock.

cerrajería f locksmith's (shop).

cerrajero m locksmith.

cerrar vt to close; (con llave) to lock; (grifo, gas) to turn off; (local, negocio, fábrica) to close down; (ir detrás de) to bring up the rear of; (impedir) to block; (pacto, trato) to strike ◆ vi (comercio) to close ▫ **cerrarse** vpr (en uno mismo) to close o.s. off; **cerrarse a** v + prep (propuestas, innovaciones) to close one's mind to.

cerro m hill.

cerrojo m bolt.

certamen m (concurso) competition; (fiesta) awards ceremony.

certeza f certainty; **tener la ~ de** to be sure that.

certidumbre f certainty.

certificado, -da adj (carta, paquete) registered ◆ m certificate.

certificar vt (documento) to certify; (carta, paquete) to register.

cervecería f (establecimiento) bar.

cerveza f beer; ~ con Casera® shandy; ~ sin alcohol alcohol-free beer; ~ negra stout; ~ rubia lager.

cesar vi to stop ♦ vt: ~ a alguien de (cargo, ocupación) to sack sb from; no ~ de hacer algo to keep doing sthg; sin ~ non-stop.

cesárea f Caesarean (section).

cese m (de empleo, cargo) sacking; (de actividad) stopping.

cesión f transfer.

césped m (superficie) lawn; (hierba) grass.

cesta f basket; ~ de la compra cost of living.

cesto m large basket.

cetro m sceptre.

cg (abrev de centigramo) cg.

chabacano, -na adj vulgar ♦ m (Amér) (fruto) apricot; (árbol) apricot tree.

chabola f shack; barrios de ~s shanty town (sg).

chacarero, -ra m, f (Amér) (agricultor) farmer; (hablador) chatterbox.

chacha f (fam) (criada) maid; (niñera) nanny.

cháchara f chatter.

chacolí m light, dry wine from the North of Spain.

chacra f smallholding.

chafar vt (aplastar) to flatten; (plan, proyecto) to ruin; (fam: desmoralizar) to depress.

chal m shawl.

chalado, -da adj (fam) crazy; estar ~ por (estar enamorado) to be crazy about.

chalé m (en ciudad) detached house; (en el campo) cottage; (en alta montaña) chalet.

chaleco m waistcoat; ~ salvavidas life jacket.

chamaco, -ca m, f (Amér) lad (f lass).

chamba f (Amér: fam) job.

chambear vi (Amér: fam) to work.

champán m champagne.

champiñón m mushroom; champiñones con jamón mushrooms fried slowly with garlic and cured ham.

champú m shampoo.

champurrado m (Amér) cocktail.

chamuscado, -da adj (madera) scorched.

chamuscarse vpr (barba, pelo, tela) to singe.

chamusquina f: oler a ~ (fig) to smell fishy.

chance m (Amér) chance.

chanchada f (Amér) (fig: grosería) rude thing; (porquería) filth.

chancho m (Amér) pig.

chancleta f (de playa) flip-flop; (de vestir) low sandal.

chanclo m (de madera) clog; (de goma) galosh.

chándal m tracksuit.

changarro m (Amér) small shop.

changurro m spider crab.

chantaje m blackmail.

chantajista m f blackmailer.

chapa f (de metal) plate; (de botella) top; (Amér: cerradura) lock; ~ de madera veneer.

chapado, -da adj (con metal)

plated; *(con madera)* veneered; ~ a la antigua old-fashioned.

chapar *vt (con metal)* to plate; *(con madera)* to veneer.

chaparrón *m* cloudburst.

chapucería *f* botch (job).

chapucero, -ra *adj (trabajo, obra)* shoddy; *(persona)* bungling.

chapuza *f* botch (job).

chaqué *m* morning coat.

chaqueta *f* jacket.

chaquetilla *f* short jacket.

chaquetón *m* three-quarter length coat.

charca *f* pond.

charco *m* puddle.

charcutería *f (tienda)* = delicatessen; *(productos)* cold cuts *(pl)* and cheese.

charla *f (conversación)* chat; *(conferencia)* talk.

charlar *vi* to chat.

charlatán, -ana *adj (hablador)* talkative; *(indiscreto)* gossipy.

charola *f (Amér)* tray.

charro *adj (Amér)* typical of Mexican cowboys ♦ *m (Amér)* Mexican cowboy.

chárter *m inv* charter flight.

chasco *m (decepción)* disappointment; *(broma)* practical joke.

chasis *m inv* chassis.

chatarra *f (metal)* scrap; *(objetos, piezas)* junk.

chatarrero, -ra *m, f* scrap dealer.

chato, -ta *adj (nariz)* snub; *(persona)* snub-nosed ♦ *m (apelativo)* love ♦ *m (de vino)* small glass of wine.

chau *interj (Amér)* bye!

chaucha *f (Amér) (patata)* new potato; *(vaina)* pod; *(moneda)* small coin.

chavo, -va *m, f (Amér: fam)* lad *(f* lass).

che *interj (Amér)* pah!

Checoslovaquia *s* Czechoslovakia.

chef *m* chef.

cheque *m* cheque; ~ de viaje traveller's cheque.

chequeo *m (médico)* check-up.

chequera *f (Amér)* cheque book.

chévere *adj (Amér)* great.

chic *adj inv* chic.

chica *f (muchacha)* girl; *(criada)* maid.

chicha *f (fam)* meat; *(Amér: bebida)* fermented maize liquor.

chícharo *m (Amér)* pea.

chicharrones *mpl* pork crackling *(sg)*.

chiche *m (Amér) (chuchería)* knick-knack; *(fam: teta)* tit.

chichón *m* bump.

chicle *m* chewing gum.

chico, -ca *adj* small ♦ *m (muchacho)* boy.

chicote *m (Amér) (látigo)* whip; *(colilla)* cigarette butt.

chifa *m (Amér)* Chinese restaurant.

chiflado, -da *adj (fam)* crazy.

chiflar *vi (Amér: aves)* to sing; me chifla *(fam)* I love it ☐ **chiflarse** *vpr (fam)* to go crazy.

chiflido *m (Amér)* whistle.

Chile *s* Chile.

chileno, -na adj & m, f Chilean.

chillar vi (gritar) to scream.

chillido m scream.

chillón, -ona adj (voz, sonido) piercing; (color) loud.

chimenea f (de casa) chimney; (de barco) funnel; (hogar) hearth.

chimpancé m chimpanzee.

china f (piedra) pebble; (Amér: criada) Indian maid; **le tocó la ~** he drew the short straw.

China f: **la ~** China.

chinche f (insecto) bedbug ◆ adj (pesado) annoying.

chincheta f drawing pin (Br), thumbtack (Am).

chinchín m (en brindis) toast; (sonido) clash (of a brass band) ◆ excl cheers!

chingado, -da adj (Amér: vulg: estropeado) fucked.

chingar vt (Amér: vulg: estropear) to fuck up.

chino, -na adj, m, f Chinese.

chip m chip.

chipirón m baby squid; **chipirones en su tinta** baby squid served in its own ink.

chirimoya f custard apple.

chirucas fpl canvas boots.

chisme m (habladuría) piece of gossip; (fam: objeto, aparato) thingy.

chismoso, -sa adj gossipy.

chispa f spark; (pizca) bit; (de lluvia) spot.

chiste m joke.

chistorra f cured pork and beef sausage typical of Aragon and Navarre.

chistoso, -sa adj funny.

chivarse vpr (fam) (niño) to tell; (delincuente) to grass.

chivatazo m (fam) tip-off.

chivato, -ta m, f (fam: acusica) telltale; (fam: delator) grass ◆ m (Amér: hombre valioso) brave man; (Amér: aprendiz) apprentice.

chocar vi (coche, camión, etc) to crash; (enfrentarse) to clash ◆ vt (las manos) to shake; (copas, vasos) to clink; (sorprender) to shock.

chocho, -cha adj (viejo) senile; (encariñado) doting.

choclo m (Amér) maize (Br), corn (Am).

chocolate m (alimento) chocolate; (bebida) drinking chocolate; **~ amargo** dark chocolate.

chocolatería f bar which serves drinking chocolate.

chocolatina f chocolate bar.

chófer m (de coche) chauffeur; (de autobús) driver.

chollo m (fam) (ganga) bargain; (trabajo) cushy number.

chompa f (Amér) jumper.

chongo m (Amér) bun.

chopitos mpl baby squid in batter (sg).

chopo m poplar.

choque m (colisión) crash; (pelea, riña) clash.

chorizo m (embutido) spiced, smoked pork sausage; (fam: ladrón) thief.

choro m (Amér) mussel.

chorrada f (fam) stupid thing.

chorrear vi (ropa) to drip.

chorro m (de líquido) jet; **salir a ~s** to gush out.

choto, -ta m, f (cabrito) kid.

choza f hut.

christmas m Christmas card.

chubasco m (heavy) shower.

chubasquero m raincoat.

chúcaro, -ra adj (Amér) (bravío) wild; (huraño) surly.

chuchería f (golosina) sweet; (trivialidad) trinket.

chucho, -cha m, f (fam) mutt.

chueco, -ca adj (Amér) (torcido) twisted; (patizambo) bow-legged.

chufa f tiger nut.

chuleta f (de carne) chop; (de examen) crib note; **~ de cerdo** pork chop; **~ de ternera** veal cutlet.

chuletón m large cutlet.

chulo, -la adj (engreído) cocky; (fam: bonito) lovely ◆ m (de prostituta) pimp.

chumbera f prickly pear.

chupachup® m lollipop.

chupado, -da adj (fig: flaco) skinny; (fam: fácil) dead easy; **está ~** (fam) it's a cinch.

chupar vt (caramelo, fruta etc) to suck; (suj: esponja, papel) to soak up; **~le algo a alguien** (fam: quitar) to milk sb for sthg.

chupe m (Amér) stew made with potatoes and meat or fish; **~ de camarones** thick potato and prawn soup.

chupete m (de bebé) dummy (Br), pacifier (Am); (de biberón) teat.

chupito m (de licor) tot.

churrasco m barbecued meat.

churrería f stall selling "churros".

churro m (dulce) stick of dough fried in oil, usually eaten with sugar or thick drinking chocolate; (fam: chapuza) botch.

chusma f mob.

chutar vi to kick.

chute m (fam: en fútbol) shot.

Cía. (abrev de compañía) Co.

cicatriz (pl **-ces**) f scar.

cicatrizar vi to heal ❑ **cicatrizarse** vpr to heal.

ciclismo m cycling.

ciclista mf cyclist.

ciclo m (periodo de tiempo) cycle; (de actos, conferencias) series.

ciclomotor m moped.

ciclón m cyclone.

ciego, -ga adj blind ◆ m, f blind person; **~ de** (pasión, ira, etc) blinded by; **los ~s** the blind.

cielo m (de la tierra) sky; (de casa, habitación, etc) ceiling; (en religión) heaven; (apelativo) darling; **como llovido del ~** (fig) out of the blue ❑ **cielos** interj good heavens!

ciempiés m inv centipede.

cien núm one ❑ a hundred, → **ciento**.

ciencia f (disciplina) science; (saber, sabiduría) knowledge; **~ ficción** science fiction; **~s económicas** economics (sg); **~s naturales** natural sciences ❑ **ciencias** fpl (en educación) science (sg).

científico, -ca adj scientific ◆ m, f scientist.

ciento núm one ❑ a hundred, → **seis**; **~ cincuenta** one hundred and fifty; **cien mil** one hundred thousand; **por ~** percent.

cierre m (mecanismo) fastener; (de local, tienda, negociación) closing; (de trato) striking; (de actividad, acto) closure; **~ centralizado** central locking.

cierto, -ta *adj* certain; *(seguro, verdadero)* true; **~ hombre** a certain man; **cierta preocupación** a degree of unease; **por ~** by the way.

ciervo, -va *m, f* deer.

CIF *m* Spanish tax code.

cifra *f* figure.

cigala *f* Dublin Bay prawn.

cigarra *f* cicada.

cigarrillo *m* cigarette.

cigarro *m (cigarrillo)* cigarette.

cigüeña *f* stork.

cilindrada *f* cylinder capacity.

cilíndrico, -ca *adj* cylindrical.

cilindro *m* cylinder.

cima *f (de montaña)* summit.

cimiento *m (de edificio)* foundations *(pl)*; *(principio, raíz)* basis.

cinco *núm* five, → **seis**.

cincuenta *núm* fifty, → **seis**.

cine *m* cinema.

cineasta *mf (film)* director.

cinematografía *f* cinematography.

cinematográfico, -ca *adj* film *(antes de s)*.

cínico, -ca *adj* cynical.

cinismo *m* cynicism.

cinta *f (de tela)* ribbon; *(de papel, plástico)* strip; *(para grabar, medir)* tape; **~ adhesiva** adhesive tape; **~ aislante** insulating tape; **~ magnética** recording tape; **~ de video** videotape.

cintura *f* waist.

cinturón *m* belt; **~ de seguridad** seat belt.

cipote, -ta *m, f (Amér) (muchacho)* boy *(f* girl*)*; *(persona rechoncha)* chubby person.

ciprés *m* cypress.

circo *m* circus.

circuito *m (recorrido)* tour; *(en competiciones)* circuit; **~ eléctrico** electrical circuit.

circulación *f (de automóviles)* traffic; *(de la sangre)* circulation.

circular *adj & f* circular ♦ *vi (automóvil)* to drive (along); *(persona, grupo)* to move along; *(información, noticia)* to circulate.

círculo *m* circle; **~ polar** polar circle.

circunferencia *f* circumference.

circunscribir *vt:* **~ algo a** to restrict sthg to.

circunscrito, -ta *pp* → **circunscribir**.

circunstancia *f* circumstance; **las ~s** the circumstances.

circunstancial *adj* chance.

cirio *m* large candle.

cirrosis *f inv* cirrhosis.

ciruela *f* plum.

ciruelo *m* plum tree.

cirugía *f* surgery; **~ plástica** plastic surgery.

cirujano, -na *m, f* surgeon.

cisma *m (en religión)* schism.

cisne *m* swan.

cisterna *f (de agua)* tank.

cita *f (con médico, jefe, etc)* appointment; *(de novios)* date; *(nota)* quotation; **tener una ~ con alguien** to have arranged to meet sb.

citación *f* summons.

citar *vt (convocar)* to summons; *(mencionar)* to quote ❑ **citarse** *vpr* to arrange to meet.

cítrico, -ca adj citric ❑ **cítricos** mpl citrus fruits.

ciudad f (población no rural) town; (población importante) city; ~ **universitaria** (university) campus.

ciudadanía f citizenship.

ciudadano, -na adj city/town (antes de s) ◆ m, f citizen.

cívico, -ca adj (de la ciudad, ciudadano) civic; (educado, cortés) public-spirited.

civil adj civil; (de la ciudad) civic.

civilización f civilization.

civilizado, -da adj civilized.

civismo m (educación, cortesía) civility.

cl (abrev de centilitro) cl.

clan m clan.

clara f (de huevo) white; (bebida) shandy.

claraboya f skylight.

clarear vt to make lighter ◆ vi to brighten up ◆ v impers (amanecer): **empezaba a ~ dawn was breaking.**

claridad f (en el hablar) clarity; (sinceridad) sincerity.

clarinete m clarinet.

clarividencia f farsightedness.

claro, -ra adj clear; (con luz) bright; (color) light; (sincero, franco) straightforward ◆ m (de tiempo) bright spell; (en el bosque) clearing ◆ adv clearly ◆ interj of course!; **poner ~** to clear up; **sacar en ~** to make out.

clase f class; (variedad, tipo) kind; (aula) classroom; **dar ~s** to teach; **de primera** ~ first-class; **toda** ~ **de** all sorts of; ~ **media** middle class; ~ **preferente** club class; ~ **turista**

tourist class; **primera/segunda** ~ first/second class.

clásico, -ca adj classical.

clasificación f (lista) classification; (DEP) league table.

clasificador m (carpeta) divider (for filing); (mueble) filing cabinet.

clasificar vt to classify ❑ **clasificarse** vpr (en competición) to qualify.

claudicar vi (rendirse) to give up.

claustro m (de iglesia, convento, etc) cloister; (de profesores) senate.

claustrofobia f claustrophobia.

cláusula f clause.

clausura f (de acto) closing ceremony; (de curso) end.

clausurar vt (acto, celebración) to close; (curso) to finish; (local, establecimiento) to close down.

clavado, -da adj (en punto) on the dot; **ser ~ a** (fam) to be the spitting image of.

clavar vt (clavo, palo) to drive in; (cuchillo) to thrust; (alfiler) to stick; (sujetar, fijar) to fix; (fam: en el precio) to rip off.

clave f (explicación, solución) key; (de enigma, secreto) code ◆ adj inv key.

clavel m carnation.

clavícula f collar bone.

clavija f (de madera) peg; (de metal) pin.

clavo m (para sujetar) nail; (especia) clove; **dar en el ~** to hit the nail on the head.

claxon m horn.

clérigo m clergyman.

clero m clergy.

cliché m (de fotografía) negative; (frase, actuación) cliché.

cliente mf (de médico, abogado) client; (de tienda, comercio) customer; (de hotel) guest.

clima m climate.

climático, -ca adj climatic.

climatizado, -da adj air-conditioned.

climatología f (tiempo) weather.

clímax m inv climax.

clínica f clinic.

clínico, -ca adj clinical.

clip m (para papeles) paper clip; (para pelo) hairclip.

cloaca f sewer.

cloro m chlorine.

club m club; ~ **náutico** yacht club.

cm (abrev de centímetro) cm.

coacción f coercion.

coaccionar vt to coerce.

coartada f alibi.

coba f: dar ~ to suck up to.

cobarde adj cowardly ◆ mf coward.

cobardía f cowardice.

cobertizo m (tejado) lean-to; (barracón) shed.

cobija f (Amér) blanket.

cobijar vt (suj: edificio) to house; (suj: persona) to put up; (proteger) to shelter ❑ **cobijarse** vpr to (take) shelter.

cobra f cobra.

cobrador, -ra m, f (de autobús) conductor (f conductress).

cobrar vt (dinero) to charge; (cheque) to cash; (en el trabajo) to earn; (importancia, fama) to acquire; ¡me **cobra, por favor!** could I have the bill, please?

cobre m copper; **no tener un ~** (Amér) not to have a penny.

cobro m (de dinero) collection; (de talón) cashing; **llamar a ~ revertido** to reverse the charges (Br), to call collect (Am).

coca f (planta) coca; (fam: cocaína) coke.

cocaína f cocaine.

cocainómano, -na m, f cocaine addict.

cocción f (en agua) boiling; (en horno) baking.

cocear vi to kick.

cocer vt (guisar) to cook; (en agua) to boil; (en horno) to bake ◆ vi (hervir) to boil ❑ **cocerse** vpr (fig: idea, plan) to be brewing.

cochayuyo m (Amér) seaweed.

coche m (automóvil) car; (de tren, caballos) carriage; ~ **de alquiler** hire car; ~ **cama** sleeper; ~ **restaurante** dining car.

cochinillo m: ~ **al horno** roast suckling pig, a speciality of Segovia.

cochino, -na adj filthy ◆ m, f (animal) pig (f sow).

cocido, -da adj boiled ◆ m stew; ~ **madrileño** stew made with meat, chickpeas, bacon and root vegetables, typical of Madrid.

cocina f (estancia, habitación) kitchen; (aparato) cooker; (arte, técnica) cooking; ~ **española** Spanish cuisine; ~ **de butano** butane gas cooker; ~ **eléctrica** electric cooker; ~ **de gas** gas cooker.

cocinar vt & vi to cook.

cocinero, -ra m, f cook.

coco m (fruto) coconut; (árbol) coconut palm; (fam: cabeza) nut.

cocodrilo m (animal) crocodile; (piel) crocodile skin.

cocotero m coconut palm.

cóctel m (bebida) cocktail; (reunión, fiesta) cocktail party.

coctelera f cocktail shaker.

codazo m poke with the elbow.

codiciar vt to covet.

codificado, -da adj coded.

código m code; **~ de barras** bar code; **~ de circulación** highway code; **~ penal** penal code; **~ postal** post code (Br), zip code (Am).

codo m elbow; **~ a ~** side by side.

codorniz (pl -ces) f quail.

coeficiente m coefficient; **~ intelectual** I.Q.

coetáneo, -a adj contemporary.

coexistencia f coexistence.

coexistir: coexistir con v + prep to coexist with.

cofia f (de tendero, camarero) cap; (de monja) coif.

cofradía f religious fraternity.

cofre m (arca) chest.

coger vt to take; (ladrón, pez, enfermedad, oír) to catch; (frutos) to pick; (suj: toro) to gore; (entender) to get ♦ vi (planta, árbol) to take; (caber) to fit; **~ algo a alguien** to take sthg (away) from sb; **coge cerca de aquí** it's not far from here; **~ a la derecha** to turn right ❑

cogerse vpr: **~se de** (agarrarse de) to hold on to.

cogida f (de toro) goring.

cogollos mpl (brotes) shoots.

cogote m nape (of the neck).

cohabitar vi to live together.

coherencia f coherence.

coherente adj coherent.

cohete m rocket.

COI m (abrev de Comité Olímpico Internacional) IOC.

coima f (Amér: fam) bribe.

coincidencia f coincidence.

coincidir vi (en un lugar) to meet; (ser igual) to coincide ❑ **coincidir con** v + prep (de la misma opinión que) to agree with; (ocurrir en el mismo momento que) to coincide with.

coito m (sexual) intercourse.

cojear vi (persona) to limp; (mueble) to wobble.

cojín m cushion.

cojo, -ja adj (persona, animal) lame; (mesa, silla) wobbly ♦ m, f lame person.

cojón m (vulg: testículo) ball ♦ **cojones** interj (vulg) balls!

cojonudo, -da adj (vulg) bloody brilliant.

cojudear vt (Amér: fam) to mess about.

cojudez f (Amér: fam) silly thing.

cojudo, -da adj (Amér: fam) silly.

col f cabbage; **~ de Bruselas** Brussels sprout.

cola f (rabo, de avión) tail; (fila) queue (Br), line (Am); (de tren) back; (de vestido) train; (para pegar) glue; (bebida) cola; **~ de caballo** ponytail; **hacer ~** to queue (Br), to stand in line (Am); **traer ~** (fig) to have repercussions.

colaboración f (en trabajo, tarea) collaboration; (en publicación) article.

colaborador, -ra m, f (en trabajo) collaborator; (en periódico) writer.

colaborar vi: ~ en (trabajo, tarea) to collaborate on; (periódico) to write for.

colada f (de ropa) laundry.

colado, -da adj: estar ~ por (fam) to have a crush on.

colador m (para líquidos) strainer; (para verduras) colander.

colar vt (líquido) to strain; (café) to filter; (lo falso, lo ilegal) to slip through ◆ vi to wash; **no cuela** it won't wash □ **colarse** vpr (en cine, metro) to jump the queue (Br), to jump the line (Am); (equivocarse) to get it wrong.

colcha f bedspread.

colchón m mattress; ~ **inflable** air bed.

colchoneta f (en la playa) beach mat.

colección f collection.

coleccionar vt to collect.

coleccionista mf collector.

colecta f collection.

colectivo, -va adj collective ◆ m group.

colega mf colleague.

colegiado, -da m, f referee.

colegial, -la m, f schoolchild.

colegio m (de estudiantes) school; (de profesionales) professional association.

cólera m (enfermedad) cholera ◆ f (enfado) rage.

colérico, -ca adj bad-tempered.

colesterol m cholesterol.

coleta f pigtail.

colgador m hanger.

colgar vt to hang; (la ropa) to hang out; (fam: abandonar) to give up ◆ vi (pender) to hang; (al teléfono) to hang up; ~ **el teléfono** to hang up.

coliflor f cauliflower.

colilla f butt.

colina f hill.

colirio m eyewash.

colitis f inv diarrhea.

collage m collage.

collar m (joya) necklace; (para animales) collar.

collarín m surgical collar.

colmado m grocer's (shop).

colmar vt (cuchara, vaso, etc) to fill to the brim; ~ **a alguien de** to shower sb with.

colmena f beehive.

colmillo m (de persona) eyetooth; (de elefante) tusk.

colmo m: ser el ~ de to be the height of; ¡eso sí es el ~! that's the last straw!

colocación f position.

colocado, -da adj (fam: drogado) high; (bebido) plastered.

colocar vt to place; ~ **a alguien** (proporcionar empleo) to give sb a job □ **colocarse** vpr (fam: drogarse) to get stoned.

Colombia s Colombia.

colombiano, -na adj & m, f Colombian.

colonia f (perfume) (eau de) cologne; (grupo de personas, territo-

rio) colony; *(Amér: barrio)* area; **~ proletaria** *(Amér)* slum area; **~ de verano** summer camp ❑ **colonias** *fpl (para niños)* holiday camp *(sg)*; **ir de ~s** to go to a holiday camp.

colonización *f* colonization.

colonizar *vt* to colonize.

colono *m* settler.

coloquial *adj* colloquial.

coloquio *m* debate.

color *m* colour; *(colorante)* dye; *(aspecto)* tone; **en ~** colour *(antes de s)*.

colorado, -da *adj (rojo)* red; **ponerse ~** to go red.

colorante *m* colouring.

colorete *m* blusher.

colorido *m (conjunto de colores)* colours *(pl)*; *(animación)* colour.

colosal *adj (extraordinario)* extraordinary; *(muy grande)* colossal.

columna *f* column; *(de objetos)* stack; **~ vertebral** spinal column.

columpiarse *vpr* to swing.

columpio *m* swing.

coma *f (signo ortográfico)* comma; *(signo matemático)* decimal point ◆ *m*: **estar en ~** to be in a coma; **cinco ~ dos** five point two.

comadreja *f* weasel.

comadrona *f* midwife.

comandante *m* major.

comando *m* commando.

comarca *f* area.

comba *f (juego)* skipping.

combate *m* fight ❑ **combates** *mpl* fighting *(sg)*.

combatir *vi* to fight ◆ *vt* to combat.

combinación *f* combination; *(de transportes)* connections *(pl)*; *(prenda femenina)* slip.

combinado *m (cóctel)* cocktail.

combinar *vt (unir, mezclar)* to combine; *(bebidas)* to mix ◆ *vi*: **~ (con)** *(colores, ropa etc)* to go together; **~ algo con** *(compaginar)* to combine sthg with.

combustible *m* fuel.

combustión *f* combustion.

comecocos *m inv (juego)* brainteaser.

comedia *f (obra humorística)* comedy; *(obra en general)* play; **hacer ~** *(fam)* to pretend.

comediante *mf (actor)* actor *(f* actress*)*; *(farsante)* fraud.

comedor *m (habitación)* dining room; *(muebles)* dining room furniture.

comensal *mf* fellow diner.

comentar *vt* to comment on.

comentario *m (observación)* comment; *(análisis)* commentary.

comentarista *mf* commentator.

comenzar *vt & vi* to begin, to start; **~ a** to begin to, to start to.

comer *vt* to eat ◆ *vi (alimentarse)* to eat; *(almorzar)* to have lunch.

comercial *adj* commercial.

comercializar *vt* to market.

comerciante *mf (negociante)* trader; *(tendero)* shopkeeper.

comerciar *vi*: **~ (con)** to trade (with).

comercio *m (negocio)* trade; *(tienda)* shop; *(actividad comercial)* business.

comestible *adj* edible.

cometa m (astro) comet ♦ f (juguete) kite.

cometer vt (delito) to commit; (error) to make.

cometido m task.

cómic m comic.

comicios mpl (formal) elections.

cómico, -ca adj (gracioso) comical; (de la comedia) comedy (antes de s) ♦ m, f comedian (f comédienne).

comida f (alimento) food; (almuerzo, cena, etc) meal; (almuerzo) lunch; ~ **rápida** fast food; ~s **caseras** home-made food (sg); ~s **para llevar** takeaway food (sg).

comienzo m beginning, start; **a** ~s **de** at the beginning of.

comillas fpl inverted commas; **entre** ~ in inverted commas.

comilón, -ona adj greedy.

comilona f (fam) blow-out.

comino m cumin; **me importa un** ~ (fam) I couldn't care less.

comisaría f police station.

comisario, -ria m, f (de policía) police superintendent; (de exposición, museo) curator.

comisión f (grupo de personas) committee; (cantidad de dinero) commission.

comisura f (de labios) corner of the mouth.

comité m committee.

comitiva f retinue.

como adv as; (comparativo) like; (aproximadamente) roughly, more or less ♦ conj (ya que) as; (si) if; **tan** ... ~ ... as ... as ...; ~ **si** as if.

cómo adv how ♦ m: **el** ~ **y el porqué** the whys and wherefores;

¡~ es? what's it like?; **¡~?** (qué dices?) sorry?; **¡~ no!** of course!

cómoda f chest of drawers.

cómodamente adv comfortably.

comodidad f comfort □ **comodidades** fpl (ventajas) advantages; **con todas las** ~**es** all mod cons.

comodín m joker.

cómodo, -da adj comfortable.

comodón, -ona adj comfortloving.

compa mf (Amér: fam) mate.

compacto, -ta adj compact ♦ m compact disc.

compadecer vt to feel sorry for □ **compadecerse de** v + prep to feel sorry for.

compadrear vi (Amér: fam) to brag.

compadreo m (Amér: fam) friendship.

compaginar vt: ~ **algo con** to reconcile sthg with.

compañerismo m comradeship.

compañero, -ra m, f (acompañante) companion; (de clase) classmate; (de trabajo) colleague; (de juego) partner; (amigo) partner.

compañía f company; **de** ~ (animal) pet; **hacer** ~ **a alguien** to keep sb company.

comparación f comparison.

comparar vt to compare □ **compararse** vpr: ~**se con** to compare with.

comparsa f (de fiesta) group of masked revellers at carnival; (de teatro) extras (pl) ♦ mf extra.

compartimiento *m* compartment.

compartir *vt* to share; ~ **algo con alguien** to share sthg with sb.

compás *m* (*en dibujo*) pair of compasses; (*ritmo*) beat.

compasión *f* compassion.

compasivo, -va *adj* compassionate.

compatible *adj* compatible; ~ **con** compatible with.

compatriota *mf* compatriot.

compenetrarse *vpr* to be in tune.

compensación *f* compensation.

compensar *vt* to compensate for ♦ *vi* (*satisfacer*) to be worthwhile; ~ **algo con** to make up for sthg with.

competencia *f* (*rivalidad*) competition; (*incumbencia*) area of responsibility; (*aptitud*) competence.

competente *adj* competent.

competición *f* competition.

competir *vi* to compete.

competitivo, -va *adj* competitive.

complacer *vt* to please ♦ *vi* to be pleasing ❏ **complacerse** *vpr*: ~**se en** to take pleasure in.

complaciente *adj* obliging.

complejidad *f* complexity.

complejo, -ja *adj & m* complex.

complementar *vt* to complement ❏ **complementarse** *vpr* to complement one another.

complementario, -ria *adj* complementary.

complemento *m* (*accesorio*) complement; (*en gramática*) complement, object.

completamente *adv* completely.

completar *vt* to complete.

completo, -ta *adj* (*con todas sus partes*) complete; (*lleno*) full; **por ~** completely; **"completo"** "no vacancies".

complexión *f* build.

complicación *f* complication.

complicado, -da *adj* complicated.

complicar *vt* (*hacer difícil*) to complicate; ~ **a alguien en** (*implicar*) to involve sb in ❏ **complicarse** *vpr* (*situación, problema*) to get complicated; (*enfermedad*) to get worse.

cómplice *mf* accomplice.

complot *m* plot.

componente *m* component.

componer *vt* (*obra literaria*) to write; (*obra musical*) to compose; (*lo roto*) to repair; (*lo desordenado*) to tidy up ❏ **componerse de** *v + prep* to consist of; **componérselas** to manage.

comportamiento *m* behaviour.

comportar *vt* to involve ❏ **comportarse** *vpr* to behave.

composición *f* composition.

compositor, -ra *m, f* composer.

compostura *f* (*buena educación*) good behaviour.

compota *f* stewed fruit; ~ **de manzana** stewed apple.

compra *f* purchase; **hacer la** ~

to do the shopping; **ir de ~s** to go shopping; **~ a plazos** hire purchase.

comprador, -ra *m, f* buyer.

comprar *vt* to buy; **~ algo a alguien** to buy sthg from sb.

comprender *vt* (*entender*) to understand; (*abarcar*) to comprise.

comprensible *adj* understandable.

comprensión *f* (*de ejercicio, texto*) comprehension; (*de problema, situación*) understanding.

comprensivo, -va *adj* understanding.

compresa *f* (*para higiene femenina*) sanitary towel; (*para uso médico*) compress.

comprimido, -da *adj* compressed ◆ *m* pill.

comprimir *vt* to compress.

comprobación *f* checking.

comprobar *vt* (*verificar*) to check; (*demostrar*) to prove.

comprometer *vt* to compromise ❏ **comprometerse** *vpr* (*novios*) to get engaged; **~se (a)** to commit o.s. (to); **~se (con)** to commit o.s. (to).

comprometido, -da *adj* (*empeñado*) committed.

compromiso *m* (*obligación*) commitment; (*acuerdo*) compromise; (*apuro*) difficult situation; **sin ~** uncompromising.

compuerta *f* sluice gate.

compuesto, -ta *adj* (*por varios elementos*) composed; (*reparado*) repaired ◆ *m* compound.

compungido, -da *adj* remorseful.

comulgar *vi* to take communion ❏ **comulgar con** *v + prep* (*ideas, sentimientos*) to agree with.

común *adj* (*frecuente*) common; (*compartido*) shared.

comuna *f* commune.

comunicación *f* (*entre personas, animales*) communication; (*escrito*) communiqué; (*por carretera, tren, etc*) communications (*pl*); **se cortó la ~** I was cut off.

comunicado, -da *adj* connected ◆ *m* statement; **bien/mal ~** (*pueblo, ciudad*) with good/bad connections.

comunicar *vt* to communicate ◆ *vi* (*al teléfono*) to get through; **está comunicando** (*teléfono*) the line's engaged.

comunicativo, -va *adj* communicative.

comunidad *f* community; **~ autónoma** Spanish autonomous region; **Comunidad Europea** European Community.

COMUNIDAD AUTÓNOMA

In Spain, the "comunidad autónoma" is a region consisting of one or more provinces which enjoys a degree of autonomy in administrative matters. There are 17 "comunidades autónomas": Andalusia, Aragon, the Principality of Asturias, the Balearic Islands, the Canary Islands, Cantabria, Castile and León, Castile and La Mancha, Catalonia, Extremadura, La Rioja, Madrid, Murcia, Navarre, Valencia, Galicia and the Basque Country.

comunión f communion.

comunismo m communism.

comunista mf communist.

comunitario, -ria adj community (antes de s).

con prep 1. (modo, medio) with; **hazlo ~ el martillo** do it with the hammer; **lo ha conseguido ~ su esfuerzo** he has achieved it through his own efforts. 2. (compañía) with; **trabaja ~ su padre** he works with his father. 3. (junto a) with; **una cartera ~ varios documentos** a briefcase containing several documents. 4. (a pesar de) in spite of; **~ lo aplicado que es lo han suspendido** for all his hard work, they still failed him; **~ todo iremos a su casa** we'll go to her house anyway. 5. (condición) by; **~ salir a las cinco será suficiente** if we leave at five we'll have plenty of time. 6. (en locuciones): **~ (tal) que** as long as.

conato m (de agresión) attempt; (de incendio) beginnings (pl).

cóncavo, -va adj concave.

concebir vt to conceive; **no ~** (no entender) to be unable to conceive of.

conceder vt (dar) to grant; (premio) to award; (asentir) to admit.

concejal, -la m, f councillor.

concentración f (de personas) gathering; (de líquido) concentration.

concentrado, -da adj (reunido) gathered; (espeso) concentrated ◆ m: **~ de ...** concentrated ...

concentrar vt (interés, atención) to concentrate; (lo desunido) to bring together ❑ **concentrarse** vpr: **~se en** (estudio, trabajo, etc) to concentrate on; (lugar) to gather in.

concepción f conception.

concepto m (idea) concept; (opinión) opinion; **en ~ de** by way of.

concernir: concernir a v + prep to concern.

concertación f agreement.

concertado, -da adj agreed.

concertar vt (precio) to agree on; (cita, entrevista) to arrange; (acuerdo) to reach.

concesión f award.

concesionario, -ria adj concessionary ◆ m licensee.

concha f (caparazón) shell; (material) tortoiseshell.

concho, -da adj (Amér: vulg) bloody stupid.

conciencia f (conocimiento) awareness; (moral) conscience; **a ~** conscientiously; **tener ~ de** to be aware of.

concienzudo, -da adj conscientious.

concierto m (actuación musical) concert; (composición musical) concerto; (convenio) agreement.

conciliación f reconciliation.

conciliar vt to reconcile; **~ el sueño** to get to sleep ❑ **conciliarse con** v + prep to be reconciled with.

concisión f conciseness.

conciso, -sa adj concise.

concluir vt to conclude ◆ vi to (come to an) end.

conclusión f conclusion.

concordancia f agreement.

concordar vt to reconcile ♦ vi (de género) to agree; (de número) to tally; **~ con** (coincidir con) to agree with.

concordia f harmony.

concretar vt (especificar) to specify; (reducir) to cut down.

concreto, -ta adj (no abstracto) concrete; (específico) specific ♦ m: **~ armado** (Amér) concrete.

concubina f concubine.

concurrencia f (público) audience; (de hechos) concurrence; (asistencia) attendance.

concurrente adj concurrent.

concurrido, -da adj crowded.

concurrir vi (asistir) to attend; (coincidir) to meet.

concursante mf contestant.

concursar vi to compete.

concurso m (de deportes, literatura) competition; (en televisión) game show.

condado m county.

condal adj county (antes de s).

conde, -desa m, f count (f countess).

condecoración f medal.

condena f sentence.

condenado, -da adj convicted ♦ m, f convicted criminal.

condenar vt (suj: juez) to sentence; (desaprobar) to condemn.

condensación f condensation.

condensar vt to condense.

condición f (supuesto) condition; (modo de ser) nature; (estado social) status ☐ **condiciones** fpl (situación) conditions; **estar en buenas/malas condiciones** to be/not to be in a fit state.

condicional adj conditional.

condimentar vt to season.

condimento m seasoning.

condominio m (Amér: viviendas) block of flats (Br), apartment block (Am); (oficinas) office block.

conducción f (de vehículos) driving; (cañerías) pipes (pl).

conducir vt (vehículo) to drive; (llevar) to lead; (dirigir) to conduct ♦ vi to drive.

conducta f behaviour.

conducto m (tubo) pipe; (vía) channel.

conductor, -ra m, f driver.

conectar vt to connect ☐ **conectar con** v + prep (contactar con) to get in touch with; (comprender) to get on well with.

conejera f (madriguera) warren.

conejo, -ja f rabbit; **~ a la cazadora** rabbit cooked in olive oil, with onion, garlic and parsley.

conexión f connection.

confección f (de vestido) dressmaking ☐ **confecciones** fpl (tienda) clothes shop (sg).

confederación f confederation.

conferencia f (disertación) lecture; (por teléfono) long-distance call.

conferenciante mf speaker (at conference).

confesar vt to confess ☐ **confesarse** vpr to take confession.

confesión f (de los pecados) con-

congregar

fession; (religión) religion.

confesionario m confessional.

confesor m confessor.

confeti m confetti.

confiado, -da adj (crédulo) trusting.

confianza f (seguridad) confidence; (fe) faith; (trato familiar) familiarity.

confiar vt (secreto) to confide; (persona, cosa) to entrust ❑ confiar en v + prep (persona) to trust; (esperar en) to have faith in; ~ en que to be confident that; confiarse vpr to be overconfident.

confidencia f confidence.

confidencial adj confidential.

confidente mf (de un secreto) confidante; (de la policía) informer.

configuración f configuration.

configurar vt to shape.

confirmación f confirmation.

confirmar vt to confirm.

confiscar vt to confiscate.

confitado, -da adj crystallized.

confite m sweet (Br), candy (Am).

confitería f (tienda) sweet shop (Br), candy store (Am).

confitura f preserve.

conflictivo, -va adj difficult.

conflicto m (desacuerdo) conflict; (situación difícil) difficulty.

confluencia f (lugar) intersection; (de ríos) confluence.

confluir: confluir en v + prep to meet at.

conformarse: conformarse

con v + prep to settle for.

conforme adj in agreement ◆ adv as; ~ a O con in accordance with.

conformidad f: dar la ~ to give one's consent.

conformismo m conformism.

conformista mf conformist.

confort m comfort; "todo ~" "all mod cons".

confortable adj comfortable.

confrontación f confrontation.

confundir vt to confuse; ~ algo/a alguien con to confuse sthg/sb with ❑ confundirse vpr (equivocarse) to make a mistake; (al teléfono) to get the wrong number; ~se de casa to get the wrong house; confundirse con v + prep (mezclarse con) to merge into.

confusión f (equivocación) mix-up; (desorden) confusion.

confuso, -sa adj (perplejo) confused; (no diferenciado) unclear.

congelación f freezing.

congelado, -da adj (alimentos, productos) frozen; (persona) freezing ❑ congelados mpl (alimentos) frozen foods.

congelador m freezer.

congelar vt to freeze ❑ congelarse vpr (persona) to freeze.

congeniar: congeniar con v + prep to get on with.

congénito, -ta adj congenital.

congestión f congestion.

conglomerado m (de madera) hardboard.

congregar vt to gather together ❑ congregarse vpr to gather.

congresista *mf* delegate.

congreso *m* (de especialistas) conference; (de diputados) parliament; **el ~ de diputados** the lower house of the Spanish Parliament.

conjetura *f* conjecture.

conjugación *f* (de verbos) conjugation; (de colores, estilos, etc) combination.

conjugar *vt* (verbos) to conjugate; (unir) to combine.

conjunción *f* (GRAM) conjunction; (unión) combining.

conjuntamente *adv* jointly.

conjuntivitis *f inv* conjunctivitis.

conjunto *m* (grupo, de rock) group; (ropa) outfit; (en matemáticas) set; **en ~** as a whole.

conmemoración *f* commemoration.

conmemorar *vt* to commemorate.

conmigo *pron* with me.

conmoción *f* shock; **~ cerebral** concussion.

conmover *vt* (impresionar) to move, to touch.

conmutador *m* (de electricidad) switch; (Amér: centralita) switchboard.

cono *m* cone.

conocer *vt* to know; (persona por primera vez) to meet; (distinguir) to recognize ♦ **conocerse** *vpr* (tratarse) to know one another; (por primera vez) to meet; (reconocerse) to recognize one another; (uno mismo) to know o.s.

conocido, -da *adj* well-known ♦ *m, f* acquaintance.

conocimiento *m* (entendimiento) knowledge; (MED) consciousness ❑ **conocimientos** *mpl* knowledge (sg).

conque *conj* so.

conquista *f* conquest.

conquistador, -ra *adj* seductive ♦ *m, f* conqueror.

conquistar *vt* (país, territorio) to conquer; (puesto, trabajo, etc) to obtain; (persona) to win over.

consagrado, -da *adj* (en religión) consecrated; (dedicado) dedicated.

consagrar *vt* (monumento, calle, etc) to dedicate; (acreditar) to confirm.

consciente *adj*: **estar ~** to be conscious; **ser ~ de** to be aware of.

consecuencia *f* consequence; **en ~** consequently.

consecuente *adj* (persona) consistent; (hecho) resultant.

consecutivo, -va *adj* consecutive.

conseguir *vt* (lograr) to obtain; (objetivo) to achieve.

consejo *m* (advertencias) advice; (advertencia concreta) piece of advice; (organismo) council; (reunión) meeting.

consenso *m* consensus.

consentido, -da *adj* spoilt.

consentir *vt* (permitir) to allow.

conserje *m* caretaker.

conserjería *f* reception (desk).

conserva *f*: **en ~** tinned ❑ **conservas** *fpl* tinned food (sg).

conservador, -ra *adj* (en ideología) conservative; (en política)

Conservative; *(que mantiene)* pre-servative.

conservadurismo *m* conservatism.

conservante *m* preservative.

conservar *vt (mantener, cuidar)* to preserve; *(guardar)* to keep ❑ **conservarse** *vpr (persona)* to look after o.s.; *(alimentos, productos)* to keep.

conservatorio *m* conservatoire.

considerable *adj (grande)* considerable; *(hecho)* notable.

consideración *f (respeto)* respect; **de ~** considerable.

considerar *vt* to consider; *(valorar)* to value.

consigna *f (orden)* instructions *(pl)*; *(depósito)* left-luggage office; **~ automática** (left-)luggage locker.

consignación *f* consignment.

consigo *pron (con él, con ella)* with him *(f* with her); *(con usted)* with you; *(con uno mismo)* with o.s.

consiguiente: por consiguiente *adv* therefore.

consistencia *f* consistency.

consistente *adj (sólido)* solid.

consistir: consistir en *v* + *prep (componerse de)* to consist of; *(estar fundado en)* to be based on.

consistorio *m* town council.

consola *f (mesa)* console table; *(de videojuegos)* console.

consolar *vt* to console ❑ **consolarse** *vpr* to console o.s.

consolidación *f* consolidation.

consolidar *vt* to consolidate.

consomé *m* consommé; **~ al**

jerez consommé made with sherry.

consonante *f* consonant.

consorcio *m* consortium.

consorte *mf* spouse.

conspiración *f* conspiracy.

conspirar *vi* to conspire.

constancia *f (tenacidad)* perseverance.

constante *adj (que dura)* constant; *(tenaz)* persistent ♦ *f* constant; **~s vitales** signs of life.

constantemente *adv* constantly.

constar: constar de *v* + *prep* to be made up of ❑ **constar en** *v* + *prep (figurar en)* to appear in; **me consta que** I know that; **que conste que** let there be no doubt that.

constelación *f* constellation.

constipado *m (formal)* cold.

constiparse *vpr (formal)* to catch a cold.

constitución *f (forma)* make-up; *(ley)* constitution.

constitucional *adj* constitutional.

constituir *vt (formar)* to make up; *(componer, fundar)* to form; *(ser)* to be ❑ **constituirse** *vpr (formarse)* to form; **~se de** *(estar compuesto de)* to be made up of.

construcción *f (edificio)* building; *(arte)* construction.

constructivo, -va *adj* constructive.

constructor *m* builder.

constructora *f* construction company.

construir *vt* to build; *(máquina)* to manufacture.

consuelo *m* consolation.

cónsul *mf* consul.

consulado *m (lugar)* consulate; *(cargo)* consulship.

consulta *f (aclaración, examen médico)* consultation; *(pregunta)* question; **~ (médica)** surgery.

consultar *vt (persona, libro)* to consult; *(dato)* to look up; **~le algo a alguien** to consult sb about sthg.

consultorio *m (de médico)* surgery; *(de revista)* problem page; *(de radio)* programme which answers listeners' questions.

consumición *f (alimento)* food; *(bebida)* drink; **"~ obligatoria"** "minimum charge".

consumidor, -ra *m, f* consumer.

consumir *vt (gastar)* to use; *(acabar totalmente)* to use up ◆ *vi (gastar dinero)* to spend □ **consumirse** *vpr (extinguirse)* to burn out.

consumismo *m* consumerism.

consumo *m* consumption.

contabilidad *f (cuentas)* accounts *(pl)*.

contable *mf* accountant.

contacto *m* contact; *(de coche)* ignition.

contador, -ra *m, f (Amér) (prestamista)* moneylender; *(contable)* accountant ◆ *m* meter.

contagiar *vt (persona)* to infect; *(enfermedad)* to pass on, to give.

contagio *m* infection; **transmitirse por ~** to be contagious.

contagioso, -sa *adj* infectious.

container *m (de mercancías)* container; *(de basuras)* wheely bin

for rubbish from blocks of flats etc.

contaminación *f* pollution.

contaminado, -da *adj* polluted.

contaminar *vt* to pollute □ **contaminarse** *vpr* to become polluted.

contar *vt* to count; *(explicar)* to tell ◆ *vi* to count □ **contar con** *v + prep (tener en cuenta)* to take into account; *(tener)* to have; *(confiar en)* to count on.

contemplaciones *fpl* indulgence *(sg)*; **sin ~** without standing on ceremony.

contemplar *vt* to contemplate.

contemporáneo, -a *adj* contemporary.

contenedor *m* container; **~ de basura** wheely bin for rubbish from blocks of flats etc.

contener *vt (llevar)* to contain; *(impedir)* to hold back □ **contenerse** *vpr* to hold back.

contenido, -da *adj* restrained ◆ *m* contents *(pl)*.

contentar *vt* to please □ **contentarse con** *v + prep* to make do with.

contento, -ta *adj (alegre)* happy; *(satisfecho)* pleased.

contestación *f* answer.

contestador *m:* **~ automático** answering machine.

contestar *vt* to answer ◆ *vi (responder)* to answer; *(responder mal)* to answer back.

contexto *m* context.

contigo *pron* with you.

contiguo, -gua *adj* adjacent.

continental *adj* continental.

continente *m* continent.

continuación *f* continuation; **a ~** then.

continuamente *adv (sin interrupción)* continuously; *(repetidamente)* continually.

continuar *vt* to continue; **continúa en la casa** it's still in the house.

continuo, -nua *adj (sin interrupción)* continuous; *(repetido)* continual.

contorno *m (silueta)* outline.

contra *prep* against ◆ *m*: **los pros y los ~s** the pros and cons; **en ~** against; **en ~ de** against.

contrabajo *m (instrumento)* double bass.

contrabandista *mf* smuggler.

contrabando *m (de mercancías, droga)* smuggling; *(mercancías)* contraband.

contracorriente *f* cross current; **a ~** against the flow.

contradecir *vt* to contradict ❏

contradecirse *vpr* to be inconsistent.

contradicción *f* contradiction.

contradicho, -cha *pp* → contradecir.

contradictorio, -ria *adj* contradictory.

contraer *vt* to contract; *(deuda)* to run up; **~ matrimonio** to marry.

contraindicado, -da *adj* not recommended.

contraluz *m* picture taken against the light; **a ~** against the light.

contrapartida *f* compensation; **en ~** as compensation.

contrapelo *m*: **a ~** against the grain.

contrapeso *m* counterbalance.

contrariar *vt (disgustar)* to upset.

contrario, -ria *adj (opuesto)* opposite; *(equipo, etc)* opposing; *(negativo)* contrary ◆ *m, f* opponent; **al ~** on the contrary; **por el ~** on the contrary; **llevar la contraria** to always take an opposing view.

contraseña *f* password.

contrastar *vt (comparar)* to contrast; *(comprobar)* to check ◆ *vi* to contrast.

contraste *m* contrast.

contratar *vt* to hire.

contratiempo *m* mishap.

contrato *m* contract.

contribuir *vi* to contribute; **~ a** to contribute to; **~ con** to contribute.

contrincante *mf* opponent.

control *m (comprobación)* inspection; *(dominio)* control; **~ de pasaportes** passport control.

controlar *vt (comprobar)* to check; *(dominar)* to control ❏ **controlarse** *vpr* to control o.s.

contusión *f* bruise.

convalidar *vt (estudios)* to recognize.

convencer *vt* to convince ❏ **convencerse de** *v + prep* to convince o.s. of.

convención *f* convention.

convencional *adj* conventional.

conveniente *adj* (*oportuno*) suitable; (*hora*) convenient; (*aconsejable*) advisable; (*útil*) useful.

convenio *m* agreement.

convenir *vt* to agree on ◆ *vi* (*ser adecuado*) to be suitable; **conviene hacerlo** it's a good idea to do it.

convento *m* (*de monjas*) convent; (*de monjes*) monastery.

conversación *f* conversation.

conversar *vi* to have a conversation.

convertir *vt*: ~ **algo/a alguien en** to turn sthg/sb into ❑ **convertirse** *vpr*: ~**se a** (*religión, ideología*) to convert to; ~**se en** (*transformarse en*) to turn into.

convicción *f* conviction.

convidado, -da *m, f* guest.

convidar *vt* to invite.

convincente *adj* convincing.

convite *m* banquet.

convivencia *f* living together.

convivir: **convivir con** *v* + *prep* to live with.

convocar *vt* (*reunión*) to convene; (*huelga, elecciones*) to call.

convocatoria *f* (*de exámenes*) diet.

convulsión *f* (*espasmo*) convulsion; (*conmoción, revolución*) upheaval.

cónyuge *mf* spouse.

coña *f* (*vulg: guasa*) joke; **estar de ~ to** be pissing around.

coñac *m* brandy.

coñazo *m* (*vulg*) pain (in the arse).

coño *interj* (*vulg*) fuck!

cooperar *vi* to cooperate.

cooperativa *f* cooperative.

coordinación *f* coordination.

coordinar *vt* to coordinate.

copa *f* (*para beber*) glass; (*trofeo*) cup; (*de árbol*) top; **invitar a alguien a una ~** to buy sb a drink; **tomar una ~** to have a drink; **ir de ~s** to go out drinking ❑ **copas** *fpl* (*de la baraja*) suit with pictures of goblets in Spanish deck of cards.

copeo *m*: **ir de ~** (*fam*) to go out drinking.

copia *f* copy.

copiar *vt* to copy.

copiloto *m* copilot.

copioso, -sa *adj* copious.

copla *f* (*estrofa*) verse; (*canción*) popular song.

copo *m* flake.

coquetear *vi* to flirt.

coqueto, -ta *adj* (*que flirtea*) flirtatious.

coraje *m* (*valor*) courage; **dar ~** to make angry.

coral *m* coral ◆ *f* (*coro*) choir.

coraza *f* (*de soldado*) cuirass.

corazón *m* heart; (*de fruta*) core; **corazones** *mpl* (*de la baraja*) hearts.

corbata *f* tie.

corchea *f* quaver.

corchete *m* (*cierre*) hook and eye; (*signo*) square bracket.

corcho *m* cork.

cordel *m* cord.

cordero, -ra *m, f* lamb; **~ asado** roast lamb.

cordial *adj* cordial.

cordialmente *adv* cordially.

cordillera *f* mountain range; **la ~ Cantábrica** the Cantabrian Mountains (*pl*).

cordón m (cuerda) cord; (de zapato) lace; (cable eléctrico) flex; ~ umbilical umbilical cord.

Corea s Korea; ~ del Norte North Korea; ~ del Sur South Korea.

coreografía f choreography.

corista mf chorus singer.

cornada f goring.

cornamenta f (de toro) horns (pl); (de ciervo) antlers (pl).

córnea f cornea.

corneja f crow.

córner m corner (kick).

cornete m cone.

cornflakes® ['konfleiks] mpl Cornflakes®

cornisa f cornice.

coro m choir; a ~ in unison.

corona f (de rey) crown; (fig: trono) throne; (de flores) garland.

coronar vt to crown.

coronel m colonel.

coronilla f crown (of the head); **estar hasta la ~** to be fed up to the back teeth.

corporal adj (olor) body (antes de s).

corpulento, -ta adj corpulent.

Corpus m Corpus Christi.

corral m (para animales) pen.

correa f (de bolso, reloj) strap; (de pantalón) belt; (del animal) lead.

corrección f (de errores) correction; (de comportamiento) correctness.

correctamente adv correctly.

correcto, -ta adj (sin errores) correct; (educado) polite.

corredor, -ra m, f (en deporte) runner; (intermediario) agent ◆ m (pasillo) corridor.

corregir vt (error, comportamiento) to correct; (exámenes) to mark ❑ **corregirse** vpr to mend one's ways.

correo m post, mail; ~ aéreo airmail; ~ certificado = registered post; ~ urgente = special delivery ❑ **Correos** m inv the Post Office; **"Correos y Telégrafos"** sign outside a major post office indicating telegram service.

correr vi (persona, animal) to run; (río) to flow; (tiempo) to pass; (noticia, rumor) to go around ◆ vt (mesa, silla, etc) to move up; (cortinas) to draw; **dejar ~ algo** to let sthg be ❑ **correrse** vpr (tintas, colores) to run.

correspondencia f correspondence; (de transporte) connection; "~s" (en metro) "to other lines".

corresponder vi: ~ a alguien (con algo) to repay sb (with sthg); **te corresponde hacerlo** it's your responsibility to do it.

correspondiente adj corresponding.

corresponsal mf correspondent.

corrida f (de toros) bullfight.

corriente adj (agua) running; (común) ordinary; (día, mes, año) current ◆ f (de aire) draught; (de mar) current; **estar al ~** to be up to date with; **ponerse al ~ de** to bring o.s. up to date with; ~ (eléctrica) (electric) current.

corro m circle.

corromper vt (pervertir) to corrupt; (sobornar) to bribe; (pudrir) to rot.

corrupción f (perversión) corruption; (soborno) bribery.

corsé m corset.

corsetería f ladies' underwear shop.

cortacésped m lawnmower.

cortado, -da adj (leche) off; (salsa) curdled; (labios, manos) chapped; (fam: persona) inhibited ♦ m small coffee with a drop of milk.

cortante adj (cuchilla, etc) sharp; (persona) cutting; (viento, frío) bitter.

cortar vt to cut; (calle) to block off; (conversación) to cut short; (luz, gas, etc) to cut off; (piel) to chap □ **cortarse** vpr (herirse) to cut o.s.; (avergonzarse) to become tongue-tied; (leche, salsa) to curdle.

cortaúñas m inv nailclippers (pl).

corte m (herida) cut; (en vestido, tela, etc) tear; (de corriente eléctrica) power cut; (vergüenza) embarrassment; **~ y confección** (para mujeres) dressmaking; **~ de pelo** haircut.

Cortes fpl: **Las ~** the Spanish parliament.

cortés adj polite.

cortesía f politeness.

corteza f (de árbol) bark; (de pan) crust; (de queso, tubería) rind; (de naranja) peel; **~s de cerdo** pork scratchings.

cortijo m farm.

cortina f curtain.

corto, -ta adj (breve) short; (fam: tonto) thick; **quedarse ~** (al calcular) to underestimate; **~ de vista** short-sighted.

cortometraje m short (film).

cosa f thing; **¿alguna ~ más?** is that everything?; **ser ~ de alguien** to be sb's business; **como si tal ~** as if nothing had happened.

coscorrón m bump on the head.

cosecha f harvest; (de vino) vintage.

cosechar vt to harvest ♦ vi to bring in the harvest.

coser vt & vi to sew.

cosmopolita adj cosmopolitan.

cosmos m cosmos.

cosquillas fpl: **hacer ~** to tickle; **tener ~** to be ticklish.

cosquilleo m tickling sensation.

costa f (orilla) coast; **a ~ de** at the expense of.

costado m side.

costar vi (valer) to cost; **me cuesta (mucho) hacerlo** it's (very) difficult for me to do it; **¿cuánto cuesta?** how much is it?

Costa Rica s Costa Rica.

costarriqueño, -ña adj & m, f Costa Rican.

coste m (de producción) cost; (de producto, mercancía) price.

costero, -ra adj coastal.

costilla f rib; **~s de cordero** lamb chops.

costo m (de producción) cost; (de producto, mercancía) price.

costoso, -sa adj expensive.

costra f (de herida) scab.

costumbre f habit; **tener la ~**

de to be in the habit of.

costura f (labor) sewing; (de vestido) seam.

costurera f seamstress.

costurero m sewing box.

cota f (altura) height (above sea level).

cotejo m comparison.

cotidiano, -na adj daily.

cotilla mf (fam) gossip.

cotilleo m (fam) gossip.

cotillón m New Year's Eve party.

cotización f (de la moneda) price.

cotizar vt (en la Bolsa) to price; (cuota) to pay.

coto m (terreno) reserve; ~ (privado) de caza (private) game preserve.

cotorra f (pájaro) parrot; (fam: charlatán) chatterbox.

COU m (abrev de curso de orientación universitaria) optional year of Spanish secondary education in which 17-18 year olds prepare for university entrance exams; a mixture of compulsory and optional subjects is studied.

coyuntura f current situation.

coz f tick.

cráneo m skull.

cráter m crater.

crawl [krol] m crawl.

creación f creation.

creador, -ra m, f creator.

crear vt (inventar) to create; (fundar) to found.

creatividad f creativity.

creativo, -va adj creative.

crecer vi to grow; (río) to rise;

(luna) to wax.

crecimiento m growth.

credencial f identification.

crédito m (préstamo) loan; (disponibilidad) credit; (confianza) confidence.

credo m (oración) Creed.

creencia f (en religión) faith; (convicción) belief.

creer vt (dar por verdadero) to believe; (suponer) to think; ¡ya lo creo! I should say so! ◊ **creer en** v + prep to believe in.

creído, -da adj (presuntuoso) vain.

crema f (nata, cosmético) cream; (betún) polish; ~ de ave cream of chicken soup; ~ de belleza beauty cream; ~ de cangrejos crab bisque; ~ catalana Catalan dessert similar to crème caramel; ~ de espárragos cream of asparagus soup; ~ de gambas shrimp bisque; ~ de marisco seafood bisque; ~ (pastelera) custard.

cremallera f zip (Br), zipper (Am).

crepe [krep] f crepe.

cresta f crest.

cretino, -na adj (estúpido) stupid.

creyente mf believer.

cría f (de ganado) breeding; (hijo de animal) young, → **crío**.

criadero m farm.

criadillas fpl bull's testicles.

criado, -da m, f servant (maid).

crianza f (de animales) breeding; (educación) bringing up; (de vino) vintage.

criar vt (animales) to breed; (educar) to bring up ♦ vi to breed.

criatura f creature.

crimen m crime.

criminal mf criminal.

crío, -a m, f kid.

criollo, -lla m, f Latin American of Spanish extraction.

crisis f inv (en política) crisis; (económica) recession; (en enfermedad) breakdown.

cristal m (sustancia) glass; (vidrio fino) crystal; (de ventana) pane.

cristalería f (tienda) glassware shop; (objetos) glassware.

cristalino, -na adj crystalline.

cristianismo m Christianity.

cristiano, -na adj & m, f Christian.

Cristo m Christ.

criterio m (regla, norma) criterion; (opinión) opinion.

crítica f (de arte, cine, etc) review; (censura) criticism, → crítico.

criticar vt (obra, película, etc) to review; (censurar) to criticize ♦ vi to criticize.

crítico, -ca adj critical ♦ m, f critic.

croar vi to croak.

croissant [krwa'san] m croissant.

croissantería f shop selling filled croissants.

crol m (front) crawl.

cromo m (estampa) transfer.

crónica f (de historia) chronicle; (en periódico) column.

cronometrar vt to time.

cronómetro m stopwatch.

croqueta f croquette.

croquis m inv sketch.

cros m inv cross-country (running).

cruce m (de calles, caminos) crossroads; (en el teléfono) crossed line.

crucero m (en barco) cruise; (de iglesia) transept.

crucial adj crucial.

crucifijo m crucifix.

crucigrama m crossword.

crudo, -da adj (no cocido) raw; (novela, película) harshly realistic; (clima) harsh.

cruel adj cruel.

crueldad f cruelty.

crujido m creak.

crujiente adj (alimento) crunchy.

crustáceo m crustacean.

cruz f cross; (de la moneda) tails; (fig: carga) burden.

cruzada f crusade.

cruzar vt to cross ❏ **cruzarse** vpr: **~se de brazos** (fig) to twiddle one's thumbs; **cruzarse con** v + prep (persona) to pass.

cta. (abrev de cuenta) a/c.

cte. (abrev de corriente) inst.

CTNE (abrev de Compañía Telefónica Nacional de España) Spanish state telephone company.

cuaderno m (libreta) notebook; (de colegial) exercise book.

cuadra f (lugar, conjunto) stable; (Amér: esquina) corner; (Amér: de casas) block.

cuadrado, -da adj & m square.

cuadriculado, -da adj squared.

cuadrilla f group, team.

cuadro m (cuadrado) square; (pintura) picture, painting; (gráfico) diagram; **a** o **de** ~s checked.

cuajada f curd; ~ **con miel** dish of curd covered in honey.

cual pron: **el/la** ~ (persona) who; (cosa) which; **lo** ~ which; **sea** ~ **sea su nombre** whatever his name may be.

cuál pron (qué) what; (especificando) which; **¿**~ **te gusta más?** which do you prefer?

cualidad f quality.

cualificado, -da adj skilled.

cualquier adj → **cualquiera**.

cualquiera adj any ◆ pron anybody ◆ adj nobody; **cualquier día iré a verte** I'll drop by one of these days.

cuando adv when ◆ conj (si) if ◆ prep: ~ **la guerra** when the war was on; **de** ~ **en** ~ from time to time; **de vez en** ~ from time to time.

cuándo adv when.

cuantía f amount.

cuanto, -ta adj 1. (todo): **despilfarra** ~ **dinero gana** he squanders all the money he earns.

2. (compara cantidades): **cuantas más mentiras digas, menos te creerán** the more you lie, the less people will believe you.

◆ pron 1. (de personas) everyone who; **dio las gracias a todos** ~s **le ayudaron** he thanked everyone who helped him.

2. (todo lo que) everything; **come** ~/~s **quieras** eat as much/as many as you like; **todo** ~ **dijo era verdad** everything she said was true.

3. (compara cantidades): ~ **más se tiene, más se quiere** the more you have, the more you want.

4. (en locuciones): **en** ~ antes as soon as possible; **en** ~ (tan pronto como) as soon as; **en** ~ **a** as regards; **unos** ~s a few.

cuánto, -ta adj (interrogativo singular) how much; (interrogativo plural) how many; (exclamativo) what a lot of ◆ pron (interrogativo singular) how much; (interrogativo plural) how many; **¿**~ **quieres?** how much do you want?

cuarenta núm forty, → **seis**.

cuaresma f Lent.

cuartel m barracks (pl); ~ **de la Guardia Civil** headquarters of the "Guardia Civil".

cuartelazo m (Amér) military uprising.

cuarteto m quartet.

cuartilla f sheet of (quarto) paper.

cuarto, -ta núm fourth ◆ m (parte, período) quarter; (habitación) room, ~ **sexto**; ~ **de baño** bathroom; ~ **de estar** living room; **un** ~ **de hora** a quarter of an hour; **un** ~ **de kilo** a quarter of a kilo.

cuarzo m quartz.

cuate mf inv (Amér: fam) mate.

cuatro núm four, → **seis**.

cuatrocientos, -tas núm four hundred, → **seis**.

Cuba s Cuba.

cubalibre m rum and Coke.

cubano, -na adj & m, f Cuban.

cubertería f cutlery.

cubeta f (Amér) bucket.

cúbico, -ca adj cubic.

cubierta

cubierta f (de libro) cover; (de barco) deck.

cubierto, -ta pp irreg → **cubrir** ♦ adj (tapado) covered; (cielo) overcast ♦ m (pieza para comer) piece of cutlery; (para comensal) place setting; **a ~** under cover.

cubito m: ~ **de hielo** ice cube.

cúbito m ulna.

cubo m (recipiente) bucket; (en geometría, matemáticas) cube; ~ **de la basura** rubbish bin (Br), trash can (Am).

cubrir vt to cover; (proteger) to protect ◆ **cubrirse** vpr to cover o.s.

cucaracha f cockroach.

cuchara f spoon.

cucharada f spoonful.

cucharilla f teaspoon.

cucharón m ladle.

cuchilla f blade; ~ **de afeitar** razor blade.

cuchillo m knife.

cuclillas fpl: **en ~** squatting.

cucurucho m cone.

cuello m (del cuerpo) neck; (de la camisa) collar.

cuenca f (de río, mar) basin.

cuenco m bowl.

cuenta f (cálculo) sum; (factura) bill; (de banco) account; (de collar) bead; **la ~, por favor** could I have the bill, please?; **caer en la ~** to catch on; **darse ~** to notice; **tener en ~** to take into account.

cuentagotas m inv dropper; **en ~** in dribs and drabs.

cuentakilómetros m inv (de distancia) ≈ mileometer; (de veloci-

dad) speedometer.

cuento m (relato) short story; (mentira) story.

cuerda f (fina, de instrumento) string; (gruesa) rope; (del reloj) spring; **~s vocales** vocal cords; **dar ~ a** (reloj) to wind up.

cuerno m horn; (de ciervo) antler.

cuero m (piel) leather; ~ **cabelludo** scalp; **en ~s** stark naked.

cuerpo m body; (de policía) force; (militar) corps.

cuervo m raven.

cuesta f slope; ~ **arriba** uphill; ~ **abajo** downhill; **a ~s** on one's back.

cuestión f question; **ser ~ de** to be a question of.

cuestionario m questionnaire.

cueva f cave.

cuidado m care ♦ interj be careful; **¡~ con la cabeza!** mind your head!; **de ~** dangerous; **estar al ~ de** to be responsible for; **tener ~** to be careful.

cuidadosamente adv carefully.

cuidadoso, -sa adj careful.

cuidar vt to look after ♦ vi: ~ **de** to look after ◆ **cuidarse** vpr to look after o.s.; **cuidarse de** v + prep (encargarse de) to look after.

culata f (de arma) butt; (de motor) cylinder head.

culebra f snake.

culebrón m (fam) soap opera.

culo m (fam) (de persona) bum (Br), butt (Am); (de botella, etc) bottom.

culpa f fault; **echar la ~ a alguien**

to blame sb; **tener la ~** to be to blame.

culpabilidad f guilt.

culpable mf guilty party ♦ adj: **~ de** guilty of.

culpar vt (echar la culpa) to blame; (acusar) to accuse; **~ a algo/a alguien de** to blame sthg/sb for.

cultivar vt (plantas) to grow; (tierra) to farm.

cultivo m (plantas) crop.

culto, -ta adj (persona) educated; (estilo) refined; (lenguaje) literary ♦ m worship.

cultura f (actividades) culture; (conocimientos) knowledge.

cultural adj cultural.

culturismo m body-building.

cumbre f summit.

cumpleaños m inv birthday.

cumplido m compliment.

cumplir vt (ley, orden) to obey; (promesa) to keep; (condena) to serve ♦ vi (plazo) to expire; **~ con** (deber) to do; (promesa) to keep; **hoy cumple 21 años** he's 21 today.

cúmulo m (de cosas) pile; (de nubes) cumulus.

cuna f (cama) cot; (origen) cradle; (patria) birthplace.

cuneta f (en carretera) ditch; (en la calle) gutter.

cuña f (calza) wedge; (en radio, televisión) commercial break.

cuñado, -da m, f brother-in-law (f sister-in-law).

cuota f (a club, etc) membership fee; (a Hacienda) tax (payment); (precio) fee.

cuplé m type of popular song.

cupo v → **caber** ♦ m (cantidad máxima) quota; (cantidad proporcional) share.

cupón m (vale) coupon; (de sorteo, lotería) ticket.

cúpula f (de edificio) dome.

cura[1] m (sacerdote) priest.

cura[2] f (restablecimiento) recovery; (tratamiento) cure; **~ de reposo** rest cure.

curandero, -ra m, f quack.

curar vt to cure; (herida) to dress; (pieles) to tan □ **curarse** vpr to recover.

curiosidad f curiosity; **tener ~ por** to be curious about.

curioso, -sa adj (de noticias, habladurías, etc) curious; (interesante, raro) strange ♦ m, f onlooker.

curita f (Amér) (sticking) plaster.

curry m curry; **al ~** curried.

cursi adj (persona) pretentious; (vestido, canción) naff.

cursillo m (curso breve) short course; (de conferencias) series of talks.

curso m course; (año académico, alumnos) year; **en ~** (año) current.

cursor m cursor.

curva f curve; (de camino, carretera, etc) bend.

curvado, -da adj curved.

custodia f (vigilancia) safekeeping; (de los hijos) custody.

cutis m inv skin, complexion.

cutre adj (fam: sucio) shabby; (fam: pobre) cheap and nasty.

cuy m (Amér) guinea-pig.

cuyo, -ya adj (de quien) whose; (de que) of which.

D

D. *abrev* = **don**.

dado *m* dice.

daga *f* dagger.

dalia *f* dahlia.

dama *f* lady ❑ **damas** *fpl* (juego) draughts (sg).

danés, -esa *adj & m* Danish ◆ *m, f* Dane.

danza *f* dance.

danzar *vt & vi* to dance.

dañar *vt (persona)* to harm; *(cosa)* to damage.

dañino, -na *adj (sustancia)* harmful; *(animal)* dangerous.

daño *m (dolor)* pain; *(perjuicio)* damage; *(a persona)* harm; **hacer ~** *(producir dolor)* to hurt; **la cena me hizo ~** the meal didn't agree with me.

dar *vt* **1.** *(entregar, regalar, decir)* to give; **da clases en la universidad** he teaches at the university; **me dio las gracias/los buenos días** she thanked me/said good morning to me.

2. *(producir)* to produce.

3. *(causar, provocar)* to give; **me da vergüenza/sueño** it makes me ashamed/sleepy; **me da risa** it makes me laugh.

4. *(suj: reloj)* to strike; **el reloj ha dado las diez** the clock struck ten.

5. *(encender)* to turn on; **por favor, da la luz** turn on the lights, please.

6. *(comunicar, emitir)* to give.

7. *(película, programa)* to show; *(obra de teatro)* to put on.

8. *(mostrar)* to show; **su aspecto daba señales de cansancio** she was showing signs of weariness.

9. *(expresa acción)* to give; **~ un grito** to give a cry; **le dio un golpe** he hit him.

10. *(banquete, baile)* to hold; **van a ~ una fiesta** they're going to throw a party.

11. *(considerar)*: **~ algo/a alguien por algo** to consider sthg/sb to be sthg.

◆ *vi* **1.** *(horas)* to strike; **han dado las tres en el reloj** the clock struck three.

2. *(golpear)*: **le dieron en la cabeza** they hit her on the head; **la piedra dio contra el cristal** the stone hit the glass.

3. *(sobrevenir)*: **le dieron varios ataques al corazón** he had several heart attacks.

4.: **~ a** *(balcón, ventana)* to look out onto; *(pasillo)* to lead to; *(casa, fachada)* to face.

5. *(proporcionar)*: **~ de comer** to feed; **~ de beber a alguien** to give sb something to drink.

6.: **~ en** *(blanco)* to hit.

7. *(en locuciones)*: **~ de sí** to stretch; **~ que hablar** to set people talking; **da igual** ○ **lo mismo** it doesn't matter; **¡qué más da!** what does it matter!

❑ **dar a** *v + prep (llave)* to turn; **dar con** *v + prep (encontrar)* to find; **darse** *vpr (suceder)* to happen; *(dilatarse)* to stretch; **~se contra** to bump into; **se le da bien/mal el latín** she is good/bad at Latin; **~se prisa** to hurry; **se las da de listo** likes to make out that he's clever; **~se por vencido** to give in; **darse a** *v* + *prep* (*entregarse*) to take to.

dardo *m* dart ▫ **dardos** *mpl* (*juego*) darts (*sg*).

dátil *m* date.

dato *m* fact, piece of information; **~s** information (*sg*); **~s personales** personal details.

dcha. (*abrev de derecha*) r.

d. de J.C. (*abrev de después de Jesucristo*) AD.

de *prep* 1. (*posesión, pertenencia*) of; **el coche ~ mi padre/mis padres** my father's/parents' car; **la casa es ~ ella** the house is hers.

2. (*materia*) (made) of; **un reloj ~ oro** a gold watch.

3. (*contenido*) of; **un vaso ~ agua** a glass of water.

4. (*en descripciones*): **~ fácil manejo** user-friendly; **la señora ~ verde** the lady in green; **difícil ~ creer** hard to believe; **una bolsa ~ deporte** a sports bag.

5. (*asunto*) about; **háblame ~ ti** tell me about yourself; **libros ~ historia** history books.

6. (*en calidad de*) as; **trabaja ~ bombero** he works as a fireman.

7. (*tiempo*): **trabaja ~ nueve a cinco** she works from nine to five; **trabaja ~ noche y duerme ~ día** he works at night and sleeps during the day; **a las tres ~ la tarde** at three in the afternoon; **llegamos ~ madrugada** we arrived early in the morning; **~ pequeño** as a child.

8. (*procedencia, distancia*) from; **vengo ~ mi casa** I've come from home; **soy ~ Zamora** I'm from Zamora; **del metro a casa voy a pie** I walk home from the under-

ground.

9. (*causa, modo*) with; **morirse ~ frío** to freeze to death; **llorar ~ alegría** to cry with joy; **~ una (sola) vez** in one go.

10. (*con superlativos*): **el mejor ~ todos** the best of all.

11. (*cantidad*): **más/menos ~** more/less than.

12. (*condición*) if; **~ querer ayudarme, lo haría** if she wanted to help me, she would.

dé *v* → **dar**.

debajo *adv* underneath; **~ de** under.

debate *m* debate.

debatir *vt* to debate.

deber *m* duty.

♦ *vt* 1. (*expresa obligación*): **debes dominar tus impulsos** you should control your impulses; **nos debemos ir a casa a las diez** we must go home at ten.

2. (*adeudar*) to owe; **me debes mil pesetas** you owe me twelve thousand pesetas; **¿cuánto o qué le debo?** how much does it come to?

3. (*en locuciones*): **debido a** due to.

❏ **deber de** *v* + *prep*: **debe de llegar a las nueve** she should arrive at nine; **deben de ser las doce** it must be twelve o'clock; **deberse a** *v* + *prep* (*ser consecuencia de*) to be due to; (*dedicarse a*) to have a responsibility towards; **deberes** *mpl* (*trabajo escolar*) homework (*sg*).

debido, -da *adj* proper; **~ a** due to.

débil *adj* (*sin fuerzas*) weak; (*voz, sonido*) faint; (*luz*) dim.

debilidad *f* weakness.

debilitar *vt* to weaken.

debut *m (de artista)* debut.

década *f* decade.

decadencia *f (declive)* decline.

decadente *adj* decadent.

decaer *vi (fuerza, energía)* to fail; *(esperanzas, país)* to decline; *(ánimos)* to flag.

decaído, -da *adj (deprimido)* gloomy.

decano, -na *m, f (de universidad)* dean; *(el más antiguo)* senior member.

decena *f* ten.

decente *adj (honesto)* decent; *(limpio)* clean.

decepción *f* disappointment.

decepcionar *vt* to disappoint ❑ **decepcionarse** *vpr* to be disappointed.

decidido, -da *adj* determined.

decidir *vt* to decide ❑ **decidirse** *vpr*: ~se a to decide to.

decimal *adj* decimal.

décimo, -ma *núm* tenth ◆ *m (en lotería)* tenth share in a lottery ticket, → **sexto**.

decir *vt (enunciar)* to say; *(contar)* to tell; ~ **a alguien que haga algo** to tell sb to do sthg; ~ **que sí** to say yes; **¿diga?, ¿dígame?** *(al teléfono)* hello?; **es** ~ that is; **¿cómo se dice ...?** how do you say ...?; **se dice ...** they say ...

decisión *f (resolución)* decision; *(de carácter)* determination; **tomar una** ~ to take a decision.

declaración *f* statement; *(de amor)* declaration; **prestar** ~ to give evidence; **tomar** ~ to take a statement; ~ **de la renta** tax return.

declarado, -da *adj* declared.

declarar *vt* to state; *(afirmar, bienes, riquezas)* to declare ◆ *vi (dar testimonio)* to give evidence ❑ **declararse** *vpr (incendio, epidemia, etc)* to break out; *(en el amor)* to declare o.s.; **me declaro a favor de ...** I'm in favour of ...

declinar *vt* to decline.

decoración *f (de casa, habitación)* décor; *(adornos)* decorations *(pl)*.

decorado *m (en teatro, cine)* set.

decorar *vt* to decorate.

decretar *vt* to decree.

decreto *m* decree.

dedal *m* thimble.

dedicación *f* dedication.

dedicar *vt (tiempo, dinero, energía)* to devote; *(libro)* to dedicate ❑ **dedicarse a** *v + prep (actividad, tarea)* to spend time on; **¿a qué se dedica Vd?** what do you do for a living?

deducción *f* deduction.

deducir *vt (concluir)* to deduce; *(restar)* to deduct.

defecar *vi (formal)* to defecate.

defecto *m (físico)* defect; *(moral)* fault.

defender *vt* to defend ❑ **defenderse** *vpr (protegerse)* to defend o.s.; ~se **de** *(ataque, insultos)* to defend o.s. against.

defensa *f* defence.

defensor, -ra m, f defender; *(abogado)* counsel for the defence.

deficiencia f *(defecto)* deficiency; *(falta, ausencia)* lack.

deficiente adj *(imperfecto)* deficient.

déficit m inv *(en economía)* deficit; *(escasez)* shortage.

definición f definition. □

definir vt to define **□ definirse** vpr *(fig)* to take a position.

definitivo, -va adj *(final, decisivo)* definitive; *(terminante)* definite; **en definitiva** in short.

deformación f deformation.

deformar vt to deform.

defraudar vt *(decepcionar)* to disappoint; *(estafar)* to defraud.

defunción f *(formal)* death.

degenerado, -da m, f degenerate.

degenerar vi to degenerate.

degustación f tasting.

dejadez f neglect.

dejar vt **1.** *(colocar, poner)* to leave; **deja el abrigo en la percha** leave your coat on the hanger; **"deje aquí su compra"** sign indicating lockers where bags must be left when entering a supermarket.
2. *(prestar)* to lend; **me dejó su pluma** she lent me her pen.
3. *(no tomar)* to leave; **deja lo que no quieras** leave whatever you don't want; **deja un poco de café para mí** leave a bit of coffee for me.
4. *(dar)* to give; **déjame la llave** give me the key; **dejé el perro a mi madre** I left the dog with my mother.

5. *(vicio, estudios)* to give up; *(casa, novia)* to leave; *(familia)* to abandon; **dejó su casa** he left home.
6. *(producir)* to leave; **este perfume deja mancha en la ropa** this perfume stains your clothing.
7. *(permitir)* to allow, to let; ~ **a alguien hacer algo** to let sb do sthg; **"dejen salir antes de entrar"** *(en metro, tren)* "let the passengers off the train first, please"; **sus gritos no me dejaron dormir** his cries prevented me from sleeping.
8. *(olvidar, omitir)* to leave out; ~ **algo por** o **sin hacer** to fail to do sthg; **déjalo para otro día** leave it for another day.
9. *(no molestar)* to leave alone; **¡déjame!** let me be!
10. *(esperar)* **dejó que acabara de llover para salir** she waited until it stopped raining before going out.
11. *(en locuciones)* ~ **algo aparte** to leave sthg to one side; ~ **algo/a alguien atrás** to leave sthg/sb behind; ~ **caer algo** *(objeto)* to drop sthg.

♦ vi **1.** *(parar)* ~ **de hacer algo** to stop doing sthg.
2. *(no olvidar)* **no** ~ **de hacer algo** to be sure to do sthg.
□ **dejarse** vpr *(olvidarse)* to leave; *(descuidarse, abandonarse)* to let o.s. go; ~ **se llevar por** to get carried away with; **apenas se deja ver** we hardly see anything of her; **dejarse de** v + prep: **¡déjate de tonterías!** stop that nonsense!

del → **de, el.**

delantal m apron.

delante adv *(en primer lugar)* in front; *(en la parte delantera)* at the front; *(enfrente)* opposite; ~ **de** in front of.

delantera f (de coche, avión, etc)
front; **coger** O **tomar la ~ to** take
the lead.

delantero, -ra adj front ♦ m
(en deporte) forward.

delatar vt (persona) to de-
nounce; (suj: gesto, acto) to betray.

delco® m distributor.

delegación f (oficina) (local)
office; (representación) delegation.

delegado, -da m, f delegate; ~
de curso student elected to represent
his/her classmates.

delegar vt to delegate.

deletrear vt to spell.

delfín m dolphin.

delgado, -da adj thin; (esbelto)
slim.

deliberadamente adv deliberately.

deliberado, -da adj deliberate.

deliberar vt to deliberate.

delicadeza f (atención, mira-
miento) consideration; (finura) delicacy; (cuidado) care.

delicado, -da adj delicate;
(respetuoso) considerate.

delicia f delight.

delicioso, -sa adj (exquisito)
delicious; (agradable) lovely.

delincuencia f crime.

delincuente mf criminal; ~
común common criminal.

delirante adj (persona) delirious; (idea) mad.

delirar vi (por la fiebre) to be
delirious; (decir disparates) to talk
rubbish.

delirio m (perturbación) ravings (pl).

delito m crime.

delta m delta.

demanda f (petición) request;
(reivindicación, de mercancías) demand; (en un juicio) action.

demandar vt (pedir) to request;
(reivindicar) to demand; (en un
juicio) to sue.

demás adj other ♦ pron: **los/las ~**
the rest; **lo ~** the rest; **por lo ~**
apart from that.

demasiado, -da adj (con sustantivos singulares) too much; (con
sustantivos plurales) too many ♦ adv
too much; **lo ~ rápido** too fast; **hace
~ frío** it's too cold.

demencia f insanity.

demente adj (formal) insane.

democracia f democracy.

demócrata adj democratic ♦
mf democrat.

democráticamente adv
democratically.

democrático, -ca adj democratic.

demoledor, -ra adj (máquina,
aparato) demolition (antes de s);
(argumento, crítica) devastating.

demoler vt to demolish.

demonio m devil; ¡qué **~s ...?**
what the hell ...?

demora f delay.

demostración f (de hecho)
proof; (de afecto, sentimiento, etc)
demonstration.

demostrar vt (probar) to prove;
(indicar) to demonstrate, to
show.

denominación f: ~ **de origen**
appellation d'origine.

densidad f density.

denso, -sa *adj* dense.

dentadura *f* teeth (pl); ~ **postiza** dentures (pl).

dentífrico *m* toothpaste.

dentista *mf* dentist.

dentro *adv* (*en el interior*) inside; ~ **de** (*en el interior*) in; (*en el plazo de*) in, within.

denunciante *mf* person who reports a crime.

denunciar *vt* (*delito, persona*) to report (to the police); (*situación irregular, escándalo*) to reveal.

departamento *m* (*de empresa, organismo*) department; (*de armario, maleta*) compartment.

dependencia *f* (*subordinación*) dependence; (*habitación*) room; (*sección, departamento*) branch.

depender *vi:* **depende ...** it depends ... ☐ **depender de** *v + prep* to depend on.

dependiente, -ta *m, f* shop assistant.

depilarse *vpr* to remove hair from; ~ **las cejas** to pluck one's eyebrows.

depilatorio, -ria *adj* hairremoving.

deporte *m* sport; **hacer** ~ to do sport; ~**s de invierno** winter sports.

deportista *mf* sportsman (*f* sportswoman).

deportivo, -va *adj* (*zapatillas, pantalón, prueba*) sports (*antes de s*); (*persona*) sporting ◆ *m* sports car.

depositar *vt* (*en un lugar*) to place; (*en el banco*) to deposit.

depósito *m* (*almacén*) store; (*de dinero*) deposit; (*recipiente*) tank; ~

de agua water tank; ~ **de gasolina** petrol tank (*Br*), gas tank (*Am*).

depresión *f* depression.

depresivo, -va *adj* (MED) depressive.

deprimido, -da *adj* depressed.

deprimir *vt* to depress ☐ **deprimirse** *vpr* to get depressed.

deprisa *adv* quickly.

depuradora *f* purifier.

depurar *vt* (*sustancia*) to purify.

derecha *f*: **la** ~ (*mano derecha*) one's right hand; (*lado derecho, en política*) the right; **a la** ~ on the right; **gira a la** ~ turn right; **ser de** ~**s** to be right wing.

derecho, -cha *adj* (*lado, mano, pie*) right; (*recto*) straight ◆ *m* (*privilegio, facultad*) right; (*estudios*) law; (*de tela, prenda*) right side ◆ *adv* straight; **todo** ~ straight on; **¡no hay** ~! it's not fair!

derivar: derivar de *v + prep* to derive from; **derivar en** *v + prep* to end in.

dermoprotector, -ra *adj* barrier (*antes de s*).

derramar *vt* (*por accidente*) to spill; (*verter*) to pour ☐ **derramarse** *vpr* to spill.

derrame *m* spillage; ~ **cerebral** brain haemorrhage.

derrapar *vi* to skid.

derretir *vt* to melt ☐ **derretirse** *vpr* (*hielo, mantequilla*) to melt; (*persona*) to go weak at the knees.

derribar *vt* (*casa, muro, adversario*) to knock down; (*gobierno*) to overthrow.

derrochar vt to waste.

derroche m (de dinero) waste; (de esfuerzo, simpatía) excess.

derrota f defeat.

derrotar vt to defeat.

derrumbar vt (casa, muro) to knock down ❑ **derrumbarse** vpr (casa, muro) to collapse; (moralmente) to be devastated.

desabrochar vt to undo ❑ **desabrocharse** vpr: **~se la camisa** to unbutton one's shirt.

desacreditar vt to discredit.

desacuerdo m disagreement.

desafiar vt (persona) to challenge; (elementos, peligros) to defy; **~ a alguien a** to challenge sb to.

desafinar vi to be out of tune ❑ **desafinarse** vpr to go out of tune.

desafío m challenge.

desafortunadamente adv unfortunately.

desafortunado, -da adj (sin suerte) unlucky; (inoportuno) unfortunate.

desagradable adj unpleasant.

desagradecido, -da adj (persona) ungrateful; (trabajo, tarea) thankless.

desagüe m (de bañera, fregadero, piscina) drain; (cañería) drainpipe.

desahogarse vpr to pour one's heart out.

desaire m snub.

desajuste m: **~ horario** jet lag.

desaliñado, -da adj (persona) unkempt.

desalojar vt (por incendio, etc) to evacuate; (por la fuerza) to evict; **~ a alguien de** to evict sb from.

desamparado, -da adj abandoned.

desangrarse vpr to lose a lot of blood.

desanimar vt to discourage ❑ **desanimarse** vpr to be discouraged.

desaparecer vi to disappear.

desaparecido, -da m, f missing person.

desaparición f disappearance.

desapercibido, -da adj: pasar **~** to go unnoticed.

desaprovechar vt to waste.

desarmador m (Amér) screwdriver.

desarrollado, -da adj developed; (persona) well-developed.

desarrollar vt to develop ❑ **desarrollarse** vpr to develop; (suceder) to take place.

desarrollo m development.

desasosiego m anxiety.

desastre m disaster; (objeto de mala calidad) useless thing.

desatar vt to untie; (sentimiento) to unleash.

desatino m (equivocación) mistake.

desavenencia f disagreement.

desayunar vt to have for breakfast ♦ vi to have breakfast.

desayuno m breakfast.

desbarajuste m disorder.

desbaratar vt to ruin.

desbordarse vpr (río, lago) to overflow; (sentimiento, pasión) to erupt.

descabellado, -da adj mad.

descafeinado adj decaffeinated ♦ m decaffeinated coffee; **café ~** decaffeinated coffee.

descalificar vt (jugador) to disqualify; (desacreditar) to discredit.

descalzarse vpr to take one's shoes off.

descalzo, -za adj barefoot; **ir ~ to** go barefoot.

descampado m open ground.

descansar vi (reposar) to rest; (dormir) to sleep.

descansillo m landing.

descanso m (reposo) rest; (pausa) break; (intermedio) interval; (alivio) relief.

descapotable m convertible.

descarado, -da adj (persona) cheeky; (intento, mentira) blatant.

descarga f (de mercancías) unloading; **~ eléctrica** electric shock.

descargar vt (camión, mercancías, equipaje) to unload; (arma) to fire ❑ **descargarse** vpr (batería) to go flat; (encendedor) to run out; (desahogarse) to vent one's frustration.

descaro m cheek.

descarrilar vi to be derailed.

descartar vt (ayuda) to reject; (posibilidad) to rule out.

descendencia f (hijos) offspring.

descender vi to go down.

descendiente mf descendent.

descenso m (bajada) drop; (de un río, montaña) descent.

descifrar vt to decipher.

descolgar vt (cortina, ropa, cuadro) to take down; (teléfono) to take off the hook ♦ vi to pick up the receiver.

descolorido, -da adj faded.

descomponer vt (Amér) to break ❑ **descomponerse** vpr (Amér) to break down.

descomposición f (de un alimento) decomposition; **~ (de vientre)** (formal) diarrhea.

descompuesto, -ta pp → **descomponer** ♦ adj (Amér) broken.

desconcertante adj disconcerting.

desconcertar vt to disconcert.

desconfianza f distrust.

desconfiar: desconfiar de v + prep to distrust.

descongelar vt (alimentos) to thaw; (nevera) to defrost ❑ **descongelarse** vpr (alimentos) to thaw; (nevera) to defrost.

descongestionarse vpr to clear.

desconocer vt not to know.

desconocido, -da m, f stranger.

desconocimiento m ignorance.

desconsiderado, -da adj inconsiderate.

desconsolado, -da adj distressed.

desconsuelo m distress.

descontar vt to deduct.

descrédito m discredit.

describir vt to describe.

descripción f description.

descrito, -ta pp → **describir**.

descuartizar vt to quarter.

descubierto, -ta pp → **cubrir** ♦ adj (sin tapar) uncovered; (sin nubes) clear; **al ~ in** the open.

descubrimiento m discovery.

descubrir vt to discover; *(averiguar, destapar)* to uncover.

descuento m discount.

descuerar vt *(Amér: fig)* to pull to pieces.

descuidado, -da adj *(persona, aspecto)* untidy; *(lugar)* neglected.

descuidar vt to neglect ◻ **descuidarse** de v + prep *(olvidarse de)* to forget to.

descuido m *(imprudencia)* carelessness; *(error)* mistake.

desde prep *(tiempo)* since; *(espacio)* from ; ~ ... **hasta** ... from ... to ...; **vivo aquí ~ hace dos años** I've been living here for two years; **~ luego** of course; **~ que** since.

desdén m disdain.

desdentado, -da adj toothless.

desdicha f *(pena)* misfortune.

desdoblar vt *(papel, servilleta)* to unfold.

desear vt *(querer)* to want; *(anhelar)* to wish for; *(amar)* to desire; **¿qué desea?** what can I do for you?

desechable adj disposable.

desechar vt *(tirar)* to throw away.

desechos mpl *(basura)* rubbish *(sg)*; *(residuos)* waste *(sg)*.

desembarcar vi to disembark.

desembocadura f *(de río)* mouth; *(de calle)* opening.

desembocar: desembocar en v + prep *(río)* to flow into; *(calle)* to lead into; *(situación, problema)* to end in.

desempeñar vt *(funciones)* to

carry out; *(papel)* to play; *(objeto empeñado)* to redeem.

desempleo m unemployment.

desencadenar vt *(provocar)* to unleash ◻ **desencadenarse** v impers *(tormenta)* to break; *(tragedia)* to strike.

desencajarse vpr *(piezas)* to come apart; *(rostro)* to become distorted.

desencanto m disappointment.

desenchufar vt to unplug.

desenfadado, -da adj *(persona)* easy-going; *(ropa)* casual; *(estilo)* light.

desenfrenado, -da adj *(ritmo)* frantic.

desengañar vt to reveal the truth to ◻ **desengañarse** vpr: **~se de** to become disillusioned with.

desengaño m disappointment.

desenlace m ending.

desenmascarar vt to expose.

desenredar vt *(pelo, madeja, ovillo)* to untangle; *(situación)* to unravel.

desentenderse: desentenderse de v + prep to refuse to have anything to do with.

desenvolver vt to unwrap ◻ **desenvolverse** vpr *(persona)* to cope.

desenvuelto, -ta pp → **desenvolver**.

deseo m desire.

desequilibrado, -da adj *(formal: loco)* (mentally) unbalanced.

desesperación f desperation.

desesperarse vpr to lose hope.

desfachatez f cheek.

desfallecer vi (debilitarse) to flag; (desmayarse) to faint.

desfigurarse vpr to be disfigured.

desfiladero m (mountain) pass.

desfile m (de militares) parade; (de carrozas, etc) procession; (de modelos) fashion show.

desgana f (falta de apetito) lack of appetite; (falta de interés) lack of enthusiasm; **con ~** unwillingly.

desgastar vt (objeto) to wear out; (fuerza) to wear down.

desgracia f (suerte contraria) bad luck; (suceso trágico) disaster; **por ~** unfortunately.

desgraciadamente adv unfortunately.

desgraciado, -da m, f poor wretch.

desgraciar vt (estropear) to spoil.

desgreñado, -da adj tousled; **ir ~** to be dishevelled.

deshacer vt (lo hecho) to undo; (cama) to mess up; (quitar las sábanas de) to strip; (las maletas) to unpack; (destruir) to ruin; (disolver) to dissolve ❑ **deshacerse** vpr (disolverse) to dissolve; (derretirse) to melt; (destruirse) to be destroyed; **deshacerse de** v + prep (desprenderse de) to get rid of.

deshecho, -cha pp → **deshacer** ♦ adj (nudo, paquete) undone; (cama) unmade; (maletas) unpacked; (estropeado) ruined; (triste, abatido) shattered.

desheredar vt to disinherit.

deshidratarse vpr to be dehydrated.

deshielo m thaw.

deshonesto, -ta adj (inmoral) indecent; (poco honrado) dishonest.

deshonra f dishonour.

deshuesar vt (carne) to bone; (fruta) to stone.

desierto, -ta adj (lugar) deserted ♦ m desert.

designar vt (persona) to appoint; (lugar) to decide on.

desigual adj (no uniforme) different; (irregular) uneven.

desigualdad f inequality.

desilusión f disappointment.

desilusionar vt to disappoint.

desinfectante m disinfectant.

desinfectar vt to disinfect.

desinflar vt (balón, globo, rueda) to let down.

desintegración f disintegration.

desinterés m lack of interest.

desinteresado, -da adj unselfish.

desistir: desistir de v + prep to give up.

desliz (pl -ces) m slip.

deslizar vt to slide ❑ **deslizarse** vpr (resbalar) to slide.

deslumbrar vt to dazzle.

desmadrarse vpr (fam) to go over the top.

desmaquillador m make-up remover.

desmaquillarse vpr to take one's make-up off.

desmayarse vpr to faint.

desmayo m (desvanecimiento)

fainting fit.

desmentir vt (negar) to deny.

desmesurado, -da adj excessive.

desmontar vt (estructura) to take down; (aparato) to take apart ♦ vi to dismount.

desmoralizar vt to demoralize.

desnatado, -da adj (leche) skimmed; (yogur) low-fat.

desnivel m (del terreno) unevenness.

desnudar vt to undress.
desnudarse vpr to get undressed.
desnudo, -da adj (sin ropa) naked; (sin adorno) bare.

desnutrición f undernourishment.

desobedecer vt to disobey.

desobediente adj disobedient.

desodorante m deodorant.

desorden m (de objetos, papeles) mess; **en ~** in disarray.

desordenar vt to mess up.

desorganización f disorganization.

desorientar vt (confundir) to confuse □ **desorientarse** vpr (perderse) to lose one's bearings; (confundirse) to get confused.

despachar vt (vender) to sell; (despedir) to sack.

despacho m (oficina) office; (estudio) study; **~ de billetes** ticket office.

despacio adv slowly ♦ interj slow down!

despampanante adj stunning.

desparpajo m self-assurance.

despecho m bitterness.

despectivo, -va adj disdainful.

despedida f goodbye.

despedir vt (decir adiós) to say goodbye to; (del trabajo) to sack; (arrojar) to fling; (producir) to give off □ **despedirse** vpr (decir adiós) to say goodbye; (del trabajo) to hand in one's notice.

despegar vt to remove ♦ vi (avión) to take off.

despegue m take-off.

despeinarse vpr to mess up one's hair.

despejado, -da adj (cielo, día, camino) clear; (persona) alert; (espacio) spacious.

despejar vt (lugar) to clear; (incógnita, dudas) to clear up □ **despejarse** vpr (cielo, día, noche) to clear up; (persona) to clear one's head.

despensa f larder.

despeñadero m precipice.

desperdiciar vt to waste.

desperdicio m waste □ **desperdicios** mpl (basura) waste (sg); (de cocina) scraps.

desperezarse vpr to stretch.

desperfecto m (daño) damage; (defecto) fault.

despertador m alarm clock.

despertar vt (persona) to wake up; (sentimiento) to arouse □ **despertarse** vpr to wake up.

despido m dismissal.

despierto, -ta adj (que no duerme) awake; (listo) alert.

despistado, -da adj absent-minded.

despistarse *vpr (desorientarse)* to get lost; *(distraerse)* to get confused.

despiste *m (olvido)* absent-mindedness; *(error)* mistake.

desplazarse *vpr (moverse)* to move; *(viajar)* to travel.

desplegar *vt (tela, periódico, mapa)* to unfold; *(bandera)* to unfurl; *(alas)* to spread; *(cualidad)* to display.

desplomarse *vpr* to collapse.

despojos *mpl (de animal)* offal *(sg)*; *(de persona)* remains; *(sobras)* leftovers.

despreciar *vt (persona, cosa)* to despise; *(posibilidad, propuesta)* to reject.

desprecio *m* contempt.

desprender *vt (desenganchar)* to unfasten; *(soltar)* to give off ▫

desprenderse *vpr (soltarse)* to come off; **desprenderse de** + *prep (deshacerse de)* to get rid of; *(deducirse de)* to be clear from.

desprendimiento *m (de tierra)* landslide.

despreocuparse: **despreocuparse de** *v* + *prep (no atender)* to neglect.

desprevenido, -da *adj* unprepared.

desproporcionado, -da *adj* disproportionate.

después *adv* 1. *(más tarde)* afterwards; *(entonces)* then; *(justo lo siguiente)* next; **lo haré ~** I'll do it later; **ya voy ~** it's my turn next; **años ~** years later; **poco/mucho ~** soon/ a long time after.

2. *(en el espacio)* next; **¿qué calle viene ~?** which street comes next?; **hay una farmacia y ~ está mi casa** there's a chemist's and then you come to my house.

3. *(en una lista)* further down.

4. *(en locuciones):* **~ de** after; **~ de que** after; **~ de todo** after all.

destacar *vt* to emphasize ♦ *vi (resaltar)* to stand out.

destajo: *m:* **trabajar a ~** to do piecework.

destapar *vt (caja, botella, etc)* to open.

destello *m (de luz)* flash.

destemplado, -da *adj (persona)* out of sorts.

desteñir *vt* to bleach ♦ *vi* to run.

desterrar *vt (persona)* to exile; *(pensamiento, sentimiento)* to banish.

destierro *m* exile.

destilación *f* distillation.

destilar *vt* to distil.

destilería *f* distillery.

destinar *vt (objeto)* to earmark; *(persona)* to appoint; *(programa, medidas)* to aim.

destinatario, -ria *m, f* addressee.

destino *m (azar)* destiny; *(de viaje)* destination; *(finalidad)* use; *(trabajo)* job; **vuelos con ~ a Londres** flights to London.

destornillador *m* screwdriver.

destornillar *vt* to unscrew.

destrozar *vt (objeto)* to smash; *(plan, proyecto)* to ruin; *(persona)* to shatter.

destrucción *f* destruction.

destruir vt to destroy; (plan, proyecto) to ruin.

desuso m disuse; **caer en ~** to become obsolete.

desvalijar vt (persona) to rob; (casa) to burgle.

desván m attic.

desvanecimiento m (desmayo) fainting fit.

desvariar vi to rave.

desvelar vt (persona) to keep awake; (secreto) to reveal □ **desvelarse** vpr (no dormir) to be unable to sleep; (Amér: quedarse levantado) to have a late night.

desventaja f disadvantage.

desvergonzado, -da adj shameless.

desvestirse vpr to get undressed.

desviar vt (de un camino) to divert □ **desviarse** vpr: **~se de** (camino) to turn off; (propósito) to be diverted from.

desvío m diversion.

detallar vt to describe in detail.

detalle m (pormenor, minucia) detail; (delicadeza) kind gesture; **al ~** (minuciosamente) in detail.

detallista adj (minucioso) painstaking.

detectar vt to detect.

detective mf detective.

detener vt (parar) to stop; (retrasar) to hold up; (arrestar) to arrest □ **detenerse** vpr (pararse) to stop.

detenido, -da m, f prisoner.

detergente m detergent.

determinación f (decisión) decision; **tomar una ~** to take a

decision.

determinado, -da adj (concreto) specific; (en gramática) definite.

determinante adj decisive ◆ m determiner.

determinar vt (fijar) to fix; (decidir) to decide; (causar, motivar) to cause.

detestable adj detestable.

detestar vt to detest.

detrás adv (en el espacio) behind; (en el orden) then; **el interruptor está ~** the switch is at the back; **~ de** behind; **por ~** at/on the back.

deuda f debt; **contraer ~s** to get into debt.

devaluación f devaluation.

devaluar vt to devalue.

devoción f devotion.

devolución f (de dinero) refund; (de objeto) return.

devolver vt (objeto, regalo comprado, favor) to return; (dinero) to refund; (cambio, objeto prestado) to give back; (vomitar) to bring up ◆ vi to be sick; **"devuelve cambio"** "change given".

devorar vt to devour.

devoto, -ta adj (en religión) devout; (aficionado) devoted.

devuelto, -ta pp → **devolver**.

dg (abrev de decigramo) dg.

DGT abrev = **Dirección General de Tráfico**.

di v → **dar**, **decir**.

día m day; **es de ~** it's daytime; **de ~** in the daytime; **al ~ siguiente** the next day; **del ~** (fresco) fresh; **el ~ seis** the sixth; **por ~** daily; **¿qué tal ~ hace?** what's the weather like today?; **todos los ~s** every day; **~ azul** day for cheap travel on trains; **~ del espectador** day on which cinema tickets are sold at a discount; **~ festivo** (public) holiday; **Día de los inocentes** 28 December, = April Fools' Day; **~ laborable** working day; **~ libre** day off; **Día de los Muertos** Day of the Dead; **~ del santo** saint's day.

DÍA DE LOS INOCENTES

On 28 December, it is traditional for Spanish people to play tricks and practical jokes known as "inocentadas" on each other, the most typical of which is to stick a paper doll to somebody's back without them realizing. It is also common for the media to run false stories aimed at duping the public.

DÍA DE LOS MUERTOS

In Mexico, "Day of the Dead" is the name given to All Souls' Day. Officially, the Day of the Dead is 2 November, although the celebrations start on 1 November. Children dress up as skeletons, mummies, vampires etc, and the shops sell brightly-coloured sugar and chocolate skulls bearing the name of a dead person. These will form part of an offering to dead friends and relatives which may also include "pan de muerto", a type of large, round cake coated in sugar.

---

diabetes f inv diabetes.
diabético, -ca m, f diabetic.

diablo m devil.
diablura f prank.
diabólico, -ca adj diabolical.
diadema f Alice band.
diagnosticar vt to diagnose.
diagnóstico m diagnosis.
dialecto m dialect.
diálogo m (conversación) conversation.
diamante m diamond ❑ **diamantes** mpl (palo de la baraja) diamonds.
diana f (blanco) bull's-eye.
diapositiva f slide.
diario, -ria adj daily ◆ m (daily) newspaper; **a ~** every day.
diarrea f diarrhea.
dibujar vt to draw.
dibujo m drawing; **~s animados** cartoons.
diccionario m dictionary.
dice v → **decir**.
dicha f (felicidad) joy.
dicho, -cha pp → **decir** ◆ m saying ◆ adj: **~ y hecho** no sooner said than done; **mejor ~** rather.
diciembre m December, → **setiembre**.
dictado m dictation.
dictador m dictator.
dictadura f dictatorship.
dictamen m opinion.
dictar vt (texto) to dictate; (decreto) to issue; (ley) to enact.
dictatorial adj dictatorial.
diecinueve núm nineteen, → **seis**.
dieciocho núm eighteen, → **seis**.
dieciséis núm sixteen, → **seis**.

diecisiete *núm* seventeen, →
seis.

diente *m* tooth; **~ de ajo** clove
of garlic; **~ de leche** milk tooth.

diera *v* → **dar**.

diéresis *f inv* diaeresis.

dieron *v* → **dar**.

diesel *m* diesel.

diestro, -tra *adj (de la derecha)*
right-hand; *(experto)* skilful ♦ *m*
matador.

dieta *f* diet ❑ **dietas** *fpl (honorarios)* expenses.

dietética *f* dietetics *(sg)*; **tienda
de ~** health food shop.

diez *núm* ten, → **seis**.

diferencia *f* difference; **a ~ de**
in contrast to.

diferenciar *vt* to distinguish.

diferente *adj* different ♦ *adv*
differently.

diferido, -da *adj*: **en ~** recorded.

diferir *vt* to defer ❑ **diferir de** *v*
+ *prep* to differ from.

difícil *adj* difficult.

dificultad *f (complejidad)* difficulty; *(obstáculo)* problem.

difundir *vt (calor, luz)* to diffuse;
(noticia, idea) to spread; *(programa)*
to broadcast.

difunto, -ta *m, f*: **el ~** the de-
ceased.

difusión *f (de noticia, idea)* dis-
semination; *(de programa)* broadcasting.

diga *v* → **decir**.

digerir *vt* to digest.

digestión *f* digestion; **hacer la
~** to digest.

digital *adj (en electrónica)* digital;

(de los dedos) finger *(antes de s)*.

dígito *m* digit.

dignarse *vpr* to deign.

dignidad *f (decoro)* dignity;
(cargo) office.

digno, -na *adj (merecedor)* worthy; *(apropiado)* appropriate; *(honrado)* honourable.

digo *v* → **decir**.

dilema *m* dilemma.

diligente *adj* diligent.

diluviar *v impers*: **diluvió** it
poured with rain.

diluvio *m* flood.

dimensión *f (medida)* dimen-
sion; *(importancia)* extent.

diminuto, -ta *adj* tiny.

dimitir *vi*: **~ (de)** to resign
(from).

dimos *v* → **dar**.

Dinamarca *s* Denmark.

dinámico, -ca *adj* dynamic.

dinamita *f* dynamite.

dinastía *f* dynasty.

dinero *m* money; **~ de bolsillo**
pocket money; **~ suelto** loose
change.

dinosaurio *m* dinosaur.

dio *v* → **dar**.

diócesis *f inv* diocese.

dios *m* god ❑ **Dios** *m* God; **como
Dios manda** properly; **¡Dios mío!**
my God!; **¡por Dios!** for God's
sake!

diploma *m* diploma.

diplomacia *f* diplomacy.

diplomado, -da *m, f* qualified
man *(f* qualified woman).

diplomarse: diplomarse en *v*
+ *prep* to get a qualification in.

diplomático, -ca adj diplomatic ◆ m, f diplomat.

diplomatura f degree awarded after three years of study.

diptongo m diphthong.

diputación f (edificio) building that houses the "diputación provincial"; ~ **provincial** governing body of each province of an autonomous region in Spain, = county council (Br).

diputado, -da m, f = MP (Br), = representative (Am).

dique m dike; ~ **seco** dry dock.

dirá v → decir.

dirección f (rumbo) direction; (domicilio) address; (de empresa) management; (de vehículo) steering; **calle de ~ única** one-way street; ~ **asistida** power steering; **Dirección General de Tráfico** Spanish traffic department.

direccionales mpl (Amér) indicators.

directa f (en el coche) top gear.

directo, -ta adj direct; **en ~** live.

director, -ra m, f (de empresa) director; (de hotel) manager (f manageress); (de orquesta) conductor; (de colegio) head.

directorio m directory.

diría v → decir.

dirigente mf (de partido) leader; (de empresa) manager.

dirigir vt (destinar) to address; (conducir, llevar) to steer; (gobernar) to run; (película, obra de teatro, enfocar) to direct; (orquesta) to conduct; (periódico) to edit; (guiar, orientar) to guide; ~ **la palabra a alguien** to

speak to sb ❑ **dirigirse** a v + prep (ir, marchar) to head for; (hablar a) to speak to.

discar vt (Amér) to dial.

disciplina f discipline.

discípulo, -la m, f disciple.

disco m (en música) record; (cilindro) disc; (semáforo) (traffic) light; (en informática) disk; (en deporte) discus; ~ **compacto** compact disc.

disconformidad f disagreement.

discoteca f disco.

discotequero, -ra adj (fam) disco (antes de s).

discreción f discretion.

discrepancia f difference.

discreto, -ta adj (diplomático) discreet; (mediano) modest.

discriminación f discrimination.

discriminar vt to discriminate against.

disculpa f (pretexto) excuse; (al pedir perdón) apology; **pedir ~s** to apologize.

disculpar vt to excuse ❑ **disculparse** vpr: ~**se (por algo)** to apologize (for sthg).

discurrir vi (pensar) to reflect.

discurso m speech.

discusión f (debate) discussion; (riña) argument.

discutible adj debatable.

discutir vt (debatir) to discuss; (contradecir) to dispute ◆ vi (reñir) to argue.

disecar vt (planta) to dry; (animal) to stuff.

diseñador, -ra m, f desi[...]

diseñar vt to design.

iseño m design; **de ~** designer.

disfraz (pl **-ces**) m disguise.

disfrazar vt to disguise □ **disfrazarse**: **~se (de)** to dress up (as).

disfrutar vi to enjoy o.s. □ **disfrutar de** v + prep to enjoy.

disgustar vt to upset □ **disgustarse** vpr to get upset.

disgusto m annoyance; **llevarse un ~** to be upset.

disidente mf dissident.

disimular vt to hide ♦ vi to pretend.

disminución f decrease.

disminuir vt to decrease.

disolvente m solvent.

disolver vt to dissolve.

disparar vt & vi to shoot □ **dispararse** vpr (actuar precipitadamente) to go over the top; (precios) to shoot up.

disparate m stupid thing.

disparo m shot.

dispensar vt: **~ a alguien de** to excuse sb from.

dispersar vt to scatter.

disponer vt (colocar) to arrange; (preparar) to lay on; (suj: ley) to stipulate □ **disponer de** v + prep (tener) to have; (usar) to make use of; **disponerse** vpr: **~se a** to get ready to.

disponible adj available.

disposición f (colocación) arrangement; (estado de ánimo) mood; (orden) order; **a ~ de** at the disposal of.

dispositivo m device.

dispuesto, -ta pp → **disponer** ♦ adj (preparado) ready; **~ a**

prepared to.

disputa f dispute.

disputar vt (competición) to compete in; (premio) to compete for ♦ vi to argue □ **disputarse** vpr (competir por) to dispute.

disquete m diskette.

disquetera f disk drive.

distancia f distance; (en tiempo) gap; **¿a qué ~?** how far away?

distanciarse vpr (perder afecto) to grow apart.

distante adj (lugar) far away; (persona) distant.

diste vi → **dar**.

distinción f (diferencia) distinction; (elegancia) refinement.

distinguido, -da adj (elegante) refined; (notable, destacado) distinguished.

distinguir vt (diferenciar) to distinguish; (lograr ver) to make out; (destacar) to pick out.

distintivo m distinctive.

distinto, -ta adj different.

distracción f (falta de atención) absent-mindedness; (descuido) slip; (diversión) entertainment.

distraer vt (entretener) to entertain □ **distraerse** vpr (descuidarse) to get distracted; (no prestar atención) to let one's mind wander; (entretenerse) to enjoy o.s.

distraído, -da adj (entretenido) entertaining; (despistado) absentminded.

distribución f (de correo, mercancías) delivery; (comercial) distribution.

distribuir vt (repartir) to distribute; (correo, mercancías) to deliver.

distrito m district; ~ **postal** postal district.

disturbio m (tumulto) disturbance; (del orden público) riot.

disuelto, -ta pp → **disolver**.

diurno, -na adj daytime.

diva f diva.

diván m couch.

diversidad f diversity.

diversión f entertainment.

diverso, -sa adj diverse; ~**s** various.

divertido, -da adj (entretenido) enjoyable; (que hace reír) funny.

divertirse vpr to enjoy o.s.

dividir vt to divide.

divino, -na adj divine.

divisar vt to spy.

divisas fpl foreign exchange (sg).

división f division.

divorciado, -da m, f divorcé (f divorcée).

divorciarse vpr to get divorced.

divorcio m divorce.

divulgar vt (secreto) to reveal; (rumor) to spread; (información) to disseminate.

DNI m (abrev de documento nacional de identidad) ID card.

dobladillo m hem.

doblaje m dubbing.

doblar vt (plegar) to fold; (duplicar) to double; (flexionar) to bend; (en cine) to dub; ~ **la esquina** to go round the corner.

doble adj & m/f double ◆ m: **el ~ (de)** twice as much ❑ **dobles** mpl (en tenis) doubles.

doce núm twelve, → **seis**.

docena f dozen.

docente adj teaching.

dócil adj obedient.

doctor, -ra m, f doctor.

doctorado m doctorate.

doctorarse vpr to get a doctorate.

doctrina f doctrine.

documentación f papers (pl); ~ **del coche** registration documents (pl).

documental m documentary.

documento m (escrito) document; (de identidad) identity card; (en historia) record.

dogma m dogma.

dogmático, -ca adj dogmatic.

dólar m dollar.

doler vi to hurt; **me duele la pierna** my leg hurts; **me duele la garganta** I have a sore throat.

dolor m (daño) pain; (pena) sorrow; **tener ~ de cabeza** to have a headache; **tener ~ de estómago** have a stomachache; **tener ~ de muelas** to have toothache.

doloroso, -sa adj painful.

domador, -ra m, f tamer.

domar vt to tame.

domesticar vt to tame.

doméstico, -ca adj domestic.

domicilio m (casa) residence; (dirección) address; **servicio a ~** home delivery.

dominante adj dominant.

dominar vt (persona, panorama) to dominate; (nación) to rule; (situación) to be in control of; (nervios, pasiones, etc) to control; (incendio) to bring under control; (idioma) to be fluent in; (divisar) to overlook ♦ vi (sobresalir, destacar) to stand out; (ser característico) to predominate ⬚ **dominarse** vpr to control o.s.

domingo m Sunday; **~ de Pascua** Easter Sunday; **~ de Ramos** Palm Sunday, → **sábado**.

dominguero, -ra m, f (fam) Sunday tripper.

dominical m Sunday supplement.

dominio m (control) control; (autoridad) authority; (de una lengua) command; (territorio) domain; (ámbito) realm.

dominó m (juego) dominoes (sg).

don m (regalo, talento) gift; (tratamiento) = Mr.

donante mf donor.

donativo m donation.

donde adv where; **el bolso está ~ lo dejaste** your bag is where you left it; **de/desde ~** from where; **por ~** wherever.
♦ pron where; **la casa ~ nací** the house where I was born; **la ciudad**

de ~ vengo the town I come from; **por ~** where.

dónde adv where; **¿~ está el niño?** where's the child?; **no sé ~ se habrá metido** I don't know where she can be; **¿de ~ eres?** where are you from?; **por ~** where.

donut® ['donut] m (ring) dough-nut.

doparse vpr to take artificial stimulants.

doping ['dopɪŋ] m doping.

dorado, -da adj golden.

dormir vi to sleep ♦ vt (niño) to put to bed; **~ con alguien** to sleep with sb ⬚ **dormirse** vpr (persona) to fall asleep; (parte del cuerpo) to go to sleep.

dormitorio m (habitación) bedroom; (mobiliario) bedroom suite.

dorsal adj back (antes de s).

dorso m back; **~ de la mano** back of the hand.

dos núm two; **cada ~ por tres** every five minutes, → **seis**.

doscientos núm two hundred, → **seis**.

dosis f inv dose.

dotado, -da adj gifted; **~ de** (persona) blessed with; (edificio, instalación) equipped with.

dotar vt (equipar, proveer) to provide; (suj: naturaleza) to endow.

doy v → **dar**.

Dr. (abrev de doctor) Dr.

Dra. (abrev de doctora) Dr.

dragón m dragon.

drama m (obra) play; (género) drama; (desgracia) tragedy.

dramático, -ca adj dramatic.

dramaturgo, -ga *m, f* playwright.

droga *f* drug; **la ~ drugs** (*pl*).

drogadicción *f* drug addiction.

drogadicto, -ta *m, f* drug addict.

droguería *f* shop selling paint, cleaning materials etc.

dto. *abrev* = **descuento**

dual *adj* (*emisión*) that can be listened to either dubbed or in the original language version.

ducha *f* shower; **darse una ~** to have a shower.

ducharse *vpr* to have a shower.

duda *f* doubt; **sin ~** doubtless.

dudar *vi* to be unsure ❏ **dudar de** *v + prep* to have one's doubts about.

duelo *m* (*pelea*) duel; (*en deporte*) contest; (*pena*) grief.

duende *m* (*de cuentos infantiles*) goblin; (*gracia, encanto*) charm; **tener ~** to have a certain something.

dueño, -ña *m, f* (*propietario*) owner; (*de piso*) landlord (*f* landlady).

dulce *adj* sweet; (*agua*) fresh ◆ *m* (*caramelo, postre*) sweet; (*pastel*) cake; **~ de membrillo** quince jelly.

dulzura *f* sweetness.

duna *f* dune.

dúo *m* duet.

dúplex *m inv* duplex.

duplicar *vt* to double.

duración *f* length.

durante *adv* during; **~ toda la semana** all week; **lo estuve haciendo ~ dos horas** I was doing it for two hours.

durar *vi* (*prolongarse*) to last;

(*resistir*) to wear well.

durazno *m* (*Amér*) peach.

dureza *f* hardness; (*callosidad*) callus; (*de carácter*) harshness.

duro, -ra *adj* hard; (*carácter, persona, clima*) harsh; (*carne*) tough ◆ *m* (*moneda*) five-peseta piece ◆ *adv* hard.

E

ébano *m* ebony.

ebrio, ebria *adj* (*formal*) drunk.

ebullición *f* boiling.

echado, -da *adj* (*acostado*) lying down.

echar *vt* **1.** (*tirar*) to throw; **echó la pelota** she threw the ball.
2. (*añadir*) **~ algo a** (*sal, azúcar*) to add sthg to; (*vino, agua*) to pour sthg into.
3. (*reprimenda, discurso*) to give; **me echaron la buenaventura** I had my fortune told.
4. (*carta, postal*) to post.
5. (*expulsar*) to throw out; (*del trabajo*) to sack; **lo echaron del colegio** they threw him out of school.
6. (*humo, vapor, chispas*) to give off.
7. (*accionar*) **~ la llave/el cerrojo** to lock/bolt the door; **~ el freno** to brake.
8. (*flores, hojas*) to sprout.
9. (*acostar*) to lie (down); **echa al niño en el sofá** lie the child down on the sofa.

10. *(calcular)*: ¿cuántos años me **echas?** how old would you say I am?

11. *(fam: en televisión, cine)* to show; **¿qué echan esta noche en la tele?** what's on telly tonight?

12. *(en locuciones)*: ~ **abajo** *(edificio)* to pull down; *(gobierno)* to bring down; *(proyecto)* to ruin; ~ **de menos** to miss.

◆ *vi* **1.** *(dirigirse)*: **echó por el camino más corto** he took the shortest route.

2. *(empezar)*: ~ **a hacer algo** to begin to do sthg; ~ **a correr** to break into a run.

❏ **echarse** *vpr (lanzarse)* to throw o.s.; *(acostarse)* to lie down; **nos echamos a la carretera** we set out on the road; **~se a hacer algo** *(empezar)* to begin to do sthg.

echarpe *m* shawl.

eclesiástico, -ca *adj* ecclesiastical.

eclipse *m* eclipse.

eco *m* echo; **tener ~** to arouse interest.

ecología *f* ecology.

ecológico, -ca *adj* ecological.

economía *f (administración)* economy; *(ciencia)* economics ❏ **economías** *fpl (ahorros)* savings.

económico, -ca *adj (situación, crisis)* economic; *(barato)* cheap; *(motor, dispositivo)* economical.

economista *mf* economist.

ecosistema *m* ecosystem.

ecu *m* ecu.

ecuación *f* equation.

ecuador *m* equator.

Ecuador *m*: **(el)** ~ Ecuador.

ecuatoriano, -na *adj & m, f* Equadorian.

edad *f* age; **tengo 15 años de** ~ I'm 15 (years old); **la Edad Media** the Middle Ages *(pl)*.

edición *f (publicación)* publication; *(ejemplares)* edition.

edificante *adj* exemplary.

edificar *vt* to build.

edificio *m* building.

editar *vt (publicar)* to publish; *(disco)* to release.

editor, -ra *m, f* publisher.

editorial *f* publishing house.

edredón *m* duvet.

educación *f (formación)* education; *(cortesía, urbanidad)* good manners *(pl)*.

educado, -da *adj* polite; **bien** ~ polite; **mal** ~ rude.

educar *vt (hijos)* to bring up; *(alumnos)* to educate; *(sensibilidad, gusto)* to refine.

educativo, -va *adj* educational; *(sistema)* education *(antes de s)*.

EEUU *mpl (abrev de Estados Unidos)* USA.

efectivo *m* cash; **en** ~ in cash.

efecto *m (resultado)* effect; *(impresión)* impression; **en** ~ indeed; **~s personales** personal belongings; ~ **secundarios** side effects.

efectuar *vt (realizar)* to carry out; *(compra, pago, viaje)* to make.

eficacia *f (de persona)* efficiency; *(de medidas, plan)* effectiveness.

eficaz *(pl -ces)* *adj (persona)* efficient; *(medidas, plan)* effective.

eficiente *adj (medicamento, solu-*

ción, etc) effective; *(trabajador)* efficient.

EGB *f (abrev de Enseñanza General Básica) Spanish primary education system for pupils aged 6-14.*

Egipto *s* Egypt.

egoísmo *m* selfishness.

egoísta *adj* selfish.

egresado, -da *m, f (Amér)* graduate.

egresar *vi (Amér)* to graduate.

egreso *m (Amér)* graduation.

ej. *(abrev de ejemplo)* eg.

eje *m (de rueda)* axle; *(centro, en geometría)* axis.

ejecución *f (de condenado)* execution.

ejecutar *vt (realizar)* to carry out; *(matar)* to execute.

ejecutivo, -va *m, f* executive.

ejemplar *adj* exemplary ♦ *m (de especie, raza)* specimen; *(de libro)* copy; *(de revista)* issue.

ejemplo *m* example; **poner un ~** to give an example; **por ~** for example.

ejercer *vt (profesión, actividad)* to practise; *(influencia, autoridad)* to have.

ejercicio *m* exercise; *(de profesión, actividad)* practising; **~ físico** physical exercise.

ejército *m* army.

ejote *m (Amér)* green bean.

el, la *(pl* los, las*) art* **1.** *(con sustantivo genérico)* the; **~ coche** the car; **las niñas** the girls; **~ agua/hacha/águila** the water/axe/eagle. **2.** *(con sustantivo abstracto)*: **~ amor** love; **la vida** life; **los celos** jealousy *(sg)*.

3. *(indica posesión, pertenencia)*: **se rompió la pierna** he broke his leg; **tiene ~ pelo oscuro** she has dark hair.

4. *(con días de la semana)*: **vuelven ~ sábado** they're coming back on Saturday.

5. *(antes de adj)*: **prefiero la blanca** I prefer the white one.

6. *(en locuciones)*: **cogeré ~ de atrás** I'll take the one at the back; **mi hermano y ~ de Juan** my brother and Juan's; **~ que** *(persona)* whoever; *(cosa)* whichever (one); **~ que más me gusta** the one I like best.

él, ella *(pl* ellos, ellas*) pron* **1.** *(sujeto, predicado)* he (f she), they *(pl)*; *(animal, cosa)* it, they *(pl)*; **mi hermano es ~** he's my brother; **ella es una amiga de la familia** she's a friend of the family.

2. *(complemento)* him (f her), them *(pl)*; *(animal, cosa)* it, them *(pl)*; **voy a ir de vacaciones con ellos** I'm going on holiday with them.

3. *(posesivo)*: **de ~** his; **de ella** hers.

elaborar *vt (preparar)* to make; *(idea)* to work out; *(plan, lista)* to draw up.

elasticidad *f* elasticity.

elástico, -ca *adj* elastic ❑ **elásticos** *mpl (para pantalones)* braces.

elección *f (de regalo, vestido, etc)* choice; *(de presidente, jefe, etc)* election ❑ **elecciones** *fpl* elections.

electricidad *f* electricity.

electricista *mf* electrician.

eléctrico, -ca *adj* electric.

electrocutar vt to electrocute.

electrodoméstico m electrical household appliance.

electrónica f electronics.

electrónico, -ca adj electronic.

elefante m elephant.

elegancia f elegance; (de comportamiento) dignity.

elegante adj elegant; (comportamiento) dignified.

elegir vt (escoger) to choose; (en votación) to elect.

elemental adj (sencillo) obvious; (fundamental) basic.

elemento m element; (factor) factor ❑ **elementos** mpl (fuerzas de la naturaleza) elements.

elevación f rise.

elevado, -da adj high; (edificio, monte) tall.

elevador m (Amér) lift (Br), elevator (Am).

elevadorista mf (Amér) lift attendant (Br), elevator operator (Am).

elevar vt to raise; (ascender) to promote ❑ **elevarse** vpr (subir) to rise.

eliminación f elimination.

eliminar vt to eliminate.

élite f elite.

ello pron neutro it.

ellos, ellas pron pl (sujeto) they; (complemento) them; **de ~/ellas** theirs.

elocuencia f eloquence.

elocuente adj eloquent.

elogiar vt to praise.

elogio m praise.

elote m (Amér) cob.

eludir vt to avoid.

emancipado, -da adj emancipated.

emanciparse vpr to become emancipated.

embajada f (lugar) embassy; (cargo) ambassadorship.

embajador, -ra m, f ambassador.

embalar vt to wrap up ❑ **embalarse** vpr to race away.

embalsamar vt to embalm.

embalse m reservoir.

embarazada adj f pregnant.

embarazo m (de mujer) pregnancy; (dificultad) obstacle.

embarcación f boat.

embarcadero m jetty.

embarcar vi to board ❑ **embarcarse** vpr (pasajeros) to board; (en asunto, negocio) to get involved.

embargar vt (bienes, propiedades) to seize.

embargo m (de bienes) seizure; **sin ~** however.

embarque m (de pasajeros) boarding; (de equipaje) embarkation.

embestir vt to attack.

emblema m (símbolo) symbol; (distintivo) emblem.

emborracharse vpr to get drunk.

emboscada f ambush.

embotellado, -da adj (vino, licor) bottled; (calle, circulación) blocked.

embotellamiento m (de tráfico) traffic jam; (de vino, agua) bot-

tling.
embotellar vt (líquido) to bottle.
embrague m clutch.
embrión m embryo.
embromar vt (Amér) to annoy.
embrujar vt to bewitch.
embudo m funnel.
embustero, -ra m, f liar.
embutidos mpl cold, cured meat (sg).
emergencia f emergency.
emigración f (de familia, pueblo) emigration; (de animales) migration.
emigrante mf emigrant.
emigrar vi (persona, pueblo) to emigrate; (animal) to migrate.
eminente adj eminent.
emisión f (de sonido) emission; (del mensaje) transmission; (programa) broadcast; (de juicio, opinión, etc) expression.
emisor, -ra adj broadcasting.
emisora f radio station.
emitir vt (palabras) to utter; (sonido) to emit; (programa, música, etc) to broadcast; (juicio, opinión, etc) to express.
emoción f emotion; ¡qué ~! how exciting!
emocionado, -da adj excited.
emocionante adj exciting.
emocionarse vpr to get excited.
empacho m (de comida) upset stomach.
empanada f pasty; ~ **gallega** pasty containing tomato, tuna and peppers.

empanadilla f small pasty.
empañarse vpr to steam up.
empapado, -da adj (mojado) soaked.
empapar vt (mojar) to soak ❑ **empaparse** vpr to get soaked.
empapelar vt to paper.
empaquetar vt to pack; "empaquetado para regalo" "gift-wrapped".
empastar vt to fill.
empaste m filling.
empatar vi to draw ✦ vt (Amér) to connect.
empate m (en juego, deporte) draw; (Amér: empalme) connection; ~ **a dos** two-two draw.
empeñar vt (joyas, bienes) to pawn ❑ **empeñarse** vpr (endeudarse) to get into debt; **empeñarse en** v + prep (insistir en) to insist on.
empeño m (constancia) determination.
empeorar vt to make worse ✦ vi to get worse.
emperador, -triz (fpl -ces) m, f emperor (f empress) ✦ m (pez) swordfish.
empezar vt & vi to begin, to start; ~ **a hacer algo** to begin to do sthg, to start to do sthg.
empinado, -da adj steep.
empleado, -da m, f employee; ~ **de banco** bank clerk.
emplear vt (trabajador) to employ; (objeto, herramienta) to use; (dinero, tiempo) to spend ❑ **emplearse en** v + prep (empresa, oficina) to get a job in.
empleo m (trabajo en general)

employment; *(puesto)* job; *(uso)* use.

emplomadura f *(Amér)* filling.

emplomar vt *(Amér)* to fill.

empotrado, -da adj built-in; **armario ~** fitted cupboard.

emprender vt *(tarea, negocio, etc)* to start; *(viaje)* to set off on.

empresa f company.

empresario, -ria m, f businessman (f businesswoman).

empujar vt to push; **~ a alguien a hacer algo** to push sb into doing sthg.

empujón m shove; **a empujones** *(bruscamente)* by pushing; *(de forma discontinua)* in fits and starts.

en prep 1. *(en el interior de)* in; **viven ~ la capital** they live in the capital. 2. *(sobre la superficie de)* on; **el plato/la mesa** on the plate/table. 3. *(en un punto concreto de)* at; **~ casa/el trabajo** at home/work. 4. *(dirección)* into; **el avión cayó ~ el mar** the plane fell into the sea; **entraron ~ la habitación** they came into the room. 5. *(tiempo)* in; *(día)* on; *(período, momento)* at; **llegará ~ mayo/ Navidades** she will arrive in May/ at Christmas; **nació ~ 1940/sábado** he was born in 1940/on a Saturday; **~ un par de días** in a couple of days. 6. *(medio de transporte)* by; **ir ~ coche/tren/avión/barco** to go by car/train/plane/boat. 7. *(modo)* in; **lo dijo ~ inglés** she said it in English; **todo se lo gasta ~ ropa** he spends it all on clothes; **~ voz baja** in a low voice; **aumentar ~ un 10%** to increase by 10%.

8. *(precio)* in; **las ganancias se calculan ~ millones** profits are calculated in millions; **te lo dejo ~ 5.000 pesetas** I'll let you have it for 5,000 pesetas. 9. *(tema)*: **es un experto ~ matemáticas** he's an expert on mathematics; **es doctor ~ medicina** he's a doctor of medicine. 10. *(cualidad)*: **rápido ~ actuar** quick to act; **le supera ~ inteligencia** she is more intelligent than he is.

enaguas fpl petticoat *(sg)*.

enamorado, -da adj: **~ (de)** in love (with).

enamorarse vpr: **~ (de)** to fall in love (with).

enano, -na adj *(verdura)* baby *(antes de s)* ◆ m, f dwarf.

encabezar vt *(lista, carta, escrito)* to head; *(grupo)* to lead.

encadenar vt *(atar)* to chain; *(enlazar)* to link ◇ **encadenarse** vpr *(hechos, sucesos)* to happen one after the other.

encajar vt *(meter)* to fit; *(aceptar)* to take ◆ vi *(caber)* to fit; *(cuadrar)* to square.

encaje m *(tejido)* lace; *(de vestido, camisa)* lace trim.

encalar vt to whitewash.

encamotarse vpr *(Amér: fam)* to fall in love.

encantado, -da adj *(satisfecho)* delighted; *(lugar, edificio)* haunted; *(persona)* bewitched ◆ **~ de conocerle** pleased to meet you.

encantador, -ra adj delightful.

encantar vt *(hechizar)* to cast a spell on; **me encanta bailar** I love dancing; ¡me **encanta**! I love it! ❑

encantarse vpr (distraerse) to be entranced.

encanto m (atractivo) charm; (hechizo) spell.

encapotado, -da adj overcast.

encapricharse vpr: ~ con (obstinarse) to set one's mind on.

encaramarse a + prep to climb up onto.

encarar vt (problema, riesgo) to face up to ♦ **encararse** vpr: ~se a to confront.

encarcelar vt to imprison.

encarecer vt (precio) to make more expensive.

encargado, -da m, f (responsable) person in charge; (de tienda, negocio) manager (f manageress).

encargar vt (pedir) to order; (poner al cuidado) to put in charge ♦ **encargarse de** v + prep to see to, to take care of.

encargo m (pedido) order; (tarea) task; (recado) errand.

encariñarse: encariñarse con v + prep to become fond of.

encarnado, -da adj (rojo) red; (personificado) incarnate.

encausar vt to prosecute.

encendedor m lighter.

encender vt (fuego, cigarrillo) to light; (luz, gas, aparato eléctrico) to turn on.

encendido m (de motor) ignition.

encerado m (pizarra) blackboard; (del suelo) polishing.

encerrar vt (recluir) to lock up; (contener) to contain ❑ **encerrarse**

vpr to shut o.s. away.

encestar vi to score a basket.

enchilarse vpr (Amér) (con chile) to eat a mouthful of very hot food; (fig: enfadarse) to get angry.

enchinar vt (Amér) to curl.

enchufar vt (aparato eléctrico) to plug in; (fam: a una persona) to pull strings for.

enchufe m (de aparato) plug; (de pared) socket; (fam: recomendación) connections (pl).

encía f gum.

enciclopedia f encyclopedia.

encierro m (de personas) sit-in; (de toros) running of the bulls to the enclosure where they are kept before a bullfight.

encima adv (arriba) on top; (en edificio) upstairs; (además) on top of that; **no llevo dinero** ~ I haven't got any money on me; ~ **de** (en lugar superior) above; (en edificio) upstairs from; (sobre) on (top of); **por** ~ (superficialmente) superficially; **por** ~ **de** (más arriba de) over; **por** ~ **de sus posibilidades** beyond his means; **por** ~ **de todo** more than anything.

encimera f worktop.

encina f holm oak.

encinta adj pregnant.

encoger vt (piernas) to pull in ♦ vi to shrink ❑ **encogerse** vpr (tejido, ropa) to shrink; (persona) to get scared; ~**se de hombros** to shrug one's shoulders.

encolar vt (pegar) to glue.

encolerizarse vpr to get angry.

encontrar vt to find; (persona)

to meet; **~ trabajo** to find work ❑

encontrarse *vpr* (*coincidir*) to meet; (*hallarse*) to be; **~se con alguien** to meet sb.

encrespado, -da *adj* (*pelo*) curly; (*mar*) rough.

encrucijada *f* crossroads (*sg*).

encuadernar *vt* to bind.

encuadre *m* (*de foto*) composition.

encubierto, -ta *pp* → encubrir.

encubrir *vt* to conceal.

encuentro *m* (*con persona*) meeting; (*partido*) match.

encuesta *f* survey.

encuestador, -ra *m, f* pollster.

enderezar *vt* (*lo torcido*) to straighten; (*lo caído*) to put upright; (*persona, negocio, trabajo*) to set right.

endeudado, -da *adj* in debt.

endivia *f* endive; **~ al roquefort** endives in a Roquefort sauce.

enemigo, -ga *m, f* enemy; **ser ~ de** to hate.

energía *f* (*en física, etc*) energy; (*de persona*) strength; **~ atómica** nuclear power.

enérgico, -ca *adj* energetic.

enero *m* January, → setiembre.

enfadado, -da *adj* angry.

enfadarse *vpr* to get angry.

enfado *m* anger.

enfermar *vi* to fall ill ◆ **enfermarse** *vpr* (*Amér*) to fall ill.

enfermedad *f* (*caso concreto*) illness; (*morbo*) disease.

enfermería *f* sick bay.

enfermero, -ra *m, f* nurse.

enfermizo, -za *adj* unhealthy.

enfermo, -ma *adj* ill, sick ◆ *m, f* (*persona enferma*) sick person; (*en el hospital*) patient; **ponerse ~** to fall ill.

enfocar *vt* (*luz, foco*) to shine; (*cámara*) to focus; (*tema, cuestión, problema*) to look at.

enfoque *m* (*de cámara*) focus; (*de cuestión, problema*) approach.

enfrentamiento *m* confrontation.

enfrentarse *vpr* to clash; **~se a** (*oponerse a*) to confront.

enfrente *adv* opposite; **~ de** opposite; **la casa de ~** the house across the road.

enfriamiento *m* cold.

enfriarse *vpr* (*comida, bebida*) to get cold; (*relación*) to cool down; (*resfriarse*) to catch a cold.

enganchar *vt* (*objeto, papel*) to hang up; (*caballos, caravana, coche*) to hitch up ❑ **engancharse** *vpr* (*ropa, persona*) to get caught.

enganche *m* (*Amér: depósito*) deposit; (*mecanismo, pieza*) hook; **$50 de ~** (*Amér*) a $50 deposit.

engañar *vt* (*decir mentiras a*) to deceive; (*timar*) to cheat; (*a cónyuge*) to cheat on ❑ **engañarse** *vpr* (*equivocarse*) to be wrong.

engaño *m* (*mentira*) deceit; (*timo*) swindle; (*infidelidad*) cheating.

engañoso, -sa *adj* (*apariencia*) deceptive; (*mirada, palabra*) deceitful.

engendrar *vt* (*persona, animal*) to give birth to; (*sentimiento*) to give rise to.

englobar *vt* to bring together.

engordar vi (persona) to put on weight; (alimento) to be fattening ❑ **engordarse** vpr to put on weight.

engorde m (Amér): **(carne de) ~** meat from domestic animals (not birds) reared for slaughter.

engranaje m (de coche) gears (pl).

engrasar vt (mecanismo, pieza) to lubricate; (ensuciar) to make greasy.

engreído, -da adj conceited.

enhorabuena f congratulations (pl) ◆ interj congratulations!; **dar la ~** to congratulate.

enigma m enigma.

enjabonar vt (ropa) to soap; (fig: persona) to butter up ❑ **enjabonarse** vpr to soap o.s. down.

enjuagar vt to rinse ❑ **enjuagarse** vpr (boca) to rinse out one's mouth.

enlace m (de trenes) connection; (de carreteras) link; (formal: matrimonio) marriage ◆ mf (intermediario) go-between.

enlazar vt (conectar) to tie; (relacionar) to connect ◆ vi: **~ con** to connect with.

enlosar vt to pave.

enmendar vt (corregir) to correct ❑ **enmendarse** vpr to mend one's ways.

enmienda f (corrección) correction; (de ley) amendment.

enmudecer vi to be struck dumb.

enojado, -da adj annoyed.

enojar vt (enfadar) to anger; (molestar) to annoy ❑ **enojarse** vpr (enfadarse) to get angry; (molestarse) to get annoyed.

enojo m (enfado) anger; (molestia) annoyance.

enorme adj huge.

enredadera f creeper.

enredar vt (lana, hilo, pelo) to tangle; **~ a alguien en** (complicar) to involve sb in.

enredo m (de lana, hilo, etc) tangle; (situación difícil, desorden) mess.

enriquecer vt to make rich ❑ **enriquecerse** vpr to get rich.

enrojecer vt to redden ◆ vi (sonrojarse) to blush.

enrollar vt to roll up ❑ **enrollarse** vpr (fam) (hablar mucho) to go on and on; (ligar) to get off with each other.

ensaimada f cake made of sweet, coiled pastry.

ensalada f salad; **~ catalana** salad of lettuce, tomato, onion and cold meats; **~ de lechuga** lettuce salad; **~ mixta** mixed salad; **~ variada** o **del tiempo** salad of lettuce, tomato, carrot and onion; **~ verde** green salad.

ensaladera f salad bowl.

ensaladilla f: **~ (rusa)** Russian salad.

ensanchar vt (camino) to widen; (falda, pantalón) to let out.

ensayar vt (espectáculo) to rehearse; (mecanismo, invento) to test.

ensayo m (de espectáculo) rehearsal; (de mecanismo, invento) test; (escrito) essay.

enseguida adv (inmediatamente) immediately; (pronto) very soon.

ensenada f cove.

enseñanza f *(método, sistema)* education; *(profesión)* teaching.

enseñar vt *(en escuela, universidad)* to teach; *(indicar, mostrar)* to show.

enseres mpl belongings.

ensopar vt *(Amér)* to soak.

ensuciar vt make dirty ☐ **ensuciarse** vpr to get dirty.

ente m *(ser)* being; *(asociación)* organization.

entender vt to understand; *(opinar)* to think ◆ vi to understand ☐ **entender de** v + prep *(saber de)* to be an expert on; **entenderse** vpr *(comprenderse)* to understand each other; *(llegar a un acuerdo)* to reach an agreement; *(fam: estar liado)* to be involved; **~se bien/mal con** to get on well/badly with.

entendido, -da m, f expert.

enterarse vpr **enterarse de** v + prep *(noticia, suceso)* to find out about; *(fam: darse cuenta de)* to realize.

entero, -ra adj whole; *(de carácter)* composed; **por ~** entirely.

enterrar vt to bury.

entidad f *(asociación)* body.

entierro m burial.

entlo abrev = **entresuelo**.

entonces adv then; **desde ~** since then.

entrada f *(lugar)* entrance; *(puerta)* doorway; *(de espectáculo)* ticket; *(plato)* starter; *(anticipo)* down payment; **"entrada"** "way in"; **"~ libre"** "admission free"; **"~ por la otra puerta"** "enter by other door"; **"prohibida la ~"** "no

entry"; **de ~** *(en principio)* from the beginning; **¿qué quiere de ~?** what would you like for starters?

entrantes mpl *(entremeses)* hors d'œuvres.

entrañable adj *(digno de afecto)* likeable; *(afectuoso)* affectionate.

entrañas fpl *(vísceras)* entrails.

entrar vt **1.** *(introducir)* to bring in; **están entrando el carbón** they're bringing in the coal; **ya puedes ~ el coche en el garaje** you can put your car in the garage now.

2. *(INFORM)* to enter.

◆ vi **1.** *(introducirse)* to enter, to come/go in; **la pelota entró por la ventana** the ball came in through the window; **entramos en el bar** we went into the bar.

2. *(penetrar)* to go in; **el enchufe no entra** the plug won't go in; **el clavo ha entrado en la pared** the nail went into the wall.

3. *(caber)* to fit; **este anillo no te entra** this ring doesn't fit you; **en el garaje entran dos coches** you can fit two cars in the garage.

4. *(incorporarse)* to join; **para ~ has de hacer un test** you have to do a test to get in; **entró en el partido en abril** she joined the party in April; **entró de secretaria** she started out as a secretary.

5. *(entender)*: **no le entra la geometría** he can't get the hang of geometry.

6. *(estado físico o de ánimo)*: **me entró mucha pena** I was filled with pity; **me entraron ganas de hablar** I suddenly felt like talking.

7. *(estar incluido)*: **~ (en)** to be included (in); **la consumición no**

entra *(en discoteca)* drinks are not included.

8. *(participar)*: ~ **(en)** to participate (in).

9. *(cantidad)*: **¿cuántas peras entran en un kilo?** how many pears do you get to the kilo?

10. *(AUTOM)* to engage; **no entra la quinta** you can't get into fifth.

11. *(empezar)*: ~ **a hacer algo** to start doing sthg.

entre *prep* 1. *(en medio de dos términos)* between; **aparcar ~ dos coches** to park between two cars; **vendré ~ las tres y las cuatro** I'll come between three and four.

2. *(en medio de muchos)* among; **estaba ~ los asistentes** she was among those present; **~ hombres y mujeres somos cien** there are a hundred of us, taking men and women together.

3. *(participación, cooperación)* between; **~ todos lo consiguieron** between them they managed it; **~ nosotros** *(en confianza)* between you and me.

4. *(lugar)* among; **encontré tu carta ~ los libros** I found your letter among the books.

entreabierto, -ta *adj (puerta, ventana)* ajar.

entreacto *m* interval.

entrecejo *m* space between the brows.

entrecot *m* entrecôte; **~ a la pimienta verde** entrecôte in a green peppercorn sauce; **~ al roquefort** entrecôte in a Roquefort sauce.

entrega *f (acto)* handing over; *(de pedido)* delivery; *(dedicación)* devotion; *(fascículo)* instalment.

entregar *vt (dar)* to hand over; *(pedido, paquete)* to deliver ❑ **entregarse a** v + prep *(rendirse)* to surrender to; *(abandonarse a)* to surrender to; *(dedicarse a)* to devote o.s. to.

entrelazar *vt* to interlace.

entremeses *mpl* hors d'œuvres.

entrenador, -ra *m, f* coach.

entrenamiento *m* training.

entrenar *vt* to train ❑ **entrenarse** *vpr* to train.

entrepierna *f* crotch.

entresuelo *m* mezzanine.

entretanto *adv* meanwhile.

entretecho *m (Amér)* attic.

entretener *vt (divertir)* to entertain; *(hacer retrasar)* to hold up ❑ **entretenerse** *vpr (divertirse)* to amuse o.s.; *(retrasarse)* to be held up.

entretenido, -da *adj (divertido)* entertaining; *(que requiere atención)* time-consuming.

entretenimiento *m (diversión)* entertainment.

entretiempo *m*: **de ~** mild-weather.

entrever *vt (ver)* to glimpse; *(sospechar)* to suspect.

entreverar *vt (Amér)* to mix up ❑ **entreverarse** *vpr (Amér)* to be mixed up.

entrevero *m (Amér)* muddle.

entrevista *f* interview.

entrevistador, -ra *m, f* interviewer.

entrevistar *vt* to interview.

entrevisto, -ta *pp* → **entrever**.

entristecer *vt* to make sad ❑

entristecerse *vpr* to become sad.

entrometerse *vpr* to interfere.

entusiasmado, -da *adj* full of enthusiasm.

entusiasmar *vt*: me entusiasma I love it ❑ **entusiasmarse** *vpr* to get excited.

entusiasmo *m* enthusiasm.

entusiasta *adj* enthusiastic.

envasar *vt* to pack.

envase *m* (recipiente) container; ~ **sin retorno** non-returnable bottle.

envejecer *vi* to grow old.

envenenamiento *m* poisoning.

envenenar *vt* to poison.

envergadura *f* (importancia) extent.

enviar *vt* to send.

envidia *f* envy.

envidiar *vt* to envy.

envidioso, -sa *adj* envious.

envío *m* (acción) delivery; (paquete) package.

enviudar *vi* to be widowed.

envolver *vt* (regalo, paquete) to wrap (up).

envuelto, -ta *pp* → envolver.

enyesar *vt* (pared, muro) to plaster; (pierna, brazo) to put in plaster.

epidemia *f* epidemic.

episodio *m* (suceso) event; (capítulo) episode.

época *f* (periodo) period; (estación) season.

equilibrado, -da *adj* balanced.

equilibrar *vt* to balance.

equilibrio *m* balance; (de persona) level-headedness.

equilibrista *mf* tightrope walker.

equipaje *m* luggage (Br), baggage (Am); ~ **de mano** hand luggage.

equipar *vt* (proveer) to equip.

equipo *m* (de personas) team; (de objetos) equipment; (de prendas) kit.

equitación *f* horse riding.

equivalente *adj & m* equivalent.

equivaler: **equivaler a** *v + prep* to be equivalent to.

equivocación *f* mistake.

equivocado, -da *adj* wrong.

equivocar *vt* (confundir) to mistake ❑ **equivocarse** *vpr* (cometer un error) to make a mistake; (no tener razón) to be wrong; ~ **de nombre** to get the wrong name; **me he equivocado** (al teléfono) sorry, wrong number.

era *v* → ser ♦ f era.

eres *v* → ser.

erguido, -da *adj* erect.

erizo *m* hedgehog; ~ **de mar** sea urchin.

ermita *f* hermitage.

erótico, -ca *adj* erotic.

erotismo *m* eroticism.

errante *adj* wandering.

errar *vi* (equivocarse) to make a mistake.

erróneo, -a *adj* wrong.

error *m* mistake, error.

eructar *vi* to belch.

eructo *m* belch.

erudito, -ta m, f erudite.

erupción f (de la piel) rash; (de volcán) eruption.

es v → ser.

esbelto, -ta adj slim.

esbozo m (dibujo) sketch; (resumen, guión) outline.

escabeche m: en ~ marinated.

escala f scale; (de barco, avión) stopover; **a gran** ~ on a large scale; ~ **musical** scale; **hacer** ~ **en** to stop over at.

escalador, -ra m, f climber.

escalar vt to climb.

escalera f (de casa, edificio) staircase, stairs (pl); (portátil) ladder; ~ **de caracol** spiral staircase; ~ **de incendios** fire escape; ~ **mecánica** escalator ▫ **escaleras** fpl stairs.

escalerilla f stairs (pl).

escalofrío m shiver.

escalón m step.

escalope m escalope.

escalopín m: **escalopines de ternera** escalope of veal (sg).

escama f (de pez, reptil) scale; (en la piel) flake.

escampar vi to clear up.

escandalizar vt to shock ▫ **escandalizarse** vpr to be shocked.

escándalo m (inmoralidad) scandal; (alboroto) uproar.

escaño m (de diputado) seat (in parliament).

escapar vi: ~ (**de**) to escape (from) ▫ **escaparse** vpr (persona) to escape; (líquido, gas) to leak.

escaparate m (shop) window.

escape m (de líquido, gas) leak; (de coche) exhaust; **a** ~ in a rush.

escarabajo m beetle.

escarbar vt to scratch.

escarcha f frost.

escarmentar vi to learn (one's lesson) ♦ vt: ~ **a alguien** to teach sb a lesson.

escarola f endive.

escasear vi to be scarce.

escasez f (insuficiencia) shortage; (pobreza) poverty.

escaso, -sa adj (recursos, número) limited; (víveres) scarce; (tiempo) (visibilidad) poor; **un metro** ~ barely a metre; **andar** ~ **de dinero** to be short of money.

escayola f plaster.

escayolar vt to put in plaster.

escena f scene; (escenario) stage.

escenario m (de teatro) stage; (de un suceso) scene.

escepticismo m scepticism.

escéptico, -ca adj sceptical.

esclavitud f slavery.

esclavo, -va m, f slave.

esclusa f lock.

escoba f broom.

escobilla f brush.

escocer vi to sting.

escocés, -esa adj Scottish ♦ m, f Scot.

Escocia s Scotland.

escoger vt to choose ♦ vi: ~ **entre** to choose between.

escolar adj school (antes de s) ♦ mf schoolboy (f schoolgirl).

escolaridad f schooling.

escollo m (roca) reef.

escolta f escort.

escombros mpl rubble (sg).

esconder vt to hide ▫ **escon-**

derse *vpr* to hide.
escondidas: a escondidas *adv* in secret.
escondite *m* *(lugar)* hiding place; *(juego)* hide-and-seek.
escopeta *f* shotgun.
escorpión *m* scorpion ☐ **Escorpión** *m* Scorpio.
escotado, -da *adj* low-cut.
escote *m* *(de vestido)* neckline.
escotilla *f* hatch.
escribir *vt & vi* to write; ~ a mano to write by hand; ~ a máquina to type ☐ **escribirse** *vpr* *(tener correspondencia)* to write to one another; **¿cómo se escribe ...?** how do you spell ...?
escrito, -ta *pp* → **escribir** ◆ *m* *(texto)* text; *(documento)* document.
escritor, -ra *m, f* writer.
escritorio *m* desk.
escritura *f* *(letra)* script; *(documento)* deed.
escrúpulo *m* scruple ☐ **escrúpulos** *mpl* *(reservas)* qualms.
escuadra *f* *(en dibujo)* set square; *(de barcos)* squadron; *(del ejército)* squad.
escuchar *vt* to listen to ◆ *vi* to listen; ~ la radio to listen to the radio.
escudella *f*: ~ catalana Catalan dish similar to "cocido madrileño".
escudo *m* *(arma defensiva)* shield; *(moneda)* escudo.
escuela *f* school; ~ privada/pública private/state school; ~ universitaria university which awards degrees after three years' study.
esculpir *vt* to sculpt.
escultor, -ra *m, f* sculptor (f

sculptress).
escultura *f* sculpture.
escupir *vt* to spit out ◆ *vi* to spit.
escurrir *vt* *(ropa)* to wring out; *(platos)* to drain; *(deslizar)* to slide ☐ **escurrirse** *vpr* *(deslizarse)* to slip.
ese, esa *adj* that.
ése, ésa *pron* that one.
esencia *f* essence.
esencial *adj* essential.
esfera *f* *(en geometría)* sphere; *(del reloj)* face; *(ámbito)* circle.
esférico, -ca *adj* spherical.
esforzarse *vpr* to make an effort.
esfuerzo *m* effort.
esfumarse *vpr* to vanish.
esgrima *f* fencing.
esguince *m* sprain.
eslabón *m* link.
eslálom *m* slalom.
eslip *(pl* eslips*)* *m* *(pieza interior)* briefs *(pl)*; *(bañador)* swimming trunks *(pl)*.
Eslovaquia *s* Slovakia.
esmalte *m* enamel; ~ de uñas nail varnish.
esmeralda *f* emerald.
esmerarse *vpr* to take great pains.
esmero *m* great care.
esmoquin *m* dinner jacket *(Br)*, tuxedo *(Am)*.
esnob *(pl* esnobs*)* *mf* person who wants to be trendy.
eso *pron neutro* that; ~ que tienes en la mano that thing in your hand; a ~ de (at) around; por ~ te

lo digo that's why I'm telling you; **y ~ que** even though.

esos, esas adj pl those.

espacial adj space (antes de s).

espacio m space; (de tiempo) period; (programa) programme; ~ **aéreo** air space; ~ **publicitario** advertising spot.

espacioso, -sa adj spacious.

espada f sword ♦ f **espadas** fpl (naipes) suit in a Spanish deck of cards bearing swords.

espaguetis mpl spaghetti (sg).

espalda f back ♦ f inv (en natación) backstroke ❑ **espaldas** fpl back (sg); **a ~s de** behind.

espantapájaros m inv scarecrow.

espanto m fright.

espantoso, -sa adj (que asusta) horrific; (muy feo, desagradable) horrible; (enorme) terrible.

España s Spain.

español, -la adj & m Spanish ♦ m, f Spaniard.

esparadrapo m (sticking) plaster.

esparcir vt (extender) to spread; (azúcar) to sprinkle; (semillas, papeles) to scatter.

espárrago m asparagus; ~**s trigueros** wild asparagus.

espasmo m spasm.

espátula f (en cocina) spatula.

especia f spice.

especial adj special; (fam: persona) odd; ~ **para** specially for.

especialidad f speciality (Br), specialty (Am); ~ **de la casa** house speciality.

especialista mf specialist.

especializado, -da adj specialized.

especializarse: especializarse en v + prep to specialize in.

especialmente adv especially.

especie f (familia) species; (fig: tipo) type; **en ~** in kind; ~ **protegida** protected species.

especificar vt to specify.

específico, -ca adj specific.

espectáculo m (en teatro, circo, etc) performance, show.

espectador, -ra m, f (en deporte) spectator; (en cine, teatro) member of the audience.

especulación f speculation.

espejismo m mirage.

espejo m mirror.

espera f wait; **en ~ de** waiting for.

esperanza f (deseo) hope; (confianza) expectation.

esperar vt (aguardar) to wait for; (confiar) to expect; (recibir, buscar) to meet; (en el futuro) to await ♦ vi (aguardar) to wait; ~ **que** to hope (that); **¡eso espero!** I hope so!; **¡espera y verás!** wait and see!; **espérate sentado** (fig) you're in for a long wait ❑ **esperarse** vpr (figurarse) to expect; (aguardar) to wait.

esperma m sperm.

espeso, -sa adj thick.

espesor m (grosor) thickness; (densidad) density.

espía mf spy.

espiar vt to spy on.

espiga f (de trigo) ear.

espina f (de planta) thorn; (de pez) bone.

espinacas fpl spinach (sg).

espinilla f (de la pierna) shin; (en la piel) blackhead.

espionaje m espionage.

espiral f spiral; en ~ in spiral.

espirar vi to breathe out.

espiritismo m spiritualism.

espíritu m (alma) spirit; (en religión) soul.

espiritual adj spiritual.

espléndido, -da adj (magnífico) splendid; (generoso) lavish.

esplendor m splendour.

espliego m lavender.

esponja f sponge.

esponjoso, -sa adj spongy.

espontaneidad f spontaneity.

espontáneo, -a adj spontaneous ◆ m spectator who takes part in bullfight on the spur of the moment.

esposas fpl handcuffs.

esposo, -sa m, f husband (f wife).

espray m spray.

esprint m sprint.

esprínter mf sprinter.

espuma f (burbujas) foam; (de jabón) lather; (de cerveza) head; ~ para el pelo (styling) mousse.

esqueleto m skeleton.

esquema m (esbozo) outline; (gráfico) diagram.

esquematizar vt to outline.

esquí m (patín) ski; (deporte) skiing; ~ acuático water skiing.

esquiador, -ra m, f skier.

esquiar vi to ski.

esquilar vt to shear.

esquimal adj & mf Eskimo.

esquina f corner.

esquivar vt to avoid.

estabilidad f stability.

estable adj stable.

establecer vt (fundar) to establish; (suj: ley, decreto) to stipulate ❑ **establecerse** vpr (con residencia) to settle.

establecimiento m (acto) setting up; (local) establishment.

establo m cowshed.

estaca f (de tienda de campaña) peg.

estación f (de tren, autobús, etc) station; (del año, temporada) season; "~ de servicio" "service station".

estacionamiento m (aparcamiento) parking; ~ indebido parking offence; "~ limitado" "restricted parking".

estacionar vt to park; "no ~" "no parking" ❑ **estacionarse** vpr to park.

estadio m (de deporte) stadium.

estadística f (censo) statistics (pl).

estado m state; estar en ~ to be expecting; en buen/mal ~ in good/bad condition; ~ civil marital status; ~ físico physical condition ❑ **Estado** m: el Estado the State.

Estados Unidos mpl: (los) ~ the United States.

estadounidense adj United States ◆ mf United States citizen.

estafa f swindle.

estafador, -ra m, f swindler.

estafar vt (engañar) to swindle; (robar) to defraud.

estalactita f stalactite.

estalagmita f stalagmite.

estallar *vi (bomba)* to explode; *(guerra, revolución)* to break out; **~ en sollozos** to burst into tears.

estallido *m (explosión)* explosion.

estambre *m* stamen.

estamento *m* class.

estampado, -da *adj* printed ◆ *m (cotton)* print.

estampida *f* stampede.

estampilla *f (Amér) (sello)* stamp; *(cromo)* transfer.

estancado, -da *adj (agua, río, etc)* stagnant; *(mecanismo)* jammed.

estancarse *vpr (agua, río, etc)* to stagnate; *(mecanismo)* to jam.

estancia *f (período)* stay; *(cuarto)* room; *(Amér: hacienda de campo)* cattle ranch.

estanciero, -ra *m, f (Amér)* ranch owner.

estanco *m* tobacconist's (shop).

estand *(pl* **estands***) m* stand, stall.

estándar *adj* standard.

estanque *m (alberca)* pond; *(para riego)* reservoir.

estante *m* shelf.

estantería *f (estantes)* shelves *(pl)*; *(para libros)* bookcase.

estaño *m* tin.

estar *vi* 1. *(hallarse)* to be; **¿está Juan?** is Juan in?; **estaré allí a la hora convenida** I'll be there at the agreed time.
2. *(con fechas)*: **¿a qué estamos hoy?** what's the date today?; **hoy estamos a martes 13 de julio** today is Tuesday the 13th of July; **estamos en febrero/primavera** it's February/spring.

3. *(quedarse)* to stay; **estaré un par de horas y me iré** I'll stay a couple of hours and then I'll go; **estuvo toda la tarde en casa** he was at home all afternoon.

4. *(hallarse listo)* to be ready; **la comida estará a las tres** the meal will be ready at three.

5. *(expresa duración)* to be; **están golpeando la puerta** they're banging on the door.

6. *(expresa valores, grados)*: **la libra está a 200 pesetas** the pound is at 200 pesetas; **estamos a 20 grados** it's 20 degrees here.

7. *(servir)*: **~ para** to be (there) for.

8. *(faltar)*: **eso está por descubrir** we have yet to discover that.

9. *(hallarse a punto de)*: **~ por hacer algo** to be on the verge of doing sthg.

◆ *v copulativo* 1. *(expresa cualidad, estado)* to be; **¿cómo estás?** how are you?; **esta calle está sucia** this street is dirty; **~ bien/mal** *(persona)* to be well/unwell; **el cielo está con nubes** the sky is cloudy; **estoy sin dinero** I'm out of money; **el jefe está que muerde** the boss is furious.

2. *(sentar)*: **el traje te está muy bien** the suit looks good on you.

3. *(expresa situación, ocupación, acción)*: **~ como camarero** to be a waiter; **~ de suerte** to be in luck; **~ de viaje** to be on a trip.

4. *(expresa permanencia)*: **~ en uso** to be in use.

5. *(consistir)*: **~ en** to lie in.

❑ **estarse** *vpr (permanecer)* to stay.

estárter *m* starter.

estatal *adj* state.

estático, -ca *adj (inmóvil)*

stock-still.

estatua f statue.

estatura f height.

estatus m status.

estatuto m (de compañía) article (of association); (de asociación) by-law.

este¹, esta adj this.

este² m east ❑ **Este**: **el Este** (de Europa) Eastern Europe.

éste, ésta pron (cercano en espacio) this one; (cercano en el tiempo) this.

estera f mat.

estéreo m stereo.

estéril adj (persona, animal) sterile; (envase, jeringuilla) sterilized.

esterilizar vt to sterilize.

esternón m breastbone.

estética f (aspecto) look.

estibador, -ra m, f stevedore.

estiércol m (excremento) dung; (abono) manure.

estilo m style; (de natación) stroke; **algo por el ~** something of the sort.

estilográfica f fountain pen.

estima f esteem.

estimación f (aprecio) esteem; (valoración) valuation.

estimado, -da adj (querido) esteemed; (valorado) valued; **Estimado señor** Dear Sir.

estimulante adj (alentador) encouraging ◆ m stimulant.

estimular vt (animar) to encourage; (excitar) to stimulate.

estímulo m incentive.

estirado, -da adj (orgulloso) haughty; (ropa) stretched.

estirar vt to stretch ◆ vi to pull ❑ **estirarse** vpr (desperezarse) to stretch.

estirpe f stock.

esto pron neutro this; **~ que dices** what you're saying.

estofado m stew.

estoico, -ca adj stoical.

estómago m stomach.

estorbar vt (obstaculizar) to hinder; (molestar) to bother ◆ vi (estar en medio) to be in the way; (molestar) to be a bother.

estorbo m (obstáculo) hindrance.

estornudar vi to sneeze.

estornudo m sneeze.

estos, -tas adj pl these.

éstos, -tas pron pl (cercano en espacio) these (ones); (cercano en el tiempo) these.

estoy v → **estar**.

estrafalario, -ria adj (fam) eccentric.

estrangulador, -ra m, f strangler.

estrangular vt to strangle.

estratega mf strategist.

estrategia f strategy.

estratégico, -ca adj strategic.

estrechar vt (camino, calle) to narrow; (ropa) to take in; (amistad, relación) to make closer; **~ la mano a alguien** to shake sb's hand ❑ **estrecharse** vpr (apretarse) to squeeze up.

estrecho, -cha adj (calle, camino, etc) narrow; (zapato, ropa, etc) tight; (amistad) close ◆ m strait; **estar ~** (en un lugar) to be cramped.

estrella f star; ~ **de cine** film star; ~ **fugaz** shooting star; ~ **de mar** starfish.

estrellarse vpr (chocar) to crash.

estremecerse: estremecerse de v + prep to tremble with.

estrenar vt (ropa) to wear for the first time; (espectáculo) to première; (coche, vajilla, sábanas) to use for the first time.

estreno m (de espectáculo) première.

estreñimiento m constipation.

estrepitoso, -sa adj (ruido, caída, etc) noisy.

estrés m stress.

estría f groove.

estribillo m (de canción) chorus.

estribo m (del jinete) stirrup; (del automóvil) step; **perder los ~s** to fly off the handle.

estribor m starboard.

estricto, -ta adj strict.

estrofa f verse.

estropajo m scourer.

estropeado, -da adj (coche) broken down; (máquina) out of order.

estropear vt (proyecto, plan, comida, etc) to spoil; (averiar) to break; (dañar) to damage ❑ **estropearse** vpr (máquina, aparato) to break down.

estructura f structure.

estuario m estuary.

estuche m case.

estudiante mf student.

estudiar vt & vi to study.

estudio m study; (de artista) stu-

dio; (piso) studio apartment ❑ **estudios** mpl (de radio, televisión) studios; (educación) education (sg).

estudioso, -sa adj studious.

estufa f heater.

estupefacto, -ta adj astonished.

estupendo, -da adj great ◆ interj great!

estupidez f (calidad) stupidity; (dicho, acto) stupid thing.

estúpido, -da adj stupid.

estuviera v → estar.

ETA f (abrev de Euskadi ta Askatasuna) ETA (terrorist Basque separatist organization).

etapa f stage.

etarra mf member of "ETA".

etc. (abrev de etcétera) etc.

etcétera adv etcetera.

eternidad f eternity; **una ~** (fam) ages (pl).

eterno, -na adj (perpetuo) eternal; (fam: que dura mucho, que se repite) interminable.

ética f ethics (pl).

ético, -ca adj ethical.

etimología f etymology.

etiqueta f (de paquete, vestido) label; (normas) etiquette; **de ~** formal.

étnico, -ca adj ethnic.

eucalipto m eucalyptus.

eucaristía f Eucharist.

eufemismo m euphemism.

eufórico, -ca adj elated.

Europa s Europe.

europeo, -a adj & m, f European.

Euskadi s the Basque Country.

euskera adj & m Basque.

eutanasia f euthanasia.

evacuación f evacuation.

evacuar vt to evacuate.

evadir vt to avoid □ **evadirse** vpr: ~se de to escape from.

evaluación f (de trabajo, examen, etc) assessment; (de casa, terreno, etc) valuation.

evaluar vt (trabajo, examen etc) to assess; (casa, terreno, etc) to value.

evangelio m gospel.

evangelización f evangelization.

evaporarse vpr to evaporate.

evasión f (distracción) amusement; (fuga) escape; ~ de capitales capital flight.

eventual adj (posible) possible; (trabajador) casual.

eventualidad f (posibilidad) possibility.

evidencia f (seguridad) obviousness; (prueba) evidence.

evidente adj evident.

evidentemente adv evidently.

evitar vt to avoid; (desastre, peligro) to avert.

evocar vt to evoke.

evolución f (desarrollo) development; (cambio) evolution; (movimiento) manoeuvre.

evolucionar vi (progresar) to evolve; (cambiar) to change; (hacer movimientos) to carry out manoeuvres.

exactamente adv exactly.

exactitud f (fidelidad) accuracy; (rigurosidad) exactness.

exacto, -ta adj (riguroso) exact; (preciso) accurate; (correcto) correct; (cantidad, hora, etc) precise; (igual) exactly the same.

exageración f exaggeration.

exagerado, -da adj (poco razonable) exaggerated; (precio) exorbitant.

exagerar vt & vi to exaggerate.

exaltarse vpr to get excited.

examen m (prueba, ejercicio) exam; (inspección) examination.

examinar vt to examine □ **examinarse** vpr: ~se (de) to take an exam (in).

excavación f (en arqueología) dig.

excavadora f (mechanical) digger.

excavar vt (en arqueología) to excavate.

excedencia f leave (of absence).

exceder vt to exceed □ **excederse** vpr (propasarse) to go too far.

excelencia f (calidad superior) excellence; (tratamiento) Excellency; **por** ~ par excellence.

excelente adj excellent.

excentricidad f eccentricity.

excéntrico, -ca m, f eccentric.

excepción f exception; **a** o **con** ~ **de** except for; **de** ~ exceptional.

excepcional adj exceptional.

excepto adv except (for).

excesivo, -va adj excessive.

exceso m excess; **en** ~ excessively; ~ **de peso** excess weight; ~ **de velocidad** speeding □ **excesos** mpl (abusos) excesses.

excitar vt (provocar nerviosismo) to agitate; (ilusionar) to excite ❑

excitarse vpr (ponerse nervioso) to get agitated; (ilusionarse) to get excited.

exclamación f (grito) cry.

excluir vt (descartar) to rule out; (no admitir) to exclude.

exclusivo, -va adj exclusive.

excursión f trip; "excursiones" "day trips".

excusa f (pretexto) excuse; (disculpa) apology.

excusar vt (disculpar) to excuse ❑ **excusarse** vpr to apologize.

exento, -ta adj exempt.

exhaustivo, -va adj exhaustive.

exhibición f (demostración) display; (deportiva, artística) exhibition; (de películas) showing.

exhibir vt (productos) to display; (cuadros, etc) to exhibit; (película) to show.

exigencia f (petición) demand; (pretensión) fussiness.

exigente adj demanding.

exigir vt (pedir) to demand; (requerir) to require.

exiliar vt to exile ❑ **exiliarse** vpr to go into exile.

exilio m exile.

existencia f existence ❑ **existencias** fpl stock (sg).

existir vi to exist; existen varias razones there are several reasons.

éxito m success; (canción) hit; **tener ~** to be successful.

exitoso, -sa adj (Amér) successful.

exótico, -ca adj exotic.

expedición f expedition; (de carne) issuing.

expediente m (de trabajador, empleado) file; (documentación) documents (pl); (de alumno) record.

expedir vt (paquete, mercancía, etc) to send; (documento) to draw up; (pasaporte, carné) to issue.

expendedor, -ra m, f (comerciante) dealer; (de lotería) vendor; **~ automático** vending machine; **"expendedora de billetes"** "ticket machine".

expensas fpl expenses; **a ~ de** at the expense of.

experiencia f experience; (experimento) experiment.

experimentado, -da adj experienced.

experimental adj experimental.

experimentar vt (en ciencia) to experiment with; (probar) to test; (sensación, sentimiento) to experience.

experimento m experiment.

experto, -ta m, f expert; **~ en** expert on.

expirar vi (formal) to expire.

explicación f explanation.

explicar vt to explain; (enseñar) to teach ❑ **explicarse** vpr (hablar) to explain o.s.; (comprender) to understand.

explícito, -ta adj explicit.

explorador, -ra m, f explorer.

explorar vt to explore.

explosión f (de bomba, artefacto) explosion; (de alegría, tristeza) outburst.

explosivo, -va adj & m explosive.

explotación f (de petróleo) drilling; (agrícola) farming; (de mina) mining; (de negocio) running; (de trabajador, obrero) exploitation; ~ **agrícola** (instalación) farm.

explotar vi to explode ♦ vt (mina) to work; (negocio) to run; (terreno) to farm; (obreros) to exploit.

exponente m (ejemplo) example.

exponer vt (explicar) to explain; (exhibir) to display; (arriesgar) to risk ◻ **exponerse a** v + prep to expose o.s. to.

exportación f export.

exportar vt to export.

exposición f (de pinturas) exhibition; (en fotografía) exposure; (en escaparate) display; (de automóviles) show; (de tema, asunto) explanation; ~ **de arte** art exhibition.

expositor, -ra m, f (persona) exhibitor ♦ m (mueble) display cabinet.

exprés adj (tren) express; (café) espresso.

expresar vt to express ◻ **expresarse** vpr to express o.s.

expresión f expression.

expresivo, -va adj (elocuente) expressive; (afectuoso) affectionate.

expreso, -sa adj (claro) clear; (tren) express ♦ m (tren) express train.

exprimidor m squeezer.

exprimir vt (limón, naranja) to squeeze.

expuesto, -ta pp → **exponer** ♦ adj: **estar ~ a** to be exposed to.

expulsar vt (de clase, local) to throw out; (de colegio) to expel; (jugador) to send off.

expulsión f (de local) throwing-out; (de colegio) expulsion; (de jugador) sending-off.

exquisitez (pl **-ces**) f delicacy.

exquisito, -ta adj (comida) delicious.

éxtasis m inv ecstasy.

extender vt (desplegar) to spread (out); (brazos, piernas) to stretch; (influencia, dominio) to extend; (documento) to draw up; (cheque) to make out; (pasaporte) to issue ◻ **extenderse** vpr (ocupar) to extend; (durar) to last; (hablar mucho) to talk at length; (difundirse) to spread.

extensión f (en espacio) area; (en tiempo) length; (alcance) extent; (de teléfono) extension.

extenso, -sa adj (espacio) extensive; (duración) long.

exterior adj (de fuera) outside; (capa) outer; (extranjero) foreign ♦ m (parte exterior) outside.

exterminar vt to exterminate.

externo, -na adj m outer ♦ m, f day boy (f day girl); "**uso ~**" "for external use only".

extinguirse vpr (luz, fuego) to go out; (vida, amor) to come to an end.

extintor m fire extinguisher.

extirpar vt (formal: órgano) to remove.

extra adj (de calidad superior) top-quality; (de más) extra ♦ m extra.

extracción f (formal: de órgano) removal; (de petróleo) drilling; (de *mineral)* mining.

extracto m *(resumen)* summary; *(sustancia)* extract; **~ de cuentas** bank statement.

extractor m extractor (fan).

extradición f extradition.

extraer vt *(echar: órgano)* to remove; *(petróleo)* to drill for.

extranjero, -ra adj foreign ◆ m, f foreigner ◆ m foreign countries *(pl)*; **en/al ~** abroad.

extrañar vt *(echar de menos)* to miss; *(sorprender)* to surprise ❑ **extrañarse de** v + prep to be surprised at.

extrañeza f surprise.

extraño, -ña adj strange ◆ m, f stranger.

extraordinario, -ria adj extraordinary.

extraterrestre mf extraterrestrial.

extravagante adj eccentric.

extraviar vt *(formal: perder)* to mislay ❑ **extraviarse** vpr *(formal: objeto)* to go missing; *(persona)* to get lost.

extremar vt to go to extremes with.

extremidades fpl extremities.

extremista mf extremist.

extremo, -ma adj *(último)* furthest; *(exagerado)* extreme ◆ m *(final)* end; *(punto máximo)* extreme; **en ~** extremely.

extrovertido, -da adj extrovert.

F

fabada f: **~ (asturiana)** Asturian stew made of beans, pork sausage and bacon.

fábrica f factory.

fabricante mf manufacturer.

fabricar vt to make, to manufacture; **"fabricado en"** "made in".

fábula f *(relato)* fable.

fabuloso, -sa adj *(extraordinario)* fabulous; *(irreal)* mythical.

faceta f facet.

fachada f *(de edificio)* façade.

fácil adj easy; *(dócil)* easy-going; *(probable)* likely.

facilidad f *(aptitud)* aptitude; *(sencillez)* ease; **tener ~ para** to have a gift for; **~es de pago** easy *(payment)* terms.

facilitar vt *(hacer fácil)* to make easy; *(hacer posible)* to make possible; *(proporcionar)* to provide.

factor m *(elemento, condición)* factor; *(empleado)* luggage clerk.

factura f *(de gas, teléfono, hotel)* bill; *(por mercancías, etc)* invoice.

facturación f *(de equipaje)* checking-in; *(de empresa)* turnover; **"facturación"** "check-in".

facturar vt *(equipaje)* to check in; *(cobrar)* to bill.

facultad f *(facultad)* faculty; *(poder)* right; **~ de ciencias/letras** faculty of science/arts.

faena f *(tarea, trabajo)* task; *(en los*

toros) bullfighter's performance.

faisán m pheasant.

faja f (ropa interior) corset; (para cintura) sash.

fajo m (de billetes) wad.

falange f (hueso) phalanx.

falda f (prenda de vestir) skirt; (de montaña) mountainside; (de persona) lap ◻ **faldas** fpl (fam: mujeres) girls.

falla f (de terreno) fault; (de cartón) cardboard frame burned during "Fallas" ◻ **Fallas** fpl celebrations in Valencia on 19 March during which "fallas" are burned.

 FALLAS

Valencia is famous for the festival known as "las Fallas". Throughout the year, people prepare grotesque papier-mâché giants ("ninots") which are decorated with ornaments called "fallas". These are displayed in the streets and squares of Valencia from 16–19 March, and a jury decides which will be spared from being burned in the "cremà" at midnight on 19 March.

fallar vi (equivocarse) to get it wrong; (no acertar) to miss; (fracasar, no funcionar) to fail.

fallecer vi (formal) to pass away.

fallo m (equivocación) mistake; (de frenos, etc) failure; (sentencia) verdict.

falsedad f falseness.

falsete m falsetto.

falsificar vt to forge.

falso, -sa adj (afirmación, noticia)

false; (puerta, salida) hidden; (joya, piel) fake; (dinero, cuadro) forged; (hipócrita) deceitful.

falta f (carencia) lack; (necesidad) need; (error) mistake; (de asistencia, puntualidad) absence; (en fútbol, etc) foul; (en tenis) fault; (infracción) offence; **echar en ~ algo/a alguien** (echar de menos) to miss sthg/sb; (notar la ausencia de) to notice sthg/sb is missing; **hacer ~** to be necessary; **me hace ~ suerte** I need some luck; **~ de educación** rudeness.

faltar vi (no haber) to be lacking; (estar ausente) to be absent; **falta aire** there isn't enough air; **falta sal** it needs some salt; **me falta un lápiz** I need a pencil; **le falta interés** she lacks interest; **falta una semana** there's a week to go; **faltan 15 km para Londres** we're 15 km away from London; **~ a clase** not to attend one's classes; **¡no faltaba más!** that's all I/we etc needed! ◻ **faltar a** v + prep (obligación) to neglect; (palabra, promesa) to break; (cita, trabajo) not to turn up at; (ofender) to offend.

fama f (renombre) fame; (reputación) reputation.

familia f family; **~ numerosa** large family.

familiar adj (de familia) family (antes de s); (conocido) familiar; (llano) informal ◻ mf relative.

familiarizarse: familiarizarse con v + prep to familiarize o.s. with.

famoso, -sa adj famous.

fanatismo m fanaticism.

fandango m fandango.

fanfarrón, -ona *adj* boastful.

fantasía *f* (*imaginación*) imagination; (*imagen, ilusión*) fantasy.

fantasma *m* (*aparición*) ghost; (*fam: persona presuntuosa*) showoff.

fantástico, -ca *adj* fantastic.

farmacéutico, -ca *m, f* chemist.

farmacia *f* chemist's (shop) (Br), pharmacy (Am); "~ de guardia" "duty chemist's".

faro *m* (*torre*) lighthouse ❑ **faros** *mpl* (*de coche*) headlights.

farol *m* (*lámpara*) street light; (*en los toros*) movement in which bullfighter throws cape towards bull before passing it over his head to rest on his shoulders.

farola *f* (*poste*) lamppost; (*farol*) street light.

farolillo *m* paper lantern.

farsa *f* farce.

farsante *adj* (*impostor*) fraudulent; (*hipócrita*) deceitful.

fascismo *m* fascism.

fascista *mf* fascist.

fase *f* phase.

fastidiar *vt* (*molestar*) to annoy; (*fiesta, planes*) to ruin; (*máquina, objeto*) to break ❑ **fastidiarse** *vpr* (*fam*) (*persona*) to put up with it; (*plan, proyecto*) to be ruined.

fastidio *m* (*molestia*) bother.

fatal *adj* (*trágico*) fatal; (*inevitable*) inevitable; (*malo*) awful ♦ *adv* (*fam*) awfully; **me siento ~** I feel awful.

fatalidad *f* (*desgracia*) misfortune; (*destino, suerte*) fate.

fatiga *f* (*cansancio*) fatigue.

fatigarse *vpr* to get tired.

fauna *f* fauna.

favor *m* favour; **estar a ~ de** to be in favour of; **hacer un ~ a alguien** to do sb a favour; **pedir un ~ a alguien** to ask sb a favour; **por ~** please.

favorable *adj* favourable.

favorecer *vt* (*quedar bien*) to suit; (*beneficiar*) to favour.

favorito, -ta *adj* favourite.

fax *m inv* fax.

fayuquero *m* (*Amér*) contraband dealer.

fe *f* faith; **de buena/mala ~** (*fig*) in good/bad faith.

fealdad *f* ugliness.

febrero *m* February, → **setiembre**.

fecha *f* date; **~ de caducidad** (*de carné etc*) expiry date; (*de alimentos*) sell-by date; (*de medicamentos*) "use-by" date; **~ de nacimiento** date of birth ❑ **fechas** *fpl* (*período, época*) time (*sg*).

fechar *vt* to date.

fecundo, -da *adj* (*mujer*) fertile; (*productivo, creativo*) prolific.

federación *f* federation.

felicidad *f* happiness ❑ **felicidades** *interj* (*enhorabuena*) congratulations!; (*en cumpleaños*) happy birthday!

felicitación *f* (*de palabra*) congratulations (*pl*); (*tarjeta*) greetings card.

felicitar *vt* to congratulate.

feligrés, -esa *m, f* parishioner.

feliz *adj* happy; (*viaje, trayecto, día*) pleasant; **¡felices Pascuas!** Happy Easter; **¡~ Año Nuevo!**

Happy New Year; **¡~ cumpleaños!** Happy Birthday; **¡~ Navidad!** Merry Christmas.

felpudo m doormat.

femenino, -na adj feminine.

feminismo m feminism.

feminista mf feminist.

fémur m thighbone.

fenomenal adj (estupendo) wonderful; (fam: muy grande) huge.

fenómeno m phenomenon ◆ adv (fam) brilliantly.

feo, -a adj (rostro, decoración) ugly; (actitud, comportamiento, tiempo) nasty.

féretro m coffin.

feria f fair; ~ **de muestras** trade fair ☐ **ferias** fpl (fiestas) festival (sg).

FERIA DE ABRIL

The "feria de abril" in Seville is Spain's most famous festival. People gather in an open-air compound to look at the hundreds of stalls and to drink, talk and dance the "sevillanas". At the same time, the first bullfights of the season are held in Seville's bullrings.

---

fermentación f fermentation.

feroz, -ces adj (animal) fierce; (cruel) savage.

ferretería f ironmonger's (shop) (Br), hardware store (Am).

ferrocarril m railway.

ferroviario, -ria adj rail (antes de s).

ferry m ferry.

fértil adj fertile.

fertilidad f fertility.

festival m festival; ~ **de cine** film festival.

FESTIVALES

The most important theatre festivals in Spain are the "Festival Internacional de Teatro de Mérida", the "Fira de Teatre al carrer de Tàrrega" and the "Sitges Teatre Internacional". Film festivals are usually held in September and October, the most important being the "Festival Internacional de Cine de San Sebastián", the "Semana Internacional de Cine de Valladolid (SEMINCI)", the "Festival de Cinema Fantàstic de Sitges" and the "Festival de Cine Iberoamericano de Huelva".

---

festividad f festivity.

festivo, -va adj (traje) festive; (humorístico) funny.

feto m foetus.

fiambre m cold meat (Br), cold cut (Am).

fiambrera f lunch box.

fianza f (de alquiler, venta) deposit; (de preso) bail.

fiar vt (vender a crédito) to sell on credit ☐ **fiarse de** v + prep to trust.

fibra f fibre.

ficción f fiction.

ficha f (de datos) card; (de datos personales) file; (de guardarropa, parking) ticket; (de casino) chip; (de dominó, parchís, etc) counter.

fichar vt (contratar) to sign up; (delincuente) to put on police files ◆

vi (empleado) to clock in/out.

fichero *m* file.

ficticio, -cia *adj* fictitious.

fidelidad *f (lealtad)* loyalty; *(exactitud)* accuracy.

fideos *mpl* noodles.

fiebre *f* fever; **tener ~** to have a temperature.

fiel *adj (amigo, seguidor)* loyal; *(cónyuge)* faithful; *(exacto)* accurate ◆ *m (cristiano)* believer.

fieltro *m* felt.

fiera *f (animal)* wild animal.

fiero, -ra *adj* savage.

fierro *m (Amér)* iron.

fiesta *f (de pueblo, etc)* festivities *(pl)*; *(reunión)* party; *(día festivo)* public holiday; *(alegría)* delight; **~ mayor** local celebrations for the festival of a town's patron saint.

 FIESTA MAYOR

All Spain's towns and villages hold a "fiesta mayor", which consists of celebrations and cultural activities in honour of their patron saint. Dances are usually held every evening of the fiesta, which may last from a weekend up to 10 days.

ⓘ **FIESTAS PATRIAS**

This is the name given to the national celebrations held across all of Spanish-speaking America to mark the day on which each country gained independence from Spain. The independence day celebrations usually last two days.

figura *f (forma exterior)* shape; *(representación)* figure.

figurar *vt (representar)* to represent; *(simular)* to feign ◆ *vi (constar)* to appear; *(ser importante)* to be important ▢ **figurarse** *vpr (imaginarse)* to imagine.

figurativo, -va *adj* figurative.

figurín *m (dibujo)* fashion sketch; *(revista)* fashion magazine.

fijador *m (de pelo)* hairspray; *(crema)* hair gel.

fijar *vt* to fix ▢ **fijarse** *vpr (prestar atención)* to pay attention; **~se en** *(darse cuenta de)* to notice.

fijo, -ja *adj* fixed; *(sujeto)* secure; *(fecha)* definite.

fila *f (hilera)* line.

filatelia *f* philately.

filete *m* fillet; *(de carne)* steak; **~ de ternera** fillet of veal; **~ de lenguado** fillet of sole.

filiación *f (datos personales)* record; *(procedencia)* relationship.

filial *adj* filial ◆ *f* subsidiary.

Filipinas *fpl:* **(las) Filipinas** the Philippines.

filmar *vt & vi* to film.

filoso, -sa *adj (Amér)* sharp.

filosofar *vi (fam)* to philosophize.

filosofía *f* philosophy.

filósofo, -fa *m, f* philosopher.

filtrar *vt (líquido)* to filter; *(noticia, información)* to leak.

filtro *m* filter; **bronceador con 15 ~s** factor 15 suntan lotion.

filudo, -da *adj (Amér)* sharp.

fin *m* end; *(objetivo)* aim; **a ~ de que** in order that; **a ~es de** at the end of; **en ~** anyway; **por ~** finally; ~ **de semana** weekend; **"~ zona de estacionamiento**" "end of parking zone".

final adj & f final ♦ m end.

finalidad f purpose.

finalista mf finalist.

finalizar vt & vi to finish.

financiación f financing.

financiar vt to finance.

financista mf (Amér) financier.

finanzas fpl finance (sg).

finca f (bienes inmuebles) property; (casa de campo) country residence.

finger m (de aeropuerto) jetway.

fingir vt to feign.

finlandés, -esa adj Finnish ♦ m, f Finn.

Finlandia s Finland.

fino, -na adj (delgado) thin; (suave) smooth; (esbelto) slim; (restaurante, hotel) posh; (persona) refined; (de calidad, sabor, olor) fine; (sutil) subtle ♦ m dry sherry; **finas hierbas** fines herbes.

fiordo m fjord.

firma f (de persona) signature; (empresa) firm.

firmar vt to sign.

firme adj firm; (bien sujeto) stable; (carácter) resolute.

firmemente adv firmly.

firmeza f (solidez) stability; (constancia) firmness; (de carácter) resolution.

fiscal adj tax (antes de s) ♦ mf public prosecutor (Br), district attorney (Am).

fiscalía f (oficio) post of public prosecutor (Br), post of district attorney (Am); (oficina) public

prosecutor's office (Br), district attorney's office (Am).

física f physics (sg), → **físico**.

físico, -ca adj physical ♦ m, f physicist ♦ m (aspecto exterior) physique.

fisioterapeuta mf physiotherapist.

fisonomía f appearance.

fisonomista adj good at remembering faces.

flaco, -ca adj thin.

flamante adj (llamativo) resplendent; (nuevo) brand-new.

flamenco, -ca adj (de Flandes) Flemish ♦ m (ave) flamingo; (cante andaluz) flamenco.

flan m crème caramel; **~ con nata** crème caramel with whipped cream.

flaqueza f weakness.

flash [flaʃ] m (en fotografía) flash.

flauta f flute.

flecha f arrow.

fleco m (de cortina, mantel) fringe □ **flecos** mpl (de pantalón, camisa) frayed edges.

flemón m gumboil.

flequillo m fringe.

flexibilidad f flexibility.

flexible adj flexible.

flexión f (ejercicio) press-up.

flojera f (fam) lethargy.

flojo, -ja adj (cuerda, clavo) loose; (carácter, persona) weak; (de poca calidad) poor.

flor f flower.

flora f flora.

florecer vi (planta) to flower; (prosperar) to flourish.

florero m vase.

florido, -da adj (árbol) blossoming; (jardín) full of flowers.

florista mf florist.

floristería f florist's (shop).

flota f fleet.

flotador m (para la cintura) rubber ring; (para los brazos) arm band.

flotar vi to float.

flote: a flote adv afloat; **salir a ~** (fig) to get back on one's feet.

fluido, -da adj (líquido) fluid; (lenguaje, estilo) fluent ♦ m fluid.

fluir vi to flow.

flúor m (en dentífrico) fluoride.

FM f (abrev de frecuencia modulada) FM.

foca f seal.

foco m (en teatro) spotlight; (en campo de fútbol) floodlight; (de infección, epidemia) centre; (Amér: bombilla) light bulb.

foi-gras m inv foie-gras.

folio m sheet (of paper).

folklore m folklore.

folklórico, -ca adj (tradición, baile) traditional, popular; (fam: ridículo) absurd.

follaje m foliage.

folleto m (turístico, publicitario) brochure; (explicativo, de instrucciones) leaflet.

fomentar vt to encourage.

fonda f boarding house.

fondo m bottom; (de dibujo, fotografía) background; (dimensión) depth; **a ~** thoroughly; **al ~ de** (calle) at the end of; (habitación) at the back of ◆ **fondos** mpl (dinero) funds; (de archivo, biblioteca) catalogue (sg).

fono m (Amér) receiver.

fontanero, -ra m, f plumber.

footing [ˈfutin] m jogging; **hacer ~** to go jogging.

forastero, -ra m, f stranger.

forense mf pathologist.

forestal adj forest (antes de s).

forfait f ski pass.

forjar vt (hierro) to forge; (crear) to build up.

forma f (figura externa) shape; (modo, manera) way; **en ~ de** in the shape of; **estar en ~** to be fit ❑ **formas** fpl (modales) social conventions.

formación f formation; (educación) training; **~ profesional** Spanish vocational training for pupils aged 14-18 who do not do "BUP" it is possible to go on to study technical subjects at university.

formal adj (de forma) formal; (de confianza) reliable; (serio) serious.

formalidad f (seriedad) seriousness; (requisito) formality.

formar vt (crear) to form; (educar) to train ❑ **formarse** vpr (educarse) to be trained.

formidable adj (estupendo) amazing; (grande) tremendous.

fórmula f formula.

formular vt to formulate.

formulario m form.

forrar vt (libro) to cover; (ropa) to line ❑ **forrarse** vpr (fam) to make a pile.

forro m (de prenda de vestir) lining; (de libro) cover.

fortaleza f (fuerza) strength; (recinto) fortress.

fortuna

fortuna f (suerte) (good) luck; (riqueza) fortune.

forzado, -da adj forced.

forzar vt to force; ~ a alguien a hacer algo to force sb to do sthg.

forzosamente adv necessarily.

fósforo m (cerilla) match.

fósil m fossil.

foso m (de castillo) moat; (de orquesta) pit; (hoyo) ditch.

foto f (fam) photo; **sacar una ~ to** take a photo.

fotocopia f photocopy.

fotocopiadora f photocopier.

fotocopiar vt to photocopy.

fotografía f (imagen) photograph; (arte) photography.

fotografiar vt to photograph.

fotográfico, -ca adj photographic.

fotógrafo, -fa m, f photographer.

fotomatón m passport photo machine.

FP abrev = **formación profesional**.

fra. (abrev de factura) inv.

fracasar vi to fail.

fracaso m failure.

fracción f fraction.

fractura f fracture.

fragancia f fragrance.

frágil adj: "frágil" "fragile".

fragmento m (pedazo) fragment; (de obra) excerpt.

fraile m friar.

frambuesa f raspberry.

francamente adv (sinceramente) frankly; (muy) really.

francés, -esa adj & m French ♦ m, f Frenchman (f Frenchwoman); **los franceses** the French.

Francia s France.

franco, -ca adj (sincero) frank; (sin obstáculos) free ♦ m (moneda) franc.

francotirador, -ra m, f sniper.

franela f flannel.

franja f (en bandera, ropa) stripe.

franqueo m postage.

frasco m small bottle.

frase f sentence.

fraternal adj fraternal.

fraternidad f brotherhood.

fraude m fraud.

fray m brother.

frazada f (Amér) blanket; ~ eléctrica electric blanket.

frecuencia f frequency; **con ~** often.

frecuente adj (repetido) frequent; (usual) common.

fregadero m (kitchen) sink.

fregado, -da adj (Amér: fam) annoying.

fregar vt (limpiar) to wash; (frotar) to scrub; (Amér: fam: molestar) to bother; ~ **los platos** to do the washing-up.

fregona f (utensilio) mop; (despec: mujer) skivvy.

freír vt to fry.

frenar vt (parar) to brake; (contener) to check ♦ vi to brake.

frenazo m: **dar un ~** to slam on the brakes.

frenético, -ca adj (rabioso) furious; (exaltado) frantic.

freno m brake; ~ **de mano** hand brake (Br), parking brake (Am); ~ **de urgencia** (en tren) emergency cord.

frente¹ m front; **estar al ~ de** (dirigir) to be at the head of.

frente² f (de la cara) forehead; **de ~ head on**; ~ **a** opposite; ~ **a** face to face.

fresa f strawberry.

fresco, -ca adj fresh; (frío) cool; (desvergonzado) cheeky; (tejido, ropa) light ♦ m, f (desvergonzado) cheeky person ♦ m (frío suave) cool; (pintura) fresco; **hace ~** it's chilly; **tomar el ~** to get a breath of fresh air.

fresno m ash (tree).

fresón m large strawberry.

fricandó m fricandeau.

fricción f friction.

frigorífico m refrigerator.

frijol m (judía) bean; (Amér: tipo de judía) pinto bean.

frío, -a adj & m cold; **hace ~** it's cold; **tener ~** to be cold.

fritada f fried dish; ~ **de pescado** dish of fried fish.

frito, -ta pp < **freír** ♦ adj fried.

fritura f fried dish.

frívolo, -la adj frivolous.

frondoso, -sa adj leafy.

frontera f border.

fronterizo, -za adj (cerca de la frontera) border (antes de s); (vecino) neighbouring.

frontón m (juego) pelota; (de edificio) pediment.

frotar vt to rub.

fruncir vt ~ **el ceño** to frown.

frustración f frustration.

frustrar vt (plan, proyecto) to thwart □ **frustrarse** vpr (persona) to get frustrated; (plan, proyecto) to fail.

fruta f fruit; ~ **del tiempo** fruit in season.

frutal m fruit tree.

frutería f fruit shop.

frutero, -ra m, f (persona) fruiterer ♦ m (plato) fruit bowl.

frutilla f (Amér) strawberry.

fruto m fruit; (nuez, avellana, etc) nut □ **frutos** mpl produce (sg); ~**s del bosque** fruits of the forest; ~**s secos** dried fruit and nuts.

fue v < **ir, ser.**

fuego m fire; **a ~ lento** over a low heat; **¿tienes ~?** do you have a light?; ~**s artificiales** fireworks.

fuelle m (de aire) bellows (pl); (entre vagones) concertina vestibule.

fuente f (manantial) spring; (en la calle) fountain; (recipiente) dish; (origen) source.

fuera v < **ir, ser** ♦ adv (en el exterior) outside; (en otro lugar) away ♦ interj get out!; **sal ~** go out; **por ~** (on the) outside; ~ **borda** outboard motor; ~ **de** (a excepción de) except for; ~ **de combate** (en boxeo) knocked out; "~ **de servicio**" "out of order".

fuerte adj strong; (frío, dolor) intense; (lluvia) heavy; (golpe, colisión) hard; (alimento) rich; (voz, sonido) loud ♦ m (fortaleza) fort; (afición) strong point ♦ adv (con fuerza, intensidad) hard; (gritar) loudly.

fuerza f force; (de persona, animal, resistencia) strength; **a ~ de** by dint of; **a la ~** by force; **por ~** (por *obligación)* by force; *(por necesidad)* of necessity; **las ~s armadas** the armed forces.

fuese v → **ir, ser.**

fuga f *(de persona)* escape; *(de gas)* leak.

fugarse vpr to escape; **~ de casa** to run away (from home).

fugaz, -ces adj fleeting.

fugitivo, -va m, f fugitive.

fui v → **ir.**

fulana f tart, → **fulano.**

fulano, -na m, f what's his/her name.

fulminante adj *(muy rápido)* sudden.

fumador, -ra m, f smoker; **"~es"** "smokers"; **"no ~es"** "non-smokers".

fumar vt & vi to smoke; **~ en pipa** to smoke a pipe; **"no ~"** "no smoking".

función f *(utilidad)* function; *(de teatro)* show.

funcionar vi to work; **funciona con diesel** it runs on diesel; **"no funciona"** "out of order".

funcionario, -ria m, f civil servant.

funda f *(cubierta)* cover; *(de almohada)* pillowcase.

fundación f foundation.

fundador, -ra m, f founder.

fundamental adj fundamental.

fundamento m *(base)* basis ❑ **fundamentos** mpl *(conocimientos)* basics.

fundar vt *(crear)* to found; *(apoyar)* to base ❑ **fundarse en** v + prep to be based on.

fundición f *(de metal)* smelting;

(fábrica) foundry.

fundir vt *(derretir)* to melt; *(aparato)* to fuse; *(bombilla, dinero)* to blow; *(unir)* to merge ❑ **fundirse** vpr *(derretirse)* to melt.

funeral m funeral.

fungir vi *(Amér)* to act.

funicular m *(por tierra)* funicular railway; *(por aire)* cable car.

furgón m *(coche grande)* van; *(vagón de tren)* wagon.

furgoneta f van.

furia f fury.

furioso, -sa adj *(lleno de ira)* furious; *(intenso)* intense.

furor m *(furia)* rage; **hacer ~** *(fam)* to be all the rage.

fusible m fuse.

fusil m rifle.

fusilar vt to shoot.

fusión m *(de metal, cuerpo sólido)* melting; *(de empresas)* merger.

fustán m *(Amér) (enaguas)* petticoat; *(falda)* skirt.

fútbol m football; **~ sala** indoor five-a-side.

futbolín m table football.

futbolista mf footballer.

futuro, -ra adj & m future.

G

g *(abrev de gramo)* g.

g/ abrev = **giro.**

gabán m overcoat.

gabardina f raincoat.

gabinete m (sala) study; (gobierno) cabinet.

gafas fpl glasses; ~ **de sol** sunglasses.

gaita f bagpipes (pl); **ser una** ~ (fam) to be a pain in the neck.

gala f (actuación) show; **de** ~ black tie (antes de) ☐ **galas** fpl (vestidos) best clothes.

galán m (hombre atractivo) handsome man; (actor) leading man; (mueble) clothes stand.

galaxia f galaxy.

galería f gallery; (corredor descubierto) verandah; ~ **de arte** art gallery ☐ **galerías** fpl (tiendas) shopping arcade (sg).

Gales s Wales.

galés, -esa adj & m Welsh ◆ m, f Welshman (f Welshwoman); **los galeses** the Welsh.

Galicia s Galicia.

gallego, -ga adj & m, f Galician.

galleta f biscuit.

gallina f (animal) hen ◆ mf (cobarde) chicken.

gallinero m (corral) henhouse; (de teatro) gods (pl).

gallo m (ave) cock; (pescado) John Dory; (fam: nota falsa) false note.

galopar vi to gallop.

galope m gallop.

gama f range.

gamba f prawn; ~**s al ajillo** prawns cooked in an earthenware dish in a sauce of oil, garlic and chilli; ~**s a la plancha** grilled prawns.

gamberro, -rra m, f hooligan.

gamonal m (Amér) village chief.

gamuza f (piel, para limpiar el coche, etc) chamois; (para quitar el polvo) duster.

gana f (apetito) appetite; **de buena** ~ willingly; **de mala** ~ unwillingly; **no me da la** ~ **de hacerlo** I don't feel like doing it ☐ **ganas** fpl: **tener** ~**s de** to feel like.

ganadería f (ganado) livestock; (actividad) livestock farming; (en toros) breed.

ganadero, -ra m, f (dueño) livestock farmer; (cuidador) cattle hand.

ganado m (animales de granja) livestock; (vacuno) cattle.

ganador, -ra m, f winner.

ganancias fpl profit (sg).

ganar vt to win; (obtener) to earn; (beneficio) to make; (aumentar) to gain; (derrotar) to beat ◆ vi (ser vencedor) to win; (mejorar) to benefit ☐ **ganarse** vpr (conseguir) to earn; ~**se la vida** to earn a living.

ganchillo m (aguja) crochet hook; (labor) crochet.

gancho m (para colgar) hook; (atractivo) sex appeal; (Amér: percha) coat hanger.

gandul, -la adj lazy.

ganga f bargain.

ganso m goose.

garabato m scribble.

garaje m garage.

garantía f guarantee.

garbanzo m chickpea.

garfio m hook.

garganta f (de persona) throat; (entre montañas) gorge.

gargantilla f (short) necklace.

gárgaras fpl: **hacer** ~ to gargle.

garra f (de animal) claw.

garrafa f large bottle usually in a wicker holder.

garrapata f tick.

garúa f (Amér) drizzle.

gas m gas ❑ **gases** mpl (del estómago) wind (sg).

gasa f gauze.

gaseosa f lemonade.

gaseoso, -sa adj fizzy.

gasfitería f (Amér) plumber's (shop).

gasfitero m (Amér) plumber.

gasóleo m diesel oil.

gasolina f petrol (Br), gas (Am); ~ **normal** = two-star petrol; ~ **sin plomo** unleaded petrol; ~ **súper** = four-star petrol.

gasolinera f petrol station (Br), gas station (Am).

gastar vt (dinero) to spend; (usar) to use; (talla, número) to take; (acabar) to use up ❑ **gastarse** vpr (acabarse) to run out; (desgastarse) to wear out.

gasto m (acción de gastar) expenditure; (cosa que pagar) expense ❑ **gastos** mpl expenditure (sg).

gastritis f inv gastritis.

gastronomía f gastronomy.

gastronómico, -ca adj gastronomic.

gatear vi to crawl.

gatillo m trigger.

gato, -ta m, f cat ♦ m (aparato) jack; **a gatas** on all fours.

gauchada f (Amér: fig) shrewd action.

gaucho m gaucho.

gavilán m sparrowhawk.

gaviota f seagull.

gazpacho m: ~ **(andaluz)** gazpacho, Andalusian soup made from tomatoes, peppers, cucumbers and bread, served chilled.

gel m gel.

gelatina f (para cocinar) gelatine; (postre) jelly.

gemelo, -la adj & m, f twin ♦ m (músculo) calf ❑ **gemelos** mpl (botones) cufflinks; (anteojos) binoculars.

gemido m moan.

Géminis m inv Gemini.

gemir vi to moan.

generación f generation.

generador m generator.

general adj & m general; **en** ~ in general; **por lo** ~ generally.

generalizar vt to make widespread ♦ vi to generalize.

generalmente adv generally.

generar vt to generate.

género m (mercancía) goods (pl); (clase, especie) type; (GRAM) gender; (en literatura) genre; ~**s de punto** knitwear.

generosidad f generosity.

generoso, -sa adj generous.

genial adj brilliant.

genio m (carácter) character; (mal carácter) bad temper; (persona inteligente) genius; **tener mal** ~ to be bad-tempered.

genitales mpl genitals.

gente f people (pl); (fam: familia) folks (pl).

gentil adj (cortés) kind; (elegante) elegant.

gentileza f (cortesía) kindness; (elegancia) elegance.

genuino, -na *adj* genuine.

geografía *f* geography; **la ~ nacional** the country.

geometría *f* geometry.

geométrico, -ca *adj* geometric.

geranio *m* geranium.

gerente *mf* manager (*f* manageress).

germen *m* germ.

gestión *f* (diligencia) step; (administración) management.

gestionar *vt* (tramitar) to work towards; (administrar) to manage.

gesto *m* (con las manos) gesture; (mueca) grimace, face.

gestor, -ra *m, f* de (gestoría) agent who deals with public bodies on behalf of private individuals; (de empresa) manager.

gestoría *f* (establecimiento) office of a "gestor".

Gibraltar *s* Gibraltar.

gibraltareño, -na *adj & m, f* Gibraltarian.

gigante, -ta *adj & m, f* giant.

gigantesco, -ca *adj* gigantic.

gimnasia *f* (deporte) gymnastics (sg); (ejercicio) exercises (pl).

gimnasio *m* gymnasium.

gimnasta *mf* gymnast.

ginebra *f* gin.

ginecólogo, -ga *m, f* gynaecologist.

gin tonic [ʒin'tonik] *m* gin and tonic.

gira *f* tour.

girar *vt* (hacer dar vueltas) to turn; (rápidamente) to spin; (letra, cheque) to draw; (paquete) to send; (dinero) to transfer ◆ *vi* (dar vueltas) to turn; (rápidamente) to spin.

girasol *m* sunflower.

giro *m* turn; (de letra, cheque) draft; (expresión, dicho) saying; **~ postal** postal order; **~ urgente** postal order delivered by the Post Office to the payee on the following day.

gitano, -na *adj & m, f* gypsy.

glaciar *m* glacier.

gladiolo *m* gladiolus.

glándula *f* gland.

global *adj* overall.

globo *m* (para jugar, volar) balloon; (cuerpo esférico) globe; (la Tierra, de lámpara) globe; **~ terráqueo** globe.

glóbulo *m* corpuscle.

gloria *f* glory; (fam: placer) bliss; (persona) star.

glorieta *f* (plaza) square; (redonda) = roundabout (Br), = traffic circle (Am); (de jardín) bower.

glorioso, -sa *adj* glorious.

glotón, -ona *adj* gluttonous, greedy.

glucosa *f* glucose.

gluten *m* gluten.

gobernador, -ra *m, f* governor.

gobernante *mf* leader.

gobernar *vt* (nación, país) to govern; (nave, vehículo) to steer.

gobierno *m* (de país) government; (edificio) governor's office; (de nave, vehículo) steering.

goce *m* pleasure.

godo, -da *m, f* Goth.

gol *m* goal.

goleador, -ra *m, f* scorer.

golf *m* golf.

golfa *f* (*prostituta*) whore, → golfo.

golfo, -fa *m, f* (*gamberro*) lout; (*pillo*) rascal ♦ *m* (*en geografía*) gulf.

golondrina *f* swallow.

golosina *f* (*dulce*) sweet.

goloso, -sa *adj* sweet-toothed.

golpe *m* (*puñetazo, desgracia*) blow; (*bofetada*) smack; (*en puerta*) knock; (*choque*) bump; (DEP) shot; (*gracia*) witticism; (*atraco, asalto*) raid; **de ~** suddenly; **~ de Estado** coup.

golpear *vt* to hit ♦ *vi* to bang.

goma *f* (*pegamento*) gum; (*material*) rubber; (*banda elástica*) elastic; (*gomita*) elastic band; **~ de borrar** rubber (Br), eraser (Am).

gomero *m* (*Amér*) rubber tree.

gomina *f* hair gel.

góndola *f* (*Amér*) bus.

gordo, -da *adj* (*obeso*) fat; (*grueso*) thick; (*grave*) big; (*importante*) important ♦ *m, f* fat person ♦ *m*: **el ~** (*de la lotería*) first prize.

ⓘ EL GORDO

This is the name given to first prize in the Spanish National Lottery, especially the one in the Christmas draw, where all the winning numbers are sung out by children on national radio.

---

gordura *f* fatness.

gorila *m* (*animal*) gorilla; (*fam: guardaespaldas*) bodyguard; (*fam: en discoteca*) bouncer.

gorjeo *m* chirping.

gorra *f* cap; **de ~** for free.

gorrión *m* sparrow.

gorro *m* cap.

gota *f* drop; (*enfermedad*) gout; **no quiero ni ~** I don't want anything □ **gotas** *fpl* (*para nariz, ojos*) drops.

gotera *f* leak; (*mancha*) stain (left by leaking water).

gótico, -ca *adj* Gothic ♦ *m* (*en arte*) Gothic (art).

gozar *vi* to enjoy o.s. □ **gozar de** *v + prep* (*disponer de*) to enjoy.

gozo *m* joy.

gr (*abrev de grado*) deg.

grabación *f* recording.

grabado *m* (*arte*) engraving; (*lámina*) print.

grabar *vt* to engrave; (*canción, voz, imágenes, etc*) to record.

gracia *f* (*humor*) humour; (*atractivo*) grace; (*talent*) (*chiste*) joke; **no me hace ~** (*no me gusta*) I'm not keen on it; **tener ~** to be funny □ **dar las ~s a** to thank; **~s a** thanks to; **~s por** thank you for; **muchas ~s** thank you very much.

gracias *fpl* thanks ♦ *interj* thank you; **dar las ~s a** to thank; **~s a** thanks to; **~s por** thank you for; **muchas ~s** thank you very much.

gracioso, -sa *adj* (*que da risa*) funny; (*con encanto*) graceful.

grada *f* (*de plaza de toros*) row; (*peldaño*) step; **las ~s** the terraces.

gradería *f* (*de plaza de toros*) rows (*pl*); (*de estadio*) terraces (*pl*); (*público*) crowd.

grado *m* (*medida*) degree; (*fase*) stage; (*de enseñanza*) level; (*del ejército*) rank; **de buen ~** willingly.

graduación *f* (*de bebida*) = proof; (*de militar*) rank; (*acto*) grading.

graduado, -da adj (persona) graduate; (regla, termómetro) graduated ♦ m, f (persona) graduate ♦ m (título) degree; **~ escolar** qualification received on completing primary school.

GRADUADO ESCOLAR

This is the qualification received on successful completion of primary education in Spain. It is needed in order to go to secondary school and is also one of the requirements for people over the age of 25 who wish to go to university.

---

gradual adj gradual.
gradualmente adv gradually.
graduar vt (calefacción, calentador) to regulate ♦ **graduarse** vpr (militar) to receive one's commission; **~se (en)** (estudiante) to graduate (in).
graffiti m graffiti.
grafía f written symbol.
gráfico, -ca adj graphic ♦ m of (dibujo) graph.
gragea f pill.
gramática f grammar.
gramatical adj grammatical.
gramo m gram.
gran adj → grande.
granada f (fruto) pomegranate; (proyectil) grenade.
granadilla f (Amér) passion fruit.
granate adj inv deep red ♦ m garnet.
Gran Bretaña s Great Britain.

grande adj (de tamaño) big; (de altura) tall; (importante) great ♦ m (noble) grandee; **le va ~** (vestido, zapato) it's too big for him; **~s almacenes** department store (sg).
grandeza f (importancia) grandeur; (tamaño) (great) size.
grandioso, -sa adj grand.
granel: a granel adv (arroz, judías, etc) loose; (líquidos) by volume; (en abundancia) in abundance.
granero m granary.
granito m granite.
granizada f hailstorm.
granizado m = Slush Puppie®, drink consisting of crushed ice with lemon juice, coffee etc.
granizar v impers: **está granizando** it's hailing.
granja f (en el campo) farm; (bar) milk bar.
granjero, -ra m, f farmer.
grano m (de cereal) grain; (de la piel) spot; (de fruto, planta) seed; (de café) bean; **ir al ~** (fam) to get to the point.
granuja mf (chiquillo) rascal.
grapa f staple.
grapadora f stapler.
grapar vt to staple.
grasa f (grease); (de persona, animal) fat.
grasiento, -ta adj greasy.
graso, -sa adj greasy.
gratificar vt (recompensar) to reward; **"se gratificará"** "reward".
gratinado m gratin.
gratinar vt to cook au gratin.
gratis adv free.
gratitud f gratitude.

grato, -ta adj pleasant.

gratuito, -ta adj (gratis) free; (sin fundamento) unfounded.

grave adj serious; (voz) deep; (tono) low; (palabra) with the stress on the penultimate syllable.

gravedad f (importancia) seriousness; (de la Tierra) gravity.

gravilla f gravel.

Grecia s Greece.

gremio m (profesión) profession, trade.

greña f mop of hair.

griego, -ga adj & m, f Greek.

grieta f crack.

grifero, -ra m, f (Amér) petrol-pump attendant.

grifo m (de agua) tap; (Amér: gasolinera) petrol station (Br), gas station (Am).

grill [gril] m grill.

grilla f (Amér: fam) plot to oust sb from their post.

grillo m cricket.

gripa f (Amér) flu.

gripe f flu.

gris adj & m grey.

gritar vi (hablar alto) to shout; (chillar) to scream.

grito m (de dolor, alegría) cry; (palabra) shout; **a ~s** at the top of one's voice.

grosella f redcurrant; **~ negra** blackcurrant.

grosería f (dicho) rude word; (acto) rude thing.

grosero, -ra adj (poco refinado) coarse; (maleducado) rude.

grosor m thickness.

grotesco, -ca adj grotesque.

grúa f (máquina) crane; (para averías) breakdown truck; (para aparcamientos indebidos) towaway truck.

grueso, -sa adj (persona) fat; (objeto) thick ♦ m (espesor, volumen) thickness; (parte principal) bulk.

grumo m lump.

gruñido m grunt.

gruñir vi to grunt.

grupa f hindquarters (pl).

grupo m group; **en ~** in a group; **~ de riesgo** high risk group; **~ sanguíneo** blood group.

gruta f grotto.

guaca f (Amér) Indian tomb.

guacal m (Amér) basket.

guacamole m (Amér) guacamole.

guachimán m (Amér) security guard.

guacho, -cha adj (Amér) (huérfano) orphaned; (solitario) solitary ♦ m, f (Amér: hijo ilegítimo) illegitimate child.

guaco m (Amér) object of pre-Colombian pottery.

guagua f (Amér) (fam: autobús) bus; (bebé) baby.

guaiño m (Amér) melancholy Indian song.

guajiro, -ra m, f (Amér: fam) peasant.

guano m (Amér) manure.

guante m glove.

guantera f glove compartment.

guapo, -pa adj (mujer) pretty; (hombre) handsome; (fam: objeto, ropa, etc) nice.

guardabarros m inv mudguard.

guardacoches m inv car park attendant.

guardaespaldas m inv bodyguard.

guardameta m goalkeeper.

guardapolvo m (prenda) overalls (pl); (funda) dust cover.

guardar vt to keep; (poner) to put (away); (cuidar) to look after; (suj: guardia) to guard; (ley) to observe ☐ **guardarse** vpr: ~se de (abstenerse de) to be careful not to.

guardarropa m (de local) cloakroom; (armario) wardrobe.

guardería f (escuela) nursery (school); (en el trabajo) crèche.

guardia mf (policía) police officer ◆ f (vigilancia) guard; (turno) duty; ~ civil member of the "Guardia Civil"; ~ municipal o urbano local police officer who deals mainly with traffic offences; ~ de seguridad security guard; farmacia f de ~ duty chemist's ☐ **Guardia Civil** f Spanish police who patrol rural areas, highways and borders.

guardián, -ana m, f guardian.

guarida f lair.

guarnición f (de comida) garnish; (del ejército) garrison.

guarro, -rra adj (despec) filthy.

guasa f (fam) (ironía) irony; (gracia) humour.

guasca f (Amér) (látigo) whip; (vulg: pene) prick.

Guatemala s Guatemala.

guatemalteco, -ca adj & m, f Guatemalan.

guateque m party.

guayaba f guava.

guayabo m guava tree.

güero, -ra adj (Amér: fam) f blonde.

guerra f war; ~ civil civil war; ~ mundial world war.

guerrera f (chaqueta) military-style jacket, → **guerrero**.

guerrero, -ra m, f warrior.

guerrilla f guerilla group.

guerrillero, -ra m, f guerrilla.

guía mf (persona) guide ◆ f (libro, folleto, indicación) guide; ~ de ferrocarriles train timetable; ~ telefónica telephone directory; ~ turística tourist guide.

guiar vt (mostrar dirección) to guide; (vehículo) to steer ☐ **guiarse** por v + prep to be guided by.

guijarro m pebble.

guillotina f guillotine.

guinda f morello cherry.

guindilla f chilli pepper.

guiñar vt: ~ un ojo to wink.

guiñol m puppet theatre.

guión m (argumento) script; (esquema) outline; (signo) hyphen.

guionista mf scriptwriter.

guiri mf (fam) bloody foreigner.

guirnalda f garland.

guisado m stew.

guisante m pea; ~s salteados o con jamón peas fried with "jamón serrano".

guisar vt & vi to cook.

guiso m dish (food).

guitarra f guitar.

guitarrista mf guitarist.

gusano m worm.

gustar vi: me gusta I like it; me gustan los pasteles I like cakes; no me gusta ese libro I don't like that book.

gusto *m* taste; *(placer)* pleasure; **a tu ~** as you wish; **vivir a ~** *(bien)* to live comfortably; **un filete al ~** a steak done the way you like it; **con mucho ~** with pleasure; **mucho ~** pleased to meet you.

h. *(abrev de hora)* h.

ha *v* → haber.

ha. *(abrev de hectárea)* ha.

haba *f* broad bean; **~s a la catalana** stew of broad beans, bacon, "butifarra" and wine.

habano *m* Havana cigar.

haber *m (bienes)* assets *(pl)*; **tiene tres pisos en su ~** he owns three flats.

♦ *v aux* 1. *(en tiempos compuestos)* to have; **los niños han comido** the children have eaten; **habían desayunado antes** they'd had breakfast earlier. 2. *(expresa reproche)*: **¡lo dicho!** why didn't you say so?

♦ *v impers* 1. *(existir, estar, tener lugar)* **hay there is, there are** *(pl)* **¿qué hay hoy para comer?** what's for dinner today?; **¡no hay nadie en casa?** isn't anyone at home?; **el jueves no habrá reparto** there will be no delivery on Thursday. 2. *(expresa obligación)*: **~ que hacer**

algo to have to do sthg; **habrá que soportarlo** we'll have to put up with it. 3. *(en locuciones)*: **habérselas con alguien** to confront sb; **¡hay que ver!** well I never!; **no hay de qué** don't mention it.

❑ **haber de** *v + prep* to have to.

habichuela *f* bean.

hábil *adj (diestro)* skilful; *(astuto)* clever; **día ~** working day.

habilidad *f (destreza)* skill; *(astucia)* cleverness.

habiloso, -sa *adj (Amér)* shrewd.

habitación *f (cuarto)* room; *(dormitorio)* bedroom; **~ doble** *(con cama de matrimonio)* double room; *(con dos camas)* twin room; **~ individual** single room.

habitante *mf* inhabitant.

habitar *vi* to live ♦ *vt* to live in.

hábito *m (costumbre)* habit.

habitual *adj (acostumbrado)* habitual; *(cliente, lector)* regular.

habitualmente *adv (generalmente)* usually; *(siempre)* regularly.

hablador, -ra *adj* talkative.

habladurías *fpl* gossip (sg).

hablar *vi* to talk; *(pronunciar discurso)* to speak ♦ *vt (saber)* to speak; *(tratar)* to discuss; **~ de** to talk about; **~ por teléfono** to talk on the telephone; **~ por ~** to talk for the sake of it; **¡ni ~!** no way!

❑ **hablarse** *vpr (relacionarse)* to speak (to each other); **"se habla inglés"** "English spoken".

habrá *v* → haber.

hacer *vt* 1. *(elaborar, crear, cocinar)* to make; **~ planes/un vestido** to

make plans/a dress; **~ un poema**
to write a poem; **~ la comida** to
make the meal.

2. *(construir)* to build.

3. *(generar)* to produce; **la carretera
hace una curva** there's a bend in
the road; **el fuego hace humo** fire
produces smoke; **llegar tarde hace
mal efecto** arriving late makes a
bad impression.

4. *(realizar)* to make; **hizo un gesto
de dolor** he grimaced with pain; **le
hice una señal con la mano** I sig-
nalled to her with my hand; **estoy
haciendo segundo** I'm in my second year; **haremos una excursión**
we'll go on a trip.

5. *(practicar)* to do; **deberías ~
deporte** you should start doing
some sport.

6. *(colada)* to do; *(cama)* to make.

7. *(dar aspecto)*: **este traje te hace
más delgado** this suit makes you
look slimmer.

8. *(transformar)* to make; **hizo pedazos el papel** she tore the paper to
pieces; **~ feliz a alguien** to make sb
happy.

9. *(en cine y teatro)* to play; **hace el
papel de reina** she plays (the part
of) the queen.

10. *(mandar)*: **haré que tiñan el
traje** I'll have this dress dyed.

11. *(comportarse como)*: **~ el tonto** to
act the fool.

12. *(ser causa de)* to make; **no me
hagas reír/llorar** don't make me
laugh/cry.

13. *(en cálculo, cuentas)* to make;
éste hace cien this one makes (it) a
hundred.

◆ vi 1. *(intervenir)*: **déjame ~ a mí**
let me do it.

2. *(en cine y teatro)*: **~ de malo** to
play the villain.

3. *(trabajar, actuar)*: **~ de cajera** to
be a checkout girl.

4. *(aparentar)*: **~ como si** to act as
if.

◆ v impers 1. *(tiempo meteorológico)*:
hace frío/calor/sol it's cold/hot/
sunny; **hace buen/mal tiempo** the
weather is good/bad.

2. *(tiempo transcurrido)*: **hace un año
que no lo veo** it's a year since I
saw him; **no nos hablamos desde
hace un año** we haven't spoken for
a year.

◻ hacerse *vpr (convertirse en)* to
become; *(formarse)* to form; *(desarrollarse, crecer)* to grow; *(cocerse)*
to get; **~se el rico** to pretend to
be rich; **hacerse a** *v + prep (acostumbrarse)* to get used to; **hacerse
con** *v + prep (apropiarse)* to take.

hacha *f* axe.

hachís *m* hashish.

hacia *prep (de dirección)* towards;
(en el tiempo) about; **~ abajo** downwards; **~ arriba** upwards; **gira ~ la
izquierda** turn left.

hacienda *f (finca)* farm; *(bienes)*
property. **◻ Hacienda** *f* the Spanish
Treasury.

hada *f* fairy.

haga *v* → **hacer**.

Haití *s* Haiti.

hala *interj (para dar prisa)* hurry
up!; *(expresa contrariedad)* you're
joking!

halago *m* flattery.

halcón *m* falcon.

hall [xol] *m* foyer.

hallar *vt (encontrar)* to find;

halógeno

(inventar) to discover ◻ **hallarse** *vpr* to be.

halógeno, -na *adj* halogen *(antes de s).*

halterofilia *f* weightlifting.

hamaca *f (en árbol, etc)* hammock; *(en la playa)* deck chair.

hambre *f* hunger; **tener ~** to be hungry.

hambriento, -ta *adj* starving.

hamburguesa *f* hamburger.

hamburguesería *f* hamburger joint.

hámster [xamster] *m* hamster.

hangar *m* hangar.

hará *v* → **hacer**.

hardware [xarwar] *m* hardware.

harina *f* flour.

hartar *vt (saciar)* to fill up; *(cansar)* to annoy ◻ **hartarse de** *v + prep (cansarse de)* to get fed up with; **~se de algo** *(hacer en exceso)* to do sthg non-stop.

harto, -ta *adj (saciado)* full; **estar ~ de** *(cansado)* to be fed up with.

hasta *prep (en el espacio)* as far as; *(en el tiempo)* until ◆ *adv (incluso)* even; **el agua llega ~ el borde** the water comes up to the edge; **desde ... ~ ...** from ... to ...; **~ luego** see you later; **~ mañana** see you tomorrow; **~ pronto** see you soon; **~ que** until.

haya *v* → **haber**.

haz *(pl* **-ces)** *v* → **hacer** ◆ *m (de luz)* beam; *(de hierba, leña)* bundle.

hazaña *f* exploit.

he *v* → **haber**.

hebilla *f* buckle.

hebra *f (de hilo)* thread; *(de legumbres)* string.

hebreo, -a *adj & m, f* Hebrew.

hechizar *vt* to bewitch.

hechizo *m (embrujo)* spell; *(fascinación)* charm.

hecho, -cha *pp* → **hacer** ◆ *adj (carne)* done ◆ *m (suceso)* event; *(dato)* fact; *(acto)* action; **muy ~** well-done; **poco ~** rare; **~ de** *(material)* made of; **de ~** in fact.

hectárea *f* hectare.

helada *f* frost.

heladería *f (tienda)* ice-cream parlour; *(quiosco)* ice-cream stall.

helado, -da *adj (muy frío)* freezing; *(congelado)* frozen; *(pasmado)* astonished ◆ *m* ice-cream; **"~s variados"** "assorted ice-creams".

helar *vt* to freeze ◆ *v impers*: **heló** there was a frost ◻ **helarse** *vpr* to freeze.

hélice *f (de barco, avión)* propeller.

helicóptero *m* helicopter.

hematoma *m* bruise.

hembra *f (animal)* female; *(de enchufe)* socket.

hemorragia *f* haemorrhage.

heno *m* hay.

hepatitis *f inv* hepatitis.

herboristería *f* herbalist's (shop).

heredar *vt* to inherit.

heredero, -ra *m, f* heir *(f* heiress).

hereje *mf* heretic.

herejía *f (en religión)* heresy; *(disparate)* silly thing.

herencia *f* inheritance.

herida *f (lesión)* injury; *(en lucha,*

atentado) wound, → **herido**.

herido, -da *adj* (*lesionado*) injured; (*en lucha, atentado*) wounded; (*ofendido*) hurt ♦ *m, f:* **hubo 20 ~s** 20 people were injured.

herir *vt* (*causar lesión*) to injure; (*en lucha, atentado*) to wound; (*ofender*) to hurt.

hermanastro, -tra *m, f* stepbrother (*f* stepsister).

hermano, -na *m, f* brother (*f* sister).

hermético, -ca *adj* airtight.

hermoso, -sa *adj* (*bello*) beautiful; (*hombre*) handsome; (*fam: grande*) large.

hermosura *f* beauty; (*de hombre*) handsomeness.

héroe *m* hero.

heroico, -ca *adj* heroic.

heroína *f* (*persona*) heroine; (*droga*) heroin.

heroinómano, -na *m, f* heroin addict.

heroísmo *m* heroism.

herradura *f* horseshoe.

herramienta *f* tool.

herrería *f* (*taller*) forge.

herrero *m* blacksmith.

hervir *vt & vi* to boil.

heterosexual *mf* heterosexual.

hice *v* → **hacer**.

hidalgo *m* nobleman.

hidratante *adj* moisturizing.

hidratar *vt* to moisturize.

hiedra *f* ivy.

hielo *m* ice.

hiena *f* hyena.

hierba *f* (*césped*) grass; (*planta*)

herb; **mala ~** weed.

hierbabuena *f* mint.

hierro *m* iron.

hígado *m* liver.

higiene *f* (*aseo*) hygiene; (*salud*) health.

higiénico, -ca *adj* hygienic.

higo *m* fig.

higuera *f* fig tree.

hijastro, -tra *m, f* stepson (*f* stepdaughter).

hijo, -ja *m, f* son (*f* daughter); **~ de la chingada** (*Amér: vulg*) son of a bitch; **~ político** son-in-law; **hija política** daughter-in-law; **~ de puta** (*vulg*) son of a bitch ❑ **hijos** *mpl* children.

hilera *f* row.

hilo *m* (*de coser, de conversación*) thread; (*tejido*) linen; (*alambre, cable*) wire; **~ musical**® piped music.

hilvanar *vt* (*coser*) to tack.

hincapié *m:* **hacer ~ en algo** (*insistir*) to insist on sthg; (*subrayar*) to emphasize sthg.

hincha *mf* fan.

hinchado, -da *adj* (*globo, colchón*) inflated; (*parte del cuerpo*) swollen.

hinchar *vt* to blow up ❑ **hincharse** *vpr* (*parte del cuerpo*) to swell up; **hincharse de** *v + prep* (*hartarse de*) to stuff o.s. with.

hinchazón *f* swelling.

híper *m* (*fam*) hypermarket.

hipermercado *m* hypermarket.

hipermetropía *f* longsightedness.

hipertensión *f* high blood

pressure.

hipertenso, -sa *adj* suffering from high blood pressure.

hípica *f (carreras de caballos)* horseracing; *(de obstáculos)* showjumping.

hipnotizar *vt* to hypnotize.

hipo *m* hiccups *(pl).*

hipocresía *f* hypocrisy.

hipócrita *adj* hypocritical.

hipódromo *m* racecourse.

hipopótamo *m* hippopotamus.

hipoteca *f* mortgage.

hipótesis *f inv (supuesto)* theory.

hipotético, -ca *adj* hypothetical.

hippy [xipi] *m* hippy.

hispánico, -ca *adj* Hispanic, Spanish-speaking.

hispano, -na *adj (hispanoamericano)* Spanish-American; *(español)* Spanish.

Hispanoamérica *s* Spanish-speaking Latin America.

hispanoamericano, -na *adj & m, f* Spanish-American.

hispanohablante *mf* Spanish speaker.

histeria *f* hysteria.

histérico, -ca *adj* hysterical.

historia *f (hechos pasados)* history; *(narración)* story.

histórico, -ca *adj (real, auténtico)* factual; *(de importancia)* historic.

historieta *f (relato)* anecdote; *(cuento con dibujos)* comic strip.

hizo *v → hacer.*

hobby [xoβi] *m* hobby.

hocico *m (de cerdo)* snout; *(de*

perro, gato) nose.

hockey [xokej] *m* hockey.

hogar *m (casa)* home; *(de chimenea)* fireplace.

hogareño, -ña *adj (persona)* home-loving.

hoguera *f* bonfire.

hoja *f (de plantas)* leaf; *(de papel)* sheet; *(de libro)* page; *(de cuchillo)* blade; **~ de afeitar** razor blade.

hojalata *f* tinplate.

hojaldre *m* puff pastry.

hola *interj* hello!

Holanda *s* Holland.

holandés, -esa *adj & m* Dutch ♦ *m, f* Dutchman *(f* Dutchwoman).

holgado, -da *adj (ropa)* loose-fitting; *(vida, situación)* comfortable.

holgazán, -ana *adj* lazy.

hombre *m* man ♦ *interj* wow!; **~ de negocios** businessman.

hombrera *f (almohadilla)* shoulder pad.

hombro *m* shoulder.

homenaje *m* tribute; **en ~ a** in honour of.

homeopatía *f* homeopathy.

homicida *mf* murderer.

homicidio *m* murder.

homosexual *mf* homosexual.

hondo, -da *adj (profundo)* deep; *(intenso)* deep.

Honduras *s* Honduras.

hondureño, -ña *adj & m, f* Honduran.

honestidad *f (sinceridad)* honesty.

honesto, -ta *adj (honrado)*

honest.

hongo *m* (*comestible*) mushroom; (*no comestible*) toadstool.

honor *m* honour; **en ~ de** in honour of.

honorario *adj* honorary ❑ **honorarios** *mpl* fees.

honra *f* honour; **¡a mucha ~!** and (I'm) proud of it!

honradez *f* honesty.

honrado, -da *adj* honest.

honrar *vt* to honour.

hora *f* (*período de tiempo*) hour; (*momento determinado*) time; **¡a qué ~ ...?** what time ...?; **¡qué ~ es?** what's the time?; **media ~** half an hour; **pedir ~ para** to ask for an appointment for; **tener ~ (con)** to have an appointment (with); **a última ~** at the last minute; **"~s convenidas**" "appointments available"; **~s de visita** visiting times; **~ punta** rush hour.

horario *m* timetable; "**~ comercial**" "opening hours".

horca *f* (*de ejecución*) gallows (*pl*); (*en agricultura*) pitchfork.

horchata *f* cold drink made from ground tiger nuts, milk and sugar.

horchatería *f* "horchata" bar.

horizontal *adj* horizontal.

horizonte *m* horizon.

horma *f* (*molde*) mould; (*para zapatos*) last.

hormiga *f* ant.

hormigón *m* concrete; **~ armado** reinforced concrete.

hormigonera *f* concrete mixer.

hormiguero *m* anthill.

hormona *f* hormone.

hornear *vt* to bake.

hornillo *m* (*para cocinar*) camping stove.

horno *m* oven; **al ~** (*carne*) roast; (*pescado*) baked.

horóscopo *m* horoscope.

horquilla *f* (*para el pelo*) hairgrip.

hórreo *m* type of granary, on stilts, found in Galicia and Asturias.

horrible *adj* (*horroroso*) horrible; (*pésimo*) awful.

horror *m* terror; **¡qué ~!** that's awful!

horrorizar *vt* to terrify.

horroroso, -sa *adj* horrible.

hortaliza *f* (*garden*) vegetable.

hortelano, -na *m, f* market gardener.

hortensia *f* hydrangea.

hortera *adj* (*fam*) tacky.

hospedarse *vpr* to stay.

hospital *m* hospital.

hospitalario, -ria *adj* (*persona*) hospitable.

hospitalidad *f* hospitality.

hospitalizar *vt* to put in hospital.

hostal *m* = two-star hotel.

hostelería *f* hotel trade.

hostia *f* (*en religión*) host; (*vulg: golpe*) whack ♦ *interj* (*vulg*) bloody hell!; **darse una ~** (*vulg*) to have a smash-up.

hostil *adj* hostile.

hotel *m* hotel; **~ de lujo** luxury hotel.

hotelero, -ra *adj* hotel (*antes de s*).

hoy *adv* (*día presente*) today;

hoyo

(*momento actual*) nowadays; **~ en día** nowadays; **~ por ~** at the moment.

hoyo m hole.

hoz f sickle.

huachafería f (*Amér*) tacky thing.

huachafo, -fa adj (*Amér*) tacky.

huachinango m (*Amér*) porgy.

hubiera v → **haber**.

hucha f moneybox.

hueco, -ca adj (*vacío*) hollow ◆ m (*agujero*) hole; (*de tiempo*) spare moment.

huelga f strike.

huella f (*de persona*) footprint; (*de animal*) track; **~s dactilares** fingerprints.

huérfano, -na m, f orphan.

huerta f market garden.

huerto m (*de hortalizas*) vegetable patch; (*de frutales*) orchard.

hueso m (*del esqueleto*) bone; (*de una fruta*) stone.

huésped, -da m, f guest.

huevada f (*Amér: fam*) stupid thing.

huevear vi (*Amér: fam*) to be stupid.

huevo m egg; **~ de la copa** o **tibio** (*Amér*) hard-boiled egg; **~ duro** hard-boiled egg; **~ escalfado** poached egg; **~ estrellado** fried egg; **~ frito** fried egg; **~ pasado por agua** soft-boiled egg; **~s a la flamenca** "huevos al plato" with fried pork sausage, black pudding and a tomato sauce; **~s al plato** eggs cooked in the oven in an earthenware dish; **~s revueltos** scrambled eggs.

huevón m (*Amér*) idiot.

huida f escape.

huir vi (*escapar*) to flee; (*de cárcel*) to escape; **~ de algo/alguien** (*evitar*) to avoid sthg/sb.

humanidad f humanity ❑ **humanidades** fpl humanities.

humanitario, -ria adj humanitarian.

humano, -na adj (*del hombre*) human; (*benévolo, compasivo*) humane ◆ m human (being).

humareda f cloud of smoke.

humedad f (*de piel*) moisture; (*de atmósfera*) humidity; (*en la pared*) damp.

humedecer vt to moisten.

húmedo, -da adj (*ropa, toalla, etc*) damp; (*clima, país*) humid; (*piel*) moist.

humilde adj humble.

humillación f humiliation.

humillante adj humiliating.

humillar vt to humiliate.

humo m (*gas*) smoke; (*de coche*) fumes (pl) ❑ **humos** mpl airs.

humor m (*estado de ánimo*) mood; (*gracia*) humour; **estar de buen ~** to be in a good mood; **estar de mal ~** to be in a bad mood.

humorismo m comedy.

humorista mf comedian (f comedienne).

humorístico, -ca adj humorous.

hundir vt (*barco*) to sink; (*edificio*) to knock down; (*techo*) to knock in; (*persona*) to devastate ❑ **hundirse** vpr (*barco*) to sink; (*edificio, techo*) to collapse; (*persona*) to be devastated.

húngaro, -ra *adj & m, f* Hungarian.

Hungría *s* Hungary.

huracán *m* hurricane.

hurtadillas: a hurtadillas *adv* stealthily.

hurto *m* theft.

I

iba *v* → **ir.**

IBERIA *f* IBERIA *(Spanish national airline).*

ibérico, -ca *adj* Iberian.

Ibiza *s* Ibiza.

iceberg *m* iceberg.

ICONA *m Spanish national conservation organization.*

icono *m* icon.

id *v* → **ir.**

ida *f* outward journey; **(billete de)** **~ y vuelta** return (ticket).

idea *f* idea; *(propósito)* intention; *(opinión)* impression; **no tengo ni ~** I've no idea.

ideal *adj & m* ideal.

idealismo *m* idealism.

idealista *mf* idealist.

idéntico, -ca *adj* identical.

identidad *f* identity.

identificación *f* identification.

identificar *vt* to identify □

identificarse *vpr (mostrar documentación)* to show one's identifi-

cation.

ideología *f* ideology.

idilio *m* love affair.

idioma *m* language.

idiota *adj (despec)* stupid ♦ *mf* idiot.

ídolo *m* idol.

idóneo, -a *adj* suitable.

iglesia *f* church.

ignorancia *f* ignorance.

ignorante *adj* ignorant.

ignorar *vt (desconocer)* not to know; *(no hacer caso)* to ignore.

igual *adj (idéntico)* the same; *(parecido)* similar; *(cantidad, proporción)* equal; *(ritmo)* steady ♦ *adv* the same; **ser ~ que** to be the same as; **da ~** it doesn't matter; **me da ~** I don't care; **es ~** it doesn't matter; **al ~ que** just like; **por ~** equally.

igualado, -da *adj* level.

igualdad *f* equality.

igualmente *adv* likewise.

ilegal *adj* illegal.

ilegítimo, -ma *adj* illegitimate.

ileso, -sa *adj* unhurt.

ilimitado, -da *adj* unlimited.

ilógico, -ca *adj* illogical.

iluminación *f (alumbrado)* lighting.

iluminar *vt (suj: luz, sol)* to light up.

ilusión *f (esperanza)* hope; *(espejismo)* illusion; **el regalo me ha hecho ~** I liked the present; **me hace ~ la fiesta** I'm looking forward to the party; **hacerse ilusiones** to get one's hopes up.

ilusionarse *vpr (esperanzarse)* to get one's hopes up; *(emo-*

cionarse) to get excited.

ilustración *f* illustration.

ilustrar *vt* to illustrate.

ilustre *adj* illustrious.

imagen *f* image; *(en televisión)* picture.

imaginación *f* imagination.

imaginar *vt (suponer)* to imagine; *(inventar)* to think up ❑ **imaginarse** *vpr* to imagine.

imaginario, -ria *adj* imaginary.

imaginativo, -va *adj* imaginative.

imán *m* magnet.

imbécil *adj (despec)* stupid ◆ *mf* idiot.

imitación *f (de persona)* impression; *(de obra de arte)* imitation.

imitar *vt* to imitate.

impaciencia *f* impatience.

impaciente *adj* impatient; **~ por** impatient to.

impar *adj* odd.

imparable *adj* unstoppable.

imparcial *adj* impartial.

impasible *adj* impassive.

impecable *adj* impeccable.

impedimento *m* obstacle.

impedir *vt (no permitir)* to prevent; *(obstaculizar)* to hinder.

impensable *adj* unthinkable.

imperativo *m (en gramática)* imperative.

imperceptible *adj* imperceptible.

imperdible *m* safety pin.

imperdonable *adj* unforgivable.

imperfecto, -ta *adj (incomple-*

to) imperfect; *(defectuoso)* faulty ◆ *m* imperfect tense.

imperial *adj* imperial.

imperio *m (territorio)* empire; *(dominio)* rule.

impermeable *adj* waterproof ◆ *m* raincoat.

impersonal *adj* impersonal.

impertinencia *f (insolencia)* impertinence; *(comentario)* impertinent remark.

impertinente *adj* impertinent.

ímpetu *m (energía)* force.

implicar *vt* to involve; *(significar)* to mean.

implícito, -ta *adj* implicit.

imponer *vt (obligación, castigo, impuesto)* to impose; *(obediencia, respeto)* to command ◆ *vi* to be imposing.

importación *f (producto)* import.

importancia *f* importance.

importante *adj (destacado)* important; *(cantidad)* large.

importar *vt (mercancías)* to import ◆ *vi (interesar)* to matter; **¿le importa que fume?** do you mind if I smoke?; **¿le importaría venir?** would you mind coming?; **no importa** it doesn't matter; **no me importa** I don't care.

importe *m (precio)* price; *(en cuenta, factura)* total; **"~ del billete"** "ticket price".

imposibilidad *f* impossibility.

imposible *adj* impossible ◆ *interj* never! ◆ *m*: **pedir un ~** to ask the impossible.

impostor, -ra *m, f* impostor.

impotencia f impotence.

impotente adj impotent.

impreciso, -sa adj vague.

impregnar vt (humedecer) to soak.

imprenta f (arte) printing; (taller) printer's (shop).

imprescindible adj indispensable.

impresión f (de un libro) edition; (sensación) feeling; (opinión) impression.

impresionante adj impressive.

impresionar vt to impress ♦ vi (causar admiración) to be impressive.

impreso, -sa pp → **imprimir** ♦ m (formulario) form.

impresora f printer.

imprevisto m unexpected event.

imprimir vt to print.

improvisación f improvisation.

improvisado, -da adj improvised.

improvisar vt to improvise.

imprudente adj rash.

impuesto, -ta pp → **imponer** ♦ m tax.

impulsar vt (empujar) to drive; ~ a alguien a to drive sb to.

impulsivo, -va adj impulsive.

impulso m (empuje) momentum; (estímulo) stimulus.

impuro, -ra adj impure.

inaceptable adj unacceptable.

inadecuado, -da adj unsuitable.

inadmisible adj unacceptable.

inaguantable adj unbearable.

inauguración f inauguration, opening.

inaugurar vt to inaugurate, to open.

incapacidad f (incompetencia) incompetence; (por enfermedad) incapacity.

incapaz, -ces adj incapable; ser ~ de to be unable to.

incendio m fire; contra ~s (medidas) fire-fighting; (seguro, brigada) fire (antes de s).

incentivo m incentive.

incidente m incident.

incineradora f incinerator.

incinerar vt to incinerate.

incitar vt (animar) to encourage; (a la violencia) to incite.

inclinación f (saludo) bow; (tendencia) tendency; (afecto) fondness.

inclinarse vpr: ~ por (preferir) to favour; (decidirse por) to decide on.

incluido, -da adj included.

incluir vt (contener) to include; (adjuntar) to enclose.

inclusive adv inclusive.

incluso adv even.

incógnita f (cosa desconocida) mystery.

incoherente adj (contradictorio) inconsistent.

incoloro, -ra adj colourless.

incómodo, -da adj uncomfortable.

incomparable adj incomparable.

incompatibilidad f incompatibility.

incompetente adj incompetent.

incomprensible adj incomprehensible.

incomunicado, -da adj (pueblo) cut off.

incondicional adj (apoyo, ayuda) wholehearted; (amigo) staunch.

inconfundible adj unmistakable.

inconsciencia f (irresponsabilidad) thoughtlessness.

inconsciente adj (sin conocimiento) unconscious; (insensato) thoughtless.

incontable adj countless.

inconveniente m (dificultad) difficulty; (desventaja) disadvantage.

incorporación f (unión) inclusion.

incorporar vt (agregar) to incorporate; (levantar) to sit up □ **incorporarse** vpr (levantarse) to sit up; ~ **a** (ingresar en) to join.

incorrecto, -ta adj (erróneo) incorrect; (descortés) impolite.

incorregible adj incorrigible.

incrédulo, -la adj sceptical.

increíble adj (inverosímil) hard to believe; (extraordinario) incredible.

incremento m increase.

incubadora f incubator.

incubar vt to incubate.

inculpado, -da m, f accused.

inculto, -ta adj (persona) uneducated.

incumbir vi: **no te incumbe hacerlo** it's not for you to do it.

incurable adj incurable.

incurrir: incurrir en v + prep (error) to make; (delito) to commit.

indecente adj indecent.

indeciso, -sa adj (falta de iniciativa) indecisive; (falto de decisión) undecided; (poco claro) inconclusive.

indefenso, -sa adj defenceless.

indefinido, -da adj indefinite; (impreciso) vague.

indemnización f compensation.

indemnizar vt to compensate.

independencia f independence.

independiente adj independent.

independizarse: independizarse de v + prep to become independent of.

indeterminado, -da adj indefinite.

India f: la ~ India.

indicación f (señal) sign □ **indicaciones** fpl (instrucciones) instructions; (para llegar a un sitio) directions.

indicador m indicator; ~ **de dirección** indicator.

indicar vt (señalar) to indicate; (lugar, dirección) to show; (suj: señal, reloj) to read.

indicativo, -va adj indicative.

índice m (de libro, precios) index; (de natalidad, mortalidad) rate; (de la mano) index finger.

indicio m (señal) sign.

indiferencia f indifference.

indiferente adj indifferent; **es**

~ it makes no difference.

indígena *mf* native.

indigestión *f* indigestion.

indigesto, -ta *adj* hard to digest.

indignación *f* indignation.

indignado, -da *adj* indignant.

indignante *adj* outrageous.

indio, -dia *adj & m, f* Indian.

indirecta *f* hint.

indirecto, -ta *adj* indirect.

indiscreto, -ta *adj* indiscreet.

indiscriminado, -da *adj* indiscriminate.

indiscutible *adj* indisputable.

indispensable *adj* indispensable.

indispuesto, -ta *adj* unwell.

individual *adj (del individuo)* individual; *(cama, habitación)* single; **~es** *(DEP)* singles.

individuo *m* individual.

índole *f (tipo)* type.

Indonesia *s* Indonesia.

indudablemente *adv* undoubtedly.

indumentaria *f* clothes *(pl)*.

industria *f (actividad)* industry; *(fábrica)* factory.

industrial *adj* industrial ◆ *mf* industrialist.

industrializado, -da *adj* industrialized.

inédito, -ta *adj (desconocido)* unprecedented.

inepto, -ta *adj* inept.

inequívoco, -ca *adj (clarísimo)* unequivocal; *(inconfundible)* unmistakable.

inesperado, -da *adj* unexpected.

inestable *adj* unstable.

inevitable *adj* inevitable.

inexperto, -ta *adj (sin experiencia)* inexperienced.

infalible *adj* infallible.

infancia *f* childhood.

infanta *f* princess.

infantería *f* infantry.

infantil *adj (para niños)* children's; *(despec: inmaduro)* childish.

infarto *m* heart attack.

infección *f* infection.

infeccioso, -sa *adj* infectious.

infectar *vt* to infect ❑ **infectarse** *vpr* to become infected.

infelicidad *f* unhappiness.

infeliz *(pl -ces) adj* unhappy ◆ *mf (desgraciado)* wretch; *(fam: ingenuo)* naive person.

inferior *adj (de abajo, menos importante, cantidad)* lower; *(de menos calidad)* inferior ◆ *mf* inferior.

inferioridad *f* inferiority.

infidelidad *f* infidelity.

infiel *adj (a la pareja)* unfaithful ◆ *mf (no cristiano)* infidel.

infierno *m* hell.

ínfimo, -ma *adj* very low.

infinito, -ta *adj* infinite ◆ *mf* infinity.

inflación *f* inflation.

inflar *vt (de aire)* to inflate; *(globo)* to blow up ❑ **inflarse de** *v + prep (comer, beber)* to stuff o.s. with.

inflexible *adj* inflexible.

influencia *f* influence; **tener ~** to have influence.

influenciar *vt* to influence.

influir: influir en *v + prep* to influence.

influjo *m* influence.

influyente *adj* influential.

información *f (datos)* information; *(noticias)* news; *(oficina)* information office; *(mostrador)* information desk; *(de teléfono)* directory enquiries *(pl) (Br)*, directory assistance *(Am)*.

informal *adj (persona)* unreliable; *(lenguaje, traje)* informal.

informalidad *f (irresponsabilidad)* unreliability.

informar *vt* to tell ❏ **informarse** *vpr* to find out.

informática *f* information technology, computing, → **informático**.

informático, -ca *m, f* computer expert.

informativo *m* news bulletin.

informe *m* report ❏ **informes** *mpl (referencias)* references.

infracción *f (delito)* offence.

infundir *vt* to inspire.

infusión *f* infusion; ~ **de tila** lime blossom tea.

ingeniería *f* engineering.

ingeniero, -ra *m, f* engineer.

ingenio *m (agudeza)* wit; *(inteligencia)* ingenuity; *(máquina)* device.

ingenioso, -sa *adj (agudo)* witty; *(inteligente)* ingenious.

ingenuidad *f* naivety.

ingenuo, -nua *adj* naive.

Inglaterra *s* England.

ingle *f* groin.

inglés, -esa *adj & m* English ♦ *m, f* Englishman *(f* English-

woman); **los ingleses** the English.

ingrato, -ta *adj (trabajo)* thankless; *(persona)* ungrateful.

ingrediente *m* ingredient.

ingresar *vt (dinero)* to deposit ♦ *vi (en hospital)* to be admitted; *(en sociedad)* to join; *(en universidad)* to enter.

ingreso *m (entrada, en universidad)* entry; *(de dinero)* deposit; *(en hospital)* admission; *(en sociedad)* joining ❏ **ingresos** *mpl (sueldo)* income *(sg)*.

inhabitable *adj* uninhabitable.

inhalar *vt* to inhale.

inhibición *f* inhibition.

inhumano, -na *adj* inhumane.

iniciación *f (comienzo)* beginning.

inicial *adj & f* initial.

iniciar *vt (empezar)* to begin, to start ❏ **iniciarse en** *v + prep (conocimiento, práctica)* to learn.

iniciativa *f* initiative; **tener ~** to have initiative.

inicio *m* beginning, start.

inimaginable *adj* unimaginable.

injerto *m* graft.

injusticia *f* injustice.

injusto, -ta *adj* unfair.

inmaduro, -ra *adj (persona)* immature; *(fruta)* unripe.

inmediatamente *adv* immediately.

inmediato, -ta *adj (tiempo)* immediate; *(contiguo)* next; **de ~** immediately.

inmejorable *adj* unbeatable.

inmenso, -sa *adj* immense.

inmigración *f* immigration.

inmigrante *mf* immigrant.

inmigrar *vi* to immigrate.

inmobiliaria *f* estate agency (Br), real-estate office (Am).

inmoral *adj* immoral.

inmortal *adj* immortal.

inmóvil *adj* (persona) motionless; (coche, tren) stationary.

inmovilizar *vt* to immobilize.

inmueble *m* building.

inmune *adj* immune.

inmunidad *f* immunity.

innato, -ta *adj* innate.

innecesario, -ria *adj* unnecessary.

innovación *f* innovation.

inocencia *f* innocence.

inocentada *f* (bobada) foolish thing; (broma) practical joke.

inocente *adj* innocent.

inofensivo, -va *adj* harmless.

inolvidable *adj* unforgettable.

inoportuno, -na *adj* (inadecuado) inappropriate; (molesto) inconvenient; (en mal momento) untimely.

inoxidable *adj* (material) rustproof; (acero) stainless.

inquietarse *vpr* to worry.

inquieto, -ta *adj* (preocupado) worried; (aventurero) restless.

inquietud *f* worry.

inquilino, -na *m, f* tenant.

Inquisición *f*: la ~ the (Spanish) Inquisition.

insaciable *adj* insatiable.

insalubre *adj* unhealthy.

insatisfacción *f* dissatisfaction.

insatisfecho, -cha *adj* dissatisfied.

inscribir: **inscribirse en** *v + prep* to enrol on.

inscripción *f* (de moneda, piedra, etc) inscription; (en registro) enrolment.

inscrito, -ta *pp* → inscribir.

insecticida *m* insecticide.

insecto *m* insect.

inseguridad *f* (falta de confianza) insecurity; (peligro) lack of safety.

inseguro, -ra *adj* (sin confianza) insecure; (peligroso) unsafe.

insensato, -ta *adj* foolish.

insensible *adj* (persona) insensitive; (aumento, subida, bajada) imperceptible.

inseparable *adj* inseparable.

insertar *vt* to insert; ~ algo en to insert sthg into.

inservible *adj* useless.

insignia *f* (distintivo) badge; (de militar) insignia; (estandarte) flag.

insignificante *adj* insignificant.

insinuar *vt* to hint at ❑ **insinuarse** *vpr* to make advances.

insípido, -da *adj* insipid.

insistencia *f* insistence.

insistir *vi*: ~ (en) to insist (on).

insolación *f* (indisposición) sunstroke.

insolencia *f* (dicho, hecho) insolent thing.

insolente *adj* (desconsiderado) insolent; (orgulloso) haughty.

insólito, -ta *adj* unusual.

insolvente *adj* insolvent.

insomnio *m* insomnia.

insonorización f soundproofing.

insoportable adj unbearable.

inspeccionar vt to inspect.

inspector, -ra m, f inspector; ~ de aduanas customs official.

inspiración f (de aire) inhalation; (de un artista) inspiration.

inspirar vt (aire) to inhale; (ideas) to inspire ◻ **inspirarse en** v + prep to be inspired by.

instalación f (acto) installation; (equipo) installations (pl); ~ eléctrica wiring ◻ **instalaciones** fpl (edificios) facilities; **instalaciones deportivas** sports facilities.

instalar vt (teléfono, antena, etc) to install; (gimnasio, biblioteca, etc) to set up; (alojar) to settle ◻ **instalarse** vpr (en nueva casa) to move in.

instancia f (solicitud) application.

instantánea f snapshot.

instantáneo, -a adj instantaneous.

instante m instant; **al ~** straight away.

instintivo, -va adj instinctive.

instinto m instinct.

institución f institution ◻ **instituciones** fpl institutions.

institucional adj institutional.

instituir vt to set up.

instituto m institute; (centro de enseñanza) state secondary school.

institutriz (pl **-ces**) f governess.

instrucción f (formación) education ◻ **instrucciones** fpl (indicaciones) instructions.

instruir vt (enseñar) to teach; (enjuiciar) to prepare.

instrumental m instruments (pl).

instrumento m instrument.

insuficiente adj insufficient ◆ m fail.

insufrible adj insufferable.

insultante adj insulting.

insultar vt to insult ◻ **insultarse** vpr to insult each other.

insulto m insult.

insuperable adj (inmejorable) unsurpassable; (problema) insurmountable.

intacto, -ta adj intact.

integración f integration.

integrarse: integrarse en v + prep to become integrated in.

íntegro, -gra adj (cosa) whole; (persona) honourable.

intelectual mf intellectual.

inteligencia f intelligence.

inteligente adj intelligent.

intemperie f: **a la ~** in the open air.

intención f intention; **con la ~ de** with the intention of; **tener la ~ de** to intend to.

intencionado, -da adj deliberate; **bien ~** well-meaning; **mal ~** ill-intentioned.

intensivo, -va adj intensive.

intenso, -sa adj intense; (luz) bright; (lluvia) heavy.

intentar vt to try; **~ hacer algo** to try to do sthg.

intento m (propósito) intention; (tentativa) try.

intercalar vt to insert.

intercambio *m* exchange.

interceder: interceder por *v* + *prep* to intercede on behalf of.

interceptar *vt* to intercept.

interés *m* interest; *(provecho)* self-interest ❑ **intereses** *mpl (dinero)* interest *(sg); (fortuna, aspiraciones)* interests.

interesado, -da *adj (que tiene interés)* interested; *(egoísta)* self-interested.

interesante *adj* interesting.

interesar *vi* to be of interest; **¿te interesa la música?** are you interested in music? ❑ **interesarse en** *v* + *prep* to be interested in; **interesarse por** *v* + *prep* to take an interest in.

interferencia *f* interference.

interina *f (criada)* cleaning lady.

interino, -na *adj (trabajador)* temporary.

interior *adj* inner; *(mercado, política)* domestic ◆ *m (parte de dentro)* inside; *(fig: mente)* inner self; *(en deporte)* inside forward; **el ~ de España** inland Spain.

interlocutor, -ra *m*, *f* speaker.

intermediario, -ria *m*, *f* middleman.

intermedio, -dia *adj* intermediate ◆ *m* interval.

interminable *adj* endless.

intermitente *m* indicator.

internacional *adj* international.

internado *m* boarding school.

interno, -na *adj* internal ◆ *m*, *f (en colegio)* boarder; *(en hospital)* intern.

interponerse *vpr* to intervene.

interpretación *f (en teatro, cine, etc)* performance; *(traducción)* interpreting.

interpretar *vt (en teatro, cine, etc)* to perform; *(traducir)* to interpret.

intérprete *mf (en teatro, cine, etc)* performer; *(traductor)* interpreter.

interpuesto, -ta *pp →* **interponer**.

interrogación *f (pregunta)* question; *(signo)* question mark.

interrogante *m o f* question mark.

interrogar *vt* to question.

interrogatorio *m* questioning.

interrumpir *vt* to interrupt.

interrupción *f* interruption.

interruptor *m* switch.

interurbano, -na *adj* long-distance.

intervalo *m (tiempo)* interval; *(espacio)* gap.

intervención *f (discurso)* speech; **~ quirúrgica** operation.

intervenir *vt (en medicina)* to operate on; *(confiscar)* to seize ◆ *vi (tomar parte)* to participate.

interviú *f* interview.

intestino *m* intestine.

intimidad *f (vida privada)* private life.

íntimo, -ma *adj (cena, pensamiento, etc)* private; *(amistad, relación)* close; *(ambiente, restaurante)* intimate.

intocable *adj* untouchable.

intolerable *adj* intolerable.

intolerante *adj* intolerant.

intoxicación *f* poisoning; ~ **alimenticia** food poisoning.

intoxicarse *vpr* to be poisoned.

intranquilo, -la *adj* (*nervioso*) restless; (*preocupado*) worried.

intransigente *adj* intransigent.

intransitable *adj* impassable.

intrépido, -da *adj* intrepid.

intriga *f* (*maquinación*) intrigue; (*trama*) plot.

intrigar *vt & vi* to intrigue.

introducción *f* introduction.

introducir *vt* to introduce; (*meter*) to put in; "~ **monedas**" "insert coins".

introvertido, -da *adj* introverted.

intruso, -sa *m, f* intruder.

intuición *f* intuition.

inundación *f* flood.

inundar *vt* to flood.

inusual *adj* unusual.

inútil *adj* useless; (*no provechoso*) unsuccessful; (*inválido*) disabled.

invadir *vt* (*país, territorio*) to invade; (*suj: alegría, tristeza*) to overwhelm.

inválido, -da *m, f* disabled person.

invasión *f* invasion.

invasor, -ra *m, f* invader.

invención *f* invention.

inventar *vt* to invent.

inventario *m* inventory.

invento *m* invention.

invernadero *m* greenhouse.

inversión *f* (*de dinero*) investment; (*de orden*) reversal.

inversionista *mf* (*Amér*) investor.

inverso, -sa *adj* opposite; **a la inversa** the other way round.

invertir *vt* (*dinero, tiempo*) to invest; (*orden*) to reverse.

investigación *f* (*de delito, crimen*) investigation; (*en ciencia*) research.

investigador, -ra *m, f* researcher.

investigar *vt* (*delito, crimen*) to investigate; (*en ciencia*) to research.

invidente *mf* blind person.

invierno *m* winter; **en ~** in (the) winter.

invisible *adj* invisible.

invitación *f* invitation; **es ~ de la casa** it's on the house.

invitado, -da *m, f* guest.

invitar *vt* (*a fiesta, boda, etc*) to invite; **os invito** (*a café, copa, etc*) it's my treat; **te invito a cenar fuera** I'll take you out for dinner; **~ a alguien a** (*incitar*) to encourage sb to.

involucrar *vt* to involve ❑ **involucrarse en** *v + prep* to get involved in.

invulnerable *adj* invulnerable.

inyección *f* injection.

ir *vi* 1. (*desplazarse*) to go; **fuimos andando** we went on foot; **iremos en coche** we'll go by car; **¡vamos!** let's go!
2. (*asistir*) to go; **nunca va a las juntas** he never goes to meetings.
3. (*extenderse*) to go; **la carretera va hasta Valencia** the road goes as far

as Valencia.

4. *(funcionar)* to work; **la televisión no va** the television's not working.

5. *(desenvolverse)* to go; **le va bien en su trabajo** things are going well (for him) in his job; **los negocios van mal** business is bad; **¿cómo te va?** how are you going?

6. *(vestir):* **~ en** O **con o** to wear; **~ de azul/de uniforme** to wear blue/a uniform.

7. *(tener aspecto físico)* to look like; **tal como voy no puedo entrar** I can't go in looking like this.

8. *(valer)* to be; **¿a cuánto va el pollo?** how much is the chicken?

9. *(expresa duración gradual):* **~ haciendo algo** to be doing sthg; **voy mejorando mi estilo** I'm working on improving my style.

10. *(sentar):* **le va fatal el color negro** black doesn't suit him at all; **le irían bien unas vacaciones** she could do with a holiday.

11. *(referirse):* **~ por o con alguien** to go for sb.

12. *(en locuciones):* **ni me va ni me viene** *(fam)* I don't care; **¡qué va!** you must be joking!; **vamos, no te preocupes** come along, don't worry; **¿vamos bien a Madrid?** is this the right way to Madrid? ❑ **ir a** *v + prep (expresa intención)* to be going to; **ir de** *v + prep (película, libro)* to be about; *(buscar)* to go and fetch; **voy por la mitad del libro** I'm halfway through the book; **irse** *vpr* to go; **~se abajo** *(edificio)* to fall down; *(negocio)* to collapse; *(proyecto)* to fall through.

ira *f* fury, rage.

Irak *s* Iraq.

Irán *s* Iran.

Irlanda *s* Ireland; **~ del Norte** Northern Ireland.

irlandés, -esa *adj* Irish ◆ *m, f* Irishman *(f* Irishwoman); **los irlandeses** the Irish.

ironía *f* irony.

irónico, -ca *adj* ironic.

IRPF *m (abrev de Impuesto sobre la Renta de las Personas Físicas)* Spanish income tax.

irracional *adj* irrational.

irrecuperable *adj* irretrievable.

irregular *adj* irregular; *(objeto, superficie)* uneven.

irregularidad *f* irregularity; *(de superficie, contorno)* unevenness.

irresistible *adj (inaguantable)* unbearable; *(apetecible)* irresistible.

irresponsable *adj* irresponsible.

irreversible *adj* irreversible.

irrigar *vt* to irrigate.

irritable *adj (persona)* irritable; *(piel, ojos)* itchy.

irritación *f* irritation.

irritante *adj* irritating.

irritar *vt* to irritate ❑ **irritarse** *vpr* to get irritated.

isla *f* island.

islam *m* Islam.

islandés, -esa *adj* Icelandic ◆ *m, f* Icelander.

Islandia *s* Iceland.

islote *m* islet.

Israel *s* Israel.

istmo *m* isthmus.

Italia *s* Italy.

italiano, -na *adj, m, f* Italian.

itinerario *m* itinerary.

IVA *m (abrev de impuesto sobre el valor añadido)* VAT.

izda *(abrev de izquierda)* l.

izquierda f: **la ~** *(lado izquierdo)* the left; *(mano izquierda)* one's left hand; **a la ~** on the left; **girar a la ~** to turn left; **ser de ~s** to be left-wing.

izquierdo, -da *adj* left.

J

jabalí *m* wild boar.

jabalina *f* javelin.

jabón *m* soap.

jabonera *f* soap dish.

jacal *m (Amér)* shack.

jacuzzi® *m* Jacuzzi®.

jade *m* jade.

jadear *vi* to pant.

jaguar *m* jaguar.

jaiba *f (Amér)* crayfish.

jalea *f* jelly; **~ real** royal jelly.

jaleo *m (barullo)* row; *(lío)* mess.

Jamaica *s* Jamaica.

jamás *adv* never; **lo mejor que he visto ~** the best I've ever seen.

jamón *m* ham; **~ de bellota** cured ham from pigs fed on acorns; **~ de jabugo** type of top-quality cured ham from Jabugo; **~ serrano** cured ham, = Parma ham; **~ (de) York** boiled ham.

Japón *s* Japan.

japonés, -esa *adj, m, f* Japanese.

jarabe *m* syrup; **~ para la tos** cough mixture.

jardín *m* garden; **~ botánico** botanical gardens *(pl)*; **~ de infancia** nursery school; **~ público** park.

jardinera *f (recipiente)* plant pot holder, → **jardinero**.

jardinero, -ra *m, f* gardener; **a la jardinera** garnished with vegetables.

jarra *f* jug; **en ~s** *(posición)* hands on hips.

jarro *m* jug.

jarrón *m* vase.

jaula *f* cage.

jazmín *m* jasmine.

jazz [ʒas] *m* jazz.

jefatura *f (lugar)* headquarters *(pl); (cargo)* leadership; **~ de policía** police headquarters.

jefe, -fa *m, f (de trabajador)* boss; *(de empresa)* manager; *(de partido, asociación)* leader; *(de departamento)* head; *(de gobierno)* head of state.

jerez *m* sherry.

jerga *f (argot)* slang; *(lenguaje difícil)* jargon.

jeringuilla *f* syringe.

jeroglífico *m (pasatiempo)* rebus.

jersey *m* sweater; **~ de cuello alto** polo neck.

Jesucristo *s* Jesus Christ.

jesús *interj (después de estornudo)* bless you!; *(de asombro)* good heavens!

jícama *f (Amér)* large, onion-shaped tuber.

jinete *m* rider.

jirafa f giraffe.

jirón m (Amér) avenue.

jitomate m (Amér) tomato.

JJOO abrev = **juegos olímpicos**.

joder vt (vulg: fastidiar) to fuck up ♦ vi (vulg: copular) to fuck ♦ interj (vulg) fucking hell!

Jordania s Jordan.

jornada f (de trabajo) working day; (de viaje, trayecto) day's journey.

jornal m day's wage.

jornalero, -ra m, f day labourer.

jota f (baile) popular dance of Aragon.

joven adj young ♦ mf young man (f young woman) ❑ **jóvenes** mpl (juventud): **los jóvenes** young people.

joya f jewel; (fig: persona) gem.

joyería f jeweller's (shop).

joyero, -ra m, f jeweller ♦ m jewellery box.

joystick m joystick.

jubilación f (retiro) retirement; (pensión) pension.

jubilado, -da m, f pensioner.

jubilarse vpr to retire.

judaísmo m Judaism.

judía f bean; ~ **tierna** young, stringless bean; ~**s blancas** haricot beans; ~**s pintas** kidney beans; ~**s verdes** green beans, → judío.

judío, -a adj Jewish ♦ m, f Jew.

judo ['ʒuðo] m judo.

juego m (entretenimiento, en tenis) game; (acción) play; (con dinero) gambling; (con algo) to match (sthg); ~ **de azar** game of chance; ~ **de manos** (conjuring) trick; ~**s de sociedad** parlour games; ~**s olímpicos** Olympic Games.

juerga f party; **irse de** ~ to go out on the town.

jueves m inv Thursday; **Jueves Santo** Maundy Thursday, → sábado.

juez (pl -ces) mf judge; ~ **de línea** (en fútbol) linesman.

jugador, -ra m, f (participante) player; (de dinero) gambler.

jugar vi (entretenerse) to play; (con dinero) to gamble ♦ vt to play ❑ **jugar a** v + prep (fútbol, parchís, etc) to play; **jugar con** v + prep (no tomar en serio) to play with; **jugarse** vpr (arriesgar) to risk; (apostar) to bet.

jugo m (líquido) juice; (interés) substance.

jugoso, -sa adj juicy.

juguete m toy.

juguetería f toy shop.

juguetón, -ona adj playful.

juicio m (sensatez) judgment; (cordura) sanity; (ante juez, tribunal) trial; (opinión) opinion, **a mi** ~ in my opinion.

julio m July, → setiembre.

junco m reed.

jungla f jungle.

junio m June, → setiembre.

junta f committee; (sesión) meeting.

juntar vt (dos cosas) to put together; (personas) to bring together; (fondos, provisiones) to get together ❑ **juntarse** vpr (ríos, caminos) to meet; (personas) to get together; (pareja) to live together.

junto, -ta *adj (unido)* together ◆
adv at the same time; **~ a** *(al lado
de)* next to; *(cerca de)* near; **todo ~**
all together.

jurado *m (de juicio)* jury; *(de concurso, oposición)* panel of judges.

jurar *vt & vi* to swear.

jurídico, -ca *adj* legal.

justicia *f* justice; *(organismo)*
law.

justificación *f* justification.

justificar *vt* to justify; *(persona)*
to make excuses for; *(demostrar)* to
prove □ **justificarse** *vpr (excusarse)* to excuse o.s.

justo, -ta *adj (equitativo)* fair;
(exacto) exact; *(adecuado)* right;
(apretado) tight ◆ *adv* just; **~ en
medio** right in the middle.

juvenil *adj (persona)* youthful.

juventud *f (etapa de la vida)*
youth; *(jóvenes)* young people *(pl)*.

juzgado *m* court; *(territorio)*
jurisdiction.

juzgar *vt (procesar)* to try; *(considerar, opinar)* to judge.

K

karaoke *m (juego)* karaoke;
(lugar) karaoke bar.

kárate *m* karate.

kg *(abrev de kilogramo)* kg.

kilo *m (fam)* kilo; **un cuarto de ~
de ...** a quarter of a kilo of ...

kilogramo *m* kilogram.

kilómetro *m* kilometre; **~s por
hora** kilometres per hour.

kimono *m* silk dressing gown.

kiwi *m* fruit.

kleenex® *m inv* tissue.

km *(abrev de kilómetro)* km.

KO *m (abrev de knock-out)* KO.

L

l *(abrev de litro)* l.

la → el, lo.

laberinto *m* labyrinth.

labio *m* lip.

labor *f (trabajo)* work; *(tarea)*
task; *(en agricultura)* farmwork; *(de
costura)* needlework.

laborable *adj (día)* working ◆
m: "**sólo ~s**" "working days only".

laboral *adj* labour *(antes de s).*

laboratorio *m* laboratory; **~
fotográfico** developer's (shop).

laborioso, -sa *adj (trabajador)*
hard-working; *(complicado, difícil)*
laborious.

labrador, -ra *m, f (agricultor)*
farmer.

labrar *vt (tierra)* to farm; *(madera, piedra, etc)* to carve.

laca *f (de cabello)* hairspray;
(barniz) lacquer.

lacio, -cia *adj (cabello)* straight.

lacón *m* shoulder of pork; **~ con
grelos** Galician dish of shoulder of

pork with turnip tops.

lácteo, -a *adj (de leche)* milk *(antes de s)*; *(producto)* dairy *(antes de s)*.

ladera *f (de cerro)* slope; *(de montaña)* mountainside.

lado *m* side; *(sitio)* place; *al ~ (cerca)* nearby; *al ~ de* beside; *al otro ~ de* on the other side of; *de ~ a* to one side; *en otro ~* somewhere else; *la casa de al ~* the house next door.

ladrar *vi* to bark.

ladrido *m* bark.

ladrillo *m* brick.

ladrón, -ona *m, f* thief ◆ *adj (enchufe)* adapter.

lagartija *f (small)* lizard.

lagarto *m* lizard.

lago *m* lake.

lágrima *f* tear.

laguna *f (de agua)* lagoon; *(de ley)* loophole; *(de memoria)* gap.

lamentable *adj* pitiful.

lamentar *vt* to be sorry about ❑ **lamentarse** *vpr:* *~se (de)* to complain (about).

lamer *vt* to lick.

lámina *f (de papel, metal, etc)* sheet; *(estampa)* plate.

lámpara *f* lamp.

lampista *m* plumber.

lana *f* wool; *(Amér: fam: dinero)* dough.

lancha *f* boat; *~ motora* motorboat.

langosta *f (crustáceo)* lobster; *(insecto)* locust.

langostino *m* king prawn; *~s al ajillo* king prawns cooked in an earthenware dish in garlic and chilli sauce; *~s a la plancha* grilled king prawns.

lanza *f (arma)* spear.

lanzar *vt (pelota, dardo, etc)* to throw; *(producto, novedad)* to launch ❑ **lanzarse** *vpr (al mar, piscina, etc)* to dive; *(precipitarse)* to rush into it.

lapa *f* limpet.

lápida *f* memorial stone.

lápiz *(pl* **-ces)** *m* pencil; *~ de labios* lipstick; *~ de ojos* eyeliner.

largo, -ga *adj* long ◆ *m* length; *tiene 15 metros de ~* it's 15 metres long; *a la larga* in the long run; *a lo ~ de (playa, carretera, etc)* along; *(en el transcurso de)* throughout; *de ~ recorrido* long-distance.

largometraje *m* feature film.

laringe *f* larynx.

las *→* el, lo.

lástima *f (compasión)* pity; *(disgusto, pena)* shame; *¡qué ~!* what a pity!

lata *f (envase, lámina)* tin; *(de bebidas)* can; *ser una ~ (fam)* to be a pain.

latido *m* beat.

látigo *m* whip.

latín *m* Latin.

Latinoamérica *s* Latin America.

latinoamericano, -na *adj & m, f* Latin American.

latir *vi* to beat.

laurel *m (hoja)* bay leaf; *(árbol)* laurel.

lava *f* lava.

lavabo *m (cuarto de baño)* toilet; *(pila)* washbasin.

lavadero *m (de coches)* carwash.

lavado m wash; ~ **automático** automatic wash.

lavadora f washing machine; ~ **automática** automatic washing machine.

lavandá f lavender.

lavandería f (establecimiento) launderette; (de hotel, residencia) laundry.

lavaplatos m inv (máquina) dishwasher ♦ mf inv (persona) dishwasher.

lavar vt (limpiar) to wash; (dientes) to clean; ~ **la ropa** to do the washing □ **lavarse** vpr to wash; ~**se las manos** to wash one's hands; ~**se los dientes** to clean one's teeth.

lavavajillas m inv (máquina) dishwasher; (detergente) washing-up liquid.

laxante m laxative.

lazo m (nudo) bow; (para animales) lasso; (vínculo) tie, link.

le pron (a él) him; (a ella) her; (a usted) you.

leal adj loyal.

lealtad f loyalty.

lección f lesson.

lechal adj: **cordero** ~ baby lamb.

leche f milk; (vulg: golpe) whack ♦ interj shit!; ~ **condensada** condensed milk; ~ **desnatada** o **descremada** skimmed milk; ~ **entera** full-cream milk (Br), whole milk; ~ **frita** sweet made from fried milk, cornflour and lemon rind; ~ **limpiadora** cleansing milk.

lechera f (jarra) milk jug, → **lechero**.

lechería f dairy.

lechero, -ra m, f milkman (f milkwoman).

lecho m bed.

lechuga f lettuce.

lechuza f owl.

lector, -ra m, f (persona) reader; (profesor) language assistant ♦ m (aparato) scanner.

lectura f reading.

leer vt & vi to read.

legal adj legal.

legalidad f (cualidad) legality; (conjunto de leyes) law.

legible adj legible.

legislación f legislation.

legislatura f term (of office).

legítimo, -ma adj (legal) legitimate; (auténtico) genuine.

legumbre f pulse.

lejano, -na adj distant.

lejía f bleach.

lejos adv (en el espacio) far (away); (en el pasado) long ago; (en el futuro) far away; ~ **de** far from; **a lo** ~ in the distance; **de** ~ from a distance.

lencería f (ropa interior) lingerie; (tienda) draper's (shop).

lengua f (órgano) tongue; (idioma) language; ~ **de gato** = chocolate finger (biscuit); ~ **materna** mother tongue; ~ **oficial** official language.

lenguado m sole; ~ **menier** sole meunière.

lenguaje m language.

lengüeta f tongue.

lentamente adv slowly.

lente m o f lens; ~ **de contacto** contact lenses □ **lentes** mpl (formal: gafas) spectacles.

lenteja f lentil; **~s estofadas** lentil stew (with wine) (sg).

lentitud f slowness.

lento, -ta adj slow ◆ adv slowly.

leña f firewood.

leñador, -ra m, f woodcutter.

leño m log.

Leo m Leo.

león, -ona m, f lion (f lioness).

leopardo m (animal) leopard; (piel) leopard skin.

leotardos mpl thick tights.

lépero, -ra adj (Amér) (vulg: malicioso) spiteful; (astuto) sharp.

les pron (a ellos, ellas) them; (a ustedes) you.

lesbiana f lesbian.

lesión f (herida) injury.

letal adj lethal.

letra f (signo) letter; (de persona) handwriting; (de canción) lyrics (pl); (de una compra) bill of exchange; **~ de cambio** bill of exchange □ **letras** fpl (en enseñanza) arts.

letrero m sign.

levantamiento m (sublevación) uprising; **~ de pesos** weightlifting.

levantar vt to raise; (caja, peso, prohibición) to lift; (edificio) to build □ **levantarse** vpr (de la cama) to get up; (ponerse de pie) to stand up; (sublevarse) to rise up.

levante m (este) (viento) east wind □ **Levante** m the east coast of Spain between Castellón and Cartagena.

léxico m vocabulary.

ley f (parlamentaria) act.

leyenda f legend.

liar vt (atar) to tie up; (envolver) to roll up; (fam: complicar) to muddle up □ **liarse** vpr (enredarse) to get muddled up; **~se a** (comenzar a) to start to.

Líbano s Lebanon.

libélula f dragonfly.

liberal adj liberal.

liberar vt to free.

libertad f freedom □ **libertades** fpl (atrevimiento) liberties.

libertador, -ra m, f liberator.

Libia s Libya.

libra f (moneda, unidad de peso) pound; **~ esterlina** pound (sterling) □ **Libra** m (zodíaco) Libra.

librar vt (de trabajo) to free; (de peligro) to save; (letra, orden de pago) to make out ◆ vi (tener fiesta) to be off work □ **librarse de** v + prep (peligro, obligación) to escape from.

libre adj free; (no ocupado) vacant; (soltero) available; **"libre"** (taxi) "for hire"; **~ de** free from; **~ de impuestos** tax-free.

librería f (establecimiento) bookshop; (mueble) bookcase.

librero m (Amér) bookshelf.

libreta f (cuaderno) notebook; **~ de ahorros** savings book.

libro m book; **~ de bolsillo** paperback; **~ de cheques** cheque book; **~ de reclamaciones** complaints book; **~ de texto** textbook.

licencia f licence.

licenciado, -da m, f graduate.

licenciarse vpr (en universidad) to graduate; (de servicio militar) to be discharged.

licenciatura f degree.

licor m liquor.

licorería f (tienda) ≈ off-licence (Br), = liquor store (Am).

licuadora f liquidizer.

líder mf leader.

lidia f (corrida) bullfight; **la ~** bullfighting.

liebre f hare.

lienzo m (tela) canvas; (pintura) painting.

liga f league; (para medias) suspender.

ligar vt (atar) to tie; (relacionar) to link ♦ vi: **~ con** (fam) to get off with.

ligeramente adv (poco) slightly.

ligero, -ra adj light; (rápido) quick; (ágil) agile; (leve) slight; (vestido, tela) thin; **a la ligera** lightly.

light adj inv (comida) low-calorie; (bebida) diet (antes de s); (cigarrillo) light.

ligue m (fam: relación) fling.

liguero m suspender belt (Br), garter belt (Am).

lija f (papel) sandpaper.

lijar vt to sandpaper.

lila adj inv & f lilac.

lima f (herramienta) file; (fruto) lime; **~ para uñas** nail file.

límite m limit; (línea de separación) boundary; **~ de velocidad** speed limit.

limón m lemon.

limonada f lemonade.

limonero m lemon tree.

limosna f alms (pl); **pedir ~** to beg.

limpiabotas m inv shoeshine.

limpiacristales m inv (detergente) window-cleaning fluid ♦ mf inv (persona) window cleaner.

limpiador, -ra m, f cleaner.

limpiaparabrisas m inv (de automóvil) windscreen wiper (Br), windshield wiper (Am) ♦ mf inv (persona) windscreen cleaner (Br), windshield cleaner (Am).

limpiar vt (quitar suciedad) to clean; (zapatos) to polish; (con trapo) to wipe; (mancha) to wipe away; (fam: robar) to pinch; **~ la casa** to do the housework.

limpieza f (cualidad) cleanliness; (acción) cleaning; (destreza) skill; (honradez) honesty; **hacer la ~** to do the cleaning.

limpio, -pia adj (sin suciedad) clean; (pulcro) neat; (puro) pure; (correcto) honest; (dinero) net; **en ~** (escrito) final.

linaje m lineage.

lince m lynx.

lindo, -da adj pretty; **de lo ~** a great deal.

línea f line; (pauta) course; (aspecto) shape; **~ aérea** airline; **~ telefónica** (telephone) line.

lingote m ingot; **~ de oro** gold ingot.

lingüística f linguistics (sg).

lingüístico, -ca adj linguistic.

lino m (tejido) linen; (planta) flax.

linterna f (utensilio) torch (Br), flashlight (Am).

lío m (paquete) bundle; (fam: desorden, embrollo) mess; (fam: relación amorosa) affair; **hacerse un ~** to get muddled up.

lionesa f large profiterole filled with cream or chocolate.

liquidación f (de cuenta) settlement; (de mercancías, género) clearance sale; "~ total" "closing down sale".

liquidar *vt (cuenta)* to settle; *(mercancías, existencias)* to sell off; *(fam: matar)* to bump off.

líquido *m* liquid.

lira *f (instrumento)* lyre.

lirio *m* iris.

liso, -sa *adj (llano)* flat; *(sin asperezas)* smooth; *(color)* plain; *(pelo)* straight ◆ *m, f (Amér)* rude person.

lista *f (enumeración)* list; *(de tela)* strip; ~ **de boda** wedding list; ~ **de correos** poste restante; ~ **de espera** waiting list; ~ **de precios** price list; ~ **de vinos** wine list.

listín *m* directory; ~ **telefónico** telephone directory.

listo, -ta *adj (inteligente, astuto)* clever; *(preparado)* ready ◆ *interj* I'm/we're/it's ready!

listón *m (de madera)* lath; *(en deporte)* bar.

lisura *f (Amér)* swearword.

litera *f (de tren)* couchette; *(de barco)* berth; *(mueble)* bunk (bed).

literal *adj* literal.

literario, -ria *adj* literary.

literatura *f* literature.

litro *m* litre.

llaga *f* wound.

llama *f (de fuego)* flame; *(animal)* llama.

llamada *f* call; **hacer una a cobro revertido** to reverse the charges (Br), to call collect (Am); ~ **automática** direct-dialled call; ~ **interprovincial** national call; ~ **interurbana** long-distance call; ~ **metropolitana** local call; ~ **provin-**

cial = local area call; ~ **telefónica** telephone call.

llamar *vt* to call ◆ *vi (a la puerta)* to knock; *(al timbre)* to ring; ~ **por teléfono** to phone ▫ **llamarse** *vpr* to be called; **¿cómo te llamas?** what's your name?

llano, -na *adj (superficie, terreno)* flat; *(amable)* straightforward ◆ *m* plain.

llanta *f (de rueda)* rim; *(Amér: rueda de coche, camión)* wheel.

llanura *f* plain.

llave *f* key; *(para tuercas)* spanner; *(signo ortográfico)* curly bracket; **echar la ~** to lock up; ~ **de contacto** ignition key; ~ **inglesa** monkey wrench; ~ **maestra** master key; ~ **de paso** mains tap.

llegada *f (de viaje, trayecto, etc)* arrival; *(en deporte)* finish ▫ **llegadas** *fpl (de tren, avión, etc)* arrivals; **"~s internacionales"** "international arrivals".

llegar *vi (a un lugar)* to arrive; *(fecha, momento)* to come; *(ser suficiente)* to be enough; ~ **a** *o* **hasta** *(extenderse)* to reach; ~ **a hacer algo** *(expresa conclusión)* to come to do sthg; *(expresa esfuerzo)* to manage to do sthg ▫ **llegar a** *v + prep (presidente, director)* to become; *(edad, altura, temperatura)* to reach; ~ **a ser** to become; ~ **a conocer** to get to know.

llenar *vt (recipiente, espacio)* to fill; *(impreso)* to fill out ▫ **llenarse** *vpr (lugar)* to fill up; *(hartarse)* to be full; **llenarse de** *v + prep (cubrirse)* to get covered with.

lleno, -na *adj (ocupado)* full; *(espectáculo, cine)* sold out ◆ *m (en* *espectáculo)* full house; **de ~** *(total-mente)* completely.

llevar *vt* 1. *(transportar)* to carry; **el barco lleva carga y pasajeros** the boat carries cargo and passengers. 2. *(acompañar)* to take; **llevó al niño a casa** she took the child home; **me llevaron en coche** they drove me there. 3. *(prenda, objeto personal)* to wear; **lleva gafas** he wears glasses; **no lle-vamos dinero** we don't have any money on us. 4. *(coche, caballo)* to handle. 5. *(conducir)*: **~ a alguien a** to lead sb to. 6. *(ocuparse, dirigir)* to be in charge of; **lleva muy bien sus estudios** he's doing very well in his studies. 7. *(tener)* to have; **~ el pelo largo** to have long hair; **llevas las manos sucias** your hands are dirty. 8. *(soportar)* to deal with. 9. *(con tiempo)*: **lleva tres semanas de viaje** he's been travelling for three weeks; **me llevó mucho tiem-po hacer el trabajo** I took a long time to get the work done. 10. *(sobrepasar)*: **te llevo seis puntos** I'm six points ahead of you; **le lleva seis años** she's six years older than him.
◆ *vi* 1. *(dirigirse)* to lead; **este camino lleva a Madrid** this road leads to Madrid. 2. *(haber)*: **llevo leída media novela** I'm halfway through the novel. 3. *(estar)*: **lleva viniendo cada día** she's been coming every day.
❏ **llevarse** *vpr (coger)* to take; *(conseguir, recibir)* to get; *(estar de moda)* to be in (fashion); **~se bien/mal (con)** to get on well/badly (with).

llorar *vi* to cry ◆ *vt* to mourn.

llorón, -ona *m, f* crybaby.

llover *v impers*: **está lloviendo** it's raining ◆ *vi (ser abundante)* to rain down; **~ a cántaros** to rain cats and dogs.

llovizna *f* drizzle.

lloviznar *v impers*: **está lloviz-nando** it's drizzling.

lluvia *f* rain; *(fig: de preguntas)* barrage.

lluvioso, -sa *adj* rainy.

lo, la *pron (cosa)* it, them *(pl)*; *(persona)* him *(f* her), them *(pl)*; *(usted, ustedes)* you ◆ *pron neutro* it ◆ *art*: **~ mejor** the best; **~ bueno del asunto** the good thing about it; **ella es guapa, él no ~ es** she's good-looking, he isn't; **siento ~ de tu padre** I'm sorry about your father; **~ que** what.

lobo, -ba *m, f* wolf.

local *adj* local ◆ *m (lugar)* prem-ises *(pl)*.

localidad *f (población)* town; *(asiento)* seat; *(entrada)* ticket.

localización *f* location.

localizar *vt (encontrar)* to locate; *(limitar)* to localize ❏ **localizarse** *vpr (situarse)* to be located.

loción *f* lotion; **~ bronceadora** suntan lotion.

loco, -ca *adj* mad ◆ *m, f* madman *(f* madwoman); **~ por** *(afi-cionado)* mad about; **a lo ~** *(sin pen-sar)* hastily; **volver ~ a alguien** to drive sb crazy.

locomotora *f* engine, loco-motive.

locura *f (falta de juicio)* madness; *(acción insensata)* folly; **tener ~ por**

to be mad about.

locutor, -ra *m, f* presenter.

locutorio *m (de emisora)* studio; *(de convento)* visiting room.

lodo *m* mud.

lógica *f* logic.

lógico, -ca *adj* logical.

logrado, -da *adj (bien hecho)* accomplished.

lograr *vt (resultado, objetivo)* to achieve; *(beca, puesto)* to obtain; **hacer algo** to manage to do sthg; **que alguien haga algo** to manage to get sb to do sthg.

logro *m* achievement.

lombriz *(pl* **-ces)** *f* earthworm.

lomo *m (de animal)* back; *(carne)* loin; *(de libro)* spine; **~ de cerdo** pork loin; **~ embuchado** pork loin stuffed with seasoned mince; **~ ibérico** cold, cured pork sausage; **~s de merluza** hake steak *(sg)*.

lona *f* canvas.

loncha *f* slice.

lonche *m (Amér)* lunch.

Londres *s* London.

longaniza *f* type of spicy, cold pork sausage.

longitud *f* length.

lonja *f (edificio)* exchange; *(loncha)* slice.

loro *m* parrot.

lote *m (porción)* share.

lotería *f* lottery; **~ primitiva** twice-weekly state-run lottery.

LOTERÍA PRIMITIVA

In this Spanish state-run lottery, participants try to guess a combi-

nation of six numbers between one and forty-nine. A ticket contains eight grids of forty-nine boxes, each grid being equivalent to one entry. The "lotería primitiva" is drawn twice a week.

lotero, -ra *m, f* lottery ticket seller.

loza *f (material)* earthenware; *(porcelana)* china; *(vajilla)* crockery.

ltda. *(abrev de limitada)* Ltd.

lubina *f* sea bass.

lubricante *m* lubricant.

lucha *f (pelea)* fight; *(oposición)* struggle; **~ libre** all-in wrestling.

luchador, -ra *m, f* fighter.

luchar *vi (pelear)* to fight; *(esforzarse)* to struggle.

luciérnaga *f* glow-worm.

lucir *vt (llevar puesto)* to wear ◆ *vi* to shine; *(Amér: verse bien)* to look good ☐ **lucirse** *vpr (quedar bien)* to shine; *(dejarse ver)* to be seen; *(fam: hacer el ridículo)* to mess things up.

lucro *m* profit.

lúdico, -ca *adj*: **actividades lúdicas** fun and games.

luego *adv (justo después)* then; *(más tarde)* later; *(Amér: pronto)* soon ◆ *conj* so; **desde ~** *(sin duda)* of course; *(para reprochar)* for heaven's sake; **luego luego** *(Amér)* straight away.

lugar *m* place; **tener ~** to take place; **en ~ de** instead of.

lujo *m* luxury; *(abundancia)* profusion; **de ~** luxury *(antes de s)*.

lujoso, -sa *adj* luxurious.

lujuria *f* lust.

lumbago *m* lumbago.

luminoso, -sa *adj* bright.

luna *f (astro)* moon; *(de vidrio)* window (pane).

lunar *m (de la piel)* mole ❑

lunares *mpl (estampado)* spots.

lunes *m inv* Monday, → **sábado**.

luneta *f (de coche)* windscreen *(Br)*, windshield *(Am)*; ~ **térmica** demister.

lupa *f* magnifying glass.

lustrabotas *m inv (Amér)* bootblack.

lustrador *m (Amér)* bootblack.

luto *m* mourning.

luz *(pl* -ces*) f* light; *(electricidad)* electricity; ~ **solar** sunlight; **dar a** ~ to give birth ❑ **luces** *fpl (de coche)* lights.

lycra® *f* Lycra®.

m *(abrev de metro)* m.

macana *f (Amér) (garrote)* club; *(fig: disparate)* stupid thing.

macanudo *adj (Amér: fam)* great.

macarrones *mpl* macaroni *(sg)*.

macedonia *f:* ~ **(de frutas)** fruit salad.

maceta *f* flowerpot.

machacar *vt* to crush.

machismo *m* machismo.

machista *mf* male chauvinist.

macho *adj (animal, pieza)* male;

(hombre) macho ◆ *m (animal)* male.

macizo, -za *adj* solid ◆ *m (de montañas)* massif; *(de flores)* flowerbed.

macramé *m* macramé.

macuto *m* backpack.

madeja *f* hank.

madera *f* wood; *(pieza)* piece of wood; **de** ~ wooden.

madrastra *f* stepmother.

madre *f* mother; ~ **política** mother-in-law; **¡~ mía!** Jesus!

madreselva *f* honeysuckle.

Madrid *s* Madrid; ~ **capital** (the city of) Madrid.

madriguera *f (de tejón)* den; *(de conejo)* burrow.

madrileño, -ña *adj* of/relating to Madrid ◆ *m, f* native/inhabitant of Madrid.

madrina *f (de bautizo)* godmother; *(de boda)* bridesmaid; *(de fiesta, acto)* patroness.

madrugada *f (noche)* early morning; *(amanecer)* dawn.

madrugador, -ra *adj* early-rising.

madrugar *vi* to get up early.

madurar *vt (proyecto, plan, idea)* to think through ◆ *vi (fruto)* to ripen; *(persona)* to mature.

madurez *f (sensatez)* maturity; *(edad adulta)* adulthood; *(de fruto)* ripeness.

maduro, -ra *adj (fruto, grano)* ripe; *(sensato, mayor)* mature; *(proyecto, plan, idea)* well thought-out.

maestría *f (habilidad)* mastery.

maestro, -tra *m, f (de escuela)* teacher; *(de arte, oficio)* master;

(músico) maestro.

mafia f mafia.

magdalena f fairy cake.

magia f magic.

mágico, -ca adj *(maravilloso)* magical; *(de la magia)* magic.

magistrado, -da m, f *(de justicia)* judge.

magistratura f *(tribunal)* tribunal; *(cargo)* judgeship.

magnate m magnate.

magnesio m magnesium.

magnético, -ca adj magnetic.

magnetófono m tape recorder.

magnífico, -ca adj magnificent.

magnitud f magnitude.

magnolia f magnolia.

mago, -ga m, f *(en espectáculo)* magician; *(personaje fantástico)* wizard.

magro, -gra adj *(carne)* lean.

maguey m *(Amér)* agave, maguey.

maicena f cornflour *(Br)*, cornstarch *(Am)*.

maillot m *(de ballet, deporte)* maillot.

maitre m maître.

maíz m maize *(Br)*, corn *(Am)*.

majestuoso, -sa adj majestic.

majo, -ja adj *(agradable)* nice; *(bonito)* pretty.

mal m *(daño)* harm; *(enfermedad)* illness ◆ adv *(incorrectamente)* wrong; *(inadecuadamente)* badly ◆ adj → **malo; el ~** evil; **encontrarse ~** to feel ill; **oír/ver ~** to have poor hearing/eyesight; **oler ~** to smell bad; **saber ~** to taste bad; **sentar ~**

a alguien *(ropa)* not to suit sb; *(comida)* to disagree with sb; *(comentario)* to upset sb; **ir de ~ en peor** to go from bad to worse.

Malasia s Malaysia.

malcriar vt to spoil.

maldad f *(cualidad)* evil; *(acción)* evil thing.

maldición f curse.

maldito, -ta adj damned; **¡maldita sea!** damn it!

maleable adj malleable.

malecón m *(atracadero)* jetty; *(rompeolas)* breakwater.

maleducado, -da adj rude.

malentendido m misunderstanding.

malestar m *(inquietud)* uneasiness; *(dolor)* discomfort.

maleta f suitcase; **hacer las ~s** to pack (one's bags).

maletero m boot *(Br)*, trunk *(Am)*.

maletín m briefcase.

malformación f malformation.

malgastar vt *(dinero, esfuerzo, tiempo)* to waste.

malhablado, -da adj foul-mouthed.

malhechor, -ra adj criminal.

malicia f *(maldad)* wickedness; *(mala intención)* malice; *(astucia)* sharpness.

malintencionado, -da adj malicious.

malla f *(tejido)* mesh; *(traje)* leotard ❏ **mallas** fpl *(pantalones)* leggings.

Mallorca s Majorca.

malo, -la *(compar & superl* **peor***)*

adj bad; *(travieso)* naughty; **estar ~** *(enfermo)* to be ill; **estar de malas** to be in a bad mood; **por las malas** by force.

malograr *vt (Amér)* to waste ❑
malograrse *(Amér)* to fail.

malpensado, -da *m, f* malicious person.

maltratar *vt (persona)* to ill-treat; *(objeto)* to damage.

mamá *f (fam)* mum; **~ grande** *(Amér)* grandma.

mamadera *f (Amér) (biberón)* (baby's) bottle; *(tetilla)* teat.

mamar *vt & vi* to suckle.

mamey *m (Amér)* mammee.

mamífero *m* mammal.

mamita *f (Amér: fam)* mum.

mampara *f* screen.

manada *f (de vacas)* herd.

mánager *m* manager.

manantial *m* spring.

mancha *f* stain.

manchar *vt (ensuciar)* to make dirty; *(con manchas)* to stain ❑ **mancharse** *vpr* to get dirty.

manco, -ca *adj* one-handed.

mancuerna *f (Amér)* cufflink.

mandar *vt (suj: ley, orden)* to decree; *(ordenar)* to order; *(dirigir)* to be in charge of; *(enviar)* to send; **~ hacer algo** to have sthg done; **¡mande?** *(Amér)* eh?

mandarina *f* mandarin.

mandíbula *f* jaw.

mando *m (autoridad)* command; *(jefe)* leader; *(instrumento)* control; **~ a distancia** remote control.

manecilla *f* hand *(of clock)*.

manejable *adj* manageable.

manejar *vt (herramienta, persona)* to handle; *(aparato)* to operate; *(dinero)* to manage; *(Amér: conducir)* to drive.

manejo *m (de instrumento)* handling; *(de aparato)* operation; *(de dinero)* management; *(engaño, astucia)* intrigue.

manera *f* way; **de cualquier ~** *(mal)* any old how; *(de todos modos)* anyway; **de esta ~** *(así)* this way; **de ninguna ~** certainly not; **de ~ que** *(así que)* so (that) ❑ **maneras** *fpl (comportamiento)* manners.

manga *f (de vestido)* sleeve; *(tubo flexible)* hosepipe; *(de campeonato)* round.

mango *m (asa)* handle; *(fruto)* mango.

manguera *f* hosepipe.

maní *m (Amér)* peanut.

manía *f (obsesión)* obsession; *(afición exagerada)* craze; *(antipatía)* dislike.

maniático, -ca *adj (tiquismiquis)* fussy ◆ *m, f*: **es un ~ del fútbol** he's football crazy.

manicomio *m* mental hospital.

manicura *f* manicure; **hacerse la ~** to have a manicure.

manifestación *f (de personas)* demonstration; *(muestra)* display; *(declaración)* expression.

manifestante *mf* demonstrator.

manifestar *vt (declarar)* to express; *(mostrar)* to show ❑ **manifestarse** *vpr* to demonstrate.

manifiesto, -ta *adj* clear ◆ *m* manifesto.

manillar *m* handlebars *(pl)*.

maniobra f (de coche, barco, tren) manoeuvre; (astucia) trick.

manipular vt (con las manos) to handle; (persona, información) to manipulate.

maniquí m (muñeco) dummy ♦ mf (persona) model.

manito m (Amér: fam) pal.

manivela f crank.

mano f hand; (capa) coat ♦ m (Amér) pal; **a ~** (sin máquina) by hand; (cerca) to hand; **a ~ derecha** on the right; **de segunda ~** second-hand; **dar la ~ a alguien** to shake hands with sb; **echar una ~ a alguien** to lend sb a hand; **~ de obra** (trabajadores) workforce.

manoletina f (zapato) type of open, low-heeled shoe, often with a bow.

manopla f mitten.

manosear vt to handle roughly.

mansión f mansion.

manso, -sa adj (animal) tame; (persona) gentle.

manta f blanket.

manteca f (de animal) fat; (de cerdo) lard; (de cacao, leche) butter.

mantecado m (dulce) short-cake; (sorbete) ice-cream made of milk, eggs and sugar.

mantel m tablecloth.

mantelería f table linen.

mantener vt to keep; (sujetar) to support; (defender) to maintain; (relación, correspondencia) to have □ **mantenerse** vpr (edificio) to be standing; (alimentarse) to support o.s.

mantenimiento m (de per-

sona) sustenance; (de edificio, coche) maintenance.

mantequería f dairy.

mantequilla f butter.

mantilla f (de mujer) mantilla.

mantón m shawl.

manual adj & m manual.

manualidad f manual labour.

manuscrito m manuscript.

manzana f (fruto) apple; (de casas) block; **~ al horno** baked apple.

manzanilla f (infusión) camomile tea; (vino) manzanilla (sherry).

manzano m apple tree.

mañana f morning ♦ adv & m tomorrow; **las dos de la ~** two o'clock in the morning; **~ por la ~** tomorrow morning; **por la ~** in the morning.

mañanitas fpl (Amér) birthday song (sg).

mapa m map.

maqueta f model.

maquillaje m (producto) make-up; (acción) making-up.

maquillar vt to make up □ **maquillarse** vpr to put on one's make up.

máquina f (aparato) machine; (locomotora) engine; (Amér: coche) car; **a ~** by machine; **~ de afeitar** electric razor; **~ de coser** sewing machine; **~ de escribir** typewriter; **~ fotográfica** camera.

maquinaria f (conjunto de máquinas) machinery.

maquinilla f razor.

maquinista mf (de metro, tren) engine driver (Br), engineer (Am).

mar *m o f* sea ❑ **Mar** *m*: **el Mar del Norte** the North Sea.

maracas *fpl* maracas.

maratón *m (carrera)* marathon; *(fig: de cine)* three or more films by the same director or on the same subject, shown consecutively.

maravilla *f (cosa extraordinaria)* marvel; *(impresión)* wonder.

maravilloso, -sa *adj* marvellous.

marc *m*: **~ de champán** champagne brandy.

marca *f (señal, huella)* mark; *(nombre)* brand; *(en deporte)* record; **de ~** *(ropa, producto)* designer *(antes de s)*; **~ registrada** registered trademark.

marcado, -da *adj* marked.

marcador *m (panel)* scoreboard; *(rotulador)* marker pen.

marcapasos *m inv* pacemaker.

marcar *vt (poner señal)* to mark; *(anotar)* to note down; *(un tanto)* to score; *(suj: termómetro, contador)* to read; *(suj: reloj)* to say; *(número de teléfono)* to dial; *(pelo)* to set; *(con el precio)* to price; **~ un gol** to score a goal; **~ un número** to dial a number.

marcha *f (partida)* departure; *(de vehículo)* gear; *(desarrollo)* progress; *(fam: animación)* life; *(pieza musical)* march; **dar ~ atrás** to reverse; **en ~** *(motor)* running; **poner en ~** to start.

marchar *vi (aparato, mecanismo)* to work; *(asunto, negocio)* to go well; *(soldado)* to march ❑ **marcharse** *vpr (irse)* to go; *(partir)* to leave.

marchitarse *vpr* to wither.

marchoso, -sa *adj (fam)* lively.

marco *m* frame; *(límite)* framework.

marea *f* tide; **~ negra** oil slick.

mareado, -da *adj (con náuseas)* sick; *(en coche)* carsick; *(en barco)* seasick; *(en avión)* airsick; *(aturdido)* dizzy.

marearse *vpr (en coche)* to be carsick; *(en barco)* to be seasick; *(en avión)* to be airsick; *(aturdirse)* to get dizzy.

marejada *f* heavy sea.

marejadilla *f* slight swell.

maremoto *m* tidal wave.

mareo *m (náuseas)* sickness; *(aturdimiento)* dizziness.

marfil *m* ivory.

margarina *f* margarine.

margarita *f* daisy.

margen *m (de página, beneficio)* margin; *(de camino)* side; *(de río)* bank; *(tiempo, de actuar)* leeway.

marginación *f* exclusion.

marginado, -da *m, f* outcast.

mariachi *m (orquesta)* mariachi band.

---

i	**MARIACHI**

Mariachi bands are groups of Mexican musicians who wear traditional Mexican dress and play their music at local "fiestas", in restaurants and in the streets. They are often hired for private functions such as birthdays or weddings.

---

maricón *m (vulg)* poof.

marido *m* husband.

marihuana f marijuana.

marina f (armada) navy; (cuadro) seascape.

marinero, -ra adj (ropa) sailor (antes de s); **a la marinera** cooked in a white wine and garlic sauce.

marino m sailor.

marioneta f (muñeco) puppet ❑ **marionetas** fpl (teatro) puppet show (sg).

mariposa f butterfly.

mariquita f ladybird (Br), ladybug (Am).

mariscada f seafood dish.

mariscos mpl seafood (sg).

marisma f salt marsh.

marítimo, -ma adj (paseo) seaside (antes de s); (barco) sea-going.

mármol m marble.

marqués, -esa m, f marquis (f marchioness).

marquesina f (de puerta, andén) glass canopy; (parada de autobús) bus shelter.

marrano, -na adj (sucio) filthy; (innoble) contemptible ◆ m, f (cerdo) pig.

marrón adj inv brown.

marroquí adj & mf Moroccan.

Marruecos s Morocco.

martes m inv Tuesday, → **sábado**.

martillo m hammer.

mártir mf martyr.

marzo m March, → **setiembre**.

más adv **1.** (comparativo) more; **Pepe es ~ alto/ambicioso** Pepe is taller/more ambitious; **tengo ~ hambre** I'm hungrier; **~ de/que** more than; **~ ... que ...** more ...

than ...; **de ~** (de sobra) left over.
2. (superlativo): **el/la ~ ...** the most ...; **el ~ listo** the cleverest.
3. (en frases negativas) any more; **no necesitas ~ trabajo** you don't need any more work.
4. (con pron interrogativo o indefinido) else; **¡quién/qué ~?** who/what else?; **nadie ~** no one else.
5. (indica intensidad): **¡qué día ~ bonito!** what a lovely day!; **¡es ~ tonto!** he's so stupid!
6. (indica suma) plus; **dos ~ dos igual a cuatro** two plus two is four.
7. (indica preferencia): **~ vale que te quedes en casa** it would be better for you to stay at home.
8. (en locuciones): **es ~** what is more; **~ bien** rather; **~ o menos** more or less; **poco ~** little more; **por ~ que** however much; **por ~ que lo intente** however hard she tries; **¿qué ~ da?** what difference does it make?
◆ **m inv**: **tiene sus ~ y sus menos** it has its good points and its bad points.

masa f mass; (de pan, bizcocho) dough; (Amér: dulce) small cake.

masaje m massage.

masajista mf masseur (f masseuse).

mascar vt to chew.

máscara f mask.

mascarilla f (crema, loción) face pack; (para nariz y boca) mask.

mascota f mascot.

masculino, -na adj (sexo) male; (viril) manly; (en gramática) masculine.

masía f farm (in Aragon or Catalonia).

masticar vt to chew.

mástil m (de barco) mast.

matadero m slaughterhouse.

matador m matador.

matambre m (Amér) cut of cold meat from between the hide and the ribs of a cow.

matamoscas m inv (palo) flyswat; (espray) flyspray.

matanza f (de personas, animales) slaughter; (de cerdo) pigkilling.

matar vt to kill; (hacer sufrir) to drive mad; (brillo, color) to tone down; (en juegos, cartas) to beat ◆ **matarse** vpr (tomarse interés, trabajo) to go to great lengths.

matarratas m inv (insecticida) rat poison; (bebida mala) rotgut.

matasellos m inv postmark.

mate adj matt ◆ m (en ajedrez) mate; (planta, infusión) maté.

---

i MATE

Maté is a herbal infusion from the southern part of South America. It is drunk from a small cup, also known as a maté, which is made from a small, hollowed-out gourd.

---

matemáticas fpl mathematics.

matemático, -ca adj mathematical.

materia f (sustancia, tema) matter; (material) material; (asignatura) subject; ~ **prima** raw material.

material adj (de materia) material; (físico) physical ◆ m (componente) material; (instrumento) equipment.

maternidad f (cualidad) motherhood; (clínica) maternity hospital.

materno, -na adj (de madre) maternal; (lengua) mother (antes de s).

matinal adj morning (antes de s).

matiz m (pl -ces) (de color) shade; (leve diferencia) nuance.

matizar vt (colores) to tinge; (concepto, idea, proyecto) to explain in detail.

matón m (guardaespaldas) bodyguard; (asesino) hired assassin.

matorral m thicket.

matrícula f (de colegio) registration; (de universidad) matriculation; (de vehículo) numberplate; ~ **de honor** top marks (pl).

matricular vt to register ❑ **matricularse** vpr to register.

matrimonio m (ceremonia) marriage; (pareja) married couple.

matutino, -na adj morning (antes de s).

maullar vi to miaow.

maullido m miaow.

máxima f (temperatura) highest temperature; (frase) maxim.

máximo, -ma superl ◆ **grande** ◆ adj (triunfo, pena, frecuencia) greatest; (temperatura, puntuación, galardón) highest ◆ m maximum; **como** ~ at the most.

maya adj Mayan ◆ mf Maya Indian ◆ m (lengua) Maya.

mayo m May, → setiembre.

mayonesa f mayonnaise.

mayor adj (en tamaño) bigger; (en

número) higher; (*en edad*) older; (*en importancia*) greater; (*adulto*) grown-up; (*anciano*) elderly ♦ **m** (*en el ejército*) major; **el/la ~** (*en tamaño*) the biggest; (*en número*) the highest; (*en edad*) the oldest; (*en importancia*) the greatest; **al por ~** wholesale; **la ~ parte (de)** most (of); **ser ~ de edad** to be an adult ☐ **mayores** *mpl*: **los ~es** (*adultos*) grown-ups; (*ancianos*) the elderly.

mayoreo *m* (Amér) wholesale.

mayoría *f* majority; **la ~ de** most of.

mayúscula *f* capital letter; **en ~s** in capitals.

mazapán *m* marzipan.

mazo *m* (*de madera*) mallet; (*de cartas*) balance (of the deck).

me *pron* (*complemento directo*) me; (*complemento indirecto*) (to) me; (*reflexivo*) myself; **~ voy** I'm going.

mear *vi* (fam) to piss.

mecánica *f* (*mecanismo*) mechanics (*pl*).

mecánico, -ca *adj* mechanical ♦ **m** mechanic.

mecanismo *m* (*funcionamiento*) procedure; (*piezas*) mechanism.

mecanografía *f* typing.

mecanógrafo, -fa *m, f* typist.

mecedora *f* rocking chair.

mecer *vt* to rock.

mecha *f* (*de vela*) wick; (*de explosivo*) fuse; (*de pelo*) streak; (*de tocino*) strip of meat used as stuffing for chicken etc.

mechero *m* (cigarette) lighter.

mechón *m* (*de pelo*) lock.

medalla *f* medal.

medallón *m* medallion; **meda-**

llones de rape médaillons of angler fish; **medallones de solomillo** médaillons of sirloin steak.

media *f* (*calcetín*) stocking; (*punto*) average ☐ **medias** *fpl* tights.

mediado, -da *adj*: **a ~s de** in the middle of.

mediana *f* (*de autopista*) central reservation (Br), median (Am).

mediano, -na *adj* (*en tamaño*) medium; (*en calidad*) average.

medianoche *f* midnight.

mediante *prep* by means of.

mediar *vi* (*llegar a la mitad*) to be halfway through; (*transcurrir*) to pass; (*interceder*) to intercede; **~ entre** to be between.

medicamento *m* medicine.

medicina *f* medicine.

medicinal *adj* medicinal.

médico, -ca *m, f* doctor; **~ de guardia** duty doctor.

medida *f* (*dimensión*) measurement; (*cantidad, disposición*) measure; (*intensidad*) extent; **tomar ~s** to take measures; **~s de seguridad** safety measures; **a la ~** (*ropa*) made-to-measure; **a ~ que** as; **en cierta ~** to some extent.

medieval *adj* medieval.

medio, -dia *adj* half; (*tamaño, estatura*) medium; (*posición, punto, clase*) middle; (*de promedio*) average ♦ **m** (*centro*) middle; (*ambiente*) environment; (*manera, medida, de transporte*) means; (*en matemáticas*) average ♦ *adv* half; **en ~ de** (*entre dos*) between; (*entre varios, en mitad de*) in the middle of; **a medias** (*partido entre dos*) half each; **hacer algo a medias** to half-do something; **~ ambiente** environment; **media hora** half an hour; **~ kilo (de)** half a kilo (of); **media docena/libra (de)** half a dozen/ pound (of); **un vaso y ~ a** glass and a half; **media pensión** half board ❑ **medios** mpl (económicos) resources; **los ~s de comunicación** the media.

mediocre adj mediocre.

mediocridad f mediocrity.

mediodía m midday.

mediopensionista mf child who has lunch at school.

medir vt (dimensión, intensidad) to measure; (comparar) to weigh up; (fuerzas) to compare; (palabras, acciones) to weigh; **¿cuánto mides?** how tall are you?

meditar vt to ponder ♦ vi to meditate.

mediterráneo, -a adj Mediterranean ❑ **Mediterráneo** m: **el (mar) Mediterráneo** the Mediterranean (Sea).

médium mf inv medium.

medusa f jellyfish.

megáfono m megaphone.

mejilla f cheek.

mejillón m mussel; **mejillones a la marinera** moules marinière.

mejor adj & adv better; **el/la ~** the best; **a lo ~** maybe.

mejora f improvement.

mejorar vt to improve; (superar) to be better than; (enfermo) to make better ♦ vi (enfermo) to get better; (tiempo, clima) to improve ❑ **mejorarse** vpr (persona) to get better; (tiempo, clima) to improve.

mejoría f improvement.

melancolía f melancholy.

melancólico, -ca adj melancholic.

melena f (de persona) long hair; (de león) mane.

mella f (en metal) nick; (en diente) chip; **hacer ~** (causar impresión) to make an impression.

mellizo, -za adj twin (antes de s) ❑ **mellizos** mpl twins.

melocotón m peach; **~ en almíbar** peaches (pl) in syrup.

melocotonero m peach tree.

melodía f tune.

melodrama m melodrama.

melodramático, -ca adj melodramatic.

melón m melon; **~ con jamón** melon with "serrano" ham.

membrillo m (fruto) quince; (dulce) quince jelly.

memorable adj memorable.

memoria f memory; (estudio) paper; (informe) report; **de ~** by heart ❑ **memorias** fpl (de persona) memoirs.

memorizar vt to memorize.

menaje m (de cocina) kitchenware.

mención f mention.

mencionar vt to mention.

mendigo, -ga m, f beggar.

menestra f: **~ (de verduras)** vegetable stew.

menor adj (en edad) younger; (en tamaño) smaller; (en número) lower; (en calidad) lesser ♦ m (persona) minor; **el/la ~** (en tamaño) the smallest; (en edad) the youngest; (en número) the lowest; **~ de edad** under age.

Menorca s Minorca.

menos *adv* 1. *(comparativo)* less; **está ~ gordo** he's not as fat; **tengo ~ hambre** I'm not as hungry; **~ leche** less milk; **~ manzanas** fewer apples; **~ de/que** fewer/less than; **~ ... que ...** fewer/less ... than ...; **me han dado 25 pesetas de ~** they've given me 25 pesetas too little.
2. *(superlativo)*: **el/la ~ ...** the least ...; **lo ~ que puedes hacer** the least you can do.
3. *(indica resta)* minus; **tres ~ dos igual a uno** three minus two is one.
4. *(con las horas)*: **son las cuatro ~ diez** it is ten to four.
5. *(en locuciones)*: **a ~ que** unless; **poco ~ de** just under; **¡~ mal!** thank God!; **eso es lo de ~** that's the least of it.
◆ *prep (excepto)* except (for); **acudieron todos ~ él** everyone came except him; **todo ~ eso** anything but that.
◆ *m inv*: **al ○ por lo ~** at least.

menospreciar *vt (despreciar)* to despise; *(apreciar poco)* to undervalue.

menosprecio *m (desprecio)* scorn; *(poco aprecio)* undervaluing.

mensaje *m* message.

mensajero, -ra *m, f (de paquetes, cartas)* courier; *(de comunicados)* messenger.

menstruación *f* menstruation.

mensual *adj* monthly.

menta *f* mint; **a la ~** with mint.

mental *adj* mental.

mente *f (inteligencia)* mind; *(forma de pensar)* mentality.

mentir *vi* to lie.

mentira *f* lie.

mentiroso, -sa *m, f* liar.

mentón *m* chin.

menú *m* menu; *(de precio reducido)* set menu; **~ de degustación** meal consisting of several small portions of different dishes; **~ (del día)** set meal.

menudeo *m (Amér)* retail.

menudo, -da *adj* small; **a ~** often; **¡~ gol!** what a goal!

meñique *m* little finger.

mercadillo *m* flea market.

mercado *m* market.

mercancía *f* merchandise.

mercantil *adj* commercial.

mercería *f* haberdasher's (shop) *(Br)*, notions store *(Am)*.

mercurio *m* mercury.

merecer *vt* to deserve ☐ **merecerse** *vpr* to deserve.

merendar *vt* = to have for tea
◆ *vi* = to have tea.

merendero *m* open air café or bar in the country or on the beach.

merengue *m* meringue.

meridiano, -na *adj (evidente)* crystal-clear; *(del mediodía)* midday *(antes de s)* ◆ *m* meridian.

meridional *adj* southern.

merienda *f (de media tarde)* tea *(light afternoon meal)*; *(para excursión)* picnic.

mérito *m* merit.

merluza *f* hake; **~ a la plancha** grilled hake; **~ a la romana** hake fried in batter.

mermelada *f* jam.

mero *m* grouper; **~ a la plancha**

grilled grouper.

mes m month; (salario mensual) monthly salary; **en el ~ de** in (the month of).

mesa f table; (escritorio) desk; (de personas) committee; **poner la ~** to lay the table; **quitar la ~** to clear the table.

mesero, -ra m, f (Amér) waiter (f waitress).

meseta f plateau.

mesilla f: **~ de noche** bedside table.

mesón m (restaurante) old, country-style restaurant and bar.

mestizo, -za m, f person of mixed race.

meta f goal; (de carrera) finishing line.

metáfora f metaphor.

metal m metal.

metálico, -ca adj (de metal) metal ◆ m cash; **en ~** in cash.

meteorito m meteorite.

meteorología f meteorology.

meter vt 1. (introducir, ingresar, invertir) to put in; **~ algo/a alguien en algo** to put sthg/sb in sthg; **lo han metido en la cárcel** they've put him in prison.
2. (hacer partícipe): **~ a alguien en algo** to get sb into sthg.
3. (fam: hacer soportar): **nos meterá su discurso** she'll make us listen to her speech.
4. (fam: imponer, echar) to give; **me han metido una multa** they've given me a fine; **le metieron una bronca** they told him off.
5. (causar): **~ miedo/prisa a alguien** to scare/rush sb.

❑ **meterse** vpr (entrar) to get in; (estar) to get to; (entrometerse) to meddle; **~se a** (dedicarse a) to become; (empezar) to start; **~se en** (mezclarse con) to get involved in; **meterse con** v + prep (molestar) to hassle; (atacar) to go for.

método m (modo ordenado) method; (de enseñanza) course.

metralla f (munición) shrapnel; (fragmento) piece of shrapnel.

metro m (unidad de longitud) metre; (transporte) underground (Br), subway (Am); (instrumento) tape measure.

metrópoli f metropolis.

mexicano, -na adj & m, f Mexican.

México s Mexico.

mezcla f mixture.

mezclar vt to mix; (confundir, involucrar) to mix up ❑ **mezclarse en** v + prep to get mixed up in.

mezquino, -na adj mean.

mezquita f mosque.

mg (abrev de miligramo) mg.

mi (pl mis) adj my.

mí pron (después de preposición) me; (reflexivo) myself; **¡a ~ qué!** so what!; **por lo que a ~ se refiere** as far as I'm concerned ...

mico m monkey.

microbio m germ.

micrófono m microphone.

microondas m inv microwave (oven).

microscopio m microscope.

miedo m fear; **tener ~ de** to be afraid of.

miedoso, -sa adj fearful.

miel f honey.

miembro *m (de grupo, asociación)* member; *(extremidad)* limb.

mientras *conj (a la vez)* while; ~ **no se apruebe** until it has been approved; ~ **(que)** whilst; ~ **(tanto)** in the meantime.

miércoles *m inv* Wednesday, → **sábado.**

mierda *f (vulg)* shit ◆ *interj (vulg)* shit!

mies *f (cereal)* ripe corn; *(siega)* harvest time.

miga *f* crumb; *(parte sustanciosa)* substance ❑ **migas** *fpl (guiso)* fried breadcrumbs.

migaja *f* crumb.

mil *núm* a thousand; **dos** ~ **two** thousand; → **seis.**

milagro *m* miracle; **de** ~ miraculously.

milenario, -ria *adj* ancient ◆ *m* millennium.

milenio *m* millennium.

milésimo, -ma *adj* thousandth.

mili *f (fam)* military service; **hacer la** ~ *(fam)* to do one's military service.

miligramo *m* milligram.

mililitro *m* millilitre.

milímetro *m* millimetre.

militante *mf* militant.

militar *adj* military ◆ *m* soldier.

milla *f (en tierra)* mile; *(en mar)* nautical mile.

millar *m* thousand.

millón *núm* million; **dos millones** two million, → **seis.**

millonario, -ria *m, f* millionaire *(f* millionairess).

mimado, -da *adj* spoilt.

mimar *vt* to spoil.

mímica *f* mime.

mimosa *f* mimosa.

min *(abrev de minuto)* min.

mina *f* mine; *(de lápiz)* lead.

mineral *adj & m* mineral.

minero, -ra *m, f* miner.

miniatura *f* miniature.

minifalda *f* mini skirt.

mínimo, -ma *superl* → **pequeño** ◆ *adj & m* minimum; **como** ~ at the very least.

ministerio *m* ministry.

ministro, -tra *m, f* minister.

minoría *f* minority.

minoritario, -ria *adj* minority *(antes de s).*

minucioso, -sa *adj (persona)* meticulous; *(trabajo)* very detailed.

minúscula *f* small letter; **en** ~ in lower-case letters.

minúsculo, -la *adj (muy pequeño)* minute.

minusválido, -da *m, f* disabled person.

minutero *m* minute hand.

minuto *m* minute.

mío, mía *adj* mine ◆ *pron*: **el** ~, **la mía** mine; **lo** *(lo que me gusta)* my thing; **un amigo** ~ a friend of mine.

miope *adj* shortsighted.

miopía *f* shortsightedness.

mirada *f* look; *(rápida)* glance; **echar una** ~ a to have a quick look at.

mirador *m (lugar)* viewpoint; *(balcón cerrado)* enclosed balcony.

mirar *vt (ver)* to look at; *(observar, vigilar)* to watch; *(considerar)* to consider ◆ vi (buscar) to look; ~ a (estar orientado) to face; **estoy mirando** (en tienda) I'm just looking ❑ **mirarse** vpr to look at o.s.

mirilla f spyhole.

mirlo m blackbird.

mirón, -ona m, f (espectador) onlooker.

misa f mass; ~ **del gallo** midnight mass.

miserable adj (muy pobre) poor; (desgraciado, lastimoso) wretched; (mezquino) mean.

miseria f (pobreza) poverty; (poca cantidad) pittance.

misericordia f compassion.

misil m missile.

misión f mission; (tarea) task.

misionero, -ra m, f missionary.

mismo, -ma adj (igual) same ◆ pron: **el ~, la misma** the same ~; **el que vi ayer** the same one I saw yesterday; **ahora ~** right now; **lo ~ (que)** the same thing (as); **da lo ~** it doesn't matter; **en este ~ cuarto** in this very room; **yo ~** I myself.

misterio m (secreto) mystery; (sigilo) secrecy.

misterioso, -sa adj mysterious.

mitad f (parte) half; (centro, medio) middle; **a ~ de camino** halfway there; **a ~ de precio** half-price; **en ~ de** in the middle of.

mitin m rally.

mito m myth.

mitología f mythology.

mitote m (Amér: fam) racket; **armar un ~** to make a racket.

mixto, -ta adj (colegio, vestuario) mixed; (comisión, agrupación) joint ◆ m ham and cheese toasted sandwich.

ml (abrev de mililitro) ml.

mm (abrev de milímetro) mm.

mobiliario m furniture.

mocasín m moccasin.

mochila f backpack.

mocho, -cha (fregona) mop.

mochuelo m little owl.

moco m mucus; **tener ~s** to have a runny nose.

moda f fashion; **a la ~** fashionable; **estar de ~** to be fashionable; **pasado de ~** unfashionable.

modalidad f (variante) type; (en deporte) discipline.

modelo m model; (vestido) number ◆ mf model.

modem (pl **modems**) m modem.

modernismo m (en arte) Modernismo.

modernista adj (en arte) Modernista.

moderno, -na adj modern.

modestia f modesty.

modesto, -ta adj modest.

modificación f alteration.

modificar vt to alter.

modisto, -ta m, f (sastre) tailor (f dressmaker).

modo m (manera) way; (en gramática) mood; **de ~ que** (de manera que) in such a way that; **de ningún ~** in no way; **de todos ~s** in any case; **en cierto ~** in some ways; ~ **de empleo** instructions (pl).

moflete m chubby cheek.

mogollón m (fam: cantidad) loads (pl).

moho m (hongo) mould.

mojado, -da adj (empapado) wet; (húmedo) damp.

mojar vt (empapar) to wet; (humedecer) to dampen; (pan) to dunk ❑ **mojarse** vpr to get wet.

molde m mould.

moldeado m (en peluquería) soft perm.

moldear vt (dar forma) to mould; (en peluquería) to give a soft perm to.

mole m (Amér) chilli sauce containing green tomatoes, spices and sometimes chocolate and peanuts.

molestar vt (incordiar) to annoy; (disgustar) to bother; (doler) to hurt ❑ **molestarse** vpr (enfadarse, ofenderse) to take offence; (darse trabajo) to bother.

molestia f (fastidio) nuisance; (dolor) discomfort.

molesto, -ta adj (fastidioso) annoying; **estar ~** (enfadado) to be annoyed.

molino m mill; **~ de viento** windmill.

molusco m mollusc.

momento m moment; (época) time; **hace un ~** a moment ago; **por el ~** for the moment; **de un ~ a otro** any minute now; **¡un ~!** just a moment!

momia f mummy.

mona: **mona de Pascua** f round sponge cake coated in chocolate with a chocolate egg on top, → **mono**.

monada f (fam) (cosa) lovely thing; (niño) little darling.

monaguillo m altar boy.

monarca m monarch.

monarquía f monarchy.

monasterio m monastery.

Moncloa f: **la ~** the Moncloa palace.

 LA MONCLOA

The Moncloa palace has been the official residence of the Spanish premier and the seat of the Spanish government since 1977. It is situated in the northwest of Madrid, near the Complutense university campus. It forms part of a complex of government buildings and has been rebuilt several times, most notably after the Spanish Civil War.

moneda f (pieza) coin; (divisa) currency; **~ de duro** five-peseta coin.

monedero m purse.

monitor, -ra m, f (persona) instructor ◆ m monitor.

monja f nun.

monje m monk.

mono, -na adj lovely ◆ m, f (animal) monkey ◆ m (con peto) dungarees (pl); (con mangas) overalls (pl); **¡qué ~!** how lovely!

monólogo m monologue.

monopatín m skateboard.

monopolio m monopoly.

monótono, -na adj monotonous.

monstruo m monster.

montacargas m inv goods lift (Br), freight elevator (Am).

montaje m (de una máquina) assembly; (de espectáculo) staging;

(de película) editing; *(estafa)* put-up job.

montaña *f* mountain; **~ rusa** roller coaster.

montañismo *m* mountaineering.

montañoso, -sa *adj* mountainous.

montar *vt (caballo, burro)* to ride; *(tienda de campaña)* to put up; *(máquina, instalación)* to assemble; *(negocio, tienda)* to set up; *(clara de huevo)* to beat; *(nata)* to whip; *(película)* to edit ♦ *vi (subir)*: **~ en** *(animal, bicicleta)* to get on; *(coche)* to get into; **~ en bicicleta** to ride a bicycle; **~ a caballo** to ride a horse.

monte *m (montaña)* mountain; *(bosque)* woodland.

montera *f* bullfighter's cap.

montón *m* heap; **un ~ de** *(fam)* loads of.

montura *f (de gafas)* frame; *(caballo, burro, etc)* mount.

monumental *adj (lugar, ciudad)* famous for its monuments; *(enorme)* monumental.

monumento *m* monument.

moño *m* bun.

MOPU *m (abrev de Ministerio de Obras Públicas y Urbanismo)* Spanish ministry of public works and town planning.

moqueta *f* (fitted) carpet.

mora *f* blackberry, → **moro**.

morado, -da *adj* purple ♦ *m (color)* purple; *(herida)* bruise.

moral *adj* moral ♦ *f* morality; *(ánimo)* morale.

moraleja *f* moral.

moralista *mf* moralist.

morcilla *f ≈* black pudding *(Br)*, *≈* blood sausage *(Am)*.

mordaza *f* gag.

mordedura *f* bite.

morder *vt* to bite.

mordida *f (Amér: fam)* bribe.

mordisco *m* bite.

moreno, -na *adj (por el sol)* tanned; *(piel, pelo)* dark.

moribundo, -da *adj* dying.

morir *vi* to die ☐ **morirse** *vpr (fallecer)* to die; *(fig: tener deseo fuerte)* to be dying.

moro, -ra *adj* Moorish ♦ *m, f* Moor.

morocho, -cha *adj (Amér) (fam: robusto)* tough; *(moreno)* dark.

moroso, -sa *m, f* defaulter.

morralla *f (Amér)* change.

morro *m (de animal)* snout; *(vulg: de persona)* thick lips *(pl)*; **por el ~** *(fam)* without asking.

morsa *f* walrus.

mortadela *f* Mortadella, *type of cold pork sausage*.

mortal *adj (vida)* mortal; *(herida, accidente)* fatal; *(fig: aburrido)* deadly.

mortero *m* mortar.

mosaico *m* mosaic.

mosca *f* fly; **por si las ~s** just in case.

moscatel *m* Muscatel.

mosquito *m* mosquito.

mostaza *f* mustard.

mostrador *m (en tienda)* counter; *(en bar)* bar; **"~ de facturación"** "check-in desk".

mostrar *vt* to show ☐ **mostrarse** *vpr*: **se mostró muy interesado** he expressed great interest.

motel m motel.

motivación f (motivo) motive.

motivar vt (causar) to cause.

motivo m (causa, razón) reason; (en música, pintura) motif; con ~ de (a causa de) because of; (con ocasión de) on the occasion of.

moto f motorbike, motorcycle; ~ acuática jet-ski.

motocicleta f motorbike, motorcycle.

motociclismo m motorcycling.

motociclista mf motorcyclist.

motocross m inv motocross.

motor m engine, motor; ~ de arranque starter.

motora f motorboat.

motorista mf motorcyclist.

mountain bike f mountain biking.

mousse f mousse; ~ de chocolate chocolate mousse; ~ de limón lemon mousse.

mover vt to move; (hacer funcionar) to drive ❑ **moverse** vpr (fam: realizar gestiones) to make an effort.

movida f (fam) scene.

movido, -da adj (persona) restless.

móvil adj mobile ◆ m (motivo) motive.

movimiento m movement; (circulación) activity; (de cuenta corriente) transactions (pl).

mozárabe adj Mozarabic ◆ m Mozarabic style.

mozo, -za m, f young boy (f young girl) ◆ m (de hotel, estación) porter; (recluta) conscript; (Amér:

camarero) waiter.

mucamo, -ma m, f (Amér) servant.

muchacha f (fam: criada) maid, → muchacho.

muchachada f (Amér) crowd of young people.

muchacho, -cha m, f boy (f girl).

muchedumbre f crowd.

mucho, -cha adj a lot of ◆ pron a lot ◆ adv a lot; (indica comparación) much; **tengo ~ sueño** I'm very sleepy; ~ antes long before; ~ gusto (saludo) pleased to meet you; como ~ at most; ¡con ~ gusto! (encantado) with pleasure!; vinieron ~s a lot of people came; ni ~ menos by no means; por ~ que no matter how much.

mudanza f (de casa) move.

mudar vt (piel, plumas) to moult ❑ **mudarse** vpr (de ropa) to change; ~se (de casa) to move (house).

mudéjar adj Mudejar ◆ m Mudejar style.

mudo, -da adj (que no habla) dumb; (película, letra) silent ◆ m, f mute.

mueble m piece of furniture; los ~s the furniture.

mueca f (gesto) face; (de dolor) grimace.

muela f (diente) tooth.

muelle m (de colchón) spring; (de puerto) dock.

muerte f (fallecimiento) death; (homicidio) murder.

muerto, -ta pp → morir ◆ adj dead ◆ m, f dead person; ~ de frío freezing; ~ **de hambre** starving.

muestra *f (de mercancía)* sample; *(señal)* sign; *(demostración)* demonstration; *(exposición)* show; *(prueba)* proof.

mugido *m* moo.

mugir *vi* to moo.

mujer *f* woman; *(esposa)* wife.

mulato, -ta *m, f* mulatto.

muleta *f (bastón)* crutch; *(de torero)* muleta, *red cape hanging from a stick used to tease the bull.*

mulo, -la *m, f* mule.

multa *f* fine.

multar *vt* to fine.

multicine *m* multiscreen cinema.

multinacional *f* multinational.

múltiple *adj* multiple □ **múltiples** *adj pl (numerosos)* numerous.

multiplicación *f* multiplication.

multiplicar *vt* to multiply □ **multiplicarse** *vpr (persona)* to do lots of things at the same time.

multitud *f (de personas)* crowd.

mundial *adj* world *(antes de s)*.

mundo *m* world; **un hombre de** ~ a man of the world; **todo el** ~ everyone.

munición *f* ammunition.

municipal *adj* municipal ♦ *m, f* local police officer who deals mainly with traffic offences.

municipio *m (territorio)* town; *(organismo)* town council.

muñeca *f (de la mano)* wrist, → **muñeco.**

muñeco, -ca *m, f* doll.

muñeira *f* type of music and dance from Galicia.

muñequera *f* wristband.

mural *m* mural.

muralla *f* wall.

murciélago *m* bat.

muro *m* wall.

musa *f* muse.

músculo *m* muscle.

museo *m* museum; ~ **de arte** art gallery.

musgo *m* moss.

música *f* music; ~ **ambiental** background music; ~ **clásica** classical music; ~ **pop** pop music, → **músico.**

musical *adj* musical.

músico, -ca *m, f* musician.

muslo *m* thigh; ~ **de pollo** drumstick.

musulmán, -ana *adj & m, f* Muslim.

mutilado, -da *m, f* cripple.

mutua *f* mutual benefit society.

muy *adv* very.

N

nabo *m* turnip.

nacer *vi (persona, animal)* to be born; *(vegetal)* to sprout; *(arroyo, río)* to rise.

nacimiento *m (de persona, animal)* birth; *(de vegetal)* sprouting; *(de río, arroyo)* source; *(belén)* Nativity scene.

nación *f* nation.

nacional adj national; (vuelo, mercado) domestic.

nacionalidad f nationality.

nada pron (ninguna cosa) nothing; (en negativas) anything ♦ adv: no me gustó ~ I didn't like it at all; de ~ (respuesta a "gracias") you're welcome; ~ más nothing else; ~ más llegar as soon as he arrived.

nadador, -ra m, f swimmer.

nadar vi to swim.

nadie pron nobody; no se lo dije a ~ I didn't tell anybody.

nailon® ['nailon] m nylon.

naipe m (playing) card.

nalga f buttock ❑ **nalgas** fpl backside (sg).

nana f lullaby.

naranja adj inv, m & f orange; ~ exprimida freshly-squeezed orange juice.

naranjada f orange squash.

naranjo m orange tree.

narcotraficante mf drug trafficker.

narcotráfico m drug trafficking.

nariz (pl -ces) f nose.

narración f (relato) story.

narrador, -ra m, f narrator.

narrar vt to tell.

narrativa f narrative.

nata f cream; ~ **montada** whipped cream.

natación f swimming.

natillas fpl custard (sg).

nativo, -va m, f native.

natural adj natural; (alimento) fresh; ser ~ de to come from; al ~ (fruta) in its own juice.

naturaleza f nature; por ~ by nature.

naufragar vi to be wrecked.

naufragio m shipwreck.

náuseas fpl nausea (sg); tener ~ to feel sick.

náutico, -ca adj (de navegación) nautical; (DEP) water (antes de s).

navaja f (pequeña) penknife; (más grande) jackknife; (de afeitar) razor; (molusco) razor clam.

naval adj naval.

nave f (barco) ship; (de iglesia) nave; (en una fábrica) plant; ~ **espacial** spaceship.

navegable adj navigable.

navegar vi (en barco) to sail.

Navidad f Christmas (Day) ❑ **Navidades** fpl Christmas (sg).

nazareno m man dressed in hood and tunic who takes part in Holy Week processions.

neblina f mist.

necedad f (cualidad) stupidity; (dicho) stupid thing.

necesario, -ria adj necessary.

neceser m toilet bag.

necesidad f need; de primera ~ essential ❑ **necesidades** fpl: hacer sus ~es to answer the call of nature.

necesitar vt to need; "se necesita ..." "... wanted".

necio, -cia adj foolish.

nécora f fiddler crab.

necrológicas fpl obituaries.

negación f (desmentido) denial; (negativa) refusal.

negado, -da adj useless.

negar vt to deny ❑ **negarse** vpr: ~se (a) to refuse (to).

negativa *f* (*negativa*) refusal; (*desmentido*) denial.

negativo, -va *adj & m* negative.

negociable *adj* negotiable.

negociación *f* negotiation.

negociador, -ra *m, f* negotiator.

negociar *vt* to negotiate ◆ *vi* (*comerciar*) to do business; ~ en to deal in.

negocio *m* business; (*transacción*) deal; (*beneficio*) good deal; **hacer ~s** to do business.

negro, -gra *adj & m* black ◆ *m, f* (*persona*) black man (*f* black woman).

nene, -na *m, f* (*fam*) baby.

nenúfar *m* water lily.

nervio *m* (*de persona*) nerve; (*de planta*) vein; (*de carne*) sinew; (*vigor*) energy ❑ **nervios** *mpl* (*estado mental*) nerves.

nerviosismo *m* nerves (*pl*).

nervioso, -sa *adj* nervous; (*irritado*) worked-up.

neto, -ta *adj* (*peso, precio*) net; (*contorno, línea*) clean.

neumático *m* tyre.

neurosis *f inv* neurosis.

neutral *adj* neutral.

neutro, -tra *adj* neutral.

nevada *f* snowfall.

nevado, -da *adj* snowy.

nevar *v impers:* **está nevando** it's snowing.

nevera *f* fridge (*Br*), icebox (*Am*).

ni *conj:* **no ... ~ ...** neither ... nor ...; **no es alto ~ bajo** he's neither tall nor short; **~ mañana ~ pasado** neither tomorrow nor the day

after; **~ un/una ...** not a single ...; **~ siquiera lo ha probado** she hasn't even tried it; **~ que** as if.

◆ *adv* not even; **está tan atareado que ~ come** he's so busy he doesn't even eat.

Nicaragua *s* Nicaragua.

nicaragüense *adj & mf* Nicaraguan.

nicho *m* niche.

nido *m* nest.

niebla *f* (*densa*) fog; (*neblina*) mist; **hay ~** it's foggy.

nieto, -ta *m, f* grandson (*f* granddaughter).

nieve *f* snow.

NIF *m* (*abrev de número de identificación fiscal*) = National Insurance number (*Br*), identification number for tax purposes.

ningún *adj* → **ninguno.**

ninguno, -na *adj no* ◆ *pron* (*ni uno*) none; (*nadie*) nobody; **no tengo ningún abrigo** I don't have a coat; **~ me gusta** I don't like any of them; **~ de los dos** neither of them.

niña *f* (*del ojo*) pupil, → **niño.**

niñera *f* nanny.

niñez *f* childhood.

niño, -ña *m, f* (*cría*) child, boy (*f* girl); (*bebé*) baby; **los ~s** the children.

níquel *m* nickel.

níspero *m* medlar.

nítido, -da *adj* clear.

nitrógeno *m* nitrogen.

nivel *m* level; **al ~ de** level with; **~ de vida** standard of living.

no *adv* (*de negación*) not; (*en respuestas*) no; **¿~ vienes?** aren't you coming?; **estamos de acuerdo ¿~?** so, we're agreed then, are we?; **~ sé** I don't know; **~ veo nada** I can't see anything; **¿cómo ~?** of course; **eso sí que ~** certainly not; **¡qué ~!** I said no!

nº (abrev de número) no.

noble adj (metal) precious; (honrado) noble ♦ mf noble.

nobleza f nobility.

noche f (más tarde) night; (atardecer) evening; **ayer por la ~** last night; **esta ~** tonight; **por la ~** at night; **las diez de la ~** ten o'clock at night.

Nochebuena f Christmas Eve.

nochero m (Amér) (vigilante nocturno) night watchman; (trasnochador) night owl; (mesita de noche) bedside table.

Nochevieja f New Year's Eve.

NOCHEVIEJA

New Year's Eve traditions in Spain include the dancing of the "cotillón" to see out the old year and the eating of twelve grapes, one for each of the twelve chimes of midnight, which supposedly brings good luck for the coming year.

---

noción f notion ❑ **nociones** fpl: **tener nociones de** to have a smattering of.

nocivo, -va adj harmful.

noctámbulo, -la m, f night owl.

nocturno, -na adj (tren, vuelo, club) night (antes de s); (clase) evening (antes de s).

nogal m walnut.

nómada mf nomad.

nombrar vt (mencionar) to mention; (para un cargo) to appoint.

nombre m name; (en gramática) noun; **a ~ de** (cheque) on behalf of; (carta) addressed to; **~ de pila** first name; **~ y apellidos** full name.

nomeolvides m inv forget-me-not.

nómina f (lista de empleados) payroll; (sueldo) wages (pl).

nopal m (Amér) prickly pear.

nórdico, -ca adj (del norte) northern; (escandinavo) Nordic.

noreste m north-east.

noria f (de feria) Ferris wheel, big wheel (Br).

norma f (principio) standard; (regla) rule.

normal adj normal.

normalmente adv normally.

noroeste m north-west.

norte m north.

Norteamérica s North America.

norteamericano, -na adj & m, f (North) American.

Noruega s Norway.

noruego, -ga adj, m, f Norwegian.

nos pron (complemento directo) us; (complemento indirecto) (to) us; (reflexivo) ourselves; (recíproco) each other; **~ vamos** we're going.

nosotros, -tras pron (sujeto) we; (complemento) us.

nostalgia f (de país, casa) homesickness.

nostálgico, -ca adj (de país, casa) homesick.

nota f note; (en educación) mark; (cuenta) bill; **tomar ~ de** to note down.

notable adj remarkable.

notar vt (darse cuenta de) to notice; (sentir) to feel.

notario, -ria m, f notary.

noticia f piece of news ☐ **noticias** fpl (telediario) news (sg).

novatada f (broma) joke (played on new arrivals).

novato, -ta m, f beginner.

novecientos, -tas núm nine hundred, → **seis**.

novedad f (cualidad) newness; (suceso) new development; (cosa) new thing; **"~es"** (discos) "new releases"; (ropa) "latest fashion" (sg).

novela f novel; **~ de aventuras** adventure story; **~ policíaca** detective story; **~ rosa** romantic novel.

novelesco, -ca adj fictional.

novelista mf novelist.

noveno, -na núm ninth, → **sexto**.

noventa núm ninety, → **seis**.

noviazgo m engagement.

noviembre m November, → **setiembre**.

novillada f bullfight with young bulls.

novillero m apprentice bull-fighter.

novillo, -lla m, f young bull (f young cow) (2-3 years old).

novio, -via m, f (prometido) fiancé (f fiancée); (amigo) boyfriend (f girlfriend) ☐ **novios** mpl (recién casados) newly weds.

nubarrón m storm cloud.

nube f cloud.

nublado, -da adj cloudy.

nublarse v impers: **se está nublando** it's clouding over.

nubosidad f cloudiness.

nuboso, -sa adj cloudy.

nuca f nape.

nuclear adj nuclear.

núcleo m (parte central) centre.

nudillos mpl knuckles.

nudismo m nudism.

nudista mf nudist.

nudo m (de cuerda, hilo) knot; (de comunicaciones) major junction; (en argumento) crux.

nuera f daughter-in-law.

nuestro, -tra adj our ♦ pron: **el ~, la nuestra** ours; **lo ~** (lo que nos gusta) our thing; **un amigo ~** a friend of ours.

nuevamente adv again.

Nueva Zelanda s New Zealand.

nueve núm nine, → **seis**.

nuevo, -va adj new; **de ~** again.

nuez (pl -ces) f (fruto seco en general) nut; (de nogal) walnut; (del cuello) Adam's apple.

nulidad f (anulación) nullity; (persona) useless idiot.

nulo, -la adj (sin valor legal) null and void; (inepto) useless.

núm. (abrev de número) no.

numerado, -da adj numbered.

número m number; (de lotería) ticket; (de una publicación) issue; (talla) size; **~ de teléfono** telephone number.

numeroso, -sa adj numerous.

numismática *f* coin-collecting.

nunca *adv* never; *(en negativas)* ever.

nupcial *adj* wedding *(antes de s)*.

nupcias *fpl* wedding *(sg)*.

nutria *f* otter.

nutrición *f* nutrition.

nutritivo, -va *adj* nutritious.

ñandú *m* rhea.

ñato, -ta *adj (Amér)* snub.

ñoñería *f* insipidness.

ñoño, -ña *adj (remilgado)* squeamish; *(quejica)* whining; *(soso)* dull.

ñoqui *m* gnocchi *(pl)*.

ñudo: al ñudo *adv (Amér)* in vain.

o *conj* or; **~ sea** in other words.

oasis *m inv* oasis.

obedecer *vt* to obey ❑ **obedecer a** *v + prep (ser motivado por)* to be due to.

obediencia *f* obedience.

obediente *adj* obedient.

obesidad *f* obesity.

obeso, -sa *adj* obese.

obispo *m* bishop.

objeción *f* objection.

objetividad *f* objectivity.

objetivo, -va *adj* objective ♦

m (finalidad) objective; *(blanco)* target; *(lente)* lens.

objeto *m* object; *(finalidad)* purpose; **con el ~ de** with the aim of; **"~s perdidos"** "lost property".

obligación *f (deber)* obligation; *(de una empresa)* bond.

obligar *vt* to force ❑ **obligarse a** *v + prep (comprometerse a)* to undertake to.

obligatorio, -ria *adj* compulsory.

obra *f (realización)* work; *(en literatura)* book; *(en teatro)* play; *(en música)* opus; *(edificio en construcción)* building site; **~ de caridad** charity; **~ (de teatro)** play ❑ **obras** *fpl (reformas)* alterations; **"obras"** *(en carretera)* "roadworks".

obrador *m* workshop.

obrero, -ra *m, f* worker.

obsequiar *vt*: **~ a alguien con algo** to present sb with sthg.

obsequio *m* gift.

observación *f* observation.

observador, -ra *adj* observant.

observar *vt* to observe; *(darse cuenta de)* to notice.

observatorio *m* observatory.

obsesión *f* obsession.

obsesionar *vt* to obsess ❑ **obsesionarse** *vpr* to be obsessed.

obstáculo *m* obstacle.

obstante: no obstante *conj* nevertheless.

obstinado, -da *adj (persistente)* persistent; *(terco)* obstinate.

obstruir *vt* to obstruct ❑ **obstruirse** *vpr (agujero, cañería)* to get blocked (up).

obtener vt to get.

obvio, -via adj obvious.

oca f (ave) goose; (juego) board game similar to snakes and ladders.

ocasión f (momento determinado) moment; (vez) occasion; (oportunidad) chance; **de ~** (rebajado) bargain (antes de e).

ocasional adj (eventual) occasional; (casual) accidental.

ocaso m (de sol) sunset; (fig: decadencia) decline.

occidental adj western.

occidente m west ❑ **Occidente** m the West.

océano m ocean.

ochenta núm eighty, → **seis**.

ocho núm eight, → **seis**.

ochocientos, -tas núm eight hundred, → **seis**.

ocio m leisure.

ocioso, -sa adj (inactivo) idle.

ocre adj inv ochre.

octavo, -va núm eighth, → **sexto**.

octubre m October, → **setiembre**.

oculista mf ophthalmologist.

ocultar vt (esconder) to hide; (callar) to cover up.

oculto, -ta adj hidden.

ocupación f occupation; (oficio) job.

ocupado, -da adj (plaza, asiento) taken; (aparcamiento) full; (lavabo) engaged; (atareado) busy; (invadido) occupied; **"ocupado"** (taxi) sign indicating that a taxi is not for hire.

ocupar vt to occupy; (habitar) to live in; (mesa) to sit at; (en tiempo)

to take up; (cargo, posición, etc) to hold; (dar empleo) to provide work for ❑ **ocuparse de** v + prep (encargarse de) to deal with; (persona) to look after.

ocurrir vi to happen ❑ **ocurrirse** vpr: **no se me ocurre la respuesta** I can't think of the answer.

odiar vt to hate.

odio m hatred.

oeste m west.

ofensiva f offensive.

oferta f (propuesta) offer; (en precio) bargain; (surtido) range.

oficial adj official ◆ m, f (militar) officer.

oficina f office; **~ de correos** post office; **~ de objetos perdidos** lost property office; **~ de turismo** tourist office.

oficinista mf office worker.

oficio m (profesión) trade; (empleo) job; (misa) service.

ofrecer vt to offer; (mostrar) to present ❑ **ofrecerse** vpr (ser voluntario) to volunteer.

oftalmología f ophthalmology.

ogro m ogre.

oído m (sentido) hearing; (órgano) ear; **hablar al ~ a alguien** to have a word in sb's ear.

oír vt (ruido, música, etc) to hear; (atender) to listen to; **¡oiga, por favor!** excuse me!

ojal m buttonhole.

ojalá interj if only!

ojeras fpl bags under the eyes.

ojo m eye; (de cerradura) keyhole ◆ interj watch out!; **~ de buey** porthole; **a ~** (fig) roughly.

OK [o'kej] *interj* OK.

okupa *mf (fam)* squatter.

ola *f* wave; **~ de calor** heatwave; **~ de frío** cold spell.

ole *interj* bravo!

oleaje *m* swell.

óleo *m* oil (painting).

oler *vt & vi* to smell; **~ bien** to smell good; **~ mal** to smell bad ❑ **olerse** *vpr* to sense.

olfato *m (sentido)* sense of smell; *(astucia)* nose.

olimpiadas *fpl* Olympics.

olímpico, -ca *adj* Olympic.

oliva *f* olive.

olivo *m* olive tree.

olla *f* pot; **~ a presión** pressure cooker.

olmo *m* elm (tree).

olor *m* smell.

olvidar *vt* to forget; *(dejarse)* to leave ❑ **olvidarse de** *v + prep (dejarse)* to leave.

olvido *m (en memoria)* forgetting; *(descuido)* oversight.

ombligo *m (de vientre)* navel; *(fig: centro)* heart.

omitir *vt* to omit.

once *núm* eleven, → **seis**.

ONCE *f* Spanish association for the blind.

ONCE

The ONCE is an independent organization which was originally set up to help the blind, although it now covers other disabled people as well. One of its main aims is to provide work for its members, and to this end it runs a daily national lottery, tickets for which are sold by the blind. The lottery is the ONCE's main source of income.

---

onda *f* wave.

ondulado, -da *adj* wavy.

ONU *f* UN.

opaco, -ca *adj* opaque.

opción *f* option; **tener ~ a** to be eligible for.

ópera *f* opera.

operación *f* operation; *(negocio)* transaction; **~ retorno/salida** *operation to assist travel of holiday-makers to/from city homes, minimizing congestion and maximizing road safety.*

operadora *f (de teléfonos)* operator.

operar *vt (enfermo)* to operate on; *(realizar)* to bring about ❑ **operarse** *vpr (del hígado, etc)* to have an operation.

operario, -ria *m, f* worker.

opinar *vt* to think ♦ *vi* to give one's opinion.

opinión *f* opinion; **la ~ pública** public opinion.

oponer *vt (obstáculo, resistencia)* to use against; *(razón, argumento, etc)* to put forward ❑ **oponerse** *vpr (contrarios, fuerzas)* to be opposed; **oponerse a** *v + prep (ser contrario a)* to oppose; *(negarse a)* to refuse to.

oportunidad *f* opportunity; **"~es"** bargains".

oportuno, -na *adj (adecuado)* appropriate; *(propicio)* timely;

(momento) right.

oposición f *(impedimento)* opposition; *(resistencia)* resistance; **la ~** the opposition ❑ **oposiciones** fpl *(para empleo)* public entrance examinations.

oprimir vt *(botón)* to press; *(reprimir)* to oppress.

optar: optar a v + prep *(aspirar a)* to go for ❑ **optar por** v + prep: **~ por algo** to choose sthg; **~ por hacer algo** to choose to do sthg.

optativo, -va adj optional.

óptica f *(ciencia)* optics; *(establecimiento)* optician's *(shop)*.

optimismo m optimism.

optimista adj optimistic.

óptimo, -ma superl → **bueno**.

opuesto, -ta pp → **oponer** ◆ adj *(contrario)* conflicting; **~ a** contrary to.

oración f *(rezo)* prayer; *(frase)* sentence.

orador, -ra m, f speaker.

oral adj oral.

órale interj *(Amér)* that's right!

orangután m orangutang.

órbita f *(de astro)* orbit; *(de ojo)* eye socket; *(ámbito)* sphere.

orca f killer whale.

orden[1] m order; **en ~** *(bien colocado)* tidy; *(en regla)* in order.

orden[2] f order.

ordenación f *(colocación)* arrangement; *(de sacerdote)* ordination.

ordenado, -da adj *(en orden)* tidy.

ordenador m computer.

ordenar vt *(colocar)* to arrange; *(armario, habitación)* to tidy up;

(mandar) to order; *(sacerdote)* to ordain.

ordeñar vt to milk.

ordinario, -ria adj *(habitual)* ordinary; *(basto, grosero)* coarse.

orégano m oregano.

oreja f ear; *(de sillón)* wing.

orgánico, -ca adj organic.

organillo m barrel organ.

organismo m *(de ser vivo)* body; *(institución)* organization.

organización f organization.

organizador, -ra m, f organizer.

organizar vt to organize; *(negocio, empresa, etc)* to set up.

órgano m organ.

orgullo m pride.

orgulloso, -sa adj proud; **~ de** proud of.

oriental adj *(del este)* eastern; *(del Lejano Oriente)* oriental ◆ mf oriental.

orientar vt *(guiar)* to direct; **~ algo hacia algo** to place sthg facing sthg.

oriente m *(punto cardinal)* east; *(viento)* east wind ❑ **Oriente** m: el **Oriente** the East.

orificio m hole.

origen m origin; *(motivo)* cause; *(ascendencia)* birth.

original adj original; *(extraño)* eccentric.

originario, -ria adj *(país, ciudad)* native; *(inicial)* original; **ser ~ de** to come from.

orilla f *(de mar, lago)* shore; *(de río)* bank; *(borde)* edge.

orillarse vpr *(Amér)* to move to one side.

orina f urine.

orinal m chamberpot.

orinar vi to urinate.

oro m (metal) gold; (riqueza) riches (pl) ❑ **oros** mpl (de la baraja) suit of Spanish cards bearing gold coins.

orquesta f (de música) orchestra; (lugar) orchestra pit.

orquestar vt to orchestrate.

orquídea f orchid.

ortiga f (stinging) nettle.

ortodoxo, -xa adj orthodox.

oruga f caterpillar.

os pron (complemento directo) you; (complemento indirecto) (to) you; (reflexivo) yourselves; (recíproco) each other.

oscilar vi (moverse) to swing; ~ (entre) (variar) to fluctuate (between).

oscuridad f (falta de luz) darkness; (confusión) obscurity.

oscuro, -ra adj dark; (confuso) obscure; (nublado) overcast; **a oscuras** in the dark.

oso, osa m, f bear; ~ **hormiguero** anteater.

osobuco m osso bucco.

ostra f oyster ❑ **ostras** interj (fam) wow!

OTAN f NATO.

otoño m autumn (Br), fall (Am).

otorrino, -na m, f (fam) ear, nose and throat specialist.

otorrinolaringólogo, -ga m, f ear, nose and throat specialist.

otro, otra adj another (sg), other (pl) ✦ pron (otra cosa) another (sg), others (pl); (otra persona) someone else; **el** ~ the other one; **los** ~**s** the others; ~ **vaso** another

glass; ~**s dos vasos** another two glasses; **el** ~ **día** the other day; **la otra tarde** the other evening.

ovalado, -da adj oval.

ovario m ovary.

oveja f sheep.

ovni ['ofni] m UFO.

óxido m (herrumbre) rust.

oxígeno m oxygen.

oyente mf listener.

ozono m ozone.

P

p. (abrev de paseo) Av.

pabellón m (edificio) pavilion; (de hospital) block; (tienda de campaña) bell tent; (de oreja) outer ear.

pacer vi to graze.

pachamama f (Amér) (mother) earth.

pacharán m liqueur made from brandy and sloes.

paciencia f patience; **perder la** ~ to lose one's patience; **tener** ~ to be patient.

paciente adj & mf patient.

pacificación f pacification.

pacífico, -ca adj peaceful ❑ **Pacífico** m: **el Pacífico** the Pacific.

pacifista mf pacifist.

pack m pack.

pacto m (entre personas) agreement.

padecer vt (enfermedad) to suf-

fer from; *(soportar)* to endure ♦ *vi*
to suffer; **padece del hígado** she
has liver trouble.

padrastro *m (pariente)* stepfather; *(pellejo)* hangnail.

padre *m* father ♦ *adj (Amér: fam:
estupendo)* brilliant ❑ **padres** *mpl
(de familia)* parents.

padrino *m (de boda)* best man;
(de bautizo) godfather ❑ **padrinos**
mpl godparents.

padrísimo *adj (Amér: fam)* brilliant.

padrote *m (Amér)* pimp.

paella *f* paella.

pág. *(abrev de página)* p.

paga *f (sueldo)* wages *(pl)*.

pagadero, -ra *adj*: ~ a 90 días
payable within 90 days.

pagano, -na *m, f* pagan.

pagar *vt (cuenta, deuda, etc)* to
pay; *(estudios, gastos, error)* to pay
for; *(corresponder)* to repay ♦ *vi* to
pay; **"pague en caja antes de retirar su vehículo"** "please pay before
leaving" *(sign in car park)*.

página *f* page.

pago *m* payment; *(recompensa)*
reward.

paila *f (Amér) (sartén)* frying pan;
(charco pequeño) small pool.

país *m* country.

paisaje *m* landscape; *(vista panorámica)* view.

paisano, -na *m, f (persona no
militar)* civilian; *(de país)* compatriot; *(de ciudad)* person from the
same city.

Países Bajos *mpl*: **los** ~ the
Netherlands.

País Vasco *m*: **el** ~ the Basque

country.

paja *f* straw; *(parte desechable)*
padding.

pajarita *f (corbata)* bow tie; ~
de papel paper bird.

pájaro *m* bird.

paje *m* page.

pala *f (herramienta)* spade; *(de
ping-pong)* bat; *(de cocina)* slice; *(de
remo, hacha)* blade.

palabra *f* word; **dar la** ~ **a
alguien** to give sb the floor; **de**
(hablando) by word of mouth ❑
palabras *fpl (discurso)* words.

palacio *m* palace; ~ **municipal**
(Amér) town hall.

**PALACIO DE LA
MONEDA**

The Palacio de la Moneda is the
official residence of the Chilean
president and the seat of the Chilean
government. It is here that the president holds Cabinet meetings and
receives State visits.

**PALACIO DE LA
ZARZUELA**

This is the current residence of
the Spanish monarch and is
situated in the El Pardo hills to the
northwest of Madrid. It was built
during the reign of Philip IV, who
used it as a country retreat and a
hunting lodge. A neoclassical building which consists of a single floor
built around an interior courtyard, it
was rebuilt in the 18th century and
redecorated in the rococo style.

paladar m palate.

paladear vt to savour.

palanca f lever; **~ de cambio** gear lever.

palangana f (para fregar) washing-up bowl; (para lavarse) wash bowl.

palco m box (at theatre).

paletilla f shoulder blade; **~ de cordero** shoulder of lamb.

pálido, -da adj pale.

palillo m (para dientes) toothpick; (para tambor) drumstick.

paliza f (zurra, derrota) beating; (esfuerzo) hard grind.

palma f (de mano, palmera) palm; (hoja de palmera) palm leaf □ **palmas** fpl applause (sg); **dar ~s** to applaud.

palmada f (golpe) pat; (ruido) clap.

palmera f (árbol) palm (tree).

palmitos mpl (de cangrejo) crab sticks; **~ a la vinagreta** crab sticks in vinegar.

palo m (de madera) stick; (de golf) club; (de portería) post; (de tienda de campaña) pole; (golpe) blow (with a stick); (de barco) mast; (en naipes) suit.

paloma f dove, pigeon.

palomar m dovecote.

palomitas fpl popcorn (sg).

palpitar vi (corazón) to beat; (sentimiento) to shine through.

palta f (Amér) avocado.

pamela f sun hat.

pampa f pampas (pl).

pan m (alimento) bread; (hogaza) loaf; **~ dulce** (Amér) (sweet) pastry; **~ integral** wholemeal bread; **~ de**

molde sliced bread; **~ de muerto** (Amér) sweet pastry eaten on All Saints' Day; **~ rallado** breadcrumbs (pl); **~ con tomate** bread rubbed with tomato and oil; **~ tostado** toast.

panadería f bakery.

panadero, -ra m, f baker.

panal m honeycomb.

Panamá s Panama.

panameño, -ña adj & m, f Panamanian.

pancarta f banner.

pandereta f tambourine.

pandilla f gang.

panecillo m (bread) roll.

panel m panel.

panera f (cesta) bread basket; (caja) bread bin.

pánico m panic.

panorama m (paisaje) panorama; (situación) overall state.

panorámica f panorama.

panorámico, -ca adj panoramic.

pantaletas fpl (Amér) knickers.

pantalla f (de cine, televisión) screen; (de lámpara) lampshade.

pantalones mpl trousers; **~ cortos** shorts; **~ vaqueros** jeans.

pantano m (embalse) reservoir; (ciénaga) marsh.

pantanoso, -sa adj marshy.

pantera f panther.

pantimedias fpl (Amér) tights.

pantorrilla f calf.

pantys mpl tights.

pañal m nappy (Br), diaper (Am); **~es higiénicos** disposable nappies.

paño m cloth; **~ de cocina** tea towel.

pañuelo m (para limpiarse) handkerchief; (de adorno) scarf.

Papa m: el ~ the Pope.

papá m (fam) dad; ~ **grande** (Amér) grandad ❑ **papás** mpl (fam: padres) parents.

papachador, -ra adj (Amér) pampering.

papachar vt (Amér) to spoil.

papagayo m parrot.

papalote m (Amér) kite.

papel m paper; (hoja) sheet of paper; (función, de actor) role; ~ **higiénico** toilet paper; ~ **pintado** wallpaper ❑ **papeles** mpl (documentos) papers.

papeleo m red tape.

papelera f wastepaper basket.

papelería f stationer's (shop).

papeleta f (de votación) ballot paper; (de examen) slip of paper with university exam results; (fig: asunto difícil) tricky thing.

paperas fpl mumps.

papilla f (alimento) baby food.

paquete m (postal) parcel; (de cigarrillos, klínex, etc) pack; ~ **turístico** package tour.

Paquistán m: el ~ Pakistan.

paquistaní adj & mf Pakistani.

par adj (número) even ◆ m (de zapatos, guantes, etc) pair; (de veces) couple; **abierto de ~ en ~** wide open; **sin ~** matchless; **un ~ de ...** a couple of ...

para prep **1.** (finalidad) for; **esta agua no es buena ~ beber** this water isn't fit for drinking; **lo he comprado ~ ti** I bought it for you; **te lo repetiré ~ que te enteres** I'll repeat it so you understand.

2. (motivación) (in order) to; **lo hecho ~ agradarte** I did it to please you.

3. (dirección) towards; **ir ~ casa** to head (for) home; **salir ~ el aeropuerto** to leave for the airport.

4. (tiempo) for; **lo tendré acabado ~ mañana** I'll have it finished for tomorrow.

5. (comparación) considering; **está muy delgado ~ lo que come** he's very thin considering how much he eats.

6. (inminencia, propósito): **la comida está lista ~ servir** the meal is ready to be served.

parabólica f satellite dish.

parabrisas m inv windscreen (Br), windshield (Am).

paracaídas m inv parachute.

parachoques m inv bumper (Br), fender (Am).

parada f stop; ~ **de autobús** bus stop; ~ **de taxis** taxi rank, → **parado**.

parado, -da adj (coche, máquina, etc) stationary; (desempleado) unemployed; (sin iniciativa) unenterprising ◆ m, f unemployed person.

paradoja f paradox.

paradójico, -ca adj paradoxical.

parador m (mesón) roadside inn; ~ **nacional** state-owned luxury hotel.

---

i **PARADOR NACIONAL**

A "parador nacional" is a building of artistic or historic interest which has been converted into a luxury four-star hotel and is run by the Spanish state. Although some may be found in cities, they are usually situated in the countryside, in places of outstanding natural beauty.

---

paraguas *m inv* umbrella.

Paraguay *s* Paraguay.

paraguayo, -ya *adj & m, f* Paraguayan.

paraíso *m* paradise.

paraje *m* spot.

paralelas *fpl* parallel bars.

paralelo, -la *adj & m* parallel.

parálisis *f inv* paralysis.

paralítico, -ca *m, f* paralytic.

paralizar *vt* to paralyse.

parapente *m* paraskiing.

parar *vt* to stop; *(Amér: levantar)* to lift ◆ *vi (detenerse)* to stop; *(hacer huelga)* to go on strike; ~ **de hacer algo** to stop doing sthg; "**para en todas las estaciones**" "stopping at all stations"; **sin** ~ non-stop.

pararse *vpr (detenerse)* to stop; *(Amér: ponerse de pie)* to stand up.

pararrayos *m inv* lightning conductor.

parasol *m* parasol.

parchís *m inv* ludo.

parcial *adj* partial; *(injusto)* biased ◆ *m (examen)* end-of-term examination.

pardo, -da *adj* dun-coloured.

parecer *m (opinión)* opinion ◆ *v copulativo* to look, to seem ◆ *v impers*: **me parece que ... I** think (that) ...; **parece que va a llover** it looks like it's going to rain; **¿qué te parece?** what do you think?; **buen** ~ good-looking ❑ **parecerse** *vpr* to look alike; ~**se a** to resemble.

parecido, -da *adj* similar ◆ *m* resemblance.

pared *f (muro)* wall.

pareja *f (conjunto de dos)* pair; *(de casados, novios)* couple; *(compañero)* partner.

parentesco *m* relationship.

paréntesis *m inv (signo de puntuación)* bracket; *(interrupción)* break; **entre** ~ in brackets.

pareo *m* wraparound skirt.

pariente, -ta *m, f* relative.

parking ['parkin] *m* car park.

parlamentario, -ria *m, f* member of parliament.

parlamento *m (asamblea legislativa)* parliament; *(discurso)* speech.

parlanchín, -ina *adj* talkative.

paro *m (desempleo)* unemployment; *(parada)* stoppage; *(huelga)* strike; **estar en** ~ to be unemployed.

parpadear *vi (ojos)* to blink.

párpado *m* eyelid.

parque *m (jardín)* park; *(de niños)* playpen; *(de automóviles)* fleet; ~ **acuático** waterpark; ~ **de atracciones** amusement park; ~ **de bomberos** fire station; ~ **infantil** children's playground; ~ **nacional** national park; ~ **zoológico** zoo.

Spanish national parks are areas of natural beauty that are pro-

parqué 202

tected by the government. Although admission is free, there are strict regulations governing what visitors may do, to minimize the damage they may cause to the surroundings. The best-known national parks are the Coto de Doñana in Huelva, the Ordesa national park in Huesca and the Delta del Ebro park in Tarragona.

parqué *m* parquet.

parquear *vt (Amér)* to park.

parquímetro *m* parking meter.

parra *f* vine.

párrafo *m* paragraph.

parrilla *f (para cocinar)* grill; *(Amér: baca)* roof rack; **a la ~** grilled.

parrillada *f* mixed grill; **~ de carne** selection of grilled meats; **~ de pescado** selection of grilled fish.

parroquia *f (iglesia)* parish church; *(conjunto de fieles)* parish; *(fig: clientela)* clientele.

parte *f (bando, lado, cara)* side ◆ *m* report; **dar ~ de algo** to report sthg; **de ~ de** *(en nombre de)* on behalf of; **¿de ~ de quién?** *(en el teléfono)* who's calling?; **en alguna ~** somewhere; **en otra ~** somewhere else; **en ~** partly; **en** O **por todas ~s** everywhere; **~ meteorológico** weather forecast; **por otra ~** *(además)* what is more.

participación *f (colaboración)* participation; *(de boda, bautizo)* notice; *(de lotería)* share.

participar *vi:* **~ (en)** to participate (in) ◆ *vt:* **~ algo a alguien** to notify sb of sthg.

partícula *f* particle.

particular *adj (privado)* private; *(propio)* particular; *(especial)* unusual; **en ~** in particular.

partida *f (marcha)* departure; *(en el juego)* game; *(certificado)* certificate; *(de género, mercancías)* consignment.

partidario, -ria *m, f* supporter; **ser ~ de** to be in favour of.

partidista *adj* partisan.

partido *m (en política)* party; *(en deporte)* game; **sacar ~ de** to make the most of; **~ de ida** away leg; **~ de vuelta** home leg.

partir *vt (dividir)* to divide; *(romper)* to break; *(nuez)* to crack; *(repartir)* to share ◆ *vi (ponerse en camino)* to set off; **a ~ de** from ❑ **partir de** *v + prep (tomar como base)* to start from.

partitura *f* score.

parto *m* birth.

parvulario *m* nursery school.

pasa *f* raisin.

pasable *adj* passable.

pasada *f (con trapo)* wipe; *(de pintura, barniz)* coat; *(en labores de punto)* row; **de ~** in passing.

pasado, -da *adj (semana, mes, etc)* last; *(viejo)* old; *(costumbre)* old-fashioned; *(alimento)* off, bad ◆ *m* past; **el año ~** last year; **bien ~** *(carne)* well-done; **~ de moda** old-fashioned; **~ mañana** the day after tomorrow.

pasaje *m (de avión, barco)* ticket; *(calle)* alley; *(conjunto de pasajeros)* passengers *(pl)*; *(de novela, ópera)* passage; **"~ particular"** "pedestrianized zone".

pasajero, -ra *adj* passing ◆ *m, f* passenger; "~s sin equipaje" "passengers with hand luggage only".

pasamanos *m inv* (*barandilla*) handrail.

pasaporte *m* passport.

pasar *vt* 1. (*deslizar, filtrar*) to pass; **me pasó la mano por el pelo** she ran her hand through my hair; **~ algo por** to pass sthg through.

2. (*cruzar*) to cross; **~ la calle** to cross the road.

3. (*acercar, hacer llegar*) to pass; **¿me pasas la sal?** would you pass me the salt?

4. (*contagiar*) **me has pasado la tos** you've given me your cough.

5. (*trasladar*) **~ algo a** to move sthg.

6. (*llevar adentro*) to show in; **nos pasó al salón** he showed us into the living room.

7. (*admitir*) to accept.

8. (*rebasar*) to go through; **no pases el semáforo en rojo** don't go through a red light.

9. (*sobrepasar*) **ya ha pasado los veinticinco** he's over twenty-five now.

10. (*tiempo*) to spend; **pasó dos años en Roma** she spent two years in Rome.

11. (*padecer*) to suffer.

12. (*adelantar*) to overtake.

13. (*aprobar*) to pass.

14. (*revisar*) to go over.

15. (*en cine*) to show.

16. (*en locuciones*) **~ lo bien/mal** to have a good/bad time; **~ lista** to call the register; **~ visita** to see one's patients.

◆ *vi* 1. (*ir, circular*) to go; **el autobús pasa por mi casa** the bus goes past my house; **el Manzanares pasa por Madrid** the Manzanares goes through Madrid; **~ de largo** to go by.

2. (*entrar*) to go in; **"no ~"** "no entry"; **¡pase!** come in!; **"pasen por caja"** "please pay at the till".

3. (*poder entrar*) to get through; **déjame más sitio, que no paso** move up, I can't get through.

4. (*ir un momento*) to pop in; **pasaré por tu casa** I'll drop by (your place).

5. (*suceder*) to happen; **¿qué (te) pasa?** what's the matter (with you)?; **¿qué pasa aquí?** what's going on here?; **pase lo que pase** whatever happens.

6. (*terminarse*) to be over; **cuando pase el verano** when the summer's over.

7. (*transcurrir*) to go by; **el tiempo pasa muy deprisa** time passes very quickly.

8. (*cambiar de acción, tema*) **~ a** to move on to.

9. (*servir*) to be all right; **puede ~** it'll do.

10. (*fam: prescindir*) **paso de política** I'm not into politics.

❏ **pasarse** *vpr* (*acabarse*) to pass; (*comida*) to go off; (*flores*) to fade; (*fam: propasarse*) to go over the top; (*tiempo*) **(omitir)** to miss out; **se me pasó decírtelo** I forgot to mention it to you; **no se le pasa nada** she doesn't miss a thing.

pasarela *f* (*de barco*) gangway; (*para modelos*) catwalk.

pasatiempo *m* pastime.

Pascua *f* (*en primavera*) Easter ◆

Pascuas *fpl (Navidad)* Christmas *(sg)*.

pase *m* pass.

pasear *vt* to take for a walk ◆ *vi* to go for a walk ❑ **pasearse** *vpr* to walk.

paseíllo *m* opening procession of bullfighters.

paseo *m (caminata)* walk; *(calle ancha)* avenue; *(distancia corta)* short walk; *(distancia larga)* to go for a walk; **ir de ~** to go for a walk; **~ marítimo** promenade.

pasillo *m* corridor.

pasión *f* passion.

pasiva *f (en gramática)* passive voice.

pasividad *f* passivity.

pasivo, -va *adj* passive ◆ *m (deudas)* debts *(pl)*.

paso *m (acción de pasar)* passing; *(manera de andar)* walk; *(ritmo)* pace; *(en montaña)* pass; **de ~** in passing; **estar de ~** to be passing through; **a dos ~s** *(muy cerca)* round the corner; **~ de cebra** zebra crossing; **~ a nivel** level crossing; **~ de peatones** pedestrian crossing; **~ subterráneo** subway *(Br)*, underpass *(Am)*.

pasodoble *m* paso doble.

pasta *f (macarrones, espagueti, etc)* pasta; *(para pastelería)* pastry; *(pastelillo)* cake; *(fam: dinero)* dough; **~ de dientes** toothpaste.

pastel *m (tarta)* cake; *(salado)* pie; *(en pintura)* pastel.

pastelería *f (establecimiento)* cake shop; *(bollos)* pastries *(pl)*.

pastelero, -ra *m, f* cake shop owner.

pastilla *f (medicamento)* pill; *(de chocolate)* bar.

pastor, -ra *m, f (de ganado)* shepherd *(f shepherdess)* ◆ *m (sacerdote)* minister.

pastoreo *m* shepherding.

pata *f (pierna, de mueble)* leg; *(pie)* foot; *(de perro, gato)* paw ◆ *m (Amér)* mate; **~ negra** type of top-quality cured ham; **estar ~s arriba** *(fig)* to be upside-down; **meter la ~** *(fig)* to put one's foot in it; **tener mala ~** *(fig)* to be unlucky, → **pato**.

patada *f* kick.

patata *f* potato; **~s fritas** *(de sartén)* chips *(Br)*, French fries *(Am)*; *(de bolsa)* crisps *(Br)*, chips *(Am)*.

paté *m* paté.

patente *adj* obvious ◆ *f* patent.

paterno, -na *adj* paternal.

patilla *f (de barba)* sideboard *(Br)*, sideburn *(Am)*; *(de gafas)* arm.

patín *m (de ruedas)* roller skate; *(de hielo)* ice skate; **~ (de pedales)** pedal boat.

patinaje *m* skating; **~ sobre hielo** ice skating.

patinar *vi (con patines)* to skate; *(resbalar)* to skid; *(fam: equivocarse)* to put one's foot in it.

patinazo *m (resbalón)* skid; *(fam: equivocación)* blunder.

patinete *m* scooter.

patio *m (de casa)* patio; *(de escuela)* playground; **~ de butacas** stalls *(pl)*; **~ interior** courtyard.

pato, -ta *m, f* duck; **~ a la naranja** duck à l'orange.

patoso, -sa *adj* clumsy.

patria *f* native country.

patriota *mf* patriot.

patriótico, -ca *adj* patriotic.

patrocinador, -ra *m, f* sponsor.

patrón, -ona *m, f (de pensión)* landlord *(f* landlady*); (jefe)* boss; *(santo)* patron saint ♦ *m (de barco)* skipper; *(en costura)* pattern; *(fig: modelo)* standard.

patronal *f (de empresa)* management.

patrono, -na *m, f (jefe)* boss; *(protector)* patron *(f patroness)*.

patrulla *f* patrol; **~ urbana** vigilante group.

pausa *f* break.

pauta *f* guideline.

pavimento *m* road surface.

pavo, -va *m, f* turkey; **~ real** peacock.

payaso, -sa *m, f* clown.

paz *(pl* **-ces)** *f* peace; **dejar en ~** to leave in peace; **hacer las paces** to make it up; **que en ~ descanse** may he/she rest in peace.

pazo *m* Galician country house.

PC *m (abrev de personal computer)* PC.

PD *(abrev de posdata)* PS.

peaje *m* toll.

peatón *m* pedestrian.

peatonal *adj* pedestrian *(antes de s)*.

peca *f* freckle.

pecado *m* sin.

pecador, -ra *m, f* sinner.

pecar *vi* to sin.

pecera *f (acuario)* fish tank.

pecho *m (en anatomía)* chest; *(de la mujer)* breast.

pechuga *f* breast *(meat)*.

pecoso, -sa *adj* freckly.

peculiar *adj (propio)* typical; *(extraño)* peculiar.

pedagogía *f* education.

pedagogo, -ga *m, f (profesor)* teacher.

pedal *m* pedal.

pedalear *vi* to pedal.

pedante *adj* pedantic.

pedazo *m* piece; **hacer ~s** to break to pieces.

pedestal *m* pedestal.

pediatra *mf* pediatrician.

pedido *m* order.

pedir *vt (rogar)* to ask for; *(poner precio)* to ask; *(en restaurante, bar)* to order; *(exigir)* to demand ♦ *vi (mendigar)* to beg; **~ a alguien que haga algo** to ask sb to do sthg; **~ disculpas** to apologize; **~ un crédito** to ask for a loan; **~ prestado algo** to borrow sthg.

pedo *m (vulg: ventosidad)* fart.

pedregoso, -sa *adj* stony.

pedrisco *m* hail.

pega *f (pegamento)* glue; *(fam: inconveniente)* hitch; **poner ~s** to find problems.

pegajoso, -sa *adj (cosa)* sticky; *(fig: persona)* clinging.

pegamento *m* glue.

pegar *vi (sol)* to beat down; *(armonizar)* to go (together) ♦ *vt (adherir, unir)* to stick; *(cartel)* to put up; *(golpear)* to hit; *(contagiar)* to give, to pass on; *(grito, salto)* to give; **~ algo a algo** *(arrimar)* to put sthg up against sthg □ **pegarse** *vpr (chocar)* to hit o.s.; *(adherirse)* to stick; *(a una persona)* to attach o.s.

pegatina f sticker.

peinado m hairstyle.

peinar vt to comb ❑ **peinarse** vpr to comb one's hair.

peine m comb.

peineta f ornamental comb.

p.ej. (abrev de por ejemplo) e.g.

peladilla f sugared almond.

pelar vt (patatas, fruta) to peel; (ave) to pluck ❑ **pelarse** vpr: ~se **de frío** to be freezing cold.

peldaño m step.

pelea f fight.

pelear vi to fight ❑ **pelearse** vpr to fight.

peletería f (tienda) furrier's (shop).

pelícano m pelican.

película f film.

peligro m (riesgo) risk; (amenaza) danger; **correr** ~ to be in danger.

peligroso, -sa adj dangerous.

pelirrojo, -ja adj red-haired.

pellejo m skin.

pellizcar vt to pinch.

pellizco m pinch.

pelma mf (fam) pain.

pelo m hair; (de animal) coat; (fig: muy poco) tiny bit; **con** ~**s y señales** in minute detail; **por un** ~ by the skin of one's teeth; **tomar el** ~ **a alguien** to pull sb's leg; ~ **rizado** curly hair.

pelota f ball ♦ mf (fam) crawler; **jugar a la** ~ to play ball; **hacer la** ~ to suck up; ~ **(vasca)** (juego) pelota.

pelotari mf pelota player.

pelotón m (de gente) crowd; (de soldados) squad.

pelotudo, -da adj (Amér: fam) thick.

peluca f wig.

peludo, -da adj hairy.

peluquería f (local) hairdresser's (salon); (oficio) hairdressing; "~-estética" "beauty salon".

peluquero, -ra m, f hairdresser.

pelvis f inv pelvis.

pena f (lástima) pity; (tristeza) sadness; (desgracia) problem; (castigo) punishment; (condena) sentence; (Amér: vergüenza) embarrassment; **me da** ~ (lástima) I feel sorry for him; (vergüenza) I'm embarrassed about it; **a duras** ~**s** with great difficulty; **vale la** ~ it's worth it; **¡qué** ~! what a pity!

penalti m penalty.

pendiente adj (por hacer) pending ♦ m earring ♦ f slope.

péndulo m pendulum.

pene m penis.

penetrar: penetrar en v + prep (filtrarse por) to penetrate; (entrar en) to go into; (perforar) to pierce.

penicilina f penicillin.

península f peninsula.

peninsular adj (de la península española) of/relating to mainland Spain.

penitencia f penance; **hacer** ~ to do penance.

penitente m (en procesión) person in Holy Week procession wearing penitent's clothing.

penoso, -sa adj (lamentable) distressing; (dificultoso) laborious; (Amér: vergonzoso) shy.

pensador, -ra m, f thinker.

pensamiento m thought.

pensar vi to think ✦ vt (meditar) to think about; (opinar) to think; (idear) to think up; ~ hacer algo to intend to do sthg; ~ en algo to think about sthg; ~ en un número to think of a number.

pensativo, -va adj pensive.

pensión f (casa de huéspedes) = guesthouse; (paga) pension; media ~ half board; ~ completa full board.

peña f (piedra) rock; (acantilado) cliff; (de amigos) group.

peñasco m large rock.

peón m (obrero) labourer; (en ajedrez) pawn.

peonza f (spinning) top.

peor adj & adv worse ✦ interj too bad!; el/la ~ the worst; el que lo hizo ~ the one who did it worst.

pepino m cucumber.

pepita f (de fruta) pip; (de metal) nugget.

pepito m (de carne) grilled meat sandwich.

pequeño, -ña adj small, little; (cantidad) low; (más joven) little.

pera f pear.

peral m pear tree.

percebe m barnacle.

percha f (coat) hanger.

perchero m (de pared) clothes' rail; (de pie) coat stand.

percibir vt (sentir, notar) to notice; (cobrar) to receive.

perdedor, -ra m, f loser.

perder vt to lose; (tiempo) to waste; (tren, oportunidad) to miss ✦ vi (en competición) to lose ✦ (empeo-

rar) to get worse; echar a ~ (fam) to spoil ❑ **perderse** vpr (extraviarse) to get lost.

pérdida f loss.

perdigón m pellet.

perdiz (pl -ces) f partridge.

perdón m forgiveness ✦ interj sorry!

perdonar vt (persona) to forgive; ~ algo a alguien (obligación, castigo, deuda) to let sb off sthg; (ofensa) to forgive sb for sthg.

peregrinación f (romería) pilgrimage.

peregrino, -na m, f pilgrim.

perejil m parsley.

pereza f (gandulería) laziness; (lentitud) sluggishness.

perezoso, -sa adj lazy.

perfección f perfection.

perfeccionista mf perfectionist.

perfectamente adv (sobradamente) perfectly; (muy bien) fine.

perfecto, -ta adj perfect.

perfil m (contorno) outline; (de cara) profile; de ~ in profile.

perforación f (MED) puncture.

perforar vt to make a hole in.

perfumar vt to perfume ❑ **perfumarse** vpr to put on perfume.

perfume m perfume.

perfumería f perfumery; "~-cosmética" "beauty products".

pergamino m parchment.

pérgola f pergola.

periferia f (de ciudad) outskirts (pl).

periódico, -ca adj periodic ✦ m newspaper.

periodismo m journalism.

periodista mf journalist.

período m period.

periquito m parakeet.

peritaje m expert's report.

perito, -ta m, f (experto) expert; (ingeniero técnico) technician.

perjudicar vt to harm.

perjuicio m harm.

perla f pearl; **me va de ~s** it's just what I need.

permanecer vi (seguir) to remain; **~ (en)** (quedarse en) to stay (in).

permanencia f continued stay.

permanente adj permanent ♦ f perm.

permiso m (autorización) permission; (documento) permit; (de soldado) leave; **~ de conducir** driving licence (Br), driver's license (Am).

permitir vt to allow.

pernoctar vi to spend the night.

pero conj but; **~ ¿no lo has visto?** you mean you haven't seen it?

perpendicular adj perpendicular ♦ f perpendicular line; **~ a** at right angles to.

perpetuo, -tua adj perpetual.

perplejo, -ja adj bewildered.

perra f (rabieta) tantrum; (dinero) penny, → **perro**.

perrito m: **~ caliente** hot dog.

perro, -rra m (perro) dog (f bitch).

persa adj & mf Persian.

persecución f (seguimiento) pursuit.

perseguir vt to pursue.

persiana f blind.

persona f person; **cuatro ~s** four people; **en ~** in person.

personaje m (celebridad) celebrity; (en cine, teatro) character.

personal adj personal ♦ m (empleados) staff; (fam: gente) people (pl); **"sólo ~ autorizado"** "staff only".

personalidad f personality.

perspectiva f (vista, panorama) view; (aspecto) perspective; (esperanzas, porvenir) prospect.

persuadir vt to persuade.

persuasión f persuasion.

pertenecer vi: **~ a** to belong to; (corresponder a) to belong in.

perteneciente adj: **~ a** belonging to.

pertenencias fpl (objetos personales) belongings.

pértiga f (deporte) pole vault.

Perú m: **(el) ~** Peru.

peruano, -na adj & m, f Peruvian.

pesa f weight □ **pesas** fpl (en gimnasia) weights.

pesadez f (molestia) drag; (sensación) heaviness.

pesadilla f nightmare.

pesado, -da adj (carga, sueño) heavy; (broma) bad; (agotador) tiring; (aburrido) boring; (persona) annoying.

pesadumbre f sorrow.

pésame m: **dar el ~** to offer one's condolences.

pesar m (pena) grief ♦ vt to weigh ♦ vi (tener peso) to weigh; (ser pesado) to be heavy; (influir) to carry weight; **me pesa tener que**

hacerlo it grieves me to have to do it; **a ~ de** in spite of.

pesca f (actividad) fishing; (captura) catch.

pescadería f fishmonger's (shop).

pescadero, -ra m, f fishmonger.

pescadilla f whiting.

pescado m fish.

pescador, -ra m, f fisherman (f fisherwoman).

pescar vt (peces) to fish for; (fam: pillar) to catch.

pesebre m (establo) manger; (belén) crib.

pesero m (Amér) small bus used in towns.

peseta f peseta.

pesimismo m pessimism.

pesimista adj pessimistic.

pésimo, -ma superl → malo ◆ adj awful.

peso m weight; (moneda) peso.

pesquero, -ra adj fishing ◆ m (barco) fishing boat.

pestañas fpl eyelashes.

peste f (mal olor) stink; (enfermedad) plague.

pesticida m pesticide.

pestillo m (cerrojo) bolt; (en verjas) latch.

petaca f (para bebidas) hip flask.

pétalo m petal.

petanca f boules, form of bowls using metal balls, played in public areas.

petardo m firecracker.

petición f (solicitud) request.

peto m (vestidura) bib.

petróleo m oil.

petrolero, -ra adj oil (antes de s) ◆ m (barco) oil tanker.

petrolífero, -ra adj oil (antes de s).

petulancia f (comentario) opinionated remark.

petulante adj opinionated.

petunia f petunia.

peúco m bootee.

pez (pl -ces) m fish; **~ espada** swordfish.

pezón m (de mujer) nipple.

pezuña f hoof.

pianista mf pianist.

piano m piano; **~ bar** piano bar.

piar vi to tweet.

pibe, -ba m, f (Amér: fam) boy (f girl).

picador, -ra m, f (torero) picador.

picadora f mincer, → picador.

picadura f (de mosquito, serpiente) bite; (de avispa, ortiga) sting; (tabaco picado) (loose) tobacco.

picante adj (comida) spicy; (broma, chiste) saucy.

picantería f (Amér) stall selling spicy food.

picar vt (suj: mosquito, serpiente, pez) to bite; (suj: avispa, ortiga) to sting; (al toro) to goad; (piedra) to hack at; (carne) to mince; (verdura) to chop; (billete) to clip ◆ vi (comer un poco) to nibble; (sal, pimienta, pimiento) to be hot; (la piel) to itch; (sol) to burn ❑ **picarse** vp (vino) to go sour; (muela) to decay; (fam: enfadarse) to get upset.

pícaro, -ra adj (astuto) crafty.

picas fpl (palo de la baraja)

spades.

pichincha f (Amér) bargain.

pichón m (young) pigeon.

picnic m picnic.

pico m (de ave) beak; (de montaña) peak; (herramienta) pickaxe; **cincuenta y ~** fifty-odd; **a las tres y ~** just after three o'clock.

picor m itch.

picoso, -sa adj (Amér) spicy.

pie m foot; (apoyo) stand; **a ~** on foot; **en ~** (válido) valid; **estar de ~** to be standing up; **no hacer ~** (en el agua) to be out of one's depth; **~s de cerdo** (pig's) trotters.

piedad f pity.

piedra f stone; (granizo) hailstone; **~ preciosa** precious stone.

piel f (de persona, animal, fruta) skin; (cuero) leather; (pelo) fur.

pierna f leg; **estirar las ~s** to stretch one's legs; **~ de cordero** leg of lamb.

pieza f piece; (en mecánica) part; (en pesca, caza) specimen; **~ de recambio** spare part.

pijama m pyjamas (pl).

pila f (de casete, radio, etc) battery; (montón) pile; (fregadero) sink; **~ alcalina** alkaline battery.

pilar m pillar.

píldora f pill.

pillar vt (agarrar) to grab hold of; (atropellar) to hit; (dedos, ropa, delincuente) to catch; **~ una insolación** (fam) to get sunstroke; **~ un resfriado** (fam) to catch a cold.

pilotar vt (avión) to pilot; (barco) to steer.

piloto mf (de avión) pilot; (de barco) navigator ♦ m (luz de coche)

tail light; **~ automático** automatic pilot.

pimentón m paprika.

pimienta f pepper (for seasoning); **a la ~ verde** in a green peppercorn sauce.

pimiento m (fruto) pepper (vegetable); **~s del piquillo** type of hot red pepper eaten baked.

pin m pin (badge).

pincel m paintbrush.

pinchar vt (con aguja, pinchos) to prick; (rueda) to puncture; (globo, balón) to burst; (provocar) to annoy; (fam: con inyección) to jab ❏ **pincharse** vpr (fam: drogarse) to shoot up.

pinchazo m (de rueda) puncture; (en la piel) prick.

pinche adj (Amér: fam) damned.

pincho m (punta) point; (tapa) aperitif on a stick, or a small sandwich; **~ moruno** shish kebab.

pinga f (Amér: vulg) prick.

ping-pong® [pin'pon] m table tennis.

pingüino m penguin.

pino m pine tree; **los Pinos** official residence of the Mexican president.

---

i LOS PINOS

L os Pinos is the official residence of the Mexican president and the seat of the Mexican government. It is here that the president holds Cabinet meetings and receives State visits.

---

pintada f graffiti.

pintado, -da adj (coloreado) coloured; (maquillado) made-up; "recién ~" "wet paint".

pintalabios m inv lipstick.

pintar vt to paint □ **pintarse** vpr to make o.s. up.

pintor, -ra m, f painter.

pintoresco, -ca adj picturesque.

pintura f (arte, cuadro) painting; (sustancia) paint.

pinza f (de tender ropa) peg; (pliegue) pleat □ **pinzas** fpl (para depilar) tweezers; (para azúcar) tongs; (de cangrejo) pincers.

piña f (ananás) pineapple; (del pino) pine cone; (fam: de gente) close-knit group; ~ **en almíbar** pineapple in syrup; ~ **natural** fresh pineapple.

piñata f pot of sweets.

ℹ️ PIÑATA

This is an earthenware pot filled with sweets and small gifts which blindfolded children break open with a stick at birthday parties. In Latin America, a papier-mâché doll is used instead of a jar.

---

piñón m (semilla) pine nut.

piojo m louse.

pipa f (de fumar) pipe; (semilla) seed □ **pipas** fpl (de girasol) sunflower seeds coated in salt.

pipí m (fam) wee.

pique m (fam: enfado) bad feeling; **irse a ~** (barco) to sink.

piragua f canoe.

piragüismo m canoeing.

pirámide f pyramid.

piraña f piranha.

pirata adj & m pirate.

piratear vt (programa informático) to hack.

Pirineos mpl: **los ~** the Pyrenees.

pirómano, -na m, f pyromaniac.

piropo m flirtatious comment.

pirueta f pirouette.

pisada f (huella) footprint; (ruido) footstep.

pisar vt to step on.

piscina f swimming pool.

Piscis m Pisces.

pisco m (Amér) strong liquor made from grapes, popular in Chile and Peru; ~ **sour** (Amér) cocktail with "pisco".

piso m (vivienda) flat (Br), apartment (Am); (suelo, planta) floor; (Amér: fig: influencia) influence; ~ **bajo** ground floor.

pisotón m stamp (on sb's foot).

pista f track; (indicio) clue; ~ **de aterrizaje** runway; ~ **de baile** dance floor; ~ **de esquí** ski slope; ~ **de tenis** tennis court.

pistacho m pistachio.

pistola f pistol.

pistolero m gunman.

pitar vi (tocar el pito) to blow a whistle; (tocar la bocina) to toot one's horn; **salir pitando** (fig) to leave in a hurry.

pitillera f cigarette case.

pitillo m cigarette.

pito m whistle.

pitón m (del toro) tip of the horn; (de botijo, jarra) spout; (serpiente) python.

pizarra f (encerado) blackboard; (roca) slate.

pizza ['pitsa] f pizza.

pizzería [pitse'ria] f pizzeria.

placa f (lámina) plate; (inscripción) plaque; (insignia) badge.

placer m pleasure; **es un ~** it's a pleasure.

plan m (proyecto, intención) plan; (programa) programme; **hacer ~es** to make plans; **~ de estudios** syllabus.

plancha f (para planchar) iron; (para cocinar) grill; (de metal) sheet; (fam: error) boob; **a la ~** grilled.

planchar vt to iron.

planeta m planet.

plano, -na adj flat ♦ m (mapa) plan; (nivel) level; (en cine, fotografía) shot; (superficie) plane.

planta f (vegetal, fábrica) plant; (del pie) sole; (piso) floor; **~ baja** ground floor; **segunda ~** second floor.

plantar vt (planta, terreno) to plant; (poste) to put in; (tienda de campaña) to stand up □ **plantarse** vpr (ponerse) to plant o.s.; (en naipes) to stick.

planteamiento m (exposición) raising; (perspectiva) approach.

plantear vt (plan, proyecto) to set out; (problema, cuestión) to raise □ **plantearse** vpr to think about.

plantilla f (personal) staff; (de zapato) insole; (patrón) template.

plástico, -ca adj & m plastic; **de ~** plastic.

plastificar vt to plasticize.

plastilina® f Plasticine®.

plata f silver; **de ~** silver.

plataforma f (tarima) platform; (del tren, autobús, etc) standing room.

plátano m (fruta) banana; (árbol platanáceo) plane tree.

platea f stalls (pl).

plateresco, -ca adj plateresque.

plática f (Amér) chat.

platicar vi (Amér) to have a chat.

platillo m (plato pequeño) small plate; (de taza) saucer; (de balanza) pan □ **platillos** mpl (en música) cymbals.

plato m (recipiente) plate; (comida) dish; (parte de una comida) course; **~ combinado** single-course meal usually of meat or fish with chips and vegetables; **~ del día** today's special; **~ principal** main course; **~s caseros** home-made food (sg); **primer ~** starter.

platudo, -da adj (Amér: fam) loaded.

playa f beach; **ir a la ~ de vacaciones** to go on holiday to the seaside; **~ de estacionamiento** (Amér) car park.

play-back ['pleiβak] m: **hacer ~** to mime (the lyrics).

playeras fpl (de deporte) tennis shoes; (para la playa) canvas shoes.

plaza f (en una población) square; (sitio, espacio) space; (puesto, vacante) job; (asiento) seat; (mercado) market; **~ de toros** bullring.

plazo m (de tiempo) period; (pago) instalment; **hay 20 días de ~** the deadline is in 20 days; **a corto ~** in the short term; **a largo ~** in the long term; **a ~s** in instalments.

plegable adj (silla) folding.

pleito m (en un juicio) lawsuit.

plenamente adv completely.

plenitud f (apogeo) peak.

pleno, -na adj complete ◆ m plenary (session); **en ~ día** in broad daylight; **en ~ invierno** in the middle of the winter.

pliegue m (en tela) pleat.

plomería f (Amér) plumbing.

plomero m (Amér) plumber.

plomo m (metal) lead; (bala) bullet; (fam: persona pesada) pain; (fusible) fuse.

pluma f (de ave) feather; (para escribir) pen; **~ estilográfica** fountain pen.

plumaje m (de ave) plumage; (adorno) plume.

plumero m (para el polvo) feather duster; (estuche) pencil case; (adorno) plume.

plumier (pl plumiers) m pencil case.

plumilla f nib.

plumón m down.

plural adj & m plural.

pluralidad f (diversidad) diversity.

plusmarca f record.

plusmarquista mf record holder.

p.m. (abrev de post meridiem) p.m.

PM (abrev de policía militar) MP.

p.n. (abrev de peso neto) nt. wt.

p.o. (abrev de por orden) by order.

población f (habitantes) population; (ciudad) town; (más grande) city; (pueblo) village.

poblado, -da adj populated ◆ m (ciudad) town; (pueblo) village.

poblar vt (establecerse en) to settle.

pobre adj poor ◆ mf (mendigo) beggar.

pobreza f (miseria) poverty; (escasez) scarcity.

pochismo m (Amér: fam) English spoken by Californian Mexicans.

pocho, -cha adj (Amér) (fam) (mejicano) Mexican American; (rechoncho) plump.

pocilga f pigsty.

poco, -ca adj & pron (en singular) little, not much; (en plural) few, not many ◆ adv (con escasez) not much; (tiempo corto) not long; **tengo ~ dinero** I don't have much money; **unos ~s días** a few days; **tengo ~s** I don't have many; **come ~** he doesn't eat much; **dentro de ~** shortly; **hace ~** not long ago; **a ~** a bit by bit; **por ~** almost; **un ~ (de)** a bit (of).

poda f (acto) pruning.

podar vt to prune.

poder m 1. (facultad, gobierno) power; **~ adquisitivo** purchasing power; **estar en el ~** to be in power.
2. (posesión): **estar en ~ de alguien** to be in sb's hands.
◆ v aux 1. (tener facultad para) can, to be able to; **puedo hacerlo** I can do it.
2. (tener permiso para) can, to be allowed to; **¿se puede fumar aquí?** can I smoke here?; **no puedo salir**

por la noche I'm not allowed to go out at night.

3. *(ser capaz moralmente de)* can; **no podemos abandonarle** we can't abandon him.

4. *(tener posibilidad)* may, can; **puedo ir en barco o en avión** I can go by boat or by plane; **podías haber cogido el tren** you could have caught the train.

5. *(expresa queja, reproche):* **¡hubiera podido invitarnos!** she could have invited us!

6. *(en locuciones):* **es tonto a o hasta más no ~** he's as stupid as can be; **no ~ más** *(estar lleno)* to be full (up); *(estar enfadado)* to have had enough; *(estar cansado)* to be too tired to carry on; **¿se puede?** may I come in?

◆ *v impers (ser posible)* may; **puede ser que llueva** it may rain; **no puede ser verdad** it can't be true; **¿vendrás mañana? - puede** will you come tomorrow? - I may do.

◆ *vt (tener más fuerza que)* to be stronger than.

❏ **poder con** *v + prep (enfermedad, rival)* to be able to overcome; *(tarea, problema)* to be able to cope with; **no puedo con los celos** I can't stand jealousy.

poderoso, -sa *adj* powerful.

podio *m* podium.

podrá *v* → **poder.**

podría *v* → **poder.**

podrido, -da *pp* → **pudrir** ◆ *adj* rotten.

poema *m* poem.

poesía *f (poema)* poem; *(arte)* poetry.

poeta *mf* poet.

poético, -ca *adj* poetic.

polar *adj* polar.

polaroid® *f* Polaroid®.

polea *f* pulley.

polémica *f* controversy.

polémico, -ca *adj* controversial.

polen *m* pollen.

polichinela *m (títere)* marionette.

policía *f (cuerpo)* police ◆ *mf* policeman *f* policewoman); ~ **municipal** o **urbana** local police who deal mainly with traffic offences and administrative matters; ~ **nacional** national police.

policíaco, -ca *adj* police *(antes de s).*

polideportivo *m* sports centre.

poliéster *m* polyester.

políglota *mf* polyglot.

polígono *m*: ~ **industrial** industrial estate.

politécnica *f* university faculty devoted to technical subjects.

política *f (arte de gobernar)* politics; *(modo de gobernar)* policy, → **político.**

político, -ca *m, f* politician ◆ *adj* political; **hermano** ~ brother-in-law.

póliza *f (de seguros)* policy *(sello)* stamp on a document proving payment of tax.

pollera *f (Amér)* loose skirt worn by Peruvian and Bolivian Indians.

pollito *m* chick.

pollo *m* chicken; ~ **al ajillo** chicken pieces fried in garlic until crunchy; ~ **asado** roast chicken; ~ **a l'ast**

chicken roasted on a spit; **~ al curry** chicken curry; **~ a la plancha** grilled chicken.

polluelo m chick.

polo m (helado) ice lolly; (de una pila) pole; (jersey) polo shirt; (juego) polo.

pololo, -la m, f (Amér: persona impertinente) cheeky person ◆ m (Amér: galán) ladies' man.

Polonia s Poland.

Polo Norte m: **el ~** the North Pole.

Polo Sur m: **el ~** the South Pole.

polución f pollution.

polvera f powder compact.

polvo m dust ❑ **polvos** mpl (en cosmética, medicina) powder (sg); **~s de talco** talcum powder (sg).

pólvora f gunpowder.

polvoriento, -ta adj dusty.

polvorón m powdery sweet made of flour, sugar and butter.

pomada f ointment.

pomelo m grapefruit.

pomo m knob.

pómulo m cheekbone.

ponchar vt (Amér) to puncture ❑ **poncharse** vpr (Amér) to get a puncture.

poner vt **1.** (colocar, añadir) to put; **pon el libro en el estante** put the book on the shelf; **pon más azúcar al café** put some more sugar in the coffee.

2. (vestir): **~ algo** to put sthg on.

3. (contribuir, invertir): **puso su capital en el negocio** he put his capital into the business.

4. (hacer estar de cierta manera): **me**

has puesto colorado you've made me blush; **lo puso de mal humor** it put him in a bad mood.

5. (radio, televisión, luz, etc) to switch on; (gas, instalación) to put in.

6. (oponer): **~ inconvenientes** to raise objections.

7. (telegrama, fax) to send; (conferencia) to make; **¿me pones con Juan?** can you put me through to Juan?

8. (asignar, imponer) to fix; **le han puesto una multa** they've fined him; **¿qué nombre le han puesto?** what have they called her?

9. (aplicar facultad) to put; **no pone ningún interés** he shows no interest.

10. (montar) to set up; (casa) to do up; (tienda de campaña) to pitch; **han puesto una tienda nueva** they've opened a new shop.

11. (en cine, teatro, televisión) to show; **¿qué ponen en la tele?** what's on (the) telly?

12. (escribir, decir) to say; **no sé qué pone ahí** I don't know what that says.

13. (suponer) to suppose; **pongamos que sucedió así** (let's) suppose that's what happened.

14. (en locuciones): **~ en marcha** (iniciar) to start.

◆ vi (ave) to lay (eggs).

❑ **ponerse** vpr (ropa, gafas, maquillaje) to put on; (estar de cierta manera) to become; (astro) to set; **ponte aquí** stand here; **se puso rojo** he went red; **~se bien** (de salud) to get better; **~se malo** to fall ill.

pongo v → **poner**.

poniente m (oeste) west.

popa

popa f stern.

popular adj (del pueblo) of the people; (arte, música) folk; (famoso) popular.

popularidad f popularity.

póquer m poker.

por prep 1. (causa) because of; **se enfadó ~ tu comportamiento** she got angry because of your behaviour.

2. (finalidad) (in order) to; **lo hizo ~ complacerte** he did it to please you; **lo compré ~ ti** I bought it for you; **luchar ~ algo** to fight for sthg.

3. (medio, modo, agente) by; ~ **mensajero/fax** by courier/fax; ~ **escrito** in writing; **el récord fue batido ~ el atleta** the record was broken by the athlete.

4. (tiempo): ~ **la mañana/tarde** in the morning/afternoon; ~ **la noche** at night; ~ **unos días** for a few days; **creo que la boda será ~ abril** I think the wedding will be some time in April.

5. (aproximadamente en): **está ~ ahí** it's round there somewhere; **¿dónde vive?** whereabouts does she live?

6. (a través de) through; **pasar ~ la aduana** to go through customs; **entramos en Francia ~ Irún** we entered France via Irún.

7. (a cambio, en lugar de) for; **cambió el coche ~ una moto** he exchanged his car for a motorbike.

8. (distribución) per; **cien pesetas ~ unidad** a hundred pesetas each; **20 km ~ hora** 20 km an hour.

9. (en matemáticas): **tres ~ dos igual a cuatro** two times two is four.

porcelana f (material) porce-

lain; (vasija) piece of porcelain.

porcentaje m percentage.

porche m porch.

porción f (cantidad) portion; (parte) share.

porno adj (fam) porno.

pornografía f pornography.

pornográfico, -ca adj pornographic.

porque conj because.

porqué m reason.

porrón m wine jar with a long spout for drinking.

portada f (de libro) title page; (de revista) cover.

portador, -ra m, f carrier; **al ~ (cheque)** to the bearer.

portaequipajes m inv boot (Br), trunk (Am).

portafolios m inv (carpeta) file.

portal m (vestíbulo) hallway; (entrada) main entrance.

portalámparas m inv socket.

portarse vpr to behave; ~ **bien/mal** to behave well/badly.

portátil adj portable.

portavoz (pl -ces) mf spokesman (f spokeswoman).

portazo m slam; **dar un ~** to slam the door.

portería f (conserjería) porter's office; (en deporte) goal.

portero, -ra m, f (conserje) porter; (en deporte) goalkeeper; ~ **electrónico** entryphone.

Portugal s Portugal.

portugués, -esa adj & m, f Portuguese.

porvenir m future.

posada f (alojamiento) accommodation; *(hostal)* guesthouse.

posarse *vpr (ave)* to perch; *(insecto)* to settle.

posavasos *m inv* coaster.

posdata *f* postscript.

pose *f* pose.

poseedor, -ra *m, f (dueño)* owner; *(de cargo, récord)* holder.

poseer *vt (ser dueño de)* to own; *(tener)* to have, to possess.

posesión *f* possession.

posesivo, -va *adj & m* possessive.

posibilidad *f* possibility.

posible *adj* possible.

posición *f* position; *(social)* status; *(económica)* situation.

positivamente *adv* positively.

positivo, -va *adj* positive ◆ *m (en fotografía)* print.

posmoderno, -na *adj* postmodern.

poso *m* sediment.

postal *f* postcard.

poste *m* post.

póster *m* poster.

posterior *adj (en tiempo, orden)* subsequent; *(en espacio)* back; **~ a** after.

postre *m* dessert; **~ de la casa** chef's special dessert.

póstumo, -ma *adj* posthumous.

postura *f* position.

potable *adj (agua)* drinkable; *(fam: aceptable)* palatable.

potaje *m* stew; **~ de garbanzos** chickpea stew.

potencia *f* power.

potenciar *vt* to foster.

potrillo *m (Amér)* large glass.

potro *m (caballo)* colt; *(en gimnasia)* vaulting horse.

pozo *m (de agua)* well.

p.p. *(abrev de por poder)* p.p.

práctica *f (de un deporte)* playing ❏ **prácticas** *fpl (de conducir)* lessons.

practicante *mf (en religión)* practising member; **~ (ambulatorio)** medical assistant.

practicar *vt (ejercer)* to practise; *(deporte)* to play ◆ *vi* to practise.

práctico, -ca *adj* practical.

pradera *f* large meadow, prairie.

prado *m* meadow.

pral. *abrev* = **principal**.

precario, -ria *adj* precarious.

precaución *f (medida)* precaution; *(prudencia)* care.

precintado, -da *adj* sealed.

precio *m* price; **¿qué ~ tiene?** how much is it?; **~ fijo** fixed price; **~ de venta al público** retail price; **~s de coste** warehouse prices.

preciosidad *f (cosa preciosa)* beautiful thing.

precioso, -sa *adj (bonito)* lovely; *(valioso)* precious.

precipicio *m* precipice.

precipitación *f (imprudencia, prisa)* haste; *(lluvia)* rainfall.

precipitado, -da *adj* hasty.

precipitarse *vpr (actuar sin pensar)* to act rashly.

precisamente *adv* precisely.

precisar *vt (especificar)* to specify; *(necesitar)* to need.

preciso, -sa *adj (detallado, exacto)* precise; *(imprescindible)* necessary.

precoz adj (persona) precocious.
predicar vt to preach.
predilecto, -ta adj favourite.
predominar vi to prevail.
preeminente adj preeminent.
preescolar adj pre-school.
preferencia f preference; (en carretera) right of way.
preferible adj preferable.
preferir vt to prefer.
prefijo m (en gramática) prefix; (de teléfono) dialling code.
pregón m (de fiesta) opening speech.
pregonar vt (noticia) to announce; (secreto) to spread about.
pregonero m town crier.
pregunta f question; **hacer una ~** to ask a question.
preguntar vt to ask □ **preguntar por** v + prep to ask after; **preguntarse** vpr to wonder.
prehistórico, -ca adj prehistoric.
prejuicio m prejudice.
prematuro, -ra adj premature.
premeditación f premeditation.
premiar vt to award a prize to.
premio m prize; (recompensa) reward; **~ gordo** first prize.
premisa f premise.
prenatal adj antenatal.
prenda f (vestido) item of clothing; (garantía) pledge.
prensa f press; **la ~** the press.
preocupación f worry.
preocupado, -da adj

worried.
preocupar vt to worry □ **preocuparse de** v + prep (encargarse de) to take care of; **preocuparse por** v + prep to worry about.
preparación f (arreglo, disposición) preparation; (formación) training.
preparar vt (disponer) to prepare; (maletas) to pack; (estudiar) to study for □ **prepararse** vpr (arreglarse) to get ready.
preparativos mpl preparations.
preparatoria f (Amér) pre-university course in Latin America.

---

i PREPARATORIA

This is the name given to the three years of pre-university education in Latin America. Students usually begin the "prepa", as it is known colloquially, at the age of 16 and finish when they are 19.

---

preponderante adj prevailing.
preposición f preposition.
prepotente adj dominant.
presa f (de un animal) prey; (embalse) dam, → **preso**.
presbiterio m chancel.
prescindir : **prescindir de** v + prep (renunciar a) to do without; (omitir) to dispense with.
presencia f presence.
presenciar vt to attend.
presentable adj presentable.
presentación f presentation;

(entre personas) introduction.

presentador, -ra *m, f* presenter.

presentar *vt* to present; *(queja)* to lodge; *(a dos personas)* to introduce; *(excusas, respetos)* to offer; *(aspecto, apariencia)* to have ☐ **presentarse** *vpr (comparecer)* to turn up; *(como candidato, voluntario)* to put o.s. forward; **~se a** *(examen)* to sit; *(elección)* to stand for.

presente *adj & m* present; **tener ~** to remember.

presentimiento *m* feeling, hunch.

preservar *vt* to protect.

preservativo *m* condom.

presidencia *f (cargo)* presidency; *(lugar)* president's office; *(grupo de personas)* board.

presidencial *adj* presidential.

presidente, -ta *m, f (de nación)* president; *(de asamblea)* chairperson.

presidiario, -ria *m, f* convict.

presidir *vt (ser presidente de)* to preside over; *(reunión)* to chair; *(predominar)* to dominate.

presión *f* pressure; **~ sanguínea** blood pressure.

preso, -sa *m, f* prisoner.

préstamo *m* loan.

prestar *vt (dinero)* to lend; *(colaboración, ayuda)* to give; *(declaración)* to make; *(atención)* to pay ☐ **prestarse a** *v + prep (ofrecerse a)* to offer to; *(dar motivo a)* to be open to.

prestigio *m* prestige.

presumido, -da *adj* conceited.

presumir *vt* to presume ◆ *vi* to show off; **~ de guapo** to think o.s. good-looking.

presunción *f (suposición)* assumption; *(vanidad)* conceit.

presunto, -ta *adj (delincuente, etc)* alleged.

presuntuoso, -sa *adj* conceited.

presupuesto *m (cálculo)* budget; *(de costo)* estimate.

pretencioso, -sa *adj* pretentious.

pretender *vt (aspirar a)* to aim at; *(afirmar)* to claim; **~ hacer algo** to try to do sthg.

pretendiente *mf (al trono)* pretender; *(a una mujer)* suitor.

pretensión *f (intención)* aim; *(aspiración)* aspiration.

pretexto *m* pretext.

prever *vt (presagiar)* to foresee; *(prevenir)* to plan.

previo, -via *adj* prior.

previsor, -ra *adj* farsighted.

previsto, -ta *adj (planeado)* anticipated.

primaria *f (enseñanza)* primary school.

primario, -ria *adj (primordial)* primary; *(elemental)* primitive.

primavera *f* spring.

primer *núm* → **primero.**

primera *f (velocidad)* first gear; *(clase)* first class; **de ~** first-class, → **primero.**

primero, -ra *núm & adv* first ◆ *m, f:* **el ~ de la clase** top of the class; **a ~s de** at the beginning of; **lo ~** the main thing; **primera clase** first class; **~s auxilios** first aid *(sg)*,

→ **sexto**.

primo, -ma *m, f (familiar)* cousin; *(fam: bobo)* sucker.

primogénito, -ta *m, f* first-born (child).

princesa *f* princess.

principado *m* principality.

principal *adj* main ◆ *m* first floor.

príncipe *m* prince.

principiante *m* beginner.

principio *m (inicio)* beginning; *(causa, origen)* origin; *(norma)* principle; **a ~s de** at the beginning of; **al ~** at the beginning; **en ~** in principle; **por ~s** on principle.

pringoso, -sa *adj (pegajoso)* sticky.

prioridad *f* priority.

prisa *f (rapidez)* speed; *(urgencia)* urgency; **darse ~** to hurry up; **tener ~** to be in a hurry.

prisión *f (cárcel)* prison.

prisionero, -ra *m, f* prisoner.

prisma *m* prism.

prismáticos *mpl* binoculars.

privado, -da *adj* private.

privar *vt* to deprive ❑ **privarse de** *v + prep* to go without.

privilegiado, -da *adj* privileged.

privilegio *m* privilege.

proa *f* bows *(pl)*.

probabilidad *f (cualidad)* probability; *(oportunidad)* chance.

probable *adj* probable.

probador *m* changing room.

probar *vt (demostrar)* to prove; *(examinar)* to check; *(comida, bebida)* to taste ◆ *vi* to try ❑ **probarse**

vpr (ropa, zapato) to try on.

probeta *f* test tube.

problema *m* problem.

problemático, -ca *adj* problematic.

procedencia *f (origen, fuente)* origin; **con ~ de** *(arriving)* from.

procedente *adj (oportuno)* appropriate; **~ de** from.

proceder *vi (actuar)* to act; *(ser oportuno)* to be appropriate ❑ **proceder de** *v + prep* to come from.

procedimiento *m (método)* procedure.

procesado, -da *m, f* accused.

procesar *vt (enjuiciar)* to try.

procesión *f* procession.

proceso *m* process; *(transcurso, evolución)* course; *(juicio)* trial.

proclamación *f* proclamation.

proclamar *vt* to proclaim; *(aclamar)* to acclaim ❑ **proclamarse** *vpr* to proclaim o.s.

procurar *vt*: **~ hacer algo** to try to do sthg.

prodigarse *vpr (esforzarse)* to put o.s. out; **~ en algo** to overdo sthg.

producción *f* production; *(producto)* products *(pl)*.

producir *vt* to produce; *(provocar)* to cause ❑ **producirse** *vpr (ocurrir)* to take place.

productividad *f* productivity.

productivo, -va *adj (que produce)* productive; *(que da beneficio)* profitable.

producto *m* product; *(de la tierra)* produce; *(beneficios)* profit.

productor, -ra *m, f* producer.

productora f (en cine) production company, → **productor**.

profecía f prophecy.

profesión f profession.

profesional adj & mf professional.

profesionista mf (Amér) professional.

profesor, -ra m, f teacher.

profeta m prophet.

profiteroles mpl profiteroles.

profundidad f depth; **tiene dos metros de ~** it's two metres deep.

profundo, -da adj deep; (notable) profound.

programa m programme; (de estudios) syllabus; (plan) schedule; (en informática) program.

programación f (en televisión, radio) programmes (pl); (en informática) programming.

programador, -ra m, f programmer.

programar vt (planear) to plan; (en televisión, radio) to put on; (en informática) to program.

progresar vi to (make) progress.

progresivo, -va adj progressive.

progreso m progress.

prohibición f ban.

prohibido, -da adj prohibited; **"~ aparcar"** "no parking"; **"~ el paso"** "no entry"; **"~ el paso a personas ajenas a la obra"** "no entry for unauthorised personnel"; **"~ fijar carteles"** "billposters will be prosecuted"; **"~ fumar"** "no smoking"; **"prohibida la entra-** da" "no entry"; **"prohibida la entrada a menores"** "adults only".

prohibir vt (vedar) to forbid; (por ley) to prohibit; (práctica existente) to ban.

prójimo m fellow human being.

proliferación f proliferation.

prólogo m (en libro, revista) introduction.

prolongar vt (alargar) to extend; (hacer durar más) to prolong ❑ **prolongarse** vpr to go on.

promedio m average.

promesa f promise.

prometer vt to promise ♦ vi to show promise ❑ **prometerse** vpr to get engaged.

prometido, -da m, f fiancé (f fiancée).

promoción f (ascenso) promotion; (curso) class.

promocionar vt to promote ❑ **promocionarse** vpr to promote o.s.

promotor, -ra m, f promoter.

pronóstico m (predicción) forecast; (en medicina) prognosis; **~ del tiempo** weather forecast.

pronto adv (temprano) early; (dentro de poco) soon; (rápidamente) quickly; **de ~** suddenly; **tan ~ como** as soon as.

pronunciación f pronunciation.

pronunciar vt to pronounce; (discurso) to make.

propaganda f advertising.

propensión f: **~ a** a tendency towards.

propenso, -sa adj: **ser ~ a** to

propicio 222

have a tendency to.

propicio, -cia adj favourable.

propiedad f property; (posesión) ownership.

propietario, -ria m, f owner.

propina f tip.

propio, -pia adj (de propiedad) own; (peculiar) characteristic; (apropiado) appropriate; (natural) natural; **el ~ presidente** the president himself.

proponer vt to propose ❑ **proponerse** vpr to intend.

proporcionado, -da adj proportionate.

proporcionar vt (facilitar) to give, to provide; (ser causa de) to add.

proposición f (propuesta) proposal.

propósito m (intención) intention; (objetivo) purpose; **a ~** on purpose; **a ~ de** with regard to.

propuesta f proposal.

propuesto, -ta pp → **proponer**.

prórroga f (aplazamiento) extension; (en deporte) extra time.

prorrogar vt to extend.

prosa f prose.

proscrito, -ta m, f exile.

prospecto m (folleto) leaflet; (de medicamento) instructions leaflet.

próspero, -ra adj prosperous.

prostíbulo m brothel.

prostitución f prostitution.

prostituta f prostitute.

protagonista mf (de libro) main character; (en cine, teatro) lead.

protección f protection.

proteger vt to protect ❑ **protegerse** vpr (resguardarse) to shelter.

protegido, -da m, f protégé (f protégée).

proteína f protein.

protesta f protest.

protestante mf Protestant.

protestar vi to protest.

protocolo m protocol.

provecho m benefit; **buen ~** enjoy your meal!; **sacar ~ de** to make the most of.

provechoso, -sa adj advantageous.

provenir: provenir de v + prep to come from.

proverbio m proverb.

provincia f province.

provisional adj provisional.

provocación f provocation.

provocar vt (incitar, enojar) to provoke; (excitar sexualmente) to arouse; (causar) to cause; (incendio) to start; **¿te provoca hacerlo?** (Amér) do you feel like doing it?

provocativo, -va adj provocative.

próximo, -ma adj (cercano) near; (ciudad, casa) nearby; (siguiente) next; **"próximas llegadas"** "arriving next".

proyección f (de película) showing.

proyectar vt (película) to show; (luz) to shine; (sombra, figura) to cast; (idear) to plan.

proyecto m (plan) plan; (propósito) project; (de ley) bill.

proyector m (de cine, diapositivas) projector.

prudencia f (cautela) caution; (moderación) moderation.

prudente adj (cauteloso) cautious; (sensato) sensible.

prueba f (testimonio) proof; (ensayo, examen) test; (competición) event.

psicoanálisis m inv psychoanalysis.

psicología f psychology.

psicológico, -ca adj psychological.

psicólogo, -ga m, f psychologist.

psicópata mf psychopath.

psiquiatra mf psychiatrist.

psiquiátrico m psychiatric hospital.

psíquico, -ca adj psychic.

pta. (abrev de peseta) pta.

púa f (de planta) thorn; (de peine) tooth.

pub [pap] m upmarket pub.

pubertad f puberty.

pubis m inv pubes (pl).

publicación f publication.

públicamente adv publicly.

publicar vt to publish; (noticia) to make public.

publicidad f (propaganda) advertising; (en televisión) adverts (pl).

publicitario, -ria adj advertising (antes de s).

público, -ca adj public; (colegio) state ♦ m (en cine, teatro, televisión) audience; (en partido) crowd; **en ~** in public.

pucha interj (Amér) good heavens!

pucho m (Amér) cigarette butt.

pudding ['puðin] m pudding.

pudiera v → poder.

pudor m (recato) modesty; (timidez) shyness.

pudrir vt to rot ❑ **pudrirse** vpr to rot.

pueblo m people; (localidad pequeña) village; (más grande) town.

pueda v → poder.

puente m bridge; **hacer ~** to take a day off between two public holidays; **~ aéreo** shuttle.

puerco, -ca adj filthy ♦ m, f pig.

puerro m leek.

puerta f door; (de jardín, ciudad) gate; (en deporte) goal; **~ de embarque** boarding gate; **~ principal** front door.

puerto m (de mar) port; (de montaña) pass; **~ deportivo** marina.

Puerto Rico s Puerto Rico.

pues conj (ya que) since; (así que) so; (uso enfático) well.

puesta f: **~ de sol** sunset.

puesto, -ta pp → poner ♦ adj (elegante) smart ♦ m (lugar) place; (cargo) job; (tienda pequeña) stall; (de la Guardia Civil) station; **~ que** as, since.

pulga f flea.

pulgar m thumb.

pulidora f polisher.

pulir vt to polish.

pulmón m lung.

pulmonía f pneumonia.

pulpa f flesh.

pulpo m octopus; **~ a la gallega** octopus cooked with red pepper and spices.

pulque m (Amér) alcoholic drink made from maguey juice.

pulquería f (Amér) bar where "pulque" is sold.

pulsar vt (timbre, botón) to press; (cuerdas de un instrumento) to play.

pulsera f bracelet.

pulso m (latido) pulse; (firmeza) steady hand.

puma m puma.

punk [pan] mf punk.

punta f (extremo agudo) point; (extremo) end; (de dedo) tip; (de tierra) spit; **en la ~ de la lengua** on the tip of one's tongue.

puntapié m kick.

puntera f toecap.

puntería f (habilidad) marksmanship.

puntiagudo, -da adj pointed.

puntilla f point lace.

punto m point; (marca) dot; (signo ortográfico) full stop; (lugar) spot, place; (momento) moment; (grado, intensidad) level; (en cirugía, costura) stitch; **estar a ~ de** to be about to; **en ~** on the dot; **hacer ~** to knit; **dos ~s** colon (sg); **~ de encuentro** meeting point; **~ muerto** neutral; **~ de vista** point of view; **~ y aparte** new paragraph; **~ y coma** semi-colon; **~ y seguido** full-stop; **~s suspensivos** suspension points.

puntuación f (en gramática) punctuation; (en competición) score; (en examen) mark.

puntual adj (persona) punctual; (detallado) detailed.

puntualidad f (de persona) punctuality.

puntualización f detailed explanation.

puntualizar vt to explain in detail.

puntuar vt (texto) to punctuate; (examen) to mark.

punzón m punch.

puñado m handful.

puñal m dagger.

puñalada f (golpe) stab; (herida) stabwound.

puñeta interj damn!

puñetazo m punch.

puñetero, -ra adj (fam) damn.

puño m (mano cerrada) fist; (de arma) hilt; (de camisa) cuff; (de bastón, paraguas) handle.

pupa f (en el labio) blister; (fam: daño) pain.

pupitre m desk.

puré m (concentrado) purée; (sopa) thick soup; **~ de patatas** mashed potatoes (pl).

puritano, -na adj puritanical.

puro, -ra adj pure; (cielo) clear; (verdad) simple ♦ m cigar.

puta f (vulg) whore.

puzzle ['puθle] m jigsaw puzzle.

PVP m abrev = **precio de venta al público**.

pza. (abrev de plaza) Sq.

Q

que pron **1.** *(cosa)* that, which; **la moto ~ me gusta** the motorbike (that) I like; **el libro ~ le regalé** the book (that) I gave her; **la playa a la ~ fui** the beach I went to; **el día en ~ me fui** the day I left.
2. *(persona: sujeto)* who, that; **el hombre ~ corre** the man who's running.
3. *(persona: complemento)* whom, that; **el hombre ~ conociste** the man you met; **la chica a la ~ lo presté** the girl to whom I lent it; **la mujer con la ~ hablas** the woman to whom you are talking.
♦ conj **1.** *(con oraciones de sujeto)* that; **es importante ~ me escuches** it's important that you listen to me.
2. *(con oraciones de complemento directo)* that; **me ha confesado ~ me quiere** he has told me that he loves me.
3. *(comparativo)* than; **es más rápido ~ tú** he's quicker than you; **antes morir ~ vivir la guerra** I'd rather die than live through a war.
4. *(expresa causa)*: **hemos de esperar, ~ todavía no es la hora** we'll have to wait, as it isn't time yet.
5. *(expresa consecuencia)* that; **tanto me lo pidió ~ se lo di** she asked for it so persistently that I gave it to her.
6. *(expresa finalidad)* so (that); **ven aquí ~ te vea** come here so (that) I can see you.
7. *(expresa deseo)* that; **espero ~ te diviertas** I hope (that) you enjoy yourself; **quiero ~ lo hagas** I want you to do it.
8. *(expresa disyunción)* or; **quieras ~ no** whether you want to or not.
9. *(en oraciones exclamativas)*: **¡~ te diviertas!** have fun!; **¡~ sí/no!** I said yes/no!

qué adj *(interrogativo)* what; *(al elegir, concretar)* which; **¿por ~ ...?** which ♦ adv how; **¿qué?** *(¿cómo?)* sorry?; **¡por ~ (...)!** why (...)?

quebrado m fraction.

quebrar vt to break ♦ vi to go bankrupt.

quedar vi *(permanecer)* to remain, to stay; *(haber suficiente, faltar)* to be left; *(llegar a ser, resultar)* to turn out; *(sentar)* to look; *(estar situado)* to be; **~ en ridículo** to make a fool of o.s.; **~ por hacer** to remain to be done; **~ bien/mal con alguien** to make a good/bad impression on sb; **~ en nada** to come to nothing ❑ **quedar con** v + prep *(citarse)* to arrange to meet; **quedar en** v + prep *(acordar)* to agree to; **quedarse** vpr *(permanecer)* to stay; *(cambio)* to keep; *(comprar)* to take; **se quedó ciego** he went blind; **quedarse con** v + prep *(preferir)* to go for; *(fam: burlarse de)* to take the mickey out of.

quehacer m task.

quejarse vpr *(protestar)* to complain; *(lamentarse)* to cry out; **~ de/por** to complain about.

quejido m cry.

quemadura f burn.

quemar vt to burn ◆ vi to be (scalding) hot ❑ **quemarse** vpr (casa, bosque, etc) to burn down; (persona) to get burnt.

quepa v → **caber.**

quepo v → **caber.**

querer m love.

◆ vt 1. (desear) to want; **quiere una bicicleta** she wants a bicycle; **queremos que las cosas vayan bien** we want things to go well; **quiero que vengas** I want you to come; **quisiera hacerlo** I would like to do it; **tal vez él quiera acompañarte** maybe he'll go with you.

2. (amar) to love; **quiere mucho a su hijo** he loves his son very much.

3. (en preguntas formales): **¿quiere pasar?** would you like to come in?

4. (precio) to want; **¿cuánto quiere por el coche?** how much does he want for the car?

5. (requerir) to need; **esta habitación quiere más luz** this room needs more light.

◆ vi 1. (apetecer) to want; **ven cuando quieras** come whenever you like ❑ want; **estoy aquí porque quiero** I'm here because I want to be.

2. (en locuciones): **queriendo** (con intención) on purpose; ~ **decir** to mean; **sin** ~ accidentally.

◆ v impers: **parece que quiere llover** it looks like rain.

❑ **quererse** vpr to love each other.

querido, -da adj dear.

queso m cheese; ~ **de bola** Dutch cheese; ~ **manchego** hard, mild yellow cheese made in La Mancha; ~ **rallado** grated cheese.

quiebra f (de empresa) bankruptcy.

quien pron (relativo sujeto) who; (relativo complemento) whom; (indefinido) whoever.

quién pron who; **¡~ pudiera verlo!** if only I could have seen it!; **¿~ es?** (en la puerta) who is it?; (al teléfono) who's speaking?

quieto, -ta adj (inmóvil) still; (inactivo) at a standstill; (de carácter) quiet.

quilla f keel.

quilo m = kilo.

química f chemistry, → **químico.**

químico, -ca m, f chemist.

quince núm fifteen, → **seis**; ~ **días** a fortnight.

quincena f fortnight.

quiniela f (juego) (football) pools (pl).

quinientos, -tas núm five hundred, → **seis.**

quinqué m oil lamp.

quinteto m quintet.

quinto, -ta núm fifth ◆ m (recluta) recruit, → **sexto.**

quiosco m (puesto) kiosk; (de periódicos) newspaper stand.

quirófano m operating theatre.

quisquilla f shrimp.

quisquilloso, -sa adj (detallista) pernickety; (susceptible) touchy.

quitamanchas m inv stain remover.

quitar vt (robar) to take; (separar, retirar, suprimir) to remove; (ropa, zapatos) to take off; **~le algo a alguien** to take sthg away from sb

❑ **quitarse** *vpr (apartarse)* to get out of the way; **~se la ropa** to take off one's clothes.

quizá(s) *adv* perhaps.

R

rábano *m* radish.

rabia *f (ira)* rage; *(enfermedad)* rabies.

rabieta *f* tantrum.

rabioso, -sa *adj (enfermo)* rabid; *(violento)* furious.

rabo *m* tail.

racha *f (de viento, aire)* gust; *(fam: época)* spell; **buena/mala ~** good/bad patch.

racial *adj* racial.

racimo *m* bunch.

ración *f* portion; *(en un bar)* large portion of a particular dish, served as a snack.

racismo *m* racism.

racista *mf* racist.

radar *m* radar.

radiación *f* radiation.

radiador *m* radiator.

radiante *adj* radiant.

radiar *vt (irradiar)* to radiate; *(en la radio)* to broadcast; *(en medicina)* to give X-ray treatment to.

radical *adj* radical.

radio *f* radio ◆ *m* radius; *(de una rueda)* spoke.

radioaficionado, -da *m, f*

radio ham.

radiocasete *m o f* radio cassette (player).

radiodespertador *m* clock radio *(with alarm)*.

radiodifusión *f* broadcasting.

radiografía *f (fotografía)* X-ray.

radiólogo, -ga *m, f* radiologist.

radionovela *f* radio soap opera.

radiorreloj *m* clock radio.

radiotaxi *m* minicab.

radioyente *mf* listener.

ráfaga *f (de viento, aire)* gust; *(de luz)* flash; *(de disparos)* burst.

rafia *f* raffia.

rafting *m* white-water rafting.

raíl *m* rail.

raíz *f* root; **a ~ de** as a result of.

raja *f (grieta)* crack; *(porción)* slice.

rajatabla: a rajatabla *adv* to the letter.

rallador *m* grater.

rallar *vt* to grate.

rally ['rali] *(pl* **rallys)** *m* rally.

rama *f* branch.

ramada *f (Amér)* shed.

rambla *f* avenue.

ramo *m (de flores)* bunch; *(de actividad)* branch.

rampa *f (pendiente)* steep incline; *(para ayudar al acceso)* ramp.

rana *f* frog.

ranchera *f (Amér)* popular Mexican song and dance.

rancho *m (granja)* ranch; *(comida)* mess.

rancio, -cia *adj (vino)* mellow; *(pasado)* rancid.

rango *m (categoría social)* standing; *(en una jerarquía)* rank.

ranura *f (surco)* groove; *(para monedas)* slot.

rape *m* angler fish; ~ **a la marinera** *angler fish cooked in a white wine and garlic sauce;* ~ **a la plancha** *grilled angler fish.*

rápidamente *adv* quickly.

rapidez *f* speed.

rápido, -da *adj (veloz)* fast; *(que dura poco)* quick ◆ *adv* quickly ◆ *m (tren)* express train ☐ **rápidos** *mpl* rapids.

raptar *vt* to abduct.

raqueta *f (de tenis)* racquet; *(para la nieve)* snowshoe.

raramente *adv* rarely.

raro, -ra *adj (poco frecuente)* unusual; *(extraño)* strange; *(escaso)* rare; *(extravagante)* odd.

rascacielos *m inv* skyscraper.

rascador *m* scraper.

rascar *vt (con las uñas)* to scratch; *(limpiar)* to scrub; *(pintura)* to scrape (off).

rasgar *vt* to tear.

rasgo *m (de rostro)* feature; *(característica)* characteristic; *(trazo)* stroke.

raso, -sa *adj (superficie)* flat; *(cucharada, etc)* level ◆ *m* satin; **al ~** in the open (air).

rastrillo *m* rake.

rastro *m (huella)* trace; *(mercadillo)* flea market.

 RASTRO

A "rastro" is a street market where antiques, second-hand

and new goods are sold. The most famous "rastro" is the one in Madrid, although they are to be found in most Spanish cities.

---

rata *f* rat.

ratero, -ra *m, f* petty thief.

rato *m* while; **a ~s** from time to time; **pasar un buen ~** to have a good time; **pasar un mal ~** to have a hard time of it; **~s libres** spare time *(sg)*.

ratón *m* mouse.

rattán *m (Amér)* wicker.

raya *f (línea)* line; *(estampado)* stripe; *(del pelo)* parting; *(de pantalón)* crease; *(arañazo)* scratch; *(pez)* ray; **a ~ o de ~s** stripy.

rayo *m* ray; *(de tormenta)* bolt of lightning; **~s** lightning *(sg)*; **~s-X** X-rays.

rayuela *f* pitch and toss.

raza *f (de personas)* race; *(de animales)* breed; **de ~** pedigree.

razón *f* reason; **dar la ~ a alguien** to say that sb is right; **entrar en ~** to see reason; **"se vende piso: ~ portería"** "flat for sale: enquire at caretaker's office"; **tener ~** to be right.

razonable *adj* reasonable.

razonamiento *m* reasoning.

razonar *vt* to reason out ◆ *vi* to reason.

reacción *f* reaction.

reaccionar *vi (responder)* to react; *(a tratamiento)* to respond.

reactor *m (avión)* jet (plane); *(motor)* jet engine.

real *adj (verdadero)* real; *(de rey)* royal.

realeza f royalty.

realidad f (existencia) reality; (verdad) truth; **en ~** in fact.

realismo m realism.

realización f (de tarea, trabajo) carrying-out; (de proyecto, plan) implementation; (de deseo, sueño) fulfilment; (de película) production.

realizar vt (tarea, trabajo) to carry out; (proyecto, plan) to implement; (deseo, sueño) to fulfil; (película) to produce.

realmente adv (en verdad) actually; (muy) really.

realquilado, -da m, f subtenant.

realquilar vt to sublet.

reanimación f (de fuerzas, energía) recovery; (de enfermo) revival; (del ánimo) cheering-up.

rebaja f (de precio) discount; (de altura, nivel, etc) reduction ➪ **rebajas** fpl sales.

rebajado, -da adj reduced.

rebajar vt (precio) to reduce; (altura, nivel, etc) to lower; (humillar) to humiliate.

rebanada f slice.

rebanar vt to slice.

rebaño m (de ovejas) flock.

rebelarse vpr to rebel.

rebelde adj rebellious; (niño, pelo) unruly; (enfermedad) persistent ◆ mf rebel.

rebeldía f (cualidad) rebelliousness; (acción) rebellion.

rebelión f rebellion.

rebozado, -da adj coated in batter or fried breadcrumbs.

recado m (mensaje) message.

recaer vi (en enfermedad) to have a relapse; (en vicio, error, etc) to relapse.

recalcar vt to stress.

recalentar vt (volver a calentar) to warm up; (calentar demasiado) to overheat ➪ **recalentarse** vpr to overheat.

recámara f (Amér) bedroom.

recamarera f (Amér) maid.

recambio m (pieza) spare (part); (de pluma) refill.

recargar vt (mechero, recipiente) to refill; (batería) to recharge; (arma) to reload; (cargar demasiado) to overload; (impuesto) to increase.

recato m (pudor) modesty; (prudencia) caution.

recepción f reception.

recepcionista mf receptionist.

receptor m receiver.

recesión f recession.

receta f (de guiso) recipe; **~ (médica)** prescription.

recetar vt to prescribe.

rechazar vt to reject; (físicamente) to push away; (denegar) to turn down.

rechazo m rejection.

recibidor m entrance hall.

recibimiento m reception.

recibir vt to receive; (dar la bienvenida a) to welcome; (ir a buscar) to meet.

recibo m receipt.

reciclado, -da adj recycled.

reciclar vt to recycle ➪ **reciclarse** vpr (persona) to retrain.

recién adv recently; **~ hecho** fresh; **~ nacido** newborn baby; **"~ pintado"** "wet paint".

reciente adj recent.

recientemente adv recently.

recinto m area.

recipiente m container.

recital m (de música pop) concert; (de música clásica) recital.

recitar vt to recite.

reclamación f (queja) complaint; (petición) claim; "reclamaciones y quejas" "complaints".

reclamar vt to demand.

recluir vt to shut away.

reclusión f (encarcelamiento) imprisonment; (voluntaria) seclusion.

recobrar vt to recover ❑ **recobrarse de** v + prep to recover from.

recogedor m dustpan.

recoger vt (coger) to pick up; (reunir) to collect; (fruta) to pick; (ir a buscar) to meet; (mesa) to clear; (acoger) to take in ❑ **recogerse** vpr (retirarse) to withdraw; (acostarse) to retire.

recogida f (de objetos, basura, etc) collection; (de frutos) harvest.

recolección f (de frutos) harvesting.

recomendar vt to recommend.

recompensa f reward.

recompensar vt to reward.

reconocer vt (reconocer; (examinar) to examine; (terreno) to survey.

reconocimiento m recognition; (agradecimiento) gratitude; (en medicina) examination.

récord ['rekor] m record.

recordar vt to remember; ~ **a alguien a** to remind sb of.

recorrer vt (país, etc) to travel across; (distancia) to cover.

recorrido m (trayecto) route; (viaje) journey; **tren de largo ~** intercity train.

recortar vt (pelo) to trim; (papel) to cut out; (tela, gastos, precio) to cut.

recostarse vpr to lie down.

recreo m (diversión) recreation; (de escolares) break.

recta f straight line.

rectangular adj rectangular.

rectángulo m rectangle.

rectitud f rectitude.

recto, -ta adj (camino, línea, etc) straight; (severo, honesto) upright; **todo ~** straight on.

rector, -ra m, f vice chancellor (Br), president (Am).

recuerdo m (del pasado) memory; (de viaje) souvenir ❑ **recuerdos** mpl (saludos) regards; **dar ~s a** to give one's regards to.

recuperación f recovery.

recuperar vt to recover; (tiempo) to make up ❑ **recuperarse** vpr (volver en sí) to come to; **recuperarse de** v + prep to recover from.

recurrir vi (en juicio) to appeal; ~ **a** (pedir ayuda) to turn to.

recurso m (medio) resort; (reclamación) appeal ❑ **recursos** mpl resources; **~s humanos** human resources.

red f (malla, en deporte) net; (de pelo) hairnet; (de carreteras, conductos, etc) network; (de tiendas, empresas, etc) chain.

redacción f (de texto, periódico) editing; (en escuela) essay; (estilo)

wording; *(conjunto de personas)* editorial team; *(oficina)* editorial office.

redactar *vt* to write.

redactor, -ra *m, f (escritor)* writer; *(editor)* editor.

redil *m* pen.

redondeado, -da *adj (material, forma, etc)* rounded; *(precio, cantidad, etc)* rounded up/down.

redondel *m* ring.

redondo, -da *adj* round; *(perfecto)* excellent.

reducción *f* reduction.

reducir *vt* to reduce; *(someter)* to suppress ❑ **reducirse a** *v + prep* to be reduced to.

reembolsar *vt (gastos)* to reimburse; *(dinero)* to refund; *(deuda)* to repay.

reembolso *m (de gastos)* reimbursement; *(de dinero)* refund; *(de deuda)* repayment; **contra ~** cash on delivery.

reemplazar *vt* to replace.

reestrenar *vt* to re-release.

reestreno *m* re-release.

reestructurar *vt* to restructure.

refacción *f (Amér)* spare (part).

refaccionar *vt (Amér)* to repair.

referencia *f* reference ❑ **referencias** *fpl* references.

referéndum *m* referendum.

referente *adj*: **~ a** concerning.

referirse: referirse a *v + prep* to refer to.

refinería *f* refinery.

reflector *m* spotlight.

reflejar *vt* to reflect ❑ **reflejarse** *vpr* to be reflected.

reflejo, -ja *adj (movimiento)* reflex ♦ *m (luz)* gleam; *(imagen)* reflection ❑ **reflejos** *mpl (reacción rápida)* reflexes; **hacerse ~s** *(en el pelo)* to have highlights put in.

reflexión *f* reflection.

reflexionar *vi* to reflect.

reforma *f* reform; *(de casa, edificio)* alteration; *(de idea, plan)* change.

reformar *vt* to reform; *(casa, edificio)* to do up; *(idea, plan)* to alter ❑ **reformarse** *vpr* to mend one's ways.

reforzar *vt* to reinforce.

refrán *m* proverb.

refrescante *adj* refreshing.

refresco *m* soft drink; **"~s"** "refreshments".

refrigerado, -da *adj (con aire acondicionado)* air-conditioned.

refrigerador *m* refrigerator.

refugiado, -da *m, f* refugee.

refugiar *vt* to give refuge to ❑ **refugiarse** *vpr* to take refuge.

refugio *m* refuge; *(de guerra)* shelter.

regadera *f (para plantas)* watering can; *(Amér: ducha)* shower head.

regadío *m* irrigated land.

regalar *vt (obsequiar)* to give (as a present); *(dar gratis)* to give away.

regaliz *m* liquorice.

regalo *m* present, gift.

regañar *vt* to tell off ♦ *vi (pelearse)* to argue.

regar *vt (campos, plantas)* to water; *(suj: río)* to flow through.

regata *f (competición)* regatta;

(canal) irrigation channel.

regatear *vt (precio)* to haggle over; *(esfuerzos, ayuda)* to be sparing with; *(en deporte)* to beat, to dribble past.

regazo *m* lap.

regenerar *vt (cosa)* to regenerate; *(persona)* to reform ❑ **regenerarse** *vpr (persona)* to mend one's ways.

regente *m (Amér)* mayor.

régimen *m (de alimentación)* diet; *(conjunto de normas)* rules *(pl)*; *(forma de gobierno)* regime.

región *f* region.

regional *adj* regional.

regir *vt (dirigir)* to run ◆ *vi* to apply.

registrar *vt (inspeccionar)* to search; *(cachear)* to frisk; *(en lista, registro, cinta)* to record ❑ **registrarse** *vpr (ocurrir)* to occur.

registro *m (libro)* register; *(inspección)* search; *(de luz, agua, etc)* cupboard containing electricity/water meter; **~ (civil)** registry office.

regla *f (norma)* rule; *(instrumento)* ruler; *(menstruación)* period; **en ~** in order; **por ~ general** as a rule.

reglamento *m* regulations *(pl)*.

regresar *vt (Amér)* to return ◆ *vi* to return ❑ **regresarse** *vpr (Amér)* to return.

regreso *m* return.

regular *adj (uniforme)* regular; *(de tamaño)* medium; *(vuelo)* scheduled; *(habitual)* normal; *(mediocre)* average ◆ *vt (reglamentar)* to regulate; *(mecanismo)* to adjust ◆ *adv* all right.

regularidad *f* regularity.

rehabilitar *vt (local, casa, etc)* to restore; *(persona)* to rehabilitate.

rehén *mf* hostage.

rehogar *vt* to fry over a low heat.

reina *f* queen.

reinado *m* reign.

reinar *vi* to reign.

reincorporar *vt* to reincorporate ❑ **reincorporarse a** *v + prep* to go back to.

reino *m* kingdom.

Reino Unido *m*: **el ~** the United Kingdom.

reintegro *m (pago)* reimbursement; *(en banco)* withdrawal; *(en lotería)* return of one's stake.

reír *vi* to laugh ◆ *vt* to laugh at ❑ **reírse de** *v + prep* to laugh at.

reivindicación *f* claim.

reivindicar *vt* to claim.

reja *f (de puerta, ventana)* bars *(pl)*.

rejilla *f (para abertura)* grid; *(de ventana)* grille; *(de horno)* gridiron; *(de silla)* wickerwork; *(para equipaje)* luggage rack.

rejuvenecer *vt & vi* to rejuvenate.

relación *f (nexo)* relation; *(trato)* relationship; *(enumeración)* list; *(narración)* account ❑ **relaciones** *fpl (amistades)* relations; *(influencias)* connections; *(noviazgo)* relationship *(sg)*.

relacionar *vt* to relate ❑ **relacionarse** *vpr (ideas, objetos, etc)* to be related; *(personas)* to mix.

relajación *f* relaxation.

relajar *vt* to relax ❑ **relajarse** *vpr* to relax.

relajo *m (Amér)* commotion.

relámpago *m* flash of lightning.

relampaguear *v impers*: **relampagueó** lightning flashed.

relatar *vt* to relate.

relativo, -va *adj* (*no absoluto*) relative; (*escaso*) limited; **~ a** concerning.

relato *m* (*cuento*) tale; (*exposición*) account.

relevo *m* (*sustitución*) relief; (*en deporte*) relay ❏ **relevos** *mpl* relay (race) (*sg*).

relieve *m* relief; (*importancia*) importance.

religión *f* religion.

religioso, -sa *adj* religious ◆ *m, f* (*monje*) monk (*f* nun).

relinchar *vi* to neigh.

rellano *m* landing.

rellenar *vt* (*volver a llenar*) to refill; (*pastel*) to fill; (*pollo, almohada*) to stuff; (*formulario, documento*) to fill in.

relleno, -na *adj* stuffed ◆ *m* stuffing; (*de pastel*) filling.

reloj *m* clock; **~ de arena** hourglass; **~ (de pared)** clock; **~ (de pulsera)** watch.

relojería *f* (*tienda*) watchmaker's (shop); (*taller*) watchmaker's workshop.

relojero, -ra *m, f* watchmaker.

remar *vi* to row.

remediar *vt* (*solucionar*) to put right; (*problema*) to solve.

remedio *m* (*solución*) solution; (*auxilio*) help; (*para enfermedad*) remedy; **no queda más ~** there's nothing for it; **no tener más ~ to** have no choice; **sin ~** hopeless.

remendar *vt* to mend.

remezón *m* (*Amér*) earth tremor.

remite *m* sender's name and address.

remitente *mf* sender.

remitir *vt* to send ❏ **remitir a** *v + prep* to refer to.

remo *m* oar.

remojar *vt* to soak.

remojo *m*: **poner en ~** to leave to soak.

remolacha *f* beetroot (*Br*), beet (*Am*).

remolcador *m* (*embarcación*) tugboat; (*camión*) breakdown lorry.

remolcar *vt* to tow.

remolque *m* (*vehículo*) trailer.

remontar *vt* to go up ❏ **remontarse a** *v + prep* to date back to.

remordimiento *m* remorse.

remoto, -ta *adj* remote.

remover *vt* (*café, sopa*) to stir; (*tierra*) to dig up; (*recuerdos*) to rake up.

remuneración *f* remuneration.

renacuajo *m* tadpole.

rencor *m* resentment.

rendición *f* surrender.

rendimiento *m* (*de motor*) performance.

rendir *vt* (*homenaje*) to pay ◆ *vi* (*máquina*) to perform well; (*persona*) to be productive; (*negocio, dinero*) to be profitable ❏ **rendirse** *vpr* (*someterse*) to surrender.

RENFE *f* Spanish state railway network.

reno m reindeer.

renovación f (de decoración, local) renovation; (de contrato, carné) renewal.

renovar vt (decoración, local) to renovate; (contrato, carné, relación) to renew; (vestuario) to clear out.

renta f (ingresos) income; (beneficio) return; (alquiler) rent.

rentable adj profitable.

rentar vt (Amér) to rent.

renunciar: renunciar a v + prep (prescindir de) to give up; (declinar) to refuse to.

reñir vt (reprender) to tell off ◆ vi (pelearse) to argue; (romper relaciones) to fall out.

reo, -a m, f offender.

reparación f (de coche, avería, etc) repair; (de daño, ofensa, etc) reparation.

reparar vt (coche, máquina, etc) to repair; (equivocación, ofensa, etc) to make amends for □ **reparar en** v + prep to notice.

repartidor, -ra m, f deliveryman (f deliverywoman).

repartir vt (dividir) to share out; (distribuir) to deliver.

reparto m (de bienes, dinero, etc) division; (de mercancías, periódicos, etc) delivery; (de actores) cast.

repasar vt to go over; (trabajo, lección) to revise; (releer) to go over; (remendar) to mend; **~ apuntes** to go over one's notes.

repaso m revision; (fam: reprensión) telling off.

repelente adj repulsive.

repente: de repente adv suddenly.

repentino, -na adj sudden.

repercusión f repercussion.

repertorio m (catálogo) list; (de actor, compañía, etc) repertoire.

repetición f repetition.

repetidor, -ra m, f (alumno) student repeating a year ◆ m (en telecomunicaciones) repeater.

repetir vt to repeat; (comida, bebida) to have seconds of ◆ vi (sabor) to repeat.

réplica f (copia) replica; (contestación) reply.

replicar vt & vi to answer back.

repoblación f (de ciudad, región, etc) repopulation; (de bosque, campos) replanting; **~ forestal** reafforestation.

repoblar vt (ciudad, región, etc) to repopulate; (bosque, campos, etc) to replant.

reponer vt to replace; (película, obra de teatro) to re-run ◆ **reponerse** vpr to recover.

reportaje m (en radio, televisión) report; (en periódico, revista) article.

reportar vt (Amér) to report □ **reportarse** (Amér) to report.

reporte m (Amér) report.

reportero, -ra m, f reporter.

reposera f (Amér) deck chair.

reposo m (descanso) rest; (quietud) calm.

repostería f confectionery.

representación f representation; (de obra de teatro) performance; **en ~ de** on behalf of.

representante mf (de actor, cantante, etc) agent; (vendedor) representative.

representar vt to represent;

(obra de teatro) to perform; *(edad)* to look; *(importar)* to mean.

representativo, -va *adj* representative.

represión *f* suppression.

reprimir *vt* to suppress ❏ **reprimirse** *vpr* to restrain o.s.

reprochar *vt* to reproach.

reproche *m* reproach.

reproducción *f* reproduction.

reproducir *vt* to reproduce ❏ **reproducirse** *vpr (seres vivos)* to reproduce.

reptar *vi* to crawl.

reptil *m* reptile.

república *f* republic.

República Dominicana *f*: la ~ the Dominican Republic.

republicano, -na *adj* republican.

repuesto, -ta *pp* → **reponer** ♦ *m (recambio)* spare (part); **de ~** spare.

repugnar *vt*: me repugna ese olor I find that smell disgusting.

reputación *f* reputation.

requerir *vt* to require.

requesón *m* cottage cheese.

resaca *f (de borrachera)* hangover; *(del mar)* undertow.

resbalada *f (Amér)* slip.

resbaladizo, -za *adj* slippery.

resbalar *vi (deslizarse)* to slide; *(caer)* to slip; *(equivocarse)* to slip up ❏ **resbalarse** *vpr* to slip.

rescatar *vt* to rescue.

rescate *m (dinero)* ransom.

resentimiento *m* resentment.

reserva[1] *f (de habitación, asiento, comedimiento)* reservation; *(cautela)*

discretion; *(de alimentos, provisiones, etc)* reserves *(pl)*; *(de animales)* reserve; *(de repuesto)* in reserve; **"~s hoteles y pensiones"** "hotel and guest house reservations"; **~ natural** nature reserve.

reserva[2] *m (vino)* vintage.

reservado, -da *adj* reserved ♦ *m (compartimiento)* reserved compartment.

reservar *vt (asiento, billete, etc)* to reserve, to book; *(callar)* to reserve; *(noticia, datos)* to keep to o.s.; *(guardar)* to set aside.

resfriado, -da *m* cold ♦ *adj*: estar ~ to have a cold.

resfriarse *vpr* to catch a cold.

resfrío *m (Amér)* cold.

resguardar *vt* to protect ❏ **resguardarse de** *v + prep* to shelter from.

resguardo *m (documento)* receipt.

residencia *f (estancia)* stay; *(casa)* residence; *(de estudiantes)* hall of residence; *(de ancianos)* old people's home; *(pensión)* guest house.

residuo *m* residue ❏ **residuos** *mpl* waste *(sg)*.

resignarse *vpr* to resign o.s.

resistencia *f* resistance; *(para correr, etc)* stamina; *(de pared, material, etc)* strength.

resistente *adj* tough.

resistir *vt (carga, dolor, enfermedad)* to withstand; *(tentación, deseo, ataque)* to resist; *(tolerar)* to stand ♦ *vi (durar)* to keep going ❏ **resistirse a** *v + prep* to refuse to.

resolver *vt (duda, crisis)* to

resolve; *(problema, caso)* to solve.

resonancia *f (de sonido)* resonance; *(repercusión)* repercussions *(pl)*.

resorte *m* spring.

respaldo *m (de asiento)* back.

respectivo, -va *adj* respective.

respecto *m*: al ~ in this respect; *(con)* ~ a regarding.

respetable *adj (digno de respeto)* respectable; *(considerable)* considerable.

respetar *vt* to respect.

respeto *m* respect.

respiración *f* breathing.

respirar *vi* to breathe; *(sentir alivio)* to breathe again.

respiro *m (alivio)* relief; **darse un ~** to have a breather.

resplandor *m* brightness.

responder *vt* to answer ♦ *vi (contestar)* to answer; *(replicar)* to answer back; *(reaccionar)* to respond; **~ a algo** to answer sthg ❑ **responder a** *v + prep (deberse a)* to be due to; **responder de** *v + prep* to answer for; **responder por** *v + prep* to answer for.

responsabilidad *f* responsibility.

responsable *adj* responsible; **~ de** responsible for.

respuesta *f (contestación)* answer; *(reacción)* response.

resta *f* subtraction.

restar *vt (quitar)* to take away; *(en matemáticas)* to subtract.

restauración *f* restoration; *(en hostelería)* restaurant trade.

restaurado, -da *adj* restored.

restaurador, -ra *m, f (de pintura, escultura, etc)* restorer; *(en hostelería)* restauranteur.

restaurante *m* restaurant.

restaurar *vt* to restore.

resto *m* ❑ **restos** *mpl* remains; *(de comida)* leftovers.

restricción *f* restriction.

resucitar *vt (persona)* to bring back to life ♦ *vi* to rise from the dead.

resuelto, -ta *pp* → **resolver** ♦ *adj (decidido)* determined.

resultado *m* result.

resultar *vi (acabar en)* to turn out to be; *(tener éxito)* to work out; *(ser)* to be ❑ **resultar de** *v + prep* to result from.

resumen *m* summary.

resumir *vt* to summarize.

retablo *m* altarpiece.

retal *m* remnant.

retención *f (de tráfico)* hold-up; *(de líquidos, grasas)* retention.

retirado, -da *adj (apartado)* secluded; *(jubilado)* retired.

retirar *vt (quitar, recoger)* to remove; *(carné, permiso, dinero, afirmación)* to withdraw ❑ **retirarse** *vpr* to retire.

reto *m* challenge.

retocar *vt (fotografía, pintura)* to touch up; *(trabajo)* to put the finishing touches to.

retorcer *vt (brazo)* to twist; *(ropa)* to wring ❑ **retorcerse de** *v + prep (dolor)* to writhe in; *(risa)* to double up with.

retórica *f* rhetoric.

retornable *adj* returnable.

retorno *m* return.

retransmisión f broadcast.

retransmitir vt to broadcast.

retrasado, -da adj (tren) delayed; (trabajo) behind; (reloj) slow; (no actual) old-fashioned; (persona) backward.

retrasar vt (aplazar) to postpone; (reloj) to put back; (hacer más lento) to hold up ❏ **retrasarse** vpr (tardar) to be late; (reloj) to lose time; (en el pago) to be behind.

retraso m (de persona, tren, etc) delay; (de reloj) slowness; (de pueblo, cultura, etc) backwardness; (deuda) arrears (pl); **con ~ late; llevar ~** to be late.

retratar vt (fotografiar) to photograph; (dibujar, pintar) to do a portrait of; (describir) to portray.

retrato m (fotografía) photograph; (dibujo, pintura) portrait; (descripción) portrayal; (imagen parecida) spitting image.

retrete m toilet.

retroceder vi to go back.

retrospectivo, -va adj retrospective.

retrovisor m rear-view mirror.

reuma m o f rheumatism.

reunión f meeting.

reunir vt (personas) to bring together; (dinero, fondos) to raise; (condiciones) to meet ❏ **reunirse** vpr to reunite.

revancha f revenge.

revelado m developing; **~ en color/blanco y negro** color/black and white developing.

revelar vt (secreto, noticia, etc) to reveal; (fotografía) to develop.

reventar vt (romper) to burst;

(fam: fastidiar) to bug ◆ vi (cansar) to get exhausted; (bomba) to explode; (globo) to burst; (fam: morir) to kick the bucket ❏ **reventarse** vpr (romperse) to burst.

reventón m puncture.

reverencia f (inclinación) bow.

reversible adj reversible.

reverso m back.

revés m (de moneda, folio, etc) back; (con raqueta) backhand; (con mano) slap; (desgracia) setback; **al ~** (en orden contrario) the other way round; (en mal orden) the wrong way round; (al contrario) on the contrary.

revestimiento m (de pintura) coat.

revisar vt (corregir) to revise; (coche) to service.

revisión f (repaso) revision; (arreglo) amendment.

revisor, -ra m, f (en tren) ticket inspector; (en autobús) conductor.

revista f (publicación) magazine; (espectáculo) revue; (inspección) inspection.

revistero m magazine rack.

revolcarse vpr to roll about.

revoltillo m (confusión) jumble; (guiso) scrambled egg, usually with fried prawns and mushrooms.

revoltoso, -sa adj (travieso) naughty; (rebelde) rebellious.

revolución f revolution.

revolucionario, -ria m, f revolutionary.

revolver vt (mezclar) to mix; (desordenar) to mess up; (líquido) to stir.

revólver m revolver.

revuelta f (rebelión) revolt.

revuelto, -ta pp → revolver ◆ adj (desordenado) in a mess; (turbio) cloudy; (tiempo) unsettled; (mar) choppy; (alborotado) turbulent ◆ m scrambled eggs (pl).

rey m king; **los Reyes Magos** the Three Wise Men ❑ **Reyes** m (fiesta) Epiphany, 6 January when Spanish children traditionally receive presents.

REYES

On 6 January, Spanish children traditionally receive presents supposedly brought by the Three Wise Men. The "roscón de reyes" is a large ring-shaped bun eaten for dessert on this day, in which a bean and a small figure are hidden. Whoever gets the slice with the bean has to pay for the "roscón", whilst the person who finds the figure is proclaimed "king of the party".

rezar vt to say ◆ vi to pray.

rezo m prayer.

ría f estuary.

riachuelo m stream.

riada f flood.

ribera f (del río) bank; (del mar) shore; (terreno) plain (irrigated by a river).

ribete m (de vestido, zapato, etc) edging; (añadido) touch.

rico, -ca adj rich; (sabroso) tasty; (fam: simpático) cute.

ridículo, -la adj (cómico) ridiculous; (escaso) laughable ◆ m: **hacer el ~** to make a fool of o.s.

riego m irrigation.

rienda f rein.

riesgo m risk; **a todo ~** comprehensive.

rifar vt to raffle.

rigidez f (de palo, tela, etc) stiffness; (de carácter) inflexibility; (de norma, regla) strictness.

rígido, -da adj (palo, tela, etc) stiff; (carácter, persona) inflexible; (norma, regla) strict.

rigor m (exactitud) accuracy; (severidad) strictness; (del clima) harshness; **de ~** essential.

riguroso, -sa adj (exacto) rigorous; (severo, normas, leyes, etc) strict; (frío, calor) harsh.

rima f rhyme.

rímel m mascara.

rincón m corner.

ring m (boxing) ring.

rinoceronte m rhinoceros.

riña f (discusión) quarrel; (pelea) fight.

riñón m kidney ❑ **riñones** mpl (parte del cuerpo) lower back (sg); **riñones al jerez** kidneys cooked in sherry.

riñonera f bum bag (Br), fanny pack (Am).

río m river.

rioja m Rioja (wine).

RIP (abrev de requiescat in pace) RIP.

riqueza f (fortuna) wealth; (cualidad) richness.

risa f laughter.

ristra f string.

ritmo m (armonía) rhythm; (velocidad) pace.

rito m rite; (costumbre) ritual.

ritual m ritual.

rival mf rival.

rizado, -da adj (pelo) curly; (papel, tela, etc) crumpled; (mar) choppy.

rizo m (de pelo) curl.

RNE (abrev de Radio Nacional de España) Spanish national radio station.

robar vt (quitar) to steal; (casa) to burgle; (cobrar demasiado) to rob; (en naipes, dominó) to draw.

roble m oak.

robo m robbery; (en casa) burglary; (estafa): **es un ~** it's daylight robbery.

robot m (de cocina) food processor.

robusto, -ta adj robust.

roca f rock.

roce m (acción) rub; (más suave) brush; (desgaste) wear; (trato) close contact; (desavenencia) brush.

rociar vt (mojar) to sprinkle; (con spray) to spray.

rocío m dew.

rock m rock.

rocoso, -sa adj rocky.

rodaballo m turbot.

rodaje m (de película) shooting; (de vehículo) running-in.

rodar vt (película) to shoot; (vehículo) to run in ◆ vi (bola, pelota, etc) to roll; (coche) to go, to travel; (caerse) to tumble; (deambular) to wander.

rodeado, -da adj surrounded; **~ de** surrounded by.

rodear vt (cercar) to surround; (dar la vuelta a) to go around ❑ **rodearse de** v + prep to surround

o.s. with.

rodeo m (camino largo, vuelta) detour; (al hablar) evasiveness; (espectáculo) rodeo; **dar ~s** to beat about the bush.

rodilla f knee; **de ~s** on one's knees.

rodillo m (de máquina) roller; (utensilio) rolling pin.

roedor m rodent.

roer vt (raspar, atormentar) to gnaw (at); (desgastar) to eat away (at).

rogar vt (pedir) to ask.

rojo, -ja adj, m, f red.

rollito m: **~ de primavera** spring roll.

rollo m (cilindro) roll; (película fotográfica) (roll of) film; (fam: persona, cosa, actividad aburrida) bore.

romana f: **a la ~** fried in batter.

románico, -ca adj (lengua) Romance; (en arte) Romanesque ◆ m Romanesque.

romano, -na adj Roman.

romántico, -ca adj (sentimental) romantic; (en arte) Romantic.

rombo m (símbolo) lozenge.

romería f (fiesta) popular religious festival combining a religious ceremony and dancing, eating etc.

romero m (planta) rosemary.

romo, -ma adj blunt.

rompecabezas m inv (juego) jigsaw; (asunto complicado) puzzle.

rompeolas m inv breakwater.

romper vt to break; (rasgar) to tear; (hacer añicos) to smash; (terminar) to break off ◆ vi (olas, día) to break; **~ con alguien** to split up with sb; **~ a hacer algo** to sudden-

ly start doing sthg ❑ **romperse**
vpr (partirse) to break; *(desgarrarse)*
to tear.

ron *m* rum.

roncar *vi (persona)* to snore;
(mar, viento, etc) to roar.

ronco, -ca *adj* hoarse.

ronda *f (paseo)* nighttime walk on
which young men serenade young
women outside their windows; *(grupo
de personas)* group of serenaders;
(vigilancia) rounds *(pl)*; *(de
copas, tapas)* round; *(de circunvalación)* ring road.

rondín *m (Amér)* guard.

ronquido *m (de persona)* snore;
(de motor, máquina) roar.

ronronear *vi* to purr.

ronroneo *m* purr.

ropa *f* clothes *(pl)*; **~ interior**
underwear.

roquefort [roke'for] *m* Roquefort; **al ~ in** a Roquefort sauce.

rosa *f* rose ♦ *adj inv* pink; **~ de
los vientos** compass.

rosado, -da *adj* pink ♦ *m* rosé.

rosal *m* rose(bush).

rosario *m* rosary.

roscón *m* **~ (de reyes)** ring-
shaped bun eaten on 6 January).

rosetón *m* rose window.

rosquilla *f* ring doughnut.

rostro *m* face.

rotativo *m* newspaper.

roto, -ta *pp →* **romper** ♦ *adj*
broken ♦ *m (en ropa)* tear.

rotonda *f (plaza)* circus; *(edificio)* rotunda.

rotulador *m (para dibujar)* felt-
tip pen; *(para marcar)* marker pen.

rótulo *m (letrero)* sign.

rotundo, -da *adj (respuesta,
negación)* emphatic.

rozar *vt (frotar)* to rub; *(tocar)* to
brush (against) ❑ **rozarse** *vpr
(desgastarse)* to get worn.

r.p.m. *(abrev de* revoluciones por
minuto)* rpm.

Rte. *abrev =* remitente.

RTVE *f* Spanish state broadcasting
company.

rubí *m* ruby.

rubio, -bia *adj* blond *(f*
blonde).

rubor *m (enrojecimiento)* blush;
(vergüenza) embarrassment.

ruborizarse *vpr* to blush.

rudimentario, -ria *adj* rudi-
mentary.

rudo, -da *adj (descortés)*
rude.

rueda *f (pieza)* wheel; *(corro)* circle; **~ de prensa** press conference;
~ de repuesto O **de recambio** spare
wheel.

ruedo *m (plaza de toros)* bullring;
(de falda) hem.

ruego *m* request.

rugby *m* rugby.

rugido *m* roar.

rugir *vi* to roar.

rugoso, -sa *adj (áspero)* rough;
(con arrugas) wrinkled.

ruido *m (sonido desagradable)*
noise; *(sonido cualquiera)* sound.

ruidoso, -sa *adj* noisy.

ruin *adj* mean.

ruina *f* ruin ❑ **ruinas** *fpl* ruins.

ruinoso, -sa *adj (edificio,
puente)* tumbledown; *(negocio, trabajo)* ruinous.

ruiseñor *m* nightingale.

ruleta f roulette.

rulo m (rizo) curl; (objeto) curler.

ruma f (Amér) pile.

rumba f rumba.

rumbo m (dirección) direction; (con) ~ a heading for.

rumiante m ruminant.

rumiar vt (masticar) to chew; (fig: reflexionar) to chew over.

rumor m (chisme) rumour; (ruido) murmur.

rumorearse v impers: **se rumorea que** ... it is rumoured that ...

ruptura f (de relaciones) breaking-off.

rural adj rural.

Rusia s Russia.

ruso, -sa adj, m, f Russian.

ruta f route.

rutina f routine.

S

s (abrev de segundo) sec.

S (abrev de San) St.

SA f (abrev de sociedad anónima) = Ltd, = PLC.

sábado m Saturday; **cada ~, todos los ~s** every Saturday; **caer en ~** to be on a Saturday; **el próximo ~, el ~ que viene** next Saturday; **viene el ~** she's coming on Saturday; **el ~ pasado** last Saturday; **el ~ por la ma-** ñana/tarde/noche (on) Saturday morning/afternoon/night; **este ~** (pasado) last Saturday; (próximo) this (coming) Saturday; **los ~s** (on) Saturdays.

sábana f sheet.

sabañón m chilblain.

saber m knowledge ◆ vt (conocer) to know; (entender de) to know about; (poder hablar) to speak ◆ vi: ~ **hacer algo** (ser capaz de) to know how to do sthg, to be able to do sthg; **¿sabes algo de él?** have you heard from him?; ~ **bien/mal** (alimento, bebida) to taste good/bad; ~ **mal a alguien** to upset sb ☐ **saber a** v + prep to taste of.

sabiduría f (prudencia) wisdom; (conocimiento profundo) knowledge.

sabio, -bia adj (prudente) wise; (con conocimientos profundos) knowledgable ◆ m, f (persona prudente) wise person; (persona sabia) knowledgable person.

sable m sabre.

sabor m (gusto) taste; (variedad) flavour; **tener ~ a** to taste of; **helado con ~ a fresa** strawberry ice cream.

saborear vt to savour.

sabotaje m sabotage.

sabrá v → saber.

sabroso, -sa adj (comida) tasty; (comentario, noticia, etc) juicy; (cantidad) substantial.

sacacorchos m inv corkscrew.

sacapuntas m inv pencil sharpener.

sacar vt (extraer, llevar) to take out; (quitar) to remove; (salvar, información) to get out; (conseguir) *obtener)* to get; *(en el juego)* to play; *(ensanchar)* to let out; *(pecho, barriga)* to stick out; *(crear, fabricar)* to bring out; *(copia)* to make ♦ vi *(en tenis)* to serve; ~ **billetes** O **entradas** to get tickets; ~ **brillo** to polish; ~ **dinero** to withdraw money; ~ **fotos** to take photos; ~ **la lengua** to stick one's tongue out; ~ **nota** to get a good mark; ~ **buenas/malas notas** to get good/bad marks; **sacan tres puntos a sus rivales** they are three points ahead of their rivals ❏ **sacarse** *vpr (carné, permiso)* to get.

sacarina *f* saccharine.

sacerdote *m* priest.

saciar *vt* to satisfy; *(sed)* to quench.

saco *m* sack, bag; *(Amér: chaqueta)* jacket; ~ **de dormir** sleeping bag.

sacramento *m* sacrament.

sacrificar *vt (renunciar a)* to sacrifice; *(animal)* to slaughter ❏ **sacrificarse** *vpr:* ~**se por** to make sacrifices for.

sacrificio *m* sacrifice; *(de animal)* slaughter.

sacristán *m* sacristan.

sacudida *f (movimiento brusco)* shake; *(de vehículo)* bump; *(terremoto)* tremor.

sacudir *vt (agitar)* to shake; *(alfombra, sábana)* to shake out; *(pegar)* to hit.

safari *m (expedición)* safari; *(parque zoológico)* safari park.

Sagitario *m* Sagittarius.

sagrado, -da *adj* sacred.

sal *f (condimento)* salt; *(fig: gracia)* wit ❏ **sales** *fpl (de baño)* bath salts;

(para reanimar) smelling salts.

sala *f (habitación)* room; *(de hospital)* ward; *(de cine)* screen, cinema; *(tribunal)* court; ~ **de espera** waiting room; ~ **de estar** living room; ~ **de fiestas** discothèque; ~ **de juegos** casino; "~ **climatizada**" "air-conditioning".

salado, -da *adj (comida)* salty; *(persona)* funny.

salamandra *f* salamander.

salar *vt (comida)* to add salt to; *(para conservar)* to salt.

salario *m* salary.

salchicha *f* sausage.

salchichón *m* = salami.

saldo *m (de cuenta)* balance; *(pago)* payment; *(mercancía)* remnant.

salero *m (recipiente)* salt cellar; *(gracia)* wit.

salida *f (de lugar)* exit; *(de tren, avión, autobús)* departure; *(excursión)* outing; *(ocurrencia)* witty remark; *(recurso)* way out; *(de productos)* market; "~ **sin compra**" sign in supermarkets etc indicating exit for people who have not bought anything; ~ **de incendios** fire escape; ~ **de socorro** O **emergencia** emergency exit; ~**s internacionales** international departures.

salina *f* saltmine ❏ **salinas** *fpl* saltworks *(sg).*

salir *vi* 1. *(ir fuera)* to go out; *(venir fuera)* to come out; **salió a la calle** he went out into the street; ¡**sal aquí fuera!** come out here!; ~ **de** to leave.

2. *(marcharse)* to leave; **el tren sale muy temprano** the train leaves very early; **él ha salido para Madrid**

he's left for Madrid.

3. *(ser novios)* to go out; **Juan y María salen juntos** Juan and María are going out together.

4. *(separarse)* to come off; **el anillo no le sale del dedo** the ring won't come off her finger.

5. *(resultar)* to turn out; **ha salido muy estudioso** he has turned out to be very studious; **ha salido perjudicado** he came off badly; **~ bien/mal** to turn out well/badly; **mi número ha salido premiado** my ticket won a prize.

6. *(resolverse)*: **este problema no me sale** I can't solve this problem.

7. *(proceder)*: **~ de** to come from.

8. *(surgir)* to come out; **ha salido el sol** *(al amanecer)* the sun has come up.

9. *(aparecer)* to appear; *(publicación, producto, disco)* to come out; **¡qué bien sales en la foto!** you look great in the photo!; **en la película sale tu actor favorito** your favourite actor is in the film.

10. *(costar)*: **la comida le ha salido por diez mil pesetas** the meal worked out at ten thousand pesetas.

11. *(sobresalir)* to stick out.

12. *(librarse)*: **~ de** to get out of.

13. *(en locuciones)*: **~ adelante** *(persona, empresa)* to get by; *(proyecto, propuesta)* to be successful.

❏ **salirse** *vpr (marcharse)* to leave; *(rebosar)* to overflow; **~se de** *(desviarse)* to come off; *(fig: escaparse)* to deviate from.

saliva *f* saliva.

salmón *m* salmon; **~ ahumado** smoked salmon; **~ fresco** fresh salmon.

salmonete *m* red mullet.

salón *m (de casa)* living room; *(de edificio público)* hall; *(muebles)* lounge suite; *(exposición)* show; **~ del automóvil** motor show; **~ recreativo** arcade.

salpicadero *m* dashboard.

salpicar *vt* to splash ♦ *vi (aceite)* to spit.

salpicón *m*: **~ de marisco** cold dish of chopped seafood with pepper, salt, oil, vinegar and onion.

salpimentar *vt* to season.

salsa *f (para comidas)* sauce; *(de carne)* gravy; *(gracia)* spice; *(baile, música)* salsa; **~ bechamel** bechamel sauce; **~ rosa** thousand island dressing; **~ de tomate** tomato sauce; **~ verde** *sauce made with mayonnaise, parsley, capers and gherkins.*

salsera *f* gravy boat.

saltamontes *m inv* grasshopper.

saltar *vi* to jump; *(tapón, corcho)* to pop out; *(levantarse)* to jump (up); *(botón, pintura)* to come off; *(enfadarse)* to flare up; *(explotar)* to explode ♦ *vt* to jump over ❏ **saltarse** *vpr (omitir)* to miss out; *(cola, semáforo)* to jump; *(ley, norma)* to break.

salteado, -da *adj (discontinuo)* unevenly spaced; *(frito)* sautéed.

saltear *vt (freír)* to sauté.

salto *m* jump; *(en el tiempo, omisión)* gap; **~ de agua** waterfall; **~ de cama** negligée.

salud *f* health; **tener buena/mala ~** to be in good/in poor health; **estar bien/mal de ~** to be healthy/in poor health; **¡(a su) ~!**

cheers!

saludable *adj* healthy; *(provechoso)* beneficial.

saludar *vt* to greet □ **saludarse** *vpr* to greet each other.

saludo *m* greeting □ **saludos** *mpl (recuerdos)* regards.

salvación *f (rescate)* rescue.

Salvador *m*: **El ~** El Salvador.

salvadoreño, -ña *adj & m, f* Salvadoran.

salvaje *adj* wild.

salvamanteles *m inv* tablemat.

salvar *vt* to save; *(rescatar)* to rescue; *(obstáculo)* to go round; *(peligro, dificultad)* to get through; *(distancia, espacio)* to cover □ **salvarse** *vpr (escapar)* to escape.

salvavidas *m inv (chaleco)* life-jacket; *(cinturón)* lifebelt.

salvo *adv* except; **a ~** safe.

san *adj* → santo.

sanatorio *m* sanatorium.

sanción *f (castigo)* punishment.

sancochado *m (Amér)* meat and vegetable stew.

sancochar *vt (Amér)* to stew.

sandalia *f* sandal.

sandía *f* watermelon.

sandwich ['sanwitʃ] *m* toasted sandwich.

sanfermines *mpl* Pamplona bullfighting festival.

 SANFERMINES

Pamplona is famous for the "sanfermines", a week-long festival starting on 7 July, in which bulls are let loose in the streets of the town and young men demonstrate their bravery by running in front of them on the way to the bullring, sometimes receiving fatal wounds in the process. Bullfights are held every afternoon of the festival.

sangrar *vi* to bleed ♦ *vt (línea, párrafo)* to indent.

sangre *f (líquido)* blood; **~ azul** blue blood; **~ fría** sangfroid.

sangría *f* sangria.

sangriento, -ta *adj* bloody.

sanidad *f (servicios de salud)* (public) health; *(higiene)* health.

sanitario, -ria *adj* health *(antes de s)* ♦ *m, f* health worker □ **sanitarios** *mpl (instalaciones)* bathroom fittings.

sano, -na *adj* healthy; *(sin daño)* undamaged; **~ y salvo** safe and sound.

santiguarse *vpr* to make the sign of the Cross.

santo, -ta *adj* holy ♦ *m, f* saint ♦ *m (festividad)* saint's day.

 SANTO

Catholic tradition dictates that each day of the year is dedicated to a particular saint. On the day in question, people with the same name as the saint celebrate by buying drinks for their friends and family and, in turn, they are given presents.

santuario *m* shrine.

sapo *m* toad.

saque *m (en tenis)* serve.

saquear vt (tienda) to loot; (vaciar) to ransack.

sarampión m measles.

sarcástico, -ca adj sarcastic.

sardana f popular Catalan dance.

sardina f sardine; ~s a la plancha grilled sardines.

sargento m sergeant.

sarna f (de persona) scabies.

sarpullido m rash.

sarro m (de dientes) tartar.

sartén f frying pan.

sastre m tailor.

sastrería f (tienda) tailor's (shop); (oficio) tailoring.

satélite m satellite.

sátira f satire.

satírico, -ca adj satirical.

satisfacción f satisfaction.

satisfacer vt to satisfy; (deuda) to pay; (duda, pregunta, dificultad) to deal with.

satisfecho, -cha pp → **satisfacer** ♦ adj satisfied.

sauce m willow.

sauna f sauna.

saxofón m saxophone.

sazonar vt to season.

se pron 1. (reflexivo) himself (f herself), themselves (pl); (usted mismo) yourself, yourselves (pl); (de cosas, animales) itself, themselves (pl); ~ lavó los dientes she cleaned her teeth.
2. (recíproco) each other; ~ aman they love each other; ~ escriben they write to each other.
3. (en construcción pasiva): ~ ha suspendido la reunión the meeting has been cancelled.
4. (en construcción impersonal): "~

habla inglés" "English spoken"; "~ prohíbe fumar" "no smoking"; "~ dice que it is said that.
5. (complemento indirecto) to him (f to her), to them (pl); (usted, ustedes) to you; (de cosa, animal) to it, to them (pl); yo ~ lo daré I'll give it to him/her/etc.

sé v → **saber**, **ser**.

sea v → **ser**.

secador m dryer; ~ de cabello hairdryer.

secadora f (tumble) dryer.

secano m dry land.

secar vt to dry; (sudor, sangre) to wipe away ❑ **secarse** vpr (río, fuente) to dry up; (planta, árbol) to wilt; (ropa, cabello, superficie) to dry.

sección f section; (de empresa, oficina) department.

seco, -ca adj dry; (planta, árbol) wilted; (delgado) lean; (ruido, sonido) dull; (brusco) brusque; a secas just, simply; parar en ~ to stop dead.

secretaría f (oficina) secretary's office; (cargo) post of secretary.

secretariado m (estudios) secretarial studies (pl); (profesión) secretaries (pl).

secretario, -ria m, f secretary; (de ministerio) Secretary of State.

secreto, -ta adj secret ♦ m secret; (reserva) secrecy; en ~ in secret.

secta f sect.

sector m sector.

secuestrador, -ra m, f (de persona) kidnapper; (de avión) hijacker.

secuestrar vt (persona) to kidnap; *(avión)* to hijack.

secuestro *m (de persona)* kidnap; *(de avión)* hijacking.

secundario, -ria *adj* secondary.

sed *v → ser ◆ f* thirst; **correr me da ~** running makes me thirsty; **tener ~** to be thirsty.

seda *f* silk.

sedante *m* sedative.

sede *f* headquarters *(pl)*.

sedentario, -ria *adj* sedentary.

sediento, -ta *adj* thirsty.

seductor, -ra *adj (persona)* seductive; *(oferta, libro)* enticing.

segador, -ra *m, f* harvester.

segadora *f (máquina)* reaping machine, *→ segador.*

segar *vt (hierba)* to mow; *(cereal)* to reap.

segmento *m* segment.

seguido, -da *adj (continuo)* continuous; *(consecutivo)* consecutive ◆ *adv (en línea recta)* straight on; **dos años ~s** two years in a row; **en seguida** straight away; **todo ~** straight ahead.

seguir *vt* to follow; *(perseguir)* to chase; *(reanudar)* to continue ◆ *vi* to continue; **~ a algo** to follow sthg; **sigue nevando** it's still snowing.

según *prep (de acuerdo con)* according to; *(dependiendo de)* depending on ◆ *adv* as; **~ yo/tú** in my/your opinion.

segunda *f (velocidad)* second (gear), *→ segundo.*

segundero *m* second hand.

segundo, -da *núm* second

◆ *m, f* second-in-command ◆ *m (de tiempo)* second, *→ sexto.*

seguramente *adv (con seguridad)* for certain; *(probablemente)* probably.

seguridad *f (falta de peligro)* safety; *(protección)* security; *(certidumbre)* certainty; *(confianza)* confidence ❑ **Seguridad Social** *f* Social Security.

seguro, -ra *adj (sin riesgo, peligro)* safe; *(confiado)* sure; *(fiable)* reliable; *(amigo)* firm ◆ *adv* definitely ◆ *m (de coche, vida, casa)* insurance; *(cierto, confiado)* to be safe; **estar ~** *(sin temor)* to be safe; *(cierto, confiado)* to be sure; **empataron a ~** they drew six-all; **~ a cero** six-nil. **~ Social** *(Amér)* Social Security.

seis *adj inv six ◆ m (día)* sixth ◆ *mpl* six; *(temperatura)* six (degrees) ◆ *fpl: (son) las ~* (it's six o'clock; **el ~ de agosto** the sixth of August; **doscientos ~** two hundred and six; **treinta y ~** thirty-six; **de ~ en ~** in sixes; **los ~** the six of them; **empataron a ~** they drew six-all; **~ a cero** six-nil.

seiscientos *núm* six hundred, *→ seis.*

selección *f* selection; *(equipo nacional)* team.

seleccionador, -ra *m, f* = manager.

seleccionar *vt* to pick.

selectividad *f (examen)* Spanish university entrance examination.

---

i SELECTIVIDAD

The "selectividad" is a series of exams which take place over two days at the end of secondary education in Spain. The mark obtained in these exams is one of the factors which determines whether or not a student is admitted to his or her preferred field of study at university.

selecto, -ta *adj* fine, choice.

selector *m* selector.

self-service *m* self-service restaurant.

sello *m* (*de correos*) stamp; (*tampón*) rubber stamp.

selva *f* (*jungla*) jungle; (*bosque*) forest.

semáforo *m* traffic lights (*pl*).

semana *f* week □ **Semana Santa** *f* Easter; (*RELIG*) Holy Week.

---

i SEMANA SANTA

Throughout Easter week in Spain, a number of processions take place. People line the streets and pray, as statues of Christ and the saints are carried past. The most famous procession is that of Seville.

---

semanal *adj* (*que sucede cada semana*) weekly; (*que dura una semana*) week-long.

semanario *m* weekly (newspaper).

sembrar *vt* to sow.

semejante *adj* (*parecido*) similar; (*tal, uso despectivo*) such; *m* fellow human being; **~ cosa** such a thing.

semejanza *f* similarity.

semen *m* semen.

semestre *m* six-month period.

semidesnatado, -da *adj* semi-skimmed.

semidirecto, -ta *adj*: **tren ~** through train, a section of which becomes a stopping train.

semifinal *f* semifinal.

semilla *f* seed.

sémola *f* semolina.

Senado *m*: **el ~** the Senate.

senador, -ra *m, f* senator.

sencillo, -lla *adj* simple; (*espontáneo*) unaffected; (*Amér: monedas*) small change.

sendero *m* track.

seno *m* (*pecho*) breast; (*interior*) heart.

sensación *f* sensation; (*premonición*) feeling.

sensacional *adj* sensational.

sensacionalismo *m* sensationalism.

sensacionalista *adj* sensationalist.

sensato, -ta *adj* sensible.

sensibilidad *f* (*don*) feel; (*sentimentalismo, de aparato*) sensitivity; (*de los sentidos*) feeling.

sensible *adj* sensitive.

sensual *adj* sensual.

sentado, -da *adj* (*persona*) sensible; **dar por ~** to take for granted.

sentar *vt* (*basar*) to base ♦ *vi*: **bien/mal a alguien** (*comida, bebida*) to agree/disagree with sb; (*ropa, zapatos, joyas*) to suit/not to suit sb; (*dicho, hecho, broma*) to go down well/badly with sb □ **sentarse** *vpr* to sit (down).

sentencia *f* (*de juez, tribunal*)

sentence; *(frase corta)* saying.

sentenciar vt to sentence.

sentido m sense; *(dirección)* direction; *(conocimiento)* consciousness; **~ común** common sense.

sentimental adj sentimental.

sentimiento m feeling; **le acompaño en el ~ mío** my deepest sympathy.

sentir m feeling ◆ vt to feel; *(lamentar)* to be sorry about, to regret; **lo siento** I'm sorry □ **sentirse** vpr to feel; **~se bien/mal** *(de salud)* to feel well/ill; *(de ánimo)* to feel good/bad.

seña f *(gesto)* sign; *(marca)* mark □ **señas** fpl *(domicilio)* address *(sg)*; **~s personales** description *(sg)*.

señal f sign; *(aviso, orden)* signal; *(fianza)* deposit; *(cicatriz)* mark; *(de teléfono)* tone; **~ de tráfico** road sign.

señalado, -da adj *(fecha, día)* special; *(persona)* distinguished.

señalar vt *(poner marca, herir)* to mark; *(con la mano, dedo)* to point out; *(lugar, precio, fecha)* to fix; *(nombrar)* to pick; *(ser indicio de)* to indicate.

señor, -ra adj *(gran)* big ◆ m *(hombre)* man; *(antes de nombre)* Mr; *(al dirigir la palabra)* Sir; *(dueño)* owner; *(caballero)* gentleman; **muy ~ mío** Dear Sir.

señora f *(mujer, dama)* lady; *(antes de nombre)* Mrs; *(al dirigir la palabra)* Madam; *(esposa)* wife; *(dueña)* owner; **muy ~ mía** Dear Madam.

señorita f *(maestra)* teacher; *(mujer joven)* young woman; *(mujer soltera)* Miss.

señorito, -ta adj *(despec)* lordly ◆ m master.

sepa v → **saber**.

separación f separation; *(espacio, distancia)* space.

separado, -da adj *(persona, matrimonio)* separated.

separar vt to separate; *(silla, etc)* to move away; *(reservar)* to put aside □ **separarse** vpr *(persona)* to leave; *(pareja)* to separate.

sepia f cuttlefish; **~ a la plancha** grilled cuttlefish.

septentrional adj northern.

septiembre m = **setiembre**.

séptimo, -ma núm seventh, → **sexto**.

sepulcro m tomb.

sequía f drought.

ser m being; **~ humano** human being.

◆ v aux *(forma la voz pasiva)* to be; **el atracador fue visto** the robber was seen.

◆ v copulativo 1. *(descripción)* to be; **mi abrigo es lila** my coat is lilac; **este señor es alto/gracioso** this man is tall/funny; **~ como** to be like.

2. *(empleo, dedicación)* to be; **su mujer es abogada** his wife is a lawyer.

3.: **~ de** *(materia)* to be made of; *(origen)* to be from; *(posesión)* to belong to; *(pertenencia)* to be a member of.

◆ vi 1. *(suceder, ocurrir)* to be; **la final fue ayer** the final was yesterday.

2. *(haber, existir)* to be.

3. *(valer)* to be; **¿cuánto es? - son doscientas pesetas** how much is it?

- two hundred pesetas, please.
4. *(día, fecha, hora)* to be; **hoy es martes** it's Tuesday today; **¿qué hora es?** what time is it?; **son las tres (de la tarde)** it's three o'clock (in the afternoon).
5. *(en locuciones)*: **a no ~ que** unless; **como sea** somehow or other; **o sea** I mean.
◆ *v impers (expresión de tiempo)* to be; **es de día/de noche** it's day-time/night; **es muy tarde** it is very late.
❑ **ser para** *v + prep (servir para, adecuarse a)* to be for.

serenar *vt* to calm ❑ **serenarse** *vpr (persona, ánimo)* to calm down; *(mar)* to become calm; *(tiempo)* to clear up.

serenidad *f* calm.

sereno, -na *adj* calm; *(tiempo)* fine.

serie *f* series; *(en deportes)* heat.

seriedad *f* seriousness; *(formalidad)* responsible nature.

serio, -ria *adj* serious; *(responsable)* responsible; *(sin adornos)* sober; **en ~** seriously; **ir en ~** to be serious; **tomar en ~** to take seriously.

sermón *m* sermon.

serpentina *f* streamer.

serpiente *f* snake.

serrar *vt* to sow.

serrín *m* sawdust.

serrucho *m* handsaw.

servicio *m* service; *(retrete)* toilet; **estar de ~** to be on duty; **~ militar** military service; **~ público** public service; **~ de revelado rápido** = developing in one hour; **~ urgente** express service; **~s míni-**mos skeleton services *(pl)* ❑ **servicios** *mpl (baño)* toilets.

servidumbre *f (criados)* servants *(pl)*; *(dependencia)* servitude.

servilleta *f* serviette.

servir *vt (bebida, comida)* to serve; *(mercancía)* to supply; *(ayudar)* to help ◆ *vi* to serve; *(ser útil)* to be useful; **no sirven** *(ropa, zapatos)* they're no good; **~ de algo** to serve as sthg; **¿en qué le puedo ~?** what can I do for you? ❑ **servirse** *vpr (bebida, comida)* to help o.s. to; **"sírvase usted mismo"** "please help yourself"; **servirse de** *v + prep* to make use of.

sesenta *núm* sixty, → **seis.**

sesión *f* session; *(de cine)* showing; *(de teatro)* performance; **~ continua** continuous showing; **~ golfa** late-night showing; **~ matinal** matinée; **~ de noche** evening showing; **~ de tarde** afternoon matinée.

sesos *mpl* brains.

seta *f* mushroom; **~s al ajillo** garlic mushrooms; **~s con gambas** *mushrooms filled with prawns and egg.*

setecientos, -tas *núm* seven hundred, → **seis.**

setenta *núm* seventy, → **seis.**

setiembre *m* September; **a principios/mediados/finales de ~** at the beginning/in the middle/at the end of September; **el nueve de ~** the ninth of September; **el pasado/próximo (mes de) ~** last/next September; **en ~** in September; **este (mes de) ~** *(pasado)* last September; *(próximo)* this (coming) September; **para ~ by**

September.

seto *m* hedge.

severidad *f* severity.

severo, -ra *adj* severe; *(estricto)* strict.

Sevilla *s* Seville.

sevillanas *fpl (baile)* dance from Andalusia; *(música)* music of the "sevillanas".

sexismo *m* sexism.

sexista *mf* sexist.

sexo *m* sex; *(órganos sexuales)* genitals *(pl)*.

sexto, -ta *adj* sixth ◆ *m, f:* el ~, la sexta *(persona, cosa)* the sixth; *(piso, planta)* the sixth floor ◆ *m:* ~ (de E.G.B.) *year six of Spanish primary education system;* llegar el ~ to come sixth; capítulo ~ chapter six; el ~ día the sixth day; en ~ lugar, en sexta posición in sixth place; la sexta parte a sixth.

sexual *adj* sexual.

sexualidad *f* sexuality.

si *conj* if.

sí *(pl* síes) *adv* yes ◆ *pron (de personas)* himself *(f* herself), themselves *(pl)*; *(usted)* yourself, yourselves *(pl)*; *(de cosas, animales)* itself, themselves *(pl)*; *(impersonal)* oneself ◆ *m* consent; creo que ~ I think so.

sida *m* AIDS.

sidecar *m* sidecar.

sidra *f* cider.

siega *f (acción)* harvesting; *(temporada)* harvest.

siembra *f (acción)* sowing; *(temporada)* sowing time.

siempre *adv* always; *(Amér: con toda seguridad)* definitely; desde ~

always.

sien *f* temple.

sierra *f (herramienta)* saw; *(de montañas)* mountain range.

siesta *f* afternoon nap; echar una ~ to have an afternoon nap.

siete *núm* seven, → seis ◆ *f:* ¡la gran ~! *(Amér: fam)* Jesus!

sifón *m (botella)* siphon; *(agua con gas)* soda water.

siglas *fpl* acronym *(sg)*.

siglo *m* century; *(fam: periodo muy largo)* ages *(pl)*.

significado *m* meaning.

significar *vt* to mean.

significativo, -va *adj* significant.

signo *m* sign; ~ de admiración exclamation mark; ~ de interrogación question mark.

siguiente *adj (en el tiempo, espacio)* next; *(a continuación)* following ◆ *mf:* el/la ~ the next one.

sílaba *f* syllable.

silbar *vi* to whistle ◆ *vt (abuchear)* to boo.

silbato *m* whistle.

silbido *m* whistle.

silenciador *m* silencer.

silencio *m* silence.

silenciosamente *adv* silently.

silencioso, -sa *adj* silent, quiet.

silla *f* chair; ~ de montar saddle; ~ de ruedas wheelchair.

sillín *m* saddle.

sillón *m* armchair.

silueta *f* figure; *(contorno)* outline.

silvestre *adj* wild.

símbolo *m* symbol.

simétrico, -ca *adj* symmetrical.

similar *adj* similar.

similitud *f* similarity.

simpatía *f* (*cariño*) affection; (*cordialidad*) friendliness.

simpático, -ca *adj* (*amable*) nice; (*amigable*) friendly.

simpatizante *mf* sympathizer.

simpatizar *vi*: ~ (**con**) (*persona*) to get on (with); (*cosa*) to sympathize (with).

simple *adj* simple; (*sin importancia*) mere ♦ *m* (*en tenis, ping-pong*) singles (*pl*).

simplicidad *f* (*sencillez*) simplicity; (*ingenuidad*) simpleness.

simular *vt* to feign.

simultáneo, -a *adj* simultaneous.

sin *prep* without; **está ~ hacer** it hasn't been done before; **estamos ~ vino** we're out of wine; **~ embargo** however.

sinagoga *f* synagogue.

sinceridad *f* sincerity.

sincero, -ra *adj* sincere.

sincronizar *vt* to synchronize.

sindicato *m* (trade) union.

sinfonía *f* symphony.

sinfónico, -ca *adj* symphonic.

singular *adj* (*único*) unique; (*extraordinario*) strange; (*en gramática*) singular ♦ *m* singular.

siniestro, -tra *adj* sinister ♦ *m* (*accidente, desgracia*) disaster; (*de coche, avión*) loss.

sinnúmero *m*: **un ~ de** countless.

sino *conj* (*para contraponer*) but; (*excepto*) except.

sinónimo *m* synonym.

síntesis *f* (*resumen*) summary.

sintético, -ca *adj* synthetic.

sintetizador *m* synthesizer.

síntoma *m* symptom.

sintonía *f* (*música, canción*) signature tune; (*de televisión, radio*) tuning.

sintonizar *vt* to tune in to.

sinvergüenza *mf* (*descarado*) cheeky person; (*estafador*) scoundrel.

siquiera *adv* at least; **ni ~** not even.

sirena *f* (*sonido*) siren; (*en mitología*) mermaid.

sirviente, -ta *m, f* servant.

sisa *f* (*robo*) pilfering; (*de vestido*) armhole.

sistema *m* system; (*medio, método*) method; **por ~** systematically.

sitiar *vt* to besiege.

sitio *m* (*lugar*) place; (*espacio*) space, room; (*de ciudad, pueblo*) siege; (*Amér: de taxis*) rank; **en otro ~** somewhere else; **hacer ~** to make room.

situación *f* (*estado, condición, localización*) position; (*circunstancias*) situation.

situar *vt* (*colocar*) to put; (*localizar*) to locate ❑ **situarse** *vpr* (*establecerse*) to get established.

skin head *m* skinhead.

SL *f* (*abrev de sociedad limitada*) = Ltd.

SM (*abrev de Su Majestad*) HM.

s/n *abrev* = **sin número**.

sobaco *m* armpit.

sobado, -da *adj (vestido)* shabby; *(libro)* dog-eared; *(chiste, broma)* old.

soberbia *f* arrogance.

soberbio, -bia *adj (orgulloso)* arrogant; *(magnífico)* magnificent.

soborno *m* bribe.

sobrar *vi (haber demasiado)* to be more than enough; *(estar de más)* to be superfluous; *(quedar)* to be left (over).

sobras *fpl (de comida)* leftovers.

sobrasada *f* spicy Mallorcan sausage.

sobre[1] *prep* 1. *(encima de)* on (top of); **el libro estaba ~ la mesa** the book was on the table. 2. *(por encima de)* over, above; **el pato vuela ~ el lago** the duck is flying over the lake. 3. *(acerca de)* about; **un libro ~ el amor** a book about love. 4. *(alrededor)* about; **llegaron ~ las diez** they arrived at about ten o'clock. 5. *(en locuciones)*: **~ todo** above all.

sobre[2] *m* envelope.

sobreático *m* penthouse.

sobrecarga *f* excess weight.

sobredosis *f inv* overdose.

sobrehumano, -na *adj* superhuman.

sobremesa *f* period of time sitting around the table after lunch; **hacer la ~** to have a chat after lunch.

sobrenombre *m* nickname.

sobrepasar *vt (exceder)* to exceed; *(aventajar)* to overtake.

sobreponer *vt (poner delante)* to put first ❑ **sobreponerse a** *v + prep* to overcome.

sobrepuesto, -ta *adj* superimposed.

sobresaliente *adj* outstanding ◆ *m (nota)* excellent.

sobresalir *vi (en altura)* to jut out; *(en importancia)* to stand out.

sobresalto *m* fright.

sobrevivir *vi* to survive.

sobrevolar *vt* to fly over.

sobrino, -na *m, f* nephew *(f niece)*.

sobrio, -bria *adj* sober; *(moderado)* restrained.

sociable *adj* sociable.

social *adj (de la sociedad)* social; *(de los socios)* company *(antes de s)*.

socialista *mf* socialist.

sociedad *f* society; *(empresa)* company.

socio, -cia *m, f (de club, asociación)* member; *(de negocio)* partner.

sociología *f* sociology.

sociólogo, -ga *m, f* sociologist.

socorrer *vt* to help.

socorrismo *m (primeros auxilios)* first aid; *(en la playa)* lifesaving.

socorrista *mf (primeros auxilios)* first aid worker; *(en la playa)* lifeguard.

socorro *m* help ◆ *interj* help!

soda *f* soda water.

sofá *m* sofa, couch.

sofisticado, -da *adj* sophisticated.

sofocante *adj* stifling.

sofoco *m (ahogo)* breathlessness; *(disgusto)* fit (of anger); *(vergüenza)* embarrassment.

sofrito *m* tomato and onion sauce.

software ['sofwer] *m* software.

sois *v* → ser.

sol *m* sun; *(de plaza de toros)* seats in the sun which are the cheapest in the bullring; **hace** ~ it's sunny; **tomar el** ~ to sunbathe.

solamente *adv* only.

solapa *f (de vestido, chaqueta)* lapel; *(de libro)* flap.

solar *adj* solar ◆ *m* (undeveloped) plot.

solárium *m* solarium.

soldado *m* soldier; ~ **raso** private.

soldador *m* soldering iron.

soldar *vt* to weld.

soleado, -da *adj* sunny.

soledad *f (falta de compañía)* solitude; *(tristeza)* loneliness.

solemne *adj* solemn; *(grande)* utter.

solemnidad *f* ceremony.

soler *vi:* ~ **hacer algo** to do sthg usually; **solíamos hacerlo** we used to do it.

solicitar *vt (pedir)* to request; *(puesto)* to apply for.

solicitud *f (petición)* request; *(de puesto)* application; *(impreso)* application form.

solidaridad *f* solidarity.

sólido, -da *adj (cimientos, casa, muro)* solid; *(argumento, conocimiento)* sound ◆ *m* solid.

solista *mf* soloist.

solitario, -ria *adj (sin compañía)* solitary; *(lugar)* lonely ◆ *m, f* loner ◆ *m (juego)* patience; *(joya)* solitaire.

sollozar *vi* to sob.

sollozo *m* sob.

solo, -la *adj (sin compañía, familia)* alone; *(único)* single; *(sin añadidos)* on its own; *(café)* black; *(whisky)* neat; *(solitario)* lonely; **a solas** on one's own.

sólo *adv* only.

solomillo *m* sirloin; ~ **a la parrilla** grilled sirloin steak; ~ **de ternera** veal sirloin.

soltar *vt (de la mano)* to let go of; *(desatar)* to undo; *(dejar libre)* to set free; *(desenrollar)* to pay out; *(decir)* to come out with; *(lanzar)* to let out.

soltero, -ra *adj* single ◆ *m, f* bachelor *(f* single woman).

solterón, -ona *m, f* old bachelor *(f* old maid).

soltura *f* fluency; **con** ~ fluently.

solución *f* solution.

solucionar *vt* to solve.

solvente *adj* solvent.

sombra *f (oscuridad)* shade; *(de un cuerpo)* shadow; *(de plaza de toros)* most expensive seats in the bullring, located in the shade; **a la** ~ in the shade; **el árbol da** ~ the tree is shady.

sombrero *m* hat.

sombrilla *f* sunshade.

someter *vt (dominar)* to subdue; *(mostrar)* to submit; ~ **a alguien a algo** to subject sb to sthg ❑ **someterse** *vpr (rendirse)* to surrender.

somier *m (de muelles)* bed springs *(pl)*.

somnífero *m* sleeping pill.

somos *v* → ser.

son *v* → ser.

sonajero m rattle.

sonar vi to sound; (teléfono, timbre) to ring; (ser conocido) to be familiar; (letra) to be pronounced ♦ vt (nariz) to blow; **suena a verdad** it sounds true ☐ **sonarse** vpr to blow one's nose.

sonido m sound.

sonoro, -ra adj resonant; (banda) sound (antes de s); (consonante, vocal) voiced.

sonreír vi to smile ☐ **sonreírse** vpr to smile.

sonriente adj smiling.

sonrisa f smile.

sonrojarse vpr to blush.

soñar vi to dream ♦ vt to dream about; ~ **con** to dream of.

sopa f soup; ~ **de ajo** garlic soup; ~ **de cebolla** onion soup; ~ **de marisco** seafood bisque; ~ **de pescado** fish soup.

sopera f soup tureen.

soplar vi to blow ♦ vt (polvo, migas) to blow away; (respuesta) to whisper.

soplete m blowlamp.

soplido m puff.

soplo m (soplido) puff; (del corazón) murmur; (fam: chivatazo) tip-off.

soportales mpl arcade (sg).

soportar vt (carga, peso) to support; (persona) to stand; (dolor, molestia) to bear.

soporte m support.

soprano f soprano.

sorber vt (beber) to sip; (haciendo ruido) to slurp; (absorber) to soak up.

sorbete m sorbet; ~ **de fram-**

buesa raspberry sorbet; ~ **de limón** lemon sorbet.

sordo, -da adj deaf; (ruido, sentimiento) dull ♦ m, f deaf person.

sordomudo, -da m, f deaf-mute.

soroche m (Amér) altitude sickness.

sorprendente adj surprising.

sorprender vt to surprise ☐ **sorprenderse** vpr to be surprised.

sorpresa f surprise; **por** ~ by surprise.

sorpresivo, -va adj (Amér) unexpected.

sortear vt (rifar) to raffle; (evitar) to dodge.

sorteo m (lotería) draw; (rifa) raffle.

sortija f ring.

sosiego m peace, calm.

soso, -sa adj bland.

sospechar vt to suspect ☐ **sospechar de** v + prep to suspect.

sospechoso, -sa adj suspicious ♦ m, f suspect.

sostén m (apoyo) support; (prenda femenina) bra.

sostener vt to support; (defender, afirmar) to defend ☐ **sostenerse** vpr (sujetarse) to stay fixed; (tenerse en pie) to stand up.

sota f = jack.

sotana f cassock.

sótano m basement.

soy v → ser.

squash ['eskwaʃ] m squash.

Sr. (abrev de señor) Mr.

Sra. (abrev de señora) Mrs.

Sres. *(abrev de señores)* Messrs.

Srta. *abrev* = **señorita**.

SSMM *abrev* = **Sus Majestades**.

Sta. *(abrev de santa)* St.

Sto. *(abrev de santo)* St.

stock [es'tok] *m* stock.

stop *m* stop sign.

su *(pl* **sus)** *adj (de él)* his; *(de ella)* her; *(de cosa, animal)* its; *(de ellos, ellas)* their; *(de usted, ustedes)* your.

suave *adj (agradable al tacto)* soft; *(liso)* smooth; *(cuesta, brisa)* gentle; *(clima, temperatura)* mild.

suavidad *f (al tacto)* softness; *(de cuesta, brisa)* gentleness; *(de clima, temperatura)* mildness.

suavizante *m* conditioner.

subasta *f* auction.

subcampeón, -ona *m, f* runner-up.

subconsciente *m* subconscious.

subdesarrollado, -da *adj* underdeveloped.

subdesarrollo *m* underdevelopment.

subdirector, -ra *m, f* assistant manager *(f* assistant manageress).

súbdito, -ta *m, f (de país)* citizen.

subida *f (de precios, temperatura)* increase; *(pendiente, cuesta)* hill.

subir *vt (escaleras, calle, pendiente)* to go up; *(montaña)* to climb; *(llevar arriba)* to take up; *(brazo, precio, volumen, persiana)* to raise; *(ventanilla)* to close* ◆ *vi* to rise; ~ **a** *(piso, desván)* to go up to; *(montaña, torre)* to go up; *(coche)* to get into; *(avión, barco, tren, bicicleta)* to get

onto; *(cuenta, factura)* to come to; ~ **de** *(categoría)* to be promoted from.

súbito, -ta *adj* sudden.

subjetivo, -va *adj* subjective.

subjuntivo *m* subjunctive.

sublevar *vt (indignar)* to infuriate ❏ **sublevarse** *vpr* to rebel.

sublime *adj* sublime.

submarinismo *m* skin-diving.

submarinista *mf* skin-diver.

submarino *m* submarine.

subrayar *vt* to underline.

subsidio *m* benefit.

subsistencia *f* subsistence.

subterráneo, -a *adj* underground* ◆ *m* underground tunnel.

subtitulado, -da *adj* with subtitles.

subtítulo *m* subtitle.

suburbio *m* poor suburb.

subvención *f* subsidy.

sucedáneo *m* substitute.

suceder *v impers* to happen ❏ **suceder a** *v + prep (en un cargo, trono)* to succeed; *(venir después de)* to follow.

sucesión *f* succession; *(descendencia)* heirs *(pl)*.

sucesivo, -va *adj (consecutivo)* successive; **en días ~s** over the next few days.

suceso *m* event.

sucesor, -ra *m, f (en un cargo, trono)* successor; *(heredero)* heir *(f* heiress).

suciedad *f (cualidad)* dirtiness; *(porquería)* dirt.

sucio, -cia *adj* dirty; *(al comer, trabajar)* messy* ◆ *adv (en juego)* dirty.

suculento, -ta adj tasty.

sucumbir vi (rendirse) to succumb; (morir) to die.

sucursal f branch.

sudadera f sweatshirt.

sudado m (Amér) stew.

Sudáfrica s South Africa.

Sudamérica s South America.

sudamericano, -na adj & m, f South American.

sudar vi to sweat.

sudeste m southeast.

sudoeste m southwest.

sudor m sweat.

Suecia s Sweden.

sueco, -ca adj & m Swedish ♦ m, f Swede.

suegro, -gra m, f father-in-law (f mother-in-law).

suela f sole.

sueldo m salary, wages (pl).

suelo m (piso) floor; (superficie terrestre) ground; (terreno) soil; (para edificar) land; **en el ~** on the ground/floor.

suelto, -ta adj loose; (separado) separate; (calcetín, guante) odd; (arroz) fluffy ♦ m (dinero) change.

sueño m (acto de dormir) sleep; (ganas de dormir) drowsiness; (imagen mental, deseo) dream; **coger el ~** to get to sleep; **tener ~** to be sleepy.

suero m (en medicina) serum.

suerte f (azar) chance; (fortuna, casualidad) luck; (futuro) fate; (en el toreo) each of the three parts of a bullfight ♦ interj good luck!; **por ~** luckily; **tener ~** to be lucky.

suéter m sweater.

suficiente adj enough ♦ m (nota) pass.

sufragio m suffrage.

sufrido, -da adj (persona) uncomplaining; (color) that does not show the dirt.

sufrimiento m suffering.

sufrir vt (accidente, caída) to have; (persona) to bear ♦ vi to suffer; **~ de** to suffer from; **~ del estómago** to have a stomach complaint.

sugerencia f suggestion.

sugerir vt to suggest; (evocar) to evoke.

suicidio m suicide.

Suiza s Switzerland.

suizo, -za adj & m, f Swiss ♦ m (bollo) type of plain bun covered in sugar.

sujetador m bra.

sujetar vt (agarrar) to hold down; (asegurar, aguantar) to fasten ❑ **sujetarse** vpr (agarrarse) to hold on.

sujeto, -ta adj fastened ♦ m subject; (despec: individuo) individual.

suma f (operación) addition; (resultado) total; (conjunto de cosas, dinero) sum.

sumar vt to add together.

sumario m (resumen) summary; (de juicio) indictment.

sumergible adj waterproof.

sumergirse vpr to plunge.

suministrar vt to supply.

suministro m (acción) supplying; (abasto, víveres) supply.

sumiso, -sa adj submissive.

súper *adj* (*fam*) great ◆ *m* (*fam*)
supermarket ◆ *f* (*gasolina*) ≃ four-
star.

superación *f* overcoming.

superar *vt* (*prueba, obstáculo*) to
overcome; (*persona*) to beat □
superarse *vpr* (*mejorar*) to better
o.s.

superficial *adj* superficial.

superficie *f* surface; (*área*) area.

superfluo, -flua *adj* superfluous.

superior *adj* (*de arriba*) top;
(*excepcional*) excellent; ~ **a** (*mejor*)
superior to; (*en cantidad, importancia*) greater than ◆ *m* superior.

supermercado *m* supermarket.

superponer *vt* (*colocar encima*)
to put on top.

superpuesto, -ta *pp* →
superponer.

superstición *f* superstition.

supersticioso, -sa *adj* superstitious.

superviviente *mf* survivor.

supiera *v* → **saber**.

suplemento *m* supplement.

suplente *adj* (*médico*) locum;
(*jugador*) substitute.

supletorio *m* (*teléfono*) extension.

súplica *f* plea.

suplir *vt* (*falta, carencia*) to compensate for; (*persona*) to replace.

supo *v* → **saber**.

suponer *vt* (*creer*) to suppose;
(*representar, implicar*) to involve;
(*imaginar*) to imagine.

suposición *f* assumption.

supositorio *m* suppository.

suprema *f* chicken breast.

suprimir *vt* (*proyecto, puesto*) to
axe; (*anular*) to abolish; (*borrar*) to
delete.

supuesto, -ta *pp* → **suponer**
◆ *adj* (*presunto*) supposed; (*delincuente*) alleged; (*falso*) false ◆ *m*
assumption; **por** ~ of course.

sur *m* south; (*viento*) south wind.

surco *m* (*en la tierra*) furrow; (*de
disco*) groove; (*de piel*) line.

sureño, -ña *adj* southern.

surf *m* surfing.

surfista *mf* surfer.

surgir *vi* (*brotar*) to spring forth;
(*destacar*) to rise up; (*producirse*) to
arise.

surtido, -da *adj* assorted ◆ *m*
range.

surtidor *m* (*de agua*) spout; (*de
gasolina*) pump.

susceptible *adj* (*sensible*) over-
sensitive; ~ **de** liable to.

suscribir *vt* (*escrito*) to sign;
(*opinión*) to subscribe to □
suscribirse a *v* + *prep* to subscribe to.

suscripción *f* subscription.

suspender *vt* (*interrumpir*) to
adjourn; (*anular*) to postpone;
(*examen*) to fail; (*de empleo, sueldo*)
to suspend; (*colgar*) to hang (up).

suspense *m* suspense.

suspenso *m* fail.

suspensores *mpl* (*Amér*)
braces.

suspirar *vi* to sigh □ **suspirar
por** *v* + *prep* to long for.

suspiro *m* to sigh.

sustancia *f* substance; (*esencia*)
essence; (*de alimento*) nutritional

value.

sustancial *adj* substantial.

sustantivo *m* noun.

sustituir *vt* to replace; **~ algo/a alguien por** to replace sthg/sb with.

susto *m* fright; **¡qué ~!** what a fright!

sustracción *f* (*robo*) theft; (*resta*) subtraction.

sustraer *vt* (*robar*) to steal; (*restar*) to subtract.

susurrar *vt & vi* to whisper.

suyo, -ya *adj* (*de él*) his; (*de ella*) hers; (*de usted, ustedes*) yours; (*de ellos, de ellas*) theirs ◆ *pron:* **el ~, la suya** (*de él*) his; (*de ella*) hers; (*de usted, ustedes*) yours; (*de ellos, de ellas*) theirs; **lo ~** his/her *etc* thing; **un amigo ~** a friend of his/hers *etc.*

T

t (*abrev de tonelada*) t.

Tabacalera *f* State tobacco monopoly in Spain.

tabaco *m* tobacco; (*cigarrillos*) cigarettes (*pl*).

tábano *m* horsefly.

tabasco® *m* Tabasco®.

taberna *f* country-style bar, usually cheap.

tabique *m* partition (wall).

tabla *f* (*de madera*) plank; (*lista, de multiplicar*) table; (*de navegar,*

surf) board; (*en arte*) panel ❑

tablas *fpl* (*en juego*) stalemate (*sg*); (*escenario*) stage (*sg*).

tablao *m:* **~ flamenco** flamenco show.

tablero *m* board.

tableta *f* (*de chocolate*) bar; (*medicamento*) tablet.

tablón *m* plank; **~ de anuncios** notice board.

tabú *m* taboo.

taburete *m* stool.

tacaño, -ña *adj* mean.

tachar *vt* to cross out.

tacho *m* (*Amér*) bin.

tácito, -ta *adj* (*acuerdo, trato*) unwritten.

taco *m* (*para pared*) plug; (*de billar*) cue; (*de jamón, queso*) hunk; (*de papel*) wad; (*fam: palabrota*) swearword; (*fam: lío*) muddle; (*Amér: tortilla*) taco.

tacón *m* heel.

tacto *m* (*sentido*) sense of touch; (*textura*) feel; (*en el trato*) tact.

taekwondo [tajˈkwondo] *m* tae kwon do.

Taiwán [taiˈwan] *s* Taiwan.

tajada *f* slice; **agarrarse una ~** to get sloshed.

tal *adj* such ◆ *pron* such a thing; **~ cosa** such a thing; **¿qué ~?** how are you doing?; **~ vez** perhaps.

taladradora *f* drill.

taladrar *vt* to drill.

taladro *m* drill.

talco *m* talc.

talento *m* (*aptitud*) talent; (*inteligencia*) intelligence.

talgo *m* Spanish intercity high-speed train.

talla f (de vestido, calzado) size; (estatura) height; (de piedra preciosa) cutting; (escultura) sculpture.

tallarines mpl tagliatelle (sg).

taller m (de coches) garage; (de trabajo manual) workshop.

tallo m stem.

talón m heel; (cheque) cheque.

talonario m cheque book.

tamal m (Amér) mixture of maize flour and meat wrapped in banana/maize leaf and cooked.

tamaño m size.

también adv also; ~ dijo que … she also said that …; **yo** ~ me too.

tambor m drum.

tampoco adv neither; **yo** ~ me neither; **si a ti no te gusta a mí** ~ if you don't like it, then neither do I.

tampón m (sello) stamp; (para la menstruación) tampon.

tan adv ~ tanto.

tanda f (turno) shift; (serie) series.

tándem m (bicicleta) tandem; (dúo) duo.

tanga m tanga.

tango m tango.

tanque m (vehículo cisterna) tanker; (de guerra) tank.

tanto, -ta adj 1. (gran cantidad) so much, so many (pl); **tiene ~ dinero** he's got so much money; **tanta gente** so many people; ~ … **que** so much … that.
2. (cantidad indeterminada) so much, so many (pl); **tantas pesetas al día** so many pesetas a day; **cincuenta y ~s** fifty-something, fifty-odd.
3. (en comparaciones): ~ … **como** as

much … as, as many … as (pl); **tiene tanta suerte como tú** she's as lucky as you.

♦ adv 1. (gran cantidad) so much; **no merece la pena disgustarse** ~ it's not worth getting so upset; ~ **que** so much that.
2. (en comparaciones): ~ … **como** as much … as; **sabe** ~ **como yo** she knows as much as I do.
3. (en locuciones): **por (lo)** ~ so, therefore; ~ **(es así) que** so much so that.

♦ pron 1. (gran cantidad) so much, so many (pl); **él no tiene** ~s he doesn't have so many.
2. (igual cantidad) as much, as many (pl); **había mucha gente allí, aquí no tanta** there were a lot of people there, but not as many here.
3. (cantidad indeterminada) so much, so many (pl); **supongamos que vengan** ~s let's suppose so many come; **a** ~s **de agosto** on such-and-such a date in August.
4. (en locuciones): **eran las tantas** it was very late.

♦ m 1. (punto) point; (gol) goal; **marcar un** ~ to score.
2. (cantidad indeterminada): **un** ~ so much; ~ **por ciento** percentage.

tapa f (de recipiente) lid; (de libro) cover; (de comida) tapa; (de zapato) heel plate; **"~s variadas"** "selection of tapas".

 TAPAS

A **"tapa"** is a small portion of food, usually eaten with a glass of wine or beer in a bar before a

tapabarro 260

main meal. Many bars specialize in
"tapas", particularly in the north of
Spain and in Andalusia.

tapabarro m (Amér) mudguard.
tapadera f (de recipiente) lid;
(para encubrir) front.
tapar vt (cofre, caja, botella) to
close; (olla) to put the lid on;
(encubrir) to cover up; (en la cama)
to tuck in; (con ropa) to wrap up ❏
taparse vpr (en la cama) to tuck
o.s. in; (con ropa) to wrap up.
tapete m mat.
tapia f (stone) wall.
tapicería f (tela) upholstery;
(tienda) upholsterer's (shop).
tapiz (pl -ces) m tapestry.
tapizado m upholstery.
tapizar vt to upholster.
tapón m (de botella) stopper; (de
rosca) top; (de bañera, fregadero)
plug; (para el oído) earplug.
taquería f (Amér) taco bar.

 TAQUERÍA

This is a type of café where traditional Mexican food, especially tacos, is eaten. In recent years,
taquerías have become popular outside Mexico, especially in the United
States.

taquigrafía f shorthand.
taquilla f (de cine, teatro) box
office; (de tren) ticket office;
(armario) locker; (recaudación) takings (pl).
taquillero, -ra adj who/that

pulls in the crowds ◆ m, f ticket
clerk.
tara f (defecto) defect; (peso) tare.
tardar vi (tiempo) to take ◆ vi
(retrasarse) to be late; **el comienzo
tardará aún dos horas** it doesn't
start for another two hours.
tarde f (hasta las cinco) afternoon; (después de las cinco) evening
◆ adv late; **las cuatro de la ~** four
o'clock in the afternoon; **por la ~**
in the afternoon/evening; **buenas
~s** good afternoon/evening.
tarea f (trabajo) task; (deberes
escolares) homework.
tarifa f (de electricidad, etc)
charge; (en transportes) fare; (lista de
precios) price list; **"~s de metro"**
"underground fares".
tarima f platform.
tarjeta f card; **"~s admitidas"**
"credit cards accepted"; **~ de
crédito** credit card; **~ de embarque**
boarding pass; **~ postal** postcard;
~ 10 viajes (en metro) underground
travelcard valid for ten journeys.
tarro m jar.
tarta f cake; (plana, con base de
pasta dura) tart; **~ de la casa** chef's
special cake; **~ de chocolate**
chocolate cake; **~ helada** ice
cream gâteau; **~ de Santiago**
sponge cake filled with almond paste;
~ al whisky whisky-flavoured ice-
cream gâteau.
tartamudo, -da m, f stam-
merer.
tasa f rate.
tasca f = pub.
tatuaje m tattoo.
taurino, -na adj bullfighting
(antes de s).

Tauro *m* Taurus.
tauromaquia *f* bullfighting.

 TAUROMAQUIA

Bullfights begin with a procession in which all the participants parade across the bullring in traditional costume. The fight itself is divided into three parts: in the first part, the "picador" goads the bull with a lance; in the second, the "banderillero" sticks barbed darts into it and in the final part, the "matador" performs a series of passes before killing the bull.

taxi *m* taxi.
taxímetro *m* taximeter.
taxista *mf* taxi driver.
taza *f* cup; *(de retrete)* bowl.
tazón *m* bowl.
te *pron (complemento directo)* you; *(complemento indirecto)* (to) you; *(reflexivo)* yourself.
té *m* tea.
teatral *adj (de teatro)* theatre *(antes de s)*; *(afectado)* theatrical.
teatro *m* theatre.
tebeo® *m* (children's) comic.
techo *m (de habitación, persona, avión)* ceiling; *(tejado)* roof.
tecla *f* key.
teclado *m* keyboard.
teclear *vi (en ordenador)* to type.
técnica *f* technique; *(de ciencia)* technology.
técnico, -ca *adj* technical.
tecnología *f* technology.
tecnológico, -ca *adj* techno-logical.

teja *f* tile.
tejado *m* roof.
tejanos *mpl* jeans.
tejer *vt (jersey, labor)* to knit; *(tela)* to weave.
tejido *m (tela)* fabric; *(del cuerpo humano)* tissue.
tejo *m (juego)* hopscotch.
tel. *(abrev de teléfono)* tel.
tela *f (tejido)* material, cloth; *(lienzo)* canvas; *(fam: dinero)* dough.
telaraña *f* spider's web.
tele *f (fam)* telly.
telearrastre *m* ski-tow.
telecabina *f* cable-car.
telecomunicación *f (medio)* telecommunication; *(estudios)* telecommunications.
telediario *m* television news.
teledirigido, -da *adj* remote-controlled.
telefax *m inv* fax.
teleférico *m* cable-car.
telefonazo *m* phone call.
telefonear *vt* to phone.
Telefónica *f Spanish national telephone monopoly.*
telefónico, -ca *adj* telephone *(antes de s)*.
telefonista *mf* telephonist.
teléfono *m* telephone; **~ móvil** mobile telephone.
telégrafo *m* telegraph.
telegrama *m* telegram; **poner un ~** to send a telegram.
telenovela *f* television soap opera.
teleobjetivo *m* telephoto lens.

telescopio m telescope.

telesilla f chair lift.

telespectador, -ra m, f viewer.

telesquí m ski lift.

teletexto m Teletext®.

teletipo m teleprinter.

televidente mf viewer.

televisado, -da adj televised.

televisión f television.

televisor m television (set).

télex m inv telex.

telón m curtain.

tema m subject; (melodía) theme.

temática f subject matter.

temático, -ca adj thematic.

temblar vi to tremble; (de frío) to shiver.

temblor m (de persona) trembling; (de suelo) earthquake.

temer vt to fear; **~ por** to fear for □ **temerse** vpr to fear.

temor m fear.

temperamento m temperament.

temperatura f temperature.

tempestad f storm.

templado, -da adj (líquido, comida) lukewarm; (clima) temperate.

templo m (pagano) temple; (iglesia) church.

temporada f (periodo concreto) season; (de una actividad) period; **de ~** seasonal.

temporal adj temporary ♦ m storm.

temprano, -na adj & adv early.

ten v → tener.

tenazas fpl pliers.

tendedero m clothes line.

tendencia f tendency.

tender vt (colgar) to hang out; (extender) to spread; (tumbar) to lay (out); (cable) to lay; (cuerda) to stretch (out); (entregar) to hand □ **tender a** v + prep to tend to; **tenderse** vpr to lie down.

tenderete m stall.

tendero, -ra m, f shopkeeper.

tendón m tendon.

tendrá v → tener.

tenedor m fork.

tener vt 1. (poseer, contener) to have; **tiene mucho dinero** she has a lot of money; **tengo dos hijos** I have two children; **~ un niño** (parir) to have a baby; **la casa tiene cuatro habitaciones** the house has four bedrooms; **tiene los ojos azules** she has blue eyes.
2. (medidas, edad) to be; **la sala tiene cuatro metros de largo** the room is four metres long; **¿cuántos años tienes?** how old are you?; **tiene diez años** he's ten (years old).
3. (padecer, sufrir) to have; **~ dolor de muelas/fiebre** to have toothache/a temperature.
4. (sujetar, coger) to hold; **tiene la olla por las asas** she's holding the pot by its handles; **¡ten!** here you are!
5. (sentir) to be; **~ frío/calor** to be cold/hot; **~ hambre/sed** to be hungry/thirsty.
6. (sentimiento): **nos tiene cariño** he's fond of us.
7. (mantener) to have; **hemos tenido una discusión** we've had an

argument.

8. *(para desear)* to have; **que tengan unas felices fiestas** have a good holiday.

9. *(deber asistir a)* to have; **hoy tengo clase** I have to go to school today; **el médico no tiene consulta hoy** the doctor is not seeing patients today.

10. *(valorar, considerar):* ~ **algo/a alguien por algo** to think sthg/sb is sthg; **ten por seguro que lloverá** you can be sure it will rain.

11. *(haber de):* **tengo mucho que contaros** I have a lot to tell you.

◆ *v aux* **1.** *(haber):* **tiene alquilada una casa en la costa** she has a rented house on the coast.

2. *(hacer estar):* **me tienes loca** you're driving me mad.

3. *(obligación):* ~ **que hacer algo** to have to do sthg; **tenemos que estar a las ocho** we have to be there at eight.

tenga *v* → tener.

tengo *v* → tener.

teniente *m* lieutenant.

tenis *m* tennis; ~ **de mesa** table tennis.

tenista *mf* tennis player.

tenor *m* tenor.

tensión *f* tension; *(de la sangre)* blood pressure; *(fuerza)* stress; *(voltaje)* voltage.

tenso, -sa *adj (persona)* tense; *(objeto, cuerda)* taut.

tentación *f* temptation.

tentáculo *m* tentacle.

tentempié *m (bebida, comida)* snack.

tenue *adj (color, luz)* faint; *(tela, cortina)* fine.

teñir *vt* to dye.

teología *f* theology.

teoría *f* theory; **en** ~ in theory.

terapeuta *mf* therapist.

tercera *f (categoría)* third class; *(velocidad)* third (gear).

tercermundista *adj* third-world.

tercero, -ra *núm* third ◆ *m (persona)* third party; *(piso)* third floor, → **sexto.**

tercio *m (tercera parte)* third; *(de corrida de toros)* each of the three parts of a bullfight.

terciopelo *m* velvet.

terco, -ca *adj* stubborn.

tergal® *m* Tergal®.

termas *fpl* hot baths, spa *(sg).*

terminado, -da *adj* finished.

terminal *adj (enfermo)* terminal; *(estación)* final ◆ *m* terminal ◆ *f (de aeropuerto)* terminal; *(de autobús)* terminus.

terminar *vt* to finish ◆ *vi* to end; *(tren)* to terminate; ~ **en** to end in; ~ **por hacer algo** to end up doing sthg.

término *m* end; *(plazo)* period; *(palabra)* term; ~ **municipal** district ❏ **términos** *mpl* terms.

terminología *f* terminology.

termita *f* termite.

termo *m* Thermos® (flask).

termómetro *m* thermometer.

termostato *m* thermostat.

ternera *f* veal; ~ **asada** roast veal.

ternero, -ra *m, f* calf.

terno *m (Amér)* suit.

ternura *f* tenderness.

terraplén *m* embankment.

terrateniente 264

terrateniente *mf* landowner.

terraza *f (balcón)* balcony; *(techo)* terrace roof; *(de bar, restaurante, cultivo)* terrace.

terremoto *m* earthquake.

terreno *m (suelo)* land; *(parcela)* plot (of land); *(fig: ámbito)* field.

terrestre *adj* terrestrial.

terrible *adj (que causa terror)* terrifying; *(horrible)* terrible.

territorio *m* territory.

terrón *m (de azúcar)* lump.

terror *m* terror.

terrorismo *m* terrorism.

terrorista *mf* terrorist.

tertulia *f (personas)* regular meeting of people for informal discussion of a particular issue of common interest; *(lugar)* area in café given over to billiard and card tables.

tesis *f inv* thesis.

tesoro *m (botín)* treasure; *(hacienda pública)* treasury.

test *m* test.

testamento *m* will.

testarudo, -da *adj* stubborn.

testículo *m* testicle.

testigo *m* witness.

testimonio *m (prueba)* proof; *(declaración)* testimony.

teta *f (fam)* tit.

tetera *f* teapot.

tetrabrick *m* tetrabrick.

textil *adj* textile.

texto *m* text; *(pasaje, fragmento)* passage.

textura *f* texture.

ti *pron (después de preposición)* you; *(reflexivo)* yourself.

tianguis *m inv (Amér)* (open-air)

market.

tibia *f* shinbone.

tibio, -bia *adj (cálido)* warm; *(falto de calor)* lukewarm.

tiburón *m* shark.

ticket *m (billete)* ticket; *(recibo)* receipt.

tiempo *m* time; *(en meteorología)* weather; *(edad)* age; *(en deporte)* half; *(en gramática)* tense; **a ~** on time; **al mismo ~ que** at the same time as; **con ~** in good time; **del ~** *(bebida)* at room temperature; **en otros ~s** in a different age; **hace ~** a long time ago; **hace ~ que no te veo** it's a long time since I saw you; **tener ~** to have time; **todo el ~** *(todo el rato)* all the time; *(siempre)* always; **~ libre** spare time.

tienda *f* shop; *(para acampar)* tent; **~ de campaña** tent; **~ de comestibles** grocery (shop); **~ de confecciones** clothes shop.

tiene *v → tener.*

tierno, -na *adj* tender; *(pan)* fresh.

tierra *f* land; *(materia)* soil; *(suelo)* ground; *(patria)* homeland; **~ adentro** inland; **tomar ~** to touch down □ **Tierra** *f:* **la Tierra** the Earth.

tieso, -sa *adj (rígido)* stiff; *(erguido)* erect; *(antipático)* haughty.

tiesto *m* flowerpot.

tigre, -gresa *m, f* tiger (*f* tigress).

tijeras *fpl* scissors.

tila *f* lime blossom tea.

tilde *f (acento)* accent; *(de ñ)* tilde.

tiliches *mpl (Amér)* bits and pieces.

timbal m kettledrum.

timbre m (aparato) bell; (de voz, sonido) tone; (sello) stamp.

tímido, -da adj shy.

timo m swindle.

timón m rudder.

tímpano m (del oído) eardrum.

tina f (vasija) pitcher; (bañera) bathtub.

tino m (juicio) good judgment; (moderación) moderation.

tinta f ink; **en su ~** cooked in its ink.

tintero m (en pupitre) inkwell.

tinto m red wine.

tintorería f dry cleaner's.

tío, -a m, f (pariente) uncle (f aunt); (fam: compañero, amigo) mate (f darling); (fam: persona) guy (f bird).

tiovivo m merry-go-round.

típico, -ca adj typical; (traje, restaurante) traditional.

tipo m (clase) type; (figura de mujer) figure; (figura de hombre) build; (en individuo) guy; (modelo) model; **~ de cambio** exchange rate.

tipografía f (arte) printing.

TIR m (abrev de transport international routier) = HGV.

tira f strip.

tirabuzón m curl.

tirada f (número de ventas) circulation; (en juegos) throw; (distancia grande) long way.

tiradero m (Amér) tip.

tirador m (de puerta, cajón) handle.

tiranía f tyranny.

tirano, -na m, f tyrant.

tirante adj (estirado) taut; (relación, situación) tense ❑ **tirantes** mpl braces (Br), suspenders (Am).

tirar vt (arrojar, lanzar) to throw; (desechar, malgastar) to throw away; (derribar) to knock down; (dejar caer) to drop; (volcar) to knock over; (derramar) to spill; (disparar) to fire ◆ vi (atraer) to be attractive; (desviarse) to head; (fam: durar) to keep going; (en juegos) to have one's go; **~ de** to pull; **voy tirando** I'm O.K., I suppose; **"tirar" "pull"** ❑ **tirar a** v + prep (parecerse a) to take after; **~ a gris** to be greyish; **tirarse** vpr to throw o.s.; (tiempo) to spend.

tirita® f (sticking) plaster (Br), Bandaid® (Am).

tiritar vi to shiver.

tiro m shot; (actividad) shooting; (herida) gunshot wound; (de chimenea) draw; (de carruaje) team.

tirón m (estirón) pull; (robo) bag-snatching.

tisú m lamé.

títere m puppet ❑ **títeres** mpl (espectáculo) puppet show (sg).

titular adj official ◆ vt to title ◆ **titularse** vpr (llamarse) to be called; (en estudios) to graduate.

título m title; (diploma) qualification; (licenciatura) degree.

tiza f chalk.

tlapalería f (Amér) shop selling paint, cleaning materials, pots and pans etc.

toalla f towel; **~ de ducha** bath towel; **~ de manos** hand towel.

tobillo m ankle.

tobogán m (en parque de atrac-

ciones) helter-skelter; *(rampa)* slide; *(en piscina)* flume; *(trineo)* toboggan.

tocadiscos *m inv* record player.

tocador *m (mueble)* dressing table; *(habitación)* powder room.

tocar *vt* to touch; *(palpar)* to feel; *(instrumento musical)* to play; *(alarma)* to sound; *(timbre, campana)* to ring; *(tratar)* to touch on ♦ *vi (a la puerta)* to knock; *(al timbre)* to ring; *(estar próximo)* to border; **te toca a ti** *(es tu turno)* it's your turn; *(es tu responsabilidad)* it's up to you; **le tocó la mitad** he got half of it; **le tocó el gordo** she won first prize; **"no ~ el género" "do not touch".**

tocino *m* bacon fat; **~ de cielo** dessert made of sugar and eggs.

todavía *adv* still; **~ no** not yet.

todo, -da *adj* all; *(cada, cualquier)* every ♦ *pron (para cosas)* everything, all of them *(pl)*; *(para personas)* everybody ♦ *m* whole; **~ el libro** all (of) the book; **~s los lunes** every Monday; **tenemos de ~** we've got all sorts of things; **ante ~** first of all; **sobre ~** above all.

toga *f (de abogado, juez)* gown.

toldo *m (de tienda)* awning; *(de playa)* sunshade.

tolerancia *f* tolerance.

tolerante *adj* tolerant.

tolerar *vt* to tolerate; *(sufrir)* to stand.

toma *f (de leche)* feed; *(de agua, gas)* inlet; *(de luz)* socket.

tomar *vt* to take; *(contratar)* to take on; *(comida, bebida, baño, luz)* to have; *(sentir)* to acquire; **~ a alguien por** to take sb for;

algo a mal to take sthg the wrong way; **~ algo** *(comer, beber)* to have sthg to eat/drink; **~ el fresco** to get a breath of fresh air; **~ el sol** to sunbathe; **~ prestado** to borrow.

tomate *m* tomato.

tómbola *f* tombola.

tomillo *m* thyme.

tomo *m* volume.

tonel *m* barrel.

tonelada *f* tonne.

tongo *m (Amér)* type of bowler hat worn by Bolivian Indians.

tónica *f (bebida)* tonic water.

tónico, -ca *adj (vigorizante)* revitalizing; *(con acento)* tonic ♦ *m (cosmético)* skin toner.

tono *m* tone; *(de color)* shade.

tontería *f (cualidad)* stupidity; *(indiscreción)* stupid thing; *(cosa sin valor)* trifle.

tonto, -ta *adj* stupid; *(ingenuo)* innocent.

tope *m (punto máximo)* limit; *(pieza)* block.

tópico, -ca *adj (medicamento)* topical ♦ *m (tema recurrente)* recurring theme; *(frase muy repetida)* cliché.

topo *m* mole.

tórax *m inv* thorax.

torbellino *m (de viento)* whirlwind; *(de sucesos, preguntas, etc)* spate.

torcer *vt (retorcer)* to twist; *(doblar)* to bend; *(girar)* to turn; *(inclinar)* to tilt ♦ *vi* to turn ❑

torcerse *vpr (fracasar)* to go wrong; *(no cumplirse)* to be frustrated; **~se el brazo** to twist one's arm; **~se el tobillo** to sprain one's ankle.

torcido, -da adj (retorcido) twisted; (doblado) bent; (inclinado) crooked.

tordo m thrush.

torear vt (toro, vaquilla) to fight; (fig: evitar) to dodge; (fig: burlarse de) to mess about ◆ vi to fight bulls.

torera f bolero (jacket).

torero, -ra m, f bullfighter.

tormenta f storm.

tormentoso, -sa adj stormy.

torneo m tournament.

tornillo m screw.

torniquete m (para hemorragia) tourniquet.

toro m bull ❏ **toros** mpl (corrida) bullfight (sg); (fiesta) bullfighting (sg).

torpe adj (poco ágil) clumsy; (poco inteligente, lento) slow.

torpedo m torpedo.

torpeza f (falta de agilidad) clumsiness; (falta de inteligencia, lentitud) slowness.

torre f tower; (de oficinas, etc) tower block; (en ajedrez) castle, rook.

torrente m torrent.

torrija f French toast.

torta f (de harina) cake; (fam: bofetada) thump; (fam: accidente) bump; **ni ~** (fam) not a thing.

tortazo m (fam) (bofetada) thump; (golpe fuerte) bump.

tortilla f omelette; (Amér: de harina) tortilla; **~ de atún** tuna omelette; **~ de champiñón** mushroom omelette; **~ (a la) francesa** plain omelette; **~ de gambas** prawn omelette; **~ de jamón** ham omelette; **~ de patatas** Spanish omelette.

tórtola f turtledove.

tortuga f (terrestre) tortoise; (marina) turtle.

torturar vt to torture.

tos f cough.

toser vi to cough.

tosta f piece of toast with a topping.

tostada f piece of toast.

tostador m toaster.

tostar vt to toast ❏ **tostarse** vpr (broncearse) to get brown.

total adj & m total ◆ adv so, anyway.

totalidad f: **la ~ de** all of.

totora f (Amér) merry-go-round.

tóxico, -ca adj poisonous.

toxicomanía f drug addiction.

toxicómano, -na m, f drug addict.

trabajador, -ra adj hard-working ◆ m, f worker.

trabajar vt & vi to work; **~ de** to work as; **~ de canguro** to babysit.

trabajo m work; (empleo) job; (esfuerzo) effort; (en el colegio) essay; **~s manuales** arts and crafts.

trabalenguas m inv tongue-twister.

traca f string of firecrackers.

tractor m tractor.

tradición f tradition.

tradicional adj traditional.

tradicionalmente adv traditionally.

traducción f translation.

traducir 268

traducir vt to translate.

traductor, -ra m, f translator.

traer vt 1. (trasladar) to bring; (llevar) to carry; **me trajo un regalo** she brought me a present; **¿qué traes ahí?** what have you got there?

2. (provocar, ocasionar) to bring; **le trajo graves consecuencias** it had serious consequences for him.

3. (contener) to have; **el periódico trae una gran noticia** the newspaper has an important piece of news in it.

4. (llevar puesto) to wear.

❑ **traerse** vpr: **se las trae** (fam) it's got a lot to it.

traficante mf trafficker.

traficar vi to traffic.

tráfico m (de vehículos) traffic; (de drogas) trafficking.

tragar vt (ingerir) to swallow; (fam: devorar, consumir) to guzzle; (soportar) to put up with ◆ vi to swallow; **no ~ a alguien** (fam) not to be able to stand sb ❑ **tragarse** vpr (fam) to swallow.

tragedia f tragedy.

trágico, -ca adj tragic.

tragicomedia f tragicomedy.

trago m (de líquido) mouthful; (fam: copa) drink; (disgusto) difficult situation.

traición f (infidelidad) betrayal; (delito) treason.

traje m (vestido) dress; (de hombre) suit; (de chaqueta) two-piece suit; (de región, época, etc) costume; **~ de baño** swimsuit; **~ (de) chaqueta** woman's two-piece suit; **~ de luces** matador's outfit.

trama f (de novela, historia) plot;

(maquinación) intrigue.

tramar vt to weave.

tramitar vt (suj: autoridades) to process (document); (suj: solicitante) to obtain.

tramo m (de camino, calle) stretch; (de escalera) flight (of stairs).

tramontana f north wind.

tramoya f (en teatro) stage machinery.

tramoyista mf stage hand.

trampa f (para cazar) trap; (engaño) trick; (en juego) cheating; (puerta) trapdoor; **hacer ~** to cheat.

trampolín m (en piscina) diving board; (en esquí) ski jump; (en gimnasia) springboard.

trance m (momento difícil) difficult situation; (estado hipnótico) trance.

tranquilidad f (de lugar) peacefulness; (de carácter) calmness; (despreocupación) peace of mind.

tranquilo, -la adj (lugar) peaceful; (de carácter, mar, tiempo) calm; (libre de preocupaciones) unworried.

transbordador m ferry.

transbordar vt to transfer.

transbordo m change (of train etc); **hacer ~** to change.

transcurrir vi to take place.

transeúnte mf passer-by.

transferencia f transfer.

transformación f transformation.

transformador m transformer.

transformar vt to transform;

~ algo/a alguien en to turn sthg/sb into ❏ **transformarse** *vpr (cambiar)* to be transformed; **~se en** to be converted into.

transfusión *f* transfusion.

transición *f* transition.

transigir *vi (ceder)* to compromise; *(ser tolerante)* to be tolerant.

transistor *m* transistor.

tránsito *m (de vehículos)* traffic.

translúcido, -da *adj* translucent.

transmitir *vt (difundir)* to broadcast; *(comunicar)* to pass on; *(contagiar)* to transmit.

transparente *adj* transparent.

transportar *vt* to transport.

transporte *m* transport; **~ público** public transport.

transversal *adj (atravesado)* transverse; *(perpendicular)* cross *(antes de s)*.

tranvía *m* tram.

trapear *vt (Amér)* to wash.

trapecio *m* trapeze.

trapecista *mf* trapeze artist.

trapo *m (trozo de tela)* rag; *(para limpiar)* cloth.

tráquea *f* windpipe.

tras *prep (detrás de)* behind; *(después de)* after.

trasero, -ra *adj* back *(antes de s)* ◆ *m (fam)* backside.

trasladar *vt (mudar)* to move; *(empleado, trabajador)* to transfer; *(aplazar)* to postpone ❏ **trasladarse** *vpr (desplazarse)* to go; *(mudarse)* to move.

traslado *m (de muebles, libros, etc)* moving; *(de puesto, cargo, etc)* transfer.

traspasar *vt (cruzar)* to cross (over); *(atravesar)* to go through; *(suj: líquido)* to soak through; *(negocio)* to sell *(as a going concern)*.

traspiés *m inv (tropezón)* trip; *(equivocación)* slip.

trasplantar *vt* to transplant.

trasplante *m* transplant.

traste *m (Amér) (trasto)* thing; *(trasero)* backside.

trasto *m (objeto inútil)* piece of junk; *(fig: persona)* nuisance ❏ **trastos** *mpl (equipo)* things.

tratado *m (acuerdo)* treaty; *(escrito)* treatise.

tratamiento *m* treatment; *(título)* title.

tratar *vt* to treat; *(discutir)* to discuss; *(conocer)* to come into contact with ❏ **tratar de** *v + prep (hablar sobre)* to be about; *(intentar)* to try to.

trato *m (de persona)* treatment; *(acuerdo)* deal; *(tratamiento)* dealings *(pl)*.

trauma *m* trauma.

través: a través de *prep (en espacio)* across; *(en tiempo)* through.

travesaño *m (de portería)* crossbar.

travesía *f (calle)* cross-street; *(por mar)* crossing; *(por aire)* flight.

travesti *m* transvestite.

travieso, -sa *adj* mischievous.

trayecto *m (camino, distancia)* distance; *(viaje)* journey; *(ruta)* route.

trayectoria *f (recorrido)* trajectory; *(desarrollo)* path.

trazado *m (de carretera, canal)* course; *(de edificio)* design.

trazar vt (línea, dibujo) to draw; (proyecto, plan) to draw up.

trazo m line; (de escritura) stroke.

trébol m (planta) clover; (en naipes) club.

trece núm thirteen, → **seis**.

tregua f (en conflicto) truce; (en trabajo, estudios) break.

treinta núm thirty, → **seis**.

tremendo, -da adj (temible) terrible; (muy grande) enormous; (travieso) mischievous.

tren m train; ~ de cercanías local train; ~ de lavado car wash.

trenza f plait.

trepar vt to climb.

tres núm three, → **seis**.

tresillo m (sofá) three-piece suite; (juego) ombre, card game for three players.

trial m trial.

triangular adj triangular.

triángulo m triangle.

tribu f tribe.

tribuna f (para orador) rostrum; (para espectadores) stand.

tribunal m court; (en examen, oposición) board of examiners.

triciclo m tricycle.

trigo m wheat.

trilladora f threshing machine.

trillar vt to thresh.

trillizos, -zas m, fpl triplets.

trimestral adj (cada tres meses) quarterly; (de tres meses) three-month.

trimestre m (periodo) quarter, three months (pl); (en escuela) term.

trinchante m (cuchillo) carving knife; (tenedor) meat fork.

trineo m sledge.

trío m trio.

tripa f (barriga) belly; (intestino) gut ◻ **tripas** fpl (interior) insides.

triple adj triple ◆ m (en baloncesto) basket worth three points; **el** ~ de three times as much as.

trípode m tripod.

tripulación f crew.

tripulante mf crew member.

triste adj sad; (color, luz) pale; (insuficiente) miserable.

tristeza f sadness.

triturar vt (desmenuzar) to grind; (mascar) to chew.

triunfal adj triumphant.

triunfar vi (vencer) to win; (tener éxito) to succeed.

triunfo m (victoria) triumph; (en encuentro) victory, win.

trivial adj trivial.

trizas fpl bits; **hacer** ~ (hacer añicos) to smash to pieces; (desgarrar) to tear to shreds.

trocha f (Amér) gauge.

trofeo m trophy.

trombón m trombone.

trombosis f inv thrombosis.

trompa f (de elefante) trunk; (instrumento) horn; **coger una** ~ (fam) to get sloshed.

trompazo m bump.

trompeta f trumpet.

tronar v impers: **tronaba** it was thundering.

tronco m trunk; ~ de merluza thick hake steak taken from the back of the fish.

trono m throne.

tropa *f (de soldados)* troops *(pl); (de personas)* crowd ❏ **tropas** *fpl* troops.

tropezar *vi* to trip; ~ **con** to run into.

tropezón *m (tropiezo)* trip; *(de jamón, pan)* small chunk; *(equivocación)* slip.

tropical *adj* tropical.

trópico *m* tropic.

tropiezo *m (tropezón)* trip; *(dificultad)* obstacle; *(equivocación)* slip.

trotar *vi (caballo)* to trot; *(persona)* to dash around.

trote *m (de caballo)* trot; *(trabajo, esfuerzo)* dashing around.

trozo *m* piece; **a ~s** in patches; **un ~ de** a piece of.

trucaje *m (en cine)* trick photography.

trucha *f* trout.

truco *m (trampa, engaño)* trick; *(en cine)* special effect.

trueno *m (durante tormenta)* (roll of) thunder; *(de arma)* boom.

trufa *f* truffle; **~s heladas** frozen chocolate truffles.

trusa *f (Amér) (traje de baño)* swimming trunks *(pl); (braga)* knickers *(pl)*.

tu *(pl* **tus**) *adj* your.

tú *pron* you; **hablar** ○ **tratar de ~ a alguien** to address sb as "tú".

tuberculosis *f inv* tuberculosis.

tubería *f* pipe.

tubo *m (de agua, gas)* pipe; *(recipiente)* tube; **~ de escape** exhaust pipe.

tuerca *f* nut.

tuerto, -ta *adj (sin un ojo)* one-eyed.

tul *m* tulle.

tulipán *m* tulip.

tullido, -da *adj* paralysed.

tumba *f* grave.

tumbar *vt (derribar)* to knock down; *(fam: suspender)* to fail ❏ **tumbarse** *vpr* to lie down.

tumbona *f (en la playa)* deck chair; *(en el jardín)* sun lounger.

tumor *m* tumour.

tumulto *m (disturbio)* riot; *(confusión)* uproar.

tuna *f* group of student minstrels.

---

i TUNA

A "tuna" is a musical group made up of university students who wear black capes and coloured ribbons. They wander the streets playing music, singing and dancing, either for pleasure or to collect money.

---

túnel *m* tunnel.

Túnez *s (país)* Tunisia.

túnica *f* tunic.

tupido, -da *adj* thick.

turbina *f* turbine.

turbio, -bia *adj (líquido, agua)* cloudy; *(asunto)* shady.

turbulencia *f* turbulence.

turco, -ca *adj, m, f* Turkish.

turismo *m* tourism; *(coche)* private car.

turista *mf* tourist.

turístico, -ca *adj* tourist *(antes de s)*.

túrmix® *f inv* blender.

turno *m (momento)* turn; *(en el trabajo)* shift; **"su ~"** "next customer, please".

Turquía *s* Turkey.

turrón *m* sweet eaten at Christmas, made with almonds and honey.

tute *m (juego)* card game similar to whist.

tutear *vt* to address as "tú" ❑ **tutearse** *vpr* to address one another as "tú".

tutor, -ra *m, f (de bienes, menor)* guardian; *(de curso)* form teacher.

tuviera *v* → **tener**.

tuyo, -ya *adj* yours ♦ *pron:* **el ~**, **la tuya** yours; **lo ~** your thing; **un amigo ~** a friend of yours.

TV *(abrev de televisión)* TV.

UCI *f (abrev de unidad de cuidados intensivos)* ICU.

Ud. *abrev* = **usted**.

Uds. *abrev* = **ustedes**.

úlcera *f* ulcer.

ultimar *vt (Amér)* to kill.

último, -ma *adj* last; *(más reciente)* latest; *(más bajo)* bottom; *(más alto)* top; **a ~s de** at the end of; **por ~** finally; **última llamada** last call.

ultramarinos *m inv (tienda)* grocer's (shop).

ultravioleta *adj* ultraviolet.

umbral *m* threshold.

un, una *art* a, an *(antes de sonido vocálico)* ♦ *adj* = **uno**; **~ hombre** a man; **una mujer** a woman; **~ águila** an eagle.

unánime *adj* unanimous.

UNED *f Spanish open university.*

únicamente *adv* only.

único, -ca *adj (solo)* only; *(extraordinario)* unique; *(precio)* single; **lo ~ que quiero** all I want.

unidad *f* unit; *(unión, acuerdo)* unity.

unido, -da *adj (cariñosamente)* close; *(físicamente)* joined.

unifamiliar *adj* detached.

unificación *f* funification.

uniforme *m* uniform ♦ *adj* even.

unión *f* union; *(coordinación, acuerdo)* unity; *(cariño)* closeness.

unir *vt (juntar)* to join; *(mezclar)* to mix; *(personas)* to unite; *(comunicar)* to link ❑ **unirse** *vpr* to join together.

unisex *adj inv* unisex.

universal *adj* universal.

universidad *f* university.

universitario, -ria *m, f (estudiante)* student; *(licenciado)* graduate.

universo *m* universe.

uno, una *adj* **1.** *(indefinido)* one, some *(pl)*; **un día volveré** one day I will return; **~s coches** some cars. **2.** *(para expresar cantidades)* one; **treinta y un días** thirty-one days. **3.** *(aproximadamente)* around, about; **había unas doce personas** there were around twelve people.

♦ *pron* **1.** *(indefinido)* one, some *(pl)*; **coge ~** take one; **dame unas** give me some; **~ de ellos** one of them; **~ ... otro** one ... another, some ... others *(pl)*.
2. *(fam: referido a personas)* someone; **ayer hablé con ~ que te conoce** I spoke to someone who knows you yesterday.
3. *(yo)* one.
4. *(en locuciones)*: **de ~ en ~** one by one; **~ a ~** one by one; **más de ~** many people, → **seis**.

untar *vt (pan, tostada)* to spread; *(manchar)* to smear ❏ **untarse** *vpr* to smear o.s.

uña *f (de persona)* nail; *(de animal)* claw; **hacerse las ~s** to do one's nails.

uralita® *f* corrugated material made from cement and asbestos, used for roofing.

urbanización *f* housing estate.

urbano, -na *adj* urban ♦ *m, f* local police officer who deals mainly with traffic offences.

urgencia *f* emergency ❏ **Urgencias** *fpl* casualty (department) *(sg)*.

urgente *adj* urgent; **"urgente"** *(en cartas)* "express".

urgentemente *adv* urgently.

urinario *m* urinal.

urna *f (de votación)* (ballot) box; *(para restos mortales)* urn; *(de exposición)* glass case.

urraca *f* magpie.

urticaria *f* nettle rash.

Uruguay *s* Uruguay.

uruguayo, -ya *adj & m, f* Uruguayan.

usado, -da *adj (gastado)* worn.

usar *vt* to use; *(llevar)* to wear; **¿qué talla usa?** what size do you take?

uso *m* use; *(costumbre)* custom.

usted *(pl -des)* *pron* you.

usual *adj* usual.

usuario, -ria *m, f* user.

utensilio *m (herramienta)* tool; *(de cocina)* utensil.

útero *m* womb.

útil *adj* useful ♦ *m* tool.

utilidad *f (cualidad)* usefulness; *(provecho)* use.

utilitario *m* run-around car.

utilizar *vt* to use.

uva *f* grape; **~s de la suerte** twelve grapes eaten for luck as midnight chimes on New Year's Eve in Spain.

va *v* → **ir**.

vaca *f (animal)* cow; *(carne)* beef.

vacaciones *fpl* holidays; **estar de ~** to be on holiday; **ir de ~** to go on holiday.

vacante *f* vacancy.

vaciar *vt* to empty; *(hacer hueco)* to hollow out.

vacilar *vi (dudar)* to hesitate; *(tambalearse)* to wobble.

vacilón *m (Amér)* party.

vacío, -a *adj* empty ♦ *m (espacio)* void; *(hueco)* gap; **envasado al ~**

vacuna 274

vacuum-packed.

vacuna f vaccine.

vacunación f vaccination.

vacunar vt to vaccinate.

vado m (en la calle) lowered kerb; (de río) ford; **"~ permanente**" "keep clear".

vagabundo, -da m, f tramp.

vagamente adv vaguely.

vagina f vagina.

vago, -ga adj (perezoso) lazy; (impreciso) vague.

vagón m (de pasajeros) carriage.

vagoneta f cart.

vaho m (vapor) steam; (aliento) breath ❑ **vahos** mpl inhalation (sg).

vaina f (de guisantes, habas) pod.

vainilla f vanilla.

vajilla f crockery.

valdrá v → **valer**.

vale m (papel) voucher; (Amér: amigo) mate ♦ interj OK!

valenciana f (Amér) turn-up.

valentía f bravery.

valer vt (costar) to cost; (tener un valor de) to be worth; (originar) to earn ♦ vi (ser eficaz, servir) to be of use; (persona) to be good; (ser válido) to be valid; (estar permitido) to be allowed; ¿**cuánto vale**? how much is it?; ¿**vale**? OK?; **vale la pena** it's worth it ❑ **valerse de** v + prep to make use of.

valeriana f (infusión) valerian tea.

valga v → **valer**.

validez f validity.

válido, -da adj (documento, ley) valid.

valiente adj (persona) brave; (actitud, respuesta) fine.

valioso, -sa adj valuable.

valla f (cercado) fence; (muro) barrier; (de publicidad) hoarding; (en deporte) hurdle.

valle m valley.

valor m value; (valentía) bravery.

valoración f (de precio) valuation.

valorar vt (tasar) to value; (evaluar) to evaluate.

vals m waltz.

válvula f valve.

vanguardista adj avant-garde.

vanidad f vanity.

vanidoso, -sa adj vain.

vano: en vano adv in vain.

vapor m vapour; (de agua) steam; (barco) steamship; **al ~** steamed.

vaporizador m spray.

vaquero, -ra adj (ropa) denim ❑ **vaqueros** mpl (pantalones) jeans.

vara f (de árbol) stick; (de metal) rod; (de mando) staff.

variable adj changeable.

variado, -da adj (que varía) varied; (bombones, dulces) assorted.

variar vt (cambiar) to change; (dar variedad) to vary ♦ vi: **~ de** (cambiar) to change; (ser diferente) to be different from.

varicela f chickenpox.

varices fpl varicose veins.

variedad f variety ❑ **variedades** fpl (espectáculo) variety (sg).

varios, -rias adj pl (algunos) several; (diversos) various.

varón m male.

varonil adj (de varón) male; (valiente, fuerte) manly.

vasallo, -lla m, f subject.

vasco, -ca adj, m, f Basque.

vasija f container (earthenware).

vaso m glass; (de plástico) cup.

vasto, -ta adj vast.

Vaticano m: El ~ the Vatican.

vaya v → ir ♦ interj well!

Vda. abrev = viuda.

ve v → ir.

vecindad f (vecindario) community; (alrededores) neighbourhood.

vecindario m community.

vecino, -na adj neighbouring ♦ m, f (de una casa) neighbour; (de barrio) resident; (de pueblo) inhabitant.

vegetación f vegetation.

vegetal adj (planta) plant (antes de s); (sandwich) salad (antes de s) ♦ m vegetable.

vegetariano, -na m, f vegetarian.

vehículo m vehicle; (de infección) carrier.

veinte núm twenty, → seis.

vejez f old age.

vejiga f bladder.

vela f (cirio) candle; (de barco) sail; (vigilia) vigil; **pasar la noche en ~** not to sleep all night.

velero m (más pequeño) sailing boat; (más grande) sailing ship.

veleta f weather vane.

vello m down.

velo m (prenda) veil; (tela) cover.

velocidad f (rapidez) speed; (marcha) gear; **"~ controlada por**

radar" = "speed cameras in operation".

velódromo m cycle track.

velomotor m moped.

velorio m (Amér) wake.

veloz adj fast.

ven v → venir.

vena f vein.

venado m (carne) venison.

vencedor, -ra m, f winner.

vencejo m swift.

vencer vt (rival, enemigo) to beat; (dificultad, suj: sueño) to overcome ♦ vi (ganar) to win; (plazo, garantía) to expire; (pago) to be due.

vencido, -da adj beaten; **darse por ~** to give in.

vencimiento m (de plazo, garantía) expiry; (de pago) due date.

venda f bandage.

vendaje m bandaging.

vendar vt to bandage.

vendaval m gale.

vendedor, -ra m, f seller.

vender vt to sell.

vendimia f grape harvest.

vendimiador, -ra m, f grape picker.

vendimiar vt to pick (grapes).

vendrá v → venir.

veneno m poison.

venenoso, -sa adj poisonous.

venezolano, -na adj & m, f Venezuelan.

Venezuela s Venezuela.

venga v → venir.

venganza f revenge.

vengarse vpr to take revenge.

vengo v → venir.

venida f (llegada) arrival; (regre-

so) return.

venir *vi* 1. *(presentarse)* to come; **vino a verme** he came to see me.

2. *(llegar)* to arrive; **vino a las doce** he arrived at twelve o'clock.

3. *(seguir en el tiempo)* to come; **el año que viene** next year; **ahora viene la escena más divertida** the funniest scene comes next.

4. *(suceder)*: **le vino una desgracia inesperada** she suffered an unexpected misfortune; **vino la guerra** the war came.

5. *(proceder)*: ~ **de** to come from.

6. *(hallarse, estar)* to be; **el texto viene en inglés** the text is in English.

7. *(ropa, zapatos)*: **el abrigo le viene pequeño** the coat is too small for her; **tus zapatos no me vienen** your shoes don't fit me.

8. *(en locuciones)*: **¿a qué viene esto?** what do you mean by that?

❑ **venirse** *vpr* *(llegar)* to come back; **~se abajo** *(edificio, persona)* to collapse; *(proyecto)* to fall through.

venta *f* sale; *(hostal)* country inn; "**~ de billetes**" "tickets on sale here"; "**en ~**" "for sale"; **~ anticipada** advance sale; **~ al detalle** retail; **~ al mayor** wholesale.

ventaja *f* advantage.

ventana *f* window.

ventanilla *f* *(de oficina, banco)* counter; *(de cine, etc)* ticket office; *(de coche)* window.

ventilación *f* ventilation.

ventilador *m* ventilator, fan.

ventisca *f* blizzard.

ventosa *f* sucker.

ventoso, -sa *adj* windy.

ventrílocuo, -cua *m, f* ventriloquist.

ver *vt* 1. *(percibir)* to see; *(mirar)* to look at; *(televisión, partido)* to watch; **desde casa vemos el mar** we can see the sea from our house; **he estado viendo tu trabajo** I've been looking at your work; **~ la televisión** to watch television.

2. *(visitar, encontrar)* to see; **fui a ~ a unos amigos** I went to see some friends.

3. *(darse cuenta de, entender)* to see; **ya veo que estás de mal humor** I see you're in a bad mood; **ya veo lo que pretendes** now I see what you're trying to do.

4. *(investigar)* to see; **voy a ~ si han venido** I'm going to see whether they've arrived.

5. *(juzgar)*: **yo no lo veo tan mal** I don't think it's that bad.

6. *(en locuciones)*: **hay que ~ qué lista es** you wouldn't believe how clever she is; **por lo visto** o **que se ve** apparently; **~ mundo** to see the world.

◆ *vi* to see; **a ~** let's see.

❑ **verse** *vpr* *(mirarse)* to see o.s.; *(encontrarse)* to meet, to see each other; **desde aquí se ve el mar** you can see the sea from here.

veraneante *mf* (summer) holidaymaker.

veranear *vi* to have one's summer holiday.

veraneo *m* summer holidays *(pl)*.

veraniego, -ga *adj* summer *(antes de s)*.

verano *m* summer; **en ~** in summer.

veras: de veras *adv* really.

verbena f (fiesta) street party (on the eve of certain saints' days); (planta) verbena.

verbo m verb; **~ auxiliar** auxiliary verb.

verdad f truth; **es ~** it's true; **de ~** (en serio) really; (auténtico) real; **está bueno ¿~?** it's good, isn't it?

verdadero, -ra adj (cierto, real) real; (no falso) true.

verde adj inv green; (obsceno) blue, dirty ◆ m green.

verdulería f greengrocer's (shop).

verdulero, -ra m, f greengrocer.

verdura f vegetables (pl), greens (pl); **~ con patatas** starter of boiled potatoes and vegetables, usually cabbage and green beans.

vereda f (Amér) pavement (Br), sidewalk (Am).

veredicto m verdict.

vergonzoso, -sa adj (persona) bashful; (acción) shameful.

vergüenza f (timidez) bashfulness; (sofoco) embarrassment; (dignidad) pride; (pudor) shame; (escándalo) disgrace; **me dio ~** I was embarrassed.

verificar vt (comprobar) to check, to verify; (confirmar) to confirm.

verja f (puerta) iron gate.

vermut m vermouth.

verosímil adj probable.

verruga f wart.

versión f version; **en ~ original** undubbed (film).

verso m (unidad) line; (poema) poem.

---

vertedero m (de basuras) (rubbish) tip.

verter vt (contenido, líquido) to pour out; (recipiente) to empty; (derramar) to spill.

vertical adj vertical.

vertido m (residuo) waste.

vertiente f slope.

vértigo m (mareo) dizziness; (fobia) vertigo.

vestíbulo m (de casa) hall; (de hotel) foyer.

vestido m (ropa) clothes (pl); (prenda de mujer) dress.

vestimenta f clothes (pl).

vestir vt (con ropa) to dress; (llevar puesto) to wear; (mantener) to clothe ◆ vi to dress ▢ **vestirse** vpr to get dressed.

vestuario m (ropa) wardrobe; (de gimnasio, etc) changing room; (de teatro) dressing room.

veterano, -na m, f veteran.

veterinario, -ria m, f vet.

vez (pl -ces) f time; (turno) turn; **a veces** sometimes; **¿lo has hecho alguna ~?** have you ever done it?; **cada ~ más** more and more; **de ~ en cuando** from time to time; **dos veces** twice; **en ~ de** instead of; **muchas veces** a lot, often; **otra ~** again; **pocas veces** hardly ever; **tres veces por día** three times a day; **una ~** once; **unas veces** sometimes.

VHF m VHF.

VHS m VHS.

vía f (rail) track; (andén) platform; (medio de transporte) route; (calzada, calle) road; (medio) channel; **en ~ de** in the process of; **por aérea/marítima** by air/sea; **por**

oral orally.

viaducto m viaduct.

viajar vi to travel.

viaje m (trayecto) journey; (excursión) trip; (en barco) voyage; **ir de ~** to go away; **¡buen ~!** have a good trip!; **~ de novios** honeymoon.

viajero, -ra m, f (persona que viaja) traveller; (pasajero) passenger.

víbora f viper.

vibrar vi to vibrate.

vicepresidente, -ta m, f vicepresident.

vichyssoise [biʃiˈswas] f vichyssoise.

viciarse vpr to get corrupted.

vicio m (mala costumbre) bad habit; (inmoralidad) vice.

vicioso, -sa adj depraved.

víctima f victim; (muerto) casualty; **ser ~ de** to be the victim of.

victoria f victory.

vid f vine.

vida f life; (medios de subsistencia) living; **de toda la ~** (amigo, etc) lifelong; **buena ~** good life; **mala ~** vice; **~ familiar** family life.

vidente mf clairvoyant.

vídeo m video.

videocámara f camcorder.

videocasete m video(tape).

videojuego m video game.

vidriera f (de iglesia) stained glass window.

vidrio m glass.

vieira f scallop.

viejo, -ja adj old ♦ m, f (anciano) old man (f old woman); (Amér: amigo) mate.

viene v → venir.

viento m wind; **hace ~** it's windy.

vientre m stomach.

viera v → ver.

viernes m inv Friday, → sábado ❑ **Viernes Santo** m Good Friday.

Vietnam s: **~ del Norte** North Vietnam; **~ del Sur** South Vietnam.

viga f (de madera) beam; (de hierro) girder.

vigencia f (de ley, documento) validity; (de costumbre) use.

vigente adj (ley, documento) in force; (costumbre) in use.

vigilante mf guard.

vigilar vt (niños, bolso) to keep an eye on; (presos, banco) to guard.

vigor m vigour; **en ~** in force.

vigoroso, -sa adj vigorous.

vil adj despicable.

villancico m Christmas carol.

vinagre m vinegar.

vinagreras fpl cruet set (sg).

vinagreta f: **(salsa) ~** vinaigrette; **a la ~** with vinaigrette.

vinculación f link.

vincular vt to link.

viniera v → venir.

vino v → venir ♦ m wine; **~ blanco** white wine; **~ de la casa** house wine; **~ corriente** cheap wine; **~ de mesa** table wine; **~ rosado** rosé; **~ tinto** red wine.

viña f vineyard.

violación f (de persona) rape.

violador, -ra m, f rapist.

violar vt (ley, acuerdo) to break; (mujer) to rape; (territorio) to violate.

violencia f (agresividad) violence; (fuerza) force; (incomodidad) embarrassment.

violento, -ta adj violent; (incómodo) awkward.

violeta f violet.

violín m violin.

violinista mf violinist.

violoncelo m cello.

VIP f VIP.

virgen adj (mujer) virgin; (cinta) blank; (película) new ❑ **Virgen** f: la **Virgen** the Virgin Mary.

Virgo s Virgo.

virtud f virtue; **en ~ de** by virtue of.

viruela f smallpox.

virus m inv virus.

viruta f shaving; **~s de jamón** small flakes of "serrano" ham.

visa m Visa®.

visado m visa.

víscera f internal organ.

viscosa f viscose.

visera f (en gorra) peak; (suelta) visor.

visible adj visible.

visillos mpl net curtains.

visita f visit; (persona) visitor; **hacer una ~ a** to visit.

visitante mf visitor.

visitar vt to visit.

vislumbrar vt (entrever) to make out; (adivinar) to get an idea of.

víspera f eve.

vista f (sentido) sight; (ojos) eyes (pl); (panorama) view; (perspicacia) foresight; (juicio) hearing; **a**

primera ~ at first sight; **a simple ~** at first sight; **¡hasta la ~!** see you!

vistazo m glance; **echar un ~ a** to have a quick look at.

visto, -ta pp → **ver** ◆ adj (pasado de moda) old-fashioned; **estar bien/mal ~** to be approved of/frowned on; **por lo ~** apparently.

vistoso, -sa adj eye-catching.

vital adj (de la vida) life (antes de s); (fundamental) vital; (con vitalidad) lively.

vitalidad f vitality.

vitamina f vitamin.

vitrina f glass cabinet.

viudo, -da m, f widower (f widow).

viva interj hurray!

víveres mpl supplies.

vivienda f (casa) dwelling.

vivir vi to live ◆ vt to experience; **~ de** to live on.

vivo, -va adj alive; (dolor, ingenio) sharp; (detallado) vivid; (ágil, enérgico) lively; (color) bright.

vizcaíno, -na adj: **a la vizcaína** in a thick sauce of olive oil, onion, tomato, herbs and red peppers.

vocabulario m vocabulary.

vocación f vocation.

vocal f vowel.

vodka ['boθka] m vodka.

vol. (abrev de volumen) vol.

volador, -ra adj flying.

volante adj flying ◆ m (de coche) steering wheel; (adorno) frill.

volar vi to fly; (desaparecer) to vanish ◆ vt to blow up.

volcán m volcano.

volcánico, -ca adj volcanic.

volcar vt (sin querer) to knock over; (vaciar) to empty out ◆ vi (recipiente) to tip over; (camión, coche) to overturn; (barco) to capsize.

voleibol m volleyball.

volquete m dumper truck.

voltaje m voltage.

voltear vt (Amér) to knock over ❑ **voltearse** vpr (Amér) to turn.

voltereta f (en el aire) somersault; (en el suelo) handspring.

volumen m volume.

voluntad f (facultad, deseo) will; (resolución) willpower.

voluntario, -ria adj voluntary ◆ m, f volunteer.

voluntarioso, -sa adj willing.

volver vt 1. (cabeza, ojos, vista) to turn; ~ **la mirada** to look round. 2. (lo de arriba abajo) to turn over; (boca abajo) to turn upside down; (lo de dentro fuera) to turn inside out; **vuelve la tortilla** turn the omelette over; **he vuelto el abrigo** I've turned the coat inside out. 3. (convertir): **lo volvió un delincuente** it turned him into a criminal; **me vuelve loco** it makes me mad.

◆ vi to return; ~ **a** (tema) to return to; ~ **a hacer algo** to do sthg again. ❑ **volverse** vpr (darse la vuelta) to turn round; (ir de vuelta) to return; (convertirse) to become; ~**se loco** to go mad; ~**se atrás** (de decisión) to back out; (de afirmación) to go back on one's word.

vomitar vt to vomit.

vos pron (Amér) you.

VOSE f (abrev de **versión original subtitulada en español**) original language version with Spanish subtitles.

vosotros, -tras pron you.

votación f vote.

votante mf voter.

votar vt to vote for ◆ vi to vote.

voto m (en elecciones) vote; (en religión) vow.

voy v → ir.

voz (pl -ces) f voice; (grito) shout; (palabra) word; (rumor) rumour; **en** ~ **alta** aloud; **en** ~ **baja** softly.

vuelo m flight; (de un vestido) fullness; ~ **chárter** charter flight; ~ **regular** scheduled flight; "~s **nacionales**" "domestic flights".

vuelta f (movimiento, de llave) turn; (acción) turning; (regreso) return; (monedas) change; (paseo) walk; (en coche) drive; (cambio) twist; **dar la** ~ **a algo** (rodear) to go round sthg; **dar una** ~ to go for a walk/drive; **dar** ~**s** to spin; **darse la** ~ to turn round; **estar de** ~ to be back; **a la** ~ (volviendo) on the way back; **a la** ~ **de la esquina** round the corner; **a** ~ **de correo** by return (of post); "~ **al colegio**" "back to school".

vuelto, -ta pp → **volver** ◆ m (Amér) change.

vuestro, -tra adj your ◆ pron: **el** ~, **la vuestra** yours; **lo** ~ your thing; **un amigo** ~ a friend of yours.

vulgar adj (popular) ordinary; (no técnico) lay; (grosero) vulgar.

W

walkman® ['walman] *m* Walkman®.
wáter ['bater] *m* toilet.
waterpolo [water'polo] *m* water polo.
WC *m* WC.
whisky ['wiski] *m* whisky.
windsurf ['winsurf] *m* windsurfing; **hacer ~** to windsurf.

X

xenofobia *f* xenophobia.
xilófono *m* xylophone.

Y

y *conj* and; *(pero)* and yet; *(en preguntas)* what about.
ya *adv (ahora, refuerza al verbo)* now; *(ahora mismo)* at once; *(denota pasado)* already; *(denota futuro)*

---

zambullirse

some time soon ◆ *interj (expresa asentimiento)* that's it!; *(expresa comprensión)* yes! ◆ *conj:* ~ ... ~ ... whether ... or ...; ~ **que** since.
yacimiento *m* deposit.
yanqui *mf (despec)* Yank.
yate *m* yacht.
yegua *f* mare.
yema *f (de huevo)* yolk; *(de dedo)* fingertip; *(de planta)* bud; *(dulce)* sweet made of sugar and egg yolk, similar to marzipan.
yerbatero *m (Amér)* herbalist.
yerno *m* son-in-law.
yeso *m* plaster.
yo *pron* I; **soy ~** it's me; **~ que tú/él/***etc* if I were you/him/*etc.*
yodo *m* iodine.
yoga *m* yoga.
yogur *m* yoghurt.
Yugoslavia *s* Yugoslavia.
yunque *m* anvil.
yunta *f (Amér)* cufflinks *(pl)*.

Z

zafacón *m (Amér)* dustbin *(Br)*, trashcan *(Am)*.
zafiro *m* sapphire.
zafra *f* container for sprinkling oil on food.
zaguán *m* entrance hall.
zambullida *f* dive.
zambullirse *vpr* to dive.

zanahoria f carrot.

zancadilla f trip.

zanco m stilt.

zancudo m (Amér) mosquito.

zanja f ditch.

zapallo m (Amér) pumpkin.

zapateado m type of flamenco foot-stamping dance.

zapatería f (tienda) shoe shop; (taller) shoemaker's (shop).

zapatero, -ra m, f cobbler ◆ m (mueble) shoe cupboard.

zapatilla f slipper; ~ de deporte trainer.

zapato m shoe; ~s de caballero/señora men's/women's shoes.

zapping m channel-hopping; **hacer** ~ to channel-hop.

zarandear vt to shake.

zarpar vi to set sail.

zarpazo m clawing.

zarza f bramble.

zarzamora f blackberry.

zarzuela f (obra musical) light opera; (guiso) spicy fish stew.

zenit m zenith.

zinc m zinc.

zíper m (Amér) zip (Br), zipper (Am).

zipizape m (fam) squabble.

zócalo m (del edificio) plinth; (de muro, pared) skirting board.

zodíaco m zodiac.

zona f area, zone; (parte) part; ~ azul restricted parking zone; "~ de estacionamiento limitado y vigilado" "restricted parking".

ZONA AZUL

In Spain, blue lines on the road surface indicate areas where parking meters are in operation. Parking in "zonas azules" is free between certain hours; these times are displayed on the parking meters.

zonzo, -za adj (Amér) stupid; **hacerse el** ~ to act dumb.

zoo m zoo.

zoología f zoology.

zoológico, -ca adj zoological ◆ m zoo.

zopenco, -ca adj stupid.

zorra f (vulg: prostituta) whore, → zorro.

zorro, -rra m, f fox ◆ m (piel) fox(fur).

zueco m clog.

zumbar vt (fam) to thump ◆ vi to buzz.

zumbido m buzzing.

zumo m juice; ~ de fruta fruit juice; ~ de naranja orange juice.

zurcir vt to darn.

zurdo, -da adj (izquierdo) left; (que usa la mano izquierda) left-handed.

zurrar vt to hit.

ENGLISH-SPANISH
INGLÉS-ESPAÑOL

ABBREVIATIONS

ABREVIATURAS

abbreviation	*abbr/abrev*	abreviatura
adjective	*adj*	adjetivo
adverb	*adv*	adverbio
American English	*Am*	inglés americano
Latin American Spanish	*Amér*	español latinoamericano
anatomy	*ANAT*	anatomía
before noun	*antes de s*	antes de sustantivo
article	*art*	artículo
automobile, cars	*AUT(OM)*	automóviles
auxiliary	*aux*	auxiliar
British English	*Br*	inglés británico
commerce, business	*COM(M)*	comercio
comparative	*compar*	comparativo
computers	*COMPUT*	informática
conjunction	*conj*	conjunción
continuous	*cont*	continuo
culinary, cooking	*CULIN*	cocina
sport	*DEP*	deporte
juridical, legal	*DER*	derecho, jurídico
pejorative	*despec*	despectivo
economics	*ECON*	economía
school, education	*EDUC*	educación
exclamation	*excl*	interjección
feminine noun	*f*	sustantivo femenino
informal	*fam*	familiar
figurative	*fig*	figurado
finance, financial	*FIN*	finanzas
formal	*fml*	formal, culto
inseparable	*fus*	inseparable
generally	*gen*	generalmente
grammar	*GRAM(M)*	gramática
informal	*inf*	familiar

computers	*INFORM*	informática
exclamation	*interj*	interjección
invariable	*inv*	invariable
juridical, legal	*JUR*	derecho, jurídico
masculine noun	*m*	sustantivo masculino
mathematics	*MATH*	matemáticas
medicine	*MED*	medicina
military	*MIL*	militar
music	*MUS/MÚS*	música
noun	*n*	sustantivo
nautical, maritime	*NAUT*	náutica, marítimo
numeral	*num/núm*	número
oneself	*o.s.*	
pejorative	*pej*	despectivo
plural	*pl*	plural
politics	*POL(IT)*	política
past participle	*pp*	participio pasado
preposition	*prep*	preposición
pronoun	*pron*	pronombre
past tense	*pt*	pasado, pretérito
registered trademark	®	marca registrada
religion	*RELIG*	religión
noun	*s*	sustantivo
someone, somebody	*sb*	
school, education	*SCH*	educación
Scottish English	*Scot*	inglés escocés
separable	*sep*	separable
singular	*sg*	singular
something	*sthg*	
subject	*subj/suj*	sujeto
superlative	*superl*	superlativo
technology	*TECH/TECN*	tecnología
television	*TV*	televisión
transport	*TRANS(P)*	transportes
verb	*vb/v*	verbo
intransitive verb	*vi*	verbo intransitivo

impersonal verb	*v impers*	verbo impersonal
pronominal verb	*vpr*	verbo pronominal
transitive verb	*vt*	verbo transitivo
vulgar	*vulg*	vulgar
cultural equivalent	$\simeq$	equivalente cultural

SPANISH ALPHABETICAL ORDER

This dictionary follows international alphabetical order. Thus entries with **ch** appear after **cg** and not at the end of **c**. Similarly, entries with **ll** appear after **lk** and not at the end of **l**. Note, however, that **ñ** *is* treated as a separate letter and follows **n**.

LA ORDENACIÓN ALFABÉTICA EN ESPAÑOL

En este diccionario se ha seguido la ordenación alfabética internacional. Esto significa que las entradas con **ch** aparecerán después de **cg** y no al final de **c**; del mismo modo las entradas con **ll** vendrán después de **lk** y no al final de **l**. Adviértase, sin embargo, que la letra **ñ** *sí* se considera letra aparte y sigue a la **n**.

ENGLISH COMPOUNDS

A compound is a word or expression which has a single meaning but is made up of more than one word, e.g. **point of view**, **kiss of life**, **virtual reality** and **West Indies**. It is a feature of this dictionary that English compounds appear in the A-Z list in strict alphabetical order. The compound **blood test** will therefore come after **bloodshot** which itself follows **blood pressure**.

LOS COMPUESTOS EN INGLÉS

En inglés se llama compuesto a una locución sustantiva de significado único pero formada por más de una palabra; p.ej. **point of view**, **kiss of life**, **virtual reality** o **West Indies**. Uno de los rasgos distintivos de este diccionario es la inclusión de estos compuestos con entrada propia y en riguroso orden alfabético. De esta forma **blood test** vendrá después de **bloodshot**, el cual sigue a **blood pressure**.

PHONETIC TRANSCRIPTION

English vowels

[ɪ] pit, big, rid
[e] pet, tend
[æ] pat, bag, mad
[ʌ] run, cut
[ɒ] pot, log
[ʊ] put, full
[ə] mother, suppose
[iː] bean, weed
[ɑː] barn, car, laugh
[ɔː] born, lawn
[uː] loop, loose
[ɜː] burn, learn, bird

English diphthongs

[eɪ] bay, late, great
[aɪ] buy, light, aisle
[ɔɪ] boy, foil
[əʊ] no, road, blow
[aʊ] now, shout, town
[ɪə] peer, fierce, idea
[eə] pair, bear, share
[ʊə] poor, sure, tour

Semi-vowels

you, spaniel   [j]
wet, why, twin   [w]

Consonants

pop, people   [p]
bottle, bib   [b]
train, tip   [t]
dog, did   [d]
come, kitchen   [k]
gag, great   [g]

TRANSCRIPCIÓN FONÉTICA

Vocales españolas

[i] piso, imagen
[e] tela, eso
[a] pata, amigo
[o] bola, otro
[u] luz, una

Vocales catalanas

[ɛ] fresc

Diptongos españoles

[ei] ley, peine
[ai] aire, caiga
[oi] soy, boina
[au] causa, aula
[eu] Europa, deuda

Semivocales

hierba, miedo   [j]
agua, hueso   [w]

Consonantes

papá, campo   [p]
vaca, bomba   [b]
curvo, caballo   [β]
toro, pato   [t]
donde, caldo   [d]
que, cosa   [k]
grande, guerra   [g]
aguijón, bulldog   [ɣ]

chain, wre**tch**ed	[tʃ]	o**ch**o, **ch**usma
jet, fri**dg**e	[dʒ]	
fib, **ph**ysical	[f]	**f**ui, a**f**án
vine, li**v**e	[v]	
think, fif**th**	[θ]	**c**era, pa**z**
this, wi**th**	[ð]	ca**d**a, par**d**o
seal, pea**c**e	[s]	**s**olo, pa**s**o
zip, hi**s**	[z]	
sheep, ma**ch**ine	[ʃ]	
u**s**ual, mea**s**ure	[ʒ]	
	[x]	**g**emir, **j**amón
how, per**h**aps	[h]	
metal, co**mb**	[m]	**m**adre, ca**m**a
night, di**nn**er	[n]	**n**o, pe**n**a
su**ng**, par**k**ing	[ŋ]	ba**n**ca, e**n**canto
	[ɲ]	ca**ñ**a
little, he**lp**	[l]	a**l**a, **l**uz
right, ca**rr**y	[r]	a**t**ar, pa**r**o
	[rr]	pe**rr**o, **r**osa
	[ʎ]	**ll**ave, co**ll**ar

The symbol ['] indicates that the following syllable carries primary stress and the symbol [,] that the following syllable carries secondary stress.

Los símbolos ['] y [,] indican que la sílaba siguiente lleva un acento primario o secundario respectivamente.

The symbol [ʳ] in English phonetics indicates that the final "r" is pronounced only when followed by a word beginning with a vowel. Note that it is nearly always pronounced in American English.

El símbolo [ʳ] en fonética inglesa indica que la "r" al final de palabra se pronuncia sólo cuando precede a una palabra que comienza por vocal. Adviértase que casi siempre se pronuncia en inglés americano.

ENGLISH-SPANISH
INGLÉS-ESPAÑOL

a [*stressed* eɪ, *unstressed* ə] *indef art*
1. *(referring to indefinite thing, person)*
un (una); **a friend** un amigo; **a
table** una mesa; **an apple** una manzana; **to be a doctor** ser médico.
2. *(instead of the number one)* un
(una); **a hundred and twenty
pounds** ciento veinte libras; **a
month ago** hace un mes; **a thousand** mil; **four and a half** cuatro y
medio.
3. *(in prices, ratios)* por; **they're £2 a
kilo** están a dos libras el kilo; **three
times a year** tres veces al año.

AA *n* (*Br: abbr of* Automobile
Association) *asociación británica del
automóvil,* ≈ RACE *m*.

aback [ə'bæk] *adj*: **to be taken ~**
quedarse atónito(-ta).

abandon [ə'bændən] *vt* abandonar.

abattoir ['æbətwɑːr] *n* matadero
m.

abbey ['æbɪ] *n* abadía *f*.

abbreviation [ə,briːvɪ'eɪʃn] *n*
abreviatura *f*.

abdomen ['æbdəmən] *n* abdomen *m*.

abide [ə'baɪd] *vt*: **I can't ~ him** no
le aguanto ❑ **abide by** *vt fus* (rule,
law) acatar.

ability [ə'bɪlətɪ] *n* (capability)
capacidad *f*, facultad *f*; (skill) dotes
fpl.

able ['eɪbl] *adj* capaz, competente; **to be ~ to do sthg** poder
hacer algo.

abnormal [æb'nɔːml] *adj* anor-
mal.

aboard [ə'bɔːd] *adv* a bordo ◆
prep (ship, plane) a bordo de; *(train,
bus)* en.

abolish [ə'bɒlɪʃ] *vt* abolir.

aborigine [,æbə'rɪdʒənɪ] *n* abori-
gen *mf* de Australia.

abort [ə'bɔːt] *vt* abortar.

abortion [ə'bɔːʃn] *n* aborto *m*;
to have an ~ abortar.

about [ə'baʊt] *adv* **1.** *(approximately)* más o menos; **~ 50** unos
cincuenta; **at ~ six o'clock** a eso de
las seis.
2. *(referring to place)* por ahí; **to
walk ~** pasearse.
3. *(on the point of):* **to be ~ to do
sthg** estar a punto de hacer algo;
it's ~ to rain va a empezar a
llover.
◆ *prep* **1.** *(concerning)* acerca de; **a
book ~ Scotland** un libro sobre

Escocia; **what's it ~?** ¿de qué (se) trata?; **what ~ a drink?** ¿qué tal si tomamos algo?
2. *(referring to place)* por; **there are lots of hotels ~** the town hay muchos hoteles por toda la ciudad.

above [ə'bʌv] *prep* por encima de ♦ *adv (higher)* arriba; **children aged ten and ~** niños mayores de diez años; **the room ~** la habitación de arriba; **~ all** sobre todo.

abroad [ə'brɔːd] *adv (be, live, work)* en el extranjero; *(go, move)* al extranjero.

abrupt [ə'brʌpt] *adj* repentino(-na).

abscess ['æbses] *n* absceso *m*.

absence ['æbsəns] *n* ausencia *f*.

absent ['æbsənt] *adj* ausente.

absent-minded [-'maɪndɪd] *adj* despistado(-da).

absolute ['æbsəluːt] *adj* absoluto(-ta).

absolutely [*adv* 'æbsəluːtlɪ, *excl* ˌæbsə'luːtlɪ] *adv (completely)* absolutamente ♦ *excl* ¡por supuesto!

absorb [əb'sɔːb] *vt (liquid)* absorber.

absorbed [əb'sɔːbd] *adj:* **to be ~ in sthg** estar absorto(-ta) en algo.

absorbent [əb'sɔːbənt] *adj* absorbente.

abstain [əb'steɪn] *vi:* **to ~ (from)** abstenerse (de).

absurd [əb'sɜːd] *adj* absurdo(-da).

ABTA ['æbtə] *n* asociación británica de agencias de viajes.

abuse [*n* ə'bjuːs, *vb* ə'bjuːz] *n (insults)* insultos *mpl*; *(wrong use,*

maltreatment) abuso *m* ♦ *vt (insult)* insultar; *(use wrongly)* abusar de; *(maltreat)* maltratar.

abusive [ə'bjuːsɪv] *adj* insultante.

AC *(abbr of alternating current)* CA.

academic [ˌækə'demɪk] *adj (educational)* académico(-ca) ♦ *n* profesor *m* universitario (profesora *f* universitaria).

academy [ə'kædəmɪ] *n* academia *f*.

accelerate [ək'seləreɪt] *vi* acelerar.

accelerator [ək'seləreɪtəʳ] *n* acelerador *m*.

accent ['æksent] *n* acento *m*.

accept [ək'sept] *vt* aceptar; *(blame, responsibility)* admitir.

acceptable [ək'septəbl] *adj* aceptable.

access ['ækses] *n* acceso *m*.

accessible [ək'sesəbl] *adj* accesible.

accessories [ək'sesərɪz] *npl (extras)* accesorios *mpl*; *(fashion items)* complementos *mpl*.

access road *n* vía *f* de acceso.

accident ['æksɪdənt] *n* accidente *m*; **by ~** por casualidad.

accidental [ˌæksɪ'dentl] *adj* accidental.

accident insurance *n* seguro *m* contra accidentes.

accident-prone *adj* propenso(-sa) a los accidentes.

acclimatize [ə'klaɪmətaɪz] *vi* aclimatarse.

accommodate [ə'kɒmədeɪt] *vt* alojar.

accommodation [əˌkɒmə'deɪʃn] *n* alojamiento *m*.

accommodations [əˌkɒmə-ˈdeɪʃnz] *npl* (*Am*) = **accommodation**.

accompany [əˈkʌmpənɪ] *vt* acompañar.

accomplish [əˈkʌmplɪʃ] *vt* conseguir, lograr.

accord [əˈkɔːd] *n*: of one's own ~ por propia voluntad.

accordance [əˈkɔːdəns] *n*: in ~ with conforme a.

according to [əˈkɔːdɪŋ-] *prep* según.

accordion [əˈkɔːdɪən] *n* acordeón *m*.

account [əˈkaʊnt] *n* (*at bank, shop*) cuenta *f*; (*spoken report*) relato *m*; to take into ~ tener en cuenta; on no ~ bajo ningún pretexto; on ~ of debido a ❑ **account for** *vt fus* (*explain*) justificar; (*constitute*) representar.

accountant [əˈkaʊntənt] *n* contable *mf*.

account number *n* número *m* de cuenta.

accumulate [əˈkjuːmjʊleɪt] *vt* acumular.

accurate [ˈækjʊrət] *adj* (*description, report*) veraz; (*work, measurement, figure*) exacto(-ta).

accuse [əˈkjuːz] *vt*: to ~ sb of sthg acusar a alguien de algo.

accused [əˈkjuːzd] *n*: the ~ el acusado *m* (la acusada *f*).

ace [eɪs] *n* as *m*.

ache [eɪk] *n* dolor *m* ♦ *vi*: my leg ~s me duele la pierna.

achieve [əˈtʃiːv] *vt* conseguir.

acid [ˈæsɪd] *adj* ácido(-da) ♦ *n* ácido *m*.

acid rain *n* lluvia *f* ácida.

acknowledge [əkˈnɒlɪdʒ] *vt* (*accept*) reconocer; (*letter*) acusar recibo de.

acne [ˈæknɪ] *n* acné *m*.

acorn [ˈeɪkɔːn] *n* bellota *f*.

acoustic [əˈkuːstɪk] *adj* acústico(-ca).

acquaintance [əˈkweɪntəns] *n* (*person*) conocido *m* (-da *f*).

acquire [əˈkwaɪəʳ] *vt* adquirir.

acre [ˈeɪkəʳ] *n* acre *m*.

acrobat [ˈækrəbæt] *n* acróbata *mf*.

across [əˈkrɒs] *prep* (*to, on other side of*) al otro lado de; (*from one side to the other of*) de un lado a otro ♦ *adv* (*to other side*) al otro lado; it's ten miles ~ tiene diez millas de ancho; we walked ~ the road cruzamos la calle; ~ from en frente de.

acrylic [əˈkrɪlɪk] *n* acrílico *m*.

act [ækt] *vi* actuar; (*behave*) comportarse ♦ *n* (*action*) acto *m*, acción *f*; (POL) ley *f*; (*of play*) acto; (*performance*) número *m*; to ~ as (*serve as*) hacer de.

action [ˈækʃn] *n* acción *f*; to take ~ tomar medidas; to put sthg into ~ poner algo en acción; out of ~ (*machine*) averiado; (*person*) fuera de combate.

active [ˈæktɪv] *adj* activo(-va).

activity [ækˈtɪvətɪ] *n* actividad *f* ❑ **activities** *npl* (*leisure events*) atracciones *fpl*.

activity holiday *n* vacaciones organizadas para niños de actividades deportivas, etc.

act of God *n* caso *m* de fuerza mayor.

actor [ˈæktəʳ] *n* actor *m*.

actress ['æktrɪs] n actriz f.

actual ['æktjʊəl] adj (exact, real) verdadero(-ra); (for emphasis) mismísimo(-ma); (final) final.

actually ['æktjʊəlɪ] adv (really) realmente; (in fact) la verdad es que.

acupuncture ['ækjʊpʌŋktʃə'] n acupuntura f.

acute [ə'kjuːt] adj (feeling, pain) intenso(-sa); (angle, accent) agudo(-da).

ad [æd] n (inf) anuncio m.

AD (abbr of Anno Domini) d.C.

adapt [ə'dæpt] vt adaptar ♦ vi adaptarse.

adapter [ə'dæptə'] n (for foreign plug) adaptador m; (for several plugs) ladrón m.

add [æd] vt (put, say in addition) añadir; (numbers, prices) sumar ▫ **add up** vt sep sumar; **add up to** vt fus (total) venir a ser.

adder ['ædə'] n víbora f.

addict ['ædɪkt] n adicto m (-ta f).

addicted [ə'dɪktɪd] adj: **to be ~ to sthg** ser adicto(-ta) a algo.

addiction [ə'dɪkʃn] n adicción f.

addition [ə'dɪʃn] n (added thing) adición f; (in maths) suma f; **in ~** además; **in ~ to** además de.

additional [ə'dɪʃənl] adj adicional.

additive ['ædɪtɪv] n aditivo m.

address [ə'dres] n (on letter) dirección f ♦ vt (speak to) dirigirse a; (letter) dirigir.

address book n agenda f de direcciones.

addressee [ædre'siː] n destinatario m (-ria f).

adequate ['ædɪkwət] adj (sufficient) suficiente; (satisfactory) acep-table.

adhere [əd'hɪə'] vi: **to ~ to** (stick to) adherirse a; (obey) observar.

adhesive [əd'hiːsɪv] adj adhesivo(-va) ♦ n adhesivo m.

adjacent [ə'dʒeɪsənt] adj adyacente.

adjective ['ædʒɪktɪv] n adjetivo m.

adjoining [ə'dʒɔɪnɪŋ] adj contiguo(-gua).

adjust [ə'dʒʌst] vt ajustar ♦ vi: **to ~ to** adaptarse a.

adjustable [ə'dʒʌstəbl] adj ajustable.

adjustment [ə'dʒʌstmənt] n ajuste m.

administration [əd,mɪnɪ'streɪʃn] n administración f.

administrator [əd'mɪnɪstreɪtə'] n administrador m (-ra f).

admiral ['ædmərəl] n almirante m.

admire [əd'maɪə'] vt admirar.

admission [əd'mɪʃn] n (permission to enter) admisión f; (entrance cost) entrada f.

admission charge n entrada f.

admit [əd'mɪt] vt admitir ♦ vi: **to ~ to sthg** admitir algo; **"~s one"** (on ticket) "válido para una persona".

adolescent [ædə'lesnt] n adolescente mf.

adopt [ə'dɒpt] vt adoptar.

adopted [ə'dɒptɪd] adj adoptivo(-va).

adorable [ə'dɔːrəbl] adj adorable.

adore [ə'dɔː'] vt adorar.

adult ['ædʌlt] n adulto m (-ta f) ♦ adj (entertainment, films) para adultos; *(animal)* adulto(-ta).

adult education *n* educación *f* para adultos.

adultery [ə'dʌltərɪ] *n* adulterio *m*.

advance [əd'vɑːns] *n (money)* anticipo *m*; *(movement)* avance *m* ♦ *adj (warning)* previo(-via); *(payment)* anticipado(-da) ♦ *vt* adelantar ♦ *vi* avanzar.

advance booking *n* reserva *f* anticipada.

advanced [əd'vɑːnst] *adj (student, level)* avanzado(-da).

advantage [əd'vɑːntɪdʒ] *n (benefit)* ventaja *f*; **to take ~ of** *(opportunity, offer)* aprovechar; *(person)* aprovecharse de.

adventure [əd'ventʃəʳ] *n* aventura *f*.

adventurous [əd'ventʃərəs] *adj (person)* aventurero(-ra).

adverb [ˈædvɜːb] *n* adverbio *m*.

adverse [ˈædvɜːs] *adj* adverso(-sa).

advert [ˈædvɜːt] = **advertisement**.

advertise [ˈædvətaɪz] *vt (product, event)* anunciar.

advertisement [əd'vɜːtɪsmənt] *n* anuncio *m*.

advice [əd'vaɪs] *n* consejos *mpl*; **a piece of ~** un consejo.

advisable [əd'vaɪzəbl] *adj* aconsejable.

advise [əd'vaɪz] *vt* aconsejar; **to ~ sb to do sthg** aconsejar a alguien que haga algo; **to ~ sb against doing sthg** desaconsejar a alguien que haga algo.

advocate [*n* ˈædvəkət, *vb* ˈædvəkeɪt] *n (JUR)* abogado *m* (-da *f*) ♦ *vt* abogar por.

aerial [ˈeərɪəl] *n* antena *f*.

aerobics [eəˈrəʊbɪks] *n* aerobic *m*.

aerodynamic [ˌeərəʊdaɪˈnæmɪk] *adj* aerodinámico(-ca).

aeroplane [ˈeərəpleɪn] *n* avión *m*.

aerosol [ˈeərəsɒl] *n* aerosol *m*.

affair [əˈfeəʳ] *n (matter)* asunto *m*; *(love affair)* aventura *f* (amorosa); *(event)* acontecimiento *m*.

affect [əˈfekt] *vt (influence)* afectar.

affection [əˈfekʃn] *n* afecto *m*.

affectionate [əˈfekʃnət] *adj* cariñoso(-sa).

affluent [ˈæfluənt] *adj* opulento(-ta).

afford [əˈfɔːd] *vt*: **to be able to ~ sthg** *(holiday, new coat)* poder permitirse algo; **I can't ~ it** no me lo puedo permitir; **I can't ~ the time** no tengo tiempo.

affordable [əˈfɔːdəbl] *adj* asequible.

afloat [əˈfləʊt] *adj* a flote.

afraid [əˈfreɪd] *adj*: **to be ~ of** *(person)* tener miedo a; *(thing)* tener miedo de; **I'm ~ so/not** me temo que sí/no.

Africa [ˈæfrɪkə] *n* África.

African [ˈæfrɪkən] *adj* africano(-na) ♦ *n* africano *m* (-na *f*).

after [ˈɑːftəʳ] *prep* después de ♦ *conj* después de que ♦ *adv* después; **a quarter ~ ten** *(US)* las diez y cuarto; **to be ~ sthg/sb** *(in search of)* buscar algo/a alguien; **~ all** *(in spite of everything)* después de todo; *(it should be remembered)* al fin y al cabo.

aftercare [ˈɑːftəkeəʳ] *n* asistencia *f* post-hospitalaria.

aftereffects [ˈɑːftərɪˌfekts] *npl* efectos *mpl* secundarios.

afternoon [ˌɑːftəˈnuːn] *n* tarde *f*; **good ~!** ¡buenas tardes!

afternoon tea *n* = merienda *f*.

aftershave [ˈɑːftəʃeɪv] *n* colonia *f* de hombre.

aftersun [ˈɑːftəsʌn] *n* aftersún *m*.

afterwards [ˈɑːftəwədz] *adv* después.

again [əˈɡen] *adv* de nuevo, otra vez; **~ and ~** una y otra vez; **never ~** nunca jamás.

against [əˈɡenst] *prep* contra; *(in disagreement with)* en contra de; **to lean ~ sthg** apoyarse en algo; **~ the law** ilegal.

age [eɪdʒ] *n* edad *f*; *(old age)* vejez *f*; **under ~** menor de edad; **I haven't seen her for ~s** *(inf)* hace siglos que no la veo.

aged [eɪdʒd] *adj*: **~ eight** de ocho años de edad.

age group *n* grupo *m* de edad.

age limit *n* edad *f* máxima/mínima.

agency [ˈeɪdʒənsɪ] *n* agencia *f*.

agenda [əˈdʒendə] *n* orden *m* del día.

agent [ˈeɪdʒənt] *n* agente *mf*.

aggression [əˈɡreʃn] *n* agresividad *f*.

aggressive [əˈɡresɪv] *adj* agresivo(-va).

agile [*Br* ˈædʒaɪl, *Am* ˈædʒəl] *adj* ágil.

agility [əˈdʒɪlətɪ] *n* agilidad *f*.

agitated [ˈædʒɪteɪtɪd] *adj* agitado(-da).

ago [əˈɡəʊ] *adv*: **a month ~** hace un mes; **how long ~?** ¿cuánto tiempo hace?

agonizing [ˈæɡənaɪzɪŋ] *adj* *(delay)* angustioso(-sa); *(pain)* atroz.

agony [ˈæɡənɪ] *n* dolor *m* intenso.

agree [əˈɡriː] *vi* *(be in agreement)* estar de acuerdo; *(consent)* acceder; *(correspond)* concordar; **it doesn't ~ with me** *(food)* no me sienta bien; **to ~ to sthg** acceder a algo; **to ~ to do sthg** acceder a hacer algo ❑ **agree on** *vt fus* *(time, price)* acordar.

agreed [əˈɡriːd] *adj* acordado(-da); **to be ~** *(person)* estar de acuerdo.

agreement [əˈɡriːmənt] *n* acuerdo *m*; **in ~ with** de acuerdo con.

agriculture [ˈæɡrɪkʌltʃə] *n* agricultura *f*.

ahead [əˈhed] *adv* *(in front)* delante; *(forwards)* adelante; **the months ~** los meses que vienen; **to be ~** *(winning)* ir ganando; **~ of** *(in front of)* delante de; *(in better position than)* por delante de; **~ of schedule** por delante de lo previsto; **go straight ~** sigue todo recto; **they're two points ~** llevan dos puntos de ventaja.

aid [eɪd] *n* ayuda *f* ◆ *vt* ayudar; **in ~ of** a beneficio de; **with the ~ of** con la ayuda de.

AIDS [eɪdz] *n* SIDA *m*.

ailment [ˈeɪlmənt] *n* *(fml)* achaque *m*.

aim [eɪm] *n* *(purpose)* propósito *m* ◆ *vt* apuntar ◆ *vi*: **to ~ (at)** apuntar (a); **to ~ to do sthg** aspirar a hacer algo.

air [eə] *n* aire *m* ◆ *vt* *(room)* ventilar ◆ *adj* aéreo(-a); **by ~** *(travel)* en avión; *(send)* por avión.

airbed [ˈeəbed] *n* colchón *m*

de aire.

airborne ['eəbɔːn] *adj* en el aire.

air-conditioned [-kən'dɪʃnd] *adj* climatizado(-da).

air-conditioning [-kən'dɪʃnɪŋ] *n* aire *m* acondicionado.

aircraft ['eəkrɑːft] (*pl inv*) *n* avión *m*.

aircraft carrier [-ˌkærɪə'] *n* portaaviones *m inv*.

airfield ['eəfiːld] *n* aeródromo *m*.

airforce ['eəfɔːs] *n* fuerzas *fpl* aéreas.

air freshener [-ˌfreʃnə'] *n* ambientador *m*.

airhostess ['eəˌhəʊstɪs] *n* azafata *f*.

airing cupboard ['eərɪŋ-] *n* armario de aire caliente para guardar la ropa.

airletter ['eəˌletə'] *n* aerograma *m*.

airline ['eəlaɪn] *n* línea *f* aérea.

airliner ['eəˌlaɪnə'] *n* avión *m* (grande) de pasajeros.

airmail ['eəmeɪl] *n* correo *m* aéreo; **by ~** por avión.

airplane ['eəpleɪn] *n* (*Am*) avión *m*.

airport ['eəpɔːt] *n* aeropuerto *m*.

air raid *n* ataque *m* aéreo.

airsick ['eəsɪk] *adj* mareado(-da) (*en avión*).

air steward *n* auxiliar *m* de vuelo.

air stewardess *n* azafata *f*.

air traffic control *n* (*people*) personal *m* de la torre de control.

airy ['eərɪ] *adj* espacioso(-sa) y bien ventilado(-da).

aisle [aɪl] *n* (*in church*) nave *f* lateral; (*in plane, cinema, supermarket*)

pasillo *m*.

aisle seat *n* (*on plane*) asiento *m* junto al pasillo.

ajar [ə'dʒɑː'] *adj* entreabierto (-ta).

alarm [ə'lɑːm] *n* alarma *f* ♦ *vt* alarmar.

alarm clock *n* despertador *m*.

alarmed [ə'lɑːmd] *adj* (*door, car*) con alarma.

alarming [ə'lɑːmɪŋ] *adj* alarmante.

Albert Hall ['ælbət-] *n*: **the ~** el Albert Hall.

i ALBERT HALL

Esta gran sala de conciertos londinense se llama así en honor al príncipe Albert, consorte de la reina Victoria. Además de conciertos, en el Albert Hall se celebran otros espectáculos, incluidos acontecimientos deportivos.

album ['ælbəm] *n* (*for photos*) álbum *m*; (*record*) elepé *m*.

alcohol ['ælkəhɒl] *n* alcohol *m*.

alcohol-free *adj* sin alcohol.

alcoholic [ˌælkə'hɒlɪk] *adj* alcohólico(-ca) ♦ *n* alcohólico *m* (-ca *f*).

alcoholism ['ælkəhɒlɪzm] *n* alcoholismo *m*.

alcove ['ælkəʊv] *n* hueco *m*.

ale [eɪl] *n* cerveza oscura de sabor amargo y alto contenido en alcohol.

alert [ə'lɜːt] *adj* atento(-ta) ♦ *vt* alertar.

A-level *n examen necesario para acceder a la universidad.*

 A-LEVEL

Los exámenes llamados "A-levels" se realizan a los 18 años normalmente y son un requisito obligatorio para acceder a la universidad en Gran Bretaña. En general, los estudiantes se examinan de tres materias, o cuatro como máximo. Las notas de los "A-levels" son muy importantes puesto que determinan si los estudiantes pueden ir a la universidad de su elección.

algebra ['ældʒɪbrə] *n* álgebra *f.*

Algeria [æl'dʒɪərɪə] *n* Argelia.

alias ['eɪlɪəs] *adv* alias.

alibi ['ælɪbaɪ] *n* coartada *f.*

alien ['eɪlɪən] *n (foreigner)* extranjero *m* (-ra *f*); *(from outer space)* extraterrestre *mf.*

alight [ə'laɪt] *adj* ardiendo ◆ *vi (fml: from train, bus):* **to ~ (from)** apearse (de).

align [ə'laɪn] *vt* alinear.

alike [ə'laɪk] *adj* parecido(-da) ◆ *adv* igual; **to look ~** parecerse.

alive [ə'laɪv] *adj* vivo(-va).

all [ɔːl] *adj* **1.** *(with singular noun)* todo(-da); **~ the money** todo el dinero; **~ the time** todo el rato; **~ day** todo el día. **2.** *(with plural noun)* todos(-das); **~ the houses** todas las casas; **~ trains stop at Tonbridge** todos los trenes hacen parada en Tonbridge; **~ three died** los tres murieron.

◆ *adv* **1.** *(completely)* completa-

mente; **~ alone** completamente solo. **2.** *(in scores):* **it's two ~** van empatados a dos. **3.** *(in phrases):* **~ but empty** casi vacío; **~ over** *adj (finished)* terminado ◆ *prep* por todo.

◆ *pron* **1.** *(everything)* todo *m* (-da *f*); **~ of the work** todo el trabajo; **is that ~?** *(in shop)* ¿algo más?; **the best of ~** lo mejor de todo. **2.** *(everybody)* todos *mpl* (-das *fpl*); **~ of us went** fuimos todos. **3.** *(in phrases):* **in ~** *(in total)* en total; **can I help you at ~?** ¿le puedo ayudar en algo?

Allah ['ælə] *n* Alá *m.*

allege [ə'ledʒ] *vt* alegar.

allergic [ə'lɜːdʒɪk] *adj:* **to be ~ to** ser alérgico(-ca) a.

allergy ['ælədʒɪ] *n* alergia *f.*

alleviate [ə'liːvɪeɪt] *vt* aliviar.

alley [ælɪ] *n (narrow street)* callejón *m.*

alligator ['ælɪgeɪtə'] *n* caimán *m.*

all-in *adj (Br: inclusive)* con todo incluido.

all-night *adj (bar, petrol station)* abierto(-ta) toda la noche.

allocate ['æləkeɪt] *vt* asignar.

allotment [ə'lɒtmənt] *n (Br: for vegetables)* parcela municipal arrendada para su cultivo.

allow [ə'laʊ] *vt (permit)* permitir; *(time, money)* contar con; **to ~ sb to do sthg** dejar a alguien hacer algo; **to be ~ed to do sthg** poder hacer algo ❑ **allow for** *vt fus* contar con.

allowance [ə'laʊəns] *n (state benefit)* subsidio *m; (for expenses)* dietas *fpl; (Am: pocket money)* dinero *m* de bolsillo.

all right adj bien ◆ adv (satisfactorily) bien; (yes, okay) vale.

ally ['ælaɪ] n aliado m (-da f).

almond ['ɑːmənd] n almendra f.

almost ['ɔːlməʊst] adv casi.

alone [ə'ləʊn] adj & adv solo(-la); **to leave sb ~** dejar a alguien en paz; **to leave sthg ~** dejar algo.

along [ə'lɒŋ] prep (towards one end of) por; (alongside) a lo largo de ◆ adv: **she was walking ~** iba caminando; **to bring sthg ~** traerse algo; **all ~** siempre, desde el principio; **~ with** junto con.

alongside [ə,lɒŋ'saɪd] prep junto a ◆ adv: **to come ~** ponerse al lado.

aloof [ə'luːf] adj distante.

aloud [ə'laʊd] adv en voz alta.

alphabet ['ælfəbet] n alfabeto m.

Alps [ælps] npl: **the ~ los** Alpes.

already [ɔːl'redɪ] adv ya.

also ['ɔːlsəʊ] adv también.

altar ['ɔːltər] n altar m.

alter ['ɔːltər] vt alterar.

alteration [,ɔːltə'reɪʃn] n alteración f.

alternate [Br ɔːl'tɜːnət, Am 'ɔːltərnət] adj alterno(-na).

alternating current ['ɔːltə-neɪtɪŋ-] n corriente f alterna.

alternative [ɔːl'tɜːnətɪv] adj alternativo(-va) ◆ n alternativa f.

alternatively [ɔːl'tɜːnətɪvlɪ] adv o bien.

alternator ['ɔːltɜːneɪtər] n alternador m.

although [ɔːl'ðəʊ] conj aunque.

altitude ['æltɪtjuːd] n altitud f.

altogether [,ɔːltə'geðər] adv

(completely) completamente; (in total) en total.

aluminium [,æljʊ'mɪnɪəm] n (Br) aluminio m.

aluminum [ə'luːmɪnəm] (Am) = **aluminium**.

always ['ɔːlweɪz] adv siempre.

am [æm] → **be**.

a.m. (abbr of ante meridiem): **at 2 ~** a las dos de la mañana.

amateur ['æmətər] n aficionado m (-da f).

amazed [ə'meɪzd] adj asombrado(-da).

amazing [ə'meɪzɪŋ] adj asombroso(-sa).

Amazon ['æməzn] n (river): **the ~ el** Amazonas.

ambassador [æm'bæsədər] n embajador m (-ra f).

amber ['æmbər] adj (traffic lights) (de color) ámbar; (jewellery) de ámbar.

ambiguous [æm'bɪgjʊəs] adj ambiguo(-gua).

ambition [æm'bɪʃn] n ambición f.

ambitious [æm'bɪʃəs] adj ambicioso(-sa).

ambulance ['æmbjʊləns] n ambulancia f.

ambush ['æmbʊʃ] n emboscada f.

amenities [ə'miːnətɪz] npl instalaciones fpl.

America [ə'merɪkə] n América f.

American [ə'merɪkən] adj americano(-na) ◆ n (person) americano m (-na f).

amiable ['eɪmɪəbl] adj amable.

ammunition [,æmjʊ'nɪʃn] n

municiones *fpl*.

amnesia [æm'ni:zɪə] *n* amnesia *f*.

among(st) [ə'mʌŋ(st)] *prep* entre.

amount [ə'maʊnt] *n* cantidad *f* □ **amount to** *vt fus* (*total*) ascender a.

amp [æmp] *n* amperio *m*; **a 13-~ plug** un enchufe con un fusible de 13 amperios.

ample ['æmpl] *adj* más que suficiente.

amplifier ['æmplɪfaɪəʳ] *n* amplificador *m*.

amputate ['æmpjʊteɪt] *vt* amputar.

Amtrak ['æmtræk] *n* organismo que regula los ferrocarriles en EEUU.

amuse [ə'mju:z] *vt* (*make laugh*) divertir; (*entertain*) entretener.

amusement arcade [ə'mju:z-mənt-] *n* salón *m* de juegos.

amusement park [ə'mju:z-mənt-] *n* parque *m* de atracciones.

amusements [ə'mju:zmənts] *npl* atracciones *fpl*.

amusing [ə'mju:zɪŋ] *adj* divertido(-da).

an [stressed æn, unstressed ən] → **a**.

anaemic [ə'ni:mɪk] *adj* (*Br: person*) anémico(-ca).

anaesthetic [ˌænɪs'θetɪk] *n* (*Br*) anestesia *f*.

analgesic [ˌænæl'dʒi:zɪk] *n* analgésico *m*.

analyse ['ænəlaɪz] *vt* analizar.

analyst ['ænəlɪst] *n* (*psychoanalyst*) psicoanalista *mf*.

analyze ['ænəlaɪz] (*Am*) = **analyse**.

anarchy ['ænəkɪ] *n* anarquía *f*.

anatomy [ə'nætəmɪ] *n* anatomía *f*.

ancestor ['ænsestəʳ] *n* antepasado *m* (-da *f*).

anchor ['æŋkəʳ] *n* ancla *f*.

anchovy ['æntʃəvɪ] *n* (*salted*) anchoa *f*; (*fresh*) boquerón *m*.

ancient ['eɪnʃənt] *adj* antiguo(-gua).

and [strong form ænd, weak form ənd, ən] *conj* y; (*before "i" or "hi"*) e; **~ you?** ¿y tú?; **a hundred ~ one** ciento uno; **more ~ more** cada vez más; **to try ~ do sthg** intentar hacer algo; **to go ~ see** ir a ver.

Andalusia [ˌændə'lu:zɪə] *n* Andalucía *f*.

Andes ['ændi:z] *npl*: **the ~** los Andes.

anecdote ['ænɪkdəʊt] *n* anécdota *f*.

anemic [ə'ni:mɪk] (*Am*) = **anaemic**.

anesthetic [ˌænɪs'θetɪk] (*Am*) = **anaesthetic**.

angel ['eɪndʒl] *n* ángel *m*.

anger ['æŋgəʳ] *n* ira *f*, furia *f*.

angina [æn'dʒaɪnə] *n* angina *f* de pecho.

angle ['æŋgl] *n* ángulo *m*; **at an ~** torcido.

angler ['æŋgləʳ] *n* pescador *m* (-ra *f*) (*con caña*).

angling ['æŋglɪŋ] *n* pesca *f* (*con caña*).

angry ['æŋgrɪ] *adj* (*person*) enfadado(-da); (*words, look, letter*) airado(-da); **to get ~ (with sb)** enfadarse (con alguien).

animal ['ænɪml] *n* animal *m*.

aniseed ['ænɪsi:d] *n* anís *m*.

ankle ['æŋkl] n tobillo m.

annex ['æneks] n (building) edificio m anejo.

annihilate [ə'naɪəleɪt] vt aniquilar.

anniversary [ˌænɪ'vɜːsərɪ] n aniversario m.

announce [ə'naʊns] vt anunciar.

announcement [ə'naʊnsmənt] n anuncio m.

announcer [ə'naʊnsər] n (on TV) presentador m (-ra f); (on radio) locutor m (-ra f).

annoy [ə'nɔɪ] vt molestar, fastidiar.

annoyed [ə'nɔɪd] adj molesto(-ta); **to get ~ (with)** enfadarse (con).

annoying [ə'nɔɪɪŋ] adj molesto (-ta), fastidioso(-sa).

annual ['ænjʊəl] adj anual.

anonymous [ə'nɒnɪməs] adj anónimo(-ma).

anorak ['ænəræk] n anorak m.

another [ə'nʌðər] adj otro (otra) ♦ pron otro m (otra f); **~ one** otro (otra); **one ~** el uno al otro (la una a la otra); **they love one ~** se quieren; **with one ~** el uno con el otro (la una con la otra); **one after ~** uno tras otro (una tras otra).

answer ['ɑːnsər] n respuesta f ♦ vt (person, question) contestar a; (letter, advert) responder a ♦ vi contestar; **to ~ the door** abrir la puerta; **to ~ the phone** coger el teléfono ❑ **answer back** vi replicar.

answering machine ['ɑːnsər-ɪŋ-] = answerphone.

answerphone ['ɑːnsəfəʊn] n contestador m automático.

ant [ænt] n hormiga f.

Antarctic [æn'tɑːktɪk] n: **the ~** el Antártico.

antenna [æn'tenə] n (Am: aerial) antena f.

anthem ['ænθəm] n himno m.

antibiotics [ˌæntɪbaɪ'ɒtɪks] npl antibióticos mpl.

anticipate [æn'tɪsɪpeɪt] vt prever.

anticlimax [ˌæntɪ'klaɪmæks] n anticlímax m inv.

anticlockwise [ˌæntɪ'klɒkwaɪz] adv (Br) en sentido contrario al de las agujas del reloj.

antidote ['æntɪdəʊt] n antídoto m.

antifreeze ['æntɪfriːz] n anticongelante m.

antihistamine [ˌæntɪ'hɪstəmɪn] n antihistamínico m.

antiperspirant [ˌæntɪ'pɜːspə-rənt] n desodorante m.

antiquarian bookshop [ˌæntɪ'kweərɪən-] n librería en que se encuentran volúmenes antiguos.

antique [æn'tiːk] n antigüedad f.

antique shop n tienda f de antigüedades.

antiseptic [ˌæntɪ'septɪk] n antiséptico m.

antisocial [ˌæntɪ'səʊʃl] adj (person) insociable; (behaviour) antisocial.

antlers ['æntləz] npl cornamenta f.

anxiety [æŋ'zaɪətɪ] n inquietud f, ansiedad f.

anxious ['æŋkʃəs] adj (worried) preocupado(-da); (eager) ansioso(-sa).

any ['enɪ] adj 1. (in questions) algún(-una); **have you got ~ money?** ¿tienes (algo de) dinero?; **have you got ~ postcards?** ¿tienes alguna postal?; **have you got ~ rooms?** ¿tienes habitaciones libres? 2. (in negatives) ningún(-una); **I haven't got ~ money** no tengo (nada de) dinero; **we don't have ~ rooms** no tenemos ninguna habitación. 3. (no matter which) cualquier; **take ~ one you like** coge el que quieras. ◆ pron 1. (in questions) alguno m (-na f); **I'm looking for a hotel - are there ~ nearby?** estoy buscando un hotel ¿hay alguno por aquí cerca? 2. (in negatives) ninguno m (-na f); **I don't want ~ (of them)** no quiero ninguno; **I don't want ~ (of it)** no quiero (nada). 3. (no matter which one) cualquiera; **you can sit at ~ of the tables** puede sentarse en cualquier mesa. ◆ adv 1. (in questions): **is that ~ better?** ¿es así mejor?; **is there ~ more cheese?** ¿hay más queso?; **~ other questions?** ¿alguna otra pregunta? 2. (in negatives): **he's not ~ better** no se siente nada mejor; **we can't wait ~ longer** ya no podemos esperar más.

anybody ['enɪˌbɒdɪ] = anyone.

anyhow ['enɪhaʊ] adv (carelessly) de cualquier manera; (in any case) en cualquier caso; (in spite of that) de todos modos.

anyone ['enɪwʌn] pron (in questions) alguien; (any person) cualquiera; **I don't like ~** no me gusta nadie.

anything ['enɪθɪŋ] pron (in questions) algo; (no matter what) cualquier cosa; **he didn't say ~** no dijo nada.

anyway ['enɪweɪ] adv de todos modos.

anywhere ['enɪweə'] adv (in questions) en/a algún sitio; (any place) en/a cualquier sitio; **I can't find it ~** no lo encuentro en ningún sitio; **~ you like** donde quieras.

apart [ə'pɑːt] adv aparte; **they're miles ~** están muy separados; **to come ~** romperse; **~ from** (except for) salvo; (as well as) además de.

apartheid [ə'pɑːteɪt] n apartheid m.

apartment [ə'pɑːtmənt] n (Am) piso m, apartamento m.

apathetic [ˌæpə'θetɪk] adj apático(-ca).

ape [eɪp] n simio m.

aperitif [əˌperə'tiːf] n aperitivo m.

aperture ['æpətʃə'] n (of camera) abertura f.

APEX ['eɪpeks] n (plane ticket) APEX f; (Br: train ticket) billete de precio reducido no transferible que se compra con dos semanas de antelación.

apiece [ə'piːs] adv cada uno (una).

apologetic [əˌpɒlə'dʒetɪk] adj lleno(-na) de disculpas.

apologize [ə'pɒlədʒaɪz] vi: **to ~ (to sb for sthg)** disculparse (con alguien por algo).

apology [ə'pɒlədʒɪ] n disculpa f.

apostrophe [ə'pɒstrəfi] n

apóstrofo m.

appal [ə'pɔːl] vt horrorizar.

appall [ə'pɔːl] (Am) = **appal**.

appalling [ə'pɔːlɪŋ] adj horrible.

apparatus [ˌæpə'reɪtəs] n aparato m.

apparently [ə'pærəntlɪ] adv (it seems) por lo visto; (evidently) aparentemente.

appeal [ə'piːl] n (JUR) apelación f; (fundraising campaign) campaña f para recaudar fondos ◆ vi (JUR) apelar; **to ~ to sb (for sthg)** hacer un llamamiento a alguien (para algo); **it doesn't ~ to me** no me atrae.

appear [ə'pɪə^r] vi (come into view) aparecer; (seem) parecer; (in play, on TV) salir; (before court) comparecer; **it ~s that** parece que.

appearance [ə'pɪərəns] n (arrival) aparición f; (look) aspecto m.

appendicitis [ə,pendɪ'saɪtɪs] n apendicitis f inv.

appendix [ə'pendɪks] (pl -dices) n apéndice m.

appetite ['æpɪtaɪt] n apetito m.

appetizer ['æpɪtaɪzə^r] n aperitivo m.

appetizing ['æpɪtaɪzɪŋ] adj apetitoso(-sa).

applaud [ə'plɔːd] vt & vi aplaudir.

applause [ə'plɔːz] n aplausos mpl.

apple ['æpl] n manzana f.

apple charlotte [-'ʃɑːlət] n postre de manzana con miga de pan envuelto completamente en rebanadas de pan y cocido al horno.

apple crumble n budín de manzana cubierto con una masa de harina, azúcar y mantequilla que se sirve caliente.

apple juice n zumo m de manzana.

apple pie n pastel de hojaldre relleno de compota de manzana.

apple sauce n compota de manzana que se suele servir con chuletas de cerdo.

apple tart n tarta f de manzana.

apple turnover [-'tɜːn,əʊvə^r] n bollo de hojaldre relleno de compota de manzana.

appliance [ə'plaɪəns] n aparato m; **electrical/domestic ~** electrodoméstico m.

applicable [ə'plɪkəbl] adj: **to be ~ (to)** ser aplicable (a); **if ~** si corresponde.

applicant ['æplɪkənt] n solicitante mf.

application [ˌæplɪ'keɪʃn] n solicitud f.

application form n impreso m de solicitud.

apply [ə'plaɪ] vt (lotion) aplicar; (brakes) pisar ◆ vi: **to ~ to sb for sthg** (make request) solicitar algo a alguien; **to ~ (to sb)** (be applicable) ser aplicable (a alguien).

appointment [ə'pɔɪntmənt] n (with businessman) cita f; (with doctor, hairdresser) hora f; **to have an ~ (with)** (businessman) tener una cita (con); (doctor, hairdresser) tener hora (con); **to make an ~ (with)** (businessman) pedir una cita (con); (doctor, hairdresser) pedir hora (a); **by ~** mediante cita.

appreciable [ə'priːʃəbl] adj apreciable.

appreciate [ə'priːʃɪeɪt] vt (be grateful for) agradecer; (understand) ser consciente de; (like, admire) apreciar.

apprehensive [ˌæprɪ'hensɪv] adj inquieto(-ta).

apprentice [ə'prentɪs] n aprendiz m (-za f).

apprenticeship [ə'prentɪsʃɪp] n aprendizaje m.

approach [ə'prəʊtʃ] n (road) acceso m; (to problem, situation) enfoque m, planteamiento m ♦ vt (come nearer to) acercarse a; (problem, situation) enfocar ♦ vi acercarse.

appropriate [ə'prəʊprɪət] adj apropiado(-da).

approval [ə'pruːvl] n (favourable opinion) aprobación f; (permission) permiso m.

approve [ə'pruːv] vi: to ~ of sthg/sb ver con buenos ojos algo/a alguien.

approximate [ə'prɒksɪmət] adj aproximado(-da).

approximately [ə'prɒksɪmətlɪ] adv aproximadamente.

apricot ['eɪprɪkɒt] n albaricoque m.

April ['eɪprəl] n abril m, → September.

April Fools' Day n = Día m de los Santos Inocentes.

ⓘ APRIL FOOLS' DAY

El primero de abril es el día en que la gente se gasta bromas (trucos, bromas prácticas, etc). No existe la tradición de los monigotes de papel, y no se permiten más bromas después del mediodía.

apron ['eɪprən] n delantal m.

apt [æpt] adj (appropriate) acertado(-da); **to be ~ to do sthg** ser propenso(-sa) a hacer algo.

aquarium [ə'kweərɪəm] (pl -ria [-rɪə]) n acuario m.

aqueduct ['ækwɪdʌkt] n acueducto m.

Arab ['ærəb] adj árabe ♦ n (person) árabe mf.

Arabic ['ærəbɪk] adj árabe ♦ n (language) árabe m.

arbitrary ['ɑːbɪtrərɪ] adj arbitrario(-ria).

arc [ɑːk] n arco m.

arcade [ɑː'keɪd] n (for shopping) centro m comercial; (of video games) salón m de juegos.

arch [ɑːtʃ] n arco m.

archaeology [ˌɑːkɪ'ɒlədʒɪ] n arqueología f.

archbishop [ˌɑːtʃ'bɪʃəp] n arzobispo m.

archery ['ɑːtʃərɪ] n tiro m con arco.

archipelago [ˌɑːkɪ'pelɪgəʊ] n archipiélago m.

architect ['ɑːkɪtekt] n arquitecto m (-ta f).

architecture ['ɑːkɪtektʃəʳ] n arquitectura f.

archive ['ɑːkaɪv] n archivo m.

Arctic ['ɑːktɪk] n: **the ~** el Ártico.

are [weak form əʳ, strong form ɑːʳ] → be.

area ['eərɪə] n (region, space, zone)

zona f, **área** f; (surface size) **área** f.

area code n (Am) prefijo m (telefónico).

arena [əˈriːnə] n (at circus) pista f; (at sportsground) campo m.

aren't [ɑːnt] = are not.

Argentina [ˌɑːdʒənˈtiːnə] n Argentina.

Argentinian [ˌɑːdʒənˈtɪnɪən] adj argentino(-na) ♦ n argentino m (-na f).

argue [ˈɑːgjuː] vi: to ~ (with sb about sthg) discutir (con alguien acerca de algo) ♦ vt: to ~ (that) sostener que.

argument [ˈɑːgjumənt] n (quarrel) discusión f; (reason) argumento m.

arid [ˈærɪd] adj árido(-da).

arise [əˈraɪz] (pt arose, pp arisen [əˈrɪzn]) vi: to ~ (from) surgir (de).

aristocracy [ˌærɪˈstɒkrəsɪ] n aristocracia f.

arithmetic [əˈrɪθmətɪk] n aritmética f.

arm [ɑːm] n (of person, chair) brazo m; (of garment) manga f.

arm bands npl (for swimming) brazaletes mpl (de brazos).

armchair [ˈɑːmtʃeəʳ] n sillón m.

armed [ɑːmd] adj armado(-da).

armed forces npl: the ~ las fuerzas armadas.

armor [ˈɑːmər] (Am) = **armour**.

armour [ˈɑːməʳ] n (Br) armadura f.

armpit [ˈɑːmpɪt] n axila f.

arms [ɑːmz] npl (weapons) armas fpl.

army [ˈɑːmɪ] n ejército m.

A-road n (Br) ≈ carretera f nacional.

aroma [əˈrəʊmə] n aroma m.

aromatic [ˌærəˈmætɪk] adj aromático(-ca).

arose [əˈrəʊz] pt → **arise**.

around [əˈraʊnd] adv (about, round) por ahí; (present) por ahí/ aquí ♦ prep (surrounding, approximately) alrededor de; (to the other side of) al otro lado de; (near, all over) por; (in the area) por aquí; to go ~ the corner doblar la esquina; to turn ~ volverse; to look ~ (turn head) volver la mirada; (visit) visitar; is Paul ~? ¿está Paul por aquí?

arouse [əˈraʊz] vt (suspicion, interest) suscitar.

arrange [əˈreɪndʒ] vt (flowers, books) colocar; (meeting, event) organizar; to ~ to do sthg (with sb) acordar hacer algo (con alguien).

arrangement [əˈreɪndʒmənt] n (agreement) acuerdo m; (layout) disposición f; by ~ sólo con cita previa; to make ~s (to do sthg) hacer los preparativos (para hacer algo).

arrest [əˈrest] n detención f ♦ vt detener; under ~ bajo arresto.

arrival [əˈraɪvl] n llegada f; on ~ al llegar; new ~ (person) recién llegado m (-da f).

arrive [əˈraɪv] vi llegar; to ~ at llegar a.

arrogant [ˈærəgənt] adj arrogante.

arrow [ˈærəʊ] n flecha f.

arson [ˈɑːsn] n incendio m provocado.

art [ɑːt] n arte m ❑ **arts** npl

(humanities) letras *fpl*; **the ~s** *(fine arts)* las bellas artes.

artefact [ˈɑːtɪfækt] *n* artefacto *m*.

artery [ˈɑːtərɪ] *n* arteria *f*.

art gallery *n (commercial)* galería *f* (de arte); *(public)* museo *m* (de arte).

arthritis [ɑːˈθraɪtɪs] *n* artritis *f inv.*

artichoke [ˈɑːtɪtʃəʊk] *n* alcachofa *f*.

article [ˈɑːtɪkl] *n* artículo *m*.

articulate [ɑːˈtɪkjʊlət] *adj* elocuente.

artificial [ɑːtɪˈfɪʃl] *adj* artificial.

artist [ˈɑːtɪst] *n* artista *mf*.

artistic [ɑːˈtɪstɪk] *adj (person)* con sensibilidad artística; *(design)* artístico(-ca).

arts centre *n* ≃ casa *f* de cultura.

arty [ˈɑːtɪ] *adj (pej)* con pretensiones artísticas.

as [*unstressed* əz, *stressed* æz] *adv (in comparisons)*: ~ ... ~ tan ... como; **he's ~ tall ~ I am** es tan alto como yo; **twice ~ big ~** el doble de grande que; **many ~** tantos como; **much ~** tanto como.
♦ *conj* **1.** *(referring to time)* mientras; **~ the plane was coming in to land** cuando el avión iba a aterrizar.
2. *(referring to manner)* como; **do you like** haz lo que quieras; **~ expected** (tal) como era de esperar.
3. *(introducing a statement)* como; **~ you know** como sabes.
4. *(because)* como, ya que.
5. *(in phrases)*: **~ for** en cuanto a; **~ from** a partir de; **~ if** como si.
♦ *prep (referring to function)* como;

(referring to job) de; **I work ~ a teacher** soy profesor.

asap *(abbr of as soon as possible)* a la mayor brevedad posible.

ascent [əˈsent] *n* ascenso *m*.

ascribe [əˈskraɪb] *vt*: **to ~ sthg to** atribuir algo a.

ash [æʃ] *n (from cigarette, fire)* ceniza *f*; *(tree)* fresno *m*.

ashore [əˈʃɔːʳ] *adv (be)* en tierra; **to go ~** desembarcar.

ashtray [ˈæʃtreɪ] *n* cenicero *m*.

Asia [Br ˈeɪʒə, Am ˈeɪʒə] *n* Asia.

Asian [Br ˈeɪʃn, Am ˈeɪʒn] *adj* asiático(-ca) ♦ *n* asiático *m* (-ca *f*).

aside [əˈsaɪd] *adv* a un lado; **to move ~** apartarse.

ask [ɑːsk] *vt (person)* preguntar; *(question)* hacer; *(request)* pedir; *(invite)* invitar ♦ *vi*: **to ~ about sthg** preguntar acerca de algo; **to ~ sb sthg** preguntar algo a alguien; **to ~ sb about sthg** preguntar a alguien acerca de algo; **to ~ sb to do sthg** pedir a alguien que haga algo; **to ~ sb for sthg** pedir a alguien algo ❑ **ask for** *vt fus (ask to talk to)* preguntar por; *(request)* pedir.

asleep [əˈsliːp] *adj* dormido(-da); **to fall ~** quedarse dormido.

asparagus [əˈspærəgəs] *n* espárragos *mpl*.

asparagus tips *npl* puntas *fpl* de espárragos.

aspect [ˈæspekt] *n* aspecto *m*.

aspirin [ˈæsprɪn] *n* aspirina *f*.

ass [æs] *n (animal)* asno *m* (-na *f*).

assassinate [əˈsæsɪneɪt] *vt* asesinar.

assault [əˈsɔːlt] *n* agresión *f* ♦ *vt* agredir.

assemble [ə'sembl] vt (bookcase, model) montar ♦ vi reunirse.

assembly [ə'sembli] n (at school) reunión cotidiana de todos los alumnos y profesores en el salón de actos.

assembly hall n (at school) salón m de actos.

assembly point n punto m de reunión.

assert [ə'sɜːt] vt (fact, innocence) afirmar; (authority) imponer; to ~ o.s. imponerse.

assess [ə'ses] vt evaluar.

assessment [ə'sesmənt] n evaluación f.

asset ['æset] n (valuable person, thing) elemento m valioso.

assign [ə'saɪn] vt: to ~ sthg to sb ceder algo a alguien; to ~ sb to do sthg asignar algo a alguien.

assignment [ə'saɪnmənt] n (task) misión f; (SCH) trabajo m.

assist [ə'sɪst] vt ayudar.

assistance [ə'sɪstəns] n ayuda f; to be of ~ (to sb) ayudar (a alguien).

assistant [ə'sɪstənt] n ayudante mf.

associate [n ə'səʊʃɪət, vb ə'səʊʃɪeɪt] n socio m (-cia f) ♦ vt: to ~ sthg/sb with asociar algo/a alguien con; to be ~d with estar asociado con.

association [əˌsəʊsɪ'eɪʃn] n asociación f.

assorted [ə'sɔːtɪd] adj surtido (-da), variado(-da).

assortment [ə'sɔːtmənt] n surtido m.

assume [ə'sjuːm] vt (suppose) suponer; (control, responsibility) asumir.

assurance [ə'ʃʊərəns] n (promise) garantía f; (insurance) seguro m.

assure [ə'ʃʊəʳ] vt asegurar; to ~ sb (that) ... asegurar a alguien que ...

asterisk ['æstərɪsk] n asterisco m.

asthma ['æsmə] n asma f.

asthmatic [æs'mætɪk] adj asmático(-ca).

astonished [ə'stɒnɪʃt] adj estupefacto(-ta), pasmado(-da).

astonishing [ə'stɒnɪʃɪŋ] adj asombroso(-sa).

astound [ə'staʊnd] vt asombrar, pasmar.

astray [ə'streɪ] adv: to go ~ extraviarse.

astrology [ə'strɒlədʒɪ] n astrología f.

astronomy [ə'strɒnəmɪ] n astronomía f.

asylum [ə'saɪləm] n hospital m psiquiátrico.

at [unstressed ət, stressed æt] prep 1. (indicating place, position) en; ~ the bottom of the hill al pie de la colina; ~ school en la escuela; ~ the hotel en el hotel; ~ home en casa; ~ my mother's en casa de mi madre.

2. (indicating direction) a; to throw sthg ~ sthg arrojar algo contra algo; to look ~ sthg/sb mirar algo/a alguien; to smile ~ sb sonreír a alguien.

3. (indicating time) a; ~ Christmas en Navidades; ~ nine o'clock a las nueve; ~ night por la noche.

4. (indicating rate, level, speed) a; it works out ~ £5 each sale a 5 libras

cada uno; ~ **60 km/h** a 60 km/h.

5. *(indicating activity)*: **to be ~ lunch** estar comiendo; **I'm good/bad ~ maths** se me dan bien/mal las matemáticas.

6. *(indicating cause)*: **shocked ~ sthg** horrorizado ante algo; **angry ~ sb** enfadado con alguien; **delighted ~ sthg** encantado con algo.

ate [Br et, Am eit] *pt* → **eat**.

atheist ['eiθiist] *n* ateo *m* (-a *f*).

athlete ['æθli:t] *n* atleta *mf*.

athletics [æθ'letiks] *n* atletismo *m*.

Atlantic [ət'læntik] *n*: **the ~ (Ocean)** el (océano) Atlántico.

atlas ['ætləs] *n* atlas *m inv*.

atmosphere ['ætməsfiər] *n* atmósfera *f*.

atom ['ætəm] *n* átomo *m*.

A to Z *n (map)* callejero *m*.

atrocious [ə'trəuʃəs] *adj* atroz.

attach [ə'tætʃ] *vt* sujetar; **to ~ sthg to sthg** sujetar algo a algo.

attachment [ə'tætʃmənt] *n (device)* accesorio *m*.

attack [ə'tæk] *n* ataque *m* ◆ *vt* atacar.

attacker [ə'tækər] *n* atacante *mf*.

attain [ə'tein] *vt (fml)* alcanzar, conseguir.

attempt [ə'tempt] *n* intento *m* ◆ *vt* intentar; **to ~ to do sthg** intentar hacer algo.

attend [ə'tend] *vt* asistir a ❑ **attend to** *vt fus* ocuparse de.

attendance [ə'tendəns] *n* asistencia *f*.

attendant [ə'tendənt] *n (in museum)* conserje *mf*; *(in car park)*

encargado *m* (-da *f*).

attention [ə'tenʃn] *n* atención *f*; **to pay ~ (to)** prestar atención (a).

attic ['ætik] *n* desván *m*.

attitude ['ætitju:d] *n* actitud *f*.

attorney [ə'tɜ:ni] *n (Am)* abogado *m* (-da *f*).

attract [ə'trækt] *vt* atraer.

attraction [ə'trækʃn] *n* atracción *f*; *(attractive feature)* atractivo *m*.

attractive [ə'træktiv] *adj* atractivo(-va).

attribute [ə'tribju:t] *vt*: **to ~ sthg to** atribuir algo a.

aubergine ['əubəʒi:n] *n (Br)* berenjena *f*.

auburn ['ɔ:bən] *adj* castaño rojizo.

auction ['ɔ:kʃn] *n* subasta *f*.

audience ['ɔ:dɪəns] *n (of play, concert, film)* público *m*; *(of TV, radio)* audiencia *f*.

audio ['ɔ:dɪəu] *adj (store, department)* de sonido.

audio-visual [-'vɪʒuəl] *adj* audiovisual.

auditorium [ˌɔ:dɪ'tɔ:rɪəm] *n* auditorio *m*.

August ['ɔ:gəst] *n* agosto *m*, → **September**.

aunt [ɑ:nt] *n* tía *f*.

au pair [ˌəu'peər] *n* au pair *f*.

aural ['ɔ:rəl] *adj* auditivo(-va).

Australia [ɒ'streilɪə] *n* Australia.

Australian [ɒ'streilɪən] *adj* australiano(-na) ◆ *n (person)* australiano *m* (-na *f*).

Austria ['ɒstrɪə] *n* Austria.

Austrian ['ɒstrɪən] *adj* austría-

co(-ca) ◆ *n (person)* austríaco *m* (-ca *f*).

authentic [ɔːˈθentɪk] *adj* auténtico(-ca).

author [ˈɔːθəʳ] *n (of book, article)* autor *m* (-ra *f*); *(by profession)* escritor *m* (-ra *f*).

authority [ɔːˈθɒrətɪ] *n* autoridad *f*; **the authorities** las autoridades.

authorization [ˌɔːθəraɪˈzeɪʃn] *n* autorización *f*.

authorize [ˈɔːθəraɪz] *vt* autorizar; **to ~ sb to do sthg** autorizar a alguien a hacer algo.

autobiography [ˌɔːtəbaɪˈɒɡrəfɪ] *n* autobiografía *f*.

autograph [ˈɔːtəɡrɑːf] *n* autógrafo *m*.

automatic [ˌɔːtəˈmætɪk] *n (car)* coche *m* automático ◆ *adj* automático(-ca); **you will receive an ~ fine** Vd. será multado en el acto.

automatically [ˌɔːtəˈmætɪklɪ] *adv* automáticamente.

automobile [ˈɔːtəməbiːl] *n (Am)* coche *m*, automóvil *m*.

autumn [ˈɔːtəm] *n* otoño *m*; **in (the) ~** en otoño.

auxiliary (verb) [ɔːɡˈzɪljərɪ-] *n* verbo *m* auxiliar.

available [əˈveɪləbl] *adj* disponible.

avalanche [ˈævəlɑːnʃ] *n* avalancha *f*.

Ave. *(abbr of avenue)* Avda.

avenue [ˈævənjuː] *n* avenida *f*.

average [ˈævərɪdʒ] *adj* medio (-dia); *(not very good)* regular ◆ *n* media *f*, promedio *m*; **on ~** por tér-

mino medio.

aversion [əˈvɜːʃn] *n* aversión *f*.

aviation [ˌeɪvɪˈeɪʃn] *n* aviación *f*.

avid [ˈævɪd] *adj* ávido(-da).

avocado (pear) [ˌævəˈkɑːdəʊ-] *n* aguacate *m*.

avoid [əˈvɔɪd] *vt* evitar; **to ~ doing sthg** evitar hacer algo.

await [əˈweɪt] *vt* esperar, aguardar.

awake [əˈweɪk] *(pt* **awoke**, *pp* **awoken)** *adj* despierto(-ta) ◆ *vi* despertarse.

award [əˈwɔːd] *n* premio *m*, galardón *m* ◆ *vt*: **to ~ sb sthg** *(prize)* otorgar algo a alguien; *(damages, compensation)* adjudicar algo a alguien.

aware [əˈweəʳ] *adj* consciente; **to be ~ of** ser consciente de.

away [əˈweɪ] *adv (move, look, turn)* hacia otra parte; *(not at home, in office)* fuera; **put your toys ~!** ¡recoge tus juguetes!; **to take sthg ~ (from sb)** quitarle algo a alguien; **far ~** lejos; **it's 10 miles ~ (from here)** está a 10 millas de aquí; **it's two weeks ~** faltan dos semanas; **to look ~** apartar la vista; **to walk/drive ~** alejarse; **we're going ~ on holiday** nos vamos de vacaciones.

awesome [ˈɔːsəm] *adj* impresionante.

awful [ˈɔːfəl] *adj (very bad)* fatal; *(very great)* tremendo(-da); **how ~!** ¡qué horror!

awfully [ˈɔːflɪ] *adv (very)* tremendamente.

awkward [ˈɔːkwəd] *adj (movement)* torpe; *(position, situation)* incómodo(-da); *(shape, size)* poco manejable; *(time)* inoportuno(-na); *(question, task)* difícil.

awning ['ɔːnɪŋ] *n* toldo *m*.

awoke [ə'wəʊk] *pt* → **awake**.

awoken [ə'wəʊkn] *pp* → **awake**.

axe [æks] *n* hacha *f*.

axle ['æksl] *n* eje *m*.

B

BA *(abbr of Bachelor of Arts) (titular de una)* licenciatura de letras.

babble ['bæbl] *vi (person)* farfullar.

baby ['beɪbɪ] *n (newborn baby)* bebé *m*; *(infant)* niño *m* (-ña *f*); **to have a ~** tener un niño; **~ sweetcorn** *pequeña mazorca de maíz usada en la cocina china*.

baby carriage *n (Am)* cochecito *m* de niños.

baby food *n* papilla *f*.

baby-sit *vi* cuidar a niños.

baby wipe *n* toallita *f* húmeda para bebés.

back [bæk] *n (of person)* espalda *f*; *(of chair)* respaldo *m*; *(of room)* fondo *m*; *(of car, book)* parte *f* trasera; *(of hand, banknote)* dorso *m* ♦ *adj* trasero(-ra) ♦ *vi (car, driver)* dar marcha atrás ♦ *vt (support)* respaldar ♦ *adv (towards the back)* hacia atrás; *(to previous position, state)* de vuelta; **to get ~** llegar; **to give ~** devolver; **to put sthg ~** devolver algo a su sitio; **to stand ~** apartarse; **to write ~** contestar; **at the ~ of** detrás de; **in ~ of** *(Am)* detrás de; **~ to front** al revés ❑

back up *vt sep (support)* apoyar ♦ *vi (car, driver)* dar marcha atrás.

backache ['bækeɪk] *n* dolor *m* de espalda.

backbone ['bækbəʊn] *n* columna *f* vertebral.

back door *n* puerta *f* trasera.

backfire [,bæk'faɪəʳ] *vi (car)* petardear.

background ['bækgraʊnd] *n (in picture, on stage)* fondo *m*; *(to situation)* trasfondo *m*; *(upbringing)* origen *m*.

backlog ['bæklɒg] *n* acumulación *f*.

backpack ['bækpæk] *n* mochila *f*.

backpacker ['bækpækəʳ] *n* mochilero *m* (-ra *f*).

back seat *n* asiento *m* trasero OR de atrás.

backside [,bæk'saɪd] *n (inf)* trasero *m*.

back street *n* callejuela en una zona periférica y deprimida.

backstroke ['bækstrəʊk] *n* espalda *f* (en natación).

backwards ['bækwədz] *adv (move, look)* hacia atrás; *(the wrong way round)* al revés.

bacon ['beɪkən] *n* panceta *f*, bacon *m*; **~ and eggs** huevos fritos con bacon.

bacteria [bæk'tɪərɪə] *npl* bacterias *fpl*.

bad [bæd] *(compar* **worse**, *superl* **worst**) *adj* malo(-la); *(accident,* *wound)* grave; *(cold)* fuerte; *(poor, weak)* débil; **not ~** *(bastante)* bien; **to go ~** echarse a perder.

badge [bædʒ] *n* chapa *f*.

badger [bædʒəʳ] *n* tejón *m*.

badly [bædlɪ] *(compar* **worse**, *superl* **worst**) *adv (poorly)* mal; *(seriously)* gravemente; *(very much)* mucho.

badly paid *adj* mal pagado (-da).

badminton [bædmɪntən] *n* bádminton *m*.

bad-tempered [-tempəd] *adj* de mal genio.

bag [bæg] *n (of paper, plastic)* bolsa *f*; *(handbag)* bolso *m*; *(suitcase)* maleta *f*; **a ~ of crisps** una bolsa de patatas fritas.

bagel [beɪgəl] *n* bollo de pan en forma de rosca.

baggage [bægɪdʒ] *n* equipaje *m*.

baggage allowance *n* equipaje *m* permitido.

baggage reclaim *n* recogida *f* de equipajes.

baggy [bægɪ] *adj* holgado(-da).

bagpipes [bægpaɪps] *npl* gaita *f*.

bail [beɪl] *n* fianza *f*.

bait [beɪt] *n* cebo *m*.

bake [beɪk] *vt* cocer al horno ♦ *n (CULIN)* gratén *m*.

baked [beɪkt] *adj* asado(-da) al horno.

baked Alaska [-ə'læskə] *n* postre de bizcocho y helado, cubierto de merengue y cocinado al horno durante breves minutos.

baked beans *npl* alubias *fpl* cocidas en salsa de tomate.

baked potato *n* patata *f*

asada OR al horno *(con piel)*.

baker [beɪkəʳ] *n* panadero *m* (-ra *f*); **~'s** *(shop)* panadería *f*.

Bakewell tart [beɪkwəl-] *n* tarta glaseada consistente en una base de masa quebrada cubierta con bizcocho de sabor a almendra con una capa de mermelada.

balance [bæləns] *n (of person)* equilibrio *m*; *(of bank account)* saldo *m*; *(remainder)* resto *m* ♦ *vt* mantener en equilibrio.

balcony [bælkənɪ] *n (small)* balcón *m*; *(big)* terraza *f*.

bald [bɔːld] *adj* calvo(-va).

bale [beɪl] *n* fardo *m*.

Balearic Islands [bælɪ'ærɪk-] *npl*: **the ~** (las) Baleares.

ball [bɔːl] *n (in tennis, golf, table tennis)* pelota *f*; *(in football)* balón *m*; *(in snooker, pool, of paper)* bola *f*; *(of wool, string)* ovillo *m*; *(dance)* baile *m*; **on the ~** *(fig)* al tanto de todo.

ballad [bæləd] *n* balada *f*.

ballerina [bælə'riːnə] *n* bailarina *f*.

ballet [bæleɪ] *n* ballet *m*.

ballet dancer *n* bailarín *m* (-ina *f*).

balloon [bə'luːn] *n* globo *m*.

ballot [bælət] *n* votación *f*.

ballpoint pen [bɔːlpɔɪnt-] *n* bolígrafo *m*.

ballroom [bɔːlrum] *n* salón *m* de baile.

ballroom dancing *n* baile *m* de salón.

bamboo [bæm'buː] *n* bambú *m*.

bamboo shoots *npl (CULIN)* brotes *mpl* de bambú.

ban [bæn] *n* prohibición *f* ♦ *vt*

prohibir; **to ~ sb from doing sthg** prohibir a alguien hacer algo.

banana [bə'nɑːnə] *n* plátano *m*.

banana split *n* banana split *m*, plátano partido por la mitad y relleno con helado y nata montada.

band [bænd] *n* (pop group) grupo *m*; (military orchestra) banda *f*; (strip of paper, rubber) cinta *f*.

bandage ['bændɪdʒ] *n* venda *f* ♦ *vt* vendar.

B and B *abbr* = bed and breakfast.

bandstand ['bændstænd] *n* quiosco *m* de música.

bang [bæŋ] *n* estruendo *m* ♦ *vt* (hit loudly) golpear; (shut loudly) cerrar de golpe; **to ~ one's head** golpearse la cabeza.

banger ['bæŋə'] *n* (Br: inf: sausage) salchicha *f*; **~s and mash** salchichas con puré de patatas.

bangle ['bæŋgl] *n* brazalete *m*.

bangs [bæŋz] *npl* (Am) flequillo *m*.

banister ['bænɪstə'] *n* barandilla *f*.

banjo ['bændʒəʊ] *n* banjo *m*.

bank [bæŋk] *n* (for money) banco *m*; (of river, lake) orilla *f*, ribera *f*; (slope) loma *f*.

bank account *n* cuenta *f* bancaria.

bank book *n* libreta *f* (del banco).

bank charges *npl* comisiones *fpl* bancarias.

bank clerk *n* empleado *m* de banco.

bank draft *n* giro *m* bancario.

banker ['bæŋkə'] *n* banquero

m (-ra *f*).

banker's card *n* tarjeta *f* de identificación bancaria.

bank holiday *n* (Br) día *m* festivo.

bank manager *n* director *m* (-ra *f*) de banco.

bank note *n* billete *m* de banco.

bankrupt ['bæŋkrʌpt] *adj* quebrado(-da).

bank statement *n* extracto *m* de cuenta.

banner ['bænə'] *n* pancarta *f*.

bannister ['bænɪstə'] = **banister**.

banquet ['bæŋkwɪt] *n* (formal dinner) banquete *m*; (at Indian restaurant etc) menú fijo para varias personas.

bap [bæp] *n* (Br) panecillo *m*, bollo *m*.

baptize [Br bæp'taɪz, Am 'bæptaɪz] *vt* bautizar.

bar [bɑː'] *n* (pub, in restaurant, hotel) bar *m*; (counter in pub, metal rod) barra *f*; (of wood) tabla *f*; (of soap) pastilla *f*; (of chocolate) tableta *f* ♦ *vt* (obstruct) bloquear.

barbecue ['bɑːbɪkjuː] *n* barbacoa *f* ♦ *vt* asar a la parrilla.

barbecue sauce *n* salsa *f* para barbacoa.

barbed wire [bɑːbd-] *n* alambre *m* de espino.

barber ['bɑːbə'] *n* barbero *m*; **~'s** (shop) barbería *f*.

bar code *n* código *m* de barras.

bare [beə'] *adj* (feet) descalzo(-za); (head) descubierto(-ta); (arms) desnudo(-da); (room, cup-

board) vacío(-a); *(facts, minimum)* esencial.

barefoot ['beəfʊt] *adv:* **to go ~** ir descalzo.

barely ['beəlɪ] *adv* apenas.

bargain ['bɑːgɪn] *n (agreement)* trato *m*, acuerdo *m*; *(cheap buy)* ganga *f* ♦ *vi* negociar ❏ **bargain for** *vt fus* contar con.

bargain basement *n* sección *f* de oportunidades.

barge [bɑːdʒ] *n* barcaza *f* ❏ **barge in** *vi:* **to ~ in (on sb)** interrumpir (a alguien).

bark [bɑːk] *n (of tree)* corteza *f* ♦ *vi* ladrar.

barley ['bɑːlɪ] *n* cebada *f*.

barmaid ['bɑːmeɪd] *n* camarera *f*.

barman ['bɑːmən] *(pl* **-men** [-mən]) *n* camarero *m*.

bar meal *n* comida sencilla en un *pub* o en el *bar* de un hotel.

barn [bɑːn] *n* granero *m*.

barometer [bə'rɒmɪtəʳ] *n* barómetro *m*.

baron ['bærən] *n* barón *m*.

baroque [bə'rɒk] *adj* barroco(-ca).

barracks ['bærəks] *npl* cuartel *m*.

barrage [bæ'rɑːʒ] *n (of questions, criticism)* lluvia *f*, alud *m*.

barrel ['bærəl] *n (of beer, wine, oil)* barril *m*; *(of gun)* cañón *m*.

barren ['bærən] *adj (land, soil)* estéril.

barricade [ˌbærɪ'keɪd] *n* barricada *f*.

barrier ['bærɪəʳ] *n* barrera *f*.

barrister ['bærɪstəʳ] *n* abogado *m (-da f) (de tribunales superiores)*.

bartender ['bɑːtendəʳ] *n (Am)* camarero *m (-ra f)*.

barter ['bɑːtəʳ] *vi* hacer trueques.

base [beɪs] *n* base *f* ♦ *vt:* **to ~ sthg on** basar algo en; **to be ~d** *(company)* tener la sede; *(person)* trabajar.

baseball ['beɪsbɔːl] *n* béisbol *m*.

baseball cap *n* gorra *f* de béisbol.

basement ['beɪsmənt] *n* sótano *m*.

bases ['beɪsiːz] *pl* → **basis**.

bash [bæʃ] *vt (door)* dar un porrazo a; **to ~ one's head** darse un porrazo en la cabeza.

basic ['beɪsɪk] *adj (fundamental)* básico(-ca); *(accommodation, meal)* simple ❏ **basics** *npl:* **the ~s** los fundamentos.

basically ['beɪsɪklɪ] *adv* en realidad.

basil ['bæzl] *n* albahaca *f*.

basin ['beɪsn] *n (washbasin)* lavabo *m; (bowl)* barreño *m*.

basis ['beɪsɪs] *(pl* **-ses**) *n* base *f;* **on a weekly ~** de forma semanal; **on the ~ of** partiendo de.

basket ['bɑːskɪt] *n* cesto *m*, cesta *f*.

basketball ['bɑːskɪtbɔːl] *n* baloncesto *m*.

basmati rice [ˌbæz'mɑːtɪ-] *n* arroz de origen pakistaní utilizado en muchos platos de cocina oriental.

Basque [bæsk] *adj* vasco(-ca) ♦ *n (person)* vasco *m (-ca f); (language)* euskera *m*.

Basque Country *n:* **the ~** el País Vasco, Euskadi.

bass[1] [beɪs] *n (singer)* bajo *m*.

bass² [bæs] n (fish) lubina f, róbalo m.

bass guitar [beis-] n bajo m.

bassoon [bə'su:n] n fagot m.

bastard [ba:stəd] n (vulg) cabrón m (-ona f).

bat [bæt] n (in cricket, baseball) bate m; (in table tennis) paleta f; (animal) murciélago m.

batch [bætʃ] n lote m.

bath [ba:θ] n (tub) bañera f ♦ vt bañar; to have a ~ bañarse.

baths npl (Br: public swimming pool) piscina f municipal.

bathe [beið] vi bañarse.

bathing [beiðiŋ] n (Br) baños mpl.

bathrobe [ba:θrəub] n (for bathroom, swimming pool) albornoz m; (dressing gown) bata f.

bathroom [ba:θrom] n (room with bath) cuarto m de baño; (Am: toilet) servicio m.

bathroom cabinet n armario m de aseo.

bathtub [ba:θtʌb] n bañera f.

baton [bætən] n (of conductor) batuta f; (truncheon) porra f.

batter [bætə] n (CULIN) masa f para rebozar ♦ vt (wife, child) maltratar.

battered [bætəd] adj (CULIN) rebozado(-da).

battery [bætərɪ] n (for radio, torch etc) pila f; (for car) batería f.

battery charger [-ˌtʃɑ:dʒə] n aparato m para recargar pilas.

battle [bætl] n (in war) batalla f; (struggle) lucha f.

battlefield [bætlfi:ld] n campo m de batalla.

battlements [bætlmənts] npl almenas fpl.

battleship [bætlʃɪp] n acorazado m.

bay [beɪ] n (on coast) bahía f; (for parking) plaza f.

bay leaf n hoja f de laurel.

bay window n ventana f salediza.

B & B abbr = bed and breakfast.

BC (abbr of before Christ) a.C.

be [bi:] (pt was, were, pp been) vi 1. (exist) ser; **there is/are** hay; **are there any shops near here?** ¿hay alguna tienda por aquí?

2. (referring to location) estar; **the hotel is near the airport** el hotel está cerca del aeropuerto.

3. (go, come) estar; **have you ever been to Ireland?** ¿has estado alguna vez en Irlanda?; **I'll ~ there in five minutes** estaré ahí dentro de cinco minutos.

4. (occur) ser; **the final is in May** la final es en mayo.

5. (describing quality, permanent condition) ser; **he's a doctor** es médico; **I'm British** soy británico.

6. (describing state, temporary condition) estar; **I'm angry** estoy enfadado; **I'm hot/cold** tengo calor/frío.

7. (referring to health) estar; **how are you?** ¿cómo estás?; **I'm fine** estoy bien; **she's ill** está enferma.

8. (referring to age): **how old are you?** ¿cuántos años tienes?; **I'm 14 (years old)** tengo 14 años (de edad).

9. (referring to cost) valer, costar; **how much is it?** ¿cuánto es?; **it's ten pounds** son diez libras.

10. (referring to time, dates) ser; **what time is it?** ¿qué hora es?; **it's ten o'clock** son las diez; **it's the 9th of April** estamos a 9 de abril.

11. (referring to measurement): **it's 2 metres wide/long** mide 2 metros de ancho/largo; **he's 2 metres tall** mide 2 metros; **I'm 60 kilos** peso 60 kilos.

12. (referring to weather) hacer; **it's hot/cold** hace calor/frío; **it's sunny/windy** hace sol/viento; **it's going to be nice today** hoy va a hacer buen tiempo.

♦ aux vb **1.** (forming continuous tense) estar; **I'm learning French** estoy aprendiendo francés; **we've been visiting the museum** hemos estado visitando el museo; **I was eating when ...** estaba comiendo cuando ...

2. (forming passive) ser; **to ~ loved** ser amado; **the flight was delayed** el avión se retrasó.

3. (with infinitive to express order): **all rooms are to ~ vacated by ten a.m.** las habitaciones han de ser desocupadas antes de las diez de la mañana.

4. (with infinitive to express future tense): **the race is to start at noon** la carrera empezará a mediodía.

5. (in tag questions): **it's cold, isn't it?** hace frío ¿no?

beach [biːtʃ] n playa f.

bead [biːd] n cuenta f, abalorio m.

beak [biːk] n pico m.

beaker ['biːkər] n taza f (sin asa).

beam [biːm] n (of light) rayo m; (of wood, concrete) viga f ♦ vi (smile) sonreír resplandeciente.

bean [biːn] n (haricot) judía f; (pod) judía f verde; (of coffee) grano m.

bean curd n pasta hecha de soja y generalmente en forma de cubo que se usa en la cocina china y vegetariana.

beansprouts ['biːnsprauts] npl brotes mpl de soja.

bear [beər] (pt bore, pp borne) n (animal) oso m (osa f) ♦ vt aguantar, soportar; **to ~ left/right** torcer a la izquierda/derecha.

bearable ['beərəbl] adj soportable.

beard [bɪəd] n barba f.

bearer ['beərər] n (of cheque) portador m (-ra f); (of passport) titular mf.

bearing ['beərɪŋ] n (relevance) relación f; **to get one's ~s** orientarse.

beast [biːst] n bestia f.

beat [biːt] (pt beat, pp beaten ['biːtn]) n (of heart, pulse) latido m; (MUS) ritmo m ♦ vt (defeat) ganar, derrotar; (hit) golpear; (eggs, cream) batir ❑ **beat down** vt sep convencer que rebaje el precio ♦ vi (rain) descargar; (sun) pegar fuerte; **beat up** vt sep dar una paliza a.

beautiful ['bjuːtɪful] adj (in appearance, very good) precioso(-sa); (person) guapo(-pa).

beauty ['bjuːtɪ] n belleza f.

beauty parlour n salón m de belleza.

beauty spot n (place) bello paraje m.

beaver ['biːvər] n castor m.

became [bɪ'keɪm] pt → **become**.

because [bɪ'kɒz] conj porque; ~ **of** a causa de.

beckon ['bekən] *vi:* to ~ (to) hacer señas para atraer la atención (a).

become [bɪ'kʌm] (*pt* became, *pp* become) *vi* hacerse; (*ill, angry, cloudy*) ponerse; (*champion, prime minister*) llegar a ser; **what became of him?** ¿qué fue de él?

bed [bed] *n* (*for sleeping in*) cama *f*; (*of river, CULIN*) lecho *m*; (*of sea*) fondo *m*; **in** ~ en la cama; **to get out of** ~ levantarse (de la cama); **to go to** ~ irse a la cama; **to go to** ~ **with** sb acostarse con alguien; **to make the** ~ hacer la cama.

bed and breakfast *n* (*Br*) casa privada donde se ofrece cama y desayuno a precios asequibles.

BED AND BREAKFAST

Los "B & B" o "guest houses" son casas particulares en lugares turísticos con una o más habitaciones para huéspedes. En el precio de la habitación se incluye el "desayuno inglés", consistente en salchichas, huevos, beicon, tostadas y té o café.

bedclothes ['bedkləʊðz] *npl* ropa *f* de cama.

bedding ['bedɪŋ] *n* ropa *f* de cama.

bed linen *n* sábanas *y* fundas de almohada.

bedroom ['bedrum] *n* (*en casa*) dormitorio *m*; (*en hotel*) habitación *f*.

bedside table ['bedsaid-] *n* mesita *f* de noche.

bedsit ['bed,sɪt] *n* (*Br*) habitación alquilada con cama e instalaciones para cocinar y lavarse.

bedspread [bedspred] *n* colcha *f*.

bedtime ['bedtaɪm] *n* hora *f* de dormir.

bee [bi:] *n* abeja *f*.

beech [bi:tʃ] *n* haya *f*.

beef [bi:f] *n* carne *f* de vaca; ~ **Wellington** ternera *f* al hojaldre.

beefburger ['bi:f,bɜ:gə'] *n* hamburguesa *f*.

beehive ['bi:haɪv] *n* colmena *f*.

been [bi:n] *pp* → be.

beer [bɪə'] *n* cerveza *f*; **to have a couple of** ~s tomarse un par de cervezas.

BEER

A grandes rasgos, la cerveza británica se puede dividir en "bitter" y "lager". La "bitter", o "heavy" en Escocia, es oscura y tiene un sabor ligeramente amargo, mientras que la "lager" es la cerveza rubia que se encuentra normalmente en España. "Real ale" es un tipo de "bitter" en barril, normalmente más cara, que frecuentemente se produce en pequeñas cervecerías utilizando métodos y recetas tradicionales. La cerveza en Estados Unidos es casi siempre "lager".

beer garden *n* patio *m* de bar.

beer mat *n* posavasos *m inv* (de bar).

beetle ['bi:tl] *n* escarabajo *m*.

beetroot ['bi:tru:t] *n* remolacha f.

before [bɪˈfɔːʳ] adv antes ◆ prep (earlier than) antes de; (in order) antes que; (fml: in front of) frente a ◆ conj antes de; ~ **you leave** antes de irte; **the day** ~ el día anterior; **the week** ~ **last** la semana pasada no, la anterior.

beforehand [bɪˈfɔːhænd] adv con antelación.

befriend [bɪˈfrend] vt hacer amistad con.

beg [beg] vi mendigar ◆ vt: **to** ~ **sb** **to** **do** **sthg** rogar a alguien que haga algo.

began [bɪˈɡæn] pt → begin.

beggar [ˈbegəʳ] n mendigo m (-ga f).

begin [bɪˈɡɪn] (pt **began**, pp **begun**) vt & vi empezar, comenzar; **to** ~ **doing** OR **to do sthg** empezar a hacer algo; **to** ~ **by doing sthg** empezar haciendo algo; **to** ~ **with** (firstly) de entrada; (in restaurant) de primero.

beginner [bɪˈɡɪnəʳ] n principiante mf.

beginning [bɪˈɡɪnɪŋ] n comienzo m; **at the** ~ **of** a principios de.

begun [bɪˈɡʌn] pp → begin.

behalf [bɪˈhɑːf] n: **on** ~ **of** en nombre de.

behave [bɪˈheɪv] vi comportarse; **to** ~ (**o.s.**) (be good) portarse bien.

behavior [bɪˈheɪvjəʳ] (Am) = **behaviour**.

behaviour [bɪˈheɪvjəʳ] n comportamiento m.

behind [bɪˈhaɪnd] adv detrás ◆ n (inf) trasero m ◆ prep (at the back of) detrás de; **to be** ~ **sb** (supporting) apoyar a alguien; **to be** ~ (schedule) ir retrasado; **to leave** **sthg** ~ dejarse algo (olvidado); **to** **stay** ~ quedarse.

beige [beɪʒ] adj beige (inv).

being [ˈbiːɪŋ] n ser m; **to come** **into** ~ nacer.

belated [bɪˈleɪtɪd] adj tardío(-a).

belch [beltʃ] vi eructar.

Belgian [ˈbeldʒən] adj belga ◆ n belga mf.

Belgian waffle n (Am) gofre m (grueso).

Belgium [ˈbeldʒəm] n Bélgica f.

belief [bɪˈliːf] n (faith) creencia f; (opinion) opinión f.

believe [bɪˈliːv] vt creer ◆ vi: **to** ~ **in** creer en; **to** ~ **in doing sthg** ser partidario de hacer algo.

believer [bɪˈliːvəʳ] n creyente mf.

bell [bel] n (of church) campana f; (of phone, door) timbre m.

bellboy [ˈbelbɔɪ] n botones m inv.

bellow [ˈbeləʊ] vi rugir.

belly [ˈbelɪ] n (inf) barriga f.

belly button n (inf) ombligo m.

belong [bɪˈlɒŋ] vi (be in right place) ir; **to** ~ **to** (property) pertenecer a; (to club, party) ser miembro de.

belongings [bɪˈlɒŋɪŋz] npl pertenencias fpl.

below [bɪˈləʊ] prep por debajo de ◆ adv (lower down) abajo; (in text) más abajo; **the flat** ~ el piso de abajo; ~ **zero** bajo cero; **children** ~ **the age of ten** niños menores de diez años.

belt [belt] n (for clothes) cinturón m; (TECH) correa f.

beltway ['belt,wei] n (Am) carretera f de circunvalación.

bench [bentʃ] n banco m.

bend [bend] (pt & pp bent) n curva f ◆ vt doblar ◆ vi torcerse ▷ **bend down** vi agacharse; **bend over** vi inclinarse.

beneath [bɪ'niːθ] adv debajo ◆ prep bajo.

beneficial [,benɪ'fɪʃl] adj beneficioso(-sa).

benefit ['benɪfɪt] n (advantage) ventaja f; (money) subsidio m ◆ vt beneficiar ◆ vi: to ~ (from) beneficiarse (de); **for the ~ of** en atención a.

benign [bɪ'naɪn] adj (MED) benigno(-na).

bent [bent] pt & pp → **bend**.

bereaved [bɪ'riːvd] adj desconsolado(-da).

beret ['bereɪ] n boina f.

Bermuda shorts [bə'mjuːdə] npl bermudas fpl.

berry ['berɪ] n baya f.

berserk [bə'zɜːk] adj: **to go** ~ ponerse hecho(-cha) una fiera.

berth [bɜːθ] n (for ship) amarradero m; (in ship, train) litera f.

beside [bɪ'saɪd] prep junto a; **it's ~ the point** no viene al caso.

besides [bɪ'saɪdz] adv además ◆ prep además de.

best [best] adj & adv mejor ◆ n: **the** ~ el mejor (la mejor); **a pint of** ~ (beer) una pinta de "bitter" de máxima calidad; **I like it** ~ me gusta más; **the** ~ **thing to do is ...** lo mejor es ...; **to make the** ~ **of it** apañárselas; **to do one's** ~ hacer lo mejor que uno puede; **"~ before**

..." "consúmase preferentemente antes de ..."; **at** ~ en el mejor de los casos; **all the** ~! (in letter) un abrazo.

best man n padrino m de boda.

best-seller [-'selə'] n (book) éxito m editorial.

bet [bet] (pt & pp bet) n apuesta f ◆ vt (gamble) apostar ◆ vi: **to** ~ **(on)** apostar (por); **I** ~ **(that)** you can't do it a que no puedes hacerlo.

betray [bɪ'treɪ] vt traicionar.

better ['betə'] adj & adv mejor; **you had** ~ **go** más vale que te vayas; **to get** ~ mejorar.

betting ['betɪŋ] n apuestas fpl.

betting shop n (Br) casa f de apuestas.

between [bɪ'twiːn] prep entre ◆ adv (in time) entremedias; **in** ~ prep entre ◆ adv (in space) en medio; (in time) entremedias; **"closed ~ 1 and 2"** "cerrado de 1 a 2".

beverage ['bevərɪdʒ] n (fml) bebida f.

beware [bɪ'weə'] vi: **to** ~ **of** tener cuidado con; **"~ of the dog"** "ojo con el perro".

bewildered [bɪ'wɪldəd] adj desconcertado(-da).

beyond [bɪ'jɒnd] prep más allá de ◆ adv más allá; **to be** ~ **doubt** estar fuera de toda duda.

biased ['baɪəst] adj parcial.

bib [bɪb] n (for baby) babero m.

bible ['baɪbl] n biblia f; **the Bible** la Biblia.

biceps ['baɪseps] n bíceps m inv.

bicycle ['baɪsɪkl] n bicicleta f.

bicycle path n camino m para bicicletas.

bicycle pump n bomba f (de bicicleta).

bid [bɪd] (pt & pp **bid**) n (at auction) puja f; (attempt) intento m ◆ vt pujar ◆ vi: **to ~ (for)** pujar (por).

bidet [ˈbiːdeɪ] n bidé m.

big [bɪg] adj grande; **a ~ problem** un gran problema; **my ~ brother** mi hermano mayor; **how ~ is it?** ¿cómo es de grande?

bike [baɪk] n (inf) (bicycle) bici f; (motorcycle) moto f.

biking [ˈbaɪkɪŋ] n: **to go ~** ir en bici.

bikini [bɪˈkiːnɪ] n biquini m.

bikini bottom n bragas fpl de biquini.

bikini top n sujetador m de biquini.

bilingual [baɪˈlɪŋgwəl] adj bilingüe.

bill [bɪl] n (for meal) cuenta f; (for electricity, hotel room) factura f; (Am: bank note) billete m; (at cinema, theatre) programa m; (POL) proyecto m de ley; **can I have the ~ please?** la cuenta, por favor.

billboard [ˈbɪlbɔːd] n cartelera f.

billfold [ˈbɪlfəʊld] n (Am) billetera f.

billiards [ˈbɪljədz] n billar m.

billion [ˈbɪljən] n (thousand million) millar m de millones; (Br: million million) billón m.

bin [bɪn] n (rubbish bin) cubo m de la basura; (wastepaper bin) papelera f; (for bread) panera f; (for flour) bote m; (on plane) maletero m superior.

bind [baɪnd] (pt & pp **bound**) vt atar.

binding [ˈbaɪndɪŋ] n (of book) encuadernación f; (for ski) fijación f.

bingo [ˈbɪŋgəʊ] n bingo m.

---

i BINGO

El "bingo" es un juego muy popular en Gran Bretaña que consiste en rellenar casillas en una tarjeta con números. El "bingo caller" canta los números elegidos al azar y la primera persona que completa una línea o toda la tarjeta es la que gana. Los premios pueden ser en metálico, pero muchas veces son regalos como osos de peluche o adornos. A menudo se juega en antiguos cines o grandes salas públicas y también en salones de juego en lugares de veraneo.

---

binoculars [bɪˈnɒkjʊləz] npl prismáticos mpl.

biodegradable [ˌbaɪəʊdɪˈgreɪdəbl] adj biodegradable.

biography [baɪˈɒgrəfɪ] n biografía f.

biological [ˌbaɪəˈlɒdʒɪkl] adj biológico(-ca).

biology [baɪˈɒlədʒɪ] n biología f.

birch [bɜːtʃ] n abedul m.

bird [bɜːd] n (smaller) pájaro m; (large) ave f; (Br: inf: woman) tía f.

bird-watching [-ˌwɒtʃɪŋ] n observación f de aves.

Biro® [ˈbaɪərəʊ] n bolígrafo m.

birth [bɜːθ] n nacimiento m; **by ~** de nacimiento; **to give ~ to** dar a luz.

birth certificate n partida f

de nacimiento.

birth control n control m de natalidad.

birthday ['bɜːθdeɪ] n cumpleaños m inv; **happy ~!** ¡feliz cumpleaños!

birthday card n tarjeta f de cumpleaños.

birthday party n fiesta f de cumpleaños.

birthplace ['bɜːθpleɪs] n lugar m de nacimiento.

biscuit ['bɪskɪt] n (Br) galleta f; (Am: scone) masa cocida al horno que se suele comer con salsa de carne.

bishop ['bɪʃəp] n (RELIG) obispo m; (in chess) alfil m.

bistro ['biːstrəʊ] n = bar-restaurante m.

bit [bɪt] pt → **bite** ◆ n (piece) trozo m; (of drill) broca f; (of bridle) bocado m, freno m; **a ~** un poco de; **a ~ un poco**; **not a ~ interested** nada interesado; **~ by ~** poco a poco.

bitch [bɪtʃ] n (vulg: woman) bruja f; (dog) perra f.

bite [baɪt] (pt bit, pp bitten ['bɪtn]) n (when eating) mordisco m; (from insect, snake) picadura f ◆ vt (subj: person, dog) morder; (subj: insect, snake) picar; **to have a ~ to eat** comer algo.

bitter ['bɪtəʳ] adj (taste, food) amargo(-ga); (lemon, grapefruit) agrio (agria); (cold, wind) penetrante; (person) resentido(-da) ◆ n (Br: beer) tipo de cerveza amarga.

bitter lemon n bíter m de limón.

bizarre [bɪˈzɑːʳ] adj extravagante.

black [blæk] adj negro(-gra); (coffee, tea) solo ◆ n (colour) negro m; (person) negro m (-gra f) ❑ **black out** vi desmayarse.

black and white adj en blanco y negro.

blackberry ['blækbrɪ] n mora f.

blackbird ['blækbɜːd] n mirlo m.

blackboard ['blækbɔːd] n pizarra f.

black cherry n variedad de cereza oscura.

blackcurrant [,blæk'kʌrənt] n grosella f negra.

black eye n ojo m morado.

Black Forest gâteau n pastel m (de chocolate) Selva Negra.

black ice n hielo transparente en el suelo.

blackmail ['blækmeɪl] n chantaje m ◆ vt chantajear.

blackout ['blækaʊt] n (power cut) apagón m.

black pepper n pimienta f negra.

black pudding n (Br) = morcilla f.

blacksmith ['blæksmɪθ] n herrero m.

bladder ['blædəʳ] n vejiga f.

blade [bleɪd] n (of knife, saw) hoja f; (of propeller, oar) aleta f; (of grass) brizna f.

blame [bleɪm] n culpa f ◆ vt echar la culpa a; **to ~ sb for sthg** culpar a alguien de algo; **to ~ sthg on sb** echar la culpa de algo a alguien.

bland [blænd] adj soso(-sa).

blank [blæŋk] adj (space, page) en blanco; (cassette) virgen; (expres-

siom) vacío(-a). ◆ n (empty space)
espacio m en blanco.
blank cheque n cheque m en
blanco.
blanket ['blæŋkɪt] n manta f.
blast [blɑːst] n (explosion) explosión f; (of air, wind) ráfaga f. ◆ excl
(inf) ¡maldita sea!; **at full ~** a todo
trapo.
blaze [bleɪz] n (fire) incendio m;
(fire) arder; (sun, light) resplande-

...ctors n junta f
...vi; **to** ... ◆ **(about**
...de algo).
...(large) barco m;
...) by ... (Br) tren de enlace
...media
...(en una capa), des-
...brío(-a).
...(hairstyle)
Pin
['bɒb]
(Am)

bliss [blɪs] n gloria f.
blister ['blɪstə'] n ampolla f.
blizzard ['blɪzəd] n ventisca f
(de nieve).
bloated ['bləʊtɪd] adj (after eating) hinchado(-da).
blob [blɒb] n gota f.
block [blɒk] n bloque m; (Am: in
town, city) manzana f. ◆ vt bloquear; **to have a ~ed (up) nose**
tener la nariz bloqueada □ **block
up** v sep obstruir.
blockage ['blɒkɪdʒ] n obstruc-
ción f.
block capitals npl mayúscu-
las fpl.
block of flats n bloque m de
pisos.
bloke [bləʊk] n (Br: inf) tipo m.
blond [blɒnd] adj & n rubio m.
blonde [blɒnd] adj rubia f.
◆ n rubia f.
blood [blʌd] n sangre f.
blood donor n donante mf de
sangre.
blood group n grupo m san-
...**poisoning** n sep-
...**sure** n presión f
... high ~ tener la
... low ~ tener la
...análisis m inv de
...j adj inyec-
...**dy** ['blʌdɪ] adj (hands, hand-

kerchief) ensangrentado(-da); (Br: vulg: damn) maldito(-ta) ◆ adv (Br: vulg) acojonantemente.

Bloody Mary n, vodka con zumo de tomate.

bloom [blu:m] n flor f ◆ vi florecer; in ~ en flor.

blossom [blɒsəm] n flor f.

blot [blɒt] n borrón m.

blotch [blɒtʃ] n mancha f.

blotting paper [blɒtɪŋ] n papel m secante.

blouse [blauz] n blusa f.

blow [bləu] (pt blew, pp blown) vt (subj: wind) hacer volar; (whistle, trumpet) tocar; (bubbles) hacer ◆ vi (wind, person) soplar; (fuse) fundirse ◆ n (hit) golpe m; to ~ one's nose sonarse la nariz □ blow up vt sep (cause to explode) volar; (inflate) inflar ◆ vi estallar.

blow-dry n secado m (con secador) ◆ vt secar (con secador).

blown [bləun] pp → blow.

BLT n (sandwich) sándwich de bacon, lechuga y tomate.

blue [blu:] adj (colour) azul; (film) porno ◆ n azul m □ blues n (MUS) blues m inv.

bluebell [blu:bel] n campanilla f.

blueberry [blu:bəri] n arándano m.

bluebottle [blu:bɒtl] n moscardón m.

blue cheese n queso m azul.

bluff [blʌf] n (cliff) peñasco m ◆ vi farolear.

blunder [blʌndə] n metedura f de pata.

blunt [blʌnt] adj (knife, pencil) desafilado(-da); (fig: person) franco(-ca).

blurred [blɜːd] adj borroso(-sa).

blush [blʌʃ] vi ruborizarse.

blusher [blʌʃə] n colorete m.

blustery [blʌstəri] adj borrascoso(-sa).

board [bɔːd] n (plank) tabla f; (notice board) tablón m; (for games) tablero m; (blackboard) pizarra f; (of company) junta f directiva; (hardboard) conglomerado m ◆ vt (plane, ship) embarcar en; (bus) subir a; ~ and lodging comida y habitación; full ~ pensión completa; half ~ media pensión; on ~ adv a bordo ◆ prep (plane, ship) a bordo (bus) dentro de.

board game n juego tablero.

boarding [bɔːdɪŋ] n e... embarque.

boarding card n t...

boardinghouse [... -hauzɪz] n casa f de...

boarding scho...

board of dire... directiva.

boast [baust...] sthg) alardea...

boat [baut...] (small) barca...

boat tra... con un barc...

bob [b... melena f...

bobb... horqu...

bodice ['bɒdɪs] n cuerpo m.

body ['bɒdɪ] n (of person, wine) cuerpo m; (corpse) cadáver m; (of car) carrocería f; (organization) organismo m.

bodyguard ['bɒdɪgɑːd] n guardaespaldas m inv.

bodywork ['bɒdɪwɜːk] n carrocería f.

bog [bɒg] n cenagal m.

bogus ['bəʊgəs] adj falso(-sa).

boil [bɔɪl] vt (water) hervir; (kettle) poner a hervir; (food) cocer ◆ vi hervir ◆ n pústula f.

boiled egg [bɔɪld-] n huevo m pasado por agua.

boiled potatoes [bɔɪld-] npl patatas fpl cocidas.

boiler ['bɔɪlə] n caldera f.

boiling (hot) ['bɔɪlɪŋ-] adj (inf: person) asado(-da) de calor; (weather) abrasador(-ra); (water) ardiendo.

bold [bəʊld] adj (brave) audaz.

Bolivia [bə'lɪvɪə] n Bolivia.

Bolivian [bə'lɪvɪən] adj boliviano(-na) ◆ n boliviano m (-na f).

bollard ['bɒlɑːd] n (Br: on road) poste m.

bolt [bəʊlt] n (on door, window) cerrojo m; (screw) tornillo m ◆ vt (door, window) echar el cerrojo a.

bomb [bɒm] n bomba f ◆ vt bombardear.

bombard [bɒm'bɑːd] vt bombardear.

bomb scare n amenaza f de bomba.

bomb shelter n refugio m antiaéreo.

bond [bɒnd] n (tie, connection)

lazo m, vínculo m.

bone [bəʊn] n (of person, animal) hueso m; (of fish) espina f.

boned [bəʊnd] adj (chicken) deshuesado(-da); (fish) limpio (-pia).

boneless ['bəʊnlɪs] adj (chicken, pork) deshuesado(-da).

bonfire ['bɒn,faɪə] n hoguera f.

bonnet ['bɒnɪt] n (Br: of car) capó m.

bonus ['bəʊnəs] (pl -es) n (extra money) paga f extra; (additional advantage) beneficio m adicional.

bony ['bəʊnɪ] adj (fish) lleno(-na) de espinas; (chicken) lleno de huesos.

boo [buː] vi abuchear.

boogie ['buːgɪ] vi (inf) mover el esqueleto.

book [bʊk] n (for reading) libro m; (for writing in) libreta f, cuaderno m; (of stamps) librillo m; (of matches) cajetilla f; (of tickets) talonario m ◆ vt (reserve) reservar ❑ **book in** vi registrarse.

bookable ['bʊkəbl] adj (seats, flight) reservable.

bookcase ['bʊkkeɪs] n estantería f.

booking ['bʊkɪŋ] n (reservation) reserva f.

booking office n taquilla f.

bookkeeping ['bʊk,kiːpɪŋ] n contabilidad f.

booklet ['bʊklɪt] n folleto m.

bookmaker's ['bʊk,meɪkəz] n casa f de apuestas.

bookmark ['bʊkmɑːk] n separador m.

bookshelf ['bʊkʃelf] (pl -shelves

[-ʃelvz] n (shelf) estante m; (bookcase) estantería f.

bookshop ['bukʃɒp] n librería f.

bookstall ['bukstɔːl] n puesto m de libros.

bookstore ['bukstɔːr] = bookshop.

book token n vale m para comprar libros.

boom [buːm] n (sudden growth) auge m ◆ vi (voice, guns) retumbar.

boost [buːst] vt (profits, production) incrementar; (confidence, spirits) estimular.

booster ['buːstər] n (injection) inyección f de revacunación.

boot [buːt] n (shoe) bota f; (Br: of car) maletero m.

booth [buːð] n (for telephone) cabina f; (at fairground) puesto m.

booze [buːz] n (inf) bebida f, alcohol m ◆ vi (inf) empinar el codo.

bop [bɒp] n (inf: dance): to have a ~ mover el esqueleto.

border ['bɔːdər] n (of country) frontera f; (edge) borde m; **the Borders** región de Escocia que linda con Inglaterra, especialmente las zonas central y oriental.

bore [bɔːr] pt → **bear** ◆ n (person) pelmazo m (-za f); (thing) rollo m ◆ vt (person) aburrir; (hole) horadar.

bored [bɔːd] adj aburrido(-da).

boredom ['bɔːdəm] n aburrimiento m.

boring ['bɔːrɪŋ] adj aburrido (-da).

born [bɔːn] adj: to be ~ nacer.

borne [bɔːn] pp → **bear**.

borough ['bʌrə] n municipio m.

borrow ['bɒrəu] vt: to ~ sthg (from sb) tomar algo prestado (de alguien).

bosom ['buzəm] n pecho m.

boss [bɒs] n jefe m (-fa f) ◆ **boss around** vt sep mangonear.

bossy ['bɒsɪ] adj mandón(-ona).

botanical garden [bə'tænɪkl-] n jardín m botánico.

both [bəuθ] adj ambos(-bas) ◆ pron los dos mpl (las dos fpl) ◆ adv: **she speaks** ~ **French and German** habla francés y alemán; ~ **of them** los dos (las dos); ~ **of us** los dos (las dos).

bother ['bɒðər] vt (worry) preocupar; (annoy, pester) molestar ◆ vi molestarse ◆ n molestia f; **I can't be** ~**ed** no tengo ganas; **it's no** ~! ¡no es molestia!

bottle ['bɒtl] n (container, contents) botella f; (of shampoo) bote m; (of medicine) frasco m; (for baby) biberón m.

bottle bank n contenedor m de vidrio (para reciclaje).

bottled ['bɒtld] adj embotellado(-da); ~ **beer** cerveza f de botella; ~ **water** agua f mineral (embotellada).

bottle opener [-ˌəupnər] n abrebotellas m inv.

bottom ['bɒtəm] adj (shelf, line, object in pile) inferior; (floor) bajo(-ja); (last, worst) peor ◆ n (of sea, bag) fondo m; (of hill, stairs, ladder) pie m; (of page) final m; (of glass, bin) culo m; (farthest part) final m, fondo m; (buttocks) trasero m.

bought [bɔːt] pt & pp → **buy**.

boulder ['bəuldər] n canto m

rodado.

bounce [baʊns] vi (rebound) rebotar; (jump) saltar; (cheque) ser rechazado por el banco.

bouncer [ˈbaʊnsəʳ] n (inf) matón m (en discoteca, bar, etc).

bouncy [ˈbaʊnsɪ] adj (person) dinámico(-ca).

bound [baʊnd] pt & pp → **bind** ♦ vi ir dando saltos ♦ adj: it's ~ to rain seguro que llueve; **to be ~ for** ir rumbo a; **to be out of ~s** estar en zona prohibida.

boundary [ˈbaʊndrɪ] n frontera f.

bouquet [buˈkeɪ] n (of flowers) ramo m; (of wine) buqué m.

bourbon [ˈbɜːbən] n bourbon m.

bout [baʊt] n (of illness) ataque m; (of activity) racha f.

boutique [buːˈtiːk] n boutique f.

bow[1] [baʊ] n (of head) reverencia f; (of ship) proa f ♦ vi inclinarse.

bow[2] [bəʊ] n (knot) lazo m; (weapon, MUS) arco m.

bowels [ˈbaʊəlz] npl intestinos mpl.

bowl [bəʊl] n (for salad, fruit, sugar) bol m, cuenco m; (for soup, of soup) tazón m; (for washing-up) barreño m; (of toilet) taza f ❑ **bowls** npl bochas fpl.

bowling alley [ˈbəʊlɪŋ-] n bolera f.

bowling green [ˈbəʊlɪŋ-] n campo de césped para jugar a las bochas.

bow tie [bəʊ-] n pajarita f.

box [bɒks] n (container, contents) caja f; (of jewels) estuche m; (on form) casilla f; (in theatre) palco m ♦ vi boxear; **a ~ of chocolates** una

caja de bombones.

boxer [ˈbɒksəʳ] n boxeador m.

boxer shorts npl calzoncillos mpl boxer.

boxing [ˈbɒksɪŋ] n boxeo m.

Boxing Day n el 26 de diciembre.

---

i BOXING DAY

El 26 de diciembre, "Boxing Day", es fiesta en toda Gran Bretaña. Tradicionalmente, era el día en el que los comerciantes y criados recibían un dinero extra que se llamaba el "Christmas box". Aún hoy, los repartidores de leche, los basureros y los niños que reparten periódicos reciben este aguinaldo.

---

boxing gloves npl guantes mpl de boxeo.

boxing ring n cuadrilátero m.

box office n taquilla f.

boy [bɔɪ] n (male) chico m, niño m; (son) hijo m ♦ excl (Am: inf): **(oh) ~!** ¡jolín!

boycott [ˈbɔɪkɒt] vt boicotear.

boyfriend [ˈbɔɪfrend] n novio m.

boy scout n (boy) scout m.

BR abbr = **British Rail**.

bra [brɑː] n sujetador m.

brace [breɪs] n (for teeth) aparato m corrector ❑ **braces** npl (Br) tirantes mpl.

bracelet [ˈbreɪslɪt] n brazalete m.

bracken [ˈbrækn] n helecho m.

bracket [ˈbrækɪt] n (written symbol) paréntesis m inv; (support) soporte m, palomilla f.

brag [bræg] vi fanfarronear.

braid [breɪd] n (hairstyle) trenza f; (on clothes) galón m.

brain [breɪn] n cerebro m.

brainy ['breɪnɪ] adj (inf) listo (-ta).

braised [breɪzd] adj cocido(-da) a fuego lento.

brake [breɪk] n freno m ◆ vi frenar.

brake block n zapata f.

brake fluid n líquido m para frenos.

brake light n luz f de freno.

brake pad n pastilla f de frenos.

brake pedal n pedal m de freno.

bran [bræn] n salvado m.

branch [brɑːntʃ] n (of tree, subject) rama f; (of bank, company) sucursal f ❏ **branch off** vi desviarse.

branch line n ramal m.

brand [brænd] n marca f ◆ vt: to ~ sb (as) tildar a alguien (de).

brand-new adj completamente nuevo(-va).

brandy ['brændɪ] n coñac m.

brash [bræʃ] adj (pej) insolente.

brass [brɑːs] n latón m.

brass band n banda f de metal.

brasserie ['bræsərɪ] n restaurante m.

brassiere [Br 'bræsɪəʳ, Am 'brəzɪəʳ] n sujetador m.

brat [bræt] n (inf) mocoso m (-sa f).

brave [breɪv] adj valiente.

bravery ['breɪvərɪ] n valentía f.

bravo [ˌbrɑːˈvəʊ] excl ¡bravo!

brawl [brɔːl] n gresca f.

Brazil [brəˈzɪl] n Brasil.

brazil nut n nuez f de Pará.

breach [briːtʃ] vt (contract) incumplir; (confidence) abusar de.

bread [bred] n pan m; ~ and butter pan con mantequilla.

bread bin n (Br) panera f.

breadboard ['bredbɔːd] n tabla f (de cortar pan).

bread box (Am) = bread bin.

breadcrumbs ['bredkrʌmz] npl pan m rallado.

breaded ['bredɪd] adj empanado(-da).

bread knife n cuchillo m de pan.

bread roll n panecillo m.

breadth [bretθ] n anchura f.

break [breɪk] (pt broke, pp broken) n (interruption) interrupción f; (in transmission) corte m; (in line) espacio m; (rest, pause) descanso m; (SCH: playtime) recreo m ◆ vt (cup, window, record) romper; (machine) estropear; (disobey) violar, infringir; (fail to fulfil) incumplir; (journey) interrumpir; (news) dar ◆ vi (cup, window, chair) romperse; (machine) estropearse; (dawn) romper; (voice) cambiar; **without a ~** sin parar; **a lucky ~** un golpe de suerte; **to ~ one's leg** romperse la pierna ❏ **break down** vi (car, machine) estropearse ◆ vt sep (door, barrier) derribar; **break in** vi entrar por la fuerza; **break off** vt (detach) partir; (holiday) interrumpir ◆ vi (stop suddenly) pararse, detenerse; **break out** vi (fire, war) desencadenarse; (panic) cundir; **he broke out in a rash** le salió un sarpullido; **break up** vi (with spouse, partner) romper;

(meeting) disolverse; *(marriage)* deshacerse; *(school, pupils)* terminar el curso.

breakage ['breɪkɪdʒ] *n* rotura *f*.

breakdown ['breɪkdaʊn] *n (of car)* avería *f*; *(in communications, negotiations)* ruptura *f*; *(acute depression)* crisis *f* nerviosa.

breakdown truck *n* camión *m* grúa.

breakfast ['brekfəst] *n* desayuno *m*; **to have ~** desayunar; **to have sthg for ~** desayunar algo.

breakfast cereal *n* cereales *mpl* (para desayuno).

break-in *n* robo *m* (con allanamiento de morada).

breakwater ['breɪkˌwɔːtər] *n* rompeolas *m inv*.

breast [brest] *n (of woman)* pecho *m*, seno *m*; *(of chicken, duck)* pechuga *f*.

breastbone ['brestbəʊn] *n* esternón *m*.

breast-feed *vt* dar el pecho a.

breaststroke ['breststrəʊk] *n* braza *f*.

breath [breθ] *n* aliento *m*; **out of ~** sin aliento; **to go for a ~ of fresh air** salir a tomar un poco de aire; **to take a deep ~** respirar hondo.

Breathalyser® ['breθəlaɪzər] *n (Br)* alcoholímetro *m*.

Breathalyzer® ['breθəlaɪzər] *(Am)* = **Breathalyser**.

breathe [briːð] *vi* respirar ❑ **breathe in** *vi* aspirar; **breathe out** *vi* espirar.

breathtaking ['breθˌteɪkɪŋ] *adj* sobrecogedor(-ra).

breed [briːd] *(pt & pp* **bred** [bred]*)*

n (of animal) raza *f*; *(of plant)* especie *f* ◆ *vt* criar ◆ *vi* reproducirse.

breeze [briːz] *n* brisa *f*.

breezy ['briːzɪ] *adj*: **it's ~** hace aire.

brew [bruː] *vt (beer)* elaborar; *(tea, coffee)* preparar ◆ *vi (tea, coffee)* reposar.

brewery ['brʊərɪ] *n* fábrica *f* de cerveza.

bribe [braɪb] *n* soborno *m* ◆ *vt* sobornar.

bric-a-brac ['brɪkəbræk] *n* baratijas *fpl*.

brick [brɪk] *n* ladrillo *m*.

bricklayer ['brɪkˌleɪər] *n* albañil *m*.

brickwork ['brɪkwɜːk] *n* enladrillado *m*.

bride [braɪd] *n* novia *f*.

bridegroom ['braɪdgrum] *n* novio *m*.

bridesmaid ['braɪdzmeɪd] *n* dama *f* de honor.

bridge [brɪdʒ] *n (across road, river)* puente *m*; *(of ship)* puente *m* de mando; *(card game)* bridge *m*.

bridle ['braɪdl] *n* brida *f*.

bridle path *n* camino *m* de herradura.

brief [briːf] *adj* breve ◆ *vt* informar; **in ~** en resumen ❑ **briefs** *npl (underpants)* calzoncillos *mpl*; *(knickers)* bragas *fpl*.

briefcase ['briːfkeɪs] *n* cartera *f*.

briefly ['briːflɪ] *adv (for a short time)* brevemente; *(in few words)* en pocas palabras.

brigade [brɪˈgeɪd] *n* brigada *f*.

bright [braɪt] *adj (light)* brillante; *(sun, smile)* radiante; *(weather)* despejado(-da); *(room)* luminoso(-sa); *(colour)* vivo(-va); *(clever)* listo(-ta), inteligente; *(idea)* genial.

brilliant ['brɪljənt] *adj (colour)* vivo(-va); *(light, sunshine)* resplandeciente; *(idea, person)* genial; *(inf: wonderful)* fenomenal.

brim [brɪm] *n (of hat)* ala *f*; **it's full to the ~** está lleno hasta el borde.

brine [braɪn] *n* salmuera *f*.

bring [brɪŋ] *(pt & pp* brought*)* vt traer; *(cause)* producir □ **bring along** vt sep traer; **bring back** vt sep *(return)* devolver; *(shopping, gift)* traer; **bring in** vt sep *(introduce)* introducir; *(earn)* ganar; **bring out** vt sep *(new product)* sacar; **bring up** vt sep *(child)* criar; *(subject)* sacar a relucir; *(food)* devolver.

brink [brɪŋk] *n*: **on the ~** al borde de.

brisk [brɪsk] *adj (quick)* rápido (-da); *(efficient)* enérgico(-ca).

bristle ['brɪsl] *n (of brush)* cerda *f*; *(on chin)* pelillo *m*.

Britain ['brɪtn] *n* Gran Bretaña.

British ['brɪtɪʃ] *adj* británico(-ca) ♦ *npl*: **the ~** los británicos.

British Rail *n* compañía ferroviaria británica.

British Telecom [-'telɪkɒm] *n* principal empresa británica de telecomunicaciones.

Briton ['brɪtn] *n* británico *m* (-ca *f*).

brittle ['brɪtl] *adj* quebradizo(-za).

broad [brɔːd] *adj (wide)* ancho(-cha); *(wide-ranging)* amplio (-plia); *(description, outline)* general; *(accent)* cerrado(-da).

B road *n (Br)* = carretera *f* comarcal.

broad bean *n* haba *f* de mayo.

broadcast ['brɔːdkɑːst] *(pt & pp* broadcast*)* n emisión *f* ♦ vt emitir.

broadly ['brɔːdlɪ] *adv* en general; **~ speaking** en líneas generales.

broccoli ['brɒkəlɪ] *n* brécol *m*.

brochure ['brəʊʃə'] *n* folleto *m*.

broiled [brɔɪld] *adj (Am)* a la parrilla.

broke [brəʊk] *pt* → **break** ♦ *adj (inf)* sin blanca.

broken ['brəʊkn] *pp* → **break** ♦ *adj (window, glass, leg)* roto(-ta); *(machine)* estropeado(-da); *(English, Spanish)* macarrónico(-ca).

bronchitis [brɒŋ'kaɪtɪs] *n* bronquitis *f inv*.

bronze [brɒnz] *n* bronce *m*.

brooch [brəʊtʃ] *n* broche *m*.

brook [brʊk] *n* arroyo *m*.

broom [bruːm] *n* escoba *f*.

broomstick ['bruːmstɪk] *n* palo *m* de escoba.

broth [brɒθ] *n* caldo *m*.

brother ['brʌðə'] *n* hermano *m*.

brother-in-law *n* cuñado *m*.

brought [brɔːt] *pt & pp* → **bring**.

brow [braʊ] *n (forehead)* frente *f*; *(eyebrow)* ceja *f*.

brown [braʊn] *adj (earth, paint, wood)* marrón *m*; *(hair, eyes)* castaño(-ña); *(skin)* moreno(-na); *(tanned)* bronceado(-da) ♦ *n* marrón *m*.

brown bread *n* pan *m* moreno.

brownie ['braʊnɪ] *n (CULIN)* pequeño bizcocho de chocolate y nueces *de forma cuadrada.*

Brownie ['braunɪ] *n* guía *f* (de 7-10 años).

brown rice *n* arroz *m* integral.

brown sauce *n* (Br) salsa *f* inglesa.

brown sugar *n* azúcar *m* moreno.

browse [brauz] *vi* (in shop) mirar, curiosear; **to ~ through** sthg hojear algo.

browser ['brauzə] *n*: "**~s welcome**" "le invitamos a curiosear".

bruise [bru:z] *n* cardenal *m*.

brunch [brʌntʃ] *n* desayuno-almuerzo que se toma por la mañana tarde.

brunette [bru:'net] *n* morena *f*.

brush [brʌʃ] *n* (for hair, teeth) cepillo *m*; (of artist) pincel *m*; (for decorating) brocha *f* ◆ *vt* (floor) barrer; (clothes) cepillar; (move with hand) quitar; **to ~** one's hair cepillarse el pelo; **to ~** one's teeth cepillarse los dientes.

Brussels sprouts ['brʌsl̩z] *npl* coles *fpl* de Bruselas.

brutal ['bru:tl] *adj* brutal.

BSc *n* (abbr of Bachelor of Science) (titular de una) licenciatura de ciencias.

BT *abbr* = **British Telecom**.

bubble ['bʌbl] *n* burbuja *f*.

bubble bath *n* espuma *f* de baño.

bubble gum *n* chicle *m* (para hacer globos).

bubbly ['bʌblɪ] *n* (inf) champán *m*.

buck [bʌk] *n* (Am: inf: dollar) dólar

m; (male animal) macho *m*.

bucket ['bʌkɪt] *n* cubo *m*.

Buckingham Palace ['bʌkɪŋəm-] *n* el palacio de Buckingham.

BUCKINGHAM PALACE

El palacio de Buckingham, construido en 1703 por el duque de Buckingham, es la residencia oficial en Londres del monarca británico. Se encuentra al final de The Mall, entre Green Park y St James's Park. La ceremonia del cambio de guardia tiene lugar a diario frente al palacio.

buckle ['bʌkl] *n* hebilla *f* ◆ *vt* (fasten) abrochar (con hebilla) ◆ *vi* (warp) combarse.

Buck's Fizz [,bʌks'fɪz] *n* bebida preparada con champán y zumo de naranja.

bud [bʌd] *n* (shoot) brote *m*; (flower) capullo *m* ◆ *vi* brotar.

Buddhist ['budɪst] *n* budista *mf*.

buddy ['bʌdɪ] *n* (inf) amiguete *m* (-ta *f*).

budge [bʌdʒ] *vi* moverse.

budgerigar ['bʌdʒərɪgɑ:ʳ] *n* periquito *m*.

budget ['bʌdʒɪt] *adj* (holiday, travel) económico(-ca) ◆ *n* presupuesto *m*; **the Budget** (Br) los presupuestos del Estado ❏ **budget for** *vt fus* contar con.

budgie ['bʌdʒɪ] *n* (inf) periquito *m*.

buff [bʌf] *n* (inf) aficionado *m* (-da *f*).

buffalo ['bʌfələu] *n* búfalo *m*.

buffalo wings npl (Am) alitas fpl de pollo fritas.

buffer ['bʌfəˠ] n (on train) tope m.

buffet [Br 'bʊfeɪ, Am bəˠfeɪ] (meal) bufé m; (cafeteria) cafetería f.

buffet car ['bʊfeɪ-] n coche m restaurante (sólo mostrador).

bug [bʌg] n (insect) bicho m; (inf: mild illness) virus m inv ◆ vt (inf: annoy) fastidiar.

buggy ['bʌgɪ] n (pushchair) silla f de niño; (Am: pram) cochecito m de niño.

bugle ['bjuːgl] n corneta f.

build [bɪld] (pt & pp built) n complexión f ◆ vt construir ❑ **build up** vt sep (strength, speed) ir aumentando ◆ vi acumularse.

builder ['bɪldəˠ] n constructor m (-ra f).

building ['bɪldɪŋ] n edificio m.

building site n solar m.

building society n (Br) = caja f de ahorros.

built [bɪlt] pt & pp → build.

built-in adj empotrado(-da).

built-up area n zona f urbanizada.

bulb [bʌlb] n (for lamp) bombilla f; (of plant) bulbo m.

Bulgaria [bʌlˈgeərɪə] n Bulgaria.

bulge [bʌldʒ] vi hacer bulto.

bulk [bʌlk] n: the ~ of la mayor parte de; **in** ~ a granel.

bulky ['bʌlkɪ] adj voluminoso(-sa).

bull [bʊl] n toro m.

bulldog ['bʊldɒg] n buldog m.

bulldozer ['bʊldəʊzəˠ] n bulldozer m.

bullet ['bʊlɪt] n bala f.

bulletin ['bʊlətɪn] n boletín m.

bullfight ['bʊlfaɪt] n corrida f (de toros).

bull's-eye n diana f.

bully ['bʊlɪ] n abusón m (-ona f) ◆ vt intimidar.

bum [bʌm] n (inf: bottom) culo m; (Am: inf: tramp) vagabundo m (-da f).

bum bag n (Br) riñonera f.

bumblebee ['bʌmblbɪ] n abejorro m.

bump [bʌmp] n (on surface) bulto m; (on road) bache m; (on head, leg) chichón m; (sound, minor accident) golpe m ◆ vt: to ~ one's head golpearse la cabeza ❑ **bump into** vt fus (hit) darse con; (meet) toparse con.

bumper ['bʌmpəˠ] n (on car) parachoques m inv; (Am: on train) tope m.

bumpy ['bʌmpɪ] adj (road) lleno(-na) de baches; (flight, journey) con muchas sacudidas.

bun [bʌn] n (cake) bollo m; (bread roll) panecillo m; (hairstyle) moño m.

bunch [bʌntʃ] n (of people) grupo m; (of flowers) ramo m; (of grapes, bananas) racimo m; (of keys) manojo m.

bundle ['bʌndl] n (of clothes) bulto m; (of notes, papers) fajo m.

bung [bʌŋ] n tapón m.

bungalow ['bʌŋgələʊ] n bungalow m.

bunion ['bʌnjən] n juanete m.

bunk [bʌŋk] n litera f.

bunk bed n litera f.

bunker ['bʌŋkəˠ] n (shelter) búnquer m; (for coal) carbonera f; (in golf) búnker m.

bunny ['bʌnɪ] n conejito m.

buoy [Br bɔɪ, Am 'buːɪ] n boya f.

buoyant ['bɔɪənt] adj (that floats) boyante.

BUPA ['buːpə] n seguro médico privado en Gran Bretaña.

burden ['bɜːdn] n carga f.

bureaucracy [bjʊə'rɒkrəsɪ] n burocracia f.

bureau de change n [ˌbjʊərəʊdə'ʃɒndʒ] n caja f de cambio.

burger ['bɜːgəʳ] n (hamburger) hamburguesa f; (made with nuts, vegetables etc) hamburguesa vegetariana.

burglar ['bɜːgləʳ] n ladrón m (-ona f).

burglar alarm n alarma f antirrobo.

burglarize ['bɜːgləraɪz] (Am) = burgle.

burglary ['bɜːglərɪ] n robo m (de una casa).

burgle ['bɜːgl] vt robar (una casa).

burial ['berɪəl] n entierro m.

burn [bɜːn] (pt & pp burnt OR burned) n quemadura f ◆ vt quemar ◆ vi (be on fire) arder; to ~ one's hand quemarse la mano ▫ **burn down** vt sep incendiar ◆ vi incendiarse.

burning (hot) ['bɜːnɪŋ-] adj muy caliente.

Burns' Night ['bɜːnz-] n el 25 de enero.

ⓘ **BURNS' NIGHT**

El 25 de enero, "Burns' Night", es el día en que se conmemora el nacimiento del poeta nacional escocés, Robert Burns (1759–96). Muchos escoceses acuden a cenas organizadas en honor a Burns ("Burns' suppers") donde tradicionalmente se comen platos típicos escoceses como "haggis", se bebe whisky, y se recitan los poemas de Burns por turno.

---

burnt [bɜːnt] pt & pp → burn.

burp [bɜːp] vi (inf) eructar.

burrow ['bʌrəʊ] n madriguera f.

burst [bɜːst] (pt & pp burst) n (of gunfire, applause) estallido m ◆ vt & vi reventar; **he ~ into the room** irrumpió en la habitación; **to ~ into tears** romper a llorar; **to ~ open** (door) abrirse de golpe.

bury ['berɪ] vt enterrar.

bus [bʌs] n autobús m; **by ~** en autobús.

bus conductor [-ˌkən'dʌktəʳ] n cobrador m (-ra f) de autobús.

bus driver n conductor m (-ra f) de autobús.

bush [bʊʃ] n arbusto m.

business ['bɪznɪs] n (commerce) negocios mpl; (shop, firm, trade) negocio m; (things to do) asuntos mpl, tareas fpl; (affair) asunto m; **mind your own ~!** ¡no te metas donde no te llaman!; **"~ as usual"** "abierto como de costumbre".

business card n tarjeta f de visita.

business class n clase f preferente.

business hours *npl* horario *m* de apertura.

businessman [ˈbɪznɪsmæn] (*pl* -men [-men]) *n* hombre *m* de negocios.

business studies *npl* empresariales *fpl*.

businesswoman [ˈbɪznɪs‚wʊmən] (*pl* -women [-‚wɪmɪn]) *n* mujer *f* de negocios.

busker [ˈbʌskəʳ] *n* (*Br*) músico *m* callejero (música *f* callejera).

bus lane *n* carril *m* de autobús.

bus pass *n* abono *m* (de autobús).

bus shelter *n* marquesina *f* (*de parada de autobús*).

bus station *n* estación *f* de autobuses.

bus stop *n* parada *f* de autobús.

bust [bʌst] *n* (*of woman*) busto *m* ◆ *adj*: to go ~ (*inf*) quebrar.

bustle [ˈbʌsl] *n* bullicio *m*.

bus tour *n* excursión *f* (en autobús).

busy [ˈbɪzɪ] *adj* (*person, telephone, line*) ocupado(-da); (*day*) ajetreado(-da); (*schedule*) lleno(-na); (*street, office*) concurrido(-da); to be ~ doing sthg estar ocupado haciendo algo.

busy signal *n* (*Am*) señal *f* de comunicando.

but [bʌt] *conj* pero ◆ *prep* menos; not just one ~ two no uno sino dos; you've done nothing ~ moan no has hecho más que quejarte; the last ~ one el penúltimo; ~ for de no ser por.

butcher [ˈbʊtʃəʳ] *n* carnicero *m*

(-ra *f*); ~'s (*shop*) carnicería *f*.

butt [bʌt] *n* (*of rifle*) culata *f*; (*of cigarette, cigar*) colilla *f*.

butter [ˈbʌtəʳ] *n* mantequilla *f* ◆ *vt* untar con mantequilla.

butter bean *n* judía *f* blanca.

buttercup [ˈbʌtəkʌp] *n* ranúnculo *m*.

butterfly [ˈbʌtəflaɪ] *n* mariposa *f*.

butterscotch [ˈbʌtəskɒtʃ] *n* dulce hecho hirviendo azúcar y mantequilla.

buttocks [ˈbʌtəks] *npl* nalgas *fpl*.

button [ˈbʌtn] *n* (*on clothing, machine*) botón *m*; (*Am: badge*) chapa *f*.

buttonhole [ˈbʌtnhəʊl] *n* (*hole*) ojal *m*.

button mushroom *n* champiñón *m* pequeño.

buttress [ˈbʌtrɪs] *n* contrafuerte *m*.

buy [baɪ] (*pt & pp* bought) *vt* comprar ◆ *n*: a good ~ una buena compra; to ~ sthg for sb, to ~ sthg comprar algo a alguien; to ~ sthg from sb comprar algo a alguien.

buzz [bʌz] *vi* zumbar ◆ *n* (*inf: phone call*): to give sb a ~ dar un telefonazo a alguien.

buzzer [ˈbʌzəʳ] *n* timbre *m*.

by [baɪ] *prep* 1. (*expressing cause, agent*) por; funded ~ the government subvencionado por el gobierno; a book ~ Joyce un libro de Joyce.
2. (*expressing method, means*): ~ car/train/plane en coche/tren/

avión; **~ post/phone** por correo/teléfono; **to pay** **~ credit card** pagar con tarjeta de crédito; **to win** **~ cheating** ganar haciendo trampa.
3. (near to, beside) junto a; **~ the sea** junto al mar.
4. (past) por delante de; **a car went** **~ the house** pasó un coche por delante de la casa.
5. (via) por; **exit ~ the door on the left** salgan por la puerta a la izquierda.
6. (with time) para; **be there ~ nine** estate allí para las nueve; **~ day/night** de día/noche; **~ now** ya.
7. (expressing quantity) por; **prices fell ~ 20%** los precios bajaron en un 20%; **we charge ~ the hour** cobramos por horas.
8. (expressing meaning) por; **what do you mean ~ that?** ¿qué quieres decir con eso?
9. (in division, multiplication) por; **two metres ~ five** dos metros por cinco.
10. (according to) según; **~ law** según la ley; **it's fine ~ me** por mí no hay problema.
11. (expressing gradual process): **one ~ one** uno a uno; **day ~ day** día a día.
12. (in phrases): **~ mistake** por equivocación; **~ oneself** (alone) solo; **he did it ~ himself** lo hizo él solo; **~ profession** de profesión.
♦ **adv** (past): **to go/drive ~** pasar.
bye(-bye) [ˌbaɪ(baɪ)] **excl** (inf) ¡hasta luego!
bypass [ˈbaɪpɑːs] **n** carretera **f** de circunvalación.

C

C (abbr of Celsius, centigrade) C.
cab [kæb] **n** (taxi) taxi **m**; (of lorry) cabina **f**.
cabaret [ˈkæbəreɪ] **n** cabaret **m**.
cabbage [ˈkæbɪdʒ] **n** col **f**.
cabin [ˈkæbɪn] **n** (on ship) camarote **m**; (of plane) cabina **f**; (wooden house) cabaña **f**.
cabin crew **n** personal **m** de cabina.
cabinet [ˈkæbɪnɪt] **n** (cupboard) armario **m**; (POL) consejo **m** de ministros.
cable [ˈkeɪbl] **n** cable **m**.
cable car **n** teleférico **m**.
cable television **n** televisión **f** por cable.
cactus [ˈkæktəs] (pl **-tuses** OR **-ti** [-taɪ]) **n** cactus **m** inv.
Caesar salad [ˌsiːzə-] **n** ensalada verde con anchoas, aceitunas, queso parmesano y croutons.
cafe [ˈkæfeɪ] **n** cafetería **f**.
cafeteria [ˌkæfɪˈtɪərɪə] **n** cantina **f**.
cafetière [kæfˈtjeɪ] **n** cafetera **f** de émbolo.
caffeine [ˈkæfiːn] **n** cafeína **f**.
cage [keɪdʒ] **n** jaula **f**.
cagoule [kəˈɡuːl] **n** (Br) chubasquero **m**.

Cajun [ˈkeɪdʒən] *adj* cajún.

---

i CAJUN

Originariamente colonos franceses en Nueva Escocia, la comunidad cajún fue deportada a Luisiana en el siglo XVIII. Allí desarrollaron una lengua y cultura propia cuya cocina, caracterizada por el uso de especias picantes, es hoy muy conocida, así como la música popular cajún que hace uso prominente del violín y acordeón.

cake [keɪk] *n* (*sweet*) pastel *m*; (*savoury*) medallón *m* empanado; (*of soap*) pastilla *f*.

calculate [ˈkælkjʊleɪt] *vt* calcular.

calculator [ˈkælkjʊleɪtər] *n* calculadora *f*.

calendar [ˈkælɪndər] *n* calendario *m*.

calf [kɑːf] (*pl* **calves**) *n* (*of cow*) ternero *m* (-ra *f*); (*part of leg*) pantorrilla *f*.

call [kɔːl] *n* (*visit*) visita *f*; (*phone call, at airport*) llamada *f*; (*of bird*) reclamo *m* ◆ *vt* llamar; (*meeting, elections, strike*) convocar; (*flight*) anunciar ◆ *vi* (*phone*) llamar; **to ~ at** (*visit*) pasarse (por); **to be ~ed** llamarse; **what is he ~ed?** ¿cómo se llama?; **could I have a ~ for eight o'clock?** por favor, llámeme a las ocho; **on ~** (*nurse, doctor*) de guardia; **she ~ed my name** me llamó; **to pay sb a ~** hacer una visita a alguien; **this train ~s at ...** este tren para en ...; **who's ~ing?** ¿de

parte de quién? ❑ **call back** *vt sep* llamar (más tarde) ◆ *vi* (*phone again*) llamar (más tarde); (*visit again*) volver a pasarse; **call for** *vt fus* (*come to fetch*) ir a buscar; (*demand*) pedir; (*require*) requerir; **call on** *vt fus* (*visit*) visitar; **to ~ on sb to do sthg** pedir a alguien que haga algo; **call out** *vt sep* (*name, winner*) anunciar; (*doctor, fire brigade*) llamar ◆ *vi* gritar; **call up** *vt sep* (MIL) llamar a filas a; (*telephone*) llamar (por teléfono).

call box *n* cabina *f* telefónica.

caller [ˈkɔːlər] *n* (*visitor*) visita *f*; (*on phone*) persona *f* que llama.

calm [kɑːm] *adj* (*person*) tranquilo(-la); (*sea*) en calma; (*weather, day*) apacible ◆ *vt* calmar ❑ **calm down** ◆ *vt* calmar ◆ *vi* calmarse.

Calor gas® [ˈkælə-] *n* butano *m*.

calorie [ˈkælərɪ] *n* caloría *f*.

calves [kɑːvz] *pl* → **calf**.

camcorder [ˈkæmˌkɔːdər] *n* cámara *f* de vídeo.

came [keɪm] *pt* → **come**.

camel [ˈkæml] *n* camello *m*.

camembert [ˈkæməmbeər] *n* camembert *m*.

camera [ˈkæmərə] *n* cámara *f*.

cameraman [ˈkæmərəmæn] (*pl* **-men** [-men]) *n* cámara *m*.

camera shop *n* tienda *f* de fotografía.

camisole [ˈkæmɪsəʊl] *n* picardías *m inv*.

camp [kæmp] *n* (*for holidaymakers*) colonia *f* de vacaciones para toda la familia, *um* parque de atracciones, *etc*; (*for soldiers*) campamento *m*; (*for prisoners*) campo *m* ◆ *vi* acampar.

campaign [kæm'peɪn] n campaña f ♦ vi: to ~ (for/against) hacer campaña (a favor de/contra).

camp bed n cama f de campaña.

camper ['kæmpər] n (person) campista mf; (van) caravana f.

camping ['kæmpɪŋ] n: to go ~ ir de camping.

camping stove n cocina f de camping.

campsite ['kæmpsaɪt] n camping m.

campus ['kæmpəs] (pl -es) n campus m inv.

can[1] [kæn] n (container) lata f.

can[2] [weak form kən, strong form kæn] (pt & conditional **could**) aux vb
1. (be able to) poder; ~ you help me? ¿puedes ayudarme?; I ~ see the sea veo el mar.
2. (know how to) saber; ~ you drive? ¿sabes conducir?; I ~ speak Spanish hablo español.
3. (be allowed to) poder; ~ I speak to the manager? ¿puedo hablar con el director?
4. (in polite requests) poder; ~ you tell me the time? ¿me puedes decir la hora?
5. (expressing occasional occurrence): it ~ get cold at night a veces hace frío por la noche.
6. (expressing possibility): I could do it podría hacerlo; they could be lost puede que se hayan perdido.

Canada ['kænədə] n Canadá m.

Canadian [kə'neɪdɪən] adj canadiense ♦ n canadiense mf.

canal [kə'næl] n canal m.

canapé ['kænəpeɪ] n canapé m.

Canaries [kə'neərɪz] npl: the ~ (las islas) Canarias.

Canary Islands [kə'neərɪ-] npl: the ~ (las islas) Canarias.

cancel ['kænsl] vt cancelar.

cancellation [ˌkænsə'leɪʃn] n cancelación f.

cancer ['kænsər] n cáncer m.

Cancer ['kænsər] n Cáncer m.

candidate ['kændɪdət] n (for parliament, job) candidato m (-ta f); (in exam) examinando m (-da f).

candle ['kændl] n vela f.

candlelit dinner ['kændlɪt-] n cena f a la luz de las velas.

candy ['kændɪ] n (Am) (confectionery) golosinas fpl; (sweet) caramelo m.

candyfloss ['kændɪflɒs] n (Br) algodón m (de azúcar).

cane [keɪn] n (for walking) bastón m; (for punishment) vara f; (for furniture, baskets) caña f.

canister ['kænɪstər] n (for tea) bote m; (for gas) bombona f.

cannabis ['kænəbɪs] n canabis m.

canned [kænd] adj (food, drink) en lata.

cannon ['kænən] n cañón m.

cannot ['kænɒt] = cannot.

canoe [kə'nu:] n (SPORT) piragua f.

canoeing [kə'nu:ɪŋ] n piragüismo m.

canopy ['kænəpɪ] n (over bed etc) dosel m.

can't [kɑ:nt] = cannot.

cantaloup(e) ['kæntəlu:p] n cantalupo m.

canteen [kæn'ti:n] n cantina f.

canvas

canvas ['kænvəs] n (for tent, bag) lona f.

cap [kæp] n (hat) gorra f; (without peak) gorro m; (of pen) capuchón m; (of bottle) tapón m; (contraceptive) diafragma m.

capable ['keɪpəbl] adj (competent) competente, hábil; **to be ~** doing sthg ser capaz de hacer algo.

capacity [kə'pæsɪtɪ] n (ability) habilidad f, facultad f; (of stadium, theatre) capacidad f.

cape [keɪp] n (of land) cabo m; (cloak) capa f.

capers ['keɪpəz] npl alcaparras fpl.

capital ['kæpɪtl] n (of country) capital f; (money) capital m; (letter) mayúscula f.

capital punishment n pena f capital.

cappuccino [kæpʊ'tʃiːnəʊ] n capuchino m.

capsicum ['kæpsɪkəm] n pimiento m.

capsize [kæp'saɪz] vi volcar.

capsule ['kæpsjuːl] n cápsula f.

captain ['kæptɪn] n capitán m (-ana f).

caption ['kæpʃn] n pie m, leyenda f.

capture ['kæptʃəˈ] vt (person, animal) capturar; (town, castle) tomar.

car [kɑːˈ] n (motorcar) coche m, carro m (Amér); (railway wagon) vagón m.

carafe [kə'ræf] n vasija sin mango para servir vino y agua.

caramel ['kærəmel] n (sweet) tofe m; (burnt sugar) azúcar m quemado.

carat ['kærət] n quilate m; **24-~**

gold oro de 24 quilates.

caravan ['kærəvæn] n (Br) caravana f.

caravanning ['kærəvænɪŋ] n (Br): **to go ~** ir de vacaciones en caravana.

caravan site n (Br) camping m para caravanas.

carbohydrate [kɑːbəʊ'haɪdreɪt] n (in foods) fécula f.

carbon ['kɑːbən] n carbono m.

carbon copy n copia f en papel carbón.

carbon dioxide [-daɪ'ɒksaɪd] n dióxido m de carbono.

carbon monoxide [-mɒ'nɒksaɪd] n monóxido m de carbono.

car boot sale n (Br) mercadillo de objetos usados exhibidos en el maletero del coche.

carburetor [kɑːbə'retəˈ] (Am) = **carburettor**

carburettor [kɑːbə'retəˈ] n (Br) carburador m.

car crash n accidente m de tráfico.

card [kɑːd] n tarjeta f; (postcard) postal f; (playing card) carta f, naipe m; (cardboard) cartulina f; **~s** (game) las cartas.

cardboard ['kɑːdbɔːd] n cartón m.

car deck n cubierta f para coches.

cardiac arrest [kɑːdɪæk-] n paro m cardíaco.

cardigan ['kɑːdɪgən] n cárdigan m.

care [keəˈ] n (attention) cuidado m ♦ vi (mind): **I don't ~** no me importa; **to take ~ of** (look after) cuidar de; (deal with) encargarse de; **would you ~ to ...?** (fml) ¿le importaría ...?; **to take ~ to do sthg** tener cuidado de hacer algo; **take ~!** (goodbye) ¡cuídate!; **with ~** con cuidado; **"handle with ~"** "frágil"; **to ~ about** (think important) preocuparse por; (person) tener aprecio a.

career [kə'rɪəʳ] n carrera f.

carefree ['keəfri:] adj despreocupado(-da).

careful ['keəful] adj (cautious) cuidadoso(-sa); (driver) prudente; (thorough) esmerado(-da); **be ~!** ¡ten cuidado!

carefully ['keəflɪ] adv (cautiously) cuidadosamente; (drive) con prudencia; (thoroughly) detenidamente, con atención.

careless ['keələs] adj (inattentive) descuidado(-da); (unconcerned) despreocupado(-da).

caretaker ['keə,teɪkəʳ] n (Br: of school, flats) conserje mf.

car ferry n transbordador m de coches.

cargo ['kɑ:gəʊ] (pl -es OR -s) n cargamento m.

car hire n (Br) alquiler m de coches.

Caribbean [Br ,kærɪ'bi:ən, Am kə'rɪbɪən] n: **the ~** el Caribe.

caring ['keərɪŋ] adj solícito(-ta).

carnation [kɑ:'neɪʃn] n clavel m.

carnival ['kɑ:nɪvl] n carnaval m.

carousel [,kærə'sel] n (for luggage) cinta f transportadora; (Am: merry-go-round) tiovivo m.

carp [kɑ:p] n carpa f.

car park n (Br) aparcamiento m.

carpenter ['kɑ:pəntəʳ] n carpintero m (-ra f).

carpentry ['kɑ:pəntrɪ] n carpintería f.

carpet ['kɑ:pɪt] n (not fitted) alfombra f; (fitted) moqueta f.

car rental n (Am) alquiler m de coches.

carriage ['kærɪdʒ] n (Br: of train) vagón m; (horse-drawn) carruaje m.

carriageway ['kærɪdʒweɪ] n (Br) carril m.

carrier (bag) ['kærɪəʳ-] n bolsa f (de papel o plástico).

carrot ['kærət] n zanahoria f.

carrot cake n pastel de bizcocho hecho con zanahoria rallada y cubierto con azúcar glaseado.

carry ['kærɪ] vt llevar; (disease) transmitir ♦ vi (voice, sound) oírse a lo lejos □ **carry on** vi continuar ♦ vt fus (continue) continuar; (conduct) realizar; **to ~ on doing sthg** seguir haciendo algo; **carry out** vt sep (perform) llevar a cabo; (fulfil) cumplir.

carrycot ['kærɪkɒt] n (Br) moisés m inv.

carryout ['kærɪaʊt] n (Am & Scot) comida f para llevar.

carsick ['kɑ:,sɪk] adj mareado(-da) (en coche).

cart [kɑ:t] n (for transport) carro m; (inf: video game cartridge) cartucho m; (Am: in supermarket) carrito m.

carton ['kɑ:tn] n cartón m, envase m.

cartoon [kɑ:'tu:n] n (drawing) chiste m (en viñeta); (film) película f de dibujos animados.

cartridge ['kɑːtrɪdʒ] n (for gun) cartucho m; (for pen) recambio m.

carve [kɑːv] vt (wood, stone) tallar; (meat) trinchar.

carvery ['kɑːvərɪ] n restaurante donde se sirve un bufé de carne que se trincha delante del cliente.

car wash n lavado m de coches.

case [keɪs] n (for suitcase) maleta f; (container) estuche m; (instance, patient) caso m; (JUR: trial) pleito m; **in any ~** de todas formas; **in ~ of** en caso de; **(just) in ~** por si acaso; **in that ~** en ese caso.

cash [kæʃ] n (coins, notes) efectivo m; (money in general) dinero m ♦ vt: **to ~ a cheque** cobrar un cheque; **to pay ~** pagar en efectivo.

cash desk n caja f.

cash dispenser n cajero m automático.

cashew (nut) ['kæʃuː-] n anacardo m.

cashier [kæ'ʃɪər] n cajero m (-ra f).

cashmere [kæʃ'mɪər] n cachemir m.

cashpoint ['kæʃpɔɪnt] n (Br) cajero m automático.

cash register n caja f (registradora).

casino [kə'siːnəʊ] (pl -s) n casino m.

cask [kɑːsk] n tonel m.

cask-conditioned [-kən-'dɪʃnd] adj fermentado en tonel.

casserole ['kæsərəʊl] n (stew) guiso m; **~ (dish)** cacerola f.

cassette [kə'set] n casete m, cinta f.

cassette recorder n casete m.

cast [kɑːst] (pt & pp cast) n (actors) reparto m; (for broken bone) escayola f ♦ vt (shadow, light) proyectar; (look) echar; (vote) emitir; **to ~ doubt on** poner en duda ❑ **cast off** vi (boat, ship) soltar amarras.

caster [kɑːstər] n ruedecilla f.

caster sugar n (Br) azúcar m extrafino.

Castile [kæs'tiːl] n Castilla.

castle [kɑːsl] n (building) castillo m; (in chess) torre f.

casual ['kæʒʊəl] adj (relaxed) despreocupado(-da); (offhand) superficial; (clothes) informal; **~ work** trabajo eventual.

casualty ['kæʒʊəltɪ] n víctima f; **~ (ward)** urgencias fpl.

cat [kæt] n gato m.

Catalan ['kætəlæn] adj catalán(-ana) ♦ n (person) catalán m (-ana f); (language) catalán m.

catalog ['kætəlɒg] (Am) = catalogue.

catalogue ['kætəlɒg] n catálogo m.

Catalonia [,kætə'ləʊnɪə] n Cataluña.

Catalonian [,kætə'ləʊnɪən] adj catalán(-ana).

catapult ['kætəpʌlt] n tirachinas m inv.

cataract ['kætərækt] n (in eye) catarata f.

catarrh [kə'tɑːr] n catarro m.

catastrophe [kə'tæstrəfi] n catástrofe f.

catch [kætʃ] (pt & pp caught) vt

coger, agarrar (*Amér*); (*fish*) pescar; (*bus, train, plane, taxi*) coger, tomar (*Amér*); (*hear*) coger, escuchar (*Amér*); (*attract*) despertar ♦ *vi* (*become hooked*) engancharse ♦ *n* (*of window, door*) pestillo *m*; (*snag*) pega *f* ◻ **catch up** *vt sep* alcanzar ♦ *vi*: **to ~ up (with)** ponerse a la misma altura (que).

catching ['kætʃɪŋ] *adj* (*inf*) contagioso(-sa).

category ['kætəgərɪ] *n* categoría *f*.

cater ['keɪtə']: **cater for** *vt fus* (*Br*) (*needs, tastes*) atender a, satisfacer; (*anticipate*) prever.

caterpillar ['kætəpɪlə'] *n* oruga *f*.

cathedral [kə'θi:drəl] *n* catedral *f*.

Catholic ['kæθlɪk] *adj* católico(-ca) ♦ *n* católico *m* (-ca *f*).

Catseyes® ['kætsaɪz] *npl* (*Br*) catafaros *mpl*.

cattle ['kætl] *npl* ganado *m* (vacuno).

caught [kɔ:t] *pt & pp* → **catch**.

cauliflower ['kɒlɪˌflaʊə'] *n* coliflor *f*.

cauliflower cheese *n* coliflor en salsa bechamel con queso.

cause [kɔ:z] *n* causa *f*; (*justification*) motivo *m* ♦ *vt* causar; **to ~ sb to do sthg** hacer que alguien haga algo.

causeway ['kɔ:zweɪ] *n* carretera *f* elevada.

caustic soda [ˌkɔ:stɪk-] *n* sosa *f* cáustica.

caution ['kɔ:ʃn] *n* (*care*) cautela *f*; (*warning*) amonestación *f*.

cautious ['kɔ:ʃəs] *adj* cauteloso(-sa).

cave [keɪv] *n* cueva *f* ◻ **cave in** *vi* hundirse, derrumbarse.

caviar(e) ['kævɪɑ:'] *n* caviar *m*.

cavity ['kævətɪ] *n* (*in tooth*) caries *f inv*.

CD *n* (*abbr of* compact disc) CD *m*.

CDI *n* (*abbr of* compact disc interactive) CDI *m*.

CD player *n* reproductor *m* de CD.

CDW *n* (*abbr of* collision damage waiver) franquicia *f*.

cease [si:s] *vt* (*fml*) suspender ♦ *vi* (*fml*) cesar.

ceasefire ['si:s,faɪə'] *n* alto *m* el fuego.

ceilidh ['keɪlɪ] *n* baile popular en Escocia e Irlanda.

---

i CEILIDH

E l "ceilidh" es un espectáculo tradicional escocés o irlandés de carácter informal que consiste en bailes y música popular. Tradicionalmente, un "ceilidh" era una pequeña reunión de amigos y familiares, pero hoy en día son normalmente grandes bailes públicos.

---

ceiling ['si:lɪŋ] *n* techo *m*.

celebrate ['selɪbreɪt] *vt* celebrar ♦ *vi*: **let's ~!** ¡hay que celebrarlo!

celebration [ˌselɪ'breɪʃn] *n* (*event*) festejo *m* ◻ **celebrations** *npl* (*festivities*) conmemoraciones *fpl*.

celebrity [sɪ'lebrətɪ] *n* (*person*)

celebridad f.

celeriac [sɪ'lerɪæk] n apio m nabo.

celery ['seləri] n apio m.

cell [sel] n (of plant, body) célula f; (in prison) celda f.

cellar ['selər] n sótano m.

cello ['tʃeləu] n violoncelo m.

Cellophane® ['seləfeɪn] n celofán® m.

Celsius ['selsɪəs] adj centígrado(-da).

cement [sɪ'ment] n cemento m.

cement mixer n hormigonera f.

cemetery ['semɪtrɪ] n cementerio m.

cent [sent] n (Am) centavo m.

center ['sentər] (Am) = centre.

centigrade ['sentɪgreɪd] adj centígrado(-da); **five degrees ~** cinco grados (centígrados).

centimetre ['sentɪ,miːtər] n centímetro m.

centipede ['sentɪpiːd] n ciempiés m inv.

central ['sentrəl] adj (in the middle) central; (near town centre) céntrico(-ca).

central heating n calefacción f central.

central locking [-'lɒkɪŋ] n cierre m centralizado.

central reservation n (Br) mediana f.

centre ['sentər] n (Br) centro m ◆ adj (Br) central; **the ~ of attention** el centro de atención.

century ['sentʃʊrɪ] n siglo m.

ceramic [sɪ'ræmɪk] adj de cerámica ❑ **ceramics** npl piezas fpl de cerámica.

cereal ['sɪərɪəl] n (breakfast food) cereales mpl.

ceremony ['serɪmənɪ] n ceremonia f.

certain ['sɜːtn] adj (sure) seguro(-ra); (particular) cierto(-ta); **she's ~ to be late** seguro que llega tarde; **to be ~ of sthg** estar seguro de algo; **to make ~ (that)** asegurarse de que.

certainly ['sɜːtnlɪ] adv desde luego.

certificate [sə'tɪfɪkət] n (of studies, medical) certificado m; (of birth) partida f.

certify ['sɜːtɪfaɪ] vt (declare true) certificar.

chain [tʃeɪn] n cadena f ◆ vt: **to ~ sthg to sthg** encadenar algo a algo.

chain store n grandes almacenes mpl.

chair [tʃeər] n silla f.

chair lift n telesilla m.

chairman ['tʃeəmən] (pl **-men** [-mən]) n presidente m.

chairperson ['tʃeə,pɜːsn] n presidente m (-ta f).

chairwoman ['tʃeə,wumən] (pl **-women** [-,wɪmɪn]) n presidenta f.

chalet ['tʃæleɪ] n chalé m.

chalk [tʃɔːk] n (for writing) tiza f; (substance) creta f; **a piece of ~** una tiza.

chalkboard ['tʃɔːkbɔːd] n (Am) pizarra f.

challenge ['tʃælɪndʒ] n desafío m ◆ vt (question) poner en tela de juicio; **to ~ sb (to sthg)** desafiar a alguien (a algo).

chamber ['tʃeɪmbər] n (room)

cámara f.

chambermaid [ˈtʃeɪmbəmeɪd] n
camarera f.

champagne [ˌʃæmˈpeɪn] n
champán m.

champion [ˈtʃæmpjən] n (of competition) campeón m (-ona f).

championship [ˈtʃæmpjənʃɪp] n
campeonato m.

chance [tʃɑːns] n (luck) azar m;
(possibility) posibilidad f; (opportunity) oportunidad f ◆ vt: to ~ it
(inf) arriesgarse; **to take a ~** correr
un riesgo; **by ~** por casualidad; **on
the off ~** por si acaso.

Chancellor of the Exchequer [ˌtʃɑːnsələrəvðəɪksˈtʃekər]
n ministro de economía y hacienda en
Gran Bretaña.

chandelier [ˌʃændəˈlɪər] n lámpara f de araña.

change [tʃeɪndʒ] n cambio m;
(coins) suelto m ◆ vt cambiar; (job)
cambiar ◆ vi (become different)
cambiar; (on bus, train) hacer transbordo; (change clothes) cambiarse; **a
~ of clothes** una muda; **do you
have ~ for a pound?** ¿tienes cambio
de una libra?; **for a ~** para variar; **to
get ~d** cambiarse; **to ~ money**
cambiar dinero; **to ~ a nappy** cambiar un pañal; **to ~ a wheel** cambiar
una rueda; **to ~ trains/planes**
cambiar de tren/avión; **all ~!** (on
train) ¡cambio de tren!

changeable [ˈtʃeɪndʒəbl] adj
(weather) variable.

change machine n máquina f
de cambio.

changing room [ˈtʃeɪndʒɪŋ-] n
(for sport) vestuario m; (in shop)
probador m.

channel [ˈtʃænl] n canal m; **the
(English) Channel** el Canal de la
Mancha.

Channel Islands npl: **the ~** las
islas del Canal de la Mancha.

Channel Tunnel n: **the ~** el
túnel del Canal de la Mancha.

---

i CHANNEL TUNNEL

La conexión férrea entre Cheriton
(cerca de Folkestone) y Coquelles (cerca de Calais) a través del
Eurotúnel se abrió en 1994. Un tren
de carga, Le Shuttle, transporta los
vehículos y frecuentes trenes con
pasajeros conectan Londres con
otras ciudades europeas.

---

chant [tʃɑːnt] vt (RELIG) cantar;
(words, slogan) corear.

chaos [ˈkeɪɒs] n caos m inv.

chaotic [keɪˈɒtɪk] adj caótico(-ca).

chap [tʃæp] n (Br: inf) chico m,
tío m.

chapatti [tʃəˈpætɪ] n tipo de pan
ázimo de origen indio.

chapel [ˈtʃæpl] n capilla f.

chapped [tʃæpt] adj agrietado(-da).

chapter [ˈtʃæptər] n capítulo m.

character [ˈkærəktər] n carácter
m; (in film, book, play) personaje m;
(inf: person, individual) tipo m.

characteristic [ˌkærəktəˈrɪstɪk]
adj característico(-ca) ◆ n característica f.

charcoal [ˈtʃɑːkəʊl] n (for barbecue) carbón m (vegetal).

charge [tʃɑːdʒ] n (price) tarifa f;
(JUR) cargo m ♦ vt (money, customer)
cobrar; (JUR) acusar; (battery) cargar
♦ vi (ask money) cobrar; she ~d in
entró en tromba; to be in ~ (of)
ser el encargado (de); to take ~
(of) hacerse cargo (de); extra ~
suplemento m; free of ~ gratis;
there is no ~ for service el servicio
está incluido.

char-grilled [tʃɑːgrɪld] adj
asado(-da) a la parrilla.

charity [tʃærɪtɪ] n (organization)
entidad f benéfica; to give to ~
hacer donaciones a entidades
benéficas.

charity shop n tienda de objetos
usados cuyas ventas se destinan a entidades benéficas.

charm [tʃɑːm] n (attractiveness)
encanto m ♦ vt encantar, hechizar.

charming [tʃɑːmɪn] adj encan-
tador(-ra).

chart [tʃɑːt] n (diagram) gráfico
m; the ~s la lista de éxitos.

chartered accountant
[tʃɑːtəd-] n contable m colegiado
(contable f colegiada).

charter flight [tʃɑːtə-] n vuelo
m chárter.

chase [tʃeɪs] n persecución f ♦ vt
perseguir.

chat [tʃæt] n charla f ♦ vi charlar;
to have a ~ (with) charlar (con) ❑
chat up vt sep (Br: inf) ligarse.

chat show n (Br) programa m
de entrevistas.

chatty [tʃætɪ] adj (letter) informal; (person) dicharrachero(-ra).

chauffeur [ʃəʊfə] n chófer mf.

cheap [tʃiːp] adj (inexpensive)
barato(-ta); (pej: low-quality) de

mala calidad.

cheap day return n (Br) billete de ida y vuelta más barato que se ha
de utilizar en el mismo día y después
de las 9.15.

cheaply [tʃiːplɪ] adv barato.

cheat [tʃiːt] n tramposo m (-sa f)
♦ vi hacer trampa ♦ vt: to ~ sb
(out of sthg) estafar (algo) a
alguien.

check [tʃek] n (inspection) inspección f; (Am: bill) cuenta f; (Am: tick)
señal f de visto bueno; (Am) =
cheque ♦ vt (inspect) revisar; (verify) comprobar ♦ vi: to ~ for sthg
comprobar algo; to ~ on sthg
comprobar algo; to ~ with sb consultar con alguien ❑ check in vt
sep (luggage) facturar ♦ vi (at hotel)
inscribirse; (at airport) facturar;
check off vt sep ir comprobando
(en una lista); check out vi dejar el
hotel; check up vi: to ~ up (on)
informarse (acerca de).

checked [tʃekt] adj a cuadros.

checkers [tʃekəz] n (Am) damas
fpl.

check-in desk n mostrador m
de facturación.

checkout [tʃekaʊt] n caja f.

checkpoint [tʃekpɔɪnt] n control m.

checkroom [tʃekrʊm] n (Am)
consigna f.

checkup [tʃekʌp] n chequeo m.

cheddar (cheese) [tʃedə-] n
cheddar m.

cheek [tʃiːk] n mejilla f; what a
~! ¡qué cara!

cheeky [tʃiːkɪ] adj descara-
do(-da).

cheer [tʃɪəʳ] n aclamación f ♦ vi gritar con entusiasmo.

cheerful ['tʃɪəful] adj alegre.

cheerio [,tʃɪərɪ'əʊ] excl (Br: inf) ¡hasta luego!

cheers [tʃɪəz] excl (when drinking) ¡salud!; (Br: inf: thank you) ¡gracias!

cheese [tʃi:z] n queso m.

cheeseboard ['tʃi:zbɔ:d] n (cheese and biscuits) tabla f de quesos.

cheeseburger ['tʃi:z,bɜ:gəʳ] n hamburguesa f de queso.

cheesecake ['tʃi:zkeɪk] n tarta f de queso (fresco, sin hornear).

chef [ʃef] n jefe m de cocina.

chef's special n especialidad f de la casa.

chemical ['kemɪkl] adj químico(-ca) ♦ n sustancia f química.

chemist ['kemɪst] n (Br: pharmacist) farmacéutico m (-ca f); (scientist) químico m (-ca f); ~'s (Br: shop) farmacia f.

chemistry ['kemɪstrɪ] n química f.

cheque [tʃek] n (Br) cheque m; to pay by ~ pagar con cheque.

chequebook ['tʃekbʊk] n talonario m de cheques.

cheque card n tarjeta f de identificación bancaria.

cherry ['tʃerɪ] n cereza f.

chess [tʃes] n ajedrez m.

chest [tʃest] n (of body) pecho m; (box) arca f.

chestnut ['tʃesnʌt] n castaña f ♦ adj (colour) castaño(-ña).

chest of drawers n cómoda f.

chew [tʃu:] vt masticar ♦ n (sweet)

gominola f.

chewing gum ['tʃu:ɪŋ-] n chicle m.

chic [ʃi:k] adj elegante.

chicken ['tʃɪkɪn] n (bird) gallina f; (meat) pollo m.

chicken breast n pechuga f de pollo.

chicken Kiev [-'ki:ev] n filete de pollo relleno con mantequilla, ajo y especias y rebozado con pan rallado.

chickenpox ['tʃɪkɪnpɒks] n varicela f.

chickpea ['tʃɪkpi:] n garbanzo m.

chicory ['tʃɪkərɪ] n achicoria f.

chief [tʃi:f] adj (highest-ranking) jefe(-fa); (main) principal ♦ n jefe m (-fa f).

chiefly ['tʃi:flɪ] adv (mainly) principalmente; (especially) por encima de todo.

child [tʃaɪld] (pl children) n (young boy, girl) niño m (-ña f); (son, daughter) hijo m (-ja f).

child abuse n maltrato m de niños.

child benefit n subsidio pagado a todas las familias británicas por cada hijo.

childhood ['tʃaɪldhʊd] n infancia f.

childish ['tʃaɪldɪʃ] adj (pej: immature) infantil.

childminder ['tʃaɪld,maɪndəʳ] n (Br) niñera f (durante el día).

children ['tʃɪldrən] pl → child.

childrenswear ['tʃɪldrənzweəʳ] n ropa f de niños.

child seat n asiento m de seguridad para niños.

Chile ['tʃɪlɪ] n Chile.

Chilean ['tʃɪlɪən] adj chileno(-na) ◆ n chileno m (-na f).

chill [tʃɪl] n (illness) resfriado m ◆ vt enfriar; **there's a ~ in the air** hace un poco de fresco.

chilled [tʃɪld] adj frío(-a); "**serve ~**" "sírvase muy frío".

chilli ['tʃɪlɪ] (pl -ies) n (vegetable) guindilla f; (dish) chilli con carne.

chilli con carne [-kɒn'kɑːnɪ] n picadillo de carne en una salsa picante de guindilla con cebolla, tomate y judías pintas.

chilly ['tʃɪlɪ] adj frío(-a).

chimney ['tʃɪmnɪ] n chimenea f.

chimneypot ['tʃɪmnɪpɒt] n cañón m de chimenea.

chimpanzee [,tʃɪmpən'ziː] n chimpancé mf.

chin [tʃɪn] n barbilla f.

china ['tʃaɪnə] n (material) porcelana f.

China ['tʃaɪnə] n la China.

Chinese [,tʃaɪ'niːz] adj chino(-na) ◆ n (language) chino m ◆ npl: **the ~** los chinos; **a ~ restaurant** un restaurante chino.

chip [tʃɪp] n (small piece) pedacito m; (mark) mella f; (counter) ficha f; (COMPUT) chip m ◆ vt desportillar.

chips npl (Br: French fries) patatas fpl fritas (de sartén) ; (Am: crisps) patatas fpl fritas (de bolsa).

chiropodist [kɪ'rɒpədɪst] n podólogo m (-ga f).

chisel ['tʃɪzl] n formón m.

chives [tʃaɪvz] npl cebollino m.

chlorine ['klɔːriːn] n cloro m.

choc-ice ['tʃɒkaɪs] n (Br) tipo de

bombón helado en forma de bloque y sin palo.

chocolate ['tʃɒkələt] n (food, drink) chocolate m; (sweet) bombón m ◆ adj de chocolate.

chocolate biscuit n galleta f de chocolate.

choice [tʃɔɪs] n (option) elección f; (person or thing chosen) opción f; (variety) variedad f ◆ adj de primera calidad; "**pizzas with the topping of your ~**" "elija los ingredientes de su pizza".

choir ['kwaɪər] n coro m.

choke [tʃəʊk] n (AUT) estárter m ◆ vt asfixiar ◆ vi (on fishbone etc) atragantarse; (to death) asfixiarse.

cholera ['kɒlərə] n cólera m.

choose [tʃuːz] (pt chose, pp chosen) vt & vi elegir; **to ~ to do sthg** decidir hacer algo.

chop [tʃɒp] n (of meat) chuleta f ◆ vt cortar ❑ **chop down** vt sep talar; **chop up** vt sep picar.

chopper ['tʃɒpər] n (inf: helicopter) helicóptero m.

chopping board ['tʃɒpɪŋ-] n tabla f de cocina.

choppy ['tʃɒpɪ] adj picado(-da).

chopsticks ['tʃɒpstɪks] npl palillos mpl (chinos).

chop suey [,tʃɒp'suːɪ] n plato chino de brotes de soja, verdura, arroz y carne de cerdo o pollo con salsa de soja.

chord [kɔːd] n acorde m.

chore [tʃɔːr] n tarea f.

chorus ['kɔːrəs] n (part of song) estribillo m; (group of singers, dancers) coro m.

chose [tʃəʊz] pt → **choose.**

chosen ['tʃəuzn] pp → choose.

choux pastry [ʃuː] n pasta d f brisa.

chowder ['tʃaudə'] n sopa espesa de pescado.

chow mein [,tʃau'meɪn] n chow mein m.

Christ [kraɪst] n Cristo m.

christen ['krɪsn] vt (baby) bautizar.

Christian ['krɪstʃən] adj cristiano(-na) ♦ n cristiano m (-na f).

Christian name n nombre m de pila.

Christmas ['krɪsməs] n (day) Navidad f; (period) Navidades fpl; Happy ~! ¡Felices Navidades!

Christmas card n tarjeta f de Navidad.

Christmas carol [-'kærəl] n villancico m.

Christmas Day n día m de Navidad.

Christmas Eve n Nochebuena f.

Christmas pudding n pudín de frutas que se come caliente el día de Navidad.

Christmas tree n árbol m de Navidad.

chrome [krəum] n cromo m.

chuck [tʃʌk] vt (inf) (throw) tirar; (boyfriend, girlfriend) mandar a paseo, dejar ❏ **chuck away** vt sep tirar.

chunk [tʃʌŋk] n trozo m.

church [tʃɜːtʃ] n iglesia f; **to go to ~** ir a misa.

churchyard ['tʃɜːtʃjɑːd] n cementerio m.

chute [ʃuːt] n vertedor m.

chutney ['tʃʌtnɪ] n salsa agridulce y picante de fruta y semillas.

cider ['saɪdə'] n sidra f.

cigar [sɪ'gɑː'] n puro m.

cigarette [,sɪgə'ret] n cigarrillo m.

cigarette lighter n mechero m.

cinema ['sɪnəmə] n cine m.

cinnamon ['sɪnəmən] n canela f.

circle ['sɜːkl] n círculo m; (in theatre) anfiteatro m ♦ vt (draw circle around) rodear con un círculo; (move round) dar vueltas alrededor de ♦ vi dar vueltas.

circuit ['sɜːkɪt] n (track) circuito m; (lap) vuelta f.

circular ['sɜːkjulə'] adj circular ♦ n circular f.

circulation [,sɜːkju'leɪʃn] n (of blood) circulación f; (of newspaper, magazine) tirada f.

circumstances ['sɜːkəmstənsɪz] npl circunstancias fpl; **in** OR **under the ~** dadas las circunstancias.

circus ['sɜːkəs] n circo m.

cistern ['sɪstən] n (of toilet) cisterna f.

citizen ['sɪtɪzn] n (of country) ciudadano m (-na f); (of town) habitante mf.

city ['sɪtɪ] n ciudad f; **the City** la City.

city centre n centro m de la ciudad.

city hall n (Am) ayuntamiento m.

civilian [sɪ'vɪljən] n civil mf.

civilized ['sɪvɪlaɪzd] adj (society) civilizado(-da); (person, evening) agradable.

civil rights [ˌsɪvl-] *npl* derechos *mpl* civiles.

civil servant [ˌsɪvl-] *n* funcionario *m* (-ria *f*).

civil service [ˌsɪvl-] *n* administración *f* pública.

civil war [ˌsɪvl-] *n* guerra *f* civil.

cl (*abbr of centilitre*) cl.

claim [kleɪm] *n* (*assertion*) afirmación *f*, declaración *f*; (*demand*) demanda *f*, reivindicación *f*; (*for insurance*) reclamación *f* ♦ *vt* (*allege*) afirmar; (*demand*) reclamar; (*credit, responsibility*) reivindicar ♦ *vi* (*on insurance*) reclamar.

claimant [ˈkleɪmənt] *n* (*of benefit*) solicitante *mf*.

claim form *n* impreso *m* de solicitud.

clam [klæm] *n* almeja *f*.

clamp [klæmp] *n* (*for car*) cepo *m* ♦ *vt* (*car*) poner un cepo a.

clap [klæp] *vi* aplaudir.

claret [ˈklærət] *n* burdeos *m inv*.

clarinet [ˌklærəˈnet] *n* clarinete *m*.

clash [klæʃ] *n* (*noise*) estruendo *m*; (*confrontation*) enfrentamiento *m* ♦ *vi* (*colours*) desentonar; (*event, date*) coincidir.

clasp [klɑːsp] *n* cierre *m* ♦ *vt* agarrar.

class [klɑːs] *n* clase *f* ♦ *vt*: to ~ sthg/sb (as) clasificar algo/a alguien (de).

classic [ˈklæsɪk] *adj* (*typical*) clásico(-ca) ♦ *n* clásico *m*.

classical [ˈklæsɪkl] *adj* clásico(-ca).

classical music *n* música *f* clásica.

classification [ˌklæsɪfɪˈkeɪʃn] *n* clasificación *f*.

classified ads [ˌklæsɪfaɪd-] *npl* anuncios *mpl* por palabras.

classroom [ˈklɑːsrʊm] *n* aula *f*.

claustrophobic [ˌklɔːstrəˈfəʊbɪk] *adj* claustrofóbico(-ca).

claw [klɔː] *n* (*of bird, cat, dog*) garra *f*; (*of crab, lobster*) pinza *f*.

clay [kleɪ] *n* arcilla *f*.

clean [kliːn] *adj* limpio(-pia); (*page*) en blanco; (*driving licence*) sin sanciones ♦ *vt* limpiar; to ~ one's teeth lavarse los dientes.

cleaner [ˈkliːnər] *n* (*person*) hombre *m* de la limpieza (mujer *f* de la limpieza); (*substance*) producto *m* de limpieza.

cleanse [klenz] *vt* limpiar.

cleanser [ˈklenzər] *n* tónico *m*.

clear [klɪər] *adj* claro(-ra); (*road, view, sky*) despejado(-da) ♦ *vt* (*remove obstructions from*) limpiar, despejar; (*jump over*) saltar; (*declare not guilty*) declarar inocente; (*authorize*) aprobar; (*cheque*) conformar ♦ *vi* (*weather, fog*) despejarse; to be ~ (*about sthg*) entender (algo); to be ~ of sthg (*not touching*) no estar en contacto con algo; to ~ one's throat carraspear; to ~ the table quitar la mesa ☐ **clear up** *vt sep* (*room, toys*) ordenar; (*problem, confusion*) aclarar ♦ *vi* (*weather*) despejarse; (*tidy up*) recoger.

clearance [ˈklɪərəns] *n* (*authorization*) permiso *m*; (*free distance*) distancia *f* de seguridad; (*for take-off*) autorización *f* (para despegar).

clearing [ˈklɪərɪŋ] *n* claro *m*.

clearly [ˈklɪəlɪ] *adv* claramente;

(obviously) obviamente.

clearway [ˈklɪəweɪ] n *(Br)* carretera donde no se puede parar.

clementine [ˈkleməntaɪn] n clementina f.

clerk [Br klɑːk, Am klɜːrk] n *(in office)* oficinista mf; *(Am: in shop)* dependiente m (-ta f).

clever [ˈklevər] adj *(person)* listo(-ta); *(idea, device)* ingenioso(-sa).

click [klɪk] n chasquido m ◆ vi *(make sound)* hacer clic.

client [ˈklaɪənt] n cliente m (-ta f).

cliff [klɪf] n acantilado m.

climate [ˈklaɪmət] n clima m.

climax [ˈklaɪmæks] n clímax m inv.

climb [klaɪm] vt *(tree)* trepar a; *(ladder)* subir; *(mountain)* escalar ◆ vi *(person)* ascender; *(plane)* subir ❑ **climb down** vt fus *(tree, mountain)* descender de; *(ladder)* bajar ◆ vi bajar; **climb up** vt fus *(tree)* trepar a; *(ladder)* subir; *(mountain)* escalar.

climber [ˈklaɪmər] n *(person)* escalador m (-ra f).

climbing [ˈklaɪmɪŋ] n montañismo m; **to go ~** ir de montañismo.

climbing frame n *(Br)* barras de metal para trepar los niños.

clingfilm [ˈklɪŋfɪlm] n *(Br)* film m de plástico adherente.

clinic [ˈklɪnɪk] n clínica f.

clip [klɪp] n *(fastener)* clip m; *(of film, programme)* fragmento m ◆ vt *(fasten)* sujetar; *(cut)* recortar; *(ticket)* picar.

cloak [kləʊk] n capa f.

cloakroom [ˈkləʊkrʊm] n *(for coats)* guardarropa m; *(Br: toilet)* servicios mpl.

clock [klɒk] n *(for telling time)* reloj m; *(mileometer)* cuentakilómetros m inv; **round the ~** día y noche.

clockwise [ˈklɒkwaɪz] adv en el sentido de las agujas del reloj.

clog [klɒg] n zueco m ◆ vt obstruir.

close¹ [kləʊs] adj *(near)* cercano(-na); *(friend)* íntimo(-ma); *(relation, family)* cercano(-na); *(contact, cooperation, link)* estrecho(-cha); *(resemblance)* grande; *(examination)* detallado(-da); *(race, contest)* reñido(-da) ◆ adv cerca; **~ by** *(near)* cerca de; **~ to** *(near)* cerca de; **~ to tears** a punto de llorar.

close² [kləʊz] vt cerrar ◆ vi *(door, jar, eyes)* cerrarse; *(shop, office)* cerrar; *(deadline, offer, meeting)* terminar ❑ **close down** vt sep & vi cerrar (definitivamente).

closed [kləʊzd] adj cerrado(-da).

closely [ˈkləʊsli] adv *(related, involved)* estrechamente; *(follow, examine)* atentamente.

closet [ˈklɒzɪt] n *(Am: cupboard)* armario m.

close-up [ˈkləʊs-] n primer plano m.

closing time [ˈkləʊzɪŋ-] n hora f de cierre.

clot [klɒt] n *(of blood)* coágulo m.

cloth [klɒθ] n *(fabric)* tela f; *(piece of cloth)* trapo m.

clothes [kləʊðz] npl ropa f.

clothesline [ˈkləʊðzlaɪn] n cuerda f para tender la ropa.

clothes peg n *(Br)* pinza f *(para*

la ropa).

clothespin [ˈkləʊðzpɪn] (Am) = clothes peg.

clothes shop n tienda f de ropa.

clothing [ˈkləʊðɪŋ] n ropa f.

clotted cream n nata f muy espesa típica de Cornualles.

cloud [klaʊd] n nube f.

cloudy [ˈklaʊdɪ] adj (sky, day) nublado(-da); (liquid) turbio(-bia).

clove [kləʊv] n (of garlic) diente m ▫ **cloves** npl (spice) clavos mpl.

clown [klaʊn] n payaso m.

club [klʌb] n (organization) club m; (nightclub) ≃ sala f de fiestas (abierta sólo de noche); (stick) garrote m ▫ **clubs** npl (in cards) tréboles mpl.

clubbing [ˈklʌbɪŋ] n: **to go ~** (inf) ir de disco.

club class n clase f club.

club sandwich n (Am) sandwich m de tres pisos.

club soda n (Am) soda f.

clue [klu:] n (information) pista f; (in crossword) clave f; **I haven't got a ~** no tengo ni idea.

clumsy [ˈklʌmzɪ] adj (person) torpe.

clutch [klʌtʃ] n (on car, motorbike) embrague m; (clutch pedal) pedal m de embrague ◆ vt agarrar.

cm (abbr of centimetre) cm.

c/o (abbr of care of) c/d.

Co. (abbr of company) Cía.

coach [kəʊtʃ] n (bus) autocar m; (of train) vagón m; (SPORT) entrenador m (-ra f).

coach party n (Br) grupo de personas en un viaje organizado en autobús.

coach station n estación f de autocares.

coach trip n (Br) excursión f en autocar.

coal [kəʊl] n carbón m.

coal mine n mina f de carbón.

coarse [kɔːs] adj (rough) áspero(-ra); (vulgar) ordinario(-ria).

coast [kəʊst] n costa f.

coaster [ˈkəʊstə] n posavasos m inv.

coastguard [ˈkəʊstgɑːd] n (person) guardacostas mf inv; (organization) guardacostas mpl.

coastline [ˈkəʊstlaɪn] n litoral m.

coat [kəʊt] n (garment) abrigo m; (of animal) pelaje m ◆ vt: **to ~ sthg (with)** rebozar algo (en).

coat hanger n percha f.

coating [ˈkəʊtɪŋ] n (of chocolate) baño m; (on surface) capa f; **with a ~ of breadcrumbs** rebozado en pan rallado.

cobbled street [ˈkɒbld-] n calle f adoquinada.

cobbles [ˈkɒblz] npl adoquines mpl.

cobweb [ˈkɒbweb] n telaraña f.

Coca-Cola® [ˌkəʊkəˈkəʊlə] n Coca-Cola® f.

cocaine [kəʊˈkeɪn] n cocaína f.

cock [kɒk] n (male chicken) gallo m.

cock-a-leekie [ˌkɒkəˈliːkɪ] n sopa de pollo y puerros.

cockerel [ˈkɒkrəl] n gallo m joven.

cockles [ˈkɒklz] npl berberechos mpl.

cockpit [ˈkɒkpɪt] n cabina f.

cockroach [ˈkɒkrəʊtʃ] n cucaracha f.

cocktail ['kɒkteɪl] n cóctel m.

cocktail party n cóctel m.

cock-up n (Br: vulg): **to make a ~ of sthg** jorobar algo.

cocoa ['kəʊkəʊ] n (drink) chocolate m.

coconut ['kəʊkənʌt] n coco m.

cod [kɒd] (pl inv) n bacalao m.

code [kəʊd] n (system) código m; (dialling code) prefijo m.

cod-liver oil n aceite m de hígado de bacalao.

coeducational [ˌkəʊedjuː-
'keɪʃənl] adj mixto(-ta).

coffee ['kɒfɪ] n café m; **black/white ~** café solo/con leche; **ground/instant ~** café molido/instantáneo.

coffee bar n (Br) cafetería f (en aeropuerto, etc).

coffee break n descanso en el trabajo, por la mañana y por la tarde.

coffeepot ['kɒfɪpɒt] n cafetera f.

coffee shop n (cafe) cafetería f.

coffee table n mesita f baja.

coffin ['kɒfɪn] n ataúd m.

cog(wheel) ['kɒg(wiːl)] n rueda f dentada.

coil [kɔɪl] n (of rope) rollo m; (Br: contraceptive) DIU m ◆ vt enrollar.

coin [kɔɪn] n moneda f.

coinbox ['kɔɪnbɒks] n (Br) teléfono m público.

coincide [ˌkəʊɪn'saɪd] vi: **to ~ (with)** coincidir (con).

coincidence [kəʊ'ɪnsɪdəns] n coincidencia f.

Coke® [kəʊk] n Coca-Cola® f.

colander ['kʌləndəʳ] n colador m.

cold [kəʊld] adj frío(-a) ◆ n (illness) resfriado m; (low temperature) frío m; **I'm ~** tengo frío; **it's ~** hace frío; **to get ~** enfriarse; **to catch (a) ~** resfriarse.

cold cuts (Am) = **cold meats**.

cold meats npl fiambres mpl.

coleslaw ['kəʊlslɔː] n ensalada de col, zanahoria, cebolla y mayonesa.

colic ['kɒlɪk] n cólico m.

collaborate [kə'læbəreɪt] vi colaborar.

collapse [kə'læps] vi (building, tent) desplomarse; (person) sufrir un colapso.

collar ['kɒləʳ] n (of shirt, coat) cuello m; (of dog, cat) collar m.

collarbone ['kɒləbəʊn] n clavícula f.

colleague ['kɒliːg] n colega mf.

collect [kə'lekt] vt (gather) reunir; (as a hobby) coleccionar; (go and get) recoger; (money) recaudar ◆ vi acumularse ◆ adv (Am): **to call (sb) ~** llamar (a alguien) a cobro revertido.

collection [kə'lekʃn] n colección f; (of money) recaudación f; (of mail) recogida f.

collector [kə'lektəʳ] n (as a hobby) coleccionista mf.

college ['kɒlɪdʒ] n (school) instituto m, escuela f; (Br: of university) colegio universitario que forma parte de ciertas universidades; (Am: university) universidad f.

collide [kə'laɪd] vi: **to ~ (with)** colisionar (con).

collision [kə'lɪʒn] n colisión f.

cologne [kə'ləʊn] n colonia f.

Colombia [kəˈlɒmbɪə] n Colombia.

Colombian [kəˈlɒmbɪən] adj colombiano(-na) ◆ n colombiano m (-na f).

colon [ˈkəʊlən] n (GRAMM) dos puntos mpl.

colonel [ˈkɜːnl] n coronel m.

colony [ˈkɒlənɪ] n (country) colonia f.

color [ˈkʌlər] (Am) = colour.

colour [ˈkʌlər] n color m ◆ adj (photograph, film) en color ◆ vt (hair) teñir; (food) colorear ❑ **colour in** vt sep colorear.

colour-blind adj daltónico(-ca).

colourful [ˈkʌləful] adj (picture, garden, scenery) de vivos colores; (fig: person, place) pintoresco(-ca).

colouring [ˈkʌlərɪŋ] n (of food) colorante m; (complexion) tez f.

colouring book n libro m de colorear.

colour supplement n suplemento m en color.

colour television n televisión f en color.

column [ˈkɒləm] n columna f.

coma [ˈkəʊmə] n coma m.

comb [kəʊm] n peine m ◆ vt: to ~ one's hair peinarse (el pelo).

combination [ˌkɒmbɪˈneɪʃn] n combinación f.

combine [kəmˈbaɪn] vt: to ~ sthg (with) combinar algo (con).

combine harvester [ˌkɒmbaɪnˈhɑːvɪstər] n cosechadora f.

come [kʌm] (pt came, pp come) vi 1. (move) venir; **we came by taxi** vinimos en taxi; ~ **here!** ¡ven aquí!

2. (arrive) llegar; **they still haven't ~** todavía no han llegado; **"coming soon"** "próximamente".

3. (in order): to ~ **first/last** (in race) llegar el primero/el último; (in exam) quedar el primero/el último.

4. (reach): **the water ~s up to my ankles** el agua me llega hasta los tobillos.

5. (become): to ~ **loose** aflojarse; to ~ **undone** deshacerse.

6. (be sold) venir; **they ~ in packs of six** vienen en paquetes de seis.

❑ **come across** vt fus encontrarse con; **come along** vi (progress) ir; (arrive) venir; ~ **along!** ¡venga!; **come apart** vi (become detached) deshacerse; **come back** vi (return) volver; **come down** vi (price) bajar; **come down with** vt fus (illness) coger, agarrar (Amér); **come from** vt fus (person) ser de; (noise, product) venir de; **come in** vi (enter) entrar; (arrive) llegar; (fig: crecer); ~ **in!** ¡adelante!; **come off** vi (become detached) desprenderse; (succeed) salir bien; **come on** vi (progress) ir; (improve) mejorar; ~ **on!** ¡venga!; **come out** vi salir; (film) estrenarse; (stain) quitarse; **come over** vi (visit) venir; **come round** vi (visit) venir; (regain consciousness) volver en sí; **come to** vt fus (subj: bill) ascender a; **come up** vi (go upstairs) subir; (be mentioned, arise) surgir; (sun, moon) salir; **come up with** vt fus: **she came up with a brilliant idea** se le ocurrió una idea estupenda.

comedian [kəˈmiːdjən] n humorista mf.

comedy [ˈkɒmədɪ] n (TV programme, film, play) comedia f; (humour) humor m.

comfort ['kʌmfət] n comodidad f; (consolation) consuelo m ♦ vt consolar.

comfortable ['kʌmftəbl] adj cómodo(-da); (after illness, operation) en estado satisfactorio; (financially) acomodado(-da).

comic ['kɒmɪk] adj cómico(-ca) ♦ n (person) humorista mf; (adult magazine) cómic m; (children's magazine) tebeo m.

comical ['kɒmɪkl] adj cómico(-ca).

comic strip n tira f cómica.

comma ['kɒmə] n coma f.

command [kə'mɑːnd] n (order) orden f; (mastery) dominio m ♦ vt (order) ordenar; (be in charge of) estar al mando de.

commander [kə'mɑːndəʳ] n comandante m.

commemorate [kə'meməreɪt] vt conmemorar.

commence [kə'mens] vi (fml) comenzar.

comment ['kɒment] n comentario m ♦ vi hacer comentarios.

commentary ['kɒməntrɪ] n (on TV, radio) comentario m.

commentator ['kɒmənteɪtəʳ] n (on TV, radio) comentarista m.

commerce ['kɒmɜːs] n comercio m.

commercial [kə'mɜːʃl] adj comercial ♦ n anuncio m (televisivo o radiofónico).

commercial break n pausa f para la publicidad.

commission [kə'mɪʃn] n comi-

sión f.

commit [kə'mɪt] vt (crime, sin) cometer; to ~ o.s. (to sthg) comprometerse (a algo); to ~ suicide suicidarse.

committee [kə'mɪtɪ] n comité m.

commodity [kə'mɒdɪtɪ] n producto m.

common ['kɒmən] adj común; (pej: vulgar) ordinario(-ria) ♦ n (Br: land) zona f de hierba abierta accesible a todo el mundo; in ~ en común.

commonly ['kɒmənlɪ] adv (generally) generalmente.

Common Market n Mercado m Común.

common room n sala f de estudiantes.

common sense n sentido m común.

Commonwealth ['kɒmənwelθ] n Commonwealth f.

communal ['kɒmjunl] adj comunal.

communicate [kə'mjuːnɪkeɪt] vi: to ~ (with) comunicarse (con).

communication [kə,mjuːnɪ-'keɪʃn] n comunicación f.

communication cord n (Br) alarma f (de un tren o metro).

communist ['kɒmjunɪst] n comunista mf.

community [kə'mjuːnətɪ] n comunidad f.

community centre n centro m social.

commute [kə'mjuːt] vi viajar diariamente al lugar de trabajo, especialmente en tren.

commuter [kə'mjuːtəʳ] n persona que viaja diariamente al lugar de trabajo, especialmente en tren.

compact [adj kəm'pækt, n 'kɒmpækt] adj compacto(-ta) ♦ n (for make-up) polvera f; (Am: car) utilitario m.

compact disc [,kɒmpækt-] n compact disc m.

compact disc player [,kɒmpækt-] n compact m (disc).

company ['kʌmpənɪ] n compañía f; **to keep sb** ~ hacer compañía a alguien.

company car n coche m de la empresa.

comparatively [kəm'pærətɪvlɪ] adv relativamente.

compare [kəm'peəʳ] vt: **to** ~ **sthg (with)** comparar algo (con); ~d **with** en comparación con.

comparison [kəm'pærɪsn] n comparación f; **in** ~ **with** en comparación con.

compartment [kəm'pɑːtmənt] n compartimento m.

compass ['kʌmpəs] n brújula f; **(a pair of)** ~es (un) compás f.

compatible [kəm'pætəbl] adj compatible.

compensate ['kɒmpənseɪt] vt compensar ♦ vi: **to** ~ **for sthg** compensar algo; **to** ~ **sb for sthg** compensar a alguien por algo.

compensation [,kɒmpən'seɪʃn] n (money) indemnización f.

compete [kəm'piːt] vi competir; **to** ~ **with sb for sthg** competir con alguien por algo.

competent ['kɒmpɪtənt] adj competente.

competition [,kɒmpɪ'tɪʃn] n

(SPORT) competición f; (of writing, music etc) concurso m; (rivalry) competencia f; **the** ~ la competencia.

competitive [kəm'petɪtɪv] adj competitivo(-va).

competitor [kəm'petɪtəʳ] n (in race, contest) participante mf; (in game show) concursante mf; (COMM) competidor m (-ra f).

complain [kəm'pleɪn] vi: **to** ~ **(about)** quejarse (de).

complaint [kəm'pleɪnt] n (statement) queja f; (illness) dolencia f.

complement ['kɒmplɪment] vt complementar.

complete [kəm'pliːt] adj (whole) completo(-ta); (finished) terminado(-da); (change, disaster) total; (idiot) consumado(-da) ♦ vt (finish) terminar; (a form) rellenar; (make whole) completar; ~ **with** con.

completely [kəm'pliːtlɪ] adv completamente.

complex ['kɒmpleks] adj complejo(-ja) ♦ n complejo m.

complexion [kəm'plekʃn] n (of skin) cutis m inv.

complicated ['kɒmplɪkeɪtɪd] adj complicado(-da).

compliment [n 'kɒmplɪmənt, vb 'kɒmplɪment] n cumplido m ♦ vt felicitar.

complimentary [,kɒmplɪ'mentərɪ] adj (seat, ticket) gratuito(-ta); (words, person) halagador(-ra).

compose [kəm'pəʊz] vt componer; **to be** ~**d of** estar compuesto de.

composed [kəm'pəʊzd] adj tranquilo(-la).

composer [kəm'pəʊzəʳ] *n* compositor *m* (-ra *f*).

composition [kɒmpə'zɪʃn] *n* (essay) redacción *f*.

compound ['kɒmpaʊnd] *n* (substance) compuesto *m*; (word) palabra *f* compuesta.

comprehensive [kɒmprɪ'hensɪv] *adj* amplio(-plia).

comprehensive (school) *n* (Br) instituto de enseñanza media no selectiva en Gran Bretaña.

compressed air [kəm'prest-] *n* aire *m* comprimido.

comprise [kəm'praɪz] *vt* comprender.

compromise ['kɒmprəmaɪz] *n* arreglo *m*, acuerdo *m*.

compulsory [kəm'pʌlsərɪ] *adj* obligatorio(-ria).

computer [kəm'pju:təʳ] *n* ordenador *m*.

computer game *n* videojuego *m*.

computerized [kəm'pju:təraɪzd] *adj* informatizado(-da).

computer operator *n* operador *m* (-ra *f*) de ordenador.

computer programmer [-'prəʊgræməʳ] *n* programador *m* (-ra *f*) (de ordenadores).

computing [kəm'pju:tɪŋ] *n* informática *f*.

con [kɒn] *n* (inf: trick) timo *m*, estafa *f*; **all mod ~s** con todas las comodidades.

conceal [kən'si:l] *vt* ocultar.

conceited [kən'si:tɪd] *adj* (pej) engreído(-da).

concentrate ['kɒnsəntreɪt] *vi* concentrarse ♦ *vt*: **to be ~d** (in one

place) concentrarse; **to ~ on sthg** concentrarse en algo.

concentrated ['kɒnsəntreɪtɪd] *adj* concentrado(-da).

concentration [kɒnsən'treɪʃn] *n* concentración *f*.

concern [kən'sɜːn] *n* (worry) preocupación *f*; (matter of interest) asunto *m*; (COMM) empresa *f* ♦ *vt* (be about) tratar de; (worry) preocupar; (involve) concernir; **to be ~ed about** estar preocupado por; **to be ~ed with** tratar de; **to ~ o.s. with sthg** preocuparse por algo; **as far as I'm ~ed** por lo que a mí respecta.

concerned [kən'sɜːnd] *adj* preocupado(-da).

concerning [kən'sɜːnɪŋ] *prep* acerca de.

concert ['kɒnsət] *n* concierto *m*.

concession [kən'seʃn] *n* (reduced price) descuento *m*.

concise [kən'saɪs] *adj* conciso(-sa).

conclude [kən'klu:d] *vt* concluir ♦ *vi* (fml: end) concluir.

conclusion [kən'klu:ʒn] *n* (decision) conclusión *f*; (end) final *m*.

concrete ['kɒŋkri:t] *adj* (building, path) de hormigón; (idea, plan) concreto(-ta) ♦ *n* hormigón *m*.

concussion [kən'kʌʃn] *n* conmoción *f* cerebral.

condensation [kɒndenˈseɪʃn] *n* (on window) vaho *m*.

condensed milk [kən'denst-] *n* leche *f* condensada.

condition [kən'dɪʃn] *n* (state) estado *m*; (proviso) condición *f*; (illness) afección *f*; **to be out of ~** no estar en forma; **on ~ that** a condición de que ▢ **conditions** *npl* (*circumstances*) condiciones *fpl*.

conditioner [kən'dɪʃnə] *n* suavizante *m*.

condo [ˈkɒndəʊ] (*Am*: *inf*) = **condominium**.

condom [ˈkɒndəm] *n* condón *m*.

condominium [ˌkɒndəˈmɪnɪəm] *n* (*Am*) apartamento *m*.

conduct [*vb* kənˈdʌkt, *n* ˈkɒndʌkt] *vt* (*investigation*, *business*) llevar a cabo; (*MUS*) dirigir ◆ *n* (*fml*) conducta *f*; **to ~ o.s.** (*fml*) comportarse.

conductor [kənˈdʌktə] *n* (*MUS*) director *m* (-ra *f*); (*on bus*) cobrador *m* (-ra *f*); (*Am*: *on train*) revisor *m* (-ra *f*).

cone [kəʊn] *n* (*shape*, *on roads*) cono *m*; (*for ice cream*) cucurucho *m*.

confectioner's [kənˈfekʃnəz] *n* (*shop*) confitería *f*.

confectionery [kənˈfekʃnərɪ] *n* dulces *mpl*.

conference [ˈkɒnfərəns] *n* conferencia *f*, congreso *m*.

confess [kənˈfes] *vi*: **to ~ (to sth)** confesar (algo).

confession [kənˈfeʃn] *n* confesión *f*.

confidence [ˈkɒnfɪdəns] *n* (*self-assurance*) seguridad *f* (en sí mismo); (*trust*) confianza *f*; **to have ~** tener confianza en.

confident [ˈkɒnfɪdənt] *adj* (*self-assured*) seguro de sí mismo (segura de sí misma); (*certain*) seguro(-ra).

confined [kənˈfaɪnd] *adj* limita-

do(-da).

confirm [kənˈfɜːm] *vt* confirmar.

confirmation [ˌkɒnfəˈmeɪʃn] *n* confirmación *f*.

conflict [*n* ˈkɒnflɪkt, *vb* kənˈflɪkt] *n* conflicto *m* ◆ *vi*: **to ~ (with)** estar en desacuerdo (con).

conform [kənˈfɔːm] *vi*: **to ~ (to)** ajustarse (a).

confuse [kənˈfjuːz] *vt* confundir; **to ~ sth with sth** confundir algo con algo.

confused [kənˈfjuːzd] *adj* confuso(-sa).

confusing [kənˈfjuːzɪŋ] *adj* confuso(-sa).

confusion [kənˈfjuːʒn] *n* confusión *f*.

congested [kənˈdʒestɪd] *adj* (*street*) congestionado(-da).

congestion [kənˈdʒestʃn] *n* (*traffic*) congestión *f*.

congratulate [kənˈgrætʃʊleɪt] *vt*: **to ~ sb (on sth)** felicitar a alguien (por algo).

congratulations [kənˌgrætʃʊˈleɪʃənz] *excl* ¡enhorabuena!

congregate [ˈkɒŋgrɪgeɪt] *vi* congregarse.

Congress [ˈkɒŋgres] *n* (*Am*) el Congreso.

conifer [ˈkɒnɪfəʳ] *n* conífera *f*.

conjunction [kənˈdʒʌŋkʃn] *n* (*GRAMM*) conjunción *f*.

conjurer [ˈkʌndʒərəʳ] *n* prestidigitador *m* (-ra *f*).

connect [kəˈnekt] *vt* conectar, (*caller on phone*) comunicar, poner ◆ *vi*: **to ~ with** (*train*, *plane*) enlazar con; **to ~ sth with sth** (*associate*) asociar algo con algo.

connecting flight [kəˈnektɪŋ-] n vuelo m de enlace.

connection [kəˈnekʃn] n (link) conexión f; (train, plane) enlace m; **a bad ~** (on phone) mala línea; **a loose ~** (in machine) un hilo suelto; **in ~ with** con relación a.

conquer [ˈkɒŋkəʳ] vt conquistar.

conscience [ˈkɒnʃəns] n conciencia f.

conscientious [ˌkɒnʃɪˈenʃəs] adj concienzudo(-da).

conscious [ˈkɒnʃəs] adj (awake) consciente; (deliberate) deliberado(-da); **to be ~ of** ser consciente de.

consent [kənˈsent] n consentimiento m.

consequence [ˈkɒnsɪkwəns] n (result) consecuencia f.

consequently [ˈkɒnsɪkwəntlɪ] adv por consiguiente.

conservation [ˌkɒnsəˈveɪʃn] n conservación f.

conservative [kənˈsɜːvətɪv] adj conservador(-ra) ❑ **Conservative** adj conservador(-ra) ♦ n conservador m (-ra f).

conservatory [kənˈsɜːvətrɪ] n pequeña habitación acristalada aneja a la casa.

consider [kənˈsɪdəʳ] vt considerar; **to ~ doing sthg** pensarse si hacer algo.

considerable [kənˈsɪdrəbl] adj considerable.

consideration [kənˌsɪdəˈreɪʃn] n consideración f; **to take sthg into ~** tener algo en cuenta.

considering [kənˈsɪdərɪŋ] prep teniendo en cuenta.

consist [kənˈsɪst]: **consist in** vt fus consistir en; **consist of** vt fus consistir en.

consistent [kənˈsɪstənt] adj (coherent) coherente; (worker, performance) constante.

consolation [ˌkɒnsəˈleɪʃn] n consuelo m.

console [ˈkɒnsəul] n consola f.

consonant [ˈkɒnsənənt] n consonante f.

conspicuous [kənˈspɪkjuəs] adj visible.

constable [ˈkʌnstəbl] n (Br) policía mf.

constant [ˈkɒnstənt] adj constante.

constantly [ˈkɒnstəntlɪ] adv (all the time) constantemente.

constipated [ˈkɒnstɪpeɪtɪd] adj estreñido(-da).

constitution [ˌkɒnstɪˈtjuːʃn] n (health) constitución f.

construct [kənˈstrʌkt] vt construir.

construction [kənˈstrʌkʃn] n construcción f; **"under ~"** "en construcción".

consul [ˈkɒnsəl] n cónsul mf.

consulate [ˈkɒnsjulət] n consulado m.

consult [kənˈsʌlt] vt consultar.

consultant [kənˈsʌltənt] n (Br: doctor) especialista mf.

consume [kənˈsjuːm] vt consumir.

consumer [kənˈsjuːməʳ] n consumidor m (-ra f).

contact [ˈkɒntækt] n contacto m ♦ vt ponerse en contacto con; **in ~ with** en contacto con.

contact lens n lentilla f.

contagious [kən'teɪdʒəs] adj contagioso(-sa).

contain [kən'teɪn] vt contener.

container [kən'teɪnə*] n (box etc) envase m.

contaminate [kən'tæmɪneɪt] vt contaminar.

contemporary [kən'tempərərɪ] adj contemporáneo(-a) ◆ n contemporáneo m (-a f).

contend [kən'tend]: **contend with** vt fus afrontar.

content [adj kən'tent, n 'kɒntent] adj contento(-ta) ◆ n (of vitamins, fibre etc) contenido m ❑ **contents** npl (things inside) contenido m; (at beginning of book) índice m (de materias).

contest [n 'kɒntest, vb kən'test] n (competition) competición f, concurso m; (struggle) contienda f ◆ vt (election, seat) presentarse como candidato a; (decision, will) impugnar.

context ['kɒntekst] n contexto m.

continent ['kɒntɪnənt] n continente m; **the Continent** (Br) la Europa continental.

continental [,kɒntɪ'nentl] adj (Br: European) de la Europa continental.

continental breakfast n desayuno m continental.

continental quilt n (Br) edredón m.

continual [kən'tɪnjʊəl] adj continuo(-nua).

continually [kən'tɪnjʊəlɪ] adv continuamente.

continue [kən'tɪnjuː] vt & vi continuar; **to ~ doing sthg** continuar haciendo algo; **to ~ with sthg** continuar con algo.

continuous [kən'tɪnjʊəs] adj continuo(-nua).

continuously [kən'tɪnjʊəslɪ] adv continuamente.

contraception [,kɒntrə'sepʃn] n anticoncepción f.

contraceptive [,kɒntrə'septɪv] n anticonceptivo m.

contract [n 'kɒntrækt, vb kən'trækt] n contrato m ◆ vt (fml: illness) contraer.

contradict [,kɒntrə'dɪkt] vt contradecir.

contraflow ['kɒntrəfləʊ] n (Br) estrechamiento en una autopista, a una vía de dos direcciones.

contrary ['kɒntrərɪ] n: **on the ~** al contrario.

contrast [n 'kɒntrɑːst, vb kən'trɑːst] n contraste m ◆ vt contrastar; **in ~ to** a diferencia de.

contribute [kən'trɪbjuːt] vt (help, money) contribuir ◆ vi: **to ~** to contribuir a.

contribution [,kɒntrɪ'bjuːʃn] n contribución f.

control [kən'trəʊl] n control m ◆ vt controlar; (restrict) restringir; **to be in ~** estar al mando; **out of ~** fuera de control; **under ~** bajo control ❑ **controls** npl (for TV, video) botones mpl de mando; (of plane) mandos mpl.

control tower n torre f de control.

controversial [,kɒntrə'vɜːʃl] adj controvertido(-da).

convenience [kən'vi:njəns] n (convenient nature) conveniencia f; (convenient thing) comodidad f; **at your ~** cuando le venga bien.

convenient [kən'vi:njənt] adj (suitable) conveniente; (well-situated) bien situado(-da); **would tomorrow be ~?** ¿le viene bien mañana?

convent ['kɒnvənt] n convento m.

conventional [kən'venʃənl] adj convencional.

conversation [ˌkɒnvə'seɪʃn] n conversación f.

conversion [kən'vɜːʃn] n (change) conversión f; (to building) reforma f.

convert [kən'vɜːt] vt convertir; **to ~ sthg into** convertir algo en.

converted [kən'vɜːtɪd] adj (barn, loft) acondicionado(-da).

convertible [kən'vɜːtəbl] n descapotable m.

convey [kən'veɪ] vt (fml: transport) transportar; (idea, impression) transmitir.

convict [n 'kɒnvɪkt, vb kən'vɪkt] n presidiario m (-ria f) ◆ vt: **to ~ sb (of)** declarar a alguien culpable (de).

convince [kən'vɪns] vt: **to ~ sb (of sthg)** convencer a alguien (de algo); **to ~ sb to do sthg** convencer a alguien para que haga algo.

convoy ['kɒnvɔɪ] n convoy m.

cook [kʊk] n cocinero m (-ra f) ◆ vt (meal) preparar; (food) guisar ◆ vi (person) guisar; (food) cocerse, hacerse.

cookbook ['kʊkbʊk] = **cookery book**.

cooker ['kʊkə'] n cocina f (aparato).

cookery ['kʊkərɪ] n cocina f (arte).

cookery book n libro m de cocina.

cookie ['kʊkɪ] n (Am) galleta f.

cooking ['kʊkɪŋ] n cocina f.

cooking apple n manzana f para asar.

cooking oil n aceite m para cocinar.

cool [kuːl] adj (temperature) fresco(-ca); (calm) tranquilo(-la); (unfriendly) frío(-a); (inf: great) chachi ◆ vt refrescar ❑ **cool down** vi (become colder) enfriarse; (become calmer) calmarse.

cooperate [kəʊ'ɒpəreɪt] vi cooperar.

cooperation [kəʊˌɒpə'reɪʃn] n cooperación f.

cooperative [kəʊ'ɒpərətɪv] adj dispuesto(-ta) a cooperar.

coordinates [kəʊ'ɔːdɪnəts] npl (clothes) conjuntos mpl.

cope [kəʊp] vi: **to ~ with** (problem, situation) hacer frente a; (work) poder con.

copilot ['kəʊˌpaɪlət] n copiloto m.

copper ['kɒpə'] n (metal) cobre m; (Br: inf: coin) moneda f de cobre de uno o dos peniques.

copy ['kɒpɪ] n copia f; (of newspaper, book) ejemplar m ◆ vt (duplicate) hacer una copia de; (imitate) copiar.

cord(uroy) ['kɔːd(ərɔɪ)] n pana f.

core [kɔː'] n (of fruit) corazón m.

coriander [ˌkɒrɪˈændəʳ] n cilantro m.

cork [kɔːk] n (in bottle) corcho m.

corkscrew [ˈkɔːkskruː] n sacacorchos m inv.

corn [kɔːn] n (Br: crop) cereal m; (Am: maize) maíz m; (on foot) callo m.

corned beef [kɔːnd-] n carne de vaca cocinada y enlatada.

corner [ˈkɔːnəʳ] n (outside angle, bend in road) esquina f; (inside angle) rincón m; (in football) córner m; **it's just around the ~** está a la vuelta de la esquina.

corner shop n (Br) pequeña tienda de ultramarinos de barrio.

cornet [ˈkɔːnɪt] n (Br: ice-cream cone) cucurucho m.

cornflakes [ˈkɔːnfleɪks] npl copos mpl de maíz.

corn-on-the-cob [-ˈkɒb] n mazorca f.

Cornwall [ˈkɔːnwɔːl] n Cornualles.

corporal [ˈkɔːpərəl] n cabo mf.

corpse [kɔːps] n cadáver m.

correct [kəˈrekt] adj correcto(-ta) ♦ vt corregir.

correction [kəˈrekʃn] n corrección f.

correspond [ˌkɒrɪˈspɒnd] vi: to ~ (to) (match) concordar (con); to ~ (with) (exchange letters) cartearse (con).

corresponding [ˌkɒrɪˈspɒndɪŋ] adj correspondiente.

corridor [ˈkɒrɪdɔːʳ] n pasillo m.

corrugated iron [ˈkɒrəɡeɪtɪd-] n chapa f ondulada.

corrupt [kəˈrʌpt] adj corrup-

to(-ta).

cosmetics [kɒzˈmetɪks] npl cosméticos mpl.

cost [kɒst] (pt & pp cost) n coste m ♦ vt costar; **how much does it ~?** ¿cuánto cuesta?

Costa Rica [ˌkɒstəˈriːkə] n Costa Rica.

Costa Rican [ˌkɒstəˈriːkən] adj costarricense ♦ n costarricense mf.

costly [ˈkɒstlɪ] adj (expensive) costoso(-sa).

costume [ˈkɒstjuːm] n traje m.

cosy [ˈkəʊzɪ] adj (Br: room, house) acogedor(-ra).

cot [kɒt] n (Br: for baby) cuna f; (Am: camp bed) cama f plegable.

cottage [ˈkɒtɪdʒ] n casita f de campo.

cottage cheese n requesón m.

cottage pie n (Br) pastel de carne de vaca picada y cebollas con una capa de puré de patatas cocinado al horno.

cotton [ˈkɒtn] adj (dress, shirt) de algodón ♦ n (cloth) algodón m; (thread) hilo m (de algodón).

cotton candy n (Am) algodón m (de azúcar).

cotton wool n algodón m (hidrófilo).

couch [kaʊtʃ] n (sofa) sofá m; (at doctor's) camilla f.

couchette [kuːˈʃet] n (bed on train) litera f; (seat on ship) butaca f.

cough [kɒf] n tos f ♦ vi toser; **to have a ~** tener tos.

cough mixture n jarabe m para la tos.

could [kʊd] pt → **can**.

couldn't ['kʊdnt] = could not.

could've ['kʊdəv] = could have.

council ['kaʊnsl] n (Br: of town) ayuntamiento m; (of county) = diputación f; (organization) consejo m.

council house n (Br) = casa f de protección oficial.

councillor ['kaʊnsələr] n (Br) concejal m.

council tax n (Br) = contribución f urbana.

count [kaʊnt] vt & vi contar ◆ n (nobleman) conde m ❏ **count on** vt fus contar con.

counter ['kaʊntər] n (in shop) mostrador m; (in bank) ventanilla f; (in board game) ficha f.

counterclockwise [,kaʊntə'klɒkwaɪz] adv (Am) en sentido opuesto a las agujas del reloj.

counterfoil ['kaʊntəfɔɪl] n matriz f.

countess ['kaʊntɪs] n condesa f.

country ['kʌntrɪ] n (state) país m; (countryside) campo m; (population) pueblo m ◆ adj campestre.

country and western n música f country.

country house n casa f de campo.

country road n camino m vecinal.

countryside ['kʌntrɪsaɪd] n campo m.

county ['kaʊntɪ] n (in Britain) condado m; (in US) división administrativa de un estado en EEUU.

couple ['kʌpl] n pareja f; **a ~ (of)** un par (de).

coupon ['ku:pɒn] n cupón m.

courage ['kʌrɪdʒ] n valor m.

courgette [kɔː'ʒet] n (Br) calabacín m.

courier ['kʊrɪər] n (for holidaymakers) guía m; (for delivering letters) mensajero m (-ra f).

course [kɔːs] n (in curso m; (of meal) plato m; (of treatment, injections) tratamiento m; (for golf) campo m (de golf); **of ~** por supuesto, claro; **of ~ not** claro que no; **in the ~ of** en el curso de.

court [kɔːt] n (JUR: building, room) juzgado m; (SPORT) cancha f; (of king, queen) corte f.

courtesy coach ['kɜːtɪsɪ-] n autocar gratuito fletado para llevar a invitados.

court shoes npl zapatos m de señora de tacón alto y sin adornos.

courtyard ['kɔːtjɑːd] n patio m.

cousin ['kʌzn] n primo m (-ma f).

cover ['kʌvər] n (soft covering) funda f; (lid) tapa f; (of book, magazine) cubierta f; (blanket) manta f; (insurance) cobertura f ◆ vt cubrir; (travel) recorrer; (apply to) afectar; (discuss) abarcar; **to be ~ed in** estar cubierto de; **to ~ sthg with sthg** (food, tray, furniture etc) cubrir algo con algo; (hole, ears) tapar algo con algo; **to take ~** refugiarse ❏ **cover up** vt sep (put cover on) cubrir; (facts, truth) encubrir.

cover charge n precio m del cubierto.

cover note n (Br) póliza f provisional.

cow [kaʊ] n vaca f.

coward ['kaʊəd] n cobarde mf.

cowboy ['kaʊbɔɪ] n vaquero m.

crab [kræb] n cangrejo m.

crack [kræk] n (in cup, glass, wood) grieta f; (gap) rendija f ◆ vt (cup, glass, wood) agrietar, rajar; (nut, egg) cascar; (inf: joke) contar; (whip) chasquear ◆ vi agrietarse, rajarse.

cracker ['krækə'] n (biscuit) galleta f salada; (for Christmas) tubo con sorpresa típico de Navidades que produce un pequeño restallido al ser abierto.

cradle ['kreidl] n cuna f.

craft [krɑːft] n (skill, trade) oficio m; (boat: pl inv) embarcación f.

craftsman ['krɑːftsmən] (pl -men [-mən]) n artesano m.

cram [kræm] vt: to ~ sthg into embutir algo en; to be crammed with estar atestado de.

cramp [kræmp] n calambres mpl; stomach ~s retortijones mpl.

cranberry ['krænbəri] n arándano m (agrio).

cranberry sauce n salsa de arándanos agrios que se suele comer con pavo.

crane [krein] n (machine) grúa f.

crap [kræp] adj (vulg) de mierda ◆ n (vulg: excrement) mierda f.

crash [kræʃ] n (accident) colisión f; (noise) estruendo m ◆ vt (car) estrellar ◆ vi (two vehicles) chocar; (into wall, ground) estrellarse ☐ **crash into** vt fus estrellarse contra.

crash helmet n casco m protector.

crash landing n aterrizaje m forzoso.

crate [kreit] n caja f (para embalaje o transporte).

crawl [krɔːl] vi (baby) gatear; (person, insect) arrastrarse; (traffic) ir a paso de tortuga ◆ n (swimming stroke) crol m.

crawler lane ['krɔːlə-] n (Br) carril m de los lentos.

crayfish ['kreifiʃ] (pl inv) n cangrejo m de río.

crayon ['kreiɒn] n lápiz m de cera.

craze [kreiz] n moda f.

crazy ['kreizi] adj loco(-ca); to be ~ about estar loco por.

crazy golf n minigolf m.

cream [kriːm] n (food) nata f; (for face, burns) crema f ◆ adj (in colour) crema inv.

cream cake n (Br) pastel m de nata.

cream cheese n queso m cremoso.

cream sherry n jerez m cream.

cream tea n (Br) merienda de té con bollos, nata cuajada y mermelada.

creamy ['kriːmi] adj cremoso(-sa).

crease [kriːs] n arruga f.

creased [kriːst] adj arrugado(-da).

create [kriː'eit] vt (make) crear; (impression, interest) producir.

creative [kriː'eitiv] adj creativo(-va).

creature ['kriːtʃə'] n criatura f.

crèche [kreʃ] n (Br) guardería f.

credit ['kredit] n (praise) mérito m; (money, for studies) crédito m; to be in ~ estar con saldo acreedor ☐ **credits** npl (of film) rótulos mpl de crédito.

credit card n tarjeta f de crédito; **to pay by ~** pagar con tarjeta de crédito; **"all major ~s accepted"** "se aceptan las principales tarjetas de crédito".

creek [kri:k] n (inlet) cala f; (Am: river) riachuelo m.

creep [kri:p] (pt & pp **crept**) vi arrastrarse ♦ n (inf: groveller) pelotillero m (-ra f).

cremate [krɪ'meɪt] vt incinerar.

crematorium [kremə'tɔ:rɪəm] n crematorio m.

crepe [kreɪp] n (thin pancake) crepe f.

crept [krept] pt & pp → **creep**.

cress [kres] n berro m.

crest [krest] n (of hill) cima f; (of wave) cresta f; (emblem) blasón m.

crew [kru:] n (of ship, plane) tripulación f.

crew neck n cuello m redondo.

crib [krɪb] n (Am: cot) cuna f.

cricket [krɪkɪt] n (game) críquet m; (insect) grillo m.

crime [kraɪm] n (serious offence) crimen m; (less serious offence) delito m; (illegal activity) delincuencia f.

criminal [krɪmɪnl] adj criminal ♦ n (serious) criminal mf; (less serious) delincuente mf; **~ offence** delito m.

cripple [krɪpl] n lisiado m (-da f) ♦ vt dejar inválido.

crisis [kraɪsɪs] (pl **crises** [kraɪsiːz]) n crisis f.

crisp [krɪsp] adj crujiente ▫

crisps npl (Br) patatas fpl fritas (de bolsa).

crispy [krɪspɪ] adj crujiente.

critic [krɪtɪk] n (reviewer) crítico m (-ca f).

critical [krɪtɪkl] adj crítico(-ca); (very serious, dangerous) grave.

criticize [krɪtɪsaɪz] vt criticar.

crockery [krɒkərɪ] n vajilla f.

crocodile [krɒkədaɪl] n cocodrilo m.

crocus [krəʊkəs] (pl **-es**) n azafrán m (flor).

crooked [krʊkɪd] adj torcido(-da).

crop [krɒp] n (kind of plant) cultivo m; (harvest) cosecha f ▫ **crop up** vi surgir.

cross [krɒs] adj enfadado(-da) ♦ n cruz f; (mixture) mezcla f ♦ vt cruzar ♦ vi cruzarse ▫ **cross out** vt sep tachar; **cross over** vt fus cruzar.

crossbar [krɒsbɑ:] n (of goal) larguero m; (of bicycle) barra f.

cross-Channel ferry n ferry que hace la travesía del Canal de la Mancha.

cross-country (running) n cross m.

crossing [krɒsɪŋ] n (on road) cruce m; (sea journey) travesía f.

crossroads [krɒsrəʊdz] (pl inv) n cruce m.

crosswalk [krɒswɔːk] n (Am) paso m de peatones.

crossword (puzzle) [krɒswɜːd-] n crucigrama m.

crotch [krɒtʃ] n entrepierna f.

crouton [kru:tɒn] n cuscurro m.

crow [krəʊ] n cuervo m.

crowbar [krəʊbɑ:] n palanca f.

crowd [kraʊd] n (large group of people) multitud f; (at match) público m.

crowded ['kraudɪd] adj atestado(-da).

crown [kraun] n corona f; (of head) coronilla f.

Crown Jewels npl joyas de la corona británica.

 CROWN JEWELS

Estas ricas joyas, que el monarca británico utiliza en ocasiones oficiales, se pueden admirar en la Torre de Londres, donde están expuestas en un edificio construido para tal fin. Las joyas de la antigua corona escocesa se pueden contemplar en el castillo de Edimburgo.

crucial ['kru:ʃl] adj crucial.

crude [kru:d] adj (rough) tosco(-ca); (rude) ordinario(-ria).

cruel [kruəl] adj cruel.

cruelty ['kruəltɪ] n crueldad f.

cruet (set) ['kru:ɪt-] n vinagreras fpl.

cruise [kru:z] n crucero m ◆ vi (car, plane, ship) ir a velocidad de crucero.

cruiser ['kru:zə'] n crucero m.

crumb [krʌm] n miga f.

crumble ['krʌmbl] n compota de fruta cubierta con una masa de harina, azúcar y mantequilla que se sirve caliente ◆ vi (building, cliff) desmoronarse; (cheese) desmenuzarse.

crumpet ['krʌmpɪt] n bollo que se come tostado y con mantequilla.

crunchy ['krʌntʃɪ] adj crujiente.

crush [krʌʃ] n (drink) zumo con

agua añadida ◆ vt (flatten) aplastar; (garlic, ice) triturar.

crust [krʌst] n corteza f.

crusty ['krʌstɪ] adj crujiente.

crutch [krʌtʃ] n (stick) muleta f; (between legs) = crotch.

cry [kraɪ] n grito m ◆ vi (weep) llorar; (shout) gritar ❑ **cry out** vi gritar.

crystal ['krɪstl] n cristal m.

cub [kʌb] n (animal) cachorro m.

Cub [kʌb] n boy scout de entre 8 y 11 años.

Cuba ['kju:bə] n Cuba.

Cuban ['kju:bən] adj cubano(-na) ◆ n cubano m (-na f).

cube [kju:b] n (shape) cubo m; (of sugar) terrón m; (of ice) cubito m.

cubicle ['kju:bɪkl] n (at swimming pool) caseta f; (in shop) probador m.

Cub Scout = Cub.

cuckoo ['kuku:] n cuclillo m.

cucumber ['kju:kʌmbə'] n pepino m.

cuddle ['kʌdl] n abrazo m.

cuddly toy ['kʌdlɪ-] n muñeco m de peluche.

cue [kju:] n (in snooker, pool) taco m.

cuff [kʌf] n (of sleeve) puño m; (Am: of trousers) vuelta f.

cuff links npl gemelos mpl.

cuisine [kwɪ'zi:n] n cocina f.

cul-de-sac ['kʌldəsæk] n callejón m sin salida.

cult [kʌlt] n culto m ◆ adj de culto.

cultivate ['kʌltɪveɪt] vt cultivar.

cultivated ['kʌltɪveɪtɪd] adj (person) culto(-ta).

cultural [ˈkʌltʃərəl] *adj* cultural.

culture [ˈkʌltʃə*ʳ*] *n* cultura *f*.

cumbersome [ˈkʌmbəsəm] *adj* aparatoso(-sa).

cumin [ˈkjuːmɪn] *n* comino *m*.

cunning [ˈkʌnɪŋ] *adj* astuto(-ta).

cup [kʌp] *n* (for drinking, cupful) taza *f*; (trophy, competition, of bra) copa *f*.

cupboard [ˈkʌbəd] *n* armario *m*.

curator [kjʊəˈreɪtə*ʳ*] *n* director *m* (-ra *f*) (de museo, biblioteca, etc).

curb [kɜːb] (Am) = **kerb**.

curd cheese [ˌkɜːd-] *n* requesón *m*.

cure [kjʊə*ʳ*] *n* cura *f* ♦ *vt* curar.

curious [ˈkjʊərɪəs] *adj* curioso(-sa).

curl [kɜːl] *n* (of hair) rizo *m* ♦ *vt* (hair) rizar.

curler [ˈkɜːlə*ʳ*] *n* rulo *m*.

curly [ˈkɜːlɪ] *adj* rizado(-da).

currant [ˈkʌrənt] *n* pasa *f* de Corinto.

currency [ˈkʌrənsɪ] *n* (money) moneda *f*.

current [ˈkʌrənt] *adj* actual ♦ *n* corriente *f*.

current account *n* (Br) cuenta *f* corriente.

current affairs *npl* temas *mpl* de actualidad.

currently [ˈkʌrəntlɪ] *adv* actualmente.

curriculum [kəˈrɪkjələm] *n* temario *m*.

curriculum vitae [-ˈviːtaɪ] *n* (Br) currículum *m* (vitae).

curried [ˈkʌrɪd] *adj* al curry.

curry [ˈkʌrɪ] *n* curry *m*.

curse [kɜːs] *vi* maldecir.

cursor [ˈkɜːsə*ʳ*] *n* cursor *m*.

curtain [ˈkɜːtn] *n* (in house) cortina *f*; (in theatre) telón *m*.

curve [kɜːv] *n* curva *f* ♦ *vi* torcer.

curved [kɜːvd] *adj* curvo(-va).

cushion [ˈkʊʃn] *n* cojín *m*.

custard [ˈkʌstəd] *n* natillas *fpl*.

custom [ˈkʌstəm] *n* (tradition) costumbre *f*; **"thank you for your ~"** "gracias por su visita".

customary [ˈkʌstəmrɪ] *adj* habitual.

customer [ˈkʌstəmə*ʳ*] *n* (of shop) cliente *m* (-ta *f*).

customer services *n* (department) servicio *m* de atención al cliente.

customs [ˈkʌstəmz] *n* aduana *f*; **to go through ~** pasar por la aduana.

customs duty *n* derechos *mpl* de aduana.

customs officer *n* empleado *m* (-da *f*) de aduana.

cut [kʌt] (pt & pp cut) *n* corte *m*; (reduction) reducción *f*, recorte *m* ♦ *vt* cortar; (reduce) reducir ♦ *vi* (knife, scissors) cortar; **to ~ and blow-dry** corte y peinado; **to ~ one's finger** cortarse el dedo; **to ~ one's nails** cortarse las uñas; **to ~ o.s.** cortarse; **to have one's hair ~** cortarse el pelo; **to ~ the grass** cortar el césped; **to ~ sthg open** abrir algo (cortándolo) ❑ **cut back** *vi*: **to ~ back on sthg** reducir algo; **cut down** *vt fus*: **to ~ down on sweets** comer menos golosinas; **cut off** *vt sep* (remove, disconnect) cortar; **I've been ~ off** (on phone) me han des-

conectado; **to be ~ off** *(isolated)*
estar aislado; **cut out** *vt sep (newspaper article, photo)* recortar ◆ *vi (engine)* calarse; **to ~ out smoking**
dejar de fumar; **~ it out!** *(inf)*
¡basta ya!; **cut up** *vt sep* desmenuzar.

cute [kju:t] *adj* mono(-na).

cut-glass *adj* de cristal labrado.

cutlery ['kʌtləri] *n* cubertería *f*.

cutlet ['kʌtlɪt] *n (of meat)* chuleta
f; *(of nuts, vegetables)* ≃ croqueta
f.

cut-price *adj* de oferta.

cutting ['kʌtɪŋ] *n (from newspaper)* recorte *m*.

CV *n (Br: abbr of curriculum vitae)*
CV *m*.

cwt *abbr* = **hundredweight**.

cycle ['saɪkl] *n (bicycle)* bicicleta *f*;
(series) ciclo *m* ◆ *vi* ir en bicicleta.

cycle hire *n* alquiler *m* de bicicletas.

cycle lane *n* carril-bici *m*.

cycle path *n* camino *m* para
bicicletas.

cycling ['saɪklɪŋ] *n* ciclismo *m*; **to
go ~** ir en bicicleta.

cycling shorts *npl* pantalones
mpl de ciclista.

cyclist ['saɪklɪst] *n* ciclista *mf*.

cylinder ['sɪlɪndər] *n (container)*
bombona *f*; *(in engine)* cilindro *m*.

cynical ['sɪnɪkl] *adj* cínico(-ca).

Czech [tʃek] *adj* checo(-ca) ◆ *n
(person)* checo *m* (-ca *f*); *(language)*
checo *m*.

Czechoslovakia [,tʃekəsləˈvækɪə] *n* Checoslovaquia *f*.

Czech Republic *n*: **the ~** la
República Checa.

D

dab [dæb] *vt (ointment, cream)* aplicar una pequeña cantidad de.

dad [dæd] *n (inf)* papá *m*.

daddy ['dædɪ] *n (inf)* papá *m*.

daddy longlegs [-'lɒŋlegz] *(pl
inv)* *n* típula *f*.

daffodil ['dæfədɪl] *n* narciso *m*.

daft [dɑ:ft] *adj (Br: inf)* tonto
(-ta).

daily ['deɪlɪ] *adj* diario(-ria) ◆ *adv*
diariamente ◆ *n*: **a ~ (newspaper)**
un diario.

dairy ['deərɪ] *n (on farm)* vaquería
f; *(shop)* lechería *f*.

dairy product *n* producto *m*
lácteo.

daisy ['deɪzɪ] *n* margarita *f*.

dam [dæm] *n* presa *f*.

damage ['dæmɪdʒ] *n (physical
harm)* daño *m*; *(fig: to reputation,
chances)* perjuicio *m* ◆ *vt (house, car)*
dañar; *(back, leg)* hacerse daño en;
(fig: reputation, chances) perjudicar.

damn [dæm] *excl (inf)* ¡maldita
sea! ◆ *adj (inf)* maldito(-ta) ◆ *n*: **I
don't give a ~** me importa un rábano.

damp [dæmp] *adj* húmedo(-da) ◆
n humedad *f*.

damson ['dæmzn] *n* ciruela *f*
damascena.

dance [dɑ:ns] *n* baile *m* ◆ *vi* bailar;
to have a ~ bailar.

dance floor *n* pista *f* de baile.

dancer ['dɑːnsər] n bailarín m (-ina f).

dancing ['dɑːnsɪŋ] n baile m; **to go ~** ir a bailar.

dandelion ['dændɪlaɪən] n diente m de león.

dandruff ['dændrʌf] n caspa f.

Dane [deɪn] n danés m (-esa f).

danger ['deɪndʒər] n peligro m; **in ~** en peligro.

dangerous ['deɪndʒərəs] adj peligroso(-sa).

Danish ['deɪnɪʃ] adj danés(-esa) ♦ n (language) danés m.

Danish pastry n pasta de hojaldre con pasas, manzanas, etc.

dare [deər] vt: **to ~ to do sthg** atreverse a hacer algo; **to ~ sb to do sthg** desafiar a alguien a hacer algo; **how ~ you!** ¡cómo te atreves!

daring ['deərɪŋ] adj atrevido(-da).

dark [dɑːk] adj oscuro(-ra); (day, weather) sombrío(-a); (person, skin) moreno(-na) ♦ n: **after ~** después del anochecer; **the ~** la oscuridad.

dark chocolate n chocolate m amargo.

dark glasses npl gafas fpl oscuras.

darkness ['dɑːknɪs] n oscuridad f.

darling ['dɑːlɪŋ] n (term of affection) querido m (-da f).

dart [dɑːt] n dardo m □ **darts** n (game) dardos mpl.

dartboard ['dɑːtbɔːd] n diana f.

dash [dæʃ] n (of liquid) gotas fpl; (in writing) guión m ♦ vi ir de prisa.

dashboard ['dæʃbɔːd] n salpicadero m.

data ['deɪtə] n datos mpl.

database ['deɪtəbeɪs] n base f de datos.

date [deɪt] n (day) fecha f; (meeting) cita f; (Am: person) pareja f (con la que se sale); (fruit) dátil m ♦ vt (cheque, letter) fechar; (person) salir con ♦ vi (become unfashionable) pasar de moda; **what's the ~?** ¿qué fecha es?; **to have a ~ with sb** tener una cita con alguien.

date of birth n fecha f de nacimiento.

daughter ['dɔːtər] n hija f.

daughter-in-law n nuera f.

dawn [dɔːn] n amanecer m.

day [deɪ] n día m; **what ~ is it today?** ¿qué día es hoy?; **what a lovely ~!** ¡qué día más bonito!; **to have a ~ off** tomarse un día libre!; **to have a ~ out** ir de excursión; **by ~** de día; **the ~ after tomorrow** pasado mañana; **the ~ before** el día anterior; **the ~ before yesterday** anteayer; **the following ~** el día siguiente; **have a nice ~!** ¡adiós y gracias!

daylight ['deɪlaɪt] n luz f del día.

day return n (Br) billete m de ida y vuelta para un día.

dayshift ['deɪʃɪft] n turno m de día.

daytime ['deɪtaɪm] n día m.

day-to-day adj cotidiano(-na).

day trip n excursión f (de un día).

dazzle ['dæzl] vt deslumbrar.

DC (abbr of direct current) CC.

dead [ded] adj (not alive) muerto(-ta); (not lively) sin vida; (telephone, line) cortado(-da); (battery) descargado(-da) ♦ adv (precisely) justo; (inf: very) la mar de; **it's ~**

ahead está justo enfrente; **"~ slow"** "al paso".

dead end n (street) callejón m sin salida.

deadline ['dedlaɪn] n fecha f tope.

deaf [def] adj sordo(-da) ♦ npl: **the ~** los sordos.

deal [diːl] (pt & pp **dealt**) n (agreement) trato m ♦ vt (cards) repartir; **to be a good/bad ~** estar bien/mal de precio; **a great ~ of** mucho; **it's a ~!** ¡trato hecho! □ **deal in** vt fus comerciar en; **deal with** vt fus (handle) hacer frente a; (be about) tratar de.

dealer ['diːləʳ] n (COMM) comerciante mf; (in drugs) traficante mf (que vende).

dealt [delt] pt & pp → **deal**.

dear [dɪəʳ] adj (loved) querido(-da); (expensive) caro(-ra) ♦ n: **my ~** querido m (-da f); **Dear Sir** Muy señor mío; **Dear Madam** Estimada señora; **Dear John** Querido John; **oh ~!** ¡vaya por Dios!

death [deθ] n muerte f.

debate [dɪ'beɪt] n debate m ♦ vt (wonder) pensar, considerar.

debit ['debɪt] n debe m ♦ vt: **to ~ sb's account with an amount** deducir una cantidad de la cuenta de alguien.

debt [det] n deuda f; **to be in ~** tener deudas.

decaff ['diːkæf] n (inf) descafeinado m.

decaffeinated [dɪ'kæfɪneɪtɪd] adj descafeinado(-da).

decanter [dɪ'kæntəʳ] n licorera f.

decay [dɪ'keɪ] n (of building, wood) deterioro m; (of tooth) caries f inv ♦ vi descomponerse.

deceive [dɪ'siːv] vt engañar.

decelerate [ˌdiː'seləreɪt] vi desacelerar.

December [dɪ'sembəʳ] n diciembre m, → **September**.

decent ['diːsnt] adj decente; (kind) amable.

decide [dɪ'saɪd] vt & vi decidir; **to ~ to do sthg** decidir hacer algo □ **decide on** vt fus decidirse por.

decimal ['desɪml] adj decimal.

decimal point n coma f decimal.

decision [dɪ'sɪʒn] n decisión f; **to make a ~** tomar una decisión.

decisive [dɪ'saɪsɪv] adj (person) decidido(-da); (event, factor) decisivo(-va).

deck [dek] n (of ship) cubierta f; (of bus) piso m; (of cards) baraja f.

deckchair ['dektʃeəʳ] n tumbona f.

declare [dɪ'kleəʳ] vt declarar; **to ~ that** declarar que; **"goods to ~"** cartel que indica la ruta para personas con objetos que declarar en la aduana; **"nothing to ~"** cartel que indica la ruta para personas sin objetos que declarar en la aduana.

decline [dɪ'klaɪn] n declive m ♦ vi (get worse) disminuir; (refuse) rehusar.

decorate ['dekəreɪt] vt (with wallpaper) empapelar; (with paint) pintar; (make attractive) decorar.

decoration [ˌdekə'reɪʃn] n (wallpaper, paint, furniture) decoración f; (decorative object) adorno m.

decorator [ˈdekəreɪtəʳ] n (painter) pintor m (-ra f); (paperhanger) empapelador m (-ra f).

decrease [n ˈdiːkriːs, vb dɪˈkriːs] n disminución f ♦ vi disminuir.

dedicated [ˈdedɪkeɪtɪd] adj dedicado(-da).

deduce [dɪˈdjuːs] vt deducir.

deduct [dɪˈdʌkt] vt deducir.

deduction [dɪˈdʌkʃn] n deducción f.

deep [diːp] adj profundo(-da); (colour) intenso(-sa); (breath, sigh) hondo(-da); (voice) grave ♦ adv hondo; **it's two metres ~** tiene dos metros de profundidad.

deep end n (of swimming pool) parte f honda.

deep freeze n congelador m.

deep-fried [-ˈfraɪd] adj frito(-ta) en aceite abundante.

deep-pan adj de masa doble.

deer [dɪəʳ] (pl inv) n ciervo m.

defeat [dɪˈfiːt] n derrota f ♦ vt derrotar.

defect [ˈdiːfekt] n defecto m.

defective [dɪˈfektɪv] adj defectuoso(-sa).

defence [dɪˈfens] n (Br) defensa f.

defend [dɪˈfend] vt defender.

defense [dɪˈfens] (Am) = **defence**.

deficiency [dɪˈfɪʃnsɪ] n (lack) deficiencia f.

deficit [ˈdefɪsɪt] n déficit m inv.

define [dɪˈfaɪn] vt definir.

definite [ˈdefɪnɪt] adj (answer, plans) definitivo(-va); (improvement) claro(-ra); (person) concluyente; **it's not ~** no es seguro.

definite article n artículo m definido.

definitely [ˈdefɪnɪtlɪ] adv (certainly) sin duda alguna.

definition [defɪˈnɪʃn] n (of word) definición f.

deflate [dɪˈfleɪt] vt (tyre) desinflar.

deflect [dɪˈflekt] vt desviar.

defogger [diːˈfɒɡəʳ] n (Am) luneta f térmica.

deformed [dɪˈfɔːmd] adj deforme.

defrost [diːˈfrɒst] vt (food, fridge) descongelar; (Am: demist) desempañar.

degree [dɪˈɡriː] n grado m; (qualification) = licenciatura f; **to have a ~ in sthg** tener una licenciatura en algo.

dehydrated [diːhaɪˈdreɪtɪd] adj deshidratado(-da).

de-ice [diːˈaɪs] vt descongelar.

de-icer [diːˈaɪsəʳ] n descongelante m.

dejected [dɪˈdʒektɪd] adj abatido(-da).

delay [dɪˈleɪ] n retraso m ♦ vt retrasar ♦ vi retrasarse; **without ~** sin demora.

delayed [dɪˈleɪd] adj: **to be ~** ir con retraso; **our train was ~ by two hours** nuestro tren llegó con dos horas de retraso.

delegate [n ˈdelɪɡət, vb ˈdelɪɡeɪt] n delegado m (-da f) ♦ vt (person) delegar.

delete [dɪˈliːt] vt borrar.

deli [ˈdelɪ] n (inf: abbr of delicatessen) = charcutería f.

deliberate [dɪˈlɪbərət] adj (inten-

tional) deliberado(-da).

deliberately [dɪ'lɪbərətlɪ] *adv* (*intentionally*) deliberadamente.

delicacy ['delɪkəsɪ] *n* (*food*) manjar *m*.

delicate ['delɪkət] *adj* delicado(-da); (*object, china*) frágil; (*taste, smell*) suave.

delicatessen [,delɪkə'tesn] *n* = charcutería *f*.

delicious [dɪ'lɪʃəs] *adj* delicioso(-sa).

delight [dɪ'laɪt] *n* (*feeling*) gozo *m* ♦ *vt* encantar; **to take (a) ~ in doing sthg** deleitarse haciendo algo.

delighted [dɪ'laɪtɪd] *adj* encantado(-da).

delightful [dɪ'laɪtfʊl] *adj* encantador(-ra).

deliver [dɪ'lɪvər] *vt* (*goods, letters, newspaper*) entregar; (*speech, lecture*) pronunciar; (*baby*) traer al mundo.

delivery [dɪ'lɪvərɪ] *n* (*of goods, letters*) entrega *f*; (*birth*) parto *m*.

delude [dɪ'luːd] *vt* engañar.

de-luxe [də'lʌks] *adj* de lujo.

demand [dɪ'mɑːnd] *n* demanda *f*; (*requirement*) requisito *m* ♦ *vt* (*request forcefully*) exigir; (*require*) requerir; **to ~ to do sthg** exigir hacer algo; **in ~** solicitado.

demanding [dɪ'mɑːndɪŋ] *adj* absorbente.

demerara sugar [demə'reərə-] *n* azúcar *m* moreno.

demist [,diː'mɪst] *vt* (*Br*) desempañar.

demister [,diː'mɪstər] *n* (*Br*) luneta *f* térmica.

democracy [dɪ'mɒkrəsɪ] *n* democracia *f*.

Democrat ['deməkræt] *n* (*Am*) demócrata *mf*.

democratic [demə'krætɪk] *adj* democrático(-ca).

demolish [dɪ'mɒlɪʃ] *vt* (*building*) demoler.

demonstrate ['demənstreɪt] *vt* (*prove*) demostrar; (*machine, appliance*) hacer una demostración de ♦ *vi* manifestarse.

demonstration [demən'streɪʃn] *n* (*protest*) manifestación *f*; (*of machine, proof*) demostración *f*.

denial [dɪ'naɪəl] *n* negación *f*.

denim ['denɪm] *n* tela *f* vaquera ❑ **denims** *npl* vaqueros *mpl*.

denim jacket *n* cazadora *f* vaquera.

Denmark ['denmɑːk] *n* Dinamarca.

dense [dens] *adj* (*crowd, smoke, forest*) denso(-sa).

dent [dent] *n* abolladura *f*.

dental ['dentl] *adj* dental.

dental floss [-flɒs] *n* hilo *m* dental.

dental surgeon *n* odontólogo *m* (-ga *f*).

dental surgery *n* (*place*) clínica *f* dental.

dentist ['dentɪst] *n* dentista *mf*; **to go to the ~'s** ir al dentista.

dentures ['dentʃəz] *npl* dentadura *f* postiza.

deny [dɪ'naɪ] *vt* (*declare untrue*) negar; (*refuse*) denegar.

deodorant [diː'əʊdərənt] *n* desodorante *m*.

depart [dɪ'pɑːt] *vi* salir; **this train**

will ~ **from platform 3** este tren efectuará su salida de la vía 3.

department [dɪˈpɑːtmənt] n departamento m; (of government) ministerio m.

department store n grandes almacenes mpl.

departure [dɪˈpɑːtʃəʳ] n salida f; "~s" "salidas".

departure lounge n (at airport) sala f de embarque; (at coach station) vestíbulo m de salidas.

depend [dɪˈpend] vi: **it ~s** depende ◻ **depend on** vt fus (be decided by) depender de; (rely on) confiar en; **~ing on** dependiendo de.

dependable [dɪˈpendəbl] adj fiable.

deplorable [dɪˈplɔːrəbl] adj deplorable.

deport [dɪˈpɔːt] vt deportar.

deposit [dɪˈpɒzɪt] n (in bank) ingreso m; (part-payment) entrada f; (against damage) depósito m; (substance) sedimento m ◆ vt (put down) depositar; (money in bank) ingresar.

deposit account n (Br) cuenta f de ahorro a plazo fijo.

depot [ˈdiːpəʊ] n (Am: for buses, trains) terminal f.

depressed [dɪˈprest] adj deprimido(-da).

depressing [dɪˈpresɪŋ] adj deprimente.

depression [dɪˈpreʃn] n depresión f.

deprive [dɪˈpraɪv] vt: **to ~ sb of sthg** privar a alguien de algo.

depth [depθ] n profundidad f; **I'm out of my ~** (when swimming) he perdido pie; (fig: unable to cope)

no puedo; **~ of field** profundidad de campo.

deputy [ˈdepjʊtɪ] adj suplente; **~ head** subdirector m (-ra f).

derailleur [dəˈreɪljəʳ] n cambio m de piñón.

derailment [dɪˈreɪlmənt] n descarrilamiento m.

derelict [ˈderəlɪkt] adj abandonado(-da).

derv [dɜːv] n (Br) gasóleo m.

descend [dɪˈsend] vt descender por ◆ vi descender.

descendant [dɪˈsendənt] n descendiente mf.

descent [dɪˈsent] n (going down) descenso m; (downward slope) pendiente f.

describe [dɪˈskraɪb] vt describir.

description [dɪˈskrɪpʃn] n descripción f.

desert [n ˈdezət, vb dɪˈzɜːt] n desierto m ◆ vt abandonar.

deserted [dɪˈzɜːtɪd] adj desierto(-ta).

deserve [dɪˈzɜːv] vt merecer.

design [dɪˈzaɪn] n diseño m ◆ vt diseñar; **to be ~ed for** estar diseñado para.

designer [dɪˈzaɪnəʳ] n diseñador m (-ra f) ◆ adj (clothes, sunglasses) de marca.

desirable [dɪˈzaɪərəbl] adj deseable.

desire [dɪˈzaɪəʳ] n deseo m ◆ vt desear; **it leaves a lot to be ~d** deja mucho que desear.

desk [desk] n (in home, office) escritorio m; (in school) pupitre m; (at airport, station, hotel) mostrador m.

desktop publishing ['desk‚tɒp] n autoedición f de textos.

despair [dɪ'speəʳ] n desesperación f.

despatch [dɪ'spætʃ] = dispatch.

desperate ['desprət] adj desesperado(-da); **to be ~ for sthg** necesitar algo desesperadamente.

despicable [dɪ'spɪkəbl] adj despreciable.

despise [dɪ'spaɪz] vt despreciar.

despite [dɪ'spaɪt] prep a pesar de.

dessert [dɪ'zɜːt] n postre m.

dessertspoon [dɪ'zɜːtspuːn] n (spoon) cuchara f de postre; (spoonful) cucharada f (de postre).

destination [‚destɪ'neɪʃn] n destino m.

destroy [dɪ'strɔɪ] vt destruir.

destruction [dɪ'strʌkʃn] n destrucción f.

detach [dɪ'tætʃ] vt separar.

detached house [dɪ'tætʃt-] n casa f individual.

detail [ˈdiːteɪl] n (minor point) detalle m; (facts, information) detalles mpl; **in ~** detalladamente ◻ **details** npl (facts) información f.

detailed ['diːteɪld] adj detallado(-da).

detect [dɪ'tekt] vt detectar.

detective [dɪ'tektɪv] n detective mf; **a ~ story** una novela policíaca.

detention [dɪ'tenʃn] n (SCH) castigo de permanecer en la escuela después de clase.

detergent [dɪ'tɜːdʒənt] n detergente m.

deteriorate [dɪ'tɪərɪəreɪt] vi deteriorarse.

determination [dɪ‚tɜːmɪ'neɪʃn]
n determinación f.

determine [dɪ'tɜːmɪn] vt determinar.

determined [dɪ'tɜːmɪnd] adj decidido(-da); **to be ~ to do sthg** estar decidido a hacer algo.

deterrent [dɪ'terənt] n fuerza f disuasoria.

detest [dɪ'test] vt detestar.

detour [‚diː'tuəʳ] n desvío m.

detrain [‚diː'treɪn] vi (fml) apearse (de un tren).

deuce [djuːs] excl (in tennis) cuarenta iguales.

devastate ['devəsteɪt] vt devastar.

develop [dɪ'veləp] vt (idea, company) desarrollar; (land) urbanizar; (film) revelar; (machine, method) elaborar; (illness) contraer; (habit, interest) adquirir ◆ vi (evolve) desarrollarse.

developing country [dɪ'veləpɪŋ-] n país m en vías de desarrollo.

development [dɪ'veləpmənt] n (growth) desarrollo m; (new event) (nuevo) acontecimiento m; **a housing ~** una urbanización.

device [dɪ'vaɪs] n dispositivo m.

devil ['devl] n diablo m; **what the ~ ...?** (inf) ¿qué demonios ...?

devise [dɪ'vaɪz] vt diseñar.

devoted [dɪ'vəʊtɪd] adj dedicado(-da), leal.

dew [djuː] n rocío m.

diabetes [‚daɪə'biːtiːz] n diabetes f inv.

diabetic [‚daɪə'betɪk] adj (person) diabético(-ca); (chocolate) para diabéticos ◆ n diabético m (-ca f).

diagnosis [daɪəgˈnəʊsɪs] (pl -oses [-əsiːz]) n diagnóstico m.

diagonal [daɪˈægənəl] adj diagonal.

diagram ['daɪəgræm] n diagrama m.

dial ['daɪəl] n (of telephone, radio) dial m; (of clock) esfera f ◆ vt marcar.

dialling code ['daɪəlɪŋ-] n (Br) prefijo m (telefónico).

dialling tone ['daɪəlɪŋ-] n (Br) señal f de llamada.

dial tone (Am) = **dialling tone**.

diameter [daɪˈæmɪtə] n diámetro m.

diamond ['daɪəmənd] n diamante m □ **diamonds** npl (in cards) diamantes mpl.

diaper ['daɪpə] n (Am) pañal m.

diarrhoea [daɪəˈrɪə] n diarrea f.

diary ['daɪərɪ] n (for appointments) agenda f; (journal) diario m.

dice [daɪs] (pl inv) n dado m.

diced [daɪst] adj cortado(-da) en cuadraditos.

dictate [dɪkˈteɪt] vt dictar.

dictation [dɪkˈteɪʃn] n dictado m.

dictator [dɪkˈteɪtə] n dictador m (-ra f).

dictionary ['dɪkʃənrɪ] n diccionario m.

did [dɪd] pt → do.

die [daɪ] (cont dying) vi morir; to be dying for sthg (inf) morirse por algo; to be dying to do sthg (inf) morirse por hacer algo □ **die away** vi desvanecerse; **die out** vi extinguirse.

diesel ['diːzl] n (fuel) gasóleo m; (car) vehículo m diesel.

diet ['daɪət] n (for slimming, health) dieta f; régimen m; (food eaten) dieta f ◆ vi estar a régimen ◆ adj bajo(-ja) en calorías.

diet Coke® n Coca-Cola® f light.

differ ['dɪfə] vi: to ~ (from) (be dissimilar) ser distinto (de); (disagree) discrepar (de).

difference ['dɪfrəns] n diferencia f; it makes no ~ da lo mismo; a ~ of opinion un desacuerdo.

different ['dɪfrənt] adj distinto(-ta); to be ~ (from) ser distinto (de).

differently ['dɪfrəntlɪ] adv de otra forma.

difficult ['dɪfɪkəlt] adj difícil.

difficulty ['dɪfɪkəltɪ] n dificultad f.

dig [dɪg] (pt & pp dug) vt (hole, tunnel) excavar; (garden, land) cavar ◆ vi cavar □ **dig out** vt sep sacar; **dig up** vt sep desenterrar.

digest [dɪˈdʒest] vt digerir.

digestion [dɪˈdʒestʃn] n digestión f.

digestive (biscuit) [dɪˈdʒestɪv-] n (Br) galleta hecha con harina integral.

digit ['dɪdʒɪt] n (figure) dígito m; (finger, toe) dedo m.

digital ['dɪdʒɪtl] adj digital.

dill [dɪl] n eneldo m.

dilute [daɪˈluːt] vt diluir.

dim [dɪm] adj (light) tenue; (room) sombrío(-a); (inf: stupid) torpe ◆ vt atenuar.

dime [daɪm] n (Am) moneda de diez

centavos.

dimensions ['dɪmenʃnz] *npl* (measurements) dimensiones *fpl*; (extent) dimensión *f*.

din [dɪn] *n* estrépito *m*.

dine [daɪn] *vi* cenar □ **dine out** *vi* cenar fuera.

diner ['daɪnə'] *n* (Am: restaurant) restaurante *m* económico; (person) cliente *mf* (en un restaurante).

[*i*] **DINER**

Los "diners" pequeños restaurantes baratos donde se sirven comidas ligeras, suelen localizarse en las carreteras principales, aunque también se dan en ciudades. La mayoría de sus clientes son camioneros y gente de paso.

dinghy ['dɪŋgɪ] *n* bote *m*.

dingy ['dɪndʒɪ] *adj* lóbrego(-ga).

dining car ['daɪnɪŋ-] *n* vagón *m* restaurante.

dining hall ['daɪnɪŋ-] *n* comedor *m*.

dining room ['daɪnɪŋ-] *n* comedor *m*.

dinner ['dɪnə'] *n* (at lunchtime) almuerzo *m*; (in evening) cena *f*; **to have ~** (at lunchtime) almorzar; (in evening) cenar.

dinner jacket *n* esmoquin *m*.

dinner party *n* cena *f* (de amigos en casa).

dinner set *n* vajilla *f*.

dinner suit *n* traje *m* de esmoquin.

dinnertime ['dɪnətaɪm] *n* (at lunchtime) hora *f* del almuerzo; (in evening) hora de la cena.

dinosaur ['daɪnəsɔ:'] *n* dinosaurio *m*.

dip [dɪp] *n* (in road, land) pendiente *f*; (food) salsa *f* ♦ *vt* (into liquid) mojar ♦ *vi* descender ligeramente; **to have a ~** darse un chapuzón; **to ~ one's headlights** (Br) poner las luces de cruce.

diploma [dɪ'pləʊmə] *n* diploma *m*.

dipstick ['dɪpstɪk] *n* varilla *f* (para medir el nivel) del aceite.

direct [dɪ'rekt] *adj* directo(-ta) ♦ *vt* dirigir; (give directions to) indicar el camino a ♦ *adv* directamente.

direct current *n* corriente *f* continua.

direction [dɪ'rekʃn] *n* dirección *f*; **to ask for ~s** pedir señas □ **directions** *npl* (instructions) instrucciones *fpl* (de uso).

directly [dɪ'rektlɪ] *adv* (exactly) directamente; (soon) pronto.

director [dɪ'rektə'] *n* director *m*.

directory [dɪ'rektərɪ] *n* guía *f* (telefónica).

directory enquiries *n* (Br) servicio *m* de información telefónica.

dirt [dɜ:t] *n* suciedad *f*; (earth) tierra *f*.

dirty ['dɜ:tɪ] *adj* sucio(-cia); (joke) verde.

disability [,dɪsə'bɪlətɪ] *n* minusvalía *f*.

disabled [dɪs'eɪbld] *adj* minusválido(-da) ♦ *npl*: **the ~** los minusválidos; **~ toilet** "aseo para minusválidos".

disadvantage [ˌdɪsədˈvɑːntɪdʒ] n desventaja f.

disagree [ˌdɪsəˈgriː] vi (people) discrepar; to ~ with sb (about) no estar de acuerdo con alguien (sobre); those mussels ~d with me los mejillones me sentaron mal.

disagreement [ˌdɪsəˈgriːmənt] n (argument) discusión f; (dissimilarity) discrepancia f.

disappear [ˌdɪsəˈpɪəʳ] vi desaparecer.

disappearance [ˌdɪsəˈpɪərəns] n desaparición f.

disappoint [ˌdɪsəˈpɔɪnt] vt decepcionar.

disappointed [ˌdɪsəˈpɔɪntɪd] adj decepcionado(-da).

disappointing [ˌdɪsəˈpɔɪntɪŋ] adj decepcionante.

disappointment [ˌdɪsəˈpɔɪntmənt] n decepción f.

disapprove [ˌdɪsəˈpruːv] vi: to ~ of censurar.

disarmament [dɪsˈɑːməmənt] n desarme m.

disaster [dɪˈzɑːstəʳ] n desastre m.

disastrous [dɪˈzɑːstrəs] adj desastroso(-sa).

disc [dɪsk] n (Br)(circular object, record) disco m; (CD) disco compacto; to slip a ~ sufrir una hernia discal.

discard [dɪsˈkɑːd] vt desechar.

discharge [dɪsˈtʃɑːdʒ] vt (prisoner) poner en libertad; (patient) dar de alta; (soldier) licenciar; (liquid, smoke, gas) emitir.

discipline [ˈdɪsɪplɪn] n disciplina f.

disc jockey n pinchadiscos mf inv.

disco [ˈdɪskəʊ] n (place) discoteca f; (event) baile m.

discoloured [dɪsˈkʌləd] adj descolorido(-da).

discomfort [dɪsˈkʌmfət] n (pain) malestar m.

disconnect [ˌdɪskəˈnekt] vt (unplug) desenchufar; (telephone, gas supply, pipe) desconectar.

discontinued [ˌdɪskənˈtɪnjuːd] adj (product) que ya no se fabrica.

discotheque [ˈdɪskətek] n (place) discoteca f; (event) baile m.

discount [ˈdɪskaʊnt] n descuento m.

discover [dɪˈskʌvəʳ] vt descubrir.

discovery [dɪˈskʌvərɪ] n descubrimiento m.

discreet [dɪˈskriːt] adj discreto(-ta).

discrepancy [dɪˈskrepənsɪ] n discrepancia f.

discriminate [dɪˈskrɪmɪneɪt] vi: to ~ against sb discriminar a alguien.

discrimination [dɪˌskrɪmɪˈneɪʃn] n discriminación f.

discuss [dɪˈskʌs] vt discutir.

discussion [dɪˈskʌʃn] n discusión f.

disease [dɪˈziːz] n enfermedad f.

disembark [ˌdɪsɪmˈbɑːk] vi desembarcar.

disgrace [dɪsˈgreɪs] n vergüenza f; it's a ~! ¡es una vergüenza!

disgraceful [dɪsˈgreɪsfʊl] adj vergonzoso(-sa).

disguise [dɪsˈgaɪz] n disfraz m ◆ vt disfrazar; in ~ disfrazado.

disgust [dɪsˈɡʌst] n asco m ◆ vt asquear.

disgusting [dɪsˈɡʌstɪn] adj asqueroso(-sa).

dish [dɪʃ] n (container) fuente f; (food) plato m; (Am: plate) plato; **to do the ~s** fregar los platos; **"~ of the day"** "plato del día" ❑ **dish up** vt sep servir.

dishcloth [ˈdɪʃklɒθ] n trapo m de fregar los platos.

disheveled [dɪˈʃevəld] (Am) = **dishevelled**.

dishevelled [dɪˈʃevəld] adj (Br: person) desaliñado(-da).

dishonest [dɪsˈɒnɪst] adj deshonesto(-ta).

dish towel n (Am) paño m de cocina.

dishwasher [ˈdɪʃˌwɒʃəʳ] n (machine) lavavajillas m inv.

disinfectant [ˌdɪsɪnˈfektənt] n desinfectante m.

disintegrate [dɪsˈɪntɪɡreɪt] vi desintegrarse.

disk [dɪsk] n (Am) = **disc**; (COMPUT) disquete m.

disk drive n disquetera f.

dislike [dɪsˈlaɪk] n (poor opinion) aversión f ◆ vt tener aversión a; **to take a ~ to** cogerle manía a.

dislocate [ˈdɪsləkeɪt] vt dislocar.

dismal [ˈdɪzml] adj (weather, place) sombrío(-a); (terrible) lamentable.

dismantle [dɪsˈmæntl] vt desmontar.

dismay [dɪsˈmeɪ] n consternación f.

dismiss [dɪsˈmɪs] vt (not consider) desechar; (from job) despedir; (from

classroom) echar.

disobedient [ˌdɪsəˈbiːdjənt] adj desobediente.

disobey [ˌdɪsəˈbeɪ] vt desobedecer.

disorder [dɪsˈɔːdəʳ] n (confusion) desorden m; (violence) disturbios mpl; (illness) afección f.

disorganized [dɪsˈɔːɡənaɪzd] adj desorganizado(-da).

dispatch [dɪsˈpætʃ] vt enviar.

dispense [dɪsˈpens]: **dispense with** vt fus prescindir de.

dispenser [dɪsˈpensəʳ] n máquina f expendedora.

dispensing chemist [dɪsˈpensɪn]- n (Br) (person) farmacéutico m (-ca f); (shop) farmacia f.

disperse [dɪsˈpɜːs] vt dispersar ◆ vi dispersarse.

display [dɪsˈpleɪ] n (of goods in window) escaparate m; (public event) demostración f; (readout) pantalla f ◆ vt (goods, information) exponer; (feeling, quality) mostrar; **on ~** expuesto.

displeased [dɪsˈpliːzd] adj disgustado(-da).

disposable [dɪsˈpəʊzəbl] adj desechable.

dispute [dɪsˈpjuːt] n (argument) disputa f; (industrial) conflicto m ◆ vt cuestionar.

disqualify [ˌdɪsˈkwɒlɪfaɪ] vt descalificar; **he has been disqualified from driving** (Br) se le ha retirado el permiso de conducir.

disregard [ˌdɪsrɪˈɡɑːd] vt hacer caso omiso de.

disrupt [dɪsˈrʌpt] vt trastornar.

disruption [dɪsˈrʌpʃn] n trastorno m.

dissatisfied [ˌdɪsˈsætɪsfaɪd] adj descontento(-ta).

dissolve [dɪˈzɒlv] vt disolver ♦ vi disolverse.

dissuade [dɪˈsweɪd] vt: **to ~ sb from doing sthg** disuadir a alguien de hacer algo.

distance [ˈdɪstəns] n distancia f; **from a ~** desde lejos; **in the ~** a lo lejos.

distant [ˈdɪstənt] adj lejano(-na); (reserved) distante.

distilled water [dɪˈstɪld-] n agua f destilada.

distillery [dɪˈstɪlərɪ] n destilería f.

distinct [dɪˈstɪŋkt] adj (separate) distinto(-ta); (noticeable) notable.

distinction [dɪˈstɪŋkʃn] n (difference) distinción f; (mark for work) sobresaliente m.

distinctive [dɪˈstɪŋktɪv] adj característico(-ca).

distinguish [dɪˈstɪŋgwɪʃ] vt distinguir; **to ~ sthg from sthg** distinguir algo de algo.

distorted [dɪˈstɔːtɪd] adj (figure, shape) deformado(-da); (sound) distorsionado(-da).

distract [dɪˈstrækt] vt distraer.

distraction [dɪˈstrækʃn] n distracción f.

distress [dɪˈstres] n (pain) dolor m; (anxiety) angustia f.

distressing [dɪˈstresɪŋ] adj angustioso(-sa).

distribute [dɪˈstrɪbjuːt] vt distribuir.

distributor [dɪˈstrɪbjutə⁰] n (COMM) distribuidor m (-ra f); (AUT)

delco m.

district [ˈdɪstrɪkt] n (region) región f; (of town) distrito m.

district attorney n (Am) fiscal mf (del distrito).

disturb [dɪˈstɜːb] vt (interrupt) molestar; (worry) inquietar; (move) mover; **"do not ~"** "no molestar".

disturbance [dɪˈstɜːbəns] n (riot) disturbio m; (small altercation) altercado m.

ditch [dɪtʃ] n zanja f.

ditto [ˈdɪtəʊ] adv idem.

divan [dɪˈvæn] n diván m.

dive [daɪv] (pt Am **-d** OR **dove**, pt Br **-d**) n (of swimmer) zambullida f ♦ vi (from divingboard, rock) zambullirse; (under water) bucear; (bird, plane) bajar en picado; (rush) lanzarse.

diver [ˈdaɪvə⁰] n (from divingboard, rock) saltador m (-ra f); (under water) buceador m (-ra f).

diversion [daɪˈvɜːʃn] n (of traffic) desvío m; (amusement) diversión f.

divert [daɪˈvɜːt] vt (traffic, river) desviar; (attention) distraer.

divide [dɪˈvaɪd] vt dividir; (share out) repartir □ **divide up** vt sep (into two parts) dividir; (share out) repartir.

diving [ˈdaɪvɪŋ] n (from divingboard, rock) salto m; (under water) buceo m; **to go ~** bucear.

divingboard [ˈdaɪvɪŋbɔːd] n trampolín m.

division [dɪˈvɪʒn] n división f.

divorce [dɪˈvɔːs] n divorcio m ♦ vt divorciarse de.

divorced [dɪˈvɔːst] adj divorciado(-da).

DIY n (abbr of do-it-yourself) bricolaje m.

dizzy ['dɪzɪ] adj mareado(-da).

DJ n (abbr of disc jockey) pinchadiscos mf inv.

do [du:] (vt did, pp done, pl dos) aux vb **1.** (in negatives): **don't ~ that!** ¡no hagas eso!; **she didn't listen** no hizo caso.

2. (in questions): **~ you like it?** ¿te gusta?; **how ~ you do it?** ¿cómo se hace?

3. (referring to previous verb): **I eat more than you ~** yo como más que tú; **~ you smoke? - yes, I ~/no, I don't** ¿fumas? - sí/no; **so I ~** yo también.

4. (in question tags): **so, you like Scotland, ~ you?** así que te gusta Escocia ¿no?

◆ vt **1.** (gen) hacer; **to ~ one's homework** hacer los deberes; **what can I ~ for you?** ¿en qué puedo servirle?; **to ~ one's hair** peinarse; **to ~ one's teeth** lavarse los dientes; **to ~ damage** hacer daño; **to ~ sb good** sentarle bien a alguien.

2. (have as job): **what do you ~?** ¿a qué te dedicas?

3. (provide, offer) hacer; **we ~ pizzas for under £4** vendemos pizzas a menos de 4 libras.

4. (study) hacer.

5. (subj: vehicle) ir a.

6. (inf: visit) recorrer.

◆ vi **1.** (behave, act) hacer; **~ as I say** haz lo que te digo.

2. (progress, get on) ir; **I did well/badly** me fue bien/mal.

3. (be sufficient) valer; **will £5 ~?** ¿llegará con cinco libras?

4. (in phrases): **how do you ~?** (greeting) ¿cómo está usted?;

(answer) mucho gusto; **what has that got to ~ with it?** ¿y eso qué tiene que ver?

◆ n (party) fiesta f; **~s and don'ts** normas fpl de conducta.

❑ **do out of** vt sep (inf) timar; **do up** vt sep (shirt, buttons) abrochar; (shoes, laces) atar; (zip) subir; (decorate) renovar; (wrap up) envolver; **do with** vt fus: **I could ~ with a drink** no me vendría mal una copa; **do without** vt fus pasar sin.

dock [dɒk] n (for ships) muelle m; (JUR) banquillo m (de los acusados)

◆ vi atracar.

doctor ['dɒktə'] n (of medicine) médico m (-ca f); (academic) doctor m (-ra f); **to go to the ~'s** ir al médico.

document ['dɒkjʊmənt] n documento m.

documentary [,dɒkjʊ'mentərɪ] n documental m.

Dodgems® ['dɒdʒəmz] npl (Br) coches mpl de choque.

dodgy ['dɒdʒɪ] adj (Br: inf: plan, car) poco fiable; (health) delicado(-da).

does [weak form dəz, strong form dʌz] → do.

doesn't ['dʌznt] = does not.

dog [dɒg] n perro m.

dog food n comida f para perros.

doggy bag ['dɒgɪ-] n bolsa que da un restaurante para llevarse las sobras.

do-it-yourself n bricolaje m.

dole [dəʊl] n: **to be on the ~** (Br) estar parado.

doll [dɒl] n muñeca f.

dollar ['dɒlə'] n dólar m.

dolphin ['dɒlfín] n delfín m.

dome [dəʊm] n cúpula f.

domestic [də'mestık] adj (of house, family) doméstico(-ca); (of country) nacional.

domestic appliance n electrodoméstico m.

domestic flight n vuelo m nacional.

domestic science n hogar m (asignatura).

dominate ['dɒmıneıt] vt dominar.

dominoes ['dɒmınəʊz] n dominó m.

donate [də'neıt] vt donar.

donation [də'neıʃn] n donación f.

done [dʌn] pp → **do** ◆ adj (finished) listo(-ta); (cooked) hecho (-cha).

donkey ['dɒŋkı] n burro m.

don't [dəʊnt] = do not.

door [dɔːr] n puerta f.

doorbell ['dɔːbel] n timbre m.

doorknob ['dɔːnɒb] n pomo m.

doorman ['dɔːmən] (pl -men [-mən]) n portero m.

doormat ['dɔːmæt] n felpudo m.

doormen ['dɔːmən] pl → **doorman**.

doorstep ['dɔːstep] n (in front of door) peldaño m de la puerta; (Br: piece of bread) rebanada de pan muy gruesa.

doorway ['dɔːweı] n portal m.

dope [dəʊp] n (inf) (any illegal drug) droga f; (marijuana) maría f.

dormitory ['dɔːmıtrı] n dormitorio m.

Dormobile® ['dɔːməbiːl] n autocaravana f.

dosage ['dəʊsıdʒ] n dosis f inv.

dose [dəʊs] n (amount) dosis f inv; (of illness) ataque m.

dot [dɒt] n punto m; on the ~ (fig) en punto.

dotted line ['dɒtıd-] n línea f de puntos.

double ['dʌbl] adj doble ◆ n (twice the amount) el doble; (alcohol) doble m ◆ vt doblar ◆ vi doblarse ◆ adv: it's ~ the size es el doble de grande; to bend sthg ~ doblar algo; a ~ whisky un whisky doble; ~ three, four, two treinta y tres, cuarenta y dos; it's spelt with a ~ "s" se escribe con dos eses □ **doubles** n pl.

double bed n cama f de matrimonio.

double-breasted [-'brestıd] adj cruzado(-da).

double cream n (Br) nata f enriquecida.

double-decker (bus) [-'dekə-] n autobús m de dos pisos.

double doors npl puerta f de dos hojas.

double-glazing [-'gleızıŋ] n doble acristalamiento m.

double room n habitación f doble.

doubt [daʊt] n duda f ◆ vt (distrust) dudar de; I ~ it lo dudo; I ~ she'll be there dudo que esté ahí; to be in ~ (person) estar dudando; (matter, outcome) ser incierto; no ~ sin duda.

doubtful ['daʊtfʊl] adj (uncertain) dudoso(-sa); it's ~ that ... es improbable que ...

dough [dəʊ] n masa f.

doughnut ['dəʊnʌt] n (without hole) buñuelo m; (with hole) dónut® m.

dove[1] [dʌv] n (bird) paloma f.

dove[2] [dəʊv] pt (Am) → dive.

Dover sole ['dəʊvə-r] n lenguado de gran calidad que proviene del Canal de la Mancha.

down [daʊn] adv 1. (towards the bottom) (hacia) abajo; ~ here/there aquí/allí abajo; to fall ~ caer.
2. (along): I'm going ~ to the shops voy a acercarme a las tiendas.
3. (downstairs) abajo; I'll come ~ later bajaré más tarde.
4. (southwards) hacia el sur; we're going ~ to London vamos a bajar a Londres.
5. (in writing): to write sthg ~ apuntar algo.
6. (in phrases): to go ~ with (illness) pillar.
◆ prep 1. (towards the bottom of): they ran ~ the hill corrieron cuesta abajo.
2. (along) por; I was walking ~ the street iba andando por la calle.
◆ adj (inf: depressed) deprimido(-da).
◆ n (feathers) plumón m.

❏ **downs** npl (Br) montes en el sur de Inglaterra.

downhill [ˌdaʊn'hɪl] adv cuesta abajo.

Downing Street ['daʊnɪŋ-] n Downing Street m.

DOWNING STREET

Esta calle de Londres es famosa por ser la residencia del Primer Ministro británico (en el número 10) y del Ministro de Economía y Hacienda (en el número 11). El nombre "Downing Street" se utiliza también para referirse al Primer Ministro y sus asistentes.

downpour ['daʊnpɔː-r] n chaparrón m.

downstairs [adj ˌdaʊnˌsteəz, adv ˌdaʊn'steəz] adj de abajo ◆ adv abajo; to go ~ bajar (la escalera).

downtown [adj ˌdaʊntaʊn, adv ˌdaʊn'taʊn] adj (hotel, train) del centro; (area) (live) en el centro; (go) al centro; ~ New York el centro de Nueva York.

down under adv (Br: inf) en/a Australia.

downwards ['daʊnwədz] adv hacia abajo.

doz. abbr = dozen.

doze [dəʊz] vi dormitar.

dozen ['dʌzn] n docena f; a ~ eggs una docena de huevos.

Dr (abbr of Doctor) Dr.

drab [dræb] adj (clothes, wallpaper) deslustrado(-da).

draft [drɑːft] n (early version) borrador m; (money order) giro m; (Am) = draught.

drag [dræg] vt arrastrar ◆ vi (along ground) arrastrase; what a ~! (inf) ¡qué rollo! ❏ **drag on** vi ser interminable.

dragonfly ['drægnflaɪ] n libélula f.

drain [dreɪn] n (sewer) desagüe m; (grating in street) sumidero m ◆ vt (tank, radiator) vaciar ◆ vi (vegetables, washing-up) escurrirse.

draining board ['dreɪnɪŋ-] n

escurridero m.

drainpipe ['dreinpaip] n tubo m de desagüe.

drama ['drɑːmə] n (play, excitement) drama m; (art) teatro m.

dramatic [drə'mætɪk] adj (impressive) dramático(-ca).

drank [dræŋk] pt → drink.

drapes [dreips] npl (Am) cortinas fpl.

drastic ['dræstɪk] adj (extreme) drástico(-ca); (change, improvement) radical.

drastically ['dræstɪklɪ] adv drásticamente.

draught [drɑːft] n (Br: of air) corriente f de aire.

draught beer n cerveza f de barril.

draughts [drɑːfts] n (Br) damas fpl.

draughty ['drɑːftɪ] adj: it's ~ hay corriente.

draw [drɔː] (pt drew, pp drawn) vt (picture, map) dibujar; (line) trazar; (pull) tirar de; (attract) atraer; (comparison) señalar; (conclusion) llegar a ♦ vi (with pen, pencil) dibujar; (SPORT) empatar ♦ n (SPORT: result) empate m; (lottery) sorteo m; **to ~ the curtains** (open) descorrer las cortinas; (close) correr las cortinas ❑ **draw out** vt sep (money) sacar; **draw up** vt sep (list, plan) preparar ♦ vi (car, bus) pararse.

drawback ['drɔːbæk] n desventaja f.

drawer [drɔːᵣ] n cajón m.

drawing ['drɔːɪŋ] n dibujo m.

drawing pin n (Br) chincheta f.

drawing room n cuarto m de

estar.

drawn [drɔːn] pp → draw.

dreadful ['dredfʊl] adj terrible.

dream [driːm] n sueño m ♦ vt (when asleep) soñar; (imagine) imaginar ♦ vi: **to ~ (of)** soñar (con); **a ~ house** una casa de ensueño.

dress [dres] n (for woman, girl) vestido m; (clothes) traje m ♦ vt (person, baby) vestir; (wound) vendar; (salad) aliñar ♦ vi (get dressed) vestirse; (in particular way) vestir; **to be ~ed in** ir vestido de; **to get ~ed** vestirse ❑ **dress up** vi (in costume) disfrazarse; (in best clothes) engalanarse.

dress circle n piso m principal.

dresser ['dresᵣ] n (Br: for crockery) aparador m; (Am: chest of drawers) cómoda f.

dressing ['dresɪŋ] n (for salad) aliño m; (for wound) vendaje m.

dressing gown n bata f.

dressing room n vestuario m.

dressing table n tocador m.

dressmaker ['dres,meɪkəᵣ] n modisto m (-ta f).

dress rehearsal n ensayo m general.

drew [druː] pt → draw.

dribble ['drɪbl] vi (liquid) gotear; (baby) babear.

drier ['draɪəᵣ] = dryer.

drift [drɪft] n (of snow) ventisquero m ♦ vi (in wind) dejarse llevar por el viento; (in water) dejarse llevar por el agua.

drill [drɪl] n (tool) taladro m; (of dentist) fresa f ♦ vt (hole) taladrar.

drink [drɪŋk] (pt drank, pp drunk) n (of water, tea etc) bebida f;

(alcoholic) copa *f* ♦ *vt & vi* beber; **to have a ~** *(alcoholic)* tomar una copa; **would you like a ~?** ¿quieres beber algo?

drinkable ['drɪŋkəbl] *adj (safe to drink)* potable; *(wine)* agradable.

drinking water ['drɪŋkɪŋ-] *n* agua *f* potable.

drip [drɪp] *n (drop)* gota *f*; *(MED)* gotero *m* ♦ *vi* gotear.

drip-dry *adj* de lava y pon.

dripping (wet) ['drɪpɪŋ-] *adj* empapado(-da).

drive [draɪv] *(pt* drove, *pp* driven) *n (journey)* viaje *m* (en coche); *(in front of house)* camino *m* (de entrada) ♦ *vt (car, bus, train)* conducir; *(take in car)* llevar (en coche); *(operate, power)* impulsar ♦ *vi (drive car)* conducir; *(travel in car)* ir en coche; **to ~ sb to do sthg** llevar a alguien a hacer algo; **to go for a ~** dar una vuelta en coche; **to ~ sb mad** volver loco a alguien.

drivel ['drɪvl] *n* tonterías *fpl*.

driven ['drɪvn] *pp → drive.*

driver ['draɪvəʳ] *n (of car, bus)* conductor *m* (-ra *f*); *(of train)* maquinista *m*.

driver's license *(Am) =* driving licence.

driveshaft ['draɪvʃɑːft] *n* eje *m* de transmisión.

driveway ['draɪvweɪ] *n* camino *m* de entrada.

driving lesson ['draɪvɪŋ-] *n* clase *f* de conducir.

driving licence ['draɪvɪŋ-] *n (Br)* permiso *m* de conducir.

driving test ['draɪvɪŋ-] *n* examen *m* de conducir.

drizzle ['drɪzl] *n* llovizna *f*.

drop [drɒp] *n (drip, small amount)* gota *f*; *(distance down)* caída *f*; *(decrease)* descenso *m*; *(in wages)* disminución *f* ♦ *vt (let fall)* dejar caer; *(reduce)* reducir; *(from vehicle)* dejar; *(omit)* omitir ♦ *vi (fall)* caer; *(decrease)* disminuir; *(price, temperature)* bajar; **to ~ a hint** lanzar una indirecta; **to ~ sb a line** escribir unas líneas a alguien □ **drop in** *vi (inf)*: **to ~ in on sb** pasarse por casa de alguien; **drop off** *vt sep (from vehicle)* dejar ♦ *vi (fall asleep)* quedarse dormido; *(fall off)* desprenderse; **drop out** *vi (of college)* abandonar los estudios; *(of race)* retirarse.

drought [draʊt] *n* sequía *f*.

drove [drəʊv] *pt → drive.*

drown [draʊn] *vi* ahogarse.

drug [drʌg] *n (MED)* medicamento *m*; *(stimulant)* droga *f* ♦ *vt* drogar.

drug addict *n* drogadicto *m* (-ta *f*).

druggist ['drʌgɪst] *n (Am)* farmacéutico *m* (-ca *f*).

drum [drʌm] *n (MUS)* tambor *m*; *(container)* bidón *m*; **~s** *(in pop music)* batería *f*.

drummer ['drʌməʳ] *n (in pop music)* batería *mf*.

drumstick ['drʌmstɪk] *n (of chicken)* muslo *m*.

drunk [drʌŋk] *pp → drink* ♦ *adj* borracho(-cha) ♦ *n* borracho *m* (-cha *f*); **to get ~** emborracharse.

dry [draɪ] *adj* seco(-ca); *(day)* sin lluvia ♦ *vt* secar ♦ *vi* secarse; **to o.s.** secarse; **to ~ one's hair** secarse el pelo; **to ~ one's hands** secarse las manos □ **dry up** *vi (become dry)* secarse; *(dry the dishes)* secar.

dry-clean *vt* limpiar en seco.

dry cleaner's *n* tintorería *f.*

dryer ['draɪə'] *n (for clothes)* secadora *f; (for hair)* secador *m.*

dry-roasted   peanuts [-ˈrəʊstɪd] *npl* cacahuetes *mpl* tostados y salados.

DSS *n (Br) ministerio británico de la seguridad social.*

DTP *n (abbr of desktop publishing)* autoed. *f.*

dual carriageway ['dju:əl-] *n (Br)* (tramo de) carretera con dos carriles en cada dirección.

dubbed [dʌbd] *adj (film)* doblado(-da).

dubious ['dju:bjəs] *adj (suspect)* sospechoso(-sa).

duchess ['dʌtʃɪs] *n* duquesa *f.*

duck [dʌk] *n (bird)* pato *m (-ta f); (food)* pato *m* ♦ *vi* agacharse.

due [dju:] *adj (bill, rent)* pagadero(-ra); **when is the train ~?** ¿cuándo debería llegar el tren?; **the money ~ to me** el dinero que se me debe; **in ~ course** a su debido tiempo; **~ to** debido a.

duet [dju:'et] *n* dúo *m.*

duffel bag ['dʌfl-] *n* morral *m.*

duffel coat ['dʌfl-] *n* trenca *f.*

dug [dʌg] *pt & pp →* **dig.**

duke [dju:k] *n* duque *m.*

dull [dʌl] *adj (boring)* aburrido(-da); *(not bright)* torpe; *(weather)* gris; *(pain)* sordo(-da).

dumb [dʌm] *adj (inf: stupid)* estúpido(-da); *(unable to speak)* mudo(-da).

dummy ['dʌmɪ] *n (Br: for baby)* chupete *m; (for clothes)* maniquí *m.*

dump [dʌmp] *n (for rubbish)* vertedero *m; (inf: place)* tugurio *m* ♦ *vt (drop carelessly)* dejar; *(get rid of)* deshacerse de.

dumpling ['dʌmplɪŋ] *n* bola *f* de masa que se guisa al vapor con carne y verduras.

dune [dju:n] *n* duna *f.*

dungarees [ˌdʌŋgə'ri:z] *npl (Br: for work)* mono *m; (fashion item)* pantalones *mpl* de peto; *(Am: jeans)* vaqueros *mpl* de tela gruesa utilizados para trabajar.

dungeon ['dʌndʒən] *n* mazmorra *f.*

duo ['dju:əʊ] *n*: **with a ~ of sauces** con dos salsas distintas.

duplicate ['dju:plɪkət] *n* copia *f.*

during ['djʊərɪŋ] *prep* durante.

dusk [dʌsk] *n* crepúsculo *m.*

dust [dʌst] *n* polvo *m* ♦ *vt* quitar el polvo a.

dustbin ['dʌstbɪn] *n (Br)* cubo *m* de la basura.

dustcart ['dʌstkɑ:t] *n (Br)* camión *m* de la basura.

duster ['dʌstə'] *n* trapo *m* (de quitar el polvo) *m.*

dustman ['dʌstmən] *(pl -men* [-mən]*) n (Br)* basurero *m.*

dustpan ['dʌstpæn] *n* recogedor *m.*

dusty ['dʌstɪ] *adj* lleno(-na) de polvo.

Dutch [dʌtʃ] *adj* holandés(-esa) ♦ *n (language)* holandés *m* ♦ *npl*: **the ~** los holandeses.

Dutchman ['dʌtʃmən] *(pl -men* [-mən]*) n* holandés *m.*

Dutchwoman ['dʌtʃˌwʊmən] *(pl -women* [-ˌwɪmɪn]*) n* holandesa *f.*

duty ['dju:tɪ] n (moral obligation) deber m; (tax) impuesto m; **to be on ~** estar de servicio; **to be off ~** no estar de servicio ❑ **duties** npl (job) tareas fpl.

duty chemist's n farmacia f de guardia.

duty-free adj libre de impuestos ◆ n (article) artículo m libre de impuestos.

duty-free shop n tienda f libre de impuestos.

duvet ['du:veɪ] n edredón m.

dwarf [dwɔ:f] (pl **dwarves** [dwɔ:vz]) n enano m (-na f).

dwelling ['dwelɪŋ] n (fml) morada f.

dye [daɪ] n tinte m ◆ vt teñir.

dying ['daɪɪŋ] cont → **die**.

dynamite ['daɪnəmaɪt] n dinamita f.

dynamo ['daɪnəməʊ] (pl **-s**) n dínamo f.

dyslexic [dɪs'leksɪk] adj disléxico(-ca).

E

E (abbr of east) E.

E111 n E111 m, impreso para obtener asistencia médica en otros países de la Unión Europea.

each [i:tʃ] adj cada ◆ pron cada uno m (cada una f); **~ one** cada uno (cada una); **~ of them** cada uno (cada una); **~ other** el uno al otro; **they hate ~ other** se odian; **we know ~ other** nos conocemos; **one ~** cada uno (una cada una); **one of ~** uno de cada.

eager ['i:gəʳ] adj (pupil) entusiasta; (expression) de entusiasmo; **to be ~ to do sthg** estar deseoso(-sa) de hacer algo.

eagle ['i:gl] n águila f.

ear [ɪəʳ] n (of person, animal) oreja f; (of corn) espiga f.

earache ['ɪəreɪk] n: **to have ~** tener dolor de oídos.

earl [ɜ:l] n conde m.

early ['ɜ:lɪ] adj temprano(-na) ◆ adv temprano; **~ last year** a principios del año pasado; **~ morning** la madrugada; **it arrived an hour ~** llegó con una hora de adelanto; **the earliest** como muy pronto; **~ on** al principio; **to have an ~ night** irse a la cama temprano.

earn [ɜ:n] vt (money) ganar; (praise, success) ganarse; **to ~ a living** ganarse la vida.

earnings ['ɜ:nɪŋz] npl ingresos mpl.

earphones ['ɪəfəʊnz] npl auriculares mpl.

earplugs ['ɪəplʌgz] npl tapones mpl para los oídos.

earrings ['ɪərɪŋz] npl pendientes mpl.

earth [ɜ:θ] n tierra f; (Br: electrical connection) toma f de tierra ◆ vt (Br) conectar a tierra; **how on ~ ...?** ¿cómo demonios ...?

earthenware ['ɜ:θnweəʳ] adj de loza.

earthquake ['ɜ:θkweɪk] n terremoto m.

ease [iːz] n facilidad f ◆ vt (pain) aliviar; (problem) atenuar; **at ~** cómodo; **with ~** con facilidad ▢ **ease off** vi (pain) calmarse; (rain) amainar.

easily [ˈiːzɪlɪ] adv (without difficulty) fácilmente; (by far) sin lugar a dudas.

east [iːst] n este m ◆ adv hacia el este; **in the ~ of England** al este de Inglaterra; **the East** (Asia) el Oriente.

eastbound [ˈiːstbaʊnd] adj con dirección este.

Easter [ˈiːstəʳ] n (day) Domingo m de Resurrección; (period) Semana f Santa.

eastern [ˈiːstən] adj del este ▢ **Eastern** adj (Asian) oriental.

Eastern Europe n Europa del Este.

eastwards [ˈiːstwədz] adv hacia el este.

easy [ˈiːzɪ] adj (not difficult) fácil; (without problems) cómodo(-da); **to take it ~** (relax) relajarse.

easygoing [ˌiːzɪˈɡəʊɪŋ] adj tranquilo(-la).

eat [iːt] (pt ate, pp eaten [ˈiːtn]) vt & vi comer ▢ **eat out** vi comer fuera.

eating apple [ˈiːtɪŋ-] n manzana f (para comer).

ebony [ˈebənɪ] n ébano m.

EC n (abbr of European Community) CE f.

eccentric [ɪkˈsentrɪk] adj excéntrico(-ca).

echo [ˈekəʊ] (pl -es) n eco m ◆ vi resonar.

ecology [ɪˈkɒlədʒɪ] n ecología f.

economic [ˌiːkəˈnɒmɪk] adj (relating to the economy) económico(-ca); (profitable) rentable ▢ **economics** n economía f.

economical [ˌiːkəˈnɒmɪkl] adj económico(-ca).

economize [ɪˈkɒnəmaɪz] vi economizar.

economy [ɪˈkɒnəmɪ] n economía f.

economy class n clase f turista.

economy size adj de tamaño económico.

ecstasy [ˈekstəsɪ] n éxtasis m inv.

ECU [ˈekjuː] n ECU m.

Ecuador [ˈekwədɔːʳ] n Ecuador.

Ecuadoran [ˌekwəˈdɔːrən] adj ecuatoriano(-na) ◆ n ecuatoriano m (-na f).

eczema [ˈeksɪmə] n eccema m.

edge [edʒ] n (border) borde m; (of table, coin, ruler) canto m; (of knife) filo m.

edible [ˈedɪbl] adj comestible.

Edinburgh [ˈedɪnbrə] n Edimburgo.

Edinburgh Festival n: **the ~** el festival de Edimburgo.

---

i **EDINBURGH FESTIVAL**

El festival de Edimburgo es un festival internacional de música y teatro que tiene lugar cada año en la capital escocesa durante el mes de agosto. El festival oficial, con lo mejor en música, baile y teatro, se complementa con el "Fringe", que incluye cientos de producciones independientes representadas en pequeños locales por toda la ciudad.

edition [ɪˈdɪʃn] n edición f.

editor [ˈedɪtəˀ] n (of newspaper, magazine) director m (-ra f); (of book) autor m (-ra f) de la edición; (of film, TV programme) montador m (-ra f).

editorial [ˌedɪˈtɔːrɪəl] n editorial m.

educate [ˈedʒʊkeɪt] vt educar.

education [ˌedʒʊˈkeɪʃn] n (field) enseñanza f; (process or result of teaching) educación f.

EEC n CEE f.

eel [iːl] n anguila f.

effect [ɪˈfekt] n efecto m; **to put sthg into** ~ hacer entrar algo en vigor; **to take** ~ (medicine) hacer efecto; (law) entrar en vigor.

effective [ɪˈfektɪv] adj (successful) eficaz; (law, system) operativo(-va).

effectively [ɪˈfektɪvlɪ] adv (successfully) eficazmente; (in fact) de hecho.

efficient [ɪˈfɪʃənt] adj eficiente.

effort [ˈefət] n esfuerzo m; **to make an** ~ **to do sthg** hacer un esfuerzo por hacer algo; **it's not worth the** ~ no merece la pena.

e.g. adv p. ej.

egg [eg] n huevo m.

egg cup n huevera f.

egg mayonnaise n relleno de bocadillo consistente en huevo duro triturado con mayonesa.

eggplant [ˈegplɑːnt] n (Am) berenjena f.

egg white n clara f (de huevo).

egg yolk n yema f (de huevo).

Egypt [ˈiːdʒɪpt] n Egipto m.

eiderdown [ˈaɪdədaʊn] n edredón m.

eight [eɪt] num ocho, → **six**.

eighteen [ˌeɪˈtiːn] num dieciocho, → **six**.

eighteenth [ˌeɪˈtiːnθ] num decimoctavo(-va), → **sixth**.

eighth [eɪtθ] num octavo(-va), → **sixth**.

eightieth [ˈeɪtɪɪθ] num octogésimo(-ma), → **sixth**.

eighty [ˈeɪtɪ] num ochenta, → **six**.

Eire [ˈeərə] n Eire.

eisteddfod [aɪˈstedfəd] n festival galés de cultura.

ℹ️ **EISTEDDFOD**

El "Eisteddfod" es un festival que tiene lugar cada agosto en Gales para celebrar el idioma y la cultura galeses, con competiciones de música, poesía, teatro y arte. Este festival se remonta al siglo XII.

---

either [ˈaɪðəˀ, ˈiːðəˀ] adj: ~ **book will do** cualquiera de los dos libros vale ♦ pron: **I'll take** ~ (of them) me llevaré cualquiera de los dos; **I don't like** ~ (of them) no me gusta ninguno (de los dos). ♦ adv: **I can't** ~ yo tampoco (puedo); ~ ... **or** o ... o; **I don't speak** ~ **French or Spanish** no hablo ni francés ni español; **on** ~ **side** a ambos lados.

eject [ɪˈdʒekt] vt (cassette) expulsar.

elaborate [ɪˈlæbrət] adj elaborado(-da).

elastic [ɪˈlæstɪk] n elástico m.

elastic band n (Br) goma f (elástica).

elbow ['elbəʊ] n codo m.

elder ['eldəʳ] adj mayor.

elderly ['eldəlɪ] adj anciano(-na)
♦ npl: the ~ los ancianos.

eldest ['eldɪst] adj mayor.

elect [ɪ'lekt] vt (by voting) elegir;
to ~ to do sthg (fml) optar por
hacer algo.

election [ɪ'lekʃn] n elección f.

electric [ɪ'lektrɪk] adj eléctri-
co(-ca).

electrical goods [ɪ'lektrɪkl-]
npl electrodomésticos mpl.

electric blanket n manta f
eléctrica.

electric drill n taladro m eléctrico.

electric fence n cercado m
electrificado.

electrician [ɪlek'trɪʃn] n electricista mf.

electricity [ɪlek'trɪsətɪ] n electricidad f.

electric shock n descarga f
eléctrica.

electrocute [ɪ'lektrəkjuːt] vt
electrocutar.

electronic [ɪlek'trɒnɪk] adj elec-
trónico(-ca).

elegant ['elɪgənt] adj elegante.

element ['elɪmənt] n (part, chemical) elemento m; (degree) toque m,
matiz m; (of fire, kettle) resistencia
f; the ~s los elementos.

elementary [ˌelɪ'mentərɪ] adj
elemental.

elephant ['elɪfənt] n elefante m.

elevator ['elɪveɪtəʳ] n (Am)
ascensor m.

eleven [ɪ'levn] num once, → six.

eleventh [ɪ'levnθ] num undéci-

mo(-ma), → sixth.

eligible ['elɪdʒəbl] adj elegible.

eliminate [ɪ'lɪmɪneɪt] vt eliminar.

Elizabethan [ɪˌlɪzə'biːθn] adj
isabelino(-na).

elm [elm] n olmo m.

El Salvador [el'sælvədɔːʳ] n El
Salvador.

else [els] adv: **I don't want anything ~** no quiero nada más; **anything ~?** ¿algo más?; **everyone ~**
todos los demás (todas las
demás); **nobody ~** nadie más;
nothing ~ nada más; **somebody ~**
otra persona; **something ~** otra
cosa; **somewhere ~** a/en otra
parte; **what ~?** ¿qué más?; **who ~?**
¿quién más?; **or ~** si no.

elsewhere [els'weəʳ] adv a/en
otra parte.

embankment [ɪm'bæŋkmənt] n
(next to river) dique m; (next to road,
railway) terraplén m.

embark [ɪm'bɑːk] vi (board ship)
embarcar.

embarkation card [ˌembɑː-
'keɪʃn-] n tarjeta f de embarque.

embarrass [ɪm'bærəs] vt avergonzar.

embarrassed [ɪm'bærəst] adj: **I
was ~** me daba vergüenza.

embarrassing [ɪm'bærəsɪŋ] adj
embarazoso(-sa).

embarrassment [ɪm'bærəs-
mənt] n vergüenza f.

embassy ['embəsɪ] n embajada f.

emblem ['embləm] n emblema
m.

embrace [ɪm'breɪs] vt abrazar.

embroidered [ɪm'brɔɪdəd] adj
bordado(-da).

embroidery [ɪmˈbrɔɪdərɪ] n bordado m.

emerald [ˈemərəld] n esmeralda f.

emerge [ɪˈmɜːdʒ] vi (from place) salir; (fact, truth) salir a la luz.

emergency [ɪˈmɜːdʒənsɪ] n emergencia f ♦ adj de emergencia; **in an ~** en caso de emergencia.

emergency exit n salida f de emergencia.

emergency landing n aterrizaje m forzoso.

emergency services npl servicios mpl de emergencia.

emigrate [ˈemɪɡreɪt] vi emigrar.

emit [ɪˈmɪt] vt emitir.

emotion [ɪˈməʊʃn] n emoción f.

emotional [ɪˈməʊʃənl] adj emotivo(-va).

emphasis [ˈemfəsɪs] (pl -ases [-əsiːz]) n énfasis m inv.

emphasize [ˈemfəsaɪz] vt enfatizar, subrayar.

empire [ˈempaɪər] n imperio m.

employ [ɪmˈplɔɪ] vt emplear.

employed [ɪmˈplɔɪd] adj empleado(-da).

employee [ɪmˈplɔɪiː] n empleado m (-da f).

employer [ɪmˈplɔɪər] n patrono m (-na f).

employment [ɪmˈplɔɪmənt] n empleo m.

employment agency n agencia f de trabajo.

empty [ˈemptɪ] adj vacío(-a); (threat, promise) vano(-na) ♦ vt vaciar.

EMU n UME f.

emulsion (paint) [ɪˈmʌlʃn-] n

pintura f mate.

enable [ɪˈneɪbl] vt: **to ~ sb to do sthg** permitir a alguien hacer algo.

enamel [ɪˈnæml] n esmalte m.

enclose [ɪnˈkləʊz] vt (surround) rodear; (with letter) adjuntar.

enclosed [ɪnˈkləʊzd] adj (space) cerrado(-da).

encounter [ɪnˈkaʊntər] vt encontrarse con.

encourage [ɪnˈkʌrɪdʒ] vt (person) animar; **to ~ sb to do sthg** animar a alguien a hacer algo.

encouragement [ɪnˈkʌrɪdʒmənt] n aliento m, ánimo m.

encyclopedia [ɪnˌsaɪkləˈpiːdjə] n enciclopedia f.

end [end] n fin m; (furthest point) extremo m; (of finger, toe) punta f ♦ vt terminar ♦ vi acabarse; **to come to an ~** acabarse; **to put an ~ to sthg** poner fin a algo; **for days on ~** día tras día; **in the ~** al final; **to make ~s meet** llegar al final de mes; **at the ~ of** (street, garden) al final de; **at the ~ of April** a finales de abril ❑ **end up** vi acabar, terminar; **to ~ up doing sthg** acabar por hacer algo.

endangered species [ɪnˈdeɪndʒəd-] n especie f en peligro.

ending [ˈendɪŋ] n (of story, film) final m; (GRAMM) terminación f.

endive [ˈendaɪv] n (curly) endibia f; (chicory) achicoria f.

endless [ˈendlɪs] adj interminable.

endorsement [ɪnˈdɔːsmənt] n (of driving licence) nota de sanción en el carné de conducir.

endurance [ɪnˈdjʊərəns] n resistencia f.

endure [ɪn'djʊəʳ] vt soportar.

enemy ['enɪmɪ] n enemigo m (-ga f).

energy ['enədʒɪ] n energía f.

enforce [ɪn'fɔːs] vt hacer cumplir.

engaged [ɪn'geɪdʒd] adj (to be married) prometido(-da); (Br phone) ocupado(-da), comunicando; (toilet) ocupado(-da); **to get ~** prometerse.

engaged tone n (Br) señal f de comunicando.

engagement [ɪn'geɪdʒmənt] n (to marry) compromiso m; (appointment) cita f.

engagement ring n anillo m de compromiso.

engine ['endʒɪn] n (of vehicle) motor m; (of train) máquina f.

engineer [ˌendʒɪ'nɪəʳ] n ingeniero m (-ra f).

engineering [ˌendʒɪ'nɪərɪŋ] n ingeniería f.

engineering works npl (on railway line) trabajos mpl de mejora en la línea.

England ['ɪŋglənd] n Inglaterra.

English ['ɪŋglɪʃ] adj inglés(-esa) ♦ n (language) inglés m ♦ npl: **the ~** los ingleses.

English breakfast n desayuno m inglés.

English Channel n: **the ~** el Canal de la Mancha.

Englishman ['ɪŋglɪʃmən] (pl -men [-mən]) n inglés m.

Englishwoman ['ɪŋglɪʃˌwʊmən] (pl -women [-wɪmɪn]) n inglesa f.

engrave [ɪn'greɪv] vt grabar.

engraving [ɪn'greɪvɪŋ] n grabado m.

enjoy [ɪn'dʒɔɪ] vt: **I ~ed the film** me gustó la película; **I ~ swimming** me gusta nadar; **to ~ o.s.** divertirse; **~ your meal!** ¡que aproveche!

enjoyable [ɪn'dʒɔɪəbl] adj agradable.

enjoyment [ɪn'dʒɔɪmənt] n placer m.

enlargement [ɪn'lɑːdʒmənt] n (of photo) ampliación f.

enormous [ɪ'nɔːməs] adj enorme.

enough [ɪ'nʌf] adj, pron & adv bastante; **~ time** bastante tiempo; **is that ~?** ¿es bastante?; **it's not big ~** no es lo bastante grande; **to have had ~ (of)** estar harto (de).

enquire [ɪn'kwaɪəʳ] vi informarse.

enquiry [ɪn'kwaɪərɪ] n (question) pregunta f; (investigation) investigación f; **"Enquiries"** "Información".

enquiry desk n información f.

enrol [ɪn'rəʊl] vi (Br) matricularse.

enroll [ɪn'rəʊl] (Am) = **enrol**.

en suite bathroom [ɒn'swiːt-] n baño m adjunto.

ensure [ɪn'ʃʊəʳ] vt asegurar.

entail [ɪn'teɪl] vt conllevar.

enter ['entəʳ] vt (room, building) entrar en; (plane, bus) subir a; (college) matricularse a; (army) alistarse en; (competition) presentarse a; (on form) escribir ♦ vi (come in) entrar; (in competition) presentarse, participar.

enterprise ['entəpraɪz] n empresa f.

entertain [ˌentəˈteɪn] *vt (amuse)* entretener.

entertainer [ˌentəˈteɪnəʳ] *n* artista *mf*.

entertaining [ˌentəˈteɪnɪŋ] *adj* entretenido(-da).

entertainment [ˌentəˈteɪnmənt] *n (amusement)* diversión *f*; *(show)* espectáculo *m*.

enthusiasm [ɪnˈθjuːzɪæzm] *n* entusiasmo *m*.

enthusiast [ɪnˈθjuːzɪæst] *n* entusiasta *mf*.

enthusiastic [ɪnˌθjuːzɪˈæstɪk] *adj* entusiasta.

entire [ɪnˈtaɪəʳ] *adj* entero(-ra).

entirely [ɪnˈtaɪəlɪ] *adv* enteramente.

entitle [ɪnˈtaɪtl] *vt*: to ~ sb to sthg dar a alguien derecho a algo; to ~ sb to do sthg autorizar a alguien a hacer algo.

entrance [ˈentrəns] *n* entrada *f*.

entrance fee *n* precio *m* de entrada.

entry [ˈentrɪ] *n* entrada *f*; *(in competition)* respuesta *f*; "no ~" "prohibido el paso".

envelope [ˈenvələʊp] *n* sobre *m*.

envious [ˈenvɪəs] *adj* envidioso(-sa).

environment [ɪnˈvaɪərənmənt] *n (surroundings)* entorno *m*; the ~ el medio ambiente.

environmental [ɪnˌvaɪərənˈmentl] *adj* medioambiental.

environmentally friendly [ɪnˌvaɪərənˈmentəlɪ] *adj* ecológico(-ca).

envy [ˈenvɪ] *vt* envidiar.

epic [ˈepɪk] *n* epopeya *f*.

epidemic [ˌepɪˈdemɪk] *n* epidemia *f*.

epileptic [ˌepɪˈleptɪk] *adj* epiléptico(-ca).

episode [ˈepɪsəʊd] *n* episodio *m*.

equal [ˈiːkwəl] *adj* igual ◆ *vt (number)* ser igual a; to be ~ to ser igual a.

equality [ɪˈkwɒlətɪ] *n* igualdad *f*.

equalize [ˈiːkwəlaɪz] *vi* marcar el empate.

equally [ˈiːkwəlɪ] *adv* igualmente; *(pay, treat)* equitativamente; *(share)* por igual.

equation [ɪˈkweɪʒn] *n* ecuación *f*.

equator [ɪˈkweɪtəʳ] *n*: the ~ el ecuador.

equip [ɪˈkwɪp] *vt*: to ~ sb with proveer a alguien (de); to ~ sthg with equipar algo (con).

equipment [ɪˈkwɪpmənt] *n* equipo *m*.

equipped [ɪˈkwɪpt] *adj*: to be ~ with estar provisto(-ta) de.

equivalent [ɪˈkwɪvələnt] *adj* equivale ◆ *n* equivalente *m*.

erase [ɪˈreɪz] *vt* borrar.

eraser [ɪˈreɪzəʳ] *n* goma *f* de borrar.

erect [ɪˈrekt] *adj (person, posture)* erguido(-da) ◆ *vt (tent)* montar; *(monument)* erigir.

ERM *n* mecanismo de tipos de cambio (del SME).

erotic [ɪˈrɒtɪk] *adj* erótico(-ca).

errand [ˈerənd] *n* recado *m*.

erratic [ɪˈrætɪk] *adj* irregular.

error [ˈerəʳ] *n* error *m*.

escalator [ˈeskəleɪtəʳ] *n* escalera *f* mecánica.

escalope [ˈeskələp] n escalope m.

escape [rˈskeɪp] n (flight) fuga f; (of gas, water) escape m ♦ vi: **to ~ (from)** (prison, danger) escaparse (de); (leak) fugarse (de).

escort [n ˈeskɔːt, vb rˈskɔːt] n (guard) escolta f ♦ vt escoltar.

espadrilles [ˈespəˌdrɪlz] npl alpargatas fpl.

especially [rˈspeʃəlɪ] adv especialmente.

esplanade [ˌespləˈneɪd] n paseo m marítimo.

essay [ˈeseɪ] n (at school) redacción f; (at university) trabajo m.

essential [rˈsenʃl] adj esencial □ **essentials** npl: **the (bare) ~s** lo (mínimo) indispensable.

essentially [rˈsenʃəlɪ] adv esencialmente.

establish [rˈstæblɪʃ] vt (set up, create) establecer; (fact, truth) verificar.

establishment [rˈstæblɪʃmənt] n (business) establecimiento m.

estate [rˈsteɪt] n (land in country) finca f; (for housing) urbanización f; (Br: car) = **estate car**.

estate agent n (Br) agente m inmobiliario (agente f inmobiliaria).

estate car n (Br) coche m familiar, coche m ranchera.

estimate [n ˈestɪmət, vb ˈestɪmeɪt] n (guess) estimación f; (for job) presupuesto m ♦ vt calcular.

estuary [ˈestjʊərɪ] n estuario m.

ethnic minority [ˈeθnɪk-] n minoría f étnica.

EU n (abbr of European Union) UE f.

Eurocheque [ˈjʊərəʊˌtʃek] n eurocheque m.

Europe [ˈjʊərəp] n Europa.

European [ˌjʊərəˈpɪən] adj europeo(-a) ♦ n europeo m (-a f).

European Community n Comunidad f Europea.

evacuate [rˈvækjʊeɪt] vt evacuar.

evade [rˈveɪd] vt eludir.

evaporated milk [rˈvæpəreɪtɪd-] n leche f evaporada.

eve [iːv] n: **on the ~** en la víspera de.

even [ˈiːvn] adj (uniform) constante, uniforme; (level, flat) llano(-na), liso(-sa); (equal) igualado(-da); (number) par ♦ adv (emphasizing surprise) hasta; (in comparisons) aun; **to break ~** acabar sin ganar ni perder; **~ so** aun así; **~ though** aunque; **not ~** ni siquiera.

evening [ˈiːvnɪŋ] n (from 5 p.m. to 8 p.m.) tarde f; (from 9 p.m. onwards) noche f; (event) velada f; **good ~!** ¡buenas tardes!, ¡buenas noches!; **in the ~** por la tarde, por la noche.

evening classes npl clases fpl nocturnas.

evening dress n (formal clothes) traje m de etiqueta; (woman's garment) traje de noche.

evening meal n cena f.

event [rˈvent] n (occurrence) suceso m; (SPORT) prueba f; **in the ~ of** (fml) en caso de.

eventual [rˈventʃʊəl] adj final, definitivo(-va).

eventually [rˈventʃəlɪ] adv finalmente.

ever [ˈevə²] adv (at any time) alguna vez; *(in negatives)* nunca; **I don't ~ do that** no hago eso nunca; **the best I've ~ seen** lo mejor que nunca he visto; **he was ~ so angry** estaba muy enfadado; **for ~** *(eternally)* para siempre; **we've been waiting for ~** hace siglos que esperamos; **hardly ~** casi nunca; **~ since** *adv* desde entonces ◆ *prep* desde ◆ *conj* desde que.

every ['evrɪ] *adj* cada; **~ day** cada día; **~ other day** un día sí y otro no; **one in ~ ten** uno de cada diez; **we make ~ effort ...** hacemos todo lo posible ...; **~ so often** de vez en cuando.

everybody ['evrɪˌbɒdɪ] = **everyone**.

everyday ['evrɪdeɪ] *adj* diario(-ria).

everyone ['evrɪwʌn] *pron* todo el mundo, todos *mpl* (-das *fpl*).

everyplace ['evrɪˌpleɪs] *(Am)* = **everywhere**.

everything ['evrɪθɪŋ] *pron* todo.

everywhere ['evrɪweəʳ] *adv* *(be, search)* por todas partes; *(with verbs of motion)* a todas partes; **~ you go** por todas partes.

evidence ['evɪdəns] *n* *(proof)* prueba *f*; *(JUR)* declaración *f*.

evident ['evɪdənt] *adj* evidente.

evidently ['evɪdəntlɪ] *adv* *(apparently)* aparentemente; *(obviously)* evidentemente.

evil ['iːvl] *adj* malvado(-da) ◆ *n* mal *m*.

ex [eks] *n* *(inf)* ex *mf*.

exact [ɪɡ'zækt] *adj* exacto(-ta); **"~ fare ready please"** "tenga listo el precio exacto del billete".

exactly [ɪɡ'zæktlɪ] *adv* exacta-

mente ◆ *excl* ¡exacto!

exaggerate [ɪɡ'zædʒəreɪt] *vt* & *vi* exagerar.

exaggeration [ɪɡˌzædʒə'reɪʃn] *n* exageración *f*.

exam [ɪɡ'zæm] *n* examen *m*; **to take an ~** examinarse, presentarse a un examen.

examination [ɪɡˌzæmɪ'neɪʃn] *n* *(exam)* examen *m*; *(MED)* reconocimiento *m*.

examine [ɪɡ'zæmɪn] *vt* *(inspect)* examinar; *(consider carefully)* considerar; *(MED)* reconocer.

example [ɪɡ'zɑːmpl] *n* ejemplo *m*; **for ~** por ejemplo.

exceed [ɪk'siːd] *vt* *(be greater than)* exceder; *(go beyond)* rebasar.

excellent ['eksələnt] *adj* excelente.

except [ɪk'sept] *prep* & *conj* salvo; **~ for** aparte de; **"~ for access"** cartel que indica que el tránsito no está permitido; **"~ for loading"** "salvo carga y descarga".

exception [ɪk'sepʃn] *n* excepción *f*.

exceptional [ɪk'sepʃnəl] *adj* excepcional.

excerpt ['eksɜːpt] *n* extracto *m*.

excess [ɪk'ses, *before noun* 'ekses] *adj* excedente ◆ *n* exceso *m*.

excess baggage *n* exceso *m* de equipaje.

excess fare *n* *(Br)* suplemento *m*.

excessive [ɪk'sesɪv] *adj* excesivo(-va).

exchange [ɪks'tʃeɪndʒ] *n* *(of telephones)* central *f* telefónica; *(of students)* intercambio *m* ◆ *vt* intercambiar; **to ~ sthg for sthg** cambiar algo por algo; **to be on an ~** estar de intercambio.

exchange rate n tipo m de cambio.

excited [ɪkˈsaɪtɪd] adj emocionado(-da).

excitement [ɪkˈsaɪtmənt] n emoción f; **~s** (exciting things) emociones fpl.

exciting [ɪkˈsaɪtɪŋ] adj emocionante.

exclamation mark [ˌeksklə-ˈmeɪʃn] n (Br) signo m de admiración.

exclamation point [ˌeksklə-ˈmeɪʃn] (Am) = **exclamation mark**.

exclude [ɪkˈskluːd] vt excluir.

excluding [ɪkˈskluːdɪŋ] prep excepto, con excepción de.

exclusive [ɪkˈskluːsɪv] adj (high-class) selecto(-ta); (sole) exclusivo(-va) ◆ n exclusiva f; **~ of** excluyendo.

excursion [ɪkˈskɜːʃn] n excursión f.

excuse [n ɪkˈskjuːs, vb ɪkˈskjuːz] n excusa f ◆ vt (forgive) perdonar; (let off) dispensar; **~ me!** (attracting attention) ¡perdone!; (trying to get past) ¿me deja pasar, por favor?; (as apology) perdone.

ex-directory adj (Br) que no figura en la guía telefónica.

execute [ˈeksɪkjuːt] vt ejecutar.

executive [ɪgˈzekjʊtɪv] adj (desk, suite) para ejecutivos ◆ n (person) ejecutivo m (-va f).

exempt [ɪgˈzempt] adj: **~ (from)** exento(-ta) (de).

exemption [ɪgˈzempʃn] n exención f.

exercise [ˈeksəsaɪz] n ejercicio m ◆ vi hacer ejercicio; **to do ~s** hacer ejercicio.

exercise book n cuaderno m de ejercicios.

exert [ɪgˈzɜːt] vt ejercer.

exhaust [ɪgˈzɔːst] vt agotar ◆ n: **~ (pipe)** tubo m de escape.

exhausted [ɪgˈzɔːstɪd] adj agotado(-da).

exhibit [ɪgˈzɪbɪt] n (in museum, gallery) objeto m expuesto ◆ vt (in exhibition) exponer.

exhibition [ˌeksɪˈbɪʃn] n (of art) exposición f.

exist [ɪgˈzɪst] vi existir.

existence [ɪgˈzɪstəns] n existencia f; **to be in ~** existir.

existing [ɪgˈzɪstɪŋ] adj existente.

exit [ˈeksɪt] n salida f ◆ vi salir.

exotic [ɪgˈzɒtɪk] adj exótico(-ca).

expand [ɪkˈspænd] vi (in size) extenderse, expandirse; (in number) aumentarse, ampliarse.

expect [ɪkˈspekt] vt esperar; **to do sthg** esperar hacer algo; **to ~ sb to do sthg** esperar que alguien haga algo; **to be ~ing** (be pregnant) estar embarazada.

expedition [ˌekspɪˈdɪʃn] n (to explore etc) expedición f; (short outing) salida f.

expel [ɪkˈspel] vt (from school) expulsar.

expense [ɪkˈspens] n gasto m; **at the ~ of** a costa de ❏ **expenses** npl (of business person) gastos mpl.

expensive [ɪkˈspensɪv] adj caro(-ra).

experience [ɪkˈspɪərɪəns] n experiencia f ◆ vt experimentar.

experienced [ɪkˈspɪərɪənst] adj experimentado(-da).

experiment [ɪkˈsperɪmənt] n experimento m ◆ vi experimentar.

expert [ˈekspɜːt] adj experto(-ta) ◆ n experto m (-ta f).

expire [ɪkˈspaɪər] vi caducar.

expiry date [ɪkˈspaɪə-] n fecha f de caducidad.

explain [ɪkˈspleɪn] vt explicar.

explanation [ekspləˈneɪʃn] n explicación f.

explode [ɪkˈspləʊd] vi estallar.

exploit [ɪkˈsplɔɪt] vt explotar.

explore [ɪkˈsplɔːr] vt explorar.

explosion [ɪkˈspləʊʒn] n explosión f.

explosive [ɪkˈspləʊsɪv] n explosivo m.

export [n ˈekspɔːt, vb ɪkˈspɔːt] n exportación f ◆ vt exportar.

exposed [ɪkˈspəʊzd] adj (place) al descubierto.

exposure [ɪkˈspəʊʒər] n exposición f; (MED) hipotermia f.

express [ɪkˈspres] adj (letter, delivery) urgente; (train) rápido(-da) ◆ n (train) expreso m ◆ vt expresar ◆ adv urgente.

expression [ɪkˈspreʃn] n expresión f.

expresso [ɪkˈspresəʊ] n café m exprés.

expressway [ɪkˈspresweɪ] n (Am) autopista f.

extend [ɪkˈstend] vt (visa, permit) prorrogar; (road, railway) prolongar; (hand) tender ◆ vi (stretch) extenderse.

extension [ɪkˈstenʃn] n (of building) ampliación f; (for phone, permit, essay) extensión f.

extension lead [-liːd] n alargador m.

extensive [ɪkˈstensɪv] adj (damage, area) extenso(-sa); (selection) amplio(-plia).

extent [ɪkˈstent] n (of damage, knowledge) extensión f; **to a certain ~** hasta cierto punto; **to what ...?** ¿hasta qué punto ...?

exterior [ɪkˈstɪərɪər] adj exterior ◆ n (of car, building) exterior m.

external [ɪkˈstɜːnl] adj externo(-na).

extinct [ɪkˈstɪŋkt] adj extinto(-ta).

extinction [ɪkˈstɪŋkʃn] n extinción f.

extinguish [ɪkˈstɪŋwɪʃ] vt (fire) extinguir; (cigarette) apagar.

extinguisher [ɪkˈstɪŋwɪʃər] n extintor m.

extortionate [ɪkˈstɔːʃnət] adj exorbitante.

extra [ˈekstrə] adj (additional) extra inv; (spare) de más ◆ n (bonus) paga f extraordinaria; (optional thing) extra m ◆ adv (more) más; **an ~ special offer** una oferta muy especial; **be ~ careful** ten mucho cuidado; **I need some ~ help** necesito más ayuda; **~ charge** suplemento m; **~ large** extra-grande ❑ **extras** npl (in price) suplementos mpl.

extract [n ˈekstrækt, vb ɪkˈstrækt] n (of yeast, malt etc) extracto m; (from book, opera) fragmento m ◆ vt (tooth) extraer.

extractor fan [ɪkˈstræktər-] n

(Br) extractor *m* (de humos).

extraordinary [ɪkˈstrɔːdnrɪ] *adj* extraordinario(-ria).

extravagant [ɪkˈstrævəgənt] *adj (wasteful)* derrochador(-ra); *(expensive)* exorbitante.

extreme [ɪkˈstriːm] *adj* extremo(-ma) ♦ *n* extremo.

extremely [ɪkˈstriːmlɪ] *adv* extremadamente.

extrovert [ˈekstrəvɜːt] *n* extrovertido *m* (da *f*).

eye [aɪ] *n* ojo *m* ♦ *vt* mirar detenidamente; **to keep an ~ on** vigilar.

eyebrow [ˈaɪbraʊ] *n* ceja *f*.

eye drops *npl* colirio *m*.

eyeglasses [ˈaɪglɑːsɪz] *npl (Am)* gafas *fpl*.

eyelash [ˈaɪlæʃ] *n* pestaña *f*.

eyelid [ˈaɪlɪd] *n* párpado *m*.

eyeliner [ˈaɪˌlaɪnər] *n* lápiz *m* de ojos.

eye shadow *n* sombra *f* de ojos.

eyesight [ˈaɪsaɪt] *n* vista *f*.

eye test *n* prueba *f* de visión.

eyewitness [ˌaɪˈwɪtnɪs] *n* testigo *mf* presencial.

F

F *(abbr of Fahrenheit)* F.

fabric [ˈfæbrɪk] *n (cloth)* tejido *m*.

fabulous [ˈfæbjʊləs] *adj* fabuloso(-sa).

facade [fəˈsɑːd] *n* fachada *f*.

face [feɪs] *n* cara *f*; *(of clock, watch)* esfera *f*; *(look towards)* mirar a; *(confront, accept)* hacer frente a; *(cope with)* soportar; **to be ~d with** enfrentarse con ❑ **face up to** *vt fus* hacer frente a.

facecloth [ˈfeɪsklɒθ] *n (Br)* toalla *f* de cara.

facial [ˈfeɪʃəl] *n* limpieza *f* de cutis.

facilitate [fəˈsɪlɪteɪt] *vt (fml)* facilitar.

facilities [fəˈsɪlɪtɪz] *npl* instalaciones *fpl*.

facsimile [fækˈsɪmɪlɪ] *n* facsímil *m*.

fact [fækt] *n (established truth)* hecho *m*; *(piece of information)* dato *m*; **in ~** *(in reality)* en realidad; *(moreover)* de hecho.

factor [ˈfæktər] *n (condition)* factor *m*; *(of suntan lotion)* factor (de protección solar); **~ ten suntan lotion** bronceador *m* con factor de protección diez.

factory [ˈfæktərɪ] *n* fábrica *f*.

faculty [ˈfækltɪ] *n (at university)* facultad *f*.

FA Cup *n* copa de fútbol británica, ≈ Copa *f* del Rey.

fade [feɪd] *vi (light, sound)* irse apagando; *(flower)* marchitarse; *(jeans, wallpaper)* descolorarse.

faded [ˈfeɪdɪd] *adj (jeans)* desteñido(-da).

fag [fæg] *n (Br: inf: cigarette)* pitillo *m*.

Fahrenheit [ˈfærənhaɪt] *adj* Fahrenheit *inv*.

fail [feɪl] *vt (exam)* suspender ♦ *vi*

(not succeed) fracasar; *(in exam)* suspender; *(engine)* fallar; **to ~ to do sth** *(not do)* no hacer algo.

failing ['feɪlɪŋ] n defecto m ♦ prep: **~ that** en su defecto.

failure ['feɪljə*] n fracaso m; *(unsuccessful person)* fracasado m (-da f); **~ to comply with the regulations** el incumplimiento de las normas.

faint [feɪnt] adj *(sound, colour)* débil; *(outline)* impreciso(-sa); *(dizzy)* mareado(-da) ♦ vi desmayarse; **I haven't the ~est idea** no tengo la más mínima idea.

fair [feə*] adj *(just)* justo(-ta); *(quite large)* considerable; *(quite good)* bastante bueno(-na); *(SCH)* satisfactorio(-ria); *(hair, person)* rubio(-bia); *(skin)* blanco(-ca); *(weather)* bueno(-na) ♦ n feria f; **~ enough!** ¡vale!

fairground ['feəgraʊnd] n recinto m de la feria.

fair-haired [-'heəd] adj rubio (-bia).

fairly ['feəlɪ] adv *(quite)* bastante.

fairy ['feərɪ] n hada f.

fairy tale n cuento m de hadas.

faith [feɪθ] n fe f.

faithfully ['feɪθfəlɪ] adv: **Yours ~** le saluda atentamente.

fake [feɪk] n *(false thing)* falsificación f ♦ vt *(signature, painting)* falsificar.

fall [fɔːl] *(pt fell, pp fallen* ['fɔːln]*)* vi caer; *(lose balance)* caerse; *(decrease)* bajar ♦ n *(accident)* caída f; *(decrease)* descenso m; *(of snow)* nevada f; *(Am: autumn)* otoño m; **to ~ asleep** dormirse; **to ~ ill** ponerse enfermo; **to ~ in love** enamorarse

□ **falls** npl *(waterfall)* cataratas fpl; **fall behind** vi *(with work, rent)* retrasarse; **fall down** vi *(lose balance)* caerse; **fall off** vi *(person)* caerse; *(handle, branch)* desprenderse; **fall out** vi *(argue)* pelearse; **my tooth fell out** se me cayó un diente; **fall over** vi caerse; **fall through** vi fracasar.

false [fɔːls] adj falso(-sa); *(artificial)* postizo(-za).

false alarm n falsa alarma f.

false teeth npl dentadura f postiza.

fame [feɪm] n fama f.

familiar [fə'mɪljə*] adj *(known)* familiar; *(informal)* demasiado amistoso(-sa); **to be ~ with** *(know)* estar familiarizado(-da) con.

family ['fæmlɪ] n familia f ♦ adj *(large)* familiar; *(film, holiday)* para toda la familia.

family planning clinic [-'plænɪŋ-] n clínica f de planificación familiar.

family room n *(at hotel)* habitación f familiar; *(at pub, airport)* habitación para familias con niños pequeños.

famine ['fæmɪn] n hambruna f.

famished ['fæmɪʃt] adj *(inf)* muerto(-ta) de hambre.

famous ['feɪməs] adj famoso (-sa).

fan [fæn] n *(held in hand)* abanico m; *(electric)* ventilador m; *(enthusiast)* admirador m (-ra f); *(supporter)* aficionado m (-da f).

fan belt n correa f del ventilador.

fancy ['fænsɪ] adj *(elaborate)* recargado(-da); *(food)* elaborado(-da) ♦

vt (*inf*) : **I ~ an ice cream** me apetece tomar un helado; **he fancies Jane** él está por Jane; **~ (that)!** ¡fíjate!

fancy dress *n* disfraz *m*.

fan heater *n* convector *m*.

fanlight ['fænlaɪt] *n* (*Br*) montante *m* de abanico.

fantastic [fæn'tæstɪk] *adj* fantástico(-ca).

fantasy ['fæntəsɪ] *n* fantasía *f*.

far [fɑːʳ] (*compar* **further** OR **farther**, *superl* **furthest** OR **farthest**) *adv* (*in distance, time*) lejos; (*in degree*) mucho; (*side*) opuesto(-ta); **have you come ~?** ¿vienes de lejos?; **how ~ is it?** ¿está lejos?; **how ~ is it to London?** ¿cuánto hay de aquí a Londres?; **as ~ as** (*place*) hasta; **as ~ as I'm concerned** por lo que a mí se refiere; **as ~ as I know** que yo sepa; **~ better** mucho mejor; **by ~** con mucho; **so ~** hasta ahora; **to go too ~** pasarse.

farce [fɑːs] *n* farsa *f*.

fare [feəʳ] *n* (*on bus, train etc*) precio *m* del billete; (*fml: food*) comida *f* ♦ *vi*: **she ~d well** le fue bien.

Far East *n*: **the ~** el Lejano Oriente.

fare stage *n* (*Br*) parada de autobús donde termina un tramo de línea con misma tarifa.

farm [fɑːm] *n* granja *f*.

farmer ['fɑːməʳ] *n* agricultor *m* (-ra *f*).

farmhouse ['fɑːmhaus, *pl* -hauzɪz] *n* caserío *m*.

farming ['fɑːmɪŋ] *n* agricultura *f*.

farmland ['fɑːmlænd] *n* tierras *fpl* de labranza.

farmyard ['fɑːmjɑːd] *n* corral *m*.

farther ['fɑːðəʳ] *compar* → **far**.

farthest ['fɑːðəst] *superl* → **far**.

fascinating ['fæsɪneɪtɪŋ] *adj* fascinante.

fascination [,fæsɪ'neɪʃn] *n* fascinación *f*.

fashion ['fæʃn] *n* (*trend, style*) moda *f*; (*manner*) manera *f*; **to be in ~** estar de moda; **to be out of ~** estar pasado de moda.

fashionable ['fæʃnəbl] *adj* de moda.

fashion show *n* desfile *m* de moda.

fast [fɑːst] *adj* (*quick*) rápido(-da); (*clock, watch*) adelantado(-da) ♦ *adv* (*quickly*) rápidamente; (*securely*) firmemente; **~ asleep** profundamente dormido; **a ~ train** un tren rápido.

fasten ['fɑːsn] *vt* (*belt, coat*) abrochar; (*two things*) sujetar.

fastener ['fɑːsnəʳ] *n* (*of window, box*) cierre *m*; (*of dress*) corchete *m*.

fast food *n* comida *f* rápida.

fat [fæt] *adj* (*person*) gordo(-da); (*meat*) con mucha grasa ♦ *n* grasa *f*; (*for cooking*) manteca *f*.

fatal ['feɪtl] *adj* (*accident, disease*) mortal.

father ['fɑːðəʳ] *n* padre *m*.

Father Christmas *n* (*Br*) Papá *m* Noel.

father-in-law *n* suegro *m*.

fattening ['fætnɪŋ] *adj* que engorda.

fatty ['fætɪ] *adj* graso(-sa).

faucet ['fɔːsɪt] *n* (*Am*) grifo *m*.

fault [fɔːlt] n (responsibility) culpa f; (flaw) defecto m; (in machine) fallo m; it's your ~ tú tienes la culpa.

faulty [ˈfɔːltɪ] adj defectuoso(-sa).

favor [ˈfeɪvər] (Am) = favour.

favour [ˈfeɪvər] n (Br: kind act) favor m ♦ vt (prefer) preferir; to be in ~ of estar a favor de; to do sb a ~ hacerle un favor a alguien.

favourable [ˈfeɪvrəbl] adj favorable.

favourite [ˈfeɪvrɪt] adj favorito(-ta) ♦ n favorito m (-ta f).

fawn [fɔːn] adj beige inv.

fax [fæks] n fax m ♦ vt (document) enviar por fax; (person) enviar un fax a.

fear [fɪər] n (sensation) miedo m; (thing feared) temor m ♦ vt (be afraid of) temer; for ~ of por miedo a.

feast [fiːst] n banquete m.

feather [ˈfeðər] n pluma f.

feature [ˈfiːtʃər] n (characteristic) característica f; (of face) rasgo m; (in newspaper) artículo m de fondo; (on radio, TV) programa m especial ♦ vt (subj: film) estar protagonizado por.

feature film n largometraje m.

Feb [feb] (abbr of February) feb.

February [ˈfebruərɪ] n febrero m, → September.

fed [fed] pt & pp → feed.

fed up adj harto(-ta); to be ~ with estar harto de.

fee [fiː] n (for entry) precio m; (for service) tarifa f; (of doctor, lawyer) honorarios mpl.

feeble [ˈfiːbəl] adj (weak) débil.

feed [fiːd] (pt & pp fed) vt (person, animal) dar de comer a; (insert) introducir.

feel [fiːl] (pt & pp felt) vt (touch) tocar; (experience) sentir; (think) pensar que ♦ vi (tired, ill, better) encontrarse; (sad, angry, safe) sentirse ♦ n (of material) tacto m; my nose ~s cold tengo la nariz fría; to ~ cold tener frío; to ~ hungry tener hambre; I ~ like a cup of tea me apetece una taza de té; to ~ up to doing sthg sentirse con ánimos de hacer algo.

feeling [ˈfiːlɪŋ] n (emotion) sentimiento m; (sensation) sensación f; (belief) impresión f; to hurt sb's ~s herir los sentimientos de alguien.

feet [fiːt] pl → foot.

fell [fel] pt → fall ♦ vt talar.

fellow [ˈfeləʊ] n (man) tío m ♦ adj: my ~ students mis compañeros de clase.

felt [felt] pt & pp → feel ♦ n fieltro m.

felt-tip pen n rotulador m.

female [ˈfiːmeɪl] adj (animal) hembra; (person) femenino(-na) ♦ n hembra f.

feminine [ˈfemɪnɪn] adj femenino(-na).

feminist [ˈfemɪnɪst] n feminista mf.

fence [fens] n valla f.

fencing [ˈfensɪŋ] n (SPORT) esgrima f.

fend [fend] vi: to ~ for o.s. valerse por sí mismo(-ma).

fender [ˈfendər] n (for fireplace) guardafuego m; (Am: on car) guardabarros m inv.

fennel [ˈfenl] n hinojo m.

fern [fɜːn] n helecho m.

ferocious [fəˈrəʊʃəs] adj feroz.

ferry ['ferɪ] n ferry m.

fertile ['fɜːtaɪl] adj fértil.

fertilizer ['fɜːtɪlaɪzə'] n abono m.

festival ['festəvl] n (of music, arts etc) festival m; (holiday) día m festivo.

feta cheese ['fetə-] n queso blando de origen griego fabricado con leche de oveja.

fetch [fetʃ] vt (person) ir a buscar; (object) traer; (be sold for) alcanzar.

fete [feɪt] n fiesta al aire libre.

FETE

Un "fete" es una especie de fiesta al aire libre, generalmente en verano, que incluye concursos, espectáculos y venta de productos caseros. Se suele celebrar un "fete" para recolectar dinero destinado a fines benéficos o a proyectos locales.

fever ['fiːvə'] n fiebre f; **to have a ~** tener fiebre.

feverish ['fiːvərɪʃ] adj febril.

few [fjuː] adj pocos(-cas) ♦ pron pocos mpl (-cas fpl); **~ people** poca gente; **a ~** adj algunos(-nas) ♦ pron unos pocos (unas pocas fpl); **quite a ~** bastantes.

fewer ['fjuːə'] adj & pron menos.

fiancé [fɪˈɒnseɪ] n prometido m.

fiancée [fɪˈɒnseɪ] n prometida f.

fib [fɪb] n (inf) bola f.

fiber ['faɪbə'] (Am) = **fibre**.

fibre ['faɪbə'] n (Br) fibra f.

fibreglass ['faɪbəɡlɑːs] n fibra f de vidrio.

fickle ['fɪkl] adj voluble.

fiction ['fɪkʃn] n ficción f.

fiddle ['fɪdl] n (violin) violín m ♦ vi: **to ~ with sthg** juguetear con algo.

fidget ['fɪdʒɪt] vi moverse inquietamente.

field [fiːld] n campo m.

field glasses npl prismáticos mpl.

fierce [fɪəs] adj (animal, person) feroz; (storm, heat) fuerte.

fifteen [fɪfˈtiːn] num quince, → **six**.

fifteenth [fɪfˈtiːnθ] num decimoquinto(-ta), → **sixth**.

fifth [fɪfθ] num quinto(-ta), → **sixth**.

fiftieth ['fɪftɪəθ] num quincuagésimo(-ma), → **sixth**.

fifty ['fɪftɪ] num cincuenta, → **six**.

fig [fɪɡ] n higo m.

fight [faɪt] (pt & pp fought) n (physical clash, argument) pelea f; (struggle) lucha f ♦ vt (enemy, crime, illness) luchar contra; (in punch-up) pelearse con ♦ vi (in war, struggle) luchar; (quarrel) discutir; **to have a ~ with sb** pelearse con alguien; **fight back** vi defenderse; **fight off** vt sep (attacker) rechazar; (illness) sanar de.

fighting ['faɪtɪŋ] n (at football match, in streets) violencia f; (in war) combate m.

figure [Br 'fɪɡə', Am 'fɪɡjər] n (number, statistic) cifra f; (shape of body) tipo m; (outline of person) figura f; (diagram) gráfico m ❑ **figure out** vt sep (answer) figurarse; **I can't ~ out how to do it** no sé cómo hacerlo.

file [faɪl] n (document holder) carpeta f; (information on person) expediente m; (COMPUT) fichero m; (tool) lima f ♦ vt (complaint, petition) presentar; (nails) limar; **in single ~** en fila india.

filing cabinet ['faɪlɪŋ-] n archivador m.

fill [fɪl] vt (make full) llenar; (hole) rellenar; (role) desempeñar; (tooth) empastar □ **fill in** vt sep (form) rellenar; **fill out** vt sep = **fill in**; **fill up** vt sep llenar (hasta el tope); **~ her up!** (with petrol) ¡llénelo!

filled roll [-fɪld-] n bocadillo m (de bollo).

fillet ['fɪlɪt] n filete m.

fillet steak n filete m de carne de vaca.

filling ['fɪlɪŋ] n (of cake, sandwich) relleno m; (in tooth) empaste m ♦ adj que llena mucho.

filling station n estación f de servicio.

film [fɪlm] n película f ♦ vt rodar.

film star n estrella f de cine.

filter ['fɪltə*] n filtro m.

filthy ['fɪlθɪ] adj (very dirty) sucísimo(-ma).

fin [fɪn] n (of fish) aleta f; (Am: of swimmer) aleta f.

final ['faɪnl] adj (last) último(-ma); (decision, offer) definitivo(-va) ♦ n final f.

finalist ['faɪnlɪst] n finalista mf.

finally ['faɪnəlɪ] adv (at last) por fin; (lastly) finalmente.

finance [n 'faɪnæns, vb faɪ'næns] n (money) fondos mpl; (management of money) finanzas fpl ♦ vt financiar □ **finances** npl finanzas fpl.

financial [fɪ'nænʃl] adj finan-

ciero(-ra).

find [faɪnd] (pt & pp found) vt encontrar ♦ n hallazgo m; **to ~ the time to do sthg** encontrar tiempo para hacer algo □ **find out** vt sep (fact, truth) averiguar ♦ vi: **to ~ out about sthg** averiguar algo.

fine [faɪn] adj (good) bueno(-na); (food, wine) excelente; (thin) fino (-na) ♦ adv (thinly) finamente; (well) bien ♦ n multa f ♦ vt multar ♦ excl vale; **I'm ~** estoy bien; **it's ~** está bien.

fine art n bellas artes fpl.

finger ['fɪŋgə*] n dedo m.

fingernail ['fɪŋgəneɪl] n uña f de la mano.

fingertip ['fɪŋgətɪp] n yema f de la mano.

finish ['fɪnɪʃ] n (end) final m; (on furniture) acabado m ♦ vt & vi acabar; **to ~ doing sthg** terminar de hacer algo □ **finish off** vt sep (complete) acabar del todo; (eat or drink) acabar; **finish up** vi acabar; **to ~ up doing sthg** acabar haciendo algo.

Finland ['fɪnlənd] n Finlandia f.

Finn [fɪn] n finlandés m (-esa f).

Finnan haddock ['fɪnən-] n tipo de eglefino ahumado escocés.

Finnish ['fɪnɪʃ] adj finlandés (-esa) ♦ n (language) finlandés m.

fir [fɜ:*] n abeto m.

fire ['faɪə*] n fuego m; (uncontrolled) incendio m; (device) estufa f ♦ vt (gun) disparar; (from job) despedir; **on ~** en llamas; **to catch ~** prender fuego; **to make a ~** encender un fuego.

fire alarm n alarma f antiincendios.

fire brigade n (Br) cuerpo m de bomberos.

fire department (Am) = **fire brigade**.

fire engine n coche m de bomberos.

fire escape n escalera f de incendios.

fire exit n salida f de incendios.

fire extinguisher n extintor m.

fire hazard n: it's a ~ podría causar un incendio.

fireman ['faɪəmən] (pl -men [-mən]) n bombero m.

fireplace ['faɪəpleɪs] n chimenea f.

fire regulations npl ordenanzas fpl en caso de incendio.

fire station n parque m de bomberos.

firewood ['faɪəwʊd] n leña f.

firework display ['faɪəwɜːk-] n espectáculo m de fuegos artificiales.

fireworks ['faɪəwɜːks] npl fuegos mpl artificiales.

firm [fɜːm] adj firme ◆ n firma f, empresa f.

first [fɜːst] adj primero(-ra) ◆ adv primero; (for the first time) por primera vez ◆ n (event) acontecimiento m sin precedentes ◆ pron: the ~ el primero (la primera); ~ (gear) primera f (marcha); ~ thing (in the morning) a primera hora (de la mañana); for the ~ time por primera vez; the ~ of January el uno de enero; at ~ al principio; ~ of all antes de nada.

first aid n primeros auxilios mpl.

first-aid kit n botiquín m (de primeros auxilios).

first class n (mail) correo que se distribuye el día siguiente; (on train, plane, ship) primera clase f.

first-class adj (stamp) para la UE o distribución al día siguiente; (ticket) de primera (clase); (very good) de primera.

first floor n (Br: floor above ground floor) primer piso m; (Am: ground floor) bajo m.

firstly ['fɜːstlɪ] adv en primer lugar.

First World War n: the ~ la Primera Guerra Mundial.

fish [fɪʃ] (pl inv) n (animal) pez m; (food) pescado m ◆ vi pescar.

fish and chips n filete de pescado blanco rebozado, con patatas fritas.

---

i FISH AND CHIPS

La tradicional comida británica para llevar, "fish and chips", consiste en pescado rebozado y frito acompañado de patatas fritas, todo ello envuelto en papel de estraza y periódico. En las tiendas de "fish and chips", que son muy comunes en Gran Bretaña, se pueden encontrar otras frituras, tales como salchichas, pollo, morcilla y pasteles de carne. A menudo, "fish and chips" se come al aire libre directamente del envoltorio.

---

fishcake ['fɪʃkeɪk] n hamburguesa f de pescado.

fisherman [ˈfɪʃəmən] (*pl* **-men** [-mən]) *n* pescador *m*.

fish farm *n* piscifactoría *f*.

fish fingers *npl* (Br) palitos *mpl* de pescado.

fishing [ˈfɪʃɪŋ] *n* pesca *f*; **to go ~** ir de pesca.

fishing boat *n* barco *m* de pesca.

fishing rod *n* caña *f* de pescar.

fishmonger's [ˈfɪʃmʌŋgəz] *n* (shop) pescadería *f*.

fish sticks (Am) = **fish fingers**.

fish supper *n* (Scot) filete *m* de pescado blanco rebozado, con patatas fritas.

fist [fɪst] *n* puño *m*.

fit [fɪt] *adj* (healthy) en forma ♦ *vt* (be right size for) sentar bien a; (a lock, kitchen, bath) instalar; (insert) insertar ♦ *vi* (clothes, shoes) estar bien de talla; (in space) caber ♦ *n* ataque *m*; **to be ~** for estar apto(-ta) para algo; **~ to eat** apto para el consumo; **it's a good ~** sienta bien; **it doesn't ~** no cabe; **to get ~** ponerse en forma; **to keep ~** mantenerse en forma □ **fit in** *vt sep* (find time to do) hacer un hueco a ♦ *vi* (belong) encajar.

fitness [ˈfɪtnɪs] *n* (health) estado *m* físico.

fitted carpet [ˌfɪtəd-] *n* moqueta *f*.

fitted sheet [ˌfɪtəd-] *n* sábana *f* ajustable.

fitting room [ˈfɪtɪŋ-] *n* probador *m*.

five [faɪv] *num* cinco, → **six**.

fiver [ˈfaɪvə] *n* (Br) (inf) (£5) cinco libras *fpl*; (£5 note) billete *m*

de cinco libras.

fix [fɪks] *vt* (attach, decide on) fijar; (mend) reparar; (drink, food) preparar; **have you ~ed anything for tonight?** ¿tienes planes para esta noche? □ **fix up** *vt sep*: **to ~ sb up with sthg** proveer a alguien de algo.

fixture [ˈfɪkstʃə] *n* (SPORT) encuentro *m*; **~s and fittings** instalaciones *fpl* domésticas.

fizzy [ˈfɪzɪ] *adj* gaseoso(-sa).

flag [flæg] *n* bandera *f*.

flake [fleɪk] *n* (of snow) copo *m* ♦ *vi* descamarse.

flame [fleɪm] *n* llama *f*.

flammable [ˈflæməbl] *adj* inflamable.

flan [flæn] *n* tarta *f*.

flannel [ˈflænl] *n* (material) franela *f*; (Br: for washing face) toalla *f* de cara □ **flannels** *npl* pantalones *mpl* de franela.

flap [flæp] *n* (of envelope, pocket) solapa *f*; (of tent) puerta *f* ♦ *vt* (wings) batir.

flapjack [ˈflæpdʒæk] *n* (Br) torta *f* de avena.

flare [fleə] *n* (signal) bengala *f*.

flared [fleəd] *adj* acampanado(-da).

flash [flæʃ] *n* (of light) destello *m*; (for camera) flash *m* ♦ *vi* (light) destellar; **a ~ of lightning** un relámpago; **to ~ one's headlights** dar las luces.

flashlight [ˈflæʃlaɪt] *n* linterna *f*.

flask [flɑːsk] *n* (Thermos) termo *m*; (hip flask) petaca *f*.

flat [flæt] *adj* (level) llano(-na); (battery) descargado(-da); (drink)

muerto(-ta); *(rate, fee)* único(-ca) ♦ *n (Br)* piso *m* ♦ *adv:* **to lie ~** estar extendido; **a ~** *(tyre)* un pinchazo; **~ out** a toda velocidad.

flatter ['flætər] *vt* adular.

flavor ['fleɪvər] *(Am)* = **flavour**.

flavour ['fleɪvər] *n (Br)* sabor *m*.

flavoured ['fleɪvəd] *adj* de sabores.

flavouring ['fleɪvərɪŋ] *n* aroma *m*.

flaw [flɔː] *n* fallo *m*.

flea [fliː] *n* pulga *f*.

flea market *n* mercado de objetos curiosos y de segunda mano, ≈ rastro *m*.

fleece [fliːs] *n (downy material)* vellón *m*.

fleet [fliːt] *n* flota *f*.

Flemish ['flemɪʃ] *adj* flamenco(-ca) ♦ *n (language)* flamenco *m*.

flesh [fleʃ] *n (of person, animal)* carne *f*; *(of fruit, vegetable)* pulpa *f*.

flew [fluː] *pt* → **fly**.

flex [fleks] *n* cable *m*.

flexible ['fleksəbl] *adj* flexible.

flick [flɪk] *vt (a switch)* apretar; *(with finger)* golpear rápidamente ❑ **flick through** *vt fus* hojear rápidamente.

flies [flaɪz] *npl* bragueta *f*.

flight [flaɪt] *n* vuelo *m*; **a ~ (of stairs)** un tramo (de escaleras).

flight attendant *n* auxiliar *mf* de vuelo.

flimsy ['flɪmzɪ] *adj (object)* frágil, poco sólido(-da); *(clothes)* ligero(-ra).

fling [flɪŋ] *(pt & pp* **flung)** *vt* arrojar.

flint [flɪnt] *n (of lighter)* piedra *f*.

flip-flop ['flɪp-] *n (Br)* chancleta *f*.

flipper ['flɪpər] *n (Br)* aleta *f*.

flirt [flɜːt] *vi:* **to ~ (with sb)** coquetear (con alguien).

float [fləʊt] *n (for swimming)* flotador *m*; *(for fishing)* corcho *m*; *(in procession)* carroza *f*; *(drink)* bebida con una bola de helado flotando ♦ *vi* flotar.

flock [flɒk] *n (of birds)* bandada *f*; *(of sheep)* rebaño *m* ♦ *vi (people)* acudir en masa.

flood [flʌd] *n* inundación *f* ♦ *vt* inundar ♦ *vi* desbordarse.

floodlight ['flʌdlaɪt] *n* foco *m*.

floor [flɔːr] *n (of room)* suelo *m*; *(storey)* piso *m*; *(of nightclub)* pista *f* de baile.

floorboard ['flɔːbɔːd] *n* tabla *f* del suelo.

floor show *n* espectáculo *m* de cabaret.

flop [flɒp] *n (inf)* fracaso *m*.

floppy disk [ˌflɒpɪ-] *n* floppy disk *m*.

floral ['flɔːrəl] *adj (pattern)* floreado(-da).

Florida Keys ['flɒrɪdə-] *npl:* **the ~** las Florida Keys.

 i **FLORIDA KEYS**

Un archipiélago de pequeñas islas que se extiende más de 100 millas frente a la costa sur de Florida, las Florida Keys incluyen lugares turísticos como las islas de Cayo Largo y Cayo Hueso. Un sistema de carreteras y puentes, la "Overseas Highway", comunica las distintas islas.

florist's ['florists] n (shop) floristería f.

flour ['flauə^r] n harina f.

flow [fləu] n corriente f ♦ vi correr.

flower ['flauə^r] n flor f.

flowerbed ['flauəbed] n arriate m.

flowerpot ['flauəppt] n tiesto m.

flown [fləun] pp → fly.

fl oz abbr = **fluid ounce**.

flu [flu:] n gripe f.

fluent ['flu:ənt] adj: **to be ~ in/to speak ~ Spanish** dominar el español.

fluff [flʌf] n pelusa f.

fluid ounce ['flu:ɪd-] n = 0,03 litros, onza f líquida.

flume [flu:m] n tobogán m acuático.

flung [flʌŋ] pt & pp → **fling**.

flunk [flʌŋk] vt (Am: inf) catear.

fluorescent [fluə'resənt] adj fluorescente.

flush [flʌʃ] vi (toilet) funcionar ♦ vt: **to ~ the toilet** tirar de la cadena.

flute [flu:t] n flauta f.

fly [flaɪ] (pt **flew**, pp **flown**) n (insect) mosca f; (of trousers) bragueta f ♦ vt (plane, helicopter) pilotar; (travel by) volar con; (transport) transportar en avión ♦ vi volar; (pilot a plane) pilotar; (flag) ondear.

fly-drive n paquete turístico que incluye vuelo y coche alquilado.

flying ['flaɪɪŋ] n: **I like ~** me gusta volar.

flyover ['flaɪˌəuvə^r] n (Br) paso m elevado.

flypaper ['flaɪˌpeɪpə^r] n papel m

insecticida.

flysheet ['flaɪʃi:t] n doble techo m.

FM n FM f.

foal [fəul] n potro m.

foam [fəum] n (bubbles) espuma f; (foam rubber) gomaespuma f.

focus ['fəukəs] n (of camera) foco m ♦ vi (with camera, binoculars) enfocar; **in ~** enfocado; **out of ~** desenfocado.

fog [fɒg] n niebla f.

fogbound ['fɒgbaund] adj (airport) cerrado(-da) a causa de la niebla.

foggy ['fɒgɪ] adj (weather) brumoso(-sa).

fog lamp n faro m antiniebla.

foil [fɔɪl] n papel m de aluminio.

fold [fəuld] n pliegue m ♦ vt (paper, material) doblar; (wrap) envolver; **to ~ one's arms** cruzarse de brazos □ **fold up** vi plegarse.

folder ['fəuldə^r] n carpeta f.

foliage ['fəulɪdʒ] n follaje m.

folk [fəuk] npl (people) gente f ♦ n: **~ (music)** folk m □ **folks** npl (inf: relatives) familia f.

follow ['fɒləu] vt seguir; (understand) comprender ♦ vi (go behind) ir detrás; (in time) seguir; (understand) comprender; **~ed by** seguido de; **as ~s** como sigue □ **follow on** vi ir detrás.

following ['fɒləuɪŋ] adj siguiente ♦ prep tras.

follow on call n nueva llamada con crédito restante, sin colgar.

fond [fɒnd] adj: **to be ~ of** (person) tener cariño a; (thing) ser aficionado(-da) a.

fondue ['fɒndu:] n fondue f.

food [fu:d] n (nourishment) comida f; (type of food) alimento m.

food poisoning [-ˌpɔɪznɪŋ] n intoxicación f alimenticia.

food processor [-ˈprəʊsesəʳ] n robot m de cocina.

foodstuffs ['fu:dstʌfs] npl comestibles mpl.

fool [fu:l] n (idiot) tonto m (-ta f); (pudding) mousse de nata y fruta ♦ vt engañar.

foolish ['fu:lɪʃ] adj tonto(-ta).

foot [fut] (pl **feet**) n pie m; (of animal, wardrobe, tripod) pata f; **by ~** a pie; **on ~** a pie.

football ['futbɔ:l] n (Br: soccer) fútbol m; (Am: American football) fútbol americano; (Br: in soccer) balón m (de fútbol); (Am: in American football) balón m de fútbol americano).

footballer ['futbɔ:ləʳ] n (Br) futbolista m.

football pitch n (Br) campo m de fútbol.

footbridge ['futbrɪdʒ] n pasarela f.

footpath ['futpɑ:θ, pl -pɑ:ðz] n sendero m.

footprint ['futprɪnt] n huella f.

footstep ['futstep] n paso m.

footwear ['futweəʳ] n calzado m.

for [fɔ:ʳ] prep **1.** (expressing intention, purpose, destination) para; **this book is ~ you** este libro es para ti; **what did you do that ~?** ¿por qué hiciste eso?; **what's it ~?** ¿para qué es?; **to go ~ a walk** dar un paseo; **"~ sale"** "se vende"; **a ticket ~**

Edinburgh un billete para Edimburgo; **the train ~ London** el tren de Londres.

2. (expressing reason) por; **a town famous ~ its wine** una ciudad famosa por sus vinos; **the reason ~ it** el motivo de ello.

3. (during) durante; **I've lived here ~ ten years** llevo diez años viviendo aquí; **we've lived here ~ years** vivimos aquí desde hace años; **we talked ~ hours** estuvimos hablando durante horas y horas.

4. (by, before) para; **be there ~ 8 p.m.** estate allí para las ocho de la tarde.

5. (on the occasion of) por; **what's ~ dinner?** ¿qué hay de cena?; **~ the first time** por primera vez.

6. (on behalf of) por; **to do sthg ~ sb** hacer algo por alguien; **to work ~ sb** trabajar para alguien.

7. (with time and space) para; **there's no room/time ~ it** no hay sitio/tiempo para eso.

8. (expressing distance) road **works ~ 20 miles** obras por espacio de 20 millas; **we walked ~ miles** andamos millas y millas.

9. (expressing price) por; **I bought it ~ five pounds** lo compré por cinco libras; **they sell ~ a pound** se venden a una libra.

10. (expressing meaning): **what's the Spanish ~ "boy"?** ¿cómo se dice "boy" en español?

11. (with regard to) por; **it's cold ~ summer** para ser verano, hace frío; **I'm sorry ~ them** me dan pena.

12. (introducing more information) para; **it's too far ~ us to walk** nos queda demasiado lejos para ir andando; **it's time ~ dinner** es hora de cenar.

forbid [fə'bɪd] (*pt* **-bade** [-'beɪd], *pp* **-bidden**) *vt* prohibir; **to ~ sb to do sthg** prohibir a alguien hacer algo.

forbidden [fə'bɪdn] *adj* prohibido(-da).

force [fɔːs] *n* fuerza *f* ♦ *vt* forzar; **to ~ sb to do sthg** forzar a alguien a hacer algo; **to ~ one's way through** abrirse camino; **the ~s** las fuerzas armadas.

ford [fɔːd] *n* vado *m*.

forecast ['fɔːkɑːst] *n* pronóstico *m*.

forecourt ['fɔːkɔːt] *n* patio *m*.

forefinger ['fɔːˌfɪŋgəʳ] *n* dedo *m* índice.

foreground ['fɔːgraund] *n* primer plano *m*.

forehead ['fɔːhed] *n* frente *f*.

foreign ['fɒrən] *adj* extranjero(-ra).

foreign currency *n* divisa *f*.

foreigner ['fɒrənəʳ] *n* extranjero *m* (-ra *f*).

foreign exchange *n* divisas *fpl*.

Foreign Secretary *n* (*Br*) ministro *m* (-tra *f*) de Asuntos Exteriores.

foreman ['fɔːmən] (*pl* **-men** [-mən]) *n* capataz *m*.

forename ['fɔːneɪm] *n* (*fml*) nombre *m* de pila.

foresee [fɔː'siː] (*pt* **-saw** [-'sɔː], *pp* **-seen** [-'siːn]) *vt* prever.

forest ['fɒrɪst] *n* bosque *m*.

forever [fə'revəʳ] *adv* (*eternally*) para siempre; (*continually*) siempre.

forgave [fə'geɪv] *pt* → **forgive**.

forge [fɔːdʒ] *vt* falsificar.

forgery ['fɔːdʒərɪ] *n* falsificación *f*.

forget [fə'get] (*pt* **-got**, *pp* **-gotten**) *vt* olvidar ♦ *vi* olvidar; **to ~ about sthg** olvidarse de algo; **to ~ how to do sthg** olvidar cómo se hace algo; **to ~ to do sthg** olvidarse de hacer algo; **~ it!** ¡ni lo menciones!

forgetful [fə'getful] *adj* olvidadizo(-za).

forgive [fə'gɪv] (*pt* **-gave**, *pp* **-given** [-'gɪvn]) *vt* perdonar.

forgot [fə'gɒt] *pt* → **forget**.

forgotten [fə'gɒtn] *pp* → **forget**.

fork [fɔːk] *n* (*for eating with*) tenedor *m*; (*for gardening*) horca *f*; (*of road, path*) bifurcación *f* ❑ **forks** *npl* (*of bike, motorbike*) horquilla *f*.

form [fɔːm] *n* (*type, shape*) forma *f*; (*piece of paper*) impreso *m*; (*SCH*) clase *f* ♦ *vt* formar ♦ *vi* formarse; **off ~** en baja forma; **on ~** en forma; **to ~ part of** formar parte de.

formal ['fɔːml] *adj* formal.

formality [fɔː'mælətɪ] *n* formalidad *f*; **it's just a ~** es una pura formalidad.

format ['fɔːmæt] *n* formato *m*.

former ['fɔːməʳ] *adj* (*previous*) antiguo(-gua); (*first*) primero(-ra) ♦ *pron*: **the ~** el primero (la primera).

formerly ['fɔːməlɪ] *adv* previamente, antiguamente.

formula ['fɔːmjʊlə] (*pl* **-as** OR **-ae** [-iː]) *n* fórmula *f*.

fort [fɔːt] *n* fortaleza *f*.

forthcoming [ˌfɔːθ'kʌmɪŋ] *adj (future)* próximo(-ma).

fortieth [ˈfɔːtɪnθ] *num* cuadragésimo(-ma), → **sixth**.

fortnight [ˈfɔːtnaɪt] *n (Br)* quincena *f.*

fortunate [ˈfɔːtʃnət] *adj* afortunado(-da).

fortunately [ˈfɔːtʃnətlɪ] *adv* afortunadamente.

fortune [ˈfɔːtʃuːn] *n (money)* fortuna *f; (luck)* suerte *f;* **it costs a ~** *(inf)* cuesta un riñón.

forty [ˈfɔːtɪ] *num* cuarenta, → **six**.

forward [ˈfɔːwəd] *adv* hacia adelante ◆ *n* delantero *m* (-ra *f*) ◆ *vt* reenviar; **to look ~ to** esperar (con ilusión).

forwarding address [ˈfɔːwədɪŋ-] *n* nueva dirección *f* para reenvío del correo.

fought [fɔːt] *pt & pp* → **fight**.

foul [faul] *adj (unpleasant)* asqueroso(-sa) ◆ *n* falta *f.*

found [faund] *pt & pp* → **find** ◆ *vt* fundar.

foundation (cream) [faun-ˈdeɪʃn-] *n* base *f* (hidratante).

foundations [faun'deɪʃnz] *npl* cimientos *mpl.*

fountain [ˈfauntɪn] *n* fuente *f.*

fountain pen *n* pluma *f.*

four [fɔːʳ] *num* cuatro, → **six**.

four-star (petrol) *n* = súper *f.*

fourteen [ˌfɔːˈtiːn] *num* catorce, → **six**.

fourteenth [ˌfɔːˈtiːnθ] *num* decimocuarto(-ta), → **sixth**.

fourth [fɔːθ] *num* cuarto(-ta), → **sixth**.

four-wheel drive *n* coche *m* con tracción a las cuatro ruedas.

fowl [faul] *(pl inv)* *n* volatería *f.*

fox [fɒks] *n* zorro *m.*

foyer [ˈfɔɪeɪ] *n* vestíbulo *m.*

fraction [ˈfrækʃn] *n* fracción *f.*

fracture [ˈfræktʃəʳ] *n* fractura *f* ◆ *vt* fracturar, romper.

fragile [ˈfrædʒaɪl] *adj* frágil.

fragment [ˈfrægmənt] *n* fragmento *m.*

fragrance [ˈfreɪgrəns] *n* fragancia *f.*

frail [freɪl] *adj* débil.

frame [freɪm] *n (of window, photo, door)* marco *m; (of glasses)* montura *f; (of tent, bicycle, bed)* armazón *m* ◆ *vt (photo, picture)* enmarcar.

France [frɑːns] *n* Francia *f.*

frank [fræŋk] *adj* franco(-ca).

frankfurter [ˈfræŋkfɜːtəʳ] *n* salchicha *f* de Francfort.

frankly [ˈfræŋklɪ] *adv* francamente.

frantic [ˈfræntɪk] *adj* frenético(-ca).

fraud [frɔːd] *n (crime)* fraude *m.*

freak [friːk] *adj* estrafalario(-ria) ◆ *n (inf: fanatic)* fanático *m* (-ca *f*).

freckles [ˈfreklz] *npl* pecas *fpl.*

free [friː] *adj* libre; *(costing nothing)* gratis *(inv)* ◆ *vt (prisoner)* liberar ◆ *adv (without paying)* gratis; **for ~** gratis; **~ of charge** gratis; **to be ~ to do sthg** ser libre de hacer algo.

freedom [ˈfriːdəm] *n* libertad *f.*

freefone [ˈfriːfəun] *n (Br)* teléfono *m* gratuito.

free gift *n* obsequio *m.*

free house *n (Br)* "pub" no controlado por una compañía cervecera.

free kick n tiro m libre.

freelance ['fri:lɑ:ns] adj autónomo(-ma).

freely ['fri:lɪ] adv (available) fácilmente; (speak) francamente; (move) libremente.

free period n hora f libre.

freepost ['fri:pəʊst] n franqueo m pagado.

free-range adj de granja.

free time n tiempo m libre.

freeway ['fri:weɪ] n (Am) autopista f.

freeze [fri:z] (pt froze, pp frozen) vt congelar ◆ vi helarse ◆ v impers helar.

freezer ['fri:zə'] n (deep freeze) arcón m congelador; (part of fridge) congelador m.

freezing ['fri:zɪŋ] adj helado(-da); **it's ~** hace un frío cortante.

freezing point n: below ~ bajo cero.

freight [freɪt] n (goods) mercancías fpl.

French [frentʃ] adj francés(-esa) ◆ n (language) francés ◆ npl: the ~ los franceses.

French bean n judía f verde.

French bread n pan m de barra.

French dressing n (in UK) vinagreta f; (in US) salsa f rosa.

French fries npl patatas fpl fritas.

Frenchman ['frentʃmən] (pl -men [-mən]) n francés m.

French toast n torrija f.

French windows npl puertaventanas fpl.

Frenchwoman ['frentʃ,wʊmən] (pl -women [-,wɪmɪn]) n francesa f.

frequency ['fri:kwənsɪ] n frecuencia f.

frequent ['fri:kwənt] adj frecuente.

frequently ['fri:kwəntlɪ] adv frecuentemente.

fresh [freʃ] adj fresco(-ca); (bread) del día; (coffee) recién hecho; (refreshing) refrescante; (water) dulce; (developments, instructions, start) nuevo(-va); (news) reciente; **to get some ~ air** tomar el aire.

fresh cream n nata f (no artificial).

freshen ['freʃn]: **freshen up** vi refrescarse.

freshly ['freʃlɪ] adv recién.

fresh orange (juice) n zumo m de naranja.

Fri (abbr of Friday) v.

Friday ['fraɪdɪ] n viernes m inv, → **Saturday**.

fridge [frɪdʒ] n nevera f.

fried egg [fraɪd-] n huevo m frito.

fried rice [fraɪd-] n arroz frito, mezclado a veces con huevo, carne o verduras, servido como acompañamiento de platos chinos.

friend [frend] n amigo m (-ga f); **to be ~s with sb** ser amigo de alguien; **to make ~s with sb** hacerse amigo de alguien.

friendly ['frendlɪ] adj (kind) amable; **to be ~ with sb** ser amigo(-ga) de alguien.

friendship ['frendʃɪp] n amistad f.

fries [fraɪz] = **French fries**.

fright [fraɪt] n terror m; **to give sb a ~** darle un susto a alguien.

frighten [fraɪtn] vt asustar.

frightened [fraɪtnd] adj asustado(-da); **I'm ~ we won't finish** me temo que no vamos a acabar; **to be ~ of** tener miedo a.

frightening [fraɪtnɪŋ] adj aterrador(-ra).

frightful [fraɪtful] adj horrible.

frilly [frɪlɪ] adj con volantes.

fringe [frɪndʒ] n (Br: of hair) flequillo m; (of clothes, curtain etc) fleco m.

frisk [frɪsk] vt cachear.

fritter [frɪtər] n buñuelo m.

fro [frəʊ] adv → **to**.

frog [frɒg] n rana f.

from [weak form frəm, strong form frɒm] prep **1.** (expressing origin, source) de; **I'm ~ Spain** soy de España; **I bought it ~ a supermarket** lo compré en un supermercado; **the train ~ Manchester** el tren (procedente) de Manchester.
2. (expressing removal, separation, deduction) de; **away ~ home** fuera de casa; **to take sthg (away) ~ sb** quitarle algo a alguien; **10% will be deducted ~ the total** se descontará un 10% del total.
3. (expressing distance) de; **five miles ~ London** a cinco millas de Londres.
4. (expressing position) de; **here you can see the valley** desde aquí se ve el valle.
5. (expressing starting point) desde; **~ now on** de ahora en adelante; **open ~ nine to five** abierto de nueve a cinco; **tickets are ~ £10** hay entradas desde 10 libras.

6. (expressing change) de; **the price has gone up ~ £1 to £2** el precio ha subido de 1 a 2 libras.
7. (expressing range): **it could take ~ two to six months** podría tardar entre dos y seis meses.
8. (as a result of) de; **I'm tired ~ walking** estoy cansado de haber andado tanto.
9. (expressing protection) de; **sheltered ~ the wind** resguardado del viento.
10. (in comparisons): **different ~** diferente a.

fromage frais [ˌfrɒmɑːʒ'freɪ] n tipo de queso fresco.

front [frʌnt] adj delantero(-ra) ◆ n (foremost part) parte f delantera; (of building) fachada f; (of weather) frente m; (by the sea) paseo m marítimo; **in ~** delante; **to be in ~** ir ganando; **in ~ of** delante de.

front door n puerta f principal.

frontier [ˈfrʌntɪər] n frontera f.

front page n portada f.

front seat n asiento m delantero.

frost [frɒst] n (on ground) escarcha f; (cold weather) helada f.

frosty [frɒstɪ] adj (morning, weather) de helada.

froth [frɒθ] n espuma f.

frown [fraʊn] n ceño m ◆ vi fruncir el ceño.

froze [frəʊz] pt → **freeze**.

frozen [frəʊzn] pp → **freeze** ◆ adj helado(-da); (food) congelado(-da).

fruit [fruːt] n fruta f; **a piece of ~** una fruta; **~s of the forest** frutas del bosque.

fruit cake n pastel de pasas y frutas confitadas.

fruiterer ['fruːtərə'] n (Br) frutero m (-ra f).

fruit juice n zumo m de fruta.

fruit machine n (Br) máquina f tragaperras.

fruit salad n macedonia f (de frutas).

frustrating [frʌ'streɪtɪŋ] adj frustrante.

frustration [frʌ'streɪʃn] n frustración f.

fry [fraɪ] vt freír.

frying pan [fraɪŋ-] n sartén f.

ft abbr = foot, feet.

fudge [fʌdʒ] n caramelo fabricado con leche, azúcar y mantequilla.

fuel [fjʊəl] n combustible m.

fuel pump n surtidor m de gasolina.

fulfil [fʊl'fɪl] vt (Br) (promise, duty, conditions) cumplir; (need) satisfacer; (role) desempeñar.

fulfill [fʊl'fɪl] (Am) = fulfil.

full [fʊl] adj (filled) lleno(-na); (complete) completo(-ta); (maximum) máximo(-ma); (busy) atareado(-da); (flavour) rico(-ca) ◆ adv de lleno; **I'm ~ (up)** estoy lleno; **~ of** lleno de; **in ~** íntegramente.

full board n pensión f completa.

full-cream milk n leche f entera.

full-length adj (skirt, dress) largo(-ga) (hasta los pies).

full moon n luna f llena.

full stop n punto m.

full-time adj de jornada completa ◆ adv a tiempo completo.

fully ['fʊlɪ] adv (completely) completamente.

fully-licensed adj autorizado para vender bebidas alcohólicas durante el horario completo establecido legalmente.

fumble ['fʌmbl] vi: **to ~ for sthg** buscar algo a tientas.

fun [fʌn] n (amusement) diversión f; **it's good ~** es muy divertido; **for ~ de broma**; **to have ~** divertirse; **to make ~ of** burlarse de.

function ['fʌŋkʃn] n (role) función f; (formal event) acto m ◆ vi funcionar.

fund [fʌnd] n fondo m ◆ vt financiar □ **funds** npl fondos mpl.

fundamental [fʌndə'mentl] adj fundamental.

funeral ['fjuːnərəl] n funeral m.

funfair ['fʌnfeə'] n parque m de atracciones.

funky ['fʌŋkɪ] adj (inf: music) funky (inv).

funnel ['fʌnl] n (for pouring) embudo m; (on ship) chimenea f.

funny ['fʌnɪ] adj (person) gracioso(-sa); (thing) divertido(-da); (strange) raro(-ra); **to feel ~** (ill) sentirse raro.

fur [fɜː'] n (on animal) pelaje m; (garment) piel f.

fur coat n abrigo m de piel.

furious ['fjʊərɪəs] adj furioso(-sa).

furnished ['fɜːnɪʃt] adj amueblado(-da).

furnishings ['fɜːnɪʃɪŋz] npl mobiliario m.

furniture ['fɜːnɪtʃə'] n muebles mpl; **a piece of ~** un mueble.

furry ['fɜːrɪ] *adj* peludo(-da).

further ['fɜːðəʳ] *compar* → **far** ◆ *adv (in distance)* más lejos; *(more)* más ◆ *adj (additional)* otro (otra); **until ~ notice** hasta nuevo aviso.

furthermore [ˌfɜːðəˈmɔːʳ] *adv* además.

furthest ['fɜːðɪst] *superl* → **far** ◆ *adj (most distant)* más lejano(-na) ◆ *adv (in distance)* más lejos.

fuse [fjuːz] *n (of plug)* fusible *m*; *(on bomb)* mecha *f* ◆ *vi (plug)* fundirse; *(electrical device)* estropearse.

fuse box *n* caja *f* de fusibles.

fuss [fʌs] *n (agitation)* jaleo *m*; *(complaints)* quejas *fpl*.

fussy ['fʌsɪ] *adj (person)* quisquilloso(-sa).

future ['fjuːtʃəʳ] *n* futuro *m* ◆ *adj* futuro(-ra); **in ~ de** ahora en adelante.

G

g *(abbr of gram)* g.

gable ['geɪbl] *n* aguilón *m*.

gadget ['gædʒɪt] *n* artilugio *m*.

Gaelic ['geɪlɪk] *n* gaélico *m*.

gag [gæg] *n (inf: joke)* chiste *m*.

gain [geɪn] *n (get more of)* ganar; *(achieve)* conseguir; *(subj: clock, watch)* adelantarse ◆ *vi (get benefit)* beneficiarse *f*; *(improvement)* mejora *f*; *(profit)* ganancia *f*.

gale [geɪl] *n* vendaval *m*.

gallery ['gælərɪ] *n (for art etc)* galería *f*; *(at theatre)* gallinero *m*.

gallon ['gælən] *n* = 4,546 litros, galón *m*; *(in US)* = 3,785 litros, galón *m*.

gallop ['gæləp] *vi* galopar.

gamble ['gæmbl] *n* riesgo *m* ◆ *vi (bet money)* apostar.

gambling ['gæmblɪŋ] *n* juego *m* *(de dinero)*.

game [geɪm] *n* juego *m*; *(of football, tennis, cricket)* partido *m*; *(of chess, cards, snooker)* partida *f*; *(wild animals, meat)* caza *f* ❑ **games** *n (SCH)* deportes *mpl* ◆ *npl (sporting event)* juegos *mpl*.

gammon ['gæmən] *n* jamón *m*.

gang [gæŋ] *n (of criminals)* banda *f*; *(of friends)* pandilla *f*.

gangster ['gæŋstəʳ] *n* gángster *m*.

gangway ['gæŋweɪ] *n (for ship)* plancha *f (de atraque)*; *(Br: in bus, plane, theatre)* pasillo *m*.

gaol [dʒeɪl] *(Br)* = **jail**.

gap [gæp] *n (space)* hueco *m*; *(of time)* intervalo *m*; *(difference)* discordancia *f*.

garage ['gærɑːʒ, 'gærɪdʒ] *n (for keeping car)* garaje *m*; *(Br: for petrol)* gasolinera *f*; *(for repairs)* taller *m* *(de reparaciones)*; *(Br: for selling cars)* concesionario *m (de automóviles)*.

garbage ['gɑːbɪdʒ] *n (Am: refuse)* basura *f*.

garbage can *n (Am)* cubo *m* de la basura.

garbage truck *n (Am)* camión *m* de la basura.

garden ['gɑːdn] *n* jardín *m* ◆ *vi*

trabajar en el jardín ❏ **gardens** *npl (public park)* jardines *mpl.*

garden centre *n* centro *m* de jardinería.

gardener ['gɑːdnəʳ] *n* jardinero *m* (-ra *f*).

gardening ['gɑːdnɪŋ] *n* jardinería *f.*

garden peas *npl* guisantes *mpl.*

garlic ['gɑːlɪk] *n* ajo *m.*

garlic bread *n* pan untado con mantequilla y ajo y cocido al horno.

garlic butter *n* mantequilla *f* con ajo.

garment ['gɑːmənt] *n* prenda *f* (de vestir).

garnish ['gɑːnɪʃ] *n (herbs, vegetables)* adorno *m; (sauce)* guarnición *f* ◆ *vt* adornar.

gas [gæs] *n* gas *m; (Am: petrol)* gasolina *f.*

gas cooker *n (Br)* cocina *f* de gas.

gas cylinder *n* bombona *f* de gas.

gas fire *n (Br)* estufa *f* de gas.

gasket ['gæskɪt] *n* junta *f* (de culata).

gas mask *n* máscara *f* antigás.

gasoline ['gæsəliːn] *n (Am)* gasolina *f.*

gasp [gɑːsp] *vi (in shock, surprise)* ahogar un grito.

gas pedal *n (Am)* acelerador *m.*

gas station *n (Am)* gasolinera *f.*

gas stove *(Br)* = **gas cooker**.

gas tank *n (Am)* depósito *m* de gasolina.

gasworks ['gæswɜːks] *n (pl inv)* n fábrica *f* de gas.

gate [geɪt] *n (to garden, field)* puer-ta *f; (at airport)* puerta *f* de embarque.

gâteau ['gætəʊ] *(pl -x [-z]) n (Br)* tarta *f (con nata).*

gateway ['geɪtweɪ] *n* entrada *f.*

gather ['gæðəʳ] *vt (collect)* recoger; *(speed)* ganar; *(understand)* deducir ◆ *vi* reunirse.

gaudy ['gɔːdɪ] *adj* chillón(-ona).

gauge [geɪdʒ] *n (for measuring)* indicador *m; (of railway track)* ancho *m* de vía ◆ *vt (calculate)* calibrar.

gauze [gɔːz] *n* gasa *f.*

gave [geɪv] *pt → **give**.

gay [geɪ] *adj (homosexual)* homosexual.

gaze [geɪz] *vi*: **to ~ at** mirar fijamente.

GB *(abbr of Great Britain)* GB.

GCSE *n* examen final de enseñanza media en Gran Bretaña.

---

[i] GCSE

Los GCSE (General Certificate of Secondary Education) se introdujeron en Gran Bretaña en 1986 en lugar de los "O-levels". Se hacen a los 15 o 16 años, y los estudiantes que deseen preparar "A-levels" han de aprobar al menos cinco asignaturas. A diferencia de los antiguos "O-levels", las notas se basan no sólo en el examen sino también en el trabajo a lo largo del curso.

---

gear [gɪəʳ] *n (wheel)* engranaje *m; (speed)* marcha *f; (equipment, clothes)* equipo *m; (belongings)* cosas *fpl;* **in ~** con una marcha metida.

gearbox ['gɪəbɒks] n caja f de cambios.

gear lever n palanca f de cambios.

gear shift (Am) = gear lever.

gear stick (Br) = gear lever.

geese [giːs] pl → goose.

gel [dʒel] n (for hair) gomina f; (for shower) gel m (de ducha).

gelatine [ˌdʒelə'tiːn] n gelatina f.

gem [dʒem] n piedra f preciosa.

Gemini ['dʒemɪnaɪ] n Géminis m inv.

gender ['dʒendə'] n género m.

general ['dʒenərəl] adj general ◆ n general m; **in ~** (as a whole) en general; (usually) generalmente.

general anaesthetic n anestesia f general.

general election n elecciones fpl generales.

generally ['dʒenərəli] adv en general.

general practitioner [-ˌpræk'tɪʃənə'] n médico m (-ca f) de cabecera.

general store n tienda f de ultramarinos.

generate ['dʒenəreɪt] vt generar.

generation [ˌdʒenə'reɪʃn] n generación f.

generator ['dʒenəreɪtə'] n generador m.

generosity [ˌdʒenə'rɒsəti] n generosidad f.

generous ['dʒenərəs] adj generoso(-sa).

genitals ['dʒenɪtlz] npl genitales mpl.

genius ['dʒiːnjəs] n genio m.

gentle ['dʒentl] adj (careful) cuidadoso(-sa); (kind) dulce, amable; (movement, breeze) suave.

gentleman ['dʒentlmən] (pl -men [-mən]) n (man) señor m; (well-behaved man) caballero m; "gentlemen" "caballeros".

gently ['dʒentlɪ] adv (carefully) con cuidado.

gents [dʒents] n (Br) caballeros mpl.

genuine ['dʒenjuɪn] adj (authentic) auténtico(-ca); (sincere) sincero (-ra).

geographical [dʒɪə'græfɪkl] adj geográfico(-ca).

geography [dʒɪ'ɒgrəfɪ] n geografía f.

geology [dʒɪ'ɒlədʒɪ] n geología f.

geometry [dʒɪ'ɒmətrɪ] n geometría f.

Georgian ['dʒɔːdʒən] adj georgiano(-na).

geranium [dʒɪ'reɪnjəm] n geranio m.

German ['dʒɜːmən] adj alemán(-ana) ◆ n (person) alemán m (-ana f); (language) alemán m.

German measles n rubéola f.

Germany ['dʒɜːmənɪ] n Alemania.

germs [dʒɜːmz] npl microbios mpl.

gesture ['dʒestʃə'] n (movement) gesto m.

get [get] (Br pt & pp got, Am pt got, pp gotten) vt **1.** (obtain) conseguir; **I got some crisps from the shop** compré unas patatas fritas en la tienda; **she got a job** consiguió un trabajo; **I ~ a lot of enjoy-**

ment from it me gusta mucho (hacerlo).

2. *(receive)* recibir; **I got a book for Christmas** me regalaron un libro por Navidades.

3. *(means of transport)* coger, tomar *(Amér)*; **let's ~ a taxi** ¡vamos a coger un taxi!

4. *(fetch)* traer; **could you ~ me the boss?** *(in shop)* ¿puede ver al jefe?; *(on phone)* ¿puede ponerme con el jefe?; **~ me a drink** tráeme algo de beber.

5. *(illness)* coger, agarrar *(Amér)*; **I've got a cold** tengo un catarro.

6. *(cause to become, do)*: **to ~ sthg done** mandar hacer algo; **to ~ sb to do sthg** hacer que alguien haga algo; **can I ~ my car repaired here?** ¿pueden arreglarme el coche aquí?; **to ~ sthg ready** preparar algo.

7. *(move)*: **to ~ sthg out** sacar algo; **I can't ~ it through the door** no puedo meterlo por la puerta.

8. *(understand)* entender; **to ~ a joke** coger un chiste.

9. *(time, chance)* tener; **we didn't ~ the chance to see everything** no tuvimos la oportunidad de verlo todo.

10. *(phone)* contestar.

11. *(in phrases)*: **you ~ a lot of rain here in winter** aquí llueve mucho en invierno, **~ have**.

♦ vi **1.** *(become)* ponerse; **it's getting late** se está haciendo tarde; **to ~ dark** oscurecer; **to ~ lost** perderse; **to ~ ready** prepararse; **~ lost!** *(inf)* ¡vete a la porra!

2. *(into particular state, position)* meterse; **how do you ~ to Luton from here?** ¿cómo se puede ir a

Luton desde aquí?; **to ~ into the car** meterse en el coche.

3. *(arrive)* llegar; **when does the train ~ here?** ¿a qué hora llega el tren?

4. *(in phrases)*: **to ~ to do sthg** llegar a hacer algo.

♦ aux vb: **to ~ delayed** retrasarse; **to ~ killed** resultar muerto.

▪ **get back** vi *(return)* volver; **get in** vi *(arrive)* llegar; *(enter)* entrar; **get off** vi *(leave train, bus)* bajarse; *(depart)* salir; **get on** vi *(enter train, bus)* subirse; *(in relationship)* llevarse; **how are you getting on?** ¿cómo te va?; **get out** vi *(of car, bus, train)* bajarse; **get through** vi *(on phone)* conseguir comunicar; **get up** vi levantarse.

get-together n *(inf)* reunión f.

ghastly ['gɑːstlɪ] adj *(inf: very bad)* horrible.

gherkin ['gɜːkɪn] n pepinillo m.

ghetto blaster ['getəʊˌblɑːstə^r] n radiocasete portátil de gran tamaño y potencia.

ghost [gəʊst] n fantasma m.

giant ['dʒaɪənt] adj gigantesco(-ca) ♦ n *(in stories)* gigante m.

giblets ['dʒɪblɪts] npl menudillos mpl.

giddy ['gɪdɪ] adj *(dizzy)* mareado(-da).

gift [gɪft] n *(present)* regalo m; *(talent)* don m.

gifted ['gɪftd] adj *(talented)* dotado(-da); *(very intelligent)* superdotado(-da).

gift shop n tienda f de souvenirs.

gift voucher n *(Br)* vale m

(para canjear por un regalo).

gig [gɪg] *n (inf)* concierto *m (de música pop).*

gigantic [dʒaɪˈgæntɪk] *adj* gigantesco(-ca).

giggle [ˈgɪgl] *vi* reírse a lo tonto.

gill [dʒɪl] *n (measurement)* = 0,142 litros.

gimmick [ˈgɪmɪk] *n* reclamo *m.*

gin [dʒɪn] *n* ginebra *f;* **~ and tonic** gin tonic *m.*

ginger [ˈdʒɪndʒəʳ] *n* jengibre *m* ♦ *adj (colour)* rojizo(-za).

ginger ale *n* ginger-ale *m.*

ginger beer *n* refresco de jengibre con bajo contenido en alcohol.

gingerbread [ˈdʒɪndʒəbred] *n* pan *m* de jengibre.

gipsy [ˈdʒɪpsɪ] *n* gitano *m* (-na *f).*

giraffe [dʒɪˈrɑːf] *n* jirafa *f.*

girdle [ˈgɜːdl] *n* faja *f.*

girl [gɜːl] *n (child, daughter)* niña *f; (young woman)* chica *f.*

girlfriend [ˈgɜːlfrend] *n (of boy, man)* novia *f; (of girl, woman)* amiga *f.*

Girl Guide *n (Br)* exploradora *f.*

Girl Scout *(Am)* = **Girl Guide**.

giro [ˈdʒaɪrəʊ] *n (pl -s) (system)* giro *m.*

give [gɪv] *(pt* **gave**, *pp* **given** [ˈgɪvn]) *vt* dar; *(a laugh, look)* echar; *(attention)* prestar; *(time)* dedicar; **to ~ sb sthg** *(hand over, convey)* dar algo a alguien; *(as present)* regalar algo a alguien; **to ~ sthg a push** empujar algo; **to ~ sb a kiss** besar a alguien; **~ or take** más o menos; **"~ way"** "ceda el paso" ❑ **give away** *vt sep (get rid of)* regalar; *(reveal)* revelar; **give back** *vt sep*

devolver; **give in** *vi* ceder; **give off** *vt fus* despedir; **give out** *vt sep (distribute)* repartir; **give up** *vt sep (seat)* ceder ♦ *vi (stop smoking)* dejar de fumar; *(admit defeat)* darse por vencido; **to ~ up cigarettes** OR **smoking** dejar de fumar.

glacier [ˈglæsjəʳ] *n* glaciar *m.*

glad [glæd] *adj* contento(-ta); **to be ~ to do sthg** tener mucho gusto en hacer algo.

gladly [ˈglædlɪ] *adv (willingly)* con mucho gusto.

glamorous [ˈglæmərəs] *adj* atractivo(-va).

glance [glɑːns] *n* vistazo *m* ♦ *vi:* **to ~ (at)** echar un vistazo (a).

gland [glænd] *n* glándula *f.*

glandular fever [ˈglændjʊlə-] *n* mononucleosis *f inv* infecciosa.

glare [gleəʳ] *vi (person)* lanzar una mirada asesina; *(sun, light)* brillar.

glass [glɑːs] *n (material)* cristal *m; (container, glassful)* vaso *m* ♦ *adj* de cristal ❑ **glasses** *npl* gafas *fpl.*

glassware [ˈglɑːsweəʳ] *n* cristalería *f.*

glen [glen] *n (Scot)* cañada *f.*

glider [ˈglaɪdəʳ] *n* planeador *m.*

glimpse [glɪmps] *vt* vislumbrar.

glitter [ˈglɪtəʳ] *vi* relucir.

global warming [ˌgləʊbl-ˈwɔːmɪŋ] *n* calentamiento *m* de la atmósfera.

globe [gləʊb] *n (with map)* globo *m* (terráqueo); **the ~** *(Earth)* la Tierra.

gloomy [ˈgluːmɪ] *adj (room, day)* oscuro(-ra); *(person)* melancólico(-ca).

glorious [ˈglɔːrɪəs] *adj (weather,*

sight) espléndido(-da); *(victory, history)* glorioso(-sa).

glory ['glɔ:rɪ] *n* gloria *f*.

gloss [glɒs] *n (shine)* brillo *m*; ~ **(paint)** pintura *f* de esmalte.

glossary ['glɒsərɪ] *n* glosario *m*.

glossy ['glɒsɪ] *adj (magazine, photo)* de papel satinado.

glove [glʌv] *n* guante *m*.

glove compartment *n* guantera *f*.

glow [gləʊ] *n* fulgor *m* ◆ *vi* brillar, lucir.

glucose ['glu:kəʊs] *n* glucosa *f*.

glue [glu:] *n* pegamento *m* ◆ *vt* pegar.

gnat [næt] *n* mosquito *m*.

gnaw [nɔ:] *vt* roer.

go [gəʊ] *(pt* went, *pp* gone, *pl* goes) *vi* 1. *(move, travel, attend)* ir; **to ~ home** irse a casa; **to ~ to Spain** ir a España; **to ~ by bus** ir en autobús; **to ~ to church/school** ir a misa/la escuela; **to ~ for a walk** ir a dar una vuelta; **to ~ and do sthg** ir a hacer algo; **to ~ shopping** ir de compras; **where does this path ~?** ¿adónde lleva este camino?

2. *(leave)* irse; *(bus)* salir; **it's time to ~** ya es hora de irse; **~ away!** ¡largo de aquí!

3. *(become)* ponerse; **she went pale** se puso pálida; **the milk has gone sour** la leche se ha cortado.

4. *(expressing intention, probability, certainty)*: **to be going to do sthg** ir a hacer algo.

5. *(function)* funcionar; **the car won't ~** el coche no funciona.

6. *(stop working)* estropearse; **the fuse has gone** se ha fundido el plomo.

7. *(pass)* pasar.

8. *(progress)* ir; **to ~ well** ir bien; **how's it going?** ¿qué tal te va?

9. *(bell, alarm)* sonar.

10. *(match, be appropriate)*: **to ~ with** ir bien con.

11. *(be sold)* venderse; **"everything must ~"** "liquidación total".

12. *(fit)* caber.

13. *(belong)* ir.

14. *(in phrases)*: **(do) ~ on!** ¡venga!; **to let ~ of sthg** soltar algo; **to ~** *(Am: to take away)* para llevar; **there are three weeks to ~** quedan tres semanas.

◆ *n* 1. *(turn)* turno *m*; **it's your ~** te toca a ti.

2. *(attempt)* jugada *f*; **to have a ~ at sthg** probar algo; **"50p a ~"** "a 50 peniques la jugada".

□ **go ahead** *vi (take place)* tener lugar; **go ~!** ¡adelante!; **go back** *vi* volver; **go down** *vi (price, standard)* bajar; *(sun)* ponerse; *(tyre)* deshincharse; **go down with** *vt fus (inf)* pillar; **go in** *vi* entrar; **go off** *vi (alarm, bell)* sonar; *(food)* estropearse; *(milk)* cortarse; *(stop operating)* apagarse; **go on** *vi (happen)* ocurrir, pasar; *(start operating)* encenderse; **to ~ on doing sthg** seguir haciendo algo; **go out** *vi (leave house)* salir; *(light, fire, cigarette)* apagarse; **to ~ out with sb)** salir *(con alguien)*; **to ~ out for a meal** cenar fuera; **go over** *vt fus (check)* repasar; **go round** *vi (revolve)* girar; **there isn't enough to ~ round** no hay bastante para todos; **go through** *vt fus (experience)* pasar *(por)*; *(spend)* gastar; *(search)* registrar; **go up** *vi (increase)* subir; **go with** *vt fus (be included with)* venir con; **go without** vt fus pasar sin.

goal [gəʊl] n (posts) portería f; (point scored) gol m; (aim) objetivo m.

goalkeeper ['gəʊl,kiːpə'] n portero m (-a f).

goalpost ['gəʊlpəʊst] n poste m (de la portería).

goat [gəʊt] n cabra f.

gob [gɒb] n (Br: inf: mouth) pico m.

god [gɒd] n dios m ❏ **God** n Dios m.

goddaughter ['gɒd,dɔːtə'] n ahijada f.

godfather ['gɒd,fɑːðə'] n padrino m.

godmother ['gɒd,mʌðə'] n madrina f.

gods [gɒdz] npl: **the ~** (Br: inf: in theatre) el gallinero m.

godson ['gɒdsʌn] n ahijado m.

goes [gəʊz] → **go**.

goggles ['gɒglz] npl (for swimming) gafas fpl submarinas; (for skiing) gafas de esquí.

going ['gəʊɪŋ] adj (available) disponible; **the ~ rate** el precio actual.

go-kart [-kɑːt] n kart m.

gold [gəʊld] n oro m ♦ adj de oro.

goldfish ['gəʊldfɪʃ] (pl inv) n pez m de colores.

gold-plated [-'pleɪtɪd] adj chapado(-da) en oro.

golf [gɒlf] n golf m.

golf ball n pelota f de golf.

golf club n (place) club m de golf; (piece of equipment) palo m de golf.

golf course n campo m de golf.

golfer ['gɒlfə'] n jugador m (-ra f)

de golf.

gone [gɒn] pp → **go** ♦ prep (Br): it's ~ ten ya pasa de las diez.

good [gʊd] (compar **better**, superl **best**) adj (gen) bueno(-na) ♦ n el bien; **that's very ~ of you** es usted muy amable por tu parte; **be ~!** ¡pórtate bien!; **to have a ~ time** pasarlo bien; **I'm ~ at maths** se me dan bien las matemáticas; **a ~ ten minutes** diez minutos por lo menos; **in ~ time** a tiempo de sobra; **to make ~ sthg** compensar algo; **for ~** para siempre; **for the ~ of** en bien de; **to do sb ~** sentarle bien a alguien; **it's no ~ (there's no point)** no vale la pena; **~ afternoon!** ¡buenas tardes!; **~ evening!** (in the evening) ¡buenas tardes!; (at night) ¡buenas noches!; **~ morning!** ¡buenos días!; **~ night!** ¡buenas noches! ❏ **goods** npl productos mpl.

goodbye [,gʊd'baɪ] excl ¡adiós!

Good Friday n Viernes m inv Santo.

good-looking [-'lʊkɪŋ] adj guapo(-pa).

goods train [gʊdz-] n tren m de mercancías.

goose [guːs] (pl **geese**) n ganso m.

gooseberry ['gʊzbərɪ] n grosella f espinosa.

gorge [gɔːdʒ] n desfiladero m.

gorgeous ['gɔːdʒəs] adj (day, meal, countryside) magnífico(-ca); **to be ~** (inf: good-looking) estar buenísimo(-ma).

gorilla [gə'rɪlə] n gorila mf.

gossip ['gɒsɪp] n (talk) cotilleo m ♦ vi cotillear.

gossip column n ecos mpl de

sociedad.

got [gɒt] pt & pp → get.

gotten ['gɒtn] pp (Am) → get.

goujons ['gu:dʒɒnz] npl fritos mpl (rebozados).

goulash ['gu:læʃ] n gulasch m.

gourmet ['guəmeɪ] n gastrónomo m (-ma f) ♦ adj para gastrónomos.

govern ['gʌvən] vt gobernar.

government ['gʌvnmənt] n gobierno m.

gown [gaun] n (dress) vestido m (de noche).

GP n (abbr of general practitioner) médico de cabecera.

grab [græb] vt (grasp) agarrar; (snatch away) arrebatar.

graceful ['greɪsful] adj elegante.

grade [greɪd] n (quality) clase f; (in exam) nota f; (Am: year at school) curso m.

gradient ['greɪdjənt] n pendiente f.

gradual ['grædʒuəl] adj paulatino(-na).

gradually ['grædʒuəlɪ] adv paulatinamente.

graduate [n 'grædʒuət, vb 'grædʒueɪt] n (from university) licenciado m (-da f); (Am: from high school) = bachiller m ♦ vi (from university) licenciarse; (Am: from high school) = obtener el título de bachiller.

graduation [grædʒu'eɪʃn] n (ceremony) graduación f.

graffiti [grə'fi:tɪ] n pintadas fpl.

grain [greɪn] n (seed, granule) grano m; (crop) cereales mpl.

gram [græm] n gramo m.

grammar ['græmər] n gramática f.

grammar school n (in UK) colegio de enseñanza secundaria tradicional para alumnos de 11 a 18 años, con examen de acceso.

gramme [græm] = gram.

gramophone ['græməfəun] n gramófono m.

gran [græn] n (Br: inf) abuelita f.

grand [grænd] adj (impressive) grandioso(-sa) ♦ n (inf) (£1,000) mil libras fpl; ($1,000) mil dólares mpl.

grandchild ['græntʃaɪld] (pl -children [-tʃɪldrən]) n nieto m (-ta f).

granddad ['grændæd] n (inf) abuelito m.

granddaughter ['græn,dɔ:tər] n nieta f.

grandfather ['grænd,fɑ:ðər] n abuelo m.

grandma ['grænmɑ:] n (inf) abuelita f.

grandmother ['græn,mʌðər] n abuela f.

grandpa ['grænpɑ:] n (inf) abuelito m.

grandparents ['græn,peərənts] npl abuelos mpl.

grandson ['grænsʌn] n nieto m.

granite ['grænɪt] n granito m.

granny ['grænɪ] n (inf) abuelita f.

grant [grɑ:nt] n (for study) beca f; (POL) subvención f ♦ vt (fml: give) conceder; **to take sthg/sb for ~ed** no saber apreciar algo/a alguien por lo que vale.

grape [greɪp] n uva f.

grapefruit ['greɪpfru:t] n pomelo m.

grapefruit juice n zumo m de pomelo.

graph [grɑ:f] n gráfico m.

graph paper n papel m cuadriculado.

grasp [grɑ:sp] vt (grip) agarrar; (understand) entender.

grass [grɑ:s] n (plant) hierba f; (lawn) césped m; **"keep off the ~"** "prohibido pisar el césped".

grasshopper ['grɑ:s,hɒpəʳ] n saltamontes m inv.

grate [greɪt] n parrilla f.

grated ['greɪtɪd] adj rallado(-da).

grateful ['greɪtfʊl] adj agradecido(-da).

grater ['greɪtəʳ] n rallador m.

gratitude ['grætɪtju:d] n agradecimiento m.

gratuity [grə'tju:ɪtɪ] n (fml) propina f.

grave[1] [greɪv] adj (mistake, news, concern) grave ♦ n tumba f.

grave[2] [grɑ:v] adj (accent) grave.

gravel ['grævl] n gravilla f.

graveyard ['greɪvjɑ:d] n cementerio m.

gravity ['grævɪtɪ] n gravedad f.

gravy ['greɪvɪ] n salsa f de carne.

gray [greɪ] (Am) = **grey**.

graze [greɪz] vt (injure) rasguñar.

grease [gri:s] n grasa f.

greaseproof paper ['gri:spru:f-] n (Br) papel m de cera.

greasy ['gri:sɪ] adj (tools, clothes, food) grasiento(-ta); (skin, hair) graso(-sa).

great [greɪt] adj grande; (very good) estupendo(-da); ~ **success**

gran éxito; (that's) ~! ¡genial!; **to have a ~ time** pasarlo genial.

Great Britain n Gran Bretaña.

GREAT BRITAIN

Gran Bretaña es la isla que comprende Inglaterra, Escocia y Gales. No debe confundirse con el Reino Unido, que incluye además Irlanda del Norte, ni tampoco con las islas Británicas, que incluyen además la República de Irlanda, la isla de Man, las Orcadas, las Shetland y las islas del Canal de la Mancha.

great-grandfather n bisabuelo m.

great-grandmother n bisabuela f.

greatly ['greɪtlɪ] adv enormemente.

Greece [gri:s] n Grecia.

greed [gri:d] n (for food) glotonería f; (for money) codicia f.

greedy ['gri:dɪ] adj (for food) glotón(-ona); (for money) codicioso(-sa).

Greek [gri:k] adj griego(-ga) ♦ n (person) griego m (-ga f); (language) griego m.

Greek salad n ensalada con lechuga, tomate, cebolla, pepino, aceitunas negras y queso de cabra.

green [gri:n] adj verde; (inf: inexperienced) novato(-ta) ♦ n (colour) verde m; (in village) pequeña zona de hierba accesible a todo el mundo; (in golf course) green m ❑ **greens** npl (vegetables) verduras fpl.

green beans npl judías fpl

verdes.

green card n (Br: for car) seguro de automóvil para viajar al extranjero; (Am: work permit) permiso m de trabajo (para EEUU).

green channel n pasillo en la aduana para la gente sin artículos que declarar.

greengage ['gri:ngeɪdʒ] n ciruela f claudia.

greengrocer's ['gri:ngrəʊsəz] n (shop) verdulería f.

greenhouse ['gri:nhaʊs, pl -haʊzɪz] n invernadero m.

greenhouse effect n efecto m invernadero.

green light n luz f verde.

green pepper n pimiento m verde.

Greens [gri:nz] npl: the ~ los Verdes.

green salad n ensalada f verde.

greet [gri:t] vt (say hello to) saludar.

greeting ['gri:tɪŋ] n saludo m.

grenade [grə'neɪd] n granada f.

grew [gru:] pt → grow.

grey [greɪ] adj (in colour) gris; (weather) nublado(-da); he's going ~ le están saliendo canas.

greyhound ['greɪhaʊnd] n galgo m.

grid [grɪd] n (grating) reja f; (on map etc) cuadrícula f.

grief [gri:f] n pena f, aflicción f; to come to ~ (plan) ir al traste.

grieve [gri:v] vi: to ~ for llorar por.

grill [grɪl] n (on cooker) grill m; (for open fire, part of restaurant) parrilla f;

(beefburger) hamburguesa f ♦ vt asar a la parrilla.

grille [grɪl] n (AUT) rejilla f.

grilled [grɪld] adj asado(-da) a la parrilla.

grim [grɪm] adj (expression) adusto(-ta); (news, reality) deprimente.

grimace ['grɪməs] n mueca f.

grimy ['graɪmɪ] adj mugriento(-ta).

grin [grɪn] n sonrisa f (amplia) ♦ vi sonreír (ampliamente).

grind [graɪnd] (pt & pp ground) vt (pepper, coffee) moler.

grip [grɪp] vt (hold) agarrar ♦ n (of tyres) adherencia f; (handle) asidero m; (bag) bolsa f de viaje; to have a ~ on sthg agarrar algo.

gristle ['grɪsl] n cartílago m.

groan [grəʊn] n gemido m ♦ vi (in pain) gemir; (complain) quejarse.

groceries ['grəʊsərɪz] npl comestibles mpl.

grocer's ['grəʊsəz] n (shop) tienda f de comestibles.

grocery ['grəʊsərɪ] n (shop) tienda f de comestibles.

groin [grɔɪn] n ingle f.

groove [gru:v] n ranura f.

grope [grəʊp] vi: to ~ around for sthg buscar algo a tientas.

gross [grəʊs] adj (weight, income) bruto(-ta).

grossly ['grəʊslɪ] adv (extremely) enormemente.

grotty ['grɒtɪ] adj (Br: inf) cochambroso(-sa).

ground [graʊnd] (pt & pp → grind ♦ n (surface of earth) suelo m; (soil) tierra f; (SPORT) campo m ♦ adj (coffee) molido(-da) ♦ vt: to be ~ed *(plane)* tener que permanecer en tierra; *(Am: electrical connection)* estar conectado a la tierra; **below ~** bajo tierra ❏ **grounds** *npl (of building)* jardines *mpl; (of coffee)* poso *m; (reason)* razones *fpl.*

ground floor *n* planta *f* baja.

groundsheet ['graʊndʃiːt] *n* lona *f* impermeable *(para tienda de campaña).*

group [gruːp] *n* grupo *m.*

grouse [graʊs] *(pl inv)* *n* urogallo *m.*

grovel ['grɒvl] *vi (be humble)* humillarse.

grow [grəʊ] *(pt* **grew,** *pp* **grown)** *vi* crecer; *(become)* volverse ♦ *vt (plant, crop)* cultivar; *(beard)* dejarse crecer ❏ **grow up** *vi* hacerse mayor.

growl [graʊl] *vi (dog)* gruñir.

grown [grəʊn] *pp → grow.*

grown-up *adj* adulto(-ta) ♦ *n* persona *f* mayor.

growth [grəʊθ] *n (increase)* aumento *m; (MED)* bulto *m.*

grub [grʌb] *n (inf: food)* papeo *m.*

grubby ['grʌbɪ] *adj* mugriento(-ta).

grudge [grʌdʒ] *n* rencor *m* ♦ *vt:* **to ~ sb sthg** dar algo a alguien de mala gana.

grueling ['gruːlɪŋ] *(Am)* = **gruelling.**

gruelling ['gruːlɪŋ] *adj (Br)* agotador(-ra).

gruesome ['gruːsəm] *adj* horripilante.

grumble ['grʌmbl] *vi* refunfuñar.

grumpy ['grʌmpɪ] *adj (inf)* cascarrabias *(inv).*

grunt [grʌnt] *vi* gruñir.

guarantee [ˌgærən'tiː] *n* garantía *f* ♦ *vt* garantizar.

guard [gɑːd] *n (of prisoner etc)* guardia *mf; (Br: on train)* jefe *m* de tren; *(protective cover)* protector *m* ♦ *vt (watch over)* guardar; **to be on one's ~** estar en guardia.

Guatemala [ˌgwɑːtə'mɑːlə] *n* Guatemala.

Guatemalan [ˌgwɑːtə'mɑːlən] *adj* guatemalteco(-ca) ♦ *n* guatemalteco *m* (-ca *f).*

guess [ges] *n* suposición *f* ♦ *vt* adivinar ♦ *vi* suponer; **I ~ (so)** me imagino (que sí).

guest [gest] *n (in home)* invitado *m* (-da *f); (in hotel)* huésped *mf.*

guesthouse ['gesthaʊs, *pl* -haʊzɪz] *n* casa *f* de huéspedes.

guestroom ['gestrʊm] *n* cuarto *m* de los huéspedes.

guidance ['gaɪdəns] *n* orientación *f.*

guide [gaɪd] *n (for tourists)* guía *mf; (guidebook)* guía *f* ♦ *vt* guiar ❏ **Guide** *n (Br)* exploradora *f.*

guidebook ['gaɪdbʊk] *n* guía *f.*

guide dog *n* perro *m* lazarillo.

guided tour ['gaɪdɪd-] *n* visita *f* guiada.

guidelines ['gaɪdlaɪnz] *npl* directrices *fpl.*

guilt [gɪlt] *n (feeling)* culpa *f; (JUR)* culpabilidad *f.*

guilty ['gɪltɪ] *adj* culpable.

guinea pig ['gɪnɪ-] *n* conejillo *m* de Indias.

guitar [gɪ'tɑːr] *n* guitarra *f.*

guitarist [gɪ'tɑːrɪst] *n* guitarrista *mf.*

gulf [gʌlf] n (of sea) golfo m.

Gulf War n: the ~ la Guerra del Golfo.

gull [gʌl] n gaviota f.

gullible ['gʌləbl] adj ingenuo (-nua).

gulp [gʌlp] n trago m.

gum [gʌm] n (chewing gum, bubble gum) chicle m; (adhesive) pegamento m ◻ **gums** npl (in mouth) encías fpl.

gun [gʌn] n (pistol) pistola f; (rifle) escopeta f; (cannon) cañón m.

gunfire ['gʌnfaɪəʳ] n disparos mpl.

gunshot ['gʌnʃɒt] n tiro m.

gust [gʌst] n ráfaga f.

gut [gʌt] n (inf: stomach) buche m ◻ **guts** npl (inf) (intestines) tripas fpl; (courage) agallas fpl.

gutter ['gʌtəʳ] n (beside road) cuneta f; (of house) canalón m.

guy [gaɪ] n (inf: man) tío m ◻ **guys** npl (Am: inf: people) tíos mpl.

Guy Fawkes Night [-'fɔːks-] n (Br) el 5 de noviembre.

En esta fiesta, que también se conoce como "Bonfire Night", se conmemora cada 5 de noviembre con hogueras y fuegos artificiales el descubrimiento del "Gunpowder Plot", una conjuración católica para volar el Parlamento y asesinar al rey Jaime I en 1605. Es tradicional que los niños hagan monigotes de uno de los conspiradores, Guy Fawkes, y los lleven por las calles recolectando dinero. Estos monigotes se queman después en las hogueras del 5 de noviembre.

guy rope n cuerda f (de tienda de campaña).

gym [dʒɪm] n (place) gimnasio m; (school lesson) gimnasia f.

gymnast ['dʒɪmnæst] n gimnasta mf.

gymnastics [dʒɪm'næstɪks] n gimnasia f.

gym shoes npl zapatillas fpl de gimnasia.

gynaecologist [ˌgaɪnə'kɒlədʒɪst] n ginecólogo m (-ga f).

gypsy ['dʒɪpsɪ] = gipsy.

H

H (abbr of hot) C (en grifo); (abbr of hospital) H.

habit ['hæbɪt] n costumbre f.

hacksaw ['hæksɔː] n sierra f para metales.

had [hæd] pt & pp → have.

haddock ['hædək] n (pl inv) eglefino m.

hadn't ['hædnt] = had not.

haggis ['hægɪs] n plato típico escocés hecho con las asaduras del cordero, harina de avena y especias.

haggle ['hægl] vi regatear.

hail [heɪl] n granizo m ◆ v impers: it's ~ing está granizando.

hailstone ['heɪlstəʊn] n granizo m.

hair [heə'] n pelo m; (on skin) vello m; to have one's ~ cut cortarse el pelo; to wash one's ~ lavarse el pelo.

hairband ['heəbænd] n turbante m (banda elástica).

hairbrush ['heəbrʌʃ] n cepillo m (del pelo).

hairclip ['heəklɪp] n prendedor m (del pelo).

haircut ['heəkʌt] n (style) corte m (de pelo); to have a ~ cortarse el pelo.

hairdo ['heəduː] n (pl -s) peinado m.

hairdresser ['heə,dresə'] n peluquero m (-ra f); ~'s (salon) peluquería f; to go to the ~'s ir a la peluquería.

hairdryer ['heə,draɪə'] n secador m (del pelo).

hair gel n gomina f.

hairgrip ['heəgrɪp] n (Br) horquilla f.

hairnet ['heənet] n redecilla f (para el pelo).

hairpin bend ['heəpɪn-] n curva f muy cerrada.

hair remover [-rɪ,muːvə'] n depilatorio m.

hair rollers [-'rəʊləz] npl tubos mpl (del pelo).

hair slide n prendedor m.

hairspray ['heəspreɪ] n laca f (para el pelo).

hairstyle ['heəstaɪl] n peinado m.

hairy ['heərɪ] adj peludo(-da).

half [Br hɑːf, Am hæf] (pl halves) n (50%) mitad f; (of match) tiempo m; (half pint) media pinta f; (child's ticket) billete m medio ◆ adj medio(-dia) ◆ adv: ~ cooked a medio cocinar; ~ full medio lleno; I'm ~ Scottish soy medio escocés; four and a ~ cuatro y medio; ~ past seven las siete y media; ~ as big as la mitad de grande que; an hour and a ~ una hora y media; ~ an hour media hora; ~ a dozen media docena; ~ price a mitad de precio.

half board n media pensión f.

half-day n media jornada f.

half fare n medio billete m.

half portion n media ración f.

half-price adj a mitad de precio.

half term n (Br) semana de vacaciones escolares a mitad de cada trimestre.

half time n descanso m.

halfway [hɑːfweɪ] adv: ~ between a mitad de camino entre; ~ through the film a mitad de la película.

halibut ['hælɪbət] (pl inv) n halibut m.

hall [hɔːl] n (of house) vestíbulo m; (large room) sala f; (building) pabellón m; (country house) mansión f.

hallmark ['hɔːlmɑːk] n (on silver, gold) contraste m.

hallo ['hæləʊ] = hello.

hall of residence n colegio m mayor.

Halloween [ˌhæləʊ'iːn] n el 31 de octubre.

i HALLOWEEN

El 31 de octubre, también conocido como "All Hallows Eve" es tradicionalmente la noche en que los fantasmas y brujas se aparecen. Los niños se disfrazan y visitan a sus vecinos jugando a "trick or treat", un juego en que amenazan con gastar una broma si no se les da dinero o golosinas. En Gran Bretaña y Estados Unidos son tradicionales las linternas que consisten en una calabaza vaciada en cuyo interior se coloca una vela que ilumina a través de una cara tallada en la corteza.

halt [hɔːlt] vi detenerse ♦ n: **to come to a ~** detenerse.

halve [Br hɑːv, Am hæv] vt (reduce by half) reducir a la mitad; (divide in two) partir por la mitad.

halves [Br hɑːvz, Am hævz] pl → **half**.

ham [hæm] n jamón m.

hamburger ['hæmbɜːgə'] n (beefburger) hamburguesa f; (Am: mince) carne f picada.

hamlet ['hæmlɪt] n aldea f.

hammer ['hæmə'] n martillo m ♦ vt (nail) clavar.

hammock ['hæmək] n hamaca f.

hamper ['hæmpə'] n cesta f.

hamster ['hæmstə'] n hámster m.

hamstring ['hæmstrɪŋ] n tendón m de la corva.

hand [hænd] n mano f; (of clock, watch, dial) aguja f; **to give sb a ~** echar una mano a alguien; **to get out of ~** hacerse incontrolable; **by ~** a mano; **in ~** (time) de sobra; **on the one ~** por una parte; **on the other ~** por otra parte ❏ **hand in** vt sep entregar; **hand out** vt sep repartir; **hand over** vt sep (give) entregar.

handbag ['hændbæg] n bolso m.

handbasin ['hændbeɪsn] n lavabo m.

handbook ['hændbʊk] n manual m.

handbrake ['hændbreɪk] n freno m de mano.

hand cream n crema f de manos.

handcuffs ['hændkʌfs] npl esposas fpl.

handful ['hændfʊl] n (amount) puñado m.

handicap ['hændɪkæp] n (physical, mental) incapacidad f; (disadvantage) desventaja f.

handicapped ['hændɪkæpt] adj disminuido(-da) ♦ npl: **the ~** los minusválidos.

handkerchief ['hæŋkətʃɪf] (pl **-chiefs** OR **-chieves** [-tʃiːvz]) n pañuelo m.

handle ['hændl] n (round) pomo m; (long) manilla f; (of knife, pan) mango m; (of suitcase) asa f ♦ vt (touch) tocar; (deal with) encargarse de; **"~ with care"** "frágil".

handlebars ['hændlbɑːz] npl manillar m.

hand luggage n equipaje m de mano.

handmade [ˌhænd'meɪd] adj hecho(-cha) a mano.

handout ['hændaʊt] n (leaflet) hoja f informativa.

handrail ['hændreɪl] n barandilla f.

handset ['hændset] n auricular m (de teléfono); **"please replace the ~"** mensaje que avisa que el teléfono está descolgado.

handshake ['hændʃeɪk] n apretón m de manos.

handsome ['hænsəm] adj (man) guapo.

handstand ['hændstænd] n pino m.

handwriting ['hænd,raɪtɪŋ] n letra f.

handy ['hændɪ] adj (useful) práctico(-ca); (good with one's hands) mañoso(-sa); (near) a mano; **to come in ~** (inf) venir de maravilla.

hang [hæŋ] (pt & pp hung) vt (on hook, wall etc) colgar; (execute: pt & pp hanged) ahorcar ◆ vi: **to get the ~ of sthg** coger el tranquillo a algo ❑ **hang about** vi (Br: inf) pasar el rato; **hang around** (inf) = **hang about**; **hang down** vi caer, estar colgado; **hang on** vi (inf: wait) esperar; **hang out** vt sep tender ◆ vi (inf: spend time) pasar el rato; **hang up** vi (on phone) colgar.

hangar ['hæŋəʳ] n hangar m.

hanger ['hæŋəʳ] n percha f.

hang gliding [-'glaɪdɪŋ] n vuelo m con ala delta.

hangover ['hæŋ,əʊvəʳ] n resaca f.

hankie ['hæŋkɪ] n (inf) pañuelo m.

happen ['hæpən] vi pasar; **I ~ed to be alone** dio la casualidad de que estaba solo.

happily ['hæpɪlɪ] adv (luckily) afortunadamente.

happiness ['hæpɪnɪs] n felicidad f.

happy ['hæpɪ] adj feliz; **to be ~ about sthg** (satisfied) estar contento(-ta) con algo; **to be ~ to do sthg** estar muy dispuesto(-ta) a hacer algo; **to be ~ with sthg** estar contento con algo; **Happy Birthday!** ¡Feliz Cumpleaños!; **Happy Christmas!** ¡Feliz Navidad!; **Happy New Year!** ¡Feliz Año Nuevo!

happy hour n (inf) tiempo en que las bebidas se venden a precio reducido en un bar.

harassment ['hærəsmənt] n acoso m.

harbor ['hɑːbəʳ] (Am) = **harbour**.

harbour ['hɑːbəʳ] n (Br) puerto m.

hard [hɑːd] adj duro(-ra); (difficult, strenuous) difícil; (blow, push, frost) fuerte ◆ adv (try, work, rain) mucho; (listen) atentamente; (hit) con fuerza.

hardback ['hɑːdbæk] n edición f en pasta dura.

hardboard ['hɑːdbɔːd] n aglomerado m.

hard-boiled egg [-bɔɪld-] n huevo m duro.

hard disk n disco m duro.

hardly ['hɑːdlɪ] adv apenas; **~ ever** casi nunca.

hardship ['hɑːdʃɪp] n (difficult conditions) privaciones fpl; (difficult circumstance) dificultad f.

hard shoulder n (Br) arcén m.

hard up adj (inf) sin un duro.

hardware ['hɑːdweəʳ] n (tools, equipment) artículos mpl de ferretería; (COMPUT) hardware m.

hardwearing [hɑːd'weərɪŋ] adj (Br) resistente.

hardworking [hɑːd'wɜːkɪŋ] adj trabajador(-a).

hare [heəʳ] n liebre f.

harm [hɑːm] n daño m ♦ vt (person) hacer daño a; (object) dañar; (chances, reputation) perjudicar.

harmful ['hɑːmful] adj perjudicial.

harmless ['hɑːmlɪs] adj inofensivo(-a).

harmonica [hɑː'mɒnɪkə] n armónica f.

harmony ['hɑːmənɪ] n armonía f.

harness ['hɑːnɪs] n (for horse) arreos mpl; (for child) andadores mpl.

harp [hɑːp] n arpa f.

harsh [hɑːʃ] adj (conditions, winter) duro(-a); (cruel) severo(-a); (weather, climate) inclemente; (sound, voice) áspero(-a).

harvest ['hɑːvɪst] n cosecha f.

has [weak form həz, strong form hæz] → **have**.

hash browns [hæʃ-] npl (Am) patatas cortadas en trozos y fritas con cebolla en forma de bola.

hasn't ['hæznt] = has not.

hassle ['hæsl] n (inf: problems) jaleo m; (annoyance) fastidio m.

hastily ['heɪstɪlɪ] adv (rashly) a la ligera.

hasty ['heɪstɪ] adj (hurried) precipitado(-a); (rash) irreflexivo(-va).

hat [hæt] n sombrero m.

hatch [hætʃ] n (for serving food) ventanilla f ♦ vi (egg) romperse.

hatchback ['hætʃˌbæk] n coche m con puerta trasera.

hatchet ['hætʃɪt] n hacha f.

hate [heɪt] n odio m ♦ vt odiar; to ~ doing sthg odiar hacer algo.

hatred ['heɪtrɪd] n odio m.

haul [hɔːl] vt arrastrar ♦ n: a long ~ un buen trecho.

haunted ['hɔːntɪd] adj (house) encantado(-a).

have [hæv] (pt & pp had) aux vb 1. (to form perfect tenses) haber; I ~ finished he terminado; have you there? – No, I haven't ¿has estado allí? – No; we had already left ya nos habíamos ido.

2. (must): to ~ (got) to do sthg tener que hacer algo; do you ~ to pay? ¿hay que pagar?
♦ vt 1. (possess): to ~ (got) tener; do you ~ OR ~ you got a double room? ¿tiene una habitación doble?; she has (got) brown hair tiene el pelo castaño.

2. (experience) tener; to ~ a cold tener catarro; to ~ a good time pasarlo bien.

3. (replacing other verbs): to ~ breakfast desayunar; to ~ dinner cenar; to ~ lunch comer; to ~ a drink tomar algo; to ~ a shower ducharse; to ~ a swim ir a nadar; to ~ a walk dar un paseo.

4. (feel) tener; I ~ no doubt about it no tengo ninguna duda.

5. (invite): to ~ sb round for dinner invitar a alguien a cenar.

6. (cause to be): to ~ sthg done hacer que se haga algo; to ~ one's hair cut cortarse el pelo.

7. *(be treated in a certain way)*: **I've had my wallet stolen** me han robado la cartera.

haversack ['hævəsæk] *n* mochila *f*.

havoc ['hævək] *n* estragos *mpl*.

hawk [hɔːk] *n* halcón *m*.

hawker ['hɔːkə^r] *n* vendedor *m* (-ra *f*) ambulante.

hay [heɪ] *n* heno *m*.

hay fever *n* alergia *f* primaveral.

haystack ['heɪˌstæk] *n* almiar *m*.

hazard ['hæzəd] *n* riesgo *m*.

hazardous ['hæzədəs] *adj* arriesgado(-da).

hazard warning lights *npl* (Br) luces *fpl* de emergencia.

haze [heɪz] *n* neblina *f*.

hazel ['heɪzl] *adj* de color miel.

hazelnut ['heɪzl,nʌt] *n* avellana *f*.

hazy ['heɪzɪ] *adj* (misty) neblinoso(-sa).

he [hiː] *pron* él; **~'s tall** (él) es alto.

head [hed] *n* cabeza *f*; (of queue, page, letter) principio *m*; (of table, bed) cabecera *f*; (of company, department, school) director *m* (-ra *f*); (of beer) espuma *f* ♦ *vt* estar a la cabeza de ♦ *vi* dirigirse hacia; **£10 a ~** diez libras por persona; **~s or tails?** ¿cara o cruz? ❑ **head for** *vt fus (place)* dirigirse a.

headache ['hedeɪk] *n* (pain) dolor *m* de cabeza; **I have a ~** me duele la cabeza.

heading ['hedɪŋ] *n* encabezamiento *m*.

headlamp ['hedlæmp] (Br) = **headlight**.

headlight ['hedlaɪt] *n* faro *m*.

headline ['hedlaɪn] *n* titular *m*.

headmaster [,hed'mɑːstə^r] *n* director *m* (de colegio).

headmistress [,hed'mɪstrɪs] *n* directora *f* (de colegio).

head of state *n* jefe *m* (-fa *f*) de estado.

headphones ['hedfəʊnz] *npl* auriculares *mpl*.

headquarters [,hed'kwɔːtəz] *npl* sede *f* central.

headrest ['hedrest] *n* apoyacabezas *m inv*.

headroom ['hedrʊm] *n* (under bridge) altura *f* libre.

headscarf ['hedskɑːf] (pl -scarves [-skɑːvz]) *n* pañoleta *f*.

head start *n* ventaja *f* (desde el comienzo).

head teacher *n* director *m* (-ra *f*) (de colegio).

head waiter *n* jefe *m* (de camareros).

heal [hiːl] *vt* curar ♦ *vi* cicatrizar.

health [helθ] *n* salud *f*; **to be in good ~** tener buena salud; **to be in poor ~** tener mala salud; **your (very) good ~!** ¡a tu salud!

health centre *n* centro *m* de salud.

health food *n* productos *mpl* de dietética.

health food shop *n* tienda *f* de dietética.

health insurance *n* seguro *m* médico.

healthy ['helθɪ] *adj* (person, skin) sano(-na); (good for one's health) saludable.

heap [hiːp] *n* montón *m*; **~s of**

(inf) montones de.

hear [hɪə*] *(pt & pp* **heard** [hɜːd])
vt oír; *(JUR)* oír ♦ *vi* oír; **to ~ about**
sth enterarse de algo; **to ~ from**
sb tener noticias de alguien; **to**
have heard of haber oído hablar
de.

hearing ['hɪərɪŋ] *n (sense)* oído *m*;
(at court) vista *f*; **to be hard of ~** ser
duro de oído.

hearing aid *n* audífono *m*.

heart [hɑːt] *n* corazón *m*; **to**
know sth (off) by ~ saberse algo
de memoria; **to lose ~** desanimarse ❑ **hearts** *npl (in cards)* corazones *mpl*.

heart attack *n* infarto *m*.

heartbeat ['hɑːtbiːt] *n* latido *m*.

heartburn ['hɑːtbɜːn] *n* ardor *m*
de estómago.

heart condition *n*: **to have a**
~ padecer del corazón.

hearth [hɑːθ] *n* chimenea *f*.

hearty ['hɑːtɪ] *adj (meal)* abundante.

heat [hiːt] *n* calor *m*; *(specific tem-*
perature) temperatura *f* ❑ **heat up**
vt sep calentar.

heater ['hiːtə*] *n* calentador *m*.

heath [hiːθ] *n* brezal *m*.

heather ['heðə*] *n* brezo *m*.

heating ['hiːtɪŋ] *n* calefacción *f*.

heat wave *n* ola *f* de calor.

heave [hiːv] *vt (push)* empujar;
(pull) tirar de.

Heaven ['hevn] *n* el cielo.

heavily ['hevɪlɪ] *adv* mucho.

heavy ['hevɪ] *adj (in weight)* pesa-
do(-da); *(rain, fighting, traffic)* inten-
so(-sa); *(losses, defeat)* grave; *(food)*
indigesto(-ta); **how ~ is it?** ¿cuánto

pesa?; **to be a ~ smoker** fumar
mucho.

heavy cream *n (Am)* nata *f*
para montar.

heavy goods vehicle *n (Br)*
vehículo *m* pesado.

heavy industry *n* industria *f*
pesada.

heavy metal *n* heavy metal *m*.

heckle ['hekl] *vt* reventar.

hectic ['hektɪk] *adj* ajetrea-
do(-da).

hedge [hedʒ] *n* seto *m*.

hedgehog ['hedʒhɒg] *n* erizo *m*.

heel [hiːl] *n (of person)* talón *m*; *(of*
shoe) tacón *m*.

hefty ['heftɪ] *adj (person)* forni-
do(-da); *(fine)* considerable.

height [haɪt] *n* altura *f*; *(of person)*
estatura *f*; *(peak period)* punto *m*
álgido; **what ~ is it?** ¿cuánto mide?

heir [eə*] *n* heredero *m*.

heiress ['eərɪs] *n* heredera *f*.

held [held] *pt & pp* → **hold**.

helicopter ['helɪkɒptə*] *n* helicóptero *m*.

Hell [hel] *n* el infierno.

he'll [hiːl] = **he will**.

hello [həˈləʊ] *excl (as greeting)*
¡hola!; *(when answering phone)*
¡diga!, ¡bueno! *(Amér)*; *(when phon-*
ing, to attract attention) ¡oiga!

helmet ['helmɪt] *n* casco *m*.

help [help] *n* ayuda *f* ♦ *vt & vi*
ayudar ♦ *excl* ¡socorro!; **I can't ~ it**
no puedo evitarlo; **to ~ sb (to) do**
sth ayudar a alguien a hacer algo;
to ~ o.s. (to sth) servirse (algo);
can I ~ you? *(in shop)* ¿en qué
puedo servirle? ❑ **help out** *vi*
echar una mano.

helper ['helpǝʳ] n (assistant) ayudante mf; (Am: cleaner) mujer f de la limpieza.

helpful ['helpfʊl] adj (person) atento(-ta), servicial; (useful) útil.

helping ['helpɪŋ] n ración f.

helpless ['helplɪs] adj (person) indefenso(-sa).

hem [hem] n dobladillo m.

hemophiliac [ˌhi:mǝ'fɪlɪæk] n hemofílico m.

hemorrhage ['hemǝrɪdʒ] n hemorragia f.

hen [hen] n (chicken) gallina f.

hepatitis [ˌhepǝ'taɪtɪs] n hepatitis f inv.

her [hɜːʳ] adj su, sus (pl) ◆ pron: I know ~ la conozco; it's ~ es ella; send it to ~ envíaselo; tell ~ to come dile que venga; he's worse than ~ él es peor que ella.

herb [hɜːb] n hierba f.

herbal tea ['hɜːbl-] n infusión f.

herd [hɜːd] n (of sheep) rebaño m; (of cattle) manada f.

here [hɪǝʳ] adv aquí; ~'s your book aquí tienes tu libro; ~ you are aquí tienes.

heritage ['herɪtɪdʒ] n patrimonio m.

heritage centre n museo en un lugar de interés histórico.

hernia ['hɜːnjǝ] n hernia f.

hero ['hɪǝrǝʊ] (pl -es) n héroe m.

heroin ['herǝʊɪn] n heroína f.

heroine ['herǝʊɪn] n heroína f.

heron ['herǝn] n garza f real.

herring ['herɪŋ] n arenque m.

hers [hɜːz] pron suyo m (-ya f), suyos mpl (-yas fpl); a friend of ~

un amigo suyo.

herself [hɜː'self] pron (reflexive) se; (after prep) sí misma; she did it ~ lo hizo ella sola.

hesitant ['hezɪtǝnt] adj indeciso(-sa).

hesitate ['hezɪteɪt] vi vacilar.

hesitation [ˌhezɪ'teɪʃn] n vacilación f.

heterosexual [ˌhetǝrǝʊ'sekʃʊǝl] adj heterosexual ◆ n heterosexual mf.

hey [heɪ] excl (inf) ¡eh!, ¡oye!

HGV abbr = heavy goods vehicle.

hi [haɪ] excl (inf) ¡hola!

hiccup ['hɪkʌp] n: to have (the) ~s tener hipo.

hide [haɪd] (pt hid [hɪd], pp hidden ['hɪdn]) vt esconder; (truth, feelings) ocultar ◆ vi esconderse ◆ n (of animal) piel f.

hideous ['hɪdɪǝs] adj horrible.

hi-fi ['haɪfaɪ] n equipo m de alta fidelidad.

high [haɪ] adj alto(-ta); (winds) fuerte; (good) bueno(-na); (position, rank) elevado(-da); (inf: from drugs) flipado(-da) ◆ n (weather front) zona f de altas presiones ◆ adv alto; how ~ is it? ¿cuánto mide?; it's 10 metres ~ mide 10 metros de alto.

high chair n silla f alta.

high-class adj de categoría.

Higher ['haɪǝʳ] n examen al final de la enseñanza secundaria en Escocia.

higher education n enseñanza f superior.

high heels npl tacones mpl

altos.

high jump n salto m de altura.

Highland Games [ˈhaɪlənd-] npl festival típico de Escocia.

 HIGHLAND GAMES

Estos festivales de música y deportes celebrados en Escocia eran originariamente reuniones de los clanes de los Highlands. Hoy en día, los juegos recogen eventos tales como carreras, salto de longitud y salto de altura así como competiciones de gaita y bailes tradicionales. Otro concurso es "tossing the caber", una prueba de fuerza en la que los participantes han de lanzar un pesado tronco de abeto.

Highlands [ˈhaɪləndz] npl: the ~ las tierras altas del norte de Escocia.

highlight [ˈhaɪlaɪt] n (best part) mejor parte f ◆ vt (emphasize) destacar ❑ **highlights** npl (of football match etc) momentos mpl más interesantes; (in hair) mechas fpl, reflejos mpl.

highly [ˈhaɪlɪ] adv (extremely) enormemente; (very well) muy bien.

high-pitched [-pɪtʃt] adj agudo (-da).

high-rise building n rascacielos m inv.

high school n ≈ instituto m de bachillerato.

high season n temporada f alta.

high-speed train n tren m de alta velocidad.

high street n (Br) calle f mayor.

high tide n marea f alta.

highway [ˈhaɪweɪ] n (Am: between towns) autopista f; (Br: any main road) carretera f.

Highway Code n (Br) código m de la circulación.

hijack [ˈhaɪdʒæk] vt secuestrar.

hijacker [ˈhaɪdʒækəʳ] n secuestrador m (-ra f).

hike [haɪk] n caminata f ◆ vi ir de excursión.

hiking [ˈhaɪkɪŋ] n: to go ~ ir de excursión.

hilarious [hɪˈleərɪəs] adj desternillante.

hill [hɪl] n colina f.

hillwalking [ˈhɪlwɔːkɪŋ] n senderismo m.

hilly [ˈhɪlɪ] adj montañoso(-sa).

him [hɪm] pron: I know ~ le conozco, lo conozco; it's ~ es él; send it to ~ envíaselo; tell ~ to come dile que venga; she's worse than ~ ella es peor que él.

himself [hɪmˈself] pron (reflexive) se; (after prep) sí mismo; he did it ~ lo hizo él solo.

hinder [ˈhɪndəʳ] vt estorbar.

Hindu [ˈhɪnduː] (pl -s) adj hindú ◆ n (person) hindú mf.

hinge [hɪndʒ] n bisagra f.

hint [hɪnt] n (indirect suggestion) indirecta f; (piece of advice) consejo m; (slight amount) asomo m ◆ vi: to ~ at sthg insinuar algo.

hip [hɪp] n cadera f.

hippopotamus [ˌhɪpəˈpɒtəməs] n hipopótamo m.

hippy [ˈhɪpɪ] n hippy mf.

HQ *abbr* = headquarters.

hub airport [hʌb-] *n* aeropuerto *m* principal.

hubcap ['hʌbkæp] *n* tapacubos *m inv.*

hug [hʌɡ] *vt* abrazar ♦ *n*: to give sb a ~ abrazar a alguien.

huge [hju:dʒ] *adj* enorme.

hull [hʌl] *n* casco *m*.

hum [hʌm] *vi (bee, machine)* zumbar; *(person)* canturrear.

human ['hju:mən] *adj* humano(-na) ♦ *n*: ~ **(being)** ser *m* humano.

humanities [hju:'mænətiz] *npl* humanidades *fpl.*

human rights *npl* derechos *mpl* humanos.

humble ['hʌmbl] *adj* humilde.

humid ['hju:mɪd] *adj* húmedo(-da).

humidity [hju:'mɪdəti] *n* humedad *f*.

humiliating [hju:'mɪlieɪtɪŋ] *adj* humillante.

humiliation [hju:,mɪli'eɪʃn] *n* humillación *f*.

hummus ['homəs] *n* puré de garbanzos, ajo y pasta de sésamo.

humor ['hju:mər] *(Am)* = **humour**.

humorous ['hju:mərəs] *adj* humorístico(-ca).

humour ['hju:mər] *n* humor *m*; a sense of ~ un sentido del humor.

hump [hʌmp] *n (bump)* montículo *m*; *(of camel)* joroba *f*.

humpbacked bridge [ˌhʌmpbækt-] *n* puente *m* peraltado.

hunch [hʌntʃ] *n* presentimiento *m*.

hundred ['hʌndrəd] *num* cien; a ~ cien; a ~ and ten ciento diez, → **six**.

hundredth ['hʌndrətθ] *num* centésimo(-ma), → **sixth**.

hundredweight ['hʌndrədweɪt] *n (in UK)* = 50,8 kg; *(in US)* = 45,3 kg.

hung [hʌŋ] *pt & pp* → **hang**.

Hungarian [hʌŋ'ɡeəriən] *adj* húngaro(-ra) ♦ *n (person)* húngaro *m* (-ra *f*); *(language)* húngaro *m*.

Hungary ['hʌŋɡəri] *n* Hungría *f*.

hunger ['hʌŋɡə*] *n* hambre *f*.

hungry ['hʌŋɡri] *adj* hambriento(-ta); to be ~ tener hambre.

hunt [hʌnt] *n (Br: for foxes)* caza *f (del zorro)* ♦ *vt (animals)* cazar ♦ *vi (for animals)* cazar; to ~ *(for sthg)* *(search)* buscar (algo).

hunting ['hʌntɪŋ] *n (for animals)* caza *f*; *(Br: for foxes)* caza del zorro.

hurdle ['hɜ:dl] *n (SPORT)* valla *f*.

hurl [hɜ:l] *vt* arrojar.

hurricane ['hʌrɪkən] *n* huracán *m*.

hurry ['hʌrɪ] *vt (person)* meter prisa a ♦ *vi* apresurarse ♦ *n*: to be in a ~ tener prisa; to do sthg in a ~ hacer algo de prisa ❑ **hurry up** *vi* darse prisa.

hurt [hɜ:t] *(pt & pp* hurt*)* *vt* hacerse daño en; *(emotionally)* herir ♦ *vi* doler; my arm ~s me duele el brazo; to ~ o.s. hacerse daño.

husband ['hʌzbənd] *n* marido *m*.

hustle ['hʌsl] *n*: ~ **and bustle** bullicio *m*.

hut [hʌt] *n* cabaña *f*.

hyacinth ['haɪəsɪnθ] *n* jacinto *m*.

hydrofoil ['haɪdrəfɔɪl] *n* hidrofoil *m*.

hygiene ['haɪdʒiːn] *n* higiene *f*.

hygienic [haɪ'dʒiːnɪk] *adj* higiénico(-ca).

hymn [hɪm] *n* himno *m*.

hypermarket ['haɪpə,mɑːkɪt] *n* hipermercado *m*.

hyphen ['haɪfn] *n* guión *m*.

hypocrite ['hɪpəkrɪt] *n* hipócrita *mf*.

hypodermic needle [,haɪpə-'dɜːmɪk-] *n* aguja *f* hipodérmica.

hysterical [hɪs'terɪkl] *adj* histérico(-ca); *(inf: very funny)* tronchante.

I [aɪ] *pron* yo; **I'm a doctor** soy médico.

ice [aɪs] *n* hielo *m*; *(ice cream)* helado *m*.

iceberg ['aɪsbɜːg] *n* iceberg *m*.

iceberg lettuce *n* lechuga *f* iceberg.

icebox ['aɪsbɒks] *n (Am)* refrigerador *m*.

ice-cold *adj* helado(-da).

ice cream *n* helado *m*.

ice cube *n* cubito *m* de hielo.

ice hockey *n* hockey *m* sobre hielo.

Iceland ['aɪslənd] *n* Islandia.

ice lolly *n (Br)* polo *m*.

ice rink *n* pista *f* de hielo.

ice skates *npl* patines *mpl* de cuchilla.

ice-skating *n* patinaje *m* sobre hielo; **to go ~** ir a patinar.

icicle ['aɪsɪkl] *n* carámbano *m*.

icing ['aɪsɪŋ] *n* glaseado *m*.

icing sugar *n* azúcar *m* glas.

icy ['aɪsɪ] *adj* helado(-da).

I'd [aɪd] = I would, I had.

ID *n (abbr of identification)* documentos *mpl* de identificación.

ID card *n* carné *m* de identidad.

IDD code *n* prefijo *m* internacional automático.

idea [aɪ'dɪə] *n* idea *f*; **I've no ~** no tengo ni idea.

ideal [aɪ'dɪəl] *adj* ideal ♦ *n* ideal *m*.

ideally [aɪ'dɪəlɪ] *adv* idealmente; *(suited)* perfectamente.

identical [aɪ'dentɪkl] *adj* idéntico(-ca).

identification [aɪ,dentɪfɪ'keɪʃn] *n* identificación *f*.

identify [aɪ'dentɪfaɪ] *vt* identificar.

identity [aɪ'dentətɪ] *n* identidad *f*.

idiom ['ɪdɪəm] *n (phrase)* locución *f*.

idiot ['ɪdɪət] *n* idiota *mf*.

idle ['aɪdl] *adj (lazy)* perezoso(-sa); *(not working)* parado(-da) ♦ *vi (engine)* estar en punto muerto.

idol ['aɪdl] *n (person)* ídolo *m*.

idyllic [ɪ'dɪlɪk] *adj* idílico(-ca).

i.e. *(abbr of id est)* i.e.

if [ɪf] *conj* si; **~ I were you** yo que tú; **~ not** *(otherwise)* si no.

ignition [ɪg'nɪʃn] *n (AUT)* ignición *f*.

ignorant [ˈɪgnərənt] *adj (pej)* ignorante; **to be ~ of** desconocer.

ignore [ɪgˈnɔː] *vt* ignorar.

ill [ɪl] *adj* enfermo(-ma); *(bad)* malo(-la).

I'll [aɪl] = **I will, I shall.**

illegal [ɪˈliːgl] *adj* ilegal.

illegible [ɪˈledʒəbl] *adj* ilegible.

illegitimate [ˌɪlɪˈdʒɪtɪmət] *adj* ilegítimo(-ma).

illiterate [ɪˈlɪtərət] *adj* analfabeto(-ta).

illness [ˈɪlnɪs] *n* enfermedad *f*.

illuminate [ɪˈluːmɪneɪt] *vt* iluminar.

illusion [ɪˈluːʒn] *n (false idea)* ilusión *f*; *(visual)* ilusión óptica.

illustration [ˌɪləˈstreɪʃn] *n* ilustración *f*.

I'm [aɪm] = **I am.**

image [ˈɪmɪdʒ] *n* imagen *f*.

imaginary [ɪˈmædʒɪnrɪ] *adj* imaginario(-ria).

imagination [ɪˌmædʒɪˈneɪʃn] *n* imaginación *f*.

imagine [ɪˈmædʒɪn] *vt* imaginar; *(suppose)* imaginarse que.

imitate [ˈɪmɪteɪt] *vt* imitar.

imitation [ˌɪmɪˈteɪʃn] *n* imitación *f* ◆ *adj* de imitación.

immaculate [ɪˈmækjʊlət] *adj (very clean)* inmaculado(-da); *(perfect)* impecable.

immature [ˌɪməˈtjʊəʳ] *adj* inmaduro(-ra).

immediate [ɪˈmiːdjət] *adj (without delay)* inmediato(-ta).

immediately [ɪˈmiːdjətlɪ] *adv (at once)* inmediatamente ◆ *conj (Br)* en cuanto.

immense [ɪˈmens] *adj* inmenso(-sa).

immersion heater [ɪˈmɜːʃn-] *n* calentador *m* de inmersión.

immigrant [ˈɪmɪgrənt] *n* inmigrante *mf*.

immigration [ˌɪmɪˈgreɪʃn] *n* inmigración *f*.

imminent [ˈɪmɪnənt] *adj* inminente.

immune [ɪˈmjuːn] *adj*: **to be ~ to** *(MED)* ser inmune a.

immunity [ɪˈmjuːnətɪ] *n (MED)* inmunidad *f*.

immunize [ˈɪmjʊnaɪz] *vt* inmunizar.

impact [ˈɪmpækt] *n* impacto *m*.

impair [ɪmˈpeəʳ] *vt (sight)* dañar; *(ability)* mermar; *(movement)* entorpecer.

impatient [ɪmˈpeɪʃnt] *adj* impaciente; **to be ~ to do sthg** estar impaciente por hacer algo.

imperative [ɪmˈperətɪv] *n* imperativo *m*.

imperfect [ɪmˈpɜːfɪkt] *n* imperfecto *m*.

impersonate [ɪmˈpɜːsəneɪt] *vt (for amusement)* imitar.

impertinent [ɪmˈpɜːtɪnənt] *adj* impertinente.

implement [*n* ˈɪmplɪmənt, *vb* ˈɪmplɪment] *n* herramienta *f* ◆ *vt* llevar a cabo.

implication [ˌɪmplɪˈkeɪʃn] *n (consequence)* consecuencia *f*.

imply [ɪmˈplaɪ] *vt (suggest)* insinuar.

impolite [ˌɪmpəˈlaɪt] *adj* maleducado(-da).

import [*n* ˈɪmpɔːt, *vb* ɪmˈpɔːt]

importación f ♦ vt importar.

importance [ɪmˈpɔːtns] n importancia f.

important [ɪmˈpɔːtnt] adj importante.

impose [ɪmˈpəʊz] vt imponer ♦ vi abusar; **to ~ sthg on** imponer algo a.

impossible [ɪmˈpɒsəbl] adj imposible; (person, behaviour) inaguantable.

impractical [ɪmˈpræktɪkl] adj poco práctico(-ca).

impress [ɪmˈpres] vt impresionar.

impression [ɪmˈpreʃn] n impresión f.

impressive [ɪmˈpresɪv] adj impresionante.

improbable [ɪmˈprɒbəbl] adj improbable.

improper [ɪmˈprɒpəʳ] adj (incorrect, illegal) indebido(-da); (rude) indecoroso(-sa).

improve [ɪmˈpruːv] vt & vi mejorar ❑ **improve on** vt fus mejorar.

improvement [ɪmˈpruːvmənt] n mejora f; (to home) reforma f.

improvise [ˈɪmprəvaɪz] vi improvisar.

impulse [ˈɪmpʌls] n impulso m; **on ~** sin pensárselo dos veces.

impulsive [ɪmˈpʌlsɪv] adj impulsivo(-va).

in [ɪn] prep 1. (expressing location, position) en; **it comes ~ a box** viene en una caja; **~ the bedroom** en la habitación; **~ Scotland** en Escocia; **~ the sun** al sol; **~ here/there** aquí/allí dentro; **~ the middle** en el medio; **I'm not ~ the photo** no

estoy en la foto. 2. (participating in) en; **who's ~ the play?** ¿quién actúa? 3. (expressing arrangement): **~ a row** en fila; **they come ~ packs of three** vienen en paquetes de tres. 4. (with time) en; **~ April** en abril; **~ the afternoon** por la tarde; **~ the morning** por la mañana; **at ten o'clock ~ the morning** a las diez de la mañana; **~ 1994** en 1994; **it'll be ready ~ an hour** estará listo en una hora; **they're arriving ~ two weeks** llegarán dentro de dos semanas. 5. (expressing means) en; **~ writing** por escrito; **they were talking ~ English** estaban hablando en inglés; **write ~ ink** escribe a bolígrafo. 6. (wearing) de; **the man ~ the suit** el hombre del traje. 7. (expressing condition) en; **~ good health** bien de salud; **to be ~ pain** tener dolor; **~ ruins** en ruinas; **a rise ~ prices** una subida de precios; **to be 50 metres ~ length** medir 50 metros de largo; **she's ~ her twenties** tiene unos veintitantos años. 8. (with numbers): **one ~ ten** uno de cada diez. 9. (with colours): **it comes ~ green or blue** viene en verde o en azul. 10. (with superlatives) de; **the best ~ the world** el mejor del mundo. ♦ adv 1. (inside) dentro; **you can go ~ now** puedes entrar ahora. 2. (at home, work): **she's not ~** no está; **to stay ~** quedarse en casa. 3. (train, bus, plane): **the train's not ~ yet** el tren todavía no ha llegado. 4. (tide): **the tide is ~** la marea está alta.

◆ adj (inf: fashionable) de moda.

inability [ˌɪnə'bɪlətɪ] n: ~ **(to do sthg)** incapacidad f (de hacer algo).

inaccessible [ˌɪnək'sesəbl] adj inaccesible.

inaccurate [ɪn'ækjurət] adj incorrecto(-ta).

inadequate [ɪn'ædɪkwət] adj (insufficient) insuficiente.

inappropriate [ˌɪnə'prəuprɪət] adj impropio(-pia).

inauguration [ɪˌnɔːgju'reɪʃn] n (of leader) investidura f; (of building) inauguración f.

incapable [ɪn'keɪpəbl] adj: **to be ~ of doing sthg** ser incapaz de hacer algo.

incense ['ɪnsens] n incienso m.

incentive [ɪn'sentɪv] n incentivo m.

inch [ɪntʃ] n = 2,5 cm, pulgada f.

incident ['ɪnsɪdənt] n incidente m.

incidentally [ˌɪnsɪ'dentəlɪ] adv por cierto.

incline ['ɪnklaɪn] n pendiente f.

inclined [ɪn'klaɪnd] adj (sloping) inclinado(-da); **to be ~ to do sthg** tener tendencia a hacer algo.

include [ɪn'kluːd] vt incluir.

included [ɪn'kluːdɪd] adj incluido(-da); **to be ~ in sthg** estar incluido en algo.

including [ɪn'kluːdɪŋ] prep inclusive.

inclusive [ɪn'kluːsɪv] adj: **from the 8th to the 16th ~** del ocho al dieciséis inclusive; **~ of VAT** incluido IVA.

income [ɪŋkʌm] n ingresos mpl.

income support n (Br) subsidio para personas con muy bajos ingresos o desempleados sin derecho a subsidio de paro.

income tax n impuesto m sobre la renta.

incoming ['ɪnˌkʌmɪŋ] adj (train, plane) que efectúa su llegada; "**~ calls only**" cartel que indica que sólo se pueden recibir llamadas en un teléfono.

incompetent [ɪn'kɒmpɪtənt] adj incompetente.

incomplete [ˌɪnkəm'pliːt] adj incompleto(-ta).

inconsiderate [ˌɪnkən'sɪdərət] adj desconsiderado(-da).

inconsistent [ˌɪnkən'sɪstənt] adj inconsecuente.

incontinent [ɪn'kɒntɪnənt] adj incontinente.

inconvenient [ˌɪnkən'viːnjənt] adj (time) inoportuno(-na); (place) mal situado(-da); **tomorrow's ~** mañana no me viene bien.

incorporate [ɪn'kɔːpəreɪt] vt incorporar.

incorrect [ˌɪnkə'rekt] adj incorrecto(-ta).

increase [n 'ɪnkriːs, vb ɪn'kriːs] n aumento m ◆ vt & vi aumentar; **an ~ in sthg** un aumento en algo.

increasingly [ɪn'kriːsɪŋlɪ] adv cada vez más.

incredible [ɪn'kredəbl] adj increíble.

incredibly [ɪn'kredəblɪ] adv increíblemente.

incur [ɪn'kɜː] vt incurrir en.

indecisive [ˌɪndɪ'saɪsɪv] adj indeciso(-sa).

indeed [ɪnˈdiːd] adv (for emphasis) verdaderamente; (certainly) ciertamente.

indefinite [ɪnˈdefɪnɪt] adj (time, number) indefinido(-da); (answer, opinion) impreciso(-sa).

indefinitely [ɪnˈdefɪnɪtlɪ] adv (closed, delayed) indefinidamente.

independence [ˌɪndɪˈpendəns] n independencia f.

independent [ˌɪndɪˈpendənt] adj independiente.

independently [ˌɪndɪˈpendəntlɪ] adv independientemente.

independent school n (Br) colegio m privado.

index [ˈɪndeks] n (of book) índice m; (in library) catálogo m.

index finger n dedo m índice.

India [ˈɪndjə] n India.

Indian [ˈɪndjən] adj indio(-dia) (de India) ◆ n indio m (-dia f) (de India); ~ restaurant restaurante indio.

Indian Ocean n océano m Índico.

indicate [ˈɪndɪkeɪt] vt & vi indicar.

indicator [ˈɪndɪkeɪtə'] n (AUT) intermitente m.

indifferent [ɪnˈdɪfrənt] adj indiferente.

indigestion [ˌɪndɪˈdʒestʃn] n indigestión f.

indigo [ˈɪndɪgəʊ] adj añil.

indirect [ˌɪndɪˈrekt] adj indirecto(-ta).

individual [ˌɪndɪˈvɪdʒʊəl] adj (tuition, case) particular; (portion) individual ◆ n individuo m.

individually [ˌɪndɪˈvɪdʒʊəlɪ] adv individualmente.

Indonesia [ˌɪndəˈniːzjə] n Indonesia.

indoor [ˈɪndɔːʳ] adj (swimming pool) cubierto(-ta); (sports) en pista cubierta.

indoors [ɪnˈdɔːz] adv dentro.

indulge [ɪnˈdʌldʒ] vi: to ~ in sthg permitirse algo.

industrial [ɪnˈdʌstrɪəl] adj industrial.

industrial estate n (Br) polígono m industrial.

industry [ˈɪndəstrɪ] n industria f.

inedible [ɪnˈedɪbl] adj no comestible.

inefficient [ˌɪnɪˈfɪʃnt] adj ineficaz.

inequality [ˌɪnɪˈkwɒlətɪ] n desigualdad f.

inevitable [ɪnˈevɪtəbl] adj inevitable.

inevitably [ɪnˈevɪtəblɪ] adv inevitablemente.

inexpensive [ˌɪnɪkˈspensɪv] adj barato(-ta).

infamous [ˈɪnfəməs] adj infame.

infant [ˈɪnfənt] n (baby) bebé m; (young child) niño m pequeño (niña f pequeña).

infant school n (Br) colegio m preescolar.

infatuated [ɪnˈfætjʊeɪtɪd] adj: to be ~ with estar encaprichado(-da) con.

infected [ɪnˈfektɪd] adj infectado(-da).

infectious [ɪnˈfekʃəs] adj contagioso(-sa).

inferior [ɪnˈfɪərɪəʳ] adj inferior.

infinite ['ɪnfɪnət] *adj* infinito(-ta).

infinitely ['ɪnfɪnətlɪ] *adv* infinitamente.

infinitive [ɪn'fɪnɪtɪv] *n* infinitivo *m*.

infinity [ɪn'fɪnətɪ] *n* infinito *m*.

infirmary [ɪn'fɜ:mərɪ] *n* hospital *m*.

inflamed [ɪn'fleɪmd] *adj* inflamado(-da).

inflammation [ˌɪnflə'meɪʃn] *n* inflamación *f*.

inflatable [ɪn'fleɪtəbl] *adj* hinchable.

inflate [ɪn'fleɪt] *vt* inflar.

inflation [ɪn'fleɪʃn] *n* inflación *f*.

inflict [ɪn'flɪkt] *vt* infligir.

in-flight *adj* proporcionado (-da) durante el vuelo.

influence ['ɪnfluəns] *vt* influenciar ◆ *n*: ~ (on) influencia *f* (en).

inform [ɪn'fɔ:m] *vt* informar.

informal [ɪn'fɔ:ml] *adj* (occasion, dress) informal.

information [ˌɪnfə'meɪʃn] *n* información *f*; **a piece of ~** un dato.

information desk *n* información *f*.

information office *n* oficina *f* de información.

informative [ɪn'fɔ:mətɪv] *adj* informativo(-va).

infuriating [ɪn'fjuərɪeɪtɪŋ] *adj* exasperante.

ingenious [ɪn'dʒi:njəs] *adj* ingenioso(-sa).

ingredient [ɪn'gri:djənt] *n* ingrediente *m*.

inhabit [ɪn'hæbɪt] *vt* habitar.

inhabitant [ɪn'hæbɪtənt] *n* habitante *mf*.

inhale [ɪn'heɪl] *vi* respirar.

inhaler [ɪn'heɪlə*r*] *n* inhalador *m*.

inherit [ɪn'herɪt] *vt* heredar.

inhibition [ˌɪnhɪ'bɪʃn] *n* inhibición *f*.

initial [ɪ'nɪʃl] *adj* inicial ◆ *vt* poner las iniciales a ❑ **initials** *npl* iniciales *fpl*.

initially [ɪ'nɪʃəlɪ] *adv* inicialmente.

initiative [ɪ'nɪʃətɪv] *n* iniciativa *f*.

injection [ɪn'dʒekʃn] *n* inyección *f*.

injure ['ɪndʒə*r*] *vt* herir; (leg, arm) lesionar; **to ~ o.s.** hacerse daño.

injured ['ɪndʒəd] *adj* herido(-da).

injury ['ɪndʒərɪ] *n* lesión *f*.

ink [ɪŋk] *n* tinta *f*.

inland [*adj* 'ɪnlənd, *adv* ɪn'lænd] *adj* interior ◆ *adv* hacia el interior.

Inland Revenue *n* (Br) = Hacienda *f*.

inn [ɪn] *n* pub decorado a la vieja usanza.

inner ['ɪnə*r*] *adj* (on inside) interior.

inner city *n* núcleo *m* urbano.

inner tube *n* cámara *f* (de aire).

innocence ['ɪnəsəns] *n* inocencia *f*.

innocent ['ɪnəsənt] *adj* inocente.

inoculate ['ɪnɒkjuleɪt] *vt*: **to ~ sb (against sthg)** inocular a alguien (contra algo).

inoculation [ɪˌnɒkju'leɪʃn] *n* inoculación *f*.

input ['ɪnput] (*pt & pp* **input** OR

-ted *vt* (COMPUT) entrar.

inquire [ɪnˈkwaɪər] = **enquire**.

inquiry [ɪnˈkwaɪərɪ] = **enquiry**.

insane [ɪnˈseɪn] *adj* demente.

insect [ˈɪnsekt] *n* insecto *m*.

insect repellent [-rəˈpelənt] *n* loción *f* antiinsectos.

insensitive [ɪnˈsensətɪv] *adj* insensible.

insert [ɪnˈsɜːt] *vt* introducir.

inside [ɪnˈsaɪd] *prep* dentro de ◆ *adv* (be, remain) dentro; (go, run) adentro ◆ *adj* interior ◆ *n*: the ~ (interior) el interior; (AUT: in UK) el carril de la izquierda; (AUT: in Europe, US) el carril de la derecha; ~ out (clothes) al revés.

inside lane *n* (AUT) (in UK) carril *m* de la izquierda; (in Europe, US) carril de la derecha.

inside leg *n* medida *f* de la pernera.

insight [ˈɪnsaɪt] *n* (glimpse) idea *f*.

insignificant [ˌɪnsɪgˈnɪfɪkənt] *adj* insignificante.

insinuate [ɪnˈsɪnjʊeɪt] *vt* insinuar.

insist [ɪnˈsɪst] *vi* insistir; to ~ on doing sthg insistir en hacer algo.

insole [ˈɪnsəʊl] *n* plantilla *f*.

insolent [ˈɪnsələnt] *adj* insolente.

insomnia [ɪnˈsɒmnɪə] *n* insomnio *m*.

inspect [ɪnˈspekt] *vt* examinar.

inspection [ɪnˈspekʃn] *n* examen *m*.

inspector [ɪnˈspektər] *n* (on bus, train) revisor *m* (-ra *f*); (in police force) inspector *m* (-ra *f*).

inspiration [ˌɪnspəˈreɪʃn] *n* (quality) inspiración *f*; (source of inspiration) fuente *f* de inspiración.

instal [ɪnˈstɔːl] (Am) = **install**.

install [ɪnˈstɔːl] *vt* (Br: equipment) instalar.

installment [ɪnˈstɔːlmənt] (Am) = **instalment**.

instalment [ɪnˈstɔːlmənt] *n* (payment) plazo *m*; (episode) episodio *m*.

instamatic (camera) [ˌɪnstəˈmætɪk-] *n* Polaroid® *f*.

instance [ˈɪnstəns] *n* ejemplo *m*; for ~ por ejemplo.

instant [ˈɪnstənt] *adj* instantáneo(-nea) ◆ *n* instante *m*.

instant coffee *n* café *m* instantáneo.

instead [ɪnˈsted] *adv* en cambio; ~ of en vez de.

instep [ˈɪnstep] *n* empeine *m*.

instinct [ˈɪnstɪŋkt] *n* instinto *m*.

institute [ˈɪnstɪtjuːt] *n* instituto *m*.

institution [ˌɪnstɪˈtjuːʃn] *n* (organization) institución *f*.

instructions [ɪnˈstrʌkʃnz] *npl* (for use) instrucciones *fpl*.

instructor [ɪnˈstrʌktər] *n* monitor *m* (-ra *f*).

instrument [ˈɪnstrʊmənt] *n* instrumento *m*.

insufficient [ˌɪnsəˈfɪʃnt] *adj* insuficiente.

insulating tape [ˈɪnsjʊleɪtɪŋ-] *n* cinta *f* aislante.

insulation [ˌɪnsjʊˈleɪʃn] *n* aislamiento *m*.

insulin [ˈɪnsjʊlɪn] *n* insulina *f*.

insult [*n* ˈɪnsʌlt, *vb* ɪnˈsʌlt] *n* insulto *m* ◆ *vt* insultar.

insurance [ɪnˈʃʊərəns] *n* seguro *m*.

insurance certificate n certificado m de seguro.

insurance company n compañía f de seguros.

insurance policy n póliza f de seguros.

insure [ɪnˈʃʊəʳ] vt asegurar.

insured [ɪnˈʃʊəd] adj: **to be ~** estar asegurado(-da).

intact [ɪnˈtækt] adj intacto(-ta).

intellectual [ˌɪntəˈlektjʊəl] adj intelectual ◆ n intelectual f.

intelligence [ɪnˈtelɪdʒəns] n (cleverness) inteligencia f.

intelligent [ɪnˈtelɪdʒənt] adj inteligente.

intend [ɪnˈtend] vt: it's ~ed as a handbook está pensado como un manual; **to ~ to do sthg** tener la intención de hacer algo.

intense [ɪnˈtens] adj intenso(-sa).

intensity [ɪnˈtensətɪ] n intensidad f.

intensive [ɪnˈtensɪv] adj intensivo(-va).

intensive care n cuidados mpl intensivos.

intent [ɪnˈtent] adj: **to be ~ on doing sthg** estar empeñado(-da) en hacer algo.

intention [ɪnˈtenʃn] n intención f.

intentional [ɪnˈtenʃənl] adj deliberado(-da).

intentionally [ɪnˈtenʃənəlɪ] adv deliberadamente.

interchange [ˈɪntətʃeɪndʒ] n (on motorway) cruce m.

Intercity® [ˌɪntəˈsɪtɪ] n (Br) tren rápido de largo recorrido en Gran Bretaña.

intercom [ˈɪntəkɒm] n portero m automático.

interest [ˈɪntrəst] n interés m ◆ vt interesar; **to take an ~ in sthg** interesarse en algo.

interested [ˈɪntrəstɪd] adj interesado(-da); **to be ~ in sthg** estar interesado en algo.

interesting [ˈɪntrəstɪŋ] adj interesante.

interest rate n tipo m de interés.

interfere [ˌɪntəˈfɪəʳ] vi (meddle) entrometerse; **to ~ with sthg** (damage) interferir en algo.

interference [ˌɪntəˈfɪərəns] n (on TV, radio) interferencia f.

interior [ɪnˈtɪərɪəʳ] adj interior ◆ n interior m.

intermediate [ˌɪntəˈmiːdjət] adj intermedio(-dia).

intermission [ˌɪntəˈmɪʃn] n descanso m.

internal [ɪnˈtɜːnl] adj (not foreign) nacional; (on the inside) interno(-na).

internal flight n vuelo m nacional.

international [ˌɪntəˈnæʃənl] adj internacional.

international flight n vuelo m internacional.

interpret [ɪnˈtɜːprɪt] vi hacer de intérprete.

interpreter [ɪnˈtɜːprɪtəʳ] n intérprete mf.

interrogate [ɪnˈterəgeɪt] vt interrogar.

interrupt [ˌɪntəˈrʌpt] vt interrumpir.

intersection [ˌɪntəˈsekʃn] n

intersección f.

interval ['ɪntəvl] n intervalo m;
(Br: at cinema, theatre) intermedio
m.

intervene [ˌɪntə'viːn] vi (person)
intervenir; (event) interponerse.

interview ['ɪntəvjuː] n entrevista f ♦ vt entrevistar.

interviewer ['ɪntəvjuːəʳ] n
entrevistador m (-ra f).

intestine [ɪn'testɪn] n intestino
m.

intimate ['ɪntɪmət] adj ínti-
mo(-ma).

intimidate [ɪn'tɪmɪdeɪt] vt intimidar.

into ['ɪntʊ] prep (inside) en;
(against) con; (concerning) en relación con; 4 ~ 20 goes 5 (times)
veinte entre cuatro a cinco; to
translate ~ Spanish traducir al
español; to change ~ sthg transformarse en algo; I'm ~ music (inf)
lo mío es la música.

intolerable [ɪn'tɒlrəbl] adj intolerable.

intransitive [ɪn'trænzətɪv] adj
intransitivo(-va).

intricate ['ɪntrɪkət] adj intrinca-
do(-da).

intriguing [ɪn'triːgɪn] adj intri-
gante.

introduce [ˌɪntrə'djuːs] vt presentar; I'd like to ~ you to Fred me
gustaría presentarle a Fred.

introduction [ˌɪntrə'dʌkʃn] n (to
book, programme) introducción f; (to
person) presentación f.

introverted ['ɪntrəvɜːtɪd] adj
introvertido(-da).

intruder [ɪn'truːdəʳ] n intruso

m (-sa f).

intuition [ˌɪntjuː'ɪʃn] n intuición
f.

invade [ɪn'veɪd] vt invadir.

invalid [adj ɪn'vælɪd, n 'ɪnvəlɪd] adj
nulo(-la) ♦ n inválido m (-da f).

invaluable [ɪn'væljʊəbl] adj
inestimable.

invariably [ɪn'veərɪəblɪ] adv
siempre.

invasion [ɪn'veɪʒn] n invasión f.

invent [ɪn'vent] vt inventar.

invention [ɪn'venʃn] n invención f.

inventory ['ɪnvəntrɪ] n (list)
inventario m; (Am: stock) existencias fpl.

inverted commas [ɪn'vɜːtɪd-]
npl comillas fpl.

invest [ɪn'vest] vt invertir ♦ vi: to
~ in sthg invertir en algo.

investigate [ɪn'vestɪgeɪt] vt
investigar.

investigation [ɪnˌvestɪ'geɪʃn] n
investigación f.

investment [ɪn'vestmənt] n
inversión f.

invisible [ɪn'vɪzɪbl] adj invisible.

invitation [ˌɪnvɪ'teɪʃn] n invitación f.

invite [ɪn'vaɪt] vt invitar; to ~ sb
to do sthg invitar a alguien a hacer
algo; to ~ sb round invitar a
alguien.

invoice ['ɪnvɔɪs] n factura f.

involve [ɪn'vɒlv] vt (entail) conllevar; what does it ~? ¿qué implica?;
to be ~d in sthg (scheme, activity)
estar metido en algo; (accident)
verse envuelto en algo.

involved [ɪn'vɒlvd] adj: what is

~? ¿qué supone?

inwards ['ɪnwədz] adv hacia dentro.

IOU n pagaré m.

IQ n C.I. m.

Iran [ɪ'rɑːn] n Irán.

Iraq [ɪ'rɑːk] n Irak.

Ireland ['aɪələnd] n Irlanda.

iris ['aɪərɪs] (pl -es) n (flower) lirio m.

Irish ['aɪrɪʃ] adj irlandés(-esa) ♦ n (language) irlandés m ♦ npl: the ~ los irlandeses.

Irish coffee n café m irlandés.

Irishman ['aɪrɪʃmən] (pl -men [-mən]) n irlandés m.

Irish stew n estofado de carne de cordero, patatas y cebolla.

Irishwoman ['aɪrɪʃˌwomən] (pl -women [-ˌwɪmɪn]) n irlandesa f.

iron ['aɪən] n (metal, golf club) hierro m; (for clothes) plancha f ♦ vt planchar.

ironic [aɪ'rɒnɪk] adj irónico(-ca).

ironing board ['aɪənɪŋ-] n tabla f de planchar.

ironmonger's ['aɪənˌmʌŋgəz] n (Br) ferretería f.

irrelevant [ɪ'reləvənt] adj irrelevante.

irresistible [ˌɪrɪ'zɪstəbl] adj irresistible.

irrespective [ˌɪrɪ'spektɪv]: irrespective of prep con independencia de.

irresponsible [ˌɪrɪ'spɒnsəbl] adj irresponsable.

irrigation [ˌɪrɪ'geɪʃn] n riego m.

irritable ['ɪrɪtəbl] adj irritable.

irritate ['ɪrɪteɪt] vt irritar.

irritating ['ɪrɪteɪtɪŋ] adj irritante.

IRS n (Am) = Hacienda f.

is [ɪz] → be.

Islam ['ɪzlɑːm] n islam m.

island ['aɪlənd] n (in water) isla f; (in road) isleta f.

isle [aɪl] n isla f.

isolated ['aɪsəleɪtɪd] adj aislado(-da).

Israel ['ɪzreɪl] n Israel.

issue ['ɪʃuː] n (problem, subject) cuestión f; (of newspaper, magazine) edición f ♦ vt (statement) hacer público; (passport, document) expedir; (stamps, bank notes) emitir.

it [ɪt] pron 1. (referring to specific thing: subj) él m (ella f); (direct object) lo m (la f); (indirect object) le m; ~'s big es grande; she hit ~ lo golpeó; give ~ to me dámelo.
2. (nonspecific) ello; ~'s nice here se está bien aquí; I can't remember ~ no me acuerdo (de ello); tell me about ~ cuéntamelo; ~'s me soy yo; who is ~? ¿quién es?
3. (used impersonally): ~'s hot hace calor; ~'s six o'clock son las seis; ~'s Sunday es domingo.

Italian [ɪ'tæljən] adj italiano(-na) ♦ n (person) italiano m (-na f); (language) italiano m; ~ restaurant restaurante italiano.

Italy ['ɪtəlɪ] n Italia.

itch [ɪtʃ] vi: my arm is ~ing me pica el brazo.

item ['aɪtəm] n artículo m; (on agenda) asunto m; a news ~ una noticia.

itemized bill ['aɪtəmaɪzd-] n factura f detallada.

its [ɪts] *adj* su, sus *(pl)*.

it's [ɪts] = **it is, it has**.

itself [ɪt'self] *pron (reflexive)* se; *(after prep)* sí mismo(-ma); **the house ~ is fine** la casa en sí está bien.

I've [aɪv] = **I have**.

ivory ['aɪvərɪ] *n* marfil *m*.

ivy ['aɪvɪ] *n* hiedra *f*.

J

jab [dʒæb] *n (Br: inf: injection)* pinchazo *m*.

jack [dʒæk] *n (for car)* gato *m*; *(playing card)* = sota *f*.

jacket ['dʒækɪt] *n (garment)* chaqueta *f*; *(of book)* sobrecubierta *f*; *(Am: of record)* cubierta *f*; *(of potato)* piel *f*.

jacket potato *n* patata *f* asada con piel.

jack-knife *vi* derrapar la parte delantera.

Jacuzzi® [dʒə'ku:zɪ] *n* jacuzzi® *m*.

jade [dʒeɪd] *n* jade *m*.

jail [dʒeɪl] *n* cárcel *f*.

jam [dʒæm] *n (food)* mermelada *f*; *(of traffic)* atasco *m*; *(inf: difficult situation)* apuro *m* ♦ *vt (pack tightly)* apiñar ♦ *vi* atascarse; **the roads are jammed** las carreteras están atascadas.

jam-packed [-'pækt] *adj (inf)*

a tope.

Jan. [dʒæn] *(abbr of January)* ene.

janitor ['dʒænɪtəʳ] *n (Am & Scot)* conserje *m*.

January ['dʒænjʊərɪ] *n* enero *m*, → **September**.

Japan [dʒə'pæn] *n* Japón *m*.

Japanese [,dʒæpə'ni:z] *adj* japonés(-esa) ♦ *n (language)* japonés *m* ♦ *npl:* **the ~** los japoneses.

jar [dʒɑ:ʳ] *n* tarro *m*.

javelin ['dʒævlɪn] *n* jabalina *f*.

jaw [dʒɔ:] *n (of person)* mandíbula *f*.

jazz [dʒæz] *n* jazz *m*.

jealous ['dʒeləs] *adj* celoso(-sa).

jeans [dʒi:nz] *npl* vaqueros *mpl*.

Jeep® [dʒi:p] *n* jeep *m*.

Jello® ['dʒeləʊ] *n (Am)* gelatina *f*.

jelly ['dʒelɪ] *n (dessert)* gelatina *f*; *(Am: jam)* mermelada *f*.

jellyfish ['dʒelɪfɪʃ] *(pl inv)* *n* medusa *f*.

jeopardize ['dʒepədaɪz] *vt* poner en peligro.

jerk [dʒɜ:k] *n (movement)* movimiento *m* brusco; *(inf: idiot)* idiota *mf*.

jersey ['dʒɜ:zɪ] *(pl -s)* *n (garment)* jersey *m*.

jet [dʒet] *n (aircraft)* reactor *m*; *(of liquid, gas)* chorro *m*; *(outlet)* boquilla *f*.

jetfoil ['dʒetfɔɪl] *n* hidroplano *m*.

jet lag *n* jet lag *m*.

jet-ski *n* moto *f* acuática.

jetty ['dʒetɪ] *n* embarcadero *m*.

Jew [dʒu:] *n* judío *m* (-a *f*).

jewel ['dʒu:əl] *n* piedra *f* preciosa

☐ **jewels** npl (jewellery) joyas fpl.

jeweler's ['dʒuːələz] (Am) = **jeweller's**.

jeweller's ['dʒuːələz] n (Br: shop) joyería f.

jewellery ['dʒuːəlrı] n (Br) joyas fpl.

jewelry ['dʒuːəlrı] (Am) = **jewellery**.

Jewish ['dʒuːɪʃ] adj judío(-a).

jigsaw (puzzle) ['dʒɪgsɔː-] n puzzle m.

jingle ['dʒɪŋgl] n (of advert) sintonía f (de anuncio).

job [dʒɒb] n trabajo m; (function) cometido m; **to lose one's ~** perder el trabajo.

job centre n (Br) oficina f de empleo.

jockey ['dʒɒkı] (pl -s) n jockey mf.

jog [dʒɒg] vt (bump) golpear ligeramente ◆ vi hacer footing ◆ n: **to go for a ~** hacer footing.

jogging ['dʒɒgɪŋ] n footing m; **to go ~** hacer footing.

join [dʒɔɪn] vt (club, organization) hacerse socio de; (fasten together) unir, juntar; (come together with, participate in) unirse a; (connect) conectar ☐ **join in** vt fus participar en ◆ vi participar.

joint [dʒɔɪnt] adj (responsibility, effort) compartido(-da); (bank account, ownership) conjunto(-ta) ◆ n (of body) articulación f; (Br: of meat) corte m; (in structure) juntura f.

joke [dʒəʊk] n chiste m ◆ vi bromear.

joker ['dʒəʊkər] n (playing card)

comodín m.

jolly ['dʒɒlı] adj (cheerful) alegre ◆ adv (Br: inf) muy.

jolt [dʒəʊlt] n sacudida f.

jot [dʒɒt]: **jot down** vt sep apuntar.

journal ['dʒɜːnl] n (magazine) revista f; (diary) diario m.

journalist ['dʒɜːnəlıst] n periodista mf.

journey ['dʒɜːnı] (pl -s) n viaje m.

joy [dʒɔɪ] n (happiness) alegría f.

joypad ['dʒɔɪpæd] n (of video game) mando m.

joyrider ['dʒɔɪraɪdər] n persona que se pasea en un coche robado y luego lo abandona.

joystick ['dʒɔɪstık] n (of video game) joystick m.

judge [dʒʌdʒ] n juez mf ◆ vt (competition) juzgar; (evaluate) calcular.

judg(e)ment ['dʒʌdʒmənt] n juicio m; (JUR) fallo m.

judo ['dʒuːdəʊ] n judo m.

jug [dʒʌg] n jarra f.

juggernaut ['dʒʌgənɔːt] n (Br) camión m grande.

juggle ['dʒʌgl] vi hacer malabarismo.

juice [dʒuːs] n zumo m; (from meat) jugo m.

juicy ['dʒuːsı] adj (food) jugoso(-sa).

jukebox ['dʒuːkbɒks] n máquina f de discos.

Jul. (abbr of July) jul.

July [dʒuː'laı] n julio m, → **September**.

jumble sale ['dʒʌmbl-] n (Br) rastrillo m benéfico.

---

i │ JUMBLE SALE

Las "jumble sales" son mercadillos muy baratos de ropa, libros y objetos domésticos de segunda mano. Normalmente se celebran en locales pertenecientes a iglesias o en centros sociales, para recaudar dinero con fines benéficos.

jumbo ['dʒʌmbəʊ] adj (inf) (pack) familiar; (sausage, sandwich) gigante.

jumbo jet n jumbo m.

jump [dʒʌmp] ◆ n salto m ◆ vi (through air) saltar; (with fright) sobresaltarse; (increase) aumentar de golpe ◆ vt (Am: train, bus) montarse sin pagar en; **to ~ the queue** (Br) colarse.

jumper ['dʒʌmpə'] n (Br: pullover) jersey m; (Am: dress) pichi m.

jump leads npl cables mpl de empalme.

junction ['dʒʌŋkʃn] n (of roads) cruce m; (of railway lines) empalme m.

June [dʒuːn] n junio m, → September.

jungle ['dʒʌŋgl] n selva f.

junior ['dʒuːnjə'] adj (of lower rank) de rango inferior; (Am: after name) júnior (inv) ◆ n: **she's my ~** es más joven que yo.

junior school n (Br) escuela f primaria.

junk [dʒʌŋk] n (inf: unwanted things) trastos mpl.

junk food n (inf) comida preparada poco nutritiva o saludable.

junkie ['dʒʌŋkɪ] n (inf) yonqui mf.

junk shop n tienda f de objetos de segunda mano.

jury ['dʒʊərɪ] n jurado m.

just [dʒʌst] adj justo(-a) ◆ adv (exactly) justamente; (only) sólo; **I'm ~ coming** ahora voy; **we were ~ leaving** justo íbamos a salir; **a ~ a bit more** un poquito más; **~ as good** igual de bueno; **~ over an hour** poco más de una hora; **passengers ~ arriving** los pasajeros que acaban de llegar; **to be ~ about to do sthg** estar a punto de hacer algo; **to have ~ done sthg** acabar de hacer algo; **~ about** casi; **(only) ~ (almost not)** por los pelos; **~ a minute!** ¡un minuto!

justice ['dʒʌstɪs] n justicia f.

justify ['dʒʌstɪfaɪ] vt justificar.

jut [dʒʌt]: **jut out** vi sobresalir.

juvenile ['dʒuːvənaɪl] adj (young) juvenil; (childish) infantil.

K

kangaroo [ˌkæŋgə'ruː] (pl -s) n canguro m.

karaoke [ˌkærɪ'əʊkɪ] n karaoke m.

karate [kə'rɑːtɪ] n kárate m.

kebab [kɪ'bæb] n (shish kebab) pincho m moruno; (doner kebab) pan árabe relleno de ensalada y carne de cordero, con salsa.

keel [ki:l] n quilla f.

keen [ki:n] adj (enthusiastic) entusiasta; (eyesight, hearing) agudo (-da); **to be ~ on** ser aficionado(-da) a; **to be ~ to do sthg** tener ganas de hacer algo.

keep [ki:p] (pt & pp **kept**) vt (change, book, object loaned) quedarse con; (job, old clothes) conservar; (store, not tell) guardar; (cause to remain) mantener; (promise) cumplir; (appointment) acudir a; (delay) retener; (record, diary) llevar ◆ vi (food) conservarse; (remain) mantenerse; **to ~ (on) doing sthg** (do continuously) seguir haciendo algo; (do repeatedly) no dejar de hacer algo; **to ~ sb from doing sthg** impedir a alguien hacer algo; **~ back!** ¡atrás!; **"~ in lane!"** señal que advierte a los conductores que se mantengan en el carril; **"~ left"** "¡circula por la izquierda!"; **"~ off the grass!"** "no pisar la hierba"; **"~ out!"** "prohibida la entrada"; **"~ your distance!"** señal que incita a mantener la distancia de prudencia; **to ~ clear (of)** mantenerse alejado (de) ❑ **keep up** vt sep mantener ◆ vi (maintain pace, level etc) mantener el ritmo.

keep-fit n (Br) ejercicios mpl de mantenimiento.

kennel ['kenl] n caseta f del perro.

kept [kept] pt & pp → **keep**.

kerb [kɜ:b] n (Br) bordillo m.

kerosene ['kerəsi:n] n (Am) queroseno m.

ketchup ['ketʃəp] n catsup m.

kettle ['ketl] n tetera f para hervir; **to put the ~ on** poner a hervir la tetera.

key [ki:] n (for lock) llave f; (of piano, typewriter) tecla f; (of map) clave f ◆ adj clave (inv).

keyboard ['ki:bɔ:d] n teclado m.

keyhole ['ki:həul] n ojo m de la cerradura.

keypad ['ki:pæd] n teclado m.

key ring n llavero m.

kg (abbr of kilogram) kg.

kick [kik] n (of foot) patada f ◆ vt (with foot) dar una patada.

kickoff ['kikɒf] n saque m inicial.

kid [kid] n (inf) (child) crío m (-a f); (young person) chico m (-ca f) ◆ vi bromear.

kidnap ['kidnæp] vt secuestrar.

kidnaper ['kidnæpər] (Am) = **kidnapper**.

kidnapper ['kidnæpər] n (Br) secuestrador m (-ra f).

kidney ['kidni] (pl -s) n riñón m.

kidney bean n judía f pinta.

kill [kil] vt matar; **my feet are ~ing me!** ¡los pies me están matando!

killer ['kilər] n asesino m (-na f).

kilo ['ki:ləu] (pl -s) n kilo m.

kilogram ['kiləgræm] n kilogramo m.

kilometre ['kilə,mi:tər] n kilómetro m.

kilt [kilt] n falda f escocesa.

kind [kaind] adj amable ◆ n tipo m; **~ of** (Am: inf) un poco, algo.

kindergarten ['kində,gɑ:tn] n jardín m de infancia.

kindly ['kaindli] adv: **would you ~ ...?** ¿sería tan amable de ...?

kindness ['kaindnis] *n* amabilidad *f*.

king [kiŋ] *n* rey *m*.

kingfisher ['kiŋ,fiʃəʳ] *n* martín *m* pescador.

king prawn *n* langostino *m*.

king-size bed *n* cama *f* gigante.

kiosk ['ki:ɒsk] *n* (*for newspapers etc*) quiosco *m*; (*Br: phone box*) cabina *f*.

kipper ['kipəʳ] *n* arenque *m* ahumado.

kiss [kis] *n* beso *m* ◆ *vt* besar.

kiss of life *n* boca a boca *m inv*.

kit [kit] *n* (*set, clothes*) equipo *m*; (*for assembly*) modelo *m* para armar.

kitchen ['kitʃin] *n* cocina *f*.

kitchen unit *n* módulo *m* de cocina.

kite [kait] *n* (*toy*) cometa *f*.

kitten ['kitn] *n* gatito *m*.

kitty ['kiti] *n* (*for regular expenses*) fondo *m* común.

kiwi fruit ['ki:wi:-] *n* kiwi *m*.

Kleenex® ['kli:neks] *n* kleenex® *m inv*.

km (*abbr of kilometre*) km.

km/h (*abbr of kilometres per hour*) km/h.

knack [næk] *n*: **I've got the ~** (**of it**) **he cogido el tranquillo.**

knackered ['nækəd] *adj* (*Br: inf*) hecho(-cha) polvo.

knapsack ['næpsæk] *n* mochila *f*.

knee [ni:] *n* rodilla *f*.

kneecap ['ni:kæp] *n* rótula *f*.

kneel [ni:l] (*Br pt & pp* **knelt**

[nelt], *Am pt & pp* **knelt** OR **-ed**) *vi* (*be on one's knees*) estar de rodillas; (*go down on one's knees*) arrodillarse.

knew [nju:] *pt* → **know**.

knickers ['nikəz] *npl* (*Br: underwear*) bragas *fpl*.

knife [naif] (*pl* **knives**) *n* cuchillo *m*.

knight [nait] *n* (*in history*) caballero *m*; (*in chess*) caballo *m*.

knit [nit] *vt* tejer.

knitted ['nitid] *adj* de punto.

knitting ['nitiŋ] *n* (*thing being knitted*) punto *m*; (*activity*) labor *f* de punto.

knitting needle *n* aguja *f* de hacer punto.

knitwear ['nitweəʳ] *n* género *m* de punto.

knives [naivz] *pl* → **knife**.

knob [nɒb] *n* (*on door etc*) pomo *m*; (*on machine*) botón *m*.

knock [nɒk] *n* (*at door*) golpe *m* ◆ *vt* (*hit*) golpear; (*one's head, leg*) golpearse ◆ *vi* (*at door etc*) llamar **a knock down** *vt sep* (*pedestrian*) atropellar; (*building*) derribar; (*price*) bajar; **knock out** *vt sep* (*make unconscious*) dejar sin conocimiento; (*of competition*) eliminar; **knock over** *vt sep* (*glass, vase*) volcar; (*pedestrian*) atropellar.

knocker ['nɒkəʳ] *n* (*on door*) aldaba *f*.

knot [nɒt] *n* nudo *m*.

know [nəu] (*pt* **knew**, *pp* **known**) *vt* (*have knowledge of*) saber; (*language*) saber hablar; (*person, place*) conocer; **to get to ~ sb** llegar a conocer a alguien; **to ~ about sthg**

(understand) saber de algo; *(have heard)* saber algo; **to ~ how to do sthg** saber hacer algo; **to ~ of** conocer; **to be ~n as** ser conocido como; **to let sb ~ sthg** avisar a alguien de algo; **you ~** *(for emphasis)* ¿sabes?

knowledge ['nɒlɪdʒ] *n* conocimiento *m*; **to my ~** que yo sepa.

known [nəʊn] *pp* → **know.**

knuckle ['nʌkl] *n (of hand)* nudillo *m; (of pork)* jarrete *m.*

Koran [kɒ'rɑːn] *n*: **the ~** el Corán.

L

l *(abbr of litre)* l.

L *(abbr of learner)* L.

lab [læb] *n (inf)* laboratorio *m.*

label ['leɪbl] *n* etiqueta *f.*

labor ['leɪbər] *(Am)* = **labour.**

laboratory *[Br* lə'bɒrətrɪ, *Am* 'læbrə,tɔːrɪ] *n* laboratorio *m.*

labour ['leɪbər] *(Br) n (work)* trabajo *m;* **in ~** *(MED)* de parto.

labourer ['leɪbərər] *n* obrero *m* (-ra *f*).

Labour Party *n (Br)* partido *m* Laborista.

labour-saving *adj* que ahorra trabajo.

lace [leɪs] *n (material)* encaje *m; (for shoe)* cordón *m.*

lace-ups *npl* zapatos *mpl* con cordones.

lack [læk] *n* falta *f* ◆ *vt* carecer de ◆ *vi*: **to be ~ing** faltar.

lacquer ['lækər] *n* laca *f.*

lad [læd] *n (inf)* chaval *m.*

ladder ['lædər] *n (for climbing)* escalera *f* (de mano); *(Br: in tights)* carrera *f.*

ladies ['leɪdɪz] *n (Br)* lavabo *m* de señoras.

ladies' room *(Am)* = **ladies.**

ladieswear ['leɪdɪz,weər] *n* ropa *f* de señoras.

ladle ['leɪdl] *n* cucharón *m.*

lady ['leɪdɪ] *n (woman)* señora *f; (woman of high status)* dama *f.*

ladybird ['leɪdɪbɜːd] *n* mariquita *f.*

lag [læg] *vi* retrasarse; **to ~ behind** *(move more slowly)* rezagarse.

lager ['lɑːgər] *n* cerveza *f* rubia.

lagoon [lə'guːn] *n* laguna *f.*

laid [leɪd] *pt & pp* → **lay.**

lain [leɪn] *pp* → **lie.**

lake [leɪk] *n* lago *m.*

Lake District *n*: **the ~** el Distrito de los Lagos al noroeste de Inglaterra.

lamb [læm] *n* cordero *m.*

lamb chop *n* chuleta *f* de cordero.

lame [leɪm] *adj* cojo(-ja).

lamp [læmp] *n (light)* lámpara *f; (in street)* farola *f.*

lamppost ['læmppəʊst] *n* farol *m.*

lampshade ['læmpʃeɪd] *n* pantalla *f.*

land [lænd] *n* tierra *f; (property)* tierras *fpl* ◆ *vi (plane)* aterrizar;

(passengers) desembarcar; *(fall)* caer.

landing ['lændɪŋ] *n (of plane)* aterrizaje *m; (on stairs)* rellano *m*.

landlady ['lænd,leɪdɪ] *n (of house)* casera *f; (of pub)* dueña *f*.

landlord ['lændlɔːd] *n (of house)* casero *m; (of pub)* dueño *m*.

landmark ['lændmɑːk] *n* punto *m* de referencia.

landscape ['lændskeɪp] *n* paisaje *m*.

landslide ['lændslaɪd] *n (of earth, rocks)* desprendimiento *m* de tierras.

lane [leɪn] *n (in town)* calleja *f; (in country, on road)* camino *m;* "**get in** ~" señal que advierte a los conductores que tomen el carril adecuado.

language ['læŋgwɪdʒ] *n (of a people, country)* idioma *m; (system of communication, words)* lenguaje *m*.

Lanzarote [,lænzə'rɒtɪ] *n* Lanzarote.

lap [læp] *n (of person)* regazo *m; (of race)* vuelta *f*.

lapel [lə'pel] *n* solapa *f*.

lapse [læps] *vi (passport, membership)* caducar.

lard [lɑːd] *n* manteca *f* de cerdo.

larder ['lɑːdəʳ] *n* despensa *f*.

large [lɑːdʒ] *adj* grande.

largely ['lɑːdʒlɪ] *adv* en gran parte.

large-scale *adj* de gran escala.

lark [lɑːk] *n* alondra *f*.

laryngitis [,lærɪn'dʒaɪtɪs] *n* laringitis *f inv*.

lasagne [lə'zænjə] *n* lasaña *f*.

laser ['leɪzəʳ] *n* láser *m*.

lass [læs] *n (inf)* chavala *f*.

last [lɑːst] *adj* último(-ma) ◆ *adv (most recently)* por última vez; *(at the end)* en último lugar ◆ *pron:* **the ~ to come** el último en venir; **the ~ but one** el penúltimo (la penúltima); **the time before ~** la penúltima vez; ~ **year** el año pasado; **the ~ year** el año pasado; **at ~** por fin.

lastly ['lɑːstlɪ] *adv* por último.

last-minute *adj* de última hora.

latch [lætʃ] *n* pestillo *m;* **to be on the ~** tener el pestillo echado.

late [leɪt] *adj (not on time)* con retraso; *(after usual time)* tardío(-a); *(dead)* difunto(-ta) ◆ *adv (not on time)* con retraso; *(after usual time)* tarde; **in ~ June** a finales de junio; **in the ~ afternoon** al final de la tarde; ~ **in June** a finales de junio; **to be (running)** ~ ir con retraso.

lately ['leɪtlɪ] *adv* últimamente.

late-night *adj* de última hora, de noche.

later ['leɪtəʳ] *adj* posterior ◆ *adv:* ~ **(on)** más tarde; **at a ~ date** en una fecha posterior.

latest ['leɪtɪst] *adj:* **the ~ fashion** la última moda; **the ~** lo último; **at the ~** como muy tarde.

lather ['lɑːðəʳ] *n* espuma *f*.

Latin ['lætɪn] *n* latín *m*.

Latin America *n* América Latina.

Latin American *adj* latinoamericano(-na) ◆ *n* latinoamericano *m (-na f)*.

latitude ['lætɪtjuːd] *n* latitud *f*.

latter ['lætəʳ] *n:* **the ~** éste *m (-ta f)*.

laugh [lɑːf] n risa f ◆ vi reírse; **to have a ~** (Br: inf) pasarlo bomba ❏ **laugh at** vt fus reírse de.

laughter ['lɑːftə'] n risa f.

launch [lɔːntʃ] vt (boat) botar; (new product) lanzar.

laund(e)rette [lɔːn'dret] n lavandería f.

laundry ['lɔːndrɪ] n (washing) ropa f sucia; (place) lavandería f.

lavatory ['lævətrɪ] n servicio m.

lavender ['lævəndə'] n lavanda f.

lavish ['lævɪʃ] adj (meal, decoration) espléndido(-da).

law [lɔː] n ley f; (study) derecho m; **the ~** (JUR: set of rules) la ley; **to be against the ~** estar en contra de la ley.

lawn [lɔːn] n césped m.

lawnmower ['lɔːnˌməʊə'] n cortacésped m.

lawyer ['lɔːjə'] n abogado m (-da f).

laxative ['læksətɪv] n laxante m.

lay [leɪ] (pt & pp laid) pt → **lie** ◆ vt (place) colocar; (egg) poner; **to ~ the table** poner la mesa ❏ **lay off** vt sep (worker) despedir; **lay on** vt sep proveer; **lay out** vt sep (display) disponer.

lay-by (pl lay-bys) n área f de descanso.

layer ['leɪə'] n capa f.

layman ['leɪmən] (pl -men [-mən]) n lego m (-ga f).

layout ['leɪaʊt] n (of building, streets) trazado m.

lazy ['leɪzɪ] adj perezoso(-sa).

lb (abbr of pound) lb.

lead¹ [liːd] (pt & pp led) vt (take) llevar; (be in charge of) estar al frente de; (be in front of) encabezar ◆ vi (be winning) ir en cabeza ◆ n (for dog) correa f; (cable) cable m; **to ~ sb to do sthg** llevar a alguien a hacer algo; **to ~ to** (go to) conducir a; (result in) llevar a; **to ~ the way** guiar; **to be in the ~** llevar la delantera.

lead² [led] n (metal) plomo m; (for pencil) mina f ◆ adj de plomo.

leaded petrol [ledɪd-] n gasolina f con plomo.

leader ['liːdə'] n líder mf.

leadership ['liːdəʃɪp] n (position of leader) liderazgo m.

lead-free [led-] adj sin plomo.

leading ['liːdɪŋ] adj (most important) destacado(-da).

lead singer [liːd-] n cantante mf (de un grupo).

leaf [liːf] (pl leaves) n (of tree) hoja f.

leaflet ['liːflɪt] n folleto m.

league [liːg] n liga f.

leak [liːk] n (hole) agujero m; (of gas, water) escape m ◆ vi (roof, tank) tener goteras.

lean [liːn] (pt & pp leant [lent] OR -ed) adj (meat) magro(-gra); (person, animal) delgado y musculoso (delgada y musculosa) ◆ vi (bend) inclinarse ◆ vt: **to ~ sthg against sthg** apoyar algo contra algo; **to ~ on** apoyarse en; **to ~ forward** inclinarse hacia delante; **to ~ over** inclinarse.

leap [liːp] (pt & pp leapt [lept] OR -ed) vi saltar.

leap year n año m bisiesto.

learn [lɜːn] (pt & pp learnt OR -ed) vt aprender; **to ~ (how) to do**

sthg aprender a hacer algo; **to ~ about sthg** *(hear about)* enterarse de algo; *(study)* aprender algo.

learner (driver) [ˈlɜːnəʳ-] *n* conductor *m* principiante.

learnt [lɜːnt] *pt & pp* → **learn**.

lease [liːs] *n* arriendo *m* ◆ *vt* arrendar; **to ~ sthg from sb** arrendar algo de alguien; **to ~ sthg to sb** arrendar algo a alguien.

leash [liːʃ] *n* correa *f*.

least [liːst] *adj* adv menos ◆ *pron*: **(the) ~** menos; **I have ~ food** soy la que menos comida tiene; **I like him ~** él es el que menos me gusta; **he paid (the) ~** es el que menos pagó; **it's the ~ you could do** es lo menos que puedes hacer; **at ~** *(with quantities, numbers)* por lo menos; *(to indicate an advantage)* al menos.

leather [ˈleðəʳ] *n* piel *f* □
leathers *npl* cazadora y pantalón de cuero utilizados por motociclistas.

leave [liːv] *(pt & pp left)* *vt* dejar; *(go away from)* salir de; *(not take away)* dejarse ◆ *vi (person)* marcharse; *(train, bus etc)* salir ◆ *n (time off work)* permiso *m*; **to ~ a message** dejar un mensaje, → **left**
leave behind *vt sep (not take away)* dejar; **leave out** *vt sep* omitir.

leaves [liːvz] *pl* → **leaf**.

Lebanon [ˈlebənən] *n* Líbano *m*.

lecture [ˈlektʃəʳ] *n (at university)* clase *f*; *(at conference)* conferencia *f*.

lecturer [ˈlektʃərəʳ] *n* profesor *m* (-ra *f*) de universidad.

lecture theatre *n* aula *f*.

led [led] *pt & pp* → **lead¹**.

ledge [ledʒ] *n (of window)* alféizar *m*.

leek [liːk] *n* puerro *m*.

left [left] *pt & pp* → **leave** ◆ *adj (not right)* izquierdo(-da) ◆ *adv* a la izquierda ◆ *n* izquierda *f*; **on the ~** a la izquierda; **there are none ~** no queda ninguno (más).

left-hand *adj* izquierdo(-da).

left-hand drive *n* vehículo *m* con el volante a la izquierda.

left-handed [-ˈhændɪd] *adj (person)* zurdo(-da); *(implement)* para zurdos.

left-luggage locker *n (Br)* consigna *f* automática.

left-luggage office *n (Br)* consigna *f*.

left-wing *adj* de izquierdas.

leg [leg] *n (of person)* pierna *f*; *(of animal, table, chair)* pata *f*; *(of trousers)* pernera *f*; **~ of lamb** pierna de cordero.

legal [ˈliːgl] *adj* legal.

legal aid *n* ayuda financiera para personas que no poseen posibilidades económicas para pagar a un abogado.

legalize [ˈliːgəlaɪz] *vt* legalizar.

legal system *n* sistema *m* jurídico.

legend [ˈledʒənd] *n* leyenda *f*.

leggings [ˈlegɪnz] *npl* mallas *fpl*.

legible [ˈledʒɪbl] *adj* legible.

legislation [ˌledʒɪsˈleɪʃn] *n* legislación *f*.

legitimate [lɪˈdʒɪtɪmət] *adj* legítimo(-ma).

leisure [*Br* ˈleʒəʳ, *Am* ˈliːʒəʳ] *n* ocio *m*.

leisure centre *n* centro *m* deportivo y cultural.

leisure pool *n* piscina *f* (recreativa).

lemon ['lemən] n limón m.

lemonade [,lemə'neɪd] n gaseosa f.

lemon curd [-kɜːd] n (Br) dulce para untar hecho con limón, huevos, mantequilla y azúcar.

lemon juice n zumo m de limón.

lemon meringue pie n tarta de masa quebrada con crema de limón y una capa de merengue.

lemon sole n platija f.

lemon tea n té m con limón.

lend [lend] (pt & pp **lent**) vt prestar; to ~ sb sthg prestarle algo a alguien.

length [leŋθ] n (in distance) longitud f; (in time) duración f; (of swimming pool) largo m.

lengthen ['leŋθən] vt alargar.

lens [lenz] n (of camera) objetivo m; (of glasses) lente f; (contact lens) lentilla f.

lent [lent] pt & pp → **lend**.

Lent [lent] n Cuaresma f.

lentils ['lentlz] npl lentejas fpl.

leopard ['lepəd] n leopardo m.

leopard-skin adj estampado(-da) en piel de leopardo.

leotard ['liːətɑːd] n body m.

leper ['lepər] n leproso m (-sa f).

lesbian ['lezbɪən] adj lesbiano(-na) ♦ n lesbiana f.

less [les] adj, adv, pron menos; ~ than 20 menos de 20; I eat ~ than her yo como menos que ella.

lesson ['lesn] n (class) clase f.

let [let] (pt & pp **let**) vt (allow) dejar; (rent out) alquilar; to ~ sb do sthg dejar hacer algo a alguien; to ~ go of sthg soltar algo; to ~ sb

have sthg prestar algo a alguien; to ~ sb know sthg avisar a alguien de algo; ~'s go! ¡vamos!; "to ~" "se alquila" ❑ **let in** vt sep dejar entrar; **let off** vt sep (not punish) perdonar; she ~ me off doing it me dejó no hacerlo; can you ~ me off at the station? ¿puede dejarme en la estación?; **let out** vt sep (allow to go out) dejar salir.

letdown ['letdaʊn] n (inf) desilusión f.

lethargic [lə'θɑːdʒɪk] adj aletargado(-da).

letter ['letər] n (written message) carta f; (of alphabet) letra f.

letterbox ['letəbɒks] n (Br) buzón m.

lettuce ['letɪs] n lechuga f.

leuk(a)emia [luː'kiːmɪə] n leucemia f.

level ['levl] adj (horizontal) plano(-na) ♦ n nivel m; (storey) planta f; to be ~ with (in height) estar a nivel de; (in standard) estar al mismo nivel que.

level crossing n (Br) paso m a nivel.

lever [Br 'liːvər, Am 'levər] n palanca f.

liability [,laɪə'bɪlətɪ] n (responsibility) responsabilidad f.

liable ['laɪəbl] adj: to be ~ to do sthg tener tendencia a hacer algo; to be ~ for sthg ser responsable de algo.

liaise [lɪ'eɪz] vi: to ~ with mantener contacto con.

liar ['laɪər] n mentiroso m (-sa f).

liberal ['lɪbərəl] adj (tolerant) liberal; (generous) generoso(-sa).

Liberal Democrat Party n partido m demócrata liberal.

liberate ['lɪbəreɪt] vt liberar.

liberty ['lɪbətɪ] n libertad f.

librarian [laɪ'breərɪən] n bibliotecario m (-ria f).

library ['laɪbrərɪ] n biblioteca f.

Libya ['lɪbɪə] n Libia.

lice [laɪs] npl piojos mpl.

licence ['laɪsəns] n (Br) permiso m ♦ vt (Am) = **license**.

license ['laɪsəns] vt (Br) autorizar ♦ vt (Am) = **licence**.

licensed ['laɪsənst] adj (restaurant, bar) autorizado(-da) para vender bebidas alcohólicas.

licensing hours ['laɪsənsɪŋ-] npl (Br) horario en que se autoriza la venta de bebidas alcohólicas al público en un "pub".

lick [lɪk] vt lamer.

lid [lɪd] n (cover) tapa f.

lie [laɪ] (pt lay, cont lying) n mentira f ♦ vi (tell lie: pt & pp **lied**) mentir; (be horizontal) estar echado; (lie down) echarse; (be situated) encontrarse; **to tell ~s** contar mentiras; **to ~ about sthg** mentir respecto a algo ❑ **lie down** vi acostarse.

lieutenant [Br lef'tenənt, Am lu:'tenənt] n teniente m.

life [laɪf] (pl **lives**) n vida f.

life assurance n seguro m de vida.

life belt n salvavidas m inv.

lifeboat ['laɪfbəʊt] n (launched from shore) bote m salvavidas; (launched from ship) lancha f de salvamento.

lifeguard ['laɪfɡɑːd] n soco-

rrista mf.

life jacket n chaleco m salvavidas.

lifelike ['laɪflaɪk] adj realista.

life preserver [-prɪ'zɜːvər] n (Am) (life belt) salvavidas m inv; (life jacket) chaleco m salvavidas.

life-size adj de tamaño natural.

lifespan ['laɪfspæn] n vida f.

lifestyle ['laɪfstaɪl] n estilo m de vida.

lift [lɪft] n (Br: elevator) ascensor m ♦ vt (raise) levantar ♦ vi (fog) despejarse; **to give sb a ~** llevar a alguien (en automóvil) ❑ **lift up** vt sep levantar.

light [laɪt] (pt & pp **lit** OR **-ed**) adj ligero(-ra); (in colour) claro(-ra); (rain) fino(-na) ♦ n luz f; (for cigarette) fuego m ♦ vt (fire, cigarette) encender; (room, stage) iluminar; **have you got a ~?** ¿tienes fuego?; **to set ~ to sthg** prender fuego a algo ❑ **lights** (traffic lights) semáforo m; **light up** vt sep (house, road) iluminar ♦ vi (inf: light a cigarette) encender un cigarrillo.

light bulb n bombilla f.

lighter ['laɪtər] n mechero m.

light-hearted [-'hɑːtɪd] adj alegre.

lighthouse ['laɪthaʊs, pl -haʊzɪz] n faro m.

lighting ['laɪtɪŋ] n iluminación f.

light meter n contador m de la luz.

lightning ['laɪtnɪŋ] n relámpagos mpl.

lightweight ['laɪtweɪt] adj (clothes, object) ligero(-ra).

like [laɪk] prep como; (typical of)

típico de ◆ vt (want) querer; **I ~ beer** me gusta la cerveza; **I ~ them** me gustan; **I ~ doing it** me gusta hacerlo; **what's it ~?** ¿cómo es?; ~ **that** así; ~ **this** así; **to look ~ sb/sthg** parecerse a alguien/a algo; **I'd ~ to come** me gustaría venir; **I'd ~ to sit down** quisiera sentarme; **I'd ~ a drink** me apetece tomar algo.

likelihood ['laɪklɪhʊd] n probabilidad f.

likely ['laɪklɪ] adj probable.

likeness ['laɪknɪs] n (similarity) parecido m.

likewise ['laɪkwaɪz] adv del mismo modo.

lilac ['laɪlək] adj lila (inv).

Lilo® ['laɪləʊ] (pl -s) n (Br) colchoneta f.

lily ['lɪlɪ] n azucena f.

lily of the valley n lirio m de los valles.

limb [lɪm] n miembro m.

lime [laɪm] n (fruit) lima f; ~ (juice) refresco m de lima.

limestone ['laɪmstəʊn] n piedra f caliza.

limit ['lɪmɪt] n límite m ◆ vt limitar; **the city ~s** los límites de la ciudad.

limited ['lɪmɪtɪd] adj limitado(-da).

limp [lɪmp] adj flojo(-ja) ◆ vi cojear.

line [laɪn] n línea f; (row) fila f; (Am: queue) cola f; (of words on page) renglón m; (of poem, song) verso m; (for fishing) sedal m; (for washing, rope) cuerda f; (railway track) vía f; (of business, work) especialidad f; (type of food) surtido m ◆ vt (coat, drawers) forrar; **in** ~ (aligned) alineado(-da); **it's a bad** ~ hay interferencias; **the** ~ **is engaged** está comunicando; **to drop sb a** ~ (inf) escribir unas letras a alguien; **to stand in** ~ (Am) hacer cola ❑ **line up** vt sep (arrange) programar ◆ vi alinearse.

lined [laɪnd] adj (paper) de rayas.

linen ['lɪnɪn] n (cloth) lino m; (tablecloths, sheets) ropa f blanca.

liner ['laɪnər] n (ship) transatlántico m.

linesman ['laɪnzmən] (pl -men [-mən]) n juez mf de línea.

linger ['lɪŋgər] vi (in place) rezagarse.

lingerie ['lænʒərɪ] n lencería f.

lining ['laɪnɪŋ] n forro m.

link [lɪŋk] n (connection) conexión f; (between countries, companies) vínculo m ◆ vt (connect) conectar; **rail** ~ enlace m ferroviario; **road** ~ conexión de carreteras.

lino ['laɪnəʊ] n (Br) linóleo m.

lion ['laɪən] n león m.

lioness ['laɪənes] n leona f.

lip [lɪp] n labio m.

lip salve [-sælv] n protector m labial.

lipstick ['lɪpstɪk] n barra f de labios.

liqueur [lɪ'kjʊər] n licor m.

liquid ['lɪkwɪd] n líquido m.

liquor ['lɪkər] n (Am) bebida f alcohólica.

liquorice ['lɪkərɪs] n regaliz m.

lisp [lɪsp] n ceceo m.

list [lɪst] n lista f ◆ vt hacer una lista de.

listen ['lɪsn] vi: **to ~ (to)** (to person, sound, radio) escuchar; (to advice) hacer caso (de).

listener ['lɪsnə] n (to radio) oyente mf.

lit [lɪt] pt & pp → light.

liter ['liːtə] (Am) = litre.

literally ['lɪtərəlɪ] adv literalmente.

literary ['lɪtərərɪ] adj literario(-ria).

literature ['lɪtrətʃə] n literatura f; (printed information) folletos mpl informativos.

litre ['liːtə] n (Br) litro m.

litter ['lɪtə] n basura f.

litterbin ['lɪtəbɪn] n (Br) papelera f (en la calle).

little ['lɪtl] adj pequeño(-ña); (distance, time) corto(-ta); (not much) poco(-ca) ◆ adv poco ◆ pron: **I have very ~** tengo muy poco; **as ~ as possible** lo menos posible; **~ by ~** poco a poco; **a ~** (sugar un poco de azúcar; **a ~ while** un rato.

little finger n meñique m.

live¹ [lɪv] vi vivir; **to ~ with sb** vivir con alguien ❑ **live together** vi vivir juntos.

live² [laɪv] adj (alive) vivo(-va); (programme, performance) en directo; (wire) cargado(-da) ◆ adv en directo.

lively ['laɪvlɪ] adj (person) vivaz; (place, atmosphere) animado(-da).

liver ['lɪvə] n hígado m.

lives [laɪvz] pl → life.

living ['lɪvɪŋ] adj (alive) vivo(-va) ◆ n: **to earn a ~** ganarse la vida; **what do you do for a ~?** ¿en qué trabajas?

living room n sala f de estar.

lizard ['lɪzəd] n lagartija f.

load [ləʊd] n (thing carried) carga f ◆ vt cargar; **~s of** (inf) un montón de.

loaf [ləʊf] (pl loaves) n: **~ (of bread)** barra f de pan.

loan [ləʊn] n préstamo m ◆ vt prestar.

loathe [ləʊð] vt detestar.

loaves [ləʊvz] pl → loaf.

lobby ['lɒbɪ] n (hall) vestíbulo m.

lobster ['lɒbstə] n langosta f.

local ['ləʊkl] adj local ◆ n (inf) (local person) vecino m (del lugar); (Br: pub) = bar m del barrio; (Am: bus) autobús m urbano; (Am: train) tren m de cercanías.

local anaesthetic n anestesia f local.

local call n llamada f urbana.

local government n administración f local.

locate [Br ləʊˈkeɪt, Am ˈləʊkeɪt] vt (find) localizar; **to be ~d** estar situado.

location [ləʊˈkeɪʃn] n (place) situación f.

loch [lɒk] n (Scot) lago m.

lock [lɒk] n (on door, drawer) cerradura f; (for bike) candado m; (on canal) esclusa f ◆ vt (fasten with key) cerrar con llave; (keep safely) poner bajo llave ◆ vi (become stuck) bloquearse ❑ **lock in** vt sep (accidentally) dejar encerrado; **lock out** vt sep (accidentally) dejar fuera accidentalmente; **lock up** vt sep (imprison) encarcelar ◆ vi cerrar con llave.

locker ['lɒkəʳ] n taquilla f.

locker room n (Am) vestuario m (con taquillas).

locket ['lɒkɪt] n guardapelo m.

locomotive [,ləʊkə'məʊtɪv] n locomotora f.

locum ['ləʊkəm] n interino m (-na f).

locust ['ləʊkəst] n langosta f (insecto).

lodge [lɒdʒ] n (for hunters, skiers) refugio m ♦ vi alojarse.

lodger ['lɒdʒəʳ] n huésped mf.

lodgings ['lɒdʒɪŋz] npl habitación f alquilada.

loft [lɒft] n desván m.

log [lɒg] n tronco m.

logic ['lɒdʒɪk] n lógica f.

logical ['lɒdʒɪkl] adj lógico(-ca).

logo ['ləʊgəʊ] (pl -s) n logotipo m.

loin [lɔɪn] n lomo m.

loiter ['lɔɪtəʳ] vi merodear.

lollipop ['lɒlɪpɒp] n chupachús m inv.

lolly ['lɒlɪ] n (inf) (lollipop) chupachús m inv; (Br: ice lolly) polo m.

London ['lʌndən] n Londres.

Londoner ['lʌndənəʳ] n londinense mf.

lonely ['ləʊnlɪ] adj (person) solo(-la); (place) solitario(-ria).

long [lɒŋ] adj largo(-ga) ♦ adv mucho (tiempo); it's 2 metres ~ mide 2 metros de largo; it's two hours ~ dura dos horas; how ~ is it? (in distance) ¿cuánto mide (de largo)?; (in time) ¿cuánto tiempo dura?; a ~ time mucho tiempo; all day ~ todo el día; as ~ as mientras (que); for ~ mucho tiempo; I'm no ~er interested ya no me interesa;

so ~! (inf) ¡hasta luego! ❑ **long for** vt fus desear vivamente.

long-distance call n conferencia f (telefónica).

long drink n combinado de alcohol y refresco.

long-haul adj de larga distancia.

longitude ['lɒndʒɪtjuːd] n longitud f.

long jump n salto m de longitud.

long-life adj de larga duración.

longsighted [,lɒŋ'saɪtɪd] adj présbita.

long-term adj a largo plazo.

long wave n onda f larga.

longwearing [,lɒŋ'weərɪŋ] adj (Am) duradero(-ra).

loo [luː] (pl -s) n (Br: inf) wáter m.

look [lʊk] n (act of looking) mirada f; (appearance) aspecto m ♦ vi (with eyes, search) mirar; (seem) parecer; you don't ~ well no tienes muy buen aspecto; to ~ onto dar a; to have a ~ (see) echar un vistazo; (search) buscar; (good) ~s atractivo m (físico); I'm just ~ing (in shop) solamente estoy mirando; ~ out! ¡cuidado! ❑ **look after** vt fus (person) cuidar; (matter, arrangements) encargarse de; **look at** vt fus (observe) mirar; (examine) examinar; **look for** vt fus buscar; **look forward to** vt fus esperar (con ilusión); **look out for** vt fus estar atento a; **look round** vt fus (city, museum) visitar; (shop) mirar ♦ vi volver la cabeza; **look up** vt sep (in dictionary, phone book) buscar.

loony ['luːnɪ] n (inf) chiflado m (-da f).

loop [lu:p] n lazo m.

loose [lu:s] adj (not fixed firmly) flojo(-ja); (sweets, sheets of paper) suelto(-ta); (clothes) ancho(-cha); **to let sthg/sb ~** soltar algo/a alguien.

loosen ['lu:sn] vt aflojar.

lop-sided ['saidid] adj ladeado(-da).

lord [lɔ:d] n (member of nobility) lord m, título de nobleza británica.

lorry ['lɒrɪ] n (Br) camión m.

lorry driver n (Br) camionero m (-ra f).

lose [lu:z] (pt & pp lost) vt perder; (subj: watch, clock) atrasarse ♦ vi perder; **to ~ weight** adelgazar.

loser ['lu:zə'] n (in contest) perdedor m (-ra f).

loss [lɒs] n pérdida f.

lost [lɒst] pt & pp → lose ♦ adj perdido(-da); **to get ~** (lose way) perderse.

lost-and-found office n (Am) oficina f de objetos perdidos.

lost property office n (Br) oficina f de objetos perdidos.

lot [lɒt] n (group of things) grupo m; (at auction) lote m; (Am: car park) aparcamiento m; **a ~** (large amount) mucho(-cha), muchos(-chas) (pl); (to a great extent, often) mucho; **a ~ of time** mucho tiempo; **a ~ of problems** muchos problemas; **~s (of)** mucho(-cha), muchos(-chas) (pl); **the ~** (everything) todo.

lotion ['ləʊʃn] n loción f.

lottery ['lɒtərɪ] n lotería f.

loud [laʊd] adj (voice, music, noise) alto(-ta); (colour, clothes) chillón(-ona).

loudspeaker [ˌlaʊd'spi:kə'] n altavoz m.

lounge [laʊndʒ] n (in house) salón m; (at airport) sala f de espera.

lounge bar n (Br) salón-bar m.

lousy ['laʊzɪ] adj (inf: poor-quality) cochambroso(-sa).

lout [laʊt] n gamberro m (-rra f).

love [lʌv] n amor m; (strong liking) pasión f; (in tennis) cero m ♦ vt querer; **I ~ music** me encanta la música; **I'd ~ a coffee** un café me vendría estupendamente; **I ~ playing tennis** me encanta jugar al tenis; **to be in ~** (with) estar enamorado (de); **(with) ~ from** (in letter) un abrazo (de).

love affair n aventura f amorosa.

lovely ['lʌvlɪ] adj (very beautiful) guapísimo(-ma); (very nice) precioso(-sa).

lover ['lʌvə'] n amante mf.

loving ['lʌvɪŋ] adj cariñoso(-sa).

low [ləʊ] adj bajo(-ja); (quality, opinion) malo(-la); (sound, note) grave; (supply) escaso(-sa); (depressed) deprimido(-da) ♦ n (area of low pressure) zona f de baja presión (atmosférica); **we're ~ on petrol** se está terminando la gasolina.

low-alcohol adj bajo(-ja) en alcohol.

low-calorie adj bajo(-ja) en calorías.

low-cut adj escotado(-da).

lower ['ləʊə'] adj inferior ♦ vt (move downwards) bajar; (reduce) reducir.

lower sixth n (Br) primer curso de enseñanza secundaria pre-

universitaria para alumnos de 17 años que preparan sus "A-levels".

low-fat *adj* de bajo contenido graso.

low tide *n* marea *f* baja.

loyal ['lɔɪəl] *adj* leal.

loyalty ['lɔɪəltɪ] *n* lealtad *f*.

lozenge ['lɒzɪndʒ] *n* (*sweet*) caramelo *m* para la tos.

LP *n* LP *m*.

L-plate ['el-] *n* (*Br*) placa *f* de la L (*de prácticas*).

Ltd (*abbr of limited*) S.L.

lubricate ['lu:brɪkeɪt] *vt* lubricar.

luck [lʌk] *n* suerte *f*; **bad ~** mala suerte; **good ~!** ¡buena suerte!; **with ~** con un poco de suerte.

luckily ['lʌkɪlɪ] *adv* afortunadamente.

lucky ['lʌkɪ] *adj* (*person, escape*) afortunado(-da); (*event, situation*) oportuno(-na); (*number, colour*) de la suerte; **to be ~** tener suerte.

ludicrous ['lu:dɪkrəs] *adj* ridículo(-la).

lug [lʌg] *vt* (*inf*) arrastrar.

luggage ['lʌgɪdʒ] *n* equipaje *m*.

luggage compartment *n* maletero *m* (*en tren*).

luggage locker *n* consigna *f* automática.

luggage rack *n* (*on train*) redecilla *f* (*para equipaje*).

lukewarm ['lu:kwɔ:m] *adj* tibio(-bia).

lull [lʌl] *n* intervalo *m*.

lullaby ['lʌləbaɪ] *n* nana *f*.

lumbago [lʌm'beɪgəu] *n* lumbago *m*.

lumber ['lʌmbər] *n* (*Am: timber*) maderos *mpl*.

luminous ['lu:mɪnəs] *adj* luminoso(-sa).

lump [lʌmp] *n* (*of coal, mud, butter*) trozo *m*; (*of sugar*) terrón *m*; (*on body*) bulto *m*.

lump sum *n* suma *f* global.

lumpy ['lʌmpɪ] *adj* (*sauce*) grumoso(-sa); (*mattress*) lleno(-na) de bultos.

lunatic ['lu:nətɪk] *n* (*pej*) loco *m* (-ca *f*).

lunch [lʌntʃ] *n* comida *f*, almuerzo *m*; **to have ~** comer, almorzar.

luncheon ['lʌntʃən] *n* (*fml*) almuerzo *m*.

luncheon meat *n* conserva de carne de cerdo y cereales.

lunch hour *n* hora *f* del almuerzo.

lunchtime ['lʌntʃtaɪm] *n* hora *f* del almuerzo.

lung [lʌŋ] *n* pulmón *m*.

lunge [lʌndʒ] *vi*: **to ~ at** arremeter contra.

lurch [lɜ:tʃ] *vi* tambalearse.

lure [ljuər] *vt* atraer con engaños.

lurk [lɜ:k] *vi* (*person*) estar al acecho.

lush [lʌʃ] *adj* exuberante.

lust [lʌst] *n* (*sexual desire*) lujuria *f*.

Luxembourg ['lʌksəmbɜ:g] *n* Luxemburgo.

luxurious [lʌg'ʒuərɪəs] *adj* lujoso(-sa).

luxury ['lʌkʃərɪ] *adj* de lujo ♦ *n* lujo *m*.

lying ['laɪɪŋ] *cont* → **lie**.

lyrics ['lɪrɪks] *npl* letra *f*.

m n (abbr of metre) m ◆ abbr = mile.

M (Br: abbr of motorway) A; (abbr of medium) M.

MA n (abbr of Master of Arts) máster en letras.

mac [mæk] n (Br: inf) gabardina f.

macaroni [,mækə'rəʊnɪ] n macarrones mpl.

macaroni cheese n macarrones mpl con queso.

machine [mə'ʃiːn] n máquina f.

machinegun [mə'ʃiːngʌn] n ametralladora f.

machinery [mə'ʃiːnərɪ] n maquinaria f.

machine-washable adj lavable a máquina.

mackerel ['mækrəl] (pl inv) n caballa f.

mackintosh ['mækɪntɒʃ] n (Br) gabardina f.

mad [mæd] adj loco(-ca); (angry) furioso(-sa); (uncontrolled) desenfrenado(-da); **to be ~ about** (inf: like a lot) estar loco por; **like ~** (run) como un loco.

Madam ['mædəm] n señora f.

made [meɪd] pt & pp → make.

madeira [mə'dɪərə] n madeira m.

made-to-measure adj hecho(-cha) a medida.

madness ['mædnɪs] n locura f.

magazine [,mægə'ziːn] n revista f.

maggot ['mægət] n gusano m (larva).

magic ['mædʒɪk] n magia f.

magician [mə'dʒɪʃn] n (conjurer) prestidigitador m (-ra f).

magistrate ['mædʒɪstreɪt] n magistrado m (-da f).

magnet ['mægnɪt] n imán m.

magnetic [mæg'netɪk] adj magnético(-ca).

magnificent [mæg'nɪfɪsənt] adj magnífico(-ca).

magnifying glass ['mægnɪfaɪŋ-] n lupa f.

mahogany [mə'hɒgənɪ] n caoba f.

maid [meɪd] n (servant) criada f.

maiden name ['meɪdn-] n nombre m de soltera.

mail [meɪl] n (letters) correspondencia f; (system) correo m ◆ vt (Am) enviar por correo.

mailbox ['meɪlbɒks] n (Am) buzón m.

mailman ['meɪlmən] (pl -men [-mən]) n (Am) cartero m.

mail order n pedido m por correo.

main [meɪn] adj principal.

main course n plato m principal.

main deck n cubierta f principal.

mainland ['meɪnlənd] n: **the ~** el continente.

main line n línea f férrea principal.

mainly ['meɪnlɪ] *adv* principalmente.

main road *n* carretera *f* principal.

mains [meɪnz] *npl*: **the ~** (for electricity) la red eléctrica; (for gas, water) la tubería principal.

main street *n* (Am) calle *f* principal.

maintain [meɪn'teɪn] *vt* mantener.

maintenance ['meɪntənəns] *n* (of car, machine) mantenimiento *m*; (money) pensión *f* de manutención.

maisonette [,meɪzə'net] *n* (Br) piso *m* dúplex.

maize [meɪz] *n* maíz *m*.

major ['meɪdʒəʳ] *adj* (important) importante; (most important) principal ♦ *n* (MIL) comandante *m* ♦ *vi* (Am): **to ~ in** especializarse en.

Majorca [mə'jɔːkə, mə'dʒɔːkə] *n* Mallorca.

majority [mə'dʒɒrɪtɪ] *n* mayoría *f*.

major road *n* carretera *f* principal.

make [meɪk] (*pt & pp* **made**) *vt* 1. (produce, construct) hacer; **to be made of** estar hecho de; **to ~ lunch/supper** hacer la comida/cena; **made in Japan** fabricado en Japón.
2. (perform, do) hacer; **to ~ a mistake** cometer un error; **to ~ a phone call** hacer una llamada.
3. (cause to be, do) hacer; **to ~ sb sad** poner triste a alguien; **to ~ sb happy** hacer feliz a alguien; **the ice made her slip** el hielo le hizo res-

balar; **to ~ sb do sthg** (force) obligar a alguien a hacer algo.
4. (amount to, total) hacer; **that ~s £5** eso hace 5 libras.
5. (calculate) calcular; **I ~ it seven o'clock** calculo que serán las siete.
6. (money) ganar; (profit) obtener; (loss) sufrir.
7. (inf: arrive in time for): **I don't think we'll ~ the 10 o'clock train** no creo que lleguemos para el tren de las diez.
8. (friend, enemy) hacer.
9. (have qualities for) ser; **this would ~ a lovely bedroom** esta habitación sería preciosa como dormitorio.
10. (bed) hacer.
11. (in phrases): **to ~ do** arreglárselas; **to ~ good** (compensate for) indemnizar; **to ~ it** (arrive in time) llegar a tiempo; (be able to go) poder ir.

❑ **make out** *vt sep* (form) rellenar; (cheque, receipt) extender; (see) divisar; (hear) entender; **make up** *vt sep* (invent) inventar; (comprise) formar; (difference) cubrir; **make up for** *vt fus* compensar.

makeshift ['meɪkʃɪft] *adj* improvisado(-da).

make-up *n* maquillaje *m*.

malaria [mə'leərɪə] *n* malaria *f*.

Malaysia [mə'leɪzɪə] *n* Malasia.

male [meɪl] *adj* (person) masculino(-na); (animal) macho ♦ *n* (animal) macho *m*.

malfunction [mæl'fʌŋkʃn] *vi* (fml) funcionar mal.

malignant [mə'lɪgnənt] *adj* (disease, tumour) maligno(-na).

mall [mɔ:l] *n* zona *f* comercial peatonal.

 MALL

Una gran zona ajardinada en el centro de Washington DC, "the Mall" se extiende desde el Capitolio al Monumento a Lincoln. A lo largo de ello se encuentran los distintos museos del Smithsonian Institute, varios museos de arte, la Casa Blanca y los monumentos a Washington y a Jefferson. En el extremo oeste se halla "the Wall", donde se han inscrito los nombres de los soldados muertos en la guerra de Vietnam.

En el Reino Unido, "the Mall" es el nombre de la larga avenida londinense que va desde el Palacio de Buckingham hasta Trafalgar Square.

mallet ['mælɪt] *n* mazo *m*.

malt [mɔ:lt] *n* malta *f*.

maltreat [,mæl'tri:t] *vt* maltratar.

malt whisky *n* whisky *m* de malta.

mammal ['mæml] *n* mamífero *m*.

man [mæn] (*pl* **men**) *n* hombre *m*; (*mankind*) el hombre ◆ *vt*: **the lines are manned 24 hours a day** las líneas están abiertas las 24 horas.

manage ['mænɪdʒ] *vt* (*company, business*) dirigir; (*suitcase, job, food*) poder con ◆ *vi* (*cope*) arreglárselas; **can you ~ Friday?** ¿te viene bien el viernes?; **to ~ to do sthg** conseguir hacer algo.

management ['mænɪdʒmənt] *n*

(*people in charge*) dirección *f*; (*control, running*) gestión *f*.

manager ['mænɪdʒə'] *n* (*of business, bank*) director *m* (-ra *f*); (*of shop*) jefe *m* (-fa *f*); (*of sports team*) = entrenador *m* (-ra *f*).

manageress [,mænɪdʒə'res] *n* (*of business, bank*) directora *f*; (*of shop*) jefa *f*.

managing director ['mænɪdʒɪŋ-] *n* director *m* (-ra *f*) general.

mandarin ['mændərɪn] *n* (*fruit*) mandarina *f*.

mane [meɪn] *n* crin *f*.

maneuver [mə'nu:vər] (*Am*) = **manoeuvre**.

mangetout [,mɒnʒ'tu:] *n* vaina de guisante tierna que se come entera.

mangle ['mæŋgl] *vt* aplastar.

mango ['mæŋgəʊ] (*pl* **-es** OR **-s**) *n* mango *m*.

Manhattan [,mæn'hætn] *n* Manhattan *m*.

 MANHATTAN

Manhattan es el distrito central de Nueva York y se divide en los tres barrios llamados "Downtown", "Midtown" y "Upper". Allí se encuentran rascacielos tan famosos como el Empire State Building y el Chrysler Building y lugares tan conocidos como Central Park, la Quinta Avenida, Broadway, la Estatua de la Libertad y Greenwich Village.

manhole ['mænhəʊl] *n* registro *m* (de alcantarillado).

maniac ['meɪnɪæk] *n* (*inf: wild per-*

son) maníaco *m* (-ca *f*).

manicure ['mænɪkjʊə'] *n* manicura *f*.

manifold ['mænɪfəʊld] *n* colector *m*.

manipulate [mə'nɪpjʊleɪt] *vt* (*person*) manipular; (*machine, controls*) manejar.

mankind [,mæn'kaɪnd] *n* la humanidad.

manly ['mænlɪ] *adj* varonil.

man-made *adj* artificial.

manner ['mænə'] *n* (*way*) manera *f* □ **manners** *npl* modales *mpl*.

manoeuvre [mə'nu:və'] *n* (*Br*) maniobra ◆ *vt* (*Br*) maniobrar.

manor ['mænə'] *n* casa *f* solariega.

mansion ['mænʃn] *n* casa *f* solariega.

manslaughter ['mæn,slɔ:tə'] *n* homicidio *m* no premeditado.

mantelpiece ['mæntlpi:s] *n* repisa *f* de la chimenea.

manual ['mænjʊəl] *adj* manual ◆ *n* manual *m*.

manufacture [,mænjʊ'fæktʃə'] *n* fabricación *f* ◆ *vt* fabricar.

manufacturer [,mænjʊ'fæktʃərə'] *n* fabricante *mf*.

manure [mə'njʊə'] *n* estiércol *m*.

many ['menɪ] (*compar* **more**, *superl* **most**) *adj* muchos(-chas) ◆ *pron* muchos *mpl* (-chas *fpl*); **as ~ as** ... tantos(-tas) como ...; **twice as ~** el doble que; **how ~?** ¿cuántos(-tas)?; **so ~** tantos; **too ~** demasiados(-das).

map [mæp] *n* (*of town*) plano *m*; (*of country*) mapa *m*.

maple syrup ['meɪpl-] *n* jarabe

de arce que se come con crepes, etc.

Mar. (*abbr of March*) mar.

marathon ['mærəθn] *n* maratón *m*.

marble ['mɑ:bl] *n* (*stone*) mármol *m*; (*glass ball*) canica *f*.

march [mɑ:tʃ] *n* (*demonstration*) manifestación *f* ◆ *vi* (*walk quickly*) dirigirse resueltamente.

March [mɑ:tʃ] *n* marzo *m*, → **September**.

mare [meə'] *n* yegua *f*.

margarine [,mɑ:dʒə'ri:n] *n* margarina *f*.

margin ['mɑ:dʒɪn] *n* margen *m*.

marina [mə'ri:nə] *n* puerto *m* deportivo.

marinated ['mærɪneɪtɪd] *adj* marinado(-da).

marital status ['mærɪtl-] *n* estado *m* civil.

mark [mɑ:k] *n* marca *f*; (*SCH*) nota *f* ◆ *vt* (*blemish*) manchar; (*put symbol on*) marcar; (*correct*) corregir; (*show position of*) señalar; (*gas*) **~ five** número cinco (del horno).

marker pen ['mɑ:kə-] *n* rotulador *m*.

market ['mɑ:kɪt] *n* mercado *m*.

marketing ['mɑ:kɪtɪŋ] *n* marketing *m*.

marketplace ['mɑ:kɪtpleɪs] *n* mercado *m*.

markings ['mɑ:kɪŋz] *npl* (*on road*) marcas *fpl* viales.

marmalade ['mɑ:məleɪd] *n* mermelada *f* de frutos cítricos.

marquee [mɑ:'ki:] *n* carpa *f*.

marriage ['mærɪdʒ] *n* (*event*) boda *f*; (*time married*) matrimonio *m*.

married ['mærɪd] *adj* casado(-da); **to get ~** casarse.

marrow ['mærəʊ] *n (vegetable)* calabacín *m* grande.

marry ['mærɪ] *vt* casarse con ♦ *vi* casarse.

marsh [mɑːʃ] *n (area)* zona *f* pantanosa.

martial arts [ˌmɑːʃl-] *npl* artes *fpl* marciales.

marvellous ['mɑːvələs] *adj (Br)* maravilloso(-sa).

marvelous ['mɑːvələs] *(Am)* = **marvellous**.

marzipan ['mɑːzɪpæn] *n* mazapán *m*.

mascara [mæs'kɑːrə] *n* rímel *m*.

masculine ['mæskjʊlɪn] *adj* masculino(-na); *(woman)* hombruno(-na).

mashed potatoes [ˌmæʃt-] *npl* puré *m* de patatas.

mask [mɑːsk] *n* máscara *f*.

masonry ['meɪsnrɪ] *n*: **falling ~** *materiales que se desprenden de un edificio*.

mass [mæs] *n (large amount)* montón *m*; *(RELIG)* misa *f*; **~es (of)** *(inf)* montones (de).

massacre ['mæsəkər] *n* masacre *f*.

massage [*Br* 'mæsɑːʒ, *Am* mə'sɑːʒ] *n* masaje *m* ♦ *vt* dar masajes a.

masseur [mæ'sɜːr] *n* masajista *m*.

masseuse [mæ'sɜːz] *n* masajista *f*.

massive ['mæsɪv] *adj* enorme.

mast [mɑːst] *n (on boat)* mástil *m*.

master ['mɑːstər] *n (at primary school)* maestro *m*; *(at secondary school)* profesor *m*; *(of servant, dog)* amo *m* ♦ *vt (skill, language)* dominar.

masterpiece ['mɑːstəpiːs] *n* obra *f* maestra.

mat [mæt] *n (small rug)* esterilla *f*; *(for plate)* salvamanteles *m inv*; *(for glass)* posavasos *m inv*.

match [mætʃ] *n (for lighting)* cerilla *f*; *(game)* partido *m* ♦ *vt (in colour, design)* hacer juego con; *(be the same as)* coincidir con; *(be as good as)* competir con ♦ *vi (in colour, design)* hacer juego.

matchbox ['mætʃbɒks] *n* caja *f* de cerillas.

matching ['mætʃɪŋ] *adj* a juego.

mate [meɪt] *n (inf)* colega *mf* ♦ *vi* aparearse.

material [mə'tɪərɪəl] *n (substance)* material *m*; *(cloth)* tela *f*; *(information)* información *f* □ **materials** *npl*: **writing ~s** objetos *mpl* de escritorio.

maternity leave [mə'tɜːnətɪ-] *n* baja *f* por maternidad.

maternity ward [mə'tɜːnətɪ-] *n* sala *f* de maternidad.

math [mæθ] *(Am)* = **maths**.

mathematics [ˌmæθə'mætɪks] *n* matemáticas *fpl*.

maths [mæθs] *n (Br)* mates *fpl*.

matinée ['mætɪneɪ] *n (at cinema)* primera sesión *f*; *(at theatre)* función *f* de tarde.

matt [mæt] *adj* mate.

matter ['mætər] *n (issue, situation)* asunto *m*; *(physical material)* materia *f* ♦ *vi*: **winning is all that ~s** lo único que importa es ganar;

it doesn't ~ no importa; **no ~ what happens** pase lo que pase; **there's something the ~ with my car** algo le pasa a mi coche; **what's the ~?** ¿qué pasa?; **as a ~ of course** rutinariamente; **as a ~ of fact** en realidad.

mattress ['mætris] n colchón m.

mature [mə'tjʊər] adj (person, behaviour) maduro(-ra); (cheese) curado(-da); (wine) añejo(-ja).

mauve [məʊv] adj malva (inv).

max. [mæks] (abbr of maximum) máx.

maximum ['mæksɪməm] adj máximo(-ma) ♦ n máximo m.

may [meɪ] aux vb 1. (expressing possibility) poder; **it ~ rain** puede que llueva; **they ~ have got lost** puede que se hayan perdido.

2. (expressing permission) **~ I smoke?** ¿puedo fumar?; **~ you sit, if you wish** puede sentarse si lo desea.

3. (when conceding a point) **it ~ be a long walk, but it's worth it** puede que sea una caminata, pero merece la pena.

May [meɪ] n mayo m, → September.

maybe ['meɪbi] adv quizás.

mayonnaise [,meɪə'neɪz] n mayonesa f.

mayor [meər] n alcalde m.

mayoress ['meəris] n esposa f del alcalde.

maze [meɪz] n laberinto m.

me [miː] pron me; **she knows ~** me conoce; **it's ~** soy yo; **send it to ~** envíamelo; **tell ~** dime; **he's worse than ~** él aún es peor que yo; **with ~** conmigo; **without ~** sin mí.

meadow ['medəʊ] n prado m.

meal [miːl] n comida f.

mealtime ['miːltaɪm] n hora f de comer.

mean [miːn] (pt & pp meant) adj (miserly) tacaño(-ña); (unkind) mezquino(-na) ♦ vt (signify, matter) significar; (intend) querer decir; (be a sign of) indicar; **I ~ it** hablo en serio; **to ~ to do sthg** pensar hacer algo; **I didn't ~ to hurt you** no quería hacerte daño; **to be meant to do sthg** deber hacer algo; **it's meant to be good** dicen que es bueno.

meaning ['miːnɪŋ] n (of word, phrase) significado m; (intention) sentido m.

meaningless ['miːnɪŋlɪs] adj (irrelevant) sin importancia.

means [miːnz] (pl inv) n (method) medio m ♦ npl (money) medios mpl; **by all ~!** ¡por supuesto!; **by ~ of** por medio de.

meant [ment] pt & pp → mean.

meantime ['miːntaɪm]: **in the meantime** adv mientras tanto.

meanwhile ['miːnwaɪl] adv mientras tanto.

measles ['miːzlz] n sarampión m.

measure ['meʒər] vt medir ♦ n medida f; **the room ~s 10 m²** la habitación mide 10 m².

measurement ['meʒəmənt] n medida f □ **measurements** npl (of person) medidas fpl.

meat [miːt] n carne f; **red ~** carnes rojas; **white ~** carnes blancas.

meatball ['miːtbɔːl] n albóndiga f.

mechanic [mɪ'kænɪk] n mecánico *m* (-ca *f*).

mechanical [mɪˈkænɪkl] *adj*
(*device*) mecánico(-ca).

mechanism [ˈmekənɪzm] *n* mecanismo *m*.

medal [ˈmedl] *n* medalla *f*.

media [ˈmiːdjə] *n or npl*: **the ~** los
medios de comunicación.

medical [ˈmedɪkl] *adj* médico(-ca) ♦ *n* chequeo *m* (médico).

medication [ˌmedɪˈkeɪʃn] *n*
medicación *f*.

medicine [ˈmedsɪn] *n* (*substance*)
medicamento *m*; (*science*) medicina
f.

medicine cabinet *n* botiquín
m.

medieval [ˌmedɪˈiːvl] *adj* medieval.

mediocre [ˌmiːdɪˈəʊkəʳ] *adj* mediocre.

Mediterranean [ˌmedɪtə-ˈreɪnjən] *n*: **the ~** (*region*) el
Mediterráneo; **the ~ (Sea)** el (Mar)
Mediterráneo.

medium [ˈmiːdjəm] *adj* (*middle-sized*) mediano(-na); (*wine*) suave,
semi; (*sherry*) medium.

medium-dry *adj* semiseco
(-ca).

medium-sized [-saɪzd] *adj* de
tamaño mediano.

medley [ˈmedlɪ] *n* (CULIN) selección *f*.

meet [miːt] (*pt & pp* **met**) *vt* (*by
arrangement*) reunirse con; (*by
chance*) encontrarse con; (*get to
know*) conocer; (*go to collect*) ir a
buscar; (*need, requirement*) satisfacer; (*cost, expenses*) cubrir ♦ *vi* (*by
arrangement*) reunirse; (*by chance*)

encontrarse; (*get to know each other*)
conocerse; (*intersect*) unirse; **~ me
at the bar** espérame en el bar ❑
meet up *vi* reunirse; **meet with**
vt fus (*problems, resistance*) encontrarse con; (*Am: by arrangement*)
reunirse con.

meeting [ˈmiːtɪŋ] *n* (*for business*)
reunión *f*.

meeting point *n* punto *m* de
encuentro.

melody [ˈmelədɪ] *n* melodía *f*.

melon [ˈmelən] *n* melón *m*.

melt [melt] *vi* derretirse.

member [ˈmembəʳ] *n* (*of group,
party, organization*) miembro *mf*; (*of
club*) socio *m* (-cia *f*).

Member of Congress *n*
miembro *mf* del Congreso (*de
EEUU*).

Member of Parliament *n*
diputado *m* (-da *f*) (*del parlamento
británico*).

membership [ˈmembəʃɪp] *n*
(*state of being a member*) afiliación *f*;
(*members*) miembros *mpl*; (*of club*)
socios *mpl*.

memorial [mɪˈmɔːrɪəl] *n* monumento *m* conmemorativo.

memorize [ˈmeməraɪz] *vt* memorizar.

memory [ˈmemərɪ] *n* (*ability to
remember, of computer*) memoria *f*;
(*thing remembered*) recuerdo *m*.

men [men] *pl* → **man**.

menacing [ˈmenəsɪŋ] *adj* amenazador(-ra).

mend [mend] *vt* arreglar.

menopause [ˈmenəpɔːz] *n*
menopausia *f*.

men's room *n* (*Am*) servicio *m*

miaow

de caballeros.

menstruate ['menstrueɪt] vi tener la menstruación.

menswear ['menzweəʳ] n confección f de caballeros.

mental ['mentl] adj mental.

mental hospital n hospital m psiquiátrico.

mentally handicapped ['mentlɪ-] adj minusválido m psíquico (disminuida f psíquica) ♦ npl: **the ~** los disminuidos psíquicos.

mentally ill ['mentlɪ-] adj: **to be ~** ser un enfermo mental (ser una enferma mental).

mention ['menʃn] vt mencionar; **don't ~ it!** ¡no hay de qué!

menu ['menju:] n menú m; **children's ~** menú infantil.

merchandise ['mɜːtʃəndaɪz] n géneros mpl.

merchant marine [,mɜːtʃənt-məˈriːn] (Am) = **merchant navy**.

merchant navy [,mɜːtʃənt-] (Br) marina f mercante.

mercury ['mɜːkjʊrɪ] n mercurio m.

mercy ['mɜːsɪ] n compasión f.

mere [mɪəʳ] adj simple; **a ~ two pounds** tan sólo dos libras.

merely ['mɪəlɪ] adv solamente.

merge [mɜːdʒ] vi (combine) mezclarse; **"merge"** (Am) cartel que indica que los coches que acceden a un autopista deben entrar en el carril de la derecha.

merger ['mɜːdʒəʳ] n fusión f.

meringue [məˈræŋ] n merengue m.

merit ['merɪt] n mérito m; (in exam) = notable m.

merry ['merɪ] adj (cheerful) alborozado(-da); (inf: tipsy) achispado(-da); **Merry Christmas!** ¡Feliz Navidad!

merry-go-round n tiovivo m.

mess [mes] n (untidiness) desorden m; (difficult situation) lío m; **in a ~** (untidy) desordenado ☐ **mess about** vi (inf) (have fun) divertirse; (behave foolishly) hacer el tonto; **to ~ about with sthg** (interfere) manosear algo; **mess up** vt sep (inf: ruin, spoil) estropear.

message ['mesɪdʒ] n mensaje m.

messenger ['mesɪndʒəʳ] n mensajero m (-ra f).

messy ['mesɪ] adj desordenado(-da).

met [met] pt & pp → **meet**.

metal ['metl] adj metálico(-ca) ♦ n metal m.

metalwork ['metlwɜːk] n (craft) metalistería f.

meter ['miːtəʳ] n (device) contador m; (Am) = **metre**.

method ['meθəd] n método m.

methodical [mɪˈθɒdɪkl] adj metódico(-ca).

meticulous [mɪˈtɪkjʊləs] adj meticuloso(-sa).

metre ['miːtəʳ] n (Br) metro m.

metric ['metrɪk] adj métrico(-ca).

mews [mjuːz] (pl inv) n (Br) calle o patio de casas de lujo reconvertidas a partir de antiguas caballerizas.

Mexican ['meksɪkn] adj mejicano(-na) ♦ n mejicano m (-na f).

Mexico ['meksɪkəʊ] n Méjico.

mg (abbr of milligram) mg.

miaow [miːˈaʊ] vi (Br) maullar.

mice [maɪs] pl → **mouse**.

microchip ['maɪkrəʊtʃɪp] n microchip m.

microphone ['maɪkrəfəʊn] n micrófono m.

microscope ['maɪkrəskəʊp] n microscopio m.

microwave (oven) ['maɪkrə-weɪv-] n microondas m inv.

midday [,mɪd'deɪ] n mediodía m.

middle ['mɪdl] n (in space) centro m; (in time) medio m ♦ adj del medio; **in the ~ of the road** en (el) medio de la carretera; **in the ~ of April** a mediados de abril; **to be in the ~ of doing sthg** estar haciendo algo.

middle-aged adj de mediana edad.

middle-class adj de clase media.

Middle East n: **the ~** el Oriente Medio.

middle name n segundo nombre m (de pila) (en un nombre compuesto).

middle school n etapa de la enseñanza secundaria británica para niños de 14 y 15 años.

midge [mɪdʒ] n mosquito m.

midget ['mɪdʒɪt] n enano m (-na f).

Midlands ['mɪdləndz] npl: **the ~** la región del centro de Inglaterra.

midnight ['mɪdnaɪt] n medianoche f.

midsummer ['mɪd'sʌmər] n pleno verano m.

midway [,mɪd'weɪ] adv (in space) a medio camino; (in time) a la mitad.

midweek [adj 'mɪdwi:k, adv mɪd'wi:k] adj de entre semana ♦ adv entre semana.

midwife ['mɪdwaɪf] (pl -wives) n comadrona f.

midwinter ['mɪd'wɪntər] n pleno invierno m.

midwives ['mɪdwaɪvz] pl → **midwife**.

might [maɪt] aux vb 1. (expressing possibility) poder; **I suppose they ~ still come** supongo que aún podrían venir.
2. (fml: expressing permission): **I have a few words?** ¿podría hablarle un momento?
3. (when conceding a point): **it ~ be expensive, but it's good quality** puede que sea caro, pero es de buena calidad.
4. (would): **I'd hoped you ~ come too** esperaba que tú vinieras también.
♦ n fuerzas fpl.

migraine ['mi:greɪn, 'maɪgreɪn] n jaqueca f.

mild [maɪld] adj (taste, weather, detergent) suave; (illness, discomfort) leve; (slight) ligero(-ra); (person, nature) apacible ♦ n (Br) cerveza de sabor suave.

mile [maɪl] n milla f; **it's ~s away** está muy lejos.

mileage ['maɪlɪdʒ] n distancia f en millas, = kilometraje m.

mileometer [maɪ'lɒmɪtər] n cuentamillas m inv, = cuentakilómetros m inv.

military ['mɪlɪtrɪ] adj militar.

milk [mɪlk] n leche f ♦ vt (cow) ordeñar.

milk chocolate n chocolate m

con leche.

milkman ['mɪlkmən] (pl **-men** [-mən]) n lechero m.

milk shake n batido m.

milky ['mɪlkɪ] adj (drink) con mucha leche.

mill [mɪl] n (flour-mill) molino m; (for grinding) molinillo m; (factory) fábrica f.

milligram ['mɪlɪgræm] n miligramo m.

millilitre ['mɪlɪˌliːtər] n mililitro m.

millimetre ['mɪlɪˌmiːtər] n milímetro m.

million ['mɪljən] n millón m; **~s** of (fig) millones de.

millionaire [ˌmɪljəˈneər] n millonario m (-ria f).

mime [maɪm] vi hacer mímica.

min. [mɪn] (abbr of minute) min.; (abbr of minimum) mín.

mince [mɪns] n (Br) carne f picada.

mincemeat ['mɪnsmiːt] n (sweet filling) dulce de fruta confitada con especias; (Am: mince) carne f picada.

mince pie n pastelillo navideño de pasta quebrada, rellena de fruta confitada y especias.

mind [maɪnd] n mente f; (memory) memoria f ◆ vt cuidar de ◆ vi: do you ~ if ...? ¿le importa si ...?; I don't ~ (don't disturb me) no me molesta; (I'm indifferent) me da igual; it slipped my ~ se me olvidó; state of ~ estado m de ánimo; to my ~ en mi opinión; to bear sthg in ~ tener algo en cuenta; to change one's ~ cambiar de opinión; to have sthg in ~ tener algo en mente; to have sthg on one's ~ estar preocupado por algo; do you ~ the noise? ¿te molesta el ruido?; to make one's ~ up decidirse; I wouldn't ~ a drink no me importaría tomar algo; "~ the gap!" advertencia a los pasajeros de tener cuidado con el hueco entre el andén y el metro; "~ the step" "cuidado con el peldaño"; never ~! (don't worry) ¡no importa!

mine¹ [maɪn] pron mío m (-a f); a friend of ~ un amigo mío.

mine² n mina f.

miner ['maɪnər] n minero m (-ra f).

mineral ['mɪnərəl] n mineral m.

mineral water n agua f mineral.

minestrone [ˌmɪnɪˈstrəʊnɪ] n minestrone f.

mingle ['mɪŋgl] vi (combine) mezclarse; (with other people) alternar.

miniature ['mɪnətʃər] adj en miniatura ◆ n (bottle of alcohol) botellín m (de bebida alcohólica).

minibar ['mɪnɪbɑːr] n minibar m.

minibus ['mɪnɪbʌs] (pl **-es**) n microbús m.

minicab ['mɪnɪkæb] n (Br) radiotaxi m.

minimal ['mɪnɪml] adj mínimo(-ma).

minimum ['mɪnɪməm] adj mínimo(-ma) ◆ n mínimo m.

miniskirt ['mɪnɪskɜːt] n minifalda f.

minister ['mɪnɪstər] n (in government) ministro m (-tra f); (in Church) pastor m.

ministry ['mɪnɪstrɪ] n (of govern-

ment) ministerio *m*.

minor ['maɪnəʳ] *adj* menor ◆ *n* (*fml*) menor *mf* de edad.

Minorca [mɪ'nɔːkə] *n* Menorca *f*.

minority [maɪ'nɒrɪtɪ] *n* minoría *f*.

minor road *n* carretera *f* secundaria.

mint [mɪnt] *n* (*sweet*) caramelo *m* de menta; (*plant*) menta *f*.

minus ['maɪnəs] *prep* (*in subtraction*) menos; **it's ~ 10°C** estamos a 10°C bajo cero.

minuscule ['mɪnəskjuːl] *adj* minúsculo(-la).

minute¹ ['mɪnɪt] *n* minuto *m*; **any ~** en cualquier momento; **just a ~!** ¡espera un momento!

minute² [maɪ'njuːt] *adj* diminuto(-ta).

minute steak ['mɪnɪt-] *n* filete muy fino que se hace rápido al cocinarlo.

miracle ['mɪrəkl] *n* milagro *m*.

miraculous [mɪ'rækjʊləs] *adj* milagroso(-sa).

mirror ['mɪrəʳ] *n* (*on wall, handheld*) espejo *m*; (*on car*) retrovisor *m*.

misbehave [,mɪsbɪ'heɪv] *vi* portarse mal.

miscarriage [,mɪs'kærɪdʒ] *n* aborto *m* (natural).

miscellaneous [,mɪsə'leɪnjəs] *adj* diverso(-sa).

mischievous ['mɪstʃɪvəs] *adj* travieso(-sa).

misconduct [,mɪs'kɒndʌkt] *n* mala conducta *f*.

miser ['maɪzəʳ] *n* avaro *m* (-ra *f*).

miserable ['mɪzrəbl] *adj* (*un-*

happy) infeliz; (*depressing, small*) miserable; (*weather*) horrible.

misery ['mɪzərɪ] *n* (*unhappiness*) desdicha *f*; (*poor conditions*) miseria *f*.

misfire [,mɪs'faɪəʳ] *vi* (*car*) no arrancar.

misfortune [mɪs'fɔːtʃuːn] *n* (*bad luck*) mala suerte *f*.

mishap ['mɪshæp] *n* contratiempo *m*.

misjudge [,mɪs'dʒʌdʒ] *vt* (*distance, amount*) calcular mal; (*person, character*) juzgar mal.

mislay [,mɪs'leɪ] (*pt & pp* -laid [-'leɪd]) *vt* extraviar.

mislead [,mɪs'liːd] (*pt & pp* -led [-'led]) *vt* engañar.

miss [mɪs] *vt* perder; (*not notice*) no ver; (*regret absence of*) echar de menos; (*appointment*) faltar a; (*programme*) perderse ◆ *vi* fallar; **you can't ~ it** no tiene pérdida ❑ **miss out** *vt sep* pasar por alto ◆ *vi*: **to ~ out on sthg** perderse algo.

Miss [mɪs] *n* señorita *f*.

missile [*Br* 'mɪsaɪl, *Am* 'mɪsl] *n* (*weapon*) misil *m*; (*thing thrown*) proyectil *m*.

missing ['mɪsɪŋ] *adj* (*lost*) perdido(-da); **to be ~** (*not there*) faltar.

missing person *n* desaparecido *m* (-da *f*).

mission ['mɪʃn] *n* misión *f*.

missionary ['mɪʃənrɪ] *n* misionario *m* (-ria *f*).

mist [mɪst] *n* neblina *f*.

mistake [mɪ'steɪk] (*vt* -took, *pp* -taken [-'teɪkən]) *n* error *m* ◆ *vt* (*misunderstand*) malentender; **by ~** por error; **to make a ~** equivocarse; **to ~ sthg/sb for** confundir algo/a alguien con.

Mister ['mɪstə^r] n señor m.

mistook [mɪ'stʊk] pt → **mistake.**

mistress ['mɪstrɪs] n (lover) amante f; (Br: primary teacher) maestra f; (Br: secondary teacher) profesora f.

mistrust [ˌmɪs'trʌst] vt desconfiar de.

misty ['mɪstɪ] adj neblinoso(-sa).

misunderstanding [ˌmɪsʌndə'stændɪŋ] n malentendido m.

misuse [ˌmɪs'juːs] n uso m indebido.

mitten ['mɪtn] n manopla f.

mix [mɪks] vt mezclar ◆ vi (socially) alternar ◆ n (for cake, sauce) mezcla f; **to ~ sthg with sthg** mezclar algo con algo ❑ **mix up** vt sep (confuse) confundir; (put into disorder) mezclar.

mixed [mɪkst] adj (school) mixto(-ta).

mixed grill n parrillada mixta de carne, champiñones y tomate.

mixed salad n ensalada f mixta.

mixed vegetables npl selección f de verduras.

mixer ['mɪksə^r] n (for food) batidora f; (drink) bebida no alcohólica que se mezcla con las bebidas alcohólicas.

mixture ['mɪkstʃə^r] n mezcla f.

mix-up n (inf) confusión f.

ml (abbr of millilitre) ml.

mm (abbr of millimetre) mm.

moan [məʊn] vi (in pain, grief) gemir; (inf: complain) quejarse.

moat [məʊt] n foso m.

mobile ['məʊbaɪl] adj móvil.

mobile phone n (teléfono) móvil m.

mock [mɒk] adj fingido(-da) ◆ vt burlarse de ◆ n (Br: exam) simulacro m de examen.

mode [məʊd] n modo m.

model ['mɒdl] n modelo m; (small copy) maqueta f; (fashion model) modelo mf.

modem ['məʊdem] n módem m.

moderate ['mɒdərət] adj moderado(-da).

modern ['mɒdən] adj moderno(-na).

modernized ['mɒdənaɪzd] adj modernizado(-da).

modern languages npl lenguas fpl modernas.

modest ['mɒdɪst] adj modesto(-ta); (price) módico(-ca); (increase, improvement) ligero(-ra).

modify ['mɒdɪfaɪ] vt modificar.

mohair ['məʊheə^r] n mohair m.

moist [mɔɪst] adj húmedo(-da).

moisture ['mɔɪstʃə^r] n humedad f.

moisturizer ['mɔɪstʃəraɪzə^r] n crema f hidratante.

molar ['məʊlə^r] n muela f.

mold [məʊld] (Am) = **mould.**

mole [məʊl] n (animal) topo m; (spot) lunar m.

molest [mə'lest] vt (child) abusar sexualmente de; (woman) acosar.

mom [mɒm] n (Am: inf) mamá f.

moment ['məʊmənt] n momento m; at the ~ en este momento; for the ~ de momento.

Mon. (abbr of Monday) lun.

monarchy ['mɒnəkɪ] n: the ~ la familia real.

monastery ['mɒnəstrɪ] n monasterio m.

Monday ['mʌndɪ] n lunes m inv, → Saturday.

money ['mʌnɪ] n dinero m.

money belt n riñonera f.

money order n giro m postal.

mongrel ['mʌngrəl] n perro m cruzado.

monitor ['mɒnɪtə'] n (computer screen) monitor m ♦ vt (check, observe) controlar.

monk [mʌŋk] n monje m.

monkey ['mʌŋkɪ] (pl monkeys) n mono m.

monkfish ['mʌŋkfɪʃ] n rape m.

monopoly [mə'nɒpəlɪ] n monopolio m.

monorail ['mɒnəʊreɪl] n monorraíl m.

monotonous [mə'nɒtənəs] adj monótono(-na).

monsoon [mɒn'suːn] n monzón m.

monster ['mɒnstə'] n monstruo m.

month [mʌnθ] n mes m; **every ~** cada mes; **in a ~'s time** en un mes.

monthly ['mʌnθlɪ] adj mensual ♦ adv mensualmente.

monument ['mɒnjʊmənt] n monumento m.

mood [muːd] n humor m; **to be in a (bad) ~** estar de mal humor; **to be in a good ~** estar de buen humor.

moody ['muːdɪ] adj (bad-tempered) malhumorado(-da); (changeable) de humor variable.

moon [muːn] n luna f.

moonlight ['muːnlaɪt] n luz f de luna.

moor [mɔː'] n páramo m ♦ vt amarrar.

moose [muːs] (pl inv) n alce m.

mop [mɒp] n (for floor) fregona f ♦ vt (floor) pasar la fregona por ▭ **mop up** vt sep (clean up) limpiar.

moped ['məʊped] n ciclomotor m.

moral ['mɒrəl] adj moral ♦ n (lesson) moraleja f.

morality [mə'rælɪtɪ] n moralidad f.

more [mɔː'] adj 1. (a larger amount of) más; **there are ~ tourists than usual** hay más turistas que de costumbre.

2. (additional) más; **are there any ~ cakes?** ¿hay más pasteles?; **there's no ~ wine** no hay más vino; **have some ~ rice** come un poco más de arroz.

3. (in phrases): **~ and more** cada vez más.

♦ adv 1. (in comparatives) más; **it's ~ difficult than before** es más difícil que antes; **speak ~ clearly** habla con más claridad.

2. (to a greater degree) más; **we ought to go to the cinema ~** deberíamos ir más al cine.

3. (longer) más; **I don't go there any ~** ya no voy más allí.

4. (again): **once ~** una vez más.

5. (in phrases): **~ or less** más o menos; **we'd be ~ than happy to help** estaríamos encantados de ayudarle.

♦ pron 1. (a larger amount) más; **I've got ~ than you** tengo más que tú;

~ than 20 types of pizza más de 20 clases de pizzas.

2. *(an additional amount)* más; **is there any ~?** ¿hay más?

moreover [mɔːˈrəʊvəʳ] *adv (fml)* además.

morning [ˈmɔːnɪŋ] *n* mañana *f*; **two o'clock in the ~** las dos de la mañana; **good ~!** ¡buenos días!; **in the ~** *(early in the day)* por la mañana; *(tomorrow morning)* mañana por la mañana.

morning-after pill *n* píldora *f* del día siguiente.

morning sickness *n* náuseas *fpl* de por la mañana.

Morocco [məˈrɒkəʊ] *n* Marruecos.

moron [ˈmɔːrɒn] *n (inf)* imbécil *mf*.

Morse (code) [mɔːs-] *n* Morse *m*.

mortgage [ˈmɔːgɪdʒ] *n* hipoteca *f*.

mosaic [məˈzeɪɪk] *n* mosaico *m*.

Moslem [ˈmɒzləm] = **Muslim**.

mosque [mɒsk] *n* mezquita *f*.

mosquito [məˈskiːtəʊ] *(pl* **-es)** *n* mosquito *m*.

mosquito net *n* mosquitero *m*.

moss [mɒs] *n* musgo *m*.

most [məʊst] *adj* **1.** *(the majority of)* la mayoría de; **~ people** la mayoría de la gente.

2. *(the largest amount of)* más; **I drank (the) ~ beer** yo fui el que bebió más cerveza.

♦ *adv* **1.** *(in superlatives)* más; **the ~ expensive hotel** el hotel más caro.

2. *(to the greatest degree)* más; **I like**

this one ~ éste es el que más me gusta.

3. *(fml: very)* muy; **we would be ~ grateful** les agradeceríamos mucho.

♦ *pron* **1.** *(the majority)* la mayoría; **~ of the villages** la mayoría de los pueblos; **~ of the time** la mayor parte del tiempo.

2. *(the largest amount)* **she earns (the) ~** es la que más gana.

3. *(in phrases)*: **at ~** como máximo; **to make the ~ of sthg** aprovechar algo al máximo.

mostly [ˈməʊstlɪ] *adv* principalmente.

MOT *n (Br: test)* revisión anual obligatoria para todos los coches de más de tres años, = ITV *f*.

motel [məʊˈtel] *n* motel *m*.

moth [mɒθ] *n* polilla *f*.

mother [ˈmʌðəʳ] *n* madre *f*.

mother-in-law *n* suegra *f*.

mother-of-pearl *n* nácar *m*.

motif [məʊˈtiːf] *n* motivo *m*.

motion [ˈməʊʃn] *n (movement)* movimiento *m* ♦ *vi*: **to ~ to sb** hacer una señal a alguien.

motionless [ˈməʊʃənlɪs] *adj* inmóvil.

motivate [ˈməʊtɪveɪt] *vt* motivar.

motive [ˈməʊtɪv] *n* motivo *m*.

motor [ˈməʊtəʳ] *n* motor *m*.

Motorail® [ˈməʊtəreɪl] *n* motorraíl *m*.

motorbike [ˈməʊtəbaɪk] *n* moto *f*.

motorboat [ˈməʊtəbəʊt] *n* lancha *f* motora.

motorcar [ˈməʊtəkɑːʳ] *n* automóvil *m*.

motorcycle [ˈməʊtəˌsaɪkl] *n* motocicleta *f*.

motorcyclist [ˈməʊtəˌsaɪklɪst] *n* motociclista *mf*.

motorist [ˈməʊtərɪst] *n* automovilista *mf*.

motor racing *n* automovilismo *m* (*deporte*).

motorway [ˈməʊtəweɪ] *n* (*Br*) autopista *f*.

motto [ˈmɒtəʊ] (*pl* **-s**) *n* lema *m*.

mould [məʊld] *n* (*Br*) (*shape*) molde *m*; (*substance*) moho *m* ◆ *vt* (*Br*) moldear.

mouldy [ˈməʊldɪ] *adj* (*Br*) mohoso(-sa).

mound [maʊnd] *n* (*hill*) montículo *m*; (*pile*) montón *m*.

mount [maʊnt] *n* (*for photo*) marco *m*; (*mountain*) monte *m* ◆ *vt* (*horse*) montar en; (*photo*) enmarcar ◆ *vi* (*increase*) aumentar.

mountain [ˈmaʊntɪn] *n* montaña *f*.

mountain bike *n* bicicleta *f* de montaña.

mountaineer [ˌmaʊntɪˈnɪəʳ] *n* montañero *m* (-ra *f*).

mountaineering [ˌmaʊntɪˈnɪərɪŋ] *n*: **to go ~** hacer montañismo.

mountainous [ˈmaʊntɪnəs] *adj* montañoso(-sa).

Mount Rushmore [-ˈrʌʃmɔːʳ] *n* el monte Rushmore.

MOUNT RUSHMORE

Este gigantesco relieve de los bustos de los presidentes Washington, Jefferson, Lincoln y Theodore Roosevelt, excavado en un lado del Monte Rushmore (Dakota del Sur), es un monumento nacional y una popular atracción turística.

---

mourning [ˈmɔːnɪŋ] *n*: **to be in ~** estar de luto.

mouse [maʊs] (*pl* **mice**) *n* ratón *m*.

moussaka [muːˈsɑːkə] *n* plato griego de berenjenas, tomate, salsa de queso y carne picada.

mousse [muːs] *n* (*food*) mousse *m*; (*for hair*) espuma *f*.

moustache [məˈstɑːʃ] *n* (*Br*) bigote *m*.

mouth [maʊθ] *n* boca *f*; (*of river*) desembocadura *f*.

mouthful [ˈmaʊθfʊl] *n* (*of food*) bocado *m*; (*of drink*) trago *m*.

mouthorgan [ˈmaʊθˌɔːgən] *n* armónica *f*.

mouthpiece [ˈmaʊθpiːs] *n* (*of telephone*) micrófono *m*; (*of musical instrument*) boquilla *f*.

mouthwash [ˈmaʊθwɒʃ] *n* elixir *m* bucal.

move [muːv] *n* (*change of house*) mudanza *f*; (*movement*) movimiento *m*; (*in games*) jugada *f*; (*turn to play*) turno *m*; (*course of action*) medida *f* ◆ *vt* (*shift*) mover; (*emotionally*) conmover ◆ *vi* (*shift*) moverse; **to ~** (*house*) mudarse; **to make a ~** (*leave*) irse ❑ **move along** *vi* hacerse a un lado; **move in** *vi* (*to house*) instalarse; **move off** *vi* (*train, car*) ponerse en marcha; **move on** *vi* (*after stopping*) reanudar la marcha; **move out** *vi* (*from house*) mudarse; **move over** *vi* hacer sitio; **move up** vi hacer sitio.

movement ['mu:vmənt] n movimiento m.

movie ['mu:vɪ] n película f.

movie theater n (Am) cine m.

moving ['mu:vɪŋ] adj (emotionally) conmovedor(-ra).

mow [məʊ] vt: to ~ the lawn cortar el césped.

mozzarella [ˌmɒtsə'relə] n mozzarella f.

MP abbr = Member of Parliament.

mph (abbr of miles per hour) mph.

Mr ['mɪstə^r] abbr Sr.

Mrs ['mɪsɪz] abbr Sra.

Ms [mɪz] abbr abreviatura que se utiliza delante del apellido cuando no se quiere decir el estado civil de la mujer.

MSc n (abbr of Master of Science) título postuniversitario de dos años en ciencias.

much [mʌtʃ] (compar more, superl most) adj mucho(-cha); **I haven't got ~ money** no tengo mucho dinero; **as ~ food as you can eat** tanta comida como puedas comer; **how ~ time is left?** ¿cuánto tiempo queda?; **they have so ~ money** tienen tanto dinero; **we have too ~ food** tenemos demasiada comida.

♦ adv mucho; **it's ~ better** es mucho mejor; **he's ~ too good** es demasiado bueno; **I like it very ~** me gusta muchísimo; **it's not ~ good** no vale mucho; **thank you very ~** muchas gracias; **we don't go there ~** no vamos mucho allí.

♦ pron mucho; **I haven't got ~** no tengo mucho; **as ~ as you like** como quieras; **how ~ is it?** ¿cuánto es?; **you've got so ~** tienes tanto; **you've got too ~** tienes demasiado.

muck [mʌk] n mugre f ☐ **muck about** vi (Br: inf) hacer el indio; **muck up** vt sep (Br: inf) fastidiar.

mud [mʌd] n barro m.

muddle ['mʌdl] n: **to be in a ~** estar hecho un lío.

muddy ['mʌdɪ] adj lleno(-na) de barro.

mudguard ['mʌdgɑːd] n guardabarros m inv.

muesli ['mjuːzlɪ] n muesli m.

muffin ['mʌfɪn] n (roll) panecillo m; (cake) especie de bollo que se come caliente.

muffler ['mʌflə^r] n (Am: silencer) silenciador m.

mug [mʌg] n (cup) tanque m, taza f grande (cilíndrica) ♦ vt asaltar.

mugging ['mʌgɪŋ] n atraco m.

muggy ['mʌgɪ] adj bochornoso(-sa).

mule [mjuːl] n mula f.

multicoloured ['mʌltɪˌkʌləd] adj multicolor.

multiple ['mʌltɪpl] adj múltiple.

multiplex cinema [ˌmʌltɪpleks-] n multicine m.

multiplication [ˌmʌltɪplɪ'keɪʃn] n multiplicación f.

multiply ['mʌltɪplaɪ] vt multiplicar ♦ vi multiplicarse.

multistorey (car park) [ˌmʌltɪ'stɔːrɪ-] n aparcamiento m de muchas plantas.

mum [mʌm] n (Br: inf) mamá f.

mummy ['mʌmɪ] n (Br: inf: mother) mamá f.

mumps [mʌmps] n paperas fpl.

munch [mʌntʃ] vt masticar.

municipal [mju:'nɪsɪpl] adj municipal.

mural ['mjuərəl] n mural m.

murder ['mɜ:dəʳ] n asesinato m ♦ vt asesinar.

murderer ['mɜ:dərəʳ] n asesino m (-na f).

muscle ['mʌsl] n músculo m.

museum [mju:'zɪəm] n museo m.

mushroom ['mʌʃrʊm] n (small and white) champiñón m; (darker and flatter) seta f.

music ['mju:zɪk] n música f.

musical ['mju:zɪkl] adj (connected with music) musical; (person) con talento para la música ♦ n musical m.

musical instrument n instrumento m musical.

musician [mju:'zɪʃn] n músico m (-ca f).

Muslim ['mʊzlɪm] adj musulmán(-ana) ♦ n musulmán m (-ana f).

mussels ['mʌslz] npl mejillones mpl.

must [mʌst] aux vb deber, tener que ♦ n (inf): it's a ~ no te lo puedes perder; I ~ go debo irme; **the room ~ be vacated by ten** la habitación debe dejarse libre para las diez; **you ~ have seen it** tienes que haberlo visto; **you ~ see that film** no te puedes perder esa película; **you ~ be joking!** estás de broma ¿no?

mustache ['mʌstæʃ] (Am) = moustache.

mustard ['mʌstəd] n mostaza f.

mustn't ['mʌsənt] = must not.

mutter ['mʌtəʳ] vt musitar.

mutton ['mʌtn] n oveja f.

mutual ['mju:tʃʊəl] adj (feeling) mutuo(-tua); (friend, interest) común.

muzzle ['mʌzl] n (for dog) bozal m.

my [maɪ] adj mi, mis (pl).

myself [maɪ'self] pron (reflexive) me; (after prep) mí mismo(-ma); I did it ~ lo hice yo solo.

mysterious [mɪ'stɪərɪəs] adj misterioso(-sa).

mystery ['mɪstərɪ] n misterio m.

myth [mɪθ] n mito m.

N

N (abbr of north) N.

nag [næg] vt regañar.

nail [neɪl] n (of finger, toe) uña f; (metal) clavo m ♦ vt (fasten) clavar.

nailbrush ['neɪlbrʌʃ] n cepillo m de uñas.

nail file n lima f de uñas.

nail scissors npl tijeras fpl para las uñas.

nail varnish n esmalte m de uñas.

nail varnish remover [-rɪ'mu:vəʳ] n quitaesmaltes m inv.

naive [naɪˈiːv] *adj* ingenuo(-nua).

naked [ˈneɪkɪd] *adj (person)* desnudo(-da).

name [neɪm] *n* nombre *m; (surname)* apellido *m; (reputation)* reputación *f* ♦ *vt (date, price)* fijar; **they ~d him John** le pusieron John de nombre; **first ~** nombre; **last ~** apellido; **what's your ~?** ¿cómo te llamas?; **my ~ is ...** me llamo ...

namely [ˈneɪmlɪ] *adv* a saber.

nan bread [næn-] *n tipo de pan indio en forma de torta, condimentado normalmente con especias.*

nanny [ˈnænɪ] *n (childminder)* niñera *f; (inf: grandmother)* abuelita *f.*

nap [næp] *n:* **to have a ~** echar una siesta.

napkin [ˈnæpkɪn] *n* servilleta *f.*

nappy [ˈnæpɪ] *n* pañal *m.*

nappy liner *n parte desechable de un pañal de gasa.*

narcotic [nɑːˈkɒtɪk] *n* narcótico *m.*

narrow [ˈnærəʊ] *adj (road, gap)* estrecho(-cha) ♦ *vi (road, gap)* estrecharse.

narrow-minded [-ˈmaɪndɪd] *adj* estrecho(-cha) de miras.

nasty [ˈnɑːstɪ] *adj (spiteful)* malintencionado(-da); *(accident, fall)* grave; *(unpleasant)* desagradable.

nation [ˈneɪʃn] *n* nación *f.*

national [ˈnæʃənl] *adj* nacional ♦ *n* súbdito *m (-ta f).*

national anthem *n* himno *m* nacional.

National Health Service *n organismo gestor de la salud pública en Gran Bretaña.*

National Insurance *n (Br: contributions)* = Seguridad *f* Social.

nationality [ˌnæʃəˈnælətɪ] *n* nacionalidad *f.*

national park *n* parque *m* nacional.

NATIONAL PARK

Los parques nacionales en Gran Bretaña y Estados Unidos son grandes extensiones naturales abiertas al público que están protegidas para conservar su interés paisajístico. Snowdonia, el Lake District y el Peak District son conocidos parques nacionales británicos; los más conocidos de Estados Unidos son Yellowstone y Yosemite. En todos ellos hay lugares donde se puede hacer camping.

---

nationwide [ˈneɪʃənwaɪd] *adj* a escala nacional.

native [ˈneɪtɪv] *adj (country)* natal; *(customs)* originario(-ria); *(population)* indígeno(-na) ♦ *n* natural *m*f; **a ~ speaker of English** un hablante nativo de inglés.

NATO [ˈneɪtəʊ] *n* OTAN *f.*

natural [ˈnætʃrəl] *adj (ability, charm)* natural; *(swimmer, actor)* nato(-ta).

natural gas *n* gas *m* natural.

naturally [ˈnætʃrəlɪ] *adv (of course)* naturalmente.

natural yoghurt *n* yogur *m* natural.

nature [ˈneɪtʃəʳ] *n* naturaleza *f.*

nature reserve *n* reserva *f* natural.

naughty ['nɔːtɪ] adj (child) travieso(-sa).

nausea ['nɔːzɪə] n náusea f.

navigate ['nævɪgeɪt] vi (in boat, plane) dirigir; (in car) guiar.

navy ['neɪvɪ] n (ships) armada f ◆ adj: ~ (blue) azul marino.

NB (abbr of nota bene) N.B.

near [nɪəʳ] adv cerca ◆ adj (place, object) cerca; (relation) cercano(-na) ◆ prep: ~ (to) (edge, object, place) cerca de; in the ~ future en el futuro próximo.

nearby [nɪə'baɪ] adv cerca ◆ adj cercano(-na).

nearly ['nɪəlɪ] adv casi.

neat [niːt] adj (writing, work) bien hecho(-cha); (room) ordenado(-da); (whisky, vodka etc) solo(-la).

neatly ['niːtlɪ] adv (placed, arranged) con pulcritud; (written) con buena letra.

necessarily [,nesə'serɪlɪ, Br 'nesəsrəlɪ] adv: not ~ no necesariamente.

necessary ['nesəsrɪ] adj necesario(-ria); it is ~ to do it es necesario hacerlo.

necessity [nɪ'sesətɪ] n necesidad f □ **necessities** npl artículos mpl de primera necesidad.

neck [nek] n (of person, jumper, shirt) cuello m; (of animal) pescuezo m.

necklace ['neklɪs] n (long) collar m; (short) gargantilla f.

nectarine ['nektərɪn] n nectarina f.

need [niːd] n necesidad f ◆ vt necesitar; to ~ to do sthg (require) necesitar hacer algo; (be obliged) tener que hacer algo.

needle ['niːdl] n aguja f.

needlework ['niːdlwɜːk] n (SCH) costura f.

needn't ['niːdənt] = need not.

needy ['niːdɪ] adj necesitado(-da).

negative ['negətɪv] adj negativo(-va) ◆ n (in photography) negativo m; (GRAMM) negación f.

neglect [nɪ'glekt] vt (child, garden, work) descuidar.

negligence ['neglɪdʒəns] n negligencia f.

negotiations [nɪ,gəʊʃɪ'eɪʃnz] npl negociaciones fpl.

negro ['niːgrəʊ] (pl -es) n negro m (-gra f).

neighbor ['neɪbər] (Am) = **neighbour**.

neighbour ['neɪbəʳ] n vecino m (-na f).

neighbourhood ['neɪbəhʊd] n barrio m.

neighbouring ['neɪbərɪŋ] adj vecino(-na).

neither ['naɪðəʳ, 'niːðəʳ] adj: ~ bag is big enough ninguna de las dos bolsas es bastante grande. ◆ pron: ~ of us ninguno m de nosotros (ninguna f de nosotras). ◆ conj: ~ do I yo tampoco; ~ ... nor ... ni ... ni ...

neon light ['niːɒn-] n luz f de neón.

nephew ['nefjuː] n sobrino m.

nerve [nɜːv] n (in body) nervio m; (courage) coraje m; what a ~! ¡qué caradura!

nervous ['nɜːvəs] adj (tense by nature) nervioso(-sa); (apprehensive) aprensivo(-va); (uneasy) preocupado(-da).

nervous breakdown n crisis f inv nerviosa.

nest [nest] n nido m.

net [net] n red f ♦ adj neto(-ta).

netball ['netbɔ:l] n deporte parecido al baloncesto femenino.

Netherlands ['neðələndz] npl: the ~ los Países Bajos.

nettle ['netl] n ortiga f.

network ['netwɜ:k] n (of streets, trains) red f; (RADIO & TV) cadena f.

neurotic [,njuə'rɒtɪk] adj neurótico(-ca).

neutral ['nju:trəl] adj (country, person) neutral; (in colour) incoloro(-ra) ♦ n (AUT): in ~ en punto muerto.

never ['nevəʳ] adv nunca; **I've been to Berlin** no he estado nunca en Berlín; **she's ~ late** (ella) nunca llega tarde; **~ mind!** ¡no importa!

nevertheless [,nevəðə'les] adv sin embargo.

new [nju:] adj nuevo(-va).

newly ['nju:lɪ] adv recién.

new potatoes npl patatas fpl nuevas.

news [nju:z] n noticias fpl; **a piece of ~** una noticia.

newsagent ['nju:zeɪdʒənt] n (shop) = quiosco m de periódicos.

newspaper ['nju:z,peɪpəʳ] n periódico m.

New Year n Año m Nuevo.

gente se reúne en la calle. Tradicionalmente, se canta "Auld Lang Syne" mientras el reloj da las doce. En Escocia, donde se conoce como "Hogmanay", es particularmente importante. El día siguiente, Año Nuevo, es fiesta en toda Gran Bretaña.

New Year's Day n día m de Año Nuevo.

New Year's Eve n Nochevieja f.

New Zealand [-'zi:lənd] n Nueva Zelanda.

next [nekst] adj (in the future, following) próximo(-ma); (room, house) de al lado ♦ adv (afterwards) después; (on next occasion) la próxima vez; **when does the ~ bus leave?** ¿a qué hora sale el próximo autobús?; **~ year/Monday** el año/el lunes que viene; **~ to** (by the side of) junto a; **the week after ~** la semana que viene no, la otra.

next door adv en la casa de al lado.

next of kin [-kɪn] n pariente m más próximo (pariente f más próxima).

NHS abbr = National Health Service.

nib [nɪb] n plumilla f.

nibble ['nɪbl] vt mordisquear.

Nicaragua [,nɪkə'rægjuə] n Nicaragua f.

Nicaraguan [,nɪkə'rægjuən] adj nicaragüense ♦ n nicaragüense mf.

nice [naɪs] adj (pleasant) agradable; (pretty) bonito(-ta); (kind) amable; **to have a ~ time** pasarlo bien; **~ to see you!** ¡encantado(-da) de

---

 NEW YEAR

En Nochevieja en Gran Bretaña se celebran fiestas públicas y la

verle!

nickel ['nɪkl] n (metal) níquel m; (Am: coin) moneda f de cinco centavos.

nickname ['nɪkneɪm] n apodo m.

niece [niːs] n sobrina f.

night [naɪt] n (time when asleep) noche f; (evening) tarde f; **at ~** de noche; **by ~** por la noche; **last ~** anoche.

nightclub ['naɪtklʌb] n = sala f de fiestas (abierta sólo por las noches).

nightdress ['naɪtdres] n camisón m.

nightie ['naɪtɪ] n (inf) camisón m.

nightlife ['naɪtlaɪf] n vida f nocturna.

nightly ['naɪtlɪ] adv cada noche.

nightmare ['naɪtmeə'] n pesadilla f.

night safe n caja f nocturna (en un banco).

night school n escuela f nocturna.

nightshift ['naɪtʃɪft] n turno m de noche.

nil [nɪl] n (SPORT) cero m.

Nile [naɪl] n: **the ~** el Nilo.

nine [naɪn] num nueve, → **six**.

nineteen [ˌnaɪn'tiːn] num diecinueve, → **six**; **~ ninety-five** mil novecientos noventa y cinco.

nineteenth [ˌnaɪn'tiːnθ] num decimonoveno(-na), → **sixth**.

ninetieth ['naɪntɪəθ] num nonagésimo(-ma), → **sixth**.

ninety ['naɪntɪ] num noventa, → **six**.

ninth [naɪnθ] num noveno(-na), → **sixth**.

nip [nɪp] vt (pinch) pellizcar.

nipple ['nɪpl] n (of breast) pezón m; (of bottle) tetilla f.

nitrogen ['naɪtrədʒən] n nitrógeno m.

no [nəʊ] adv no ♦ adj ninguno(-na) ♦ n no m; **I've got ~ time** no tengo tiempo; **I've got ~ money left** no me queda (ningún) dinero.

noble ['nəʊbl] adj noble.

nobody ['nəʊbədɪ] pron nadie.

nod [nɒd] vi (in agreement) asentir con la cabeza.

noise [nɔɪz] n ruido m.

noisy ['nɔɪzɪ] adj ruidoso(-sa).

nominate ['nɒmɪneɪt] vt proponer.

nonalcoholic [ˌnɒnælkə'hɒlɪk] adj sin alcohol.

none [nʌn] pron ninguno m (-na f); **there's ~ left** no queda nada.

nonetheless [ˌnʌnðə'les] adv no obstante.

nonfiction [ˌnɒn'fɪkʃn] n no ficción f.

non-iron adj que no necesita plancha.

nonsense ['nɒnsəns] n tonterías fpl.

nonsmoker [ˌnɒn'sməʊkə'] n no fumador m (-ra f).

nonstick [ˌnɒn'stɪk] adj antiadherente.

nonstop [ˌnɒn'stɒp] adj (talking, arguing) continuo(-nua); (flight) sin escalas ♦ adv (run, rain) sin parar; (fly, travel) directamente.

noodles ['nuːdlz] npl fideos mpl.

noon [nuːn] n mediodía m.

no one = nobody.

nor [nɔː'] conj tampoco; **~ do I** yo

tampoco, → neither.

normal [ˈnɔːml] *adj* normal.

normally [ˈnɔːməlɪ] *adv* normalmente.

north [nɔːθ] *n* norte *m* ◆ *adv (fly, walk)* hacia el norte; *(be situated)* al norte; **in the ~ of England** en el norte de Inglaterra.

North America *n* Norteamérica.

northbound [ˈnɔːθbaund] *adj* con dirección norte.

northeast [ˌnɔːθˈiːst] *n* nordeste *m*.

northern [ˈnɔːðən] *adj* del norte.

Northern Ireland *n* Irlanda del Norte.

North Pole *n* Polo *m* Norte.

North Sea *n* Mar *m* del Norte.

northwards [ˈnɔːθwədz] *adv* hacia el norte.

northwest [ˌnɔːθˈwest] *n* noroeste *m*.

Norway [ˈnɔːweɪ] *n* Noruega.

Norwegian [nɔːˈwiːdʒən] *adj* noruego(-a) ◆ *n (person)* noruego *m* (-ga *f*); *(language)* noruego *m*.

nose [nəuz] *n (of person)* nariz *f*; *(of animal)* hocico *m*; *(of plane, rocket)* morro *m*.

nosebleed [ˈnəuzbliːd] *n*: **he had a ~** le sangraba la nariz.

nostril [ˈnɒstrəl] *n (of person)* ventana *f* de la nariz; *(of animal)* orificio *m* nasal.

nosy [ˈnəuzɪ] *adj* fisgón(-ona).

not [nɒt] *adv* no; **she's ~ there** no está allí; **I hope ~** espero que no; **~ yet** todavía no; **~ at all** *(pleased, interested)* en absoluto; *(in reply to*

thanks) no hay de qué.

notably [ˈnəutəblɪ] *adv* especialmente.

note [nəut] *n* nota *f*; *(bank note)* billete *m* ◆ *vt (notice)* notar; *(write down)* anotar; **to take ~s** tomar apuntes.

notebook [ˈnəutbuk] *n* libreta *f*.

noted [ˈnəutɪd] *adj* célebre.

notepaper [ˈnəutpeɪpər] *n* papel *m* de escribir *(para cartas)*.

nothing [ˈnʌθɪŋ] *pron* nada; **he did ~** no hizo nada; **~ new/interesting** nada nuevo/interesante; **~ for (free)** gratis; *(in vain)* para nada.

notice [ˈnəutɪs] *vt* notar ◆ *n (written announcement)* anuncio *m*; *(warning)* aviso *m*; **to take ~ of** hacer caso de; **to hand in one's ~** presentar la dimisión.

noticeable [ˈnəutɪsəbl] *adj* perceptible.

notice board *n* tablón *m* de anuncios.

notion [ˈnəuʃn] *n* noción *f*.

notorious [nəuˈtɔːrɪəs] *adj* de mala reputación.

nougat [ˈnuːgɑː] *n* turrón de frutos secos y frutas confitadas.

nought [nɔːt] *n* cero *m*.

noun [naun] *n* nombre *m*, sustantivo *m*.

nourishment [ˈnʌrɪʃmənt] *n* alimento *m*.

novel [ˈnɒvl] *n* novela *f* ◆ *adj* original.

novelist [ˈnɒvəlɪst] *n* novelista *mf*.

November [nəˈvembər] *n* noviembre *m*, → **September**.

now [naʊ] *adv* ahora ♦ *conj:* ~
(that) ahora que; ~ and then o
again ahora y de vez en cuando, de
cuando en cuando; right ~ (at the
moment) en este momento; (immediately) ahora
mismo; by ~ ya; from ~ on de
ahora en adelante.

nowadays ['naʊədeɪz] *adv* hoy
en día.

nowhere ['nəʊweə'] *adv* en ninguna parte.

nozzle ['nɒzl] *n* boquilla *f*.

nuclear ['nju:klɪə'] *adj* nuclear.

nude [nju:d] *adj* desnudo(-da).

nudge [nʌdʒ] *vt* dar un codazo a.

nuisance ['nju:sns] *n:* it's a real
~! ¡es una lata!; he's such a ~! ¡es
tan pelma!

numb [nʌm] *adj* (person) entume-
cido(-da); (leg, arm) dormido(-da).

number ['nʌmbə'] *n* número *m*
♦ *vt* (give number to) numerar.

numberplate ['nʌmbəpleɪt] *n*
matrícula *f*.

numeral ['nju:mərəl] *n* número
m.

numerous ['nju:mərəs] *adj* nu-
meroso(-sa).

nun [nʌn] *n* monja *f*.

nurse [nɜ:s] *n* enfermera *f* ♦ *vt*
(look after) cuidar de; **male** ~ enfermero *m*.

nursery ['nɜ:sərɪ] *n* (in house)
cuarto *m* de los niños; (for plants)
vivero *m*.

nursery (school) *n* escuela *f*
de párvulos.

nursery slope *n* pista *f* para
principiantes.

nursing ['nɜ:sɪŋ] *n* (profession)
enfermería *f*.

nut [nʌt] *n* (to eat) nuez *f* (frutos

secos en general); (of metal) tuerca *f*.

nutcrackers ['nʌt,krækəz] *npl*
cascanueces *m inv*.

nutmeg ['nʌtmeg] *n* nuez *f* mos-
cada.

nylon ['naɪlɒn] *n* nylon *m* ♦ *adj*
de nylon.

o' [ə] *abbr* = of.

O [əʊ] *n* (zero) cero *m*.

oak [əʊk] *n* roble *m* ♦ *adj* de
roble.

OAP *abbr* = old age pensioner.

oar [ɔ:'] *n* remo *m*.

oatcake ['əʊtkeɪk] *n* galleta *f* de
avena.

oath [əʊθ] *n* (promise) juramento
m.

oatmeal ['əʊtmi:l] *n* harina *f* de
avena.

oats [əʊts] *npl* avena *f*.

obedient [ə'bi:djənt] *adj* obediente.

obey [ə'beɪ] *vt* obedecer.

object [*n* 'ɒbdʒɪkt, *vb* əb'dʒekt] *n*
objeto *m*; (GRAMM) objeto *m*,
complemento *m* ♦ *vi:* to ~ (to) oponerse (a).

objection [əb'dʒekʃn] *n* objeción *f*.

objective [əb'dʒektɪv] *n* objetivo
m.

obligation [,ɒblɪ'geɪʃn] *n* obliga-

odds

obligatory [ə'blɪgətrɪ] adj obligatorio(-ria).

oblige [ə'blaɪdʒ] vt: to ~ sb to do sthg obligar a alguien a hacer algo.

oblique [ə'bli:k] adj oblicuo(-cua).

oblong ['ɒblɒŋ] adj rectangular ♦ n rectángulo m.

obnoxious [əb'nɒkʃəs] adj detestable.

oboe ['əubəu] n oboe m.

obscene [əb'si:n] adj obsceno(-na).

obscure [əb'skjuər] adj (difficult to understand) oscuro(-ra); (not well-known) desconocido(-da).

observant [əb'zɜ:vnt] adj observador(-ra).

observation [ˌɒbzə'veɪʃn] n observación f.

observatory [əb'zɜ:vətrɪ] n observatorio m.

observe [əb'zɜ:v] vt observar.

obsessed [əb'sest] adj obsesionado(-da).

obsession [əb'seʃn] n obsesión f.

obsolete ['ɒbsəli:t] adj obsoleto(-ta).

obstacle ['ɒbstəkl] n obstáculo m.

obstinate ['ɒbstənət] adj obstinado(-da).

obstruct [əb'strʌkt] vt (road, path) obstruir.

obstruction [əb'strʌkʃn] n (in road, path) obstáculo m.

obtain [əb'teɪn] vt obtener.

obtainable [əb'teɪnəbl] adj asequible.

obvious ['ɒbvɪəs] adj obvio(-via).

obviously ['ɒbvɪəslɪ] adv (of course) evidentemente; (clearly) claramente.

occasion [ə'keɪʒn] n (instance) vez f; (important event) acontecimiento m; (opportunity) ocasión f.

occasional [ə'keɪʒənl] adj esporádico(-ca).

occasionally [ə'keɪʒnəlɪ] adv de vez en cuando.

occupant ['ɒkjupənt] n (of house) inquilino m (-na f); (of car, plane) ocupante mf.

occupation [ˌɒkju'peɪʃn] n (job) empleo m; (pastime) pasatiempo m.

occupied ['ɒkjupaɪd] adj (toilet) ocupado(-da).

occupy ['ɒkjupaɪ] vt ocupar; (building) habitar.

occur [ə'kɜ:r] vi (happen) ocurrir; (exist) encontrarse.

occurrence [ə'kʌrəns] n acontecimiento m.

ocean ['əuʃn] n océano m; the ~ (Am: sea) el mar.

o'clock [ə'klɒk] adv: it's one ~ es la una; it's two ~ son las dos; at one/two ~ a la una/las dos.

Oct. (abbr of October) oct.

October [ɒk'təubər] n octubre m, → September.

octopus ['ɒktəpəs] n pulpo m.

odd [ɒd] adj (strange) raro(-ra); (number) impar; (not matching) sin pareja; (occasional) ocasional; **sixty ~ miles** sesenta y pico millas; **some ~ bits of paper** algunos que otros cachos de papel; **~ jobs** chapuzas fpl.

odds [ɒdz] npl (in betting) apuestas *fpl*; (*chances*) probabilidades *fpl*; ~ **and ends** chismes *mpl*.

odor ['əʊdər] (*Am*) = **odour**.

odour ['əʊdər] *n* (*Br*) olor *m*.

of [ɒv] *prep* **1.** (*gen*) de; **the handle** ~ **the door** el pomo de la puerta; **fear** ~ **spiders** miedo a las arañas; **he died** ~ **cancer** murió de cáncer; **the city** ~ **Glasgow** la ciudad de Glasgow; **that was very kind** ~ **you** fue muy amable por tu parte.

2. (*describing amounts, contents*) de; **a piece** ~ **cake** un trozo de pastel; **a glass** ~ **beer** un vaso de cerveza; **a fall** ~ **20%** un descenso del 20%.

3. (*made from*) de; **it's made** ~ **wood** es de madera.

4. (*referring to time*) de; **the summer** ~ **1969** el verano de 1969; **the 26th** ~ **August** el 26 de agosto.

5. (*Am: in telling the time*): **it's ten** ~ **four** son las cuatro menos diez.

off [ɒf] *adv* **1.** (*away*): **to drive/walk** ~ **alejarse; to get** ~ (*bus, train etc*) bajarse; **we're** ~ **to Austria next week** nos vamos a Austria la semana que viene.

2. (*expressing removal*): **to take sthg** ~ (*clothes, shoes*) quitarse algo; (*lid, wrapper*) quitar algo; (*money*) descontar algo.

3. (*so as to stop working*): **to turn sthg** ~ (*TV, radio, engine*) apagar; (*tap*) cerrar.

4. (*expressing distance or time away*): **it's a long way** ~ (*in distance*) está muy lejos; **Christmas is a long way** ~ queda mucho para las Navidades.

5. (*not at work*) libre; **I'm taking a week** ~ voy a tomar una semana libre; **she's** ~ **ill** está de baja por enfermedad.

6. (*expressing completion*): **to finish sthg** ~ terminar algo.

◆ *prep* **1.** (*away from*): **to get** ~ **sthg** bajarse de algo; **she fell** ~ **the chair** se cayó de la silla.

2. (*indicating removal*): **take the lid** ~ **the jar** quita la tapa del tarro; **we'll take £20** ~ **the price** le descontaremos 20 libras del precio.

3. (*adjoining*): **it's just** ~ **the main road** está al lado de la carretera principal.

4. (*absent from*): **to be** ~ **work** no estar en el trabajo.

5. (*inf: from*): **I bought it** ~ **her** se lo compré a ella.

6. (*inf: no longer liking*): **I'm** ~ **my food** no me apetece comer estos días.

◆ *adj* **1.** (*meat, cheese*) pasado(-da); (*milk*) cortado(-da); (*beer*) agrio (agria).

2. (*not working*) apagado(-da); (*tap*) cerrado(-da).

3. (*cancelled*) suspendido(-da).

4. (*not available*): **the soup's** ~ no hay sopa.

offence [ə'fens] *n* (*Br*) (*crime*) delito *m*; (*upset*) ofensa *f*.

offend [ə'fend] *vt* ofender.

offender [ə'fendər] *n* delincuente *mf*.

offense [ə'fens] (*Am*) = **offence**.

offensive [ə'fensɪv] *adj* (*insulting*) ofensivo(-va).

offer ['ɒfər] *n* oferta *f* ◆ *vt* ofrecer; **on** ~ (*available*) disponible; (*reduced*) en oferta; **to** ~ **to do sthg** ofrecerse a hacer algo; **to** ~ **sb sthg** ofrecer algo a alguien.

office ['ɒfɪs] *n* oficina *f*.

office block *n* bloque *m* de oficinas.

officer ['ɒfɪsə'] n (MIL) oficial mf; (policeman) agente mf de policía.

official [ə'fɪʃl] adj oficial ◆ n (of government) funcionario m (-ria f).

officially [ə'fɪʃəlɪ] adv oficialmente.

off-licence n (Br) tienda de bebidas alcohólicas para llevar.

off-peak adj de tarifa reducida.

off sales npl (Br) venta de bebidas alcohólicas para llevar en un pub.

off-season n temporada f baja.

offshore ['ɒfʃɔː'] adj (breeze) costero(-ra).

off side n (for right-hand drive) lado m izquierdo; (for left-hand drive) lado derecho.

off-the-peg adj confeccionado(-da).

often ['ɒfn, 'ɒftn] adv a menudo, con frecuencia; **how ~ do the buses run?** ¿cada cuánto tiempo pasan los autobuses?; **every so ~** cada cierto tiempo.

oh [əʊ] excl ¡ah!, ¡oh!

oil [ɔɪl] n aceite m; (fuel) petróleo m.

oilcan ['ɔɪlkæn] n aceitera f.

oil filter n filtro m del aceite.

oil rig n plataforma f petrolífera.

oily ['ɔɪlɪ] adj (cloth, hands) grasiento(-ta); (food) aceitoso(-sa).

ointment ['ɔɪntmənt] n pomada f.

OK [,əʊ'keɪ] n (inf) adv (expressing agreement) vale; (satisfactorily, well) bien ◆ adj: **is that ~ with you?** ¿te parece bien?; **everyone's ~** todos están bien; **the film was ~** la película estuvo bien.

okay [,əʊ'keɪ] = OK.

old [əʊld] adj viejo(-ja); (former) antiguo(-gua); **how ~ are you?** ¿cuántos años tienes?; **I'm 36 years ~** tengo 36 años; **to get ~** hacerse viejo.

old age n vejez f.

old age pensioner n pensionista mf.

O-level n antiguo examen estatal en una materia que se solía hacer a los 16 años en Inglaterra y Gales.

olive ['ɒlɪv] n aceituna f.

olive oil n aceite m de oliva.

Olympic Games [ə'lɪmpɪk-] npl Juegos mpl Olímpicos.

omelette ['ɒmlɪt] n tortilla f; **mushroom ~** tortilla de champiñones.

ominous ['ɒmɪnəs] adj siniestro(-tra).

omit [ə'mɪt] vt omitir.

on [ɒn] prep 1. (indicating position) en; (on top of), sobre; **it's ~ the table** está en OR sobre la mesa; **it's ~ the floor** está en el suelo; **a picture ~ the wall** un cuadro en la pared; **the exhaust ~ the car** el tubo de escape del coche; **the left/right** a la izquierda/derecha; **we stayed ~ a farm** estuvimos en una granja; **~ the banks of the river** a orillas del río; **the instructions ~ the packet** las instrucciones en el paquete. 2. (with forms of transport): **~ the train/plane** en el tren/avión; **to get ~ a bus** subirse a un autobús. 3. (expressing means, method) en; **~ foot** a pie; **to lean ~ one's elbows** apoyarse en los codos; **~ the radio** en la radio; **~ TV** en la televisión;

it runs ~ unleaded petrol funciona con gasolina sin plomo.

4. *(about)*: sobre, acerca de; **a book ~ Germany** un libro sobre Alemania.

5. *(expressing time)*: ~ **arrival** al llegar; ~ **Tuesday** el martes; ~ **Tuesdays** los martes; ~ **25th August** el 25 de agosto.

6. *(with regard to)* en, sobre; **a tax ~ imports** un impuesto sobre las importaciones; **the effect ~ Britain** el impacto en Gran Bretaña.

7. *(describing activity, state)*: ~ **holiday** de vacaciones; ~ **offer** *(reduced)* en oferta; ~ **sale** en venta.

8. *(in phrases)*: **do you have any money ~ you?** *(inf)* ¿llevas dinero?; **the drinks are ~ me** (la as copas) invito yo.

♦ *adv* **1.** *(in place, covering)*: **put the lid ~** pon la tapa; **to put one's clothes ~** vestirse.

2. *(film, play, programme)*: **the news is ~** están dando las noticias; **what's ~ at the cinema?** ¿qué ponen en el cine?

3. *(with transport)*: **to get ~** subirse.

4. *(functioning)*: **to turn sthg ~** *(TV, radio, engine)* encender algo; *(tap)* abrir algo.

5. *(taking place)*: **the match is already ~** ya ha empezado el partido.

6. *(indicating continuing action)*: **to keep ~ doing sthg** seguir haciendo algo; **to drive ~** seguir (conduciendo).

7. *(in phrases)*: **have you anything ~ tonight?** ¿haces algo esta noche?

♦ *adj* *(TV, radio, light, engine)* encendido(-da); *(tap)* abierto(-ta); **is the game ~?** ¿se va a celebrar el partido?

once [wʌns] *adv* *(one time)* una vez; *(in the past)* en otro tiempo ♦ *conj* una vez que; **at ~** *(immediately)* inmediatamente; *(at the same time)* a la vez; **for ~** por una vez; **a month** una vez al mes; ~ **more** *(one more time)* una vez más; *(again)* otra vez.

oncoming ['ɒn,kʌmɪŋ] *adj* *(traffic)* que viene en dirección contraria.

one [wʌn] *num* uno (una) ♦ *adj* **1.** *(only)* único(-ca) ♦ *pron* *(fml: you)* uno *m* (una *f*); **the green ~** el verde (la verde); **I want a blue ~** quiero uno azul; **thirty-~** treinta y uno; **a hundred and ~** ciento uno; ~ **fifth** un quinto; **that ~** *(ésa f)*; **this ~** éste *m* (-ta *f)*; **which ~?** ¿cuál?; **the ~ I told you about** aquél que te conté; ~ **of my friends** uno de mis amigos; ~ **day** *(in past)* un día; *(in future)* algún día.

one-piece (swimsuit) *n* traje *m* de baño de una pieza.

oneself [wʌn'self] *pron* *(reflexive)* se; *(after prep)* uno mismo *m* (una misma *f)*; **to wash ~** lavarse.

one-way *adj* *(street)* de dirección única; *(ticket)* de ida.

onion ['ʌnjən] *n* cebolla *f*.

onion bhaji [-'bɑ:dʒɪ] *n* buñuelo de cebolla picada, rebozada y muy frita preparado al estilo indio.

onion rings *npl* anillos *mpl* de cebolla rebozados.

only ['əʊnlɪ] *adj* único(-ca) ♦ *adv* sólo; **an ~ child** hijo único; **I ~ want one** sólo quiero uno; **we've ~ just arrived** acabamos de llegar; **there's ~ just enough** apenas hay lo justo; **"members ~"** "miembros sólo"; **not** ~ no sólo.

onto ['ɒntu:] *prep (with verbs of movement)* encima de, sobre; **to get ~ sb** *(telephone)* ponerse en contacto con alguien.

onward ['ɒnwəd] *adv* = **onwards ♦ adj: your ~ journey** el resto de su viaje.

onwards ['ɒnwədz] *adv (forwards)* adelante; **from ~** de ahora en adelante; **from October ~** de octubre en adelante.

opal ['əʊpl] *n* ópalo *m*.

opaque [əʊ'peɪk] *adj* opaco(-ca).

open ['əʊpn] *adj* abierto(-ta); *(honest)* sincero(-ra) **♦** *vt* abrir; *(start)* dar comienzo a **♦** *vi (door, window, lock)* abrirse; *(shop, office, bank)* abrir; *(start)* dar comienzo a; **are you ~ at the weekend?** ¿abres el fin de semana?; **wide ~** abierto de par en par; **in the ~ (air)** al aire libre ❑ **open onto** *vt fus* dar a; **open up** *vi* abrir.

open-air *adj* al aire libre.

opening ['əʊpnɪŋ] *n (gap)* abertura *f*; *(beginning)* comienzo *m*; *(opportunity)* oportunidad *f*.

opening hours *npl* horario *m* de apertura.

open-minded [-'maɪndɪd] *adj* sin prejuicios.

open-plan *adj* de plano abierto.

open sandwich *n* rebanada de pan cubierta con relleno habitual de bocadillos.

opera ['ɒpərə] *n* ópera *f*.

opera house *n* teatro *m* de la ópera.

operate ['ɒpəreɪt] *vt (machine)* hacer funcionar **♦** *vi (work)* funcionar; **to ~ on sb** operar a alguien.

operating room ['ɒpəreɪtɪŋ-] *n (Am)* = **operating theatre**.

operating theatre ['ɒpəreɪtɪŋ-] *n (Br)* quirófano *m*.

operation [ˌɒpə'reɪʃn] *n* operación *f*; **to be in ~** *(law, system)* estar en vigor; **to have an ~** operarse.

operator ['ɒpəreɪtə*] *n (on phone)* operador *m* (-ra *f*).

opinion [ə'pɪnjən] *n* opinión *f*; **in my ~** en mi opinión.

opponent [ə'pəʊnənt] *n (SPORT)* contrincante *mf*; *(of idea, policy, party)* adversario *m* (-ria *f*).

opportunity [ˌɒpə'tju:nətɪ] *n* oportunidad *f*.

oppose [ə'pəʊz] *vt* oponerse a.

opposed [ə'pəʊzd] *adj*: **to be ~ to** oponerse a.

opposite [ˈɒpəzɪt] *adj (facing)* de enfrente; *(totally different)* opuesto(-ta) **♦** *prep* enfrente de **♦** *n*: **the ~ (of)** lo contrario (de).

opposition [ˌɒpə'zɪʃn] *n (objections)* oposición *f*; *(SPORT)* oponentes *mfpl*; **the Opposition** la oposición.

opt [ɒpt] *vt*: **to ~ to do sthg** optar por hacer algo.

optician's [ɒp'tɪʃnz] *n (shop)* óptica *f*.

optimist ['ɒptɪmɪst] *n* optimista *mf*.

optimistic [ˌɒptɪ'mɪstɪk] *adj* optimista.

option ['ɒpʃn] *n* opción *f*.

optional ['ɒpʃənl] *adj* opcional.

or [ɔː*] *conj* o, u *(before "o" or "ho")*;

(after negative) ni; **I can't read ~ write** no sé (ni) leer ni escribir.

oral [ˈɔːrəl] *adj* (*spoken*) oral; (*of the mouth*) bucal ♦ n **examen** m **oral.**

orange [ˈɒrɪndʒ] *adj* naranja (*inv*) ♦ n **naranja** f.

orange juice n **zumo** m de naranja.

orange squash n (*Br*) naranjada f.

orbit [ˈɔːbɪt] n **órbita** f.

orbital (motorway) [ˈɔːbɪtl] n (*Br*) **ronda** f **de circunvalación.**

orchard [ˈɔːtʃəd] n **huerto** m.

orchestra [ˈɔːkɪstrə] n **orquesta** f.

ordeal [ɔːˈdiːl] n **calvario** m.

order [ˈɔːdə] n (*sequence, neatness, discipline*) **orden** m; (*command, in restaurant*) **orden** f; (*COMM*) **pedido** m ♦ vt (*command*) **ordenar;** (*food, drink, taxi*) **pedir;** (*COMM*) **encargar** ♦ vi (*in restaurant*) **pedir; in ~ to** para; **out of ~** (*not working*) **estropeado; in working ~** en funcionamiento; **to ~ sb to do sthg ordenar** a alguien que haga algo.

order form n **hoja** f **de pedido.**

ordinary [ˈɔːdənrɪ] *adj* **corriente.**

ore [ɔː] n **mineral** m.

oregano [ˌɒrɪˈɡɑːnəʊ] n **orégano** m.

organ [ˈɔːɡən] n **órgano** m.

organic [ɔːˈɡænɪk] *adj* **orgánico(-ca).**

organization [ˌɔːɡənaɪˈzeɪʃn] n **organización** f.

organize [ˈɔːɡənaɪz] vt **organizar.**

organizer [ˈɔːɡənaɪzə] n (*person*) **organizador** m (**-ra** f); (*diary*)

agenda f.

oriental [ˌɔːrɪˈentl] *adj* **oriental.**

orientate [ˈɔːrɪenteɪt] vt: **to ~ o.s. orientarse.**

origin [ˈɒrɪdʒɪn] n **origen** m.

original [əˈrɪdʒənl] *adj* (*first*) **originario(-ria);** (*novel*) **original.**

originally [əˈrɪdʒənəlɪ] *adv* **originalmente.**

originate [əˈrɪdʒəneɪt] vi: **to ~ (from) nacer** (de).

ornament [ˈɔːnəmənt] n **adorno** m.

ornamental [ˌɔːnəˈmentl] *adj* **ornamental.**

ornate [ɔːˈneɪt] *adj* **recargado(-da).**

orphan [ˈɔːfn] n **huérfano** m (**-na** f).

orthodox [ˈɔːθədɒks] *adj* **ortodoxo(-xa).**

ostentatious [ˌɒstenˈteɪʃəs] *adj* **ostentoso(-sa).**

ostrich [ˈɒstrɪtʃ] n **avestruz** m.

other [ˈʌðə] *adj* **otro** (**otra**) ♦ *adv:* **~ than** excepto; **the ~ (one)** el otro (la otra); **the ~ day** el otro día; **one after the ~** uno después del otro ❏ **others** *pron* (*additional ones*) **otros** *mpl* (**otras** *fpl*); **the ~s** (*remaining ones*) **los demás** (**las demás**), **los otros** (**las otras**).

otherwise [ˈʌðəwaɪz] *adv* (*or else*) **sino;** (*apart from that*) **por lo demás;** (*differently*) **de otra manera.**

otter [ˈɒtə] n **nutria** f.

ought [ɔːt] *aux vb* **deber; it ~ to be ready debería de estar listo; you ~ to do it deberías hacerlo.**

ounce [aʊns] n = 28,35g, **onza** f.

our [ˈaʊə] *adj* **nuestro(-tra).**

ours ['auəz] *pron* nuestro *m* (-tra *f*); **a friend of ~** un amigo nuestro.

ourselves ['auə'selvz] *pron* (*reflexive*) nos; (*after prep*) nosotros *mpl* mismos (nosotras *fpl* mismas); **we did it ~** lo hicimos nosotros mismos.

out [aut] *adj* (light, cigarette) apagado(-da).

♦ *adv* **1.** (*outside*) fuera; **to get ~** (of) (car) bajar (de); **to go ~** (of) salir (de); **it's cold ~ today** hace frío hoy.

2. (*not at home, work*) fuera; **to go ~** salir; **she's ~** está fuera.

3. (*extinguished*): **put your cigarette ~** apaga tu cigarrillo.

4. (*expressing removal*): **to take sthg ~** (of) sacar algo (de); **to pour sthg ~** (liquid) echar algo.

5. (*outwards*) hacia fuera; **to stick ~** sobresalir.

6. (*expressing exclusion*) fuera; **"keep ~"** "prohibido el paso".

7. (*wrong*): **the bill's £10 ~** hay un error de 10 libras en la cuenta.

8. (*in phrases*): **stay ~ of the sun** no te expongas al sol; **made ~ of wood** (hecho) de madera; **five ~ of ten women** cinco de cada diez mujeres; **I'm ~ of cigarettes** no tengo (más) cigarrillos.

outback ['autbæk] *n*: **the ~ los** llanos del interior australiano.

outboard (motor) ['autbɔːd] *n* fueraborda *m*.

outbreak ['autbreɪk] *n* (of war) comienzo *m*; (of illness) epidemia *f*.

outburst ['autbɜːst] *n* explosión *f*.

outcome ['autkʌm] *n* resultado *m*.

outcrop ['autkrɒp] *n* afloramiento *m*.

outdated [,aut'deɪtd] *adj* anticuado(-da).

outdo [,aut'duː] *vt* aventajar.

outdoor ['autdɔːʲ] *adj* (swimming pool, activities) al aire libre.

outdoors [aut'dɔːz] *adv* al aire libre.

outer ['autəʲ] *adj* exterior.

outer space *n* el espacio exterior.

outfit ['autfɪt] *n* (clothes) traje *m*.

outing ['autɪŋ] *n* excursión *f*.

outlet ['autlet] *n* (pipe) desagüe *m*; **"no ~"** (Am) señal que indica que una carretera no tiene salida.

outline ['autlaɪn] *n* (shape) contorno *m*; (description) esbozo *m*.

outlook ['autluk] *n* (for future) perspectivas *fpl*; (of weather) pronóstico *m*; (attitude) enfoque *m*.

out-of-date *adj* (old-fashioned) anticuado(-da); (passport, licence) caducado(-da).

outpatients' (department) ['aut,peɪʃnts-] *n* departamento *m* de pacientes externos.

output ['autput] *n* (of factory) producción *f*; (COMPUT: printout) impresión *f*.

outrage ['autreɪdʒ] *n* (cruel act) atrocidad *f*.

outrageous [aut'reɪdʒəs] *adj* (shocking) indignante.

outright [,aut'raɪt] *adv* (tell, deny) categóricamente; (own) totalmente.

outside [adv ,aut'saɪd, adj, prep & n 'autsaɪd] *adv* fuera ♦ *prep* fuera de ♦ *adj* (exterior) exterior; (help, ad-

vice) independiente ◆ *n:* **the** ~ *(of building, car, container)* el exterior; *(AUT: in UK)* carril m de adelantamiento; *(AUT: in Europe, US)* carril lento; **an** ~ **line** una línea exterior; ~ **of** *(Am) (on the outside of)* fuera de; *(apart from)* aparte de.

outside lane *n (in UK)* carril m de adelantamiento; *(in Europe, US)* carril lento.

outsize ['aʊtsaɪz] *adj (clothes)* de talla grande.

outskirts ['aʊtskɜːts] *npl* afueras *fpl.*

outstanding [aʊt'stændɪŋ] *adj (remarkable)* destacado(-da); *(problem, debt)* pendiente.

outward ['aʊtwəd] *adj (journey)* de ida; *(external)* visible.

outwards ['aʊtwədz] *adv* hacia afuera.

oval ['əʊvl] *adj* oval.

ovation [əʊ'veɪʃn] *n* ovación *f.*

oven ['ʌvn] *n* horno *m.*

oven glove *n* guante *m* de horno.

ovenproof ['ʌvnpruːf] *adj* refractario(-ria).

oven-ready *adj* listo(-ta) para hornear.

over ['əʊvəʳ] *prep* **1.** *(above)* encima de; **a lamp** ~ **the table** una lámpara encima de la mesa.

2. *(across)* por encima de; **to walk/drive** ~ **sthg** cruzar algo; **it's just** ~ **the road** está enfrente.

3. *(covering)* sobre; **to smear the cream** ~ **the wound** untar la herida con la crema.

4. *(more than)* más de; **it cost** ~ **£1,000** costó más de mil libras.

5. *(during)* durante; ~ **the past two**

years en los dos últimos años.

6. *(with regard to)* sobre; **an argument** ~ **the price** una discusión sobre el precio.

◆ *adv* **1.** *(downwards)* **to fall** ~ caerse; **to push sthg** ~ empujar algo.

2. *(referring to position, movement):* **to drive/walk** ~ cruzar; ~ **here** aquí; ~ **there** allí.

3. *(round to other side):* **to turn sthg** ~ dar la vuelta a algo.

4. *(more):* **children aged 12 and** ~ niños de 12 años en adelante.

5. *(remaining):* **to be (left)** ~ quedar.

6. *(to one's house):* **to invite sb** ~ **for dinner** invitar a alguien a cenar.

7. *(in phrases):* **all** ~ *adj (finished)* terminado(-da) ◆ *prep (throughout)* por todo.

◆ *adj (finished):* **to be** ~ haber terminado.

overall [*adv* ,əʊvər'ɔːl, *n* 'əʊvərɔːl] *adv* en conjunto ◆ *n (Br: coat)* guardapolvo *m; (Am: boiler suit)* mono *m;* **how much does it cost** ~? ¿cuánto cuesta en total? ❑ **overalls** *npl (Br: boiler suit)* mono *m; (Am: dungarees)* pantalones *mpl* de peto.

overboard ['əʊvəbɔːd] *adv (from ship)* por la borda.

overbooked [,əʊvə'bʊkt] *adj:* **to be** ~ tener overbooking.

overcame [,əʊvə'keɪm] *pt* → overcome.

overcast [,əʊvə'kɑːst] *adj* cubierto(-ta).

overcharge [,əʊvə'tʃɑːdʒ] *vt* cobrar en exceso.

overcoat ['əʊvəkəʊt] *n* abrigo *m.*

overcome [,əʊvə'kʌm] *(pt* -came,

overtake

overcooked [ˌəuvəˈkukt] adj
demasiado hecho(-cha).

overcrowded [ˌəuvəˈkraudid]
adj atestado(-da).

overdo [ˌəuvəˈduː] (pt **-did** [-ˈdid],
pp **-done**) vt (exaggerate) exagerar;
to ~ it exagerar.

overdone [ˌəuvəˈdʌn] pp →
overdo ♦ adj (food) demasiado
hecho(-cha).

overdose [ˈəuvədəus] n sobredosis f inv.

overdraft [ˈəuvədrɑːft] n (money
owed) saldo m deudor; (credit limit)
descubierto m.

overdue [ˌəuvəˈdjuː] adj (bus,
flight) retrasado(-da); (rent, payment) vencido(-da).

over easy adj (Am: egg)
frito(-ta) por ambos lados.

overexposed [ˌəuvərɪkˈspəuzd]
adj sobreexpuesto(-ta).

overflow [vb ˌəuvəˈfləu, n ˈəuvəfləu] vi desbordarse ♦ n (pipe)
cañería f de desagüe.

overgrown [ˌəuvəˈgrəun] adj
cubierto(-ta) de matojos.

overhaul [ˌəuvəˈhɔːl] n (of machine, car) revisión f.

overhead [adj ˈəuvəhed, adv
ˌəuvəˈhed] adj aéreo(-a) ♦ adv por lo
alto.

overhead locker n maletero
m superior.

overhear [ˌəuvəˈhɪər] (pt & pp
-heard [-ˈhɜːd]) vt oír por casualidad.

overheat [ˌəuvəˈhiːt] vi recalentarse.

overland [ˈəuvəlænd] adv por vía
terrestre.

overlap [ˌəuvəˈlæp] vi superponerse.

overleaf [ˌəuvəˈliːf] adv al dorso.

overload [ˌəuvəˈləud] vt sobrecargar.

overlook [vb ˌəuvəˈluk, n ˈəuvəluk] vt (subj: building, room) dar a;
(miss) pasar por alto ♦ n: (scenic) ~
(Am) mirador m.

overnight [adv ˌəuvəˈnaɪt, adj
ˈəuvənaɪt] adv (during the night)
durante la noche; (until next day)
toda la noche ♦ adj (train, journey)
de noche.

overnight bag n bolso m de
mano.

overpass [ˈəuvəpɑːs] n paso m
elevado.

overpowering [ˌəuvəˈpauərɪŋ]
adj arrollador(-ra).

oversaw [ˌəuvəˈsɔː] pt → oversee.

overseas [adv ˌəuvəˈsiːz, adj
ˈəuvəsiːz] adv (go) al extranjero; (live)
en el extranjero ♦ adj (holiday,
branch) en el extranjero; (student)
extranjero(-ra).

oversee [ˌəuvəˈsiː] (pt **-saw**, pp
-seen [-ˈsiːn]) vt supervisar.

overshoot [ˌəuvəˈʃuːt] (pt & pp
-shot [-ˈʃɒt]) vt pasarse.

oversight [ˈəuvəsaɪt] n descuido
m.

oversleep [ˌəuvəˈsliːp] (pt & pp
-slept [-ˈslept]) vi dormirse, no despertarse a tiempo.

overtake [ˌəuvəˈteɪk] (pt **-took**,
pp **-taken** [-ˈteɪkən]) vt & vi adelantar; **"no overtaking"** "prohibido
adelantar".

overtime ['əʊvətaɪm] n horas fpl extra.

overtook [əʊvə'tʊk] pt → **overtake**.

overture ['əʊtjʊ‚əvə] n (MUS) obertura f.

overturn [əʊvə'tɜːn] vi volcar.

overweight [əʊvə'weɪt] adj gordo(-da).

overwhelm [əʊvə'welm] vt abrumar.

owe [əʊ] vt deber; **to ~ sb sthg** deber algo a alguien; **owing to** debido a.

owl [aʊl] n búho m.

own [əʊn] adj propio(-pia) ◆ vt poseer ◆ pron: **my ~** el mío (la mía); **her ~** la suya; **his ~** el suyo; **on my ~** solo(-la); **to get one's ~ back** tomarse la revancha □ **own up** vi: **to ~ up (to sthg)** confesar (algo).

owner ['əʊnəʳ] n propietario m (-ria f).

ownership ['əʊnəʃɪp] n propiedad f.

ox [ɒks] (pl **oxen** ['ɒksən]) n buey m.

oxtail soup ['ɒksteɪl-] n sopa f de rabo de buey.

oxygen ['ɒksɪdʒən] n oxígeno m.

oyster ['ɔɪstəʳ] n ostra f.

oz abbr = **ounce**.

ozone-friendly ['əʊzəʊn-] adj que no daña la capa de ozono.

P

P abbr = **penny, pence**; (abbr of page) pág.

pace [peɪs] n paso m.

pacemaker ['peɪs‚meɪkəʳ] n (for heart) marcapasos m inv.

Pacific [pə'sɪfɪk] n: **the ~ (Ocean)** el (océano) Pacífico.

pacifier ['pæsɪfaɪəʳ] n (Am: for baby) chupete m.

pacifist ['pæsɪfɪst] n pacifista mf.

pack [pæk] n (packet) paquete m; (of crisps) bolsa f; (Br: of cards) baraja f; (rucksack) mochila f ◆ vt (suitcase, bag) hacer; (clothes, camera etc) meter en la maleta; (to package) empaquetar ◆ vi hacer la maleta; **a ~ of lies** una sarta de mentiras; **to ~ sthg into sthg** meter algo en algo; **to ~ one's bags** hacerse las maletas □ **pack up** vi (pack suitcase) hacer las maletas; (tidy up) recoger; (Br: inf: machine, car) fastidiarse.

package ['pækɪdʒ] n paquete m ◆ vt envasar.

package holiday n vacaciones fpl con todo incluido.

package tour n tour m con todo incluido.

packaging ['pækɪdʒɪŋ] n embalaje m.

packed [pækt] adj (crowded) repleto(-ta).

packed lunch n almuerzo preparado que se lleva al colegio, trabajo, etc.

packet ['pækɪt] *n* paquete *m*; **it cost a ~** (*Br: inf*) costó un dineral.

packing ['pækɪŋ] *n* (*material*) embalaje *m*; **to do one's ~** hacer el equipaje.

pad [pæd] *n* (*of paper*) bloc *m*; (*of cloth, cotton wool*) almohadilla *f*; **shoulder ~s** hombreras *fpl*.

padded ['pædɪd] *adj* acolchado(-da).

padded envelope *n* sobre *m* acolchado.

paddle ['pædl] *n* (*pole*) pala *f* ◆ *vi* (*wade*) pasear por la orilla; (*in canoe*) remar.

paddling pool ['pædlɪŋ] *n* (*in park*) estanque *m* para chapotear.

paddock ['pædək] *n* (*at racecourse*) paddock *m*.

padlock ['pædlɒk] *n* candado *m*.

page [peɪdʒ] *n* página *f* ◆ *vt* llamar por megafonía; **"paging Mr Hill"** "llamando a Mr Hill".

paid [peɪd] *pt & pp* → **pay** ◆ *adj* pagado(-da).

pain [peɪn] *n* (*physical*) dolor *m*; (*emotional*) pena *f*; **to be in ~** sufrir dolor; **he's such a ~!** (*inf*) ¡es un plasta! □ **pains** *npl* (*trouble*) esfuerzos *mpl*.

painful ['peɪnful] *adj* doloroso(-sa); **my leg is ~** me duele la pierna.

painkiller ['peɪn,kɪlər] *n* calmante *m*.

paint [peɪnt] *n* pintura *f* ◆ *vt & vi* pintar; **to ~ one's nails** pintarse las uñas □ **paints** *npl* (*tubes, pots etc*) pinturas *fpl*.

paintbrush ['peɪntbrʌʃ] *n* (*of decorator*) brocha *f*; (*of artist*)

pincel *m*.

painter ['peɪntər] *n* pintor *m* (-ra *f*).

painting ['peɪntɪŋ] *n* (*picture*) cuadro *m*; (*artistic activity, trade*) pintura *f*.

pair [peər] *n* (*of two things*) par *m*; **in ~s** por pares; **a ~ of pliers** unos alicates; **a ~ of scissors** unas tijeras; **a ~ of shorts** unos pantalones cortos; **a ~ of tights** un par de medias; **a ~ of trousers** unos pantalones.

pajamas [pə'dʒɑːməz] (*Am*) = **pyjamas**.

Pakistan [*Br* ˌpɑːkɪ'stɑːn, *Am* ˌpækɪ'stæn] *n* Paquistán.

Pakistani [*Br* ˌpɑːkɪ'stɑːnɪ, *Am* ˌpækɪ'stænɪ] *adj* paquistaní ◆ *n* paquistaní *mf*.

pakora [pə'kɔːrə] *npl* verduras rebozadas muy fritas y picantes, al estilo indio.

pal [pæl] *n* (*inf*) colega *mf*.

palace ['pælɪs] *n* palacio *m*.

palatable ['pælətəbl] *adj* sabroso(-sa).

palate ['pælət] *n* paladar *m*.

pale [peɪl] *adj* (*not bright*) claro (-ra); (*skin*) pálido(-da).

pale ale *n* tipo de cerveza rubia.

palm [pɑːm] *n* (*of hand*) palma *f*; **~ (tree)** palmera *f*.

palpitations [ˌpælpɪ'teɪʃnz] *npl* palpitaciones *fpl*.

pamphlet ['pæmflɪt] *n* folleto *m*.

pan [pæn] *n* cazuela *f*.

Panama [ˌpænə'mɑː] *n* Panamá.

Panamanian [ˌpænə'meɪnjən] *adj* panameño(-ña) ◆ *n* panameño *m* (-ña *f*).

pancake ['pænkeɪk] n crepe f.

pancake roll n rollito m de primavera.

panda ['pændə] n panda m.

panda car n (Br) coche m patrulla.

pane [peɪn] n cristal m.

panel ['pænl] n (of wood, on TV, radio) panel m; (group of experts) equipo m.

paneling ['pænəlɪŋ] (Am) = panelling.

panelling ['pænəlɪŋ] n (Br) paneles mpl.

panic ['pænɪk] (pt & pp -ked, cont -king) n pánico m ◆ vi aterrarse.

panniers ['pænɪəz] npl (for bicycle) bolsas fpl para equipaje.

panoramic [,pænə'ræmɪk] adj panorámico(-ca).

pant [pænt] vi jadear.

panties ['pæntɪz] npl (inf) bragas fpl.

pantomime ['pæntəmaɪm] n (Br) musical humorístico infantil de Navidades.

---

i PANTOMIME

Inspiradas normalmente en cuentos de hadas tradicionales, las "pantomimes" son musicales cómicos para niños que se representan durante las Navidades. Es costumbre que una actriz joven haga el papel del héroe y un actor cómico el de anciana.

---

pantry ['pæntri] n despensa f.

pants [pænts] npl (Br: underwear) calzoncillos mpl; (Am: trousers) pantalones mpl.

panty hose ['pæntɪ-] npl (Am) medias fpl.

paper ['peɪpə'] n (material) papel m; (newspaper) periódico m; (exam) examen m ◆ adj de papel ◆ vt empapelar; **a piece of ~** (sheet) un papel; (scrap) un trozo de papel ❑ **papers** npl (documents) documentación f.

paperback ['peɪpəbæk] n libro m en rústica.

paper bag n bolsa f de papel.

paperboy ['peɪpəbɔɪ] n repartidor m de periódicos.

paper clip n clip m.

papergirl ['peɪpəgɜːl] n repartidora f de periódicos.

paper handkerchief n pañuelo m de papel.

paper shop n = quiosco m de periódicos.

paperweight ['peɪpəweɪt] n pisapapeles m inv.

paprika ['pæprɪkə] n pimentón m.

par [pɑː'] n (in golf) par m.

paracetamol [,pærə'siːtəmɒl] n paracetamol m.

parachute ['pærəʃuːt] n paracaídas m inv.

parade [pə'reɪd] n (procession) desfile m; (of shops) hilera f.

paradise ['pærədaɪs] n paraíso m.

paraffin ['pærəfɪn] n parafina f.

paragraph ['pærəgrɑːf] n párrafo m.

Paraguay ['pærəgwaɪ] n (el) Paraguay.

Paraguayan [,pærə'gwaɪən] adj

paraguayo(-ya) ◆ *n* paraguayo *m* (-ya *f*).

parallel ['pærəlel] *adj*: ~ (to) paralelo(-la) (a).

paralysed ['pærəlaɪzd] *adj* (*Br*) paralizado(-da).

paralyzed ['pærəlaɪzd] (*Am*) = **paralysed**.

paramedic [,pærə'medɪk] *n* auxiliar *m* sanitario (auxiliar *f* sanitaria).

paranoid ['pærənɔɪd] *adj* paranoico(-ca).

parasite ['pærəsaɪt] *n* (*animal*) parásito *m*; (*pej: person*) parásito *m* (-ta *f*).

parasol ['pærəsɒl] *n* sombrilla *f*.

parcel ['pɑːsl] *n* paquete *m*.

parcel post *n* servicio *m* de paquete postal.

pardon ['pɑːdn] *excl*: ~? ¡perdón?; ~ (me)! ¡perdone!; I beg your ~! (*apologizing*) ¡le ruego me perdone!; I beg your ~? (*asking for repetition*) ¿cómo dice?

parents ['peərənts] *npl* padres *mpl*.

parish ['pærɪʃ] *n* (*of church*) parroquia *f*; (*village area*) municipio *m*.

park [pɑːk] *n* parque *m* ◆ *vt* & *vi* aparcar.

park and ride *n* aparcamiento en las afueras de la ciudad en donde hay autobuses al centro.

parking ['pɑːkɪŋ] *n* aparcamiento *m*.

parking brake *n* (*Am*) freno *m* de mano.

parking lot *n* (*Am*) aparcamiento *m* (al aire libre).

parking meter *n* parquí-

parking space *n* sitio *m* (para aparcar).

parking ticket *n* multa *f* por aparcamiento indebido.

parkway ['pɑːkweɪ] *n* (*Am*) avenida *f* (*con zona ajardinada en el medio*).

parliament ['pɑːləmənt] *n* parlamento *m*.

Parmesan (cheese) [,pɑːmɪ'zæn-] *n* parmesano *m*.

parrot ['pærət] *n* loro *m*.

parsley ['pɑːslɪ] *n* perejil *m*.

parsnip ['pɑːsnɪp] *n* chirivía *f*.

parson ['pɑːsn] *n* párroco *m*.

part [pɑːt] *n* parte *f*; (*of machine, car*) pieza *f*; (*in play, film*) papel *m*; (*Am: in hair*) raya *f* ◆ *adv* en parte ◆ *vi* (*couple*) separarse; in this ~ of France en esta parte de Francia; to form ~ of formar parte de; to play a ~ in desempeñar un papel en; to take ~ in tomar parte en; for my ~ por mi parte; for the most ~ en su mayoría; in these ~s por aquí.

partial ['pɑːʃl] *adj* (*not whole*) parcial; to be ~ to sthg ser aficionado(-da) a algo.

participant [pɑː'tɪsɪpənt] *n* participante *mf*.

participate [pɑː'tɪsɪpeɪt] *vi*: to ~ (in) participar (en).

particular [pə'tɪkjʊləʳ] *adj* (*specific, fussy*) particular; (*special*) especial; in ~ en particular; nothing in ~ nada en particular ❑ **particulars** *npl* (*details*) datos *mpl* personales.

particularly [pə'tɪkjʊləlɪ] *adv* especialmente.

parting ['pɑːtɪŋ] n (Br: in hair) raya f.

partition [pɑːˈtɪʃn] n (wall) tabique m.

partly ['pɑːtlɪ] adv en parte.

partner ['pɑːtnəʳ] n pareja f; (COMM) socio m (-cia f).

partnership ['pɑːtnəʃɪp] n asociación f.

partridge ['pɑːtrɪdʒ] n perdiz f.

part-time adj & adv a tiempo parcial.

party ['pɑːtɪ] n (for fun) fiesta f; (POL) partido m; (group of people) grupo m; **to have a** ~ hacer una fiesta.

pass [pɑːs] vt pasar; (house, entrance etc) pasar por delante de; (person in street) cruzarse con; (test, exam) aprobar; (overtake) adelantar; (law) aprobar ◆ vi pasar; (overtake) adelantar; (in test, exam) aprobar ◆ n (document, SPORT) pase m; (in mountain) desfiladero m; (in exam) aprobado m; **to ~ sb sthg** pasarle algo a alguien ❑ **pass by** vt fus (building, window etc) pasar por ◆ vi pasar cerca; **pass on** vt sep transmitir; **pass out** vi (faint) desmayarse; **pass up** vt sep (opportunity) dejar pasar.

passable ['pɑːsəbl] adj (road) transitable; (satisfactory) pasable.

passage ['pæsɪdʒ] n (corridor) pasadizo m; (in book) pasaje m; (sea journey) travesía f.

passageway ['pæsɪdʒweɪ] n pasadizo m.

passenger ['pæsɪndʒəʳ] n pasajero m (-ra f).

passerby [pɑːsəˈbaɪ] n transeúnte mf.

passing place ['pɑːsɪŋ-] n (for cars) apartadero m.

passion ['pæʃn] n pasión f.

passionate ['pæʃənət] adj apasionado(-da).

passive ['pæsɪv] n pasiva f.

passport ['pɑːspɔːt] n pasaporte m.

passport control n control m de pasaportes.

passport photo n foto f de pasaporte.

password ['pɑːswɜːd] n contraseña f.

past [pɑːst] adj (at earlier time) anterior; (finished) terminado(-da); (last) último(-ma); (former) antiguo(-gua) ◆ prep (further than) más allá de; (in front of) por delante de ◆ n pasado m ◆ adv: **to run** ~ pasar corriendo; ~ (tense) pasado m; **the** ~ **month** el mes pasado; **twenty-four** las cuatro y veinte; **in the** ~ en el pasado.

pasta ['pæstə] n pasta f.

paste [peɪst] n (spread) paté m; (glue) engrudo m.

pastel ['pæstl] n pastel m.

pasteurized ['pæstʃəraɪzd] adj pasteurizado(-da).

pastille ['pæstɪl] n pastilla f.

pastime ['pɑːstaɪm] n pasatiempo m.

pastry ['peɪstrɪ] n (for pie) pasta f; (cake) pastel m.

pasture ['pɑːstʃəʳ] n pasto m.

pasty ['pæstɪ] n (Br) empanada f.

pat [pæt] vt golpear ligeramente.

patch [pætʃ] n (for clothes) remiendo m; (of colour, damp, for eye) parche m; (for skin) esparadrapo *m*; **a bad ~** (*fig*) un mal momento.

pâté ['pætei] *n* paté *m*.

patent [*Br* 'peitənt, *Am* 'pætənt] *adj* patente *f*.

path [pɑ:θ, *pl* pɑ:ðz] *n* (*in garden, park, country*) camino *m*.

pathetic [pə'θetik] *adj* (*pej: useless*) inútil.

patience ['peiʃns] *n* (*quality*) paciencia *f*; (*Br: card game*) solitario *m*.

patient ['peiʃnt] *adj* paciente ◆ *n* paciente *mf*.

patio ['pætiəu] *n* patio *m*.

patriotic [*Br* ˌpætri'ɒtik, *Am* ˌpeitri'ɒtik] *adj* patriótico(-ca).

patrol [pə'trəul] *vt* patrullar ◆ *n* patrulla *f*.

patrol car *n* coche *m* patrulla.

patron ['peitrən] *n* (*fml: customer*) cliente *mf*; "**~s only**" "sólo para clientes".

patronizing ['pætrənaizɪŋ] *adj* paternalista.

pattern ['pætn] *n* (*of shapes, colours*) diseño *m*; (*for sewing*) patrón *m*.

patterned ['pætənd] *adj* estampado(-da).

pause [pɔ:z] *n* pausa *f* ◆ *vi* (*when speaking*) hacer una pausa; (*in activity*) detenerse.

pavement ['peivmənt] *n* (*Br: beside road*) acera *f*; (*Am: roadway*) calzada *f*.

pavilion [pə'viljən] *n* pabellón *m*.

paving stone ['peivɪŋ-] *n* losa *f*.

pavlova [pæv'ləuvə] *n* postre de merengue relleno de fruta y nata montada.

paw [pɔ:] *n* pata *f*.

pawn [pɔ:n] *vt* empeñar ◆ *n* (*in chess*) peón *m*.

pay [pei] (*pt & pp* **paid**) *vt* pagar ◆ *vi* (*give money*) pagar; (*be profitable*) ser rentable ◆ *n* paga *f*; **to ~ sb for sthg** pagar a alguien por algo; **to ~ money into an account** ingresar dinero en una cuenta; **to ~ attention (to)** prestar atención (a); **to ~ sb a visit** hacer una visita a alguien; **to ~ by credit card** pagar con tarjeta de crédito ❑ **pay back** *vt sep* (*money*) devolver; (*person*) devolver el dinero a; **pay for** *vt fus* pagar; **pay in** *vt sep* ingresar; **pay out** *vt sep* (*money*) pagar; **pay up** *vi* pagar.

payable ['peiəbl] *adj* (*bill*) pagadero(-ra); **~ to** (*cheque*) a favor de.

payment ['peimənt] *n* pago *m*.

payphone ['peifəun] *n* teléfono *m* público.

PC *n* (*abbr of* personal computer) ordenador personal, PC *m*; (*Br: abbr of* police constable) policía *mf*.

PE *abbr* = physical education.

pea [pi:] *n* guisante *m*.

peace [pi:s] *n* paz *f*; **to leave sb in ~** dejar a alguien en paz; **~ and quiet** tranquilidad *f*.

peaceful ['pi:sful] *adj* (*place, day, feeling*) tranquilo(-la); (*demonstration*) pacífico(-ca).

peach [pi:tʃ] *n* melocotón *m*.

peach melba [-'melbə] *n* postre de melocotones en almíbar con helado y jarabe de frambuesa.

peacock ['pi:kɒk] *n* pavo *m* real.

peak [pi:k] *n* (*of mountain*) pico *m*; (*of hat*) visera *f*; (*fig: highest point*) apogeo *m*.

peak hours npl horas fpl punta.

peak rate n (on telephone) tarifa f de hora punta.

peanut ['pi:nʌt] n cacahuete m.

peanut butter n manteca f de cacahuete.

pear [peəʳ] n pera f.

pearl [pɜ:l] n perla f.

peasant ['peznt] n campesino m (-na f).

pebble ['pebl] n guijarro m.

pecan pie [pɪ'kæn-] n tartaleta f de pacanas.

peck [pek] vi picotear.

peculiar [pɪ'kju:lɪəʳ] adj (strange) peculiar; **to be ~ to** ser propio(-pia) de.

peculiarity [pɪˌkju:lɪ'ærəɪ] n (special feature) peculiaridad f.

pedal ['pedl] n pedal m ♦ vi pedalear.

pedal bin n cubo m de basura con tapadera de pedal.

pedalo ['pedələʊ] (pl -s) n patín m (de agua).

pedestrian [pɪ'destrɪən] n peatón m.

pedestrian crossing n paso m de peatones.

pedestrianized [pɪ'destrɪənaɪzd] adj peatonal.

pedestrian precinct n (Br) zona f peatonal.

pedestrian zone (Am) = pedestrian precinct.

pee [pi:] vi (inf) mear ♦ n: **to have a ~** (inf) echar una meada.

peel [pi:l] n piel f ♦ vt pelar ♦ vi (paint) descascarillarse; (skin) pelarse.

peep [pi:p] n: **to have a ~** echar una ojeada.

peer [pɪəʳ] vi mirar con atención.

peg [peg] n (for tent) estaca f; (hook) gancho m; (for washing) pinza f.

pelican crossing [pelɪkən-] n (Br) paso de peatones con semáforo que el usuario puede accionar apretando un botón.

pelvis ['pelvɪs] n pelvis f.

pen [pen] n (ballpoint pen) bolígrafo m; (fountain pen) pluma f (estilográfica); (for animals) corral m.

penalty ['penltɪ] n (fine) multa f; (in football) penalti m.

pence [pens] npl (Br) peniques mpl.

pencil ['pensl] n lápiz m.

pencil case n estuche m.

pencil sharpener ['-ʃɑ:pnəʳ] n sacapuntas m inv.

pendant ['pendənt] n colgante m.

pending ['pendɪŋ] prep (fml) a la espera de.

penetrate ['penɪtreɪt] vt (pierce) penetrar en.

penfriend ['penfrend] n amigo m (-ga f) por correspondencia.

penguin ['peŋgwɪn] n pingüino m.

penicillin [ˌpenɪ'sɪlɪn] n penicilina f.

peninsula [pə'nɪnsjʊlə] n península f.

penis ['pi:nɪs] n pene m.

penknife ['pennaɪf] (pl -knives [-naɪvz]) n navaja f.

penny ['penɪ] (pl pennies) n (in UK) penique m; (in US) centavo m.

permission

pension ['penʃn] n pensión f.

pensioner ['penʃənəʳ] n pensionista mf.

penthouse ['penthaʊs, pl -haʊzɪz] n ático m.

penultimate [pe'nʌltɪmət] adj penúltimo(-ma).

people ['piːpl] npl (persons) personas fpl; (in general) gente f ♦ n (nation) pueblo m; the ~ (citizens) el pueblo.

pepper ['pepəʳ] n (spice) pimienta f; (vegetable) pimiento m.

peppercorn ['pepəkɔːn] n grano m de pimienta.

peppermint ['pepəmɪnt] adj de menta ♦ n (sweet) caramelo m de menta.

pepper pot n pimentero m.

pepper steak n bistec m a la pimienta.

Pepsi® ['pepsɪ] n Pepsi-Cola f.

per [pɜːʳ] prep por; ~ person por persona; ~ week por semana; £20 ~ night 20 libras por noche.

perceive [pə'siːv] vt percibir.

per cent adv por ciento.

percentage [pə'sentɪdʒ] n porcentaje m.

perch [pɜːtʃ] n (for bird) percha f.

percolator ['pɜːkəleɪtəʳ] n percolador m.

perfect [adj & n 'pɜːfɪkt, vb pə'fekt] adj perfecto(-ta) ♦ vt perfeccionar ♦ n: the ~ (tense) el perfecto.

perfection [pə'fekʃn] n: to do sthg to ~ hacer algo a la perfección.

perfectly ['pɜːfɪktlɪ] adv (very well) perfectamente.

perform [pə'fɔːm] vt (task, operation) realizar; (play) representar; (concert) interpretar ♦ vi (actor, singer) actuar.

performance [pə'fɔːməns] n (of play, concert, film) función f; (by actor, musician) actuación f; (of car) rendimiento m.

performer [pə'fɔːməʳ] n intérprete mf.

perfume ['pɜːfjuːm] n perfume m.

perhaps [pə'hæps] adv quizás.

perimeter [pə'rɪmɪtəʳ] n perímetro m.

period ['pɪərɪəd] n período m; (SCH) hora f; (Am: full stop) punto m ♦ adj de época; **sunny ~s** intervalos mpl de sol.

periodic [ˌpɪərɪ'ɒdɪk] adj periódico(-ca).

period pains npl dolores mpl menstruales.

periphery [pə'rɪfərɪ] n periferia f.

perishable ['perɪʃəbl] adj perecedero(-ra).

perk [pɜːk] n beneficio m adicional.

perm [pɜːm] n permanente f ♦ vt: **to have one's hair ~ed** hacerse una permanente.

permanent ['pɜːmənənt] adj permanente.

permanent address n domicilio m fijo.

permanently ['pɜːmənəntlɪ] adv permanentemente.

permissible [pə'mɪsəbl] adj (fml) lícito(-ta).

permission [pə'mɪʃn] n permiso *m*.

permit [*vb* pə'mɪt, *n* 'pɜːmɪt] *vt* permitir ♦ *n* permiso *m*; **to ~ sb to do sthg** permitir a alguien hacer algo; **"~ holders only"** "aparcamiento prohibido a personas no autorizadas".

perpendicular [,pɜːpən'dɪkjʊlə‹] *adj* perpendicular.

persevere [,pɜːsɪ'vɪə‹] *vi* perseverar.

persist [pə'sɪst] *vi* persistir; **to ~ in doing sthg** empeñarse en hacer algo.

persistent [pə'sɪstənt] *adj* persistente; *(person)* tenaz.

person ['pɜːsn] *(pl* **people**) *n* persona *f*; **in ~** en persona.

personal ['pɜːsənl] *adj* personal; *(life, letter)* privado(-da); *(rude)* ofensivo(-va); **a ~ friend** un amigo íntimo.

personal assistant *n* asistente *m* (-ta *f*) personal.

personal belongings *npl* efectos *mpl* personales.

personal computer *n* ordenador *m* personal.

personality [,pɜːsə'nælətɪ] *n* personalidad *f*.

personally ['pɜːsnəlɪ] *adv* personalmente.

personal property *n* bienes *mpl* muebles.

personal stereo *n* walkman® *m*.

personnel [,pɜːsə'nel] *npl* personal *m*.

perspective [pə'spektɪv] *n* perspectiva *f*.

Perspex® ['pɜːspeks] *n* (*Br*) =

plexiglás® *m inv*.

perspiration [,pɜːspə'reɪʃn] *n* transpiración *f*.

persuade [pə'sweɪd] *vt*: **to ~ sb (to do sthg)** persuadir a alguien (para que haga algo); **to ~ sb that** ... persuadir a alguien de que ...

persuasive [pə'sweɪsɪv] *adj* persuasivo(-va).

Peru [pə'ruː] *n* Perú.

Peruvian [pə'ruːvjən] *adj* peruano(-na) ♦ *n* peruano *m* (-na *f*).

pervert ['pɜːvɜːt] *n* pervertido *m* (-da *f*).

pessimist ['pesɪmɪst] *n* pesimista *mf*.

pessimistic [,pesɪ'mɪstɪk] *adj* pesimista.

pest [pest] *n* (*insect*) insecto *m* nocivo; (*animal*) animal *m* nocivo; (*inf*: *person*) pelma *mf*.

pester ['pestə‹] *vt* incordiar.

pesticide ['pestɪsaɪd] *n* pesticida *m*.

pet [pet] *n* animal *m* de compañía; **the teacher's ~** el favorito (la favorita) del maestro.

petal ['petl] *n* pétalo *m*.

pet food *n* alimentos *mpl* para animales de compañía.

petition [pɪ'tɪʃn] *n* petición *f*.

petits pois [,pətɪ'pwɑː] *npl* guisantes *mpl* pequeños.

petrified ['petrɪfaɪd] *adj* (*frightened*) aterrado(-da).

petrol ['petrəl] *n* (*Br*) gasolina *f*.

petrol can *n* (*Br*) lata *f* de gasolina.

petrol cap *n* (*Br*) tapón *m* del depósito.

petrol gauge *n* (*Br*) indicador

m del nivel de carburante.

petrol pump *n (Br)* surtidor *m* de gasolina.

petrol station *n (Br)* gasolinera *f*.

petrol tank *n (Br)* depósito *m* de gasolina.

pet shop *n* tienda *f* de animales de compañía.

petticoat ['petɪkəʊt] *n* combinación *f*.

petty ['petɪ] *adj (pej: person, rule)* mezquino(-na).

petty cash *n* dinero *m* para pequeños gastos.

pew [pju:] *n* banco *m (de iglesia).*

pewter ['pju:tə^r] *n* peltre *m*.

PG *(abbr of parental guidance)* con algunas escenas no aptas para menores de 15 años.

pharmacist ['fɑ:məsɪst] *n* farmacéutico *m* (-ca *f*).

pharmacy ['fɑ:məsɪ] *n (shop)* farmacia *f*.

phase [feɪz] *n* fase *f*.

PhD *n (degree)* doctorado *m*.

pheasant ['feznt] *n* faisán *m*.

phenomena [fɪ'nɒmɪnə] *pl* → **phenomenon**.

phenomenal [fɪ'nɒmɪnl] *adj* fenomenal.

phenomenon [fɪ'nɒmɪnən] *(pl* -**mena**) *n* fenómeno *m*.

Philippines ['fɪlɪpi:nz] *npl*: **the ~** (las) Filipinas.

philosophy [fɪ'lɒsəfɪ] *n* filosofía *f*.

phlegm [flem] *n (in throat)* flema *f*.

phone [fəʊn] *n* teléfono *m* ♦ *vt & vi (Br)* telefonear; **on the ~** *(talking)*

al teléfono; **to be on the ~** *(connected)* tener teléfono ❏ **phone up** *vt sep & vi* llamar (por teléfono).

phone book *n* guía *f* telefónica.

phone booth *n* teléfono *m* público.

phone box *n (Br)* cabina *f* de teléfono.

phone call *n* llamada *f* telefónica.

phonecard ['fəʊnkɑ:d] *n* tarjeta *f* telefónica.

phone number *n* número *m* de teléfono.

photo ['fəʊtəʊ] *n* foto *f*; **to take a ~ of** *(person)* sacar una foto a; *(thing)* sacar una foto de.

photo album *n* álbum *m* de fotos.

photocopier [ˌfəʊtəʊ'kɒpɪə^r] *n* fotocopiadora *f*.

photocopy ['fəʊtəʊˌkɒpɪ] *n* fotocopia *f* ♦ *vt* fotocopiar.

photograph ['fəʊtəgrɑ:f] *n* fotografía *f* ♦ *vt* fotografiar.

photographer [fə'tɒgrəfə^r] *n* fotógrafo *m* (-fa *f*).

photography [fə'tɒgrəfɪ] *n* fotografía *f*.

phrase [freɪz] *n* frase *f*.

phrasebook ['freɪzbʊk] *n* libro *m* de frases.

physical ['fɪzɪkl] *adj* físico(-ca) ♦ *n* reconocimiento *m* médico.

physical education *n* educación *f* física.

physically handicapped *adj* disminuido físico (disminuida física).

physics ['fɪzɪks] *n* física *f*.

physiotherapy [ˌfɪzɪəʊˈθerəpɪ]
n fisioterapia f.

pianist [ˈpiːənɪst] n pianista mf.

piano [pɪˈænəʊ] (pl -s) n piano m.

pick [pɪk] vt (select) escoger; (fruit, flowers) coger ♦ n (pickaxe) piqueta f; **to ~ a fight** buscar camorra; **to ~ one's nose** hurgarse la nariz; **to take one's ~** escoger lo que uno quiera ❏ **pick on** vt fus meterse con; **pick out** vt sep (select) escoger; (see) distinguir; **pick up** vt sep recoger; (lift up) recoger (del suelo); (bargain, habit) adquirir; (language, hints) aprender; (inf: woman, man) ligar con ♦ vi (improve) mejorar.

pickaxe [ˈpɪkæks] n piqueta f.

pickle [ˈpɪkl] n (Br: food) condimento hecho con trozos de frutas y verduras maceradas hasta formar una salsa agridulce; (Am: pickled cucumber) pepinillo m encurtido.

pickled onion [ˈpɪkld-] n cebolleta f en vinagre.

pickpocket [ˈpɪkˌpɒkɪt] n carterista mf.

pick-up (truck) n camioneta f.

picnic [ˈpɪknɪk] n comida f campestre.

picnic area n = área f de descanso.

picture [ˈpɪktʃər] n (painting) cuadro m; (drawing) dibujo m; (photograph) foto f; (on TV) imagen f; (film) película f ❏ **pictures** npl: **the ~s** (Br) el cine.

picture frame n marco m (para fotos).

picturesque [ˌpɪktʃəˈresk] adj pintoresco(-ca).

pie [paɪ] n (savoury) empanada f; (sweet) tarta f (cubierta de hojaldre).

piece [piːs] n (in part, bit) trozo m; (component, in chess, of music) pieza f; **a 20p ~** una moneda de 20 peniques; **a ~ of advice** un consejo; **a ~ of clothing** una prenda de vestir; **a ~ of furniture** un mueble; **a ~ of paper** una hoja de papel; **to fall to ~s** deshacerse; **in one ~** (intact) intacto; (unharmed) sano y salvo.

pier [pɪər] n paseo m marítimo (sobre malecón).

pierce [pɪəs] vt perforar; **to have one's ears ~d** hacerse agujeros en las orejas.

pig [pɪg] n (animal) cerdo m; (inf: greedy person) tragón m (-ona f).

pigeon [ˈpɪdʒɪn] n paloma f.

pigeonhole [ˈpɪdʒɪnhəʊl] n casilla f.

pigskin [ˈpɪgskɪn] adj de piel de cerdo.

pigtail [ˈpɪgteɪl] n trenza f.

pike [paɪk] n (fish) lucio m.

pilau rice [pɪˈlaʊ-] n arroz de distintos colores, condimentado con especias orientales.

pilchard [ˈpɪltʃəd] n sardina f.

pile [paɪl] n (heap) montón m; (neat stack) pila f ♦ vt amontonar; **~s of** (inf: a lot) un montón de ❏ **pile up** vt sep amontonar ♦ vi (accumulate) acumularse.

piles [paɪlz] npl (MED) almorranas fpl.

pileup [ˈpaɪlʌp] n colisión f en cadena.

pill [pɪl] n pastilla f; **the ~** la píldora.

pillar [ˈpɪlər] n pilar m.

pillar box n (Br) buzón m.

pillion ['pɪljən] n: **to ride** ~ ir sentado atrás (en moto).

pillow ['pɪləʊ] n (for bed) almohada f; (Am: on chair, sofa) cojín m.

pillowcase ['pɪləʊkeɪs] n funda f de la almohada.

pilot ['paɪlət] n piloto mf.

pilot light n piloto m.

pimple ['pɪmpl] n grano m.

pin [pɪn] n (for sewing) alfiler m; (drawing pin) chincheta f; (safety pin) imperdible m; (Am: brooch) broche m; (Am: badge) chapa f, pin m ♦ vt (fasten) prender; **a two-plug** un enchufe de dos clavijas; **~s and needles** hormigueo m.

pinafore ['pɪnəfɔː] n (apron) delantal m; (Br: dress) pichi m.

pinball ['pɪnbɔːl] n flipper m.

pincers ['pɪnsəz] npl (tool) tenazas fpl.

pinch [pɪntʃ] vt (squeeze) pellizcar; (Am: inf: steal) mangar ♦ n (of salt) pizca f.

pine [paɪn] n pino m ♦ adj de pino.

pineapple ['paɪnæpl] n piña f.

pink [pɪŋk] adj rosa inv ♦ n (colour) rosa m.

pinkie ['pɪŋki] n (Am) dedo m meñique.

PIN number ['pɪn-] n número m personal.

pint [paɪnt] n (in UK) = 0,568 litros, pinta f (in US) = 0,473 litros, pinta; **a ~ (of beer)** (Br) una jarra de cerveza.

pip [pɪp] n (of fruit) pepita f.

pipe [paɪp] n (for smoking) pipa f; (for gas, water) tubería f.

pipe cleaner n limpiapipas m inv.

pipeline ['paɪplaɪn] n (for oil) oleoducto m.

pipe tobacco n tabaco m de pipa.

pirate ['paɪrət] n pirata m.

Pisces ['paɪsiːz] n Piscis m inv.

piss [pɪs] vi (vulg) mear ♦ n: **to have a ~** (vulg) echar una meada; **it's ~ing down** (vulg) está lloviendo que te cagas.

pissed [pɪst] adj (Br: vulg: drunk) mamado(-da); (Am: vulg: angry) cabreado(-da).

pissed off adj (vulg) cabreado(-da).

pistachio [pɪˈstɑːʃɪəʊ] n pistacho m ♦ adj de pistacho.

pistol ['pɪstl] n pistola f.

piston ['pɪstən] n pistón m.

pit [pɪt] n (hole) hoyo m; (coalmine) mina f; (for orchestra) foso m de la orquesta; (Am: in fruit) hueso m.

pitch [pɪtʃ] n (Br: SPORT) campo m ♦ vt (throw) lanzar; **to ~ a tent** montar una tienda de campaña.

pitcher ['pɪtʃə] n (large jug) cántaro m; (Am: small jug) jarra f.

pitfall ['pɪtfɔːl] n escollo m.

pith [pɪθ] n (of orange) parte blanca de la corteza.

pitta (bread) ['pɪtə-] n fina torta de pan ácimo.

pitted ['pɪtɪd] adj (olives) deshuesado(-da).

pity ['pɪti] n (compassion) lástima f; **to have ~ on sb** compadecerse de alguien; **it's a ~ (that)** ... es una pena que ...; **what a ~!** ¡qué pena!

pivot ['pɪvət] n eje m.

pizza ['piːtsə] n pizza f.

pizzeria [ˌpiːtsəˈriːə] n pizzería f. Pl. (abbr of Place) nombre de ciertas calles en Gran Bretaña.

placard ['plækaːd] n pancarta f.

place [pleɪs] n (location) sitio m, lugar m; (house, flat) casa f; (seat) asiento m; (proper position) sitio m; (in race, list) lugar m; (at table) cubierto m ◆ vt (put) colocar; (an order, bet) hacer; **in the first ~** en primer lugar; **to take sb's ~** sustituir a alguien; **all over the ~** por todas partes; **in ~ of** en lugar de.

place mat n mantel m individual.

placement ['pleɪsmənt] n colocación f temporal.

place of birth n lugar m de nacimiento.

plague [pleɪg] n peste f.

plaice [pleɪs] n platija f.

plain [pleɪn] adj (not decorated) liso(-sa); (simple) sencillo(-lla); (clear) claro(-ra); (paper) sin rayas; (pej: not attractive) sin ningún atractivo ◆ n llanura f.

plain chocolate n chocolate m amargo.

plainly ['pleɪnlɪ] adv (obviously) evidentemente; (distinctly) claramente.

plait [plæt] n trenza f ◆ vt trenzar.

plan [plæn] n (scheme, project) plan m; (drawing) plano m ◆ vt (organize) planear; **have you any ~s for tonight?** ¿tienes algún plan para esta noche?; **according to ~** según

lo previsto; **to ~ to do sthg, to ~ on doing sthg** pensar hacer algo.

plane [pleɪn] n (aeroplane) avión m; (tool) cepillo m.

planet ['plænɪt] n planeta m.

plank [plæŋk] n tablón m.

plant [plaːnt] n planta f ◆ vt (seeds, tree) plantar; (land) sembrar; **"heavy ~ crossing"** cartel que indica peligro por salida de vehículos pesados.

plantation [plænˈteɪʃn] n plantación f.

plaque [plaːk] n placa f.

plaster ['plaːstə] n (Br: for cut) tirita® f; (for walls) escayola f; **in ~** escayolado.

plaster cast n (for broken bones) escayola f.

plastic ['plæstɪk] n plástico m ◆ adj de plástico.

plastic bag n bolsa f de plástico.

Plasticine® ['plæstɪsiːn] n (Br) plastilina® f.

plate [pleɪt] n (for food) plato m; (of metal) placa f.

plateau ['plætəʊ] n meseta f.

plate-glass adj de vidrio cilindrado.

platform ['plætfɔːm] n (at railway station) andén m; (raised structure) plataforma f; **~ 12** la vía 12.

platinum ['plætɪnəm] n platino m.

platter ['plætə] n (CULIN) combinado, especialmente de mariscos, servido en una fuente alargada.

play [pleɪ] n (sport, game) jugar a; (music, instrument) tocar; (opponent) jugar contra; (CD, tape, record) poner; *(role, character)* representar ♦ *vi (child, in sport, game)* jugar; *(musician)* tocar ♦ *n (in theatre, on TV)* obra *f (de teatro); (button on CD, tape recorder)* botón *m* del "play" □ **play back** *vt sep* volver a poner; **play up** *vi* dar guerra.

player ['pleɪəʳ] *n (of sport, game)* jugador *m (-ra f); (of musical instrument)* intérprete *mf*.

playful ['pleɪful] *adj* juguetón (-ona).

playground ['pleɪgraʊnd] *n (in school)* patio *m* de recreo; *(in park etc)* zona *f* recreativa.

playgroup ['pleɪgruːp] *n* guardería *f*.

playing card ['pleɪɪŋ-] *n* carta *f*.
playing field ['pleɪɪŋ-] *n* campo *m* de deportes.

playroom ['pleɪrum] *n* cuarto *m* de los juguetes.

playschool ['pleɪskuːl] = **playgroup**.

playtime ['pleɪtaɪm] *n* recreo *m*.

playwright ['pleɪraɪt] *n* dramaturgo *m (-ga f)*.

plc *(Br: abbr of public limited company)* = S.A.

pleasant ['pleznt] *adj* agradable.

please [pliːz] *adv* por favor ♦ *vt* complacer; **yes ~!** ¡sí, gracias!; **whatever you ~** lo que desee.

pleased [pliːzd] *adj* contento(-ta); **to be ~ with** estar contento con; **~ to meet you!** ¡encantado(-da) de conocerle!

pleasure ['pleʒəʳ] *n* placer *m*; **with ~** con mucho gusto; **it's a ~!** ¡es un placer!

pleat [pliːt] *n* pliegue *m*.

pleated ['pliːtɪd] *adj* plisado (-da).

plentiful ['plentɪful] *adj* abundante.

plenty ['plentɪ] *pron* de sobra; **~ of money** dinero de sobra; **~ of chairs** sillas de sobra.

pliers ['plaɪəz] *npl* alicates *mpl*.

plimsoll ['plɪmsəl] *n (Br)* playera *f*.

plonk [plɒŋk] *n (Br: inf: wine)* vino *m* peleón.

plot [plɒt] *n (scheme)* complot *m*; *(of story, film, play)* trama *f; (of land)* parcela *f*.

plough [plaʊ] *n (Br)* arado *m* ♦ *vt (Br)* arar.

ploughman's (lunch) ['plaʊmənz-] *n (Br)* tabla de queso servida con pan, cebolla, ensalada y salsa agridulce.

plow [plaʊ] *(Am)* = **plough**.

ploy [plɔɪ] *n* estratagema *f*.

pluck [plʌk] *vt (eyebrows)* depilar *(con pinzas); (chicken)* desplumar.

plug [plʌg] *n (ELEC)* enchufe *m; (for bath, sink)* tapón *m* □ **plug in** *vt sep* enchufar.

plughole ['plʌghəʊl] *n* agujero *m* del desagüe.

plum [plʌm] *n* ciruela *f*.

plumber ['plʌməʳ] *n* fontanero *m (-ra f)*.

plumbing ['plʌmɪŋ] *n (pipes)* tuberías *fpl*.

plump [plʌmp] *adj* regordete.

plunge [plʌndʒ] *vi (fall, dive)* zambullirse; *(decrease)* caer vertiginosamente.

plunge pool *n* piscina *f (muy pequeña)*.

plunger ['plʌndʒəʳ] n (for un-
blocking pipe) desatascador m.

pluperfect (tense) [‚plu-
'pɜ:fɪkt] n: the ~ el pluscuamper-
fecto.

plural ['pluərəl] n plural m; in the
~ en plural.

plus [plʌs] prep más ♦ adj: 30 ~
treinta o más.

plush [plʌʃ] adj lujoso(-sa).

Pluto ['plu:təu] n Plutón m.

plywood ['plaɪwʊd] n contra-
chapado m.

p.m. (abbr of post meridiem): at 4 ~
a las cuatro de la tarde; at 10 ~ a
las diez de la noche.

PMT n (abbr of premenstrual tension) SPM m.

pneumatic drill [nju:'mætɪk-]
n taladradora f neumática.

pneumonia [nju:'məunjə] n pulmonía f.

poached egg [pəutʃt-] n huevo
m escalfado.

poached salmon [pəutʃt-] n
salmón m hervido.

poacher ['pəutʃəʳ] n (hunting)
cazador m furtivo; (fishing) pescador m furtivo.

PO Box n (abbr of Post Office Box)
apdo. m.

pocket ['pɒkɪt] n bolsillo m; (on
car door) bolsa f ♦ adj de bolsillo.

pocketbook ['pɒkɪtbʊk] n
(notebook) libreta f; (Am: handbag)
bolso m.

pocket money n (Br) propina
f semanal.

podiatrist [pə'daɪətrɪst] n (Am)
podólogo m (-ga f).

poem ['pəuɪm] n poema m.

poet ['pəuɪt] n poeta m (-tisa f).

poetry ['pəuɪtrɪ] n poesía f.

point [pɔɪnt] n punto m; (tip)
punta f; (most important thing) razón
f; (in time) momento m; (in score)
tanto m; (fine detail) detalle m; (purpose) sentido m; (on compass) punta
f; (Br: electric socket) enchufe m ♦ vi:
to ~ to señalar; **five ~ seven** cinco
coma siete; **what's the ~?** ¿para
qué?; **there's no ~** no vale la pena;
to be on the ~ of doing sthg estar a
punto de hacer algo; **to come to
the ~** ir al grano ❑ **points** npl (Br:
on railway) agujas fpl; **point out** vt
sep (object, person) señalar; (fact,
mistake) hacer notar.

pointed ['pɔɪntɪd] adj (in shape)
puntiagudo(-da).

pointless ['pɔɪntlɪs] adj sin sentido.

point of view n punto m de
vista.

poison ['pɔɪzn] n veneno m ♦ vt
(intentionally) envenenar; (uninten-
tionally) intoxicar.

poisoning ['pɔɪznɪŋ] n (intentional) envenenamiento m; (unintentional) intoxicación f.

poisonous ['pɔɪznəs] adj (food,
gas, substance) tóxico(-ca); (snake,
spider) venenoso(-sa).

poke [pəuk] vt (with finger, stick)
dar; (with elbow) dar un codazo.

poker ['pəukəʳ] n (card game)
póker m.

Poland ['pəulənd] n Polonia f.

polar bear ['pəulə-] n oso m
polar.

Polaroid® ['pəulərɔɪd] n (photograph) fotografía f polaroid; (camera) cámara f polaroid.

pole [pəul] n (of wood) palo m.

Pole [pəul] n (person) polaco m

(-ca f).

police [pə'li:s] npl: **the ~** la policía.

police car n coche m patrulla.

police force n cuerpo m de policía.

policeman [pə'li:smən] (pl **-men** [-mən]) n policía m.

police officer n agente mf de policía.

police station n comisaría f de policía.

policewoman [pə'li:s,wumən] (pl **-women** [-,wimin]) n mujer f policía.

policy ['pɒləsi] n (approach, attitude) política f; (for insurance) póliza f.

policy-holder n asegurado m (-da f).

polio ['pəuliəu] n polio f.

polish ['pɒliʃ] n (for cleaning) abrillantador m ◆ vt sacar brillo a.

Polish ['pəuliʃ] adj polaco(-ca) ◆ n (language) polaco m ◆ npl: **the ~** los polacos.

polite [pə'lait] adj educado(-da).

political [pə'litikl] adj político(-ca).

politician [,pɒli'tiʃn] n político m (-ca f).

politics ['pɒlitiks] n política f.

poll [pəul] n (survey) encuesta f; **the ~s** (election) los comicios.

pollen ['pɒlən] n polen m.

Poll Tax n (Br: formerly) = contribución f urbana.

pollute [pə'lu:t] vt contaminar.

pollution [pə'lu:ʃn] n (of sea, air) contaminación f; (substances) agentes mpl contaminantes.

polo neck ['pəuləu-] n (Br: jumper) jersey m de cuello de cisne.

polyester [,pɒli'estər] n poliéster m.

polystyrene [,pɒli'stairi:n] n poliestireno m.

polytechnic [,pɒli'teknik] n centro de enseñanza superior especialmente de materias técnicas que concede diplomas universitarios; casi todos los "polytechnics" se han convertido en universidades.

polythene ['pɒliθi:n] n polietileno m.

pomegranate ['pɒmi,grænit] n granada f.

pompous ['pɒmpəs] adj (person) engreído(-da).

pond [pɒnd] n estanque m.

pontoon [pɒn'tu:n] n (Br: card game) veintiuna f.

pony ['pəuni] n poni m.

ponytail ['pəuniteil] n cola f de caballo (peinado).

pony-trekking [-,trekiŋ] n (Br) excursión f en poni.

poodle ['pu:dl] n caniche m.

pool [pu:l] n (for swimming) piscina f; (of water, blood, milk) charco m; (small pond) estanque m; (game) billar m americano ❑ **pools** npl (Br): **the ~s** las quinielas.

poor [pɔ:r] adj pobre; (bad) malo(-la) ◆ npl: **the ~** los pobres.

poorly ['pɔ:li] adj (Br) pachucho(-cha) ◆ adv mal.

pop [pɒp] n (music) música f pop ◆ vt (inf: put) meter ◆ vi (balloon) reventar; **my ears popped** me estallaron los oídos ❑ **pop in** vi (Br) entrar un momento.

popcorn ['pɒpkɔːn] n palomitas fpl (de maíz).

Pope [pəʊp] n: the ~ el Papa.

pop group n grupo m de música pop.

poplar (tree) ['pɒplə*] n álamo m.

pop music n música f pop.

poppadom ['pɒpədəm] n torta fina de pan indio, frito y crujiente.

popper ['pɒpə*] n (Br) corchete m.

poppy ['pɒpɪ] n amapola f.

Popsicle® ['pɒpsɪkl] n (Am) polo m.

pop socks npl calcetines cortos de cristal.

pop star n estrella f del pop.

popular ['pɒpjʊlə*] adj (person, activity) popular; (opinion, ideas) generalizado(-da).

popularity [,pɒpjʊˈlærətɪ] n popularidad f.

populated ['pɒpjʊleɪtɪd] adj poblado(-da).

population [,pɒpjʊˈleɪʃn] n población f.

porcelain ['pɔːsəlɪn] n porcelana f.

porch [pɔːtʃ] n porche m.

pork [pɔːk] n carne f de cerdo.

pork chop n chuleta f de cerdo.

pork pie n empanada redonda de carne de cerdo.

pornographic [,pɔːnəˈgræfɪk] adj pornográfico(-ca).

porridge ['pɒrɪdʒ] n papilla f de avena.

port [pɔːt] n (town, harbour) puer-

to m; (drink) oporto m.

portable ['pɔːtəbl] adj portátil.

porter ['pɔːtə*] n (at hotel, museum) conserje mf; (at station, airport) mozo m.

porthole ['pɔːthəʊl] n ojo m de buey.

portion ['pɔːʃn] n (part) porción f; (of food) ración f.

portrait ['pɔːtreɪt] n retrato m.

Portugal ['pɔːtʃʊgl] n Portugal.

Portuguese [,pɔːtʃʊˈgiːz] adj portugués(-esa) ♦ n (language) portugués m ♦ npl: the ~ los portugueses.

pose [pəʊz] vt (problem) plantear; (threat) suponer ♦ vi (for photo) posar.

posh [pɒʃ] adj (inf) (person, accent) de clase alta; (hotel, restaurant) de lujo.

position [pəˈzɪʃn] n (situation) posición f; (situation) situación f; (rank, importance) rango m; (fml: job) puesto m; "~ closed" "cerrado".

positive ['pɒzətɪv] adj positivo(-va); (certain, sure) seguro(-ra); (optimistic) optimista.

possess [pəˈzes] vt poseer.

possession [pəˈzeʃn] n posesión f.

possessive [pəˈzesɪv] adj posesivo(-va).

possibility [,pɒsəˈbɪlətɪ] n posibilidad f.

possible ['pɒsəbl] adj posible; it's ~ that we may be late puede (ser) que lleguemos tarde; would it be ~ for me to use the phone? ¿podría usar el teléfono?; as much as ~ tanto como sea posible; if ~

si es posible.

possibly ['pɒsəblɪ] *adv (perhaps)* posiblemente.

post [pəʊst] *n (system, letters etc)* correo *m; (delivery)* reparto *m; (pole)* poste *m; (fml: job)* puesto *m* ◆ *vt (letter, parcel)* echar al correo; **by ~** por correo.

postage ['pəʊstɪdʒ] *n* franqueo *m;* **~ and packing** gastos *mpl* de envío; **~ paid** franqueo pagado.

postage stamp *n (fml)* sello *m.*

postal order ['pəʊstl-] *n* giro *m* postal.

postbox ['pəʊstbɒks] *n (Br)* buzón *m.*

postcard ['pəʊstkɑːd] *n* postal *f.*

postcode ['pəʊstkəʊd] *n (Br)* código *m* postal.

poster ['pəʊstər] *n* póster *m.*

poste restante [,pəʊst-'restɑːnt] *n (Br)* lista *f* de correos.

post-free *adv* con porte pagado.

postgraduate [,pəʊst-'grædʒʊət] *n* posgraduado *m* (-da *f*).

postman ['pəʊstmən] *(pl -men* [-mən]) *n* cartero *m.*

postmark ['pəʊstmɑːk] *n* matasellos *m inv.*

post office *n (building)* oficina *f* de correos; **the Post Office ≈** Correos *m inv.*

postpone [,pəʊst'pəʊn] *vt* aplazar.

posture ['pɒstʃər] *n* postura *f.*

postwoman ['pəʊst,wʊmən] *(pl -women* [-,wɪmɪn]) *n* cartera *f.*

pot [pɒt] *n (for cooking)* olla *f; (for*

jam) tarro *m; (for paint)* bote *m; (for tea)* tetera *f; (for coffee)* cafetera *f; (inf: cannabis)* maría *f;* **a ~ of tea** una tetera.

potato [pə'teɪtəʊ] *(pl -es) n* patata *f.*

potato salad *n* ensalada *f* de patatas.

potential [pə'tenʃl] *adj* potencial ◆ *n* potencial *m.*

pothole ['pɒthəʊl] *n (in road)* bache *m.*

pot plant *n* planta *f* de interior.

pot scrubber [-'skrʌbər] *n* estropajo *m.*

potted ['pɒtɪd] *adj (meat, fish)* en conserva; *(plant)* en maceta.

pottery ['pɒtərɪ] *n* cerámica *f.*

potty ['pɒtɪ] *adj* chalado(-da).

pouch [paʊtʃ] *n (for money)* monedero *m* de atar; *(for tobacco)* petaca *f.*

poultry ['pəʊltrɪ] *n (meat)* carne *f* de pollería ◆ *npl (animals)* aves *fpl* de corral.

pound [paʊnd] *n (unit of money)* libra *f; (unit of weight) =* 453,6 *g,* libra *f* ◆ *vi (heart, head)* palpitar.

pour [pɔːr] *vt (liquid etc)* verter; *(drink)* servir ◆ *vi (flow)* manar; **it's ~ing (with rain)** está lloviendo a cántaros ❑ **pour out** *vt sep (drink)* servir.

poverty ['pɒvətɪ] *n* pobreza *f.*

powder ['paʊdər] *n* polvo *m.*

power ['paʊər] *n (control, authority)* poder *m; (ability)* capacidad *f; (strength, force)* fuerza *f; (energy)* energía *f; (electricity)* corriente *f* ◆ *vt* impulsar; **to be in ~** estar en el poder.

power cut n apagón m.

power failure n corte m de corriente.

powerful ['pauəful] adj (having control) poderoso(-sa); (physically strong, forceful) fuerte; (machine, drug, voice) potente; (smell) intenso(-sa).

power point n (Br) toma f de corriente.

power station n central f eléctrica.

power steering n dirección f asistida.

practical ['præktɪkl] adj práctico(-ca).

practically ['præktɪklɪ] adv (almost) prácticamente.

practice ['præktɪs] n (training, training session) práctica f; (SPORT) entrenamiento m; (of doctor) consulta f; (of lawyer) bufete m; (regular activity, custom) costumbre f ♦ vt (Am) = **practise**; **to be out of ~** tener falta de práctica.

practise ['præktɪs] vt (sport, music, technique) practicar ♦ vi (train) practicar; (doctor, lawyer) ejercer ♦ n (Am) = **practice**.

praise [preɪz] n elogio m ♦ vt elogiar.

pram [præm] n (Br) cochecito m de niño.

prank [præŋk] n travesura f.

prawn [prɔːn] n gamba f.

prawn cocktail n cóctel m de gambas.

prawn cracker n pan m de gambas.

pray [preɪ] vi rezar; **to ~ for sthg** (fig) rogar por algo.

prayer [preə'] n (to God) oración f.

precarious [prɪ'keərɪəs] adj precario(-ria).

precaution [prɪ'kɔːʃn] n precaución f.

precede [prɪ'siːd] vt (fml) preceder.

preceding [prɪ'siːdɪŋ] adj precedente.

precinct ['priːsɪŋkt] n (Br: for shopping) zona f comercial peatonal; (Am: area of town) distrito m.

precious ['preʃəs] adj precioso(-sa); (memories) entrañable; (possession) de gran valor sentimental.

precious stone n piedra f preciosa.

precipice ['presɪpɪs] n precipicio m.

precise [prɪ'saɪs] adj preciso(-sa), exacto(-ta).

precisely [prɪ'saɪslɪ] adv (accurately) con precisión; (exactly) exactamente.

predecessor ['priːdɪsesə'] n predecesor m (-ra f).

predicament [prɪ'dɪkəmənt] n apuro m.

predict [prɪ'dɪkt] vt predecir.

predictable [prɪ'dɪktəbl] adj (foreseeable) previsible; (pej: unoriginal) poco original.

prediction [prɪ'dɪkʃn] n predicción f.

preface ['prefɪs] n prólogo m.

prefect ['priːfekt] n (Br: at school) alumno de un curso superior elegido por los profesores para mantener el orden fuera de clase.

prefer [prɪˈfɜːʳ] *vt*: to ~ sthg (to) preferir algo (a); to ~ to do sthg preferir hacer algo.

preferable [ˈprefrəbl] *adj* preferible.

preferably [ˈprefrəblɪ] *adv* preferiblemente.

preference [ˈprefərəns] *n* preferencia *f*.

prefix [ˈpriːfɪks] *n* prefijo *m*.

pregnancy [ˈpregnənsɪ] *n* embarazo *m*.

pregnant [ˈpregnənt] *adj* embarazada.

prejudice [ˈpredʒʊdɪs] *n* prejuicio *m*.

prejudiced [ˈpredʒʊdɪst] *adj* parcial.

preliminary [prɪˈlɪmɪnərɪ] *adj* preliminar.

premature [ˈpremətjʊəʳ] *adj* prematuro(-ra); (arrival) anticipado(-da).

premier [ˈpremjəʳ] *adj* primero(-ra) ♦ *n* primer ministro *m* (primera ministra *f*).

premiere [ˈpremɪeəʳ] *n* estreno *m*.

premises [ˈpremɪsɪz] *npl* local *m*.

premium [ˈpriːmjəm] *n* (for insurance) prima *f*.

premium-quality *adj* (meat) de calidad superior.

preoccupied [priːˈɒkjʊpaɪd] *adj* preocupado(-da).

prepacked [ˌpriːˈpækt] *adj* preempaquetado(-da).

prepaid [ˈpriːpeɪd] *adj* (envelope) con porte pagado.

preparation [ˌprepəˈreɪʃn] *n* (preparing) preparación *f* ❑ **prepa-**

rations *npl* (arrangements) preparativos *mpl*.

preparatory school [prɪˈpærətrɪ-] *n* (in UK) colegio privado que prepara a alumnos de 7 a 12 años para la enseñanza secundaria; (in US) colegio privado de enseñanza media que prepara a sus alumnos para estudios superiores.

prepare [prɪˈpeəʳ] *vt* preparar ♦ *vi* prepararse.

prepared [prɪˈpeəd] *adj* (ready) preparado(-da); to be ~ to do sthg estar dispuesto(-ta) a hacer algo.

preposition [ˌprepəˈzɪʃn] *n* preposición *f*.

prep school [ˈprep-] = preparatory school.

prescribe [prɪˈskraɪb] *vt* prescribir.

prescription [prɪˈskrɪpʃn] *n* receta *f*.

presence [ˈprezns] *n* presencia *f*; in sb's ~ en presencia de alguien.

present [adj & n ˈpreznt, vb prɪˈzent] *adj* (in attendance) presente; (current) actual ♦ *n* (gift) regalo *m* ♦ *vt* (give as present) obsequiar; (problem, challenge, play) representar; (portray, on radio or TV) presentar; the ~ (tense) el presente; at ~ actualmente; the ~ el presente; to ~ sb to sb presentar a alguien a alguien.

presentable [prɪˈzentəbl] *adj* presentable.

presentation [ˌpreznˈteɪʃn] *n* (way of presenting) presentación *f*; (ceremony) ceremonia *f* de entrega.

presenter [prɪˈzentəʳ] *n* (of TV, radio programme) presentador *m* (-ra *f*).

presently ['prezntlı] adv (soon) dentro de poco; (now) actualmente.

preservation [,prezə'veɪʃn] n conservación f.

preservative [prɪ'zɜ:vətɪv] n conservante m.

preserve [prɪ'zɜ:v] n (jam) confitura f ♦ vt conservar.

president ['prezɪdənt] n presidente m (-ta f).

press [pres] vt (push) apretar; (iron) planchar ♦ n: **the ~** la prensa; **to ~ sb to do sthg** presionar a alguien para que haga algo.

press conference n rueda f de prensa.

press-stud n automático m.

press-up n flexión f.

pressure ['preʃə'] n presión f.

pressure cooker n olla f exprés.

prestigious [pre'stɪdʒəs] adj prestigioso(-sa).

presumably [prɪ'zju:məblɪ] adv probablemente.

presume [prɪ'zju:m] vt suponer.

pretend [prɪ'tend] vt: **to ~ to do sthg** fingir hacer algo.

pretentious [prɪ'tenʃəs] adj pretencioso(-sa).

pretty ['prɪtɪ] adj (person) guapo(-pa); (thing) bonito(-ta) ♦ adv (inf) (quite) bastante; muy.

prevent [prɪ'vent] vt prevenir; **to ~ sb/sthg from doing sthg** impedir que alguien/algo haga algo.

prevention [prɪ'venʃn] n prevención f.

preview ['pri:vju:] n (of film) preestreno m; (short description) repor-

taje m (sobre un acontecimiento futuro).

previous ['pri:vjəs] adj (earlier) previo(-via); (preceding) anterior.

previously ['pri:vjəslı] adv anteriormente.

price [praɪs] n precio m ♦ vt: **attractively ~d** con un precio atractivo.

priceless ['praɪslɪs] adj (expensive) de un valor incalculable; (valuable) valiosísimo(-ma).

price list n lista f de precios.

pricey ['praɪsɪ] adj (inf) caro(-ra).

prick [prɪk] vt (skin, finger) pinchar; (sting) picar.

prickly ['prɪklɪ] adj (plant, bush) espinoso(-sa).

prickly heat n sarpullido causado por el calor.

pride [praɪd] n orgullo m ♦ vt: **to ~ o.s. on sthg** estar orgulloso de algo.

priest [pri:st] n sacerdote m.

primarily ['praɪmərɪlɪ] adv primordialmente.

primary school ['praɪmərɪ-] n escuela f primaria.

prime [praɪm] adj (chief) primero(-ra); (quality, beef, cut) de calidad superior.

prime minister n primer ministro m (primera ministra f).

primitive ['prɪmɪtɪv] adj (simple) rudimentario(-ria).

primrose ['prɪmrəʊz] n primavera f.

prince [prɪns] n príncipe m.

Prince of Wales n Príncipe m de Gales.

princess [prɪn'ses] n princesa f.

principal ['prɪnsəpl] *adj* principal ◆ *n* (*of school, university*) director *m* (-ra *f*).

principle ['prɪnsəpl] *n* principio *m*; **in ~** en principio.

print [prɪnt] *n* (*words*) letras *fpl* (de imprenta); (*photo*) foto *f*; (*of painting*) reproducción *f*; (*mark*) huella *f* ◆ *vt* (*book, newspaper, photo*) imprimir; (*publish*) publicar; (*write*) escribir en letra de imprenta; **out of ~** agotado ☐ **print out** *vt sep* imprimir.

printed matter [,prɪntɪd-] *n* impresos *mpl*.

printer ['prɪntər] *n* (*machine*) impresora *f*; (*person*) impresor *m* (-ra *f*).

printout ['prɪntaut] *n* copia *f* de impresora.

prior ['praɪər] *adj* (*previous*) anterior; **~ to** (*fml*) con anterioridad a.

priority [praɪ'ɒrətɪ] *n* prioridad *f*; **to have ~ over** tener prioridad sobre.

prison ['prɪzn] *n* cárcel *f*.

prisoner ['prɪznər] *n* preso *m* (-sa *f*).

prisoner of war *n* prisionero *m* (-ra *f*) de guerra.

prison officer *n* funcionario *m* (-ria *f*) de prisiones.

privacy [Br 'prɪvəsɪ, Am 'praɪvəsɪ] *n* intimidad *f*.

private ['praɪvɪt] *adj* privado(-da); (*class, lesson*) particular; (*matter, belongings*) personal; (*quiet*) retirado(-da) ◆ *n* (MIL) soldado *m* raso; **in ~** en privado.

private health care *n* asistencia *f* sanitaria privada.

private property *n* propiedad *f* privada.

private school *n* colegio *m* privado.

privilege ['prɪvɪlɪdʒ] *n* privilegio *m*; **it's a ~!** ¡es un honor!

prize [praɪz] *n* premio *m*.

prize-giving [-,gɪvɪŋ] *n* entrega *f* de premios.

pro [prəu] (*pl* **-s**) *n* (*inf: professional*) profesional *mf* ☐ **pros** *npl*: **the ~s and cons** los pros y los contras.

probability [,prɒbə'bɪlətɪ] *n* probabilidad *f*.

probable ['prɒbəbl] *adj* probable.

probably ['prɒbəblɪ] *adv* probablemente.

probation officer [prə'beɪʃn-] *n* oficial encargado de la vigilancia de presos en libertad condicional.

problem ['prɒbləm] *n* problema *m*; **no ~!** (*inf*) ¡no hay problema!

procedure [prə'si:dʒər] *n* procedimiento *m*.

proceed [prə'si:d] *vi* (*fml*) (*continue*) proseguir; (*act*) proceder; (*advance*) avanzar; **"~ with caution"** "conduzca con precaución".

proceeds ['prəusi:dz] *npl* recaudación *f*.

process ['prəuses] *n* proceso *m*; **to be in the ~ of doing sthg** estar haciendo algo.

processed cheese ['prəusest-] *n* queso *m* para sandwiches.

procession [prə'seʃn] *n* desfile *m*.

prod [prɒd] *vt* empujar repetidamente.

produce [vb prə'dju:s, n 'prɒdju:s]
vt producir; (show) mostrar; (play)
poner en escena ♦ n productos
mpl agrícolas.

producer [prə'dju:sə²] n (manufacturer) fabricante mf; (of film) productor m (-ra f); (of play) director
m (-ra f) de escena.

product ['prɒdʌkt] n producto
m.

production [prə'dʌkʃn] n
(manufacture) producción f; (of film,
play) realización f; (play) representación f.

productivity [,prɒdʌk'tɪvəti] n
productividad f.

profession [prə'feʃn] n profesión f.

professional [prə'feʃənl] adj
profesional ♦ n profesional mf.

professor [prə'fesə²] n (in UK)
catedrático m (-ca f); (in US) profesor m (-ra f) de universidad.

profile ['prəʊfaɪl] n (silhouette,
outline) perfil m; (description) corta
biografía f.

profit ['prɒfɪt] n (financial) beneficio m ♦ vi: to ~ (from) sacar provecho (de).

profitable ['prɒfɪtəbl] adj rentable.

profiteroles [prə'fɪtə,rəʊlz] npl
profiteroles mpl.

profound [prə'faʊnd] adj pro-
fundo(-da).

program ['prəʊɡræm] n (COMPUT)
programa m; (Am) = **programme**
♦ vt (COMPUT) programar.

programme ['prəʊɡræm] n programa m.

progress [n 'prəʊɡres, vb prə'ɡres]

n (improvement) progreso m; (forward movement) avance m ♦ vi
(work, talks, student) progresar;
(day, meeting) avanzar; **to make** ~
(improve) progresar; (in journey)
avanzar; **in** ~ en curso.

progressive [prə'ɡresɪv] adj
(forward-looking) progresista.

prohibit [prə'hɪbɪt] vt prohibir;
"smoking strictly ~ed" "está terminantemente prohibido fumar".

project ['prɒdʒekt] n (plan) proyecto m; (at school) trabajo m.

projector [prə'dʒektə²] n proyector m.

prolong [prə'lɒŋ] vt prolongar.

prom [prɒm] n (Am: dance) baile
m de gala (en colegios).

promenade [,prɒmə'nɑːd] n (Br:
by the sea) paseo m marítimo.

prominent ['prɒmɪnənt] adj
(person) eminente; (noticeable) prominente.

promise ['prɒmɪs] n promesa f ♦
vt prometer ♦ vi: **I** ~ te lo prometo; **to show** ~ ser prometedor; **I** ~
(that) **I'll come** te prometo que
vendré; **to** ~ **sb sthg** prometer
algo a alguien; **to** ~ **to do sthg**
prometer hacer algo.

promising ['prɒmɪsɪŋ] adj pro-
metedor(-ra).

promote [prə'məʊt] vt (in job)
ascender.

promotion [prə'məʊʃn] n (in
job) ascenso m; (of product) promoción f.

prompt [prɒmpt] adj inmedia-
to(-ta) ♦ adv: **at six o'clock** ~ a las
seis en punto.

prone [prəʊn] adj: **to be** ~ **to**
sthg ser propenso(-sa) a algo; **to**

be ~ to do sthg tender a hacer algo.

prong [proŋ] *n* diente *m*.

pronoun ['prəʊnaʊn] *n* pronombre *m*.

pronounce [prə'naʊns] *vt (word)* pronunciar.

pronunciation [prə,nʌnsɪ'eɪʃn] *n* pronunciación *f*.

proof [pruːf] *n (evidence)* prueba *f*; it's 12% ~ tiene 12 grados.

prop [prop]: **prop up** *vt sep (support)* apuntalar.

propeller [prə'pelə'] *n* hélice *f*.

proper ['propə'] *adj (suitable)* adecuado(-da); *(correct, socially acceptable)* correcto(-ta).

properly ['propəlɪ] *adv (suitably)* bien; *(correctly)* correctamente.

property ['propətɪ] *n* propiedad *f*; *(land)* finca *f*; *(fml: building)* inmueble *m*.

proportion [prə'pɔːʃn] *n* porción *f*.

proposal [prə'pəʊzl] *n (suggestion)* propuesta *f*.

propose [prə'pəʊz] *vt (suggest)* proponer ♦ *vi*: to ~ to sb pedir la mano a alguien.

proposition [,propə'zɪʃn] *n (offer)* propuesta *f*.

proprietor [prə'praɪətə'] *n (fml)* propietario *m* (-ria *f*).

prose [prəʊz] *n (not poetry)* prosa *f*; *(SCH)* traducción *f* inversa.

prosecution [,prosɪ'kjuːʃn] *n (JUR: charge)* procesamiento *m*.

prospect ['prospekt] *n (possibility)* posibilidad *f*; **I don't relish the** ~ no me apasiona la perspectiva ❑

prospects *npl (for the future)* perspectivas *fpl*.

prospectus [prə'spektəs] *(pl -es)* *n* folleto *m* informativo.

prosperous ['prospərəs] *adj* próspero(-ra).

prostitute ['prostɪtjuːt] *n* prostituta *f*.

protect [prə'tekt] *vt* proteger; to ~ sthg/sb against proteger algo/a alguien contra; to ~ sthg/sb from proteger algo/a alguien de.

protection [prə'tekʃn] *n* protección *f*.

protection factor *n* factor *m* de protección solar.

protective [prə'tektɪv] *adj* protector(-ra).

protein ['prəʊtiːn] *n* proteína *f*.

protest [*n* 'prəʊtest, *vb* prə'test] *n (complaint)* protesta *f*; *(demonstration)* manifestación ♦ *vt (Am: protest against)* protestar contra ♦ *vi*: to ~ (against) protestar (contra).

Protestant ['protɪstənt] *n* protestante *mf*.

protester [prə'testə'] *n* manifestante *mf*.

protractor [prə'træktə'] *n* transportador *m*.

protrude [prə'truːd] *vi* sobresalir.

proud [praʊd] *adj (pleased)* orgulloso(-sa); *(pej: arrogant)* soberbio(-bia); to be ~ of estar orgulloso de.

prove [pruːv] *(pp -d OR proven* [pruːvn]*) vt (show to be true)* probar; *(turn out to be)* resultar.

proverb ['provɜːb] *n* proverbio *m*.

provide [prə'vaɪd] *vt* proporcionar; **to ~ sb with sthg** proporcionar algo a alguien □ **provide for** *vt fus* (person) mantener.

provided (that) [prə'vaɪdɪd-] *conj* con tal de que.

providing (that) [prə'vaɪdɪŋ-] = **provided (that)**.

province ['prɒvɪns] *n* provincia *f*.

provisional [prə'vɪʒənl] *adj* provisional.

provisions [prə'vɪʒnz] *npl* provisiones *fpl*.

provocative [prə'vɒkətɪv] *adj* provocador(-ra).

provoke [prə'vəʊk] *vt* provocar.

prowl [praʊl] *vi* merodear.

prune [pruːn] *n* ciruela *f* pasa ◆ *vt* podar.

PS *(abbr of postscript)* P.D.

psychiatrist [saɪ'kaɪətrɪst] *n* psiquiatra *mf*.

psychic ['saɪkɪk] *adj* clarividente.

psychological [ˌsaɪkə'lɒdʒɪkl] *adj* psicológico(-ca).

psychologist [saɪ'kɒlədʒɪst] *n* psicólogo *m* (-ga *f*).

psychology [saɪ'kɒlədʒɪ] *n* psicología *f*.

psychotherapist [ˌsaɪkəʊ-'θerəpɪst] *n* psicoterapeuta *mf*.

pt *(abbr = pint)*.

PTO *(abbr of please turn over)* sigue.

pub [pʌb] *n* = bar *m*.

 PUB

El "pub" es una institución muy importante en la vida social británica, y es el principal lugar de encuentro en las comunidades rurales. El acceso para menores es restringido, aunque las condiciones varían de un "pub" a otro. Hasta recientemente, su horario de apertura estaba estrictamente regulado, pero hoy día la mayoría de los "pubs" abre de las once de la mañana a las once de la noche. Además de bebidas, los "pubs" suelen ofrecer comidas ligeras.

puberty ['pjuːbətɪ] *n* pubertad *f*.

public ['pʌblɪk] *adj* público(-ca) ◆ *n*: **the ~** el público; **in ~** en público.

publican ['pʌblɪkən] *n* (Br) patrón de un "pub".

publication [ˌpʌblɪ'keɪʃn] *n* publicación *f*.

public bar *n* (Br) bar cuya decoración es más sencilla y cuyos precios son más bajos.

public convenience *n* (Br) aseos *mpl* públicos.

public footpath *n* (Br) camino *m* público.

public holiday *n* fiesta *f* nacional.

public house *n* (Br: fml) = bar *m*.

publicity [pʌb'lɪsɪtɪ] *n* publicidad *f*.

public school *n* (in UK) colegio *m* privado; (in US) escuela *f* pública.

public telephone *n* teléfono *m* público.

public transport *n* transporte *m* público.

publish ['pʌblɪʃ] *vt* publicar.

publisher ['pʌblɪʃəʳ] n (person) editor m (-ra f); (company) editorial f.

publishing ['pʌblɪʃɪŋ] n (industry) industria f editorial.

pub lunch n almuerzo generalmente sencillo en un "pub".

pudding ['pudɪŋ] n (sweet dish) pudín m; (Br: course) postre m.

puddle ['pʌdl] n charco m.

puff [pʌf] vi (breathe heavily) resollar ♦ n (of air) soplo m; (of smoke) bocanada f; **to ~ at** dar caladas a.

puff pastry n hojaldre m.

pull [pul] vt tirar de; (trigger) apretar ♦ vi tirar ♦ n: **to give sthg a ~** dar algo un tirón; **to ~ a face** hacer muecas; **to ~ a muscle** dar un tirón en un músculo; **"pull"** (on door) "tirar" ❑ **pull apart** vt sep (machine) desmontar; **pull down** vt sep (lower) bajar; (demolish) derribar; **pull in** vi pararse; **pull out** vt sep sacar ♦ vi (train, car) salir; (withdraw) retirarse; **pull over** vi (car) hacerse a un lado; **pull up** vt sep (socks, trousers, sleeve) subirse ♦ vi parar.

pulley ['puli] (pl **pulleys**) n polea f.

pull-out n (Am) área f de descanso.

pullover ['pul,əuvəʳ] n jersey m.

pulpit ['pulpit] n púlpito m.

pulse [pʌls] n (MED) pulso m.

pump [pʌmp] n (device, bicycle pump) bomba f; (for petrol) surtidor m ❑ **pumps** npl (sports shoes) zapatillas fpl de tenis; **pump up** vt sep inflar.

pumpkin ['pʌmpkɪn] n calabaza f.

pun [pʌn] n juego m de palabras.

punch [pʌntʃ] n (blow) puñetazo m; (drink) ponche m ♦ vt (hit) dar un puñetazo; (ticket) picar.

Punch and Judy show [-'dʒu:dɪ-] n teatro de guiñol para niños que se representa en la playa.

punctual ['pʌnktʃuəl] adj puntual.

punctuation [,pʌnktʃu'eɪʃn] n puntuación f.

puncture ['pʌnktʃəʳ] n pinchazo m ♦ vt pinchar.

punish ['pʌnɪʃ] vt: **to ~ sb** (for sthg) castigar a alguien (por algo).

punishment ['pʌnɪʃmənt] n castigo m.

punk [pʌŋk] n (person) punki mf; (music) punk m.

punnet ['pʌnɪt] n (Br) canasta f pequeña.

pupil ['pju:pl] n (student) alumno m (-na f); (of eye) pupila f.

puppet ['pʌpɪt] n títere m.

puppy ['pʌpɪ] n cachorro m.

purchase ['pɜ:tʃəs] vt (fml) comprar ♦ n (fml) compra f.

pure [pjuəʳ] adj puro(-ra).

puree ['pjuəreɪ] n puré m.

purely ['pjuəlɪ] adv puramente.

purity ['pjuərətɪ] n pureza f.

purple ['pɜ:pl] adj morado(-da).

purpose ['pɜ:pəs] n propósito m; **on ~** a propósito.

purr [pɜ:ʳ] vi (cat) ronronear.

purse [pɜ:s] n (Br: for money) monedero m; (Am: handbag) bolso m.

pursue [pə'sju:] vt (follow) perseguir; (study, inquiry, matter) continuar con.

pus [pʌs] n pus m.

push [puʃ] vt (shove) empujar; (press) apretar; (product) promocionar ◆ vi (shove) empujar ◆ n: **to give sb/sthg a ~** dar un empujón a alguien/algo; **to ~ sb into doing sthg** obligar a alguien a hacer algo; **"push"** (on door) "empujar" ❑ **push in** vi (in queue): colarse; **push off** vi (inf: go away) largarse.

push-button telephone n teléfono m de botones.

pushchair [ˈpuʃtʃeəʳ] n (Br) silla f (de paseo).

pushed [puʃt] adj (inf): **to be ~ (for time)** andar corto(-ta) de tiempo.

push-ups npl flexiones fpl.

put [put] (pt & pp put) vt poner; (pressure) ejercer; (blame) echar; (express) expresar; (a question) hacer; **to ~ sthg at** (estimate) estimarse algo en; **to ~ a child to bed** acostar a un niño; **to ~ money into sthg** invertir dinero en algo ❑ **put aside** vt sep (money) apartar; **put away** vt sep (tidy up) poner en su sitio; **put back** vt sep (replace) volver a poner en su sitio; (postpone) aplazar; (clock, watch) atrasar; **put down** vt sep (on floor, table, from vehicle) dejar; (Br: animal) matar; (deposit) pagar como depósito; **put forward** vt sep (clock, watch) adelantar; (suggest) proponer; **put in** vt sep (insert) meter; (install) instalar; **put off** vt sep (postpone) posponer; (distract) distraer; (repel) repeler; (passenger) dejar; **put on** vt sep (clothes, glasses, make-up) ponerse; (weight) ganar; (television, light, radio) encender; (CD, tape, record) poner; (play, show) representar; **to ~ the kettle on** poner la tetera a

hervir; **put out** vt sep (cigarette, fire, light) apagar; (publish) hacer público; (hand, arm, leg) extender; (inconvenience) causar molestias a; **to ~ one's back out** fastidiarse la espalda; **put together** vt sep (assemble) montar; (combine) juntar; **put up** vt sep (tent, statue, building) construir; (umbrella) abrir; (a notice, sign) pegar; (price, rate) subir; (provide with accommodation) alojar ◆ vi (Br: in hotel) alojarse; **put up with** vt fus aguantar.

putter [ˈpʌtəʳ] n (club) putter m.

putting green [ˈpʌtɪŋ-] n minigolf m (con césped y sin obstáculos).

putty [ˈpʌtɪ] n masilla f.

puzzle [ˈpʌzl] n (game) rompecabezas m inv; (jigsaw) puzzle m; (mystery) misterio m ◆ vt desconcertar.

puzzling [ˈpʌzlɪŋ] adj desconcertante.

pyjamas [pəˈdʒɑːməz] npl (Br) pijama m.

pylon [ˈpaɪlən] n torre f de alta tensión.

pyramid [ˈpɪrəmɪd] n pirámide f.

Pyrenees [ˌpɪrəˈniːz] npl: **the ~** los Pirineos.

Pyrex® [ˈpaɪreks] n pírex® m.

Q

quail [kweɪl] n codorniz f.

quail's eggs npl huevos mpl de codorniz.

quaint [kweɪnt] adj pintoresco(-ca).

qualification [ˌkwɒlɪfɪˈkeɪʃn] n (diploma) título m; (ability) aptitud f.

qualified [ˈkwɒlɪfaɪd] adj (having qualifications) cualificado(-da).

qualify [ˈkwɒlɪfaɪ] vi (for competition) clasificarse; (pass exam) sacar el título.

quality [ˈkwɒlətɪ] n (standard, high standard) calidad f; (feature) cualidad f ◆ adj de calidad.

quarantine [ˈkwɒrəntiːn] n cuarentena f.

quarrel [ˈkwɒrəl] n riña f ◆ vi reñir.

quarry [ˈkwɒrɪ] n (for stone, sand) cantera f.

quart [kwɔːt] n cuarto m de galón.

quarter [ˈkwɔːtər] n (fraction) cuarto m; (Am: coin) cuarto de dólar; (4 ounces) cuatro onzas fpl; (three months) trimestre m; (part of town) barrio m; (a) ~ to five (Br) las cinco menos cuarto; (a) ~ of five (Am) las cinco menos cuarto; (a) ~ past five (Br) las cinco y cuarto; (a) ~ after five (Am) las cinco y cuarto; (a) ~ of an hour un cuarto de hora.

quarterpounder [ˌkwɔːtə

paʊndər] n hamburguesa f de un cuarto de libra.

quartet [kwɔːˈtet] n cuarteto m.

quartz [kwɔːts] adj de cuarzo.

quay [kiː] n muelle m.

queasy [ˈkwiːzɪ] adj (inf) mareado(-da).

queen [kwiːn] n reina f; (in cards) dama f.

queer [kwɪər] adj (strange) raro(-ra); (inf: ill) pachucho(-cha) ◆ n (inf) marica m.

quench [kwentʃ] vt: to ~ one's thirst apagar la sed.

query [ˈkwɪərɪ] n pregunta f.

question [ˈkwestʃn] n (query, in exam, on questionnaire) pregunta f; (issue) cuestión f ◆ vt (person) interrogar; **it's out of the ~** es imposible.

question mark n signo m de interrogación.

questionnaire [ˌkwestʃəˈneər] n cuestionario m.

queue [kjuː] n (Br) cola f ◆ vi (Br) hacer cola ◻ **queue up** vi (Br) hacer cola.

quiche [kiːʃ] n quiche f.

quick [kwɪk] adj rápido(-da) ◆ adv rápidamente.

quickly [ˈkwɪklɪ] adv de prisa.

quid [kwɪd] (pl inv) n (Br: inf) libra f.

quiet [ˈkwaɪət] adj (silent, not noisy) silencioso(-sa); (calm, peaceful) tranquilo(-la); (voice) bajo(-ja) ◆ n tranquilidad f; **keep ~!** ¡silencio!; **to keep ~** quedarse callado(-da); **to keep ~ about sthg** callarse algo.

quieten [ˈkwaɪətn]: **quieten**

down vi tranquilizarse.

quietly ['kwaɪətlɪ] adv (silently) silenciosamente; (not noisily) sin hacer ruido; (calmly) tranquilamente.

quilt [kwɪlt] n (duvet) edredón m; (eiderdown) colcha f.

quince [kwɪns] n membrillo m.

quirk [kwɜ:k] n manía f, rareza f.

quit [kwɪt] (pt & pp quit) vi (resign) dimitir; (give up) rendirse ♦ vt (Am: school, job) abandonar; **to ~ doing sthg** dejar de hacer algo.

quite [kwaɪt] adv (fairly) bastante; (completely) totalmente; **there's not ~ enough** no alcanza por poco; **~ a lot (of children)** bastantes (niños); **~ a lot of money** bastante dinero.

quiz [kwɪz] (pl -zes) n concurso m.

quota ['kwəʊtə] n cuota f.

quotation [kwəʊ'teɪʃn] n (phrase) cita f; (estimate) presupuesto m.

quotation marks npl comillas fpl.

quote [kwəʊt] vt (phrase, writer) citar; (price) dar ♦ n (phrase) cita f; (estimate) presupuesto m.

R

rabbit ['ræbɪt] n conejo m.

rabies ['reɪbi:z] n rabia f.

RAC n asociación británica del auto-

móvil, ≃ RACE m.

race [reɪs] n (competition) carrera f; (ethnic group) raza f ♦ vi (compete) competir; (go fast) ir corriendo; (engine) acelerarse ♦ vt (compete against) competir con.

racecourse ['reɪskɔ:s] n hipódromo m.

racehorse ['reɪshɔ:s] n caballo m de carreras.

racetrack ['reɪstræk] n (for horses) hipódromo m.

racial ['reɪʃl] adj racial.

racing ['reɪsɪŋ] n: **(horse) ~** carreras fpl de caballos.

racing car n coche m de carreras.

racism ['reɪsɪzm] n racismo m.

racist ['reɪsɪst] n racista mf.

rack [ræk] n (for coats) percha f; (for plates) escurreplatos m inv; (for bottles) botellero m; (luggage) ~ portaequipajes m inv; **~ of lamb** costillar m de cordero.

racket ['rækɪt] n (SPORT) raqueta f; (noise) jaleo m.

racquet ['rækɪt] n raqueta f.

radar ['reɪdɑ:ʳ] n radar m.

radiation [reɪdɪ'eɪʃn] n radiación f.

radiator ['reɪdɪeɪtəʳ] n radiador m.

radical ['rædɪkl] adj radical.

radii ['reɪdɪaɪ] pl → **radius**.

radio ['reɪdɪəʊ] (pl -s) n radio f ♦ vt radiar; **on the ~** (hear, be broadcast) por la radio.

radioactive [reɪdɪəʊ'æktɪv] adj radiactivo(-va).

radio alarm n radiodespertador m.

radish ['rædɪʃ] n rábano m.

radius ['reɪdɪəs] (pl **radii**) n radio m.

raffle ['ræfl] n rifa f.

raft [rɑ:ft] n (of wood) balsa f; (inflatable) bote m.

rafter ['rɑ:ftə*] n par m.

rag [ræg] n (old cloth) trapo m.

rage [reɪdʒ] n rabia f.

raid [reɪd] n (attack) incursión f; (by police) redada f; (robbery) asalto m ♦ vt (subj: soldiers) hacer una redada en; (subj: thieves) asaltar.

rail [reɪl] n (bar) barra f; (for curtain, train) carril m; (on stairs) barandilla f ♦ adj ferroviario(-ria); **by ~** por ferrocarril.

railcard ['reɪlkɑ:d] n (Br) tarjeta que da derecho a un descuento al viajar en tren.

railings ['reɪlɪŋz] npl reja f.

railroad ['reɪlrəʊd] (Am) = **railway**.

railway ['reɪlweɪ] n (system) ferrocarril m; (track) vía f (férrea).

railway line n (route) línea f de ferrocarril; (track) vía f (férrea).

railway station n estación f de ferrocarril.

rain [reɪn] n lluvia f ♦ v impers llover; **it's ~ing** está lloviendo.

rainbow ['reɪnbəʊ] n arco m iris.

raincoat ['reɪnkəʊt] n impermeable m.

raindrop ['reɪndrɒp] n gota f de lluvia.

rainfall ['reɪnfɔ:l] n pluviosidad f.

rainy ['reɪnɪ] adj lluvioso(-sa).

raise [reɪz] vt (lift) levantar; (increase) aumentar; (money) recaudar; (child, animals) criar; (question,

subject) plantear ♦ n (Am: pay increase) aumento m.

raisin ['reɪzn] n pasa f.

rake [reɪk] n (tool) rastrillo m.

rally ['rælɪ] n (public meeting) mitin m; (motor race) rally m; (in tennis, badminton, squash) peloteo m.

ram [ræm] n carnero m ♦ vt (bang into) chocar con.

Ramadan [,ræmə'dæn] n Ramadán m.

ramble ['ræmbl] n paseo m por el campo.

ramp [ræmp] n (slope) rampa f; (Br: in roadworks) rompecoches m inv; (Am: to freeway) acceso m; **"ramp"** (Br) "rampa".

ramparts ['ræmpɑ:ts] npl murallas fpl.

ran [ræn] pt → **run**.

ranch [rɑ:ntʃ] n rancho m.

ranch dressing n (Am) aliño cremoso y algo picante.

rancid ['rænsɪd] adj rancio(-cia).

random ['rændəm] adj fortuito(-ta) ♦ n: **at ~** al azar.

rang [ræŋ] pt → **ring**.

range [reɪndʒ] n (of radio, telescope) alcance m; (of aircraft) autonomía f; (of prices, temperatures, ages) escala f; (of goods, services) variedad f; (of hills, mountains) sierra f; (for shooting) campo m de tiro; (cooker) fogón m ♦ vi (vary) oscilar.

ranger ['reɪndʒə*] n guardabosques m inv.

rank [ræŋk] n (in armed forces, police) grado m ♦ adj (smell, taste) pestilente.

ransom ['rænsəm] n rescate m.

rap [ræp] n (music) rap m.

rape [reɪp] *n (crime)* violación *f* ◆ *vt* violar.

rapid [ˈræpɪd] *adj* rápido(-da) ❏

rapids *npl* rápidos *mpl.*

rapidly [ˈræpɪdlɪ] *adv* rápidamente.

rapist [ˈreɪpɪst] *n* violador *m.*

rare [reəʳ] *adj (not common)* raro(-ra); *(meat)* poco hecho(-cha).

rarely [ˈreəlɪ] *adv* raras veces.

rash [ræʃ] *n (on skin)* sarpullido *m* ◆ *adj* precipitado(-da).

rasher [ˈræʃəʳ] *n* loncha *f.*

raspberry [ˈrɑːzbərɪ] *n* frambuesa *f.*

rat [ræt] *n* rata *f.*

ratatouille [ˌrætəˈtwiː] *n* guiso de tomate, cebolla, pimiento, calabacín, berenjenas, etc.

rate [reɪt] *n (level)* índice *m; (of interest)* tipo *m; (charge)* precio *m; (speed)* velocidad *f* ◆ *vt (consider)* considerar; *(deserve)* merecer; ~ **of exchange** tipo de cambio; **at any** ~ de todos modos; **at this** ~ a este paso.

rather [ˈrɑːðəʳ] *adv (quite)* bastante; **I'd ~ have a beer** prefiero tomar una cerveza; **I'd ~ not** mejor que no; **would you ~ ...?** ¿preferirías ...?; **~ a lot** bastante; ~ **than** antes que.

ratio [ˈreɪʃɪəʊ] *(pl* **-s)** *n* proporción *f.*

ration [ˈræʃn] *n* ración *f* ❏ **rations** *npl (food)* víveres *mpl.*

rational [ˈræʃənl] *adj* racional.

rattle [ˈrætl] *n (of baby)* sonajero *m* ◆ *vi* golpetear.

rave [reɪv] *n (party)* fiesta multitudinaria en locales muy amplios con

música bakalao y, generalmente, drogas.

raven [ˈreɪvn] *n* cuervo *m.*

ravioli [ˌrævɪˈəʊlɪ] *n* raviolis *mpl.*

raw [rɔː] *adj (uncooked)* crudo (-da); *(sugar)* sin refinar.

raw material *n* materia *f* prima.

ray [reɪ] *n* rayo *m.*

razor [ˈreɪzəʳ] *n (with blade)* navaja *f; (electric)* maquinilla *f* de afeitar.

razor blade *n* hoja *f* de afeitar.

Rd *abbr* = Road.

re [riː] *prep* con referencia a.

RE *n (abbr of religious education)* religión *f (materia).*

reach [riːtʃ] *vt* llegar a; *(manage to touch)* alcanzar; *(contact)* contactar con ◆ *n:* **out of** ~ fuera de alcance; **within** ~ **of the beach** a poca distancia de la playa ❏ **reach out** *vi:* **to** ~ **out (for)** alargar la mano (para).

react [rɪˈækt] *vi* reaccionar.

reaction [rɪˈækʃn] *n* reacción *f.*

read [riːd] *(pt & pp* **read** [red]) *vt* leer; *(subj: sign, note)* decir; *(subj: meter, gauge)* marcar ◆ *vi* leer; **I read about it in the paper** lo leí en el periódico ❏ **read out** *vt sep* leer en voz alta.

reader [ˈriːdəʳ] *n (of newspaper, book)* lector *m (-ra f).*

readily [ˈredɪlɪ] *adv (willingly)* de buena gana; *(easily)* fácilmente.

reading [ˈriːdɪŋ] *n* lectura *f.*

reading matter *n* lectura *f.*

ready [ˈredɪ] *adj (prepared)* listo (-ta); **to be ~ for sthg** *(prepared)* estar listo para algo; **to be ~ to do sthg** *(willing)* estar dispuesto(-a) a hacer algo; (likely) estar a punto de hacer algo; **to get ~** prepararse; **to get sthg ~** preparar algo.

ready cash n dinero m contante.

ready-cooked [-kʊkt] adj precocinado(-da).

ready-to-wear adj confeccionado(-da).

real ['rɪəl] adj (existing) real; (genuine) auténtico(-ca); (for emphasis) verdadero(-ra) ◆ adv (Am) muy.

real ale n cerveza criada en toneles, a la manera tradicional.

real estate n propiedad f inmobiliaria.

realistic [ˌrɪə'lɪstɪk] adj realista.

reality [rɪ'ælətɪ] n realidad f; **in ~** en realidad.

realize ['rɪəlaɪz] vt (become aware of, know) darse cuenta de; (ambition, goal) realizar.

really ['rɪəlɪ] adv realmente; **not ~** en realidad no; **~?** (expressing surprise) ¿de verdad?

realtor ['rɪəltər] n (Am) agente m inmobiliario (agente f inmobiliaria).

rear [rɪər] adj trasero(-ra) ◆ n (back) parte f de atrás.

rearrange [ˌriːə'reɪndʒ] vt (room, furniture) colocar de otro modo; (meeting) volver a concertar.

rearview mirror [ˈrɪəvjuː-] n espejo m retrovisor.

rear-wheel drive n coche m con tracción trasera.

reason ['riːzn] n (motive, cause) razón f; (justification) razones fpl; **for some ~** por alguna razón.

reasonable ['riːznəbl] adj razonable.

reasonably ['riːznəblɪ] adv (quite) razonablemente.

reasoning ['riːznɪŋ] n razonamiento m.

reassure [ˌriːə'ʃɔːr] vt tranquilizar.

reassuring [ˌriːə'ʃɔːrɪŋ] adj tranquilizador(-ra).

rebate ['riːbeɪt] n devolución f.

rebel [n 'rebl, vb ri'bel] n rebelde mf ◆ vi rebelarse.

rebound [rɪ'baʊnd] vi rebotar.

rebuild [ˌriː'bɪld] (pt & pp rebuilt [ˌriː'bɪlt]) vt reconstruir.

rebuke [rɪ'bjuːk] vt reprender.

recall [rɪ'kɔːl] vt (remember) recordar.

receipt [rɪ'siːt] n (for goods, money) recibo m; **on ~ of** al recibo de.

receive [rɪ'siːv] vt recibir.

receiver [rɪ'siːvər] n (of phone) auricular m.

recent ['riːsnt] adj reciente.

recently ['riːsntlɪ] adv recientemente.

receptacle [rɪ'septəkl] n (fml) receptáculo m.

reception [rɪ'sepʃn] n recepción f.

reception desk n recepción f.

receptionist [rɪ'sepʃənɪst] n recepcionista mf.

recess ['riːses] n (in wall) hueco m; (Am: SCH) recreo m.

recession [rɪ'seʃn] n recesión f.

recipe ['resɪpɪ] n receta f.

recite [rɪ'saɪt] vt (poem) recitar; (list) enumerar.

reckless ['reklɪs] *adj* imprudente.

reckon ['rekn] *vt* (*inf: think*) pensar □ **reckon on** *vt fus* contar con; **reckon with** *vt fus* (*expect*) contar con.

reclaim [rɪ'kleɪm] *vt* (*baggage*) reclamar.

reclining seat [rɪ'klaɪnɪŋ-] *n* asiento *m* reclinable.

recognition [,rekəg'nɪʃn] *n* reconocimiento *m*.

recognize ['rekəgnaɪz] *vt* reconocer.

recollect [,rekə'lekt] *vt* recordar.

recommend [,rekə'mend] *vt* recomendar; **to ~ sb to do sthg** recomendar a alguien hacer algo.

recommendation [,rekəmen'deɪʃn] *n* recomendación *f*.

reconsider [,ri:kən'sɪdər] *vt* reconsiderar.

reconstruct [,ri:kən'strʌkt] *vt* reconstruir.

record [*n* 'rekɔ:d, *vb* rɪ'kɔ:d] *n* (MUS) disco *m*; (*best performance, highest level*) récord *m*; (*account*) anotación *f* ♦ *vt* (*keep account of*) anotar; (*on tape*) grabar.

recorded delivery [rɪ'kɔ:dɪd-] *n* (*Br*) correo *m* certificado.

recorder [rɪ'kɔ:dər] *n* (*tape recorder*) magnetófono *m*; (*instrument*) flauta *f*.

recording [rɪ'kɔ:dɪŋ] *n* grabación *f*.

record player *n* tocadiscos *m* inv.

record shop *n* tienda *f* de música.

recover [rɪ'kʌvər] *vt* (*stolen goods,*

lost property) recuperar ♦ *vi* recobrarse.

recovery [rɪ'kʌvərɪ] *n* recuperación *f*.

recovery vehicle *n* (*Br*) grúa *f* remolcadora.

recreation [,rekrɪ'eɪʃn] *n* recreo *m*.

recreation ground *n* campo *m* de deportes.

recruit [rɪ'kru:t] *n* (*to army*) recluta *mf* ♦ *vt* (*staff*) contratar.

rectangle ['rektæŋgl] *n* rectángulo *m*.

rectangular [rek'tæŋgjulər] *adj* rectangular.

recycle [,ri:'saɪkl] *vt* reciclar.

red [red] *adj* rojo(-ja) ♦ *n* (*colour*) rojo *m*; **she has ~ hair** es pelirroja; **in the ~** en números rojos.

red cabbage *n* lombarda *f*.

Red Cross *n* Cruz *f* Roja.

redcurrant ['redkʌrənt] *n* grosella *f*.

redecorate [,ri:'dekəreɪt] *vt* cambiar la decoración de.

redhead ['redhed] *n* pelirrojo *m* (-ja *f*).

red-hot *adj* al rojo vivo.

redial [,ri:'daɪəl] *vi* volver a marcar.

redirect [,ri:dɪ'rekt] *vt* (*letter*) reexpedir; (*traffic, plane*) redirigir.

red pepper *n* pimiento *m* rojo.

reduce [rɪ'dju:s] *vt* (*make smaller*) reducir; (*make cheaper*) rebajar ♦ *vi* (*Am: slim*) adelgazar.

reduced price [rɪ'dju:st-] *n* precio *m* rebajado.

reduction [rɪ'dʌkʃn] *n* (*in size*) reducción *f*; (*in price*) descuento *m*.

redundancy [rɪˈdʌndənsɪ] n (Br: job loss) despido m.

redundant [rɪˈdʌndənt] adj (Br): to be made ~ perder el empleo.

red wine n vino m tinto.

reed [riːd] n carrizo m.

reef [riːf] n arrecife m.

reek [riːk] vi apestar.

reel [riːl] n carrete m.

refectory [rɪˈfektərɪ] n refectorio m.

refer [rɪˈfɜːʳ] : **refer to** vt fus (speak about, relate to) referirse a; (consult) consultar.

referee [ˌrefəˈriː] n (SPORT) árbitro m.

reference [ˈrefrəns] n (mention) referencia f; (letter for job) referencias fpl ◆ adj (book, library) de consulta; **with** ~ **to** con referencia a.

referendum [ˌrefəˈrendəm] n referéndum m.

refill [n ˈriːfɪl, vb ˌriːˈfɪl] vt volver a llenar ◆ n (for pen) cartucho m de recambio; **would you like a** ~? (inf: drink) ¿quieres tomar otra copa de lo mismo?

refinery [rɪˈfaɪnərɪ] n refinería f.

reflect [rɪˈflekt] vt reflejar ◆ vi (think) reflexionar.

reflection [rɪˈflekʃn] n (image) reflejo m.

reflector [rɪˈflektəʳ] n reflector m.

reflex [ˈriːfleks] n reflejo m.

reflexive [rɪˈfleksɪv] adj reflexivo(-va).

reform [rɪˈfɔːm] n reforma f ◆ vt reformar.

refresh [rɪˈfreʃ] vt refrescar.

refreshing [rɪˈfreʃɪŋ] adj refrescante.

refreshments [rɪˈfreʃmənts] npl refrigerios mpl.

refrigerator [rɪˈfrɪdʒəreɪtəʳ] n refrigerador m.

refugee [ˌrefjuˈdʒiː] n refugiado m (-da f).

refund [n ˈriːfʌnd, vb rɪˈfʌnd] n reembolso m ◆ vt reembolsar.

refundable [rɪˈfʌndəbl] adj reembolsable.

refusal [rɪˈfjuːzl] n negativa f.

refuse[1] [rɪˈfjuːz] vt (not accept) rechazar; (not allow) denegar ◆ vi negarse; **to** ~ **to do sthg** negarse a hacer algo.

refuse[2] [ˈrefjuːs] n (fml) basura f.

refuse collection [ˈrefjuːs-] n (fml) recogida f de basuras.

regard [rɪˈgɑːd] vt (consider) considerar ◆ n: **with** ~ **to** respecto a; **as** ~**s** por lo que se refiere a ❑ **regards** npl (in greetings) recuerdos mpl; **give them my** ~**s** salúdales de mi parte.

regarding [rɪˈgɑːdɪŋ] prep respecto a.

regardless [rɪˈgɑːdlɪs] adv a pesar de todo; ~ **of** sin tener en cuenta.

reggae [ˈregeɪ] n reggae m.

regiment [ˈredʒɪmənt] n regimiento m.

region [ˈriːdʒən] n región f; **in the** ~ **of** alrededor de.

regional [ˈriːdʒənl] adj regional.

register [ˈredʒɪstəʳ] n (official list) registro m ◆ vt registrar ◆ vi (be officially recorded) inscribirse; (at hotel) registrarse.

registered [ˈredʒɪstəd] adj (letter,

parcel) certificado(-da).

registration [ˌredʒɪˈstreɪʃn] *n (for course)* inscripción *f; (at conference)* entrega *f* de documentación.

registration (number) *n (of car)* número *m* de matrícula.

registry office [ˈredʒɪstrɪ-] *n* registro *m* civil.

regret [rɪˈɡret] *n* pesar *m* ◆ *vt* lamentar; **to ~ doing sthg** lamentar haber hecho algo; **we ~ any inconvenience caused** lamentamos las molestias ocasionadas.

regrettable [rɪˈɡretəbl] *adj* lamentable.

regular [ˈreɡjʊləʳ] *adj* regular; *(frequent)* habitual; *(normal, of normal size)* normal ◆ *n* cliente *mf* habitual.

regularly [ˈreɡjʊləlɪ] *adv* con regularidad.

regulate [ˈreɡjʊleɪt] *vt* regular.

regulation [ˌreɡjʊˈleɪʃn] *n (rule)* regla *f*.

rehearsal [rɪˈhɜːsl] *n* ensayo *m*.

rehearse [rɪˈhɜːs] *vt* ensayar.

reign [reɪn] *n* reinado *m* ◆ *vi* reinar.

reimburse [ˌriːɪmˈbɜːs] *vt (fml)* reembolsar.

reindeer [ˈreɪnˌdɪəʳ] *(pl inv)* *n* reno *m*.

reinforce [ˌriːɪnˈfɔːs] *vt* reforzar.

reinforcements [ˌriːɪnˈfɔːsmənts] *npl* refuerzos *mpl*.

reins [reɪnz] *npl (for horse)* riendas *fpl; (for child)* andadores *mpl*.

reject [rɪˈdʒekt] *vt* rechazar.

rejection [rɪˈdʒekʃn] *n* rechazo *m*.

rejoin [ˌriːˈdʒɔɪn] *vt (motorway)* reincorporarse a.

relapse [rɪˈlæps] *n* recaída *f*.

relate [rɪˈleɪt] *vt (connect)* relacionar ◆ *vi*: **to ~ to** *(be connected with)* estar relacionado con; *(concern)* referirse a.

related [rɪˈleɪtɪd] *adj (of same family)* emparentado(-da); *(connected)* relacionado(-da).

relation [rɪˈleɪʃn] *n (member of family)* pariente *mf; (connection)* relación *f*; **in ~ to** en relación con ☐ **relations** *npl (international etc)* relaciones *fpl*.

relationship [rɪˈleɪʃnʃɪp] *n* relación *f*.

relative [ˈrelətɪv] *adj* relativo (-va) ◆ *n* pariente *mf*.

relatively [ˈrelətɪvlɪ] *adv* relativamente.

relax [rɪˈlæks] *vi* relajarse.

relaxation [ˌriːlækˈseɪʃn] *n* relajación *f*.

relaxed [rɪˈlækst] *adj (person)* tranquilo(-la); *(atmosphere)* desenfadado(-da).

relaxing [rɪˈlæksɪŋ] *adj* relajante.

relay [ˈriːleɪ] *n (race)* carrera *f* de relevos.

release [rɪˈliːs] *vt (set free)* liberar; *(hand, brake, catch)* soltar; *(film)* estrenar; *(record)* sacar ◆ *n (film)* estreno *m; (record)* lanzamiento *m*.

relegate [ˈreləɡeɪt] *vt*: **to be ~d** *(SPORT)* descender.

relevant [ˈreləvənt] *adj (connected, appropriate)* pertinente; *(important)* importante.

reliable [rɪˈlaɪəbl] *adj (person, machine)* fiable.

relic [ˈrelɪk] *n (vestige)* reliquia *f*.

relief [rɪ'li:f] n (gladness) alivio m; (aid) ayuda f.

relief road n carretera f auxiliar de descongestión.

relieve [rɪ'li:v] vt (pain, headache) aliviar.

relieved [rɪ'li:vd] adj aliviado(-da).

religion [rɪ'lɪdʒn] n religión f.

religious [rɪ'lɪdʒəs] adj religioso(-sa).

relish ['relɪʃ] n (sauce) salsa f picante.

reluctant [rɪ'lʌktənt] adj reacio(-cia).

rely [rɪ'laɪ]: **rely on** vt fus (trust) contar con; (depend on) depender de.

remain [rɪ'meɪn] vi (stay) permanecer; (continue to exist) quedar ❑ **remains** npl restos mpl.

remainder [rɪ'meɪndər] n resto m.

remaining [rɪ'meɪnɪŋ] adj restante.

remark [rɪ'mɑ:k] n comentario m ♦ vt comentar.

remarkable [rɪ'mɑ:kəbl] adj excepcional.

remedy ['remədɪ] n remedio m.

remember [rɪ'membər] vt recordar ♦ vi acordarse; **to ~ doing sthg** acordarse de haber hecho algo; **to ~ to do sthg** acordarse de hacer algo.

remind [rɪ'maɪnd] vt: **to ~ sb of sthg** recordarle a alguien algo; **to ~ sb to do sthg** recordar a alguien hacer algo.

reminder [rɪ'maɪndər] n (for bill, library book) notificación f.

remittance [rɪ'mɪtns] n giro m.

remnant ['remnənt] n resto m.

remote [rɪ'məut] adj remoto(-ta).

remote control n (device) mando m (de control remoto).

removal [rɪ'mu:vl] n (taking away) extracción f.

removal van n camión m de mudanzas.

remove [rɪ'mu:v] vt quitar.

renew [rɪ'nju:] vt renovar.

renovate ['renəveɪt] vt reformar.

renowned [rɪ'naund] adj renombrado(-da).

rent [rent] n alquiler m ♦ vt alquilar.

rental ['rentl] n alquiler m.

repaid [ri:'peɪd] pt & pp → repay.

repair [rɪ'peər] vt reparar ♦ n: **in good ~** en buen estado ❑ **repairs** npl reparaciones fpl.

repair kit n caja f de herramientas.

repay [ri:'peɪ] (pt & pp **repaid**) vt (money, favour) devolver.

repayment [ri:'peɪmənt] n devolución f.

repeat [rɪ'pi:t] vt repetir ♦ n (on TV, radio) reposición f.

repetition [repɪ'tɪʃn] n repetición f.

repetitive [rɪ'petɪtɪv] adj repetitivo(-va).

replace [rɪ'pleɪs] vt (substitute) sustituir; (faulty goods) reemplazar; (put back) poner en su sitio.

replacement [rɪ'pleɪsmənt] n (substitute) sustituto m (-ta f).

replay [ri:'pleɪ] n (rematch) parti-

reply

do m de desempate; *(on TV)* repetición f.

reply [rɪˈplaɪ] n respuesta f ♦ vt & vi responder.

report [rɪˈpɔːt] n *(account)* informe m; *(in newspaper, about event)* reportaje m; *(Br: SCH)* boletín m de evaluación ♦ vt *(announce)* informar; *(theft, disappearance, person)* denunciar ♦ vi informar; **to ~ to sb** *(go to)* presentarse a alguien.

report card n boletín m de evaluación.

reporter [rɪˈpɔːtəʳ] n reportero m *(-ra f)*.

represent [ˌreprɪˈzent] vt representar.

representative [ˌreprɪˈzentətɪv] n representante mf.

repress [rɪˈpres] vt reprimir.

reprieve [rɪˈpriːv] n *(delay)* tregua f.

reprimand [ˈreprɪmɑːnd] vt reprender.

reproach [rɪˈprəʊtʃ] vt reprochar.

reproduction [ˌriːprəˈdʌkʃn] n reproducción f.

reptile [ˈreptaɪl] n reptil m.

republic [rɪˈpʌblɪk] n república f.

Republican [rɪˈpʌblɪkən] n *(in US)* republicano m *(-na f)* ♦ adj *(in US)* republicano(-na).

repulsive [rɪˈpʌlsɪv] adj repulsivo(-va).

reputable [ˈrepjʊtəbl] adj de buena reputación.

reputation [ˌrepjʊˈteɪʃn] n reputación f.

reputedly [rɪˈpjuːtɪdlɪ] adv según se dice.

238

request [rɪˈkwest] n petición f ♦ vt solicitar; **to ~ sb to do sthg** rogar a alguien que haga algo; **available on ~** disponible a petición del interesado.

request stop n *(Br)* parada f discrecional.

require [rɪˈkwaɪəʳ] vt *(need)* necesitar; **passengers are ~d to show their tickets** los pasajeros han de mostrar los billetes.

requirement [rɪˈkwaɪəmənt] n requisito m.

resat [ˌriːˈsæt] pt & pp → resit.

rescue [ˈreskjuː] vt rescatar.

research [rɪˈsɜːtʃ] n investigación f.

resemblance [rɪˈzembləns] n parecido m.

resemble [rɪˈzembl] vt parecerse a.

resent [rɪˈzent] vt tomarse a mal.

reservation [ˌrezəˈveɪʃn] n *(booking)* reserva f; *(doubt)* duda f; **to make a ~** hacer una reserva.

reserve [rɪˈzɜːv] n *(SPORT)* suplente mf; *(for wildlife)* reserva f ♦ vt reservar.

reserved [rɪˈzɜːvd] adj reservado(-da).

reservoir [ˈrezəvwɑːʳ] n pantano m.

reset [ˌriːˈset] *(pt & pp reset)* vt *(watch, meter, device)* reajustar.

reside [rɪˈzaɪd] vi *(fml)* residir.

residence [ˈrezɪdəns] n *(fml)* residencia f; **place of ~** *(fml)* domicilio m.

residence permit n permiso m de residencia.

resident [ˈrezɪdənt] n *(of country)*

residente mf; (of hotel) huésped mf; (of area, house) vecino m (-na f); "~s only" (for parking) "sólo para residentes".

residential [ˌrezɪˈdenʃl] adj (area) residencial.

residue [ˈrezɪdjuː] n residuo m.

resign [rɪˈzaɪn] vi dimitir ♦ vt: to ~ o.s. to sthg resignarse a algo.

resignation [ˌrezɪgˈneɪʃn] n (from job) dimisión f.

resilient [rɪˈzɪlɪənt] adj resistente.

resist [rɪˈzɪst] vt (fight against) resistir a; (temptation) resistir; **I can't ~ cream cakes** me encantan los pasteles de nata; **to ~ doing sthg** resistirse a hacer algo.

resistance [rɪˈzɪstəns] n resistencia f.

resit [ˌriːˈsɪt] (pt & pp resat) vt volver a presentarse a.

resolution [ˌrezəˈluːʃn] n (promise) propósito m.

resolve [rɪˈzɒlv] vt (solve) resolver.

resort [rɪˈzɔːt] n (for holidays) lugar m de vacaciones; **as a last ~** como último recurso ❑ **resort to** vt fus recurrir a; **to ~ to doing sthg** recurrir a hacer algo.

resource [rɪˈsɔːs] n recurso m.

resourceful [rɪˈsɔːsful] adj habilidoso(-sa).

respect [rɪˈspekt] n respeto m; (aspect) aspecto m ♦ vt respetar; **in some ~s** en algunos aspectos; **with ~ to** con respecto a.

respectable [rɪˈspektəbl] adj respetable.

respective [rɪˈspektɪv] adj res-

pectivo(-va).

respond [rɪˈspɒnd] vi responder.

response [rɪˈspɒns] n respuesta f.

responsibility [rɪˌspɒnsəˈbɪlətɪ] n responsabilidad f.

responsible [rɪˈspɒnsəbl] adj responsable; **to be ~ (for)** (accountable) ser responsable (de).

rest [rest] n (relaxation, for foot) descanso m; (for head) respaldo m ♦ vi (relax) descansar; **the ~** el resto; **to have a ~** descansar; **to ~ against** apoyarse contra.

restaurant [ˈrestərɒnt] n restaurante m.

restaurant car n (Br) vagón m restaurante.

restful [ˈrestful] adj tranquilo(-la).

restless [ˈrestlɪs] adj (bored, impatient) impaciente; (fidgety) inquieto(-ta).

restore [rɪˈstɔː] vt (reintroduce) restablecer; (renovate) restaurar.

restrain [rɪˈstreɪn] vt controlar.

restrict [rɪˈstrɪkt] vt restringir.

restricted [rɪˈstrɪktɪd] adj limitado(-da).

restriction [rɪˈstrɪkʃn] n (rule) restricción f; (limitation) limitación f.

rest room n (Am) aseos mpl.

result [rɪˈzʌlt] n resultado m ♦ vi: **to ~ in** resultar en; **as a ~ of** como resultado de ❑ **results** npl (of test, exam) resultados mpl.

resume [rɪˈzjuːm] vi volver a empezar.

résumé [ˈrezjuːmeɪ] n (summary) resumen m; (Am: curriculum vitae) f.

currículum m.

retail ['ri:teil] n venta f al por menor ♦ vt vender (al por menor) ♦ vi: to ~ at venderse a.

retailer ['ri:teilə^r] n minorista mf.

retail price n precio m de venta al público.

retain [ri'tein] vt (fml) retener.

retaliate [ri'tælieit] vi desquitarse.

retire [ri'taiə^r] vi (stop working) jubilarse.

retired [ri'taiəd] adj jubilado(-da).

retirement [ri'taiəmənt] n (leaving job) jubilación f; (period after retiring) retiro m.

retreat [ri'tri:t] vi retirarse ♦ n (place) refugio m.

retrieve [ri'tri:v] vt recobrar.

return [ri'tɜ:n] n (arrival back) vuelta f; (Br: ticket) billete m de ida y vuelta ♦ vt (put back) volver a poner; (ball, serve) restar; (give back) devolver ♦ vi (go back, come back) volver; (happen again) reaparecer ♦ adj (journey) de vuelta; to ~ sthg (to sb) devolver algo (a alguien); by ~ of post (Br) a vuelta de correo; many happy ~s! ¡y que cumplas muchos más!; in ~ (for) en recompensa (por).

return flight n vuelo m de regreso.

return ticket n (Br) billete m de ida y vuelta.

reunite [,ri:ju:'nait] vt reunir.

reveal [ri'vi:l] vt revelar.

revelation [,revə'leiʃn] n revelación f.

revenge [ri'vendʒ] n venganza f.

reverse [ri'vɜ:s] adj inverso(-sa) ♦ n (AUT) marcha f atrás; (of coin, film) reseña f; (of document) dorso m ♦ vt (car) dar marcha atrás a; (decision) revocar ♦ vi dar marcha atrás; the ~ (opposite) lo contrario; in ~ order al revés; to ~ the charges (Br) llamar a cobro revertido.

reverse-charge call n (Br) llamada f a cobro revertido.

review [ri'vju:] n (of book, record, film) reseña f; (examination) repaso m ♦ vt (Am: for exam) repasar.

revise [ri'vaiz] vt revisar ♦ vi (Br) repasar.

revision [ri'viʒn] n (Br) repaso m.

revive [ri'vaiv] vt (person) reanimar; (economy, custom) resucitar.

revolt [ri'vəult] n rebelión f.

revolting [ri'vəultiŋ] adj asqueroso(-sa).

revolution [,revə'lu:ʃn] n revolución f.

revolutionary [,revə'lu:ʃnəri] adj revolucionario(-ria).

revolver [ri'vɒlvə^r] n revólver m.

revolving door [ri'vɒlviŋ-] n puerta f giratoria.

revue [ri'vju:] n revista f teatral.

reward [ri'wɔːd] n recompensa f ♦ vt recompensar.

rewind [,ri:'waind] (pt & pp rewound [,ri:'waund]) vt rebobinar.

rheumatism ['ru:mətizm] n reumatismo m.

rhinoceros [rai'nɒsərəs] (pl inv OR -es) n rinoceronte m.

rhubarb ['ru:bɑ:b] n ruibarbo m.

rhyme [raim] n (poem) rima f ♦ vi rimar.

rhythm ['rɪðm] n ritmo m.

rib [rɪb] n costilla f.

ribbon ['rɪbən] n cinta f.

rice [raɪs] n arroz m.

rice pudding n arroz m con leche.

rich [rɪtʃ] adj rico(-ca) ◆ npl: **the ~** los ricos mpl; **to be ~ in sthg** abundar en algo.

ricotta cheese [rɪ'kɒtə-] n queso m de ricotta.

rid [rɪd] vt: **to get ~ of** deshacerse de.

ridden ['rɪdn] pp → **ride**.

riddle ['rɪdl] n (puzzle) acertijo m; (mystery) enigma m.

ride [raɪd] (pt **rode**, pp **ridden**) n (on horse, bike) paseo m; (in vehicle) vuelta f ◆ vt (horse) montar a; (bike) montar en ◆ vi (on horse) montar a caballo; (bike) ir en bici; (in car) ir en coche; **to go for a ~** (in car) darse una vuelta en coche.

rider ['raɪdər] n (on horse) jinete m (amazona f); (on bike) ciclista mf.

ridge [rɪdʒ] n (of mountain) cresta f; (raised surface) rugosidad f.

ridiculous [rɪ'dɪkjʊləs] adj ridículo(-la).

riding ['raɪdɪŋ] n equitación f.

riding school n escuela f de equitación.

rifle ['raɪfl] n fusil m.

rig [rɪg] n torre f de perforación ◆ vt amañar.

right [raɪt] adj **1.** (correct) correcto(-ta); **to be ~** tener razón; **have you got the ~ time?** ¿tienes buena hora?; **to be ~ to do sthg** hacer bien en hacer algo.

2. (most suitable) adecuado(-da); **is**

this the **~** way? ¿así está bien?

3. (fair) justo(-ta); **that's not ~!** ¡eso no es justo!

4. (on the right) derecho(-cha); **the ~ side of the road** la derecha de la carretera.

◆ n **1.** (side): **the ~** la derecha.

2. (entitlement) derecho m; **to have the ~ to do sthg** tener el derecho a hacer algo.

◆ adv **1.** (towards the right) a la derecha; **turn ~** tuerza a la derecha.

2. (correctly) bien; **am I pronouncing it ~?** ¿lo pronuncio bien?

3. (for emphasis) justo; **~ here** aquí mismo; **~ the way down the road** por toda la calle abajo.

4. (immediately): **I'll be ~ back** vuelvo enseguida; **~ after** justo después; **~ away** enseguida.

right angle n ángulo m recto.

right-hand adj derecho(-cha).

right-hand drive n vehículo m con el volante a la derecha.

right-handed [-'hændɪd] adj (person) diestro(-tra); (implement) para personas diestras.

rightly ['raɪtlɪ] adv (correctly) correctamente; (justly) debidamente.

right of way n (AUT) prioridad f; (path) camino m público.

right-wing adj derechista.

rigid ['rɪdʒɪd] adj rígido(-da).

rim [rɪm] n borde m.

rind [raɪnd] n corteza f.

ring [rɪŋ] (pt **rang**, pp **rung**) n (for finger) anillo m; (circle) círculo m; (sound) timbrazo m; (on cooker) quemador m; (for boxing) cuadrilátero m; (in circus) pista f ◆ vt (Br: on phone) llamar (por teléfono); (bell) tocar ◆ vi (bell, telephone) sonar; (Br: make

ringing tone

phone call) llamar (por teléfono); **to give sb a ~** llamar a alguien (por teléfono); **to ~ the bell** tocar el timbre □ **ring back** vt sep & vi (Br) volver a llamar; **ring off** vi (Br) colgar; **ring up** vt sep & vi (Br) llamar (por teléfono).

ringing tone ['rɪŋɪŋ-] n tono m de llamada.

ring road n carretera f de circunvalación.

rink [rɪŋk] n pista f.

rinse [rɪns] n aclarar □ **rinse out** vt sep enjuagar.

riot ['raɪət] n disturbio m.

rip [rɪp] n rasgón m ♦ vt rasgar ♦ vi rasgarse □ **rip up** vt sep desgarrar.

ripe [raɪp] adj maduro(-a).

ripen ['raɪpn] vi madurar.

rip-off n (inf) estafa f.

rise [raɪz] (pt **rose**, pp **risen** ['rɪzn]) vi (move upwards) elevarse; (sun, moon) salir; (increase) aumentar; (stand up) levantarse ♦ n (increase) ascenso m; (Br: pay increase) aumento m; (slope) subida f.

risk [rɪsk] n (danger) peligro m; (in insurance) riesgo m ♦ vt arriesgar; **to take a ~** arriesgarse; **at your own ~** bajo su cuenta y riesgo; **to ~ doing sthg** exponerse a hacer algo; **to ~ it** arriesgarse.

risky ['rɪskɪ] adj peligroso(-sa).

risotto [rɪ'zɒtəʊ] (pl -s) n arroz con carne, marisco o verduras.

ritual ['rɪtʃʊəl] n ritual m.

rival ['raɪvl] adj rival ♦ n rival mf.

river ['rɪvər] n río m.

river bank n orilla f del río.

riverside ['rɪvəsaɪd] n ribera f del río.

Riviera [rɪvɪ'eərə] n: **the (French) ~** la Riviera (francesa).

roach [rəʊtʃ] n (Am) cucaracha f.

road [rəʊd] n (major, roadway) carretera f; (minor) camino m; (street) calle f; **by ~** por carretera.

road book n libro m de carreteras.

road map n mapa m de carreteras.

road safety n seguridad f en carretera.

roadside ['rəʊdsaɪd] n: **the ~** el borde de la carretera.

road sign n señal f de tráfico.

road tax n impuesto m de circulación.

roadway ['rəʊdweɪ] n calzada f.

road works npl obras fpl (en la carretera).

roam [rəʊm] vi vagar.

roar [rɔːr] n (of crowd, aeroplane) estruendo m ♦ vi rugir.

roast [rəʊst] n asado m ♦ adj asado(-da); **~ beef** rosbif m; **~ chicken** pollo m asado; **~ lamb** cordero m asado; **~ pork** cerdo m asado; **~ potatoes** patatas fpl asadas.

rob [rɒb] vt robar; **to ~ sb of sthg** robar a alguien algo.

robber ['rɒbər] n ladrón m (-ona f).

robbery ['rɒbərɪ] n robo m.

robe [rəʊb] n (Am: bathrobe) bata f.

robin ['rɒbɪn] n petirrojo m.

robot ['rəʊbɒt] n robot m.

rock [rɒk] n (boulder) peñasco m; (Am: stone) guijarro m; (substance) roca f; (music) rock m; (Br: sweet) palo m de caramelo ♦ vt (baby, boat) mecer; **on the ~s** (drink) con hielo.

rock climbing n escalada f (de rocas); **to go ~** ir de escalada.

rocket ['rɒkɪt] n cohete m.

rocking chair ['rɒkɪŋ-] n mecedora f.

rock 'n' roll ['rɒkən'rəʊl] n rock and roll m.

rocky ['rɒkɪ] adj rocoso(-sa).

rod [rɒd] n (wooden) vara f; (metal) barra f; (for fishing) caña f.

rode [rəʊd] pt → **ride**.

roe [rəʊ] n hueva f.

role [rəʊl] n papel m.

roll [rəʊl] n (of bread) bollo m, panecillo m; (of film, paper) rollo m ♦ vi (ball, rock) rodar; (vehicle) avanzar; (ship) balancearse ♦ vt (ball, rock) hacer rodar; (cigarette) liar; (dice) rodar ❏ **roll over** vi (person, animal) darse la vuelta; (car) volcar; **roll up** vt sep (map, carpet) enrollar; (sleeves, trousers) remangar.

roller coaster ['rəʊlə,kəʊstə] n montaña f rusa.

roller skate ['rəʊlə-] n patín m (de ruedas).

roller-skating ['rəʊlə-] n patinaje m sobre ruedas.

rolling pin ['rəʊlɪŋ-] n rodillo m.

Roman ['rəʊmən] adj romano(-na) ♦ n romano (-na f).

Roman Catholic n católico m romano (católica f romana).

romance [rəʊˈmæns] n (love) lo romántico; (love affair) amorío m; (novel) novela f romántica.

Romania [ruːˈmeɪnjə] n Rumanía.

romantic [rəʊˈmæntɪk] adj romántico(-ca).

romper suit ['rɒmpə-] n pelele m.

roof [ruːf] n (of building, cave) tejado m; (of car, caravan, tent) techo m.

roof rack n baca f.

room [ruːm, rʊm] n habitación f; (larger) sala f; (space) sitio m.

room number n número m de habitación.

room service n servicio m de habitación.

room temperature n temperatura f ambiente.

roomy ['ruːmɪ] adj espacioso(-sa).

root [ruːt] n raíz f.

rope [rəʊp] n cuerda f ♦ vt atar con cuerda.

rose [rəʊz] pt → **rise** ♦ n rosa f.

rosé ['rəʊzeɪ] n rosado m.

rosemary ['rəʊzmərɪ] n romero m.

rot [rɒt] vi pudrirse.

rota ['rəʊtə] n lista f (de turnos).

rotate [rəʊˈteɪt] vi girar.

rotten ['rɒtn] adj (food, wood) podrido(-da); (inf: not good) malísimo(-ma); **I feel ~** (ill) me siento fatal.

rouge [ruːʒ] n colorete m.

rough [rʌf] adj (surface, skin, wine) áspero(-ra); (sea, crossing) agitado(-da); (person) bruto(-ta); (approximate) aproximado(-da); (conditions) básico(-ca); (area, town) peligroso(-sa); (inf: not good) rough m; **to have a ~ time** pasar por un momento difícil.

roughly ['rʌflɪ] adv (approximately) aproximadamente; (push, handle) brutalmente.

roulade [ruːˈlɑːd] n rollo m.

roulette [ruːˈlet] n ruleta f.

round [raund] *adj* redondo(-da).
◆ *n* **1.** (of drinks) ronda *f*; **it's my ~** es mi ronda.
2. (of sandwiches) sándwich cortado en cuartos.
3. (of toast) tostada *f*.
4. (of competition) vuelta *f*.
5. (in golf) partido *m*.
6. (in boxing) asalto *m*.
7. (of policeman, milkman) recorrido *m*.
◆ *adv* **1.** (in a circle) en redondo; **to spin ~** girar.
2. (surrounding) alrededor; **it had a wall all ~ (it)** estaba todo rodeado por un muro; **all ~** por todos lados.
3. (near): **~ about** alrededor.
4. (to one's house): **to ask some friends ~** invitar a unos amigos a casa.
5. (continuously): **all year ~** durante todo el año.
◆ *prep* **1.** (surrounding) alrededor de; **they stood ~ the car** estaban alrededor del coche.
2. (circling) alrededor de; **to go ~ the corner** doblar la esquina; **we walked ~ the lake** fuimos andando alrededor del lago.
3. (visiting): **to go ~ a town** recorrer una ciudad.
4. (approximately) sobre; **~ (about) 100** unos 100; **~ ten o'clock** a eso de las diez.
5. (near): **~ here** por aquí.
6. (in phrases): **it's just ~ the corner** (nearby) está a la vuelta de la esquina; **~ the clock** las 24 horas.
❑ **round off** *vt sep* (meal, day, visit) terminar.

roundabout ['raundabaut] *n* (Br) (in road) raqueta *f* (de tráfico); (in

playground) plataforma giratoria donde juegan los niños; (at fairground) tiovivo *m*.

rounders ['raundaz] *n* (Br) juego parecido al béisbol.

round trip *n* viaje *m* de ida y vuelta.

route [ru:t] *n* ruta *f* ◆ *vt* dirigir.

routine [ru:'ti:n] *n* rutina *f* ◆ *adj* rutinario(-ria).

row[1] [rəu] *n* fila *f* ◆ *vt* (boat) remar
◆ *vi* remar; **four in a ~** cuatro seguidos.

row[2] [rau] *n* (argument) pelea *f*; (inf: noise) estruendo *m*; **to have a ~** tener una pelea.

rowboat ['rəubəut] (Am) = rowing boat.

rowdy ['raudi] *adj* ruidoso(-sa).

rowing ['rəuɪŋ] *n* remo *m*.

rowing boat *n* (Br) bote *m* de remos.

royal ['rɔɪəl] *adj* real.

royal family *n* familia *f* real.

 ROYAL FAMILY

Este es el nombre que reciben el monarca británico y su familia; la actual cabeza de la Familia Real es la reina Isabel. Otros miembros importantes son su esposo el príncipe Felipe (duque de Edimburgo), sus hijos los príncipes Carlos (Príncipe de Gales), Andrés y Eduardo, la princesa Ana y la reina madre. El himno nacional británico se toca cuando alguno de sus miembros acude a un acontecimiento oficial y la bandera británica se despliega en sus palacios cuando se encuentran ahí.

royalty [ˈrɔɪəltɪ] n realeza f.

RRP (abbr of recommended retail price) P.V.P.

rub [rʌb] vt (back, eyes) frotar; (polish) sacar brillo a ♦ vi (with hand, cloth) frotar; (shoes) rozar □ **rub in** vt sep (lotion, oil) frotar; **rub out** vt sep borrar.

rubber [ˈrʌbəʳ] adj de goma ♦ n (material) goma f; (Br: eraser) goma f de borrar; (Am: inf: condom) goma f.

rubber band n elástica f.

rubber gloves npl guantes mpl de goma.

rubber ring n flotador m.

rubbish [ˈrʌbɪʃ] n (refuse) basura f; (inf: worthless thing) porquería f; (inf: nonsense) tonterías fpl.

rubbish bin n (Br) cubo m de la basura.

rubbish dump n (Br) vertedero m de basura.

rubble [ˈrʌbl] n escombros mpl.

ruby [ˈruːbɪ] n rubí m.

rucksack [ˈrʌksæk] n mochila f.

rudder [ˈrʌdəʳ] n timón m.

rude [ruːd] adj (person) maleducado(-da); (behaviour, joke, picture) grosero(-ra).

rug [rʌg] n (for floor) alfombra f; (Br: blanket) manta f de viaje.

rugby [ˈrʌgbɪ] n rugby m.

ruin [ˈruːɪn] vt estropear □ **ruins** npl ruinas fpl.

ruined [ˈruːɪnd] adj (building) en ruinas; (clothes, meal, holiday) estropeado(-da).

rule [ruːl] n regla f ♦ vt gobernar; **to be the ~** ser la norma; **against the ~s** contra las normas; **as a ~** por regla general □ **rule out** vt sep

descartar.

ruler [ˈruːləʳ] n (of country) gobernante mf; (for measuring) regla f.

rum [rʌm] n ron m.

rumor [ˈruːmər] (Am) = rumour.

rumour [ˈruːməʳ] n (Br) rumor m.

rump steak [ˌrʌmp-] n filete m (grueso) de lomo.

run [rʌn] (pt ran, pp run) vi 1. (on foot) correr.

2. (train, bus) circular; **the bus ~s every hour** hay un autobús cada hora; **the train is running an hour late** el tren va con una hora de retraso.

3. (operate) funcionar; **to ~ on sthg** funcionar con algo; **leave the engine running** deja el motor en marcha.

4. (tears, liquid) correr.

5. (road, river, track) pasar; **the path ~s along the coast** el camino sigue la costa.

6. (play) estar en cartelera; (event) durar; **"now running at the Palladium"** "en cartelera en el Palladium".

7. (tap): **to leave the tap running** dejar el grifo abierto.

8. (nose) moquear; (eyes) llorar.

9. (colour, dye, clothes) desteñir.

10. (remain valid) ser válido.

♦ vt 1. (on foot) correr; **to ~ a race** participar en una carrera.

2. (manage, organize) llevar.

3. (car) mantener; **it's cheap to ~** es económico.

4. (bus, train): **we're running a special bus to the airport** hemos puesto un autobús especial al aeropuerto.

5. (take in car) llevar en coche.

6. (bath): **to ~ a bath** llenar la bañera.

runaway

◆ n 1. (on foot) carrera f; **to go for a ~** ir a correr.

2. (in car) paseo m en coche; **to go for a ~** dar un paseo en coche.

3. (of play, show): **it had a two-year ~** estuvo dos años en cartelera.

4. (for skiing) pista f.

5. (of success) racha f.

6. (Am: in tights) carrera f.

7. (in phrases): **in the long ~** a largo plazo.

❑ **run away** vi huir; **run down** vt sep (run over) atropellar; (criticize) hablar mal de ◆ vi (clock) pararse; (battery) acabarse; **run into** vt fus (meet) tropezarse con; (hit) chocar con; (problem, difficulty) encontrarse con; **run out** vi (be used up) acabarse; (lease) caducar; **run out of** vt fus quedarse sin; **run over** vt sep atropellar.

runaway ['rʌnəweɪ] n fugitivo m (-va f).

rung [rʌŋ] pp → ring ◆ n escalón m.

runner ['rʌnə*] n (person) corredor m (-ra f); (for door, drawer) corredera f; (of sledge) patín m.

runner bean n judía f escarlata.

runner-up (pl **runners-up**) n subcampeón m (-ona f).

running ['rʌnɪŋ] n (SPORT) carreras fpl; (management) dirección f ◆ adj: **three days ~** durante tres días seguidos; **to go ~** hacer footing.

running water n agua f corriente.

runny ['rʌnɪ] adj (egg, omelette) poco hecho(-cha); (sauce) líquido(-da); (nose) que moquea; (eye) lloroso(-sa).

runway ['rʌnweɪ] n pista f.

rural ['rʊərəl] adj rural.

rush [rʌʃ] n (hurry) prisa f; (of crowd) tropel m de gente ◆ vi (move quickly) ir de prisa; (hurry) apresurarse ◆ vt (work) hacer de prisa; (meal) comer de prisa; (transport quickly) llevar urgentemente; **to be in a ~** tener prisa; **there's no ~!** ¡no corre prisa!; **don't ~ me!** ¡no me metas prisa!

rush hour n hora f punta.

Russia ['rʌʃə] n Rusia.

Russian ['rʌʃn] adj ruso(-sa) ◆ n (person) ruso m (-sa f); (language) ruso m.

rust [rʌst] n óxido m ◆ vi oxidarse.

rustic ['rʌstɪk] adj rústico(-ca).

rustle ['rʌsl] vi susurrar.

rustproof ['rʌstpruːf] adj inoxidable.

rusty ['rʌstɪ] adj oxidado(-da).

RV n (Am: abbr of recreational vehicle) casa remolque.

rye [raɪ] n centeno m.

rye bread n pan m de centeno.

S

S (abbr of south) S.; (abbr of small) P.

saccharin ['sækərɪn] n sacarina f.

sachet ['sæʃeɪ] n bolsita f.

sack [sæk] n saco m ◆ vt despedir; **to get the ~** ser despedido.

sacrifice ['sækrɪfaɪs] n (fig) sacrificio m.

sad [sæd] adj triste; (unfortunate)

lamentable.

saddle ['sædl] *n (on horse)* silla *f* de
montar; *(on bicycle, motorbike)* sillín
m.

saddlebag ['sædlbæg] *n (on bicycle, motorbike)* cartera *f*; *(on horse)*
alforja *f*.

sadly ['sædlɪ] *adv (unfortunately)*
desgraciadamente; *(unhappily)* tris-
temente.

sadness ['sædnɪs] *n* tristeza *f*.

s.a.e. *n (Br: abbr of stamped addressed envelope)* sobre con señas y
franqueo.

safari park [sə'fɑːrɪ-] *n* safari *m*
(reserva).

safe [seɪf] *adj (not dangerous, risky)*
seguro(-ra); *(out of harm)* a salvo ◆ *n*
caja *f* de caudales; **a ~ place** un
lugar seguro; **(have a) ~ journey!**
¡feliz viaje!; **~ and sound** sano y
salvo.

safe-deposit box *n* caja *f* de
seguridad.

safely ['seɪflɪ] *adv (not dangerously)*
sin peligro; *(arrive)* a salvo; *(out of
harm)* seguramente.

safety ['seɪftɪ] *n* seguridad *f*.

safety belt *n* cinturón *m* de
seguridad.

safety pin *n* imperdible *m*.

sag [sæg] *vi* combarse.

sage [seɪdʒ] *n (herb)* salvia *f*.

Sagittarius [,sædʒɪ'teərɪəs] *n* Sagitario *m*.

said [sed] *pt & pp* → **say**.

sail [seɪl] *n* vela *f* ◆ *vi (boat, ship)*
navegar; *(person)* ir en barco; *(depart)* zarpar ◆ *vt:* **to ~ a boat**
gobernar un barco; **to set ~** zarpar.

sailboat ['seɪlbəʊt] *(Am)* = **sailing
boat**.

sailing ['seɪlɪŋ] *n (activity)* vela *f*;
(departure) salida *f*; **to go ~** ir a practicar la vela.

sailing boat *n* barco *m* de vela.

sailor ['seɪlər] *n* marinero *m* (-ra *f*).

saint [seɪnt] *n* santo *m* (-ta *f*).

sake [seɪk] *n:* **for my/their ~** por
mí/ellos; **for God's ~!** ¡por el amor
de Dios!

salad ['sæləd] *n* ensalada *f*.

salad bar *n (Br: area in restaurant)*
bufé *m* de ensaladas; *(restaurant)*
restaurante que sirve platos de ensaladas variados.

salad bowl *n* ensaladera *f*.

salad cream *n (Br)* salsa parecida
a la mayonesa, aunque de sabor más
dulce, utilizada para aderezar ensaladas.

salad dressing *n* aliño *m*.

salami [sə'lɑːmɪ] *n* salami *m*.

salary ['sælərɪ] *n* sueldo *m*.

sale [seɪl] *n (selling)* venta *f*; *(at
reduced prices)* liquidación *f*; **"for ~"**
"se vende"; **on ~** en venta □ **sales**
npl (COMM) ventas *fpl*; **the ~s** las
rebajas.

sales assistant ['seɪlz-] *n* dependiente *m* (-ta *f*).

salesclerk ['seɪlzklɜːrk] *(Am)* =
sales assistant.

salesman ['seɪlzmən] *(pl* **-men**
[-mən]) *n (in shop)* dependiente *m*;
(rep) representante *m* de ventas.

sales rep(resentative) *n*
representante *m* de ventas.

saleswoman ['seɪlz,wʊmən] *(pl*
-women [-,wɪmɪn]) *n* dependienta *f*.

saliva [sə'laɪvə] *n* saliva *f*.

salmon ['sæmən] *(pl inv)* *n* salmón m.

salon ['sælɒn] n salón m.

saloon [sə'luːn] n (Br: car) turismo m; (Am: bar) bar m; ~ (**bar**) (Br) bar de un hotel o "pub", decorado lujosamente, que sirve bebidas a precios más altos que en el "public bar".

salopettes [sælə'pets] npl pantalones mpl de peto para esquiar.

salt [sɔːlt, sɒlt] n sal f.

saltcellar ['sɔːltˌselə] n (Br) salero m.

salted peanuts ['sɔːltɪd-] npl cacahuetes mpl salados.

salt shaker [-ˌʃeɪkə] (Am) = saltcellar.

salty ['sɔːltɪ] adj salado(-da).

salute [sə'luːt] n saludo m ◆ vi hacer un saludo.

Salvadorean [ˌsælvə'dɔːrɪən] adj salvadoreño(-ña) ◆ n salvadoreño m (-ña f).

same [seɪm] adj mismo(-ma) ◆ pron: **the ~** (unchanged) el mismo (la misma); (in comparisons) lo mismo; **they look the ~** parecen iguales; **I'll have the ~ as her** yo voy a tomar lo mismo que ella; **you've got the ~ book as me** tienes el mismo libro que yo; **it's all the ~ to me** me da igual.

samosa [sə'məʊsə] n empanadilla india picante en forma triangular, rellena de carne picada y verduras.

sample [ˈsɑːmpl] n muestra f ◆ vt probar.

sanctions ['sæŋkʃnz] npl sanciones fpl.

sanctuary ['sæŋktʃʊərɪ] n (for birds, animals) reserva f.

sand [sænd] n arena f ◆ vt lijar □

sands npl playa f.

sandal ['sændl] n sandalia f.

sandcastle ['sændˌkɑːsl] n castillo m de arena.

sandpaper ['sændˌpeɪpə] n papel m de lija.

sandwich ['sænwɪdʒ] n (made with roll) bocadillo m; (made with freshly sliced bread) sándwich m frío.

sandwich bar n tienda donde se venden bocadillos y refrescos.

sandy ['sændɪ] adj (beach) arenoso(-sa); (hair) de color rubio rojizo.

sang [sæŋ] pt → sing.

sanitary ['sænɪtrɪ] adj (conditions, measures) sanitario(-ria); (hygienic) higiénico(-ca).

sanitary napkin (Am) = sanitary towel.

sanitary towel n (Br) compresa f.

sank [sæŋk] pt → sink.

sapphire ['sæfaɪə] n zafiro m.

sarcastic [sɑːˈkæstɪk] adj sarcástico(-ca).

sardine [sɑːˈdiːn] n sardina f.

SASE n (Am: abbr of self-addressed stamped envelope) sobre con señas y franqueo.

sat [sæt] pt & pp → sit.

Sat. (abbr of Saturday) sáb.

satchel ['sætʃəl] n cartera f (para escolares).

satellite ['sætəlaɪt] n (in space) satélite m; (at airport) sala f de embarque auxiliar.

satellite dish n antena f parabólica.

satellite TV n televisión f por vía satélite.

satin ['sætɪn] n raso m.

satisfaction [ˌsætɪsˈfækʃn] *n* satisfacción *f*.

satisfactory [ˌsætɪsˈfæktən] *adj* satisfactorio(-ria).

satisfied [ˈsætɪsfaɪd] *adj* satisfecho(-cha).

satisfy [ˈsætɪsfaɪ] *vt* satisfacer.

satsuma [ˌsætˈsuːmə] *n* (*Br*) satsuma *f*.

saturate [ˈsætʃəreɪt] *vt* (*with liquid*) empapar.

Saturday [ˈsætədɪ] *n* sábado *m*; **it's** ~ es sábado; ~ **morning** el sábado por la mañana; **on** ~ el sábado; **on** ~s los sábados; **last** ~ el sábado pasado; **this** ~ este sábado; **next** ~ el sábado de la semana que viene; ~ **week, a week on** ~ del sábado en ocho días.

sauce [sɔːs] *n* salsa *f*.

saucepan [ˈsɔːspən] *n* (*with one long handle*) cazo *m*; (*with two handles*) cacerola *f*.

saucer [ˈsɔːsə²] *n* platillo *m*.

Saudi Arabia [ˌsaʊdɪəˈreɪbjə] *n* Arabia Saudí.

sauna [ˈsɔːnə] *n* sauna *f*.

sausage [ˈsɒsɪdʒ] *n* salchicha *f*.

sausage roll *n* salchicha pequeña envuelta en hojaldre y cocida al horno.

sauté [*Br* ˈsəʊteɪ, *Am* səʊˈteɪ] *adj* salteado(-da).

savage [ˈsævɪdʒ] *adj* salvaje.

save [seɪv] *vt* (*rescue*) salvar; (*money*) ahorrar; (*time, space*) ganar; (*reserve*) reservar; (*SPORT*) parar; (*COMPUT*) guardar ◆ *n* parada *f* □ **save up** *vi* ahorrar; **to** ~ **up** (**for sthg**) ahorrar (para comprarse algo).

saver [ˈseɪvə²] *n* (*Br: ticket*) billete *m*

económico.

savings [ˈseɪvɪŋz] *npl* ahorros *mpl*.

savings and loan association *n* (*Am*) = caja *f* de ahorros.

savings bank *n* = caja *f* de ahorros.

savory [ˈseɪvərɪ] (*Am*) = **savoury**.

savoury [ˈseɪvərɪ] *adj* (*Br*) salado(-da).

saw [sɔː] (*Br pt* -ed, *pp* sawn, *Am pt* & *pp* -ed) *pt* → **see** ◆ *n* sierra *f* ◆ *vt* serrar.

sawdust [ˈsɔːdʌst] *n* serrín *m*.

sawn [sɔːn] *pp* → **saw**.

saxophone [ˈsæksəfəʊn] *n* saxofón *m*.

say [seɪ] (*pt* & *pp* **said**) *vt* decir; (*subj: clock, meter*) marcar ◆ *n*: **to have a** ~ **in sthg** tener voz y voto en algo; **could you** ~ **that again?** ¿puede repetir?; ~ **we met at nine?** ¿pongamos que nos vemos a las nueve?; **to** ~ **yes** decir que sí; **what did you** ~? ¿qué has dicho?

saying [ˈseɪɪŋ] *n* dicho *m*.

scab [skæb] *n* postilla *f*.

scaffolding [ˈskæfəldɪŋ] *n* andamios *mpl*.

scald [skɔːld] *vt* escaldar.

scale [skeɪl] *n* escala *f*; (*extent*) extensión *f*; (*of fish, snake*) escama *f*; (*in kettle*) costra *f* caliza □ **scales** *npl* (*for weighing person*) báscula *f*; (*for weighing food*) balanza *f*.

scallion [ˈskæljən] *n* (*Am*) cebolleta *f*.

scallop [ˈskɒləp] *n* vieira *f*.

scalp [skælp] *n* cuero *m* cabelludo.

scampi [ˈskæmpɪ] *n*: (**breaded**) ~ gambas *fpl* rebozadas.

scan [skæn] *vt* (*consult quickly*)

scandal

echar un vistazo a ◆ *n (MED)* escáner *m*.

scandal ['skændl] *n (disgrace)* escándalo *m*; *(gossip)* habladurías *fpl*.

Scandinavia [ˌskændɪ'neɪvjə] *n* Escandinavia.

scar [skɑːʳ] *n* cicatriz *f*.

scarce [skeəs] *adj* escaso(-sa).

scarcely ['skeəslɪ] *adv* apenas.

scare [skeəʳ] *vt* asustar.

scarecrow ['skeəkrəʊ] *n* espantapájaros *m inv*.

scared [skeəd] *adj* asustado(-da).

scarf [skɑːf] *(pl* **scarves***) n (woollen)* bufanda *f*; *(for women)* pañoleta *f*.

scarlet ['skɑːlət] *adj* escarlata.

scarves [skɑːvz] *pl* → **scarf**.

scary ['skeərɪ] *adj (inf)* espeluznante.

scatter ['skætəʳ] *vt (seeds, papers)* esparcir; *(birds)* dispersar ◆ *vi* dispersarse.

scene [siːn] *n (in play, film, book)* escena *f*; *(of crime, accident)* lugar *m*; *(view)* panorama *m*; **the music** ~ el mundo de la música; **to make a** ~ armar un escándalo.

scenery ['siːnərɪ] *n (countryside)* paisaje *m*; *(in theatre)* decorado *m*.

scenic ['siːnɪk] *adj* pintoresco(-ca).

scent [sent] *n (smell)* fragancia *f*; *(of animal)* rastro *m*; *(perfume)* perfume *m*.

sceptical ['skeptɪkl] *adj (Br)* escéptico(-ca).

schedule [*Br* 'ʃedjuːl, *Am* 'skedʒʊl] *n (of work, things to do)* plan *m*; *(timetable)* horario *m*; *(list)* lista *f* ◆ *vt* programar; **according to** ~ según lo previsto; **behind** ~ con retraso; **on**

~ **a la hora prevista**.

scheduled flight [*Br* 'ʃedjuːld-, *Am* 'skedʒʊld-] *n* vuelo *m* regular.

scheme [skiːm] *n (plan)* proyecto *m*; *(pej: dishonest plan)* estratagema *f*.

scholarship ['skɒləʃɪp] *n (award)* beca *f*.

school [skuːl] *n* escuela *f*; *(institute)* academia *f*; *(university department)* facultad *f*; *(Am: university)* universidad *f* ◆ *adj* escolar; **at** ~ en la escuela.

schoolbag ['skuːlbæg] *n* cartera *f*.

schoolbook ['skuːlbʊk] *n* libro *m* de texto.

schoolboy ['skuːlbɔɪ] *n* alumno *m*.

school bus *n* autobús *m* escolar.

schoolchild ['skuːltʃaɪld] *(pl* **-children** [-tʃɪldrən]*) n* alumno *m* (-na *f*).

schoolgirl ['skuːlgɜːl] *n* alumna *f*.

schoolmaster ['skuːlˌmɑːstəʳ] *n (Br) (primary)* maestro *m*; *(secondary)* profesor *m*.

schoolmistress ['skuːlˌmɪstrɪs] *n (Br) (primary)* maestra *f*; *(secondary)* profesora *f*.

schoolteacher ['skuːlˌtiːtʃəʳ] *n (primary)* maestro *m* (-tra *f*); *(secondary)* profesor *m* (-ra *f*).

school uniform *n* uniforme *m* escolar.

science ['saɪəns] *n* ciencia *f*; *(SCH)* ciencias *fpl*.

science fiction *n* ciencia *f* ficción.

scientific [ˌsaɪən'tɪfɪk] *adj* científico(-ca).

scientist ['saɪəntɪst] *n* científico *m* (-ca *f*).

scissors ['sɪzəz] *npl:* **(a pair of)** ~ unas tijeras.

scold [skəʊld] *vt* regañar.

scone [skɒn] *n* pastelillo redondo hecho con harina, manteca y a veces pasas, que suele tomarse a la hora del té.

scoop [sku:p] *n (for ice cream)* pinzas *fpl* de helado; *(for flour)* paleta *f; (of ice cream)* bola *f; (in media)* exclusiva *f.*

scooter ['sku:tə] *n (motor vehicle)* Vespa® *f.*

scope [skəʊp] *n (possibility)* posibilidades *fpl; (range)* alcance *m.*

scorch [skɔ:tʃ] *vt* chamuscar.

score [skɔ:ʳ] *n (final result)* resultado *m; (points total)* puntuación *f; (in exam)* calificación *f* ◆ *vt (sport)* marcar; *(in test)* obtener una puntuación de ◆ *vi (sport)* marcar; **what's the ~?** ¿cómo va?

scorn [skɔ:n] *n* desprecio *m.*

Scorpio ['skɔ:pɪəʊ] *n* Escorpión *m.*

scorpion ['skɔ:pjən] *n* escorpión *m.*

Scot [skɒt] *n* escocés *m* (-esa *f*).

scotch [skɒtʃ] *n* whisky *m* escocés.

Scotch broth *n* sopa espesa con caldo de carne, verduras y cebada.

Scotch tape® *n (Am)* celo®*m.*

Scotland ['skɒtlənd] *n* Escocia.

Scotsman ['skɒtsmən] *(pl* -men [-mən]) *n* escocés *m.*

Scotswoman ['skɒtswʊmən] *(pl* -women [-wɪmɪn]) *n* escocesa *f.*

Scottish ['skɒtɪʃ] *adj* escocés(-esa).

scout [skaʊt] *n (boy scout)* explorador *m.*

SCOUTS

Los "scouts" son miembros de la "Scouting Association", fundada en Gran Bretaña en 1908 por Lord Baden-Powell para promover el sentido de la responsabilidad y de la aventura entre la juventud. Pequeños grupos de niños de 11 a 16 años se organizan bajo el mando de un adulto. Sus miembros adquieren conocimientos de primeros auxilios y técnicas de supervivencia al aire libre. Los niños de menos de 11 años pueden hacerse miembros de los "Cub Scouts", y también existen organizaciones paralelas para niñas, llamadas "Girl Guides" y "Brownies".

scowl [skaʊl] *vi* fruncir el ceño.

scrambled eggs [,skræmbld-] *npl* huevos *mpl* revueltos.

scrap [skræp] *n (of paper, cloth)* trozo *m; (old metal)* chatarra *f.*

scrapbook ['skræpbʊk] *n* álbum *m* de recortes.

scrape [skreɪp] *vt (rub)* raspar; *(scratch)* rasguñar.

scrap paper *n (Br)* papel *m* usado.

scratch [skrætʃ] *n (cut)* arañazo *m; (mark)* rayazo *m* ◆ *vt (cut)* arañar; *(mark)* rayar; *(rub)* rascar; **to be up to** ~ tener un nivel aceptable; **to start from** ~ empezar desde el principio.

scratch paper *(Am)* = **scrap paper.**

scream [skri:m] *n* grito *m* ◆ *vi* gritar.

screen [skri:n] *n (of TV, computer,*

for film) pantalla f; *(hall in cinema)* sala f (de proyecciones); *(panel)* biombo m ♦ vt *(film)* proyectar; *(programme)* emitir.

screening ['skri:nɪŋ] n *(of film)* proyección f.

screen wash n líquido m limpiaparabrisas.

screw [skru:] n tornillo m ♦ vt *(fasten)* atornillar; *(twist)* enroscar.

screwdriver ['skru:,draɪvəʳ] n destornillador m.

scribble ['skrɪbl] vi garabatear.

script [skrɪpt] n *(of play, film)* guión m.

scrub [skrʌb] vt restregar.

scruffy ['skrʌfɪ] adj andrajoso(-sa).

scrumpy ['skrʌmpɪ] n sidra de alta graduación procedente del suroeste de Inglaterra.

scuba diving ['sku:bə-] n buceo m (con botellas de oxígeno).

sculptor ['skʌlptəʳ] n escultor m (-ra f).

sculpture ['skʌlptʃəʳ] n *(statue)* escultura f.

sea [si:] n mar m o f; **by ~** en barco; **by the ~** a orillas del mar.

seafood ['si:fu:d] n mariscos mpl.

seafront ['si:frʌnt] n paseo m marítimo.

seagull ['si:gʌl] n gaviota f.

seal [si:l] n *(animal)* foca f; *(on bottle, container)* precinto m; *(official mark)* sello m ♦ vt *(envelope, container)* cerrar.

seam [si:m] n *(in clothes)* costura f.

search [sɜ:tʃ] n búsqueda f ♦ vt *(place)* registrar; *(person)* cachear ♦ vi: **to ~ for** buscar.

seashell ['si:ʃel] n concha f (marina).

seashore ['si:ʃɔːʳ] n orilla f del mar.

seasick ['si:sɪk] adj mareado(-da) *(en barco)*.

seaside ['si:saɪd] n: **the ~** la playa.

seaside resort n lugar m de veraneo *(junto al mar)*.

season ['si:zn] n *(division of year)* estación f; *(period)* temporada f ♦ vt sazonar; *(holiday)* en temporada alta; **strawberries are in ~** ahora es la época de las fresas; **out of ~** *(fruit, vegetables)* fuera de temporada; *(holiday)* en temporada baja.

seasoning ['si:znɪŋ] n condimento m.

season ticket n abono m.

seat [si:t] n *(place, chair)* asiento m; *(for show)* entrada f; *(in parliament)* escaño m ♦ vt *(sub: building, vehicle)* tener cabida para; **"please wait to be ~ed"** cartel que ruega a los clientes que esperen hasta que les sea asignada una mesa.

seat belt n cinturón m de seguridad.

seaweed ['si:wi:d] n alga f marina.

secluded [sɪ'klu:dɪd] adj aislado(-da).

second ['sekənd] n segundo m ♦ num segundo(-da), → **sixth**; **~ gear** segunda marcha f □ **seconds** npl *(goods)* artículos mpl defectuosos; **who wants ~s?** *(inf: food)* ¿quién quiere repetir?

secondary school ['sekəndrɪ-] n instituto m de enseñanza media.

second-class adj *(ticket)* de segunda clase; *(stamp)* para el correo *nacional ordinario; (inferior)* de segunda categoría.

second-hand *adj* de segunda mano.

Second World War *n*: the ~ la segunda Guerra Mundial.

secret ['si:krɪt] *adj* secreto(-ta) ♦ *n* secreto *m*.

secretary [Br 'sekrətrɪ, Am 'sekrə,terɪ] *n* secretario *m* (-ria *f*).

Secretary of State *n* (Am: foreign minister) ministro *m* (-tra *f*) de Asuntos Exteriores; (Br: government minister) ministro *m* (-tra *f*).

section ['sekʃn] *n* sección *f*.

sector ['sektə'] *n* sector *m*.

secure [sɪ'kjuə'] *adj* seguro(-ra) ♦ *vt (fix)* fijar; *(fml: obtain)* conseguir.

security [sɪ'kjuərətɪ] *n* seguridad *f*.

security guard *n* guardia *mf* jurado.

sedative ['sedətɪv] *n* sedante *m*.

seduce [sɪ'dju:s] *vt* seducir.

see [si:] (*pt* saw, *pp* seen) *vt* ver; *(friends)* visitar; *(understand)* entender; *(accompany)* acompañar; *(find out)* ir a ver; *(undergo)* experimentar ♦ *vi* ver; **I ~ ya veo; to ~ if** one can do sthg ver si uno puede hacer algo; **to ~ to sthg** *(deal with)* encargarse de algo; *(repair)* arreglar algo; **~ you!** ¡hasta la vista!; **~ you later!** ¡hasta luego!; **~ you soon!** ¡hasta pronto!; **~ p 14** véase p. 14 ❑ **see off** *vt sep (say goodbye to)* despedir.

seed [si:d] *n* semilla *f*.

seedy ['si:dɪ] *adj* sórdido(-da).

seeing (as) ['si:ɪŋ] *conj* en vista de que.

seek [si:k] (*pt & pp* sought) *vt (fml*

(look for) buscar; *(request)* solicitar.

seem [si:m] *vi* parecer ♦ *v impers*: **it ~s (that)** ... parece que ...; **to ~** like parecer.

seen [si:n] *pp* → see.

seesaw ['si:sɔ:] *n* balancín *m*.

segment ['segmənt] *n (of fruit)* gajo *m*.

seize [si:z] *vt (grab)* agarrar; *(drugs, arms)* incautarse de ❑ **seize up** *vi* agarrotarse.

seldom ['seldəm] *adv* rara vez.

select [sɪ'lekt] *vt* seleccionar ♦ *adj* selecto(-ta).

selection [sɪ'lekʃn] *n (selecting)* selección *f*; *(range)* surtido *m*.

self-assured [,selfə'ʃuəd] *adj* seguro de sí mismo (segura de sí misma).

self-catering [,self'keɪtərɪŋ] *adj* con alojamiento sólo.

self-confident [,self-] *adj* seguro de sí mismo (segura de sí misma).

self-conscious [,self-] *adj* cohibido(-da).

self-contained [,selfkən'teɪnd] *adj (flat)* autosuficiente.

self-defence [,self-] *n* defensa *f* personal.

self-employed [,self-] *adj* autónomo(-ma).

selfish ['selfɪʃ] *adj* egoísta.

self-raising flour [,self'reɪzɪŋ-] *n (Br)* harina *f* con levadura.

self-rising flour [,self'raɪzɪŋ-] *(Am)* = self-raising flour.

self-service [,self-] *adj* de autoservicio.

sell [sel] (*pt & pp* sold) *vt & vi* vender; **to ~ for** venderse a; **to ~ sb**

sthg vender algo a alguien.

sell-by date n fecha f de caducidad.

seller ['selə^r] n vendedor m (-ra f).

Sellotape® ['seləteɪp] n (Br) = celo® m.

semester [sɪ'mestə^r] n semestre m.

semicircle ['semɪˌsɜːkl] n semicírculo m.

semicolon [ˌsemɪ'kəʊlən] n punto m y coma.

semidetached [ˌsemɪdɪ'tætʃt] adj adosado(-da).

semifinal [ˌsemɪ'faɪnl] n semifinal f.

seminar ['semɪnɑː^r] n seminario m.

semolina [ˌsemə'liːnə] n sémola f.

send [send] (pt & pp **sent**) vt mandar; (TV or radio signal) transmitir; **to ~ sthg to sb** mandar algo a alguien □ **send back** vt sep devolver; **send off** vt sep (letter, parcel) mandar (por correo); (SPORT) expulsar ◆ vi: **to ~ off (for sthg)** solicitar (algo) por escrito.

sender ['sendə^r] n remitente mf.

senile ['siːnaɪl] adj senil.

senior ['siːnjə^r] adj superior ◆ n (SCH) senior mf.

senior citizen n persona f de la tercera edad.

sensation [sen'seɪʃn] n sensación f.

sensational [sen'seɪʃənl] adj sensacional.

sense [sens] n sentido m ◆ vt sentir; **to make ~** tener sentido; **~ of direction** sentido de la orientación; **~ of humour** sentido del humor.

sensible ['sensəbl] adj (person) sensato(-ta); (clothes, shoes) práctico(-ca).

sensitive ['sensɪtɪv] adj (skin, eyes, device) sensible; (easily offended) susceptible; (emotionally) comprensivo(-va); (subject, issue) delicado(-da).

sent [sent] pt & pp → **send**.

sentence ['sentəns] n (GRAMM) oración f; (for crime) sentencia f ◆ vt condenar.

sentimental [ˌsentɪ'mentl] adj (pej) sentimental.

Sep. (abbr of September) sep.

separate [adj 'seprət, vb 'sepəreɪt] adj (different, individual) distinto(-ta); (not together) separado(-da) ◆ vt (divide) dividir; (detach) separar ◆ vi separarse □ **separates** npl (Br) prendas de vestir femeninas combinables.

separately ['seprətlɪ] adv (individually) independientemente; (alone) por separado.

separation [ˌsepə'reɪʃn] n separación f.

September [sep'tembə^r] n septiembre m; **at the beginning of ~** a principios de septiembre; **at the end of ~** a finales de septiembre; **during ~** en septiembre; **every ~** todos los años en septiembre; **in ~** en septiembre; **last ~** en septiembre del año pasado; **next ~** en septiembre del próximo año; **this ~** en septiembre de este año; **2 ~ 1994** (in letters etc) 2 de septiembre de 1994.

septic ['septɪk] adj séptico(-ca).

septic tank n fosa f séptica.

sequel ['siːkwəl] n continuación f.

sequence ['siːkwəns] n (series)

sucesión f; (order) orden m.

sequin ['siːkwɪn] n lentejuela f.

sergeant ['sɑːdʒənt] n (in police force) ≈ subinspector m (-ra f) de policía; (in army) sargento m.

serial ['sɪərɪəl] n serial m.

series ['sɪəriːz] (pl inv) n serie f.

serious ['sɪərɪəs] adj serio(-ria); (very bad) grave; **I'm ~** hablo en serio.

seriously ['sɪərɪəslɪ] adv (really) en serio; (badly) gravemente.

sermon ['sɜːmən] n sermón m.

servant ['sɜːvənt] n sirviente m (-ta f).

serve [sɜːv] vt servir ♦ vi (SPORT) sacar; (work) servir ♦ n saque m; to ~ **as** (be used for) servir de; **the town is ~d** by two airports la ciudad está provista de dos aeropuertos; **"~s two"** "para dos personas"; **it ~s you right** te está bien empleado.

service ['sɜːvɪs] n servicio m; (at church) oficio m; (SPORT) saque m; (of car) revisión f ♦ vt (car) revisar; **"out of ~"** "no funciona"; **"~ included"** "servicio incluido"; **"~ not included"** "servicio no incluido"; **to be of ~ to sb** (fml) ayudar a alguien □ **services** npl (on motorway) área f de servicios; (of person) servicios mpl.

service area n área f de servicios.

service charge n servicio m.

service department n departamento m de servicio al cliente.

service station n estación f de servicio.

serviette [,sɜːvɪ'et] n servilleta f.

serving ['sɜːvɪŋ] n ración f.

serving spoon n cucharón m.

sesame seeds ['sesəmɪ-] npl sésamo m.

session ['seʃn] n sesión f.

set [set] (pt & pp set) adj 1. (fixed) fijo(-ja); **a ~ lunch** el menú del día.

2. (text, book) obligatorio(-ria).

3. (situated) situado(-da).

♦ n 1. (collection) juego m; (of stamps, stickers) colección f.

2. (TV) aparato m; **a TV ~** un televisor.

3. (in tennis) set m.

4. (of play) decorado m.

5. (at hairdresser's): **a shampoo and ~** lavado m y marcado.

♦ vt 1. (put) colocar, poner.

2. (cause to be): **to ~ a machine going** poner una máquina en marcha; **to ~ fire to** prender fuego a.

3. (clock, alarm, controls) poner; **the alarm for 7 a.m.** pon el despertador para las 7 de la mañana.

4. (fix) fijar.

5. (essay, homework, the table) poner.

6. (a record) marcar.

7. (broken bone) componer.

8. (play, film, story): **to be ~ in** desarrollarse en.

♦ vi 1. (sun) ponerse..

2. (glue) secarse; (jelly) cuajar.

□ **set down** vt sep (Br: passengers) dejar; **set off** vt sep (alarm) hacer saltar ♦ vi ponerse en camino; **set out** vt sep (arrange) disponer ♦ vi ponerse en camino; **set up** vt sep (barrier, cordon) levantar; (equipment) preparar; (meeting, interview) organizar; (committee) crear.

set meal n menú m (plato).

set menu n menú m del día.

settee [se'tiː] n sofá m.

setting ['setɪŋ] n (on machine) posición f; (surroundings) escenario m.

settle ['setl] vt (argument) resolver; (bill) saldar; (stomach) asentar; (nerves) calmar; (arrange, decide on) acordar ♦ vi (start to live) establecerse; (come to rest) posarse; (sediment, dust) depositarse ❏ **settle down** vi (calm down) calmarse; (sit comfortably) acomodarse; **settle up** vi saldar las cuentas.

settlement ['setlmənt] n (agreement) acuerdo m; (place) asentamiento m.

seven ['sevn] num siete, → six.

seventeen [,sevn'ti:n] num diecisiete, → six.

seventeenth [,sevn'ti:nθ] num decimoséptimo(-ma), → sixth.

seventh ['sevnθ] num séptimo(-ma), → sixth.

seventieth ['sevntιəθ] num septuagésimo(-ma), → sixth.

seventy ['sevntɪ] num setenta, → six.

several ['sevrəl] adj varios(-rias) ♦ pron varios mpl (-rias fpl).

severe [sɪ'vɪə] adj severo(-ra); (illness) grave; (pain) fuerte.

Seville [sə'vɪl] n Sevilla.

sew [səʊ] vt & vi coser.

sewage ['su:ɪdʒ] n aguas fpl residuales.

sewing ['səʊɪŋ] n costura f.

sewing machine n máquina f de coser.

sewn [səʊn] pp → sew.

sex [seks] n (gender) sexo m; to have ~ (with) tener relaciones sexuales (con).

sexist ['seksɪst] n sexista mf.

sexual ['sekʃʊəl] adj sexual.

sexy ['seksɪ] adj sexi inv.

shabby ['ʃæbɪ] adj (clothes, room) desastrado(-da); (person) desharrapado(-da).

shade [ʃeɪd] n (shadow) sombra f; (lampshade) pantalla f; (of colour) tonalidad f ♦ vt (protect) proteger ❏ **shades** npl (inf: sunglasses) gafas fpl de sol.

shadow ['ʃædəʊ] n (dark shape) sombra f; (darkness) oscuridad f.

shady ['ʃeɪdɪ] adj (place) sombreado(-da); (inf: person) sospechoso(-sa); (inf: deal) turbio(-bia).

shaft [ʃɑ:ft] n (of machine) eje m; (of lift) pozo m.

shake [ʃeɪk] (vt shook, pp shaken ['ʃeɪkn]) vt (tree, rug, packet, etc) sacudir; (bottle) agitar; (person) zarandear; (dice) mover; (shock) conmocionar ♦ vi temblar; to ~ hands with sb estrechar la mano a alguien; to ~ one's head (saying no) negar con la cabeza.

shall [weak form ʃəl, strong form ʃæl] aux vb 1. (expressing future): I ~ be ready soon estaré listo enseguida.
2. (in questions): ~ I buy some wine? ¿compro vino?; where ~ we go? ¿adónde vamos?
3. (fml: expressing order): payment ~ be made within a week debe efectuarse el pago dentro de una semana.

shallot [ʃə'lɒt] n chalote m.

shallow ['ʃæləʊ] adj poco profundo(-da).

shallow end n (of swimming pool) parte f poco profunda.

shambles ['ʃæmblz] n desbarajuste m.

shame [ʃeɪm] n (remorse) vergüenza f; (disgrace) deshonra f; **it's a ~ es** una lástima; **what a ~!** ¡qué lástima!

shampoo [ʃæm'pu:] n (liquid) champú m; (wash) lavado m.

shandy ['ʃændɪ] n cerveza f con gaseosa.

shape [ʃeɪp] n (form) forma f; (object, person, outline) figura f; **to be in good/bad ~** estar en (buena) forma/baja forma.

share [ʃeəʳ] n (part) parte f; (in company) acción f ♦ vt (room, work, cost) compartir; (divide) repartir ❑ **share out** vt sep repartir.

shark [ʃɑːk] n tiburón m.

sharp [ʃɑːp] adj (knife, razor, teeth) afilado(-da); (pin, needle) puntiagudo(-da); (clear) nítido(-da); (quick, intelligent) inteligente; (rise, bend) marcado(-da); (change) brusco(-ca); (painful) agudo(-da); (food, taste) ácido(-da) ♦ adv (exactly) en punto.

sharpen ['ʃɑːpn] vt (knife) afilar; (pencil) sacar punta a.

shatter ['ʃætəʳ] vt (break) hacer añicos ♦ vi hacerse añicos.

shattered ['ʃætəd] adj (Br: inf: tired) hecho(-cha).

shave [ʃeɪv] vt afeitar ♦ vi afeitarse ♦ n: **to have a ~** afeitarse.

shaver ['ʃeɪvəʳ] n maquinilla f de afeitar.

shaver point n enchufe m para maquinilla de afeitar.

shaving brush ['ʃeɪvɪŋ-] n brocha f de afeitar.

shaving cream ['ʃeɪvɪŋ-] n crema f de afeitar.

shaving foam ['ʃeɪvɪŋ-] n espuma f de afeitar.

shawl [ʃɔːl] n chal m.

she [ʃiː] pron ella f; **~'s tall** (ella) es alta.

sheaf [ʃiːf] (pl **sheaves**) n (of paper, notes) fajo m.

shears [ʃɪəz] npl (for gardening) tijeras fpl de podar.

sheaves [ʃiːvz] pl → **sheaf**.

shed [ʃed] (pt & pp **shed**) n cobertizo m ♦ vt (tears, blood) derramar.

she'd [weak form ʃɪd, strong form ʃiːd] = **she had**, **she would**.

sheep [ʃiːp] (pl inv) n oveja f.

sheepdog ['ʃiːpdɒg] n perro m pastor.

sheepskin ['ʃiːpskɪn] adj piel f de carnero; **~ jacket** zamarra f.

sheer [ʃɪəʳ] adj (pure, utter) puro(-ra); (cliff) escarpado(-da); (stockings) fino(-na).

sheet [ʃiːt] n (for bed) sábana f; (of paper) hoja f; (of glass, metal, wood) lámina f.

shelf [ʃelf] (pl **shelves**) n estante m.

shell [ʃel] n (of egg, nut) cáscara f; (on beach) concha f; (of animal) caparazón m; (bomb) proyectil m.

she'll [ʃiːl] = **she will**, **she shall**.

shellfish ['ʃelfɪʃ] n (food) mariscos mpl.

shell suit n (Br) chándal m de Táctel®.

shelter ['ʃeltəʳ] n refugio m ♦ vt (protect) proteger ♦ vi resguardarse; **to take ~** cobijarse.

sheltered [ˈʃeltəd] *adj* protegido(-da).

shelves [ʃelvz] *pl* → **shelf**.

shepherd [ˈʃepəd] *n* pastor *m*.

shepherd's pie [ˈʃepədz-] *n* plato consistente en carne picada de vaca, cebolla y especias cubierta con una capa de puré de patata dorada al grill.

sheriff [ˈʃerɪf] *n* sheriff *m*.

sherry [ˈʃerɪ] *n* jerez *m*.

she's [ʃiːz] = she is, she has.

shield [ʃiːld] *n* escudo *m* ◆ *vt* proteger.

shift [ʃɪft] *n* (change) cambio *m*; (period of work) turno *m* ◆ *vt* mover ◆ *vi* (move) moverse; (change) cambiar.

shin [ʃɪn] *n* espinilla *f*.

shine [ʃaɪn] (*pt & pp* shone) *vi* brillar ◆ *vt* (shoes) sacar brillo a; (torch) enfocar.

shiny [ˈʃaɪnɪ] *adj* brillante.

ship [ʃɪp] *n* barco *m*; **by ~** en barco.

shipwreck [ˈʃɪprek] *n* (accident) naufragio *m*; (wrecked ship) barco *m* náufrago.

shirt [ʃɜːt] *n* camisa *f*.

shit [ʃɪt] *n* (vulg) mierda *f* ◆ *excl* (vulg) ¡mierda!

shiver [ˈʃɪvəʳ] *vi* temblar.

shock [ʃɒk] *n* (surprise) susto *m*; (force) sacudida *f* ◆ *vt* (surprise) conmocionar; (horrify) escandalizar; **to be in ~** (MED) estar en estado de shock.

shock absorber [-əbˌzɔːbəʳ] *n* amortiguador *m*.

shocking [ˈʃɒkɪŋ] *adj* (very bad) horroroso(-sa).

shoe [ʃuː] *n* zapato *m*.

shoelace [ˈʃuːleɪs] *n* cordón *m* (de zapato).

shoe polish *n* betún *m*.

shoe repairer's [-rɪˌpeərəz] *n* zapatero *m* (remendón).

shoe shop *n* zapatería *f*.

shone [ʃɒn] *pt & pp* → **shine**.

shook [ʃʊk] *pt* → **shake**.

shoot [ʃuːt] (*pt & pp* shot) *vt* (kill) matar a tiros; (injure) herir (con arma de fuego); (gun, arrow) disparar; (film) rodar ◆ *vi* (with gun) disparar; (move quickly) pasar disparado; (SPORT) chutar ◆ *n* (of plant) brote *m*.

shop [ʃɒp] *n* tienda *f* ◆ *vi* hacer compras.

shop assistant *n* (Br) dependiente *m* (-ta *f*).

shop floor *n* (place) taller *m*.

shopkeeper [ˈʃɒpˌkiːpəʳ] *n* tendero *m* (-ra *f*).

shoplifter [ˈʃɒpˌlɪftəʳ] *n* ratero *m* (-ra *f*) de tiendas.

shopper [ˈʃɒpəʳ] *n* comprador *m* (-ra *f*).

shopping [ˈʃɒpɪŋ] *n* compras *fpl*; **I hate ~** odio hacer las compras; **to do the ~** hacer las compras; **to go ~** ir de compras.

shopping bag *n* bolsa *f* de la compra.

shopping basket *n* cesta *f* de la compra.

shopping centre *n* centro *m* comercial.

shopping list *n* lista *f* de la compra.

shopping mall *n* centro *m* comercial.

shop steward n enlace m sindical.

shop window n escaparate m.

shore [ʃɔːˀ] n orilla f; **on ~** en tierra.

short [ʃɔːt] adj (not tall) bajo(-ja); (in length, time) corto(-ta) ♦ adv (cut hair) corto ♦ n (Br: drink) licor m; (film) cortometraje m; **to be ~ of sthg** andar escaso de algo; **to be ~ for sthg** (be abbreviation of) ser el diminutivo de algo; **I'm ~ of breath** me falta el aliento; **in ~** en resumen ❏ **shorts** npl (short trousers) pantalones mpl cortos; (Am: underpants) calzoncillos mpl.

shortage [ˈʃɔːtɪdʒ] n escasez f.

shortbread [ˈʃɔːtbred] n especie de torta dulce y quebradiza hecha con harina, azúcar y mantequilla.

short-circuit vi tener un cortocircuito.

shortcrust pastry [ˈʃɔːtkrʌst-] n pasta f quebrada.

short cut n atajo m.

shorten [ˈʃɔːtn] vt acortar.

shorthand [ˈʃɔːthænd] n taquigrafía f.

shortly [ˈʃɔːtlɪ] adv (soon) dentro de poco; **~ before** poco antes de.

shortsighted [ˌʃɔːtˈsaɪtɪd] adj miope.

short-sleeved [-ˌsliːvd] adj de manga corta.

short-stay car park n aparcamiento m para estancias cortas.

short story n cuento m.

short wave n onda f corta.

shot [ʃɒt] pt & pp → **shoot** ♦ n (of gun, in football) tiro m; (in tennis, golf) golpe m; (photo) foto f; (in film)

plano m; (inf: attempt) intento m; (drink) trago m.

shotgun [ˈʃɒtgʌn] n escopeta f.

should [ʃod] aux vb 1. (expressing desirability) deber; **we ~ leave now** deberíamos irnos ahora.

2. (asking for advice): **~ I go too?** ¿yo también voy?

3. (expressing probability) deber de; **she ~ arrive soon** debe de estar a punto de llegar.

4. (ought to have) deber; **they ~ have won the match** deberían haber ganado el partido.

5. (in clauses with "that"): **we decided that you ~ do it** decidimos que lo hicieras tú.

6. (fml: in conditionals): **~ you need anything, call reception** si necesita alguna cosa, llame a recepción.

7. (fml: expressing wish): **I ~ like to come with you** me gustaría ir contigo.

shoulder [ˈʃəoldəˀ] n (of person) hombro m; (of meat) espaldilla f; (Am: of road) arcén m.

shoulder pad n hombrera f.

shouldn't [ˈʃodnt] = **should not**.

should've [ˈʃodəv] = **should have**.

shout [ʃaot] n grito m ♦ vt & vi gritar ❏ **shout out** vt sep gritar.

shove [ʃʌv] vt (push) empujar; (put carelessly) poner de cualquier manera.

shovel [ˈʃʌvl] n pala f.

show [ʃəo] (pp -ed OR shown) n (at theatre) función f; (on TV, radio) programa m; (exhibition) exhibició n ♦ vt mostrar; (undergo) registrar; (represent, depict) representar; (ac-

company) acompañar; *(film)* proyectar; *(TV programme)* emitir ◆ *vi (be visible)* verse; *(film)* proyectarse; **to ~ sthg to sb** enseñar algo a alguien; **to ~ sb how to do sthg** enseñar a alguien cómo se hace algo ❑ **show off** *vi* presumir; **show up** *vi (come along)* aparecer; *(be visible)* resaltar.

shower ['ʃaʊəʳ] *n (for washing)* ducha *f; (of rain)* chubasco ◆ *vi* ducharse; **to have a ~** darse una ducha.

shower gel *n* gel *m* de baño.

shower unit *n* ducha *f (cubículo).*

showing ['ʃəʊɪŋ] *n (of film)* proyección *f.*

shown ['ʃəʊn] *pp* → **show**.

showroom ['ʃəʊrʊm] *n* sala *f* de exposición.

shrank [ʃræŋk] *pt* → **shrink**.

shrimp [ʃrɪmp] *n* camarón *m.*

shrine [ʃraɪn] *n* santuario *m.*

shrink [ʃrɪŋk] *(pt* shrank, *pp* shrunk) *n (inf)* loquero *m (-ra f)* ◆ *vi (become smaller)* encoger; *(diminish)* reducirse.

shrub [ʃrʌb] *n* arbusto *m.*

shrug [ʃrʌg] *vi* encogerse de hombros ◆ *n:* **she gave a ~** se encogió de hombros.

shrunk [ʃrʌŋk] *pp* → **shrink**.

shuffle ['ʃʌfl] *vt (cards)* barajar ◆ *vi* andar arrastrando los pies.

shut [ʃʌt] *(pt & pp* shut) *adj* cerrado(-da) ◆ *vt* cerrar ◆ *vi (door, mouth, eyes)* cerrarse; *(shop, restaurant)* cerrar ❑ **shut down** *vt* sep cerrar; **shut up** *vi (inf)* callarse la boca.

shutter ['ʃʌtəʳ] *n (on window)*

contraventana *f; (on camera)* obturador *m.*

shuttle ['ʃʌtl] *n (plane)* avión *m* de puente aéreo; *(bus)* autobús *m* de servicio regular.

shuttlecock ['ʃʌtlkɒk] *n* volante *m.*

shy [ʃaɪ] *adj* tímido(-da).

sick [sɪk] *adj (ill)* enfermo(-ma); *(nauseous)* mareado(-da); **to be ~** *(vomit)* devolver; **to feel ~** estar mareado; **to be ~ of** *(fed up with)* estar harto (-ta) de.

sick bag *n* bolsa *f* para el mareo.

sickness ['sɪknɪs] *n* enfermedad *f.*

sick pay *n* = subsidio *m* de enfermedad.

side [saɪd] *n* lado *m; (of hill, valley)* ladera *f; (of river)* orilla *f; (of paper, coin, tape, record)* cara *f; (team)* equipo *m; (Br: TV channel)* canal *m; (page of writing)* página *f* ◆ *adj* lateral; **at the ~ of** al lado de; **on the other ~** al otro lado; **on this ~** en este lado; **by ~** juntos.

sideboard ['saɪdbɔːd] *n* aparador *m.*

sidecar ['saɪdkɑːʳ] *n* sidecar *m.*

side dish *n* plato *m* de acompañamiento.

side effect *n* efecto *m* secundario.

sidelight ['saɪdlaɪt] *n (Br)* luz *f* lateral.

side order *n* guarnición *f (no incluida en el plato).*

side salad *n* ensalada *f* de acompañamiento.

side street *n* travesía *f.*

sidewalk ['saɪdwɔːk] *n (Am)* acera *f.*

sideways ['saɪdweɪz] *adv (move)* de lado; *(look)* de reojo.

sieve [sɪv] *n* tamiz *m*.

sigh [saɪ] *n* suspiro *m* ♦ *vi* suspirar.

sight [saɪt] *n (eyesight)* vista *f*; *(thing seen)* imagen *f*; **at first ~** a primera vista; **to catch ~ of** divisar; **in ~** a la vista; **to lose ~ of** perder de vista; **out of ~** fuera de vista ❏ **sights** *npl (of city, country)* lugares *mpl* de interés turístico.

sightseeing ['saɪt,siːɪŋ] *n*: **to go ~** ir a visitar los lugares de interés turístico.

sign [saɪn] *n* señal *f*; *(on shop)* letrero *m*; *(symbol)* signo *m* ♦ *vt & vi* firmar; **there's no ~ of her** no hay señales de ella ❏ **sign in** *vi* firmar en el registro de entrada.

signal ['sɪgnl] *n* señal *f*; *(Am: traffic lights)* semáforo *m* ♦ *vi* señalizar.

signature ['sɪgnətʃə*r*] *n* firma *f*.

significant [sɪg'nɪfɪkənt] *adj* significativo(-va).

signpost ['saɪnpəʊst] *n* letrero *m* indicador.

Sikh [siːk] *n* sij *mf*.

silence ['saɪləns] *n* silencio *m*.

silencer ['saɪlənsə*r*] *n (Br)* silenciador *m*.

silent ['saɪlənt] *adj* silencioso(-sa).

silk [sɪlk] *n* seda *f*.

sill [sɪl] *n* alféizar *m*.

silly ['sɪlɪ] *adj* tonto(-ta).

silver ['sɪlvə*r*] *n (substance)* plata *f*; *(coins)* monedas *fpl* plateadas ♦ *adj* de plata.

silver foil *n* papel *m* de aluminio.

silver-plated [-'pleɪtɪd] *adj* chapado(-da) en plata.

similar ['sɪmɪlə*r*] *adj* similar; **to be ~ to** ser parecido(-da) a.

similarity [,sɪmɪ'lærətɪ] *n (resemblance)* parecido *m*; *(similar point)* similitud *f*.

simmer ['sɪmə*r*] *vi* hervir a fuego lento.

simple ['sɪmpl] *adj* sencillo(-lla).

simplify ['sɪmplɪfaɪ] *vt* simplificar.

simply ['sɪmplɪ] *adv (just)* simplemente; *(easily, not elaborately)* sencillamente.

simulate ['sɪmjʊleɪt] *vt* simular.

simultaneous [*Br* ,sɪml'teɪnjəs, *Am* ,saɪml'teɪnjəs] *adj* simultáneo (-a).

simultaneously [*Br* ,sɪml'teɪnjəslɪ, *Am* ,saɪml'teɪnjəslɪ] *adv* simultáneamente.

sin [sɪn] *n* pecado *m* ♦ *vi* pecar.

since [sɪns] *adv* desde entonces ♦ *prep* desde ♦ *conj (in time)* desde que; *(as)* ya que; **ever ~** *prep* desde ♦ *conj* desde que.

sincere [sɪn'sɪə*r*] *adj* sincero(-ra).

sincerely [sɪn'sɪəlɪ] *adv* sinceramente; **Yours ~** (le saluda) atentamente.

sing [sɪŋ] (*pt* sang, *pp* sung) *vt & vi* cantar.

singer ['sɪŋə*r*] *n* cantante *mf*.

single ['sɪŋgl] *adj (just one)* solo (-la); *(not married)* soltero(-ra) ♦ *n (Br:* ticket*)* billete *m* de ida; *(record)* disco *m* sencillo; **every ~** cada uno (una) de ❏ **singles** *n (Br)* modalidad *f* individual ♦ *adj (bar, club)* para solteros.

single bed *n* cama *f* individual.

single cream *n (Br)* nata *f* líquida.

single parent n padre m soltero (madre f soltera).

single room n habitación f individual.

single track road n carretera f de una sola vía.

singular ['sɪŋgjʊləʳ] n singular m; **in the ~** en singular.

sinister ['sɪnɪstəʳ] adj siniestro(-tra).

sink [sɪŋk] (pt sank, pp sunk) n (in kitchen) fregadero m; (washbasin) lavabo m ◆ vi (in water, mud) hundirse; (decrease) descender.

sink unit n fregadero m (con mueble debajo).

sinuses ['saɪnəsɪz] npl senos mpl frontales.

sip [sɪp] n sorbo m ◆ vt beber a sorbos.

siphon ['saɪfn] n sifón m ◆ vt sacar con sifón.

sir [sɜːʳ] n señor m; **Dear Sir** Muy Señor mío; **Sir Richard Blair** Sir Richard Blair.

siren ['saɪərən] n sirena f.

sirloin steak [ˌsɜːlɔɪn-] n solomillo m.

sister ['sɪstəʳ] n hermana f; (Br: nurse) enfermera f jefe.

sister-in-law n cuñada f.

sit [sɪt] (pt & pp sat) vi sentarse; (be situated) estar situado ◆ vt (place) poner; (Br: exam) presentarse a; **to be sitting** estar sentado ❑ **sit down** vi sentarse; **to be sitting down** estar sentado; **sit up** vi (after lying down) incorporarse; (stay up late) quedarse levantado.

site [saɪt] n (place) sitio m; (building site) obra f de construcción.

sitting room ['sɪtɪŋ-] n sala f de estar.

situated ['sɪtjʊeɪtɪd] adj: **to be ~** estar situado(-da).

situation [ˌsɪtjʊˈeɪʃn] n situación f; **"~s vacant"** "ofertas de empleo".

six [sɪks] num adj seis inv ◆ num n seis m inv; **to be ~ (years old)** tener seis años (de edad); **it's ~ (o'clock)** son las seis; **a hundred and ~** ciento seis; **~ Hill St** Hill St, número seis; **it's minus ~ (degrees)** hay seis grados bajo cero; **~ out of ten** seis sobre diez.

sixteen [sɪksˈtiːn] num dieciséis, → **six**.

sixteenth [sɪksˈtiːnθ] num decimosexto(-ta), → **sixth**.

sixth [sɪksθ] num adj sexto(-ta) ◆ pron sexto m (-ta f) ◆ num n (fraction) sexto m ◆ num adv sexto; **a ~ (of)** la sexta parte (de); **the ~ (of September)** el seis (de septiembre).

sixth form n (Br) curso de enseñanza media que prepara a alumnos de 16 a 18 años para los "A-levels".

sixth-form college n (Br) centro de enseñanza que prepara a alumnos de 16 a 18 años para los "A-levels" o exámenes de formación profesional.

sixtieth ['sɪkstɪəθ] num sexagésimo(-ma), → **sixth**.

sixty ['sɪkstɪ] num sesenta, → **six**.

size [saɪz] n tamaño m; (of clothes, hats) talla f; (of shoes) número m; **what ~ do you take?** ¿qué talla/número usas?; **what ~ is this?** ¿de qué talla es esto?

sizeable ['saɪzəbl] adj considerable.

skate [skeɪt] n (ice skate, roller skate) patín m; (fish) raya f ♦ vi patinar.

skateboard ['skeɪtbɔ:d] n monopatín m.

skater ['skeɪtə'] n (ice-skater) patinador m (-ra f).

skating ['skeɪtɪŋ] n: **to go** ~ ir a patinar.

skeleton ['skelɪtn] n esqueleto m.

skeptical ['skeptɪkl] (Am) = **sceptical**.

sketch [sketʃ] n (drawing) bosquejo m; (humorous) sketch m ♦ vt hacer un bosquejo de.

skewer ['skjuə'] n brocheta f.

ski [ski:] (pt & pp **skied**, cont **skiing**) n esquí m ♦ vi esquiar.

ski boots npl botas fpl de esquí.

skid [skɪd] n derrape m ♦ vi derrapar.

skier ['ski:ə'] n esquiador m (-ra f).

skiing ['ski:ɪŋ] n esquí m; **to go** ~ ir a esquiar; **a** ~ **holiday** unas vacaciones de esquí.

skilful ['skɪlful] adj (Br) experto(-ta).

ski lift n telesilla m.

skill [skɪl] n (ability) habilidad f; (technique) técnica f.

skilled [skɪld] adj (worker, job) especializado(-da); (driver, chef) cualificado(-da).

skillful ['skɪlful] (Am) = **skilful**.

skimmed milk [,skɪmd-] n leche f desnatada.

skin [skɪn] n piel f; (on milk) nata f.

skin freshener [-,freʃnə'] n tónico m.

skinny ['skɪnɪ] adj flaco(-ca).

skip [skɪp] vi (with rope) saltar a la comba; (jump) ir dando brincos ♦ vt saltarse ♦ n (container) contenedor m.

ski pants npl pantalones mpl de esquí.

ski pass n forfait m.

ski pole n bastón m para esquiar.

skipping rope ['skɪpɪŋ-] n cuerda f de saltar.

skirt [skɜ:t] n falda f.

ski slope n pista f de esquí.

ski tow n remonte m.

skittles ['skɪtlz] n bolos mpl.

skull [skʌl] n (of living person) cráneo m; (of skeleton) calavera f.

sky [skaɪ] n cielo m.

skylight ['skaɪlaɪt] n tragaluz m.

skyscraper ['skaɪ,skreɪpə'] n rascacielos m inv.

slab [slæb] n (of stone, concrete) losa f.

slack [slæk] adj (rope) flojo(-ja); (careless) descuidado(-da); (not busy) inactivo(-va).

slacks [slæks] npl pantalones mpl (holgados).

slam [slæm] vt cerrar de golpe ♦ vi cerrarse de golpe.

slander ['slɑ:ndə'] n calumnia f.

slang [slæŋ] n argot m.

slant [slɑ:nt] n (slope) inclinación f ♦ vi inclinarse.

slap [slæp] n bofetada f ♦ vt abofetear.

slash [slæʃ] vt (cut) cortar; (fig:

prices) recortar drásticamente ◆ *n (written symbol)* barra *f* (oblicua).

slate [sleɪt] *n* pizarra *f*.

slaughter ['slɔːtəʳ] *vt (kill)* matar; *(fig: defeat)* dar una paliza.

slave [sleɪv] *n* esclavo *m* (-va *f*).

sled [sled] = **sledge**.

sledge [sledʒ] *n* trineo *m*.

sleep [sliːp] *(pt & pp slept)* *n (rest)* descanso *m*; *(nap)* siesta *f* ◆ *vi* dormir ◆ *vt*: **the house ~ six** la casa tiene seis plazas; **did you ~ well?** ¿dormiste bien?; **I couldn't get to ~** no pude conciliar el sueño; **to go to ~** dormirse; **to ~ with sb** acostarse con alguien.

sleeper ['sliːpəʳ] *n (train)* tren *m* nocturno *(con literas)*; *(sleeping car)* coche-cama *m*; *(Br: on railway track)* traviesa *f*; *(Br: earring)* aro *m*.

sleeping bag ['sliːpɪŋ-] *n* saco *m* de dormir.

sleeping car ['sliːpɪŋ-] *n* coche-cama *m*.

sleeping pill ['sliːpɪŋ-] *n* pastilla *f* para dormir.

sleeping policeman ['sliːpɪŋ-] *n* (Br) rompecoches *m inv*.

sleepy ['sliːpɪ] *adj* soñoliento(-ta).

sleet [sliːt] *n* aguanieve *f* ◆ *v impers*: **it's ~ing** cae aguanieve.

sleeve [sliːv] *n (of garment)* manga *f*; *(of record)* cubierta *f*.

sleeveless ['sliːvlɪs] *adj* sin mangas.

slept [slept] *pt & pp* → **sleep**.

slice [slaɪs] *n (of bread)* rebanada *f*; *(of meat)* tajada *f*; *(of cake, pizza)* trozo *m*; *(of lemon, sausage, cucumber)* rodaja *f*; *(of cheese, ham)* loncha *f* ◆ *vt* cortar.

sliced bread [slaɪst-] *n* pan *m* en rebanadas.

slide [slaɪd] *(pt & pp slid* [slɪd]*)* *n (in playground)* tobogán *m*; *(of photograph)* diapositiva *f*; *(Br: hair slide)* prendedor *m* ◆ *vi (slip)* resbalar.

sliding door [ˌslaɪdɪŋ-] *n* puerta *f* corredera.

slight [slaɪt] *adj (minor)* leve; **the ~est** el menor (la menor); **not in the ~est** en absoluto.

slightly ['slaɪtlɪ] *adv* ligeramente.

slim [slɪm] *adj* delgado(-da) ◆ *vi* adelgazar.

slimming ['slɪmɪŋ] *n* adelgazamiento *m*.

sling [slɪŋ] *(pt & pp slung)* *n (for arm)* cabestrillo *m* ◆ *vt (inf)* tirar.

slip [slɪp] *vi* resbalar ◆ *n (mistake)* descuido *m*; *(of paper)* papelito *m*; *(petticoat)* enaguas *fpl* ❑ **slip up** *vi (make a mistake)* cometer un error.

slipper ['slɪpəʳ] *n* zapatilla *f*.

slippery ['slɪpərɪ] *adj* resbaladizo(-za).

slip road *n (Br) (for joining motorway)* acceso *m*; *(for leaving motorway)* salida *f*.

slit [slɪt] *n* ranura *f*.

slob [slɒb] *n (inf)* guarro *m* (-rra *f*).

slogan ['sləʊgən] *n* eslogan *m*.

slope [sləʊp] *n (incline)* inclinación *f*; *(hill)* cuesta *f*; *(for skiing)* pista *f* ◆ *vi* inclinarse.

sloping ['sləʊpɪŋ] *adj* inclinado(-da).

slot [slɒt] *n (for coin)* ranura *f*; *(groove)* muesca *f*.

slot machine *n (vending machine)* máquina *f* automática; *(for* *gambling)* máquina *f* tragaperras.

Slovakia [slə'vækɪə] *n* Eslovaquia.

slow [sləʊ] *adj (not fast)* lento(-ta); *(clock, watch)* atrasado(-da); *(business)* flojo(-ja); *(in understanding)* corto(-ta) ♦ *adv despacio;* **"slow"** cartel que aconseja a los automovilistas ir despacio; **a ~ train** un tren tranvía ❑ **slow down** *vt sep* reducir la velocidad de ♦ *vi (vehicle)* reducir la velocidad; *(person)* reducir el paso.

slowly ['sləʊlɪ] *adv (not fast)* despacio; *(gradually)* poco a poco.

slug [slʌg] *n* babosa *f*.

slum [slʌm] *n (building)* cuchitril *m* ❑ **slums** *npl (district)* barrios *mpl* bajos.

slung [slʌŋ] *pt & pp →* sling.

slush [slʌʃ] *n* nieve *f* medio derretida.

sly [slaɪ] *adj (cunning)* astuto(-ta); *(deceitful)* furtivo(-va).

smack [smæk] *n (slap)* cachete *m* ♦ *vt* dar un cachete.

small [smɔːl] *adj* pequeño(-ña).

small change *n* cambio *m*.

smallpox ['smɔːlpɒks] *n* viruela *f*.

smart [smɑːt] *adj (elegant, posh)* elegante; *(clever)* inteligente.

smart card *n* tarjeta *f* con banda magnética.

smash [smæʃ] *n (SPORT)* mate *m*; *(inf: car crash)* choque *m* ♦ *vt (plate, window)* romper ♦ *vi (plate, vase etc)* romperse.

smashing ['smæʃɪŋ] *adj (Br: inf)* fenomenal.

smear test ['smɪə-] *n* citología *f*.

smell [smel] *(pt & pp* **-ed** OR

smelt) *n* olor *m* ♦ *vt & vi* oler; **to ~ of sthg** oler a algo.

smelly ['smelɪ] *adj* maloliente.

smelt [smelt] *pt & pp →* smell.

smile [smaɪl] *n* sonrisa *f* ♦ *vi* sonreír.

smoke [sməʊk] *n* humo *m* ♦ *vt & vi* fumar; **to have a ~** echarse un cigarro.

smoked [sməʊkt] *adj* ahumado(-da).

smoked salmon *n* salmón *m* ahumado.

smoker ['sməʊkə*r*] *n* fumador *m* (-ra *f*).

smoking ['sməʊkɪŋ] *n* el fumar; **"no ~"** "prohibido fumar".

smoking area *n* área *f* de fumadores.

smoking compartment *n* compartimento *m* de fumadores.

smoky ['sməʊkɪ] *adj (room)* lleno (-na) de humo.

smooth [smuːð] *adj (surface, road)* liso(-sa); *(skin)* terso(-sa); *(flight, journey)* tranquilo(-la); *(mixture, liquid)* sin grumos; *(wine, beer)* suave; *(pej: suave)* meloso(-sa) ❑ **smooth down** *vt sep* alisar.

smother ['smʌðə*r*] *vt (cover)* cubrir.

smudge [smʌdʒ] *n* mancha *f*.

smuggle ['smʌgl] *vt* pasar de contrabando.

snack [snæk] *n* piscolabis *m inv*.

snack bar *n* cafetería *f*.

snail [sneɪl] *n* caracol *m*.

snake [sneɪk] *n (smaller)* culebra *f*; *(larger)* serpiente *f*.

snap [snæp] *vt (break)* partir (en dos) ♦ *vi (break)* partirse (en dos) ♦

n (inf: photo) foto *f*; *(Br: card game)* guerrilla *f*.

snare [sneə^r] *n* trampa *f*.

snatch [snætʃ] *vt (grab)* arrebatar; *(steal)* dar el tirón.

sneakers ['sni:kəz] *npl (Am)* zapatos *mpl* de lona.

sneeze [sni:z] *n* estornudo *m* ◆ *vi* estornudar.

sniff [snɪf] *vi (from cold, crying)* sorber ◆ *vt* oler.

snip [snɪp] *vt* cortar con tijeras.

snob [snɒb] *n* esnob *mf*.

snog [snɒg] *vi (Br: inf)* morrearse.

snooker ['snu:kə^r] *n* snooker *m*, juego parecido al billar.

snooze [snu:z] *n* cabezada *f*.

snore [snɔ:^r] *vi* roncar.

snorkel ['snɔ:kl] *n* tubo *m* respiratorio.

snout [snaʊt] *n* hocico *m*.

snow [snəʊ] *n* nieve *f* ◆ *v impers:* it's ~ing está nevando.

snowball ['snəʊbɔ:l] *n* bola *f* de nieve.

snowdrift ['snəʊdrɪft] *n* montón *m* de nieve.

snowflake ['snəʊfleɪk] *n* copo *m* de nieve.

snowman ['snəʊmæn] *(pl* -men [-men]) *n* muñeco *m* de nieve.

snowplough ['snəʊplaʊ] *n* quitanieves *m inv*.

snowstorm ['snəʊstɔ:m] *n* tormenta *f* de nieve.

snug [snʌg] *adj (person)* cómodo y calentito *(m,* cómoda y calentita); *(place)* acogedor(-ra).

so [səʊ] *adv* **1.** *(emphasizing degree)* tan; it's ~ difficult (that ...) es tan difícil (que ...); ~ many tantos; ~

much tanto.

2. *(referring back):* ~ you knew already así que ya lo sabías; I don't think ~ no creo; I'm afraid ~ me temo que sí; if ~ en ese caso.

3. *(also)* también; ~ do I yo también.

4. *(in this way)* así.

5. *(expressing agreement):* ~ I see ya lo veo.

6. *(in phrases):* or ~ más o menos; ~ as to do sthg para hacer algo; come here ~ that I can see you ven acá para que te vea.

◆ *conj* **1.** *(therefore)* así que.

2. *(summarizing)* entonces; ~ what have you been up to? entonces ¿qué has estado haciendo?

3. *(in phrases):* ~ what? *(inf)* ¿y qué?; ~ there! *(inf)* ¡y si no te gusta te aguantas!

soak [səʊk] *vt (leave in water)* poner en remojo; *(make very wet)* empapar ◆ *vi:* to ~ through sthg calar algo ❑ **soak up** *vt sep* absorber.

soaked [səʊkt] *adj* empapado(-da).

soaking ['səʊkɪŋ] *adj* empapado(-da).

soap [səʊp] *n* jabón *m*.

soap opera *n* culebrón *m*.

soap powder *n* detergente *m* en polvo.

sob [sɒb] *n* sollozo *m* ◆ *vi* sollozar.

sober ['səʊbə^r] *adj (not drunk)* sobrio(-bria).

soccer ['sɒkə^r] *n* fútbol *m*.

sociable ['səʊʃəbl] *adj* sociable.

social ['səʊʃl] *adj* social.

social club *n* club *m* social.

socialist ['səʊʃəlɪst] *adj* socialista ◆ *n* socialista *mf*.

social life *n* vida *f* social.

social security n seguridad f social.

social worker n asistente m (-ta f) social.

society [sə'saɪətɪ] n sociedad f.

sociology [səʊsɪ'ɒlədʒɪ] n sociología f.

sock [sɒk] n calcetín m.

socket ['sɒkɪt] n (for plug, light bulb) enchufe m.

sod [sɒd] n (Br: vulg) cabrón m (-ona f).

soda ['səʊdə] n (soda water) soda f; (Am: fizzy drink) gaseosa f.

soda water n soda f.

sofa ['səʊfə] n sofá m.

sofa bed n sofá-cama m.

soft [sɒft] adj (not firm, stiff) blando(-da); (not rough, loud) suave; (not forceful) ligero(-ra).

soft cheese n queso m blando.

soft drink n refresco m.

software ['sɒftweə] n software m.

soil [sɔɪl] n tierra f.

solarium [sə'leərɪəm] n solario m.

solar panel ['səʊlə-] n panel m solar.

sold [səʊld] pt & pp → **sell**.

soldier ['səʊldʒə] n soldado m.

sold out adj agotado(-da).

sole [səʊl] adj (only) único(-ca); (exclusive) exclusivo(-va) ◆ n (of shoe) suela f; (of foot) planta f; (fish: pl inv) lenguado m.

solemn ['sɒləm] adj solemne.

solicitor [sə'lɪsɪtə] n (Br) abogado que actúa en los tribunales de primera instancia y prepara casos para los tribunales superiores.

solid ['sɒlɪd] adj sólido(-da); (table,

gold, oak) macizo(-za).

solo ['səʊləʊ] (pl -s) n solo m; "~ m/cs" (traffic sign) "sólo motocicletas".

soluble ['sɒljʊbl] adj soluble.

solution [sə'luːʃn] n solución f.

solve [sɒlv] vt resolver.

some [sʌm] adj 1. (certain amount of): would you like ~ coffee? ¿quieres café?; can I have ~ cheese? ¿me dejas un poco de queso?; ~ money algo de dinero.

2. (certain number of) unos (unas); ~ sweets unos caramelos; have ~ grapes coge uvas; ~ people alguna gente.

3. (large amount of) bastante; I had ~ difficulty getting here me resultó bastante difícil llegar aquí.

4. (large number of) bastante; I've known him for ~ years hace bastantes años que lo conozco.

5. (not all) algunos(-nas); ~ jobs are better paid than others algunos trabajos están mejor pagados que otros.

6. (in imprecise statements) un (una); ~ man phoned llamó un hombre.

◆ pron 1. (certain amount) un poco; can I have ~? ¿puedo coger un poco?

2. (certain number) algunos mpl (-as fpl); can I have ~? ¿puedo coger algunos?; ~ (of them) left early algunos (de ellos) se fueron pronto.

◆ adv aproximadamente; there were ~ 7,000 people there había unas 7.000 personas allí.

somebody ['sʌmbədɪ] = **someone**.

somehow ['sʌmhaʊ] adv (some way or other) de alguna manera; (for some reason) por alguna razón.

someone ['sʌmwʌn] *pron* alguien.

someplace ['sʌmpleɪs] *(Am)* = somewhere.

somersault ['sʌməsɔːlt] *n* salto *m* mortal.

something ['sʌmθɪŋ] *pron* algo; it's really ~ es algo impresionante; or ~ *(inf)* o algo así; ~ like algo así como.

sometime ['sʌmtaɪm] *adv* en algún momento.

sometimes ['sʌmtaɪmz] *adv* a veces.

somewhere ['sʌmweə*] *adv* (in or to unspecified place) en/a alguna parte; (approximately) aproximadamente.

son [sʌn] *n* hijo *m*.

song [sɒŋ] *n* canción *f*.

son-in-law *n* yerno *m*.

soon [suːn] *adv* pronto; how ~ can you do it? ¿para cuándo estará listo?; as ~ as tan pronto como; as ~ as possible cuanto antes; ~ after poco después; ~er or later tarde o temprano.

soot [sʊt] *n* hollín *m*.

soothe [suːð] *vt* (pain, sunburn) aliviar; (person, anger, nerves) calmar.

sophisticated [sə'fɪstɪkeɪtɪd] *adj* sofisticado(-da).

sorbet ['sɔːbeɪ] *n* sorbete *m*.

sore [sɔː*] *adj* (painful) dolorido (-da); (Am: inf: angry) enfadado (-da) ♦ *n* úlcera *f*; to have a ~ throat tener dolor de garganta.

sorry ['sɒrɪ] *adj*: I'm ~ ¡lo siento!; I'm ~ I'm late siento llegar tarde; I'm ~ you failed lamento que hayas suspendido; ~? (pardon?) ¿perdón?; to feel ~ for sb sen-

tir lástima por alguien; to be ~ about sthg sentir algo.

sort [sɔːt] *n* tipo *m*, clase *f* ♦ *vt* clasificar; ~ of más o menos; it's ~ of difficult es algo difícil □ **sort out** *vt sep* (classify) clasificar; (resolve) resolver.

so-so *adj & adv* (inf) así así.

soufflé ['suːfleɪ] *n* suflé *m*.

sought [sɔːt] *pt & pp* → seek.

soul [səʊl] *n* (spirit) alma *f*; (soul music) música *f* soul.

sound [saʊnd] *n* sonido *m*; (individual noise) ruido *m* ♦ *vt* (horn, bell) hacer sonar ♦ *vi* (make a noise) sonar; (seem to be) parecer ♦ *adj* (health, person) bueno(-na); (heart) sano(-na); (building, structure) sólido(-da); to ~ like (make a noise like) sonar como; (seem to be) sonar.

soundproof ['saʊndpruːf] *adj* insonorizado(-da).

soup [suːp] *n* sopa *f*.

soup spoon *n* cuchara *f* sopera.

sour ['saʊə*] *adj* (taste) ácido(-da); (milk) agrio(agria); to go ~ agriarse.

source [sɔːs] *n* (supply, origin) fuente *f*; (cause) origen *m*; (of river) nacimiento *m*.

sour cream *n* nata *f* amarga.

south [saʊθ] *n* sur *m* ♦ *adv* al sur; in the ~ of England en el sur de Inglaterra.

South Africa *n* Sudáfrica.

South America *n* Sudamérica.

southbound ['saʊθbaʊnd] *adj* con rumbo al sur.

southeast [saʊθ'iːst] *n* sudeste *m*.

southern ['sʌðən] *adj* del sur.

South Pole *n* Polo *m* Sur.

southwards ['saυθwədz] *adv* hacia el sur.

southwest [,saυθ'west] *n* suroeste *m*.

souvenir [,su:və'nɪəʳ] *n* recuerdo *m*.

Soviet Union [,səυviət-] *n*: the ~ la Unión Soviética.

sow¹ [səυ] (*pp* sown [səυn]) *vt* sembrar.

sow² [saυ] *n* (*pig*) cerda *f*.

soya ['sɔɪə] *n* soja *f*.

soya bean *n* semilla *f* de soja.

soy sauce [,sɔɪ-] *n* salsa *f* de soja.

spa [spa:] *n* balneario *m*.

space [speɪs] *n* espacio *m* ◆ *vt* espaciar.

spaceship ['speɪsʃɪp] *n* nave *f* espacial.

space shuttle *n* transbordador *m* espacial.

spacious ['speɪʃəs] *adj* espacioso(-sa).

spade [speɪd] *n* (*tool*) pala *f* ▢

spades *npl* (*in cards*) picas *fpl*.

spaghetti [spə'getɪ] *n* espaguetis *mpl*.

Spain [speɪn] *n* España.

span [spæn] *pt* → spin ◆ *n* (*length*) duración *f*; (*of time*) periodo *m*.

Spaniard ['spænjəd] *n* español *m* (-la *f*).

spaniel ['spænjəl] *n* perro *m* de aguas.

Spanish ['spænɪʃ] *adj* español(-la) ◆ *n* (*language*) español *m*.

spank [spæŋk] *vt* zurrar.

spanner ['spænəʳ] *n* llave *f* (de tuercas).

spare [speəʳ] *adj* (*kept in reserve*) de sobra; (*not in use*) libre ◆ *n* (spare part) recambio *m*; (*spare wheel*) rueda *f* de recambio ◆ *vt*: **I can't ~ the time** no tengo tiempo; **with ten minutes to ~** con diez minutos de sobra.

spare part *n* pieza *f* de recambio.

spare ribs *npl* costillas *fpl* (sueltas).

spare room *n* habitación *f* de invitados.

spare time *n* tiempo *m* libre.

spare wheel *n* rueda *f* de repuesto.

spark [spa:k] *n* chispa *f*.

sparkling ['spa:klɪŋ] *adj* (*drink*) con gas.

sparkling wine *n* vino *m* espumoso.

spark plug *n* bujía *f*.

sparrow ['spærəυ] *n* gorrión *m*.

spat [spæt] *pt & pp* (*Br*) → spit.

speak [spi:k] (*pt* spoke, *pp* spoken) *vt* (*language*) hablar; (*say*) decir ◆ *vi* hablar; **who's ~ing?** (*on phone*) ¿quién es?; **can I ~ to Sarah? - ~ing!** ¿puedo hablar con Sara? - ¡soy yo!; **to ~ to sb about sthg** hablar con alguien sobre algo □ **speak up** *vi* (*more loudly*) hablar más alto.

speaker ['spi:kəʳ] *n* (*at conference*) conferenciante *mf*; (*loudspeaker, of stereo*) altavoz *m*; **a Spanish ~** un hispanohablante.

spear [spɪəʳ] *n* lanza *f*.

special ['speʃl] *adj* (*not ordinary*) especial; (*particular*) particular ◆ *n* *(dish)* plato *m* del día; **"today's ~"** "plato del día".

special delivery *n (Br)* = correo *m* urgente.

special effects *npl* efectos *mpl* especiales.

specialist ['speʃəlɪst] *n (doctor)* especialista *mf*.

speciality [ˌspeʃɪ'ælətɪ] *n* especialidad *f*.

specialize ['speʃəlaɪz] *vi:* **to ~ (in)** especializarse (en).

specially ['speʃəlɪ] *adv* especialmente; *(particularly)* particularmente.

special offer *n* oferta *f* especial.

special school *n (Br)* escuela *f* especial.

specialty ['speʃltɪ] *(Am)* = **speciality**.

species ['spiːʃiːz] *(pl inv)* n especie *f*.

specific [spə'sɪfɪk] *adj* específico(-ca).

specifications [ˌspesɪfɪ'keɪʃnz] *npl (of machine, building etc)* datos *mpl* técnicos.

specimen ['spesɪmən] *n (MED)* espécimen *m; (example)* muestra *f*.

specs [speks] *npl (inf)* gafas *fpl*.

spectacle ['spektəkl] *n* espectáculo *m*.

spectacles ['spektəklz] *npl* gafas *fpl*.

spectacular [spek'tækjulər] *adj* espectacular.

spectator [spek'teɪtər] *n* espectador *m* (-ra *f*).

sped [sped] *pt & pp* → **speed**.

speech [spiːtʃ] *n (ability to speak)*

habla *f; (manner of speaking)* manera *f* de hablar; *(talk)* discurso *m*.

speech impediment [-ɪm.pedɪmənt] *n* impedimento *m* al hablar.

speed [spiːd] *(pt & pp* **-ed** OR **sped)** *n* velocidad *f* ♦ *vi (move quickly)* moverse de prisa; *(drive too fast)* conducir con exceso de velocidad; **"reduce ~ now"** "reduzca su velocidad" ❏ **speed up** *vi* acelerarse.

speedboat ['spiːdbəʊt] *n* lancha *f* motora.

speeding ['spiːdɪŋ] *n* exceso *m* de velocidad.

speed limit *n* límite *m* de velocidad.

speedometer [spɪ'dɒmɪtər] *n* velocímetro *m*.

spell [spel] *(Br pt & pp* **-ed** OR **spelt,** *Am pt & pp* **-ed)** *vt (word, name)* deletrear; *(subj: letters)* significar ♦ *n (time spent)* temporada *f; (of weather)* racha *f; (magic)* hechizo *m*.

spelling ['spelɪŋ] *n* ortografía *f*.

spelt [spelt] *pt & pp (Br)* → **spell**.

spend [spend] *(pt & pp* **spent** [spent]) *vt (money)* gastar; *(time)* pasar.

sphere [sfɪər] *n* esfera *f*.

spice [spaɪs] *n* especia *f* ♦ *vt* condimentar.

spicy ['spaɪsɪ] *adj* picante.

spider ['spaɪdər] *n* araña *f*.

spider's web *n* telaraña *f*.

spike [spaɪk] *n (metal)* clavo *m*.

spill [spɪl] *(Br pt & pp* **-ed** OR **spilt** [spɪlt], *Am pt & pp* **-ed)** *vt* derramar ♦ *vi* derramarse.

spin [spɪn] (*pt* **span** OR **spun**, *pp* **spun**) *vt* (*wheel, coin, chair*) hacer girar; (*washing*) centrifugar ◆ *n* (*on ball*) efecto *m*; **to go for a ~** (*inf*) ir a dar una vuelta.

spinach ['spɪnɪdʒ] *n* espinacas *fpl*.

spine [spaɪn] *n* (*of back*) espina *f* dorsal; (*of book*) lomo *m*.

spinster ['spɪnstə'] *n* soltera *f*.

spiral ['spaɪərəl] *n* espiral *f*.

spiral staircase *n* escalera *f* de caracol.

spire ['spaɪə'] *n* aguja *f*.

spirit [spɪrɪt] *n* (*soul*) espíritu *m*; (*energy*) vigor *m*; (*courage*) valor *m*; (*mood*) humor *m* ◻ **spirits** *npl* (*Br: alcohol*) licores *mpl*.

spit [spɪt] (*Br pt & pp* **spat**, *Am pt & pp* **spit**) *vi* escupir ◆ *n* (*saliva*) saliva *f*; (*for cooking*) asador *m* ◆ *v impers*: **it's spitting** está chispeando.

spite [spaɪt] : **in spite of** *prep* a pesar de.

spiteful ['spaɪtful] *adj* rencoroso(-sa).

splash [splæʃ] *n* (*sound*) chapoteo *m* ◆ *vt* salpicar.

splendid ['splendɪd] *adj* (*beautiful*) magnífico(-ca); (*very good*) espléndido(-da).

splint [splɪnt] *n* tablilla *f*.

splinter ['splɪntə'] *n* astilla *f*.

split [splɪt] (*pt & pp* **split**) *n* (*tear*) rasgón *m*; (*crack*) grieta *f*; (*in skirt*) abertura *f* ◆ *vt* (*wood, stone*) agrietar; (*tear*) rasgar; (*bill, profits, work*) dividir ◆ *vi* (*wood, stone*) agrietarse; (*tear*) rasgarse ◻ **split up** *vi* (*group, couple*) separarse.

spoil [spɔɪl] (*pt & pp* **-ed** OR **spoilt** [spɔɪlt]) *vt* (*ruin*) estropear; (*child*) mimar.

spoke [spəʊk] *pt* → **speak** ◆ *n* radio *m*.

spoken ['spəʊkn] *pp* → **speak**.

spokesman ['spəʊksmən] (*pl* **-men** [-mən]) *n* portavoz *m*.

spokeswoman ['spəʊks-ˌwʊmən] (*pl* **-women** [-ˌwɪmɪn]) *n* portavoz *f*.

sponge [spʌndʒ] *n* (*for cleaning, washing*) esponja *f*.

sponge bag *n* (*Br*) neceser *m*.

sponge cake *n* bizcocho *m*.

sponsor ['spɒnsə'] *n* (*of event, TV programme*) patrocinador *m* (-ra *f*).

sponsored walk [ˌspɒnsəd-] *n* marcha *f* benéfica.

spontaneous [spɒn'teɪnjəs] *adj* espontáneo(-nea).

spoon [spuːn] *n* cuchara *f*.

spoonful ['spuːnful] *n* cucharada *f*.

sport [spɔːt] *n* deporte *m*.

sports car [spɔːts-] *n* coche *m* deportivo.

sports centre [spɔːts-] *n* centro *m* deportivo.

sports jacket [spɔːts-] *n* chaqueta *f* de esport.

sportsman ['spɔːtsmən] (*pl* **-men** [-mən]) *n* deportista *m*.

sports shop [spɔːts-] *n* tienda *f* de deporte.

sportswoman ['spɔːtsˌwʊmən] (*pl* **-women** [-ˌwɪmɪn]) *n* deportista *f*.

spot [spɒt] *n* (*of paint, rain*) gota *f*; (*on clothes*) lunar *m*; (*on skin*) grano *m*; (*place*) lugar *m* ◆ *vt* notar; **on the**

spotless 272

~ (at once) en el acto; (at the scene) en el lugar.

spotless ['spɒtlɪs] *adj* inmaculado(-da).

spotlight ['spɒtlaɪt] *n* foco *m*.

spotty ['spɒtɪ] *adj* (skin, person, face) lleno(-na) de granos.

spouse [spaʊs] *n* (fml) esposo *m* (-sa *f*).

spout [spaʊt] *n* pitorro *m*.

sprain [spreɪn] *vt* torcerse.

sprang [spræŋ] *pt* → **spring**.

spray [spreɪ] *n* (of aerosol, perfume) espray *m*; (droplets) rociada *f*; (of sea) espuma *f* ♦ *vt* rociar.

spread [spred] (pt & pp **spread**) *vt* (butter, jam, glue) untar; (map, tablecloth, blanket) extender; (legs, fingers, arms) estirar; (disease) propagar; (news, rumour) difundir ♦ *vi* (disease, fire, stain) propagarse; (news, rumour) difundirse ♦ *n* (food) pasta *f* para untar □ **spread out** *vi* (disperse) dispersarse.

spring [sprɪŋ] (pt **sprang**, pp **sprung**) *n* (season) primavera *f*; (coil) muelle *m*; (of water) manantial *m* ♦ *vi* (leap) saltar; **in** (the) ~ en (la) primavera.

springboard ['sprɪŋbɔːd] *n* trampolín *m*.

spring-cleaning [-'kliːnɪŋ] *n* limpieza *f* general.

spring onion *n* cebolleta *f*.

spring roll *n* rollito *m* de primavera.

sprinkle ['sprɪŋkl] *vt* rociar.

sprinkler ['sprɪŋklər] *n* aspersor *m*.

sprint [sprɪnt] *n* (race) esprint *m* ♦ *vi* (run fast) correr a toda velo-

cidad.

Sprinter® ['sprɪntər] *n* (Br: train) tren de corto recorrido.

sprout [spraʊt] *n* (vegetable) col *f* de Bruselas.

spruce [spruːs] *n* picea *f*.

sprung [sprʌŋ] *pp* → **spring** ♦ *adj* (mattress) de muelles.

spud [spʌd] *n* (inf) patata *f*.

spun [spʌn] *pt & pp* → **spin**.

spur [spɜːr] *n* (for horse rider) espuela *f*; **on the** ~ **of the moment** sin pensarlo dos veces.

spurt [spɜːt] *vi* salir a chorros.

spy [spaɪ] *n* espía *mf*.

squall [skwɔːl] *n* turbión *m*.

squalor ['skwɒlər] *n* miseria *f*.

square [skweər] *adj* (in shape) cuadrado(-da) ♦ *n* (shape) cuadrado *m*; (in town) plaza *f*; (of chocolate) onza *f*; (on chessboard) casilla *f*; **2 metres** ~ 2 metros cuadrados; **it's 2 metres** ~ tiene 2 metros cuadrados; **we're (all)** ~ **now** quedamos en paz.

squash [skwɒʃ] *n* (game) squash *m*; (Br: drink) refresco *m*; (Am: vegetable) calabaza *f* ♦ *vt* aplastar.

squat [skwɒt] *adj* achaparrado(-da) ♦ *vi* (crouch) agacharse.

squeak [skwiːk] *vi* chirriar.

squeeze [skwiːz] *n* (orange) exprimir; (hand) apretar; (tube) estrujar □ **squeeze in** *vi* meterse.

squid [skwɪd] *n* (food) calamares *mpl*.

squint [skwɪnt] *n* estrabismo *m* ♦ *vi* bizquear.

squirrel [Br 'skwɪrəl, Am 'skwɜːrəl] *n* ardilla *f*.

squirt [skwɜːt] *vi* salir a chorro.

St *(abbr of Street)* c; *(abbr of Saint)* Sto., Sta.

stab [stæb] *vt (with knife)* apuñalar.

stable ['steɪbl] *adj (unchanging)* estable; *(firmly fixed)* fijo(-ja) ◆ *n* cuadra *f*.

stack [stæk] *n (pile)* pila *f*; **~s of** *(inf: lots)* montones de.

stadium ['steɪdjəm] *n* estadio *m*.

staff [stɑːf] *n (workers)* empleados *mpl*.

stage [steɪdʒ] *n (phase)* etapa *f*; *(in theatre)* escenario *m*.

stagger ['stægə'] *vt (arrange in stages)* escalonar ◆ *vi* tambalearse.

stagnant ['stægnənt] *adj* estancado(-da).

stain [steɪn] *n* mancha *f* ◆ *vt* manchar.

stained glass window [,steɪnd-] *n* vidriera *f*.

stainless steel ['steɪnlɪs-] *n* acero *m* inoxidable.

staircase ['steəkeɪs] *n* escalera *f*.

stairs [steəz] *npl* escaleras *fpl*.

stairwell ['steəwel] *n* hueco *m* de la escalera.

stake [steɪk] *n (share)* participación *f*; *(in gambling)* apuesta *f*; *(post)* estaca *f*; **at ~** en juego.

stale [steɪl] *adj (food)* pasado(-da); *(bread)* duro(-ra).

stalk [stɔːk] *n (of flower, plant)* tallo *m*; *(of fruit, leaf)* pecíolo *m*.

stall [stɔːl] *n (in market, at exhibition)* puesto *m* ◆ *vi (car, plane, engine)* calarse ❑ **stalls** *npl (Br: in theatre)* platea *f*.

stamina ['stæmɪnə] *n* resistencia *f*.

stammer ['stæmə'] *vi* tartamudear.

stamp [stæmp] *n* sello *m* ◆ *vt (passport, document)* sellar ◆ *vi*: **to ~ on sth** pisar algo; **to ~ one's foot** patear.

stamp-collecting [-kə,lektɪŋ] *n* filatelia *f*.

stamp machine *n* máquina *f* expendedora de sellos.

stand [stænd] *(pt & pp* **stood***) vi (be on feet)* estar de pie; *(be situated)* estar *(situado)*; *(get to one's feet)* ponerse de pie ◆ *vt (place)* colocar; *(bear, withstand)* soportar ◆ *n (stall)* puesto *m*; *(for coats)* perchero *m*; *(for umbrellas)* paragüero *m*; *(for bike, motorbike)* patín *m* de apoyo; *(at sports stadium)* tribuna *f*; **to be ~ing** estar de pie; **to ~ sb a drink** invitar a alguien a beber algo; **"no ~ing"** *(Am: AUT)* "prohibido aparcar" ❑ **stand back** *vi* echarse para atrás; **stand for** *vt fus (mean)* significar; *(tolerate)* tolerar; **stand in** *vi*: **to ~ in for sb** sustituir a alguien; **stand out** *vi (be conspicuous)* destacar; *(be superior)* sobresalir; **stand up** *vi (be on feet)* estar de pie; *(get to one's feet)* levantarse ◆ *vt sep (inf: boyfriend, girlfriend etc)* dar plantón a; **stand up for** *vt fus* salir en defensa de.

standard ['stændəd] *adj (normal)* normal ◆ *n (level)* nivel *m*; *(point of comparison)* criterio *m*; **up to ~** al nivel requerido ❑ **standards** *npl (principles)* valores *mpl* morales.

standard-class *adj (Br)* de segunda clase.

standby ['stændbaɪ] *adj* sin

reserva.

stank [stæŋk] *pt* → **stink**.

staple ['steɪpl] *n (for paper)* grapa f.

stapler ['steɪplər] *n* grapadora f.

star [stɑːr] *n* estrella f ◆ *vt (subj: film, play etc)* estar protagonizado por ◻ **stars** *npl (horoscope)* horóscopo m.

starboard ['stɑːbəd] *adj* de estribor.

starch [stɑːtʃ] *n (for clothes)* almidón m; *(in food)* fécula f.

stare [steər] *vi* mirar fijamente; **to ~ at** mirar fijamente.

starfish ['stɑːfɪʃ] *n (pl inv)* estrella f de mar.

starling ['stɑːlɪŋ] *n* estornino m.

Stars and Stripes *n*: the ~ la bandera de las barras y estrellas.

 STARS AND STRIPES

Esto es uno de los muchos nombres que recibe la bandera estadounidense, junto con "Old Glory", "Star-Spangled Banner" y "Stars and Bars". Las 50 estrellas representan los 50 estados de hoy día y las 13 barras rojas y blancas los 13 estados fundadores de la Unión. Los estadounidenses están muy orgullosos de su bandera y muchos particulares la hacen ondear frente a su casa.

start [stɑːt] *n (beginning)* principio m; *(starting place)* salida f ◆ *vt (begin)* empezar; *(car, engine)* arrancar; *(business, club)* montar ◆ *vi (begin)* empezar; *(car, engine)* arrancar; *(begin journey)* salir; **at the ~ of**

the year a principios del año; prices ~ at OR from £5 precios desde cinco libras; **to ~ doing sthg** OR **to do sthg** empezar a hacer algo; **to ~ with** *(in the first place)* para empezar; *(when ordering meal)* de primero ◻ **start out** *vi (on journey)* salir; *(be originally)* empezar; **start up** *vt sep (car, engine)* arrancar; *(business, shop)* montar.

starter ['stɑːtər] *n (Br: of meal)* primer plato m; *(of car)* motor m de arranque; **for ~s** *(in meal)* de primero.

starter motor *n* motor m de arranque.

starting point ['stɑːtɪŋ-] *n* punto m de partida.

startle ['stɑːtl] *vt* asustar.

starvation [stɑː'veɪʃn] *n* hambre f.

starve [stɑːv] *vi (have no food)* pasar hambre; **I'm starving!** ¡me muero de hambre!

state [steɪt] *n* estado m ◆ *vt (declare)* declarar; *(specify)* indicar; **the State** el Estado; **the States** los Estados Unidos.

statement ['steɪtmənt] *n (declaration)* declaración f; *(from bank)* extracto m.

state school *n* = instituto m.

statesman ['steɪtsmən] *(pl -men* [-mən]) *n* estadista m.

static ['stætɪk] *n* interferencias fpl.

station ['steɪʃn] *n* estación f; *(on radio)* emisora f.

stationary ['steɪʃnərɪ] *adj* inmóvil.

stationer's ['steɪʃnəz] *n (shop)* papelería f.

stationery [ˈsteɪʃnərɪ] n objetos mpl de escritorio.

station wagon n (Am) furgoneta f familiar.

statistics [stəˈtɪstɪks] npl datos mpl.

statue [ˈstætʃuː] n estatua f.

Statue of Liberty n: the ~ la Estatua de la Libertad.

---

i **STATUE OF LIBERTY**

Esta gigantesca estatua de una mujer con una antorcha f ♦ vi mano se alza sobre una pequeña isla situada a la entrada del puerto de Nueva York y puede ser visitada por el público. La estatua es un obsequio que Francia hizo a Estados Unidos en 1884.

---

status [ˈsteɪtəs] n (legal position) estado m; (social position) condición f; (prestige) prestigio m.

stay [steɪ] n (remain) quedarse; (as guest) alojarse; (Scot: reside) vivir; **to ~ the night** pasar la noche □ **stay away** vi (not attend) no asistir; (not go near) no acercarse; **stay in** vi quedarse en casa; **stay out** vi (from home) quedarse fuera; **stay up** vi quedarse levantado.

STD code n (abbr of subscriber trunk dialling) prefijo para llamadas interurbanas.

steady [ˈstedɪ] adj (not shaking, firm) firme; (gradual) gradual; (stable) constante; (job) estable ♦ vt (stop from shaking) mantener firme.

steak [steɪk] n (type of meat) bis-tec m; (piece of meat, fish) filete m.

steak and kidney pie n empanada de bistec y riñones.

steakhouse [ˈsteɪkhaʊs, pl -haʊzɪz] n parrilla f (restaurante).

steal [stiːl] (pt stole, pp stolen) vt robar; **to ~ sthg from sb** robar algo a alguien.

steam [stiːm] n vapor m ♦ vt (food) cocer al vapor.

steamboat [ˈstiːmbəʊt] n buque m de vapor.

steam engine n máquina f de vapor.

steam iron n plancha f de vapor.

steel [stiːl] n acero m ♦ adj de acero.

steep [stiːp] adj (hill, path) empinado(-da); (increase, drop) considerable.

steeple [ˈstiːpl] n torre f coronada con una aguja.

steer [stɪər] vt (car, boat, plane) conducir, dirigir.

steering [ˈstɪərɪŋ] n dirección f.

steering wheel n volante m.

stem [stem] n (of plant) tallo m; (of glass) pie m.

step [step] n paso m; (stair, rung) peldaño m; (measure) medida f ♦ vi: **to ~ on sthg** pisar algo; **"mind the ~"** "cuidado con el escalón" □ **steps** npl (stairs) escaleras fpl; **step aside** vi (move aside) apartarse; **step back** vi (move back) echarse atrás.

step aerobics n step m.

stepbrother [ˈstepˌbrʌðər] n hermanastro m.

stepdaughter [ˈstepˌdɔːtər] n

hijastra f.

stepfather ['step,fɑ:ðəʳ] n padrastro m.

stepladder ['step,lædəʳ] n escalera f de tijera.

stepmother ['step,mʌðəʳ] n madrastra f.

stepsister ['step,sɪstəʳ] n hermanastra f.

stepson ['stepsʌn] n hijastro m.

stereo ['steriəʊ] (pl -s) adj estéreo inv ◆ n (hi-fi) equipo m estereofónico; (stereo sound) estéreo m.

sterile ['steraɪl] adj (germ-free) esterilizado(-da).

sterilize ['steralaɪz] vt esterilizar.

sterling ['stɜ:lɪŋ] adj (pound) esterlina ◆ n la libra esterlina.

sterling silver n plata f de ley.

stern [stɜ:n] adj severo(-ra) ◆ n popa f.

stew [stju:] n estofado m.

steward ['stjʊəd] n (on plane) auxiliar m de vuelo; (on ship) camarero m; (at public event) ayudante mf de organización.

stewardess ['stjʊədɪs] n auxiliar f de vuelo.

stewed [stju:d] adj (fruit) en compota.

stick [stɪk] (pt & pp stuck) n (of wood, for sport) palo m; (thin piece) barra f; (walking stick) bastón m ◆ vt (glue) pegar; (push, insert) meter; (inf: put) poner ◆ vi (become attached) pegarse; (jam) atrancarse ❑ **stick out** vi sobresalir; **stick to** vt fus (decision) atenerse a; (principles) ser fiel a; (promise) cumplir con; **stick up** vt sep (poster, notice) pegar ◆ vi salir; **stick up for** vt fus defender.

sticker ['stɪkəʳ] n pegatina f.

sticking plaster ['stɪkɪŋ-] n esparadrapo m.

stick shift n (Am: car) coche m con palanca de cambios.

sticky ['stɪkɪ] adj (substance, hands, sweets) pegajoso(-sa); (label, tape) adhesivo(-va); (weather) húmedo(-da).

stiff [stɪf] adj (firm) rígido(-da); (back, neck) agarrotado(-da); (door, latch, mechanism) atascado(-da) ◆ adv: **to be bored ~** (inf) estar muerto de aburrimiento; **to feel ~** tener agujetas.

stile [staɪl] n escalones mpl para pasar una valla.

stiletto heels [stɪ'letəʊ] npl (shoes) tacones mpl de aguja.

still [stɪl] adv todavía; (despite that) sin embargo; (even) aún ◆ adj (motionless) inmóvil; (quiet, calm) tranquilo(-la); (not fizzy) sin gas: **we've ~ got ten minutes** aún nos quedan diez minutos; **~ more** aún más; **to stand ~** estarse quieto.

Stilton ['stɪltn] n queso inglés de sabor fuerte y amargo.

stimulate ['stɪmjʊleɪt] vt (encourage) estimular; (make enthusiastic) excitar.

sting [stɪŋ] (pt & pp stung) vt picar ◆ vi: **my eyes are ~ing** me pican los ojos.

stingy ['stɪndʒɪ] adj (inf) roñoso(-sa).

stink [stɪŋk] (pt stank OR stunk, pp stunk) vi (smell bad) apestar.

stipulate ['stɪpjʊleɪt] vt estipular.

stir [stɜːʳ] vt (move around, mix) remover.

stir-fry n plato que se fríe en aceite muy caliente y removiendo constantemente.

stirrup ['stɪrəp] n estribo m.

stitch [stɪtʃ] n (in sewing, knitting) punto m; **to have a ~** sentir pinchazos ❑ **stitches** npl (for wound) puntos mpl.

stock [stɒk] n (of shop, business) existencias fpl; (supply) reserva f; (FIN) capital m; (in cooking) caldo m ♦ vt (have in stock) tener, vender; **in ~** en existencia; **out of ~** agotado.

stock cube n pastilla f de caldo.

Stock Exchange n bolsa f.

stocking ['stɒkɪŋ] n media f.

stock market n mercado m de valores.

stodgy ['stɒdʒɪ] adj (food) indigesto(-ta).

stole [stəʊl] pt → steal.

stolen ['stəʊln] pp → steal.

stomach ['stʌmək] n (organ) estómago m; (belly) vientre m.

stomachache ['stʌmækeɪk] n dolor m de estómago.

stomach upset [-'ʌpset] n trastorno m gástrico.

stone [stəʊn] n (substance, pebble) piedra f; (in fruit) hueso m; (measurement) = 6,35 kilos; (gem) piedra f preciosa ♦ adj de piedra.

stonewashed ['stəʊnwɒʃt] adj lavado(-da) a la piedra.

stood [stʊd] pt & pp → stand.

stool [stuːl] n taburete m.

stop [stɒp] n parada f ♦ vt parar; (prevent) impedir ♦ vi pararse;

(cease) parar; (stay) quedarse; **to ~ sb/sthg from doing sthg** impedir que alguien/algo haga algo; **to ~ doing sthg** dejar de hacer algo; **to put a ~ to sthg** poner fin a algo; "stop" (road sign) "stop"; "stopping at ..." (train, bus) "con paradas en ..." ❑ **stop off** vi hacer una parada.

stopover ['stɒp,əʊvəʳ] n parada f.

stopper ['stɒpəʳ] n tapón m.

stopwatch ['stɒpwɒtʃ] n cronómetro m.

storage ['stɔːrɪdʒ] n almacenamiento m.

store [stɔːʳ] n (shop) tienda f; (supply) provisión f ♦ vt almacenar.

storehouse ['stɔːhaʊs, pl -haʊzɪz] n almacén m.

storeroom ['stɔːrʊm] n almacén m.

storey ['stɔːrɪ] (pl -s) n (Br) planta f.

stork [stɔːk] n cigüeña f.

storm [stɔːm] n tormenta f.

stormy ['stɔːmɪ] adj (weather) tormentoso(-sa).

story ['stɔːrɪ] n (account, tale) cuento m; (news item) artículo m; (Am) = storey.

stout [staʊt] adj (fat) corpulento(-ta) ♦ n (drink) cerveza f negra.

stove [stəʊv] n (for cooking) cocina f; (for heating) estufa f.

straight [streɪt] adj (not curved) recto(-ta); (upright, level) derecho(-cha); (hair) liso(-sa); (consecutive) consecutivo(-va); (drink) solo(-la) ♦ adv (in a straight line) en línea recta; (upright) derecho;

(directly) directamente; *(without delay)* inmediatamente; **~ ahead** todo derecho; **~ away** enseguida.

straightforward [,stret'fɔːwəd] *adj (easy)* sencillo(-lla).

strain [streɪn] *n (force)* presión *f*; *(nervous stress)* tensión *f* nerviosa; *(tension)* tensión; *(injury)* torcedura *f* ♦ *vt (muscle)* torcerse; *(eyes)* cansar; *(food, tea)* colar.

strainer ['streɪnər] *n* colador *m*.

strait [streɪt] *n* estrecho *m*.

strange [streɪndʒ] *adj (unusual)* raro(-ra); *(unfamiliar)* extraño(-ña).

stranger ['streɪndʒər] *n (unfamiliar person)* extraño *m*; *(person from different place)* forastero *m* (-ra *f*).

strangle ['stræŋgl] *vt* estrangular.

strap [stræp] *n (of bag, camera, watch)* correa *f*; *(of dress, bra)* tirante *m*.

strapless ['stræplɪs] *adj* sin tirantes.

strategy ['strætɪdʒɪ] *n* estrategia *f*.

Stratford-upon-Avon [,strætfədəpɒn'eɪvn] *n* Stratford-upon-Avon.

STRATFORD-UPON-AVON

Esta localidad en Warwickshire es famosa por ser el lugar de origen del dramaturgo y poeta William Shakespeare (1564-1616). Hoy, la Royal Shakespeare Company tiene allí su sede y sus representaciones de obras de Shakespeare y otros auto-res hacen del lugar un centro del teatro británico.

straw [strɔː] *n* paja *f*.

strawberry ['strɔːbərɪ] *n* fresa *f*.

stray [streɪ] *adj (ownerless)* callejero(-ra) ♦ *vi* vagar.

streak [striːk] *n (stripe, mark)* raya *f*; *(period)* racha *f*.

stream [striːm] *n (river)* riachuelo *m*; *(of traffic, people, blood)* torrente *m*.

street [striːt] *n* calle *f*.

streetcar ['striːtkɑː] *n (Am)* tranvía *m*.

street light *n* farola *f*.

street plan *n* callejero *m* (mapa).

strength [streŋθ] *n (of person, food, drink)* fuerza *f*; *(of structure)* solidez *f*; *(influence)* poder *m*; *(strong point)* punto *m* fuerte; *(of feeling, smell)* intensidad *f*; *(of drug)* potencia *f*.

strengthen ['streŋθn] *vt* reforzar.

stress [stres] *n (tension)* estrés *m inv*; *(on word, syllable)* acento *m* ♦ *vt (emphasize)* recalcar; *(word, syllable)* acentuar.

stretch [stretʃ] *n (of land, water)* extensión *f*; *(of road)* tramo *m*; *(of time)* periodo *m* ♦ *vt (rope, material, body)* estirar; *(elastic, clothes)* estirar (demasiado) ♦ *vi (land, sea)* extenderse; *(person, animal)* estirarse; **to ~ one's legs** *(fig)* dar un paseo ♦.

stretch out *vt sep (hand)* alargar ♦ *vi (lie down)* tumbarse.

stretcher ['stretʃər] *n* camilla *f*.

strict [strɪkt] *adj* estricto(-ta).

(exact) exacto(-ta).

strictly ['strɪktlɪ] *adv (absolutely)* terminantemente; *(exclusively)* exclusivamente; **~ speaking** realmente.

stride [straɪd] *n* zancada *f.*

strike [straɪk] *(pt & pp* **struck)** *n (of employees)* huelga *f ◆ vt (fml: hit)* pegar; *(fml: collide with)* chocar contra; *(a match)* encender *◆ vi (refuse to work)* estar en huelga; *(happen suddenly)* sobrevenir; **the clock struck eight** el reloj dio las ocho.

striking ['straɪkɪŋ] *adj (noticeable)* chocante; *(attractive)* atractivo(-va).

string [strɪŋ] *n* cuerda *f; (of pearls, beads)* sarta *f; (series)* serie *f;* **a piece of ~** una cuerda.

strip [strɪp] *n (of paper, cloth etc)* tira *f; (of land, water)* franja *f ◆ vt (paint, wallpaper)* quitar *◆ vi (undress)* desnudarse.

stripe [straɪp] *n (of colour)* raya *f.*

striped [straɪpt] *adj* a rayas.

strip-search *vt* registrar exhaustivamente, haciendo que se quite la ropa.

strip show *n* espectáculo *m* de striptease.

stroke [strəʊk] *n (MED)* derrame *m* cerebral; *(in tennis, golf)* golpe *m; (swimming style)* estilo *m ◆ vt* acariciar; **a ~ of luck** un golpe de suerte.

stroll [strəʊl] *n* paseo *m.*

stroller ['strəʊlər] *n (Am: pushchair)* sillita *f* (de niño).

strong [strɒŋ] *adj* fuerte; *(structure, bridge, chair)* resistente; *(influential)* poderoso(-sa); *(possibility)* serio(-ria); *(drug)* potente;

(accent) marcado(-da); *(point, subject)* mejor.

struck [strʌk] *pt & pp* → **strike.**

structure ['strʌktʃər] *n (arrangement, organization)* estructura *f; (building)* construcción *f.*

struggle ['strʌgl] *n (great effort)* lucha *f ◆ vi (fight)* luchar; *(in order to get free)* forcejear; **to ~ to do sthg** esforzarse en hacer algo.

stub [stʌb] *n (of cigarette)* colilla *f; (of cheque)* matriz *f; (of ticket)* resguardo *m.*

stubble ['stʌbl] *n (on face)* barba *f* de tres días.

stubborn ['stʌbən] *adj* terco (-ca).

stuck [stʌk] *pt & pp* → **stick** *◆ adj (unable to continue)* atascado(-da); *(stranded)* colgado(-da).

stud [stʌd] *n (on boots)* taco *m; (fastener)* automático *m; (earring)* pendiente *m* (pequeño).

student ['stjuːdnt] *n* estudiante *mf.*

student card *n* carné *m* de estudiante.

students' union [ˌstjuːdnts-] *n (place)* club *m* de alumnos.

studio ['stjuːdɪəʊ] *(pl* **-s)** *n* estudio *m.*

studio apartment *(Am)* = **studio flat.**

studio flat *n (Br)* estudio *m.*

study ['stʌdɪ] *n* estudio *m ◆ vt (learn about)* estudiar; *(examine)* examinar *◆ vi* estudiar.

stuff [stʌf] *n (inf) (substance)* cosa *f,* sustancia *f; (things, possessions)* cosas *fpl ◆ vt (put roughly)* meter; *(fill)* rellenar.

stuffed [stʌft] adj (food) relleno(-na); (inf: full up) lleno(-na); (dead animal) disecado(-da).

stuffing ['stʌfɪŋ] n relleno m.

stuffy ['stʌfɪ] adj (room, atmosphere) cargado(-da).

stumble ['stʌmbl] vi (when walking) tropezar.

stump [stʌmp] n (of tree) tocón m.

stun [stʌn] vt aturdir.

stung [stʌŋ] pt & pp → sting.

stunk [stʌŋk] pt & pp → stink.

stunning ['stʌnɪŋ] adj (very beautiful) imponente; (very surprising) pasmoso(-sa).

stupid ['stju:pɪd] adj (foolish) estúpido(-da); (inf: annoying) puñetero(-ra).

sturdy ['stɜːdɪ] adj robusto(-ta).

stutter ['stʌtəʳ] vi tartamudear.

sty [staɪ] n pocilga f.

style [staɪl] n (manner) estilo m; (elegance) clase f; (design) modelo m ◆ vt (hair) peinar.

stylish ['staɪlɪʃ] adj elegante.

stylist ['staɪlɪst] n (hairdresser) peluquero m (-ra f).

sub [sʌb] n (inf) (substitute) reserva mf; (Br: subscription) suscripción f.

subdued [səb'dju:d] adj (person, colour) apagado(-da); (lighting) tenue.

subject [n 'sʌbdʒekt, vb səb'dʒekt] n (topic) tema m; (at school, university) asignatura f; (GRAMM) sujeto m; (fml: of country) ciudadano m (-na f) ◆ vt: to ~ sb to sthg someter a alguien a algo; ~ to availability hasta fin de existencias;

they are ~ to an additional charge están sujetos a un suplemento.

subjunctive [səb'dʒʌŋktɪv] n subjuntivo m.

submarine [ˌsʌbmə'ri:n] n submarino m.

submit [səb'mɪt] vt presentar ◆ vi rendirse.

subordinate [sə'bɔːdɪnət] adj (GRAMM) subordinado(-da).

subscribe [səb'skraɪb] vi (to magazine, newspaper) suscribirse.

subscription [səb'skrɪpʃn] n suscripción f.

subsequent ['sʌbsɪkwənt] adj subsiguiente.

subside [səb'saɪd] vi (ground) hundirse; (noise, feeling) apagarse.

substance ['sʌbstəns] n sustancia f.

substantial [səb'stænʃl] adj (large) sustancial.

substitute ['sʌbstɪtju:t] n (replacement) sustituto m (-ta f); (SPORT) suplente mf.

subtitles ['sʌbˌtaɪtlz] npl subtítulos mpl.

subtle ['sʌtl] adj (difference, change) sutil; (person, plan) ingenioso(-sa).

subtract [səb'trækt] vt restar.

subtraction [səb'trækʃn] n resta f.

suburb ['sʌbɜːb] n barrio m residencial; the ~s las afueras.

subway ['sʌbweɪ] n (Br: for pedestrians) paso m subterráneo; (Am: underground railway) metro m.

succeed [sək'si:d] vi (be successful) tener éxito ◆ vt (fml) suceder a; to ~ in doing sthg conseguir hacer algo.

success [sək'ses] n éxito m.

successful [sək'sesful] adj (plan, attempt) afortunado(-da); (film, book, person) de éxito; (politician, actor) popular.

succulent ['sʌkjulənt] adj suculento(-ta).

such [sʌtʃ] adj (of stated kind) tal, semejante; (so great) tal ♦ adv: ~ a lot tanto; ~ a lot of books tantos libros; it's ~ a lovely day hace un día tan bonito; ~ a thing should never have happened tal cosa nunca debería de haber pasado; ~ as tales como.

suck [sʌk] vt chupar.

sudden ['sʌdn] adj repentino(-na); all of a ~ de repente.

suddenly ['sʌdnlɪ] adv de repente.

sue [su:] vt demandar.

suede [sweɪd] n ante m.

suffer ['sʌfə'] vt sufrir ♦ vi sufrir; (experience bad effects) salir perjudicado; to ~ from (illness) padecer.

suffering ['sʌfrɪŋ] n (mental) sufrimiento m; (physical) dolor m.

sufficient [sə'fɪʃnt] adj (fml) suficiente.

sufficiently [sə'fɪʃntlɪ] adv (fml) suficientemente.

suffix ['sʌfɪks] n sufijo m.

suffocate ['sʌfəkeɪt] vi asfixiarse.

sugar ['ʃʊgə'] n azúcar m.

suggest [sə'dʒest] vt (propose) sugerir; to ~ doing sthg sugerir hacer algo.

suggestion [sə'dʒestʃn] n (proposal) sugerencia f; (hint) asomo m.

suicide ['suːɪsaɪd] n suicidio m; to commit ~ suicidarse.

suit [suːt] n (man's clothes) traje m; (woman's clothes) traje de chaqueta; (in cards) palo m; (JUR) pleito m ♦ vt (subj: clothes, colour, shoes) favorecer; (be convenient for) convenir; (be appropriate for) ser adecuado para; to be ~ed to ser apropiado para.

suitable ['suːtəbl] adj adecuado(-da); to be ~ for ser adecuado para.

suitcase ['suːtkeɪs] n maleta f.

suite [swiːt] n (set of rooms) suite f; (furniture) juego m.

sulk [sʌlk] vi estar de mal humor.

sultana [səl'tɑːnə] n (Br: raisin) pasa f de Esmirna.

sultry ['sʌltrɪ] adj (weather, climate) bochornoso(-sa).

sum [sʌm] n suma f ❑ **sum up** vt sep (summarize) resumir.

summarize ['sʌməraɪz] vt resumir.

summary ['sʌmərɪ] n resumen m.

summer ['sʌmə'] n verano m; in (the) ~ en verano; ~ holidays vacaciones fpl de verano.

summertime ['sʌmətaɪm] n verano m.

summit ['sʌmɪt] n (of mountain) cima f; (meeting) cumbre f.

summon ['sʌmən] vt (send for) llamar; (JUR) citar.

sumptuous ['sʌmptʃʊəs] adj suntuoso(-sa).

sun [sʌn] n sol m ♦ vt: to ~ o.s. tomar el sol; to catch the ~ coger color; in the ~ al sol; out of the ~ en la sombra.

Sun. *(abbr of Sunday)* dom.

sunbathe ['sʌnbeɪð] *vi* tomar el sol.

sunbed ['sʌnbed] *n* camilla *f* de rayos ultravioletas.

sun block *n* pantalla *f* solar.

sunburn ['sʌnbɜːn] *n* quemadura *f* de sol.

sunburnt ['sʌnbɜːnt] *adj* quemado(-da) (por el sol).

sundae ['sʌndeɪ] *n* helado con salsa, nata montada y nueces.

Sunday ['sʌndɪ] *n* domingo *m*, → Saturday.

Sunday school *n* catequesis *f* inv.

sundress ['sʌndres] *n* vestido *m* de playa.

sundries ['sʌndrɪz] *npl* artículos *mpl* diversos.

sunflower ['sʌn,flaʊə^r] *n* girasol *m*.

sunflower oil *n* aceite *m* de girasol.

sung [sʌŋ] *pt* → **sing**.

sunglasses ['sʌn,glɑːsɪz] *npl* gafas *fpl* de sol.

sunhat ['sʌnhæt] *n* pamela *f*.

sunk [sʌŋk] *pp* → **sink**.

sunlight ['sʌnlaɪt] *n* luz *f* del sol.

sun lounger [-,laʊndʒə^r] *n* tumbona *f*.

sunny ['sʌnɪ] *adj* soleado(-da); it's ~ hace sol.

sunrise ['sʌnraɪz] *n* amanecer *m*.

sunroof ['sʌnruːf] *n* (on car) techo *m* corredizo.

sunset ['sʌnset] *n* anochecer *m*.

sunshine ['sʌnʃaɪn] *n* luz *f* del sol; in the ~ al sol.

sunstroke ['sʌnstrəʊk] *n* insolación *f*.

suntan ['sʌntæn] *n* bronceado *m*.

suntan cream *n* crema *f* bronceadora.

suntan lotion *n* loción *f* bronceadora.

super ['suːpə^r] *adj* fenomenal ♦ *n* (petrol) gasolina *f* súper.

superb [suː'pɜːb] *adj* excelente.

superficial [,suːpə'fɪʃl] *adj* superficial.

superfluous [suː'pɜːfluəs] *adj* superfluo(-flua).

Superglue® ['suːpəgluː] *n* pegamento *m* rápido.

superior [suː'pɪərɪə^r] *adj* superior ♦ *n* superior *mf*.

supermarket ['suːpə,mɑːkɪt] *n* supermercado *m*.

supernatural [,suːpə'nætʃrəl] *adj* sobrenatural.

Super Saver® *n* (Br) billete de tren de precio muy reducido.

superstitious [,suːpə'stɪʃəs] *adj* supersticioso(-sa).

superstore ['suːpəstɔː^r] *n* hipermercado *m*.

supervise ['suːpəvaɪz] *vt* supervisar.

supervisor ['suːpəvaɪzə^r] *n* supervisor *m* (-ra *f*).

supper ['sʌpə^r] *n* cena *f*.

supple ['sʌpl] *adj* flexible.

supplement [*n* 'sʌplɪmənt, *vb* 'sʌplɪment] *n* suplemento *m*; (of diet) complemento *m* ♦ *vt* complementar.

supplementary [,sʌplɪ'mentərɪ] *adj* suplementario(-ria).

supply [sə'plaɪ] *n* suministro *m* ♦

vt suministrar; **to ~ sb with sthg** proveer a alguien de algo □ **supplies** *npl* provisiones *fpl*.

support [sə'pɔːt] *n (backing, encouragement)* apoyo *m; (supporting object)* soporte *m* ◆ *vt (cause, campaign, person)* apoyar; *(SPORT)* seguir; *(hold up)* soportar; *(financially)* financiar.

supporter [sə'pɔːtə^r] *n (SPORT)* hincha *mf; (of cause, political party)* partidario *m* (-ria *f*).

suppose [sə'pəʊz] *vt* suponer ◆ *conj* = **supposing; I ~ so** supongo que sí; **it's ~d to be good** se dice que es bueno; **it was ~d to arrive yesterday** debería haber llegado ayer.

supposing [sə'pəʊzɪŋ] *conj* si, suponiendo que.

supreme [sʊ'priːm] *adj* supremo(-ma).

surcharge ['sɜːtʃɑːdʒ] *n* recargo *m*.

sure [ʃʊə^r] *adj* seguro(-ra) ◆ *adv (inf)* por supuesto; **to be ~ of o.s.** estar seguro de sí mismo; **to make ~ (that)** asegurarse de que; **for ~** a ciencia cierta.

surely ['ʃʊəlɪ] *adv* sin duda.

surf [sɜːf] *n* espuma *f* ◆ *vi* hacer surf.

surface ['sɜːfɪs] *n* superficie *f*.

surface area *n* área *f* de la superficie.

surface mail *n* correo *m* por vía terrestre y marítima.

surfboard ['sɜːfbɔːd] *n* tabla *f* de surf.

surfing ['sɜːfɪŋ] *n* surf *m*; **to go ~** hacer surf.

surgeon ['sɜːdʒən] *n* cirujano *m* (-na *f*).

surgery ['sɜːdʒərɪ] *n (treatment)* cirujía *f; (Br: building)* consultorio *m; (Br: period)* consulta *f*.

surname ['sɜːneɪm] *n* apellido *m*.

surplus ['sɜːpləs] *n* excedente *m*.

surprise [sə'praɪz] *n* sorpresa *f* ◆ *vt (astonish)* sorprender.

surprised [sə'praɪzd] *adj* asombrado(-da).

surprising [sə'praɪzɪŋ] *adj* sorprendente.

surrender [sə'rendə^r] *vi* rendirse ◆ *vt (fml: hand over)* entregar.

surround [sə'raʊnd] *vt* rodear.

surrounding [sə'raʊndɪŋ] *adj* circundante ◆ **surroundings** *npl* alrededores *mpl*.

survey ['sɜːveɪ] *(pl -s) n (investigation)* investigación *f; (poll)* encuesta *f; (of land)* medición *f; (Br: of house)* inspección *f*.

surveyor [sə'veɪə^r] *n (Br: of houses)* perito *m* tasador de la propiedad; *(of land)* agrimensor *m* (-ra *f*).

survival [sə'vaɪvl] *n* supervivencia *f*.

survive [sə'vaɪv] *vi* sobrevivir ◆ *vt* sobrevivir a.

survivor [sə'vaɪvə^r] *n* superviviente *mf*.

suspect [*vb* sə'spekt, *n & adj* 'sʌspekt] *vt (believe)* imaginar; *(mistrust)* sospechar ◆ *n* sospechoso *m* (-sa *f*) ◆ *adj* sospechoso(-sa); **to ~ sb of sthg** considerar a alguien sospechoso de algo.

suspend [sə'spend] *vt* suspender; *(from team, school, work)* expulsar temporalmente.

suspender belt [sə'spendə] n liguero m.

suspenders [sə'spendəz] npl (Br: for stockings) ligas fpl; (Am: for trousers) tirantes mpl.

suspense [sə'spens] n suspense m.

suspension [sə'spenʃn] n (of vehicle) suspensión f; (from team, school, work) expulsión f temporal.

suspicion [sə'spiʃn] n (mistrust) recelo m; (idea) sospecha f; (trace) pizca f.

suspicious [sə'spiʃəs] adj (behaviour, situation) sospechoso(-sa); to be ~ (of) ser receloso(-sa) (de).

swallow ['swɒləʊ] n (bird) golondrina f ♦ vt & vi tragar.

swam [swæm] pt → swim.

swamp [swɒmp] n pantano m.

swan [swɒn] n cisne m.

swap [swɒp] vt (possessions, places) cambiar; (ideas, stories) intercambiar; to ~ sthg for sthg cambiar algo por algo.

swarm [swɔːm] n (of bees) enjambre m.

swear [sweər] (pt swore, pp sworn) vi jurar ♦ vt: to ~ to do sthg jurar hacer algo.

swearword ['sweəwɜːd] n palabrota f.

sweat [swet] n sudor m ♦ vi sudar.

sweater ['swetər] n suéter m.

sweatshirt ['swetʃɜːt] n sudadera f.

swede [swiːd] n (Br) nabo m sueco.

Swede [swiːd] n sueco m (-ca f).

Sweden ['swiːdn] n Suecia.

Swedish ['swiːdɪʃ] adj sueco(-ca) ♦ n (language) sueco m ♦ npl: the ~ los suecos.

sweep [swiːp] (pt & pp swept) vt (with brush, broom) barrer.

sweet [swiːt] adj (food, drink) dulce; (smell) fragante; (person, nature) amable ♦ n (Br) (candy) caramelo m; (dessert) postre m.

sweet-and-sour adj agridulce.

sweet corn n maíz m.

sweetener ['swiːtnər] n (for drink) edulcorante m.

sweet potato n batata f.

sweet shop n (Br) confitería f.

swell [swel] (pt -ed, pp swollen OR -ed) vi (ankle, arm etc) hincharse.

swelling ['swelɪŋ] n hinchazón f.

swept [swept] pt & pp → sweep.

swerve [swɜːv] vi virar bruscamente.

swig [swɪg] n (inf) trago m.

swim [swɪm] (pt swam, pp swum) n baño m ♦ vi nadar; to go for a ~ ir a nadar.

swimmer ['swɪmər] n nadador m (-ra f).

swimming ['swɪmɪŋ] n natación f; to go ~ ir a nadar.

swimming baths npl (Br) piscina f municipal.

swimming cap n gorro m de baño.

swimming costume n (Br) traje m de baño.

swimming pool n piscina f.

swimming trunks npl bañador m.

swimsuit ['swɪmsuːt] n traje m

de baño.

swindle ['swɪndl] n estafa f.

swing [swɪŋ] (pt & pp swung) n (for children) columpio m ◆ vt (move from side to side) balancear ◆ vi (move from side to side) balancearse.

swipe [swaɪp] vt (credit card etc) pasar por el datáfono.

Swiss [swɪs] adj suizo(-za) ◆ n (person) suizo m (-za f) ◆ npl: the ~ los suizos.

Swiss cheese n queso m suizo.

swiss roll n brazo m de gitano.

switch [swɪtʃ] n (for light, power, television) interruptor m ◆ vt (change) cambiar de; (exchange) intercambiar ◆ vi cambiar ▸ **switch off** vt sep apagar; **switch on** vt sep encender.

switchboard ['swɪtʃbɔːd] n centralita f.

Switzerland ['swɪtsələnd] n Suiza.

swivel ['swɪvl] vi girar.

swollen ['swəʊlən] pp → swell ◆ adj hinchado(-da).

swop [swɒp] = swap.

sword [sɔːd] n espada f.

swordfish ['sɔːdfɪʃ] (pl inv) n pez m espada.

swore [swɔːʳ] pt → swear.

sworn [swɔːn] pp → swear.

swum [swʌm] pp → swim.

swung [swʌŋ] pt & pp → swing.

syllabi ['sɪləbaɪ] pl → syllabus.

syllable ['sɪləbl] n sílaba f.

syllabus ['sɪləbəs] (pl -buses or -bi) n programa m (de estudios).

symbol ['sɪmbl] n símbolo m.

sympathetic [ˌsɪmpə'θetɪk] adj (understanding) comprensivo(-va).

sympathize ['sɪmpəθaɪz] vi: to ~ (with) (feel sorry) compadecerse (de); (understand) comprender.

sympathy ['sɪmpəθɪ] n (understanding) comprensión f; (compassion) compasión f.

symphony ['sɪmfənɪ] n sinfonía f.

symptom ['sɪmptəm] n síntoma m.

synagogue ['sɪnəgɒg] n sinagoga f.

synthesizer ['sɪnθəsaɪzəʳ] n sintetizador m.

synthetic [sɪn'θetɪk] adj sintético(-ca).

syringe [sɪ'rɪndʒ] n jeringa f.

syrup ['sɪrəp] n (for fruit etc) almíbar m.

system ['sɪstəm] n sistema m; (for gas, heating etc) instalación f.

T

ta [taː] excl (Br: inf) ¡gracias!

tab [tæb] n (of cloth, paper etc) lengüeta f; (bill) cuenta f; **put it on my ~** póngalo en mi cuenta.

table ['teɪbl] n (piece of furniture) mesa f; (of figures etc) tabla f.

tablecloth ['teɪblklɒθ] n mantel m.

tablemat ['teɪblmæt] n salvamanteles m inv.

tablespoon ['teɪblspuːn] n

(spoon) cuchara f grande (para servir); (amount) cucharada f grande.

tablet ['tæblɪt] n pastilla f.

table tennis n tenis m de mesa.

table wine n vino m de mesa.

tabloid ['tæblɔɪd] n periódico m sensacionalista.

tack [tæk] n (nail) tachuela f.

tackle ['tækl] n (SPORT) entrada f; (for fishing) aparejos mpl ♦ vt (SPORT) entrar; (deal with) abordar.

tacky ['tækɪ] adj (inf: jewellery, design etc) cutre.

taco ['tækəʊ] (pl -s) n taco m.

tact [tækt] n tacto m.

tactful ['tæktful] adj discreto(-ta).

tactics ['tæktɪks] npl táctica f.

tag [tæg] n (label) etiqueta f.

tagliatelle [ˌtæglɪə'telɪ] n tallarines mpl.

tail [teɪl] n cola f □ **tails** n (of coin) cruz f ♦ npl (formal dress) frac m.

tailgate ['teɪlgeɪt] n portón m.

tailor ['teɪlə'] n sastre m.

Taiwan [ˌtaɪ'wɑːn] n Taiwán.

take [teɪk] (pt took, pp taken) vt
1. (gen) tomar.
2. (carry, drive) llevar.
3. (hold, grasp) coger, agarrar (Amér).
4. (do, make): to ~ a bath bañarse; to ~ an exam hacer un examen; to ~ a photo sacar una foto.
5. (require) requerir; how long will it ~? ¿cuánto tiempo tardará?
6. (steal) quitar.
7. (size in clothes, shoes) usar; what size do you ~? ¿qué talla/número usas?

8. (subtract) restar.
9. (accept) aceptar; do you ~ traveller's cheques? ¿acepta cheques de viaje?; to ~ sb's advice seguir los consejos de alguien.
10. (contain) tener cabida para.
11. (react to) tomarse.
12. (tolerate) soportar.
13. (assume): I ~ it that ... supongo que ...
14. (rent) alquilar.
□ **take apart** vt sep desmontar; (subtract) restar; **take back** vt sep (return) devolver; (accept) aceptar la devolución de; (statement) retirar; **take down** vt sep (picture, curtains) descolgar; **take in** vt sep (include) abarcar; (understand) entender; (deceive) engañar; ~ this dress in mete un poco en este vestido; **take off** vt sep (remove) quitar; (clothes) quitarse; (as holiday) tomarse libre ♦ vi (plane) despegar; **take out** vt sep (from container, pocket, library) sacar; (insurance policy) hacerse; (loan) conseguir; to ~ sb out to dinner invitar a alguien a cenar; **take over** vi tomar el relevo; **take up** vt sep (begin) dedicarse a; (use up) ocupar; (trousers, skirt, dress) acortar.

takeaway ['teɪkəˌweɪ] n (Br) (shop) tienda f de comida para llevar; (food) comida f para llevar.

taken ['teɪkn] pp → take.

takeoff ['teɪkɒf] n (of plane) despegue m.

takeout ['teɪkaʊt] (Am) = takeaway.

takings ['teɪkɪŋz] npl recaudación f.

talcum powder ['tælkəm-] n

talco m.

tale [teɪl] n (story) cuento m; (account) anécdota f.

talent ['tælənt] n talento m.

talk [tɔːk] n (conversation) conversación f; (speech) charla f ◆ vi hablar; **to ~ to sb** (about sthg) hablar con alguien (sobre algo); **to ~ with sb** hablar con alguien ◆ **talks** npl conversaciones fpl.

talkative ['tɔːkətɪv] adj hablador(-ra).

tall [tɔːl] adj alto(-ta); **how ~ are you?** ¿cuánto mides?; **I'm 2 metres ~** mido dos metros.

tame [teɪm] adj (animal) doméstico(-ca).

tampon ['tæmpɒn] n tampón m.

tan [tæn] n (suntan) bronceado m ◆ vi broncearse ◆ adj (colour) de color marrón claro.

tangerine [,tændʒə'riːn] n mandarina f.

tank [tæŋk] n (container) depósito m; (vehicle) tanque m.

tanker ['tæŋkə'] n (truck) camión m cisterna.

tanned [tænd] adj (suntanned) bronceado(-da).

tap [tæp] n (for water) grifo m ◆ vt (hit) golpear ligeramente.

tape [teɪp] n cinta f; (adhesive material) cinta adhesiva ◆ vt (record) grabar; (stick) pegar.

tape measure n cinta f métrica.

tape recorder n magnetófono m.

tapestry ['tæpɪstrɪ] n tapiz m.

tap water n agua f del grifo.

tar [tɑː'] n alquitrán m.

target ['tɑːgɪt] n (in archery, shooting) blanco m; (MIL) objetivo m.

tariff ['tærɪf] n (price list) tarifa f, lista f de precios; (Br: menu) menú m; (at customs) arancel m.

tarmac ['tɑːmæk] n (at airport) pista f ◻ **Tarmac®** n (on road) alquitrán m.

tarpaulin [tɑː'pɔːlɪn] n lona f alquitranada.

tart [tɑːt] n (sweet) tarta f.

tartan ['tɑːtn] n tartán m.

tartare sauce [,tɑːtə-] n salsa f tártara.

task [tɑːsk] n tarea f.

taste [teɪst] n (flavour) sabor m; (discernment, sense) gusto m ◆ vt (sample) probar; (detect) notar un sabor a ◆ vi: **to ~ of sthg** saber a algo; **it ~s bad** sabe mal; **it ~s good** sabe bien; **to have a ~ of sthg** probar algo; **bad ~** mal gusto; **good ~** buen gusto.

tasteful ['teɪstfʊl] adj de buen gusto.

tasteless ['teɪstlɪs] adj (food) soso(-sa); (comment, decoration) de mal gusto.

tasty ['teɪstɪ] adj sabroso(-sa).

tattoo [tə'tuː] n (pl -s) (on skin) tatuaje m; (military display) desfile m militar.

taught [tɔːt] pt & pp → **teach**.

Taurus ['tɔːrəs] n Tauro m.

taut [tɔːt] adj tenso(-sa).

tax [tæks] n impuesto m ◆ vt (goods, person) gravar.

tax disc n (Br) pegatina del impuesto de circulación.

tax-free adj libre de impuestos.

taxi ['tæksɪ] n taxi m ◆ vi (plane) rodar por la pista.

taxi driver n taxista mf.

taxi rank n (Br) parada f de taxis.

taxi stand *(Am)* = **taxi rank**.

T-bone steak [ti:-] *n* chuleta de carne de vaca con un hueso en forma de T.

tea [ti:] *n* té *m*; *(herbal)* infusión *f*; *(afternoon meal)* = merienda *f*; *(evening meal)* = merienda cena.

tea bag *n* bolsita *f* de té.

teacake ['ti:keɪk] *n* bollo *m* con pasas.

teach [ti:tʃ] *(pt & pp* **taught)** *vt* enseñar ♦ *vi* ser profesor; **to ~ sb sthg, to ~ sthg to sb** enseñar algo a alguien; **to ~ sb (how) to do sthg** enseñar a alguien a hacer algo.

teacher ['ti:tʃəʳ] *n (in secondary school)* profesor *m* (-ra *f*); *(in primary school)* maestro *m* (-ra *f*).

teaching ['ti:tʃɪŋ] *n* enseñanza *f*.

tea cloth *n* = **tea towel**.

teacup ['ti:kʌp] *n* taza *f* de té.

team [ti:m] *n* equipo *m*.

teapot ['ti:pɒt] *n* tetera *f*.

tear¹ [teəʳ] *(pt* **tore,** *pp* **torn)** *vt (rip)* rasgar ♦ *vi (rip)* romperse; *(move quickly)* ir a toda pastilla ♦ *n (rip)* rasgón *m* ❏ **tear up** *vt sep* hacer pedazos.

tear² [tɪəʳ] *n* lágrima *f*.

tearoom ['ti:rum] *n* salón *m* de té.

tease [ti:z] *vt* tomar el pelo.

tea set *n* juego *m* de té.

teaspoon ['ti:spu:n] *n (utensil)* cucharilla *f*; *(amount)* = **teaspoonful**.

teaspoonful ['ti:spu:n,fʊl] *n* cucharadita *f*.

teat [ti:t] *n (of animal)* teta *f*; *(Br: of bottle)* tetina *f*.

teatime ['ti:taɪm] *n* hora *f* de la merienda cena.

tea towel *n* paño *m* de cocina.

technical ['teknɪkl] *adj* técnico(-ca).

technical drawing *n* dibujo *m* técnico.

technicality [,teknɪ'kælətɪ] *n (detail)* detalle *m* técnico.

technician [tek'nɪʃn] *n* técnico *m* (-ca *f*).

technique [tek'ni:k] *n* técnica *f*.

technological [,teknə'lɒdʒɪkl] *adj* tecnológico(-ca).

technology [tek'nɒlədʒɪ] *n* tecnología *f*.

teddy (bear) ['tedɪ-] *n* oso *m* de peluche.

tedious ['ti:djəs] *adj* tedioso(-sa).

tee [ti:] *n* tee *m*.

teenager ['ti:n,eɪdʒəʳ] *n* adolescente *mf*.

teeth [ti:θ] *pl* → **tooth**.

teethe [ti:ð] *vi*: **to be teething** estar echando los dientes.

teetotal [ti:'təʊtl] *adj* abstemio(-mia).

telegram ['telɪgræm] *n* telegrama *m*.

telegraph ['telɪgrɑ:f] *n* telégrafo *m* ♦ *vt* telegrafiar.

telegraph pole *n* poste *m* de telégrafos.

telephone ['telɪfəʊn] *n* teléfono *m* ♦ *vt & vi* telefonear; **to be on the ~ (talking)** estar al teléfono; *(connected)* tener teléfono.

telephone booth *n* teléfono *m* público.

telephone box *n* cabina *f* telefónica.

telephone call *n* llamada *f* telefónica.

telephone directory *n* guía *f* telefónica.

telephone number *n* número *m* de teléfono.

telephonist [tɪˈlefənɪst] *n* (Br) telefonista *mf*.

telephoto lens [ˌtelɪˈfəʊtəʊ-] *n* teleobjetivo *m*.

telescope [ˈtelɪskəʊp] *n* telescopio *m*.

television [ˈtelɪˌvɪʒn] *n* televisión *f*; **on (the)** ~ en la televisión.

telex [ˈteleks] *n* télex *m inv*.

tell [tel] (pt & pp **told**) vt decir; (story, joke) contar ♦ vi: **I can't** ~ no lo sé; **can you** ~ **me the time?** ¿me puedes decir la hora?; **to** ~ **sb sthg** decir algo a alguien; **to** ~ **sb about sthg** contar a alguien acerca de algo; **to** ~ **sb how to do sthg** decir a alguien cómo hacer algo; **to** ~ **sb to do sthg** decir a alguien que haga algo; **to be able to** ~ **sthg** saber algo ❑ **tell off** vt sep reñir.

teller [ˈtelər] *n* (in bank) cajero *m* (-ra *f*).

telly [ˈtelɪ] *n* (Br: inf) tele *f*.

temp [temp] *n* secretario *m* eventual (secretaria *f* eventual) ♦ vi trabajar de eventual.

temper [ˈtempər] *n* (character) temperamento *m*; **to be in a** ~ estar de mal humor; **to lose one's** ~ perder la paciencia.

temperature [ˈtemprətʃər] *n* (heat, cold) temperatura *f*; (MED) fiebre *f*; **to have a** ~ tener fiebre.

temple [ˈtempl] *n* (building) templo *m*; (of forehead) sien *f*.

temporary [ˈtempərərɪ] *adj* temporal.

tempt [tempt] vt tentar; **to be ~ed to do sthg** sentirse tentado de hacer algo.

temptation [tempˈteɪʃn] *n* tentación *f*.

tempting [ˈtemptɪŋ] *adj* tentador(-ra).

ten [ten] *num* diez, → **six**.

tenant [ˈtenənt] *n* inquilino *m* (-na *f*).

tend [tend] vi: **to** ~ **to do sthg** soler hacer algo.

tendency [ˈtendənsɪ] *n* (trend) tendencia *f*; (inclination) inclinación *f*.

tender [ˈtendər] *adj* tierno(-na); (sore) dolorido(-da) ♦ vt (fml: pay) pagar.

tendon [ˈtendən] *n* tendón *m*.

tenement [ˈtenəmənt] *n* bloque de viviendas modestas.

Tenerife [ˌtenəˈriːf] *n* Tenerife.

tennis [ˈtenɪs] *n* tenis *m*.

tennis ball *n* pelota *f* de tenis.

tennis court *n* pista *f* de tenis.

tennis racket *n* raqueta *f* de tenis.

tenpin bowling [ˈtenpɪn-] *n* (Br) bolos *mpl*.

tenpins [ˈtenpɪnz] (Am) = **tenpin bowling**.

tense [tens] *adj* tenso(-sa) ♦ *n* tiempo *m*.

tension [ˈtenʃn] *n* tensión *f*.

tent [tent] *n* tienda *f* de campaña.

tenth [tenθ] *num* décimo(-ma), → **sixth**.

tent peg *n* estaca *f*.

tepid [ˈtepɪd] *adj* tibio(-bia).

tequila [tɪˈkiːlə] *n* tequila *m*.

term [tɜːm] *n* (word, expression) término *m*; (at school, university) trimestre *m*; **in the long** ~ a largo plazo; **in the short** ~ a corto plazo; **in** ~**s of** por lo que se refiere a; **in business** ~**s** en términos de negocios ❑ **terms** *npl* (of contract) condiciones *fpl*; *(price)* precio *m*.

terminal ['tɜːmɪnl] *adj* terminal ♦ *n (for buses, at airport)* terminal *f*; *(COMPUT)* terminal *m*.

terminate ['tɜːmɪneɪt] *vi (train, bus)* finalizar el trayecto.

terminus ['tɜːmɪnəs] *(pl* -ni [-naɪ] OR -nuses) *n* terminal *f*.

terrace ['terəs] *n (patio)* terraza *f*; **the ~s** *(at football ground)* las gradas.

terraced house ['terəst-] *n (Br)* casa *f* adosada.

terrible ['terəbl] *adj (very bad, very ill)* fatal; *(very great)* terrible.

terribly ['terəblɪ] *adv (extremely)* terriblemente; *(very badly)* fatalmente.

terrier ['terɪə*] *n* terrier *m*.

terrific [tə'rɪfɪk] *adj (inf) (very good)* estupendo(-da); *(very great)* enorme.

terrified ['terɪfaɪd] *adj* aterrorizado(-da).

territory ['terɪtrɪ] *n (political area)* territorio *m*; *(terrain)* terreno *m*.

terror ['terə*] *n (fear)* terror *m*.

terrorism ['terərɪzm] *n* terrorismo *m*.

terrorist ['terərɪst] *n* terrorista *mf*.

terrorize ['terəraɪz] *vt* aterrorizar.

test [test] *n (exam)* examen *m*; *(check)* prueba *f*; *(of blood)* análisis *m inv*; *(of eyes)* revisión *f* ♦ *vt (check, try out)* probar; *(give exam to)* examinar.

testicles ['testɪklz] *npl* testículos *mpl*.

tetanus ['tetənəs] *n* tétanos *m inv*.

text [tekst] *n (written material)* texto *m*; *(textbook)* libro *m* de texto.

textbook ['tekstbuk] *n* libro *m* de texto.

textile ['tekstaɪl] *n* textil *m*.

texture ['tekstʃə*] *n* textura *f*.

Thai [taɪ] *adj* tailandés(-esa).

Thailand ['taɪlænd] *n* Tailandia.

Thames [temz] *n*: **the ~** el Támesis.

than *(weak form* ðən, *strong form* ðæn) *prep, conj* que; **you're better ~ me** eres mejor que yo; **I'd rather stay in ~ go out** prefiero quedarme antes que salir; **more ~ ten** más de diez.

thank [θæŋk] *vt*: **to ~ sb (for sthg)** agradecer a alguien (algo) ♦ **thanks** *npl* agradecimiento *m* ♦ *excl* ¡gracias!; **~s to** gracias a; **many ~s** muchas gracias.

Thanksgiving ['θæŋksgɪvɪn] *n* Día *m* de Acción de Gracias.

ⓘ THANKSGIVING

El cuarto jueves de cada noviembre se celebra en EEUU la fiesta nacional del Día de Acción de Gracias como signo de gratitud de la cosecha y otros beneficios recibidos a lo largo del año. Sus orígenes se remontan al año 1621 cuando los "Pilgrims" (colonizadores británicos) recogieron su primera cosecha. El menú tradicional de Acción de Gracias consiste en pavo asado y pastel de calabaza.

---

thank you *excl* ¡gracias!; **~ very much** muchísimas gracias; **no ~** gracias.

that [ðæt, *weak form of pron sense 3 & conj* ðət] (*pl* **those**) *adj* (*referring to thing, person mentioned*) ese (esa), esos (esas) (*pl*); (*referring to thing, person further away*) aquel (aquella), aquellos (aquellas) (*pl*); **I prefer ~ book** prefiero ese libro; **~ one** ése (ésa)/aquél (aquélla).

◆ *pron* 1. (*referring to thing, person mentioned*) ése *m* (ésa *f*), ésos *mpl* (ésas *fpl*); (*indefinite*) eso; **who's ~?** ¿quién es?; **is ~ Lucy?** (*on the phone*) ¿eres Lucy?; (*pointing*) ¿es ésa Lucy?; **what's ~?** ¿qué es eso?; **~'s interesting** qué interesante.

2. (*referring to thing, person further away*) aquél *m* (aquélla *f*), aquéllos *mpl* (aquéllas *fpl*); (*indefinite*) aquello; **I want those at the back** quiero aquéllos del fondo.

3. (*introducing relative clause*) que; **a shop ~ sells antiques** una tienda que vende antigüedades; **the film ~ I saw** la película que vi; **the room ~ I sleep in** el cuarto en (el) que duermo.

◆ *adv* tan; **it wasn't ~ bad/good** no estuvo tan mal/bien; **it doesn't cost ~ much** no cuesta tanto.

◆ *conj* que; **tell him ~ I'm going to be late** dile que voy a llegar tarde.

thatched [θætʃt] *adj* (*building*) con techo de paja.

that's [ðæts] = **that is.**

thaw [θɔː] *vi* (*snow, ice*) derretir ◆ *vt* (*frozen food*) descongelar.

the [*weak form* ðə, *before vowel* ðɪ, *strong form* ðiː] *definite article* 1. (*gen*) el (la), los (las) (*pl*); **~ book** el libro; **~ woman** la mujer; **~ girls** las chicas; **~ Wilsons** los Wilson; **to play ~ piano** tocar el piano; **give it to ~**

man dáselo al hombre; **the cover of ~ book** la tapa del libro.

2. (*with an adjective to form a noun*) el (la); **~ British** los británicos; **~ impossible** lo imposible.

3. (*in dates*): **~ twelfth of May** el doce de mayo; **~ forties** los cuarenta.

4. (*in titles*): **Elizabeth ~ Second** Isabel segunda.

theater [ˈθɪətər] *n* (*Am*) (*for plays, drama*) = **theatre**; (*for films*) cine *m*.

theatre [ˈθɪətər] *n* (*Br*) teatro *m*.

theft [θeft] *n* robo *m*.

their [ðeər] *adj* su, sus (*pl*).

theirs [ðeəz] *pron* suyo *m* (-ya *f*), suyos *mpl* (-yas *fpl*); **a friend of ~** un amigo suyo.

them [*weak form* ðəm, *strong form* ðem] *pron*: **I know ~** los conozco; **it's ~** son ellos; **send it to ~** envíaselo; **tell ~ to come** diles que vengan; **he's worse than ~** él es peor que ellos.

theme [θiːm] *n* (*topic*) tema *m*; (*tune*) sintonía *f*.

theme park *n* parque de atracciones basado en un tema específico.

themselves [ðəmˈselvz] *pron* (*reflexive*) se; (*after prep*) sí; **they did it ~** lo hicieron ellos mismos.

then [ðen] *adv* entonces; (*next, afterwards*) luego; **from ~ on** desde entonces; **until ~** hasta entonces.

theory [ˈθɪərɪ] *n* teoría *f*; **in ~** en teoría.

therapist [ˈθerəpɪst] *n* terapeuta *mf*.

therapy [ˈθerəpɪ] *n* terapia *f*.

there [ðeər] *adv* ahí; (*further away*) allí ◆ *pron*: **~ is** hay; **~ are**

hay; **is Bob ~, please?** *(on phone)* ¿está Bob?; **over ~ por alli; ~ you are** *(when giving)* aquí lo tienes.

thereabouts [ˌðeərəˈbaʊts] *adv*: **or ~** o por ahí.

therefore [ˈðeəfɔːʳ] *adv* por lo tanto.

there's [ðeaz] = **there is**.

thermal   underwear [ˈθɜːml-] *n* ropa *f* interior térmica.

thermometer [θəˈmɒmɪtəʳ] *n* termómetro *m*.

Thermos (flask)® [ˈθɜːməs-] *n* termo *m*.

thermostat [ˈθɜːməstæt] *n* termostato *m*.

these [ðiːz] *pl* → **this**.

they [ðeɪ] *pron* ellos *mpl* (ellas *fpl*); **~'re good** son buenos.

thick [θɪk] *adj* *(in size)* grueso(-sa); *(dense)* espeso(-sa); *(inf: stupid)* necio(-cia); **it's 3 metres ~** tiene 3 metros de grosor.

thicken [ˈθɪkn] *vt* espesar ◆ *vi* espesarse.

thickness [ˈθɪknɪs] *n* espesor *m*.

thief [θiːf] *(pl* **thieves** [θiːvz]) *n* ladrón *m* (-ona *f*).

thigh [θaɪ] *n* muslo *m*.

thimble [ˈθɪmbl] *n* dedal *m*.

thin [θɪn] *adj* *(in size)* fino(-na); *(not fat)* delgado(-da); *(soup, sauce)* claro(-ra).

thing [θɪŋ] *n* cosa *f*; **the ~ is** el caso es que ❑ **things** *npl* *(clothes, possessions)* cosas *fpl*; **how are ~s?** *(inf)* ¿qué tal van las cosas?

thingummyjig [ˈθɪŋəmɪdʒɪg] *n* *(inf)* chisme *m*.

think [θɪŋk] *(pt & pp* **thought**) *vt* *(believe)* creer, pensar; *(have in* mind, expect) pensar ◆ *vi* pensar; **to ~ that** creer que; **to ~ about** *(have in mind)* pensar en; *(consider)* pensar; **to ~ of** *(have in mind, consider)* pensar en; *(invent)* pensar; *(remember)* acordarse de; **to ~ of doing sthg** pensar en hacer algo; **I ~ so** creo que sí; **I don't ~ so** creo que no; **do you ~ you could ...?** ¿cree que podría ...?; **to ~ highly of sb** apreciar mucho a alguien ❑ **think over** *vt sep* pensarse; **think up** *vt sep* idear.

third [θɜːd] *num* *(after noun, as pronoun)* tercero(-ra); *(before noun)* tercer(-ra), → **sixth**.

third party insurance *n* seguro *m* a terceros.

Third World *n*: **the ~** el Tercer Mundo.

thirst [θɜːst] *n* sed *f*.

thirsty [ˈθɜːstɪ] *adj*: **to be ~** tener sed.

thirteen [ˌθɜːˈtiːn] *num* trece, → **six**.

thirteenth [ˌθɜːˈtiːnθ] *num* decimotercero(-ra), → **sixth**.

thirtieth [ˈθɜːtɪəθ] *num* trigésimo(-ma), → **sixth**.

thirty [ˈθɜːtɪ] *num* treinta, → **six**.

this [ðɪs] *(pl* **these**) *adj* **1.** *(referring to thing, person)* este (esta), estos (estas) *(pl)*; **I prefer ~ book** prefiero este libro; **these chocolates are delicious** estos bombones son riquísimos; **~ morning/week** esta mañana/semana; **~ one** éste (ésta).

2. *(inf: when telling a story)*: **~ big dog appeared** apareció un perro grande.

◆ *pron* este *m* (ésta *f*), éstos *mpl*

(éstas *fpl*); *(indefinite)* esto; ~ **is for you** esto es para ti; **what are these?** ¿qué son estas cosas?; ~ **is David Gregory** *(introducing someone)* te presento a David Gregory; *(on telephone)* soy David Gregory.
♦ *adv*: **it was** ~ **big** era así de grande; **I need** ~ **much** necesito un tanto así; **I don't remember it being** ~ **hard** no recordaba que fuera tan difícil.

thistle [ˈθɪsl] *n* cardo *m*.

thorn [θɔːn] *n* espina *f*.

thorough [ˈθʌrə] *adj (check, search)* exhaustivo(-va); *(person)* minucioso(-sa).

thoroughly [ˈθʌrəlɪ] *adv (completely)* completamente.

those [ðəʊz] *pl* →**that**.

though [ðəʊ] *conj* aunque ♦ *adv* sin embargo; **even** ~ aunque.

thought [θɔːt] *pt & pp* →**think** ♦ *n (idea)* idea *f*; **I'll give it some** ~ lo pensaré ❑ **thoughts** *npl (opinion)* opiniones *fpl*.

thoughtful [ˈθɔːtfʊl] *adj (quiet and serious)* pensativo(-va); *(considerate)* considerado(-da).

thoughtless [ˈθɔːtlɪs] *adj* desconsiderado(-da).

thousand [ˈθaʊznd] *num* mil; **a** OR **one** ~ mil; **two** ~ **dos** mil; ~**s of** miles de, →**six**.

thrash [θræʃ] *vt (inf: defeat heavily)* dar una paliza a.

thread [θred] *n (of cotton etc)* hilo *m* ♦ *vt (needle)* enhebrar.

threadbare [ˈθredbeəʳ] *adj* raído(-da).

threat [θret] *n* amenaza *f*.

threaten [ˈθretn] *vt* amenazar;

to ~ **to do sthg** amenazar con hacer algo.

threatening [ˈθretnɪŋ] *adj* amenazador(-ra).

three [θriː] *num* tres, →**six**.

three-D [-ˈdiː] *adj* en tres dimensiones.

three-piece suite [-piːs-] *n* tresillo *m*.

three-quarters [-ˈkwɔːtəz] *n* tres cuartos *mpl*; ~ **of an hour** tres cuartos de hora.

threshold [ˈθreʃhəʊld] *n (fml: of door)* umbral *m*.

threw [θruː] *pt* →**throw**.

thrifty [ˈθrɪftɪ] *adj (person)* ahorrativo(-va).

thrilled [θrɪld] *adj* encantado(-da).

thriller [ˈθrɪləʳ] *n (film)* película *f* de suspense.

thrive [θraɪv] *vi (plant, animal)* crecer mucho; *(person, business, place)* prosperar.

throat [θrəʊt] *n* garganta *f*.

throb [θrɒb] *vi (head, pain)* palpitar; *(noise, engine)* vibrar.

throne [θrəʊn] *n* trono *m*.

throttle [ˈθrɒtl] *n (of motorbike)* válvula *f* reguladora.

through [θruː] *prep (to other side of, by means of)* a través de; *(because of)* a causa de; *(from beginning to end of)* durante; *(across all of)* por todo ♦ *adv (from beginning to end)* hasta el final ♦ *adj*: **to be** ~ **(with sthg)** *(finished)* haber terminado (algo); **you're** ~ *(on phone)* ya puedes hablar; **Monday** ~ **Thursday** *(Am)* de lunes a jueves; **to let sb** ~ dejar pasar a alguien; **to go** ~

(sthg) pasar (por algo); **to soak ~** penetrar; **~ traffic** tráfico *m* de tránsito; **a ~ train** un tren directo; **"no ~ road"** (Br) "carretera cortada".

throughout [θru:'aut] *prep* (day, morning, year) a lo largo de; (place, country, building) por todo ♦ *adv* (all the time) todo el tiempo; (everywhere) por todas partes.

throw [θrəʊ] (*pt* threw, *pp* thrown [θrəʊn]) *n* (of ball, javelin, person) lanzar; (a switch) apretar; **to ~ sthg in the bin** tirar algo a la basura □ **throw away** *vt sep* (get rid of) tirar; **throw out** *vt sep* (get rid of) tirar; (person) echar; **throw up** *vi* (inf: vomit) echar la pastilla.

thru [θru:] (*Am*) = through.

thrush [θrʌʃ] *n* tordo *m*.

thud [θʌd] *n* golpe *m* seco.

thug [θʌg] *n* matón *m*.

thumb [θʌm] *n* pulgar *m* ♦ *vt*: **to ~ a lift** hacer dedo.

thumbtack [ˈθʌmtæk] *n* (Am) chincheta *f*.

thump [θʌmp] *n* puñetazo *m*; (sound) golpe *m* seco ♦ *vt* dar un puñetazo a.

thunder [ˈθʌndəʳ] *n* truenos *mpl*.

thunderstorm [ˈθʌndəstɔ:m] *n* tormenta *f*.

Thurs. (abbr of Thursday) jue.

Thursday [ˈθɜ:zdɪ] *n* jueves *m inv*, → Saturday.

thyme [taɪm] *n* tomillo *m*.

tick [tɪk] *n* (written mark) marca *f* de visto bueno; (insect) garrapata *f* ♦ *vt* marcar (con una señal de visto bueno) ♦ *vi* hacer tictac □

tick off *vt sep* (mark off) marcar (con una señal de visto bueno).

ticket [ˈtɪkɪt] *n* (for travel) billete *m*; (for cinema, theatre, match) entrada *f*; (label) etiqueta *f*; (speeding ticket, parking ticket) multa *f*.

ticket collector *n* revisor *m* (-ra *f*).

ticket inspector *n* revisor *m* (-ra *f*).

ticket machine *n* máquina *f* automática de venta de billetes.

ticket office *n* taquilla *f*, boletería *f* (Amér).

tickle [ˈtɪkl] *vt* (touch) hacer cosquillas a ♦ *vi* hacer cosquillas.

ticklish [ˈtɪklɪʃ] *adj* (person) cosquilloso(-sa).

tick-tack-toe *n* (Am) tres *fpl* en raya.

tide [taɪd] *n* (of sea) marea *f*.

tidy [ˈtaɪdɪ] *adj* (room, desk, person) ordenado(-da); (hair, clothes) arreglado(-da) □ **tidy up** *vt sep* ordenar.

tie [taɪ] (*pt & pp* tied, *cont* tying) *n* (around neck) corbata *f*; (draw) empate *m*; (Am: on railway track) traviesa *f* ♦ *vt* atar; (knot) hacer ♦ *vi* (draw) empatar □ **tie up** *vt sep* atar; (delay) retrasar.

tiepin [ˈtaɪpɪn] *n* alfiler *m* de corbata.

tier [tɪəʳ] *n* (of seats) hilera *f*.

tiger [ˈtaɪgəʳ] *n* tigre *m*.

tight [taɪt] *adj* (difficult to move) apretado(-da); (clothes, shoes) estrecho(-cha); (rope, material) tirante; (bend, turn) cerrado(-da); (schedule) ajustado(-da); (inf: drunk) cocido(-da) ♦ *adv* (hold) con fuerza; **my**

chest feels ~ tengo el pecho cogido.

tighten ['taɪtn] vt apretar.

tightrope ['taɪtrəup] n cuerda f floja.

tights [taɪts] npl medias fpl; **a pair of ~** unas medias.

tile [taɪl] n (for roof) teja f; (for floor) baldosa f; (for wall) azulejo m.

till [tɪl] n caja f registradora ◆ prep hasta ◆ conj hasta que.

tiller ['tɪlə'] n caña f del timón.

tilt [tɪlt] vt inclinar ◆ vi inclinarse.

timber ['tɪmbə'] n (wood) madera f (para construir); (of roof) viga f.

time [taɪm] n tiempo m; (measured by clock) hora f; (moment) momento m; (occasion) vez f; (in history) época f ◆ vt (measure) cronometrar; (arrange) programar; **I haven't got (the) ~** no tengo tiempo; **it's ~ to go** es hora de irse; **what's the ~?** ¿qué hora es?; **do you have the ~?** ¿tiene hora?; **two ~s two** dos por dos; **five ~s as much** cinco veces más; **in a month's ~** dentro de un mes; **to have a good ~** pasárselo bien; **all the ~** todo el tiempo; **every ~** cada vez; **from ~ to ~** de vez en cuando; **for the being** de momento; **in ~** (arrive) a tiempo; **in good ~** con tiempo de sobra; **last ~** la última vez; **most of the ~** la mayor parte del tiempo; **on ~** puntualmente; **some of the ~** parte del tiempo; **this ~** esta vez; **two at a ~** de dos en dos.

time difference n diferencia f horaria.

time limit n plazo m.

timer ['taɪmə'] n temporizador m.

time share n copropiedad f.

timetable ['taɪm,teɪbl] n horario m; (of events) programa m.

time zone n huso m horario.

timid ['tɪmɪd] adj tímido(-da).

tin [tɪn] n (metal) estaño m; (container) lata f ◆ adj de hojalata.

tinfoil ['tɪnfɔɪl] n papel m de aluminio.

tinned food [tɪnd-] n (Br) conservas fpl.

tin opener [-,əupnə'] n (Br) abrelatas m inv.

tinsel ['tɪnsl] n oropel m.

tint [tɪnt] n tinte m.

tinted glass [,tɪntɪd-] n cristal m ahumado.

tiny ['taɪnɪ] adj diminuto(-ta).

tip [tɪp] n (point, end) punta f; (to waiter, taxi driver etc) propina f; (piece of advice) consejo m; (rubbish dump) vertedero m ◆ vt (waiter, taxi driver etc) dar una propina; (tilt) inclinar; (pour) vaciar ❑ **tip over** vt sep volcar ◆ vi volcarse.

tire ['taɪə'] vi cansarse ◆ n (Am) = tyre.

tired ['taɪəd] adj (sleepy) cansado(-da); **to be ~ of** estar cansado de.

tired out adj agotado(-da).

tiring ['taɪərɪŋ] adj cansado(-da).

tissue ['tɪʃuː] n (handkerchief) pañuelo m de papel.

tissue paper n papel m de seda.

tit [tɪt] n (vulg: breast) teta f.

title ['taɪtl] n título m; (Dr, Mr, Lord etc) tratamiento m.

T-junction ['tiː-] n cruce m (en

forma de T).

to [unstressed before consonant tə, unstressed before vowel tʊ, stressed tuː] prep **1.** (indicating direction, position) a; **to go ~ France** ir a Francia; **to go ~ school** ir a la escuela; **the road ~ Leeds** la carretera de Leeds; **~ the left/right** a la izquierda/derecha.

2. (expressing indirect object) a; **to give sthg ~ sb** dar algo a alguien; **give it ~ me** dámelo; **to listen ~ the radio** escuchar la radio.

3. (indicating reaction, effect): **~ my surprise** para sorpresa mía; **it's ~ your advantage** va en beneficio tuyo.

4. (until) hasta; **to count ~ ten** contar hasta diez; **we work from 9 ~ 5** trabajamos de 9 a 5.

5. (in stating opinion): **~ me, he's lying** para mí que miente.

6. (indicating change of state): **it could lead ~ trouble** puede ocasionar problemas.

7. (Br: in expressions of time) menos; **it's ten ~ three** son las tres menos diez.

8. (in ratios, rates) por; **40 miles ~ the gallon** un galón por cada 40 millas.

9. (of, for): **the key ~ the car** la llave del coche; **a letter ~ my daughter** una carta a mi hija.

10. (indicating attitude) con; **to be rude ~ sb** tratar a alguien con grosería.

◆ with infinitive **1.** (forming simple infinitive): **~ walk** andar.

2. (following another verb): **to begin ~ do sthg** empezar a hacer algo; **to try ~ do sthg** intentar hacer algo.

3. (following an adjective) de; difficult ~ **do** difícil de hacer; **ready ~ go** listo para marchar.

4. (indicating purpose) para; **we came here ~ look at the castle** vinimos a ver el castillo; **I'm phoning ~ ask you something** te llamo para preguntarte algo.

toad [təʊd] n sapo m.

toadstool [ˈtəʊdstuːl] n seta f venenosa.

toast [təʊst] n (bread) pan m tostado; (when drinking) brindis m inv ◆ vt (bread) tostar; **a piece** OR **slice of ~** una tostada.

toasted sandwich [ˈtəʊstɪd-] n sandwich m (a la plancha).

toaster [ˈtəʊstəʳ] n tostador m.

toastie [ˈtəʊstɪ] (inf) = **toasted sandwich.**

tobacco [təˈbækəʊ] n tabaco m.

tobacconist's [təˈbækənɪsts] n (shop) estanco m.

toboggan [təˈbɒgən] n tobogán m (de deporte).

today [təˈdeɪ] n hoy m ◆ adv hoy.

toddler [ˈtɒdləʳ] n niño m pequeño (niña f pequeña).

toe [təʊ] n (of person) dedo m del pie.

toe clip n calzapiés m inv.

toenail [ˈtəʊneɪl] n uña f del dedo del pie.

toffee [ˈtɒfɪ] n tofe m.

together [təˈgeðəʳ] adv juntos(-tas); **~ with** junto con.

toilet [ˈtɔɪlɪt] n (room: in public place) servicios mpl; (at home) wáter m; (bowl) retrete m; **to go to the ~** ir al wáter; **where's the ~?** ¿dónde está el servicio?

toilet bag n neceser m.

toilet paper n papel m higiénico.

toiletries ['tɔɪlɪtrɪz] npl artículos mpl de tocador.

toilet roll n (paper) papel m higiénico.

toilet water n agua f de colonia.

token ['təʊkn] n (metal disc) ficha f.

told [təʊld] pt & pp → **tell**.

tolerable ['tɒlərəbl] adj tolerable.

tolerant ['tɒlərənt] adj tolerante.

tolerate ['tɒləreɪt] vt tolerar.

toll [təʊl] n (for road, bridge) peaje m.

tollbooth ['təʊlbuːθ] n cabina f de peaje.

toll-free adj (Am) gratuito(-ta).

tomato [Br təˈmɑːtəʊ, Am təˈmeɪtəʊ] (pl -es) n tomate m.

tomato juice n zumo m de tomate.

tomato ketchup n ketchup m.

tomato puree n puré m de tomate concentrado.

tomato sauce n ketchup m.

tomb [tuːm] n tumba f.

tomorrow [təˈmɒrəʊ] n mañana f ◆ adv mañana; **the day after ~** pasado mañana; **~ afternoon** mañana por la tarde; **~ morning** mañana por la mañana; **~ night** mañana por la noche.

ton [tʌn] n (in Britain) = 1016 kilos; (in U.S.) = 907 kilos; (metric tonne) tonelada f; **~s of** (inf) un montón de.

top [top]

tone [təʊn] n tono m; (on phone) señal f.

tongs [tɒŋz] npl (for hair) tenazas fpl; (for sugar) pinzas fpl.

tongue [tʌŋ] n lengua f.

tonic ['tɒnɪk] n (tonic water) tónica f; (medicine) tónico m.

tonic water n agua f tónica.

tonight [təˈnaɪt] n esta noche f ◆ adv esta noche.

tonne [tʌn] n tonelada f (métrica).

tonsillitis [ˌtɒnsɪˈlaɪtɪs] n amigdalitis f inv.

too [tuː] adv (excessively) demasiado; (also) también; **it's not ~ good** no está muy bien; **it's ~ late to go out** es demasiado tarde para salir; **~ many** demasiados(-das); **~ much** demasiado(-da).

took [tʊk] pt → **take**.

tool [tuːl] n herramienta f.

tool kit n juego m de herramientas.

tooth [tuːθ] (pl teeth) n diente m.

toothache ['tuːθeɪk] n dolor m de muelas.

toothbrush ['tuːθbrʌʃ] n cepillo m de dientes.

toothpaste ['tuːθpeɪst] n pasta f de dientes.

toothpick ['tuːθpɪk] n palillo m.

top [top] adj (highest) de arriba; (best, most important) mejor ◆ n (highest part) parte f superior; (best point) cabeza f; (of box, jar) tapa f; (of bottle, tube) tapón m; (of pen) capuchón m; (garment) camiseta f; (of street, road) final m; **at the ~ (of)** (stairway, pile) en lo más alto (de);

(list, page) al principio (de); **on ~ of** *(on highest part of)* en lo alto de; *(in hill, mountain)* en lo alto de; *(in addition to)* además de; **at ~ speed** a toda velocidad; **~ gear** directa f ❑ **top up** vt sep *(glass, drink)* volver a llenar ♦ vi *(with petrol)* repostar.

top floor n último piso m.

topic ['tɒpɪk] n tema m.

topical ['tɒpɪkl] adj actual.

topless ['tɒplɪs] adj topless *(inv)*.

topped ['tɒpt] adj: **~ with** cubierto(-ta) con.

topping ['tɒpɪŋ] n: **with a ~ of** cubierto con; **the ~ of your choice** los ingredientes que Vd. elija.

torch [tɔːtʃ] n *(Br: electric light)* linterna f.

tore [tɔː] pt → tear.

torment [tɔː'ment] vt *(annoy)* fastidiar.

torn [tɔːn] pp → tear ♦ adj *(ripped)* desgarrado(-da).

tornado [tɔː'neɪdəʊ] *(pl* **-es** OR **-s)** n tornado m.

torrential rain [tə,renʃl-] n lluvia f torrencial.

tortoise ['tɔːtəs] n tortuga f *(de tierra)*.

tortoiseshell ['tɔːtəʃel] n carey m.

torture ['tɔːtʃə'] n tortura f ♦ vt torturar.

Tory ['tɔːrɪ] n conservador m (-ra f).

toss [tɒs] vt *(throw)* tirar; *(salad)* mezclar; **to ~ a coin** echar a cara o cruz; **~ed in butter** con mantequilla.

total ['təʊtl] adj total ♦ n total m; **in ~** en total.

touch [tʌtʃ] n *(sense)* tacto m; *(small amount)* pizca f; *(detail)* toque m ♦ vt tocar; *(move emotionally)* conmover ♦ vi tocarse; **to get in ~ (with sb)** ponerse en contacto (con alguien); **to keep in ~ (with sb)** mantenerse en contacto (con alguien) ❑ **touch down** vi aterrizar.

touching ['tʌtʃɪŋ] adj *(moving)* conmovedor(-ra).

tough [tʌf] adj *(resilient)* fuerte; *(hard, strong)* resistente; *(meat, regulations, policies)* duro(-ra); *(difficult)* difícil.

tour [tʊə'] n *(journey)* viaje m; *(of city, castle etc)* recorrido m; *(of pop group, theatre company)* gira f ♦ vt recorrer; **on ~** en gira.

tourism ['tʊərɪzm] n turismo m.

tourist ['tʊərɪst] n turista mf.

tourist class n clase f turista.

tourist information office n oficina f de turismo.

tournament ['tɔːnəmənt] n torneo m.

tour operator n touroperador m (-ra f).

tout [taʊt] n revendedor m (-ra f).

tow [təʊ] vt remolcar.

toward [tə'wɔːd] *(Am)* = towards.

towards [tə'wɔːdz] prep *(Br)* hacia; *(to help pay for)* para.

towaway zone ['təʊəweɪ-] n *(Am)* zona en la que está prohibido estacionar y los vehículos son retirados por la grúa.

towel ['taʊəl] n toalla f.

toweling ['taʊəlɪŋ] *(Am)* = towelling.

towelling ['tauəlıŋ] n (Br) toalla f (tejido).

towel rail n toallero m.

tower ['tauə'] n torre f.

tower block n (Br) bloque m alto de pisos.

Tower Bridge n puente londinense.

 TOWER BRIDGE

Construido en el siglo XIX, este puente neogótico extiende sobre el Támesis sus características ramas gemelas que se izan para permitir el paso de los barcos de mayor altura.

Tower of London n: the ~ la Torre de Londres.

 TOWER OF LONDON

Situada al norte del Támesis, la Torre de Londres es una fortaleza construida en el siglo XI que fue utilizada como residencia real hasta el siglo XVII. Hoy en día, la Torre y el museo que alberga son una popular atracción turística.

town [taun] n (smaller) pueblo m; (larger) ciudad f; (town centre) centro m.

town centre n centro m.

town hall n ayuntamiento m.

towpath ['taupa:θ, pl -pa:ðz] n camino m de sirga.

towrope ['taurəup] n cuerda f de remolque.

tow truck n (Am) grúa f.

toxic ['tɒksɪk] adj tóxico(-ca).

toy [tɔɪ] n juguete m.

toy shop n juguetería f.

trace [treɪs] n (sign) rastro m; (small amount) pizca f ♦ vt (find) localizar.

tracing paper ['treɪsɪŋ-] n papel m de calco.

track [træk] n (path) sendero m; (of railway) vía f; (SPORT) pista f; (song) canción f ❑ **track down** vt sep localizar.

tracksuit ['træksu:t] n chándal m.

tractor ['træktə'] n tractor m.

trade [treɪd] n (COMM) comercio m; (job) oficio m ♦ vt cambiar ♦ vi comerciar.

trade-in n artículo viejo que se da como entrada al comprar uno nuevo.

trademark ['treɪdma:k] n marca f (comercial).

trader ['treɪdə'] n comerciante mf.

tradesman ['treɪdzmən] (pl -men [-mən]) n (deliveryman) repartidor m; (shopkeeper) tendero m.

trade union n sindicato m.

tradition [trə'dɪʃn] n tradición f.

traditional [trə'dɪʃənl] adj dicional.

traffic ['træfɪk] (pt & pp -ked) n tráfico m ♦ vi: to ~ in traficar con.

traffic circle n (Am) raqueta f.

traffic island n isla f de peatones.

traffic jam n atasco m.

traffic lights npl semáforos mpl.

traffic warden n (Br) = guardia mf de tráfico.

tragedy ['trædʒədɪ] n tragedia f.

tragic ['trædʒɪk] adj trágico(-ca).

trail [treɪl] n (path) sendero m; (marks) rastro m ◆ vi (be losing) ir perdiendo.

trailer ['treɪləʳ] n (for boat, luggage) remolque m; (Am: caravan) caravana f; (for film, programme) trailer m.

train [treɪn] n tren m ◆ vt (teach) enseñar ◆ vi (SPORT) entrenar; **by ~** en tren.

train driver n maquinista mf (de tren).

trainee [treɪ'niː] n aprendiz m (-za f).

trainer ['treɪnəʳ] n (of athlete etc) entrenador m (-ra f) ❑ **trainers** npl (Br) zapatillas fpl de deporte.

training ['treɪnɪŋ] n (instruction) formación f; (exercises) entrenamiento m.

training shoes npl (Br) zapatillas fpl de deporte.

tram [træm] n (Br) tranvía m.

tramp [træmp] n vagabundo m (-da f).

trampoline ['træmpəliːn] n cama f elástica.

trance [trɑːns] n trance m.

tranquilizer ['træŋkwɪlaɪzəʳ] (Am) = **tranquillizer**.

tranquillizer ['træŋkwɪlaɪzəʳ] n (Br) tranquilizante m.

transaction [træn'zækʃn] n transacción f.

transatlantic [,trænzət'læntɪk] adj transatlántico(-ca).

transfer [n 'trænsfɜːʳ, vb træns-

'fɜːʳ] n (of money, power) transferencia f; (of sportsman) traspaso m; (picture) calcomanía f; (Am: ticket) clase de billete que permite hacer transbordos durante un viaje ◆ vt transferir ◆ vi (change bus, plane etc) hacer transbordo; **"~s"** (in airport) "transbordos".

transfer desk n mostrador m de tránsito.

transform [træns'fɔːm] vt transformar.

transfusion [træns'fjuːʒn] n transfusión f.

transistor radio [træn'zɪstəʳ-] n transistor m.

transit ['trænzɪt]: **in transit** adv de tránsito.

transitive ['trænzɪtɪv] adj transitivo(-va).

transit lounge n sala f de tránsito.

translate [træns'leɪt] vt traducir.

translation [træns'leɪʃn] n traducción f.

translator [træns'leɪtəʳ] n traductor m (-ra f).

transmission [trænz'mɪʃn] n transmisión f.

transmit [trænz'mɪt] vt transmitir.

transparent [træns'pærənt] adj transparente.

transplant ['trænsplɑːnt] n trasplante m.

transport [n 'trænspɔːt, vb træns'pɔːt] n transporte m ◆ vt transportar.

transportation [,trænspɔː'teɪʃn] n (Am) transporte m.

trap [træp] n trampa f ◆ vt: **to be**

trapped estar atrapado.

trapdoor ['træp,dɔ:] n trampilla f.

trash [træʃ] n (Am) basura f.

trashcan ['træʃkæn] n (Am) cubo m de la basura.

trauma ['trɔ:mə] n trauma m.

traumatic [trɔ:'mætɪk] adj traumático(-ca).

travel ['trævl] n viajes mpl ◆ vt (distance) recorrer ◆ vi viajar.

travel agency n agencia f de viajes.

travel agent n empleado m (-da f) m de una agencia de viajes; ~'s (shop) agencia f de viajes.

Travelcard ['trævlkɑ:d] n billete, normalmente de un día, para el metro, tren y autobús de Londres.

travel centre n oficina f de información al viajero.

traveler ['trævlər] (Am) = traveller.

travel insurance n seguro m de viaje.

traveller ['trævlər] n (Br) viajero m (-ra f).

traveller's cheque ['trævləz-] n cheque m de viaje.

travelsick ['trævlsɪk] adj mareado(-da) por el viaje.

trawler ['trɔ:lər] n trainera f.

tray [treɪ] n bandeja f.

treacherous ['tretʃərəs] adj (person) traidor(-ra); (roads, conditions) peligroso(-sa).

treacle ['tri:kl] n (Br) melaza f.

tread [tred] (pt trod, pp trodden) n (of tyre) banda f ◆ vi: to ~ on sthg pisar algo.

treasure ['treʒər] n tesoro m.

treat [tri:t] vt tratar ◆ n: he bought me a meal for a ~ me invitó a cenar; to ~ sb to sthg invitar a alguien a algo.

treatment ['tri:tmənt] n (MED) tratamiento m; (of person, subject) trato m.

treble ['trebl] adj triple.

tree [tri:] n árbol m.

trek [trek] n viaje m largo y difícil.

tremble ['trembl] vi temblar.

tremendous [trɪ'mendəs] adj (very large) enorme; (inf: very good) estupendo(-da).

trench [trentʃ] n zanja f.

trend [trend] n (tendency) tendencia f; (fashion) moda f.

trendy ['trendɪ] adj (inf) (person) moderno(-na); (clothes, bar) de moda.

trespasser ['trespəsər] n intruso m (-sa f); "~s will be prosecuted" "los intrusos serán sancionados por la ley".

trial ['traɪəl] n (JUR) juicio m; (test) prueba f; a ~ period un periodo de prueba.

triangle ['traɪæŋgl] n triángulo m.

triangular [traɪ'æŋgjulər] adj triangular.

tribe [traɪb] n tribu f.

tributary ['trɪbjutrɪ] n afluente m.

trick [trɪk] n (deception) truco m; (in magic) juego m (de manos) ◆ vt engañar; to play a ~ on sb gastarle una broma a alguien.

trickle ['trɪkl] vi resbalar (formando un hilo).

tricky ['trɪkɪ] *adj* difícil.

tricycle ['traɪsɪkl] *n* triciclo *m*.

trifle ['traɪfl] *n* (*dessert*) postre de bizcocho con frutas, nata, natillas y gelatina.

trigger ['trɪgə'] *n* gatillo *m*.

trim [trɪm] *n* (*haircut*) recorte *m* ♦ *vt* recortar.

trinket ['trɪŋkɪt] *n* baratija *f*.

trio ['triːəʊ] (*pl* **-s**) *n* trío *m*.

trip [trɪp] *n* viaje *m* ♦ *vi* tropezar ❑ **trip up** *vi* tropezar.

triple ['trɪpl] *adj* triple.

tripod ['traɪpɒd] *n* trípode *m*.

triumph ['traɪəmf] *n* triunfo *m*.

trivial ['trɪvɪəl] *adj* (*pej*) trivial.

trod [trɒd] *pt* → **tread**.

trodden ['trɒdn] *pp* → **tread**.

trolley ['trɒlɪ] (*pl* **-s**) *n* (*Br*: in supermarket, at airport, for food etc) carrito *m*; (*Am*: tram) tranvía *m*.

trombone [trɒm'bəʊn] *n* trombón *m*.

troops [truːps] *npl* tropas *fpl*.

trophy ['trəʊfɪ] *n* trofeo *m*.

tropical ['trɒpɪkl] *adj* tropical.

trot [trɒt] *vi* trotar ♦ *n*: **three on the ~** (*inf*) tres seguidos.

trouble ['trʌbl] *n* (*difficulty, problems, malfunction*) problemas *mpl*; (*pain*) dolor *m*; (*illness*) enfermedad *f* ♦ *vt* (*worry*) preocupar; (*bother*) molestar; **to be in ~** tener problemas; **to get into ~** meterse en líos; **to take the ~ to do sthg** tomarse la molestia de hacer algo; **it's no ~** no es molestia.

trough [trɒf] *n* (*for drinking*) abrevadero *m*.

trouser press ['traʊzə'-] *n* prensa *f* para pantalones.

trousers ['traʊzəz] *npl* pantalones *mpl*; **a pair of ~** un pantalón.

trout [traʊt] (*pl inv*) *n* trucha *f*.

trowel ['traʊəl] *n* (*for gardening*) desplantador *m*.

truant ['truːənt] *n*: **to play ~** hacer novillos.

truce [truːs] *n* tregua *f*.

truck [trʌk] *n* camión *m*.

true [truː] *adj* verdadero(-ra); (*genuine, sincere*) auténtico(-ca); **it's ~** es verdad.

truly ['truːlɪ] *adv*: **yours ~** le saluda atentamente.

trumpet ['trʌmpɪt] *n* trompeta *f*.

trumps [trʌmps] *npl* triunfo *m*.

truncheon ['trʌntʃən] *n* porra *f*.

trunk [trʌŋk] *n* (*of tree*) tronco *m*; (*Am*: of car) maletero *m*; (*case, box*) baúl *m*; (*of elephant*) trompa *f*.

trunk call *n* (*Br*) llamada *f* interurbana.

trunk road *n* (*Br*) = carretera *f* nacional.

trunks [trʌŋks] *npl* bañador *m* (*de hombre*).

trust [trʌst] *n* (*confidence*) confianza *f* ♦ *vt* (*believe, have confidence in*) confiar en; (*fml: hope*) confiar.

trustworthy ['trʌst,wɜːðɪ] *adj* digno(-na) de confianza.

truth [truːθ] *n* (*true facts*) verdad *f*; (*quality of being true*) veracidad *f*.

truthful ['truːθfʊl] *adj* (*statement, account*) verídico(-ca); (*person*) sincero(-ra).

try [traɪ] *n* (*attempt*) intento *m* ♦ *vt* (*attempt*) intentar; (*experiment with, test*) probar; (*seek help from*) acudir a; (*JUR*) procesar ♦ *vi* intentar; **to try to do sthg** intentar hacer algo ❑

try on *vt sep* probarse; **try out** *vt sep* poner a prueba.

T-shirt ['ti:-] *n* camiseta *f*.

tub [tʌb] *n* (of margarine etc) tarrina *f*; (inf: bath) bañera *f*.

tube [tju:b] *n* tubo *m*; (Br: inf: underground) metro *m*; **by ~** en metro.

tube station *n* (Br: inf) estación *f* de metro.

tuck [tʌk]: **tuck in** *vt sep* (shirt) meterse; (child, person) arropar ◆ *vi* (inf) comer con apetito.

tuck shop *n* (Br) confitería *f* (en un colegio).

Tudor ['tju:dər] *adj* (architecture) Tudor.

Tues. (abbr of Tuesday) mar.

Tuesday ['tju:zdɪ] *n* martes *m inv*, → **Saturday**.

tuft [tʌft] *n* (of grass) matojo *m*; (of hair) mechón *m*.

tug [tʌg] *vt* tirar de.

tuition [tju:'ɪʃn] *n* clases *fpl*.

tulip ['tju:lɪp] *n* tulipán *m*.

tumble-dryer ['tʌmbldraɪər] *n* secadora *f*.

tumbler ['tʌmblər] *n* (glass) vaso *m*.

tummy ['tʌmɪ] *n* (inf) barriga *f*.

tummy upset ['-ʌpset] *n* (inf) dolor *m* de barriga.

tumor ['tu:mər] (Am) = **tumour**.

tumour ['tju:mər] *n* (Br) tumor *m*.

tuna (fish) [Br 'tju:nə, Am 'tu:nə] *n* atún *m*.

tuna melt *n* (Am) tostada con atún y queso suizo fundido.

tune [tju:n] *n* melodía *f* ◆ *vt* (radio, TV) sintonizar; (engine) poner a punto; (instrument) afinar;

in ~ afinado; **out of ~** desafinado.

tunic ['tju:nɪk] *n* túnica *f*.

Tunisia [tju:'nɪzɪə] *n* Túnez.

tunnel ['tʌnl] *n* túnel *m*.

turban ['tɜ:bən] *n* turbante *m*.

turbo ['tɜ:bəʊ] (pl -s) *n* (car) turbo *m*.

turbulence ['tɜ:bjʊləns] *n* turbulencia *f*.

turf [tɜ:f] *n* (grass) césped *m*.

Turk [tɜ:k] *n* turco *m* (-ca *f*).

turkey ['tɜ:kɪ] (pl -s) *n* pavo *m*.

Turkey ['tɜ:kɪ] *n* Turquía.

Turkish ['tɜ:kɪʃ] *adj* turco(-ca) ◆ *n* (language) turco *m* ◆ *npl*: **the ~** los turcos.

Turkish delight *n* rahat lokum *m*, dulce gelatinoso cubierto de azúcar glas.

turn [tɜ:n] *n* (in road) curva *f*; (of knob, key, switch) vuelta *f*; (go, chance) turno *m* ◆ *vt* (car, page, omelette) dar la vuelta a; (head) volver; (knob, key, switch) girar; (corner, bend) doblar; (become) volverse; (cause to become) poner ◆ *vi* girar; (milk) cortarse; **to ~ into** convertirse en algo; **to ~ sthg into sthg** transformar algo en algo; **to ~ left/right** torcer a la derecha (a ti); **at the ~ of the century** a finales de siglo; **to take it in ~s** to do sthg hacer algo por turnos; **to ~ sthg inside out** darle la vuelta a algo (de dentro para afuera) ❑ **turn back** *vt sep* hacer volver ◆ *vi* volver; **turn down** *vt sep* (radio, volume, heating) bajar; (offer, request) rechazar; **turn off** *vt sep* (light, TV) apagar; (water, gas, tap) cerrar; (engine) parar ◆ *vi* (leave road) salir;

turn on vt sep (light, TV, engine) encender; (water, gas, tap) abrir; **turn out** vt fus (be in the end) resultar ◆ vt sep (light, fire) apagar ◆ vi (come, attend) venir; **to ~ out to be sthg** resultar ser algo; **turn over** vi (in bed) darse la vuelta; (Br: change channels) cambiar ◆ vt sep (page, card, omelette) dar la vuelta a; **turn round** vt sep dar la vuelta a ◆ vi (person) darse la vuelta; **turn up** vt sep (radio, volume, heating) subir ◆ vi aparecer.

turning ['tɜːnɪŋ] n bocacalle f.

turnip ['tɜːnɪp] n nabo m.

turn-up n (Br: on trousers) vuelta f.

turps [tɜːps] n (Br: inf) trementina f.

turquoise ['tɜːkwɔɪz] adj turquesa (inv).

turtle ['tɜːtl] n tortuga f (marina).

turtleneck ['tɜːtlnek] n jersey m de cuello de cisne.

tutor ['tjuːtər] n (private teacher) tutor m (-ra f).

tuxedo [tʌkˈsiːdəʊ] (pl -s) n (Am) esmoquin m.

TV n televisión f; **on ~** en la televisión.

tweed [twiːd] n tweed m.

tweezers ['twiːzəz] npl pinzas fpl.

twelfth [twelfθ] num duodécimo(-ma), → sixth.

twelve [twelv] num doce, → six.

twentieth ['twentɪəθ] num vigésimo(-ma); **the ~ century** el siglo XX, → sixth.

twenty ['twentɪ] num veinte, → six.

twice [twaɪs] adj & adv dos veces; **it's ~ as good** es el doble de bueno; **~ as much** el doble.

twig [twɪg] n ramita f.

twilight ['twaɪlaɪt] n crepúsculo m.

twin [twɪn] n gemelo m (-la f).

twin beds npl dos camas fpl.

twine [twaɪn] n bramante m.

twin room n habitación f con dos camas.

twist [twɪst] vt (wire) torcer; (thread, rope) retorcer; (hair) enroscar; (bottle top, lid, knob) girar; **to ~ one's ankle** torcerse el tobillo.

twisting ['twɪstɪŋ] adj con muchos recodos.

two [tuː] num dos, → six.

two-piece adj de dos piezas.

tying ['taɪɪŋ] cont → tie.

type [taɪp] n (kind) tipo m ◆ vt teclear ◆ vi escribir a máquina.

typewriter ['taɪpˌraɪtər] n máquina f de escribir.

typhoid ['taɪfɔɪd] n fiebre f tifoidea.

typical ['tɪpɪkl] adj típico(-ca).

typist ['taɪpɪst] n mecanógrafo m (-fa f).

tyre ['taɪər] n (Br) neumático m.

U

U [juː] adj (Br: film) para todos los públicos.

UFO n (abbr of unidentified flying

object) OVNI *m*.

ugly ['ʌglɪ] *adj* feo(-a).

UHT *adj (abbr of ultra heat treated)* uperizado(-da).

UK *n*: the ~ el Reino Unido.

ulcer ['ʌlsər] *n* úlcera *f*.

ultimate ['ʌltɪmət] *adj (final)* final; *(best, greatest)* máximo (-ma).

ultraviolet [ˌʌltrə'vaɪələt] *adj* ultravioleta.

umbrella [ʌm'brelə] *n* paraguas *m inv*.

umpire ['ʌmpaɪər] *n* árbitro *m*.

UN *n (abbr of United Nations)*: the ~ la ONU.

unable [ʌn'eɪbl] *adj*: to be ~ to do sthg ser incapaz de hacer algo.

unacceptable [ˌʌnək'septəbl] *adj* inaceptable.

unaccustomed [ˌʌnə'kʌstəmd] *adj*: to be ~ to sthg no estar acostumbrado(-da) a algo.

unanimous [juː'nænɪməs] *adj* unánime.

unattended [ˌʌnə'tendɪd] *adj* desatendido(-da).

unattractive [ˌʌnə'træktɪv] *adj* poco atractivo(-va).

unauthorized [ʌn'ɔːθəraɪzd] *adj* no autorizado(-da).

unavailable [ˌʌnə'veɪləbl] *adj* no disponible.

unavoidable [ˌʌnə'vɔɪdəbl] *adj* inevitable.

unaware [ˌʌnə'weər] *adj* inconsciente; to be ~ of sthg no ser consciente de algo.

unbearable [ʌn'beərəbl] *adj* insoportable.

unbelievable [ˌʌnbɪ'liːvəbl] *adj* increíble.

unbutton [ˌʌn'bʌtn] *vt* desabrocharse.

uncertain [ʌn'sɜːtn] *adj (not definite)* incierto(-ta); *(not sure)* indeciso(-sa).

uncertainty [ʌn'sɜːtntɪ] *n* incertidumbre *f*.

uncle ['ʌŋkl] *n* tío *m*.

unclean [ʌn'kliːn] *adj* sucio (-cia).

unclear [ˌʌn'klɪər] *adj* poco claro (-ra); *(not sure)* poco seguro(-ra).

uncomfortable [ˌʌn'kʌmftəbl] *adj* incómodo(-da).

uncommon [ʌn'kɒmən] *adj* poco común.

unconscious [ʌn'kɒnʃəs] *adj*: to be ~ *(after accident)* estar inconsciente; *(unaware)* ser inconsciente.

unconvincing [ˌʌnkən'vɪnsɪŋ] *adj* poco convincente.

uncooperative [ˌʌnkəʊ'ɒpərətɪv] *adj* que no quiere cooperar.

uncork [ˌʌn'kɔːk] *vt* descorchar.

uncouth [ʌn'kuːθ] *adj* grosero(-ra).

uncover [ʌn'kʌvər] *vt (discover)* descubrir; *(swimming pool)* dejar al descubierto; *(car)* descapotar.

under ['ʌndər] *prep (beneath)* debajo de; *(less than)* menos de; *(according to)* según; *(in classification)* en; ~ the water bajo el agua; children ~ ten niños menores de diez años; ~ the circumstances dadas las circunstancias; to be ~ pressure *(from a person)* estar presionado; *(stressed)* estar en tensión.

underage [ˌʌndərˈeɪdʒ] adj menor de edad.

undercarriage [ˈʌndəˌkærɪdʒ] n tren m de aterrizaje.

underdone [ˌʌndəˈdʌn] adj poco hecho(-cha).

underestimate [ˌʌndərˈestɪmeɪt] vt subestimar.

underexposed [ˌʌndərɪkˈspəʊzd] adj (photograph) subexpuesto(-ta).

undergo [ˌʌndəˈgəʊ] (pt -went, pp -gone [-ˈgɒn]) vt (change, difficulties) sufrir; (operation) someterse a.

undergraduate [ˌʌndəˈɡrædjuət] n estudiante m universitario (no licenciado) (estudiante f universitaria (no licenciada)).

underground [ˈʌndəɡraʊnd] adj (below earth's surface) subterráneo(-a); (secret) clandestino(-na) ♦ n (Br: railway) metro m.

undergrowth [ˈʌndəɡrəʊθ] n maleza f.

underline [ˌʌndəˈlaɪn] vt subrayar.

underneath [ˌʌndəˈniːθ] prep debajo de ♦ adv debajo ♦ n superficie f inferior.

underpants [ˈʌndəpænts] npl calzoncillos mpl.

underpass [ˈʌndəpɑːs] n paso m subterráneo.

undershirt [ˈʌndəʃɜːt] n (Am) camiseta f.

underskirt [ˈʌndəskɜːt] n enaguas fpl.

understand [ˌʌndəˈstænd] (pt & pp -stood) vt entender; (believe) tener entendido que ♦ vi entender; **I don't ~** no entiendo; **to**

make o.s. understood hacerse entender.

understanding [ˌʌndəˈstændɪŋ] adj comprensivo(-va) ♦ n (agreement) acuerdo m; (knowledge) entendimiento m; (interpretation) impresión f; (sympathy) comprensión f mutua.

understatement [ˌʌndəˈsteɪtmənt] n: that's an ~ eso es quedarse corto.

understood [ˌʌndəˈstʊd] pt & pp → understand.

undertake [ˌʌndəˈteɪk] (pt -took, pp -taken [-ˈteɪkn]) vt emprender; **to ~ to do sthg** comprometerse a hacer algo.

undertaker [ˈʌndəˌteɪkər] n director m (-ra f) de funeraria.

undertaking [ˌʌndəˈteɪkɪŋ] n (promise) promesa f; (task) empresa f.

undertook [ˌʌndəˈtʊk] pt → undertake.

underwater [ˌʌndəˈwɔːtər] adj submarino(-na) ♦ adv bajo el agua.

underwear [ˈʌndəweər] n ropa f interior.

underwent [ˌʌndəˈwent] pt → undergo.

undesirable [ˌʌndɪˈzaɪərəbl] adj indeseable.

undo [ˌʌnˈduː] (pt -did [-ˈdɪd], pp -done) vt (coat, shirt) desabrochar; (tie, shoelaces) desatarse; (parcel) abrir.

undone [ˌʌnˈdʌn] adj (coat, shirt) desabrochado(-da); (tie, shoelaces) desatado(-da).

undress [ˌʌnˈdres] vi desnudarse ♦ vt desnudar.

undressed [ʌnˈdrest] *adj* desnudo(-da); **to get ~** desnudarse.

uneasy [ʌnˈiːzɪ] *adj* intranquilo(-la).

uneducated [ʌnˈedjukeɪtɪd] *adj* inculto(-ta).

unemployed [ʌnɪmˈplɔɪd] *adj* desempleado(-da) ♦ *npl*: **the ~** los parados.

unemployment [ʌnɪmˈplɔɪmənt] *n* paro *m*.

unemployment benefit *n* subsidio *m* de desempleo.

unequal [ʌnˈiːkwəl] *adj* desigual.

uneven [ʌnˈiːvn] *adj* desigual; *(road)* lleno(-na) de baches.

uneventful [ʌnɪˈventful] *adj* sin incidentes destacables.

unexpected [ʌnɪkˈspektɪd] *adj* inesperado(-da).

unexpectedly [ʌnɪkˈspektɪdlɪ] *adv* inesperadamente.

unfair [ʌnˈfeəʳ] *adj* injusto(-ta).

unfairly [ʌnˈfeəlɪ] *adv* injustamente.

unfaithful [ʌnˈfeɪθful] *adj* infiel.

unfamiliar [ʌnfəˈmɪljəʳ] *adj* desconocido(-da); **to be ~ with** no estar familiarizado(-da) con.

unfashionable [ʌnˈfæʃnəbl] *adj* pasado(-da) de moda.

unfasten [ʌnˈfɑːsn] *vt* *(button, belt)* desabrochar(se); *(tie, knot)* desatarse.

unfavourable [ʌnˈfeɪvrəbl] *adj* desfavorable.

unfinished [ʌnˈfɪnɪʃt] *adj* incompleto(-ta).

unfit [ʌnˈfɪt] *adj*: **to be ~** *(not healthy)* no estar en forma; **to be ~ for sthg** no ser apto(-ta) para algo.

unfold [ʌnˈfəuld] *vt* desdoblar.

unforgettable [ʌnfəˈgetəbl] *adj* inolvidable.

unforgivable [ʌnfəˈgɪvəbl] *adj* imperdonable.

unfortunate [ʌnˈfɔːtʃnət] *adj* *(unlucky)* desgraciado(-da); *(regrettable)* lamentable.

unfortunately [ʌnˈfɔːtʃnətlɪ] *adv* desgraciadamente.

unfriendly [ʌnˈfrendlɪ] *adj* huraño(-ña).

unfurnished [ʌnˈfɜːnɪʃt] *adj* sin amueblar.

ungrateful [ʌnˈgreɪtful] *adj* desagradecido(-da).

unhappy [ʌnˈhæpɪ] *adj* *(sad)* triste; *(wretched)* desgraciado(-da); *(not pleased)* descontento(-ta); **I'm ~ about that idea** no me gusta esa idea.

unharmed [ʌnˈhɑːmd] *adj* ileso(-sa).

unhealthy [ʌnˈhelθɪ] *adj* *(person)* enfermizo(-za); *(food, smoking)* perjudicial para la salud; *(place)* insalubre.

unhelpful [ʌnˈhelpful] *adj* *(person)* poco servicial; *(advice)* inútil.

unhurt [ʌnˈhɜːt] *adj* ileso(-sa).

unhygienic [ʌnhaɪˈdʒiːnɪk] *adj* antihigiénico(-ca).

unification [juːnɪfɪˈkeɪʃn] *n* unificación *f*.

uniform [ˈjuːnɪfɔːm] *n* uniforme *m*.

unimportant [ʌnɪmˈpɔːtənt] *adj* sin importancia.

unintelligent [ʌnɪnˈtelɪdʒənt] *adj* poco inteligente.

unintentional [ˌʌnɪnˈtenʃən]
adj no intencional(-da).

uninterested [ˌʌnˈɪntrəstɪd] *adj*
indiferente.

uninteresting [ˌʌnˈɪntrəstɪŋ] *adj*
poco interesante.

union [ˈjuːnjən] *n* (of workers) sindicato *m*.

Union Jack *n*: the ~ la bandera
del Reino Unido.

unique [juːˈniːk] *adj* único(-ca);
to be ~ to ser peculiar de.

unisex [ˈjuːnɪseks] *adj* unisex
(inv).

unit [ˈjuːnɪt] *n* unidad *f*; (department, building) sección *f*; (piece of
furniture) módulo *m*; (group) equipo
m.

unite [juːˈnaɪt] *vt* (people) unir;
(country, party) unificar ♦ *vi* unirse.

United Kingdom [juːˈnaɪtɪd-]
n: the ~ el Reino Unido.

United Nations [juːˈnaɪtɪd-]
npl: the ~ las Naciones Unidas.

**United States (of
America)** [juːˈnaɪtɪd-] *npl*: the ~
los Estados Unidos (de América).

unity [ˈjuːnɪtɪ] *n* unidad *f*.

universal [ˌjuːnɪˈvɜːsl] *adj* universal.

universe [ˈjuːnɪvɜːs] *n* universo
m.

university [ˌjuːnɪˈvɜːsətɪ] *n* universidad *f*.

unjust [ˌʌnˈdʒʌst] *adj* injusto(-ta).

unkind [ʌnˈkaɪnd] *adj* desagradable.

unknown [ˌʌnˈnəʊn] *adj* desco-
nocido(-da).

unleaded (petrol) [ˌʌnˈledɪd-]
n gasolina *f* sin plomo.

unless [ənˈles] *conj* a menos que.

unlike [ˌʌnˈlaɪk] *prep* (different to)
diferente a; (in contrast to) a diferencia de; (not typical of) poco
característico de.

unlikely [ʌnˈlaɪklɪ] *adj* (not probable) poco probable; she's ~ to do
it es poco probable que lo haga.

unlimited [ʌnˈlɪmɪtɪd] *adj* ilimi-
tado(-da); ~ mileage sin límite de
recorrido.

unlisted [ʌnˈlɪstɪd] *adj* (Am:
phone number) que no figura en la
guía telefónica.

unload [ˌʌnˈləʊd] *vt* descargar.

unlock [ˌʌnˈlɒk] *vt* abrir (con
llave).

unlucky [ʌnˈlʌkɪ] *adj* (unfortunate)
desgraciado(-da); (bringing bad
luck) de la mala suerte.

unmarried [ˌʌnˈmærɪd] *adj* no
casado(-da).

unnatural [ʌnˈnætʃrəl] *adj* (unusual) poco normal; (behaviour, person) afectado(-da).

unnecessary [ʌnˈnesəsərɪ] *adj*
innecesario(-ria).

unobtainable [ˌʌnəbˈteɪnəbl]
adj inasequible.

unoccupied [ˌʌnˈɒkjʊpaɪd] *adj*
(place, seat) libre.

unofficial [ˌʌnəˈfɪʃl] *adj* extraofi-
cial.

unpack [ˌʌnˈpæk] *vt* deshacer ♦
vi deshacer el equipaje.

unpleasant [ʌnˈpleznt] *adj*
(smell, weather, surprise etc) desagradable; (person) antipático(-ca).

unplug [ˌʌnˈplʌg] *vt* desenchufar.

unpopular [ˌʌnˈpɒpjʊləʳ] *adj*
impopular.

unpredictable [ʌnprɪˈdɪktəbl] adj imprevisible.

unprepared [ʌnprɪˈpeəd] adj: to be ~ no estar preparado(-da).

unprotected [ʌnprəˈtektɪd] adj desprotegido(-da).

unqualified [ʌnˈkwɒlɪfaɪd] adj (person) no cualificado(-da).

unreal [ʌnˈrɪəl] adj irreal.

unreasonable [ʌnˈriːznəbl] adj (unfair) poco razonable (excessive) excesivo(-va).

unrecognizable [ʌnrekəgˈnaɪzəbl] adj irreconocible.

unreliable [ʌnrɪˈlaɪəbl] adj poco fiable.

unrest [ʌnˈrest] n malestar m.

unroll [ʌnˈrəʊl] vt desenrollar.

unsafe [ʌnˈseɪf] adj (dangerous) peligroso(-sa); (in danger) inseguro(-ra).

unsatisfactory [ʌnsætɪsˈfæktərɪ] adj insatisfactorio(-ria).

unscrew [ʌnˈskruː] vt (lid, top) desenroscar.

unsightly [ʌnˈsaɪtlɪ] adj feo(-a).

unskilled [ʌnˈskɪld] adj (worker) no cualificado(-da).

unsociable [ʌnˈsəʊʃəbl] adj insociable.

unsound [ʌnˈsaʊnd] adj (building, structure) inseguro(-ra); (argument, method) erróneo(-a).

unspoiled [ʌnˈspɔɪlt] adj no erosionado(-a) (por el hombre).

unsteady [ʌnˈstedɪ] adj inestable; (hand) tembloroso(-sa).

unstuck [ʌnˈstʌk] adj: to come ~ despegarse.

unsuccessful [ʌnsəkˈsesful] adj fracasado(-da).

unsuitable [ʌnˈsuːtəbl] adj inadecuado(-da).

unsure [ʌnˈʃɔːʳ] adj: to be ~ (about) no estar muy seguro(-ra) (de).

unsweetened [ʌnˈswiːtnd] adj no edulcorado(-da).

untidy [ʌnˈtaɪdɪ] adj (person) desaliñado(-da); (room, desk) desordenado(-da).

untie [ʌnˈtaɪ] (cont untying) vt desatar.

until [ənˈtɪl] prep hasta ♦ conj hasta que; don't start ~ I tell you no empieces hasta que no te lo diga.

untrue [ʌnˈtruː] adj falso(-sa).

untrustworthy [ʌnˈtrʌstwɜːðɪ] adj poco fiable.

untying [ʌnˈtaɪɪŋ] cont → untie.

unusual [ʌnˈjuːʒl] adj (not common) poco común; (distinctive) peculiar.

unusually [ʌnˈjuːʒəlɪ] adv (more than usual) extraordinariamente.

unwell [ʌnˈwel] adj indispuesto(-ta); to feel ~ sentirse mal.

unwilling [ʌnˈwɪlɪŋ] adj: to be ~ to do sthg no estar dispuesto(-ta) a hacer algo.

unwind [ʌnˈwaɪnd] (pt & pp **unwound** [ʌnˈwaʊnd]) vt desenrollar ♦ vi (relax) relajarse.

unwrap [ʌnˈræp] vt desenvolver.

unzip [ʌnˈzɪp] vt abrir la cremallera de.

up [ʌp] adv 1. (towards higher position, level) hacia arriba; **we walked ~ to the top** fuimos andando hasta arriba del todo; **to pick sthg ~** coger algo; **prices are going ~** los precios están subiendo.

2. *(in higher position)* arriba; **she's in her bedroom** está arriba, en su cuarto; **~ there** allí arriba.

3. *(into upright position)*: **to sit ~** sentarse derecho; **to stand ~** ponerse de pie.

4. *(northwards)*: **we're going ~ to Dewsbury** vamos a subir a Dewsbury.

5. *(in phrases)*: **to walk ~ and down** andar de un lado para otro; **to jump ~ and down** dar brincos; **~ to six weeks/ten people** hasta seis semanas/diez personas; **are you ~ to travelling?** ¿estás en condiciones de viajar?; **what are you ~ to?** ¿qué andas tramando?; **it's ~ to you** depende de ti; **~ until ten o'clock** hasta las diez.

◆ *prep* **1.** *(towards higher position)*: **to walk ~ a hill** subir por un monte; **I went ~ the stairs** subí las escaleras.

2. *(in higher position)* en lo alto de; **~ a hill** en lo alto de una colina.

3. *(at end of)*: **they live ~ the road from us** viven al final de nuestra calle.

◆ *adj* **1.** *(out of bed)* levantado(-da); **I was ~ at six today** hoy, me levanté a las seis.

2. *(at an end)* terminado(-da); **time's ~** se acabó el tiempo.

3. *(rising)*: **the ~ escalator** el ascensor que sube.

◆ *n*: **~s and downs** altibajos *mpl*.

update ['ʌp'deɪt] *vt* poner al día.

uphill [ʌp'hɪl] *adv* cuesta arriba.

upholstery [ʌp'həʊlstərɪ] *n* tapicería *f*.

upkeep ['ʌpkiːp] *n* mantenimiento *m*.

up-market *adj* de mucha categoría.

upon [ə'pɒn] *prep* *(fml: on)* en, sobre; **~ hearing the news ...** al oír la noticia ...

upper ['ʌpər] *adj* superior ◆ *n* *(of shoe)* pala *f*.

upper class *n* clase *f* alta.

uppermost ['ʌpəməʊst] *adj* *(highest)* más alto(-ta).

upper sixth *n* *(Br: SCH)* segundo año del curso optativo de dos que prepara a los alumnos de 18 años para los *"A-levels"*.

upright ['ʌpraɪt] *adj* *(person)* erguido(-da); *(object)* vertical ◆ *adv* derecho.

upset [ʌp'set] *(pt & pp* **upset)** *adj* disgustado(-da) ◆ *vt* *(distress)* disgustar; *(cause to go wrong)* estropear; *(knock over)* volcar; **to have an ~ stomach** tener el estómago revuelto.

upside down [ʌpsaɪd-] *adj & adv* al revés.

upstairs [ʌp'steəz] *adj* de arriba ◆ *adv* arriba; **to go ~** ir arriba.

up-to-date *adj* *(modern)* moderno(-na); *(well-informed)* al día.

upwards ['ʌpwədz] *adv* hacia arriba; **~ of 100 people** más de 100 personas.

urban ['ɜːbən] *adj* urbano(-na).

urban clearway [-'klɪəweɪ] *n* *(Br)* carretera donde no está permitido parar ni estacionar.

Urdu ['ʊədu:] *n* urdu *m*.

urge [ɜːdʒ] *vt*: **to ~ sb to do sthg** incitar a alguien a hacer algo.

urgent ['ɜːdʒənt] *adj* urgente.

urgently ['ɜːdʒəntlɪ] *adv* *(im-*

*mediately) urgentemente.

urinal [juˈraɪnl] *n (apparatus)* orinal *m*; *(fml: place)* urinario *m*.

urinate [ˈjʊərɪneɪt] *vi (fml)* orinar.

urine [ˈjʊərɪn] *n* orina *f*.

Uruguay [ˈjʊərəɡwaɪ] *n* Uruguay.

Uruguayan [ˌjʊərəˈɡwaɪən] *adj* uruguayo(-ya) ♦ *n* uruguayo *m* (-ya *f*).

us [ʌs] *pron* nos; **they know ~** nos conocen; **it's ~** somos nosotros; **send it to ~** envíanoslo; **tell ~** dinos; **they're worse than ~** son peores que nosotros.

US *n (abbr of United States)*: **the ~** los EEUU.

USA *n (abbr of United States of America)*: **the ~** los EEUU.

usable [ˈjuːzəbl] *adj* utilizable.

use [*n* juːs, *vb* juːz] *n* uso *m* ♦ *vt* usar; *(exploit)* utilizar; **to be of ~** ser útil; **to have the ~ of sthg** poder hacer uso de algo; **to make ~ of sthg** aprovechar algo; **"out of ~"** "no funciona"; **to be in ~** usarse; **it's no ~** es inútil; **what's the ~?** ¿de qué vale?; **to ~ sthg as sthg** usar algo como algo; **"~ before ..."** "consumir preferentemente antes de ..." ❑ **use up** *vt sep* agotar.

used [*adj* juːzd, *aux vb* juːst] *adj* usado(-da) ♦ *aux vb*: **I ~ to live near here** antes vivía cerca de aquí; **I ~ to go there every day** solía ir allí todos los días; **to be ~ to sthg** estar acostumbrado(-da) a algo; **to get ~ to sthg** acostumbrarse a algo.

useful [ˈjuːsfʊl] *adj* útil.

useless [ˈjuːslɪs] *adj* inútil; *(inf: very bad)* pésimo(-ma).

user [ˈjuːzəʳ] *n* usuario *m* (-ria *f*).

usher [ˈʌʃəʳ] *n (at cinema, theatre)* acomodador *m*.

usherette [ˌʌʃəˈret] *n* acomodadora *f*.

USSR *n*: **the (former) ~** la (antigua) URSS.

usual [ˈjuːʒəl] *adj* habitual; **as ~** *(in the normal way)* como de costumbre; *(as often happens)* como siempre.

usually [ˈjuːʒəlɪ] *adv* normalmente.

utensil [juːˈtensl] *n* utensilio *m*.

utilize [ˈjuːtɪlaɪz] *vt (fml)* utilizar.

utmost [ˈʌtməʊst] *adj* mayor ♦ *n*: **to do one's ~** hacer todo cuanto sea posible.

utter [ˈʌtəʳ] *adj* completo(-ta) ♦ *vt (word)* pronunciar; *(sound)* emitir.

utterly [ˈʌtəlɪ] *adv* completamente.

U-turn *n* giro *m* de 180°.

V

vacancy [ˈveɪkənsɪ] *n (job)* vacante *f*; **"vacancies"** "hay camas"; **"no vacancies"** "completo".

vacant [ˈveɪkənt] *adj* libre; **"vacant"** "libre".

vacate [vəˈkeɪt] *vt (fml: room, house)* desocupar.

vacation [vəˈkeɪʃn] *n (Am)* vacaciones *fpl* ◆ *vi* (*Am*) estar de vacaciones; **to go on ~** ir de vacaciones.

vacationer [vəˈkeɪʃənər] *n* (*Am*) (*throughout the year*) persona *f* de vacaciones; (*in summer*) veraneante *mf*.

vaccination [ˌvæksɪˈneɪʃn] *n* vacunación *f*.

vaccine [*Br* ˈvæksiːn, *Am* vækˈsiːn] *n* vacuna *f*.

vacuum [ˈvækjʊəm] *vt* pasar la aspiradora por.

vacuum cleaner *n* aspiradora *f*.

vague [veɪɡ] *adj* (*plan, letter, idea*) vago(-ga); (*memory, outline*) borroso(-sa); (*person*) impreciso(-sa).

vain [veɪn] *adj* (*pej: conceited*) engreído(-da); **in ~** en vano.

Valentine card [ˈvæləntaɪn-] *n* tarjeta *f* del día de San Valentín.

Valentine's Day [ˈvæləntaɪnz-] *n* día *m* de San Valentín.

valet [ˈvæleɪ, ˈvælɪt] *n* ayuda *m* de cámara.

valet service *n* (*in hotel*) servicio *m* de ayuda de cámara; (*for car*) servicio *m* de limpieza de automóviles.

valid [ˈvælɪd] *adj* (*ticket, passport*) valedero(-ra).

validate [ˈvælɪdeɪt] *vt* validar.

Valium® [ˈvælɪəm] *n* Valium® *m*.

valley [ˈvælɪ] (*pl* -**s**) valle *m*.

valuable [ˈvæljʊəbl] *adj* valioso(-sa) ◻ **valuables** *npl* objetos *mpl* de valor.

value [ˈvæljuː] *n* (*financial*) valor *m*; (*usefulness*) sentido *m*; **a ~ pack** un paquete económico; **to be**

good ~ (for money) estar muy bien de precio ◻ **values** *npl* valores *mpl* morales.

valve [vælv] *n* válvula *f*.

van [væn] *n* furgoneta *f*.

vandal [ˈvændl] *n* vándalo *m* (-la *f*).

vandalize [ˈvændəlaɪz] *vt* destrozar.

vanilla [vəˈnɪlə] *n* vainilla *f*.

vanish [ˈvænɪʃ] *vi* desaparecer.

vapor [ˈveɪpər] (*Am*) = **vapour**.

vapour [ˈveɪpər] *n* vapor *m*.

variable [ˈveərɪəbl] *adj* variable.

varicose veins [ˈværɪkəʊs-] *npl* varices *fpl*.

varied [ˈveərɪd] *adj* variado(-da).

variety [vəˈraɪətɪ] *n* variedad *f*.

various [ˈveərɪəs] *adj* varios (-rias).

varnish [ˈvɑːnɪʃ] *n* (*for wood*) barniz *m* ◆ *vt* (*wood*) barnizar.

vary [ˈveərɪ] *vt & vi* variar; **to ~ from sthg to sthg** variar entre algo y algo; **"prices ~"** "los precios varían".

vase [*Br* vɑːz, *Am* veɪz] *n* florero *m*.

Vaseline® [ˈvæsəliːn] *n* vaselina® *f*.

vast [vɑːst] *adj* inmenso(-sa).

vat [væt] *n* cuba *f*.

VAT [væt, ˌviːeɪˈtiː] *n* (*abbr of value added tax*) IVA *m*.

vault [vɔːlt] *n* (*in bank*) cámara *f* acorazada; (*in church*) cripta *f*; (*roof*) bóveda *f*.

VCR *n* (*abbr of video cassette recorder*) vídeo *m*.

VDU *n* (*abbr of visual display unit*) monitor *m*.

veal [viːl] n ternera f.

veg [vedʒ] n (abbr of vegetable) verdura f.

vegan ['viːgən] adj de tipo vegetariano puro ♦ n persona vegetariana que no consume ningún producto de procedencia animal, como leche, huevos, etc.

vegetable ['vedʒtəbl] n vegetal m; **~s** verduras fpl.

vegetable oil n aceite m vegetal.

vegetarian [,vedʒɪ'teəɪən] adj vegetariano(-na) ♦ n vegetariano m (-na f).

vegetation [,vedʒɪ'teɪʃn] n vegetación f.

vehicle ['viːəkl] n vehículo m.

veil [veɪl] n velo m.

vein [veɪn] n vena f.

Velcro® ['velkrəʊ] n velcro® m.

velvet ['velvɪt] n terciopelo m.

vending machine ['vendɪŋ-] n máquina f de venta automática.

venetian blind [vɪ,niːʃn-] n persiana f veneciana.

Venezuela [,venɪz'weɪlə] n Venezuela.

Venezuelan [,venɪz'weɪlən] adj venezolano(-na) ♦ n venezolano m (-na f).

venison ['venɪzn] n carne f de venado.

vent [vent] n (for air, smoke etc) rejilla f de ventilación.

ventilation [,ventɪ'leɪʃn] n ventilación f.

ventilator ['ventɪleɪtə'] n ventilador m.

venture ['ventʃə'] n empresa f ♦ vi (go) aventurarse a ir.

venue ['venjuː] n lugar m (de un acontecimiento).

veranda [və'rændə] n porche m.

verb [vɜːb] n verbo m.

verdict ['vɜːdɪkt] n (JUR) veredicto m; (opinion) juicio m.

verge [vɜːdʒ] n (of road, lawn, path) borde m; **"soft ~s"** señal que avisa del peligro de estancarse en los bordes de la carretera.

verify ['verɪfaɪ] vt verificar.

vermin ['vɜːmɪn] n bichos mpl.

vermouth ['vɜːməθ] n vermut m.

versa → vice versa.

versatile ['vɜːsətaɪl] adj (person) polifacético(-ca); (machine, food) que tiene muchos usos.

verse [vɜːs] n (of song, poem) estrofa f; (poetry) versos mpl.

version ['vɜːʃn] n versión f.

versus ['vɜːsəs] prep contra.

vertical ['vɜːtɪkl] adj vertical.

vertigo ['vɜːtɪgəʊ] n vértigo m.

very ['verɪ] adv muy ♦ adj mismísimo(-ma); **~ much** mucho; **not ~ big** no muy grande; **my ~ own room** mi propia habitación; **the ~ best** el mejor de todos; **the ~ person** justo la persona.

vessel ['vesl] n (fml: ship) nave f.

vest [vest] n (Br: underwear) camiseta f; (Am: waistcoat) chaleco m.

vet [vet] n (Br) veterinario m (-ria f).

veteran ['vetrən] n veterano m (-na f).

veterinarian [,vetərɪ'neərɪən] (Am) = **vet.**

veterinary surgeon ['vetərɪnrɪ-] (Br: fml) = **vet.**

VHF n (abbr of very high frequency) VHF m.

VHS n (abbr of video home system) VHS m.

via ['vaɪə] prep (place) pasando por; (by means of) por medio de.

viaduct ['vaɪədʌkt] n viaducto m.

vibrate [vaɪ'breɪt] vi vibrar.

vibration [vaɪ'breɪʃn] n vibración f.

vicar ['vɪkə'] n párroco m (-ca f).

vicarage ['vɪkərɪdʒ] n casa f parroquial.

vice [vaɪs] n vicio m; (Br: tool) torno m de banco.

vice-president n vicepresidente m (-ta f).

vice versa [,vaɪsɪ'vɜːsə] adv viceversa.

vicinity [vɪ'sɪnətɪ] n: in the ~ en las proximidades.

vicious ['vɪʃəs] adj (attack) brutal; (animal) sañoso(-sa); (comment) hiriente.

victim ['vɪktɪm] n víctima f.

Victorian [vɪk'tɔːrɪən] adj victoriano(-na).

victory ['vɪktərɪ] n victoria f.

video ['vɪdɪəʊ] (pl -s) n vídeo ◆ vt (using video recorder) grabar en vídeo; (using camera) hacer un vídeo de; **on** ~ en vídeo.

video camera n videocámara f.

video game n videojuego m.

video recorder n vídeo m.

video shop n tienda f de vídeos.

videotape ['vɪdɪəʊteɪp] n cinta f de vídeo.

Vietnam [Br ,vjet'næm, Am ,vjet'nɑːm] n Vietnam.

view [vjuː] n (scene, line of sight) vista f; (opinion) opinión f; (attitude) visión f ◆ vt (look at) observar; **in my** ~ desde mi punto de vista; **in** ~ **of** (considering) en vista de; **to come into** ~ aparecer; **you're blocking my** ~ no me dejas ver nada.

viewer ['vjuːə'] n (of TV) telespectador m (-ra f).

viewfinder ['vjuː,faɪndə'] n visor m.

viewpoint ['vjuːpɔɪnt] n (opinion) punto m de vista; (place) mirador m.

vigilant ['vɪdʒɪlənt] adj (fml) alerta.

villa ['vɪlə] n (in countryside, by sea) casa f de campo; (Br: in town) chalé m.

village ['vɪlɪdʒ] n (larger) pueblo m; (smaller) aldea f.

villager ['vɪlɪdʒə'] n aldeano m (-na f).

villain ['vɪlən] n (of book, film) malo m (-la f); (criminal) criminal mf.

vinaigrette [,vɪnɪ'gret] n vinagreta f.

vine [vaɪn] n (grapevine) vid f; (climbing plant) parra f.

vinegar ['vɪnɪgə'] n vinagre m.

vineyard ['vɪnjəd] n viña f.

vintage ['vɪntɪdʒ] adj (wine) añejo(-ja) ◆ n (year) cosecha f (de vino).

vinyl ['vaɪnɪl] n vinilo m.

viola [vɪ'əʊlə] n viola f.

violence ['vaɪələns] n violencia f.

violent ['vaɪələnt] adj violento(-ta); *(storm)* fuerte.

violet [vaɪələt] *adj* violeta *(inv)* ♦ *n (flower)* violeta *f.*

violin [ˌvaɪəˈlɪn] *n* violín *m.*

VIP *n (abbr of very important person)* gran personalidad.

virgin [vɜːdʒɪn] *n* virgen *mf.*

Virgo [vɜːgəʊ] *(pl -s) n* Virgo *m.*

virtually [vɜːtʃʊəlɪ] *adv* prácticamente.

virtual reality [vɜːtʃʊəl-] *n* realidad *f* virtual.

virus [vaɪrəs] *n* virus *m inv.*

visa [viːzə] *n* visado *m.*

viscose [vɪskəʊs] *n* viscosa *f.*

visibility [ˌvɪzɪˈbɪlɪtɪ] *n* visibilidad *f.*

visible [vɪzəbl] *adj* visible.

visit [vɪzɪt] *vt* visitar ♦ *n* visita *f.*

visiting hours [vɪzɪtɪŋ-] *npl* horas *fpl* de visita.

visitor [vɪzɪtəʳ] *n (to person)* visita *f; (to place)* visitante *mf.*

visitor centre *n* establecimiento en un lugar de interés turístico donde suele haber una exhibición, cafetería, tienda, etc.

visitors' book [vɪzɪtəz-] *n* libro *m* de visitas.

visitor's passport [vɪzɪtəz-] *n (Br)* pasaporte *m* provisional.

visor [vaɪzəʳ] *n* visera *f.*

vital [vaɪtl] *adj* esencial.

vitamin [*Br* vɪtəmɪn, *Am* vaɪtəmɪn] *n* vitamina *f.*

vivid [vɪvɪd] *adj* vivo(-va).

V-neck [viː-] *n (design)* cuello *m* de pico.

vocabulary [vəˈkæbjʊlərɪ] *n* vocabulario *m.*

vodka [vɒdkə] *n* vodka *m.*

voice [vɔɪs] *n* voz *f.*

volcano [vɒlˈkeɪnəʊ] *(pl -es OR -s) n* volcán *m.*

volleyball [vɒlɪbɔːl] *n* voleibol *m.*

volt [vəʊlt] *n* voltio *m.*

voltage [vəʊltɪdʒ] *n* voltaje *m.*

volume [vɒljuːm] *n* volumen *m.*

voluntary [vɒləntrɪ] *adj* voluntario(-ria).

volunteer [ˌvɒlənˈtɪəʳ] *n* voluntario *m (-ria f)* ♦ *vt:* **to ~ to do sthg** ofrecerse voluntariamente a hacer algo.

vomit [vɒmɪt] *n* vómito *m* ♦ *vi* vomitar.

vote [vəʊt] *n (choice)* voto *m; (process)* votación *f; (number of votes)* votos *mpl* ♦ *vi:* **to ~ (for)** votar (a).

voter [vəʊtəʳ] *n* votante *mf.*

voucher [vaʊtʃəʳ] *n* bono *m.*

vowel [vaʊəl] *n* vocal *f.*

voyage [vɔɪɪdʒ] *n* viaje *m.*

vulgar [vʌlgəʳ] *adj (rude)* grosero(-ra); *(in bad taste)* chabacano(-na).

vulture [vʌltʃəʳ] *n* buitre *m.*

W *(abbr of west)* O.

wad [wɒd] *n (of paper)* taco *m; (of banknotes)* fajo *m; (of cotton)* bola *f.*

waddle [wɒdl] *vi* anadear.

wade [weɪd] *vi* caminar dentro del agua.

wading pool [ˈweɪdɪŋ-] *n (Am)* piscina *f* infantil.

wafer [ˈweɪfəʳ] *n* barquillo *m*.

waffle [ˈwɒfl] *n (pancake)* gofre *m* ♦ *vi (inf)* enrollarse.

wag [wæg] *vt* menear.

wage [weɪdʒ] *n (weekly)* salario *m* ❑ **wages** *npl (weekly)* salario *m*.

wagon [ˈwægən] *n (vehicle)* carro *m; (Br: of train)* vagón *m*.

waist [weɪst] *n* cintura *f*.

waistcoat [ˈweɪskəʊt] *n* chaleco *m*.

wait [weɪt] *n* espera *f* ♦ *vi* esperar; **to ~ for sb to do sthg** esperar a que alguien haga algo; **I can't ~!** ¡me muero de impaciencia! ❑ **wait for** *vt fus* esperar.

waiter [ˈweɪtəʳ] *n* camarero *m*.

waiting room [ˈweɪtɪŋ-] *n* sala *f* de espera.

waitress [ˈweɪtrɪs] *n* camarera *f*.

wake [weɪk] *(pt* woke, *pp* woken) *vt* despertar ♦ *vi* despertarse ❑ **wake up** *vt sep* despertar ♦ *vi* despertarse.

Waldorf salad [ˈwɔːldɔːf-] *n* ensalada de manzana, nueces y apio con mayonesa.

Wales [weɪlz] *n* (el país de) Gales.

walk [wɔːk] *n (journey on foot)* paseo *m; (path)* ruta *f* paisajística (a pie) ♦ *vi* andar; *(as hobby)* caminar ♦ *vt (distance)* andar; **to go for a ~** ir a dar un paseo; **it's a short ~** está a poca distancia a pie; **to take the dog for a ~** pasear el perro; **"walk"** *(Am)* señal que autoriza a los peatones a cruzar;

"don't ~" *(Am)* señal que prohibe cruzar a los peatones ❑ **walk away** *vi* marcharse; **walk in** *vi* entrar; **walk out** *vi (leave angrily)* marcharse enfurecido.

walker [ˈwɔːkəʳ] *n* caminante *mf*.

walking boots [ˈwɔːkɪŋ-] *npl* botas *fpl* de montaña.

walking stick [ˈwɔːkɪŋ-] *n* bastón *m*.

Walkman® [ˈwɔːkmən] *n* walkman® *m*.

wall [wɔːl] *n (of building, room)* pared *f; (in garden, countryside, street)* muro *m*.

wallet [ˈwɒlɪt] *n* billetero *m*.

wallpaper [ˈwɔːlˌpeɪpəʳ] *n* papel *m* de pared.

wally [ˈwɒlɪ] *n (Br: inf)* imbécil *mf*.

walnut [ˈwɔːlnʌt] *n (nut)* nuez *f (de nogal)*.

waltz [wɔːls] *n* vals *m*.

wander [ˈwɒndəʳ] *vi* vagar.

want [wɒnt] *vt (desire)* querer; *(need)* necesitar; **to ~ to do sthg** querer hacer algo; **to ~ sb to do sthg** querer que alguien haga algo.

war [wɔːʳ] *n* guerra *f*.

ward [wɔːd] *n (in hospital)* sala *f*.

warden [ˈwɔːdn] *n (of park)* guarda *mf; (of youth hostel)* encargado *m (-da f)*.

wardrobe [ˈwɔːdrəʊb] *n* armario *m*, guardarropa *m*.

warehouse [ˈweəhaʊs, *pl* -haʊzɪz] *n* almacén *m*.

warm [wɔːm] *adj (pleasantly hot)* caliente; *(lukewarm)* templado (-da); *(day, weather, welcome)* caluroso(-sa); *(clothes, blankets)* que abriga; *(person, smile)* afectuoso(-sa) ◆ *vt* calentar; **I'm ~** tengo calor; **it's ~** hace calor; **are you ~ enough?** no tienes frío ¿verdad?

warm up *vt sep* calentar ◆ *vi (get warmer)* entrar en calor; *(do exercises)* hacer ejercicios de calentamiento; *(machine, engine)* calentarse.

war memorial *n* monumento *m* a los caídos de una guerra.

warmth [wɔːmθ] *n* calor *m*.

warn [wɔːn] *vt* advertir; **to ~ sb about sthg** prevenir a alguien sobre algo; **to ~ sb not to do sthg** advertir a alguien que no haga algo.

warning [wɔːnɪŋ] *n* aviso *m*.

warranty [wɒrəntɪ] *n (fml)* garantía *f*.

warship [wɔːʃɪp] *n* buque *m* de guerra.

wart [wɔːt] *n* verruga *f*.

was [wɒz] *pt → be*.

wash [wɒʃ] *vt* lavar ◆ *vi* lavarse ◆ *n*: **to give sthg a ~** lavar algo; **to have a ~** lavarse; **to ~ one's hands/face** lavarse las manos/la cara □ **wash up** *vi (Br: do washing-up)* fregar los platos; *(Am: clean o.s.)* lavarse.

washable [wɒʃəbl] *adj* lavable.

washbasin [wɒʃˌbeɪsn] *n* lavabo *m*.

washbowl [wɒʃbəʊl] *n (Am)* lavabo *m*.

washer [wɒʃəʳ] *n (ring)* arandela *f*.

washing [wɒʃɪŋ] *n (activity, clean clothes)* colada *f*; *(dirty clothes)* ropa *f* sucia.

washing line *n* tendedero *m*.

washing machine *n* lavadora *f*.

washing powder *n* detergente *m* (en polvo).

washing-up *n (Br)*: **to do the ~** fregar los platos.

washing-up bowl *n (Br)* barreño *m*.

washing-up liquid *n (Br)* lavavajillas *m inv*.

washroom [wɒʃrʊm] *n (Am)* aseos *mpl*.

wasn't [wɒznt] = **was not**.

wasp [wɒsp] *n* avispa *f*.

waste [weɪst] *n (rubbish)* desperdicios *mpl*; *(toxic, nuclear)* residuos *mpl* ◆ *vt (energy, opportunity)* desperdiciar; *(money)* malgastar; *(time)* perder; **a ~ of money** un derroche de dinero; **a ~ of time** una pérdida de tiempo.

wastebin [weɪstbɪn] *n* cubo *m* de la basura.

waste ground *n* descampado *m*.

wastepaper basket [ˌweɪst-ˈpeɪpəʳ] *n* papelera *f*.

watch [wɒtʃ] *n (wristwatch)* reloj *m* (de pulsera) ◆ *vt (observe)* ver; *(spy on)* vigilar; *(be careful with)* tener cuidado con □ **watch out** *vi (be careful)* tener cuidado; **~ out for a big hotel** estate al tanto de un hotel grande.

watchstrap [wɒtʃstræp] *n* correa *f* de reloj.

water [wɔːtəʳ] *n* agua *f* ◆ *vi* regar; **my eyes are ~ing** me lloran los ojos; **my mouth is ~ing** se me está haciendo la boca agua.

water bottle n cantimplora f.

watercolour ['wɔ:tə,kʌlə*] n acuarela f.

watercress ['wɔ:təkres] n berro m.

waterfall ['wɔ:təfɔ:l] n (small) cascada f; (large) catarata f.

watering can ['wɔ:tərɪŋ-] n regadera f.

watermelon ['wɔ:tə,melən] n sandía f.

waterproof ['wɔ:təpru:f] adj impermeable.

water purification tablets [-pjuərɪ'keɪʃn-] npl pastillas fpl para depurar el agua.

water skiing n esquí m acuático.

watersports ['wɔ:təspɔ:ts] npl deportes mpl acuáticos.

water tank n depósito m del agua.

watertight ['wɔ:tətaɪt] adj hermético(-ca).

watt [wɒt] n vatio m; **a 60-~ bulb** una bombilla de 60 vatios.

wave [weɪv] n (in sea, of crime) ola f; (in hair, of light, sound) onda ♦ vt (hand) saludar con; (flag) agitar ♦ vi (when greeting) saludar con la mano; (when saying goodbye) decir adiós con la mano.

wavelength ['weɪvleŋθ] n longitud f de onda.

wavy ['weɪvɪ] adj ondulado(-da).

wax [wæks] n cera f.

way [weɪ] n (manner, means) modo m, manera f; (route, distance travelled) camino m; (direction) dirección f; **it's the wrong ~ round** es al revés; **which ~ is the station?** ¿por

dónde se va a la estación?; **the town is out of our ~** la ciudad no nos queda de camino; **to be in the ~** estar en medio; **to be on the ~ (coming)** estar de camino; **to get out of the ~** quitarse de en medio; **to get under ~** dar comienzo; **there's a long ~ to go** nos queda mucho camino; **a long ~ away** muy lejos; **to lose one's ~** perderse; **on the ~ back** a la vuelta; **on the ~ there** a la ida; **that ~ (like that)** así; **(in that direction)** por allí; **this ~ (like this)** así; **(in this direction)** por aquí; **"give ~"** "ceda el paso"; **"~ in"** "entrada"; **"~ out"** "salida"; **no ~!** (inf) ¡ni hablar!

WC [,dʌblju:'si:] n (abbr of water closet) aseos mpl.

we [wi:] pron nosotros mpl (-tras fpl); **we're young** (nosotros) somos jóvenes.

weak [wi:k] adj débil; (not solid) frágil; (drink) poco cargado(-da); (soup) líquido(-da); (poor, not good) mediocre.

weaken ['wi:kn] vt debilitar.

weakness ['wi:knɪs] n (weak point) defecto m; (fondness) debilidad f.

wealth [welθ] n riqueza f.

wealthy ['welθɪ] adj rico(-ca).

weapon ['wepən] n arma f.

wear [weə*] (pt **wore**, pp **worn**) vt llevar ♦ n (clothes) ropa f; **~ and tear** desgaste m ▫ **wear off** vi desaparecer; **wear out** vi gastarse.

weary ['wɪərɪ] adj fatigado(-da).

weasel ['wi:zl] n comadreja f.

weather ['weðə*] n tiempo m; **what's the ~ like?** ¿qué tiempo hace?; **to be under the ~** *(inf)* no encontrarse muy bien.

weather forecast *n* pronóstico *m* del tiempo.

weather forecaster [-fɔːkɑːstəʳ] *n* hombre *m* del tiempo (mujer *f* del tiempo).

weather report *n* parte *m* meteorológico.

weather vane [-veɪn] *n* veleta *f*.

weave [wiːv] *(pt* wove, *pp* woven) *vt* tejer.

web [web] *n* telaraña *f*.

Wed. *(abbr of Wednesday)* miér.

wedding [wedɪŋ] *n* boda *f*.

wedding anniversary *n* aniversario *m* de boda.

wedding dress *n* vestido *m* de novia.

wedding ring *n* anillo *m* de boda.

wedge [wedʒ] *n (of cake)* trozo *m*; *(of wood etc)* cuña *f*.

Wednesday [wenzdɪ] *n* miércoles *m* *inv*, → **Saturday**.

wee [wiː] *adj (Scot)* pequeño(-ña) ♦ *n (inf)* pipí *m*.

weed [wiːd] *n* mala hierba *f*.

week [wiːk] *n* semana *f*; *(week-days)* días *mpl* laborables; **a ~ today** de hoy en ocho días; **in a ~'s time** dentro de una semana.

weekday [wiːkdeɪ] *n* día *m* laborable.

weekend [wiːk'end] *n* fin *m* de semana.

weekly [wiːklɪ] *adj* semanal ♦ *adv* cada semana ♦ *n* semanario *m*.

weep [wiːp] *(pt & pp* wept) *vi* llorar.

weigh [weɪ] *vt* pesar; **how much does it ~?** ¿cuánto pesa?

weight [weɪt] *n* peso *m*; **to lose ~** adelgazar; **to put on ~** engordar ▯

weights *npl (for weight training)* pesas *fpl*.

weightlifting [weɪt,lɪftɪŋ] *n* halterofilia *f*.

weight training *n* ejercicios *mpl* de pesas.

weir [wɪəʳ] *n* presa *f*.

weird [wɪəd] *adj* raro(-ra).

welcome [welkəm] *adj (guest)* bienvenido(-da); *(freely allowed)* muy libre; *(appreciated)* grato(-ta) ♦ *n* bienvenida *f* ♦ *vt (greet)* dar la bienvenida a; *(be grateful for)* agradecer ♦ *excl* ¡bienvenido!; **to make sb feel ~** recibir bien a alguien; **you're ~!** de nada.

weld [weld] *vt* soldar.

welfare [welfeəʳ] *n (happiness, comfort)* bienestar *m*; *(Am: money)* subsidio *m* de la Seguridad Social.

well [wel] *(compar* better, *superl* best) *adj & adv* bien ♦ *n* pozo *m*; **to get ~** reponerse; **to go ~** ir bien; **before the start** mucho antes del comienzo; **~ done!** ¡muy bien!; **it may ~ happen** es muy probable que ocurra; **it's ~ worth it** sí que merece la pena; **as ~** también; **as ~ as** además de.

we'll [wiːl] = **we shall**, **we will**.

well-behaved [-bɪ'heɪvd] *adj* bien educado(-da).

well-built *adj* fornido(-da).

well-done *adj* muy hecho (-cha).

well-dressed [-'drest] *adj* bien vestido(-da).

wellington (boot) [ˈwelɪŋtən]
n bota *f* de agua.

well-known *adj* conocido
(-da).

well-off *adj* (*rich*) adinerado(-da).

well-paid *adj* bien remunerado(-da).

welly [ˈwelɪ] *n* (*Br: inf*) bota *f* de
agua.

Welsh [welʃ] *adj* galés(-esa) ◆ *n*
(*language*) galés *m* ◆ *npl*: the ~ los
galeses.

Welshman [ˈwelʃmən] (*pl* -men
[-mən]) *n* galés *m*.

Welsh rarebit [-ˈreəbɪt] *n* tostada con queso gratinado.

Welshwoman [ˈwelʃˌwʊmən] (*pl*
-women [-ˌwɪmɪn]) *n* galesa *f*.

went [went] *pt* → **go**.

wept [wept] *pt & pp* → **weep**.

were [wɜːʳ] *pt* → **be**.

we're [wɪəʳ] = we are.

weren't [wɜːnt] = were not.

west [west] *n* oeste *m* ◆ *adv* (*fly,
walk*) hacia el oeste; (*be situated*) al
oeste; **in the ~ of England** en el
oeste de Inglaterra.

westbound [ˈwestbaʊnd] *adj*
con dirección oeste.

West Country *n*: **the ~** el sudoeste de Inglaterra, especialmente los
condados de Somerset, Devon y
Cornualles.

West End *n*: **the ~** (*of London*)
zona occidental del centro de Londres,
muy conocida por sus tiendas, cines y
teatros.

western [ˈwestən] *adj* occidental
◆ *n* película *f* del oeste.

West Indies [-ˈɪndɪːz] *npl*: **the ~**

las Antillas.

Westminster [ˈwestmɪnstəʳ] *n*
Westminster.

_i_ WESTMINSTER

En esta zona de Londres cercana
al río Támesis se hallan el Parlamento y la abadía de Westminster.
La palabra "Westminster" también
se usa para referirse al propio parlamento británico.

Westminster Abbey *n* la
abadía de Westminster.

_i_ WESTMINSTER ABBEY

La abadía de Westminster es una
iglesia londinense donde se
corona al monarca británico. Varios
personajes ilustres están ahí enterrados, y hay una zona especial conocida
como "Poets' Corner" que alberga
los sepulcros de escritores como
Chaucer, Dickens y Hardy.

---

westwards [ˈwestwədz] *adv*
hacia el oeste.

wet [wet] (*pt & pp* wet OR -ted)
adj (*soaked*) mojado(-da); (*damp*)
húmedo(-da); (*rainy*) lluvioso(-sa)
◆ *vt* (*soak*) mojar; **to get ~** mojarse; "~ **paint**" "recién pintado".

wet suit *n* traje *m* de submarinista.

we've [wiːv] = we have.

whale [weɪl] *n* ballena *f*.

wharf [wɔːf] (*pl* -s OR wharves

[wɔːvz]) *n* muelle *m*.

what [wɒt] *adj* 1. *(in questions)* qué; ~ colour is it? ¿de qué color es?; ~ shape is it? ¿qué forma tiene?; he asked me ~ colour it was me preguntó de qué color era.

2. *(in exclamations)* qué; ~ a surprise! ¡qué sorpresa!; ~ a beautiful day! ¡qué día más bonito!

♦ *pron* 1. *(in questions)* qué; ~ is going on? ¿qué pasa?; ~ are they doing? ¿qué hacen?; ~ is it called? ¿cómo se llama?; ~ are they talking about? ¿de qué están hablando?; she asked me ~ happened me preguntó qué había pasado.

2. *(introducing relative clause)* lo que; I didn't see ~ happened no vi lo que pasó; take ~ you want coge lo que quieras.

3. *(in phrases)*: ~ for? ¿para qué?; ~ about going out for a meal? ¿qué tal si salimos a comer?

♦ *excl* ¡qué!

whatever [wɒt'evəʳ] *pron*: take ~ you want coge lo que quieras; ~ I do, I'll lose haga lo que haga, saldré perdiendo; ~ that may be eso lo que sea eso.

wheat [wiːt] *n* trigo *m*.

wheel [wiːl] *n* rueda *f*; *(steering wheel)* volante *m*.

wheelbarrow ['wiːl,bærəʊ] *n* carretilla *f*.

wheelchair ['wiːl,tʃeəʳ] *n* silla *f* de ruedas.

wheelclamp [wiːl'klæmp] *n* cepo *m*.

wheezy ['wiːzɪ] *adj*: to be ~ resollar.

when [wen] *adv* cuándo ♦ *conj* cuando.

whenever [wen'evəʳ] *conj* siempre que; ~ you like cuando quieras.

where [weəʳ] *adv* dónde ♦ *conj* donde.

whereabouts ['weərəbaʊts] *adv* (por) dónde ♦ *npl* paradero *m*.

whereas [weər'æz] *conj* mientras que.

wherever [weər'evəʳ] *conj* dondequiera que; ~ that may be dondequiera que esté eso; ~ you like donde quieras.

whether ['weðəʳ] *conj* si; ~ you like it or not tanto si te gusta como si no.

which [wɪtʃ] *adj* qué; ~ room do you want? ¿qué habitación quieres?; she asked me ~ room I wanted me preguntó qué habitación quería; ~ one? ¿cuál?

♦ *pron* 1. *(in questions)* cuál; ~ is the cheapest? ¿cuál es el más barato?; he asked me ~ was the best me preguntó cuál era el mejor.

2. *(introducing relative clause)* que; the house ~ is on the corner la casa que está en la esquina; the television ~ I bought la televisión que compré; the settee on ~ I'm sitting el sofá en el que estoy sentado.

3. *(referring back)* lo cual; she denied it, ~ surprised me lo negó, lo cual me sorprendió.

whichever [wɪtʃ'evəʳ] *pron* el que *m* (la que *f*) ♦ *adj*: take ~ chocolate you like best coge el bombón que prefieras; ~ way you do it lo hagas como lo hagas.

while [waɪl] *conj* *(during the time that)* mientras; *(although)* aunque; *(whereas)* mientras que ♦ *n*: a ~ un rato; **a ~ ago** hace tiempo; **for a ~** un rato; **in a ~** dentro de un rato.

whim [wɪm] n capricho m.

whine [waɪn] vi (make noise) gimotear; (complain) quejarse.

whip [wɪp] n látigo m ♦ vt azotar.

whipped cream [wɪpt-] n nata f montada.

whirlpool [ˈwɜːlpuːl] n (Jacuzzi) jacuzzi m.

whisk [wɪsk] n batidor m (de varillas) ♦ vt (eggs, cream) batir.

whiskers [ˈwɪskəz] npl (of person) patillas fpl; (of animal) bigotes mpl.

whiskey [ˈwɪskɪ] (pl -s) n whisky m (de Irlanda o EEUU).

whisky [ˈwɪskɪ] n whisky m (de Escocia).

ⓘ WHISKY

El whisky, considerado la bebida nacional escocesa, es un fuerte licor elaborado con cebada y malta. El whisky siempre madura en barriles de madera y presenta distintas características dependiendo de los métodos de producción y tipos de agua utilizados. El whisky de malta conocido como "single malt", que en muchos casos se elabora en pequeñas destilerías regionales, se considera superior a otros tipos normalmente más baratos, llamados "blended".

---

whisper [ˈwɪspər] vt susurrar ♦ vi cuchichear.

whistle [ˈwɪsl] n (instrument) silbato m; (sound) silbido m ♦ vi silbar.

white [waɪt] adj blanco(-ca); (coffee, tea) con leche ♦ n (colour) blanco m; (of egg) clara f; (person) blanco m (-ca f).

white bread n pan m blanco.

White House n: **the ~** la Casa Blanca.

white sauce n salsa f bechamel.

white spirit n especie de aguarrás.

whitewash [ˈwaɪtwɒʃ] vt blanquear.

white wine n vino m blanco.

whiting [ˈwaɪtɪŋ] (pl inv) n pescadilla f.

Whitsun [ˈwɪtsn] n Pentecostés m.

who [huː] pron (in questions) quién, quiénes (pl); (in relative clauses) que.

whoever [huːˈevər] pron quienquiera que; **~ it is** quienquiera que sea; **~ you like** quien quieras.

whole [həʊl] adj entero(-ra) ♦ n: **the ~ of the journey** todo el viaje; **on the ~** en general.

wholefoods [ˈhəʊlfuːdz] npl alimentos mpl integrales.

wholemeal bread [ˈhəʊlmiːl-] n (Br) pan m integral.

wholesale [ˈhəʊlseɪl] adv al por mayor.

wholewheat bread [ˈhəʊl‚wiːt-] (Am) = **wholemeal bread**.

whom [huːm] pron (fml: in questions) quién, quiénes (pl); (in relative clauses) que.

whooping cough [ˈhuːpɪŋ-] n tos f ferina.

whose [huːz] adj (in questions) de

quién; *(in relative clauses)* cuyo(-ya) ◆ *pron* de quién; ~ **book is this?** ¿de quién es este libro?

why [waɪ] *adv & conj* por qué; **this is** ~ **we can't do it** esta es la razón por la que no podemos hacerlo; **explain the reason** ~ explícame por qué; ~ **not?** *(in suggestions)* ¿por qué no?; *(all right)* por supuesto (que sí).

wick [wɪk] *n* mecha *f*.

wicked [ˈwɪkɪd] *adj (evil)* perverso(-sa); *(mischievous)* travieso(-sa).

wicker [ˈwɪkəʳ] *adj* de mimbre.

wide [waɪd] *adj (in distance)* ancho(-cha); *(range, variety)* amplio(-plia); *(difference, gap)* grande ◆ *adv*: **to open sthg** ~ abrir bien algo; **how** ~ **is the road?** ¿cómo es de ancha la carretera?; **it's 12 metres** ~ tiene 12 metros de ancho; ~ **open** *(door, window)* abierto de par en par.

widely [ˈwaɪdlɪ] *adv (known, found)* generalmente; *(travel)* extensamente.

widen [ˈwaɪdn] *vt (make broader)* ensanchar ◆ *vi (gap, difference)* aumentar.

widespread [ˈwaɪdspred] *adj* general.

widow [ˈwɪdəʊ] *n* viuda *f*.

widower [ˈwɪdəʊəʳ] *n* viudo *m*.

width [wɪdθ] *n* anchura *f*; *(of swimming pool)* ancho *m*.

wife [waɪf] *(pl* **wives)** *n* mujer *f*.

wig [wɪg] *n* peluca *f*.

wild [waɪld] *adj (plant)* silvestre; *(animal)* salvaje; *(land, area)* agreste; *(uncontrolled)* frenético(-ca); *(crazy)* alocado(-da); **to be** ~ **about** *(inf)* estar loco(-ca) por.

wild flower *n* flor *f* silvestre.

wildlife [ˈwaɪldlaɪf] *n* fauna *f*.

will[1] [wɪl] *aux vb* **1.** *(expressing future tense)*: **I** ~ **see you next week** te veré la semana que viene; **you be here next Friday?** ¿vas a venir el próximo viernes?; **yes I** ~ sí; **no I won't** no.

2. *(expressing willingness)*: **I won't do it** no lo haré; **no one** ~ **do it** nadie quiere hacerlo.

3. *(expressing polite question)*: ~ **you have some more tea?** ¿le apetece más té?

4. *(in commands, requests)*: ~ **you please be quiet!** ¡queréis hacer el favor de callaros!; ~ **close the window,** ~ **you?** cierra la ventana, por favor.

will[2] [wɪl] *n (document)* testamento *m*; **against one's** ~ contra la voluntad de uno.

willing [ˈwɪlɪŋ] *adj*: **to be** ~ **(to do sthg)** estar dispuesto(-ta) (a hacer algo).

willingly [ˈwɪlɪŋlɪ] *adv* de buena gana.

willow [ˈwɪləʊ] *n* sauce *m*.

win [wɪn] *(pt & pp* **won)** *n* victoria *f* ◆ *vt & vi* ganar.

wind[1] [wɪnd] *n* viento *m*; *(in stomach)* gases *mpl*.

wind[2] [waɪnd] *(pt & pp* **wound)** *vi* serpentear ◆ *vt*: **to** ~ **sthg round sthg** enrollar algo alrededor de algo ❑ **wind up** *vt sep (Br: inf: annoy)* vacilar; *(car window)* subir; *(clock, watch)* dar cuerda a.

windbreak [ˈwɪndbreɪk] *n* lona *f* de protección contra el viento.

windmill [ˈwɪndmɪl] *n* molino *m* de viento.

window [ˈwɪndəʊ] n ventana f; (of car, plane) ventanilla f; (of shop) escaparate m.

window box n jardinera f (de ventana).

window cleaner n limpiacristales mf inv.

windowpane [ˈwɪndəʊpeɪn] n cristal m.

window seat n asiento m junto a la ventanilla.

window-shopping n: to go ~ mirar los escaparates.

windowsill [ˈwɪndəʊsɪl] n alféizar m.

windscreen [ˈwɪndskriːn] n (Br) parabrisas m inv.

windscreen wipers npl (Br) limpiaparabrisas m inv.

windshield [ˈwɪndʃiːld] n (Am) parabrisas m inv.

Windsor Castle [ˈwɪnzəˈ-] n el castillo de Windsor.

WINDSOR CASTLE

Los orígenes del castillo de Windsor, en Berkshire, se remontan al siglo XI cuando Guillermo el Conquistador inició su construcción. Hoy, es una de las residencias oficiales del monarca británico, y una parte está abierta al público.

---

windsurfing [ˈwɪndˌsɜːfɪŋ] n windsurf m; to go ~ ir a hacer windsurf.

windy [ˈwɪndɪ] adj (day, weather) de mucho viento; it's ~ hace viento.

wine [waɪn] n vino m.

wine bar n (Br) bar de cierta distinción, especializado en la venta de vinos y que suele servir comidas.

wineglass [ˈwaɪnglɑːs] n copa f (de vino).

wine list n lista f de vinos.

wine tasting [-ˈteɪstɪŋ] n cata f de vinos.

wine waiter n sommelier m.

wing [wɪŋ] n ala f; (Br: of car) guardabarros m inv ❑ **wings** npl: the ~s los bastidores.

wink [wɪŋk] vi guiñar el ojo.

winner [ˈwɪnəˈ] n ganador m (-ra f).

winning [ˈwɪnɪŋ] adj (person, team) vencedor(-ra); (ticket, number) premiado(-da).

winter [ˈwɪntəˈ] n invierno m; in (the) ~ en invierno.

wintertime [ˈwɪntətaɪm] n invierno m.

wipe [waɪp] vt limpiar; to ~ one's feet limpiarse los zapatos (en el felpudo); to ~ one's hands limpiarse las manos ❑ **wipe up** vt sep (liquid) secar; (dirt) limpiar ✦ vi (dry the dishes) secar (los platos).

wiper [ˈwaɪpəˈ] n (windscreen wiper) limpiaparabrisas m inv.

wire [waɪəˈ] n alambre m; (electrical wire) cable m ✦ vt (plug) conectar el cable a.

wireless [ˈwaɪəlɪs] n radio f.

wiring [ˈwaɪərɪŋ] n instalación f eléctrica.

wisdom tooth [ˈwɪzdəm-] n muela f del juicio.

wise [waɪz] adj (person) sabio(-bia); *(decision, idea)* sensato(-ta).

wish [wɪʃ] n deseo m ◆ vt desear; **I ~ I was younger** ¡ojalá fuese más joven!; **best ~es** un saludo; **to ~ for sthg** pedir algo (como deseo); **to ~ to do sthg** *(fml)* desear hacer algo; **to ~ sb luck/happy birthday** desear a alguien buena suerte/feliz cumpleaños; **if you ~** *(fml)* si usted lo desea.

witch [wɪtʃ] n bruja f.

with [wɪð] prep **1.** *(in company of)* con; **I play tennis ~ her** juego al tenis con ella; **~ me** conmigo; **you** contigo; **~ himself/herself** consigo; **we stayed ~ friends** estuvimos en casa de unos amigos.
2. *(in descriptions)* con; **the man ~ the beard** el hombre de la barba; **a room ~ a bathroom** una habitación con baño.
3. *(indicating means, manner)* con; **I washed it ~ detergent** lo lavé con detergente; **they won ~ ease** ganaron con facilidad; **topped ~ cream** cubierto con crema; **to tremble ~ fear** temblar de miedo.
4. *(regarding)* con; **be careful ~ that!** ¡ten cuidado con eso!
5. *(indicating opposition)* contra; **to argue ~ sb** discutir con alguien.

withdraw [wɪð'drɔː] *(pt -drew, pp -drawn)* vt *(take out)* retirar; *(money)* sacar ◆ vi retirarse.

withdrawal [wɪð'drɔːəl] n *(from bank account)* reintegro m.

withdrawn [wɪð'drɔːn] pp → **withdraw**.

withdrew [wɪð'druː] pt → **withdraw**.

wither ['wɪðər] vi marchitarse.

within [wɪð'ɪn] prep *(inside)* dentro de; *(certain distance)* dentro de; *(certain time)* en menos de ◆ adv dentro; **it's ~ ten miles of ...** está a menos de diez millas de ...; **it's walking distance** se puede ir andando; **it arrived ~ a week** llegó en menos de una semana; **~ the next week** durante la próxima semana.

without [wɪð'aʊt] prep sin; **~ me knowing** sin que lo supiera.

withstand [wɪð'stænd] *(pt & pp -stood* [-'stʊd]*)* vt resistir.

witness ['wɪtnɪs] n testigo mf ◆ vt *(see)* presenciar.

witty ['wɪtɪ] adj ocurrente.

wives [waɪvz] pl → **wife**.

wobbly ['wɒblɪ] adj *(table, chair)* cojo(-ja).

wok [wɒk] n sartén china profunda de base redondeada para cocinar con fuego intenso.

woke [wəʊk] pt → **wake**.

woken ['wəʊkn] pp → **wake**.

wolf [wʊlf] *(pl* **wolves** [wʊlvz]*)* n lobo m.

woman ['wʊmən] *(pl* **women**) n mujer f.

womb [wuːm] n matriz f.

women ['wɪmɪn] pl → **woman**.

won [wʌn] pt & pp → **win**.

wonder ['wʌndər] vi *(ask o.s.)* preguntarse ◆ n *(amazement)* asombro m; **to ~ if** preguntarse si; **I ~ if I could ask you a favour?** ¿le importaría hacerme un favor?

wonderful ['wʌndəful] adj maravilloso(-sa).

won't [wəʊnt] = will not.

wood [wʊd] n *(substance)* madera f.

f; (small forest) bosque *m; (golf club)* palo *m* de madera.

wooden ['wʊdn] *adj* de madera.

woodland ['wʊdlənd] *n* bosque *m.*

woodpecker ['wʊd,pekəʳ] *n* pájaro *m* carpintero.

woodwork ['wʊdwɜːk] *n* carpintería *f.*

wool [wʊl] *n* lana *f.*

woolen ['wʊlən] *(Am)* = **woollen.**

woollen ['wʊlən] *adj (Br)* de lana.

woolly ['wʊlɪ] *adj* de lana.

wooly ['wʊlɪ] *(Am)* = **woolly.**

Worcester sauce ['wʊstəʳ-] *n* salsa *f* Perrins®.

word [wɜːd] *n* palabra *f; in other ~s es decir; to have a ~ with sb* hablar con alguien.

wording ['wɜːdɪŋ] *n* formulación *f.*

word processing [-'prəʊsesɪŋ] *n* procesamiento *m* de textos.

word processor [-'prəʊsesəʳ] *n* procesador *m* de textos.

wore [wɔːʳ] *pt* → **wear.**

work [wɜːk] *n* trabajo *m; (painting, novel etc)* obra *f* ◆ *vi* trabajar; *(operate, have desired effect)* funcionar; *(take effect)* hacer efecto ◆ *vt (machine, controls)* hacer funcionar; *out of ~* desempleado; *to be at ~ (at workplace)* estar en el trabajo; *(working)* estar trabajando; *to be off ~* estar ausente del trabajo; *the ~s (inf: everything)* todo; *how does it ~? ¿cómo funciona?; it's not ~ing* no funciona; *to ~ as* trabajar de ❑ **work out** *vt sep (price, total)* calcular; *(solution, reason)* deducir; *(method, plan)* dar con; *(understand)*

entender ◆ *vi (result, turn out)* salir; *(be successful)* funcionar; *(do exercise)* hacer ejercicio; *it ~s out at £20 each* sale a 20 libras cada uno.

worker [ˈwɜːkəʳ] *n* trabajador *m* (-ra *f*).

working class [ˈwɜːkɪŋ-] *n: the ~* la clase obrera.

working hours [ˈwɜːkɪŋ-] *npl* horario *m* de trabajo.

workman [ˈwɜːkmən] *(pl* **-men** [-mən]) *n* obrero *m.*

work of art *n* obra *f* de arte.

workout [ˈwɜːkaʊt] *n* sesión *f* de ejercicios.

work permit *n* permiso *m* de trabajo.

workplace [ˈwɜːkpleɪs] *n* lugar *m* de trabajo.

workshop [ˈwɜːkʃɒp] *n* taller *m.*

work surface *n* encimera *f.*

world [wɜːld] *n* mundo *m* ◆ *adj* mundial; *the best in the ~* el mejor del mundo.

worldwide [ˌwɜːldˈwaɪd] *adv* a escala mundial.

worm [wɜːm] *n* gusano *m.*

worn [wɔːn] *pp* → **wear** ◆ *adj* gastado(-da).

worn-out *adj (tired)* agotado(-da); *to be ~ (clothes, shoes etc)* ya estar para tirar.

worried [ˈwʌrɪd] *adj* preocupado(-da).

worry [ˈwʌrɪ] *n* preocupación *f* ◆ *vt* preocupar ◆ *vi: to ~ (about)* preocuparse (por).

worrying [ˈwʌrɪɪŋ] *adj* preocupante.

worse [wɜːs] *adj & adv* peor; *to get ~* empeorar; *~ off (in worse* *position)* en peor situación; *(poorer)* peor de dinero.

worsen ['wɜːsn] *vi* empeorar.

worship ['wɜːʃɪp] *n (church service)* oficio *m* ♦ *vt* adorar.

worst [wɜːst] *adj & adv* peor ♦ *n:* **the ~** *(person)* el peor (la peor); *(thing)* lo peor.

worth [wɜːθ] *prep:* **how much is it ~?** ¿cuánto vale?; **it's ~ £50** vale 50 libras; **it's ~ seeing** merece la pena verlo; **it's ~ the pena;** **£50 ~ of traveller's cheques** cheques de viaje por valor de 50 libras.

worthless ['wɜːθlɪs] *adj* sin valor.

worthwhile [ˌwɜːθ'waɪl] *adj* que vale la pena.

worthy ['wɜːðɪ] *adj* digno(-na); **to be ~ of sthg** merecer algo.

would [wʊd] *aux vb* **1.** *(in reported speech):* **she said she ~ come** dijo que vendría.

2. *(indicating condition):* **what ~ you do?** ¿qué harías?; **what ~ you have done?** ¿qué habrías hecho?; **I ~ be most grateful** le estaría muy agradecido.

3. *(indicating willingness):* **she ~n't go** no quería irse; **he ~ do anything for her** haría cualquier cosa por ella.

4. *(in polite questions):* **~ you like a drink?** ¿quieres tomar algo?; **~ you mind closing the window?** ¿te importaría cerrar la ventana?

5. *(indicating inevitability):* **he ~ say that** sí él ¿qué va a decir?

6. *(giving advice):* **I ~ report it if I were you** yo en tu lugar lo denunciaría.

7. *(expressing opinions):* **I ~ prefer** yo preferiría; **I ~ have thought (that) ...** hubiera pensado que ...

wound[1] [wuːnd] *n* herida *f* ♦ *vt* herir.

wound[2] [waʊnd] *pt & pp* → **wind**[2].

wove [wəʊv] *pt* → **weave**.

woven ['wəʊvn] *pp* → **weave**.

wrap [ræp] *vt (package)* envolver; **to ~ sthg round sthg** liar algo alrededor de algo ♦ **wrap up** *vt sep (package)* envolver ♦ *vi* abrigarse.

wrapper ['ræpəʳ] *n* envoltorio *m*.

wrapping ['ræpɪŋ] *n* envoltorio *m*.

wrapping paper *n* papel *m* de envolver.

wreath [riːθ] *n* corona *f* (de flores).

wreck [rek] *n (of plane, car)* restos *mpl* del siniestro; *(of ship)* restos *mpl* del naufragio ♦ *vt (destroy)* destrozar; *(spoil)* echar por tierra; **to be ~ed** *(ship)* naufragar.

wreckage ['rekɪdʒ] *n (of plane, car)* restos *mpl*; *(of building)* escombros *mpl*.

wrench [rentʃ] *n (Br: monkey wrench)* llave *f* inglesa; *(Am: spanner)* llave *f* de tuercas.

wrestler ['reslər] *n* luchador *m* (-ra *f*).

wrestling ['reslɪŋ] *n* lucha *f* libre.

wretched ['retʃɪd] *adj (miserable)* desgraciado(-da); *(very bad)* pésimo(-ma).

wring [rɪŋ] *(pt & pp* **wrung)** *vt* retorcer.

wrinkle ['rɪŋkl] n arruga f.

wrist [rɪst] n muñeca f.

wristwatch ['rɪstwɒtʃ] n reloj m de pulsera.

write [raɪt] (pt wrote, pp written) vt escribir; (cheque) extender; (prescription) hacer; (Am: send letter to) escribir a ♦ vi escribir; **to ~ (to sb)** (Br) escribir (a alguien) □ **write back** vi contestar; **write down** vt sep apuntar; **write off** vt sep (Br: inf: car) cargarse ♦ vi: **to ~ off for sthg** hacer un pedido de algo (por escrito); **write out** vt sep (list, essay) escribir; (cheque, receipt) extender.

write-off n: **the car was a ~** el coche quedó hecho un estropicio.

writer ['raɪtəʳ] n (author) escritor m (-ra f).

writing ['raɪtɪŋ] n (handwriting) letra f; (written words) escrito m; (activity) escritura f.

writing desk n escritorio m.

writing pad n bloc m.

writing paper n papel m de escribir.

written ['rɪtn] pp → **write** ♦ adj (exam) escrito(-ta); (notice, confirmation) por escrito.

wrong [rɒŋ] adj (incorrect) equivocado(-da); (unsatisfactory) malo (-la); (moment) inoportuno(-na); (person) inapropiado(-da) ♦ adv mal; **to be ~** (person) estar equivocado; (immoral) estar mal; **what's ~?** ¿qué pasa?; **something's ~ with the car** el coche no marcha bien; **to be in the ~** haber hecho mal; **to get sthg ~** confundirse con algo; **to go ~** (machine) estropearse; **"~ way"** señal que indica a los conductores que existe el peligro de ir en la dirección contraria.

wrongly ['rɒŋlɪ] adv equivocadamente.

wrong number n: **sorry, I've got the ~** perdone, me he equivocado de número.

wrote [rəʊt] pt → **write**.

wrought iron [rɔːt-] n hierro m forjado.

wrung [rʌŋ] pt & pp → **wring**.

xing (Am: abbr of crossing): **"ped ~"** señal que indica un paso de peatones.

XL (abbr of extra-large) XL.

Xmas ['eksmas] n (inf) Navidad f.

X-ray ['eks-] n (picture) radiografía f ♦ vt hacer una radiografía a; **to have an ~** hacerse una radiografía.

yacht [jɒt] n (for pleasure) yate m; (for racing) balandro m.

yard [jɑːd] n (unit of measurement)

= 91,44 cm, yarda *f*; *(enclosed area)*
patio *m*; *(Am: behind house)* jardín
m.

yard sale *n (Am)* venta de objetos
de segunda mano organizada por una
sola persona frente a su casa.

yarn [jɑːn] *n* hilo *m*.

yawn [jɔːn] *vi* bostezar.

yd *abbr* = **yard**.

yeah [jeə] *adv (inf)* sí.

year [jɪəʳ] *n* año *m*; *(at school)*
curso *m*; **next** ~ el año que viene;
this ~ este año; **I'm 15 ~s old**
tengo 15 años; **I haven't seen her
for** ~**s** *(inf)* hace siglos que no la
veo.

yearly [ˈjɪəlɪ] *adj* anual.

yeast [jiːst] *n* levadura *f*.

yell [jel] *vi* chillar.

yellow [ˈjeləʊ] *adj* amarillo(-lla)
♦ *n* amarillo *m*.

yellow lines *npl* líneas *fpl* amarillas (de tráfico).

YELLOW LINES

En Gran Bretaña, líneas amarillas
dobles o individuales pintadas a
lo largo del borde de una carretera
indican una zona de aparcamiento
restringido. Una única línea prohíbe
aparcar entre las 8 de la mañana y
las 6.30 de la tarde en días laborables, y una línea amarilla doble prohíbe aparcar en todo momento. Se
puede aparcar sobre una línea amarilla después de las 6.30 de la tarde o
en domingo.

Yellow Pages® *n*: **the** ~ las
Páginas Amarillas®.

yes [jes] *adv* sí; **to say** ~ decir que
sí.

yesterday [ˈjestədɪ] *n* ayer *m* ♦
adv ayer; **the day before** ~ anteayer; ~ **afternoon** ayer por la
tarde; ~ **evening** anoche; ~ **morning** ayer por la mañana.

yet [jet] *adv* aún, todavía ♦ *conj*
sin embargo; **have they arrived** ~?
¿ya han llegado?; **the best one** ~ el
mejor hasta ahora; **not** ~ todavía
no; **I've** ~ **to do it** aún no lo he
hecho; ~ **again** otra vez más; ~
another delay otro retraso más.

yew [juː] *n* tejo *m*.

yield [jiːld] *vt (profit, interest)* producir ♦ *vi (break, give way)* ceder;
"**yield**" *(Am: AUT)* "ceda el paso".

YMCA *n* asociación internacional
de jóvenes cristianos.

yob [jɒb] *n (Br: inf)* gamberro *m*
(¡rra *f*).

yoga [ˈjəʊgə] *n* yoga *m*.

yoghurt [ˈjɒgət] *n* yogur *m*.

yolk [jəʊk] *n* yema *f*.

York Minster [jɔːkˈmɪnstəʳ] *n* la
catedral de York.

YORK MINSTER

Esta catedral, famosa por sus
paredes de piedra clara y su
rosetón, está situada en la amurallada ciudad de York, en el norte de
Inglaterra. Fue construida en el siglo
XII, y ha sido recientemente restaurada tras los daños producidos en
1984 por un rayo.

Yorkshire pudding [ˈjɔːkʃə-]
n masa de harina, huevos y leche, coci-

da al horno hasta formar un pastel
ligero y esponjoso, que se sirve tradicionalmente con el rosbif.

you [juː] *pron* **1.** *(subject: singular)*
tú, vos *(Amér)*; *(subject: plural)*
vosotros *mpl* (-tras *fpl*), ustedes
mfpl (*Amér*); *(subject: polite form)*
usted, ustedes *(pl)*; ~ **French** voso-
tros los franceses. **2.** *(direct object: singular)* te; *(direct
object: plural)* os, les *(Amér)*; *(direct
object: polite form)* lo m (la f) *(pl)*; **I hate
~!** te odio. **3.** *(indirect object: singular)* te; *(indirect object: plural)* os, les *(Amér)*;
(indirect object: polite form) le, les
(pl); **I told ~** te lo dije. **4.** *(after prep: singular)* ti; *(after prep:
plural)* vosotros *mpl* (-tras *fpl*),
ustedes *mfpl* (*Amér*); *(after prep:
polite form)* usted, ustedes *(pl)*; **we'll
go without ~** iremos sin ti. **5.** *(indefinite use)* uno m (una f); ~
never know nunca se sabe.

young [jʌŋ] *adj* joven ♦ *npl:* **the
~ los** jóvenes.

younger ['jʌŋgəʳ] *adj (brother, sister)* menor.

youngest ['jʌŋgəst] *adj (brother,
sister)* menor.

youngster ['jʌŋstəʳ] *n* joven *mf*.

your [jɔːʳ] *adj* **1.** *(singular subject)*
tu; *(polite form)* su; ~ **dog** tu perro; ~
children tus hijos. **2.** *(indefinite subject):* **it's good for ~
teeth** es bueno para los dientes ~

yours [jɔːz] *pron (singular subject)*
tuyo m (-ya f); *(plural subject)* vuestro
(-tra f); *(polite form)* suyo m
(-ya f); **a friend of ~** un amigo
tuyo.

yourself [jɔːˈself] *(pl* **-selves**
[-ˈselvz]) *pron* **1.** *(reflexive: singular)*
te; *(reflexive: plural)* os; *(reflexive:
polite form)* se. **2.** *(after prep: singular)* ti mismo
(-ma); *(after prep: plural)* vosotros
mismos (vosotras mismas); *(after
prep: polite form)* usted mismo
(-ma), ustedes mismos (-mas) *(pl)*;
did you do it ~? *(singular)* ¿lo hiciste
tú mismo?; *(polite form)* ¿lo hizo
usted mismo?; **did you do it yourselves?** ¿lo hicisteis vosotros/uste-
des mismos?

youth [juːθ] *n* juventud f; *(young
man)* joven m.

youth club *n* club m juvenil.

youth hostel *n* albergue m
juvenil.

Yugoslavia [ˌjuːgəˈslɑːvɪə] *n* Yugoslavia.

yuppie ['jʌpɪ] *n* yuppy *mf*.

YWCA *n* asociación internacional
de jóvenes cristianas.

Z

zebra [*Br* 'zebrə, *Am* 'ziːbrə] *n*
cebra f.

zebra crossing *n (Br)* paso m
de cebra.

zero ['zɪərəʊ] *(pl* **-es**) *n* cero m;
five degrees below ~ cinco grados
bajo cero.

zest [zest] *n (of lemon, orange)*
ralladura f.

zigzag ['zɪgzæg] *vi* zigzag m.

zinc [zɪŋk] n zinc m.

zip [zɪp] n (Br) cremallera f ◆ vt cerrar la cremallera de ❑ **zip up** vt sep subir la cremallera de.

zip code n (Am) código m postal.

zipper ['zɪpəʳ] n (Am) cremallera f.

zit [zɪt] n (inf) grano m.

zodiac ['zəʊdɪæk] n zodiaco m.

zone [zəʊn] n zona f.

zoo [zu:] (pl -s) n zoo m.

zoom (lens) [zu:m-] n zoom m.

zucchini [zu:'ki:nɪ] (pl inv) n (Am) calabacín m.

guía de conversación

En el hotel

- Quisieramos una habitación doble/dos habitaciones individuales.
- Tengo una reserva a nombre de Galante.
- ¿Con ducha o con baño?
- ¿A qué hora sirven el desayuno/la cena?
- ¿Pueden despertarme a las siete de la mañana?

At the hotel

- We'd like a double room/two single rooms.
- I have a reservation in the name of Galante.
- With shower or bath?
- What time is breakfast /dinner served?
- Could I have a wake-up call at seven a.m.?

En las tiendas

- ¿Puedo ayudarlo/ ayudarla?
- No, gracias. Sólo estoy mirando.
- ¿Cuánto cuesta? ¿Cuánto es?
- ¿Cuánto mide?
- Calzo 38.
- Mido 38.
- ¿Puedo probarme este abrigo?
- ¿Es posible cambiarlo?

At the shops

- Can I help you?
- No, thanks. I'm just looking.
- How much is this?
- What size are you?
- I take size 38.
- I'm size 38.
- Can I try this coat on?
- Can it be exchanged?

En el banco

- Quisiera cambiar 50 pesos en OR por dólares.

- En billetes pequeños, por favor.
- ¿A cuánto está la libra esterlina?
- ¿Cuánto sería en euros?

- ¿Acepta cheques de viajero?

En la oficina de correos

- ¿Cuánto cuesta enviar una carta/una postal a Inglaterra/México?
- Quisiera 10 sellos OR estampillas (Amer) para Canadá.
- Quisiera enviar este paquete certificado.

- ¿Cuánto tiempo tardará en llegar la carta?

At the bank

- I'd like to change 50 pesos into dollars.

- In small denominations, please.
- What is the rate for the pound?
- How much is that in euros?
- Do you take traveller's cheques?

At the post office

- How much is it to send a letter/postcard to England/Mexico?
- I'd like ten stamps for Canada.

- I'd like to send this parcel by registered post (Br) O mail (Am).
- How long will it take for the letter to arrive?

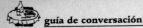 **guía de conversación**

En el café

- ¿Está libre esta mesa/este asiento?
- Dos cafés solos/cafés con leche, por favor.

- ¿Me sirve otra cerveza, por favor?

En el restaurante

- Quisiera reservar una mesa para cenar.
- ¿Podemos ver el menú/la carta de vinos?
- ¿Tienen un menú fijo/un menú para niños?
- ¿Qué quiere tomar?

- ¿A qué punto de cocción quiere la carne?
- Vuelta y vuelta/ cocida/bien cocida, por favor.
- La cuenta, por favor.

At the café

- Is this table/seat free?

- Two black coffees/ white coffees (*Br*) O coffees with cream (*Am*), please.
- Can I have another beer, please?

At the restaurant

- I'd like to reserve a table for tonight.
- Can we see the menu/the wine list?
- Do you have a set menu/a children's menu?
- What would you like to drink?
- How would you like your meat?
- Rare/medium/well done, please.

- Can I have the bill (*Br*) O the check (*Am*)?

En el consultorio del médico

- No me siento bien y tengo diarrea.
- Me duele la cabeza/la garganta/la barriga.
- Mi hijo tose y tiene fiebre.
- ¿Es usted alérgico a la penicilina?
- Una pastilla dos veces al día con las comidas.

En la farmacia

- Quisiera algún medicamento contra el dolor de cabeza/el dolor de garganta/la diarrea.
- Quisiera aspirinas/ unas tiritas® (*Esp*) OR unas curitas® (*Amer*).
- ¿Puede recomendarme un doctor?

At the doctor's

- I don't feel well and I have diarrhoea.
- I have a headache/a sore throat/ stomach ache.
- My son has a cough and is running a fever.
- Are you allergic to penicillin?
- One tablet twice a day with meals.

At the chemist's (*Br*) O drugstore (*Am*)

- I'd like something for a headache/a sore throat/diarrhoea.
- I'd like some aspirin/some sticking plasters (*Br*) ou Band-Aid® (*Am*)
- Could you recommend a doctor?

MINI PLUS

Hablar por teléfono

- ¿Oiga? (*Esp*)
  ¡Hola! (*Amer*)
  [Person phoning]
  ¿Dígame? ¿Diga? (*Esp*)
  ¿Sí? ¿Hola? ¿Bueno?
  (*Amer*) [Person answering]
- Habla Jean Brown.
- Me gustaría hablar con
  Eduardo Ortega, por
  favor.
- No cuelgue. Aguarde.
- No contesta nadie.
- La línea está ocupada.

- ¿Puede llamar de vuelta
  en 10 minutos?
- ¿Quiere dejar algún
  mensaje?
- Tiene el número
  equivocado.

Telephoning

- Hello.

- Jean Brown speaking.
- I'd like to speak to
  Eduardo Ortega, please.

- Hold the line.
- There's no answer.
- The line's engaged (*Br*)
  O busy (*Am*).
- Can you call back in ten
  minutes?
- Would you like to leave
  a messsage?
- You have the wrong
  number.

Felicitaciones y saludos

- Buena suerte.
- Diviértete. Pásatelo bien.
- ¡Que te diviertas!
  ¡Que lo pases bien!
- Buen provecho.

Wishes and greetings

- Good luck.
- Have fun.
- Enjoy yourself.

- Enjoy your meal.